JONATHAN D. SPENCE

THE SEARCH FOR MODERN CHINA

Second Edition

In this Second Edition of his widely acclaimed history of modern China, Jonathan Spence achieves a fine blend of narrative richness and efficiency. The text is tighter throughout and up-to-date on the most important scholarship in the field. The new discussions in this thorough revision include the extension of imperial power into central Asia by the eighteenth-century emperors, women's literacy and education in the Qing, the early development of Chinese nationalism, the roots of Chinese communism and alternatives to Mao, the early stages of the Great Leap Forward and of the Cultural Revolution. There is a new chapter at the end of the book on economic, cultural, and political developments since 1989. Praised as a "miracle of readability and scholarly authority,"* *The Search for Modern China* offers students a matchless introduction to China's history.

Accompanying the Second Edition is a collection of primary documents, *The Search for Modern China: A Documentary Collection,* edited by Pei-kai Cheng and Michael Lestz with Jonathan D. Spence.

Jonathan D. Spence is Sterling Professor of History at Yale University. He is the author of a distinguished body of work on the history of modern China. Among his most recent books are *God's Chinese Son: The Taiping Heavenly Kingdom of Hong Xiuquan* and *The Chan's Great Continent: China in Western Minds.*

* Jonathan Mirsky

Also by JONATHAN D. SPENCE

THE SEARCH FOR
MODERN
CHINA
SECOND EDITION

JONATHAN D. SPENCE

W·W·NORTON & COMPANY | New York · London

THE SEARCH FOR
MODERN
CHINA

SECOND EDITION

Copyright © 1999, 1990 by Jonathan D. Spence

The text of this book is composed in Granjon
Composition by Binghamton Valley Composition
Printed by Maple-Vail, Binghamton
Book design by Antonina Krass

Cover art: Ren Yi (1840–1896), *Portrait of Ge Chonghua at the Age of Twenty-seven* (1873), courtesy, The Palace Museum, Beijing, China (front); Chen Hongshou (1598–1652), untitled (*Man with Butterfly*) and undated, courtesy, Liaoning Fine Arts Museum, Shenyang, China (back).

Library of Congress Cataloging-in-Publication Data

Spence, Jonathan D.
    The search for modern China / Jonathan D. Spence. — 2nd ed.
        p.   cm.
    Includes bibliographical references and index.
    ISBN 0-393-97351-4 (pbk.)
    1. China—History—Ch'ing dynasty, 1644–1912.   2. China—
    History—20th century.   I. Title.
    DS754.S65   1999
    951'.03—dc21   98-22145

ISBN 0-393-97351-4 (pbk.)

W. W. Norton & Company, Inc., 500 Fifth Avenue, New York, N.Y. 10110
www.wwnorton.com

W. W. Norton & Company Ltd., Castle House, 75/76 Wells Street, London W1T 3QT

20 19 18 17 16 15 14 13 12 11

FOR MY STUDENTS

Contents

APPENDIXES A1

Illustrations appear following pages 38, 132, 228, 372, 484, 662, 718

Maps

Tables

Preface to the Second Edition

The first edition of *The Search for Modern China* was completed while the Chinese government crackdown against the Tiananmen democracy demonstrators was at its height in June 1989. One can see with hindsight that these events emphasized in my mind the fragility of the individual Chinese voices in their confrontations with the state, and made the chances for constructive change seem elusive. Nine years later, as I complete the second edition, the state of affairs in China and the world is vastly different. Deng Xiaoping, the man held most responsible for the violence of the 1989 repression, died early in 1997; his loyal lieutenant and fellow hard-liner, premier Li Peng, retired from the premiership in early 1998. The Soviet Union has disintegrated into a number of constituent republics, and the member states of its former satellite empire in Eastern Europe have gone their wildly different ways. The most prominent of the 1989 student leaders are now out of prison and living in exile in the United States, as is Wei Jingsheng, the best-known and most tenacious spokesman for the democracy experimenters of 1978.

China's government seems to have made its peace with the ghosts of both movements largely by denying their significance. Moreover, the country as a whole has become absorbed with the challenges, rewards, and ambiguities of domestic economic growth and participation in the international financial scene. These changes in focus have made it hard for human rights activitists—whether indigenous, exiled, or foreign—to keep alive the key issues concerning the Chinese leadership's rejection of representative government and its ongoing harassment of dissidents. And with Hong Kong reintegrated peacefully with China in the summer of 1997, Taiwan now attracts greater attention: China's policies there serve as a barometer to gauge the possibilities of some future pattern of economic reintegration.

During the same nine-year stretch of time, our knowledge of China's past has been prodigiously extended. Rich archaeological discoveries inside China are transforming our view of early Chinese society and the early texts on the theory of government. And also in countless areas closer to our current age, studies by Chinese and foreign scholars have profoundly altered what we thought we knew.

In attempting to incorporate these findings into this second edition, I have been compelled to alter many old ideas, and to introduce many new ones. Prominent among these for the Qing dynasty itself would be the following: the ways that the eighteenth-century Manchu emperors of China transformed themselves into central Asian rulers; the stages by which secret societies came to play such a dominant role in challenging the state in China from the late eighteenth century onward; the nature of women's literacy and education in the Qing, and the uses made of imagery of women in the loyalist politics of the time; the typologies of Chinese nationalism as they developed in the late Qing, and the impact of new forms of print media in circulating them widely.

For the period of the Republic of China (1912–1949) there is an equally wide array of topics that now have to be rethought: the antecedents of Chinese Communism, especially its connections to anarchism and voluntarism; the major career paths and survival strategies of the many Communist activists who did not agree with Mao Zedong; the nature of Chinese commercial and social life in the cities, and the shifting patterns there in the interpretations and expressions of modernity; the specifics of Mao's construction—through manipulation of history and through coercion—of his own heroic image; the underground war fought between the Communists and the Guomindang nationalists both before and after the outbreak of war with Japan in 1937.

And for the People's Republic since 1949, one can point to the revelations through recent archival disclosures of the relations between Mao and Stalin in Moscow in 1949 and at the outbreak of the Korean War in 1950; the domestic imperatives that can be seen as leading up to the Great Leap Forward of 1957; the psychology (of both the leaders and the led) that helped precipitate the Cultural Revolution of 1966; the slow development of the policies of economic flexibility under Deng Xiaoping; the relationship between the Communist government's stated agrarian policies and the initiatives taken by the farmers themselves; and the development of renewed diversity in thought and culture over the last two decades.

I have incorporated as much as I could of these new findings in this second edition, as well as adding an entire new chapter to cover the period from 1989 to 1998. To do this without making the book any bulkier than it already was, I made many hundreds of cuts, some brief, but others of whole pages or even entire sections when I felt they could be dispensed with. The result is a text that is not only up-dated, but also somewhat shorter than the first edition. I have also made a number of structural changes within the text to make it easier to follow, by introducing basic economic and geographical analysis earlier in the book, changing the organization of the chapters on the Nationalist and Communist parties, presenting foreign policy issues in a different form, and redesigning the sections marking the transition from the Great Leap Forward of 1958 to the Cultural Revolution of 1966.

Some readers and reviewers of the first edition expressed a wish that the book had been organized along topical or conceptual lines, rather than on chronological ones, and that it had paid even more attention to broad social trends and the experiences of those completely divorced from the various political centers. They also sought more attention to various current Western theories, such as postmodernism, subaltern studies, or various derivatives of those schools that claim neo-Marxist credentials. On these points I remain unrepentant. Both teachers and students of history need to know *when* things happened before they begin to understand why. Of course the forces generated within Chinese society affected the ideas and lives of the leaders or would-be leaders, just as did the might or the ideas imposed on China by foreign powers. But I still feel that the attempt to make sense of these varying impulses can most fittingly—in a historical introduction of this kind—be undertaken from the center, looking out. As to imposing stronger theoretical criteria for the selection or organization of information, though this might be of interest to some readers, it will puzzle or deter others; and given the nature of the current Western cultural world, any theory chosen would in addition be speedily outdated.

In the structure of this volume, accordingly, the center provides the lens by which we can start to give a general focus to the multiple blips of light radiating out from the universe of Chinese experience. Any reader wishing to get a sharper sense of individual sources can do so swiftly through the lists of further readings in the Appendix. China's troubled quest to find its place in the world is still continuing, in 1998 as it was in 1989. It is my hope that this new edition of the *Search* will lead a fresh group of readers to follow that quest with sympathy, and with a certain understanding of the issues that are the most compelling to the Chinese people themselves.

Preface to the First Edition

No country, over the past few centuries, has been free of turmoil and tragedy. It is as if there were a restlessness and a capacity for violence at the center of the human spirit that can never be contained, so that no society can achieve a perfect tranquility. Yet in every country, too, humans have shown a love of beauty, a passion for intellectual adventure, a gentleness, an exuberant sensuality, and a yearning for justice that have cut across the darkness and filled their world with light. They have struggled constantly to understand the world, to protect themselves from its ravages, to organize it more effectively, and to make it a place in which their children might live without hunger or fear.

The history of China is as rich and strange as that of any country on earth, and its destiny as a nation is now entwined with all others in the search for scarce resources, the exchange of goods, and the expansion of knowledge. Yet for a long time China was a completely unknown quantity to those living in the West, and even today seems set apart by differences of language, custom, and attitude. Now that China has over 1 billion people within its borders, it suffers internal pressures that the rest of us can only guess at; and the swings of its political life, the switches in its cultural moods, the lurches in its economy, the fact that its stated hostility to foreign influences is so often accompanied by the flashes of a welcoming smile, all combine to keep us in a state of bewilderment as to China's real nature.

There is no easy way to understand China, any more than there is an easy way to understand any culture, or even to understand ourselves. But the attempt is worth making, for China's story is an astonishing one and has much to teach us. It is the contention of this book that in trying to understand China today we need to know about China in the past; but how far back we carry that search remains, in a sense, the central question. China's history is enormously long; indeed no other society has maintained its vitality or kept so meticulous a record of its own doings over such a long span—close to four thousand years—as has China. One can plunge into that record at any point and find events, personalities, moods that appear to echo the present in haunting ways.

My narrative begins around the year 1600 because it is only by starting at this time that I feel we can get a full sense of how China's current problems have arisen, and of what resources—intellectual, economic, and emotional—the Chinese can call upon to solve them. In entitling this story *The Search for Modern China* I wish to emphasize a number of themes.

First, both China's rulers and Chinese critics of those rulers have sought repeatedly over this long time span to formulate strategies that would strengthen their country's borders, streamline bureaucratic institutions, make the most of their own resources so as to keep free from foreign interference, and sharpen the rigor of the intellectual tools needed to analyze the efficacy and the morality of political actions.

Second, even though it was not necessarily on any parallel "track" to the developing Western powers or to Japan, China was constantly adapting and changing in important ways, even as it was struggling to preserve certain immutable values. Much of the history we will be examining here is made up of overlapping cycles of collapse and reconsolidation, of revolution and evolution, of conquest and movements for progress.

Third, this remains a book about an ongoing search rather than about the conclusion of a search. I understand a "modern" nation to be one that is both integrated and receptive, fairly sure of its own identity yet able to join others on equal terms in the quest for new markets, new technologies, new ideas. If it is used in this open sense, we should have no difficulty in seeing "modern" as a concept that shifts with the times as human life unfolds, instead of simply relegating the sense of "modern" to our own contemporary world while consigning the past to the "traditional" and the future to the "postmodern." I like to think that there were modern countries—in the above sense—in A.D. 1600 or earlier, as at any moment in the centuries thereafter. Yet at no time in that span, nor at the end of the twentieth century, has China been convincingly one of them.

Fourth, I hope that the focus on the "search" for modern China as an ongoing act will make it clear how much China's history illuminates its present. China's Communist government can claim, with validity, revolutionary credentials. But it is also a giant bureaucracy whose leaders insist on their right, in the name of a higher truth, to define people's aspirations in virtually all spheres of life. So it was in the late Ming and early Qing states of the seventeenth century. In relating to the outside world, China can also rightfully claim it is charting its own course. But in attempting to adapt certain aspects of advanced foreign technologies to solve its own pressing needs while preserving its people from corrupting influences, it is re-exploring ground surveyed with care in the nineteenth century. Governing 1 billion citizens inside a single political entity is also something no state has attempted before. But it was in the eighteenth century that China's population pressures first became acute; and the effects of these growing numbers on the land, the economy, and the administration of civil society can be observed in detail from that time on.

The presence of the past can also be seen in many other areas. The customs and practices that ensured the low social and economic status of women, the educational methods that were used to instill in children certain patterns of generational deference and concepts of obligation, the power of the family as an organizational unit, the ability of certain people within local communities to gain and preserve an abusive level of control—all of these aspects of Chinese society and culture can be seen in various forms from 1600 onward. So can the aesthetic aspirations and linguistic innovations in art and literature, the probing scrutiny of administrative structures and procedures, all of which have brought deep changes to China and have endured to the present time.

By starting our story at the end of the sixteenth century, too, we can achieve one other goal. We can see how often the Chinese people, operating in difficult or even desperate circumstances, seized their own fate and threw themselves against the power of the state. We can see how in 1644, again in 1911, and yet again in 1949, disillusion with the present and a certain nostalgia for the past could combine with a passionate hope for the future to bring the old order crashing down, opening the way for an uncertain passage to the new. And armed with knowledge of those earlier struggles, we can gain a sharper understanding of the forces now confronting each other inside China, and of the chances for or against the troubled nation at last claiming its place in a modern world.

Autumn, 1989

Acknowledgments for the Second Edition

In preparing this second edition of *The Search for Modern China* I have benefited greatly from those who reviewed the first edition, or wrote to me with comments or criticisms. Though I did not always feel compelled to accept their suggestions, cumulatively they have sharpened my thinking and led me to make many changes and emendations. Especially helpful were suggestions made by T. K. Chang, Frank Ching, Chou Wan-yao, Ralph Covell, Justus Doenecke, Jaap Engelsman, the late John King Fairbank, Dolores Filandro, Erwin Fuchs, Jing Li, Jing Luo, Angus McDonald, W. Scott Morton, Shao Dongfang, Jan Stuart, Britt Towery, Arthur Waldron, Renqiu Yu, and Linong Zhou. I would also like to thank the many students at Yale, both undergraduate and graduate, with whom I have discussed the book at length, and in particular wrestled with the problems of what to cut and what to add. I hope they will find in this second edition adequate responses to the many shrewd questions that they raised. As with the first edition, Steven Forman at Norton has been consistently encouraging, while keeping an eye on the clock. And Annping, Mei, Yar, and Maddux have each helped in their own way to make this protracted task as joyful as possible.

JDS
August 1, 1997

Acknowledgments for the First Edition

In the years that were spent writing *The Search for Modern China* I have incurred countless debts of gratitude. My deepest is to my Norton editor Steven Forman, who was my partner throughout the entire enterprise, cajoling, exhorting, encouraging and occasionally, in moments of greatest need, politely threatening. He not only read every fragment of draft at every stage, with bewildering speed and thoroughness, but worked on picture selection and captions, on the maps, on details of rights acquisition, and on every detail of placement and design. But Steven Forman also always acknowledged the help of those who helped him, as I too do here: Rachel Lee for locating and securing illustrations, Roberta Flechner for careful work on the art layout, Carol Flechner for tough copy editing, Wang Lianwu for help with correspondence and manuscript material in Chinese, David Lindroth for cartography of elegance and clarity, Antonina Krass and Hugh O'Neill for their impeccable design sense, and Roy Tedoff for efficiently producing the whole.

Help with art work and illustrations was graciously given by Caron Smith, Maxwell Hearn, and James C. Y. Watt at the Metropolitan Museum of Art in New York, by the collector Robert Ellsworth and the photographer Shin Hada, by Pan Gongkai of the Pan Tianshou Museum in Hangzhou, by Charles Moyer of the International Arts Council, and by Nancy Jervis of the China Institute. The painter Liang Minwei created all the calligraphy, in a wide variety of styles, for the title pages, jacket, and seal designs. The journalist Shi Zhimin provided his photographs, and Chin Annping helped with textual problems ranging from Confucian texts to 1989 street posters. Ruth Rogaski compiled the glossary with enormous care, while Cheng Peikai and Michael Lestz (who are compiling a companion volume of sources and documents) provided valuable materials. Herbert Behrstock of the United Nations Development Programme, Peking, and Leon Segal of the United Nations Programme of Actions for African Economic Recovery and Development, New York, both supplied helpful sources and information. Four typists of patience and grace coped with my often inscrutable drafts— Karin Weng, Elna Godburn, Ethel Himberg, and above all Florence Thomas, who, as she has done so often in the past, treated my recurrent crises as if they were her own.

The aid given by outside readers in reading draft sections of the manuscript was invaluable to me, and this book would have been immeasurably weaker without their criticisms and suggestions. Herewith my sincere thanks to Parks Coble (University of Nebraska), Jerry Dennerline (Amherst College), Joseph Esherick (University of Oregon), Michael Gasster (Rutgers University), Kent Guy (University of Washington), Philip Huang (UCLA), William Kirby (Washington University), Kenneth Lieberthal (University of Michigan), Andrew Nathan (Columbia University), Lucia Pierce (Freer Gallery of Art), Vera Schwarcz (Wesleyan University), John Bryan Starr (Yale University), Frederic Wakeman (University of California, Berkeley), and John Wills (University of Southern California). I am also grateful to some shrewd and careful outside readers who chose to retain their anonymity. But because these scholars only saw sections of the manuscript, and I did not always accept (and perhaps sometimes misinterpreted) their comments, I must underline that the faults or lacunae in the book remain mine. A number of other friends and former students generously read through the draft and offered me their thoughts: Beatrice Bartlett (and four of *her* students, Victoria Caplan, Patrick Cheng, Gabrielle Shek, and Anne Wyman), Sherman Cochran, Susan Naquin, Jonathan Ocko, Kenneth Pomeranz, and Joanna Waley-Cohen. In the broadest sense, I'm also indebted to all the scholars working in the field of modern Chinese history. I hope that the "Further Readings" will suggest how much I've gained from them and how much their work is transforming our knowledge of China's past.

This book was written, in just about equal parts, either in Yale's Cross Campus Library, or in Naples Pizza on Wall Street, New Haven. I would like to thank the entire staffs of those two admirable establishments for providing two complementary worlds in which to mull over, and then to pen, this record of the past four hundred years of China's history.

JDS
Naples and CCL
October 30, 1989

The Use of Pinyin

The pinyin system for romanizing Chinese has its origins in a system of romanization developed in Soviet east Asia in the early 1930s and employed later that decade in parts of China. With some modifications, pinyin itself was introduced by the Chinese in the 1950s. It is now the official romanization system in the People's Republic of China, has been adopted by the United Nations and other world agencies, and has become the system most commonly used in scholarship and journalism, largely supplanting the older Wade-Giles system. The pinyin system is pronounced as it looks, in most cases, the most important exceptions being the pinyin "c," pronounced like "ts," and the "q," which is pronounced like "ch." In some cases where the consonant break is unclear, an apostrophe is used to aid in pronunciation: hence the cities of Xi'an and Yan'an (to distinguish them from xian or ya-nan) or the name Hong Ren'gan (not reng-an).

The Search for Modern China uses pinyin romanization throughout, with some exceptions for place names and personal names that are long familiar in the West or difficult to recognize in pinyin. Thus Peking and Canton are retained in preference to Beijing and Guangzhou, and Chiang Kai-shek is used rather than Jiang Jieshi.

There follows a table of conversions between pinyin and Wade-Giles romanizations. The index to this book includes the Wade-Giles equivalents for all personal names entered there. Most personal names entered in the Glossary are followed by their pronunciations.

Pinyin	Wade-Giles	Pinyin	Wade-Giles	Pinyin	Wade-Giles	Pinyin	Wade-Giles
a	a	cong	ts'ung	gong	kung	kei	k'ei
ai	ai	cou	ts'ou	gou	kou	ken	k'en
an	an	cu	ts'u	gu	ku	keng	k'eng
ang	ang	cuan	ts'uan	gua	kua	kong	k'ung
ao	ao	cui	ts'ui	guai	kuai	kou	k'ou
		cun	ts'un	guan	kuan	ku	k'u
ba	pa	cuo	ts'o	guang	kuang	kua	k'ua
bai	pai			gui	kuei	kuai	k'uai
ban	pan	da	ta	gun	kun	kuan	k'uan
bang	pang	dai	tai	guo	kuo	kuang	k'uang
bao	pao	dan	tan			kui	k'uei
bei	pei	dang	tang	ha	ha	kun	k'un
ben	pen	dao	tao	hai	hai	kuo	k'uo
beng	peng	de	te	han	han		
bi	pi	deng	teng	hang	hang		
bian	pien	di	ti	hao	hao	la	la
biao	piao	dian	tien	he	ho	lai	lai
bie	pieh	diao	tiao	hei	hei	lan	lan
bin	pin	die	tieh	hen	hen	lang	lang
bing	ping	ding	ting	heng	heng	lao	lao
bo	po	diu	tiu	hong	hung	le	le
bou	pou	dong	tung	hou	hou	lei	lei
bu	pu	dou	tou	hu	hu	leng	leng
		du	tu	hua	hua	li	li
ca	ts'a	duan	tuan	huai	huai	lia	lia
cai	ts'ai	dui	tui	huan	huan	lian	lien
can	ts'an	dun	tun	huang	huang	liang	liang
cang	ts'ang	duo	to	hui	hui	liao	liao
cao	ts'ao			hun	hun	lie	lieh
ce	ts'e	e	o	huo	huo	lin	lin
cen	ts'en	en	en			ling	ling
ceng	ts'eng	er	erh	ji	chi	liu	liu
cha	ch'a			jia	chia	long	lung
chai	ch'ai	fa	fa	jian	chien	lou	lou
chan	ch'an	fan	fan	jiang	chiang	lu	lu
chang	ch'ang	fang	fang	jiao	chiao	lü	lü
chao	ch'ao	fei	fei	jie	chieh	luan	luan
che	ch'e	fen	fen	jin	chin	lüan	lüan
chen	ch'en	feng	feng	jing	ching	lüe	lüeh
cheng	ch'eng	fo	fo	jiong	chiung	lun	lun
chi	ch'ih	fou	fou	jiu	chiu	luo	lo
chong	ch'ung	fu	fu	ju	chü		
chou	ch'ou			juan	chüan	ma	ma
chu	ch'u	ga	ka	jue	chüeh	mai	mai
chua	ch'ua	gai	kai	jun	chün	man	man
chuai	ch'uai	gan	kan			mang	mang
chuan	ch'uan	gang	kang	ka	k'a	mao	mao
chuang	ch'uang	gao	kao	kai	k'ai	mei	mei
chui	ch'ui	ge	ko	kan	k'an	men	men
chun	ch'un	gei	kei	kang	k'ang	meng	meng
chuo	ch'o	gen	ken	kao	k'ao	mi	mi
ci	tz'u	geng	keng	ke	k'o	mian	mien

*From *People's Republic of China: Administrative Atlas* (Washington, D.C.: Central Intelligence Agency, 1975), pp. 46–47.

Pinyin	Wade-Giles	Pinyin	Wade-Giles	Pinyin	Wade-Giles	Pinyin	Wade-Giles
miao	miao	qi	ch'i	shuo	shuo	ya	ya
mie	mieh	qia	ch'ia	si	ssu	yai	yai
min	min	qian	ch'ien	song	sung	yan	yen
ming	ming	qiang	ch'iang	sou	sou	yang	yang
miu	miu	qiao	ch'iao	su	su	yao	yao
mo	mo	qie	ch'ieh	suan	suan	ye	yeh
mou	mou	qin	ch'in	sui	sui	yi	i
mu	mu	qing	ch'ing	sun	sun	yin	yin
		qiong	ch'iung	suo	so	ying	ying
		qiu	ch'iu			yong	yung
na	na	qu	ch'ü			you	yu
nai	nai	quan	ch'üan	ta	t'a	yu	yü
nan	nan	que	ch'üeh	tai	t'ai	yuan	yüan
nang	nang	qun	ch'ün	tan	t'an	yue	yüeh
nao	nao			tang	t'ang	yun	yün
nei	nei	ran	jan	tao	t'ao		
nen	nen	rang	jang	te	t'e		
neng	neng	rao	jao	teng	t'eng		
ni	ni	re	je	ti	t'i		
nian	nien	ren	jen	tian	t'ien	za	tsa
niang	niang	reng	jeng	tiao	t'iao	zai	tsai
niao	niao	ri	jih	tie	t'ieh	zan	tsan
nie	nieh	rong	jung	ting	t'ing	zang	tsang
nin	nin	rou	jou	tong	t'ung	zao	tsao
ning	ning	ru	ju	tou	t'ou	ze	tse
niu	niu	ruan	juan	tu	t'u	zei	tsei
nong	nung	rui	jui	tuan	t'uan	zen	tsen
nou	nou	run	jun	tui	t'ui	zeng	tseng
nu	nu	ruo	jo	tun	t'un	zha	cha
nü	nü			tuo	t'o	zhai	chai
nuan	nuan	sa	sa			zhan	chan
nüe	nüeh	sai	sai	wa	wa	zhang	chang
nuo	no	san	san	wai	wai	zhao	chao
		sang	sang	wan	wan	zhe	che
		sao	sao	wang	wang	zhen	chen
ou	ou	se	se	wei	wei	zheng	cheng
		sen	sen	wen	wen	zhi	chih
		seng	seng	weng	weng	zhong	chung
pa	p'a	sha	sha	wo	wo	zhou	chou
pai	p'ai	shai	shai	wu	wu	zhu	chu
pan	p'an	shan	shan			zhua	chua
pang	p'ang	shang	shang	xi	hsi	zhuai	chuai
pao	p'ao	shao	shao	xia	hsia	zhuan	chuan
pei	p'ei	she	she	xian	hsien	zhuang	chuang
pen	p'en	shen	shen	xiang	hsiang	zhui	chui
peng	p'eng	sheng	sheng	xiao	hsiao	zhun	chun
pi	p'i	shi	shih	xie	hsieh	zhuo	cho
pian	p'ien	shou	shou	xin	hsin	zi	tzu
piao	p'iao	shu	shu	xing	hsing	zong	tsung
pie	p'ieh	shua	shua	xiong	hsiung	zou	tsou
pin	p'in	shuai	shuai	xiu	hsiu	zu	tsu
ping	p'ing	shuan	shuan	xu	hsü	zuan	tsuan
po	p'o	shuang	shuang	xuan	hsüan	zui	tsui
pou	p'ou	shui	shui	xue	hsüeh	zun	tsun
pu	p'u	shun	shun	xun	hsün	zuo	tso

I | CONQUEST AND CONSOLIDATION

IN THE LATE sixteenth century the Ming dynasty seemed at the height of its glory. Its achievements in culture and the arts were remarkable, urban and commercial life were spreading new levels of prosperity, while Chinese skills in printing and the manufacture of porcelain and silk exceeded anything that could be found in Europe at the time. But even though it is commonplace to see this period as marking the birth of "modern Europe," it is less easy to see it as the obvious starting point of a modern China. For while the West was at this time the hub of global explorations that brought it extensive knowledge of the world as a whole, the Ming rulers not only had drawn back from overseas ventures and the knowledge that might have come from them, but had begun a pattern of self-defeating behavior that within fifty years brought their dynasty to a violent end.

The loosely woven fabric of late Ming China's state and economy began to unravel at many points. Falling tax revenues led to failures to pay the army promptly. Troop desertions encouraged border penetration by hostile tribes. A flow of silver from the West brought unexpected stresses in the Chinese economy. Poor state granary supervision and harsh weather conditions led to undernourishment and a susceptibility to pestilence among rural populations. Random gangs of the disaffected coalesced into armies whose only ideology was survival. By 1644 all of these elements combined in such a virulent fashion that the last Ming emperor committed suicide.

Those who brought order out of this chaos were neither peasant rebels nor estranged scholar-officials, but Jürchen tribesmen from across China's northern frontiers who called themselves Manchus. Their victory was based on their success in forming a system of military and administrative units and the nucleus of a bureaucracy long before they were ready to conquer China. With these institutions in place, and with large numbers of surrendered or captured Chinese serving these tribesmen as political advisers, soldiers, craftsmen, and farmers, the Manchus were ready to seize the opportunity to invade China when it came in 1644.

The movement of these hundreds of thousands of troops across China can serve to introduce us, as it introduced the Manchus, to the broad features of China's geography. China's indigenous peasant rebels and the various Ming survivors chose different areas of the country as the bases for their attempted resistance to the Manchu sweep. The patterns of Manchu advance from north to south and from east to west followed the logic of the terrain and the need to incorporate areas of critical political and economic importance firmly into the structures of the new state. (Both the timing and direction of the Manchu advance were startlingly echoed by the Communists when they united China in 1949, after the country's long period of fragmentation in the twentieth century.)

The conquest of as vast a country as China could be achieved only by incorporating millions of Chinese supporters into the Manchu ranks, and by relying on Chinese administrators to rule in the Manchus' name. While some descendants of the Ming ruling house fought on with tenacity, most Chinese accepted the new rulers because the Manchus promised—with only a few exceptions—to uphold China's traditional beliefs and social structures. If the Manchu conquest had ever opened the possibility for social upheaval, it was soon over, and the Manchus' newly founded Qing dynasty, firmly entrenched, was destined to rule China until 1912.

Consolidation of the Chinese state required—for the Qing as for their predecessors and successors—that attention be devoted to a wide range of strategic, economic, and political necessities. The main architect of the Qing consolidation was Emperor Kangxi, who reigned from 1661 to 1722. Moving in measured sequence to fortify China's southern, eastern, northern, and northwestern borders, he also strengthened the institutions of rule that his Manchu forebears had tentatively designed before the conquest. Kangxi concentrated especially on restoring an effective national examination system, improving the flow of state information through reliable and secret communications channels, attracting the support of potentially dissident scholars through state-sponsored projects, and easing the latent tensions between Manchus and ethnic Chinese in both government posts and society at large. In the economic realm he was less successful. Although commerce and agriculture both flourished during his reign, they were not adequately taxed, a failure that became a permanent flaw of the dynasty.

Kangxi's son struggled intelligently with aspects of this legacy, and paid particular attention to reform of the tax system, the organization of cultural life, the elimination of certain social inequalities, and the strengthening of the central bureaucracy. But as China's population rose dramatically in the later eighteenth century and new pressures on the land brought serious social disturbances, morale at the center began to crack. Inefficiency and corruption impaired the responses of the state, which evaded rather than confronted these domestic problems. In the realm of foreign policy as well, China's established institutions for handling foreigners began to suffer new challenges as aggressive Western merchants sailed their vessels to China's shores and tested the restrictions China imposed on them. Here too the Qing state's response was sluggish and largely ineffective; its inability to adapt creatively in this as in other areas laid the groundwork for the catastrophic events of the nineteenth century. Western writers and political philosophers of the eighteenth century, who for a time had been caught in a cycle of admiration for China, began to study China's weaknesses with a sharper eye, arguing that if the Chinese could not adapt to living in the world, there was a real chance that their country would be destroyed.

CHAPTER 1

The Late Ming

THE GLORY OF THE MING

In the year A.D. 1600, the empire of China was the largest and most sophisticated of all the unified realms on earth. The extent of its territorial domains was unparalleled at a time when Russia was only just beginning to coalesce as a country, India was fragmented between Mughal and Hindu rulers, and a grim combination of infectious disease and Spanish conquerors had laid low the once great empires of Mexico and Peru. And China's population of some 120 million was far larger than that of all the European countries combined.

There was certainly pomp and stately ritual in capitals from Kyoto to Prague, from Delhi to Paris, but none of these cities could boast of a palace complex like that in Peking, where, nestled behind immense walls, the gleaming yellow roofs and spacious marble courts of the Forbidden City symbolized the majesty of the Chinese emperor. Laid out in a meticulous geometrical order, the grand stairways and mighty doors of each successive palace building and throne hall were precisely aligned with the arches leading out of Peking to the south, speaking to all comers of the connectedness of things personified in this man the Chinese termed the Son of Heaven.

Rulers in Europe, India, Japan, Russia, and the Ottoman Empire were all struggling to develop systematic bureaucracies that would expand their tax base and manage their swelling territories effectively, as well as draw to new royal power centers the resources of agriculture and trade. But China's massive bureaucracy was already firmly in place, harmonized by a millennium of tradition and bonded by an immense body of statutory laws and provisions that, in theory at least, could offer pertinent advice on any problem that might arise in the daily life of China's people.

One segment of this bureaucracy lived in Peking, serving the emperor in an elaborate hierarchy that divided the country's business among six ministries dealing respectively with finance and personnel, rituals and laws, military affairs and public works. Also in Peking were the senior scholars and academicians who advised the emperor on ritual matters, wrote the official histories, and supervised the education of the imperial children. This concourse of official functionaries worked in uneasy proximity with the enormous palace staff who attended to the emperor's more personal needs: the court women and their eunuch watchmen, the imperial children and their nurses, the elite bodyguards, the banquet-hall and kitchen staffs, the grooms, the sweepers and the water carriers.

The other segment of the Chinese bureaucracy consisted of those assigned to posts in the fifteen major provinces into which China was divided during the Ming dynasty. These posts also were arranged in elaborate hierarchies, running from the provincial governor at the top, down through the prefects in major cities to the magistrates in the counties. Below the magistrates were the police, couriers, militiamen, and tax gatherers who extracted a regular flow of revenue from China's farmers. A group of officials known as censors kept watch over the integrity of the bureaucracy both in Peking and in the provinces.

The towns and cities of China did not, in most cases, display the imposing solidity in stone and brick of the larger urban centers in post-Renaissance Europe. Nor, with the exception of a few famous pagodas, were Chinese skylines pierced by towers as soaring as those of the greatest Christian cathedrals or the minarets of Muslim cities. But this low architectural profile did not signify an absence of wealth or religion. There were many prosperous Buddhist temples in China, just as there were Daoist temples dedicated to the natural forces of the cosmos, ancestral meeting halls, and shrines to Confucius, the founding father of China's ethical system who had lived in the fifth century B.C. A scattering of mosques dotted some eastern cities and the far western areas, where most of China's Muslims lived. There were also some synagogues, where descendants of early Jewish travelers still congregated, and dispersed small groups with hazy memories of the teachings of Nestorian Christianity, which had reached China a millennium earlier. The lesser grandeur of China's city architecture and religious centers represented not any absence of civic pride or disesteem of religion, but rather a political fact: the Chinese state was more effectively centralized than those elsewhere in the world; its religions were more effectively controlled; and the growth of powerful, independent cities was prevented by a watchful government that would not tolerate rival centers of authority.

With hindsight we can see that the Ming dynasty, whose emperors had ruled China since 1368, was past its political peak by the early seventeenth century; yet in the years around 1600, China's cultural life was in an ebullient condition that few, if any, other countries could match. If one points to the figures of exceptional brilliance or insight in late sixteenth-century European society, one will easily find their near equivalents in genius and imagination working away in China at just the same time. There was no Chinese dramatist with quite the range of Shakespeare, but in the 1590s Tang Xianzu was writing plays of thwarted, youthful love, of family drama and social dissonance, that were every bit as rich and complex as *A Midsummer Night's Dream* or *Romeo and Juliet*. And if there was no precise equal to Miguel de Cervantes, whose *Don Quixote* was to become a central work of Western culture, it was in the 1590s that China's most beloved novel of religious quest and picaresque adventure, *The Journey to the West*, was published. This novel's central hero, a mischievous monkey with human traits who accompanies the monk-hero on his action-filled travels to India in search of Buddhist scriptures, has remained a central part of Chinese folk culture to this day. Without pushing further for near parallels, within this same period in China, essayists, philosophers, nature poets, landscape painters, religious theorists, historians, and medical scholars all produced a profusion of significant works, many of which are now regarded as classics of the civilization.

Perhaps in all this outpouring, it is the works of the short-story writers and the popular novelists that make the most important commentary about the vitality of Ming society, for they point to a new readership in the towns, to new levels of literacy, and to a new focus on the details of daily life. In a society that was largely male-dominated, they also indicate a growing audience of literate women. The larger implications of expanding female literacy in China were suggested in the writings of late Ming social theorists, who argued that educating women would enhance the general life of society by bringing improvements in morals, child rearing, and household management. Other critics countered that too much independence for women was harmful, and threatened to corrode the good order of society and the family.

These many themes run together in another of China's greatest novels, *Golden Lotus*, which was published anonymously in the early 1600s. In this socially elaborate and sexually explicit tale, the central character (who draws his income both from commerce and from his official connections) is analyzed through his relationships with his five consorts, each of whom speaks for a different facet of human nature. In many senses, *Golden Lotus* can be read as allegory, as a moral fable of the way greed and selfishness destroy those with the richest opportunities for happiness; yet it also has a deeply realistic side, and illuminates the tensions and cruelties within elite Chinese family life as few other works have ever done.

Novels, paintings, plays, along with the imperial compendia on court life and bureaucratic practice, all suggest the splendors—for the wealthy—of China in the late Ming. Living mainly in the larger commercial towns rather than out in the countryside, the wealthy were bonded together in elaborate clan or lineage organizations based on family descent through the male line. These lineages often held large amounts of land that provided income for support of their own schools, charity to those fallen on hard times, and the maintenance of ancestral halls in which family members offered sacrifices to the dead. The spacious compounds of the rich, protected by massive gates and high walls, often contained large and elaborate gardens, which not only served decorative and recreational functions, but also produced fruit, food, and flowers for the owners and their families. The homes of the wealthy were filled with the products of Chinese artisans, who were sometimes employed in state-directed manufactories but more often grouped in small, guild-controlled workshops. Embroidered silks that brought luster to the female form were always in demand by the rich, along with the exquisite blue and white porcelain that graced the elaborate dinner parties so beloved at the time. Glimmering lacquer, ornamental jade, feathery latticework, delicate ivory, cloisonné, and shining rosewood furniture made the homes of the rich places of beauty. And the elaborately carved brush holders of wood or stone, the luxurious paper, even the ink sticks and the stones on which they were rubbed and mixed with water to produce the best and blackest ink, all combined to make of every scholar's desk a ritual and an aesthetic world before he had even written a word. In the late years of the Ming, an elaborate system of connoisseurship had grown around such objects, and the newly rich sought out prestigious art dealers to help them stock their homes in a fitting manner. Not surprisingly, this generated an underground system of faking and false attributions, to confound the unwary.

Complementing the domestic decor, the food and drink of these wealthier Chinese would be a constant delight: pungent shrimp and bean curd, crisp duck and water chestnuts, sweetmeats, clear teas, smooth alcohol of grain or grape, fresh and preserved fruits and juices—all of these followed in stately sequence at parties during which literature, religion, and poetry were discussed over the courses. After the meal, as wine continued to flow, prize scroll paintings might be produced from the family collection, and new works of art, seeking to capture the essence of some old master, would be created by the skimming brushes of the inebriated guests.

At its upper social and economic levels, this was a highly educated society, held together intellectually by a common group of texts that reached back before the time of Confucius to the early days of the unification of a northern Chinese state in the second millennium B.C. While theorists debated its merits for women, education was rigorous and protracted for the boys of wealthy families, introducing them to the rhythms of classical Chinese around the age of six. They then kept at their studies in school or with private tutors every day, memorizing, translating, drilling until, in their late twenties or early thirties, they might be ready to tackle the state examinations. Success in these examinations, which rose in a hierarchy of difficulty from those held locally to those conducted in the capital of Peking, allegedly under the supervision of the emperor himself, brought access to lucrative bureaucratic office and immense social prestige. Women were barred by law from taking the state examinations; but those of good family often learned to write classical poetry from their parents or brothers, and courtesans in the city pleasure quarters were frequently well trained in poetry and song, skills that heightened their charms in the eyes of their educated male patrons. Women from elite families could also choose private female tutors, and engage in a varied intellectual life with other women through correspondence, the exchange of poems, and social visits—often across great distances. Since book printing with wooden blocks had been developing in China since the tenth century, the maintenance of extensive private libraries was feasible, and the wide distribution of works of philosophy, poetry, history, and moral exhortation was taken for granted.

Though frowned on by some purists, the dissemination of popular works of entertainment was also accelerating in the late sixteenth century, making for a rich and elaborate cultural mix. City dwellers could call on new images of tamed nature to contrast with their own noise and bustle, and find a sense of order in works of art that interpreted the world for them. The possibilities for this sense of contentment were caught to perfection by the dramatist Tang Xianzu in his play *The Peony Pavilion* of 1598. Tang puts his words into the mouth of a scholar and provincial bureaucrat named Du Bao. One side of Du Bao's happiness comes from the fact that administrative business is running smoothly:

> The mountains are at their loveliest
> and court cases dwindle,
> "The birds I saw off at dawn,
> at dusk I watch return,"
> petals from the vase cover my seal box,
> the curtains hang undisturbed.

This sense of peace and order, in turn, prompts a more direct response to nature, when official duties can be put aside altogether, the literary overlays forgotten, and nature and the simple pleasures enjoyed on their own terms:

> Pink of almond fully open,
> iris blades unsheathed,
> fields of spring warming to season's life.
> Over thatched hut by bamboo fence juts a tavern flag,
> rain clears, and the smoke spirals from kitchen stoves.[1]

It was a fine vision, and for many these were indeed glorious days. As long as the country's borders remained quiet, as long as the bureaucracy worked smoothly, as long as the peasants who did the hard work in the fields and the artisans who made all the beautiful objects remained content with their lot—then perhaps the splendors of the Ming would endure.

TOWN AND FARM

The towns and cities of Ming China, especially in the more heavily populated eastern part of the country, had a bustling and thriving air. Some were busy bureaucratic centers, where the local provincial officials had their offices and carried out their tax gathering and administrative tasks. Others were purely commercial centers, where trade and local markets dictated the patterns of daily life. Most were walled, closed their gates at night, and imposed some form of curfew.

As with towns and cities elsewhere in the world, those in China could be distinguished by their services and their levels of specialization. Local market towns, for instance, were the bases for coffinmakers, ironworkers, tailors, and noodle makers. Their retail shops offered for sale such semispecial goods as tools, wine, headgear, and religious supplies, including incense, candles, and special paper money to burn at sacrifices. Such market towns also offered winehouses for customers to relax in. Larger market towns, which drew on a flow of traders and wealthy purchasers from a wider region, could support cloth-dyeing establishments, shoemakers, iron foundries, firecracker makers, and sellers of bamboo, fine cloth, and teas. Travelers here found bathhouses and inns, and could buy the services of local prostitutes. Rising up the hierarchy to the local cities that coordinated the trade of several regional market towns, there were shops selling expensive stationery, leather goods, ornamental lanterns, altar carvings, flour, and the services of tinsmiths, seal cutters, and lacquer-ware sellers. Here, too, visitors could find pawnshops and local "banks" to handle money exchanges, rent a sedan chair, and visit a comfortably appointed brothel.[2] As the cities grew larger and their clientele richer, one found ever more specialized luxury goods and services, along with the kinds of ambience in which wealth edged—sometimes dramatically, sometimes unobtrusively—into the realms of decadence, snobbery, and exploitation.

At the base of the urban hierarchy, below the market towns, there were the small local townships where the population was too poor and scattered to support many shops and artisans, and where most goods were sold only by traveling peddlers at periodic markets. Such townships housed neither the wealthy nor any government officials; as a result, the simplest of tea-houses, or perhaps a roadside stall, or an occasional temple fair would be the sole focus for relaxation. Nevertheless, such smaller townships performed a vast array of important functions, for they served as the bases for news and gossip, matchmaking, simple schooling, local religious festivals, traveling theater groups, tax collection, and the distribution of famine relief in times of emergency.

Just as the towns and cities of Ming China represented a whole spectrum of goods and services, architecture, levels of sophistication, and administrative staffing, making any simple generalization about them risky, so, too, was the countryside apparently endless in its variety. Indeed the distinction between town and country was blurred in China, for suburban areas of intensive farming lay just outside and sometimes even within the city walls, and artisans might work on farms in peak periods, or farmers work temporarily in towns during times of dearth.

It was south of the Huai River, which cuts across China between the Yellow River and the Yangzi, that the country was most prosperous, for here climate and soil combined to make intensive rice cultivation possible. The region was crisscrossed by myriad rivers, canals, and irrigation streams that fed lush market gardens and paddies in which the young rice shoots grew, or flowed into lakes and ponds where fish and ducks were raised. Here the seasonal flooding of the paddy fields returned needed nutrients to the soil. In the regions just south of the Yangzi River, farmers cultivated mulberry trees for the leaves on which silk worms fed, as well as tea bushes and a host of other products that created extra resources and allowed for a richly diversified rural economy. Farther to the south, sugarcane and citrus were added to the basic crops; and in the mountainous southwest, forests of bamboo and valuable hardwood lumber brought in extra revenue. Water transport was fast, easy, and cheap in south China. Its villages boasted strong lineage organizations that helped to bond communities together.

Although there were many prosperous farming villages north of the Huai

River, life there was harsher. The cold in winter was extreme, as icy winds blew in from Mongolia, eroding the land, filling the rivers with silt, and swirling fine dust into the eyes and noses of those who could not afford to shelter behind closed doors. The main crops were wheat and millet, grown with much toil on overworked land, which the scattered farming communities painstakingly fertilized with every scrap of human and animal waste they could recycle. Fruit trees such as apple and pear grew well, as did soybeans and cotton; but by the end of the sixteenth century, much of the land was deforested, and the Yellow River was an unpredictable force as its silt-laden waters meandered across the wide plains to the sea. Unhindered by the dikes, paddies, and canals of the South, bandit armies could move men and equipment easily across the northern countryside, while cavalry forces could race ahead and to the flanks, returning to warn the slower foot soldiers of any danger from opposing forces or sorties from garrison towns. Lineage organizations were weaker here, villages more isolated, social life often more fragmented, and the tough-minded owner-cultivator, living not far above subsistence level, more common than either the prosperous landlord or the tenant farmer.

China's rural diversity meant that "landlords" could not be entirely distinguished from "peasants." For every wealthy absentee landlord living in one of the larger towns, for example, there might be scores of smaller-scale local landlords living in the countryside, perhaps renting out some of their land or hiring part-time labor to till it. Similarly, there were millions of peasant proprietors who owned a little more land than they needed for subsistence, and they might farm their own land with the help of some seasonal laborers. Others, owning a little *less* land than they needed for subsistence, might rent an extra fraction of an acre or hire themselves out as casual labor in the busy seasons. And in most peasant homes, there was some form of handicraft industry that connected the rural family to a commercial network.

The social structure was further complicated by the bewildering variety of land-sale agreements and rental contracts used in China. While the state sought extra revenue by levying a tax on each land deal, in return for which it granted an official contract with a red seal, many farmers—not surprisingly—tried to avoid these surcharges by drawing up their own unofficial contracts. The definition of a land sale, furthermore, was profoundly ambiguous. Most land sales were conducted on the general understanding that the seller might at some later date reclaim the land from the buyer at the original purchase price, or that the seller retained "subsurface" rights to the soil while the purchaser could till the land for a specified period. If land rose in price, went out of cultivation, became waterlogged, or was built upon, a maze of legal and financial problems resulted, leading often to family feuds and even to murder.

For centuries, whether in the north or the south, the peasantry of China had shown their ability to work hard and to survive even when sudden natural calamities brought extreme deprivation. In times of drought or flood, there were various forms of mutual aid, loans, or relief grain supplies that could help to tide them and their families over. Perhaps some sort of part-time labor could be secured, as a porter, an irrigation worker, or barge puller. Children could be indentured, on short-or long-term contracts, for domestic service with the rich. Female children could be sold in the cities; and even if they ended up in brothels, at least they were alive and the family freed of an extra mouth to feed. But if, on top of all the other hardships, the whole fabric of law and order within the society began to unravel, then the situation became hopeless indeed. If the market towns closed their gates, if bands of desperate men began to roam the countryside, seizing the few stores that the rural families had laid in against the coming winter's cold, or stealing the last seed grain carefully hoarded for the next spring's plant-ing, then the poor farmers had no choice but to abandon their fields—whether the land was rented or privately owned—and to swell the armies of the homeless marchers.

In the early 1600s, despite the apparent prosperity of the wealthier elite, there were signs that this dangerous unraveling might be at hand. Without state-sponsored work or relief for their own needy inhabitants, then the very towns that barred their gates to the rural poor might erupt from within. Driven to desperation by high taxes and uncertain labor prospects, thousands of silk weavers in the Yangzi delta city of Suzhou went on strike in 1601, burnt down houses, and lynched hated local tyrants. That same year, south-west of Suzhou, in the Jiangxi province porcelain-manufacturing city of Jingdezhen, thousands of workers rioted over low wages and the Ming court's demand that they meet heightened production quotas of the exquisite "dragon bowls" made for palace use. One potter threw himself into a blazing kiln and perished to underline his fellows' plight. A score of other cities and towns saw some kind of social and economic protest in the same period.

Instability in the urban world was matched by that in the countryside. There were incidents of rural protest in the late Ming, as in earlier periods, that can be seen as having elements of class struggle inherent in them. These incidents, often accompanied by violence, were of two main kinds: protests by indentured laborers or "bondservants" against their masters in attempts to regain their free status as farmers, and strikes by tenants who refused to pay their landlords what they regarded as unjust rents.

Even if they were not common, there were enough such incidents to offer a serious warning to the wealthier Chinese. In that same play, *The Peony Pavilion*, in which he speaks glowingly of the joys of the official's life, Tang Xianzu gently mocks the rustic yokels of China, putting into deliberately inelegant verse the rough-and-ready labor of their days:

> Slippery mud,
> sloppery thud,
> short rake, long plough, clutch 'em as they slide.
> After rainy night sow rice and hemp,
> when sky clears fetch out the muck,
> then a stink like long-pickled fish
> floats on the breeze.[3]

The verses sounded amusing. But Tang's audience had not yet begun to think through the implications of what might happen when those who labored under such conditions sought to overthrow their masters.

CORRUPTION AND HARDSHIP

In the midst of the rich cultural and economic life of the late Ming, therefore, there were dangerous hints of weakness in the social structure. Part of the trouble sprang from the very center of the state. The emperor Wanli, who reigned across the long span from 1572 to 1620, had started out as a conscientious young ruler, guided by intelligent and experienced advisers. But from the 1580s onward, Emperor Wanli spent more and more time behind the innermost walls of the Forbidden City. He had grown aggravated by quarrels with bureaucrats about which of his sons should be named heir apparent to the throne, frustrated by overprotective courtiers from carrying out his desires to travel widely and command his troops in person, and disgusted by the constant bickering among his own senior advisers. For years on end he held no court audiences to discuss key political events, gave up his studies of the historical and philosophical texts that lay at the heart of Confucian learning, refused to read state papers, and even stopped filling the vacancies that occurred in the upper levels of officialdom.

The result was that considerable power accrued to the court eunuchs— the castrated male attendants whose official job was to supervise the management of day-to-day business in the palace. The practice of using eunuchs in Chinese courts had existed for more than two thousand years, but Ming rulers employed many more than their predecessors, and by Wanli's time there were over ten thousand in the capital. Since the emperor would not come out from the inner recesses of the Forbidden City—an area closed to all save the imperial family and their personal attendants—the eunuchs became crucial intermediaries between the outer bureaucratic world and the inner imperial one. Any senior official with business that demanded the emperor's attention had to persuade a eunuch to carry the message for him; the eunuchs, naturally enough, asked for fees in return for such service, and soon the more powerful ones were flattered and bribed by ambitious officials.

In the 1590s, the eunuchs, many of whom were identified with certain court factions, began to play a central role in the political life of the country. Their influence grew as Emperor Wanli assigned them to collect revenues in the provinces. In many cases they acted in a high-handed way, tyrannizing wealthy provincial families, and using an elite group of military guards to enforce their will and to imprison—even torture or kill—their political enemies. The most spectacular example of these abuses occurred in the person of the eunuch Wei Zhongxian, who cleverly rose to power by obtaining a position as purveyor of food to the concubine of Emperor Wanli's son, and later, in the 1620s, dominated the court life of Wanli's grandson. At the peak of his influence, Wei was able to publish historical works belittling his bureaucratic enemies, and to order that temples in his honor be erected all across China.

Although it was always dangerous to criticize the emperor and his favorites, certain officials and prominent scholars were deeply disturbed by the situation. As scholars will, they sought a theoretical cause for the trouble: many of them concluded that the corruption sprang from a breakdown of the general ethical standards, from flaws in the educational system, and from the growth of an unbridled individualism. The villain, to many of these critics, was the earlier Ming philosopher Wang Yangming, who had argued in his writings that the keys to ethical understanding lay in our own moral nature and, hence, that any person had the power, through innate knowledge, to understand the meaning of existence. As Wang expressed this in a letter to a friend:

> Innate knowledge is identical with the Way. That it is present in the mind is true not only in the cases of the sages and worthies, but even in that of ordinary people. When one is free from the driving force and observations of material desires, and just follows innate knowledge and leaves it to continue to function and operate, everything will be in accord with the Way.[4]

"To learn," Wang added, "simply means to learn to follow innate knowledge." But Wang also advocated a creative blending of knowledge with action, and, in the teachings and practice of some of his more extreme followers, Wang's doctrine led to eccentric behavior, the rejection of normative forms of education, and the call for a new egalitarianism.

To combat these trends, certain late sixteenth-century scholars who held a rigorously moral view of the significance of Confucian thought began to gather in philosophical societies. Here they prepared for the state examinations and heard lectures on ethics; from ethics, their debates inevitably spread to politics; and political debate, in turn, began to generate a desire for political reform. By 1611, the most famous of these societies—founded in 1604 and known as the "Donglin Society"—had become a major force in politics. Donglin partisans used all their influence to have corrupt officials removed from their Peking posts. Their status rose enormously after Emperor Wanli's death in 1620, when many of them were called to serve in the bureaucracy under Wanli's son and grandson. Their task was to put their moral premises into practice and to strengthen China's frontier defense and internal economy. But their constant moral exhortations wearied the new emperor: after a Donglin leader criticized the most notorious of the eunuchs, Wei Zhongxian, and Wei had a senior official at court beaten to death in retaliation, the emperor did not censure Wei.

Emboldened by the emperor's tacit acquiescence, between 1624 and 1627 Wei and a group of court officials led a concerted campaign of terror against the Donglin members, many of whom were killed or driven to suicide. Although Wei himself was eventually condemned, and took his own life in 1627, the damage to the state's prestige had been severe, and was perhaps irreparable. As one of the Donglin leaders—having heard that mounted guards from the eunuch's inner circle had come to arrest him, and knowing that this could only mean his death—wrote in a farewell letter to his friends: "I formerly was a great minister, and when a great minister accepts disgrace the state is also disgraced."[5]

All this intellectual and political ferment exacerbated an already dangerous situation in the fields of foreign policy and the economy. China had faced a number of threats during the sixteenth century, most prominently from the nomadic tribes of Mongols who raised their horses and flocks of sheep on the steppes to the north and northwest of Peking, and from pirates on the southeast coast. Mongol forces, which earlier in the dynasty had been controlled through trade and diplomacy, now raided China regularly. On one occasion they captured a Ming emperor campaigning against them, and on another they rode almost to the gates of Peking. By the late sixteenth century, despite imperial attempts to strengthen the Great Wall and its military garrisons, the Chinese managed to hold the Mongol raiders in check only by paying them regular subsidies. On the southeast coast, Chinese cities were ravaged by pirate groups, sometimes numbering in the hundreds and including a great many Japanese as well as Chinese fugitives, and even black slaves who had escaped from the Portuguese outpost at Macao. These pirate groups looted almost at will, seizing men and women for ransom.

Although the worst of these pirate attacks had been stopped by the 1570s, Japanese military power grew stronger, and in the 1590s a major Japanese army invaded Korea. Fighting was heavy; and since the Ming regarded Korea as a loyal and dependent ally to be protected at all costs, Chinese troops were sent in force to help the hard-pressed Koreans. The war might have continued, at terrible cost to all three countries, had not domestic turmoil in Japan, coupled with effective disruption of Japanese supply lines by the Korean navy, led to the recall of Japanese troops from Korea in 1598.

Macao also represented a new kind of problem for China. This town, on the tip of a peninsula to the southwest of Canton, had been occupied by the Portuguese with China's tacit consent in the 1550s. By the 1600s, following the emperor's ban of direct trade by Chinese merchants with belligerent Japan, the Portuguese had moved into the resulting commercial vacuum as middlemen. They made fortunes by buying up Chinese silk in local markets and shipping it to Japan, where they traded it for silver from Japanese mines.

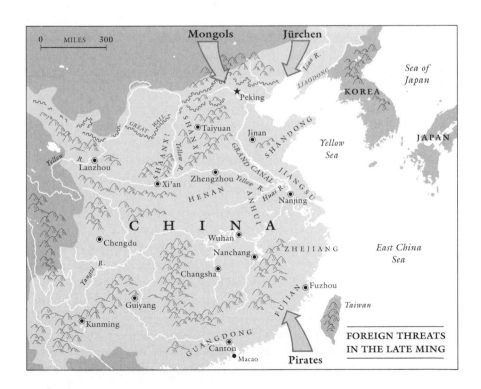

FOREIGN THREATS IN THE LATE MING

With this silver, which was valued more highly in China than in Japan, the Portuguese returned and bought larger stocks of Chinese silk. The steady flow of silver brought by the Portuguese into China was itself just one element in the larger pattern of silver shipments that brought major economic effects to all parts of the world in the sixteenth century.

At the heart of this global network lay the fantastic silver riches of the mines in Mexico and Peru, which were being exploited under royal license by the Spanish conquerors of those territories. Silver from the Americas began to reach China in the 1570s, when Spain established a new base at Manila in the Philippines. Eager to profit from this new silver supply, thousands of Chinese traders began to congregate in Manila, selling cloth and silk in bulk and speeding the flow of specie back to their homeland. As silver circulated more widely, commercial activity spread, more and more Westerners joined in the profitable trade with China, and the silver-bullion deposits available to Emperor Wanli grew impressively. At the same time, however, the massive influx of silver to China brought not only new wealth to Chinese merchants but also a range of problems that included inflation and an erratic economic growth in certain cities that disrupted traditional economic patterns. Late Ming attempts at currency stabilization were not successful.

Thus, before Wanli's reign ended with his death in 1620, China was beginning a complicated economic slide. The thriving world of the Ming merchants, which had led to the efficient distribution of luxury goods on a countrywide basis and had spawned an effective proto-banking system based on notes of exchange, suffered from the military troubles of the times. And China's trade—while never effectively taxed by the state, which concentrated mainly on the agricultural sector—was extremely vulnerable to extortion and confiscation by corrupt eunuch commissioners in the provinces, or by their agents. Government inefficiencies in flood control and famine relief led to further local crises, which, in turn, reduced the amount of prosperous land that could be taxed effectively.

During the last years of Emperor Wanli's reign and under his successors, the situation for China's peasants grew critical. International trade patterns changed as raiders from the Protestant Dutch and British nations sought to expand their own trading empires by wrecking those of the Catholic Spaniards and Portuguese. This led to a drop in silver imports into China, which encouraged hoarding and forced the ratio of copper to silver into a decline. A string of one thousand small copper coins that had been worth around an ounce of silver in the 1630s had become worth half an ounce by 1640, and perhaps one-third of an ounce by 1643. The effect on peasants was disastrous, since they had to pay their taxes *in silver,* even though they conducted local trade and sold their own harvests for copper.[6]

Famines became common, especially in north China, worsened by unusually cold and dry weather that shortened the growing season for crops by as much as two weeks. (Sometimes termed the "little ice age" of the seventeenth century, similar effects were felt in farming areas around the world during this period.) When these natural disasters and tax increases are set alongside the constant strains of military recruitment and desertions, a declining relief system for the indigent, and the abandonment of virtually all major irrigation and flood-control projects, the pressures on the country and the tensions they began to engender can be well imagined. And as rapidly became apparent, neither the court nor the bureaucracy in Peking or the countryside seemed to have the ability, the resources, or the will to do very much about it.

THE MING COLLAPSE

In the early decades of the seventeenth century, the Ming court slowly lost control of its rural bureaucracy and, as a result, of its tax structure. Pressed at the same time for more money to pay and supply the troops needed to counter the attacks of the Jürchen tribesmen who were growing in power and seizing great areas of land in Manchuria, the court both increased extra levies on those populated areas that it still controlled and laid off many employees in the northwest, where the danger to the state seemed less pressing. One of those laid off in this economy move was a post-station attendant from a rural family named Li Zicheng.

Li had worked previously in a wine shop and as an ironworker's apprentice, and was typical of a number of rootless, violent men who lived in Shaanxi province at the time. Shaanxi, a barren province of northwest China, covered the area within the great bend of the Yellow River and ran through bleak mountain countryside up to the Great Wall. About as far from Peking as Chicago is from Washington, D.C., but ringed by mountains and difficult of access, Shaanxi province had in the past proved a natural bastion where groups of rebels had built up their forces prior to breaking out and attacking the richer and more populated lands to the east and the south.

In 1630 Li Zicheng enrolled in a military unit in western Shaanxi, but once again the government let him down. Deprived of promised supplies, Li and other soldiers mutinied, and over the next few years Li slowly emerged as a natural leader among a group of uprooted men that numbered in the thousands, proving himself an intuitively skillful tactician. In 1634 Li was captured near the southern Shaanxi border by a capable Ming general, who bottled up the rebel forces in a mountain gorge. Li was released after promising that he would take his troops back into the barren northern part of the province, but the agreement fell apart after a local magistrate executed thirty-six of the surrendered rebels. Li and his men retaliated by killing the local officials and taking once more to the hills. By 1635 he was stronger than ever, and was a leading representative at an extraordinary conclave of rebel leaders that took place at the town of Rongyang in central Henan province, just south of the Yellow River.

At this conclave, some of the most powerful rebel leaders assigned different regions of north China to their armies and tried to coordinate an attack on the Ming capital of Peking. But coordinated military activity proved difficult with such motley and undisciplined forces. By the end of the year the alliance was breaking apart, though not before the rebels had captured and looted some of the imperial Ming burial grounds outside the capital and imprisoned the attendants who worked there. The emperor now on the throne, Wanli's grandson Chongzhen, responded by donning mourning, apologizing to his ancestors in special temple ceremonies, arresting several of his commanding officers, and executing the eunuch guardian of the royal tombs. For his part, in a bitter quarrel that showed how swiftly violence flared and how easily the rebel alliance could fragment, Li Zicheng demanded of his fellow rebels that he be given the captured eunuch musicians whose job had been to play ritual music at the tombs. The rebel leader who held the musicians, Zhang Xianzhong, reluctantly complied, but smashed all their instruments first. Li then killed the unfortunate musicians.

Over the next few years, the armies of these two leaders, Li and Zhang, roamed over much of northern and central China, shifting from base to base, occasionally cooperating with each other but more often feuding as they competed with both the Ming and other rebel bands for terrain and followers. By the early 1640s, each had seized a base area for himself: Zhang Xianzhong, who like Li had once served in the Ming forces in Shaanxi before deserting, was in the city of Chengdu in the prosperous heartland of Sichuan province, deep inland along the Yangzi River; Li was established in Hubei, but his jurisdiction included most of Shaanxi and Henan provinces as well.

The ravages caused by the armies of Li and Zhang were augmented by epidemics that struck China at this same time. Some estimates, noted by Chinese observers, suggest that these epidemics caused many communities to suffer losses of half or more of their inhabitants. One scholar wrote of Zhejiang province in 1642 that "the symptoms of pestilence arose again on a large scale, affecting eight or nine out of every ten households. It even

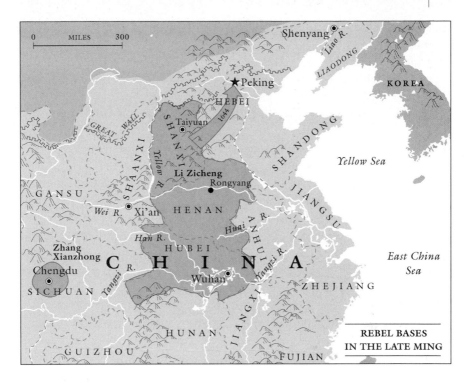

REBEL BASES
IN THE LATE MING

reached the point where in a household of ten or twenty people a single uninfected person could not be found, or where in such a household there was not one saved. Therefore at first the bodies were buried in coffins, and next in grasses, but finally they were left on the beds." An observer in Henan province noted that in one big city there in the summer of 1643 "there were few signs of human life in the streets and all that was heard was the buzzing of flies."[7]

So serious was the loss of life that it prompted a rethinking of traditional Chinese theories of medicine, and although no solutions were found, medical books of the time began to develop a new theory of epidemics. One doctor, living near the Yangzi delta area, wrote in 1642 that China was obviously being affected not just by variants in weather or temperature but by a change in the balance of Heaven and Earth caused by "deviant *Qi*," *Qi* being the normally neutral forces within nature. Such deviant *Qi*, he wrote, "appear mainly in years of war and famine." Unseen and unheard, they struck apparently at will; any response by the people was in vain. "If the people clash against them, they produce the various diseases, each according to its nature. As for the diseases produced, sometimes everyone has swollen neck glands and sometimes everyone's face and head swell up. . . . Sometimes everyone suffers from diarrhoea and intermittent fever. Or it might be cramps, or pustules, or a rash, or itching scabs, or boils."[8] The weight of description and analysis suggests that China suffered some form of plague during the 1640s, although its exact nature cannot be determined. Possibly the Jürchen tribesmen, by this time known as "Manchus," in their earlier raids introduced microbes for which the Chinese had no natural antibodies, leading to a catastrophic loss of life similar to that caused by the Europeans' spread of measles or smallpox among the indigenous Indian populations of Mexico and North America.

The Ming dynasty, during these closing years, was not completely without resources. There were loyal generals who led their troops against the rebels and occasionally inflicted defeats on them—or at least forced them to retreat or into temporary surrender. There were also semi-independent naval and military leaders, with bases in Shandong or on offshore islands, who launched damaging raids on the Manchu forces in Liaodong. And in many areas the wealthy local elites recruited and armed their own militia forces so that they could defend their estates and hometowns from rebel assaults. Emperor Chongzhen himself did try to bring some order to the Peking government; he sought to repress the worst excesses of the eunuchs, and unlike his grandfather Wanli, he met regularly with his ministers. But much of his attention was focused on Manchuria, where the Manchu-Jürchen leader Nurhaci and his son had been steadily widening their power base, seizing Shenyang (Mukden) in 1625, taking much of Inner Mongolia in 1632, and subduing Korea in 1638. During this period China produced some remarkable generals who fought bravely in Manchuria, especially in the mid-1620s, inflicting heavy losses on Manchu forces and recapturing several cities. But factional fighting in Peking and a constant shortage of funds hampered the Ming cause.

Foremost among the Ming generals was Yuan Chonghuan, whose career may be seen as exemplifying some of these late Ming tensions. A classically educated scholar from south China, Yuan entered the Peking bureaucracy as a young man. In 1622 he went on an inspection tour of southern Manchuria and grew convinced that he could defend the crucial passes that led to Peking. As a staff member in the ministry of war, with a good knowledge of European firearms apparently garnered from his cook, who knew some Westerners, Yuan was able to hold the Liao River against Nurhaci. In 1628 he was named field marshal of all northeastern forces, but for reasons of jealousy he executed one of his most talented subordinates the following year. When, in 1630, Manchu raiding parties appeared near Peking, Yuan was falsely accused of colluding with them and was tried on a trumped-up charge of treason. With hostile courtiers, friends of the man he had killed, and groups of eunuchs all arrayed against him, Yuan had no chance of clearing himself. Instead he was condemned to death by way of the most publicly humiliating and painful punishment that the Chinese penal code allowed for: being cut to pieces in the marketplace of Peking. Later scholars mourned him as one of China's greatest generals. No one of his talents came forward to succeed him; on the contrary, though some northern generals remained loyal to the Ming cause after his death, many others began to surrender to the Manchus, taking their troops over to the enemy with them. The charges falsely leveled at Yuan now began to come true in earnest.

Finally it was not the Manchus, but the rebel Li Zicheng who brought down the Ming dynasty. In 1644 Li mounted a huge attack on Peking, moving across north China with hundreds of thousands of troops, sacking the towns that resisted him, and incorporating into his own army the forces of those that surrendered. He waged a skillful propaganda war, pointing to the excesses and cruelties of the Ming regime and promising a new era of peace and prosperity to the exhausted Chinese people. In April 1644 his armies entered Peking without a fight, the city gates having been treach-erously opened at his coming. It is recorded that Emperor Chongzhen, after hearing that the rebels had entered the city, rang a bell to summon his ministers in order to get their advice or assistance. When none of them appeared, the emperor walked to the imperial garden just outside the walls of the Forbidden City. In this garden was a hill, from the crest of which the emperor and his consorts had been wont to look out over the panorama of Peking. This time the emperor did not mount the hill, but attached a cord to a tree at its foot, and there hanged himself. So died the last ruler of the dynasty that, for better or worse, had ruled China since 1368.

CHAPTER 2 | # The Manchu Conquest

THE RISE OF THE QING

While the Ming dynasty was sliding into a final decline, its eventual successor was rising in the northeast. The people known now as the Manchus were originally tribes of Jürchen stock who lived in the areas currently designated as Heilongjiang and Jilin provinces. In the distant past, between A.D. 1122 and 1234, the Jürchen had conquered northern China and combined it with their own territory under the name of Jin—or "golden"—dynasty. After their defeat in 1234, they had retreated northward to the Sungari River region, but by the late Ming they were once more pressing on the borders of China and Korea. The policy of the Ming was to control the Jürchen by formally defining their territory as a part of China's frontier defensive system, by offering them honorific titles, and by granting them trading privileges.

By the late sixteenth century the Jürchen had followed various paths. Some of them had stayed in the Sungari region and lived mainly by fishing and hunting. Others had established a firm base along the northern edge of the Korean border in the region of the Changbai Shan (Long White Mountain), where they developed a mixed agricultural and hunting economy. Yet others had moved to more fertile, open land east of the Liao River, where they mingled with Chinese emigrants and practiced a settled, arable agriculture, or thrived as traders in furs, horses, and luxury goods. Those in this third group had essentially become detribalized: they largely adopted Chinese ways, even though the towns in which they prospered, such as Fushun and Shenyang, had been in the very heartland of the old Jin Empire.

Nurhaci, who was to lay the groundwork for the Manchu conquest of

26

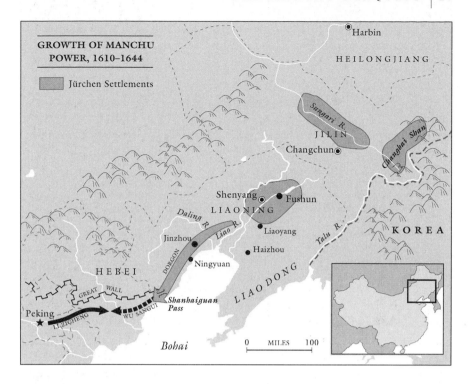

Ming China, was born in 1559 to a noble family of the Long White Mountain group of Jürchens. As a young man he traveled to Peking to pay ritual homage to the Ming rulers and to trade, and received honorific Ming titles in return for his offer to help them against the Japanese in Korea. But around 1610, he broke his relations with the Ming on the grounds that they had attacked or humiliated members of his family and had tried to wreck his own economic base.

A Korean diplomatic envoy who visited Nurhaci's base camp around this time noted the rude simplicity of the Jürchen weapons and defensive stockades, Nurhaci's own bluff manner and tough physique, and the distinctive hairstyle, clothing, and massive silver earrings worn by some of his attendant generals. But if initially Nurhaci seemed uncouth to such a visitor, he soon showed his abilities. Between 1610 and 1620 Nurhaci steadily increased his power at the expense of neighboring Jürchen and Mongol tribes, either dominating them by warfare or allying with them through marriage contracts. He organized his troops and their families into eight different groups of "banners," which were distinguished according to color (yellow, red, blue, and white, four plain and four bordered). The banners served as identification devices in battle, and membership in a given banner was used as the

basis for population registration in daily life. He also assembled large numbers of craftsmen to manufacture weapons and armor, and, developed a
written script for transcribing the Jürchen language. In 1616 he took the
important symbolic step of declaring himself the "khan," or ruler, of a
second "Jin" dynasty, thus evoking the past glory of the Jürchen people and
issuing a provocative challenge to the Ming state. Two years later he
launched a series of shattering military blows at mixed Chinese and "detribalized" Jürchen settlements east of the Liao River, in the region known as
Liaodong.*

The Ming rulers had regarded Liaodong as essentially Chinese territory
and maintained strong garrisons there under their own generals. But Nurhaci used a mixture of threats and blandishments to induce the garrison
commanders to surrender, sending them elaborate messages written out for
him by Chinese advisers in his employ. As he wrote to the Chinese officer
commanding Fushun, for instance: "Even if you fight, you certainly will not
win . . . if you do not fight, but surrender, I shall let you keep your former
office and shall care benevolently for you. But if you fight, how can our
arrows know who you are?"[1] Nurhaci also tried to undermine Ming influence in Liaodong by posing as a reformist ruler who had come to bring a
better life to the Chinese, and he urged those who lived west of the Liao
River to join him in his new kingdom. "Do not think that the land and
houses will not be yours, that they will belong to a master," he wrote in
another message that was distributed out in the countryside. "All will
equally be the Khan's subjects and will live and work the fields on an equal
basis."[2] On other occasions, Nurhaci claimed he would take over the charitable functions of the ideal ruler that had so obviously been neglected by
Wanli in his waning years, saying that he would never let "the rich accumulate their grain and have it rot away," but would "nourish the begging
poor."

Nurhaci rigidly disciplined his troops and tried to stop all looting or
harming of the Liaodong civilian population, publicly punishing guilty soldiers. To those Chinese with education who surrendered, he offered a
chance of serving in the growing Jürchen bureaucracy, and senior Chinese
officials who came over to his side were offered marriage into his family,
honorific titles, and high office. Shenyang and Liaoyang fell to his troops in
1621, and in 1625 he made Shenyang (the modern Mukden) his capital.
Soon all the territory east of the Liao River and some land west of the river
were in his hands.

*_Dong_ is Chinese for "east."

Despite his orders that males who surrendered to him must imitate Jürchen practice and shave the fronts of their foreheads and braid their hair into a long pigtail or "queue," Nurhaci initially faced little overt opposition from the conquered Chinese settlers, though receptions were often mixed. While some Chinese welcomed the Jürchen with flutes and drums, others poisoned the wells in a desperate attempt to kill Nurhaci's troops. Nor is there any easy way to categorize the fates of those Chinese or detribalized Jürchen who were now in Nurhaci's power. Some were rewarded as promised, others were moved from their city homes to work for the Jürchen on the land. Some were enslaved or forced to work under contract, others—most notably those with some knowledge of artillery—were placed in new military units and incorporated as a "Chinese martial" banner unit. Although still in an embryonic state, these artillery units were later to play a critical role in the Manchu victories.

As early as 1622, Nurhaci had expressed his intention of attacking China by sending an army down through the strategic pass of Shanhaiguan, where the Great Wall ends at the North China Sea. He might well have done so the following year had not a serious rebellion against his rule broken out among the Chinese in Liaodong. What prompted the uprising is not known, but there were many possible causes. With the arrival of large numbers of Jürchen troops in Liaodong, there was intense pressure on the available farmland. Shortages of grain and salt grew to crisis proportions, and famine was reported in some areas. Compulsory grain rationing was introduced, and Chinese under Jürchen control had to spend a portion of their time giving free labor to their masters, working in squads of three on specially designated five-acre parcels of land. In many areas of Liaodong, partly as a control measure and partly because there was a housing shortage, the Jürchen moved into Chinese homes to live and eat as co-occupants. The Chinese responded by setting fires, poisoning wells once again, killing Jürchen women and children, hiding their grain from the Jürchen, and fleeing into the mountains. Some Chinese killed border guards and tried to escape to the south; those caught were killed in turn by the Jürchen.

The Ming court did not try to take advantage of the uprising, however, and it was soon suppressed by Nurhaci's troops. The Jürchen were warned to "be on their guard day and night and not associate with the Chinese of the villages."[3] They were now lodged in separate quarters in the towns, and even forbidden to walk down Chinese streets or visit Chinese homes. The Jürchen were ordered to carry arms at all times, while possession of any weapons by the Chinese was made illegal. In criminal cases Nurhaci urged leniency for all Jürchen, while full rigor was to be used against convicted

Chinese, including death sentences for them and their families in cases of theft. A second revolt of the Chinese took place in 1625, and was even more savagely repressed.

The Ming generals had failed to respond to either of these uprisings, but late in 1625 these generals began a series of vigorous counterattacks and won their first serious victories over Nurhaci in 1626. Later that same year, Nurhaci died. In accordance with Jürchen custom—a custom derived from the Mongols of central Asia—he had not left his dominions and the title of khan to any one man, but instead had ordered them divided among his most able sons and nephews.

Not surprisingly, there followed a protracted struggle for power. The victor was Nurhaci's eighth son, Hong Taiji, who had been the general commanding the plain yellow and bordered yellow banners. This son was helped to power by Chinese advisers, and he responded by taking a more favorable view of the Chinese and their traditional institutions than his father had done. Six ministries, in exact imitation of those at the Ming court, were established, and Chinese were employed throughout this new bureaucracy. Nominally, the senior ministers were all Jürchen notables, but they were often absent on military or other business, leaving the practical running of affairs to their Chinese subordinates.

On the grounds that it was punitive to the Chinese, Hong Taiji abolished the registration system instituted by Nurhaci; he also held competitive examinations for the civil service in Liaodong, again following the traditional Chinese model; and he ordered reforms in the Jürchen written language to make it more serviceable in a new era of record keeping, census taking, and tax gathering. A swelling number of Chinese defectors from the Ming cause, many of them officers who had brought their own troops along with them, sought service with the new khan, who responded generously—too generously, thought some of his advisers, who protested that Chinese "boors without character" were filling the court.

Boors or not, the defection to the Jürchen of the senior Chinese generals assigned by the Ming to defend the area near the mouth of the Yalu River, and the northern areas of Shandong province, brought new power to Hong Taiji. In 1637 he established two full Chinese "banners" on the lines of Nurhaci's earlier system, increasing the number to four in 1639 and to eight in 1642. There was already a parallel structure of eight Mongol banners, formed in 1635, from Mongols who had turned against the Ming and pledged themselves to Hong Taiji's service. So by the early 1640s, the Jürchen leader had constructed a complete military and administrative structure, which was used to provide soldiers for active combat on a rotating system, to register and protect their wives and children, and to supervise work on the land.

Even before this, in 1636, Hong Taiji had taken a symbolic step that went beyond that taken by Nurhaci in establishing the Jin dynasty in 1616: Hong Taiji decided to abolish his fledgling state's connection with the tribal past that was associated with the Jürchen name, and the memories it evoked of servitude to the Ming dynasty. He declared the formation of a new dynasty called the Qing, which henceforth would rule over the Manchu and neighboring peoples, claiming greater power and a wider mandate than the Jin had done. *Qing* (pronounced "Ching") literally means "pure" or "clear" and, from 1636 until the final abdication of the Manchus in 1912, was used as the dynastic term for the successive Manchu rulers and for the China over which they ruled. Instead of Jürchen, Hong Taiji's people were now to be called Manchus. *Manchu* was a new term; though its exact meaning is not known, it was probably taken from a Buddhist term for "great good fortune," and implied a new measure of universality for the Qing state.

Hong Taiji now seemed poised for wider conquests. He had conquered Korea in 1638, forcing the king to renounce his loyalty to the Ming and to give his sons to the Manchus as hostages. Inside China, the Ming failures were everywhere evident, with the rebels Li Zicheng and Zhang Xianzhong in control of much of the western and northern parts of the country. Manchu raiding parties had crossed the Great Wall north of Peking and looted the area near the capital, along with wide swathes of land in Shandong province. They seized women and children, draft animals, silk, and silver, and left burnt-out, devastated cities in their wake.

Yet at the same time, there was disturbing evidence that the Manchus, despite their newly coined name with its grand pretensions, were themselves turning soft. Some of them were growing weary of war and used to the pleasures of Liaodong city life. Luxuries they had never known surrounded them, while agriculture faltered because the men-at-arms, although not fighting as well as before, still did not deign to work in the fields. The young men did not even like to go hunting anymore, sighed Hong Taiji, but "hang around the marketplaces and simply amuse themselves." If summoned to battle, "the soldiers stay in camp and just let the flunkies go."[4]

When the strategic Ming city of Jinzhou, south of the Daling River, fell to the Manchus in 1642, it was only after a sporadic ten-year siege in which the Manchus had been repulsed again and again by the Ming garrison troops. The victory came none too soon to boost Manchu morale. Two of the last few talented Ming generals surrendered after the battle and were suitably rewarded. But the mainland route to Peking through the pass at Shanhaiguan was still guarded by the redoubtable Ming general Wu Sangui, and in 1643 Hong Taiji suddenly died, leaving his younger brother Dorgon as a regent for the compromise choice as heir, Hong Taiji's ninth son, a five-year-old boy.

The chance for further Manchu expansion looked frail indeed, but in the spring of 1644 Li Zicheng led his rebel army out of the Peking he had just seized and advanced across the plains east of the city to attack General Wu Sangui, whom Li saw as the last major defender of the Ming cause. General Wu turned from the Shanhaiguan pass and marched westward to confront Li. Seizing the incredible opportunity, the regent Dorgon rallied the troops of the boy Manchu emperor and led the armies of the Manchu, Mongol, and Chinese banners swiftly down the coast, crossing the border into China unopposed. Nurhaci's dream had suddenly become a reality.

CONQUERING THE MING

With the Manchu armies to his east and Li Zicheng's forces to his west, General Wu Sangui was in a desperate situation. His only hope to survive was by allying with one of his opponents. Among arguments for joining Li were the fact that he was Chinese, that he seemed to have the support of the local people, that he promised to end the abuses that had marked the late Ming state, and that he held Wu's father as a hostage. Otherwise, Li was an unknown quantity, violent and uneducated; moreover, the behavior of his army in Peking after he had seized the city in April 1644 was not encouraging to a wealthy and cultured official like General Wu. Li's troops had looted and ravaged the city, attacking and pillaging the homes of senior officials, seizing their relatives for ransom, or demanding enormous payoffs in "protection money." Even though Li had declared the formal founding of a new dynasty, he was unable to control his own generals in Peking, and Wu might well have wondered how effective Li would be in unifying China.

As for allying with the Manchus, there was the disadvantage that they were ethnically non-Chinese, and their Jürchen background included them in a history of semicivilized frontier people whom the Chinese had traditionally despised; furthermore, they had terrorized parts of north China in their earlier raids and had virtually wiped out some of the cities they had occupied. Yet in their favor was the early development of their embryonic regime, the Qing, which offered a promise of order: the six ministries, the examination system, the formation of the Chinese banners, the large numbers of Chinese advisers in senior positions—all were encouraging signs to

Wu. And their treatment of senior Chinese officials who surrendered had been good.

For a combination of these reasons and, according to popular tales, because Li had seized one of Wu's favorite concubines and had made her his own, General Wu Sangui threw in his lot with the Manchus, fought off the army that Li sent against him, and invited Dorgon to join him in recapturing Peking. Li retaliated by executing Wu's father and displaying the head on the walls of Peking. But the morale of Li's troops was fading fast, and not even his formal assumption of imperial rank on June 3, 1644, could shore him up. The next day he and his troops, weighed down by booty, fled to the west. On the sixth of June, the Manchus and Wu entered the capital, and the boy emperor was enthroned in the Forbidden City with the reign title of Shunzhi, meaning "obedience in rule." The adopting of such a traditional Chinese title by the young emperor showed that the Manchus now formally claimed the mandate of heaven to rule China.

Although the reigning Ming emperor had hanged himself in April, and the Manchu Shunzhi now sat on the throne, this did not mean the Ming cause was dead. Many members of the imperial family had fled the capital at Li's coming, and hundreds of princes of various collateral branches of the family were living on their vast estates throughout China. The sanctity of their dynastic name, which had endured since 1368, was not to be lightly dismissed. Wu Sangui, in desperation, might have allied himself with the Manchus; but for hundreds of thousands of Chinese scholars and officials, the Ming name remained worth fighting and dying for.

It was to take the Manchus seventeen years to hunt down the last Ming pretenders, but since they also claimed to have entered Peking as the righteous avengers of the martyred Ming emperor, they also had to hunt down and destroy the leading anti-Ming rebels. Li Zicheng was their first target, as he fled southwest with his army to the Shaanxi city of Xi'an, where his career as a military rebel had commenced some twenty years earlier. After consolidating their hold on Shanxi* province, the Qing forces, in the spring of 1645, closed in on Li with a skillfully executed pincer movement. Forced out of Xi'an, Li fled with a dwindling number of followers southeast along the Han River to the city of Wuchang, crossed the Yangzi, and was finally cornered by the pursuing Manchus in the mountains on the northern border of Jiangxi province. In the summer of 1645, he died there—either by suicide, according to one source, or beaten to death by peasants from whom he was trying to steal food, according to another.

---

*Note the similarity of *Shanxi* and *Shaanxi*—highly confusing in English. The Chinese characters for the first syllable are quite different, though in both names *-xi* stands for "west."

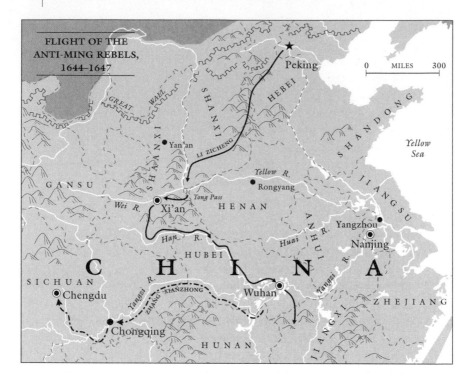

While this campaign was under way, the second major rebel leader, Zhang Xianzhong, had moved away from his base in central China and traveled westward up the Yangzi River, through its steep gorges, and into Sichuan province. After briefly seizing the river town of Chongqing, he made his capital in the wealthy and well-protected city of Chengdu. It was there, in December 1644, that he declared the formation of a new "Great Western Kingdom." But Zhang was not destined to rule much longer than Li had done, although he did establish a civilian bureaucracy staffed by scholars (many of whom were coerced into service), held examinations, and minted coinage. Zhang also set up a complex system of 120 armed military camps for the protection of his kingdom, which initially was threatened more by the armies of fleeing Ming princes than by the Manchus.

But in the ensuing years, Zhang seems to have gradually drifted into some bizarre private world of megalomania and cruelty. He laid long-range "plans" for his armies to conquer not only southern and eastern China, but also Mongolia, Korea, the Philippines, and Annam (the present Vietnam). He inflicted terrible punishments on those he believed were trying to betray him in Sichuan, beheading or maiming thousands of local scholars and their families, and even decimating whole regiments of his own armies. He finally abandoned the city of Chengdu in late 1646, burning much of it to the ground, and conducted a scorched-earth campaign of appalling thoroughness as he marched eastward. In January 1647, he was killed by Manchu troops.

The elimination of Li and Zhang was essential to the long-range success of Manchu conquest plans, but most of the energies of the Manchus had to be spent on suppressing those members of the Ming ruling house who might be able to rally a viable national resistance to the conquest. Considering the strong sense of loyalty that Chinese scholars were taught to feel toward their ruling dynasty, and their natural inclination to protect their ancestral homes and estates from foreign aggressors, a skillful survivor of the Ming ruling house should have been able to assemble millions of supporters. The first man who tried to rally the Ming armies against the Manchus was one of Emperor Wanli's grandsons, the prince of Fu. The prince tried to make a deal with the regent Dorgon, offering the Manchus enormous presents and an annual subsidy if they would return beyond the Great Wall to Liaodong. Dorgon responded by saying he would allow the prince to maintain a small independent kingdom if he abandoned his imperial claims. The prince of Fu rejected this offer on the advice of his most patriotic generals.

Over the next few months, when the prince of Fu should have been preparing Nanjing's defenses, his court was torn by the bitter quarrels, recriminations, and inefficiencies that had so plagued Emperor Wanli, including internecine struggles for power between pro- and anti-eunuch factions that echoed the battles between the Donglin partisans and Wei Zhongxian. While the Ming generals and senior officials bickered, a Manchu army advanced south down the line of China's great man-made inland waterway, the Grand Canal, and besieged the wealthy commercial city of Yangzhou in May 1645. The Ming troops, who had carefully prepared batteries of cannon to defend the city walls, held out there for one week. But they were finally defeated by the superior cannon power and the remarkable courage of the Manchus, and the city was sacked for ten terrible days as a warning to the rest of China. The defenders of Nanjing, by contrast, put up almost no resistance, and the city surrendered to the Manchus in early June. The prince of Fu was captured and sent to Peking, where he died the following year.

With the prince of Fu's death, the situation grew more complicated as new claimants to the throne appeared. Two brothers, who were descendants of the founding Ming emperor, attempted successively to lead resistance against the Manchus on the eastern coast, first in Fuzhou (across from the island of Taiwan) and then in the rich southern trading entrepôt of Canton. The Fuzhou ruler was caught and executed in late 1646; his younger brother

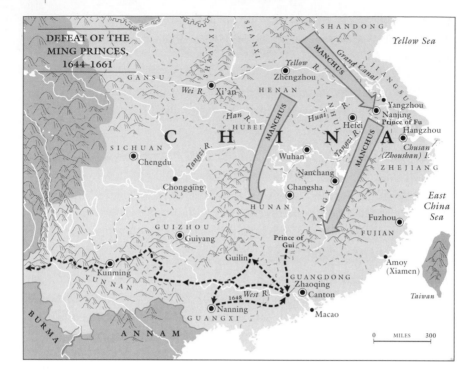

was executed in 1647, when Canton fell to the Manchus. Another descendant of the Ming founder led a series of unsuccessful attempts to rally resistance against the Manchus up and down the east coast, basing his court for a time at Amoy (Xiamen), as well as on Chusan (Zhoushan) Island, and even for a short period on a boat. He abandoned his title in 1653, and thereafter resistance to the Qing on the east coast passed into the hands of supporters of the last Ming claimant, the prince of Gui.

After the failure of the Yangzi valley and coastal regimes, this prince of Gui became the final hope of the Ming imperial cause. The last known surviving grandson of Wanli, the prince was a pampered twenty-one year old when Peking fell, and had no experience in governmental or military affairs. Forced to flee from his ancestral estates in Hunan* when the rebel Zhang Xianzhong attacked the area, he moved south to Zhaoqing, west of Canton. Over the objections of his mother, who warned that he was too young and delicate for the role, a group of fugitive officials named him emperor there in late 1646. Forced out of Guangdong province by Qing

---

*Note also in English the closeness of *Henan* and *Hunan*. In Chinese, *He* means "river," *Hu* means "lake." In both names, the syllable *nan* means "south."

forces, the prince of Gui and his court spent the next year and a half roaming across Guangxi province, based most often in either Guilin or Nanning (near the border of Annam), as a number of Qing armies pursued him.

Despite the amazing feats of the Qing armies, which had campaigned successfully over the fifteen hundred miles separating Peking from Canton, their conquest of this huge area was inevitably partial, and patriotic Chinese who bitterly resented the Manchu invasion and the Ming humiliation had time to collect their forces. In 1648 a number of former Ming officials who had been collaborating with the Manchus threw off their allegiance to the Qing and declared themselves dedicated to the cause of Ming restoration. The prince of Gui, whose southern court had been described by a contemporary as being filled with "all manner of betel-nut chewers, brine-well workers, and aborigine whorehouse owners,"[5] suddenly found himself welcomed back to Zhaoqing by numerous and enthusiastic supporters, while the Manchu troops in Canton were massacred. As had earlier fugitive regimes, this "emperor" sought to reassemble a working bureaucracy organized on hierarchical lines, to hold examinations, to set up a viable military command, and to construct some kind of provincial administration that could control the countryside and collect taxes. But his court, like all the others, was torn by factional strife among rival groupings of ministers, generals, and eunuchs, and failed to lead a concerted opposition to the Manchus.

By early 1650 the Qing forces had rallied and suppressed the key central China areas of declared support for the prince of Gui's regime, and had launched a two-pronged counterattack on his southern base. In December 1650, the Ming court of the prince of Gui fled from Guangdong province, traveling down the West River into Guangxi. For the next decade, no longer a court in any institutional sense but simply a band of fugitives held together by a shared wish to resist the domination of China by a foreign power, they retreated steadily westward—from Guangxi into Guizhou province, from Guizhou to mountainous Yunnan, and finally across the Chinese border into Burma.

The king of Burma, who initially offered sanctuary to the Ming but changed his mind, massacred most of the prince of Gui's followers, and thereafter held the "emperor" and his family virtual prisoners. It was General Wu Sangui, once the Ming guardian of the Shanhaiguan passes, who in 1661 spearheaded a final attack by the Qing armies into Burma. The Burmese handed over the sad remnants of the Ming court to Wu, who had them transported back into Chinese territory. There, in Yunnan province early in 1662, the last "emperor" of the Ming and his only son were executed by strangulation. The Qing state needed to fear no more "legitimate" rivals to its rule.

ADAPTING TO CHINA

The Manchus had seized Peking in 1644 with startling ease, and by 1662 had killed the last Ming claimants, but the succession of military victories did not mean that they had solved the problem of how to rule China. Dorgon, as regent for the child emperor Shunzhi, inherited a hybrid system of government, developed in Liaodong, in which a tentative version of China's six ministries was combined with the military and administrative eight-banner organization of the Manchus. He now had to adapt these institutions to the task of controlling a continent-sized country.

On one issue at least—that of Manchu dress and hairstyle—Dorgon was determined to make the Chinese adapt, rather than the reverse. Only a day after entering Peking, he issued a decree stating that, henceforth, all Chinese men should shave their foreheads and have their hair braided in back in the Manchu-style queue, just as Nurhaci had ordered in Liaodong. A storm of protest led Dorgon to cancel the decree, but the following June another order was issued that Chinese *military* men must adopt the queue; this was to make it easier for the Manchus to identify their enemies in battle, and assure them that those who had surrendered would remain loyal to them in the future. But senior advisers of Dorgon's felt that this did not go far enough; in July 1645, Dorgon reissued the order that every Chinese man must shave his forehead and begin to grow the queue within ten days or face execution. The Chinese faced a stark choice: "Keep your hair and lose your head," as this order was summarized in popular parlance, "or lose your hair and keep your head."[6]

Ming Chinese men had prized long and elaborately dressed hair as a sign of masculinity and elegance, and they bitterly resented Dorgon's decree. In many areas the order led them to take up arms against the Manchus even when they had already formally surrendered, but this time Dorgon stayed firm. Further decrees ordered the Chinese to adopt the Manchu style of dress—high collar and tight jacket fastened at the right shoulder—rather than wear the loosely hanging robes of the Ming. In another departure from Chinese custom, Manchu women were forbidden to bind their feet to make them smaller, as Chinese girls and women had been doing for centuries. Despite the pain caused by this practice, the custom had spread from the elite to the peasantry, and tiny feet had become the measure of feminine beauty to the Chinese. Millions of women suffered as a result. In refusing to go along with the custom, the Manchus both asserted their cultural independence and created an effective barrier to the intermarriage of Manchus

Anonymous, Two figures studying bamboo painting, Ming dynasty

Inkstone, late Ming dynasty   The inscription on its
side reads: "I give myself to you / To be treated
like jade. / To place me among gold and / grain
would be to insult me."

Inkstick, late Ming dynasty   Composed of molded
pine soot and animal glue, this inkstick shows a
plum blossom on one side and on the other the
title of a poem, "Falling Are the Plums."

Brush and cover of lacquered wood, late Ming dynasty

瓷器汶水

*Woodblock prints of porcelain production at Jingde-
zhen, Jiangxi province, late Ming dynasty*
Although the distinctive blue-and-white porcelains
they fashioned became valuable export commodities, low wages drove porcelain workers in Jingdezhen to riot in 1601. Workers decorating porcelain
with painted cobalt designs (top); two men dip-
ping the painted porcelain into a bowl of glaze
before firing (bottom)

打圈

青畫圖

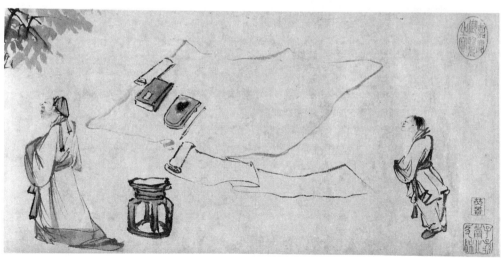

The lofty scholars   In a handscroll dated to 1520, the artist Tang Yin employs a satirical touch in his depiction of proud scholars.

Wu Wei (1459–1508), Strolling entertainers

Nurhaci, chieftain of the Jürchen tribesmen, organized both Mongol and Jürchen tribes in a united front against the Ming. *Nurhaci, on horseback, attacking a neighboring tribe, 1586 (top); Nurhaci ascending the throne as the ruler of the Jin dynasty (bottom)*

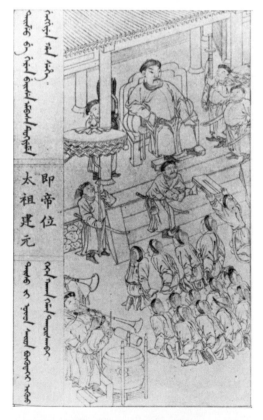

Western engravings, published in London in 1673, showing the Jesuit missionaries Matteo Ricci and Johann Adam Schall von Bell Matteo Ricci (top left) is depicted with one of his Chinese converts; Father Johann Adam Schall von Bell wears the badge of office of a senior Chinese official (bottom)

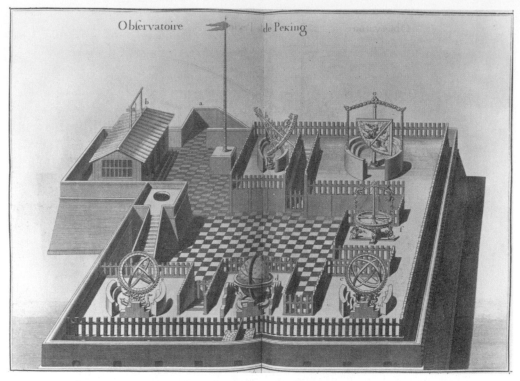

The Peking Observatory Schall's Jesuit colleague Ferdinand Verbiest refitted the observatory on Peking's eastern wall with a sextant, quadrant, and other astronomical instruments.

"Kangxi Southern Inspection Tour" (detail), by Wang Hui and assistants, c. 1695 A scroll showing Kangxi about to disembark at Suzhou.

A portrait of the emperor Kangxi at his studies   Through his study of the Confucian classics, Kangxi took on the aura of a "sage ruler."

Candidates for scholarly degrees anxiously await their examination results, Ming dynasty It was critical for the early Qing emperors to inspire scholars to confer on the new dynasty the loyalty they had given the Ming.

A scene from "The Peony Pavilion," a play by the Ming dramatist Tang Xianzu, in which the heroine paints her self-portrait while her maid looks on

Bada Shanren's "Birds and Rock," 1692 Bada Shanren and other painters of this period expressed their defiance of the Qing obliquely through their art.

Anonymous, The Yongzheng emperor offering sacrifices at the altar of agriculture　This detail of a handscroll shows the Yongzheng emperor performing the springtime sacrifices in Peking at the altar of agriculture during the ritual start of the growing season.

and Chinese, since Chinese men professed to find the Manchu women's normal-sized feet sexually unattractive.

At the Peking court, the Manchus cut back on the thousands of eunuchs who had filled the Ming palaces and whose intrigues had been so harmful to the regime. Though eunuchs remained as supervisers in the imperial women's quarters, other court duties and special financial tasks were assigned to Chinese bondservants who had been captured and enslaved in Liaodong in the 1620s and 1630s. The eunuchs were also deprived of the quasi-military status they had had as palace guards under the Ming; instead, an elite corps of bannermen, many of them descendants of warriors who had helped found the original Jürchen state under Nurhaci, were appointed to special guards divisions to patrol the palaces.

Each of the eight banners was settled in a territorial zone outside the Peking palace walls, so that the emperor and his family lived literally surrounded by their most loyal troops. The Chinese inhabitants of Peking were forcibly relocated to the southern part of the city; although this initially caused much suffering, the southern area swiftly became a thriving commercial and residential quarter. In addition, the Manchus confiscated hundreds of thousands of acres of good farmland in northern China to provide food and rewards for the garrison armies. Much of this land had belonged to members of the Ming imperial family, although estates of wealthy former Ming officials were also confiscated. In all, some forty thousand Manchu bannermen received approximately six acres each, with much larger estates being granted to senior Manchu officers.

In a further attempt to segregate the Chinese from the Manchus, Dorgon ordered the removal of many Chinese farmers in this north China area. Shrewd Chinese landlords, realizing the possibilities of exploiting this period of dynastic transition, seized unclaimed or abandoned land for themselves. The result was widespread chaos and devastation. Thousands of former farmers became vagabonds or bandits, or fled the area altogether. Many Manchus, however, were incapable of farming the land themselves, and they soon made their plots over to Chinese tenants on various types of contracts. Some of these contracts reduced the Chinese to an almost serflike dependency on their masters, and when draft animals were not available, the tenant farmers were forced to drag the plows themselves. Within twenty-five years of the Manchu invasion, about 5 million acres of land in a huge swathe some 150 miles in radius around Peking had been taken over by the Manchus. Still, neither a full-fledged feudal system nor any form of slave labor ever grew ensconced, and traditional Chinese patterns of agricultural work, tenancy, and even independent ownership slowly revived.

In most areas of governmental and intellectual organization, the Manchus were content to follow Chinese precedents. The six ministries, which were in charge respectively of civil affairs, finance, rituals, war, justice, and public works, were retained intact, although the leadership of each ministry was placed in the hands of two presidents, one a Manchu and one a Chinese bannerman or a civilian Chinese. A similar multiethnic dyarchy of four men (two Manchus and two Chinese) held the title of vice-president in each ministry. As liaison between the ministries and the emperor's immediate circle, the senior positions known as "grand secretaries" were also perpetuated. There were seven grand secretaries serving together in the early years of Shunzhi's reign: two were Manchu, two were Chinese bannermen, and three were former senior Ming officials who had recently surrendered.

Accomplished Chinese scholars who offered their loyalty to the Manchus were given staff positions in the various ministries and in the Grand Secretariat. To bring new men into the bureaucracy, the national examinations on the classical literary tradition were reinstituted in 1646, when 373 degrees were awarded, mainly to candidates in the Peking area or the bordering provinces of Shanxi and Shandong. To broaden the geographical spread another 298 degrees were given in 1647, mainly to candidates from the reconquered provinces of Jiangsu and Anhui. The choice of senior examiners showed Dorgon's awareness of Chinese sensibilities: although two were Chinese bannermen and one a scholarly Manchu, the fourth was a classical Chinese scholar and official who had surrendered only in 1644.

The Manchus could consolidate their administration in the provinces only after their armies had destroyed the Ming opposition, but slowly they installed their own officials on a system similar to that of the Ming. They initially subdivided the fifteen main provinces that had existed under the Ming into twenty-two units, but eventually they cut back that number and simply divided in two each of the three largest Ming provinces, so as to make them easier to administer. Each of these eighteen provinces was under a governor, and in the early Qing most of these governors were Chinese bannermen. Dorgon clearly believed these men had proven their loyalty to his regime, and the fact that they were ethnically Chinese and spoke the Chinese language would make them more acceptable to their compatriots across the country. Under each governor were two officials who supervised respectively the economy and the practice of justice in his province, and a number of supervisory censors and intendants. Then came the prefects, based in the larger cities, who supervised, in their turn, the local county officials—known to Westerners as "magistrates"—who were in charge of day-to-day administration and tax gathering in the towns and countryside.

Manchu power was spread very thinly over China's vast territory, and though the Qing established military garrisons in most of the key provincial cities, the new dynasty survived basically by maintaining a tenuous balance of power among three components of its state. First were the Manchus themselves, the former Jürchen, who had their own language and their own aristocratic rankings based on earlier Jürchen connections or on descent from Nurhaci. The Manchus tried to maintain their martial superiority through such practices as hunting and mounted archery; and they emphasized their natural cultural distinctness by using the Manchu spoken and written language. Though for practical reasons they had to let Chinese officials use Chinese for administrative documents, all important documents were translated into Manchu. The Manchus also kept to their own private religious practices, which were conducted by shamanic priests and priestesses in temple compounds to which the Chinese were denied access.

Second came the other bannermen, both Mongol and Chinese, most of whom were from families that had surrendered well before the conquest of 1644. With the Mongol bannermen posted mainly on the north and northwestern border regions, it was the Chinese bannermen who played the greater part in ruling China. They had their own elaborate hierarchies, based partly on noble titles granted by Nurhaci or Hong Taiji and partly by the date on which they had surrendered—those who had surrendered earliest often had the highest status. Many of these bannermen spoke both Manchu and Chinese, and had absorbed the martial culture of the former while retaining the social mores of the latter. Their support was invaluable to the Manchus; without these bannermen, there would probably have been no conquest and certainly no consolidation.

Third came the ethnic Chinese—usually known as the "Han" Chinese—raised in China proper. These Chinese essentially had four choices: they could be either active or passive collaborators, or they could choose to be resisters, again either actively or passively. Some of them, like Wu Sangui, were active collaborators with the Manchus (though never enrolled as bannermen); some defied the Manchus as active resisters and died fighting them; some, as we will see, chose passive resistance. But most, seeing the way the wind was blowing, passively collaborated with the new order.

Those from wealthy backgrounds tried to make sure that they could hold onto their ancestral lands and, if successful, proceeded to enroll their sons in the state examinations and to apply for lucrative bureaucratic office under the new regime. But the Manchus had reason to be cautious about the loyalty of this group, as they had learned in 1648 when thousands of surrendered Chinese had risen to defend the Ming cause against the Manchus in the Canton area. Millions more in the rich farmland south of the Yangzi sought to cast off their allegiance when the famous warrior general Zheng Chenggong (often called Koxinga by Westerners using a romanized form of his honorific name) launched an attack on the crucial city of Nanjing in the late 1650s. Though their resistance was rapidly suppressed by Qing troops, it had been a dangerous moment. In the south, the Manchus initially made no attempt to establish a strong presence. Instead, once the Ming claimants were dead, they let Wu Sangui and two other Chinese generals who had long before gone over to the Manchus administer the huge territories as virtually independent fiefdoms.

The Manchus were conscious that the Ming dynasty had fallen in part because of factional battles and court intrigues, but they were not immune to the same weaknesses. For instance, both of the nobly born generals who had been pivotal in the suppression of the rebel regimes of Zhang Xianzhong and Li Zicheng were later arrested on trumped-up charges of inefficiency and treachery, and died mysteriously in Manchu prisons in Peking. The regent Dorgon himself behaved extravagantly and outrageously, arrogating to himself nearly imperial powers, seizing control of several banners and ousting their generals, marrying the widow of one of his dead rivals, demanding concubines from Korea, and planning to build a palace fortress in Rehe (Jehol), north of Peking. When Dorgon died in 1650 on a hunting trip, the Manchu nobles fell to fighting over his inheritance, and the Qing regime was in danger of fragmenting.

By clever maneuvering, however, the young emperor Shunzhi, now aged thirteen, was able to consolidate his hold on the throne. Though raised as a Manchu in a Manchu court, Shunzhi seems to have been far more adaptable to Chinese ways than most of the senior Manchus around him. Astute enough to avoid being dominated by the magnates who succeeded Dorgon, and militarily shrewd enough to push the attacks on the last Ming supporters through to a successful conclusion, he also studied the Chinese language carefully, became a lover of Chinese novels and plays, and was deeply influenced by a number of devout Chinese Buddhist monks with whom he studied at court. For the last year of his life, Shunzhi grew passionately enamoured of one of his junior consorts and completely neglected the reigning empress. At the same time he returned considerable power to the palace eunuchs and revived several eunuch bureaus that had been disbanded at the time of the Qing conquest. The reasons for this are not clear, but possibly Shunzhi wanted to make the inner court more privately his own, without Manchu bodyguards and bondservants to report his movements back to the nobles of his entourage.

In another unusual development, Shunzhi became close friends with a Catholic Jesuit missionary, Father Johann Adam Schall von Bell. Jesuits from Europe had been actively preaching and seeking converts in China since the late Ming. Some Jesuits had been captured by Zhang Xianzhong and marched with his armies in Sichuan; others had accompanied the fleeing troops of the southern Ming pretenders. Schall von Bell was one of a small group that had been in Peking in 1644 and had decided to risk staying there. Because he had a high level of scientific skill, Dorgon appointed him to direct the Imperial Bureau of Astronomy. Since the imperial court was expected to determine the calendar for the entire country, it would greatly reinforce Shunzhi's claim to be Son of Heaven if the calculations were as precise as possible. Schall von Bell's favored status may also have been another way for Emperor Shunzhi to express his independence, or even to rediscover the father that he had lost so young. For Shunzhi called the sixty-year-old Schall von Bell "Grandpa" (mafa), summoned him regularly for conferences on religion and politics, and even allowed him to build a church in Peking.

Shunzhi died suddenly in 1661, probably from smallpox, not long after his beloved consort. But far from mourning his passing, the four senior Manchus who took over as regents for Shunzhi's young son almost immediately vilified his memory. Claiming that they had Shunzhi's last will and testament in their possession, they publicized this document to the country at large. According to the regents, Shunzhi blamed himself for betraying the military norms of his Manchu ancestors, for favoring the eunuchs, and for valuing Chinese advisers more than Manchus. "One reason that the Ming lost the empire," said the document, "was that they made the error of relying on eunuchs. I was clearly aware of their corruption, but I was unable to heed this warning. . . . I have caused the Manchu statesmen to have no desire to serve and their zeal has been dissipated."[7]

The four regents—among whom Oboi, a veteran general, rapidly became the most powerful—moved decisively to change the policies of Shunzhi. They executed the leading eunuch and abolished the eunuch offices, establishing in their place an effective imperial-household system supervised by Manchus. They insisted on much tougher tax-collection policies throughout the Chinese countryside. In one famous case in Jiangsu, they ordered the investigation of over 13,000 wealthy Chinese declared delinquent in their tax payments; at least 18 were publicly executed and thousands more deprived of their scholarly degrees.

In other developments, Schall von Bell was arrested and thrown into prison, Manchus were promoted to high positions, and senior Chinese scholars were humiliated. In an attempt to starve out the last anti-Manchu rebels on the island of Taiwan by depriving them of all support from allies living along China's eastern coast, the regents rammed through a savage policy of moving the Chinese coastal population twenty miles inland, despite all the suffering such an order caused. In Fujian province, for example, 8,500 farmers and fishermen were reported to have died between 1661 and 1663 as a direct result of this order. By the end of the 1660s, it looked as though the policy of peaceful adaptation to China that in various ways had been developed by Nurhaci, Hong Taiji, Dorgon, and Shunzhi was about to be abandoned in the name of a new Manchu nativism.

CLASS AND RESISTANCE

During these early years of Qing dynasty consolidation, there were numerous occasions when different economic and social groups seem to have been pitted against each other. We noted briefly how Li Zicheng spoke of a new era of peace and prosperity for the Chinese, and how both he and Zhang Xianzhong, hating the scholars and officials, had many of them killed. In other parts of China, the news of the Ming emperor's suicide in 1644 had been enough to trigger actions that point to deep and underlying levels of hostility: peasants killed their landlords, for example, and sacked or burned the homes of the wealthy; townsmen turned on the officials within their walls or fought openly with peasant armies in the countryside. The indentured servants in some great households rioted in groups, killing their masters, looting their property, terrorizing the local communities. Poor soldiers mutinied. Fishermen joined pirate groups and raided up and down the coast. Scattered squads of peasant irregulars fought on long after leaders like Li Zicheng had been killed, continuing to cause panic and trouble throughout Shunzhi's reign. Women emerged as military leaders and won brief moments of fame. Junior officials turned on their seniors, and insisted on policies of resistance that led to the sack of the towns they defended.

But the idea of class warfare presumes a level of economic cohesion and self-consciousness concerning one's role in society that seems to have been lacking in China at the time. For each occasion on which one can find social tension, one can point to others in which the lines were crossed. Li Zicheng had several successful scholars from wealthy backgrounds on the staff of his regime. Rich landowners fighting off peasant rebels might be protected by peasant militias. Scholars escaping to the hills used local villagers to develop defensive networks against the advancing Manchus. Fleeing Ming princes were aided by the dispossessed and the poor in the mountainous coastal terrain of the east. Townsmen defended their magistrates. On some of the Ming estates they seized, the Manchus gave the land to the poor tenants who had worked it, offering them hope for economic advancement that they had never dreamed of before. In the case of women military leaders, the situation was equally complex. One such woman leader, Qin Liangyu, was the wife of a native tribal chieftain in the western province of Sichuan. Qin had been taught to read and given military training by her father; after her husband's death she led her Sichuan troops all the way to Peking to fight the Manchus, and later fought the rebel leader Zhang Xianzhong. Her daughter-in-law was also a military commander, and was killed in action in Henan province. In her old age, Qin was given the special honorary rank of marquis by the fugitive prince of Gui.[8]

As we have seen, class lines in seventeenth-century China are difficult to unravel. They blurred and crossed in ways that are confusing to those of us whose historical sense of "class" may come largely from the study of the transition from feudalism to capitalism by means of an urban bourgeoisie who gradually won power—through force and representative institutions—from a reluctant nobility.

In Ming and Qing China, there was almost no aristocracy as such. The descendants of the ruling families of even the greatest dynasties did not retain their titles and prestige once their dynasties had fallen. Thus during the life of the dynasty the descendants of the Ming founder, as well as all other male children of the successive Ming emperors, had enjoyed honorific titles and lives of leisure on great estates—the prince of Fu and the prince of Gui were two such men—but they had not coexisted with aristocratic survivors of the previous Yuan dynasty (1271–1368). Similarly, after 1644, the former Ming aristocracy was not preserved. The Manchus had their own aristocracy of a kind, formed from the descendants of Nurhaci and other famous warriors, and from the powerful Chinese generals who had submitted early to the rising Qing state. But the Manchus' ingenious policy held that, within a system of nine aristocratic ranks, a given family dropped one rung on the ladder with each noble incumbent's death: thus, a title of the third rank would be inherited as a fourth-rank title and then drop to the fifth. Ultimately—unless the emperor repromoted a member for conspicuous merit—the once-noble family would re-enter the ranks of the commoners.

Yet there was certainly an "upper class" in China—even if this class cannot be defined in terms of aristocratic connections, nor in terms of precise economic status—and the Manchus chose to perpetuate the system that they encountered when they conquered the country. Upper-class status came from an amalgam of four factors: wealth, lineage, education, and bureaucratic position. The type of wealth most valued continued to be agricultural land, but the Qing upper class might also possess large amounts of silver ingots (which served as China's official means of exchange), large libraries of classical works, collections of paintings, jade, porcelain, bolts of silk, large homes, holdings in urban real estate, or interests in commercial ventures ranging from pawnshops to pharmacies.

Lineage systems—sometimes called clans or common-descent groups—bound extended families together in a network of mutual support. A certain amount of wealth might be pooled and transmitted to later generations in the form of lineage land, the income from which would pay for the upkeep of ancestral temples and graveyards, and for teachers who served as instructors in lineage schools. Marriages between the children of powerful lineages were carefully negotiated by the parents, and the survival of large numbers of meticulous genealogies shows how seriously the whole system was perpetuated and supervised.

The dominant role of education in Qing China was the result of the power and prestige attached to holding office in the bureaucracy, entrance into which was governed almost entirely through competitive examinations run by the state. In normal times few people rose to high office via a military career, and fewer still just because their families had money or imperial connections. Qing rulers perpetuated the Ming curriculum for the examinations. It was a difficult one, based on memorization and analysis of a group of prescribed texts attributed to the sage Confucius, or to some of his early followers, and a small number of approved commentaries on those texts. The texts were written in classical Chinese, which was different grammatically and structurally from the everyday spoken language. Hence if a family had the money to send their sons to a good teacher who had himself passed the higher examinations with distinction, or if they ran a lineage school and hired their own private teachers of similar status, then obviously their children had a better chance of passing the examinations and entering high office. Even if they did not get official posts, passing the examinations brought them exemption from corvée labor dues and from corporal punishment in the courts.

Finally, even though it might be risky to hold bureaucratic office in a faction-torn court, or in a countryside threatened by bandits or civil war, it was still possible in a few years of officeholding to make enough money from salary, perquisites, special fees, and perhaps outright graft to repay all the costs one had incurred in obtaining the position, and retain a hefty surplus to invest in more land and in educating one's own children. Furthermore, the mere fact of prior membership in the bureaucracy was enough to bring a measure of protection from other local officials whom one could meet as social equals after retiring and returning home to enjoy the fruits of one's labors.

Since this upper class drew much of its wealth from land, there was always a chance for friction with tenants on that land. As Ming officials had discovered, if rents grew too high, tenants might practice rent strikes or even take up arms against their landlords. If evicted, they might turn to banditry or other forms of social violence. But there was no simple landlord-tenant warfare in seventeenth-century China, since there were so many different strata of people working the land. Thus whenever the "peasants" took up arms against the "gentry" in the 1640s, the reasons have to be sought in precise gradations of local economic and personal relationships. The rage of Li Zicheng and Zhang Xianzhong and their followers against the privileged came from a diffuse sense of frustration and a desire to share in the good life, rather than from a landless/landlord antagonism.

And yet there were some broad shifts in social and economic relationships during these transitional years. The Oboi regents might employ intimidation or force to coerce the local gentry of Jiangsu into paying their taxes on time, but the Manchus conspicuously failed in their attempt to have an efficient, up-to-date survey made of the landholdings of the wealthy Chinese, a survey that alone might have enabled the Manchus to institute an equitable land-tax system. The task was a vast one, and the paradox was that it depended on local Chinese, knowledgeable about local conditions, to carry it out. By means of endless delaying tactics, evasions, and complaints of the cost involved, the landlords prevented an adequate survey from being made. The failure to reform the land-tax system left those families who had been able to accumulate large landholdings during the era of turbulence in the position of acquiring yet larger holdings in the years that followed.

Some modern Chinese historians have argued that there was essentially an alliance between the Manchu conquerors and the Chinese upper class that led to the perpetuation of a set of "feudal relationships" in the countryside, and that quashed latent "sprouts of capitalism" that had been developing in the cities. This is hard to prove. Although Manchu policies did allow some families to grow far richer, many Chinese gentry reformers—often intellectually linked to those earlier Donglin reformers of the late Ming—protested these policies and sought to gain fairer tax systems in the areas where they held office, even at the expense of their own class. The initial failure of these gentry reformers can be traced to the fact that the post-1644 Peking bureaucracy was no longer staffed by their friends, many of whom had died in 1645. But later, in the eighteenth century, some of their recommendations were implemented, even if the reformers were not given the credit.

Especially in the area of Jiangsu, the lower Yangzi River province which was China's richest and where educated scholar-officials were concentrated in great numbers, opposition to the Manchus was mainly ideological. In this region, the leaders of that opposition were sometimes able to rally the local peasantry and townspeople behind them. With charismatic upper-class leadership, in other words, class divisions could be bridged in the name of ethnic solidarity. The Manchu haircutting order was a catalyst, in many cases, but beyond that there was a pervasive sense among some scholars that loyalty was due the Ming whatever the cost: an ethos of service and duty to the dynastic ideal had developed that transcended the shortcomings of any dynastic incumbent and united, even if fleetingly, the rich and the poor. The idea of romantic love was even invoked by some scholars to underline their sense of commitment: the love for the fallen Ming dynasty was likened to the love of the well-born scholarly youth for the woman of his dreams, and in some cases young couples made the metaphor literal, whether by resorting to arms in a hopeless anti-Manchu cause, or by taking their own lives. It was this type of ethos that the Manchus had to banish forever if they were to feel completely secure in their conquest; yet it was precisely this type of ethos that the Manchus seemed once again to encourage by their tough anti-Chinese policies of the 1660s.

CHAPTER 3 | # Kangxi's Consolidation

THE WAR OF THE THREE FEUDATORIES, 1673–1681

Qing emperors had to grow up fast if they were to grow up at all. Shunzhi had been thirteen when, taking advantage of Dorgon's sudden death, he put himself in power. Shunzhi's son, Kangxi, was also thirteen when he first moved to oust the regent Oboi; and he was fifteen when, with the help of his grandmother and a group of Manchu guard officers, he managed to arrange for Oboi's arrest in 1669 on charges of arrogance and dishonesty. Oboi soon died in prison, and Kangxi began a reign that was to last until 1722 and to make him one of the most admired rulers in China's history.

The most important of the many problems facing the young ruler was that of unifying China under Manchu control. Although in 1662 Wu Sangui had eliminated the last Ming pretender in the southwest, the region had not been fully integrated into Peking's administrative structure. The enormous distances, the mountainous semitropical country that made cavalry campaigning difficult, the presence of hundreds of non-Chinese border tribes who fought tenaciously for their own terrain, the shortage of administrators of proven loyalty—all these made both Shunzhi and Oboi unwilling to commit further Manchu forces to the area. Instead, the whole of south and southwest China was left under the control of the three Chinese generals who had directed most of the fighting there in the late 1650s.

Two of these men, Shang Kexi and Geng Jimao, were Chinese bannermen of distinction who had surrendered to the Manchus in 1633 and thereafter been essential allies in the conquest; both had repeatedly proven their loyalty to the Qing, especially in 1650 when they had recaptured Canton from the Ming supporters and massacred the city's defenders. The third was Wu Sangui himself. These three were named as princes by the Manchu court and honored by having their sons married to the daughters of Manchu nobles; each of the three was granted what amounted to an almost independent domain, and in Western histories Shang, Geng, and Wu are named the "Three Feudatories." Wu controlled the provinces of Yunnan and Guizhou as well as sections of Hunan and Sichuan; Shang ruled Guangdong and parts of Guangxi from his base in Canton; and Geng controlled Fujian from the coastal city of Fuzhou.

Together they were virtual masters over a region equivalent in size to France and Spain combined, or to America's southern states from the Georgia coast to Texas. Within these areas, despite the nominal presence of Qing bureaucrats, the Three Feudatories supervised all aspects of military and civil government, the examination systems, relations with the indigenous peoples, and the collection of taxes. Not only did they keep the local revenues for themselves and control lucrative trade monopolies, they also constantly demanded lavish subsidies from the Qing court as the price of their continued loyalty. By the 1660s, they were receiving more than 10 million ounces of silver every year.

It soon became apparent that they also considered their feudatories hereditary. When Shang Kexi fell ill in 1671, he passed the supervision of military affairs in Guangdong over to his son, Shang Zhixin. That same year Geng Jimao died, and his son, Geng Jingzhong, took over Fujian province. Although the records are fragmentary, it is clear that Emperor Kangxi began discussing what to do about the Three Feudatories early in his reign and that his advisers, both Chinese and Manchu, were torn about how to proceed. Unlike many of his more cautious advisers, Kangxi was bold enough to recommend confrontation if it became necessary for the long-run strength of the country. Thus when Shang Kexi, who was indeed old and ill, inquired in 1673 if he might be allowed to retire back to Manchuria, Kangxi leaped at the chance and graciously gave his permission. He responded with equal enthusiasm when Wu Sangui and Geng Jingzhong made similar requests as feelers. These requests were intended to test Kangxi's general feelings about the continued existence of the feudatories; after his answer, it was obvious that an open break was coming.

Despite an attempt by some of Kangxi's most trusted confidants to persuade Wu Sangui to leave his base peacefully, Wu threw off his allegiance to the Qing in December 1673, declaring the formation of a new dynasty, the Zhou, and driving his armies deep into Hunan. Geng Jingzhong rebelled in 1674, and his armies consolidated their hold in Fujian and moved into

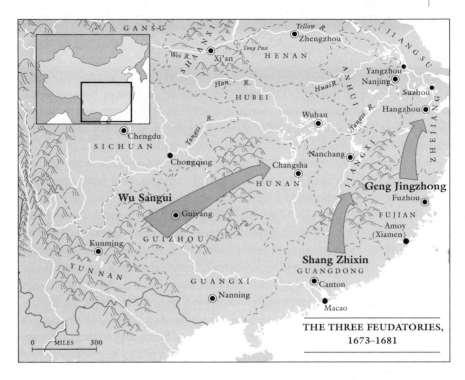

GANSU
Yellow R.
Zhengzhou
Wei R.
Tong Pass
Xi'an
HENAN
SHANXI
JIANGSU
Yangzhou
Nanjing
Han R.
Huai R.
ANHUI
Suzhou
HUBEI
Wuhan
Hangzhou
ZHEJIANG
Yangzi R.
Chengdu
SICHUAN
Nanchang
Chongqing
Changsha
JIANGXI
Geng Jingzhong
HUNAN
Fuzhou
Wu Sangui
FUJIAN
Guiyang
Amoy
(Xiamen)
Kunming
GUIZHOU
Shang Zhixin
GUANGDONG
YUNNAN
GUANGXI
Canton
Nanning
Macao

0   MILES   300

**THE THREE FEUDATORIES,
1673–1681**

Zhejiang province. Shang Zhixin imprisoned his father (who stayed stead-
fast in his loyalty to the Qing) and joined the rebellion in 1676, consolidating
Guangdong and sending troops northward to Jiangxi.

This War of the Three Feudatories confronted the Chinese in the south
and southwest with an agonizing test of loyalties. Those who had survived
the years of fighting in the 1640s and 1650s and had made their peace with
the Qing now had to decide whether to remain true to that allegiance, or
to pin their hopes on Wu's Zhou dynasty. Wu played on their sense of
Chinese loyalty by ordering the restoration of Ming customs and the cutting
of queues. He also left open the question of who the first emperor of the
Zhou should be, implying that if a survivor of the Ming ruling house could
be found, that man would be enthroned. Furthermore, the name "Zhou"
itself evoked one of China's most revered earlier dynasties, which had ruled
over northern China in the first millennium B.C. and was celebrated in
several of the basic Confucian texts. Wu offered Emperor Kangxi an
amnesty if he would only leave Chinese soil altogether and found a new
kingdom in Manchuria and Korea. Predictably, Kangxi refused, and to
underscore his anger he executed Wu's son, who was being held hostage in
Peking.

With their huge standing armies and sound administrative and economic base, Wu and his supporters had a better chance of success than the Ming loyalist princes of Fu and Gui before them. Furthermore, throughout the south and west, the Chinese loyal to the Qing were surrounded and outnumbered; although there is evidence that many tried to resist service to the rulers of the Three Feudatories—some by fleeing to the mountains, others by feigning illness or even by mutilating themselves—most felt they had no choice but to submit. The result was that the rebellion almost succeeded in destroying the Qing. At the very least, it looked as if the Manchus would lose control of all of China south of the Yangzi River, and that permanent partition of the kingdom would be the result.

China remained a unified country (with all the significance that has for later world history) as the result of five crucial factors. One was Wu Sangui's indecisiveness in not driving across the Hunan border and up to the north when he first held the initiative in 1674. A second was Kangxi's ability, despite his youth, to rally his court behind him and to develop a long-range strategy for conquest and retrenchment. A third was the courage and tenacity of a number of Manchu generals—some also young and untried in battle—who spearheaded the Qing counterattacks. (Kangxi did not campaign in person.) A fourth was the inability of the Three Feudatories to coordinate their endeavors and to mount a sustained campaign against the Qing on any one front. A fifth was their inability to appeal to the most loyal of the Ming supporters, who were fully aware that the Three Feudatories had previously been active collaborators with the Manchus.

Nor were the Three Feudatories well suited for their new roles as restorationists. Wu Sangui grew ever more absorbed by luxurious living and the trappings of grandeur, while Shang Zhixin exhibited much of the crazed cruelty of the earlier rebel Zhang Xianzhong, going so far as to have his personal enemies torn apart by hunting dogs. Geng Jingzhong seems to have been incompetent and ineffective, and it was he who ruined any chance of concerted action when he surrendered independently to the Qing in 1676. Shang Zhixin did the same the following year, apparently because Wu Sangui insisted on making appointments of officials to posts in Guangdong province, which Shang considered his own preserve.

Wu finally declared himself emperor of the new Zhou dynasty in 1678, but the gesture came too late to be meaningful. Wu died of dysentery later that same year, ending a stormy sixty-six years of life. His grandson fought on in his name for three more years, but committed suicide in the Yunnan capital of Kunming when a number of Manchu generals trapped him there. Wu's followers were executed, as were Geng and Shang, despite the fact that Emperor Kangxi had accepted their surrenders and restored their princely titles to them. The emperor could not afford to leave such men around.

At the war's end, in 1681, the advisers who had urged the "hard" line against the Three Feudatories became Kangxi's close advisers: although he and they had nearly lost the kingdom, their final victory meant that China would henceforth be stronger. Kangxi was ruthless to those in senior positions who had supported the rebels, but ordered more compassionate treatment to those who had been caught up in the fighting through no fault of their own. As he put it, they had just shown "a natural desire to hang on to life and avoid being killed. If my armies arrive and execute them all, this contradicts my desire to save the people, and denies them any chance to reform." The emperor showed similar sympathy for women and children trapped in the fighting with the "bandits" (as he usually called the rebels): "The women in the bandits' camps were often initially taken there by force—so after the bandits themselves have been destroyed, let the other local people have a chance to identify and reclaim the refugees and their children—don't just arrest everyone indiscriminately."[1]

With the leaders dead, all traces of the feudatories were abolished. New governors-general and governors—mostly Chinese bannermen—were appointed to the rebellious provinces to integrate them firmly into Kangxi's realm. Revenues once again began to flow from these areas to Peking, and with the revenues came a resumption of the examination system in the south and southwest, and the beginning of a trickle of successful candidates. But life had been too seriously disrupted to be speedily repaired. Hunan, Guangxi, Yunnan, and Guizhou all remained peripheral to the main life of China for the rest of Kangxi's reign, and distrust still ran deep. Few men from those provinces were given higher degrees, and even fewer were appointed to high office. Kangxi himself, although a great traveler, never ventured more than a few miles south of the Yangzi. It was the now-prosperous Yangzi delta towns of Nanjing and Suzhou that he referred to as "the South," with the implication that the more truly southern and western provinces remained somehow beyond his range. Throughout his life he reminisced about how shaken the war had left him, and how bitterly he regretted the loss of life that had followed his decision to let the heads of the Three Feudatories "retire." But he never regretted the decision itself.

TAIWAN AND MARITIME CHINA

The integration of Taiwan into China's history dates from the early seventeenth century. In the later years of the Ming dynasty, Taiwan was still largely unknown: dangerous seas, typhoons, and sand shoals protected its coasts; flat, malarial plains along the west, backed by inhospitable mountain ranges, sealed its isolation. Taiwan's unfriendly aboriginal populations further discouraged exploration or settlement by outsiders. But a few Chinese traders from the harbors of Guangdong and Fujian braved the dangers and made a decent profit from Taiwanese deer hides and crushed deerhorns (believed to be a potent aphrodisiac), and established small settlements in the southwest of the island. Chinese and Japanese pirates also found havens along the same coast.

In the 1620s Taiwan began to feature in global politics. At one time, shipwrecked sailors and missionaries had been the island's only European visitors. The Portuguese then explored the island and gave it the name of "Beautiful Isle" ("Ilha Formosa"); but they withdrew, deciding to keep Macao as their own main base of operations in east Asia. Not so the Spaniards, who established a small base in the north at Keelung, nor the Protestant Dutch, who in 1624 established a fort they named Zeelandia in the little town of Anping (present-day Tainan) in the south. By the 1640s the Dutch had driven out both the Spaniards and the last Japanese pirates, and a profitable trade developed among the island, the Dutch Empire in the East Indies (now Indonesia), and the merchants and administrators in China's east coast. Drawn by the island's possibilities, clusters of Chinese settlers congregated around first the Spanish and then the Dutch enclaves, while others came to drain and farm the land on Taiwan's western plains. The Dutch encouraged Chinese traders, though initially few settled permanently; they would return to the mainland coast in the winters, leaving the Dutch to work out their own economic and organizational system by a divide-and-rule strategy with the island's native inhabitants.

The Dutch stayed largely aloof from the fighting by the Ming loyalists in the 1640s and 1650s, but the development of the coastal war and its interconnections with Ming loyalists eventually made Dutch isolation impossible. The fighting escalated when the leader of the powerful and wealthy Zheng family, a pirate and trader who plied the waters between Fujian, Taiwan, and southern Japan, was finally made an official by the desperate Ming. Although he went over to the Qing court in 1646, his impetuous son, Zheng Chenggong, refused to do so. Instead he made his troops and ships available to the fleeing Ming, and continued to support them in name and deed even after they had been driven inland.

This remarkable naval warrior, known to history as Koxinga,* had been

---

*The Ming gave him their imperial surname, a title pronounced in Fujian dialect as "Kok-seng-ia," transformed by Westerners into the word *Koxinga*.

born in 1624 to a Japanese mother, and his upbringing suitably reflected the polyglot world of international trade and cultural relations. His father's trade networks extended from Nagasaki to Macao, and in their fortified home near Amoy (Xiamen) could be found a chapel with both Christian and Buddhist images, as well as a bodyguard of black slaves, fugitives from the Portuguese in Macao. Access to the inner living quarters of the compound was made directly by boat.

Koxinga's fleets fought the Manchus along China's east coast all through the 1650s, and under his control Amoy became an international entrepôt. Koxinga even organized ten trading companies that dealt in silks and other luxury goods, as well as sugar, in exchange for the naval supplies and gunpowder he needed to keep his fleet in fighting shape. It was not until he tried a decisive frontal assault on Nanjing in 1659 that he was seriously defeated. As the Qing armies closed in on his main Amoy base, Koxinga made the bold decision to attack the Dutch fortress of Zeelandia. Probably aided by a former Chinese interpreter who had worked for the Dutch and knew the details of Zeelandia's defensive system, Koxinga pressed the siege; but although he conquered the surrounding countryside easily enough, killing the Dutchmen there and enslaving their women, the Dutch defenders of the fort held out for an astonishing nine months. Only in February 1662 did they surrender, under an agreement that allowed them to retire to Batavia in the Dutch East Indies, leaving Koxinga trade goods and cash estimated to be worth over 1 million ounces of silver.

Koxinga did not enjoy his success for long. The news that his father and brothers had been executed in Peking because of his intransigence (his Japanese mother had been killed long before by Qing troops) perhaps exacerbated his already unstable mental condition. He began to follow a destructive pattern of abusing his subordinates and directing passionate rages against his own children, and died later in 1662.

Despite the savage efficiency of their policy of removing the Chinese coastal population, initiated in 1661, the Oboi regents failed to bring Taiwan into submission. They did form a brief alliance with the Dutch to smoke out the last Zheng-family holdouts on the Fujian coast, but two expeditions against Taiwan planned in 1664 and 1665 both fizzled out. The Manchus, after all, were inexperienced at naval warfare and, after 1673, were largely preoccupied with the civil war of the Three Feudatories. This allowed the Zhengs in Taiwan to continue developing a prosperous trade and commercial empire: first Koxinga's sons and then his grandson supervised a Chinese population that swelled through emigration and flight from the mainland to over 100,000, produced large quantities of rice and sugarcane, and conducted considerable business in salt, refined sugar, and shipbuilding.

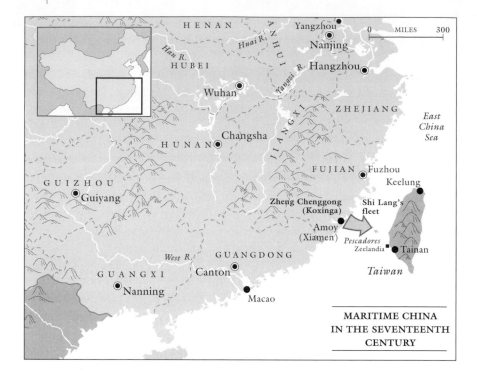

MARITIME CHINA
IN THE SEVENTEENTH
CENTURY

Even after the war of the Three Feudatories was over, Kangxi still found it hard to assemble the necessary forces to capture the island from the Zheng family. The emperor's final strategy was to appoint one of Koxinga's father's former admirals, Shi Lang—who had surrendered long before, in the 1650s—to be the senior admiral of an expeditionary force. The choice was an excellent one, for not only was Shi Lang a fine commander, but his father, brother, and son had all been vengefully killed by Koxinga when Shi joined the Manchus; he could be counted on to push the battle to its limits.

Shi Lang planned methodically for his campaign, and the scale of his fleet—three hundred war vessels—reminds us of how strong a potential sea power China was, even though its naval resources were not usually exploited. Leading his fleet from Fujian province in early July 1683, Admiral Shi won a crushing victory in the Pescadores over the last Zheng forces.

Taiwan surrendered three months later, and Kangxi, perhaps wearied by the bloodbaths of the earlier civil-war period, treated the fallen Zheng family and their leading officers graciously, ennobling some and allowing them to settle in Peking. Most of Koxinga's troops were moved from Taiwan and used to strengthen the garrisons against the Russians in northern China.

There were heated debates at the Qing court about what should be done with the island. Some courtiers suggested that it be abandoned altogether, whereas Admiral Shi urged that it be made a fortified base to protect China from the "strong, huge and invincible" warships of the Dutch. Kangxi decided to incorporate Taiwan into his empire. It became a prefecture of Fujian province, with a capital at Tainan, and was divided into three counties, each under a civilian magistrate. At the same time, Kangxi ordered that a strong Qing garrison of 8,000 troops be left permanently on the island, and that the tribal lands and hunting grounds of the aboriginal inhabitants be respected. Further Chinese emigration to Taiwan was to be carefully limited.

By these rather conflicting responses, Kangxi was reflecting the ambivalence that the Qing state (like the Ming before it) felt about overseas trade and colonization. There was a basic distrust of trade among China's leaders, who saw it as conducive to unrest and disorder. They feared it would lead to the dissemination of secret information about China's defenses to foreign powers, cause a drain of precious silver from the country, and encourage piracy and other forms of crime. Accordingly, even though the coastal-evacuation policy was abandoned after the fall of the Zheng family, Qing officials continued to control contact with Taiwan through licensing rules and limits on ship size, enforced by government agents in Amoy and other coastal cities.

But this policy was unrealistic in the vigorous entrepreneurial world of east-coast China. Its main result was to allow huge profits to flow into the hands of the senior east-coast bureaucrats who were in a position to control the maritime and coastal trade. A Chinese bondservant in the early 1680s allegedly paid bribes well in excess of 10,000 ounces of silver in order to win the post of governor-general of Guangdong and Guangxi, which would allow him to supervise most of the trade out of Canton city. In a massive relocation of the population back to the coastal regions, this man, with the aid of special commissioners appointed to the task, reassigned almost half a million acres of land to more than 30,000 people. The fortune accumulated by this one merchant-official was apparently in excess of 400,000 ounces of silver.

The potential returns of careful state-run taxation of legitimate foreign trade were clearly vast and had been effectively exploited by some rulers in earlier dynasties. But beyond setting up four maritime customs offices (one each in Guangdong, Fujian, Zhejiang, and Jiangsu) and trying to enforce an across-the-board tariff of 20 percent on foreign imports, the Qing state failed to develop the necessary mechanisms, preferring instead to work through systems of kickbacks or purchased monopolies. With the arrival of more powerful Western traders in the eighteenth century, this decision was to be a fateful one.

Similarly, by restricting emigration to Taiwan but failing to enforce the order adequately, the Qing ensured Taiwan's development as an unruly dependency, a kind of rough-and-tumble frontier society, only peripherally bound to the administrative structure of the Qing state. Records from the Kangxi reign give a few glimpses of the men who developed the island: a group of immigrant brothers from Fujian who rented land cheap from local aborigines and improved it spectacularly by applying Chinese irrigation procedures; a relative of Admiral Shi who settled in north Taiwan and spent his own money to open up virgin land there, using the labor of vagrants from the more crowded south; and a young Chinese from Guangdong who married an aborigine chieftain's daughter and became his father-in-law's interpreter, profiting thereafter from renting tribal lands to other Chinese immigrants. These were not exactly exemplars of conventional Chinese behavior, but they helped make an important addition to China's traditional empire.

WOOING THE INTELLECTUALS

The protracted resistance of the Ming claimants, the support given to Koxinga and his descendants, the swift spread and near success of the Three Feudatories: all these pointed to a lack of support for the Qing among the Chinese. From the beginning of his reign, Emperor Kangxi addressed himself to this problem by trying to strike a balance in which he reassured the Manchu nobles as to his martial vigor and political firmness on the one hand, and tried to convince the Chinese of his respect for their traditional culture on the other.

Appealing to the Manchus turned out to be comparatively simple. Kangxi was a strong young man whose survival of a childhood bout of smallpox was a factor that led to his being chosen as Shunzhi's heir. He early developed a passion for hunting and for archery, and his skill at riding meant he could go on long excursions into the ancestral homelands of Manchuria. The elite guards-officers and Manchu nobles who accompanied him on these journeys were bonded in loyalty to their ruler; and though there were serious differences of opinion over national policy, they stood behind him in all his early crises. His grandmother, Hong Taiji's widow, who doted on him, was also a powerful political figure through her family connections, and the family of Kangxi's successive empresses and consorts (he had first been married, at eleven, to the granddaughter of one of the regents opposed to Oboi) gave him valuable contacts. He was meticulous, too, in carrying out ceremonies at the Manchu shamanic temples in Peking, in promoting Manchus to high office along with the Chinese, and in holding back eunuch power by placing the imperial-household organization in the hands of Manchu nobles and by using Chinese bondservants rather than eunuchs for many menial palace functions.

Appealing to the Chinese was more complex. The Manchus claimed that they had entered China in 1644 to avenge the Ming emperor Chongzhen, but numerous Chinese did not accept this. Even if they did, the ties of loyalty to one's ruler were so strong that many Chinese committed suicide when they heard of Chongzhen's death; many took up arms, though certain that resistance would ultimately prove fatal; and many more simply removed their talents from the Qing state, refusing to serve the government in any form.

This refusal to serve was rationalized on grounds of Confucian principle, and it was on these grounds that Kangxi chose to meet the opposition. The teachings of Confucius had an undisputed place in Chinese society, although by the mid-seventeenth century there was considerable difference of opinion about what those teachings were. In essence, during the fifth century B.C. Confucius had been the spokesman in China for the values of morality and dignity in private life and in government. He had argued for the importance of righteousness and loyalty, reinforced by correct rituals that would place a given individual in proper relationship with the cosmos and with his contemporaries. He had stated that worthy men should not serve unworthy rulers and must be ready to sacrifice their lives, if necessary, in the defense of principle. He argued further that humans should concentrate on the problems of this world and, while paying proper respect to the memory of their own deceased ancestors, should not seek to understand the forces of heaven and the realm of the spirits.

A collection of dialogues that Confucius held with statesmen and students, known as the *Analects,* portrayed him as a shrewd and vigorous man, constantly testing himself and those around him for flaws of character while never losing faith in the possibilities of virtuous action. His belief in the powers of moral example and in the central importance of education was absolute. Confucius held that humans did gain in wisdom as they grew older, and charted the steps for this development of self-knowledge. Some centuries after Confucius's death, five of the works he was believed to have edited were bunched together as the "Five Classics" of the Confucian canon. One of these works was on rituals, two were on history, one on poetry, and one—the *Book of Changes* or *Yijing (I-ching)*—on cosmology and divination.

Subsequently, in the twelfth century A.D., the *Analects,* along with the sayings of Confucius's later follower Mencius and two selections from the ritual classic that dealt with human nature and moral development, were similarly grouped together as the "Four Books." Cumulatively, these nine works were believed to contain the basic precepts needed for leading a moral life, and to offer a valid record of an earlier utopian period of Chinese history that had reached its apogee of enlightened government and popular contentment during the early Zhou dynasty, some fifteen hundred years in the past.

Over the ensuing centuries this body of material was swollen by floods of commentaries, glosses, and reinterpretations, and modified in subtle ways by elements drawn from the Buddhist faith—which flourished in China after the fifth century A.D.—and from other traditions within Chinese philosophy. At the same time, this diversity of "Confucian" material was turned into "doctrine," and the Four Books and Five Classics became the basis for the state examinations that led to government service. Confucianism was now construed in a hierarchical way and used to support the absolute rights of parents over their children, of husbands over their wives, and of rulers over their subjects. This hierarchy was reinforced by restricting the examinations to male candidates, and by not allowing women to serve in the bureaucracy, however good their scholarly knowledge. The prevailing school of Confucianism in the Qing was one that emphasized the force of principle or reason *(li)* in the world but placed it outside and above life energy *(qi),* leading to a dualistic interpretation of human nature and of the whole metaphysical structure of the Chinese world.

From the moment he imprisoned the regent Oboi, Kangxi showed the utmost respect for this complex legacy. In 1670 he issued to the nation a series of sixteen maxims that were designed to be a summation of Confucian moral values. Known as the "Sacred Edict," these maxims emphasized hierarchical submission in social relations, generosity, obedience, thrift, and hard work. Kangxi subsequently named a team of Manchu and Chinese tutors, with whom he read meticulously through the Four Books and then the Five Classics. In the official court diaries, one can chart his progress from chapter to chapter and watch him debate knotty points with his teachers. Judiciously "leaked" to the court, the news of these studies, along with Kangxi's intensive work on Chinese calligraphy, gave the young monarch the aura of a "sage ruler." At the same time, popular versions of the Sacred Edict, prepared in a homely, colloquial style by Manchu and Chinese scholars, ensured the wide dissemination of Kangxi's ethical views to the people as a whole.

One of the great powers of the Chinese state lay in its control of the examination system. Shunzhi had revived this system, and Kangxi continued to hold the exams every three years—even during the civil-war period.

But he was vexed at the number of accomplished scholars who refused even to sit for the examinations on the grounds that to do so would be to betray the memory of the Ming dynasty under which they had grown up. As an ingenious solution to this predicament, Kangxi, in 1679, ordered that nominations be sent from the provinces for a special examination—separate from the triennial national exams—to be held for men of outstanding talent. Although some austere scholars still refused to come to Peking for this exam, and others would not permit themselves to be nominated, the venture was a success. Fifty special degrees were awarded, mostly to scholars from the Yangzi delta provinces; and, in a tactful gesture to their past loyalties, these scholars were put to work helping compile the official history of the defunct Ming dynasty.

Despite these gestures, many Chinese retained an ambivalent attitude toward the new dynasty. Some scholars privately accumulated materials on the Ming so they could write their own histories away from government supervision. The heroic, though futile, resistance to the Manchus of cities such as Yangzhou and Jiangyin were written up and clandestinely preserved for posterity. Some philosophers who had taken part in the defense of their native regions retreated from political life and wrote careful accounts of the moralistic and reformist scholars who had been members of the Donglin and similar societies in the late Ming.

Three scholars stand out both for their actions and their writings in this period. One was the Hunanese Wang Fuzhi, who spent years with the fugitive court of the prince of Gui in the southwest before returning home in 1650. He devoted much effort thereafter to attacking the individualistic philosophy of the followers of the mid-Ming scholar Wang Yangming, claiming that their insistence on finding the source of morality within the individual conscience had wrecked the moral fiber of the time. Wang Fuzhi also wrote a history of the prince of Gui's court as well as critical appraisals of former "barbarian" regimes, which would have led to his execution had the Manchus discovered them.

The second scholar, Huang Zongxi, a Zhejiang native whose father had been killed in 1626 on the orders of the eunuch Wei Zhongxian, was a passionate partisan of the Donglin and other reformers. Huang Zongxi fought for years alongside the Ming claimants on the east coast and built barricades in the mountains to slow the advance of Manchu troops. Finally, after 1649, he retired to a life of scholarship. Not only did he write careful historical biographies of major Ming figures, he also tried to analyze the structure of government itself. Huang suggested that an alternative to the overcentralization of the present lay in an earlier ideal Chinese society that had been governed by the moral force of scholars working as administrators in their own communities. Whereas most other Chinese political thinkers tended to ponder ways of reforming the behavior of the eunuchs and officials who stood between the emperor and the people, Huang believed that the emperors themselves should have less power.

Most famous of the three scholars was Gu Yanwu, born in 1613 in Jiangsu and raised by his widowed foster mother, a remarkable woman of great moral rectitude who was determined that Gu follow correct Confucian ethical precepts. In the late Ming, Gu Yanwu passed the lower-level examinations and responded to what he saw as the political and moral collapse of his times by a program of intensive study of traditional Chinese economics, government, and military defense. In 1644 he served briefly with the prince of Fu against the Manchus, and was deeply moved by the example of his foster mother, who starved herself to death rather than submit to the new conquerors. In her dying words to Gu, she declared: "Although only a woman, I have received favor from the [Ming] dynasty. To perish with the dynasty is no more than my duty. Do not serve another dynasty."[2]

Though Gu declined to emulate her action, he took her words to heart and spent the rest of his life (he died in 1682) in travel, reflection, and scholarship. He even abandoned the lush Yangzi plains of his native Jiangsu for the harsh northwest terrain of Shaanxi province. Gu sought to develop a body of writings that would counter what he—like his contemporary Wang Fuzhi—saw as the moral hollowness of the dominant schools of Confucianism, with their emphases on metaphysical dualisms and intuition. Gu traveled over much of north China on horseback, examining farming practices, mining technology, and the banking systems of local merchants. In a series of essays drawn from his observations, he tried to lay the basis for a new kind of rigorous and pragmatic scholarship.

In his voluminous writings, Gu focused on such themes as government, ethics, economics, geography, and social relations, and paid special attention to philology, which he saw as a fundamental tool for evaluating the exact meaning of China's earlier scholarly legacy. He especially praised the scholars of the Han dynasty (206 B.C.–A.D. 220) for their absence of literary adornment, their intellectual rigor, and their lack of metaphysical pretensions. Despite Gu's growing fame, he refused all invitations to take the Qing examinations—including the honorific one of 1679—or to work on the Ming history sponsored by Kangxi. After his death, Gu was revered by many scholars who saw him as a model of scholarly precision and integrity; and in the eighteenth century, his works came to have a profound influence on Chinese thought.

It was not only soldiers and scholars who resisted the Manchus. Many early Qing painters used their art to show their agitation and lack of faith in the regime. Through boldly innovative and eccentric brushwork, and the use of empty space in their compositions, they portrayed a world that was bleak or out of balance. Lone and twisted pine trees, desolate, angular mountain ranges, images of tangled foliage laid on paper in thick, wet strokes, isolated birds or fish—such were the subjects these artists often chose. Some of the most brilliant of these painters, like Shitao or Bada Shanren, were related to members of the fallen Ming ruling house and retired to isolated monasteries in the conquest period. Bada Shanren (his self-selected name, meaning "one who dwells in the eight great mountains") made silence his gesture of defiance to the Qing. After writing the Chinese character for "dumb" upon his door, he refused to speak anymore, though he would still laugh or weep extravagantly when drunk or caught in creative fever. But Shitao slowly edged back into society, began to mingle with other scholars and artists even if they had served with the Qing, accepted occasional commissions designing landscape gardens for wealthy urbanites, and ended up on the outer edges of court circles.

One could, indeed, write a history of the period by tracing the coopting of the intellectuals by the Qing court. Those who would not serve in administrative office and would not take the examinations could still be lured by the promise of good company and hard cash. Literary compilations especially proved a fine focus for their energies. Kangxi assembled several groups of scholars and hired them to write dictionaries, encyclopedias, records of imperial tours, and collections of classical prose and poetry. Other senior ministers sponsored massive geographical studies and local histories, which enabled restless scholars to travel the country in search of material and then to return to a comfortable home base to write it down. Yet other officials gave promising writers jobs as private secretaries with light duties, which allowed them ample time for pursuing their own creative paths, whether as novelists, short-story writers, poets, or dramatists. The result was a flowering of Chinese culture in the later seventeenth century, despite the recent bloody imposition of alien rule.

Finally, the very act of Ming resistance and loyalty became an accepted topic at Kangxi's court through the artistry of Kong Shangren. A descendant of Confucius in the sixty-fourth generation, Kong was born in 1648, after the Qing conquest. His father had been a prominent Ming scholar, and Kong Shangren became fascinated with the Ming dynasty's fall and the people who had been caught up in it. During his forties, he composed a popular drama, *The Peach Blossom Fan,* about an upright scholar, the woman he loves, and their travails in the Ming court of the prince of Fu. The heroine resists the advances of a wicked Ming minister, attacking him with her fan, which gets spattered with blood. A painter transforms the blood drops into part of a design of peach blossoms, giving the play its title and providing a brilliant metaphor for the mixture of violence and beauty that Kong saw as lying at the heart of late Ming moral and intellectual life. At the play's end, with the Ming resistance in ruins, the lovers agree to take monastic vows, while the surviving virtuous officials retreat deep into the mountains to escape a summons from the Qing that they take up office. In one of the last scenes, the lovers and a friend join in a grand aria:

> This tale of the southern court will resound forever,
> And tears of blood will swell the streams with woe,
> We raise to Heaven our "summons to the soul"
> As mists obscure the mighty river's flow.[3]

By the 1690s, this aria was being sung at Kangxi's court, and Kong Shang-ren's play had become a palace favorite. In an essay written at this time, Kong caught the emotion of the audience:

> Famous aristocrats, high officials, and talented literati gathered in such a crowd that it was impossible to find space for one's legs. The furnishings formed an embroidered universe, and the banquet a landscape of jewelled delicacies. . . . Yet in the midst of this dazzling theater, there were a few who sat quietly weeping behind their sleeves—former officials and 'survivors'. When the lanterns had flickered out and the drinking was over, they uttered sighs and went their ways.[4]

Such men might still be nostalgic, but they had made their peace.

DEFINING THE BORDERS

Foreign pressure, and at least some elements of foreign technology, were becoming commonplace in early Qing China. Even those Chinese with no knowledge or interest in foreign lands could have their lives abruptly changed. Kong Shangren, for instance, had been slowly losing his eyesight for some years before he wrote *The Peach Blossom Fan;* he recorded his resumption of scholarly activity in an ecstatic poem:

> White glass from across the Western Seas
> Is imported through Macao:
> Fashioned into lenses big as coins,
> They encompass the eyes in a double frame.
> I put them on—it suddenly becomes clear;

I can see the very tips of things!
And read fine print by the dim-lit window
Just like in my youth.[5]

Kong gained this clarity of vision, fruit of a European technology exported through Macao, thanks to the Qing decision not to destroy the Portuguese base. During the 1660s, as part of the coastal-withdrawal policy linked to the suppression of Taiwan, Qing naval forces blockaded Macao, and all Chinese were ordered to leave. Portuguese ships were banned, and there was a threat that their buildings would be razed. But for reasons of local economic self-interest, Qing officials in charge of carrying out these orders failed to do so. Through subsequent diplomatic embassies, the support of the Jesuits in Peking (now returned to favor), and the judicious gift in 1678 of an African lion—which fascinated Kangxi—the Portuguese persuaded the Qing to allow them to retain Macao as the base for their east Asian trade.

The same tolerance was not extended to the Russians. Late Ming officials and advisers to Emperor Shunzhi were aware of the spread of Russian hunters and settlers into the northeast border region. A Russian embassy had negotiated with the Manchus for permission to send regular trade caravans into China, but Kangxi, too, was uneasy about the influence the Russians were having on the allegiance of the border tribes. An attempt to withdraw several border tribes south of the Russian line of advance, and to establish a kind of no man's land to isolate the Russians from China—perhaps in deliberate imitation of the coastal policy to destroy the Zhengs—was abandoned as being too costly and impractical.

Kangxi had in fact been preparing for some years to launch an attack on the Russian outpost of Albazin, on the Amur River. When Taiwan was finally captured by the Qing in 1683, as we saw above, some of the surviving Zheng family troops were sent to the north to participate in the border campaign against the Russians. The maritime skills of the Zheng troops were valuable to Kangxi, who needed naval forces to navigate the northern rivers. With the southern wars safely over, Kangxi ordered a concerted assault on Albazin, which, after stiff fighting, was seized by Manchu forces in 1685. Abandoning the town—really more a large, fortified stockade in those days—and pulling back as the emperor had instructed, the Qing commander inexplicably disobeyed the order that he destroy the abundant crops planted by the Russian settlers in the area. Accordingly the garrison commander of Nerchinsk, the second Russian trading base located to the west down the river Shilka, sent men to gather in the crops before the winter and to reoccupy the city.

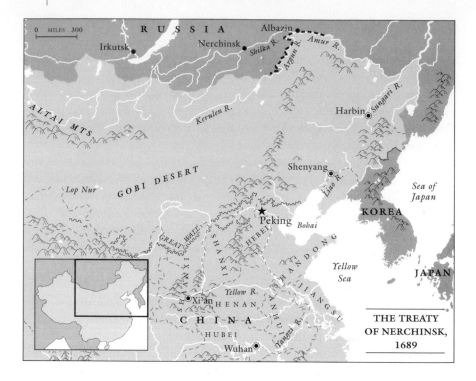

Furious, Kangxi ordered a second attack on Albazin in 1686, which met stiffer Russian opposition. The Russian rulers were worried, however, over their ability to hold the huge territory in the face of determined Manchu opposition, and had already decided to sue for peace. The two sides, with the Jesuits using their knowledge of Latin and Manchu to act as interpreters, met at Nerchinsk in 1689 and hammered out a treaty that, in its long-term effects, was one of the most important in China's history, fixing the northern border in substantially the same place it is today. In the most disputed area, the basic north-south demarcation line between the countries was fixed at the Gorbitsa and the Argun rivers. Albazin was to be abandoned by the Russians and destroyed, and the whole watershed area of the Amur River was to be Chinese. Fugitives from each side were to be extradited, and trade was to be permitted, though only to those merchants who had been issued valid documents by the Qing.

So whereas Taiwan had been reduced to Chinese territory by conquest, and the Portuguese in Macao were allowed their semi-independent status by an act of generosity unsubstantiated by treaty, in the Russian case the Chinese signed a treaty between equal sovereign states. Though this was a major departure from traditional Chinese practices, it is worth noting that from the foundation of the Qing dynasty dealings with the Russians had been conducted not through the Ministry of Rituals, which handled the so-called tributary relations with such countries as Holland, Spain, and Portugal, but through a special bureau, the Lifan Yuan. This bureau had been an invention of Hong Taiji and dealt originally with problems of diplomacy and commerce with the Mongols. By putting Russian affairs under this bureau, the Manchus tacitly admitted that their northern neighbors were a special case and that matters on the long northern land frontier required different handling from those in the southeast.

Much of the impetus for the Qing to sign a Russian treaty had come from the danger posed by the Zunghar tribes in western China: the Qing feared that the Russians might ally themselves with these dangerous nomadic warriors. Under a brilliant leader, Galdan, and drawing added unity from their deep devotion to the Dalai Lama in Tibet (whom they regarded as their spiritual leader), the Zunghars had been roaming at will over the largely unsettled lands known now as Outer Mongolia and Qinghai. In the late 1670s, by seizing Kashgar, Hami, and Turfan in turn, Galdan imposed his rule over the largely Muslim inhabitants of those cities and over their prosperous caravan routes linking China and the Mediterranean. The tribes hostile to Galdan and defeated by him in battle fled eastward, pressing into the western Qing province of Gansu. This massive migration of warriors deeply worried the emperor, who feared the possibility of a Russian-Zunghar alliance.

But such an alliance was not made, and after the Treaty of Nerchinsk was safely signed Kangxi sent an army (under his own brother) to attack Galdan. After several more years of inconclusive fighting between Galdan and certain rival tribes to his east, Kangxi decided to lead a major campaign in person, apparently prompted to such daring by his feeling that it was he—not his generals—who had correctly conceived the successful Russian war. In a logistical triumph for the Qing armies, some 80,000 men advanced westward on three fronts; Kangxi's army crossed the Gobi and pushed the Zunghars north of the Kerulen River, where Galdan was cornered and defeated at the great battle of Jao Modo in 1696. He died the following year, abandoned by most of his followers.

This successful campaign marked the pinnacle of Kangxi's career as emperor. Now forty-two years old, he took an active delight in the excitement and danger of the war; after it was over he wrote back to his court favorites in Peking that the sparkling weather, the new foods, the unexpected scenery—all filled him with joy. "Now Galdan is dead, and his followers have come back to our allegiance," the emperor wrote in a letter in the spring of 1697. "My great task is done. . . . Heaven, earth, and ances-

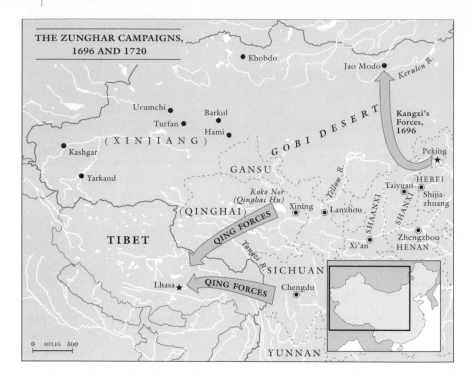

THE ZUNGHAR CAMPAIGNS,
1696 AND 1720

Khobdo

Jao Modo ●

Kerulen R.

Kangxi's
Forces,
1696

GOBI DESERT

Urumchi ●
Barkul ●
Turfan ●
Hami ●

(X I N J I A N G)

Kashgar ●

Yarkand ●

GANSU

Peking ★

Yellow R.

HEBEI
Taiyuan ●
Shijia-
zhuang ●

Koko Nor
(Qinghai Hu)
Xining ●
Lanzhou ●

SHAANXI

SHANXI

QING FORCES

(Q I N G H A I)

TIBET

Yangzi R.

Xi'an ●

Zhengzhou ●
HENAN

SICHUAN

Lhasa ★
QING FORCES
Chengdu ●

0   MILES   300

YUNNAN

tors have protected me and brought me this achievement. As for my own life, one can say it is happy. One can say it's fulfilled. One can say I've got what I wanted. In a few days, in the palace, I'll tell you all about it myself. It's hard to tell it with brush and ink."[6]

But in foreign policy, each solution leads to a fresh problem. The power politics of the region were not resolved by Galdan's death, and Kangxi found himself drawn into complex struggles with other Zunghar leaders when the Dalai Lama was murdered and an improperly chosen successor named in his place. This gave Kangxi the opportunity to invade Tibet in the name of righteous retribution (just as the Manchus had entered China in 1644); he dispatched two armies, one of which entered Tibet through Koko Nor, the other through Sichuan province. In the autumn of 1720, the two armies joined forces in the Tibetan capital of Lhasa, and a new Dalai Lama, loyal to the Qing, was installed. Thus began the Chinese military intervention in the politics of Tibet.

At about the same time, the unsettled nature of life in Taiwan and serious misgovernment there by the Qing prompted a Fujian native named Zhu Yigui, who had traveled to the island as an official's servant, to raise a flag of revolt along with some fifty blood brothers. Aided by the turbulent conditions of the time and by the fact that he had the same surname—Zhu—as the former Ming imperial family, Zhu Yigui attracted hundreds of followers and seized the prefectural capital, declaring himself king of Taiwan. His reign lasted only two months, until he was captured by an expeditionary force led by one of the sons of the same Admiral Shi who had first captured the island thirty-eight years before.

The Qing had shown that they could respond with alacrity and efficiency to two crises on distant fronts, even if they had not solved some of the basic problems that made trouble endemic. When Kangxi died, in 1722, the Tibetan and Taiwan campaigns effectively marked the limits of Qing power to the southwest and east. With the Treaty of Nerchinsk holding firm and Manchuria securely engrafted as their ancestral homeland, the Qing had reached a depth and extent of power matched by only a few rulers in times of China's earlier greatness.

A MIXED LEGACY

Kangxi owed much of his fame to the firmness with which he pursued national unity and to the vigor of his foreign policy. Priding himself on his decisiveness, he often overrode his senior advisers, both Manchu and Chinese; and when he was successful, he claimed the credit. In several important ways, however, the results were less happy, and he left a tangled legacy to his successors. This was especially true in three areas: the dispute surrounding Yinreng, the heir apparent to the throne; relations with the Catholic missionaries; and rural administration.

From early in his reign, Kangxi clearly wanted to avoid a repetition of the regency interlude that had led to the domination of the court by Dorgon in the 1640s and by Oboi in the 1660s. Accordingly, when his first empress bore him a son, Yinreng, in 1674, Kangxi moved rapidly to have the boy named heir apparent. Since Yinreng's mother died in childbirth, his birth had an aura of fate around it and set Yinreng even further apart from his half brothers, whom Kangxi was to father with other consorts or concubines.

The upbringing of Yinreng was designed to be a model in which all the precepts of moralistic Confucian education would be followed, and the Manchu virtues instilled. Venerable tutors were chosen, and the heir's progress was watched with close attention, as were his deportment and literary skills. He was introduced slowly to the problems of governance, and was left as acting ruler in Peking while Kangxi was away on the long campaigns against Galdan in 1696–1697. Kangxi even announced his intention of abdicating early so that Yinreng could take over the kingdom as emperor.

But on his return from the west, Kangxi began to hear disquieting rumors about his son's behavior: Yinreng showed signs of being erratic, violent, and cruel. When the emperor took his various sons with him on the imperial tours he loved to make—to the west, to Manchuria, or to the once again prosperous towns on the Grand Canal and on the Yangzi River—Yinreng again began to disturb others with his willful behavior.

One difficulty Kangxi faced was getting accurate information about the situation. Not surprisingly, factions began to develop at court around either Yinreng or one of the seven other imperial sons who were old enough and shrewd enough to be possible rival candidates for the throne. In these conditions, few courtiers and officials, Manchu or Chinese, were willing to speak frankly. As a result Kangxi began to use a new communications system so that he could cut through the haze of rumor.

Information for the emperor from his capital and provincial officials came, most commonly, in the form of "memorials." These were carefully written documents that were carried to the court by government couriers and processed in the Grand Secretariat, where they were copied and evaluated before being passed on to the emperor with suggestions as to the responses he might suitably make. But this was a relatively public system, and Kangxi, in the 1690s, had begun to develop a truly secret system of "palace memorials," which would be delivered to the palace by the writers' own household couriers, brought unopened to the emperor by his most trusted eunuchs, and read, annotated, and sealed by him in private. The route was then reversed, the writers' couriers carrying the memorial, which now bore the emperor's secret rescript on it in vermilion ink, back to the original writer.

Kangxi had first used this system in an informal way, telling certain trusted bondservants stationed in the provinces to send him lists of current grain prices, so that he could check the accuracy of his senior officials' reports and follow up on possible causes of future unrest. Early in the eighteenth century Kangxi began to expand the system; by 1707, a handful of trusted advisers were using palace memorials to tell the emperor secretly the details of Yinreng's conduct. They reported how Yinreng preened himself on his future role as emperor, how he tyrannized his subordinates and household, and how he ordered his agents to buy both boys and girls in the south and to bring them to his palace for his private sexual delectation. Though it took Kangxi a long time to act, by 1708 so much negative evidence had piled up that he could delay no longer. Hysterical with anger, Kangxi ordered Yinreng disbarred forever from his heir-apparent status and placed under house arrest, to be guarded by Kangxi's fourth son, Yinzhen; several of Yinreng's close friends, as well as senior courtiers involved in his misdeeds, were arrested and executed.

What followed was an anguished circle of indecision, guilt, and recrimination on the emperor's part. Believing that Yinreng could not be guilty as charged and instead had been bewitched, Kangxi released him in 1709. But in 1712 fresh evidence—including the spread of the news that Yinreng had been planning to assassinate the emperor, who obviously would not abdicate in his favor—led Kangxi to order his son's rearrest. Thereafter, for the remaining ten years of his reign, Kangxi refused to name any other heir and ruthlessly punished any officials who urged him to do so. The court was awash with rumors, factions grew around many of Kangxi's other sons, and the whole future of the Manchu dynasty was clouded with uncertainty.

The problems with the Catholic missionaries also involved questions of imperial power and prerogative. Ever since he overthrew the Oboi regency, Kangxi had favored the Jesuits in court: he placed them once again in charge of the astronomy bureau, used them as his advisers in matters of cartography and engineering, and allowed them opportunities to practice their religion in Peking and the provinces. Especially for a decade after 1692, when the emperor issued an edict granting toleration to the Christian religion, the Jesuits began to hope that they had a real chance for mass conversion. Kangxi insisted, however, that the Jesuits agree to abide by his stipulation that the Chinese rites of ancestor worship and public homage to Confucius were civil rather than religious ceremonies and, thus, could continue to be practiced by Christian converts. Since Kangxi drew this definition from the position taken by the famous Jesuit missionary Matteo Ricci in the late Ming dynasty, a majority of the Jesuits in China found nothing controversial in it.

However, many other Catholic churchmen as well as missionaries from different religious orders, both in east Asia and in Rome, disagreed profoundly. They believed that Kangxi was essentially claiming paramountcy in matters of church doctrine and that the Jesuits were fatally weakening the integrity of the Christian faith. To rectify this, Pope Clement XI dispatched a young but trusted emissary, Maillard de Tournon, to investigate. In a series of meetings between legate and emperor held in Peking during 1705 and 1706, it became clear how bitterly the two men disagreed. When de Tournon forbade Catholic missionaries to follow Kangxi's orders, under pain of excommunication, the emperor responded with an order of expulsion against all those who refused to sign a certificate accepting Kangxi's position. Though most of the China Jesuits signed, more than a dozen Franciscan, Dominican, and other missionaries refused to do so and were duly expelled from China. This mutual hard line wrecked the power base of the missions in China and effectively prevented the spread of Western teaching and science. Had either side been more flexible, then later in the eighteenth century, when the Catholic church accepted the findings of Galileo and the missionaries started to introduce up-to-date Western astronomy to the Chinese, the new knowledge and techniques might have led to significant changes in Chinese attitudes about thought and nature.

In the crucial realm of taxation and rural administration, finally, Kangxi failed to make constructive changes. He seems to have accepted the position that no comprehensive new survey of landholdings was possible under existing social circumstances; he also perpetuated the late Ming system in which the taxes formerly paid in kind and through labor services were commuted to silver. Only a small amount of this money stayed in the counties to pay for the salaries of local magistrates and their staffs, and for the carrying out of local relief and construction measures. Local officials sought to supplement their resources with a wide range of extra surcharges, much of which they pocketed for themselves, gave to their superiors as gifts, or sent as presents to Peking to make sure that the relevant ministries did not investigate their conduct too closely. This laxness coincided with a prolonged period of economic depression in which both land and crop prices dropped sharply. Contemporary Chinese agonized over the deflation and stagnation that made Shunzhi's reign appear, in retrospect, as an economic golden age.[7]

As a consequence, despite Kangxi's dramatic successes in political unification and border consolidation, life in the rural areas remained a grim struggle for millions of Chinese. Small gangs of bandits could roam almost unopposed in many parts of China, since there was no paid and armed militia to oppose them. Corrupt junior staff from the magistrates' offices could bully farming families into paying a variety of taxes for which receipts were never issued. Legal battles over land contracts dragged on for decades, and there was little recourse for minors or widows when harassed by the adult males of their clans. Private feuds led often to violence and homicides that harried officials had neither the time nor the staff to investigate.

Perhaps because he recalled the strong support that Koxinga had received from the local Chinese in his 1659 campaign or because the area was regarded as the central heartland of Confucian culture, Kangxi was particularly lax about prosecuting tax delinquents in the rich provinces of Jiangsu and Zhejiang. To preserve an appearance of harmony, he was constantly urging leniency in tax-delinquency cases and regularly gave generous tax rebates to large areas that were not suffering serious hardship. Although he did continue to enforce the "law of avoidance," which stipulated that senior officials could never serve in their home provinces (so as to avoid their abusing their position while in office), he often ignored confidential reports that pointed to flagrant abuses by the family members of his favored officials, or by those who had retired home after years of service in the capital.

Paradoxically, in the last decade of his reign, Kangxi seems to have genuinely believed that the restoration of prosperity in rural China was now complete, and that the bureaucracy could handle its assignments with the resources at hand. The court itself appeared comfortably solvent, since along with the land-tax revenues it received considerable extra income from monopoly control over salt, ginseng, and jade, as well as from allegedly "voluntary" payments by wealthy merchants, and from transit dues on commerce. Since Kangxi also believed that China's prosperity was measured by the size of its population, and that the true size of that population was being hidden by local officials who feared that if they reported rising numbers the Ministry of Revenue would respond by raising their tax payments, he decided to take dramatic action. In 1712 he froze the assessments of able-bodied men registered as working a given area of agricultural land and decreed that however much the population increased in a particular area, the state would not thereby raise that area's taxes. Local officials could thus report population increases accurately, without fearing the burden of a raised assessment at a future date.

Since Kangxi—like Shunzhi before him—had given up on attempting a national survey of landholdings, China's land-tax system was now doubly frozen: land in the provinces remained registered according to the last reasonably full survey made in 1581 during Emperor Wanli's reign, and the numbers of per capita units subject to tax assessment were henceforth based on the 1712 figures. This was seriously to impede any attempt by Kangxi's successors to rationalize China's finances. Although higher population estimates did now begin to flow into Peking, gratifying the emperor with a sense of China's prosperity, none of the basic fiscal inefficiencies had been eliminated.

"Now that I am ill I am querulous and forgetful," Kangxi told his kneeling courtiers and officials in a self-revelatory edict of 1717, "and terrified of muddling right with wrong, and leaving my work in chaos. I exhaust my mind for the country's sake, and fragment my spirits for the world."[8] Kangxi lived on for another five years after these melancholy words, the longest rule in the history of China up to that time; but longevity brought him diminishing solace. He had still not publicly named an heir when he died in December 1722, of natural causes, in his Peking palace. It is hard, in retrospect, to gauge the level of despair that had led him to neglect such a fundamental obligation.

CHAPTER 4 | # Yongzheng's Authority

ECONOMIC STRUCTURES

The brief reign of Emperor Yongzheng, successor to Kangxi, was stormy, complicated, and important. It was clouded in controversy from the first, when Yongzheng himself announced that he was the dying emperor's choice as heir. Since his other brothers and half brothers were not present at the scene, and since Yongzheng's close friend was commander of the Peking guards division, there was no one to dispute his claim publicly; but throughout his reign (1723–1735), he was troubled by charges that he was a usurper.

There is little evidence that he had usurped the throne, however, and some evidence to show that Kangxi had trusted Yongzheng more than he had most of his other sons. Kangxi and Yongzheng (then known by his ordinary family name of Yinzhen) frequently discussed policy matters together and shared mutual entertainments. As we've seen, Yongzheng, for a time, was even made the jailer of his elder half brother, the deposed heir apparent—a delicate and dangerous task, considering the politics of the time.

Once installed as emperor, Yongzheng did expend considerable effort cementing his position by arresting those of his brothers whom he believed most resented his rule. (He had quieted their suspicions by promoting them first!) The former heir apparent, Yinreng, and two other brothers died in prison shortly after their arrests (whether they were killed or died from mistreatment is not known). Several others were put under house arrest or close surveillance. Yongzheng completely trusted only Kangxi's thirteenth son, Yinxiang, whom he promoted and retained in the highest offices.

Whether one interprets these actions as evidence of a guilty conscience or as practical steps taken to prevent later trouble, Yongzheng showed himself deeply committed to the craft of government. He had a passion for detail and a willingness to spend long hours every day at work, usually reading history texts from 4:00 A.M. until 7:00 A.M., when he breakfasted, meeting with his advisers into the early afternoon, then reading documents and commenting on them, often until midnight. He took neither lengthy hunting excursions to the north nor leisurely tours of the Yangzi delta cities, as his father had loved to do. His main recreation seems to have been the practice of Buddhism, of which he was a devoted and scholarly adherent, and relaxing in the scenic garden of his palace in northwest Peking. Whereas his father had often written in Manchu, and had written Chinese slowly and carefully, Yongzheng seems to have preferred Chinese. His Chinese calligraphy, clearly written with great speed, was accurate and idiomatic.

But this apparent routinization of imperial life should not blind us to the fact that Yongzheng's China was still far from being a fully integrated or homogenous country. China's vast expanses allowed for endless variations in such areas as pace of economic change, types of lineage organization, efficiency of transportation, religious practices, sophistication of commerce, and patterns of land use and landholding. A complete history of China would ideally include information on all these variables on a district-by-district basis, so that precise patterns of change could be charted and connected with political decisions made at the center.

Daunting though this task is, various studies have begun to show that it is feasible. In particular, by analyzing late imperial China in terms of units of economic integration rather than through the traditional provincial and prefectural subdivisions, we gain a different perspective on the society based on a body of data that was not available to the rulers and bureaucrats of the time. Scholars employing this approach have identified nine "macroregions" (as they term them), each embracing parts of several provinces. Each macroregion had a "core" defined by heightened economic activity in major cities, high population density, and comparatively sophisticated transportation networks for conveyance of food and merchandise. And each core was surrounded by a "periphery" of less populated and developed areas, which isolated the core of a given macroregion from the cores of its neighbors, and also provided a loosely policed area where illegal sects or bandit elements could develop in comparative freedom.[1]

Of these nine macroregions one was in the northeast, in the area coterminus with southern Manchuria, the Qing's preconquest heartland. Two were in the north, in the Xi'an region of Shaanxi and the Peking–western Shandong area. Three extended at different points along the Yangzi River—

one on the east coast around Nanjing, one halfway upriver around Hankou, and one deeper up the river in Sichuan. A seventh was on the lower east coast in the Fujian region. An eighth was in the far southeast, centered around Canton. And the last was in the southwest, in the provinces of Yunnan and Guizhou. Without launching a detailed exploration of all nine macroregions, we can take a brief look at three of them to determine what kinds of factors were affecting their patterns of social and economic development in the eighteenth century.

First, the northern macroregion—centered around Peking and western Shandong, and extending into Henan and northern Jiangsu—was, despite the presence of the capital, less urban than most other macroregions: small independent holdings were the economic norm. Flooding was common, brought on by the silt-filled Yellow River, but flood-relief measures and emergency grain distribution in times of famine were more effective than in regions farther from the capital. Cotton was becoming a valuable cash crop of this macroregion as both spinning and weaving techniques grew more efficient, often carried out in home-based cellar workshops that provided a "climatized" environment of controlled dampness to prevent the fragile strands from breaking. Tobacco cultivation was spreading, too, along with glassmaking, coal mining, and brewing. Shifting social conditions, the presence of the many laborers and boatmen who serviced the grain barges on the Grand Canal, overworked soil, and fragmented landholdings all contributed to make this an area where crime and local violence were common.

By contrast, the middle Yangzi macroregion, with its comparatively low population density and its untilled land, was at this time experiencing a massive in-migration from other regions. The area developed a population of "sojourners" with divided loyalties to their new base and their old ancestral homes, and of disaffected local minorities pushed off their former lands. The booming Yangzi River city of Hankou, a commercial rather than an administrative center with complex systems of banks and guilds, was becoming the focus for a truly interregional long-distance grain trade. To the southeast, Jingdezhen expanded as an industrial city, making porcelain for the export markets of the West as well as for the Chinese elite. Yet along with this commercial growth, peasant strategies of building new dikes in the area of Dongting Lake to protect their tiny plots of farmland from floods, along with larger-scale land-reclamation projects engineered by the elite, led ultimately to terrible flooding by the rivers, which had been deprived of their natural runoff areas by man's hard work and ingenuity.

A different series of factors dominated our third example, the lower-east-coast macroregion that centered around Fujian province and incorporated

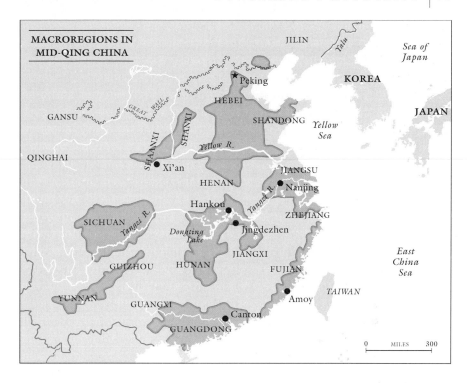

parts of southern Zhejiang and eastern Guangdong. The coastal location gave this macroregion's merchants a host of profitable trade contacts with Taiwan and Southeast Asia, which brought a certain cosmopolitanism and a highly developed system of credit and banking particularly to the port of Amoy (Xiamen). Further prosperity came from the rich tea farms of the region. But for a mixture of historical and geographical reasons, this macroregion was also riven by fierce localisms. Powerful lineages controlled whole villages, and feuds between them were deadly and frequent. Many richer homes were heavily fortified. Tenancy rates were high, and there were violent tensions involving recent immigrants or the poorer inland farmers on their terraced mountainsides. Strong local accents and dialects made contact with outsiders difficult. The region's elite were sliding in the scale of national prestige, as the area produced fewer and fewer holders of the coveted highest examination degree, the *jinshi*. The Qing government identified the region as a potential trouble spot and kept it heavily garrisoned with both banner forces and local Chinese troops known as the Green Standard armies.

Since each of the macroregions had its own internal economic logic, there was always danger that differences with other macroregions might escalate into conflict. If the centralizing state proved unable to mediate or control these conflicts, the result might be either fragmentation or civil war. Something close to this had occurred between the 1630s and 1680s, when peasant rebels, Ming loyalists, Koxinga's forces, and the Three Feudatories had each found temporary bases in different macroregional cores. The task of the state, therefore, was to bond the macroregions together by ideological and administrative means—backed if necessary by military force. This task would be eased if trade links between separate macroregions also developed, as began to happen in the eighteenth century. With economic bonds reinforcing political ones, the nature of Qing state and society might eventually be transformed.

Another factor complicating the mid-Qing society and economy was China's rapidly rising population. Despite Kangxi's attempts through the head-tax registration reforms of 1712 to get a more accurate count of his country's inhabitants, the figures still remain shadowy, and comparisons with earlier periods are hard to make with precision. We can be fairly sure, however, that China's population in the early Ming dynasty, around 1390, was somewhere between 65 million and 80 million. By the end of the reign of Yongzheng's son Qianlong in the 1790s, it had passed the 300 million mark. But the demographic significance of the Ming-Qing transition period is that it interrupted any pattern of steady, moderate growth. In fact the period from just after the Ming emperor Wanli's death in 1620 to the end of Kangxi's war against the Three Feudatories (1681) witnessed a catastrophic drop in China's population overall, the result of foreign invasion, civil war, bandit upheavals, natural disaster, irrigation-system failures, and virulent epidemics. How catastrophic the drop was we cannot say. In the late Ming, China may have had well over 150 million people; in the 1670s, the population might not have been much over 100 million. Precision is impossible.

What does seem clear is that these demographic catastrophes made possible the economic revival and population rise of the eighteenth century, for in many areas there was good land going begging for tenants and cultivators. During Kangxi's rule, there was a resettlement of the devastated areas of north China and of the war-ravaged parts of once-prosperous Sichuan. In Yongzheng's reign, settlers began to push down into southwest China. Under his son Qianlong, Chinese began to defy government prohibitions and move into southern Manchuria in large numbers, and also to populate the uplands of the Yangzi and Han river drainage areas. Others sailed from east China to Taiwan or farther afield—to Manila or Southeast Asia.

The picture we get for eighteenth-century China is of a rapidly expanding population across the country as a whole. If, by the end of Kangxi's reign,

China's population had climbed *back* to a late Ming level of around 150 million, there is no doubt that it had doubled by the end of his grandson's. The table below gives us sample figures for the two northern provinces of Hebei and Shandong as well as for the whole of China, rounded out to the nearest thousand.

The population growth traced in these figures had some major social and political implications. Although old lands were being resettled and new ones constantly opened up in this period, the crude figures suggest that while the population may have tripled from the mid-Kangxi period to the late Qianlong, the acreage of arable land only doubled; the size of individual holdings therefore shrank. Moreover, since the Chinese did not follow the practice of leaving the bulk of a family's land to the eldest son, but divided all land equally among the sons under the system known as "partible inheritance," new, large landowning families tended not to emerge. Family holdings in the north China–Peking macroregion, for which we have good figures in the eighteenth century, were only around 2.5 acres on average; a holding of over 20.0 acres was rare, and a quarter or more of the rural households were landless. China remained a nation of small landholders engaged in highly labor-intensive agriculture without the aid of significant technological innovations.

Following traditional practice, the families moving onto upland areas along the Yangzi and Han rivers, or into the forests of southern Manchuria, cleared these areas for agriculture without understanding the ecological effects of their actions. Although yields on virgin lands were high, intensive agriculture was rapidly followed by soil erosion and deforestation. Massive hillside runoffs into the rivers caused corresponding silting problems and the danger of serious flooding in settled farming areas downstream. Fur-

POPULATION FIGURES: HEBEI, SHANDONG,
AND ALL OF CHINA[2]

Year	Hebei	Shandong	China
1573 (est)	4,625,000	5,644,000	150,000,000
1685 (est)	3,297,000	2,111,000	100,000,000
1749	13,933,000	24,012,000	177,495,000
1767	16,691,000	25,635,000	209,840,000
1776	20,291,000	26,019,000*	268,238,000
1790	23,497,000	23,359,000	301,487,000

*This figure is for 1773. The fact that Shandong province showed a drop in population between 1776 and 1790 is an anomaly, probably caused by natural disasters and outbreaks of rebellion in that same period.

AGE OF WOMEN GIVING
BIRTH: DAOYI, 1792*[3]

Age of Women Giving Birth	Number of Sons Born
15–19	87
20–24	226
25–29	255
30–34	191
35–39	118
40–44	68
45–49	23

thermore, with human wastes constituting much of the fertilizer source, exhausted soil in isolated upland areas could not be replenished easily (as, for instance, farms near heavily urban areas could be) and often had to be abandoned.

Much of the country's population growth in the eighteenth century was speeded up by a massive ecological change: the introduction of new crops into China from the New World. Sweet potatoes, for example, were widespread in coastal China by the mid-eighteenth century, while maize and the Irish potato became common in the north and in the southwest in the same period. Peanuts had spread rapidly in south and southwestern China in the late Ming, and were also becoming an important crop in north China. All these crops helped to boost the caloric intake of China's rural workers; but because the crops also grew well in poor, hilly, or sandy soil, they enabled the population to rise rapidly in areas of otherwise marginal productivity, where alternate sources of food or gainful employment were rare.

Surviving documents from the rural village of Daoyi, north of Shenyang in southern Manchuria, enable us to get a closer look at local population figures and age profiles, and suggest some of the rhythms of family life at the end of the century. Since birth dates in Daoyi were recorded monthly and were most common during February and March, we can tell that conception most often occurred in early summer, during the lull between spring planting and harvesting. One-third of the males died in their first year of life, and half before they were twenty. The average life expectancy for the men of Daoyi was around thirty-two years, and some 4 percent lived past

---

*These detailed figures are for the birth of sons only. Since Daoyi was a village owing military service in the banner system, the focus of census takers was on potential recruits. But elsewhere in China also, more attention was paid to accurate counting of males than females.

sixty-five. The age span for women was comparable.

An unusual aspect of the Daoyi figures is that they enable us to see the ages at which women bore their male children. Surprisingly, these figures indicate that women in their later twenties were the most likely to have children. This suggests that because of scarce food supplies there was parental and economic pressure to hold off having children during the early years of maximum female fertility. The subsequent spacing of all childbirths, and the high ratio of recorded male to female births, provides further evidence of systematic patterns of family planning among rural Chinese.

The social and cultural consequences of one final demographic factor can be drawn from these figures. Because of childhood illnesses, a less-than-adequate diet, even infanticide in time of famine—and because wealthy men tended to keep several female consorts—there were many fewer marriageable women than men in Daoyi, as in so many other areas of China. The effects of this on family patterns are telling: although almost every woman in Daoyi over thirty was married or widowed, 20 percent of the adult men never married at all. The Chinese idealization of the family, the attention paid to children, and the insistence that descendants practice ancestor worship to keep forebears from suffering in the afterworld—all these deeply held beliefs must have seemed a cruel jest to these millions of men. For women, any attempt to avoid marriage must have been out of the question. This was just one more of the many areas in which sources of social discontent were always present, and yet could seldom be articulated because of China's prevailing social beliefs.

THE QUESTION OF TAXES

During his brief twelve-year reign (1723–1735) Emperor Yongzheng concentrated on a number of central problems in Chinese government that were crucial in his own day and have remained so to the present. These included the structure of Chinese bureaucracy and finance in the countryside, the development of an effective and confidential information system, and the strengthening of the central executive branch of the state. These three were (and are) tightly interconnected; success in managing them would go far to ensure more efficient control of China's enormous territory.

From the beginning of his reign, Yongzheng seems to have had a clear vision of how to proceed. He was not a child under the supervision of regents when he ascended the throne, as his father and grandfather had been, but an experienced man of forty-five who had watched his father's reign begin to fall apart. The system of secret palace memorials was made to measure for him, and he extended and coordinated the informal structure that Kangxi had initiated. Apart from routine matters, which were reported, as in the past, in open memorials to the ministries and to the Grand Secretariat, most senior provincial officials now reported confidentially to Yongzheng on the details of their administration and on each other. As the emperor began to realize the size of the tax deficits and the casualness with which the fiscal crisis had been treated in his father's reign, he urged his officials to suggest means of reforming the financial structure, and established a small executive office of financial review to stand separate from and above the Ministry of Revenue. In charge of this office he placed Kangxi's thirteenth son, Yinxiang.

The financial crisis was too complicated for even an absolute ruler to solve with an edict or two. The central budget of China in 1723 was about 35 million taels (ounces of silver), of which about 6 million came from commercial taxes of various kinds and 29 million from the "land and head tax" *(diding)*. Anywhere from 15 to 30 percent of this 29 million was retained in each province for "local use," while the rest was sent to Peking; but nearly all that "local use" percentage was spent on projects that were really national ones, such as military supplies and imperial post stations. Less than one-sixth of the total was available to local officials for projects in their own areas. One might have thought it simple to increase income by raising the number of land-tax and head-tax units; but here the obligations of filiality to Emperor Kangxi were too strong, and Yongzheng did not attempt to change his father's 1712 ruling. Moreover the central premise of Chinese political theory, which the Manchus had also made their own, was that a low tax base was essential to the well-being of the country and the true proof of an emperor's benevolence. Another obstacle to reform was posed by the officials in the Ministry of Revenue, who had their own procedures and protocols, and drew large sums in "gifts" from the accepted practices, which they were understandably loath to change.

The current tax system was not only entrenched but full of abuses. Members of the upper class were often wealthy landowners, and, as in Kangxi's reign, many of them concealed their tax responsibilities in a maze of false names, misregistrations, transferred holdings, mortgages, and so on, which made it almost impossible to trace their exact holdings. Furthermore, much of the economic power in the countryside was in the hands of small land-holders who tyrannized the local villagers. These landholders colluded with the clerks in the provincial magistrates' offices in order to evade paying their own taxes and to force the poorer peasants to assume a disproportionate amount of the tax burden for the whole community. In such situations, the peasants had little redress, and money that had in fact been embezzled was counted as being in "arrears"—that is, owed by delinquent farmers.

Between 1725 and 1729, Yongzheng reversed his father's casual approach and made a concerted effort to reform the land tax and to break the power of the local intermediate groups. He was determined to extend the power of the Qing state more effectively into the countryside. As he expressed himself in an edict of 1725: "When the flesh and blood of the common people is used to rectify the deficits of the officials, how can there not be hardship in the countryside? I am deeply concerned about these abuses."[4]

He began by slowly accumulating accurate information through palace memorials and by appointing new men—often Manchus or Chinese bannermen who would be less influenced by the local elites—to the key offices of provincial governor and financial commissioner. Yongzheng then moved to establish an official consensus that a fixed rate of surcharge should be levied on the basic land-tax (di) and head-tax (ding) quotas, that all of this surcharge should be passed on to the provincial financial commissioners' offices, and that all other supplementary fees and gifts should be declared illegal. The tax money gathered by the financial commissioners' offices would then be reallocated within the province on an equitable basis. Part would be used to give far higher salaries to the local officials than they had ever received before (this was called "money to nourish honesty"), and part would go into county funds for the support of irrigation works, road and school building, and other worthy or necessary local needs that did not come under the purview of the central Ministry of Revenue budget. These included provision of draft animals for disaster victims, jail improvement or gazetteer printing, city sewers or charity graveyards, examination cubicles, and candles and incense for local temples.

In assessing the effects of these reforms, one can get a brief overview of China's regional variations at this time. The reforms were most successful in the northern macroregions comprising the provinces of Shanxi, Henan, and Hebei, where independent landholding peasant cultivators were common, land registration was comparatively easy, and magistrates could be closely supervised and forced to give up their traditional perquisites. Virtually everyone in this region benefited from the reforms except for the corrupt middlemen landlords and some of the ruthlessly greedy clerks and magistrates. The flat surcharge of 15 to 20 percent on the basic land tax proved much less burdensome to the peasants and even to the larger landholders than the endless rounds of overlapping fees that had prevailed. And the new salaries gave the officials a more regular and higher-level income than they had previously enjoyed: 600 to 1,000 taels a year in the case of county magistrates, as opposed to 45 taels before the reforms. Offices were now better-run, business was conducted faster, and there was real local autonomy and initiative for dealing with specific projects.

In the south and southwest macroregions, however, the reforms went much less smoothly. Here the basic tax-quota figures were far lower because there were many recently settled, sparsely populated areas; but since the number of officials was still high, the surcharges did not bring in enough money to pay the same high levels of salary as in the north. The system could be made to work only by granting the local officials some of the tax revenues from such commercial enterprises as mining, salt production, or transit dues at checkpoints on China's roads, canals, and rivers. Even so, because of the great distances and expense involved, many magistrates failed to forward all their surcharge money to the financial commissioners of their provinces, pleading instead to be allowed to withdraw their new salaries and the local expense money *before* they forwarded the rest. Predictably this led to renewed local graft, and precluded the commissioners' making a full and equitable distribution of revenues based on true need.

It was in the central Yangzi provinces, however—especially Jiangsu and Anhui, but also Zhejiang and Jiangxi—that the system ran into the most trouble. Here lived countless retired but still powerful former officials and their relatives, whose lands had never been properly registered and who could intimidate the local magistrates through connections in the capital. Kangxi had been especially lenient to the wealthy elites in this area, and they were not about to submit meekly to tougher central control. Opposition to Yongzheng's reform was so obvious and so concentrated that the emperor finally appointed a special Manchu commissioner, backed by a staff of seventy experienced auditors from the Peking bureaucracy, to push through a thorough examination of the provinces' finances and to make a complete and accurate registration of land.

The malfeasance they found was incredible, and the examples of false and overlapping registrations so complex that they despaired of ever unraveling them. In some cases, the auditors found, landowners had divided their holdings under literally hundreds of false names, confident that in each of these tiny units the tax liability was so low that no magistrate or clerk would take the time to chase up arrears. The auditors' attempts at on-the-spot examination were met by delays, hostility, blocked roads, cut bridges, even riots and physical assault. Those imprisoned for questioning were often rescued by jail-storming crowds. Coded logbooks confiscated by the auditors showed how, generation after generation, local financial clerks had exempted wealthy families from nearly all their tax obligations in return for payoffs. Yet even with this evidence, the auditors still found it hard to pin down the guilty parties and even harder to collect more than a small percentage of the 10 million taels they found was owed from the area to the government.

The very tenacity of this opposition showed that the attempted reforms were a step in the right direction. For the reforms suggested that with persistence, the efforts of officials of integrity, and the emperor's encouragement, the Qing state could reach a new level of centralized bureaucratic efficiency. Thus China might be able to build on the achievements of national reunification gained between 1644 and 1683, and the foreign-policy successes that had followed, to create a genuinely lasting and viable governmental system. In particular, if the center could control and exploit the rich resources of China's most prosperous provinces, that would surely benefit and strengthen the country as a whole.

THE CENTER AND CHANNELS OF POWER

Rulers are rarely free to concentrate on one problem at a time, and Yongzheng was never able to give his full attention to the problems of rural taxation and administration in China's central provinces. It became necessary again to reinforce Qing power on the borders. Zhu Yigui's rebellion in Taiwan had been swiftly suppressed in 1721, but effective pacification was complex. After lengthy consultations, Yongzheng decided to strengthen local control there by subdividing several of Taiwan's counties into smaller units, and by allowing the pioneer emigrants in Taiwan to be joined by their wives and children to make for a more settled social environment. He also permitted Chinese to rent land on contract from the original Taiwanese inhabitants, while setting aside certain formal reservations for the aborigines.

There was need as well for careful new negotiations with Russia to prevent the Treaty of Nerchinsk from falling apart over arguments concerning the border tribes, trade caravans, and clashes sparked by the discovery of gold in southern Siberia. A senior negotiating team, consisting entirely of Manchus, worked with the Lifan Yuan to draw up a supplementary treaty, signed at Kiakhta in 1727. The Treaty of Kiakhta drew a line between the two countries from Kiakhta to the Argun, and stated which tribes should be based in Chinese territory. Kiakhta was to be one of two new border trading towns, one Russian caravan was to be allowed to trade in Peking every three years, and a Russian Orthodox church was to be maintained in Peking. Most members of the small Russian community in the capital had been captured in earlier wars and were now incorporated in the banners. (The treaty specifically stipulated that they were to be encouraged to learn the Chinese language.) Yongzheng also consolidated his hold over the last of the Manchu banners still controlled by Manchu princes and noblemen, and began to take serious note of problems in Tibet and among the Miao aborigines in China's southwest.

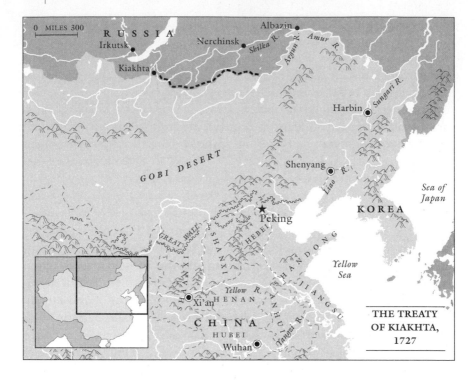

Yongzheng saw the renewed Zunghar threat as the most serious one in the long term, despite their defeat by Kangxi's forces in 1696. He was convinced that the Zunghars could be suppressed only if he meticulously prepared a major military buildup in the far west. But the supply lines were immensely long, and it was hard to keep the preparations secret. The court was full of ears, and the emperor's main policy discussion group—the Deliberative Council of Princes and High Officials—proved unable to keep its proceedings confidential. Peking was also full of Mongol princes and princesses, banner generals, traveling merchants, and lamas loyal to the Tibetan Buddhist church, any of whom might spread news of Qing intentions. So Yongzheng initially kept much of his military planning private by limiting discussions to a small group of his most trusted grand secretaries, whom he came to call the "inner grand secretaries." (The title distinguished them from those who worked in the "outer" court with the regular bureaucracy.)

The three key members of this group were his trusted younger brother Yinxiang (who was also running the revenue-auditing bureau) and two Chinese grand secretaries, Zhang Tingyu and Jiang Tingxi. Zhang Tingyu, son of one of Kangxi's most trusted advisers, was fluent in Manchu and had served as minister of revenue; Jiang had also been in charge of that ministry and was a nationally prominent painter as well. Both men also held the senior (*jinshi*) examination degree, had served in the prestigious imperial Hanlin Academy on the basis of their scholarly excellence, and came from the prosperous Yangzi delta provinces, Zhang from Anhui and Jiang from Jiangsu. They may be seen, therefore, as representing the most talented upper levels of the traditional Chinese bureaucracy who now, more than eighty years after the conquest, were firmly loyal to their Chinese-seeming Manchu emperor. By 1729 the three men were overseeing a secret new bureau, the Office of Military Finance, aided by a small group of experienced middle-echelon officials, both Manchu and Chinese, who were drawn from various ministries—especially the Ministry of Revenue—and were trusted to be discreet. Not even all the other grand secretaries knew the details of their work, and only in the reign of Yongzheng's son, Qianlong, was this office to gain public notice and prominence as the Grand Council.[5]

So once again, as he had in the matter of finance, Yongzheng created an informal yet efficient network to enhance his own power and to deflect certain information and decisions away from the regular six ministries and their staffs. Why the secretive departure from conventional channels? Part of the answer is probably that Yongzheng and his advisers feared there would be questionable financial dealings in the complicated and expensive logistical preparations for the western campaigns, and wanted to keep their inquiries concealed from the formal ministries. It is also likely that they wanted to keep the scale of their operations secret. Hence we find the Office of Military Finance keeping the most detailed accounts on such items as the number of mules or camels and carts that might be needed to transport the supplies for a given number of troops.

Another reason for these new arrangements was that the inner grand secretaries frequently needed to deliberate over secret palace memorials. In some cases these had to be filed; for the emperor, after all, could not keep all these details in his head, and the only safe place to file them was in a specially staffed office under tight security. Yongzheng could also communicate with his generals at the front through so-called "court letters" drafted for him, after discussion, by the inner grand secretaries, and dispatched swiftly and secretly to the recipient. This saved time for the emperor, who was already rescripting in person, and often at great length, from fifty to a hundred palace memorials a day. With court letters drafted for him in secrecy, the emperor could now take the time to add personal notes to show his frontier generals how he trusted them. "How are you after riding your horse through wind and snow?" the emperor wrote to General Yue Zhongqi, stationed in the far western provinces. "Are the officers, troops and animals in good condition?" Or, again to Yue: "I have made a selection of auspicious days for you to start on your journey from Xi'an to the front, and am sending it to you."[6]

Finally the new measures were prompted by considerations of state security as they related to the safety of the emperor from his own forces. Potential threats abounded. For instance, one of Yongzheng's least trusted brothers had been serving as a general in the Tibetan campaigns when Yongzheng ascended the throne. One of Yongzheng's closest friends, while serving as commanding general in Sichuan and Gansu, had also been implicated in the plots of Yongzheng's brothers and ordered to commit suicide in 1727. And the new commanding general in the region, Yue Zhongqi, though given the just-quoted marks of affection and appreciation by the emperor, was a descendant of Yue Fei, famous to all Chinese as a great patriot who, in the twelfth century, was killed in prison by his own Song dynasty rulers despite his courage in fighting Jürchen invaders. To avoid any or all of these potential threats from his own military, Yongzheng would have had cause to tread cautiously.

The long-planned campaign against the Zunghars went badly. In 1732 General Yue Zhongqi, from his forward headquarters at Barkul, was able to raid the enemy in Urumchi but could not protect his own forces in Hami from enemy counterattacks. Yue's fellow senior general rashly led his army of ten thousand troops into an ambush near Khobdo; although he escaped, he lost four-fifths of his men and most of his officers. Both generals were sentenced to death by Yongzheng for these failures and related charges of corruption, although he later commuted the death sentences. As a result of these failures, it would take another thirty years to settle the border problems in this region.

Yongzheng also employed some of his new communication channels to coordinate the fighting in southwest China against the indigenous Miao peoples. Chinese settlers had been pressing into the provinces of Yunnan and Guizhou since the suppression of the Three Feudatories, pushing the local valley dwellers up into the hills and disrupting local society by opening silver and copper mines. In 1726 Yongzheng made Oertai governor-general of the entire region. An experienced administrator, from a warrior family in the blue banner, and fluent in Chinese as well as Manchu, Oertai kept constantly in touch with the emperor through his palace memorials. These traced his efforts to break the power of the local Miao chieftains, to confiscate their tribal lands, and to have them reregistered and administered as part of the Chinese prefectural system. Those who resisted were surrounded and killed by Qing armies; those who submitted still lost the rights to their land but were often reinstated as administrators with their own stipends.

In 1728, in a highly unusual move, Oertai was also named governor-

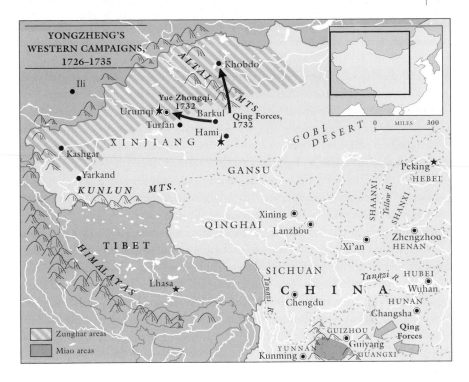

YONGZHENG'S
WESTERN CAMPAIGNS,
1726–1735

Khobdo

Ili

Yue Zhongqi,
1732
Urumqi Barkul Qing Forces,
Turfan 1732
Hami

XINJIANG

Kashgar

GOBI DESERT

0 MILES 300

Yarkand

KUNLUN MTS.

GANSU

Peking
HEBEI

Xining
QINGHAI Lanzhou

SHANXI   Yellow R.   SHANXI

TIBET

HIMALAYAS

Lhasa

SICHUAN

Chengdu

CHINA

Xi'an

Zhengzhou
HENAN

Yangzi R. HUBEI
Wuhan
HUNAN
Changsha

Qing
Forces

Yangzi R.

GUIZHOU
YUNNAN
Kunming

Guiyang
GUANGXI

Zunghar areas

Miao areas

general of Guangxi to speed the suppression of the tribesmen there. Yongzheng's long comments on the palace memorials constantly spurred Oertai
on, debated knotty problems, and discussed the performance of other officials in the area. In 1732 Oertai, having been largely successful in pacifying
the southwest, was recalled to Peking to serve concurrently in the Office of
Military Finance. He took the place of Prince Yinxiang and Jiang Tingxi,
both of whom had died while Oertai was in the southwest. Thus he and
Zhang Tingyu became Yongzheng's most trusted advisers in the capital.

Surveying these developments in the supervision of finance, the communication system, and military affairs, we can see how the Qing Empire
was developing in terms of unity and autocracy. In the near century since
the Qing conquest, the power of great Manchu regents or noblemen to rule
the country—or even their own banners—had waned. Royal brothers could
still be a danger to the emperor, but they could be manipulated or suppressed. The regular bureaucracy was considered useful in many ways but
a hindrance in others, especially when speed and confidentiality were
required. Yet Yongzheng did not take the route, as autocrats so often do,
of simply forming an important new office, staffing it with his own men,
and insisting on its monopoly over important decision making. Instead he

chose a more roundabout way, establishing an undramatic-looking office with a nondescript title, and having those who worked in it hold other jobs at the same time; thus their salaries and official ranks derived from other, more conventional bureaucratic functions. Yongzheng was a remarkable tactician with a flair for—and a belief in—informal and secret structures. Dominance of those structures was, to him, the essence of power.

MORAL AUTHORITY

Emperor Yongzheng's interests took in more than matters of administration. He had a far-ranging concern for moral and cultural values, and many of his major decisions were affected by his moral convictions. He was a man who seems to have been convinced of his own rectitude, and his pronouncements indicate a link between his basic conception of power and his idea of the emperor's superiority. One can gauge this in his handling of a wide range of issues: the Catholic church, the Lu Liuliang affair, his amplification of the Sacred Edict of his father, the printing of the great encyclopedia *Gujin tushu jicheng,* his interest in Buddhism, the problems of industrial laborers and of opium addiction, and his emancipation of the so-called "mean people." At one level, he was playing the role of Confucian monarch; at another, he still bore the autocratic impatience of his conquering Manchu forebears.

With the Catholic missionaries, Yongzheng was even sterner than his father had been in the later years of his life. Not only was the rites controversy still splitting the Catholic community in China, but at least two Jesuits, perhaps believing there was a chance of converting the emperor, had been in correspondence with one of the brothers Yongzheng most distrusted, using the Roman alphabet as a form of code. When Yongzheng discovered this, his anger spread to other scholars who knew the missionaries and to the Catholic church as a whole. Except for the few missionaries on duty at the court in Peking, all the others living in various provinces were ordered to assemble in Canton or Macao; several of the provincial churches were converted to use as schools or as hostels. Since Yongzheng had committed himself publicly against political in-groups and parties by his often-repeated attacks on the whole idea of "factions," he spoke out angrily against the factional influence of the church. Still, he held back from a final ban, taking a high moral stand: "The distant barbarians come here attracted by our culture," he noted in 1726. "We must show them generosity and virtue."[7] Although only one missionary was actually executed in this period, the missionaries as a group had to be extraordinarily circumspect in their behavior. Their influence waned to the point that their only remaining roles of significance at court were as directors of the astronomical bureau and as painters in the imperial studios.

The Lu Liuliang affair produced a similarly complex imperial reaction, involving both vengeance and compassion. Lu was a bitterly anti-Manchu scholar, medical doctor, and monk who had died in 1683 stipulating in his will that he not be buried in clothes of Manchu design. Some of his writings, containing sneering remarks about Manchus and other barbarians, circulated in central China and were read by, among others, an impressionable young schoolteacher named Zeng Jing. Fired with anti-Manchu ardor by Lu's writings and believing the rumors that Yongzheng was a usurper, in 1728 Zeng tried to convince General Yue Zhongqi, who was in Sichuan preparing for the anti-Zunghar campaign, to rebel against Emperor Yongzheng. Yue responded by feigning sympathy until he had unraveled the details of the plot, and then informed Yongzheng of what he had learned.

Checking into the case, Yongzheng was enraged to discover Lu's writings, and how widely rumors of his usurpation had circulated. The imperial response was threefold: to order the exhumation and dismemberment of Lu's corpse and the enslavement or exile of all his surviving family members; to write an angry and detailed rebuttal, attempting to prove that he was indeed his father's chosen successor, a rebuttal that every holder of a state examination degree was required to read; and to make a dramatic gesture of pardoning Zeng with no more than a reprimand on the grounds that he had been young and gullible.

Yongzheng deliberately projected this image linking Confucian benevolence to paternal sternness in other ways, including his amplifications to the Sacred Edict of his father. Kangxi had been content to give a brief summary of sixteen moral points to help his subjects lead obedient and peaceful lives. But Yongzheng elaborated on each of his father's maxims at great length, preparing lectures that were to be delivered by local scholars twice a month right down to the village level. In his elaborations, Yongzheng especially emphasized the need for integrated local communities that would pay their taxes promptly, avoid feuds, and protect themselves from outlaws; the role of thrift and hard work in an agricultural economy; avoidance of litigation; and the fostering of an educational system that taught moral conduct and orthodoxy while renouncing "false doctrines." All examination candidates at the county level had to know the expanded maxims and the emperor's commentaries on them. Simplified versions were also prepared, composed by some of Yongzheng's officials, so that the homilies could be delivered even by those with limited education and to minority peoples who spoke their own non-Han languages. It was a serious and thorough attempt at nationwide indoctrination, which, Yongzheng believed, would improve people's thoughts and behavior, and intensify their loyalty to the state. Such patterns of moral indoctrination would become a recurrent theme in later Chinese history, both after the great rebellions of the mid-nineteenth century and under the successive governments of the Chinese Nationalists and the Chinese Communists.

The emperor Yongzheng's behavior over the publication of the *Gujin tushu jicheng* marked an apparently petty side of the imperial nature, but the seriousness with which the emperor pursued the project is an important indicator of the interconnection of political and cultural values during the Qing. The *Gujin tushu jicheng* ("Complete Collection of Illustrations and Writings from the Earliest to Current Times") was an enormous encyclopedia, the fruit of decades of scholarship by the scholar Chen Menglei. Chen, helped by scores of other scholars, by Emperor Kangxi's third son—who became his patron—and finally by the patronage of Kangxi himself, sought to assemble all the finest past writings on natural phenomena, geography, history, literature, and government. The result, surely one of the largest books in the history of the world, filled 800,000 pages and contained over 100,000,000 Chinese characters. The copper type for printing this vast work was already set when Kangxi died.

Yongzheng, determined to ensure that credit for this great undertaking should not go to this particular brother, whom he hated, used the fact that Chen had once served with one of the Three Feudatories to declare him a traitor and have him banished to Manchuria. Yongzheng then erased all signs of Chen's editorship and all mention of his elder brother's involvement with the project. After a lapse of four years, which allegedly was used to "correct" the encyclopedia, it was issued as the work of Kangxi himself; one of Yongzheng's most trusted inner grand secretaries was listed as editor-in-chief of the "revision."

In the realm of Buddhism, one can again see the polarities in Yongzheng's behavior as he played out the dual roles of ardent believer and autocrat. The school of Buddhism that most attracted Yongzheng was Chan, which had first begun to flourish in China a millennium earlier. Chan devotees practiced an austere program of meditation and introspection so that they would ultimately understand that the so-called "practical" world they inhabited was in truth a realm of illusion. They believed, too, that the Buddha nature was immanent in all beings and that enlightenment could be obtained by all individuals with the requisite faith and concentration. True to this set of beliefs, Yongzheng met regularly in his Peking palace with a fourteen-person Chan study group, consisting of the five brothers he still trusted, select senior officials, one Daoist, and five Buddhist monks. He also authorized a Buddhist press to print sutras—passages from Buddhist scripture.

Yet when Yongzheng disagreed with the doctrinal interpretations that had been put forth by two Buddhist monks of the late Ming and were still adhered to by many Chan believers in his own day, he ordered the two monks' controversial books burned and compelled their later followers to renounce the monks and their works.

One can see Yongzheng's social values emerge in the area of labor relations as well. The territory around Suzhou, south of the Yangzi, was famous in eighteenth-century China as a center of the silk-and cotton-cloth trades. Among the area's large labor force were men, legendary for their great physical strength, who used huge rollers, weighing a thousand pounds or more, to press and finish the cloth. These "calenderers," as they were called, worked furiously hard for poor wages: it took almost a day to process a 68-foot length of cloth, for which each worker received 11 copper cash, or just over one-hundredth of a silver tael. This was barely enough to survive on at a time when the basic price for a picul of grain (approximately 130 pounds weight) was around 1 tael on the open market.

In Kangxi's reign these calenderers went on strike several times, demanding not only better wages, but also the right to build a hospital, an orphanage, and a meeting hall. The strikers got nowhere and their leaders were beaten, but the calenderers rose in protest once more in 1723 and again in 1729. Since there were more than eight thousand of these tough and committed laborers around Suzhou, Yongzheng took the matter seriously, but he was much more concerned with their possible links to outside rebels and agitators than he was about their poor economic conditions. He praised the governor who arrested and interrogated twenty-two of the workers.

Through surviving palace memorials bearing his lengthy interlinear inscriptions, we can see how carefully Yongzheng followed the investigation, which yielded the unsettling news that some of the workers were involved with martial-arts experts, fortunetellers, physicians, owners of male and female brothels, and even some alleged allies of a claimant to the Ming throne who had fled to the Philippines. Only when all these elements had been unraveled in 1730 and the conspirators punished did the emperor write his informant the vermilion notation "Good, now you can send a public memorial." In other words, only now would the ministries in Peking and the grand secretaries be allowed to share in the full details that the emperor and a few favored officials had been brooding about for seven years.

In the area of opium addiction, the emperor was on new and untested terrain. Although some use of opium for its medicinal and narcotic properties had been recorded since the eleventh century, it was only after tobacco smoking had become popular in China during the seventeenth century, and after knowledge of opium-smoking techniques had been brought back from

Taiwan by the soldiers who had been sent to suppress the Zhu Yigui rebellion of 1721, that opium addiction spread to the Chinese mainland. Yongzheng was alerted to the extent of the problem early in his reign and determined to ban opium smoking, but since there was no clear precedent in the Chinese legal code, a number of different clauses had to be invoked by analogy. Thus opium dealers were to be sentenced, like those selling contraband goods, to wear the heavy wooden collar called the "cangue" for one month and then to be banished to a military frontier garrison. Those who lured the innocent into their opium dens were to be punished, like those preaching heterodox religions, to strangulation (subject to mitigation after review). Those smoking or growing opium were to be beaten with one hundred strokes in accordance with penalties for those who violated imperial orders.

But in 1729 a long memorial reached Yongzheng and persuaded him to think the whole opium problem through with greater care. The memorial concerned an opium seller named Chen, who had been sentenced under the laws to have all his stock confiscated, to wear the cangue, and to be banished. But the opium seller protested his innocence on the grounds that he had only been selling *medicinal* opium for health reasons and not for smoking. Reviewing the evidence, Yongzheng acknowledged that this was indeed a valid distinction and that officials should always ascertain motivation in actions under investigation. This Chen, a Fujian shopkeeper who had traded his "dried orange cakes" with a merchant in Guangdong for some forty pounds of opium, might well be a legitimate businessman or pharmacist, not a crook. As the emperor sensibly observed: "If the opium is contraband, then Chen should not be graciously pardoned. If it is not contraband, then why have you stored it in the provincial treasure? This is the hard-earned capital of the common people. How can you deal with an error by committing another error, and thus deprive him of his livelihood?"[8] Here was a concrete example of a situation in which the absolute ruler of the world's largest empire could still keep a close watch on social problems, attempt to enforce a measure of economic equity, and pose as a supreme cultural arbiter.

Perhaps Yongzheng's most dramatic gesture in this direction was his decision to emancipate the "mean people" of China. This designation was applied to several groups who were considered social outcasts and were forbidden to serve in any government capacity or take the state exams: the "singing people" of Shaanxi and Shanxi, who sang and played music at weddings and funerals; the so-called "fallen people" of Zhejiang; the hereditary servants of Anhui and the hereditary beggars of Jiangsu; the boatmen, oyster gatherers, and pearl fishers from certain local tribes who worked in the dangerous seas off the southeast coast; the humble "hut dwellers" who gathered hemp and indigo on the Zhejiang-Fujian border; and others who worked as domestic slaves. Perhaps Yongzheng was moved to change their lowly status more from his desire to establish a unified code of public morals than from genuine compassion, but the fact that he issued a whole series of edicts between 1723 and 1731 to free them shows his consistency and tenacity in seeking to end this type of discrimination.

In the short run the edicts had less effect than he hoped. Many of the "mean people" stayed in their lowly occupations out of choice, while many others were used to their degraded status and simply accepted it even though the laws had changed. Members of the general public were not eager to accept these outcasts as equals, despite the emperor's edicts. But over the long term his pronouncements had the desired effect, and slowly many of the despised groups were able to take a more settled place in Qing society.

Here, as at other times in his reign, Yongzheng had a chance to learn that human nature could be obdurate, and that public pronouncements of moralistic concern did not necessarily change ingrown patterns of behavior; but we cannot tell if he took the lesson to heart. His belief in his own powers of persuasion remained intact, and he continued to exhort his officials and his subjects until the day he died. His practical moralism is a sign of how deeply the conventional Confucian virtues had been internalized by the Manchu rulers of the Qing state.

CHAPTER 5

Chinese Society and
the Reign of Qianlong

"LIKE THE SUN AT MIDDAY"

The reign of Qianlong, from 1736 to 1799, was the longest in the history of China. When one combines this period with the almost equally long reign of Kangxi, and adds Yongzheng's reign, one sees that just three emperors ruled over China during the entire span extending from 1661 to 1799. Comparing the events of their reigns with the developments in North America over a similar stretch of time, from the founding of New York as an English colony to the death of George Washington, or in Britain from the Restoration of Charles II to the industrial revolution, one can see why China has presented such an extraordinary picture of stability and continuity to foreign observers.

Emperor Qianlong began his long reign in a spirit of forceful optimism. Yongzheng's fourth son, Qianlong came peacefully to the throne at the age of twenty-five, having been spared the factional battles that plagued his father's youth. Yongzheng had had the foresight to write down his choice of heir in secret and to lock the designated name in a casket in the palace so that there could be no dispute. Qianlong had been carefully groomed for the role of emperor, and had no doubts about his abilities nor the grandeur of the dynasty over which he presided. But he brought an added dimension to Qing rule by conceiving of himself not merely as the emperor of China, but as the ruler of a multicultural Asian empire. To the political dimensions of rule he thus added new religious, linguistic, and racial elements, which forced a reconsideration of the Manchu heritage and of the nature of power.

Qianlong's most important achievement was the conquest and integration of huge areas of western territory—the region later known as Xinjiang, the "New Territories"—into the Chinese state. By doing this he doubled the territorial extent of China, finally ended the Zunghar troubles, and fixed a firm western border with Russia to go along with the northern borders settled by treaties at Nerchinsk and Kiakhta. The achievement of this vast task took much time and money, and was linked (as it had been in Kangxi's and Yongzheng's time) to the progress of campaigns in western Sichuan and northeastern Tibet.

Qianlong put much of his faith for leadership of the western battles in a previously obscure Manchu bannerman named Zhaohui, who had risen through the bureaucratic ranks in the Grand Secretariat during the 1730s and become quartermaster of the Qing armies in Sichuan before being sent to the Zunghar front in the same capacity. There he volunteered for active duty. After a series of extraordinary adventures between 1756 and 1759 that included the defection of his key allies, the murder of his emissaries by Muslims in Turkistan, deprivations that reduced his troops to cannibalism, and forced marches of hundreds of miles in difficult terrain, Zhaohui was able to capture the cities of Kashgar and Yarkand in 1759. Qing troops slaughtered the last Zunghar forces with great cruelty. The new territories were henceforth run by a military governor stationed in Ili and a second-in-command based in Urumchi, and the tribes of Mongolia were drawn closer in their allegiance to the Qing. When General Zhaohui returned to Peking, Qianlong came out beyond the city gates to welcome him in person, an almost unparalleled honor.

Just as all the diplomatic negotiations with the Zunghars and the Mongols had been handled by the Manchu staff of the Lifan Yuan, so now the administration of the new territories in the west was kept in the hands of the Manchus and a few experienced Chinese bannermen. The region was not thrown open to Chinese colonization and settlement, but was maintained as a strategic frontier zone. It was occupied by massive Manchu and Chinese banner garrisons of 15,000 to 20,000 troops, with 100,000 dependents, at an annual cost to the Qing of at least 3 million taels. The largely Muslim inhabitants kept their own religious leaders and followed their own strict dietary practices; the Manchus also excused them from shaving their heads and growing the queue. The civilian Muslim leaders, known as the Begs, were bound by salaries and titles to the Qing state. Trade was expanded in such items as copper, precious stones, saltpeter, shawl wool, and slaves, although the Manchu court preserved a virtual monopoly over the mining of jade and gold, the most valued minerals from the region. As added proof of his new reach into Asia, Qianlong took a woman from a wealthy Xinjiang Muslim family to be one of his concubines. She was

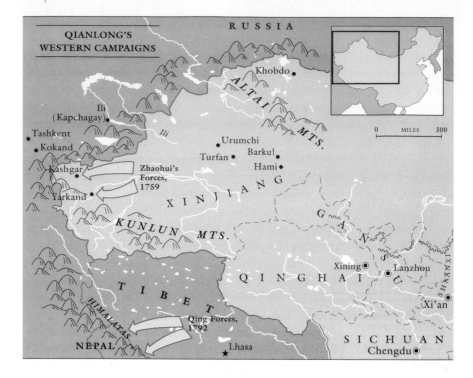

allowed to follow Muslim religious and dietary practices to the letter, and accompanied the emperor on several of his leisurely tours of north and central China. When she died in the 1780s she was buried in a special tomb, with passages from the Koran incised in Arabic on her stone sarcophagus.[1]

Qianlong's immense campaigns had not been conducted from the small, secretive Office of Military Finance, as in Yongzheng's reign. Although the office through which the campaigns were coordinated bore the same name in Chinese as Yongzheng's, its scope and personnel had vastly expanded, as had its power and visibility in the government as a whole. For this reason, from Qianlong's reign onward the office is translated as the "Grand Council" in English, for it now transcended in power all the six ministries and even the Grand Secretariat itself. Among the first of Qianlong's grand councilors were his father Yongzheng's two trusted advisers, Oertai and Zhang Tingyu. They gave continuity to the government, and were gradually joined by a small number of hand-picked ministers, the total remaining at around six or seven during most of Qianlong's reign. The grand councilors were backed by a secretarial staff of 250 or more, who served in rotation and round the clock so that the key offices were never empty.

The Grand Council now became the filing center for the crucial palace memorials conveyed by senior officials throughout China. As these memorials were copied out, evaluated by a wider circle of advisers, and often passed on to the ministries for discussion, both their symbolic and their real functions as special devices bonding official and ruler began to fade. As if recognizing this, Qianlong's comments in vermilion ink on the memorials were usually perfunctory—"Noted," "Read," "Send to the relevant Ministry," etc.—and conveyed little of the sense of warmth and intimacy, nor indeed of anger or concern, that had characterized the comments of his father and grandfather.

This is not to say Qianlong was not a conscientious ruler, for he was. He met senior officials regularly in audience, read the documents submitted to him, traveled extensively both to the Yangzi delta cities and in Manchuria, coordinated military campaigns, and issued numerous edicts on important policy matters. It was rather that he left a great deal of the actual decision making to his grand councilors, and allowed the sense of dynamic central leadership that had characterized the reigns of Kangxi and Yongzheng to fade away.

This loss of impulse can be seen in his approach to the reform of rural tax collection that had featured so largely in Yongzheng's thinking. Although Qianlong had ordered all candidates for the senior level *jinshi* exams in 1742 to write essays on the provincial revenue retention system, and asked the same of his senior officials, slowly—almost casually—the key elements of that tax strategy faded. The wealthy provinces that had surplus local revenue were made to hand it over to the poorer provinces. The result was that the rich provinces lost the opportunity to take important local initiatives that might have strengthened their government, while the poorer provinces lost any incentive to expand their collection system or reform their economic base.

More and more often, magistrates kept the local taxation surpluses to themselves rather than forwarding them to the provincial financial commissioner. The old abuses of extra fees, payments, and illegal surcharges crept back in. The Ministry of Revenue slowly instituted a system by which every item of local expenditure had to be approved by members of its Peking staff before the money could be spent. This led to an avalanche of paper work and an absurd system in which trivial matters were held up for years and important ones never got done at all. One Ministry of Revenue document of this time from the capital province of Hebei shows that provincial officials had to clear such items as 48 taels to pay some guards on a bridge, 105 taels for sailors' wages, and 12 taels as pension allowance for two widows.

In cultural affairs, Qianlong's approach was similar to his father's. He made a public show of his filial piety, particularly in his ritualized treatment of his own mother, the dowager empress. He pampered and flattered her to an extraordinary degree, taking her with him on lavish tours to the Yangzi delta region and even building a copy of southern streets in the northern palace after she was no longer able to go on her travels. Claiming filial loyalty to his insulted father, he reversed Yongzheng's edict of clemency and ordered the unfortunate Zeng Jing—that inept popularizer of Lu Liu-liang's ideas back in 1728—sliced to pieces in the market square of Peking. He gave additional examinations to scholars of outstanding caliber who had been unsuccessful in the regular state exams, made much of the local lecture systems that promulgated Confucian values and the Sacred Edict, celebrated the aged in special festivals, and praised virtuous wives and widows.

In some areas he took new initiatives. He expanded the imperial collection of painting and calligraphy enormously, drawing into the court many of the finest works from the previous millennium. (He has been blamed, by later connoisseurs, for writing elaborate poems on many great paintings in his neat but undistinguished calligraphy, thus ruining the subtlety of the orig-inal compositions.) He patronized a number of Jesuit painters at the court, especially the talented Italian Giuseppe Castiglione, whose royal portraits and large panoramas of hunts and processions marked a unique blend of Chinese composition with Western perspective and coloration. Qianlong employed Jesuit architects and designers to work on a magnificent European-style summer palace, the Yuan Ming Yuan, erected in a lakeside park just outside Peking. He ordered the compilation of a number of impor-tant works—genealogies, histories, accounts of rituals—that would accu-rately preserve and enshrine the Manchu heritage. And to emphasize the power of the Qing as religious patrons, he had a replica of the great Tibetan lamaist temple, the Potala, built on the grounds of his extensive summer palace in Rehe (Jehol).

To preserve the greatness of Chinese culture, Qianlong also ordered a massive compilation to be made of the most famous literary and historical works of the past. Known as the *Four Treasuries* from its four main com-ponents of classics, histories, philosophy, and miscellaneous literary works, this was not just a selection of passages on given topics, as was the *Gujin tushu jicheng,* (the encyclopedia brought forth under Qianlong's grandfather and father); rather, it was a complete anthology, with learned introductions, into which the works selected were copied in their entirety. The assembling of this collection, which ended up comprising 3,450 complete works and commentaries on 6,750 others, filled 36,000 manuscript volumes and took ten years to complete. It is one of the great achievements of Chinese bibli-ography.

Compiling the *Four Treasuries* also served some of the functions of a literary inquisition, since private libraries were searched and those people owning works considered to be slighting to the Manchus were strictly punished. Such books, along with volumes of geography or travel containing information considered harmful to China's defenses, were destroyed. So thorough was this campaign that over 2,000 works that we know were scheduled for destruction by Qianlong's cultural advisers have never been rediscovered. Some of Qianlong's senior editors on the *Four Treasuries* project were also able to support the schools of philosophy they espoused by omitting the works of major rivals, or by emphasizing their own philosophical views in their commentaries.

One can trace, running through many of Qianlong's pronouncements and actions, an undercurrent—faint yet disturbing. It is that of a man who has been praised too much and has thought too little, of someone who has played to the gallery in public life, mistaken grandeur for substance, sought confirmation and support for even routine actions, and is not really equipped to make difficult or unpopular decisions. In the midst of Qianlong's many glories, signs of decay and even collapse were becoming apparent. One of the five Chinese classics, the *Book of Changes,* had anticipated this, as any educated Chinese would have known. The fifty-fifth hexagram of the *Changes* is *feng*, meaning "abundance" or "fullness," and its main description says:

> ABUNDANCE has success.
> The king attains abundance.
> Be not sad.
> Be like the sun at midday.[2]

But the ancient commentary on this passage adds:

> When the sun stands at midday, it begins to set; when the moon is full it begins to wane. The fullness and emptiness of heaven and earth wane and wax in the course of time. How much truer is this of men, or of spirits and gods!

EIGHTEENTH-CENTURY CONFUCIANISM

If questioned, Qianlong would surely have insisted that he presided over a Confucian system of government with Confucian means, and there were many ways in which he could have justified such a claim: the works of Confucius were regarded by the emperor and his officials as the key repositories of ethical wisdom; the Confucian Classics formed the basic curriculum in schools and were central to the competitive state examination system; Confucian values of loyalty and filial piety bonded officials to rulers and children to parents, just as lectures on Confucian topics by scholars and officials in the countryside were aimed at unifying the populace in obedience to the state. Yet "Confucianism" was constantly changing as accretions were adopted or swept away. In the eighteenth century, the doctrine began to develop in new directions, paralleling changes in the society and the economy.

During the second half of the seventeenth century, scholars had been absorbed in searching out the reason for the collapse of the Ming dynasty, and many of them found a satisfactory explanation in the extreme individualism and belief in innate moral knowledge that had been so popular in the late Ming. Senior scholar-officials under the early Qing emperors Shunzhi and Kangxi—as well as those emperors themselves—sought to counter what they considered decadent Ming trends by reasserting the central values of Song-dynasty (960–1279) Confucianism. They emphasized the Song because it was then that the philosopher Zhu Xi (d. 1200) had given prominence to the view that there were indeed underlying principles (*li*) that explained heaven's actions and guided human conduct. Understanding such principles, Zhu Xi and his later followers believed, would help men to live rationally and in tune with heaven, and would justify the attempts of moral men to find meaning in a public career. Thus there was a state-oriented tilt to Song Confucianism, even though the elaboration of such beliefs demanded multifaceted levels of cosmological speculation as individual thinkers probed for heaven's purposes. Furthermore, the realization that even the most moral of men might never be able to fathom the dictates of heaven and would, therefore, inevitably fail in their duties to state and community led to complex levels of anxiety and guilt among Confucian thinkers.

Just as early Qing scholars in state positions had rejected elements of Ming thought and had found security in the earlier texts and interpretations of the twelfth-century Song dynasty, so did later Qing thinkers reject those Song norms and search for certainty elsewhere. By the time of Qianlong, many scholars had begun to find a new security not so much in particular texts as in a methodology. This methodology, which they called *kaozheng* has been usefully translated as "practicing evidential research," because it involved the meticulous evaluation of data based on rigorous standards of precision. *Kaozheng* scholars sought to get away from speculation altogether, to root their studies in "hard facts." They devoted their energies to studies in linguistics, mathematics, astronomy, and geography, confident that these would lead to greater certainty about what the true words and intentions of China's ancient sages had been and, hence, to a better understanding of how to live in the present.[3]

The most important precursors of the *kaozheng* movement, and those its followers spoke of with greatest awe, were men who had lived during Kangxi's reign. One of the *kaozheng* heroes was Gu Yanwu, the Ming loyalist who had sought to defend his home territory against the Manchu forces. As noted above, Gu eventually made a tacit peace with the new Qing dynasty, and spent the last part of his life traveling across north China to study aspects of local technology as well as to track down old steles, from which he took careful rubbings that would help scholars with their philological research. Gu also kept the most careful record of his work in notebooks which, unlike the moralistic or metaphysical "diaries" of speculative Confucians, were jammed with precise notes on texts, rare sources, geographical observations, and ancient artifacts. (It is worth noting that elements of Western scholarship brought by the seventeenth-century Jesuit missionaries, especially in the realms of mathematics and computational astronomy, may have affected the *kaozheng* scholars' research methodologies and given them confidence that there was a realm of "certainty" that lay above individual philosophical schools.)

Yan Ruoju, a friend of Gu's, applied similar techniques to collating the chronology and linguistic structures of part of the Confucian classic of historical documents. His conclusions, though circulated only in manuscript until the 1740s, had a shattering effect on many intellectuals of the time. Yan proved, with carefully marshaled evidence, that several sections of this major work (on which generations of state examination questions had been based) were a later forgery and thus did not deserve the reverence that scholars ascribed to it.

By the 1740s the examinations as a whole were coming under attack as sterile exercises that failed to select the finest scholars for office, and Yan's work heightened this sense of state Confucianism's weakness. Social tensions further undermined confidence in this system, for by the mid-eighteenth century the state had not increased quotas of examination candidates proportionately to the rise in China's population. The consequent pressures on students and the difficulties of finding employment even if one passed the exams brought frustration and disillusionment to many members of the educated elite.

Eighteenth-century scholars used *kaozheng* insights and methodologies to begin a profound exploration of the Confucian past. Many spent much of their time reading texts and commentaries from the Han dynasty (206 B.C.–A.D. 220), since these were so much nearer to Confucius's time than the Song texts still used in the state's schools and, hence, were believed to be nearer to the true sentiments of the sage himself. Partisans of the Han texts subsequently divided into groups, according to whether they placed more faith in scholarship done earlier or later in the Han dynasty. These were not just abstruse debates, but explorations of the past that began to approach the Classics as history and to treat history itself with a sharp and penetrating skepticism. The work of the *kaozheng* scholars also had major implications for eighteenth-century policy, since the scholars' "ant-like accumulation of facts"—as one of them described his studies—brought insights into hydraulics, astronomy, cartography, and ancient texts on government that enabled the scholars to evaluate Qing reality with a shrewder eye.

Kaozheng scholarship became so influential by the mid-Qianlong reign that it was supported by an interlocking infrastructure of book dealers and publishers, printers, library owners, and professional teachers of the many skills needed for advanced research of this kind. Often the lines between scholars and the commercial world blurred, since many merchants became patrons of *kaozheng* learning and accumulated huge libraries that they put at the scholars' disposal. Other *kaozheng* scholars were descended directly from merchant families, reflecting the growth of new urban centers in China and the blurring of previously sharp occupational categories.

In Emperor Qianlong's massive compilation project of the *Four Treasuries, kaozheng* scholars dominated the editorial process, using their new learning to denigrate speculative Confucian theories of the Song period (even though those theories remained "orthodox" in the examinations as a whole) and to boost the reputations of writers working in a *kaozheng* vein. Qianlong, in return, was so grateful for the amount of rare material that these scholars made available to him that he ordered officials to write out three extra manuscript sets of the rarest works included in the *Four Treasuries* compendium. These were to be deposited in libraries at the three main centers of *kaozheng* learning—Yangzhou, Zhenjiang, and Hangzhou—so that area scholars could consult them.

There was something highly intellectualized and even ingrown about all this work. It was extraordinarily difficult, for one thing, and hence enabled *kaozheng* scholars to reformulate a vision of a scholarly elite that had become endangered by the swelling number of unemployed degree candidates in the eighteenth century. (The plight of that elite, and the corruptibility and pomposity of many self-satisfied scholars, were poignantly and amusingly caught in a novel entitled *Unofficial History of the Scholars* [*Rulin waishi*], written between 1740 and 1750 and first published in 1768.) At the same time, by late in Qianlong's reign, even devotees of the *kaozheng* tradition were beginning to find that their techniques had limitations. One of the most brilliant scholars, Dai Zhen, while allegedly staying within the *kao-*

zheng camp, also began to write in purely philosophical terms, returning to an era of speculation about human goals, motivations, passions, and the meaning of moral action. It is significant that his closest friends refused to acknowledge the importance of this work, although exploration of these problems was central to his vision of himself.

One aspect of the eighteenth-century fascination with scholarship was a renewed interest in women's education, both among male scholars and in the discussions of women themselves. These discussions were not without their polemical sides. Some men who ran schools for young women were accused of doing so only from reasons of laciviousness, and were bitterly criticized by more puritanical contemporaries. The more acute critics pointed out that women's writing had been deflected—by the overall structural values of society—away from the broader channels of debate over moral, philosophical, and historiographical issues, where it had once been strong. Instead, women responded to being confined in the inner chambers by developing a literature of inwardness, especially one focused on certain aspects of romantic love and its accompanying frustrations. To these critics, the late Ming had not been a valuable period for women's consciousness. What was now needed was a broadening of women's minds so that they could become comprehensive analysts of the intellectual world. The large numbers of anthologies of women's poems that were being published were too circumscribed in content to be truly admirable, these critics felt.[4]

Confucianism was not just a matter of philosophy. Painting and calligraphy had always been essential adjuncts to the Confucian value system, and here again there were significant eighteenth-century shifts in style and matter. Conventional techniques of Chinese painting had been put in the hands of just about any moderately educated person by the production of "how to do it" painting manuals like the *Mustard Seed Garden* of 1701. From such a book, one could quickly learn to render a passable branch of plum blossom, a thatched cottage, or a distant mountain range, allowing any member of the educated public to produce a reasonable painting. In response, the literati painters now began to cultivate a greater sense of eccentricity, deliberately violating the norms of composition and color to show an "amateurism" that was in fact highly planned. Such eccentricity had been a feature of Ming loyalist painting in the seventeenth century, when it was used to convey a political position; by the eighteenth century, it showed a more class-conscious face.

Significant changes also took place in calligraphy. *Kaozheng* scholars' discoveries and reprintings of archaic scripts, and the circulation of careful rubbings of stone engravings, enabled the cult of the far past to dominate the present. At some extremes, painters would render the calligraphy on their paintings as if it were carved with a chisel, managing to be evocative and erudite at the same time. Thus by the end of Qianlong's reign, as literacy spread in the largely peaceful and cultivated Chinese world, it was perhaps no coincidence that the most highly educated men developed new modes of cultured expression that were out of the reach of almost everyone else.

THE DREAM OF THE RED CHAMBER

The Dream of the Red Chamber, China's greatest novel, was written in the middle of Emperor Qianlong's reign. The author, Cao Xueqin, was descended from one of the Chinese bannerman-bondservants who had enjoyed wealth and influence as a favorite of Emperor Kangxi. But the Cao family, which had lived for years on a grand scale in Nanjing, was subsequently punished for dishonesty and incompetence by Emperor Yongzheng and suffered confiscation of most of its holdings. Cao Xueqin was thus thoroughly familiar with the Sino-Manchu tensions that persisted through the Qing dynasty and, by the time of his death in 1763, had tasted the nectar of luxurious living and the gall of bankrupt gentility.

The Dream of the Red Chamber—often known by its alternate title, *The Story of the Stone*—presents a meticulous description of the Jias, a wealthy Chinese extended family who occupy a series of linked mansions in an unnamed big city that seems to have some elements of Nanjing and some of Peking. Many aspects of the fictional Jia family's story are clearly drawn from the history of Kangxi's reign: the Jias are aware of Manchu culture and deportment, carry out confidential financial assignments for the emperor, and have a favored relationship with the court, where one of the Jia daughters is a secondary consort. Yet the novel is not content to offer a realistic portrayal of Qing life. Each of the novel's two titles points to different and complex elements in the novel's structure: the "dream" that is ascribed to the "red chamber" constitutes an elaborate yet mysterious foretelling of the fates of the main female protagonists who are related or linked to the Jias in some way; the "stone" whose "story" is to be told is a miraculous artifact, empowered by the gods with a magical life of its own, and living out its existence on this earth through the religious mediation of a Buddhist and a Daoist priest.

In simple outline, *The Dream of the Red Chamber* is a love story. The fate of the novel's hero, Jia Baoyu ("Jia of the Precious Jade"), is closely entwined with the lives of two young women, Lin Daiyu and Xue Baochai, each of whom bears one of the elements of his name in her own. The three grow up in the Jia family mansions with a host of other young companions, but their idyllic relations come to a sharp end when Jia Baoyu, who deeply loves Lin Daiyu, is tricked by his parents into marrying the wealthier and stronger Xue Baochai. This deceit leads to Lin Daiyu's death; at the novel's end, Jia Baoyu—although he has just passed the highest level of the state examinations—leaves his young wife and the spacious grounds of his crumbling estate to seek the pure life of a religious pilgrim.

Cao Xueqin had a serious purpose in writing the novel, as well as the simple desire to entertain. Beyond its plot, the *Dream* is a story of the quest for identity and for an understanding of the human purpose on earth. The novel also explores the different levels of reality and illusion that lie entwined inside so-called success and failure. In Cao's words in the introduction to the book, "From the Void (which is Truth) we come to the contemplation of Form (which is Illusion); from Form is engendered Passion; by communicating Passion we enter again into Form; and from Form awake to the Void (which is Truth)."[5] Or, put another way in the same introduction, "Truth becomes fiction when the fiction's true."

Although this suggests that Cao intends to disavow "realism," so rich are the texture and structure of the novel—which is 120 chapters long and contains hundreds of richly drawn characters in addition to the main protagonists—that it can nevertheless be seen as a kind of summation of the many elements of mid-Qing elite life, including family structure, politics, economics, religion, aesthetics, and sexuality. Even allowing for all the freedoms of the creative writer's imagination and for the rich allegorical overtones that pervade the whole work, a look at each of these six categories can still tell us much about the grandeur of Qing society in the mid-eighteenth century, and about its underside.

In the realm of family structure, Cao Xueqin points to the immense power of the father over his children, especially on questions of their moral growth and education. It is the Jia father who chooses the schoolteacher for the local lineage school, who grills Jia Baoyu over the progress of his studies in the Confucian classics, and who punishes him for negligence or immorality. So terrible is the father's anger that the mere mention of it reduces the son to abject fear. The mother, in this context, is comparatively powerless; but the matriarch of the family, Jia Baoyu's grandmother, is shown as having great economic and intellectual strength, and as being able to moderate family behavior on the basis of the respect owed her for her advanced age and generational seniority. Similarly, generational hierarchies give Jia Baoyu prestige over younger siblings or cousins, while forcing him to defer to those older than he.

In political terms, the Jias are powerful not just because a member of their family is a consort to the emperor, nor because they hold high office in the bureaucracy and undertake imperial commissions. Their real power is local, in that they can use their prestige to bend the judicial system to their advantage. Any country magistrate knows better than to prosecute one of the Jias or their friends—it would be more than his job is worth. The family is thus subject to a kind of corrupting influence, which leads its younger members to believe they can break the law with impunity, even to the extent of hushing up homicides in which family members have been involved. This political power is potentially self-perpetuating, since the web of princely friends and the patterns of examination success will propel the younger men of the lineage into positions of influence, and the young women of the family into powerful marriages.

Economically, the Jia family can call on resources that would be beyond the imagination of most Chinese families. Their home is full of silver bullion, bolts of silk, paintings, and scrolls. Their grounds and buildings are spacious, and their coffers constantly replenished with the rents brought by loyal bailiffs from urban holdings and from far-off farms that the Jias own as absentee landlords. They indulge in profitable business deals of great complexity, and gain additional income from carrying out imperial commissions and acquiring exotic goods from merchants who trade with Western countries. They also have scores of indentured servants, male and female, who perform all duties in the family compound and act as retainers whenever the Jias go outside the walls.

In matters of religion, the Jia family are as eclectic as Qing society was. Central to the family's prestige and sense of fulfillment is the meticulous worship, in the Confucian tradition, of their own ancestors. Funerals, like marriages, are occasions for intense, careful pomp and ritual performance. But the Jias also call, as necessary, on priests of the Daoist and Buddhist religions; they follow the prescribed ceremonies of these religions, and even keep a group of young female Buddhist novices in the purlieus of their own home. The Jias practice both Buddhist and Daoist rites in times of fear or illness, and on occasion have priests conduct exorcisms to rid the family houses of harmful spirits and malignant influences. Jia Baoyu himself is, for a long period in the novel, immobilized by an enemy's use of black magic, against which not even his precious jade can protect him. One senior member of the family has withdrawn to a temple to follow his own pattern of religious enlightenment. (He later dies from imbibing too many magical Daoist elixirs of immortality.)

Aesthetically, the life in the Jia mansions is a joy, recalling the range and elegance that typified elite life in the late Ming dynasty. The high level of literacy of the young men and women makes possible an endless array of poetry games and the exchange of erudite jokes and riddles. The clothes, decor, gardens, and accouterments of the main characters are exquisite; the preparation of tea, drinking of wine, and eating of an evening meal are a triumphant blending of taste and artifice. Music and drama are also an integral part of life for the Jias: the family keeps its own troupe of actors and actresses who, whenever they are requested to do so, perform scenes from now-classic works such as *The Peony Pavilion,* by the Ming dramatist Tang Xianzu.

Finally, in the realm of sexuality, there are few limitations on the behavior of the Jia family members. The children and adolescents may live together in a youthful world where banter is essentially innocent even if full of sexual innuendo, but their elders are lustful creatures, and the children are growing up to be like them. Both men and women use their powers in the family hierarchy to obtain their sexual pleasures. Jealousy goes with adultery, love affairs lead to murders. Servants and bondslaves become sexual objects and are powerless to protest except by flight or suicide. Erotic paintings stir up great passions, as in the case of Jia Baoyu's initiation into sexual life. Jia Baoyu falls asleep after viewing a sensual painting and has a complex yet graphic erotic dream. His awakening is followed by a re-enactment of the dream experience, but this time in literal terms with his own favored serv-ing-maid. Novice nuns or young male actors are also caught up in the patterns of seduction and deceit, and even in the schoolroom, where Con-fucian precepts are allegedly being internalized, homosexual liaisons flourish among the young male scholars.

Cao Xueqin had not completed his novel when he died in 1763, and for several decades it circulated in various manuscript editions among his family and friends. Only in 1792 did a "full" version, with lacunae filled in by later hands, appear in published form, and it became an immediate success. One may speculate that the novel's wide readership was composed of men and women from the upper class, of underemployed scholars, and also of those with some education who lived and worked as merchants and traders in the flourishing cities of the largely peaceful mid-Qing world.

Although *The Dream of the Red Chamber* is full of echoes from the great plays and novels of the late Ming and from earlier Chinese poetic traditions, and although we cannot be sure which sections of the last forty chapters were the author's personal work, the novel remains a dazzling and original triumph, anticipating in its subtlety and scale many of the great works of the nineteenth-century Western tradition. Cao himself was tongue-in-cheek about his achievement, and in a speech that he puts into the mouth of the Jia family grandmother, he speculates on why most conventional Chinese tales and dramas written prior to his novel were so repetitive and uncon-vincing:

'There's always a reason for it,' the old lady went on, 'In some cases it's because the writer is envious of people so much better off than himself, or disappointed because he has tried to obtain their patronage and failed, and deliberately portrays them in this unfavourable light as a means of getting his own back on them. In other cases the writers have been corrupted by reading this sort of stuff before they begin to write any themselves, and, though totally ignorant of what life in educated, aristocratic families is really like portray their heroines in this way simply because everyone else does so and they think it will please their readers. I ask you now, never mind *very* grand families like the ones they pretend to be writing about, even in average well-to-do families like ours when do you ever hear of such carryings-on? It's a wonder their jaws don't drop off, telling such dreadful lies!'[6]

Cao Xueqin might have been disappointed in his life, but it is unlikely that he was envious of those in power and certain that he was not corrupted by the fiction of the past. His triumph was his own. The only real irony, perhaps, is that his great novel adds luster to the reign of Qianlong, although Cao's own sharp gaze was able to see that so much was wrong underneath all that grandeur.

QIANLONG'S LATER YEARS

As if echoing the warning note sounded by the *feng* hexagram, in Emperor Qianlong's later years a series of crises erupted. There was no particular pattern to these troubles; it was rather that a series of misjudgments on the government's part coincided with previously unsuspected levels of domestic resentment to produce a tense situation overall. Bungled military border campaigns, local rebellions, bureaucratic corruption, and imperial favoritism were all part of the story, which took place in a context of intellectual uneasiness over traditional scholarly values, the state's failure to address pressing financial and administrative needs, and a steadily growing population that put unprecedented pressures on the land.

In public pronouncements, Qianlong prided himself on his sagacity as a coordinator of military campaigns, and the conquest of Xinjiang in the 1750s—although owing a good deal to luck—had indeed been a great achievement. But a campaign against Burma in the 1760s was badly mismanaged, in sharp contrast to the efficiency with which Wu Sangui had pursued the last Ming prince in the same region a century before. And the brief war that China waged against Vietnam in 1788 and 1789 throws a sharp light on the inadequacies of Qing policy.

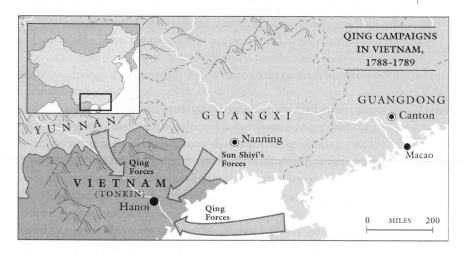

In 1788 the ruler of Vietnam's Le dynasty fled with his family from usurpers who had seized Hanoi. Taking refuge in Guangxi province, he begged for Qing protection. Qianlong responded swiftly, ordering a three-pronged attack on Vietnam, with one army marching south from Guangxi under General Sun Shiyi, a second southeast from Yunnan, and a third transported by sea from Guangdong. The Chinese armies under General Sun entered Hanoi in December 1788 and declared total victory and the restoration of the Le dynasty. Qianlong at once promoted General Sun to ducal rank. But just one month later, while Sun and his troops were in Hanoi celebrating the Chinese new year festival, the rebels counterattacked, killing over 1,000 of Sun's troops and forcing his ignominious flight back to Guangxi. Qianlong pragmatically commented that the Le had been fated to fall, and he acknowledged the succession of the victor as Vietnam's legitimate ruler. At one level this showed that China still had the prestige to confer title on border rulers; at the same time, however, Chinese military leadership was called into question. (This misadventure marked the end of China's attempts at direct military involvement in Vietnam until their equally unsuccessful invasion of 1979.)

That some Manchu generals could still muster amazing military skills was shown by the Qing victories over the Gurkhas of Nepal, who attacked Tibet in 1790 and 1791. Qing troops under Manchu generals reached Tibet in 1792 and defeated the Gurkhas in a series of battles, forcing them back into Nepal through the Himalayan passes. The Qing troops showed remarkable skills at logistics and at fighting in some of the harshest terrain in the world. In the ensuing peace treaty, Nepal agreed to send tribute to China every five years, a promise that they kept up until the year 1908. But the campaign had been extremely expensive for the Qing, and a great deal of the money expended was never accounted for satisfactorily. The man in charge of writing up the accounts was that same General Sun Shiyi who had bungled the Vietnam campaign. Despite Sun's failure there, Qianlong had transferred him to Lhasa, demonstrating more the strength of the emperor's will than the shrewdness of his evaluation of character.

These long-range campaigns against foreign states were conducted in an unsettling context of indigenous rebellions, which began to occur in different parts of the Chinese Empire during the later eighteenth century. Some of these uprisings were more imaginary than real, and served to demonstrate the emperor's suspicious nature rather than any genuine threat to the throne. Such was the case with the sorcery scare of 1768 in which the emperor grew convinced that a group of plotters were clipping the queues of hair from unsuspecting victims in order to develop magical potions that could steal away a man's soul and conjure up whole armies of spirit troops. Only after scores of arrests and many interrogations under torture—from which many innocent vagrants died—did the emperor decide that he had been misled and that no true plot against him existed. Other cases however were more serious, and fully grounded in reality. One such major uprising took place not far from Peking, in Shandong province near the city of Linqing, a key point on the north-south grain-transportation axis along the Grand Canal. This was an area near the periphery of the northeast macroregion, where population had been rising sharply and where disaffected peasants mingled easily with the restless barge pullers and coolies who kept the Grand Canal in operation. In 1774 Chinese rebels under the leadership of a martial-arts and herbal-healing expert named Wang Lun rose up against the Qing, invoking the support of an "Eternal Venerable Mother" goddess. In this way the revolt showed its links to a tradition of underground or sectarian White Lotus folk-Buddhism, which venerated the same female deity and was based on a millenarian view of catastrophe on earth that reached back to ideological roots at least five centuries earlier. Wang drew his followers from a wide variety of occupations: many were peasants or other rural laborers, but there were also traveling actresses, carters, fish sellers and dealers in bean curd, monks, vegetable-oil retailers, and a moneylender. We cannot say that Wang Lun had a firm political agenda: although some peasants did support him, he never talked of abolishing rent, or helping the poor, or dividing the land equally. His followers rose in rebellion not in response to some specific political program for social and economic amelioration, but from general feelings of antagonism to the dominant forces of society, reinforced by simple forms of spiritual euphoria.

Wang Lun's teachings convinced the rebels that they could withstand all

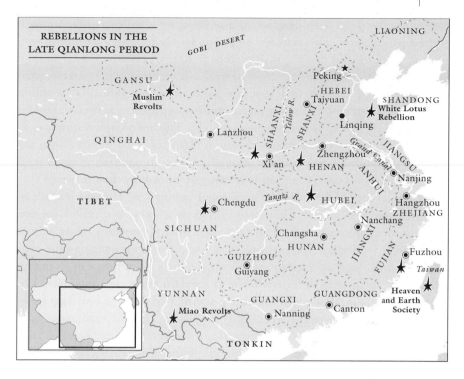

Qing attacks. As he told them, "If I call on Heaven, Heaven will assist me; if I call on Earth, Earth will give me magical strength. Their guns will not fire. What men will dare impede me?"[7] In early fighting, some of Wang's predictions seemed correct: he captured several small towns and even parts of Linqing city, and many Manchu and Chinese troops sent against him fled or deserted. But the state called up massive forces, including banner troops and local armies of Chinese soldiers known as the Green Standard troops; Wang Lun and his various "soldiers," armed mainly with spears or knives, could not withstand the coordinated attacks of these Qing troops. Despite brave street fighting, often house to house, the rebels were pinned down and slaughtered with their families. A vivid rendition of Wang Lun's final apocalypse was given to Qing authorities by a captured rebel who fled his leader's burning headquarters. Wang Lun, he testified, met his death wearing a long purple robe and two silver bracelets, his dagger and double-bladed sword beside him. He sat cross-legged in the corner of the room, motionless, his clothes and beard aflame.

Wang Lun's uprising was more important as a symptom of deep underlying discontents than for its immediate effects, and it should be considered along with other rebellions that erupted elsewhere in China, often with no precisely stated grievances or goals. In the 1780s, members of a group known as the Heaven and Earth Society, which had its own religious rituals and social bondings through oaths of allegiance, rose in revolt on Taiwan, seizing several cities and declaring a new dynasty. The uprising seems to have been as much a battle between different groups of emigrants from Fujian province for dominance over Taiwan's economy as it was an assault on the Qing state, but the government responded swiftly. The rebels were suppressed and their leaders executed in 1788.

Also in the 1780s, in Gansu province, there were two major revolts of the Muslim communities, sparked by adherents of a fundamentalist "new sect" who opposed the local Muslim officials appointed by the Qing. Both Muslim uprisings were suppressed after heavy fighting, as were a series of revolts by Miao tribesmen in southwest China. But the fighting was costly to the Qing, who despite their victories did not eradicate the underlying causes of religious, economic, and ethnic resentments. In 1799, as Qianlong's reign ended, rebels claiming the same White Lotus affiliation that had animated the followers of Wang Lun were rising up all across central China and were actively fighting Qing troops in many areas of Sichuan, Hubei, Shaanxi, and Henan.

Can one link these outbreaks to specific Manchu policies that alienated the people? The evidence is not clear on this, but it is certain that in the late eighteenth century many Qing government institutions began to falter: the emergency granaries were often empty, sections of the Grand Canal silted up, regular banner troops behaved with incompetence or brutality, efforts to stop ecologically dangerous land-reclamation projects were abandoned, the bureaucracy was faction-ridden, and corruption ran deep. It is also possible that Qing reluctance to create new county governments in areas of new settlement or dense population put impossible stresses on officials in the bureaucracy. Moreover, the intense pressure for jobs meant that those who had finally obtained office sought a swift return for all their waiting and anxiety, pressing local peasants in their jurisdictions for speedy tax payments and for supplementary charges. The White Lotus insurgents of the 1790s, for instance, stated categorically that "the officials have forced the people to rebel."[8] It is also true that in the conduct of the border campaigns, as in the suppression of local rebellions, Qing officials indulged in an unusually high level of graft. This was made possible by collusion between high figures in military and civil government, who often hid the real situation from Emperor Qianlong. And Qianlong, having allowed the secret palace memorial system of his father Yongzheng to become impersonal and routine, now had no reliable, confidential sources from which to learn of his officials' malfeasance.

There is no doubt that this pattern of corruption grew worse after 1775, when a young Manchu guards officer named Heshen became entrenched as the elderly emperor's court favorite, although Heshen was not responsible for everything that was going awry. At that time Heshen was twenty-five and the emperor sixty-five, and the following year the favorite received an extraordinary series of promotions: Qianlong named Heshen a deputy lieutenant general of the Manchu plain blue banner, a minister of the imperial household, vice-minister of revenue, and a grand councilor. There were no parallels in Qing history for giving so many powerful appointments to a young man, and Qianlong later piled honor on honor. Heshen was made minister of revenue (and, for a time, minister of civil office), a grand secretary, a director of the *Four Treasuries* compilation project, commanding officer of the Peking troops, superviser of transit dues at the Peking gates, and a baron. His son was married to Emperor Qianlong's tenth daughter in 1790.

It is not surprising that rumors swirled around the emperor's relations with his favorite. A homosexual liaison was implied in popular stories, such as one suggesting Heshen was the reincarnation of one of Emperor Yongzheng's concubines, with whom Qianlong had been infatuated as a youth. A Korean diplomatic official on a visit to China, perhaps influenced by such rumors, described Heshen at thirty as "elegant in looks, sprucely handsome in a dandified way that suggested a lack of virtue." In 1793 Lord Macartney, who was visiting China as ambassador for King George III, described Heshen as "a handsome, fair man about forty to forty-five years old, quick and fluent."[9]

There is, in fact, no clear evidence about the relationship one way or the other. Certainly Qianlong trusted Heshen implicitly for the rest of his life. It is possible that Qianlong initially wanted Heshen to be the emperor's "ears and eyes" that Kangxi and Yongzheng had found in the bondservants and officials who used the palace memorial system in its earlier days. Thus in 1780 the emperor sent Heshen on a confidential mission to Yunnan province to investigate corruption charges against the governor-general there, and in 1781 sent him to assist in suppressing the Muslim uprisings in Gansu. But Heshen, who was often ill, mainly stayed in Peking as Qianlong's chief minister and confidant. Heshen's physicians concluded that his "symptoms were owing to a malignant vapour or spirit which had infused itself into, or was generated in his flesh, which shifted itself from place to place," and were unable to help him. Boldly turning to Western medicine as an alternative, Heshen summoned Lord Macartney's Scottish doctor Hugh Gillan for a consultation. Gillan found that Heshen was suffering from acute rheumatism and a serious hernia, conditions that had plagued him since childhood, and arranged for him to be fitted with a truss.[10]

In various comments on Heshen, both Macartney and Gillan showed that they found him to be forceful and intelligent, if evasive. Moreover, miscellaneous Chinese sources also show that Heshen possessed a lively intelligence, keen curiosity, tact, and a high level of literacy. But he did use his offices to make prodigious amounts of money for himself and his cronies. He took on himself nearly imperial pretensions, coerced favors, and demanded fees for all services. He raked in extra millions by misreporting the needs for supplies and services on the numerous campaigns conducted during Qianlong's later years, especially the protracted, savage, and badly executed forays against the White Lotus rebels. By all these actions, Heshen compounded the problems of the time and contributed to a growing demoralization among the bureaucracy and the people.

Heshen's dominance was even stronger after 1796. In that year, Qianlong "abdicated," an action devised as a "filial" one to show that he did not consider himself worthy to reign longer than the sixty-one years of his famous grandfather, Kangxi. But Qianlong did not allow his son to exercise power, and during this twilight period, even though Qianlong's name was not used in dynastic titles, it was his will that was manifested through Heshen's continuing official power. When Qianlong died at last in 1799, Heshen's base crumbled. He was charged with corruption by Qianlong's son and forced to commit suicide. It was a melancholy yet somehow fitting end to one of the richest centuries in China's long history, an end that highlighted the curious mix of strength and weakness that was now emerging as lying at the heart of the Qing dynasty.

CHAPTER 6

China and the Eighteenth-Century World

MANAGING THE FOREIGNERS

The Qing state had no Ministry of Foreign Affairs. Relations with non-Chinese peoples were instead conducted by a variety of bureaus and agencies that, in different ways, implied or stated the cultural inferiority and geographical marginality of foreigners, while also defending the state against them.

In the north and northwest, relations with the Mongols, Zunghars, and Russians were handled mainly by the Lifan Yuan, or Office of Border Affairs, which had been founded by Hong Taiji in 1638. Staffed exclusively by Manchus and Mongols, the Lifan Yuan's task was to keep things quiet in China's dangerous northwest crescent, whence so many of her conquerors in the past had come. To this end, the office forged an elaborate system of agreements regulating the visits of central Asian caravan traders to China. Imperial daughters were commonly married off to influential Mongol princes, forming a protective network of personal alliances, bolstered by Qing garrisons located at strategic points in the region. Muslims, some of whom were of central Asian origin and some Chinese, were watched with care but generally allowed to practice their religion in peace; and after a Qing military presence in Lhasa became established under Yongzheng, the tribes that owed religious allegiance to the lamaist Buddhist hierarchy of Tibet ceased to be a grave threat. The variety of tasks coordinated by officials in the Lifan Yuan did, therefore, give the bureaucrats considerable skill and breadth of experience in dealing with "foreign policy" problems, and made the Great Wall largely redundant as an aspect of northwest frontier defense.

European missionary contact with China was supervised mainly by the imperial household, an autonomous bureaucratic institution in Peking. This agency managed a wide range of the emperor's affairs, including the stockpiling of bullion and food reserves, the maintenance of imperial estates and palaces, the manufactures for precious silks and porcelain, and the collection of extra revenues from such items as the salt monopoly and the transit dues on internal and foreign trade. It was most commonly the bondservants in the imperial household—often men of considerable wealth and power—who dealt directly with the missionaries and escorted papal embassies. Their general role in missionary business underlined the prevailing view that this dimension of foreign affairs was an aspect of the court's prestige rather than of national policy. The Jesuits especially found their role much constricted by this arrangement and tried to emphasize their independence in letters back to European colleagues. Some of the Jesuits, along with other Catholic missionaries and Chinese priests, worked secretly inside China, sheltered by their converts. All faced serious punishment if caught by the authorities.

Interaction with non-Chinese peoples in Korea and on the southern crescent of China's coastal and land frontiers, in countries such as Burma, Thailand, Vietnam, and the Ryukyu Islands, was supervised by officials in the Ministry of Rituals. These countries shared many of the basic values of Chinese culture, a Chinese-style calendrical system, some form of script adapted from Chinese models, similar types of food and dress, the practice of Confucianism and Buddhism, and the outlines of Chinese bureaucratic organization. By freighting its international relations with the weight of custom and symbol prescribed by this ministry, China tried to control these states without excessive military expenditures. Emissaries from these countries were expected to make a formal acknowledgment of China's cultural and political prestige by employing a language of subservience in diplomatic documents and by making the ritual prostrations (kowtow) before the Chinese emperor in royal audiences. In return these countries were allowed to conduct a controlled volume of trade with China, mainly through special delegations, termed "tribute missions" by the Chinese, which the countries were permitted to send on a fixed annual schedule to Peking. After ritual gifts had been offered to the emperor, both the diplomatic personnel and the merchants accompanying these embassies to Peking were allowed to trade, although all of them had to live in hostels managed by the Ministry of Rituals and had to leave China with their goods at the end of each stipulated visit.

Within this system, there was considerable flexibility. The most frequent missions were those from Korea, which came every year; Korean visitors mingled freely with Qing scholars and officials, and left vivid accounts of the social and cultural life in Peking and of the political attitudes of the Confucian literati. Embassies from Japan, however, had completely ceased during the later Ming, and Japan's continuing refusal to acknowledge China's ritual superiority, when combined with the Tokugawa government's decision to restrict all foreign residence and trade to Nagasaki, meant that formal Qing relations with Japan were minimal. The military dimension of "tributary" relations emerged in 1788, when the Chinese invoked their right and obligation to go to the aid of the ruling Le in Vietnam. As we have seen, the Chinese swiftly switched their support from the Le when the rebels accepted the traditional tributary position of deference to the Qing state. In the Ryukyu Islands, there was a curious case of divided loyalties. The islanders were in fact controlled by the southern Japanese lords of Satsuma, but on ritual occasions continued to profess themselves loyal tributary subjects of the Qing. Contemporary eighteenth-century accounts show Japanese ships retreating discreetly out of sight when Chinese diplomatic missions visited the islands, only to return promptly as soon as the Chinese left.

Despite Qianlong's own pretensions to universal Asian overlordship, these three broad patterns of foreign management—with the northwest, the missionaries, and the south—shared some fundamental Chinese premises of great importance. At their root was the assumption that China was the "central" kingdom and that other countries were, by definition, peripheral, removed from the cultural center of the universe. The Chinese, therefore, showed little interest in precise information or detailed study of foreign countries. Even during the peak periods of eighteenth-century "evidential" *kaozheng* research, the interest of scholars in geography and linguistics was largely concentrated on Chinese territory. Chinese descriptions of foreign countries continued to contain an exotic blend of mystical tales and fantasy in which foreigners were often likened to animals or birds and were described in patronizing or deliberately belittling language.

Those Chinese who chose to leave China and go overseas for trade or travel were seen as having abandoned their country; and even though an extensive Chinese trade developed with Southeast Asia, the Qing state showed no interest in standing up for Chinese rights there or elsewhere in the world. (An exception was the case of Taiwan, but that had been formally incorporated as a part of Fujian province.) The Qing were basically uninterested in the potential governmental gains to be made from foreign trade, although they were willing to skim a certain amount off for themselves through the imperial household. They distrusted traders and—as in the 1660s—were willing to take harsh measures against their coastal populations in order to achieve military or diplomatic goals. They reserved for themselves the absolute right to regulate foreigners trading with China, not only as to location and frequency, but down to the smallest details of personnel and goods involved.

This body of Qing beliefs and practices was bound to clash with those of the Western powers, especially after the newly expanding states of Britain, France, and Holland all began to develop major overseas empires at the expense of the earlier dominant partners, Spain and Portugal. One can trace this process of cultural opposition through the gradual emergence in China of a fourth type of "foreign management" structure, commonly known as the "Canton System." In the early Qing, Dutch and Portuguese embassies both tried to establish broad trading privileges with China but had to be content with the status of "tributary nations," registered with the Ministry of Rituals and permitted to send trade missions only at stipulated intervals. British ships sporadically appeared off the east China coast beginning in 1635; and under the Qing, perhaps because the British had the sense not to seek formal relations, British merchants were permitted to trade with the Chinese in Zhoushan (Chusan), Xiamen (Amoy), and Canton. All the Western powers benefited when the Qing ended the coastal trade-restriction policy in the 1680s and the idea of their "tributary" status was generally dropped. In an attempt to control foreign trade and increase their profits by regulating prices, in 1720 Chinese merchants in Canton formed their own monopolistic guild called the Cohong (from *gonghang,* or "combined merchant companies"). In 1754 these "Hong" merchants were each ordered by the Qing to stand surety for the foreign crews' good behavior and for the payment of transit dues.

The British East India Company, founded in 1600 and granted a monopoly of east Indian trade by the British government, was now rising rapidly from a small operation to a position of global significance as it attracted sizable new investments and started to conquer territories in the subcontinent of India itself. During the Qianlong reign, its directors began to chafe at Qing restrictions, as did the British government itself. In 1741, the British discovered the importance of having a Far Eastern base (the Portuguese already had Macao, the Spaniards Manila, and the Dutch Batavia) when a commodore in the Royal Navy, George Anson, on assignment to attack Spanish shipping in the East, put into Canton harbor after his flagship suffered severe storm damage. Anson apparently believed that the Chinese, following the international laws of the sea now prevalent in the West, would treat him hospitably as a benevolent neutral. But the Canton bureaucracy erected dozens of administrative hurdles, refused to meet with him or acknowledge his messages for weeks on end, charged him what he considered outrageous prices for the shoddy supplies they provided, and refused to let him make many of the repairs he wanted. Anson's published account of his alleged mistreatment was widely circulated and translated into several European languages, helping to build a ground swell of anti-Chinese feeling in Britain and elsewhere in the West.

The East India Company tried to enlarge the scope for China trade and negotiation in 1759 by sending James Flint, a company trader who had learned Chinese, to present complaints to the Qing court concerning the restrictions on trade in Canton and the rampant corruption there. By dint of tenacity and a certain amount of bribery, Flint, sailing first to Ningbo and then to Tianjin in a small 70-ton vessel, the *Success,* was able to have his complaints carried to Peking. The emperor initially seemed to show flexibility, and agreed to send a commission of investigation to the south. But after the *Success,* sailing back to Canton, was lost at sea with all hands except for Flint (he had traveled south independently), the emperor changed his mind. Flint was arrested and imprisoned for three years for breaking Qing regulations against sailing to northern ports, for improperly presenting petitions, and for having learned Chinese.

The Qing response to the growing number of foreign traders who began to push at their doors in the later eighteenth century was to reinforce all the preceding rules, while protesting that they wished justice done to all foreigners. All European trade was restricted to the one port of Canton after 1760, and foreigners were forbidden residence there except during the trading season, which ran each year from October to March. The Europeans now had to deal exclusively with the licensed Chinese Hong merchants— of whom there were normally around ten—despite the indulgence of many in sharp business practices and the considerable number who went bankrupt by overextending their resources. Westerners could communicate their grievances or petitions only to these Hong merchants, who in turn forwarded any written materials to the Hoppo, the court-appointed trade official. (Like *Cohong, Hoppo* derived from the Western pronunciation of a Chinese word—in this case, for Qing government personnel.) The Hoppo, if he chose, might then communicate with the provincial governor or with Peking; or he might, on a myriad grounds of procedure or impropriety, refuse to forward the documents at all.

It was a complex and exasperating procedure, far from the kind of diplomatic and commercial equality among nations that Western powers were beginning to take for granted. Tensions on both sides increased after the 1770s as British traders in particular, worried by the trade deficits that forced them to offer hundreds of thousands of pounds' worth of silver bullion each year in exchange for Chinese silks, porcelains, and teas, began to ship opium grown in India to southern Chinese ports and to exchange it there for Chinese manufactures and produce. The stakes became higher each year as the passion for tea drinking grew in both Britain and America: by 1800, the East India Company was buying over 23 million pounds of China tea at a cost of £3.6 million. (From 1784 onward, merchants in the newly independent United States, free now to trade where they chose, began to send their ships to the lucrative China tea market directly; but they too were subjected to the restrictions that bound Europeans.)

It was near the end of Qianlong's reign that the British East India Company, acting in agreement with King George III's government, decided to try to rectify the situation in a direction they believed was consonant with the new dignity of Britain as a world power. They selected as their emissary to China Lord George Macartney, a politically well-connected peer from Northern Ireland who had had diplomatic experience at the court of Russia's Catherine the Great. Macartney had also gained practical experience as governor of Grenada in the Caribbean and administrator of the region of Madras in eastern India. The British embassy traveled in a man-of-war of 66 guns, with two support vessels, each loaded with expensive gifts designed to show the finest aspects of British manufacturing technology. Macartney was accompanied by a retinue of almost 100, including scientists, artists, guards, valets, and Chinese language teachers from the Catholic college in Naples.

Leaving London in September 1792, Macartney's ships touched briefly at Canton in June 1793, but were allowed to proceed directly to Tianjin and land there since they claimed to be saluting Qianlong on his eightieth birthday. Once ashore, the embassy was escorted to Peking with much pomp but with the official status of "tribute emissaries." Macartney managed to persist in his refusal to prostrate himself full-length on the ground before the emperor in the ritual kowtow, agreeing instead to kneel on one knee and make a series of bows. This compromise satisfied the Qing, and Macartney was courteously received in September 1793 by Heshen and by the emperor at the northern summer palace of Rehe (Jehol). In his audience, Macartney asked for British rights of diplomatic residence in Peking, the ending of the restrictive Canton trading system, the opening of new ports for international commerce, and the fixing of fair and equitable tariffs. Unfailingly bland, neither the Qing emperor nor his minister would yield to any of the British requests.

Qianlong instead sent an edict to George III explaining that China would not increase its foreign commerce because it needed nothing from other countries. As Qianlong wrote, "We have never valued ingenious articles, nor do we have the slightest need of your country's manufactures. Therefore,

O king, as regards your request to send someone to remain at the capital, while it is not in harmony with the regulations of the Celestial Empire we also feel very much that it is of no advantage to your country."[1]

Macartney had no counterforce to employ. He could only leave China by the designated land route to Canton, taking as many notes about the country as he could along the way and jotting in his journal his personal view that this awesome-appearing country had grave internal weaknesses that threatened to destroy it. He drew his main metaphor, suitably enough, from the sea across which he had traveled with such cost of time and discomfort. "The Empire of China," he wrote in his journal, "is an old, crazy, first rate man-of-war, which a fortunate succession of able and vigilant officers has contrived to keep afloat for these one hundred and fifty years past, and to overawe their neighbors merely by her bulk and appearance." But with lesser men at the helm, Macartney added, China would slowly drift until "dashed to pieces on the shore." China's opposition to British goals was ultimately futile, wrote Macartney, since it was "in vain to attempt arresting the progress of human knowledge," as the Qing were doing. "The human mind is of a soaring nature and having once gained the lower steps of the ascent, struggles incessantly against every difficulty to reach the highest."[2]

The entire venture had cost the East India Company a small fortune, for which the company had received no return. It was not an auspicious opening to the era of face-to-face diplomatic relations, although Macartney himself did nicely. He had insisted on an annual allowance of £15,000 before undertaking the venture, and had cleared a profit of over £20,000 from his mission. At least China had not stood in the way of his own personal progress.

ALIENS AND CHINESE LAW

One of Lord Macartney's more interesting acquisitions in China was a copy of the Qing dynasty's legal code. When this code was brought back to England and translated by a scholar who had learned his Chinese as a member of Macartney's retinue, it made clear what had seemed probable to generations of British traders—namely, that the Chinese and the Europeans had very different views of what constituted "the law" and, accordingly, that recourse to legal expedients might exacerbate rather than lessen international tensions.

Although based on a wide range of prior experience and precedent, Chinese law was codified and interpreted by the state. There was no independent judiciary either in the provinces or in Peking: it was the county magistrate who acted as the local representative of justice. A series of reviews by the prefect and the judicial intendant of a given province could bring a case to the Ministry of Punishments in Peking. Appeals by plaintiffs were also possible but only within a rigorous hierarchy that culminated in a "court" of senior officials. Death sentences did have to be reviewed by the magistrate's superiors, and technically the emperor himself passed final judgment on all crimes meriting execution. But that was not always possible in practice and often arbitrary. In local insurrections, rebels were customarily executed immediately to discourage their followers and to prevent the possibility of their being freed from jail by other dissidents. In cases involving foreigners, summary executions were also common.

The county magistrates acted essentially as detectives, judges, and jury. They accumulated the evidence, then evaluated it, and finally passed sentence. Punishments for particular crimes were prescribed in the legal code, which magistrates had to follow. Although these officials often relied on a member of their clerical staff who was allegedly "expert" in the law, there was no independent profession of law and no lawyers. Those who tried to intervene from outside in criminal cases were castigated for their interference. Suspects were routinely treated with great harshness in jail, and often beaten or tortured with wooden presses if they refused to confess. Confession always preceded the "trial," the result of which was therefore a foregone conclusion unless some startling new exonerating evidence could be produced. Since the beatings with a heavy wooden pole sometimes used to extract confessions could lead to a suspect's death or cripple him for life, it is not surprising that many Chinese feared the legal structure, although they did use the magistrates' courts in serious disagreements over real estate, inheritances, and other economic matters.

In most other disputes the Chinese had recourse to mediators who were either respected members of the local community or leaders of influential lineage organizations. Those threatened with suit in such cases might well pay to hush a case up; and the junior personnel of the magistrate's official staff—the so-called "yamen runners"—routinely supplemented their meager incomes by accepting bribes to keep matters quiet. Those accused of committing criminal acts such as theft, rape, or homicide would also try to pay their way free, with gifts to the magistrate's staff or even to the magistrate himself. The grim and possibly fatal experience of a stay in prison (which description, of course, applied as well to the filthy, crowded prisons of Europe at the time) could be ameliorated by regular payments to one's jailers and by distribution of food to one's fellow inmates.

The Qing penal system also maintained the hierarchical social values that were propagated through the state's Confucian teachings. Crimes against the emperor and his family were the most serious, and crimes against bureaucrats or state property were also severely punished—by execution or prolonged periods of exile. Within the family structure, fathers committing a given crime against their sons were punished far more lightly than sons who committed the same crime against their fathers, and the same was true of husbands harming their wives, or older relatives their younger ones. In one case in which a father killed his son by burying him alive, the Ministry of Punishments carefully reviewed the facts and concluded that the governor had acted wrongly in sentencing the father to be beaten for the crime. Fathers who killed sons should be beaten only if they had acted "unreasonably," argued the ministry. In this case, the son had used foul language at his father, an act that deserved the death penalty: "Thus, although the killing was done intentionally, it was the killing of a son who had committed a capital crime by reviling his father."[3] The father was acquitted.

Had the Ministry of Punishments not intervened, the father could have avoided punishment nonetheless. After trial and sentencing, a great many punishments could be commuted for cash, depending on the severity of the offense: ½ tael of silver for twenty blows with the bamboo, 3 taels for sixty blows, 10 taels for one-and-a-half year's exile, 720 taels for perpetual banishment, and 1,200 taels and up for strangulation or beheading. Although such commutations were based on sliding scales according to an individual's official rank or assumed ability to pay, the system clearly benefited the wealthy, to whom such sums were comparatively trivial. For a poor peasant or urban worker they might constitute several weeks or even years of income. Furthermore, those scholars who had passed the lower-level Confucian examinations were exempt from corporal punishment and, hence, escaped the fearsome beatings that often forced confessions from terrified commoners.

The Qing judicial structure received reinforcement from a community mutual-responsibility system known as the *baojia*. A *bao*, a group of 1,000 households, consisted of 10 *jia*, each of which contained 100 households. All Chinese households were supposed to be registered in *jia* and *bao* groups and supervised by a "headman" chosen from among their own number on a rotating system. These headmen were expected to check on the accuracy of each household's registration forms, which listed family members by gender, age, relationship, and occupation, and to ensure local law and order. The headmen also supervised community projects such as dike repairs, crop watching, or militia operations. In cases of serious crime or suspected rebellion, these men called in help from the magistrate's office. The headmen were also meant to enforce prompt tax payments from the members of their own *baojia*. Their job was difficult, frustrating, and sometimes dangerous; in many communities, the system grew moribund because no one wanted to serve as headman. But of most importance to foreigners was the overall concept represented by the *baojia*—namely, that members of a given community were *all* responsible for the good order of that community and that neighbors or friends of guilty parties might be held equally liable for illegal acts and penalized for them.

Although China's penal system was harsh, its standard of law and order was probably comparable to that prevalent in Europe or the United States at the time. But there was really no room within the system for special treatment of foreigners. In all routine matters, foreigners fell within the jurisdiction either of the Lifan Yuan, the Ministry of Rituals, the Hoppos, or the imperial household. If they transgressed, the Chinese assumption, at least initially, was that they would be handled by the Chinese courts in the conventional way.

Several cases in which the crews of foreign ships accidentally killed Chinese show that the local Qing authorities were at first content to accept cash payments in restitution. In Kangxi's reign, Qing authorities demanded 5,000 taels after the crew of a British ship killed a Chinese near Canton harbor in 1689. When the British counteroffer of 2,000 taels was rejected, the ship abandoned its trading plans and sailed away. At the end of the reign, in 1722, the Chinese accepted 2,000 taels from the captain of the *King George* after his gunner's mate accidentally killed a Chinese boy while out hunting. In 1754, when an English sailor was killed by a Frenchman in Canton, Qing officials showed their determination to intervene in cases occurring within their jurisdiction even when no Chinese were involved. All trade with France was stopped until the French officers yielded up the killer. Ironically, the killer was shortly thereafter released because the emperor Qianlong, to celebrate the twentieth year of his reign and the Qing victories in the Zunghar wars, had ordered a general amnesty for all convicted criminals.

More ominous for Westerners were a number of legal cases that occurred in the later years of Qianlong's reign, after the cementing of the Cohong monopoly. In 1773 the Portuguese authorities in Macao tried an Englishman who had allegedly killed a Chinese; they found him innocent and released him. But Qing officials, insisting on their right to intervene in homicide cases in which the victim was Chinese, retried the Englishman and had him executed. Seven years later, Qing authorities successfully reasserted their right to intervene in cases in which foreigners killed foreigners on Chinese soil: a Frenchman who had killed a Portuguese sailor in a fight was forced out of his refuge with the French consul and publicly executed by strangulation.

The two cases that made the greatest impact on Western thinking and forced a serious reconsideration of how to deal with the Qing at the international diplomatic level were those involving two trading vessels, the *Lady Hughes* and the *Emily.* The first of these occurred in 1784, nine years before Lord Macartney's embassy arrived in China. The *Lady Hughes,* one of the so-called "country ships"—that is, owned by private business interests but trading between India and China under license to the British East India Company—fired a salute near Canton, and the discharge from the shot killed two Chinese bystanders. When the captain of the *Lady Hughes* declared to the Chinese that he could not tell which gunner had fired the fatal shot, the Chinese, following their ideas concerning mutual responsibility, arrested the ship's business manager. They also threatened to cancel all trade with the West. In an attempt to cow the Chinese, the crews of most foreign ships then trading at Canton—British, French, Danish, Dutch, and the first Americans in Chinese waters, from the New York–registered *Empress of China*—took up arms and posted themselves around their warehouses on shore. But the Chinese stood firm. Facing disruption of all trade and the possible execution of the business manager, the *Lady Hughes* surrendered the gunner probably responsible. He was strangled in January 1785.

The case of the United States merchant ship *Emily,* which occurred in 1821, was the first to involve American interests in a central way. A crew member on the *Emily* (ironically, he was named Terranova, "New World" in English) dropped an earthenware pitcher onto the head of a Chinese fruit seller in a boat below; she fell overboard and drowned. When the Chinese demanded Terranova's surrender, the Americans at first held firm, insisting that the trial be held on the ship. But after the Qing ordered the cessation of all American trade in the Canton region, the captain of the *Emily* wavered, perhaps because his ship had a hold full of illegal opium, which he feared would be confiscated. Terranova was handed over to the Chinese authorities. At a trial at which no Westerners were allowed, he was found guilty, and executed the next day. This sentence and the rapidity of the execution violated Qing procedures in cases of accidental homicide.

Cumulatively these trials, clashes, and executions convinced Western nations that the Chinese must be compelled to yield up jurisdiction over cases involving foreign nationals. Yet this was the very point on which the Chinese sought to hold firm. Misunderstanding helped fuel the dispute, for the complexity of the Qing legal position could not be fully gauged from a quick perusal of their statutes; it demanded careful study, which few Westerners were then equipped to give. Moreover, the legal position of foreigners in China had evolved over time. Under Ming-dynasty law, for instance, it had been declared that "all aliens who commit offenses shall be sentenced according to the Chinese Penal Code," if such offenses took place on Chinese soil. The Qing, in 1646, amended this to read that "all aliens who come to submit themselves to the government of the empire shall, when they commit offenses, be sentenced according to the Chinese Penal Code," implying full obedience from all foreigners who sought to trade with China. In Emperor Yongzheng's reign, another change placed those aliens in areas supervised by the Lifan Yuan—Zunghars, Mongols, Russians—under that bureau's legal control, leaving all other aliens subject to the Chinese penal code on the grounds that since "they have attached themselves to the empire, when they commit offenses they should be punished just as ordinary Chinese subjects."[4]

Finally, in an attempt to streamline cases involving foreigners, the Ministry of Punishments, while pledging itself to fairness under the law, added in 1743 that in alien cases the procedures "concerning detention and obtaining a confession" need not "conform to the pattern followed in the interior."[5] Chinese officials believed that by making these changes they were "deferring to barbarian wishes," and such might indeed have been the case in the 1740s and 1750s. By the 1820s, however, the law as amended was perceived by Westerners as depriving them of the appellate review, and the mitigations and commutations that ordinary Chinese defendants could expect as a right under the conventional code.

It was not only foreigners who began to protest that Chinese law was inadequate. From a diametrically opposite point of view, Chinese gentry and commoners grew exasperated by Qing officials' weakness in the face of foreign demands for certain exemptions and special treatment. When in 1807 brawling sailors from the British ship *Neptune* killed two Chinese, Qing officials and the British taipan (trade supervisor) worked out a compromise by which a scapegoat was produced. They subsequently charged him with accidental homicide and permitted him to redeem his sentence for 12.42 taels in accordance with the commutation table of the Qing code. In what seems to have been a concerted campaign, placards were posted all over Canton accusing the Qing of selling out to the "foreign devils." The initiators of that campaign are unknown, but they were sounding a theme that was to become a central one in the gradual emergence of a new force in Chinese history: antiforeign nationalism.

OPIUM

The captain of the *Emily,* in offering up the sailor Terranova to Chinese justice so that the ship's cargo of opium could be safeguarded, was very much a figure of his times. Over the previous century, the growing demand in Europe and America for Chinese teas, porcelain, silks, and decorative goods had not been matched by any growth in Chinese demand for Western exports such as cotton and woolen goods, furs, clocks and other mechanical curiosities, tin, and lead. The result was a serious balance-of-payments problem for the West. Westerners had to pay for Chinese goods mainly in silver, and this steady flow of silver into China—one of the causes of the general prosperity in Qianlong's reign—became a source of alarm to the British government. In the decade of the 1760s, for example, silver flow into Qing China exceeded 3.0 million taels; in the 1770s, the total grew to 7.5 million, and by the 1780s, 16.0 million taels. By the late eighteenth century, however, the British had developed an alternative product to exchange in China for Chinese goods: opium. Although the trade was subject to severe fluctuations, figures for sales of opium to China show the overall trend with bleak clarity. Each chest contained between 130 and 160 pounds of opium, depending on the area of origin, so that by the 1820s enough opium was coming into China to sustain the habits of around 1 million addicts. When one adds to this supply a certain amount of domestically grown opium (although this was still on a very small scale), one can begin to sense the extent of China's opium problem.

For opium to sell steadily in China, several factors were necessary: the narcotic had to be available in large quantities; there had to be a developed means of consuming it; enough people had to want to smoke it to make the trade viable, and government attempts at prohibitions had to be ineffectual. It was the conjunction of all these elements that brought China into this particularly agonizing cycle of its modern history.

The British conquest of large areas of India first spurred the organized production and sale of opium. At the instigation of the East India Company's directors, and speeded by the brilliant generalship of Robert Clive and the administrative skills of Governor-General Warren Hastings, between 1750 and 1800 the British had gained control of much of northern India, from Bombay in the west to Calcutta in the east, and with additional bases in the south at Madras (where Lord Macartney had once served as governor). Eager to find a cash crop that would earn revenue through export sales, the British discovered that the opium poppy grew especially luxuriantly in certain areas of India. Moreover, there was an abundant supply of labor to collect the sap from the incised poppy pods and to process it (by boiling) into the thick paste that was best for smoking.

The East India Company established a monopoly for the purchase of Indian opium and then sold licenses to trade in opium to selected Western

BRITISH SALES OF OPIUM
TO CHINA[6]

Year	Number of chests
1729	200
1750	600 (est.)
1773	1,000
1790	4,054
1800	4,570
1810	4,968
1816	5,106
1823	7,082
1828	13,131
1832	23,570

merchants known as the "country traders," preferring this indirect means of profit making to getting directly involved in the shipment of the narcotic. Having sold their opium in China, the country traders deposited the silver they received in payment with company agents in Canton in exchange for letters of credit; the company, in turn, used the silver to buy tea, porcelain, and other Chinese goods for sale in Britain. Thus a triangular trade of goods from Britain to India, India to China, and China to Britain developed, at each step of which high profits could be made.

The consumption of opium was perhaps a simpler aspect of the process. History offers examples of many ways of taking opium derivatives—from steeping them in potions or smoking them mixed with other herbs, to the concentrated morphine tablets of the late nineteenth century and the heroin injections of our own day. The style of opium smoking favored in China— heating a tiny globule of refined opium paste over a flame and then smoking it from the bowl of a long-stemmed pipe—may have been initially popular because tobacco smoking had become a craze in the early Qing. Tobacco plants had been introduced into Fujian province from Latin America and had spread swiftly from there to Shandong and other parts of China. In scrolls from Kangxi's reign, scores of Chinese smoking tobacco pipes can be seen strolling down city streets; and the brand names of popular varieties were displayed in front of stores. The practice of smoking opium mixed with tobacco probably came to China in the 1720s, brought there by troops returning home from Taiwan after having suppressed Zhu Yigui's rebellion of 1721. By the middle of Qianlong's reign, detailed accounts of the drug and how to prepare it for consumption were available to anyone who could read. Small public rooms where, for a few coppers, people could get a pipeful of opium and smoke it as they reclined in comfort brought the drug in reach of urban dwellers and the poor.

Why did the Chinese of the mid- and late Qing begin to smoke so much opium? Since there is no contemporary Chinese literature on this, we can only speculate; but we know that the taking of opium derivatives has the effect of slowing down and blurring the world around one, of making time stretch and fade, of shifting complex or painful realities to an apparently infinite distance. Chinese documents of the time suggest that opium appealed initially to groups confronting boredom or stress. Eunuchs caught in the ritualized web of court protocol smoked opium, as did some of the Manchu court officials, who often had sinecures or virtually pointless jobs in the palace bureaucracy. Women in wealthy households, deprived of opportunities for education and forbidden to travel outside the walls of their homes, smoked opium. Secretaries in the harried magistrates' offices smoked, as did merchants preparing for business deals and students preparing for—and even taking—the state examinations. Soldiers on their way into combat against groups of rural rebels smoked.

Later on in the nineteenth century the practice spread, especially among the leisured classes seeking a means of social relaxation. Coolie laborers also began to take opium, either by smoking it or by licking tiny pellets of the drug, to overcome the drudgery and pain of hauling huge loads day after day. (Shrewd yet ruthless employers, observing that the coolies could carry heavier loads if they were under the influence of opium, even made the drug available to their workers.) By the end of the nineteenth century, many peasants also became addicts, particularly those who themselves had begun to grow the poppies as a cash crop to supplement their tiny incomes.

The Qing government was not sure how to handle the problem. As we saw above, Yongzheng, the first emperor to pronounce on the narcotic, was aware that there was a legitimate need for opium as a medicinal drug—it could be particularly valuable in stemming the effects of diarrhea or dysentery—but that nonmedicinal uses of opium seemed to be harmful. His compromise was an uneasy one in which "pushing" the drug to potential users and running public opium dens were strictly punished, while "medicinal" sales continued openly.

During the eighteenth century, most of the wholesale opium purchases were handled by the Cohong merchants. But the trade became more indirect after 1800, when an edict forbade both opium imports and domestic opium production in China, and especially after 1813, when further edicts banned opium smoking altogether. Chinese smokers could be punished with 100 blows of the bamboo and with the public wearing of the "cangue," a heavy wooden collar, for a month or more. The Cohong merchants no longer dared deal in opium, but foreign traders found that if they anchored at selected spots off the China coast, there were plenty of Chinese adventurers willing to come out and purchase their opium stocks. Large fortified hulks anchored off Lintin Island in the bay below Canton also formed a convenient distribution point for the drug. Sailing or rowing in swift, shallow-draft boats, Chinese dealers could elude all attempts by the sparse provincial Qing naval forces to intercept them. Thereafter they distributed the opium through the network of local trade routes, by road, river, and track.

As the Qing government tried to enforce its ban by punishing pushers severely and rigorously questioning smokers as to their sources of supply, those involved in opium deals grew more circumspect, covering their trail through numerous intermediaries. The 1831 transcript of an arrested court eunuch's testimony to officials in the imperial household succinctly illustrates this:

> At first we bought the opium we smoked in small quantities directly from the Muslim Zhu Da. Then I learned that when the sea vessels came into Tianjin the opium pills got cheaper, so I asked Kekesibuku for a loan of 100 strings of local cash, and I also sold my mule cart for money. I took my servant Qin Baoquan with me to Tianjin, and got Qin's old friend Yang Huiyuan to act as my agent. Yang bought 160 ounces of opium from Zhang for 240 strings of cash. I gave Yang a commission of 3.8 strings of cash.[7]

If the Qing authorities ever did pursue this case with vigor, they might have gotten past the two intermediaries and reached the local pusher, Zhang. But Zhang himself was probably only a small dealer, and by the time he was arrested the larger distributors and the foreign vessels that supplied them would long since have gone on their way.

WESTERN IMAGES OF CHINA

Until the middle of the eighteenth century, China generally received favorable attention in the West. In large part this stemmed from the wide dissemination of books and published correspondence by Catholics, especially the Jesuits, who saw in the huge population of China a potential harvest of souls for the Christian faith. Although mindful of some of China's problems, most Catholic observers followed the example of the Jesuit missionary Matteo Ricci, who had lived in China from 1583 to 1610 and admired the industry of China's population, the sophistication of the

"Machang Chasing the Enemy," detail of a handscroll by Giuseppe Castiglione   Castiglione (1688–1766), a talented Jesuit painter at the court of Qianlong, depicts here a Qing general famous for his victories over the Uighurs in Xinjiang.

Qianlong's greatest achievement was the conquest and integration of huge territories in the west now known as Xinjiang. This engraving shows Qing forces encamped during their drive to take Kashgar and Yarkand in 1759.

The Yuan Ming Yuan, the summer palace designed by Jesuits in China for Qianlong, located just outside Peking This engraving shows the Hall of Peaceful Seas.

乾隆元年八月吉日

Giuseppe Castiglione (Lang Shining), *In My Heart There Is the Power to Reign Peaceably*, detail of Emperor Qianlong (1736)

Interview between the Emperor of China & Lord Macartney.
Pub by Richard Phillips, 6 New Bridge St 1806

A satirical cartoon of Lord Macartney and Emperor Qianlong done at the time of the mission's departure from England in 1792 (top); a more reflective view of the meeting, from an 1806 edition of Macartney's journal (bottom)

A chinoiserie *view of China from the eighteenth century; the central figure is loosely modeled on Emperor Kangxi*

The Canton factories   Western merchants created their own small world in a restricted area southwest of Canton, where the Chinese granted them residence. The entire factory area depicted here was looted by the Chinese during the warfare of 1841 and burnt to the ground the following year.

"The Decline of an Opium Smoker," c. 1860   From a series of twelve Chinese watercolors. Top: "This is the first step toward the vice of opium smoking accompanied by women, music, and singing"; bottom: "While his [the opium smoker's] mother is belaying him with a cane to the great delight of his father, his wife is cutting the opium-smoking pipe to the great horror of his child."

The Taiping Northern Campaign of 1853–55 In the fall of 1853, the Taiping Army reached the suburbs of Tianjin, less than seventy miles from the Qing capital of Peking. There they were checked and slowly driven back by Qing forces, as depicted in this painting by a local artist.

Qing Victory over the Taiping   In 1854, Qing forces finally suppressed Hong Xiuquan's Taiping uprising. This painting, honoring Zeng Guofan and his armies, shows the Qing victory on Dongting Lake in Hunan, July 1854.

Zeng Guofan, organizer of the Xiang Army and
architect of the Taiping suppression

General Charles "Chinese" Gordon, the British artillery officer who led the Ever-Victorious Army against
the Taiping

Interior of the Dagu forts, August 1860 (photograph by Felix Beato)   Continuing to resist European incursions even after signing the Tianjin treaty (1858), the Qing repulsed British forces at the strategic Dagu forts in 1859, but succumbed to Anglo-French attacks the following year. This is the earliest "news-photo" taken in China.

Ruins of the Yuan Ming Yuan (photograph by Thomas Childe, c. 1875)   On October 18, 1860, Britain's Lord Elgin ordered his troops to destroy the summer palace designed by Jesuit architects for Qianlong. That same day, the Qing capitulated to further British demands.

The first great impetus for Chinese immigration to the United States came with the California Gold Rush of 1848–49. In the 1860s, thousands of Chinese worked on the final stages of the great railroad-building boom that extended the lines from California to Utah.

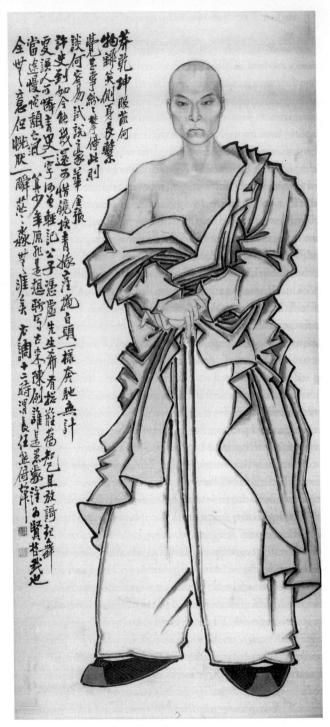

Ren Xiong (1820–1857), *Self-Portrait*

country's bureaucracy, the philosophical richness of its cultural traditions, and the strength of its rulers.

The French Jesuits, who dominated the China missions late in Kangxi's reign, presented an even more laudatory picture of the early Qing state, one deliberately designed to appeal to the "Sun King," Louis XIV, and to persuade him to back the missionaries with money and personnel. Central to these flattering presentations was the idea that the ethical content of the Confucian Classics proved the Chinese were a deeply moral nation and had once practiced a form of monotheism not so different from that found in the Judaeo-Christian tradition. With a little effort, therefore, the Chinese could be brought back to the true values they had once espoused, and did not have to be forced to convert.

Although the Jesuits rapidly lost influence in China during the last years of Kangxi's reign, and declined in prestige in Europe during the eighteenth century until suppressed altogether in 1773, their books on Chinese government and society remained far the most detailed available. The German philosopher Gottfried Wilhelm von Leibnitz read them and became deeply interested in the structure of the hexagrams in the *Book of Changes.* Even the anticlerical philosopher Voltaire was intrigued by what he read about the Chinese. Since Voltaire was intent on attacking the power of the Catholic church in eighteenth-century France, he cleverly used the information about China provided by the Catholics to disprove their more extreme claims. If, argued Voltaire, the Chinese really were so moral, intelligent, ethical, and well governed, and if this was largely attributable to the influence of Confucius, it followed that since Confucius had not been a Christian it was obviously possible for a country to get along admirably without the presence of Catholic clerical power.

In a series of influential works written between 1740 and 1760, Voltaire expounded his ideas about China. In one novel he presented his views on the parallelism of moral values in different societies, European and Asian. In a play he suggested that the innate moral strength of the Chinese had been able to calm even the Mongol conquerors led by Genghis Khan. And in an unusual historiographical gesture, Voltaire *began* his review of world history—*Essai sur les moeurs et l'esprit des nations* ("An Essay on the Customs and Spirit of Nations")—with a lengthy section on China. He did this to emphasize the values of differing civilizations and to put European arrogance in perspective: "The great misunderstanding over Chinese rites sprang from our judging their practices in light of ours: for we carry the prejudices that spring from our contentious nature to the ends of the world."[8] Unable to find a "philosopher-king" in Europe to exemplify his views of religion and government, Voltaire believed Emperor Qianlong would fill the gap, and he wrote poems in the distant emperor's honor.

Voltaire's praise for Chinese institutions appeared in a cultural context that was intensely sympathetic to China. During this same brief period in the mid-eighteenth century, Europe was swept by a fascination with China that is usually described by the French word *chinoiserie,* an enthusiasm drawn more to Chinese decor and design than to philosophy and government. In prints and descriptions of Chinese houses and gardens, and in Chinese embroidered silks, rugs, and colorful porcelains, Europeans found an alternative to the geometrical precision of their neoclassical architecture and the weight of baroque design. French rococo was a part of this mood, which tended to favor pastel colors, asymmetry, a calculated disorder, a dreamy sensuality. Its popular manifestations could be found everywhere in Europe, from the "Chinese" designs on the new wallpapers and furnishings that graced middle-class homes to the pagodas in public parks, the sedan chairs in which people were carried through the streets, and the latticework that surrounded ornamental gardens.

Yet this cult of China, whether intellectual or aesthetic, faded swiftly as angry and sarcastic accounts like George Anson's became available. Voltaire's very enthusiasms made him the object of sarcasm or mockery as other great figures among the French Enlightenment philosophers began to find his picture of China unconvincing. Jean-Jacques Rousseau and the Baron de Montesquieu worried that the Chinese did not seem to enjoy true liberty, that their laws were based on fear rather than on reason, and that their elaborate educational system might lead to the corruption of Chinese morals rather than to their improvement. Other writers declared that China did not seem to be progressing, had indeed no notion of progress; from this it was but a short step to see the Chinese as, in fact, retrogressing. In the somber words of the French historian Nicolas Boulanger, written in 1763 and translated from the French the following year by the English radical John Wilkes:

> All the remains of her ancient institutions, which China now possesses, will necessarily be lost; they will disappear in the future revolutions; as what she hath already lost of them vanished in former ones; and finally, as she acquires nothing new, she will always be on the losing side.[9]

Reflecting on these arguments concerning China and the Chinese, some leading European thinkers labored to assess the country's prospects. One of these was the Scottish philosopher Adam Smith, who wrote on China in *The Wealth of Nations,* first published in 1776. In his analysis of the productive capacities of different countries, Smith found China useful for comparative purposes, especially with the nations of Europe and the developing societies of North America. Examining population growth as an index of development, he concluded that in Europe, where countries doubled their populations every five hundred years, growth was steady if undramatic. In North America, where the population doubled every twenty or twenty-five years, there was instant employment for the entire new work force; the New World was therefore "much more thriving, and advancing with much greater rapidity to the further acquisition of riches."[10]

China, however, "long one of the richest, that is, one of the most fertile, best cultivated, most industrious, and most populous countries in the world," had reached that stage in the cycle of growth where it had "acquired that full complement of riches which the nature of its laws and institutions permits it to acquire." In such a situation, continued population growth brought serious economic repercussions: "If in such a country the wages of labour had ever been more than sufficient to maintain the labourer, and to enable him to bring up a family, the competition of the labourers and the interest of the masters would soon reduce them to this lowest rate which is consistent with common humanity." The result was that "the poverty of the lower ranks of people in China far surpasses that of the most beggarly nations in Europe" and infanticide became an integral social practice. As Smith acidly phrased it: "Marriage is encouraged in China, not by the profitableness of children, but by the liberty of destroying them." China was exacerbating these problems, according to Smith, by refusing to consider change. By staying aloof from the growth of the world economy, China was sealing its fate: "A country which neglects or despises foreign commerce, and which admits the vessels of foreign nations into one or two of its ports only, cannot transact the same quantity of business which it might do with different laws and institutions."[11]

In a famous series of lectures delivered by the German philosopher Georg Wilhelm Friedrich Hegel in the early 1820s, the various critical analyses explored by Boulanger, Rousseau, Montesquieu, and Smith were synthesized in such a way that "Oriental Civilizations"—China pre-eminent among them—came to be seen as an early and now by-passed stage of history. The view of "Asiatic Society" synthesized by Hegel was to have a profound influence on the young Karl Marx and other later nineteenth-century thinkers. History, to Hegel, was the development of what he called the ideas and practices of freedom throughout the world. Freedom was the expression of the self-realization of the "World Spirit," and that spirit was reaching its fullest manifestations in the Christian states of Europe and North America. Optimistic about his own time,

Hegel developed a theory that downplayed China's past. He described China as dominated by its emperors or despots, as typical of the "oriental nations" that saw only *one* man as free. In the West, the Greeks and Romans had come to see that *some* men were free; and, centuries later, Hegel's generation had come to see that *all* humans were free. Lacking an understanding of the march of Spirit in the world, even the Chinese emperor's "freedom" was "caprice," expressed as either "ferocity—brutal recklessness of passion—or a mildness and tameness of the desires, which is itself only an accident of Nature."[12]

Part of China's fate, Hegel wrote, turned on geographical factors: "The extensive tract of eastern Asia is severed from the general historical development." In a powerfully worded passage, Hegel explained that China had lacked the great boldness of the Europeans in exploring the seas and instead had stayed tied to the agricultural rhythms of her great plains. The soil presented only "an infinite multitude of dependencies," whereas the sea carried people "beyond these limited circles of thought and action. . . . This stretching out of the sea beyond the limitations of the land, is wanting to the splendid political edifices of Asiatic States, although they themselves border on the sea—as for example, China. For them the sea is only the limit, the ceasing of the land; they have no positive relation to it."[13] Though such a statement would have startled the wealthy ocean-going merchants of Fujian had they seen it, Hegel was basically correct that the Qing state itself was not interested in maritime exploration.

In a series of bleak conclusions, Hegel consigned the Chinese permanently to their space outside the development of the World Spirit. Although China had historians galore, they studied their country within their own limited preconceptions, not realizing that China itself lay "outside the World's History, as the mere presupposition of elements whose combination must be waited for to constitute their vital progress." Although Chinese emperors may speak words of "majesty and paternal kindness and tenderness to the people," the Chinese people "cherish the meanest opinion of themselves, and believe that men are born only to drag the car of Imperial Power." In a passage that moved beyond anything Lord Macartney had opined about the fate of the Qing dynasty, Hegel mourned for the Chinese people themselves: "The burden which presses them to the ground, seems to them to be their inevitable destiny: and it appears nothing terrible to them to sell themselves as slaves, and to eat the bitter bread of slavery."

Yet perhaps China was not caught forever in a metaphysical and geographical isolation. In one of his most ambiguous asides, Hegel added that "a relation to the rest of History could only exist in their case, through their being sought out, and their character investigated by others."[14] The question of by whom or how that seeking out was to be done was left open by Hegel, but the Western powers, with their ships, their diplomatic missions, and their opium, were rapidly beginning to provide an answer.

II | FRAGMENTATION AND REFORM

CHINA'S CONFUCIAN-TRAINED scholars were aware of the moral and economic pressures on their society in the early nineteenth century. Drawing on the intellectual tradition in which they had been raised, they proposed administrative and educational reforms, warned about the rapidly rising population, and urged greater fairness in the distribution of wealth. Some also pointed to the social inequities separating men and women, and pleaded for greater sensitivity toward the status of women in daily life.

The spread of opium addiction posed a particularly complex social dilemma. Scholars, officials, and the emperor himself were torn over whether to legalize the drug or ban it absolutely. At the same time, massive British investments in the drug's manufacture and distribution, and the critical part that opium revenues played in Britain's international balance-of-payments strategy, made the opium trade a central facet of that nation's foreign policy. The Qing, believing the problem to be a domestic one, decided to ban the drug. The British responded with force of arms. Defeating the Qing, they imposed a treaty in 1842 that fundamentally altered the structure of Qing relations with foreign powers, and ended the long cycle of history in which China's rulers had imposed effective controls over all foreigners resident on their soil.

This new foreign presence in China coincided with—and doubtless contributed to—new waves of domestic turbulence. Uprisings against the Qing had been growing in frequency during the later eighteenth century. The widening social dislocations of the nineteenth century brought even greater unrest, until in mid-century four major rebellions erupted, at least two of which—the Taiping and Nian—had the potential to overthrow the dynasty. The Taiping was based on fundamentalist Christian and egalitarian principles that cut at the heart of Confucian and imperial values; the Nian introduced new patterns of mobile guerrilla warfare that threatened the prestige of the state's basic military institutions. The other two rebellions, both led by Muslims, broke out in China's far southwest and northwest, and challenged the hold of the Qing over the non-Chinese peoples in its more inaccessible regions. Only an extraordinary series of military campaigns led by Confucian-trained scholars who put their loyalty to traditional Chinese values above all else, and were determined to perpetuate the prevailing social, educational, and family systems, enabled the Qing dynasty to survive.

The irony was that, in winning their great victories, Confucian statesmen were drawn to emulate and adopt certain elements of foreign military technology and international law that were ultimately to undermine the sanctity of the very values they endeavored to preserve. But initially such consequences could not be foreseen, and in the name of self-strengthening the Qing not only established new arsenals for arms manufacture and shipbuilding, they also set up schools to teach foreign languages, hired foreigners to collect customs dues on an equitable basis, tried to hire a small fleet of Western ships and seamen, and established the equivalent of a Foreign Ministry, the first such institution in China.

Relations between Chinese and foreigners remained strained, however. Antimissionary outbreaks in China were matched by anti-Chinese outrages in the United States, and the flow of Chinese immigrants was ultimately slashed back by a series of unilateral American restrictions. In both cases, misunderstandings of the other's culture and goals abounded, even though personal efforts made clear the possibilities for tenderness, compassion, and imaginative adaptation between the races.

By the late nineteenth century, despite the foreign pressures and domestic turbulence, it looked as if the Qing might construct a viable new synthesis. But the many achievements in the application of foreign technology to China's military and industrial needs were shattered by two defeats that the Chinese suffered in brief yet bitter wars—one with the French and one with the Japanese—that left much of China's vaunted "modern" navy at the bottom of the sea. When a burst of reforming zeal in 1898 was stillborn because of conservative opposition, the stage was set for the Boxer Uprising of 1900, in which a profound anti-Westernism led to widespread attacks on foreign missionaries and their converts. The Boxers were suppressed by foreign force, but in their wake came the first signs of a growing anti-Manchu Chinese nationalism, expressed in newspaper articles and pamphlets, in economic boycotts, and in a flurry of insurrectionary activity aimed at undercutting the power of the Qing state from within.

The final attempt of the Qing to rally their dynastic forces was a potentially effective mix of political, military, and economic reform: there were experiments in constitutional government on Western models, efforts at rearming and reorganizing the army along Western lines, and a move to gain a stronger hold over China's economy by developing a centralized railway network. Yet the combination, instead of bringing stability, brought confrontations and new layers of misunderstanding. The constitutional assemblies established in each province provided a focus for criticisms of the Qing and for the emergence of local interests. The vision of a tough, modernized army under skilled Manchu direction could not but be threatening to Chinese nationalists dreaming of their own future independence from the Qing. And the government's attempts to centralize railways and use foreign loans to do so angered provincial investors and patriots alike. When these flames of dissent were skillfully fanned by radical leaders and their impatient followers, the Qing found its foundations seriously undermined.

Helpless in the face of a military mutiny that erupted in late 1911, the Manchus saw no choice by early 1912 but to abdicate their power and declare the Qing dynasty at an end. There remained a crucial vacuum at the center of the Chinese state and no specially talented leaders able to fill it, only various groupings with rival ideologies and claims. The legacy of dynastic collapse was not a confident new republic, but a period of civil war and intellectual disorder that, tragically for the Chinese people, was even harsher than the period that had followed the fall of the Ming 268 years before. Yet amid the confusion, the dreams for a strong China held out by statecraft thinkers, self-strengtheners, constitutional reformers, and revolutionaries were never wholly eclipsed. The constructive aspect of the last century of Qing rule was that the idea of China's greatness was not allowed to die.

CHAPTER 7

The First Clash
with the West

THE RESPONSE OF CHINA'S SCHOLARS

Even before the death of Emperor Qianlong in 1799, Confucian scholars were becoming aware of the severity of the problems confronting the dynasty, both domestic and foreign. From within the *kaozheng* tradition of evidential research new trends began to emerge. Several Chinese scholars began to plead with their fellows to pay more attention to current needs and administrative problems; others began to speculate boldly on China's future and to wonder if, in the Confucian tradition itself, elements encouraging change could not be found; yet others thought that the *kaozheng* school was growing sterile and formalistic, and they worked to develop a new political focus for their writings.

Still it remained dangerous for scholars even to hint at criticism of the ruling Qing. One scholar who learned this was Hong Liangji. A friend of many *kaozheng* scholars, a member of the *Four Treasuries* compilation staff, and a tenacious examination taker who failed the top-level *jinshi* exams four times before finally passing in 1790 at the age of forty-four, Hong spent three years as inspector of education in Guizhou province, which enabled him to add intimate knowledge of the distant southwest to his ongoing analysis of political factions in the capital. In a series of essays written in the 1790s, he discussed a number of problems facing China. One of these was unchecked population growth and the difficulties it would cause as it outraced China's productive capacity. Hong also addressed the growth of luxury in the cities, the spread of corruption in local government, and the problems attendant on the attempts to suppress the White Lotus and other rebels. These essays were not censored, but when, in 1799, Hong ventured to criticize the policies of the just-deceased emperor Qianlong and his favorite Heshen, Hong was promptly sentenced to death on a charge of "extreme indecorum." Only the personal intervention of the new emperor Jiaqing (ruled 1799–1820)* commuted the sentence to exile in Ili, a barren settlement in China's far northwest.

As if conscious that Hong had true insights into the difficulties facing China, Emperor Jiaqing, who had been investigating the web of corruption surrounding Heshen and his clique, pardoned Hong altogether in 1800, and Hong returned to a life of scholarship and writing in Anhui. Hong died in 1809, but the kind of probing yet practical work for which he had become known was continued by many others. One of the best known was He Changling, who compiled a massive collection of documents on Qing statecraft. This was not just a theoretical work, but one that included the finest memorials of earlier and contemporary Qing administrators, and ranged widely over such fields as personnel evaluation, salaries, banditry, taxes, the *baojia* mutual security system, stipends for military bannermen, granaries and famine relief, salt monopolies, currency, folk religions, and flood control. The model for He's statecraft compendium was a collection produced in the late Ming by emulators of the Donglin Society activists. When the full edition of He's work appeared in 1827, many contemporaries read its descriptions with a real sense of urgency about a faltering dynasty.

He Changling was himself not just an exponent of statecraft thinking, but also an administrator of experience and insight. It is ironic that at just the same time that Hegel was discussing China's rejection of the sea, He Changling was trying to develop an elaborate plan to circumvent the decaying Grand Canal system by transporting government grain supplies from central and southern China to the north by sea. In 1826, on his advice, 4.5 million bushels of rice were shipped successfully in this way, on a fleet of over 1,500 junks. But He's plan was soon canceled, mainly in response to the vested interests of those who worked on the Grand Canal system. Had it been allowed to continue, the plan might have led to considerable growth of China's commercial ocean shipping.

Other scholars were seeking a theoretical justification for change. One of these was Gong Zizhen, born in 1792 to the family of a wealthy scholar-official in the beautiful Zhejiang city of Hangzhou. Initially Gong was in many ways a mainstream scholar of his time; he was involved in the training and scholarship needed for evidential research, and was drawn to the early commentaries and texts studied by advocates of the "Han Learning" school.

*Jiaqing technically began his reign in 1796 when his father abdicated; but, as we saw above, Qianlong did not relinquish power until he died in 1799.

But his critical feelings about Chinese society and government led him particularly to one set of documents, the Gongyang commentaries on the Confucian Classic *The Spring and Autumn Annals*. These commentaries were unlike most Chinese historical texts, which seemed to imply a cyclical view of history and thus to preclude any linear conception of "progress" in China, as European critics had pointed out. The Gongyang commentaries instead posited a genuine theory of historical development through a sequence of three ages: an age of chaos, an age of ascending peace, and a final period of universal peace.

Gong Zizhen was an emotionally complex and cantankerous man who in some ways echoed the behavior patterns of the early Qing "eccentrics": he paid no attention to dress or deportment, wrote wild calligraphy, consorted with all social classes, gambled recklessly, and insulted his elders. Yet the range of his social commentary was even wider than Hong Liangji's had been. Not only did Gong attack official corruption, court rituals such as the kowtow, and the clichés of the state examination system, he also underlined the sense that China was currently in the lowest of the three epochs—the age of chaos—with his criticisms of the judicial system, the unequal distribution of wealth, foot-binding of women, opium smoking, and all trade with foreigners.

On the redistribution of wealth, Gong was eloquent. In some forgotten early period, he wrote, rulers and subjects had been like guests at a feast to which all have contributed and in which all share alike. But in the Shang and Zhou dynasties (some three thousand years ago), "it was as if people were sitting around a bowl of soup; the rulers filled a dish as their share, the ministers used a large spoon, the ordinary people a small one." Pursuing the metaphor, Gong pointed to the development of a Chinese society in which those with large and small spoons began to attack each other, while the ruler tried to appropriate the entire kettle. Not surprisingly, the kettle "often dried up or toppled over." Now the time had come once again to spoon things out fairly.

> [For] when the wealthy vie with each other in splendor and display while the poor squeeze each other to death; when the poor do not enjoy a moment's rest while the rich are comfortable; when the poor lose more and more while the rich keep piling up treasures; when in some ever more extravagant desires awaken, and in others an ever more burning hatred; when some become more and more arrogant and overbearing in their conduct, and others ever more miserable and pitiful until gradually the most perverse and curious customs arise, bursting forth as though from a hundred springs and impossible to stop, all of this will finally congeal in an ominous vapor which will fill the space between heaven and earth with its darkness.[1]

If scholars like Gong could move from an interest in evidential research via the study of the new texts to a blunt form of social criticism, others took a more indirect route. One of China's greatest satiric novels, *Flowers in the Mirror,* was written during the critical years between 1810 and 1820. Its author, Li Ruzhen, was a conventionally educated Confucian scholar from Peking whose first intellectual passion was for phonetics. But the crises of his times led Li to re-examine not only the world of philosophy and its relation to politics, but also the particularly sensitive question of the relationship between the sexes. In central sections of his novel, he presented a world in which all conventional gender roles were completely reversed. In a chapter entitled "Country of the Women," it is the man who must taste the life of humiliation, pain, and subjugation as he has his ears pierced with needles, endures the agony of binding his feet, and spends hours over his make-up to please his female lords. Although other Chinese writers had toyed with such ideas before, no one had pursued them as vigorously as Li, and surely few Qing men could have read of the travails of the merchant Lin without at least a shudder of sympathy for their pain-racked female contemporaries:

> In due course, his feet lost much of their original shape. Blood and flesh were squeezed into a pulp and then little remained of his feet but dry bones and skin, shrunk, indeed, to a dainty size. Responding to daily anointing, his hair became shiny and smooth, and his body, after repeated ablutions of perfumed water, began to look very attractive indeed. His eyebrows were plucked to resemble a new moon. With blood-red lipstick, and powder adorning his face, and jade and pearl adorning his coiffure and ears, Merchant Lin assumed, at last, a not unappealing appearance.[2]

Li's sense of social dislocation must have been common among scholars living in Jiaqing's reign who found it difficult to pass the state examinations or to find a job. Despite the swelling numbers of educated men in early nineteenth-century China, the government still refused to increase examination quotas or enlarge the size of the bureaucracy. If these scholars had no private incomes, no interest in reform, no satiric power, and no great artistic talent, their lives took on a certain melancholy. One such man, Shen Fu, in a brief and poignant memoir written around 1807 when he was in his forties, gives a haunting picture of what it was like to be an educated Chinese without prospects at this time. Born in Suzhou in the middle of Qianlong's reign, Shen had drifted through a number of roles as part-time scholar, part-time merchant, part-time secretary. His memoirs, appropriately entitled *Six Records from a Floating Life,* show him wandering around

China in search of patrons, completely subordinate to his dictatorial father or the whims of various short-term employers.

Not that Shen's life was entirely somber. He saw something of the world on his business trips, even traveling as far south as Canton. He had a loving wife, his companion for twenty-three years until her death, with whom he shared aesthetic, sensual, and culinary joys. She was a good poet, imaginative and gentle, and did everything she could to stretch their small and erratic income. Shen's portrayal of their life together shows that it was indeed possible to have a close and affectionate marriage despite the rigorous views of the superiority of husband to wife—and the legal and philosophical justifications for that superiority—that had become part of the Confucian tradition. Ultimately, however, the couple were worn down by their poverty and his failures, though to the last Shen could not understand why fate did not allow them to be happier. "Why is it that there are sorrows and hardships in this life?" he asked. "Usually they are due to one's own fault, but this was not the case with me. I was fond of friendship, proud of keeping my word, and by nature frank and straightforward."[3] But the society he was living in did not seem to reward those quiet, conventional virtues anymore.

CHINA'S POLITICAL RESPONSE

Apart from some British sparring to make sure Macao did not fall into French hands, China enjoyed a respite from foreign pressure during Jiaqing's reign. But the reason for this was not, as many Manchus and Chinese must have believed if they thought about the problem at all, because King George III had been awed into submission after receiving Emperor Qianlong's complacent edict of 1793. Rather, the explanation lay in the Napoleonic Wars in Europe, which left the British and French few resources for an expansive policy in east Asia at a time when no other enemies of China were powerful. When there was a similar situation a century later during the First World War of 1914–1918, Japan was able to exploit the absence of Westerners to develop its own territorial ambitions in China; but in the early nineteenth century, Japan's Tokugawa rulers were still pursuing a policy of isolation and had no interest in putting pressures on the Chinese.

Within a year of Napoleon's defeat at Waterloo in 1815, however, the British East India Company dispatched another embassy to China under the leadership of William Pitt, Lord Amherst. The Amherst mission, which like Lord Macartney's sought expanded trading privileges, additional open harbors, and diplomatic residence in China, was received with considerable rudeness by the Qing. Amherst, exhausted by the long journey and by Chinese insistence that he perform the kowtow, was harried into attending an imperial audience before he had had a day's rest in Peking. When he requested more time to prepare, he was first threatened and then humiliatingly expelled from China.

Although this episode was used by the British to show that the Qing were unwilling to deal rationally with foreigners, in fact the political complexities of relations with the West were slowly becoming apparent to Qing officials. One indication of this was the growing importance that began to attach to Canton and to the officials who governed the Guangxi-Guangdong region. The sums of money circulating in the southeast because of the opium trade and the stockpiling of silks and teas for export in turn brought heightened official corruption and a rise in state revenues from transit dues and from taxation of legitimate foreign trade. The Cohong merchants were forced to make immense "donations" to the court and to local officials in order to assure continued imperial favor. Their base of security was always frail, and many of them ran up enormous debts by buying on credit from Western firms, or went bankrupt altogether, to be replaced by new—often reluctant—nominees. It is likely that the Cohong system lasted as long as it did because of the establishment of a mutual guarantee system known as the "Consoo fund," into which each major Hong merchant paid 10 percent of his trading profits, to be used as a cushion in times of emergency. Initially a secret shared only by the merchants, the fund was publicly supported by the Qing after 1780 with a 3 percent surcharge on foreign imports. By 1810, payments to the Qing government out of the Consoo fund reached a level of around 1 million taels a year.

As Canton became a major financial center, scholars were attracted there and academies began to proliferate. Ruan Yuan, the influential governor-general of the region from 1817 to 1826, founded the Xuehai Tang, the name literally meaning "Sea-of-Learning Hall." The academy became a famous center of scholarship, producing among other works a history of the Canton region. Ruan had earlier published a study on the important mathematicians of the Qing dynasty, among whom he included thirty-seven European missionaries who had lived in China and written treatises there; as this work circulated, it stimulated some interest in Western scientific accomplishments. Ruan Yuan also took a hard line against the opium trade. In one show of strength in 1821, he rounded up a number of opium dealers in Macao and tried to stop opium smoking in Canton.

The taking of a hard or soft line on the problem of opium addiction now became a central issue in China's foreign affairs and domestic economy. Moreover the controversy began to affect the formation of factions and alliances within the metropolitan and the provincial bureaucracy. Jiaqing's successor, Emperor Daoguang, who reigned from 1821 to 1850, seems to have been a well-meaning but ineffective man, anxious to shore up imperial prestige that had been weakened since the Heshen episode in Qianlong's reign and never successfully restored by Jiaqing. The strict prohibitions that Jiaqing had imposed on opium dealing in 1800 and 1813 had not been effective, and Daoguang now sought a more successful alternative.

By 1825, Daoguang was aware from censors' reports that so much Chinese silver was going to pay for Western opium that the national economy was being damaged. Although this phenomenon was still mainly restricted to the southeast coastal regions of China, its effects were being felt far inland. A scarcity of silver meant that its price rose in relation to copper; since peasants used copper currency in their everyday transactions but still had to pay their taxes to the state in silver, a rise in the value of silver meant that the peasants were in fact paying steadily higher taxes, and that unrest was sure to follow. The situation worsened in 1834 when the British Parliament ended the East India Company's monopoly of trade with Asia. The action threw open the China trade to all comers, with a predictable rise in opium sales and in the numbers of foreign traders from elsewhere in Europe and from the United States. The crisis for China was exacerbated by a worldwide silver shortage that caused foreigners to use specie less frequently when buying Chinese goods.[4] In the 1820s, about 2 million taels of silver were flowing out of China each year; by the early 1830s, the annual figure was 9 million taels. A string of 1,000 copper cash had been roughly equivalent to 1 tael of silver in Qianlong's reign; in Shandong province, 1,500 copper cash was needed per tael in Jiaqing's reign, and 2,700 in Daoguang's.

The 1834 arrival in Canton of Lord Napier, the British government's first superintendent of trade in China following the end of the East India Company monopoly, led to new confrontations. Napier refused to conduct relations through the Cohong merchants, but wished to deal directly with the governor-general of the region. After the Qing pointed out to him that "the great ministers of the Celestial Empire are not permitted to have private intercourse by letter with outside barbarians,"[5] Napier forced his fleet up the Bogue to Canton; only his death from malarial fever prevented the outbreak of serious fighting. Opium imports meanwhile continued to rise, passing 30,000 chests in 1835 and 40,000 in 1838.

In 1836 the emperor Daoguang asked his senior officials to advise him on the opium issue. The advice was split. Those who advocated legalization of the opium trade pointed out that it would end the corruption and blackmailing of officials and bring in a steady revenue through tariffs. It would also allow domestically grown Chinese opium—believed to be of better quality than Indian opium and cheaper to market—gradually to squeeze out that of the foreigners. Many officials, however, considered this view pernicious. They argued that foreigners were cruel and greedy, and that the Chinese did not need opium, domestic or foreign. They thought the prohibitions made by Emperor Jiaqing, far from being abandoned, should be pursued with even greater rigor.

In 1838, after evaluating the evidence, Emperor Daoguang made his decision. The opium trade must be stopped. To enforce this decree he chose a Fujian scholar-official of fifty-four named Lin Zexu, and ordered Lin to proceed to Canton as a specially appointed imperial commissioner to end the practice of the opium trade. On paper, the choice was a fine one. Lin was a *jinshi* degree holder of 1811 who had served in the Hanlin Academy— the prestigious government center for Confucian studies in Peking—and in a wide range of posts in Yunnan, Jiangsu, Shaanxi, and Shandong provinces. As governor-general of Hubei and Hunan, he had launched vigorous campaigns against opium smokers. One of his confidants was the outspoken scholar Gong Zizhen, who wrote in a letter to Lin that he believed all smokers of opium should be strangled, while pushers and producers should be beheaded. When Lin reached Canton in early March 1839, he took as his base not the Xuehai academy, which Ruan Yuan's successors had made a center for debating the merits of opium legalization, but a rival academy whose members were in favor of harsh repression of the opium trade.

To stamp out opium, Commissioner Lin (as the English came to call him) tried to mobilize all the traditional forces and values of the Confucian state. In public proclamations, he emphasized the health dangers of opium consumption and ordered all smokers to hand over their opium and pipes to his staff within two months. Educational officials were ordered to double-check whether any degree holders were opium smokers; all those who smoked were to be punished, and the rest were to be organized into five-man mutual-responsibility teams—like miniature *baojia* units—pledged to guarantee that no one in the group would smoke. In an ingenious adaptation of the traditional examination system, Lin summoned over 600 local students to a special assembly. There, in addition to being asked conventional questions on the Confucian classics, they were asked to name—anonymously, if they so chose—the major opium distributors and to suggest means of stopping their trade. Similar groups were formed among military and naval personnel. Lin also mobilized the local Confucian gentry, who formed an expanded version of the *baojia* system to spot addicts in the community. By mid-May 1839, over 1,600 Chinese had been arrested and about 35,000 pounds of opium and 43,000 opium pipes had been confiscated; in the following two months, Lin's forces seized a further 15,000 pounds of the drug and another 27,500 pipes.

With the foreigners, Lin used a similar combination of reason, moral suasion, and coercion, and we know from numerous statements of his that he did not wish his policies to lead to armed conflict. He moved first against the Chinese Cohong merchants, interviewing them personally in March. Lin scolded them for posting false bonds in which they stated that certain prominent British merchants—such as William Jardine and James Innes— were not opium traders, when everyone knew they were. He ordered the merchants to pass on a command to the foreigners to hand over the thousands of chests of opium they had stored in the hulks at Lintin Island and elsewhere, and to sign pledges that they would cease all further trade in opium. Foreign residents in Canton were also told to state in writing the number of weapons they owned. Lin did not wish to move rashly against foreign ships with the weak navy at his disposal, but felt he could bring enough pressure to bear on the local foreign community to force them to yield. He did not offer compensation for the opium they were to hand over.

Lin also tried to reason with the foreigners, urging them to stick to their legitimate trade in tea, silk, and rhubarb (he believed this last to be essential to the health of foreigners) and to desist from harming the Chinese people. The Guangxi-Guangdong governor-general, with whom Lin cooperated closely, had already optimistically told the Westerners that "the smokers have all quit the habit and the dealers have dispersed. There is no more demand for the drug and henceforth no profit can be derived from the traffic." In a carefully phrased letter to Queen Victoria, Lin tried to appeal to her moral sense of responsibility. "We have heard that in your honorable nation, too," wrote Lin, "the people are not permitted to smoke the drug, and that offenders in this particular expose themselves to sure punishment. ... In order to remove the source of the evil thoroughly, would it not be better to prohibit its sale and manufacture rather than merely prohibit its consumption?"[6] Opium in fact was *not* prohibited in Britain and was taken—often in the form of laudanum—by several well-known figures, Samuel Taylor Coleridge among them. Many Englishmen regarded opium as less harmful than alcohol, and Lin's moral exhortations fell on deaf ears.

Although they were begged to yield by the panic-stricken Hong merchants, the foreign traders first explained that they handled opium on consignment for others and so were not empowered to hand it over, and then offered to give up a token 1,000 chests. Lin, furious, ordered the arrest of Lancelot Dent, one of the leading British opium traders. When the foreign community refused to yield up Dent for trial, on March 24, 1839, Lin ordered the Hoppo to stop foreign trade completely. All Chinese staff and servants were ordered to leave foreign employ; and the 350 foreigners in Canton, including the senior British official, Superintendent Elliot, were blockaded in their factories. Although food and water were available to the foreigners, and some extra goods and messages were smuggled in, it was a nerve-wracking time for them, made worse by the din of gongs and horns that Chinese troops kept up throughout the nights. After six weeks, when the foreigners had agreed to give up over 20,000 chests of opium and Commissioner Lin had taken delivery, the blockade was lifted and all but sixteen foreigners were allowed to leave.

Lin had carefully supervised the transfer of the foreign opium to Chinese hands, even living on a boat in April and May to be near the action and to prevent cheating and theft. He was now faced with the remarkable challenge of destroying close to 3 million pounds of raw opium. His solution was to order the digging of three huge trenches, 7 feet deep and 150 feet long. Thereafter, five hundred laborers, supervised by sixty officials, broke up the large balls of raw opium and mixed them with water, salt, and lime until the opium dissolved. Then, as large crowds of Chinese and foreigners looked on, the murky mixture was flushed out into a neighboring creek, and so reached the sea.

In a special prayer to the spirit of the Southern Sea, "you who wash away all stains and cleanse all impurities," Lin brooded over the fact that "poison has been allowed to creep in unchecked till at last barbarian smoke fills the market." He apologized to the spirit for filling its domain with this noxious mixture and, he wrote in his diary, advised it "to tell the creatures of the water to move away for a time, to avoid being contaminated." As to the foreigners who had lived through the blockade and now watched the solemn proceedings, Lin wrote in a memorial to Emperor Daoguang, they "do not dare show any disrespect, and indeed I should judge from their attitudes that they have the decency to feel heartily ashamed."[7]

BRITAIN'S MILITARY RESPONSE

Commissioner Lin Zexu and Emperor Daoguang were conscientious, hard-working men who had fully internalized the Confucian structures of hierarchy and control. They seem to have believed that the citizens of Canton and the foreign traders there had simple, childlike natures that would respond to firm guidance and statements of moral principles set out in simple, clear terms. The reality was unfortunately more complex, as plenty of their contemporaries saw. Even before the opium had been washed out to sea, one Chinese official had dared to point out that Lin had not really solved the opium problem, just one of its immediate manifestations. And a British opium trader, reflecting on his experiences during the blockade, noted dryly to a friend that the blockade "is even fortunate as adding to the account for which we have to claim redress."[8]

The buildup toward war between China and Britain was now gaining momentum. Some of the broader causes have been noted already: the social dislocations that began to appear in the Qing world, the spread of addiction, the growth of a hard-line mentality toward foreigners, foreign refusal to accept Chinese legal norms, changes in international trade structures, and the ending of Western intellectuals' admiration for China. Other elements were more precisely tied to the background of Lin's negotiations and had ramifications that he did not understand. One of these was the fact that the foreign dealers, having followed the Qing debates at court between 1836 and 1838, had grown convinced that opium consumption was about to be legalized in China. As a result, they had stockpiled large amounts and had placed additional orders with Indian growers. When the tough prohibitions of 1838 began to take effect, the market diminished and dealers found themselves dangerously oversupplied.

A second contributing factor was that the new British post of superintendent of foreign trade in China was held by a deputy of the British crown, not by an employee of the East India Company. If the Chinese crossed the superintendent, they would be insulting the British nation rather than a business corporation, a distinction they did not fully see. The superintendent, in turn, lacked clear legal powers over the British traders and had no control over nationals from other European nations or from the United States. He could, however, call directly on the aid of British armed forces and the Royal Navy in times of serious trouble.

The third element in the picture on the British side was a crucial combination of these previous two: British opium dealers, suffering from a glut of the unsold drug, had handed their supply over to Charles Elliot, Napier's successor as the superintendent of foreign trade, and Elliot, in turn, had handed it over to Lin Zexu. Thus, far from being properly "ashamed" as their opium drifted out to sea, the merchants could anticipate putting pressure on the British government to make sure that they got financial recompense.

The unfolding events in China were monitored as closely in England as time and distance allowed. In the early summer of 1839, Elliot had sent messages to London asking for assistance, and the foreign secretary, Lord Palmerston, initially unsympathetic to British merchants who would not abide by Chinese laws, now swung in their favor. As Palmerston wrote in a letter addressed to "The Minister of the Emperor of China," he had heard "with extreme surprise" that Chinese officers had "committed violent outrages against the British Residents at Canton, who were living peaceably in that city, trusting to the good faith of the Chinese Government." Although the queen did not condone opium selling, she "cannot permit that her subjects residing abroad be treated with violence, and be exposed to insult and injustice."[9]

After news of the blockade and opium seizures reached England, China trade interests and chambers of commerce in the larger manufacturing areas launched intensive lobbying efforts to pressure Parliament into taking retaliatory action. The wealthy opium merchant William Jardine even traveled back to England from China to add his voice to the chorus, and to ensure that the moral objections to the opium traffic being raised by various Protestant missionary societies did not gain too wide an influence. China merchants had raised $20,000 for his lobbying expenses, and he was promised more if necessary, "as the magnitude of the object can well bear any amount of expense that may be considered necessary or desirable." He was also told "to secure, at a high price, the services of some leading newspaper to advocate the cause." Parliament did not, however, declare war on China. It merely authorized the dispatch of a fleet and the mobilization of further troops in India in order to obtain "satisfaction and reparation" and, if necessary, to "hold in custody the ships of the Chinese and their cargoes."[10] The total force, under the command of Charles Elliot's cousin, Admiral George Elliot, consisted of 16 warships carrying 540 guns, 4 newly designed armed steamers, 28 transports, and 4,000 troops, along with 3,000 tons of coal for the steamers and 16,000 gallons of rum for the men.

Lin Zexu, meanwhile, continued his cleansing of Guangdong province. Arrests and investigations of addicts and dealers went on apace, with opium now commanding "famine prices" of up to $3,000 a chest instead of the usual $500. When the British merchants refused to sign bonds pledging that they would not indulge in any opium traffic under penalty of Chinese law, Lin had them ousted from Macao as they had been from Canton. It was in response to this expulsion order that Charles Elliot inaugurated a new phase in east Asian history by settling his group on the almost deserted rocky island of Hong Kong. Trade in Canton by no means came to a standstill, since the Americans especially were delighted to profit from the new opportunity to operate as middlemen for the British. The American vice-consul Warren Delano let his countrymen sign bonds promising not to violate Chinese regulations. As one American merchant explained, "We Yankees had no Queen to guarantee our losses"; and even if the Chinese closed other ports of access, he would continue "retreating step by step, but buying and selling just as long as I found parties to operate with."[11]

But even as the trade continued, Lin was fortifying the waterways into Canton, buying new cannon for the forts and immense chains to block the channel, and commencing the training and drilling of his forces. The British who had retreated to Hong Kong were harried by the local Chinese, who poisoned many wells and refused to sell the foreigners food. Armed clashes between British and Chinese war junks in Hong Kong harbor and in the Bogue outside Canton occurred in September and October 1839, with casualties on both sides. Chinese ships were sunk, and the possibilities of further negotiation faded. In a surprising gesture for Qing officials usually so wary of popular manifestations, Lin even encouraged mobilization of local "braves" against the British, who had grown even more unpopular since a group of drunken seamen had killed a Chinese villager on Kowloon, across from Hong Kong island, and Elliot had refused to hand the accused over to the Chinese courts. "Assemble yourselves together for consideration," ran one proclamation; "Purchase arms and weapons; join together the stoutest of your villagers and thus be prepared to defend yourselves."[12]

The full British fleet under George Elliot arrived off Canton in June 1840. To Lin's chagrin they did not try to storm his new defenses, but

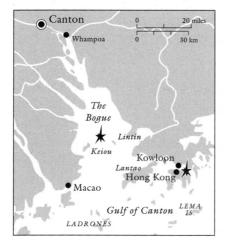

**THE OPIUM WAR,
1839–1842**

contented themselves with leaving four ships to blockade the entrance to the harbor and sailing north with the bulk of their force. In July, the British blockaded Ningbo with two ships and seized the main town on the island of Zhoushan (Chusan) off the Zhejiang coast, from which they could interdict sea traffic to the Yangzi delta region. Leaving a garrison force on Zhoushan with a missionary-interpreter standing in for the Qing magistrate who had committed suicide, the fleet sailed on unopposed to the mouth of the Bai He (White River), near the Dagu forts that guarded the approaches to the city of Tianjin. Here, in August and September 1840, serious negotiations began with Qishan, the governor-general of the region, a senior Manchu, and a grand secretary trusted by Emperor Daoguang. Qishan persuaded the British to leave north China and return to Canton to complete the negotiations, for which he was lavishly praised by the emperor and named governor-general of Guangxi and Guangdong. Lin Zexu, who had been named to that post earlier in the year, was now dismissed for his inadequate policies and banished to Ili.

In January 1841 Qishan reached an agreement with the British in which he ceded up Hong Kong, agreed to pay $6 million* in indemnities, allowed the British direct official contacts with the Qing state, and promised to reopen the Canton trade to them within ten days. This so enraged Daoguang when he heard of it that he ordered Qishan dismissed and executed, a sentence later commuted to banishment.

Lord Palmerston was equally furious with Charles Elliot for not exacting *better* terms from the Chinese. In a blistering private letter of April 1841, he dismissed Elliot and refused to ratify the agreement, scolding the former superintendent of foreign trade: "You have disobeyed and neglected your instructions; you have deliberately abstained from employing, as you might have done, the force placed at your disposal; and you have without any sufficient necessity accepted terms which fall far short of those which you were instructed to obtain." Palmerston was especially angry that Elliot had given up Zhoushan, had not insisted on repayment for the opium destroyed, and had merely gotten modified rights over Hong Kong, "a barren island with hardly a house upon it." A new plenipotentiary, Sir Henry Pottinger, was named to deal with China. In his final instructions to Pottinger, Palmerston insisted that the new agreement must be with the emperor himself. "Her Majesty's Government cannot allow that, in a transaction between Great Britain and China, the unreasonable practice of the Chinese should supersede the reasonable practice of all the rest of mankind."[13]

---

*The Mexican silver dollar was now so widely circulated that it was accepted as standard silver currency in China. The Chinese themselves used silver ingots, not coins.

With these new instructions, Pottinger reached China in August 1841 to find the situation even more volatile. There had been renewed fighting in the countryside around Canton, much of it by aroused bands of Chinese militia under local gentry leaders, and British troops had been killed and wounded. The British had responded by destroying the Bogue forts, sinking Chinese junks, razing part of the waterfront, and occupying sections of Canton. Although the British occupying troops subsequently withdrew from the city after Canton officials had paid them $6 million, there was no agreement about whether this sum was a "ransom" to save the city from sack, a response to the sum named in Elliot's earlier convention with Qishan, or recompense for the opium destroyed two years before.

In late August 1841, Pottinger proceeded north with the British fleet, seizing Xiamen (Amoy) and Ningbo, and recapturing Zhoushan. When reinforcements reached him from India in late spring 1842, he launched a campaign to force Qing capitulation by cutting China's main river and canal communications routes. The British captured Shanghai in June and took Zhenjiang in July, even though the Manchus fought with savage desperation. Scores of Qing officers committed suicide with their families when defeat was certain. The traffic on the Grand Canal and lower Yangzi was now blocked. Pottinger, ignoring Qing requests for a parley, pushed on to the great city and former Ming dynasty capital of Nanjing, taking up attack positions outside the walls on August 5. The Qing quickly sued for peace, and on August 29 the terms of the Treaty of Nanjing, translated into Chinese, were signed by the Manchu commissioners and the governor-general of Liangjiang.* Daoguang accepted the treaty in September, and Queen Victoria ratified it at the end of December.

Before turning to the precise stipulations of this treaty and its supplements, it is worth re-emphasizing that in military terms the Opium War of 1839–1842 marked an important historical moment. It was not only the most decisive reversal the Manchus had ever received, it also saw innovations in Western military technology and tactics. The emergence of the steam-driven vessel as a considerable force in naval battles was perhaps the most important of these, as shown by the campaign record of the British ship *Nemesis*. The *Nemesis* was an uncoppered paddle-wheel iron ship that used sails in favorable winds and six boilers fired by wood or coal for making seven to eight knots even in heavy seas. Drawing only five feet, the ship could operate in shallow coastal waters in virtually any wind or tidal condition. In the Canton Bogue campaigns, the *Nemesis* roamed the shallows firing grapeshot, heavy shells, and explosive rockets, grappling and towing junks, ferrying troops,

*The name of the administrative unit comprising the three provinces of Jiangsu, Anhui, and Jiangxi.

and towing the sailing vessels on calm days. In the Shanghai campaign, the ship towed the men-of-war with their heavy guns into firing range on the city and served as a transport that could unload the British directly onto the docks. Well before the war's end, new steamers of similar design were being sent to China's waters; if the British could only keep enough fuel stockpiled, they had discovered a formidable supplement to their powers.

The Qing, however, were not merely passive targets of Western technology and fire power. While still in Canton, Commissioner Lin had deputed a special task force of scholars to furnish him with all the information they could on Western nations, culled mainly from foreign publications in Canton and Singapore. He had also asked an American missionary to translate some brief passages of international law for him. Moreover, as the British proceeded with their campaigns in 1842, they found much evidence of the speed with which the Qing officials were trying to respond to the West's new technology. In Xiamen, for instance, they found a nearly completed replica of a British two-decker man-of-war with thirty guns; it was almost ready to sail, and work on several other similar vessels was well under way. In Wusong, they discovered five new Chinese paddle-wheel boats armed with newly cast brass guns. In Shanghai, they seized sixteen new, beautifully made eighteen-pound ship's guns, perfect in detail down to the sights cast on the barrels and the pierced vents for flintlocks. All were mounted on sturdy wooden trucks with iron axles.[14] At least some people in China had clearly found the barbarian challenge to be a stimulus as well as an outrage.

THE NEW TREATY SYSTEM

The Treaty of Nanjing was signed on August 29, 1842, aboard Her Majesty's ship *Cornwallis* moored in the Yangzi River, and ratified in Hong Kong ten months later after formal approval by Queen Victoria and Emperor Daoguang. It was the most important treaty settlement in China's modern history. The treaty contained twelve main articles that cumulatively had significant ramifications for China's ideas of commerce and society:

Article 1. Stipulated peace and friendship between Britain and China, and "full security and protection for their persons and property within the dominions of the other."

Article 2. Determined the opening of five Chinese cities—Canton, Fuzhou, Xiamen, Ningbo, and Shanghai—to residence by British subjects and their families "for the purpose of carrying on their mercantile pursuits,

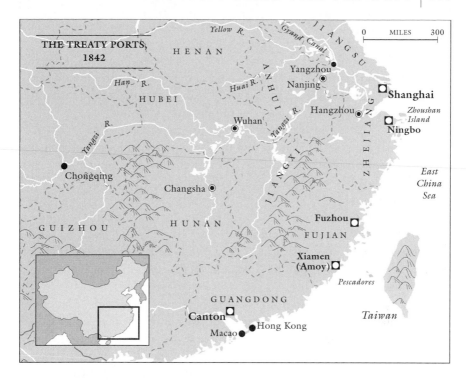

without molestation or restraint." It also permitted the establishment of consulates in each of those cities.

Article 3. "The Island of Hong Kong to be possessed in perpetuity" by Victoria and her successors, and ruled as they "shall see fit."

Article 4. Payment of $6 million by the Qing "as the value of the opium which was delivered up in Canton."

Article 5. Abolition of the Canton Cohong monopoly system and permission at the five above-named ports for British merchants "to carry on their mercantile transactions with whatever persons they please." The Qing were to pay $3 million in settlement of outstanding Cohong debts.

Article 6. Payment to the British of a further $12 million "on account of the expenses incurred" in the recent fighting, minus any sums already received "as ransom for cities and towns in China" since August 1, 1841.

Article 7. The $21 million stipulated in Articles 4 through 6 were to be paid in four installments before the end of 1845, with a 5 percent interest charge per annum on late payments.

Article 8. Immediate release of any prisoners who were British subjects, whether Indian or European.

Article 9. An unconditional amnesty for all Chinese subjects who had resided with, dealt with, or served the British.

Article 10. At the five treaty ports listed in Article 2, all merchants should pay "a fair and regular Tariff of Export and Import Customs and other Dues." Once those fees were paid, only fair and stipulated transit dues should be paid on goods conveyed to the interior of China.

Article 11. Instead of terminology such as "petition" or "beg" that foreigners had previously been forced to use, nonderogatory and nonsubordinate terms of address such as "communication," "statement," and "declaration" were to be used in future official correspondence between Britain and China.

Article 12. On receiving the first installment of the indemnity money, British forces would leave Nanjing and the Grand Canal, and "no longer molest or stop the trade of China." Troops would continue to hold Zhoushan until all money was paid and the "opening [of] the Ports to British merchants be completed."[15]

Apart from the stipulation of a $6 million payment as compensation for the opium destroyed in 1839, the narcotic was nowhere mentioned in the treaty, nor was it discussed in the supplementary tariff treaty of 1843, which fixed the rates for tea, silk, cotton, woolens, ivory, metals, and spirits. Opium was again ignored in the complicated procedures agreed to for conducting, supervising, and protecting foreign trade in the five ports. In private talks with the chief Manchu negotiator Qiying, Pottinger mentioned the British hope that the Qing would allow a legalized opium on a barter basis—to end the outflow of silver. When Qiying replied that he dared not raise the question, Pottinger said that he, too, had been ordered not to press the matter.

The clauses of the Treaty of Nanjing and its supplements were studied carefully by other powers. In 1843, President John Tyler acted on behalf of the United States and its considerable China-trade interests by dispatching Caleb Cushing—a congressman from coastal Massachusetts, where many of America's wealthiest China merchants lived—to China as minister plenipotentiary. Arriving at Macao in February 1844, Cushing at once began negotiations with Qiying, who had been promoted to governor-general of Guangxi and Guangdong. Despite tensions caused by the death of a Chinese who had tried to assault a group of Americans (the jurisdictional issue raised brought back unhappy memories of the *Emily* and Terranova), Qiying and Cushing moved rapidly to the signing of a treaty between the two countries, called the Treaty of Wanghia after the small village near Macao where it was concluded.

The American treaty followed the same lines as the British, but was much longer and had a number of important additions. Article 17, for instance, was of great potential importance to American Protestant missionaries eager to work in China, for it gave Americans in the five treaty ports rights to hire sites for the construction of "hospitals, churches, and cemeteries." Article 18 ended a long-standing attempt by Chinese rulers to prevent foreigners from learning the Chinese language fluently; it allowed United States citizens "to employ scholars and people of any part of China . . . to teach any of the languages of the Empire." The jurisdictional question was settled by the statement in Article 21 that Americans committing crimes in China could be tried and punished only by the consuls or other duly empowered American officials "according to the laws of the United States." Rejecting Britain's evasions, Article 33 stated that any Americans "who shall trade in opium or any other contraband" would be "dealt with" by the Chinese, without being entitled to protection from the United States government. Finally, Article 34 stated that in matters of "commerce and navigation," the treaty should be reviewed in twelve years' time.[16]

In October 1844, the French followed with their own treaty, modeled closely on the American agreement. Their main additions were to stipulate that if, in times of trouble, no French consul were present, French nationals might appeal to the consuls of any friendly power; and to re-emphasize the principle of extraterritoriality—the right to be judged by one's own national law in criminal cases on Chinese soil—with even greater force than had Caleb Cushing. Yielding to French pressure, Qiying obtained an imperial rescript granting full toleration to the Catholics and reversing Yongzheng's edicts against missionaries; in a supplementary proclamation of 1845, Qiying extended the same rights to Protestants.

So within six years of Lin Zexu's appointment as imperial commissioner, the Qing, instead of defending their integrity against all comers, had lost control of vital elements of China's commercial, social, and foreign policies. A host of other nations followed where Britain, the United States, and France had shown the way. The British did not have to worry about these other negotiations, because any new concessions offered up by the Chinese came also to them. In an ingenious article—number 8—to their own supplementary treaty of 1843, they had stipulated a "most-favored nation" clause: "Should the Emperor hereafter, from any cause whatever, be pleased to grant additional privileges or immunities to any of the subjects or citizens of such foreign countries, the same privileges or immunities will be extended to and enjoyed by British subjects." The Qing had agreed to this clause in the belief that it would limit foreign pressures. But in fact this clause prevented the Qing from forming alliances or playing off one foreign power against another, seriously hampering China's foreign-policy initiatives.

Surprisingly, however, the short-term commercial results of the Opium War turned out to be disappointing for the British and most other foreign merchants. Although the five treaty port cities had been carefully chosen, trade at Fuzhou and Ningbo grew so slowly that there was talk of trying to swap them for other cities with better prospects. By 1850 only nineteen adult foreigners were living in Ningbo; at Fuzhou the total was ten, of whom seven were missionaries. Prospects were not much better in Xiamen, where trade had traditionally been conducted with Taiwan or the Philippines and was difficult to integrate with European or American needs. Only traffic in human labor brought some prosperity when British ships began to transport coolie laborers to work in the sugar plantations of Cuba.

Canton had held the promise of enormous profits once the Cohong monopoly was abolished and trade was thrown open to all, but so strong was the local antipathy to the British and other foreigners that the Westerners found it impossible to establish residence and to conduct business or open their consulates in the city. The 1840s and early 1850s were marked by constant rioting and a bitter cycle of anti-British attacks by rural militias and urban mobs that were met by British reprisals and reciprocal atrocities. The Qing court condoned the anti-British violence since it could not afford to alienate Cantonese sensibilities any further.

Of the five new treaty ports, only Shanghai became a boom town when extensive "concession" areas of marshy and largely uninhabited countryside were made available for British, French, and other foreign settlements. By 1850, with the land drained and the river banks shored up, there were over one hundred merchants in residence there, supported by consular staffs, five physicians, and seventeen missionaries, many of whom were married. Whereas 44 foreign ships had entered the port in 1844, the number for 1849 was 133, and by 1855 it was 437. The silk trade expanded prodigiously, reaching a value of over $20 million by the mid-1850s. Opium, still illegal, was coming in at a rate of at least 20,000 chests a year.

The Qing attitude to the new treaty-port structure was ambiguous. Qiying's view, shared by many at court, was that the Westerners' prior motivation was commercial greed and that they could probably be stalled on most other demands if their trade kept moving. In their confidence about this and their feeling that even concessions such as extraterritoriality were insignificant, both Qiying and his emperor were probably drawing on the only near precedent they possessed—namely, the Qing handling of foreign policy in central Asia during the 1830s. In 1835, for example, the Qing had allowed the aggressive khanate of Kokand the right to station a political resident in Kashgar and commercial residents in Yarkand and other key trading cities. This political resident had both consular and judicial powers

over other foreigners in the Altishahr region, and the right to collect customs dues on goods that other foreigners brought into the area. Furthermore, the Qing agreed that Muslims would pay only half the rate paid by non-Muslims in tariffs (2½ percent instead of 5 percent) and that goods exported to Kokand from Altishahr were to be tax-free. The Qing apparently found that making such concessions, far from being an abandonment of sovereignty, was in fact a cheap and simple way of solving the Kokand khans' endless, bellicose demands for further trading privileges. Several of the senior Qing officials who took part in these negotiations—or were heroes of the wars that preceded them—were posted to the southeast coast in the late 1830s or early 1840s, suggesting that the Qing were indeed seeking continuities in policy making between China's far western and its southeastern frontiers.[17]

As he might have done with unruly potentates in central Asia, Qiying continued to woo Sir Henry Pottinger well after the Nanjing treaty and its supplements had been signed: he bestowed the status of honorary adoption on Pottinger's son, exchanged keepsakes (including pictures of their wives), fed sugarplums with his own hands into the astonished plenipotentiary's mouth, and created a new word—*yin-di-mi-te* in Chinese—to express his insistence that Pottinger was his "intimate" friend. But to the emperor Dao-guang, Qiying confided that this was his personal way of "subduing and conciliating" the British. He was not going to "fight with them over empty names"; instead, he would "pass over these small matters and achieve our larger scheme."[18] The trouble with this analysis was that to the British and other foreign powers, the hard-won treaty stipulations were far from being "empty names." They were the very stuff of international and commercial life. The fact that neither Qiying nor his emperor could accept this is, with hindsight, not surprising. For to the Manchus the "larger scheme" was now nothing less than the survival of the Qing dynasty itself. To those holding power in China, the mounting pressures of domestic discontent made all problems of foreign policy appear, indeed, peripheral.

CHAPTER 8 | # The Crisis Within

SOCIAL DISLOCATION NORTH AND SOUTH

The damaging defeats inflicted on China by the British during the first half of the nineteenth century were part cause and part consequence of China's own growing domestic instability. Many of the elements of that instability have been discussed above: the growing population that put new pressures on the land, the outflow of silver, the difficulty the educated elite found in gaining official employment, the mounting incidences of opium addiction, the waning abilities of the regular banner armies, the demoralization in the bureaucracy caused by Heshen and his faction, the wide-scale suffering that accompanied the spread and eventual suppression of the White Lotus rebellion.

Other abuses, already apparent in the late eighteenth century, became more serious in the early nineteenth century. The enormous bureaucracies that allegedly managed the Yellow River dike works and the Grand Canal grew ineffective, swelling their own ranks with sinecure appointments and using for their own private purposes the government money allotted to them. The consequent silting up of stretches of the Grand Canal, and the failure to regulate water levels on the Yellow and Huai rivers at the points where they were crossed by the Grand Canal, crucially weakened the system of government rice transport from the south. That disruption, in turn, led to trouble with the workers along the canal who pulled the government barges for a living; many of these workers now banded into their own secret associations, both to protect their jobs and to tyrannize the local farming communities among whom they lived.

The massive government system of salt distribution also became ineffective. Salt sales were, in theory, a government monopoly in which the Qing supervised salt production, either by seashore evaporation or from inland brine wells and salt mines, and then sold the produce to a small group of licensed merchants, each of whom transported the salt for sale to certain designated areas. By the early nineteenth century, inefficiencies and corruption in this system had led to a phenomenal rise in salt smuggling, which threatened to wreck the complex system. These economic and organizational problems spurred the growth of competing factions within the post-Heshen bureaucracy, as vested interests contended for profits and sought to recruit supporters into their own ranks. Many senior officials began to form their own bureaucratic subnetworks of clients and assistants, whose salaries they paid by further exploiting their own public sources of income.

During these same years of the early nineteenth century, there was also a great increase in local paramilitary or formally organized militia units led by local scholars or landlords who sought to protect their communities from marauding groups, whether of White Lotus rebels, of the jobless and the desperate, or of coastal or riverine pirates. In other areas, local leaders formed secret societies to spread esoteric religious doctrines and to defend themselves when the state proved incapable.

In much of China, one can say, private interests were encroaching on formerly governmental spheres, and the imperial system seemed incapable of reasserting its former powers. Emperor Jiaqing, who ruled China from 1799 to 1820, relied on rhetoric more than specific policies to cleanse his empire. His pleas for frugality on the part of his bureaucracy were poignant but did little to cut costs. And even though Heshen's cronies were effectively purged, other courtiers emerged and formed their own factions. Jiaqing and his son Daoguang (reigned 1821–1850) both promoted senior ministers who presented a purist view of the fundamental Confucian virtues, even if those ministers had nothing substantive to say about the many problems—domestic and foreign—that plagued the dynasty. By the end of Daoguang's reign, a series of popular uprisings began that were to last for twenty-three years and were almost to bring about the fall of the Qing dynasty.

But just as those uprisings must be seen in the context of China's foreign-policy crises, so must they be seen as the culminating stage in a pattern of protest that began with the White Lotus and continued through less dramatic but still significant crises in both north and south China. One such early nineteenth-century uprising in the north was led by Lin Qing in 1813. Lin was born in 1770, and his early life suggests a case study of the rootlessness endemic to that portion of Qing society that hovered just above the urban poverty line. The son of a clerk in Peking, Lin Qing, who had learned to read and write, took an apprenticeship in an herbal-medicine shop, but he worked at this trade for only a short period before being fired and becoming a night watchman. When his father died, Lin managed to get himself appointed clerk in his father's place; thereupon he embezzled some Grand Canal repair funds stored in his new office and used the money to open a tea shop. Gambling away the shop's profits, he moved north to Manchuria, where he held a construction job for a time. Still restless, he traveled south across China to Suzhou, where he worked first as attendant to a local grain official, then on the junior staff of a magistrate's office. He returned north, earning money as a coolie pulling grain boats up the Grand Canal. Back home near Peking, he ran a business selling songbirds.

Now equipped with some knowledge of the world, Lin Qing joined a religious sect that drew its beliefs from millenarian Buddhism, and he learned a number of mystical slogans. "Every day at dawn we pay respects to the sun and recite the sacred words," he told one of his early followers, a waiter at a local inn. "By doing this we can escape the dangers of fire, flood, and war, and if there should come a time of calamity and disorder, then we can use this opportunity to plan and organize the Great Undertaking."[1] Lin was able to inspire confidence in hundreds of local villagers and—more surprisingly—in a number of poverty-stricken Chinese bannermen and bondservants as well as eunuchs in Peking palace service. "He was very convincing," his nephew later told Qing officials. "He said that making contributions was the same as sowing seeds for future blessings and that in the future such gifts would be multiplied tenfold. So people believed and gave him money. I never saw him give any back."[2] Some of the promises were dramatic: 100 copper cash given to Lin brought a promise of 100 *mou* of land in the future, when the sect would triumph (100 *mou,* around 16 acres, represented a munificent estate to any poor north China peasant).

Growing more grandiose as he allied with other powerful leaders, Lin began to term himself the future Buddha, or Maitreya, sent by the Eternal Mother to prepare his followers to survive the catastrophes of the coming *kalpa,* the new great cycle of human history. Rhymes recited by his followers seemed to suggest that an anti-Manchu element was also becoming stronger: "We wait only for the northern region to be returned to a Han emperor/ Then all-that-is will again be under a single line."[3] By 1813, Lin Qing had laid plans to move on Peking and kill Emperor Jiaqing.

At this point the plot began to unravel: officials were warned of trouble by a suspicious lower degree holder from Shandong and by two fathers worried about their sons' involvement in the illegal sect. Arrests of some sectarians, interrogations under torture, and a number of sporadic but bitter clashes followed during that summer; late in 1813, the planned attack on the palace was launched by a handful of Lin's disciples, but it was a disastrous failure. Oddly fatalistic, Lin Qing stayed at home in his village during his "uprising," and it was there that local police officials arrested him. Emperor Jiaqing was so curious about this unknown man who had sought to kill him that he summoned him to a private interrogation. Lin refused to give any further explanations and was executed by slicing. His severed head was displayed in Henan as a warning to his followers who were still holding out in rebellion there.

Lin Qing's life and rebellion are well documented because the action was so near Peking and the emperor himself was a target. But Lin's casual accumulation of followers and money, the generalized grievances, and the broad religious claims were typical of many other such groups formed in north China over subsequent decades. These groups constituted a kind of latent potential for rebellion, but one that could often stay on peaceful, semilegal tracks if not galvanized by a particularly effective leader or a natural disaster of unusual proportions.

In south China there was also a simmering discontent, but its focus was different. Here the dominant force was the Triads, also called the Heaven and Earth Society, comprising groups with their own blood oaths, religious rituals, and brotherhoods. The Triads developed in Taiwan and Fujian in the later eighteenth century—though they were to claim much earlier origins once their power grew—and then gathered strength in Guangdong and Guangxi. Many early Triad members seem to have been sailors on ocean junks or on the myriad river craft of the interlacing southern waterways; others were poor city dwellers. They often engaged in criminal activities— extortion, robbery, and kidnapings—all the while protecting themselves through society members in the magistrates' own yamens (offices). By the 1830s, Triad lodges were also attracting numerous peasant recruits, perhaps because in south China, where powerful lineages often controlled entire villages, the Triads offered an alternative form of protection and an organizational focus to those living on the edge of destitution. Women were often recruited into Triad ranks, as they were into the White Lotus, giving them a prestige and function in society otherwise largely denied to them. According to some accounts, women who joined Triad lodges in advance of their husbands might claim precedence within the household over their own spouses. Others were members without their husbands' knowledge.

The Triads also claimed it as their cause to oust the Qing and restore the Ming. Their anti-Manchu stance was probably fueled by the inability of the Qing to control the foreigners in Canton, and the repeated occupations of that city by foreign troops. These pressures in turn made it hard for the court to mobilize for drastic action against potential rebels among its own people. And since the more dangerous rebel groups tended to assemble in rugged, hard-to-control border regions such as that between Guangxi and Guangdong, local officials could not easily coordinate their suppression activities.

The Triad lodges, and their affiliates and contacts in the local bureaucracy, enhanced their power through involvement in local militia organizations. Lin Zexu had encouraged the formation of such groups to defend Canton against the British, just as gentry in the late Ming had done to protect their bases against peasant rebels or Manchus. The Canton militia groups became complicated mixtures of gentry leaders, local thugs, bona fide peasant volunteers, members of other martial-arts organizations, and groups of men from common trades. In May 1841, such a mélange of forces had confronted a British patrol outside Canton at the village of Sanyuanli. Armed with spears and hoes—some even with guns—they had forced the British to retreat, killing one British soldier and wounding fifteen others. The Chinese made the encounter a symbol for the possibility of a united resistance to foreign pressures.

For the Qing state, as for the Ming, such assemblages were a two-edged sword. Some gentry developed regular, well-organized militia groups that could effectively keep order in the countryside or patrol the city; other groups saw militiamen melt away, perhaps with arms and some rudimentary training, to return to their original bandit gangs or bring new skills to their Triad comrades. The groups of irregulars gradually grew after 1842 as the Treaty of Nanjing began to have its effect, swelling the trade of Shanghai and drawing resources away from the intransigent region of Canton. Out-of-work boatmen and coolies, poverty-stricken artisans, destitute peasants—all swelled the groups of disaffected who sought some kind of mooring in baffling times.

Emperor Daoguang tried to think this through when responding to the xenophobic attacks on the British in the Canton region, which reached a pinnacle during 1848: "The only important thing is to appease the people's emotions. If the people's loyalties are not lost, then the foreign bandits can be handled."[4] The trouble was that appeasing popular violence was a dangerous gamble for the Qing.

THE TAIPING

In the immense upheaval known as the Taiping Uprising, which ravaged much of China between 1850 and 1864, we see many elements similar to those just mentioned: the restlessness and religious self-identification of a man like Lin Qing, the underlying social discord in the southeast, the growing strength and variety of secret society organizations among the poor, and the dislocation caused by the British and the Opium trade. But at the same time, it was one individual's personal life story and state of mind that gave the movement its particular shape. This was Hong Xiuquan, one of those who in this period had such a difficult time trying to push their way onto the lowest rung of the ladder of Qing gentility. Hong was born in 1814, the fourth of five children in a hard-working rural family of Guangdong. His parents were from the Hakka minority (the so-called "guest peoples" who had migrated southward from central China), and they sacrificed to get Hong a decent education that would win him a place in the local elite. But even though he passed the initial examinations permitting him to qualify for the licentiate's *shengyuan* degree, in the early 1830s he failed at his first two attempts to obtain the degree, which would have given him the right to wear the scholars' robes, to be exempt from physical punishment, and to receive a small stipend from the state.

For any ambitious young Chinese, such failure was humiliating, but for Hong it seems to have been unusually so. He took solace only in the chance to travel and study in Canton itself. In 1836 Hong was just about to enter the examination hall yet again in pursuit of the elusive degree when a Chinese Protestant evangelist pressed a collection of translated passages from the Bible called "Good Words for Exhorting the Age" into Hong's hands. Such a moment was possible, and such tracts were available, because of many new historical circumstances that were to distinguish Hong's uprising from all those that had come before. Western Protestant missionaries—mainly British and American—had been working since the early 1800s to translate the entire Bible into Chinese, and had printed numerous copies, which they distributed while traveling up the coast and in the interior. They and their Chinese converts also tried to distill the message of the scriptures into simple tracts like the "Good Words," which reached even more readers.

Hong Xiuquan neither studied the tracts nor threw them away. Instead he seems to have glanced at them quickly and then kept them at home. He initially made no connection between these tracts and a strange dream and delirium he experienced after a third examination failure in 1837. In those visions, Hong conversed with a bearded, golden-haired man who gave him a sword, and a younger man who instructed him on how to slay evil spirits and whom Hong addressed as "Elder Brother." For six years after his visions, Hong worked as a village schoolteacher, and tried once again to pass the examinations. But after he failed the *shengyuan* examinations for the fourth time, he opened the Christian tracts and read them fully. In a sudden shock of realization, Hong saw that the two men in his vision must have been the God and Jesus of the tracts, and that therefore he, Hong, must also be the Son of God, younger brother to Jesus Christ.

Like Lin Qing in north China thirty years before, Hong was able to persuade people of his spiritual powers through a charismatic manner and a strong religious conviction. But unlike Lin, Hong did not work secretly through a network of local sectarian cells. Instead he began to preach his message publicly, baptize converts, and openly destroy Confucian and ancestral shrines. Although these activities prompted local anger, which caused Hong to flee his village temporarily for Guangxi, they did not provoke the local authorities, and he continued to teach. In 1847 he returned to Canton and studied the Bible with Isaacher Roberts, an American southern Baptist. Late that year Hong left Canton and joined a close friend, one of his first converts, who had formed a Society of God Worshipers in the rugged area of eastern Guangxi province called Thistle Mountain.

In this isolated region—far from a county seat—Hong's movement spread, drawing converts from Hakkas and from mountain tribesmen. By 1849 he had attracted around 10,000 followers. Perhaps influenced by members of Triad organizations who joined him, Hong's ideology came to embrace both the creation of a new Christian community and the destruction of the Manchus, against whose wickedness and deceit he cried out in moving and powerful terms. When one recalls Lu Liuliang's posthumous fate after daring to attack the ruling dynasty with much milder language, Hong's courage and recklessness can be appreciated. But for Hong, the ruling dynasty represented a special challenge: to him the Manchus were demons fighting against the true God, a God whose purity and presence had existed in China until the forces of Confucian belief swayed the Chinese away from the true path of righteousness.

Hong's rhetorical passion drew a devoted following. Among Hong's closest advisers were an illiterate, orphaned charcoal maker from the Thistle Mountain area who proved to be an intuitively brilliant military tactician, and a nineteen-year-old member of a wealthy local landlord lineage who persuaded most members of his lineage to throw in their lot with Hong, bringing an estimated 100,000 taels into Hong's treasury. Another important group of converts was the local miners whose skills with explosives and tunneling, developed in the mountains of eastern Guangxi, were later to be used in the demolition of city walls. With the miners came many others who contributed a variety of forms of expertise: pawnbrokers (who ran the treasury), legal clerks (who developed bureaucratic structures), ex-soldiers of the Qing forces or local militias, as well as at least two well-known women bandit leaders and several gangs of river pirates.

By 1850 Hong's recruits and converts had passed the 20,000 mark. His movement was now sufficiently organized to drill troops, manufacture arms, and assemble military tables of organization; it could enforce rigorous instructions against corruption, sensuality, and opium smoking, conduct ceremonies of Christian worship, pool all money and valuables in a central treasury, convince its men to abandon their queues and wear their flowing hair long, and segregate the women—mothers, wives, daughters—into a separate camp run by female officers. Through these actions, the God worshipers finally attracted enough notice to be singled out from the scores of other bandit groups that roamed different parts of China.

In December 1850, Qing government forces sent to oust Hong from the Thistle Mountain area were badly defeated, and their Manchu commander killed. On January 11, 1851, Hong Xiuquan assembled his God worshipers and declared himself the Heavenly King of the Taiping Tianguo, "Heavenly Kingdom of Great Peace"(commonly abbreviated to Taiping). Forced out of their base by larger government armies, the Taiping campaigned on the Guangxi-Guangdong border until autumn 1851, when they swung north and seized the city of Yongan along with great stores of cash, food, and new recruits, who swelled their numbers to 60,000 or more.

Guiding their destinies now by a newly created Christian solar calendar

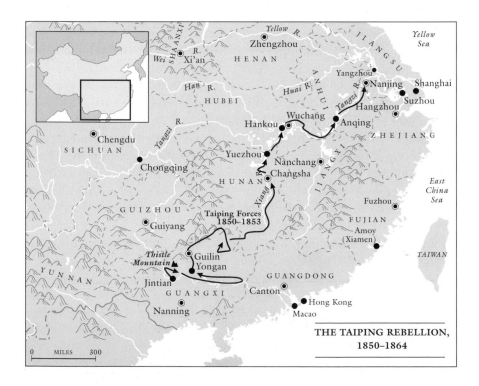

THE TAIPING REBELLION,
1850–1864

with a seven-day week (although an initial error in calculation caused the Taiping "Sunday" in fact to fall on the Christian Saturday), the Taiping advanced again in the spring of 1852. They attacked the Guangxi capital of Guilin, which they failed to capture despite the heroic exploits of their new regiments of Hakka women, who fought with exemplary courage. (Used to the life of hard farming in the mountains, the Hakka women had never bound their feet as other Chinese females did.) In the summer they crossed into Hunan, but were frustrated in their two-month attempt to take Changsha. Here the Taiping proclamations became more fiery in an attempt to win fresh recruits: "Can the Chinese still consider themselves men? Ever since the Manchus poisoned China, the flame of oppression has risen up to heaven, the poison of corruption has defiled the emperor's throne, the offensive odor has spread over the four seas, and the influence of demons has distressed the empire while the Chinese with bowed heads and dejected spirits willingly became subjects and servants."[5]

A breakthrough came in December 1852, when almost unopposed the Taiping army entered Yuezhou on the east side of Dongting Lake. Yuezhou was a wealthy, long-settled town, unlike the poorer areas through which the Taiping had hitherto ranged, and here they seized vast amounts of booty, 5,000 boats, and stockpiles of arms and gunpowder. (Some of the guns had been abandoned there by Wu Sangui after the failure of his Three Feudatories rebellion almost two centuries before, but were still serviceable.) Thereafter an incredible string of successes followed: Hankou fell in December and Wuchang in January 1853, bringing Hong a further large fleet of boats and 1.6 million taels from the provincial treasury. Anqing fell almost without opposition in February 1853, bringing 300,000 taels more, 100 large cannon, and huge stores of food. In March the great center of Nanjing, defended by only a small force, its walls undermined by explosive charges, its center bombarded by artillery, its streets infiltrated by Taiping soldiers disguised as Buddhist or Daoist priests, fell to the rebels.

Nanjing's Manchu population of some 40,000, of whom about 5,000 were combat troops, retreated into the city's inner citadel, but were overwhelmed by the charges of wave after wave of Taiping troops. All Manchus who did not die in the battle—men, women, and children—were rounded up and systematically killed by burning, stabbing, or drowning. It was Hong's way of showing that the devils would be driven from the face of China. At the end of March, wearing a crown and an embroidered dragon robe, Hong was carried into the city in a golden palanquin on the backs of sixteen men, and took up residence in a former Ming dynasty imperial palace.

The Taiping ruled their Nanjing-based Heavenly Kingdom for eleven years (1853–1864) under the formal authority of Hong Xiuquan as Heavenly

King. The policies of the Taiping remained, on paper and often in practice, startlingly radical. One facet of their rule was an asceticism that required segregation of the sexes and absolute bans on opium smoking, prostitution, dancing, and drinking of alcohol. Money was held in a common treasury, theoretically to be shared by all; and since the Taiping had acquired more than 18 million taels along their route of march and within Nanjing itself, their prosperity seemed assured. Examinations were reinstituted, based now on Chinese translations of the Bible and on the transcribed versions of Hong Xiuquan's religious revelations and literary works. Women, organized into special residential and administrative units, were allowed to hold supervisory offices in the bureaucracy and to sit for their own special examinations.

Most remarkable was the Taiping land law, which, linked to a local system of military recruitment, constituted perhaps the most utopian, comprehensive, and authoritarian scheme for human organization ever seen in China up to that time. All land was to be divided among all families of the Taiping and their supporters according to family size, with men and women receiving equal shares. After keeping the produce they needed for their own sustenance, each family would place the rest in great common granaries. Every twenty-five families were supervised by a "sergeant" who kept records of production, adjudicated squabbles, oversaw education of the young in the Bible and Taiping doctrines, and held Christian services every Sabbath. The sergeants selected men from the families under their care for service with local military units. Men selected for service were subject to rigid drill and training, taught to use signals, weapons, and booby traps, and succored in combat by medical squads for the wounded and the sick. From their Nanjing base, huge armies foraged forth, either to extend the Taiping dominions to the east and north or to bring fresh supplies and recruits back to sustain the garrison armies. The results would surely be, ran a Taiping proclamation, "that nowhere will inequality exist, and no one not be well fed and clothed."[6]

Yet for all their military and ideological passion, and their utopian dreams of perfect governance, the Taiping failed to overthrow the Qing and were ultimately eliminated, with terrible slaughter. Why did the Taiping not succeed, after achieving so many triumphs with such speed in the name of such a utopian ideology?

One reason was the failure of Taiping collective leadership. From the original brotherhood, Hong Xiuquan had gone on to name some key Taiping followers as "kings," who ruled jointly under his supervision. But two of the most talented leaders were killed in the campaigns of 1852, and the most brilliant survivors—especially Yang Xiuqing and Shi Dakai, who had

been among Hong's earliest followers during the Thistle Mountain days—
ultimately lost faith in him. Yang, who had arrogated enormous powers to
himself, was assassinated in a murderous palace coup in 1856—on Hong's
orders. Shi, who lived up to his early promise and became the Taiping's
greatest general, left Nanjing the same year, after his wife and mother were
killed by feuding Taiping generals. He tried to set up an independent kingdom in Sichuan but was trapped and killed there by Qing troops in 1863.

Shorn of his most talented advisers, Hong faltered as a leader once he
had won a measure of power. He demonstrated a dangerous inefficiency
and lack of clear goals. Just as in Wuchang he had missed a chance to strike
north to Peking, so did he fail to push the initiative after his seizure of
Nanjing. Instead he withdrew into a palace world of sensual pleasures and
religious mysticism, surrounding himself with concubines and perusing the
Bible for all references to himself and his "mission," which he found underlined everywhere from the Book of Genesis to the Book of Revelation. He
failed to exploit the potentially popular issue of an anti-Manchu crusade and
squandered his reputation as a serious religious leader.

Hong's failure to appeal to anti-Manchu sentiment was symptomatic of
the Taiping's isolation, even when they were holding power in Nanjing. If
they had maintained the city as a thriving metropolitan center, and had
Hong enshrined himself there on a firm base of popular support, the Taiping
might have been unbeatable. But the Chinese residents of Nanjing found
the Taiping occupiers—many of whom were Hakkas, with their strange
dress and accents, and their large-footed women—as bizarre as any foreigners or Manchus. The residents resented the Taiping for their alterations
of economic life, their attempt to establish a common treasury and regulate
markets, their segregation of the civil population by sex and occupation, and
their attempt to enforce a strict code of conduct. Passive resistance to the
Taiping was endemic, and flight, spying, and defections to the Qing common.[7] Dorgon's more flexible policies in the early Qing, by contrast, had
been far more successful in winning general popular acceptance.

Beyond Nanjing, the Taiping failed in the countryside, where their
dreams of a common treasury for all believers and an equitable system of
landholding remained largely unrealized. Even though they controlled large
areas of Jiangsu, Anhui, and Zhejiang for years, and areas farther north and
west intermittently, they lacked the commitment or personnel to push
through their dramatic land reforms, and ended up as yet another tax-
collection agency on the backs of a despondent peasantry. Their constant
need for food and supplies to maintain their huge armies meant that Taiping
foraging squads scoured the country for hundreds of miles. These logistical

demands, when coupled with the constant fighting with Qing forces—who also needed food and lodging—left huge areas of what had once been China's most prosperous region as barren wastes.

The Taiping failed as well to coordinate their uprising with two other upheavals occurring at the same time: the revolt of the Nian to the north and the Red Turbans to the south. Had some kind of concerted action been arranged—as the anti-Ming rebels Li Zicheng and Zhang Xianzhong had tried to do with other bandit leaders in the 1630s—the Qing could not have survived, especially when suffering a series of damaging blows from the Western powers at the same time. But Taiping asceticism and the extreme nature of their religious claims made constructive alliance with other rebels difficult.

Nor did the Taiping manage to enlist Western sympathy in their cause. Foreigners, especially missionaries, had been initially excited by the prospect of a Christian revolutionary force that promised social reforms and the defeat of the moribund and intransigent Manchus. But the eccentricities of Hong Xiuquan's Christianity eventually became apparent to the missionaries, and traders came to fear the Taiping's zealous hatred of opium. Finally, the Western powers decided to back the Qing in order to prevent a Taiping seizure of Shanghai, which might threaten the West's newly won treaty gains. With members of Triad secret societies controlling the Chinese areas of the city from 1853 to early 1855, a Taiping seizure seemed likely. In the closing years of the rebellion, a foreign-officered mercenary army supported by steam-driven, shallow-draft gunboats fought alongside Qing forces against the Taiping. This was the so-called "Ever-Victorious Army," led first by the American adventurer from Massachusetts, Frederick Townsend Ward, and after his death by the deeply religious British artillery officer, Charles "Chinese" Gordon.

The Qing cause was also bolstered by the loyalty, tenacity, and courage of senior Chinese officials who fought on against the Taiping even though the regular Manchu-led banner armies seemed unable to defeat the enemy. These Confucian-educated scholars were alarmed by the Taiping threat to their ancestral homes and distraught at the Taiping's use of Christianity to attack the whole structure of Chinese values. The greatest of these leaders was the Hunanese official Zeng Guofan, who had first raised local troops to defend his own estates when he was on mourning leave from the court in 1852. Zeng went on with his brothers to raise and equip an efficient and honestly administered army of tough Hunanese peasant conscripts officered by local Confucian gentry. Given the weakness of the Qing banner forces in the region and the proven ineptitude of the local bureaucrats in maintaining militia forces, Zeng's troops formed a crucial addition to the state's defensive resources. Named the Xiang Army, after the river that cuts through Hunan, this army became one of the Taiping's deadliest enemies and played a critical part in the eventual recapture of Nanjing.

The formation of the Xiang Army suggests more broadly the surprising flexibility and effectiveness of local forces in resisting the Taiping. Failing to attract many gentry to their cause, the Taiping encountered opposition all over central and eastern China from the hundreds of local militia forces organized by the gentry to defend their homes and fields. Accepted as essential by the Qing even if they seemed to underline the ineffectiveness of the state, these militia brought new levels of power to the gentry landlords. When the *likin* tax—a supplement on the transit dues—was permitted so that these militia leaders could finance their military ventures, it enabled them to continue their success in the long war of attrition. The Taiping found it harder and harder to obtain supplies or new recruits as whole communities solidified in resistance against them.

The fatal inflexibility of Hong's regime is evident in the failure of a bold attempt by the Taiping to alter and "Westernize" their rule. The author of this venture was Hong Ren'gan, a younger relation of Hong Xiuquan who had also studied with missionaries in Canton and been a member of the first God worshipers. During the early years of the Taiping rebellion, Hong Ren'gan lived and worked in Hong Kong, and became familiar with Britain's colonial government there. Finally in 1859 he made his way overland to Nanjing, disguised as a physician, and was enthusiastically received by the Heavenly King, who named him prime minister. Hong Ren'gan prepared an elaborate document entitled "A New Treatise on Aids to Administration," which he presented to the Heavenly King in late 1859. His program called for the development of legal and banking systems in the Taiping domains; the construction of highways, railways, and steam-driven freight ships; the introduction of a postal service; the publication of newspapers; and the abandonment of geomancy and infanticide. Hong Xiuquan endorsed all these proposals as "correct," except for those suggesting the spread of information through newspapers, on which he noted: "It will not be too late to carry out this proposal after the remnant demons are annihilated."[8] But in the event, no concrete steps were taken to initiate these reforms. And once Hong Ren'gan's attempt to develop a new grand strategy to regain the upper Yangzi for the Taiping failed, and a massive counterattack he ordered against Suzhou and Hangzhou was beaten back, the last elements of popular support for the Taiping were dashed.

As Zeng Guofan complacently told the Qing emperor, "Now when the people hear of the rebels, pain and regret pierce their hearts, men as well as women flee, and kitchen fires no longer burn. The tillers do not have harvests of a single grain, and one after another they abandon their occupations. When the rebels travel through a territory without people, it is like fish trying to swim in a place without water." Yet when the end came in July 1864, after Hong Xiuquan's death—either by suicide or from illness, it was never made clear—and Qing troops stormed into Nanjing, Zeng wrote to the emperor in some awe: "Not one of the 100,000 rebels in Nanjing surrendered themselves when the city was taken but in many cases gathered together and burned themselves and passed away without repentance. Such a formidable band of rebels has been rarely known from ancient times to the present."[9]

FOREIGN PRESSURES

One of many factors that helped the Qing overthrow the Taiping was the assistance of foreigners in the early 1860s, whether in the form of customs dues collected through the foreign-managed Shanghai Inspectorate of Customs or in the form of the Ever-Victorious Army, led in the field by Western officers. The reasons for that support had mainly to do with international affairs, in which, once again, the primary actors were the British. Disappointed at the results of the Nanjing treaty and frustrated by continued Qing intransigence, the British reacted with scant sympathy when the Qing were threatened by the spread of the Taiping rebellion. Instead the British made the highly legalistic decision to apply the most-favored-nation clause to the American treaty of 1844, which had stipulated that that treaty be renegotiated in twelve years. By applying that renewal stipulation to their own Nanjing treaty of 1842, British authorities forced the Chinese to renegotiate in 1854.

The British foreign secretary saw the speciousness of this argument, writing to the governor of Hong Kong that "the Chinese Authorities may perhaps and with some degree of plausibility object that the circumstances of the time are unsuitable for the commencement of such a work."[10] But he nevertheless suggested that the Qing be presented with the following formidable list of requests: access for the British to the entire interior of China or, failing that, to all of coastal Zhejiang and the lower Yangzi up to Nanjing; legalization of the opium trade; cancellation of internal transit dues on foreign imports; suppression of piracy; regulation of Chinese labor emigration; residence in Peking for a British ambassador; and reliance on the English version rather than the Chinese in all disputed interpretations of the revised treaty.

Despite some caution because of their involvement in the Crimean War against Russia, the British moved jointly with the Americans and French to press for treaty revision, which the beleaguered Qing continued to oppose. The British finally took advantage of an allegedly illegal Qing search of a ship formerly of Hong Kong registry, the *Arrow,* to recommence military actions at Canton in late 1856. After some delays in getting reinforcements—the Indian mutiny was now raging, and the idea of a war in east Asia was not popular with the British people—the British seized Canton in December 1857 and exiled the consistently hostile governor-general of the region to Calcutta. Sailing north in a near repeat of the 1840 campaign, they took the strategic Dagu forts in May 1858 and threatened to seize Tianjin. In June, with the way to Peking now open to the British forces, the Qing capitulated and agreed to sign a new treaty. By the terms of the most-favored-nation clause, all British gains would also be shared by the other major foreign powers.

This "Treaty of Tianjin" of 1858 imposed extraordinarily strict terms on China. A British ambassador was henceforth to reside in Peking, accompanied by family and staff, and housed in a fitting residence. The open preaching of Christianity was protected. Travel anywhere inside China was permitted to those with valid passports, and within thirty miles of treaty

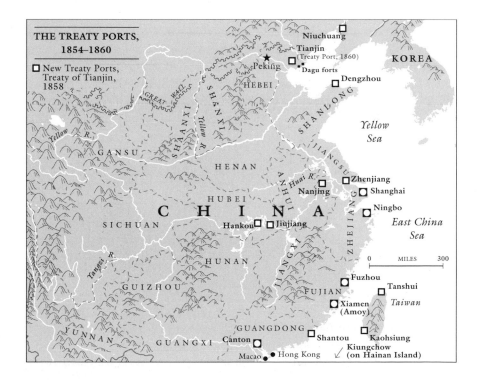

ports without passports. Once the rebellions currently raging in China were suppressed, trade was to be allowed up the Yangzi as far as Hankou, and four new Yangzi treaty ports (Hankou, Jiujiang, Nanjing, and Zhenjiang) would be opened. An additional six treaty ports were to be opened immediately: one in Manchuria, one in Shandong, two on Taiwan, one in Guangdong, and one on Hainan Island in the far south.

The Tianjin treaty also stipulated that all further interior transit taxes on foreign imports be dropped upon payment of a flat fee of 2.5 percent. Standard weights and measures would be employed at all ports and customshouses. Official communications were to be in English. The character for *barbarian (yi)* must no longer be used in Chinese documents describing the British. And British ships hunting pirates would be free to enter any Chinese port. A supplementary clause accompanying the various commercial agreements stated explicitly: "Opium will henceforth pay thirty taels per picul [approximately 130 pounds] Import Duty. The importer will sell it only at the port. It will be carried into the interior by Chinese only, and only as Chinese property; the foreign trader will not be allowed to accompany it." This condition was imposed despite the prohibition in the Chinese penal code on the sale and consumption of opium. Virtually the only British concession was to pull back from Tianjin and return the Dagu forts to Qing control.

The British evidently expected China's rulers to abandon the struggle at this point, but the Qing would not, and showed no intention of following the treaty clause that permitted foreign ambassadors to live in Peking. In June 1859, to enforce the new treaty terms, the British once more attacked the Dagu forts, now strengthened and reinforced by Qing troops. Fighting was heavy and the British were beaten back, even though the American naval commodore Josiah Tattnall, despite his country's declared neutrality, came to the aid of wounded British Admiral Hope with the ringing cry "Blood is thicker than water."[11] Repulsed from the Dagu forts, the British sent a team of negotiators to Peking by a different route in 1860, but they were arrested by the Qing and some were executed. Determined now to teach the Qing a lesson they could not ignore, Lord Elgin, Britain's chief treaty negotiator, ordered his troops to march on Peking. On October 18, 1860, following Elgin's orders, the British burnt to the ground the Yuan Ming Yuan—the exquisite summer palace in the Peking suburbs built for Qianlong's pleasure using the plans of Jesuit architects. The British, however, spared the Forbidden City palaces within Peking, calculating that destruction of those hallowed buildings would be a disgrace so profound that the Qing dynasty would inevitably fall.

The emperor had already fled the city for Manchuria and named his younger brother, Prince Gong, to act as negotiator. But there was nothing left to negotiate, and on the very day the summer palace burned, Prince Gong reaffirmed the terms of the 1858 Tianjin treaty. In an additional "Convention of Peking," the emperor was stated to express his "deep regret" at the harassment of the British queen's representatives. He also promised a further 8 million taels in indemnity, permitted Chinese emigration on British ships, made Tianjin itself a treaty port, and ceded part of the mainland Kowloon peninsula to Hong Kong. Thus did the "treaty system" reach its fruition.

THE NIAN REBELLION

The outbreak of the Nian rebellion is usually dated to 1851, the same year as the formal declaration of the Taiping Heavenly Kingdom. But the origins of the Nian can be traced back to the 1790s among roving groups of bandits who operated north of the Huai River, especially in the border-region area that comprised southwest Shandong, northwest Jiangsu, east-central Henan, and northern Anhui. The name *Nian* probably referred simply to the rebels' status as mobile bands, although the ambiguity of the term in Chinese is such that it can also refer to the martial disguises they sometimes adopted, or to the twisted paper torches by whose light they robbed houses at night.

Unlike the Taiping, the Nian had no clear-cut religious affiliation, political ideology, strategic goals, or unified leadership. Yet for the first fifty years of the nineteenth century, they steadily grew in numbers and strength. Some Nian had connections with White Lotus groups, Eight Trigrams followers, or Triad societies, while others were connected with the smugglers who made money by evading the government monopoly on salt sales. But most were poor peasants or ex-peasants struggling to survive in a bleak environment of worked-out soil, harsh winters, and unstable river systems subject to appalling floods. The prevalence of female infanticide in the area also meant that there was a profound imbalance in the region's sex ratios. As many as 20 percent of the men were unable to find wives and start families, making of them a rootless and volatile group capable of swinging into action with a raiding party at any time. The settled local communities tried to guarantee some security by establishing small protective militias, walled villages, and crop-watching associations, but the Nian nevertheless launched raids to seize crops from nearby villages, to rob the transport vehicles of government salt merchants, to kidnap wealthy landlords for ransom, or even to attack a local jail where a fellow Nian gang member was being held.

After 1851, when serious floods in northern Jiangsu brought fresh hard-

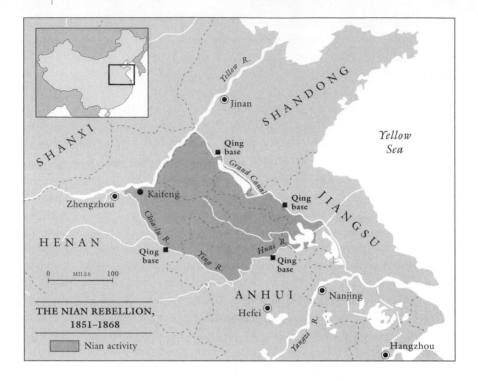

THE NIAN REBELLION,
1851–1868

Nian activity

ship, affiliation with Nian groups rose dramatically, and the Qing officially took note of them as rebels. In 1855, two years after the Taiping seized Nanjing, the Yellow River climaxed a long series of floods by breaking out of its main restraining dikes east of Kaifeng and carving a new channel into the gulf north of the Shandong peninsula; the ensuing misery brought ever more recruits to the Nian gangs. At the same time, Nian organization tightened: in 1852 leaders of eighteen separate Nian groups had proclaimed as their head Zhang Luoxing, a northern Anhui landlord who had supported sheep stealers and had run the local salt smugglers' protection racket. In 1856 Zhang was elected "Lord of the Alliance," with the honorific title "Great Han Prince with the Heavenly Mandate." The Nian forces organized themselves into five main banners, named for different colors, each of which grouped together rebels of common surnames from neighboring communities.

The veteran forces of Nian warriors may only have numbered 30,000 to 50,000 troops, but their effect was disproportionate to their size. Many of them were cavalrymen, many had firearms, and they could cut at will across the lines of communication between the Qing capital of Peking and the government forces besieging Nanjing. By developing strongly walled or moated communities, often armed with cannon, in the area north of the river Huai, they established dozens of secure bases to which their troops could retire after their forays across the countryside. Other villages and market towns also fortified themselves to keep the rebels *out,* so that much of the area north of the Huai became crisscrossed with defensive communities. Sometimes "peace treaties" were signed between defensive villages and neighboring Nian fortresses in which each agreed not to attack the other. In other cases, stipends in cash or opium were paid as "protection money."

The extent of rural misery in the region cannot be assessed precisely, but it must have been great. In one proclamation, Zhang Luoxing explained that the local people made their lives worse by fleeing the Nian. "Wherever our troops go, you grab your treasures and run away in terror. Ruffians then take advantage of the situation to plunder freely. Left unattended, your houses are burned to the ground and nothing is left standing when you return. Although your actions are intended to protect, in reality they bring nothing but disaster."[12] Although the Nian leaders issued numerous proclamations banning looting and rape, these had little effect on the rank and file. For them it was common practice to scavenge for vegetables and roots in deserted farms, hunt down wild animals, kidnap members of rich families, and seize local trade convoys. Sometimes on their return to their home base, the Nian sold cheaply the food they had looted elsewhere, to increase their popularity locally.

Although Zhang Luoxing was killed in combat, other able Nian leaders soon emerged to replace him. They developed an intensely successful form of guerrilla strategy in which Nian forces would retreat steadily from the Qing troops until those troops were tired and forced by terrain into smaller and smaller units. The Nian, regrouping, would then attack these scattered units with an overwhelming force of long-speared infantry and sword-bearing cavalry. Often the Nian conducted a grim scorched-earth policy, luring Qing forces into areas where all the crops had been rooted up, houses and boats burned, and wells filled with stones.

The Qing court's response was to appoint Zeng Guofan, hailed as a great victor after the fall of Nanjing, as supreme commander of military affairs for Nian suppression. But Zeng could not finish off the Nian, despite a careful plan that involved the formation of four provincial military bases— one each in the provinces of Jiangsu, Anhui, Henan, and Shandong, and each on a major river or canal to assist in moving supplies. The plan also entailed the digging of canals and trenches to curb the mobility of the Nian cavalry, and a systematic attempt to win local villages back to Qing allegiance by means of conciliatory policies and the selection of new headmen.

The strategy failed in part because the governors of the four provinces could not cooperate fully, and because Zeng had disbanded many of his best Xiang Army troops after the fall of Nanjing. Accordingly he was dependent on troops from the army of his protégé Li Hongzhang, who had been appointed governor-general of Liangjiang (i.e., the provinces of Jiangsu, Jiangxi, and Anhui). While Li Hongzhang was able to supply Zeng with a steady revenue for the troops, who were recruited from Anhui province and named the Huai Army after the river that cuts through the north of the province, the troops did not give their full loyalty to Zeng. The court thereupon switched the offices of the two men, making Li commander of the campaign and Zeng governor-general of Liangjiang.

These switches emphasized the complexity of the new political world that was emerging in China as more power devolved on local regional commanders. Li Hongzhang owed his political career to Zeng, who had recruited him for his own semiprivate bureaucracy while Li was still a young man. Li and Zeng not only had complicated, interlocking careers, they ran their own military systems. Still, Li Hongzhang initially had as hard a time suppressing the Nian as had Zeng Guofan. The Nian forces seemed always to elude him, breaking across the defensive barriers, even roaming as far afield in the northwest as Shaanxi province, where they entered the cities of Xi'an and Yan'an. "Our troops had to run after them," as Li put it, "while they moved as freely as mercury."[13] But a slow, steady war of attrition brought the collapse of the now divided Nian forces by 1868. Li's armies were well paid by Chinese standards and generally loyal to him and their personal commanders. They used rifles and artillery they had purchased from the foreigners, and began the systematic use of gunboats on the northern waterways. Foreign armored ships—two of them aptly named the *Confucius* and the *Plato*—patrolled the coastal waters off Shandong to prevent a Nian breakaway that might threaten foreign trade, now flourishing under the terms of the Tianjin treaty and the Convention of Peking.

In August 1868, after heavy fighting brought final Qing victories in Shandong and the execution of the cornered Nian survivors, the court offered sacrifices of thanks to heaven in the temple of their ancestors and the temple of the god of war. Li Hongzhang was ennobled and given the honorific title Grand Guardian of the Heir Apparent. Like Zeng Guofan, who had been named to the highest possible honorific rank after recapturing Nanjing, Li Hongzhang had consolidated his career on the backs of defeated rebels. Zeng died in 1872 and hence did not have much time to enjoy his fame and prestige, but Li Hongzhang was granted a long life. For the next thirty-three years he was to be one of the most powerful officials in China.

MUSLIM REVOLTS

There had been settlements of Muslims in China since the Tang dynasty (A.D. 618–907), both at the termini of the central Asian trade routes in Gansu and Shaanxi, and in certain southeast coastal towns of Fujian and Guangdong frequented by Arab traders. By the late Ming period, so many Muslims had intermarried with Chinese families that there were now large settled communities of Chinese Muslims (known as *hui*) providing a new level of complexity to local administration. The Jesuit Matteo Ricci noted the number of Chinese Muslims living in China in the early seventeenth century. Chinese Muslims had launched several uprisings during Qianlong's reign; and the jihads (holy wars) declared by the khans of Kokand, west of Chinese Turkistan, had kept the outermost areas of Qing control in Kashgar and Yarkand in constant turmoil during the early nineteenth century. In the more settled agricultural areas of north China ravaged by the Nian rebellion, there were also sizable Muslim communities, containing perhaps 1 million or more of the faithful: prosperous mosques stood in Henan and Anhui, and Muslims controlled their own branches of the salt-smuggling rackets. Discriminatory legislation protected Chinese involved in violence with Muslims, and religious riots and feuds were commonplace.

But the areas of greatest Muslim concentration, besides Gansu-Shaanxi, were in China's southwest, particularly the province of Yunnan. The Muslim settlements here dated back to the time of the Mongol conquest of China in the thirteenth century, and friction with other Chinese settlers pushing into the region had been endemic. It was in Yunnan in 1855, as the Taiping strengthened their hold on Nanjing and the Nian began to organize their grand alliance, that a third major rebellion erupted against the Qing. The triggers for this rebellion were the heavy land taxes and extra levies imposed by Peking on the Yunnanese Muslims, whose plight was exacerbated by disputes over the gold and silver mines that gave the province much of its scarce wealth. The Chinese, having exhausted their own mines, tried to oust the Muslims from theirs. Violence and rioting led to a large-scale Chinese attack on the Muslims, who fought back, seizing the important city of Dali in the west of the province and besieging Kunming, the capital. Kunming was in rebel Muslim hands only for a brief period in 1863 before being recaptured by the Qing. In Dali, however, the Muslim rebel Du Wenxiu, taking the name "Sultan Suleiman," created a new state named *Pingnan guo,* "Kingdom of the Pacified South," his variation of the Taiping Heavenly Kingdom's title.

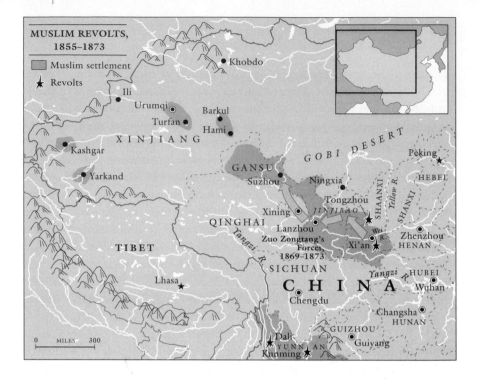

The Qing officials in the area were inept, and the terrain made campaigning difficult, especially after fighting by Miao tribesmen, religious sectarians, and Muslims spread to the mountainous border area where Yunnan, Sichuan, and Guizhou provinces meet. But the Qing managed to turn the tide by splitting the Muslim forces and rewarding the turncoats, developing local defense groups, and relying on a handful of talented local Chinese generals. In 1873 Dali fell after heavy fighting, and Du Wenxiu, failing in his attempt at suicide, was captured and executed.

Difficulties of terrain and the huge distances involved made it difficult for the Yunnan Muslims to coordinate their struggle with another Muslim rebellion that broke out far to the north—in Shaanxi and Gansu. This rebellion, commencing in 1862, had been encouraged by Taiping generals trying to deflect the Qing from their siege of Nanjing, and Nian troops marched to the region in the mid-1860s to see if some anti-Qing alliance could be forged. Several areas of Gansu and southern Shaanxi province had sizable Muslim populations, many of them followers of the "New Teachings" derived from the central Asian mystical school of Sufism. The Qing had attempted to ban these New Teachings following a series of Muslim uprisings between 1781 and 1783, but had only deepened local bitterness.

The northwest Muslim revolt of 1862, however, seems to have arisen from local tensions between Chinese and Muslims rather than from any particular religious or anti-Qing focus. A volatile situation of rioting and harassment was intensified by the Taiping foray into the area. Following the pattern now long established in east and north China, the local population responded to the threat by forming militia units to defend their homes; in doing so, it was natural for Muslim militia groups to form in some areas and Chinese ones in others. Since most banner troops had been drafted away to fight the Taiping and the Nian, and since many of the local garrison Green Standard troops were themselves Muslim, Qing authority in the region was weak, leaving the situation ripe for trouble. The revolt began with a tiny incident—a quarrel between a group of Muslims and a Chinese merchant over the price of some bamboo poles. Arguments led to blows, Chinese crowds gathered and, with gentry leadership, attacked and burned Muslim villages along the Wei River, killing innocent Muslim families. The Muslims in turn formed armed bands, retaliated against the Chinese (and against their coreligionists who refused to take up arms), and in late June besieged the two most prosperous cities in southern Shaanxi—Tongzhou and Xi'an.

The Qing forces in the area were initially plagued with inadequate leadership, but even when more efficient generals were appointed, their troops suffered from low morale, disease, and wages constantly in arrears. There were many desertions. Although Qing troops were able to hold Xi'an and Tongzhou, they lost control of much of the surrounding countryside. And when, in late 1862, Qing forces began to achieve some victories, the Muslims simply retreated west into Gansu, where they formed new armed bands whose rallying cry was that the Qing were planning to exterminate all Muslims in China.

The few banner garrisons, based mainly in Ningxia and Lanzhou, were powerless to pacify the rebels, and the only hope of the Qing seemed to be to spread dissension *within* the Muslim ranks. As a senior Manchu official pointed out to the court in words that seemed to justify a Muslim fear of total extermination: "Among the Muslims, there are certainly evil ones, but doubtless there are also numerous peaceful, law-abiding people. If we decide to destroy them all, we are driving the good ones to join the rebels, and create for ourselves an awesome, endless job of killing the Muslims." The overall problem was complex, he added, since in Gansu, "with a few rare exceptions, there are Muslims living in every city; [and] in the army, there are proportionately even more Muslims than Chinese among the rank and file." A murky sequence of negotiations, pitched battles, trickery, false surrenders, and reprisals followed throughout 1863 and 1864, while the only advice the Qing court offered its officials was to "talk softly to them and be ready for any incident."[14] By 1866 gunpowder supplies had run out, rice was too expensive to buy, and even local wheat prices were scores of times their usual level. There was no fuel, and horses died for lack of fodder. Soldiers lived on "soup" of diluted flour, and many civilians starved or committed suicide.

In desperation, the Qing court turned to a scholar who had emerged as one of the most effective anti-Taiping leaders—Zuo Zongtang. Like Zeng Guofan, Zuo was born and raised in Hunan province. In 1830, when he was eighteen, his father died, and he spent some time studying with the powerful official and statecraft scholar He Changling; but although he was a conscientious scholar, Zuo failed the senior-level *jinshi* examinations three times in the 1830s and decided never to try for them again. Instead he worked as a tutor, studied geography and the history of China's western regions, and trained himself to be a successful experimental farmer, specializing in tea and silk production. During the Taiping uprising, he emerged as a talented military leader, fighting first in his native Hunan— where he raised, trained, and equipped his own volunteer army of five thousand men in emulation of Zeng Guofan's Xiang Army—and subsequently in Anhui, Zhejiang, and Fujian. As well as being a good general, Zuo proved to be an expert in the rehabilitation of reconquered areas, encouraging agriculture, grain storage, education, cotton growing, and the building of ships. In September 1866 Zuo was named governor-general of Shaanxi and Gansu, and ordered to suppress the Muslim uprisings there. He reached Shaanxi in the summer of 1867, only to be deflected by counterorders that he join the fight against the Nian, which he did with distinction. He finally settled in the Shaanxi capital of Xi'an in November 1868 to plan his campaign.

Zuo approached the task of defeating the northwest Muslims, which had baffled his predecessors, with a practical and patient mind. He took advantage of his own studies of the western regions of China and benefitted, too, from talks he had had long before with Commissioner Lin Zexu after Lin's return from post–Opium War exile in Ili. But of greatest benefit to Zuo, besides his experiences as army commander and practical farmer, were the long discussions and the exchanges of letters he had with a local scholar who had served as Lin Zexu's secretary and had long lived in Shaanxi. This man told Zuo Zongtang: "You must take your time. Advance only when you have plenty of food and well-trained soldiers. You may just as well plan your campaign on a three-year basis. . . . Once you are ready to strike, hit the meanest Muslim leader hard. Deal with him firmly, without mercy. When the others become quite frightened by the punishment he receives, then you can accept their surrender."[15]

From Zuo's subsequent actions, we can tell that he fastened on Ma Hua-long as that "meanest Muslim leader" who had to be broken first. Ma had established a powerful base in the region of Jinjibao, south of Ningxia, protected by a network of ditches and over five hundred forts. Ma was revered as a leading exponent of the New Teachings and regarded by many of his followers as an incarnation of the holy spirit, equal in power to the prophet Muhammad himself. Accordingly, the Muslims fought with devoted tenacity. Even after Zuo had assembled and supplied adequate troops, the siege of Jinjibao took sixteen months and cost Zuo the life of his finest commander. Only when the Muslim defenders had been reduced to eating grasses, then hides, and finally the bodies of dead comrades did Ma Hualong surrender in March 1871. He and his family were executed by slicing; more than eighty of his "officials" were also killed; and thousands of Muslim merchants, women, and children were transported to other cities or exiled to northern Manchuria. Settlement in Jinjibao was forbidden to all Muslims.

Thereafter the campaign moved inexorably to its conclusion. Zuo was now subsidized with money that he persuaded the court to divert from other provinces to himself, by substantial loans he floated with foreign trad-ers or with the customs service, and with soldiers' rations and horses' fodder supplied by the military farms he had insisted on founding. He marched his forces westward along the well-traveled caravan trade route to Lanzhou, where he established an arsenal and planted more crops to feed his armies. Still refusing the court's order that he hurry, Zuo prepared with meticulous calm for the final assault on the northwest Gansu city of Suzhou, which he took in November 1873, killing most of the defenders and burning large areas within the walls. Although some of the Muslim rebels fled even farther west to Hami and would take years more to conquer, the provinces of China proper were now pacified. For the first time since 1850, China could once again, with the ambiguous exception of the treaty ports, be considered uni-fied under Qing rule.

CHAPTER 9

Restoration
through Reform

CONFUCIAN REFORM

What was truly remarkable, after this long series of challenges, was that the Qing dynasty did not collapse right away, but managed to survive for the whole of the nineteenth century and on until 1912. In partial explanation, Qing statesmen described this survival as a "restoration" *(zhongxing),* a venerable phrase frequently applied to other dynasties that had managed to weather waves of crises and restore moral and political order to the empire. The idea of restoration had both a nostalgic and a bittersweet ring to it: those past restorations, although significant, had been impermanent, for each of the "restored" dynasties had eventually passed away. Unlike those of the past, moreover, the Qing restoration took place without strong imperial leadership. Emperor Tongzhi, whose name is given to this restoration period, was only five years old at his accession to the throne in 1861, and died in 1875 before having had a chance to exercise personal power. His "reign" was presided over by his mother Cixi, acting as regent, by his uncle Prince Gong (who had been forced to negotiate with the Westerners in 1860 when the rest of the court fled Peking), by one or two influential grand councilors, but above all by an exceptional group of provincial officials who had risen to prominence fighting the Taiping, the Nian, or the Muslim rebels. Zeng Guofan, Li Hongzhang, and Zuo Zong-tang were probably the best known of these, but there were scores of others of comparable skill. Acting sometimes in concert and sometimes independently, these officials managed to reinvest the Qing dynasty with a sense of purpose, shore up the economy, and develop significant new institutions.

This was a remarkable achievement in the context of what had appeared to be a disintegrating Chinese state.

Qing officials, as we have seen, had explored all varieties of military mobilization in order to crush the rebel regimes: they had used the Eight Banner and Green Standard armies, local gentry-led militia, and semiprivate regional armies like the Xiang and the Huai; they had also developed military-agricultural bases as well as defensive perimeters of waterways and forts, and had made selective use of Western officers and mercenary troops. But all that was mere preamble to what was considered the great central task: the Tongzhi Restoration statesmen sought nothing less than the re-establishment of the basic values of Confucian government.

The most important representative of this restoration attitude was the Hunanese scholar-general Zeng Guofan. Born in 1811 to a minor gentry family of modest means, Zeng studied the Chinese classical canon tenaciously and managed to obtain the *jinshi* degree in 1838. He was admitted to the Hanlin Academy in Peking and soon became known as an expert on problems of ritual and deportment. Zeng lived a simple life on a small salary, often having to borrow money from the wealthier Hunanese in the capital to pay for the expenses of his own household and to ensure the adequate education of his younger brothers. It was only when he was appointed to supervise the provincial examinations in Sichuan that he became financially well off: so many eager families gave him "gifts" that he was able to pay off all his debts.

The Confucian doctrine that Zeng espoused was an austere yet eclectic one that sought to reconcile three approaches to Confucian truth. One approach insisted on the primacy of moral principle and personal ethical values acquired through education; one espoused the methods of textual scrutiny and rigor that had come to dominate *kaozheng* thinking in Qianlong's reign; one believed in the "practical" learning of statecraft thinkers like He Changling, seeking a sturdy foundation on which to rebuild a sound and honest administrative structure.

Zeng's synthesis was arrived at after years of study and reflection during the dark days that followed China's defeat in the Opium War. Over these years, he engaged in prolonged periods of meditation and kept a meticulous diary in which he jotted notes on his readings along with reflections on his own behavior and attitudes. A sample passage shows the frankness of Zeng's Confucian self-assessments:

> Got up too late, and felt restless all day long. Read the *Book of Changes,* but could not concentrate. Then I decided to practice quiet sitting. But after a little while, I fell asleep. How could I have become so lazy? Some friends came

in the afternoon to show me some of their literary work. I praised them very highly, but deep in my heart I didn't think they were well written at all. I have done this many times lately. I must be sick. How can people value my words anymore if I praise them every day? I have not only deceived my friends but have also deceived myself. I must get rid of this bad habit. At night, read *The Book of Changes*. Wrote two poems before going to bed.[1]

The endless demands of the Taiping war destroyed the pattern of moral reflection and scholarship to which Zeng would have liked to devote his life, and he was now forced to think through his values in a new way. Convinced that a kind of spiritual collapse lay behind the mid-Qing crises, Zeng's approach to restoration was to rebuild schools and reinstitute a strict Confucian curriculum. He wished to encourage able students to take the conventional exams rather than purchase honorary degrees and titles from the Qing government, which had been selling them by the thousands in an attempt to raise more revenue to meet military costs. He compiled and published lists of those who had died righteously opposing the rebels, so that their example would live on for future generations. Like other provincial leaders of the time, he also tried to restore order to agricultural work. His plan was to return ousted landlords to their original holdings and reassess land taxes, while attempting to prevent exploitation of long-term tenants. He aimed also to resettle the millions of refugees whose lives had been wrecked over the years by counter-marching armies. So great had been the devastation in east and central China that for decades thereafter what had been the most densely populated and prosperous parts of China were drawing numerous emigrants from western and northern provinces.

These policies had the general support of the central government in Peking, but since revenues were short and many problems clamored for attention, Zeng and his colleagues in the provinces were left a free hand. Still there was an obvious coherence to their programs, since so many of these officials owed their careers to Zeng Guofan himself. He had originally hired some to help him manage his Xiang Army and others to assist in running local finances or rebuilding judicial systems and famine-relief services. Zeng had developed a careful system of interviews and rankings to help him choose these staff members: true to his principles, he tried to gauge their honesty, efficiency, and intellectual prowess before hiring them; he always rejected those who were opium addicts, boastful, shifty-eyed, or coarse in speech and manner. By the 1870s, dozens of Zeng's former staff had been promoted by the central government to substantive office. It was a tribute to Zeng's loyalty to the Qing that he did not try to exploit this situation and build up his own power base, or seize power in his own name.

Despite the weight Zeng placed on traditional scholarly and moral values, he was not a simple-minded conservative. For instance, he not only encouraged the use of the Western-officered Ever-Victorious Army, he was also quick to see the value of making selective use of Western technology. The first person to present Zeng with convincing arguments for such a policy was the scholar Feng Guifen. The two men had a good deal in common, since Feng was also a *jinshi* degree holder (class of 1840) who had served in the Hanlin Academy. Feng's experience of warfare had developed during the mid-1850s, when he led a volunteer corps against the Taiping in defense of his native Suzhou; in 1860 he had moved to Shanghai, where he was impressed by the fire power wielded by the Westerners.

In a series of essays written in 1860, which he presented to Zeng the following year, Feng argued that China must learn to "strengthen itself" *(ziqiang)* by including foreign languages, mathematics, and science in the curriculum: Chinese students excelling in these subjects should be granted the provincial examination degree. China was a hundred times larger than France and two hundred times larger than England, Feng wrote, so "why are they small and yet strong? Why are we large and yet weak?" The answer lay in the greater skills of foreigners in four main areas: utilizing all their manpower resources, exploiting their soil to the full, maintaining close bonds between ruler and subjects, and ensuring "the necessary accord of word with deed." In order to start building China's strength, Feng argued, "what we then have to learn from the barbarians is only one thing, solid ships and effective guns."[2] This could be achieved by establishing shipyards and arsenals in selected ports, and by hiring foreign advisers to train Chinese artisans to manufacture such wares in China. Since Feng felt that "the intelligence and wisdom of the Chinese are necessarily superior to those of the various barbarians," the conclusion was clear: China would first learn from foreigners, then equal them, and finally surpass them.

A year later, in a diary entry of June 1862, Zeng Guofan recorded that he had told his staff members: "If we wish to find a method of self-strengthening, we should begin by considering the reform of government service and the securing of men of ability as urgent tasks, and then regard learning to make explosive shells and steamships and other instruments as the work of first importance."[3] Later that year, Zeng directed the staff at his military camp at Anqing to experiment with building a small steamboat. Its performance was disappointing, but Zeng did not give up. Instead, making a remarkable mental leap for someone of his background, he ordered thirty-five-year-old Yung Wing* to travel to the United States and buy the

---

*This is the Cantonese romanization that Yung himself used during his life.

machinery necessary for establishing a small arsenal in China. The choice of Yung was a shrewd one, for this man, born to a poor family near Macao and educated at missionary schools there and in Hong Kong, had first traveled to the United States in 1847. After three years of preparatory school in Massachusetts, Yung had worked his way through Yale and received his B.A. in 1854, becoming the first Chinese to graduate from an American university.

True to his proven methods of assessing character, Zeng had begun his first interview with Yung by simply staring at him for minutes on end, in total silence, a slight smile on his face. But once he had decided to trust Yung, Zeng went all the way, giving him 68,000 taels in cash from the Canton and Shanghai treasuries to purchase the basic tools needed to establish a machine shop in China. After Yung Wing had traveled to Europe and made preliminary estimates and enquiries—en route he saw the Suez Canal being built and realized how much it would speed travel to China— he continued on to the United States, which he reached in the spring of 1864.

With the Civil War raging, it was hard to find an American firm that would fill the Chinese order, but at last the Putnam Machine Company in Fitchburg, Massachusetts, agreed to take on the work. Leaving an American engineer he had met in China to supervise the technical details, Yung attended his tenth class reunion and, as a naturalized American citizen, volunteered his services to the Union in the Civil War. His offer was courteously declined. He then arranged for the shipment of the machinery from New York directly to Shanghai, although he himself returned to China via San Francisco, Hawaii, and Yokohama. Yung's circumnavigation of the globe while on official business marked a new stage for an employee of the Qing.

Zeng Guofan, who had been appointed to suppress the Nian rebels after defeating the Taiping, came to inspect the new machine tools, which had been combined with other equipment purchased by his former staff members and installed at a new arsenal near Shanghai. According to Yung Wing, Zeng "stood and watched [the machine's] automatic movement with unabashed delight, for this was the first time he had seen machinery and how it worked."[4] The machines were first used to make guns and cannon; but by 1868, with the help of Western technicians and special grants from the foreign customs dues, a Chinese-built hull and boiler were successfully combined with a refurbished foreign steam engine, and the SS *Tianqi* ("The Auspicious") was launched. A second arsenal and shipyard was established at Fuzhou in Fujian province by Zuo Zongtang, shortly before he was transferred to the northwest to suppress the Muslim rebels. At both the

Shanghai and Fuzhou arsenals, schools for the study of mechanical skills and navigation were founded under the direction of foreign advisers, and translation projects for technical works were started on an ambitious scale.

An English visitor to the arsenals, despite a sarcastic note, could not conceal his surprise at the success of these ventures and their applicability to China's needs in both peace and war: "Already several transports carrying guns, and gunboats, have been successfully launched from the dockyard, and others are rapidly approaching completion. The former vessels have been employed in carrying the imperial grain to the north, and although they are manned and officered by natives, it is noteworthy that no accident has yet befallen any of them."[5] It seemed as if a methodical program of such self-strengthening might indeed combine with Confucian inner values to produce a revivified state and economy for the Qing.

DEFINING FOREIGN POLICY

The events of the 1850s had forced China's leaders to acknowledge the existence of a wider world, and they slowly developed a number of devices to help them interact with it. The first of these had been the foreign-managed Inspectorate of Customs, created in 1854 as a response to the threat of Taiping attack on Shanghai, and designed to collect tariffs equitably and generate new revenues for the Qing from the import dues on foreign goods. The allied occupation of Peking in 1860 and the court's flight to Manchuria necessitated a second institution that would provide some more formal means of negotiating with foreigners. The Qing solution, after protracted debate, was to establish a special new agency in 1861: the Office for the Management of the Business of All Foreign Countries, usually known by its Chinese abbreviation, the Zongli Yamen. This was the first significant institutional innovation in the central Peking bureaucracy that the Qing had made since Emperor Yongzheng created the nucleus of the Grand Council in 1729.

The Zongli Yamen was supervised by a controlling board of five senior officials (initially all Manchus), among whom the emperor's uncle, Prince Gong, was the *de facto* leader. They were aided by twenty-four secretaries, sixteen of whom were drawn from the various ministries in Peking and eight from the Grand Council staff. In their discussions on establishing the new agency, Qing officials reiterated that it was only to be a temporary institution, maintained until the current foreign and domestic crises had passed. Prince Gong had also assured the emperor that he would keep the premises of the new agency modest, like a residence for the emissaries of tributary states. So although foreigners would be conducting business there, the new Zongli Yamen would carry, in Gong's words, "the hidden meaning that it cannot have a standing equal to that of other traditional government offices, thus preserving the distinction between China and foreign countries."[6] In keeping with this decision, the building finally chosen was a dilapidated one, small and old, a former office of the Department of Iron Coins located in the eastern part of the imperial city. But with an imposing new front gate added to reassure foreigners that the Zongli Yamen would indeed perform important functions, the structure was opened for business on November 11, 1861.

Prince Gong, the most important Manchu to emerge as a reformer in the Tongzhi Restoration period, was only twenty-eight. Bitterly antiforeign as a youth, he had moved gradually to a position of patient wariness and eventually to open respect for the West. He was particularly impressed that Western troops had abandoned Peking after looting the Summer Palace and forcing him to sign the Convention of Peking. "This shows," he felt, "that they do not covet our territory and people. Hence we can still through faithfulness and justice tame and control them while we ourselves strive towards recovery."[7] As an uncle of the reigning boy emperor Tongzhi and a trusted adviser to the empress dowager and regent Cixi, he endowed the new Zongli Yamen with considerable prestige. The bulk of the brainwork, however, was probably carried out by his talented second-in-command, Wenxiang. Born in 1818, the son of a lowly clerk in the plain-red Manchu banner, Wenxiang had passed his *jinshi* exams in 1845, and been active in the defense of Peking against both the anticipated Taiping attack of 1853 and the disastrous British one of 1860. His prestige was also great, despite his humble beginnings, since he served concurrently as grand councilor and minister of war.

Two early examples of Prince Gong's and Wenxiang's work in the Zongli Yamen show different aspects of the new foreign-policy methods of the Qing, and how much things had changed since the era of the *Lady Hughes* and the *Emily:* one, the hiring of the Lay-Osborn Flotilla, was something of a disaster; the other, the adjudication of rights over Prussia, was a considerable triumph.

The Lay-Osborn Flotilla had its origins in 1862, when a series of Taiping victories in coastal Zhejiang made the Qing court fear they might lose control at sea to the rebels. Accordingly, the Zongli Yamen was ordered to purchase a fleet in England and to hire the officers and crew necessary to man it. As their intermediary, the Zongli Yamen chose the current head of the Inspectorate of Customs, Horatio Nelson Lay, and made available to him a sum of 1,295,000 taels. With this money Lay arranged the purchase of seven steamers and one store ship, to be commanded by a captain in the Royal Navy, Sherard Osborn. Britain's Foreign Office was willing to allow its seamen to serve with the fleet only if they were under a specific foreign flag. Since the Qing, like all prior Chinese dynasties, had no national flag, Prince Gong informed the British that the Qing would create a flag—a triangular yellow one with a dragon at the center.

Captain Osborn reached Shanghai with his fleet in September 1863, but was confronted at once with a complex problem. Prince Gong instructed Osborn to serve as assistant commander in chief of the fleet, under the direction of a Chinese admiral. In tactical operations, Osborn would obey the orders of the Qing field commanders—who at this time were Zeng Guofan and Li Hongzhang—although Osborn himself would be in control of all foreigners within the fleet. The trouble here was that under the initial agreement with Lay, signed in England and assumed to coincide with Qing intentions, Osborn was "to have entire control over all vessels of European construction." He was also to draw his orders only from the emperor, as those were relayed via Lay, and undertook "not to attend to any orders conveyed through any other channel."[8]

The result was an impasse, since none of the parties would yield. Osborn was a man of high principles who felt he had been made a firm promise of command. Lay was a man of immense conceit and arrogance (one of his most famous remarks was that "the notion of a gentleman acting *under* an Asiatic barbarian is preposterous").[9] And the Zongli Yamen could not afford to be seen as weak toward foreigners. After weeks of inconclusive bargaining, the Zongli Yamen acknowledged the hopelessness of the situation by paying off Captain Osborn and his crews and sending them home. Both the Americans and the Qing shared fears that the ships might fall into the wrong hands—either to the Southern Confederacy or to the Taiping. Accordingly the British undertook to sell the ships to their own merchant companies. Lay was given a generous cash settlement and dismissed from his service with the Inspectorate of Customs.

The second experiment of the Zongli Yamen in the realm of international sovereignty was more successful. Since its publication in 1836, Henry Wheaton's *Elements of International Law* had become a standard text in the Western diplomatic community. In 1862 the Zongli Yamen had studied a translation of the section on foreign legations. One year later they were offered a draft of the entire work, translated into Chinese by W. A. P. Martin, a missionary from Indiana with long service in Ningbo and Shanghai. After some discussion, they accepted the translation, although Prince Gong ordered his staff to revise it stylistically into a more elegant literary form.

Prince Gong, discussing the translation with the court, observed that he had told the Westerners "that China had her own institutions and systems, and did not feel free to consult foreign books." He took this line, said Gong, "to forestall their demand that we act according to the said book."[10] But when a conflict from the other side of the world—the Prussian-Danish War of 1864—spread into Chinese territorial waters with the seizure by a Prussian warship of three Danish merchant ships at the Dagu anchorage, Prince Gong and his colleagues used Wheaton to good effect. By combining their new knowledge of the accepted definitions of a nation's territorial waters (which Martin had translated as "ocean area within the jurisdiction of a nation") with an examination of China's existing treaties with Prussia, they forced the Prussian minister not only to release the three Danish ships, but to pay China compensation of $1,500. Now noting that although "the said book on foreign laws and regulations is not basically in agreement with the Chinese systems, it nevertheless contains sporadic useful points,"[11] Prince Gong put up 500 taels to publish Wheaton and distributed three hundred copies to provincial officials. Perhaps from fear of conservative backlash, he still declined to write a preface to the volume in his own name.

In 1862 Wenxiang and Prince Gong also obtained the court's permission to open an interpreter's school in Peking. Its small body of students, aged fourteen or less, would be chosen from each of the eight banners and paid a stipend to learn English and French. (Russian had been taught for many years in Peking in a small separate school.) The decision to draw students from the eight banners reflected ongoing attempts to reassure the more conservative Manchus that the former conquerors of the Ming would continue to have a guiding hand over the dictates of foreign-policy work. But in fact the system spread rapidly and was not confined to Manchus. New government-sponsored language schools opened in Shanghai, Canton, and Fuzhou, and in 1867 Prince Gong and Wenxiang began a campaign to transform the Peking school for interpreters into a full-fledged college. They proposed adding to the curriculum such subjects as mathematics, chemistry, geology, mechanics, and international law, and hiring foreigners as instructors. Despite vigorous protests from conservative senior officials that the Chinese had no need for "barbarians as teachers" to instruct them in "trifling arts," and that even the great emperor Kangxi two hundred years before had "used their methods [but] actually hated them," the reformers carried the day. The college, with its new curriculum, was opened in February 1867 under the direction of one of China's pioneering geographers and historians, Xu Jiyu.

The choice of Xu was a good one, and again showed that a new kind of thinking was gaining some ground in China. Xu had learned about the

West from American missionaries in Fujian province in the 1840s, and had been one of the earliest appointees to the Zongli Yamen staff. Xu had written glowingly about the West, especially the United States, with its curious kingless government: "The public organs are entrusted to public opinion. There has never been a system of this sort in ancient or modern times. This is really a wonder." Xu had also praised George Washington as "an extraordinary man," superior even to China's own cultural heroes in valor and strategic cunning: "Of all the famous Westerners of ancient and modern times," Xu asked rhetorically, "can Washington be placed in any position but first?"[12] Not surprisingly, the Americans in China were delighted at his appointment, which seemed an excellent omen for future diplomatic relations. The United States' minister to China, Anson Burlingame, gave Xu a copy of Gilbert Stuart's famous portrait of Washington, and Xu's praises of Washington were inscribed on a block of granite from Fujian province and placed at the three-hundred-foot level of the Washington Monument. When Xu retired for health reasons in 1869, he was succeeded by W. A. P. Martin, the missionary scholar who had translated Wheaton on international on international law in 1863, and had assembled an able group of Chinese scientists and mathematicians to help translate other Western works.

Because it provided much needed funds, the parallel development of the Qing Imperial Maritime Customs was essential to these projects. Under the direction of the capable Robert Hart, who was born in Northern Ireland and had served in the British consulates at Ningbo and Canton before transferring his services to the Qing, the Imperial Maritime Customs was erected on the foundation of the small foreign Inspectorate of 1854, and in the 1860s became an internationally staffed bureaucracy with agencies in all the treaty ports. Hart was able to make huge sums of money available to the Peking government, some of which supported the college and other modernizing projects. Equally important, his staff accumulated accurate statistics on trade patterns and local conditions all over China.

After so many years of warfare and misunderstanding, the later 1860s seemed to be promising ones for cooperation between China and the foreign powers. With revision of the Tianjin treaty of 1858 stipulated to take place in 1868, the Zongli Yamen officials (with the court's cooperation) moved carefully and skillfully in their discussions with the British, who were represented by their articulate, intelligent minister Rutherford Alcock. Both Alcock and Hart submitted position papers to the Zongli Yamen on the types of change they thought China should undertake in administration, education, and budgetary planning. The ministers of the foreign diplomatic community moved peacefully into spacious quarters in Peking, and the question of audiences and kowtowing was shelved by the simple fact that

Tongzhi, because of his youth, gave no audiences. (Only in 1873 was the problem solved, without crisis, when the Qing allowed the foreigners to follow their own customs in paying homage to the emperor.) A group of senior Qing officials traveled to Europe with Hart to observe government systems there, and the Qing court assigned Anson Burlingame, the former U.S. minister to China, as the Chinese representative in treaty discussions in the United States and Europe.

Hosts of difficult questions remained, however, concerning missionary and trading rights, the building of railways and telegraphs, the control of opium sales, the exact status of foreign courts on Chinese soil, and the navigation of internal waterways. After the opening of the Suez Canal in 1869, China was suddenly much nearer to Europe, and old greeds and antagonisms that had seemed to slumber appeared once again. To the anger and disappointment of both Alcock and the veteran Zongli Yamen official Wenxiang, their delicate compromises for treaty revision were rejected by a majority vote in the British House of Commons in 1870, wasting years of work. Hart was dismayed and Alcock depressed. Alcock went to call on Wenxiang, to whom he complained of the constant accusations by the British merchant community of being too pliable with the Chinese. With the Zongli Yamen's own plans also lying in ruins, Wenxiang responded: "Yes, no doubt; I see what your newspapers say sometimes. I, too, am accused of being a renegade and only wearing Chinese clothes."[13]

THE MISSIONARY PRESENCE

Throughout the 1860s, as officials from the Zongli Yamen struggled to understand their new world and to adjust to it, violence by the Chinese against the Western missionaries formed a harsh accompaniment. In Sichuan and Guizhou and Guangdong, in the rich Grand Canal commercial city of Yangzhou and the barren hills of Shaanxi, missionaries and their converts were harassed, beaten, and occasionally killed, their property threatened or destroyed. Finally, in the summer of 1870 in Tianjin, the very city that had given its name to the 1858 treaties and where many foreign diplomats had made their homes during the protracted negotiations over residence in Peking, the violence burst into hideous prominence.

For months rumors had spread through the city that the Christians had been maiming and torturing children, and practicing every kind of sexual aberration. The Catholics, whose huge new Tianjin church had been built— despite public protest—on the site of a former imperial park and temple, came in for the worst abuse. Seeing himself as the Catholics' main protector,

the French consul Henri Fontanier protested several times to the city officials: but they did little to calm the agitation, and large crowds of Chinese
continued to menace the foreigners. Frustrated and angry, Fontanier, two
pistols tucked into his belt and accompanied by an aide with a drawn sword,
rushed into the magistrate's yamen. Furious at the Chinese magistrate's
bland prevarication, Fontanier drew one pistol and fired; missing the magistrate, he killed a bystander. A crowd of hostile Chinese, already assembled
outside the office, exploded with their own rage. Fontanier and his aide
were killed along with several French traders and their wives. The church
was burned. The convent of the Catholic Sisters of Mercy was broken into
by a mob, and the ten sisters there were attacked, stripped, and killed. By
day's end, sixteen French men and women were dead, along with three
Russians whom the crowd had thought were French.

The French demand for vengeance came swiftly, and the Qing were
forced to respond. Involved in the investigations were Prince Gong and
officials of the Zongli Yamen, along with the ailing Zeng Guofan, who as
governor-general of the Hebei region had titular jurisdiction over Tianjin,
and Li Hongzhang, who was to succeed Zeng. After investigation under
torture, sixteen Chinese were found guilty of the attacks and executed. The
exact matching of the number of these "criminals" to the French dead was
too neat, suggesting the concept of "an eye for an eye" rather than any
thorough search for proof of guilt. The Chinese also agreed to pay reparations of 250,000 taels, the money to go in part to the rebuilding of the church
and in part to the families of the dead civilians. The prefect and magistrate
of the Tianjin region were condemned to exile for life on the Amur River,
and the Qing agreed to send a mission of apology to France. It was generally
felt that the French would have held out for harsher terms had they not,
since that same summer of 1870, been wholly distracted from Asian events
by the outbreak of the Franco-Prussian War.

The Tianjin "massacre," as the foreigners soon came to call it, was but
the bloodiest example of a series of clashes that continued throughout the
century. These violent outbreaks revealed the deep fissures that lay between
the Christian effort at conversion and the Chinese Confucian gentry's sense
of their own worth and authority. It was often highly educated Chinese
who wrote the scurrilous, provocative posters and pamphlets attacking the
missionaries, and who assembled the crowds prior to many incidents. Behind
Chinese exaggerations of Christian excesses lay a complex web of truths that
made their exhortations effective: the Christian missionaries did preach a
new doctrine at variance with Confucianism, they did seek to penetrate ever
deeper into China's interior, they protected Chinese converts engaged in
lawsuits with non-Christian Chinese, they developed their own educational

system, and they often misrepresented real-estate deals in which they adapted private homes to churches. Furthermore, in their zeal to save souls, missionaries often accepted, or even sought out, fatally ill infants abandoned by their parents, so that they could baptize them before they died. When the burial grounds of these tiny corpses were dug up by hostile Chinese, it inevitably led to highly charged emotional responses.

Yet the story of the Christian mission movement in China was not just one of exploitation, misunderstanding, and hostility. The missionaries in China represented a wide range of nationalities and religious backgrounds. Besides the Jesuits, other Catholic priests, and members of the mendicant orders, there were a bewildering number of Protestant groupings—over thirty by 1865. These ranged from the original London Missionary Society of 1795 and the American Board of Commissioners for Foreign Missions, founded in 1810, to separate organizations of Baptists, Southern Baptists, Presbyterians, Methodists, Episcopalians, and Wesleyans. The home bases of these groups were established variously in England, the United States, Sweden, France, the German states, Switzerland, and Holland. Cumulatively, the Catholics and Protestants had deep and subtle effects on Chinese society, particularly in relation to education and in the efforts that they made to raise the status of Chinese women.

In education, the impact of the mission movement came through the spread of Christian texts, the publication of general historical or scientific works, the development of schools, and the introduction of new techniques of medicine. Christian texts spread swiftly in parts of China; we have seen how the future Taiping leader Hong Xiuquan received inspiration from the tracts handed out in and around Canton. Preliminary Chinese translations of the Bible had been finished as early as the 1820s. Careful revisions, supervised by groups of missionaries, were circulating widely in China by 1850, along with a full Manchu version of the New Testament. Special editions of the Bible, in romanization, were prepared for use in the Ningbo, Amoy, and Fuzhou dialect areas and among the Hakkas of the southeast. The development of Western-style printing presses (but using Chinese movable type) greatly aided the task of dissemination undertaken by both Catholics and Protestants.

The wide circulation of works on Western government and history began in the later 1830s, often by way of journals printed by missionary groups in Canton or Shanghai. These works systematically placed China in a world context and made it possible for Chinese scholars to view their country's history in a new way. From such works, introduced to him by the American missionary David Abeel in Amoy during the mid-1840s, the future head of the Peking college, Xu Jiyu, received his first idea of the range of Western history.

The introduction of scientific and technical texts in translation was given extra impetus by the training schools that were developed along with the new arsenals opened during the first phase of the self-strengthening movement. In 1865 Zeng Guofan himself wrote an approving preface to Euclid's *Elements of Geometry,* translated jointly by the Chinese mathematician Li Shanlan and by the British missionary Alexander Wylie. Zeng noted that this work completed the pioneering translation of Euclid's first six books done by the Jesuit Matteo Ricci over two hundred fifty years before. The completed translation, wrote Zeng, made a crucial supplement to preexisting Chinese works on mathematics: although traditional Chinese mathematical learning could not be dispensed with, one could not deny that the student "sticking blindly" to it "after a lifetime spent in practical mathematics knows his rules indeed, but knows nothing of the reason for them, so that mathematics are thought by some an impossible study." Euclid, as presented by Ricci, Li, and Wylie, traced not methods but *principles,* "presented under the headings of point, line, surface and solid." A clear understanding of these elements, said Zeng, "will enable the student to solve the manifold problems of number."[14] During the 1860s, Wylie and various collaborators also wrote, or translated into Chinese, treatises on mechanics, algebra, differential calculus, astronomy, and logarithmic tables. Equally important and productive was the long collaboration between the English missionary John Fryer and the Chinese scholar-mathematician Xu Shou. Working patiently together over decades, they were able to compile and publish a systematic and logical rendering of the entire vocabulary of chemistry into the Chinese language, backing this labor up with study guides and a journal, and making possible a rapid growth in many areas of industrial applied chemistry. By the late 1870s, other Western scholars had prepared Chinese texts on electricity, the steam engine, photography, lathes, trigonometrical surveying, and navigation.

The number of mission schools in China increased steadily throughout the nineteenth century, spreading upcoast and inland with the opening of each new treaty port. Often run by individual missionaries or by a tiny handful of teachers, these schools not only prepared young Chinese for English-speaking jobs in the treaty ports, but were designed to lead Chinese children to an understanding of Christian principles and, if possible, to convert the youngsters and train them for later work alongside the Western missionaries. Although viewed with suspicion by traditional Chinese teachers, the great significance of these schools was that they offered some form of basic education to poor Chinese, both boys and girls, who otherwise would have received none. Reciprocal benefits were also achieved. It was by working closely with Chinese scholarly collaborators that the Scottish missionary scholar James Legge was able to complete the first full translation of the Chinese Four Books and Five Classics into fluent and accurate English, immeasurably aiding the growth of Sinological studies overseas.

Because the mission schools were unfamiliar and objects of local fears, the missionary-teachers often had to lure students with offers of free food and housing, medical care, and even clothing and cash subsidies. Such was the case at the mission school in the early treaty port of Ningbo, which admitted thirty boys in 1844 and managed to graduate a first class of eight in 1850. Of these eight, one stayed to teach in the school, one went on to study medicine, and four were hired to work with the Presbyterian printing press. Qilu School in Shandong province opened with only eight pupils in 1864 and graduated its first three in 1877. Their studies had included a grounding in Chinese classics and Christian ethics, along with English, mathematics, music, and geography, and all three graduates went on to teach or become missionary assistants. Yung Wing, later to become Zeng's assistant in buying foreign machinery, had been tutored from the age of seven to twelve by a missionary's wife in a mixed primary school in Macao. He then enrolled in a Macao missionary school at the age of thirteen to study English, Chinese, geography, and arithmetic with five others. By 1847 Yung was well enough prepared to travel to the United States, with funds provided by local Western merchants and free passage on a tea clipper.

Like other young Chinese of his day, Yung Wing had been impressed by what he saw of Western medicine and initially hoped to become a doctor. Western missionaries were quick to note the impact of medical knowledge on the Chinese, and it was the "medical missionaries" who had the greatest early successes in gaining converts. It was not that China lacked medical sophistication of its own—there was a long tradition of diagnosis by study of the pulses, and of treatment through extracts of plants, animal derivatives, minerals, and acupuncture—but by the early nineteenth century the West had much greater knowledge of anatomy and more sophisticated skills in surgery. Although there were always some fatalities, which could cause local hostility or lawsuits, Western doctors proved especially successful in removing tumors and curing diseases of the eyes such as cataracts. By the 1860s, both missionary and unaffiliated doctors were beginning to build hospitals with money given by Western philanthropists or raised by subscription from local Chinese. Initially, these buildings were concentrated, of necessity, in the treaty ports, as were such accompanying centers as homes for the blind, for lepers, and for the insane. Other missionaries introduced new seed strains to Chinese farmers, and new varieties of fruits and plants; some also applied their energies to reforestation projects, attempting to halt the serious erosion that had been causing havoc on China's now barren hillsides.

Through their texts, their presses, their schools, and their hospitals, the efforts of missionaries affected Chinese thought and practice. The strength of that influence is impossible to calculate, but the missionaries did offer the Chinese a new range of options, a new way of looking at the world. The same was true in the broader world of family structures and the roles of women. Several of the early missionaries were women, and the wives of dozens of male missionaries also played an active role in their communities. Yung Wing recalled his first teacher, a white woman whom he encountered in 1835, as having "prominent features which were strong and assertive; her eyes were of clear blue lustre, somewhat deep set. She had thin lips, supported by a square chin . . . . Her features taken collectively indicated great determination and will power. As she came forward to welcome me in her long and full flowing white dress (the interview took place in the summer), surmounted by two large globe sleeves which were fashionable at the time and which lent her an exaggerated appearance, I remember most vividly I was no less puzzled than stunned. I actually trembled all over with fear at her imposing proportions—having never in my life seen such a peculiar and odd fashion. I clung to my father in fear."[15]

Yet the fear could be transcended. Thousands of Chinese learned to study from, work with, be treated by, even become friends of Westerners. The Western women presented options of public work and careers that had seemed impossible to Chinese women. As the century progressed and mission families moved deep into the interior, they created their own versions of Western domestic worlds and values. They shared these with Chinese women, introducing them to new ideas of hygiene, cuisine, and child raising. They protested foot-binding, commiserated over opium addiction, offered religion and education as sources of solace and change. Some of the bolder ones offered a new perspective on social hierarchies and sexual subordination.

Robert Hart, later the revered inspector-general of the Imperial Maritime Customs, as a young man in the Ningbo and Canton of the 1850s had kept a Chinese mistress who bore him three children. It was "a common practice for unmarried Englishmen resident in China to keep a Chinese girl," he wrote later in a confidential legal deposition, "and I did as others did."[16] When it came time for him to wed a lady of good British family, he paid off the Chinese woman with $3,000 and shipped their children off to England so they would not embarrass him with their presence. Yet such double standards did not always prevail in personal relations between Westerners and Chinese. Yung Wing married an American woman from Hartford, who bore him two children, both of whom enrolled at Yale University. And in his memoirs Yung recalled vividly how his first formidable Western teacher had also been helping three blind Chinese girls to read in Braille, doing everything she could to save them from the bleak life that would have been their probable lot. By century's end, the options for some Chinese women had become broader than either Yung Wing or Robert Hart could have foreseen. In 1892 two young Chinese mission-school graduates, their names Westernized as Ida Kahn and Mary Stone, sailed to the United States and earned their medical degrees at the University of Michigan. By 1896 they were back in China and had opened their own practices. The success of these women and the faith that inspired it were a startling tribute to the power of one side of the missionary dream.

OVERSEAS CHINESE

Tens of millions of Chinese were killed or left homeless in the waves of internal rebellions, and the accompanying famine and social dislocation, that marked the mid-nineteenth century. Yet the pressures on the land continued to be unrelenting. China's population had probably reached 430,000,000 by 1850, and even though it must have dipped sharply in the 1860s, it began to climb once more in the 1870s.

One response to the scarcity of arable land was internal migration, but the Chinese had no alternative as straightforward as that of the westward migrations to the Great Plains and the Pacific Coast that marked the same period in United States history. Chinese settlers moving west or northwest came either to the high, arid plateaus of Tibet or to the vast deserts of Xinjiang, which was finally incorporated as a province of the Qing in 1884 but remained forbidding territory. Those moving southwest encountered hostile mountain tribes or the settled borders of already established kingdoms in Vietnam and Burma. Millions chose to move northeast, first to the settled arable regions of Liaodong—the staging area long before for the Manchu conquest—and then, defying all bans by the Qing state, north again into the wooded mountains and bitter cold of what is now Jilin and Heilongjiang provinces. Others braved the short sea passage to swell the number of immigrants on Taiwan, which had become thoroughly opened to Chinese settlement and agriculture by the 1850s and was named a full province in 1885. And some chose to leave the countryside and try their luck in the expanding cities—such as Hankou, Shanghai, or Tianjin—where new industries and the need for transport workers offered chances for employment, even if at pitifully low wages.

The other main response to the demographic crisis was to move out of the known Chinese world altogether and to try one's fortunes elsewhere. Those who made this choice were mostly from southeast China, and used Canton or Macao as their points of debarkation. Some were destitute farmers, some fugitives from rebel regimes, some the ambitious children of large families who saw few opportunities for advancement in Qing society. Most were men who often married just before they left China and dreamed of returning someday to their native villages, loaded with riches, so they could buy more land and expand their families' waning fortunes. They tended to focus their hopes initially on three main regions: Southeast Asia and Indonesia, the Caribbean and the northern countries of Latin America, and the western coast of the United States.

Emigration to Southeast Asia was cheapest and easiest, and many Chinese settled quickly into rice-farming or fishing communities, and into retail and commercial businesses. Even though the upper levels of economic life might be dominated by the British, the French, or the Dutch (according to the region chosen), Chinese emigrants found ample room for their entrepreneurial skills. They branched out successfully into tin mines and rubber plantations, and into shipping. Under Dutch rule in Indonesia, the Chinese served profitably as tax collectors, working under contract, and as managers of the Dutch-controlled opium monopoly.

Because so many of these new settlers came from Fujian or the Canton delta region, local community bondings and dialect groups remained important, and Chinese from similar neighborhoods tended to cluster together and support each other. Triads and other secret-society groups also flourished, setting up protection rackets, channeling opium sales, arranging cheap passages on credit, and running prostitution rings; as late as 1890, there were still few married Chinese women in the Southeast Asian communities. Despite their uneasiness about the extent of the emigration, the Qing set up a consulate in Singapore in 1873 so that they could keep closer watch on the half a million or more Chinese settlers in that area. They also tried to retain the loyalty of the richer emigrants by selling them honorary titles in the Qing hierarchy.

Latin America, too, drew large numbers of Chinese settlers, especially after 1840, when several countries in the region experienced rapid economic growth. Along with increasing opposition there to the use of slave labor, and the availability of cheap passages on steam vessels, this rapid development beckoned to the Chinese with the promise of jobs. Close to 100,000, for instance, had come to Peru by 1875, often lured by promoters and hand-bills promising them great riches. Instead of making great fortunes, most of these Chinese laid railway lines, toiled on the cotton plantations, and labored in the guano pits, where conditions were particularly vile. There, the Chinese worked in boiling heat to clear as much as 4 to 5 tons of the bird droppings in a single day, which often led to infections, lung disease, and premature death. Others worked as domestics, cigar makers, and mill-ers. Many of the Chinese had signed labor contracts without understanding their full implications, and those who fled from the areas where they were contracted to work were, if caught, forced to work in chains. There were many suicides. In Cuba, where tens of thousands of Chinese were working on the sugar plantations by the 1860s, conditions were equally bad. The Chinese were often treated more like slaves than free labor, forced to work inhuman hours on docked pay, and were similarly punished if they fled their workplaces or argued with their employers. Conditions were little better on the sugarcane and pineapple plantations of Hawaii, where thousands of Chinese had also settled.

In 1873 the Zongli Yamen initiated a new phase of foreign-policy activism by authorizing investigation commissions to report on the conditions of life and work for Chinese in both Peru and Cuba. (Yung Wing, who had just successfully concluded the purchase of $100,000 of Gatling repeating guns for the Tianjin arsenal, was a delegate on the Peruvian commission.) The two commission reports gave startling evidence of the abuses that existed not only in working conditions, but in the original procurement of the Chinese laborers. Thousands had clearly been tricked into signing up or cheated once they had done so. A great many had literally been kidnaped by procurers for the plantation owners, and held incommunicado in hulks at Macao or Canton before being shipped off. Conditions of passage were so bad—often amounting to less than 6 square feet of space per coolie "passenger"—that scores died on every voyage and Chinese "mutinies" were commonplace. From 1876 on, mainly in response to these reports, the worst abuses of the contract-labor practices were abolished and shipping proce-dures were more carefully regulated.

The first great impetus for Chinese emigration to the United States came with the gold rush of 1848–1849 in California; indeed, the first name in Chinese for San Francisco was *Jinshan,* meaning "mountain of gold." But few Chinese arrived in time to make lucrative strikes, and most of them, after working over mines already abandoned by less tenacious forerunners, slowly drifted into other lines of work. They flourished as market gardeners, storekeepers, and laundrymen, spreading along the coast from Los Angeles to Seattle. Thousands worked on the final stages of the great railway-building boom that extended the lines from California to Utah in the 1860s. The gradual Chinese migration eastward across the United States subsequently coincided with the later stages of the American move west: startled travelers on the Oregon Trail reported in their diaries seeing their first Chinese eating with chopsticks. Portland had a large Chinese population by 1880, while other settlements arose in the mountains of Wyoming Territory and along the Snake River in Idaho. After the Civil War, southern plantation owners lured many Chinese to Mississippi, Alabama, and Tennessee and tried to induce them to work fields now abandoned by freed black slaves. By the later 1880s, there were Chinese working in shoe factories in Massachusetts, cutlery plants in Pennsylvania, and steam laundries in New Jersey, and there was a sizable group of Chinese merchants in Boston.

The process of Chinese settlement in the United States was not an easy one. From early on, hostility toward the Chinese settlers was complex and profound. Part of the trouble lay in the stated desire of many Chinese, echoing those who had gone to Southeast Asia and Peru, simply to work for a few years in the United States before returning home to their families. This led the Chinese to be regarded as "sojourners" rather than true immigrants. Part of the difficulty also lay in the industrious work habits of the Chinese, which caused them to be envied for making a profit where others had failed. There was a common belief among white workers that the Chinese would always work for lower wages than those of other races and, hence, would drag down pay scales across the board. Although there was little truth in that assertion, there were occasions when employers used the Chinese as strikebreakers. Knowing little or no English, the Chinese were often ignorant of the social and economic battles into which they had been projected.

The Chinese—or "Mongols," as many whites began to call them—were also disliked or feared by Westerners because of the relative strangeness of their social customs. The Qing queues that many of the men still wore looked bizarre in the United States. Americans noted the extremely high proportion of men over women in the Chinese communities—more than 100,000 male Chinese were living in the western United States in 1880, but only 3,000 women—and, without seeking to understand the reasons, condemned the Chinese as unnatural. The singsong sound of Chinese speech, the opium-smoking proclivities of some and the yearning for drink or gambling of others, their willingness to eat what appeared to be odd or unappetizing food—all combined to build a rumor-filled climate of opinion in which Chinese wickedness and depravity were given prominence.

Two unfortunate facts lent some appearance of validity to the wilder charges. First, like Chinese emigrants in other areas, the Chinese in the

United States clung together according to dialect and locality groups. The majority of them came from within a hundred miles of Canton, and when they landed in San Francisco, most were at once incorporated into subgroups controlled by the "Six Companies." These companies had ties to Chinese secret societies and, like them, had overlapping functions as protection systems and as economic exploiters. Rival Chinese groups became involved in numerous "tong wars," battles between feuding gangs that gave the Chinese as a whole a reputation for lawlessness. Second, the crowding of Chinese into "Chinatowns" in the United States—whether in San Francisco, Los Angeles, Portland, or later in New York—compounded by scarce housing and the loneliness of thousands of single males, led to an explosive social situation, sexual frustrations, and the prevalence of disease. The irony was that anti-Chinese discriminatory legislation concerning housing, schooling, work permits, and eating establishments tended all the more to force the Chinese into Chinatowns and keep them there. Redress was not easy to find. Chinese in many states were not allowed to testify against whites in court and were forbidden to hold public-service jobs. Most had to struggle for even basic educational opportunities.

Within a few years of the first settlements in 1849, underlying tensions burst into open violence, deliberately fanned by the racist rhetoric of white workers and their political supporters. The worst examples were in California and Wyoming. In October 1871, after two policemen had been killed trying to intervene in a tong battle, a crowd smashed through the Chinatown in Los Angeles, looting shops, burning houses, and beating up any Chinese they found. The crowd ultimately killed nineteen Chinese men, women, and children and injured hundreds before the civic authorities checked them. (By a macabre coincidence the Chinese fatalities in Los Angeles exactly matched in number the French and Russians killed in the "Tianjin massacre" of 1870.) Fourteen years later in Rock Springs, Wyoming Territory, groups of poorly-off white miners first beat a Chinese miner to death with a shovel, then burned the camps of Chinese migrant workers and killed at least twenty-eight. Scores of lesser incidents occurred in the same period, playing an integral, if unfortunate, part in the "opening of the West."

Unaccustomed to recognizing the rights of any Chinese who traveled overseas, the Qing reacted slowly, although officials in the Zongli Yamen were aware of the kinds of problems that existed. In 1867 they had obtained the services of the former American minister, Anson Burlingame, as ambassador-at-large. The next year Burlingame, in language echoing the most optimistic promises of the French philosophers of a century before, passionately pleaded the cause of the Chinese in his tour across the United States and Europe. "The present enlightened Government of China has advanced steadily along the path of progress," Burlingame told his audiences. "She says now: 'Send us your wheat, your lumber, your coal, your silver, your goods from everywhere—we will take as many of them as we can. We will give you back our tea, our silk, free labor which we have sent so largely out into the world.' " His power of persuasion led the United States to sign a treaty in 1868 guaranteeing continued Chinese rights of immigration. But Burlingame also muddled the issue by promising that the Qing state was ripe for conversion to Christianity: it would only be a short while, he cried, before China invited the Western missionaries "to plant the shining cross on every hill and in every valley, for she is hospitable to fair argument."[17] Following up on Burlingame's initiative, the Qing sent diplomatic representatives to France and England in 1871 and had a full ambassador in the United States by 1878.

But political pressures against the Chinese spread from California to Washington, D.C. In a series of closely contested electoral battles between Democrats and Republicans, there was growing preoccupation with the need to limit Chinese immigration before it became a flood. In 1879 President Rutherford B. Hayes stayed true to the sense of the 1868 treaty by vetoing a bill to limit Chinese emigrants to fifteen per ship. In 1880, however, the Qing were persuaded to agree to a new treaty that authorized the United States to "regulate, limit or suspend" the flow of Chinese laborers if the American government considered such restriction "reasonable." In 1882 President Chester A. Arthur agreed to a suspension of the immigration of Chinese skilled and unskilled "laborers" for ten years, forced all Chinese then in the United States to obtain special registration certificates, and banned them from obtaining United States citizenship. In 1884 he accepted further legislation that broadened the term *laborers* to include "peddlers, hucksters and fishermen" and applied the restrictions to all those of the "Chinese race," whether they were Qing subjects or not.

So ended the dream of making the United States a haven for all the poor and oppressed of the world regardless of race, religion, or background. The passing of that dream was confirmed by successive presidents. Grover Cleveland in 1888 proclaimed the Chinese "an element ignorant of our constitution and laws, impossible of assimilation with our people, and dangerous to our peace and welfare," and endorsed new legislation that forbade reentry to Chinese laborers who had returned to China on temporary visits.[18] Benjamin Harrison, accepting the Republican nomination in the same year, spoke of his "duty to defend our civilization by excluding alien races whose ultimate assimilation with our people is neither possible nor desirable." After his election, Harrison chose as secretary of state a man committed to the view that, far from helping to develop the U.S. economy, the Chinese had brought with them "the seeds of moral and physical disease, of destitution, and of death."[19] Americans were now choosing to make judgments about Chinese inferiority that were as harsh and comprehensive as any that Qing statesmen had made about the rest of the world in the days of Qing glory.

CHAPTER 10

New Tensions in the Late Qing

SELF-STRENGTHENING AND THE JAPANESE WAR

The Confucian statesmen whose skill, integrity, and tenacity helped suppress the rebellions of the mid-nineteenth century showed how imaginatively the Chinese could respond to new challenges. Under the general banner of restoring order to the Qing Empire, they had managed to develop new structures to handle foreign relations and collect custom dues, to build modern ships and weapons, and to start teaching international law and the rudiments of modern science. "Self-strengthening" had not proved an empty slogan, but an apparently viable road to a more secure future. Progressive-minded Chinese and Manchus seemed able to work together in order to preserve the most cherished aspects of their traditional cultures by selectively adapting elements of Western learning and technology to China's needs. It was true that there remained complex problems of continuing rural militarization, new local autonomy over taxation, landlord abuses and bureaucratic corruption, and bellicose foreign powers with their military, diplomatic, and missionary encroachments. But with forceful imperial leadership and a resolute Grand Council, it appeared that the Qing dynasty might regain some of its former strength.

Unfortunately for the survival of the dynasty, forceful leadership was not forthcoming. Tongzhi, in the name of whose rule the Tongzhi Restoration of central and provincial government had been undertaken, died suddenly at the age of eighteen in January 1875, shortly after taking up power in person. The official cause of death was smallpox, but it was widely rumored that he had exhausted himself with wild living and overindulgence in the pleasure quarters of Peking. His young empress was pregnant when he died, but seems to have been excluded from the crucial meetings called by Tongzhi's mother, the empress dowager Cixi, to decide on the imperial succession.

The only way for Cixi to preserve her own power was to continue in her role as regent; accordingly she appointed her three-year-old nephew, Guangxu, as emperor, thus assuring herself of years more activity as the power behind the throne. The success of this stratagem was assured when Tongzhi's pregnant wife died that spring, her baby still unborn.* The choice of Guangxu, however, violated a fundamental law of Qing succession: Guangxu was from the same generation as Tongzhi, not from a later one, and so could not properly perform the filial ancestral ceremonies in Tongzhi's memory. Cixi silenced any overt opposition on this point by promising that when a son was born to Guangxu, that son would be adopted as Tongzhi's heir and so would be able to perform the necessary rites. One upright Confucian official committed suicide outside Tongzhi's tomb to protest Cixi's decision, but no other scholars made as dramatic an issue of their discontent. Senior bureaucrats on the whole were silent, apparently resigned to another protracted period of indirect rule by the powerful female regent.

Cixi was a complex and able woman, though also tough-minded and ruthless when she considered it necessary. She was the only woman to attain a high level of political power in China during the Qing, and was consequently blamed for many of the dynasty's woes by men who thought she should not have been in power at all. Born in 1835—her father was descended from a distinguished Manchu lineage, but held only a minor official position in the bureaucracy—Cixi was named one of Emperor Xianfeng's consorts in 1851 and became his favorite in 1856, when she bore him a son. Xianfeng discussed policy matters with her and allowed her to read incoming memorials. She accompanied him to Rehe when he fled the advancing Allies in 1860, and had herself named coregent of China in a palace coup following Xianfeng's death in 1861. Cixi's political power thenceforth sprang from her position as coregent for her son Tongzhi from 1861 to 1873, and as coregent for her nephew Guangxu from 1875 to 1889. She also was the ultimate political authority while Guangxu languished in palace seclusion—on her orders—from 1898 to 1908. Highly literate and a competent painter, Cixi kept herself well informed on all affairs of state as she sat behind a screen (for propriety's sake) and listened to her male ministers' reports. Politically conservative and financially extravagant, she nev-

---

*It is almost certain that the pregnant widow of Tongzhi was driven to suicide by Cixi, but the evidence remains disputed.

ertheless approved many of the self-strengtheners' restoration ventures; at the same time, she tried jealously to guard the prerogatives of the ruling Manchu imperial line.

Since foreign-policy issues were going to be at the fore in all decision making, it was unfortunate that Cixi had clashed badly in 1869 with Prince Gong after he had caused the execution of one of her favorite eunuchs, who was convicted of grossly abusing his power. The growth of uncontrolled power in the hands of the eunuchs, and its attendant corruption, had traditionally been a hallmark of declining dynastic competence, and early Qing rulers had vowed never to repeat the late Ming mistake of allowing eunuchs to dominate the court. Prince Gong may have been trying to prevent the re-emergence of such a situation, but empress dowager Cixi took the killing personally and thereafter managed to block Prince Gong from holding positions of power.

Further diluting the strength of the Qing, the powerful provincial statesman Zeng Guofan died in 1872, the skillful Wenxiang died in 1876, and Zuo Zongtang remained preoccupied with the pacification of the Muslims in China's far northwest. The grand councilors in Peking, though worthy enough men with distinguished careers behind them, tended to be conservative and lacked the skill or initiative to direct China on a new course. Although self-strengthening programs continued to be implemented during the last decades of the nineteenth century, a disproportionate number of them were initiated by one man, Li Hongzhang. Li was trusted by the empress dowager Cixi; after the suppression of the Taiping and Nian rebellions, and the negotiations in the aftermath of the Tianjin massacre, he was posted to north China in the dual capacity of governor-general of the Hebei region and commissioner of trade for the northern ports. More than any person, he put his imprint on the closing years of the century in China.

Li Hongzhang's political endeavors fell largely into three broad areas: entrepreneurial, educational, and diplomatic. As an entrepreneur he built on the foundations laid during the earlier phase of the self-strengthening movement. He sought to diversify China's enterprise into areas that would have long-range effects on the country's overall development. These initiatives would involve the Qing government and individual merchant capitalists in joint operations under a formula called "government supervision and merchant management." One such project, founded by Li Hongzhang in 1872, was the China Merchant Steamship Navigation Company, which was designed to stop the domination of China's coastal shipping by foreign powers. The company, in which Li himself was a principal shareholder, drew much of its income from contracts to transship the government taxation grain from central China to the Peking region. After 1877 the Kaiping coal mines near Tianjin were enormously expanded, on Li's orders, to give China more control over its own mineral resources and to provide fuel for China's expanding navy of steamships. Li also founded a sizable cotton mill at Shanghai in 1878 to cut into the rising imports of textiles.

In the 1880s Li went on to develop arsenals in Tianjin, which manufactured the bullets and shells for the Remington and Krupp guns that he now began to buy from abroad. A start was soon made on manufacturing the Remington rifles themselves with purchased American equipment. Li developed a national telegraph system by linking the international cables—which had terminated at Shanghai—first to Tianjin and then to Peking; branch wires were then extended to many large inland cities. He also directed the construction of new dock facilities in the south Manchurian city of Lüshun and a seven-mile stretch of railway line to carry coal from the Kaiping mines to a nearby canal, whence it could be shipped to Tianjin and used by the new fleet. Originally the cars were pulled down the tracks by mules, but in 1881 one of Li's assistants used Western scrap parts to build China's first steam engine, which was employed successfully on the line.

Li Hongzhang carried forward earlier efforts at educational reform as well. He originally threw his support behind the proposal for an educational mission in the United States, an idea first formulated by Yung Wing and backed by Zeng Guofan. The court gave its consent, and in 1872 the first group of Chinese boys aged twelve to fourteen—many of them the children of employees in China's new arsenals and shipyards at Fuzhou, Tianjin, and Shanghai—were sent to Hartford, Connecticut. There they lived with local American families and plunged into a busy round of English-language training, general education, and Chinese studies. By 1875 there were 120 in all. But in the school and social environments of this American city, it was hard for the Chinese students to maintain the traditional cultural values that Qing officials insisted on. The boys began to dress in Western style, abandoning their robes, and several of them cut off their queues under local pressure or mockery. Many were attracted to Christianity. Yung Wing's own marriage to one of the Hartford teachers was a further example of the strong attraction the West had on these students.

But the final blow to Li's mission was the belated discovery that the United States government would not permit a select group of the students, once having completed their high-school education, to enroll in the naval and military academies at Annapolis and West Point, as Li had hoped. So in 1881 he acquiesced in the decision made by conservative Qing officials to close the educational mission and bring the students home. They returned to China by sea from San Francisco in August 1881. Their final triumph on American soil was their defeat of the local Oakland baseball team, which had expected a walkover but was routed by the wicked curveball of the Chinese pitcher. Upon their return to China, many of the students became influential in the armed services, engineering, and business; but Li Hongzhang henceforth dispatched his most promising students to France, Germany, or Great Britain, where the governments did not object to their receiving technically advanced military and naval training. He also established both a naval and a military academy in Tianjin itself.

The world of international diplomacy was even more inhospitable to the Qing. Here Li Hongzhang worked—sometimes on his own, sometimes in conjunction with Robert Hart, and sometimes with the Zongli Yamen—to try to handle a wide range of difficult problems. In the 1870s these included negotiations with the Japanese over the international status of the Ryukyu Islands and Korea. In neither of these cases were the Qing able to make a convincing claim for special Chinese rights, for the old system of "tributary relationships," designed so many centuries ago to show China's cultural superiority over these nearby territories, was now seriously weakened. The Qing court, indeed, was totally unprepared to respond to the extraordinary expansion of Japanese power in this period. It was only since 1854 that the American commodore Matthew C. Perry had forced the Japanese to end their isolation and to acknowledge the realities of international relations and foreign trade. Yet so effective had been the sweeping economic and institutional reforms of the Meiji Restoration beginning in 1868 that Japan could now bring superior military force to bear on China. In 1879 the Japanese annexed the Ryukyus, and Korea might well have suffered a similar fate in the 1880s had not Li persuaded the Korean king to sign treaties with the United States, Britain, France, and Germany (which, since 1871, had become a unified state).

In 1876 Li also had to conduct complex negotiations with the British after one of their consuls, Augustus Margary, was murdered by local tribesmen in Yunnan. Margary had been on assignment with a British survey team exploring the feasibility of road or railway routes from Burma into Yunnan. In the resulting convention, Li, representing the Qing, essentially acknowledged the dynasty's weakness by agreeing to pay an indemnity of 700,000 taels, to send a mission of apology to Queen Victoria, and to open four more treaty ports. More beneficial to China's interests were the negotiations with Russia conducted in the late 1870s by the Zongli Yamen and Zeng Guofan's son, now the Qing minister to Great Britain. By the Treaty of St. Petersburg of 1881, the Russians agreed to abrogate an earlier unequal treaty and to return to Qing rule the sections of Ili that had been under Russian occupation since the outbreak of the Muslim rebellions. Although Russia still held huge areas of former Qing territory north of the Amur and Ussuri rivers, the St. Petersburg treaty assured China control of her far western borders, a sovereignty confirmed when the Qing declared Xinjiang a province in 1884.

Success with Russia bred false confidence at court and among Qing scholar-officials. When the French expanded their colonial empire by occupying Hanoi and Haiphong in 1880—despite Chinese claims to special rights in the area—and began to pressure China for new concessions in Annam (now Vietnam), Li Hongzhang urged caution. But his pleas were swept aside by the excited urging of belligerent Chinese and Manchus, who insisted that the Qing take a strong stand on this matter of principle. While Li was attempting negotiations with France in 1884 to avoid the outbreak of hostilities, those in favor of strong measures continued to fight with the French in Annam and in neighboring Tonkin. The admiral in command of the French fleet in the region responded to these intermittent hostilities by moving his forces into the harbor at Fuzhou and anchoring near the Chinese fleet.

Li Hongzhang had urged a negotiated settlement with the French, however humiliating it might seem, because he knew how frail the newly developed Chinese navy was. When negotiations broke down in August 1884 and the French fleet in Fuzhou opened fire, Li was catastrophically proved correct, and the disparities between a developed industrial power and Qing China made once more clear to all. The Chinese flagship was sunk by torpedoes in the first minute of battle; within seven minutes, most of the Chinese ships were hit; within one hour every Chinese ship was sunk or on fire and the arsenal and docks destroyed. The French counted 5 dead, the Chinese 521 dead and 51 missing. Although the Qing subsequently won some indecisive land battles in the southwest, French control over Indochina was now assured. A year later the British emulated French aggressiveness and declared Burma a protectorate.

Li Hongzhang could have sent the northern segment of the Qing navy to reinforce the southern segment in Fuzhou; instead he chose to conserve those forces and strengthen them further, as well as use them to bolster his own bureaucratic and administrative power base. Besides bearing testimony to his power and prestige, the most important task of this fleet was to hold open the sea lanes to Korea. The Qing had created a new senior post, that of Chinese "resident" in Seoul, charged with the difficult task of maintaining warm relations with the Korean court, and making sure that Korean "independence" did not mean the weakening of China's privileged status in the country. The Qing wished to ensure that Japan did not gain a permanent foothold there. During the 1890s tensions heightened as Japanese designs on the peninsula became apparent. In 1894, when the outbreak of a domestic

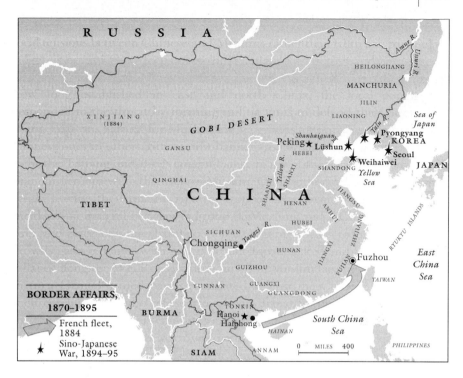

rebellion threatened the Korean king, both China and Japan seized the opportunity to send troops to protect the royal family. The Japanese, who were able to move more troops faster than the Chinese, seized the Korean palace on July 21 and appointed a "regent" loyal to their interests.

That same day the Qing commissioned a British transport to convey some 1,200 Chinese reinforcements to Korea. Intercepted by a Japanese cruiser and refusing to surrender, the transport was fired on by the Japanese and sunk; fewer than 200 men survived. By the end of the month, Japanese land troops had defeated the Chinese in a series of battles around Seoul and Pyongyang; in October the Japanese crossed the Yalu River and entered Qing territory. The following month another Japanese army seized the strongly fortified harbor at Lüshun, massacring many of the Chinese in the city. Japan's land forces were now poised to enter China proper through Shanhaiguan, as Dorgon had done two and a half centuries before.

The north China navy, despite Li's efforts to conserve it, was now to suffer a fate similar to the southern navy's, with yet more damaging consequences to China's self-strengthening goals. This northern fleet, consisting of 2 battleships, 10 cruisers, and 2 torpedo boats, had already been badly damaged by the Japanese in a September battle off the mouth of the Yalu, and had retreated to the heavily defended port of Weihaiwei on the northern side of the Shandong peninsula. There the Chinese admiral retired his fleet behind a protective curtain of contact mines and took no further part in the fighting. But in a brilliant maneuver carried through in January 1895, a Japanese force of 20,000 troops and 10,000 field laborers marched across the Shandong promontory and seized the Weihaiwei defensive forts from the landward side. Turning the guns on the Chinese fleet and simultaneously penetrating the mine fields with torpedo boats, they destroyed one of the battleships and four cruisers. The two senior Chinese admirals and the senior Qing commandants of the forts all committed suicide.

Desperate, the court turned to the disgraced Prince Gong to help with negotiations, just as it had thirty-five years before when the summer palace had been burned during the disastrous Tianjin treaty negotiations. The prince sadly told a Western diplomat that he had been given the job of "piecing together the cup which the present ministers have smashed to the floor."[1] To assist Prince Gong the Qing chose the most visible of those ministers, Li Hongzhang, and it was he who was made to go to Japan in person and negotiate with the victors.

The terms of the ensuing Treaty of Shimonoseki, made final in April 1895, were disastrous for China. They would have been even worse had a Japanese assassin not fired at Li, wounding him in the face below the left eye and shaming the Japanese government before the world. China had to recognize "the full and complete independence and autonomy of Korea," which, under the circumstances, effectively made Korea a Japanese protectorate. The Qing also promised to pay Japan 200 million taels in war indemnities, added four more treaty ports—including Chongqing, far up the Yangzi in Sichuan province—and ceded to Japan "in perpetuity" all of Taiwan, the Pescadores, and the Liaodong region of southern Manchuria. The Japanese were also to be allowed to build factories and other industrial enterprises in any of the treaty port areas. Russian, German, and French protests forced the Japanese to relinquish the claim to Liaodong in exchange for an additional indemnity of 30 million taels, but all the other treaty stipulations were confirmed. Many of China's brightest young scholars, assembled in Peking for the triennial *jinshi* examinations, braved the court's wrath by passionately denouncing the Treaty of Shimonoseki and calling for a new, bolder program of economic growth and governmental reform to offset China's tragic losses. But the Qing court seemed paralyzed. It was a dark conclusion to the brightest hopes of the era of self-strengthening.

THE REFORM MOVEMENT OF 1898

During the closing decade of the nineteenth century, China was in a curious, ambiguous position. Elements of old and new existed side by side. At many levels the pace of change seemed overwhelming and irreversible. Steamboats plied the Yangzi, huge new banks lined the waterfront in Shanghai, military academies were training young officers in Western tactics, scientific textbooks were rolling off the presses, and memorials flashed by telegraph from the provinces to the Grand Council. Victorious in a series of wars, the Western powers had imposed their presence on China and were now beginning to invest heavily in the country, especially in mines, modern communications, and heavy industry. The impact of foreign imperialism was profound, intensifying tensions already generated by the self-strengthening movement.

Yet much of this apparent change was confined to the treaty port cities and within them to the Western concession areas. Penetration of the Chinese countryside by even the most aggressive foreign businesses was slow, and in nearly all cases the Westerners relied on their Chinese-merchant intermediaries—the so-called compradors—to open up markets for their products through the traditional trade and distribution routes. For most young Chinese men from well-to-do families, the patterns of education remained unchanged: they memorized the Confucian classics, and labored to obtain their local *shengyuan* degrees before proceeding to the provincial *juren* and national *jinshi* examinations. In town and country, girls still had little access to formal education, their feet were still bound, and their marriages arranged by their parents. In the fields, sowing and harvesting were done by hand, the produce laboriously carried to market. Foreigners, if seen at all, were regarded as exotic or menacing. Chinese diplomats, posted overseas, received little prestige from the appointments and were often humiliated on their return and forced into early retirement.

Where a true interpenetration of tradition and change occurred, it was often a long-term, almost invisible development. Chinese farmers, responding to new domestic demands for cash crops such as tobacco or cotton, could make much greater profits than before, but were also more vulnerable to local market swings. Those growing tea or producing silk were in fact responding to world market demands, and sudden unexplained swoops of prosperity and dearth were the effects of world price fluctuations. The refined technology of machine silk weaving in Japan and the United States required a greater evenness of thread, which meant that peasant families, who for generations had spun silk thread by hand from the cocoons, faced a shrinking market for their product. The technology of the printing press and the spread of a new urban readership spurred the growth of journals and newspapers. These began to introduce their readers to political commentary and to paid advertisements for health and beauty products, providing a new awareness of options for the individual. A growing sense that China was just one country among others began to lead to the view that it was, therefore, also a nation among nations, and that no nation could survive without involved citizens, both male and female. China's first regularly printed newspapers began to champion these views, which found a ready response among scholars shamed and disheartened by the Japanese war and the terms of the Shimonoseki treaty.

In the years after the Sino-Japanese War, a formulation became widespread that gave philosophical reassurance to those worried about the value of "self-strengthening": "Chinese learning should remain the essence, but Western learning be used for practical development." Generally abbreviated as the *ti-yong* idea (from the Chinese words for "essence" and "practical use"), this was a culturally reassuring position in a time of ambiguous, often painful, change. It affirmed that there was indeed a fundamental structure of Chinese moral and philosophical values that gave continuity and meaning to the civilization. Holding on to that belief, China could then afford to adopt quickly and dramatically all sorts of Western practices, and to hire Western advisers.

This was the favorite formulation of the Confucian scholar-official Zhang Zhidong, once a forceful voice among bellicose Chinese conservatives. Zhang capped a distinguished civil-service career by serving for almost eighteen consecutive years as the governor-general of Hunan and Hubei provinces. After Li Hongzhang, he was perhaps the most effective of the provincial reformers. Zhang pressed vigorously and successfully for the development of a railway line from Hankou to Peking—funded with foreign loans—and built up China's first great coal, iron, and steel complex at the Han-Ye-Ping mines in east Hubei. Yet he continued to ingratiate himself with the empress dowager Cixi and her advisers by his conservative pronouncements on the need for gradual reform and his ringing declarations on the essential values of the traditional Confucian ethical system.

Echoing Zhang Zhidong's general *ti-yong* stance, many of the brightest and most successful of China's younger generation of Confucian scholars collaborated together in righteous indignation after learning the terms of the Treaty of Shimonoseki and presented a long memorial to the throne, urging continued resistance to Japan and requesting a wide range of economic, industrial, and administrative reforms. These men were assembled in Peking for the spring 1895 *jinshi* examinations, and were coordinated by two scholars of great intelligence and courage—Kang Youwei and Liang Qichao. Kang was a brilliant classical scholar of thirty-seven from the Canton region who had gained fame but also drawn criticism for his eccentric approach to Confucian scholarship. In earlier writings, Kang had drawn on his great classical learning to try to prove that Confucius had not resisted social change and that Confucianism did not negate the basic ideas of human development and progress. In this he was influenced by the ideas of Confucianism first made popular by Chinese scholars studying the Gongyang commentaries early in the nineteenth century. Liang Qichao, the second scholar, was twenty-two years old and had been a student of Kang's. He was already actively involved in provincial academies and newly formed national societies that advocated a speeded-up program of radical reform for China. Despite his radicalism, he, like Kang, was also seeking the *jinshi* degree, which remained the most prestigious route to elite status.

Influenced also by Buddhism, and of a highly emotional frame of mind, Kang Youwei saw himself as a new sage capable of saving the Chinese people. His visits to Hong Kong and Shanghai, where he examined manifestations of Western technical and urban development, when coupled with his readings on physics, electricity, and optics, convinced him of the possibilities of a true *ti-yong* synthesis. Liang shared that confidence and sense of excitement. They were overjoyed when the long reform memorial, after being shunted from bureau to bureau by worried senior bureaucrats, was at last read by the emperor Guangxu himself. Now aged twenty-four, Guangxu was just emerging from the shadow of his aunt Cixi, who had gone into semiretirement in the rebuilt summer palace. He had a strong interest in reform and was moved by the words of Kang, Liang, and the other candidates.

The *jinshi* candidates' reform memorial of 1895 raised many issues that were troubling China's more farsighted scholars. China needed a modernized army, they wrote, equipped with the most advanced Western firearms and artillery. To develop a national industrial base, the court should call on the technical skills of the Chinese in Southeast Asia. It should raise taxes, develop a state banking system, establish a railway network, build a commercial fleet, and install a modern postal system. China should improve the quality of its agriculture through training schools and build centers to foster industrial innovation and encourage the kind of creative ingenuity that led inventors in the United States to apply for over 13,000 patents a year. Resettlement programs in poor and backward rural areas should be developed to lure back the thousands of productive Chinese emigrants who had been leaving every year. Previously it was only rebels like the Taiping leader Hong Ren'gan who had publicly espoused such far-reaching changes, but now the brightest Confucian youth in China were exploring the same ideas.

These would-be reformers had made their demands for change within the accepted traditional channels, but the effects were negligible. The young emperor Guangxu, even though he seemed interested, had no overt political power, and other conservative senior bureaucrats made sure that the proposals were safely filed away. But by the 1890s, demands for change could not be confined to these comparatively orthodox and polite channels. Other reformers, such as the young Sun Yat-sen,* took a different path. Sun, from a poor rural family in the Canton area, had none of the advantages of education and status held by the Kang family. Instead, like thousands of poor Chinese in the southeast, some of the Suns had emigrated during the nineteenth century. Two had died in the California gold rush; others had settled in Hawaii. There Sun Yat-sen joined an elder brother in the early 1880s and received an education in the mission schools, which introduced him to ideas about democracy and republican government as well as Christianity, before transferring to medical school in Hong Kong. A cultural hybrid with great ambitions and a deep sense of alarm over China's impending fate, Sun offered his services to Governor-General Li Hongzhang in 1894 as an adviser to help with China's defense and development. Distracted by the crises in Korea and elsewhere, Li ignored him.

Sun was disappointed and frustrated. The British did not consider his training good enough to allow him to practice medicine in their dominions, nor did the Chinese seem adequately to admire his new skills. Sun's response was to form a secret society in Hawaii in late 1894 that he named the Revive China Society, which pledged itself to the overthrow of the Manchus and to the establishment of a new Chinese ruler or even a republican form of government. Raising some money from his brother and other friends, he moved to Hong Kong and, in 1895, tried to combine with local secret societies near Canton to stage a military uprising that would spread and overthrow the dynasty. Badly organized, hampered by poor security and inadequate weapons and funds, the plan was discovered by Qing authorities and the local ringleaders executed.

Sun fled from Hong Kong to Japan, and eventually to San Francisco and London. In this last city he settled and began to read widely in Western political and economic theory. His studies were interrupted in 1896, when the staff of the Qing legation in London made a clumsy (but nearly successful) attempt to kidnap him and ship him back to China for trial and execution. Sun became a famous figure when this dramatic story was widely

---

*This is the romanized style in which the Cantonese form of Sun's name was always written.

written up in the Western press. Returning to the East and setting up a series of bases in Southeast Asia and Japan, Sun continued to labor, through the secret societies and his own sworn brethren, to achieve a military coup against the Qing.

Sun Yat-sen found support among restless, adventurous Chinese who felt little allegiance to the Qing and had tasted some of the opportunities and risks of life overseas. One such backer was "Charlie" Soong, whose children were later to play significant roles in twentieth-century Chinese politics. Charlie Soong grew up in a fishing and trading family on the southern Chinese island of Hainan. Leaving Hainan to live with relatives in Java, Soong then shipped to Boston in 1878, where he apprenticed himself to a Chinese merchant family. Bored by his life there, Charlie Soong ran away to sea, enlisted as a crewman on a U.S. revenue-service cutter, and was finally passed on by the ship's captain to generous friends in North Carolina who put him through college and prepared him for life as a Christian missionary. Returning to China in 1886, he worked briefly as a preacher but in circumstances he found humiliating and badly paid. In 1892 he found a focus for his entrepreneurial energies and made a substantial fortune by printing Bibles for the Western missionaries to disseminate. Before long he branched out into the factory production of noodles, using advanced Western machinery, and moved into a comfortable foreign-style house in the suburbs of Shanghai. At this point, through shared secret-society contacts, he also began to funnel money to Sun Yat-sen's illegal organization.

By the late 1890s, the Chinese, who were becoming more knowledgeable about foreigners, could seize on a whole range of potential models from Japanese Meiji reformers to George Washington, Napoléon Bonaparte, and Peter the Great. Chinese language newspapers and didactic histories proliferated, extolling various Western thinkers of the past and holding up as warning mirrors to China the examples of such countries as Poland, Turkey, and India, which had been respectively partitioned, economically ruined, and politically subjugated. Simultaneously, the Western powers renewed their demands for special economic and residence rights in China—often called "the scramble for concessions"—which placed the Qing in greater jeopardy. In this context, the emperor Guangxu, who undoubtedly had a wider view of the options facing China than any of his predecessors and had even been studying English, decided to assert his own independence as ruler, and to act on the country's behalf. Between June and September 1898 he issued an extraordinary series of edicts, earning for this period the name of the "Hundred Days' Reforms." Although most of the edicts dealt with proposals that had already been raised by self-strengthening reformers and by the *jinshi* protestors of 1895, there had never before been such a coherent body of reform ideas presented on imperial initiative and backed by imperial prestige.

Guangxu called for changes in four main areas of Qing life and government. To reform China's examination system, he ordered the abolition of the highly stylized format known as the "eight-legged essay," which had structured the exams for centuries. He also urged that fine calligraphy and knowledge of poetry no longer be major criteria in grading degree candidates; instead he ordered the use of more questions related to practical governmental problems. Also in the area of education, he ordered the upgrading of the Peking college and the addition to it of a medical school, the conversion of the old academies (along with unnecessary rural shrines) to modern schools offering both Chinese and Western learning, and the opening of vocational institutes for the study of mining, industry, and railways. In the broader area of economic development, the emperor ordered local officials to coordinate reforms in commerce, industry, and agriculture, and to increase the production of tea and silk for export. New bureaus in Peking were established to supervise such growth, along with mines and railways, and the Ministry of Revenue was to design an overall annual budget for the country as a whole.

Guangxu also addressed the strengthening of the armed forces. Much of the money that had been needed by the navy had gone into the rebuilding of the empress dowager's summer palace, which included construction of a marble "boat" for her lake-viewing pleasure. Now a fleet of thirty-four modern warships was to be assembled, by purchase or by local construction. Army drill was to be standardized along Western lines. Training and discipline of local militias were to be improved. Emperor Guangxu even promised to take the empress dowager to review the new armies in Tianjin. Finally, he tried to strengthen the bureaucracy by streamlining it and simplifying its procedures. He sought to abolish the more obvious sinecure appointments and to move some of the displaced officials to positions in the new economic planning bureaus.

In developing this reform program, several important personnel changes were made. Li Hongzhang had steadily lost influence since the Japanese war disasters and was now removed from the Zongli Yamen. Guangxu's own tutor was also dismissed for being cautious about the scale of reform. Several reformist thinkers, among them Kang Youwei, were appointed as secretaries in the Grand Council or the Zongli Yamen so they could be in on important discussions and memorialize the emperor through their superiors. Kang was granted an imperial audience and submitted two works of historical analysis to the emperor: one on the fate of Poland; the other on

Ren Bonian, 1840–1895, *Portrait of a Down-and-Out Man*   Ren Bonian, who served in the army of Hong Xiuquan's Taiping Heavenly Kingdom, portrays a friend's plight as a low-paid, minor government official.

One of the main streets of Peking, 1907

Interior courtyard of a mandarin's house, Peking, c. 1871–72 (photograph by John Thomson)

Woman with bound feet The tradition of binding feet to three-inch points caused women intense pain and hindered walking but aided in securing a husband. When women unbound their feet during Qing reforms, they experienced pain equal to that of when their feet were first bound.

Empress Dowager Cixi with her attendants

Li Hongzhang

Prince Gong

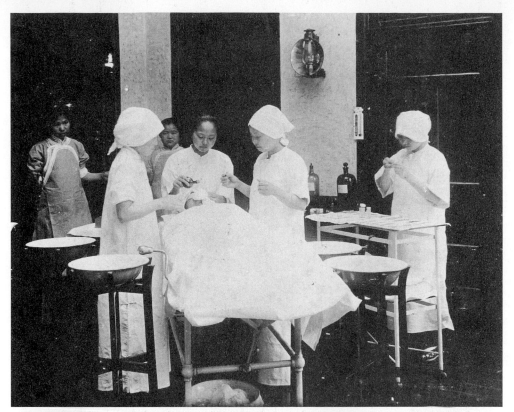

The story of the Christian mission movement in China is not just one of exploitation, misunderstanding, and hostility. Mission schools and publications opened new opportunities for Chinese. *Mary Stone, a Chinese mission-school graduate who earned her medical degree at the University of Michigan, performing surgery at a missionary hospital, Zhenjiang (top); Dr. Stone with a Methodist mission group (bottom)*

Zou Rong, author of "The Revolutionary Army" (1903)

Qiu Jin, a spirited radical and early supporter of Sun's Revolutionary Alliance

Sun Yat-sen (second from left) with radical student friends in Hong Kong, 1887

Boxer Uprising, Peking Gate   In August 1900, a foreign expeditionary column of some 20,000 troops quelled the Boxer Uprising and raised the siege on the foreign compounds in Peking. *One of the main gates to Peking, partially destroyed in the fighting (top); U.S. troops near the tombs of the Ming emperors (bottom)*

Kang Youwei (left) and Liang Qichao (right)   Kang and Liang were prominent scholars who coordinated the reform efforts of the *jinshi* candidates in Peking, spring 1895.

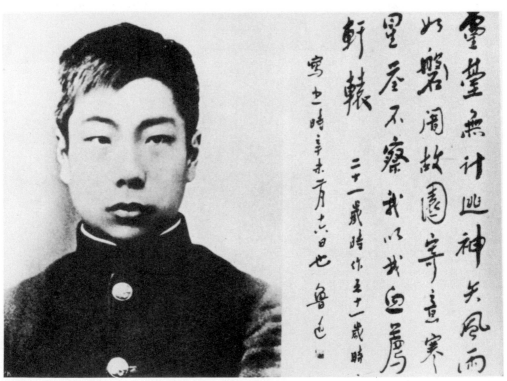

Lu Xun in Japan, aged twenty (1904), after removing his queue

Troops of the Northern Standing Army were trained in Western equipment and tactics under the command of Yuan Shikai, 1903

Revolutionary troops, Hankou, 1911

*"Charlie" Soong, one of Sun Yat-sen's earliest
supporters*   Soong's three daughters married Sun
Yat-sen, Chiang Kai-shek, and the Guomindang
finance minister, H. H. Kong.

*Yuan Shikai took office as president of the republic
on February 13, 1912, after Sun Yat-sen relinquished
claims to the title*

Sun Yat-sen (center), 1912

In Nanjing, soldiers of the Revolutionary Army cutting the queues that symbolized the old Manchu order

Young Chinese learning Western secretarial and language skills at the Government Teachers College, Nanjing

the triumphs of Japanese reforms in the Meiji Restoration. But many senior officials, viewing Guangxu's reform program with a jaundiced eye, saw it as detrimental to the long-term good of China and destructive of China's true inner values. Guangxu seems to have mistakenly thought that his aunt Cixi would support his vision of a new China and would help him override this opposition. In fact she was disturbed by some of the proposed changes that threatened to weaken the Qing ruling house, and was worried that the faction supporting Guangxu seemed dangerously subordinate to pressures and influences from both the British and the French.

Although the evidence is contradictory, it seems that a number of the reformers feared there might be a coup against the emperor, and accordingly approached some leading generals in an attempt to win their support. This led to a backlash when news of the scheming was reported to the empress dowager, who, on September 19, 1898, suddenly returned to the Forbidden City. Two days later, she issued an edict claiming that the emperor had asked her to resume power. She put Guangxu under palace detention and arrested six of his reputedly radical advisers. Before they could even be tried on the vague conspiracy charges, her order that they be executed was carried out, to the dismay of the reform party and of many foreigners in China. Kang Youwei had left Peking on assignment just before the coup, but his younger brother was among the victims. Now with a price on his head, Kang Youwei was carried to safety in Hong Kong on a British vessel, whence he made his way first to Japan and then to Canada. Liang Qichao also fled China and began a life of exile. His and Kang's dreams for a coherent program of reform, to be coordinated by the emperor in the name of a new China, had ended in disaster.

THREE SIDES OF NATIONALISM

During 1898 and 1899, as part of their general wave of imperialist expansion, the foreign powers intensified their pressures and outrages on China. The Germans used the pretext of an attack on their missionaries to occupy the Shandong port city of Qingdao and to claim mining and railway rights in the countryside nearby. The British took over the harbor at Weihaiwei on the north of the Shandong peninsula (where the Qing fleet had been sunk at anchor by the Japanese three years before), and forced the Qing to yield a ninety-nine-year lease on a large area of fertile farmland on the Kowloon peninsula north of Hong Kong, which the British henceforth called "The New Territories." The Russians stepped up their presence in Manchuria and occupied Lüshun, where they erected massive fortifications. The French claimed special rights in the Tonkin border provinces of Yunnan, Guangxi, and Guangdong, and on the island of Hainan. The Japanese, already masters of Taiwan, continued to put pressure on Korea and intensified their economic penetration of central China. Attempts by the United States to declare an "open door" policy for China, under the terms of which all countries would agree not to deny others access to their spheres of influence, may, through some moral effect, have slowed the slicing up of China, but there were no sanctions to enforce such a policy. Some Chinese began to fear—rightly enough—that their country was about to be "carved up like a melon."

In this atmosphere of hostility and fear, a vigorous force began to develop in China. The many guises in which it appeared can be encompassed under the blanket term *nationalism,* which for the Chinese comprised a new, urgent awareness of their relationship to foreign forces and to the Manchus. It carried as well a corresponding sense of the Chinese people as a unit that must be mobilized for its own survival. One can see the growth of this phenomenon in three examples: the Boxer Uprising of 1900, the publication of *The Revolutionary Army* by Zou Rong in 1903, and the anti-American boycott of 1905.

The Boxers United in Righteousness, as they called themselves, began to emerge as a force in northwest Shandong during 1898. They drew their name and the martial rites they practiced from a variety of secret-society and self-defense units that had spread in southern Shandong during the previous years, mainly in response to the provocations of Western missionaries and their Chinese converts. Some Boxers believed they were invulnerable to swords and bullets in combat, and they drew on an eclectic pantheon of spirits and protectors from folk religion, popular novels, and street plays. Although they lacked a unified leadership, Boxers recruited local farmers and other workers made desperate by the disastrous floods that had been followed by droughts in Shandong; they began to call for the ending of the special privileges enjoyed by Chinese Christian converts and to attack both converts and Christian missionaries. By early 1899 they had destroyed or stolen a good deal of property from Chinese Christians and had killed several converts in the Shandong-Hebei border area, seriously alarming the foreigners, who demanded that the Qing suppress the Boxers and their supporters. The Boxers responded with a popular slogan, "Revive the Qing, destroy the foreign," which was soon expanded into catchy jingles in doggerel verse, some of which were hung as wall posters near Boxer altars or on street corners:

> Their men are all immoral;
> Their women truly vile.

For the Devils it's mother-son sex
That serves as the breeding style.

No rain comes from Heaven,
The earth is parched and dry.
And all because the churches
Have bottled up the sky.

When at last all the Foreign Devils
Are expelled to the very last man,
The Great Qing, united, together,
Will bring peace to this our land.[2]

By spring 1900, the year their leaders had predicted as the dawn of a new religious age, the Boxers had expanded dramatically. Perhaps 70 percent were poor peasants, male and young. The rest were drawn from a broad mixture of itinerants and artisans, as had been the case with so many earlier uprisings against the Qing. In the Boxer ranks there were peddlers and rickshaw men, sedan-chair carriers, canal boatmen, leather workers, knife sharpeners, and barbers; some were dismissed soldiers and salt smugglers. They were joined by female Boxer groups, the most important of which was named the Red Lanterns Shining, girls and women usually aged twelve to eighteen whose female powers were invoked to fight the "pollution" of the Chinese Christian women, which was believed to erode the strength of Boxer men. Best known among these women was "Lotus" Huang, daughter of a poor boatman and herself a former prostitute, who was believed to have unique spiritual powers. Other women were banded together in teams called the Cooking-Pan Lanterns and fed the Boxer troops from pots that were allegedly replenished magically after every meal.

Still without any coordinated leadership, Boxer groups began to drift into Peking and Tianjin in early June. Roaming the streets, dressed in motley uniforms of red, black, or yellow turbans and red leggings, and with white charms on their wrists, they harried—and sometimes killed—Chinese converts and even those who possessed foreign objects—lamps, clocks, or matches. The Boxers also killed four French and Belgian engineers and two English missionaries, ripped up railway tracks, burned the stations, and cut telegraph lines. Powerful provincial officials wavered, as did the Qing court, sometimes protecting foreigners by meeting Boxer force with force of their own, at other times seeming to condone or even approve the Boxer show of antiforeign "loyalty."

On June 17, the Westerners seized the forts at Dagu from Qing forces in order to provide cover for a troop landing should full-scale war break out. Two days later in Peking, news of the battle at the Dagu forts arrived, the

German minister was shot dead in the street as he went to an interview at the Zongli Yamen, and Boxer forces laid siege to the foreign-legation areas. Praising the Boxers now as a loyal militia, on June 21, 1900, the empress dowager issued a "declaration of war" against the foreign powers, which stated in part:

> The foreigners have been aggressive towards us, infringed upon our territorial integrity, trampled our people under their feet.... They oppress our people and blaspheme our gods. The common people suffer greatly at their hands, and each one of them is vengeful. Thus it is that the brave followers of the Boxers have been burning churches and killing Christians.[3]

With the empress dowager and senior Manchu officials now clearly behind them, the Boxers launched a series of attacks on mission compounds and on foreigners. The attacks were particularly vicious in Shanxi, Hebei, and Henan, with the worst atrocity occurring in Shanxi. There, the Manchu governor Yuxian summoned the missionaries and their families to the provincial capital of Taiyuan, promising to protect them from the Boxers. But once they arrived, he ordered all forty-four men, women, and children killed.

In Peking, the foreign diplomatic corps and their families retreated into a defensive area composed mainly of the British, Russian, German, Japanese, and American compounds, hastily defended with makeshift barricades of furniture, sandbags, timber, and mattresses. Had the Boxers been better organized or had large numbers of regular Qing army troops joined in the attack, the Westerners would surely all have been killed. But the attack was not pressed with coordinated vigor, the modernized Qing armies stood outside the fray, and the powerful governors-general of central China such as Zhang Zhidong stalled for time and refused to commit their newly trained troops to the conflict.

On August 4, 1900, a foreign expeditionary column of about 20,000 troops, consisting mainly of soldiers from Japan, Russia, Britain, the United States, and France, and operating under a complex joint-command structure, left Tianjin. Boxer resistance quickly crumbled, key Qing commanders committed suicide, and the Western troops entered Peking and raised the Boxer siege on August 14. As they came into the city from the east, the empress dowager and her nephew Guangxu fled to the west, establishing a temporary capital in the Wei River valley city of Xi'an. After a protracted, often bitter campaign, conducted primarily by a newly arrived expeditionary force of German troops, and complex negotiations with the fugitive court and Li Hongzhang (once again indispensable as a mediator), a formal peace treaty

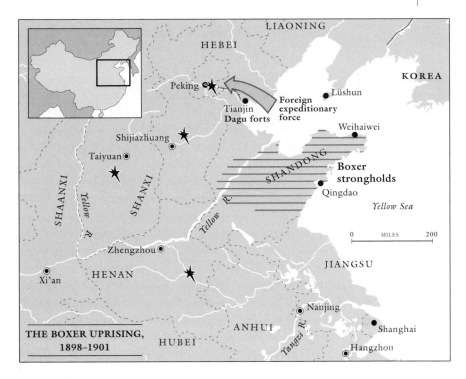

LIAONING

HEBEI

KOREA

Peking

Tianjin
Dagu forts

Foreign
expeditionary
force

Lüshun

Weihaiwei

Shijiazhuang

Taiyuan

Boxer
strongholds

Qingdao

Yellow Sea

SHAANXI

Yellow R.

SHANXI

SHANDONG

Yellow R.

0   MILES   200

Zhengzhou

JIANGSU

Xi'an

HENAN

Nanjing

THE BOXER UPRISING,
1898–1901

ANHUI

HUBEI

Yangzi R.

Shanghai

Hangzhou

known as the Boxer Protocol was signed in September 1901.

In this protocol, the Qing agreed to erect monuments to the memory of the more than two hundred Western dead, to ban all examinations for five years in cities where antiforeign atrocities had taken place, to forbid all imports of arms into China for two years, to allow permanent foreign guards and emplacements of defensive weapons to protect the legation quarter in perpetuity, to make the Zongli Yamen into a fully prestigious Ministry of Foreign Affairs, and to execute the leading Boxer supporters, including the Shanxi governor Yuxian. They also agreed to pay an indemnity for damages to foreign life and property of 450 million taels (around £67 million or $333 million at the then current exchange rates), a staggering sum at a time when the entire annual Qing income was estimated at around 250 million taels. The Chinese were to pay the indemnity in gold, on an ascending scale, with 4 percent interest charges, until the debt was amortized on December 31, 1940. With all interest charges factored in, total Chinese payments over the thirty-nine-year period would amount to almost 1 billion taels (precisely 982,238,150).

In January 1902, the empress dowager and her nephew Guangxu returned by train from Xi'an to Peking, where Li Hongzhang had just died from illness at the age of seventy-eight. Cixi re-established her residence in the Forbidden City, which for over a year had been the headquarters for the foreign expeditionary force. At the end of that month, in an apparently genuine gesture of reconciliation, she received the senior members of the foreign diplomatic corps in person at her palace; on February 1, in another unprecedented action, she held a reception for their ladies. But Emperor Guangxu was still not allowed to play any open political role.

The two exiled reformers, Sun Yat-sen and Kang Youwei, both tried to exploit the disruption caused by the Boxer Uprising by launching their own attacks against the Qing during 1900. Kang's took place in Hubei and Anhui in August and Sun's in Huizhou, east of Canton, in October. Kang's goal was to restore Guangxu to power as a constitutional monarch, whereas Sun wanted to found a Chinese republic. Neither plan was well financed or well coordinated, and both were suppressed by Qing troops without difficulty.

The forms of protest now passed back to the manipulators of the written word. The most articulate of these turned out to be an eighteen-year-old student named Zou Rong, whose work provides a second case study of the new forms of nationalism. Zou Rong was one of a growing number of young Chinese who, in the years after the Sino-Japanese War, had gone to study in Japan; awed by Japan's power, these students sought to observe it at the source. Zou grew dismayed at the apparent inability of the Qing to react creatively in their time of crisis. Like certain secret society and Taiping leaders before him, he singled out the Manchus for blame, but unlike those earlier rebels he moved beyond slogans to draw up a lengthy and careful indictment of the Manchus' weakness. Ironically, he was able to do this because he had returned from Japan to live in the foreign-concession area of Shanghai, where, according to complex jurisdictional agreements concerning "extraterritoriality," residents were subject to the so-called "mixed" courts dominated by Western legal practices. Such residents could write, and disseminate their writings, with a freedom impossible to those living in ordinary towns supervised by the Qing magistrates and police.

Zou Rong drew his anti-Manchu ideas together in a short book entitled *The Revolutionary Army* (1903). In ringing language, he called on his Chinese countrymen to reject the Manchu yoke and seize their own destiny. The Chinese had become a race of slaves, declared Zou, and such men as Zeng Guofan, destroyer of the Taiping, far from being heroes, were the lackeys of the Manchus and the butchers of their own countrymen. The Chinese should learn from Western examples that it is possible to overthrow domestic tyranny and free a country from foreign domination if the people are conscious of their unity and struggle together. As Zou wrote:

I do not begrudge repeating over and over again that internally we are the slaves of the Manchus and suffering from their tyranny, externally we are being harassed by the Powers, and we are doubly enslaved. The reason why our sacred Han race, descendants of the Yellow Emperor, should support revolutionary independence, arises precisely from the question of whether our race will go under and be exterminated.[4]

And he called dramatically on his Han countrymen to reclaim their destiny:

You possess government, run it yourselves; you have laws, guard them yourselves; you have industries, administer them yourselves; you possess armed forces, order them yourselves; you possess lands, watch over them yourselves; you have inexhaustible resources, exploit them yourselves. You are qualified in every way for revolutionary independence.[5]

These challenging calls, inserted in the midst of Zou Rong's other demands for such reforms as elected assemblies, equality of rights for women, and guarantees for freedom of the press and assembly, made an exciting mix. The tract spread widely, and Sun Yat-sen in particular seized on it as a means to outflank the more cautious Kang Youwei, distributing thousands of copies to his own supporters in San Francisco and Singapore. Qing officials put powerful pressures on the Western authorities in Shanghai to yield up Zou and those writers and journalists who had collaborated with him to publish and circulate his work. The Westerners refused, and in 1904 Zou was tried in the Shanghai Mixed Court on a charge of distributing inflammatory writings. There he received a two-year sentence, whereas a Qing court would swiftly have had him executed. By a cruel irony, Zou, spared humiliating and painful death at Qing hands, fell ill in prison and died in early 1905. Even though he was only nineteen, he had managed to make an extraordinary mark on his times.

During the period of Zou's trial, another wave of protest against foreign abuses had been building. Ever since the passage in the United States of the 1882 anti-Chinese exclusion laws and their enforced ratification by treaty, Americans had performed numerous hostile acts against Chinese immigrants. Immigration officers of the United States Treasury Department broke into Chinese homes in American cities allegedly to check registrations; harassments and deportations were common; and Chinese arriving at United States ports—including visitors of high status such as the delegations coming by invitation to the St. Louis Exposition in 1904—were roughly handled and abused. Further bitterness developed when America's exclusionary policies were extended to Chinese residing in Hawaii and the Philippines.

By 1905, a new sort of response was developing in China, providing a third expression of nationalist feeling. The newly established Qing Ministry of Foreign Affairs, urged on by China's minister in Washington, was so outraged by the stories of mistreatment of Chinese that it refused to renew the immigration treaty with the United States. To strengthen China's position, merchants in Canton, Shanghai, Xiamen, Tianjin, and elsewhere declared a total boycott of American goods in June 1905. There had been such boycotts before, most notably by merchants in Hankou in the 1880s, but nothing so widespread and ideologically charged. Although the American government protested and some local Qing officials stepped in, especially in north China ports, the boycott was effective in many cities, particularly Canton and Shanghai. The Qing court eventually yielded to American pressure and issued a proclamation against the action; but since the copies of the proclamation were posted upside down in many cities, the Chinese boycotters correctly guessed that the court was ambivalent about the ban. Supported by funds from Chinese communities in California and Oregon, and by the patriotic excitement of Chinese students—many recently returned from studies in Japan—Chinese merchants refused to handle such goods as American cigarettes, cotton, kerosene, and flour. Only in late September did their solidarity crack and trade slowly return to normal. Although it was not as dramatic on the surface as Boxer violence or Zou Rong's fiery rhetoric, this attempt to respond to national humiliation by means of concerted economic action marked a new kind of popular movement in Chinese history.

EMERGING FORCES

The growing strength and complexity of Chinese nationalism was but one aspect of a new search for self-identity that cut across the whole of society in the later Qing. Economic, political, educational, and social pressures now began to impinge on virtually everyone in China, except perhaps for those bound to traditional patterns of rural toil far from the cities. Even such poor farmers, however, learned that taxes had to go up if new reforms were to be paid for, and they gathered in protest in many parts of the country only to be roughly suppressed by Qing troops or the agents of newly founded police forces. Among those who would once have been ignored but who now made their voices heard with ever greater effect in the closing years of the dynasty were the overseas students, women, merchants, and urban workers.

After the recall of the official Qing student mission from Hartford, Connecticut, in the 1880s, a new surge of Chinese students left for Europe, where Britain and France were especially popular destinations. A pioneer of this movement was Yan Fu, who had been educated in the Fuzhou shipyard school during the 1860s and sent in 1877 to England, where he enrolled in the naval schools at Portsmouth and in Greenwich. There he studied British naval technology, still the best in the world despite a vigorous challenge by the Germans. He also spent much time examining Western legal practices and began a broad reading of Western political theory. In the course of this he developed an interest in the so-called "Social Darwinists"—those who sought to apply Charles Darwin's theories of species evolution to the fate of social units.

Such theories, which spoke of the "survival of the fittest" and the need for creative adaptation if species were to avoid extinction, seemed to Chinese to have a melancholy relevance to their nation's plight. Yan Fu's translations of such works into Chinese circulated widely. After his return to China in 1879, Yan also worked as an academic administrator in Li Hongzhang's Beiyang naval academy, becoming superintendent in 1890. In addition to his many other duties, he embarked on a series of translations of such influential works as Thomas Huxley's *Evolution and Ethics,* John Stuart Mill's *On Liberty,* Montesquieu's *Defense of the Spirit of the Laws,* and Adam Smith's *Wealth of Nations.* Although he was often depressed and unsuccessful in his professional career at the Beiyang academy—extreme depression led him to opium addiction—Yan nevertheless managed to introduce an electrifying range of ideas to China's students.

When the Qing court ordered the abolition of the traditional Confucian examination system in 1905, the way to a successful intellectual or academic career was thrown wide open and new options arose for China's youth. One young man, Zhou Shuren, who subsequently became China's most famous short-story writer under the pseudonym of "Lu Xun," was caught up by these new currents. Initially trained in local Confucian schools in Zhejiang, Lu Xun read Yan Fu's Social Darwinist works in his late teens and subsequently joined the great exodus of Chinese students to Japan, which had become a magnet for young Chinese. So much nearer and cheaper than the United States or Europe, sharing a common script and not as culturally distant in dress or diet, Japan offered an attractive model after its defeat of the Chinese in 1894 and became even more enticing after its shattering defeat of Russian forces at Lüshun in 1904. The means by which the Japanese had managed to graft a constitutional structure onto the existing imperial system deeply interested reform-minded young Chinese. It was also in Japanese periodicals that Chinese began to discover a new vocabulary, recently created by the Japanese to express major concepts imported from the West, such as "human rights," "constitutions," "democracy," "representation," and "parliament." Since Japan used Chinese characters in its own writing system, these new linguistic coinages could be transferred to China with apparent ease, even though in reality the original Chinese characters used in these neologisms often had their own resonance in China that conflicted with the intended new meanings. Japanese law and medical schools, military academies, departments of political science and economics—all seemed to offer Chinese new hope at a time when that traditional Chinese "essence" seemed every year more fragile in the face of the West's overwhelming practical power.

It was while studying medicine in Japan in 1905 that Lu Xun was shocked by a lantern slide he was shown of triumphant Japanese executing an alleged Chinese traitor in the midst of a large, apathetic circle of Chinese onlookers. He resolved then to give up medicine and concentrate on literature, which, he believed, could in turn shock the Chinese into an awareness of their plight. While China's cultural and spiritual life was in such chaos, there was, thought Lu Xun, little sense in worrying about the health of Chinese bodies. He began a program of translating into Chinese important works of social realism from Europe and Russia so that China's students would understand the great issues that had dominated other parts of the world over the preceding half century.

The thousands of Chinese students in Japan could only be loosely supervised by the Qing authorities, if at all, even though many were supported by government stipends and technically could be returned home for improper behavior. In their excitable, energetic ranks, Sun Yat-sen found ready recruits for his anti-Qing organizations, and in 1905 he allied his revolutionary organization with a number of other radical groups to form the "Revolutionary Alliance" (Tongmeng hui). The alliance tried to infiltrate student members back into China once their education was completed, there to work toward eventual military insurrection. Its ideology was a mixture of Sun's republican ideas—developed during his period of European study and in subsequent reading—and socialist theories on land-tax equalization and the need to control capitalist development. Sun Yat-sen's bold call for revolutionary activism was steadily becoming more compelling than Kang Youwei's more cautious call for constitutional monarchy and protection of the emperor Guangxu.

Among the students in Japan were many young women, and this marked a drastic change in Chinese social and political life. Although some Chinese "revolutionaries" still brought their bound-footed concubines to Japan, many independent young women were, with the encouragement of their own parents or brothers, unbinding their feet and struggling to obtain an adequate or even advanced education. They found moral and social support in sisterhoods that promised lodging and economic help if they remained unmarried, in groups of men who pledged to marry young women with the still unfashionable "large feet," and in schools that actively encouraged their pursuit of learning. These women now had new role models in the guise of famous Western figures like Joan of Arc, Mme. Roland, Florence Nightingale, and Catharine Beecher, whose biographies were translated, printed, and reprinted in magazines. There were also stark new images such as that of the young Russian radical Sophia Perofskaya, whose successful assassination of Tsar Alexander II, even though it led to her arrest and execution, made her a model for female intransigence and courage in the face of autocratic misrule.

Although the scale was still small—by 1909, only around 13,000 girls were enrolled in schools in the whole of China, and a few hundred more overseas—for these thousands of young Chinese women this was a period for the steady development of literary skills and cautious reflection on China's weakness and the restrictions of family life. But a vivid example of the literal acting out of the more revolutionary female goals was offered by Qiu Jin, a young woman from the same part of Zhejiang as the writer Lu Xun. Married young, by her parents' arrangement, to a merchant's son whom she disliked, she bore him two children before suddenly leaving her family and sailing alone for Japan in 1904. There, supporting herself by selling her jewelry and assisted by friends, she began to study a wide range of Western subjects and to speak out publicly on the need for reform.

Drawn to the orbit of Sun Yat-sen's Revolutionary Alliance, Qiu Jin liked to dress in men's clothes on occasion and to experiment with explosives. Returning to China in 1906, she became a radical teacher in a small school in Zhejiang, keeping up her contacts with members of the Revolutionary Alliance and meeting members of local secret societies. Often practicing military drills and riding her horse astride, she inevitably drew criticism from more conservative townsfolk, but she managed to retain her position. It was at her school, in July 1907, in attempted conjunction with a revolutionary friend in Anhui, that she tried to launch an uprising against the Qing. Local troops captured her with little trouble, and after a brief trial she was executed. A short, unhappy, futile life, some might have said; yet the example she left was one of courage and initiative in the face of deep national frustrations, and other Chinese women were to press forward and take up the struggle for political freedoms.

The commercial world of China's merchants was also roiling with change during this period. We have noted that Qing "self-strengthening" statesmen had sought to expand China's economic base by developing "government-supervised merchant-management companies" and that some of these had succeeded in fields such as shipping and mining. But problems of over-lapping jurisdiction and lack of capital slowed these efforts, and by the 1890s there had come to be greater interest in so-called "officials' and merchants' joint-management companies." Many of these were promoted by officials in Shanghai or by Governor-General Zhang Zhidong in Hunan-Hubei, and they included several new spinning and weaving mills, capitalized at 500,000 taels or more. The capital was raised by wealthy officials acting in conjunc-tion with local gentry and merchants, although in some cases merchants were essentially forced to "contribute" by provincial officials. From this level of activity, it was only a short step for some provincial officials to act as inde-pendent entrepreneurs or for some wealthy local figures to develop their own industries without state support. Zeng Guofan's son-in-law Nie was one senior official who invested in the new Shanghai cotton mills; Nie's two English-speaking sons, in turn, without holding office, became significant capitalist developers, bringing in profits to the family of over 100,000 taels in 1904.

Since the Qing court, the metropolitan Peking bureaucracy, the provincial officials, and the merchants each had their own interests and constituencies, it proved impossible to develop the kind of coordinated economic policy that had been so successful in Japan during the Meiji Restoration. Some leaders at court made gestures in that direction, however. Prince Chun, for example, Emperor Guangxu's brother, met large numbers of overseas Chinese mer-chants during his diplomatic journey to apologize to the Western govern-ments for the massacres in the Boxer Uprising. He returned to China a strong backer of vigorous economic intervention by the state. Partly on his urging, the Qing in 1903 founded a Ministry of Commercial Affairs (Shangbu) with similar ranking to the old six ministries and the new Foreign Affairs Ministry. The Commercial Affairs Ministry had four main bureaus: one to deal with trade (including patents and monopolies); one for agriculture and forestry; one for industry, and one for "auditing" (which included such areas as bank-ing, trade fairs, weights and measures, and commercial litigation).

At the same time, the state urged the formation of chambers of commerce in the hope that they might facilitate central control over merchants. The Qing do not seem to have realized that chambers of commerce might also give commercial Chinese a greater sense of local initiative and autonomy. Drawing members from traditional urban trade guilds, from local banking institutions, and among the newly wealthy entrepreneurs, the Shanghai Chamber of Commerce was organized in 1903, although it remained dominated by financial figures from the city of Ningbo in Zhejiang province. The Canton chamber was slower to grow because of local unwillingness to allow central supervision, but it was an economic force by 1905. Both chambers played an important part in leading the anti-American boycott of later 1905. As overseas Chinese merchants in Southeast Asia (and, to a lesser extent, in Canada and the United States) grew wealthier, they also began to invest in certain Chinese enterprises or to make capital available for investment by others.

These new forms of commerce and industrial development became, like foreign imperialism, sources of dislocation in the lives of urban workers. Scattered records allow glimpses of the responses of these workers. In the earlier Qing period, there had been examples of urban market stoppages and labor strikes among such workers as the porcelain furnace men in Jiangxi and the grain-barge pullers on the Grand Canal. But a letter of 1897, written in Shanghai by a twenty-five-year-old American salesman for the Winchester Repeating Arms Company, shows urban tensions escalating in the midst of new social realities, and how swiftly foreigners could become involved.

The writer describes a conflict in late March 1897 over a decision by the Municipal Council of Shanghai to raise the tax on wheelbarrow coolies from 400 copper cash to 600 copper cash a month (a jump from 25 cents to 37.5 at contemporary rates). In protest, the coolies managed to organize and get all wheelbarrows off the streets by April 1. When one lone coolie, a few days later, tried to cross from the French Concession to the English Concession with a wheelbarrow full of offal, a crowd of workers beat him up and smashed his wheelbarrow. A policeman, coming to aid the beaten coolie, was beaten in turn. Westerners in their club, seeing the policeman in trouble, came to help him, and mounted policemen rode to their aid but were forced to dismount because their ponies were too frightened of the crowd. The coolies fought the policemen's drawn swords with poles and bricks pulled from nearby walls. Four blasts from the ship's siren on a British gunboat brought Western "volunteers" to the scene in twenty minutes, and the coolies were dispersed, leaving behind three of their number dead and having wounded two policemen. Within thirty minutes, "Blue Jackets" from several foreign ships had arrived and occupied key bridges and public spaces. Peace returned to the streets, and the Municipal Council decided to postpone the tax increase until July.[6]

Hankou was also undergoing dramatic industrial development under Zhang Zhidong, with well over 10,000 workers employed in modern industrial plants by the 1890s. Here, too, an expansion of resident foreigners and the opening of new foreign-concession areas heightened social tensions. Labor conditions were bleak, wages low, and housing conditions atrocious as rural workers migrated to the already crowded city in search of either long-term or part-time employment. Copper workers struck in 1905, mint employees in 1907, and thousands of street vendors, hawkers, and stall keepers, along with piece-goods shop assistants, struck in 1908. In China's other large cities, the new cotton mills, cement works, cigarette factories, iron works, paper mills, and other plants that were being built—often with foreign capital—all showed the prospects of exploitation and unrest.

No larger patterns in these industrial protests were yet perceived by most people, but news of the attempted Russian Revolution of 1905 had a strong impact in east Asia. Japanese radicals close to Sun Yat-sen drew a new kind of Russo-Chinese parallel, and put Sun himself in contact with Russian revolutionaries. As one Japanese explained it with graphic simplicity, China and Russia were the two greatest autocracies in the world, and the repression they enforced was a block to freedom everywhere. The solution was clear: "For the advance of civilization it was necessary to overthrow these autocracies."[7]

CHAPTER 11

The End of the Dynasty

THE QING CONSTITUTION

Between 1860 and 1905, the Qing court and Chinese provincial officials had tried to adapt a wide range of Western techniques and ideas to China's proven needs: artillery, ships, the telegraph, new schools, factories, chambers of commerce, and international law. Although the focus constantly shifted, the goal was always to learn certain practices from the West that would make China stronger and better able to protect itself from the pressures and demands of those same foreigners. It was, therefore, logical after the debacle of the Boxer uprising that the Qing try to take over elements of the constitutional structures that seemed to lie at the heart of Western power.

In the 1850s, scholar-officials like Xu Jiyu had especially praised the flexibility and openness of the American congressional and presidential system, and it was initially to the United States that the Qing had sent their students for training. Other scholars were drawn to the ideology of the French Revolution and admired the dramatic expansion of French power in the nineteenth century. But since the idea of a republic that would entail their own demise could hardly be to the Qing court's taste, they also began to look seriously at various examples of constitutional monarchy that might both strengthen the country and shore up their own dynasty. Great Britain, still the world's paramount industrial and military power, was one obvious example; another was Germany, rapidly rising to global prominence; and a third—and most dramatic—was Japan, which in less than twenty years since the establishment of a joint imperial and parliamentary structure had transformed its economy, its industry, its military and navy, and its entire system of landholding. The most astonishing proof of the strength these changes brought Japan were its victory over China in the war of 1894 and over Russia in 1904–1905.

The first dramatic gesture in the direction of constitutional reform was made by the empress dowager Cixi in 1905, when she ordered the formation of a small study group of five princes and officials—three Manchus and two Chinese—who would travel to Japan, the United States, Britain, France, Germany, Russia, and Italy to study their governments. The realization that the mission might so strengthen the Qing state that it would be impossible to overthrow dismayed certain radical Chinese nationalists, some of whom resorted to terrorist tactics in an attempt to stop this new Qing gesture toward change. One young revolutionary student tried to blow up the train carrying the constitutional mission as it was leaving Peking station in September. The explosion was mistimed, and the would-be assassin was killed, but he did manage to injure two of the commissioners and to delay matters for four months until substitute commissioners could be named.

The revised mission traveled to the United States via Japan, reaching Washington, D.C., in January 1906 before proceeding to Europe, where they stayed until spring. When they returned to China, they recommended to the empress dowager that some kind of constitutional reform be implemented and suggested Japan as the most effective model, since there the reigning imperial family had been maintained in power. In November 1906, the empress dowager issued an edict promising to prepare a constitution and reform the administrative structure of China by reshaping the existing ministries and adding new ones, by curbing the powers of the governors-general, and by convening a national assembly. It was only eight years since Emperor Guangxu and his supporters had been prevented from pushing through much milder reforms, but the crisis was now so clear that the empress dowager's decision was widely accepted by both Manchu and Chinese officials.

Even before these policy decisions had been made at the central-government level, a reassessment of the nature of Qing local government and its accessibility to the people was being made by some Chinese officials. As early as 1902 the governor of Shanxi province, Zhao Erxun, was formulating proposals that would redesign the *baojia* mutual-security system into a local government network spanning small towns or groups of villages under carefully chosen local headmen. This would create much smaller administrative units than the current counties *(xian)* controlled by magistrates, and would allow greater popular participation in local administration and financial planning. Other proposed reforms were to establish women's schools, to develop an urban police system, and, in particular, to redirect

funds from local community organizations—such as temples or lineages—
to the needs of reforming local government and education. Zhao Erxun felt
that a new level of local structure was essential, since magistrates were
swamped with paperwork and the "majority of the officials in Shanxi are
used to taking no initiative. In poor and far away districts these men are
contentedly at ease with despicable people of their own type."[1] The newly
formed Bureau of Government Affairs officially publicized these reform
attempts, and in 1905 the court formally encouraged subcounty administrative offices.

The problems that became manifest in such reform attempts suggest the
frailty of protodemocratic institutions and the difficulty of establishing them
in an unprepared context. Members of the Confucian-educated Chinese
elite, whether officeholding, landholding, or involved in trade (and in some
cases the same family was engaged in all three), enjoyed a natural dominance
in the countryside and the cities. Their power had long been stabilized by
various institutions of the Chinese state, including the bureaucratic hierarchies, the office of county magistrate, the state examinations, the *baojia,* and
the system of rural taxation. But constitutional change would not necessarily
diminish the power of this elite; it might, indeed, perpetuate or increase it
if the elite could adjust to change intelligently and gain control of the new
organs of government.

A case in point was the "law of avoidance," under which Qing officials
were forbidden to serve in their own native provinces so that they could not
use their office to bolster their economic interests at home. But if, as the
governor of Shanxi had proposed, local men were to be appointed to local
office, they would be able to consolidate and abuse their power in their own
communities. Another example of the ambiguity of reform was the abolition
in 1905 of the state examination system. In one sense this could be seen as
offering greater opportunities to the talented of all social classes and occupational groups, but in fact it was largely the sons (and occasionally the
daughters) of the traditional elite groups who had the money and ambition
to enroll in the new schools, whether in China or overseas; thus constitutional change that demanded fairly advanced education as a criterion for
the vote or for officeholding might also strengthen certain wealthy local
families.

In Tianjin, which had emerged in the late Qing as a cosmopolitan center
for foreign trade and the headquarters of China's modern military and naval
units, the reformist governor Yuan Shikai proposed a different path for
local change. Unlike the Shanxi reformers, his plan was to abolish *baojia*
systems altogether and institute a police force staffed, trained, and paid along
Western lines so as to strengthen local control. Yuan and his staff, in inter-

preting Qing decrees on local government, were also influenced by Japanese models, and they moved swiftly to set up a "self-government bureau" to explore the possibilities of limited representation in local administration. A purpose of the bureau was to strengthen the emergent urban constituency rather than increase already entrenched rural gentry power. One of Yuan's own advisers admitted that "Western scholars have said that the tide of civilization in the past came from the East to the West. Now it comes from the West to the East. We can see that after these next few years there will certainly be no more autocratic countries."[2] The adviser's solution was the election of subcounty assemblies. Although this was too swift a change for Yuan, by 1906 he had established local self-government schools to educate residents of northern Chinese cities for the changes that lay ahead, and in 1907 authorized an election for a council in Tianjin.

Elsewhere in China, with varying degrees of speed and thoroughness, the country edged toward constitutional change. In late 1908 the court announced that full constitutional government would be established over the next nine-year period, the same time span for change that had been followed by the Japanese after the Meiji Restoration of 1868. Although the Qing emperor was to maintain almost total power over the new parliamentary structure, the budget, the armed forces, foreign policy, and the judicial system, the need for a working system of electoral government at the central, provincial, and local levels was now accepted. The death of the empress dowager Cixi in November 1908, which followed by one day the death of the unfortunate emperor Guangxu—still under palace detention after his failed reform attempt of a decade before—did not deflect the general direction of reform. If anything it increased the sense of urgency, since the Manchu regents for the new emperor, Puyi—a baby at his accession, like his two predecessors—formed an advisory cabinet packed with Manchus, foolishly failing to see that this would heighten Chinese suspicions that the whole system of constitutional reform was going to be manipulated to protect the ruling dynasty.

The provincial assemblies, which met for the first time in October 1909, were a startlingly new institution and had a volatile effect on the political life of the country. Although these were still elite bodies, open only to males, with careful criteria as to age, wealth, and education, they drew together in public forums men who cared not only about their own families and local interests, but also about the fate of their country. Election turnouts were high for such a thoroughly new institution. The Chinese state had always looked with disfavor on public gatherings, especially those with a political flavor, as was shown by the late Ming treatment of the Donglin party or Kangxi's and Yongzheng's attempts to focus political thinking around the moralistic and hierarchical Sacred Edict. Now such gatherings received official backing. Moreover the assemblies were immediately suffused with new viewpoints expressed in political magazines and newspapers, and strengthened by the breadth of experience of members who had been trained in military academies or universities overseas, or worked as entrepreneurs in new industries. By early 1910, these provincial assemblymen had exerted so much pressure on the Qing court that it agreed to speed up the reform program and convene the provisional national assembly in Peking that October.

The range of expertise within these provincial assemblies is apparent in the men who emerged as their leaders. In Guangdong, the focus of foreign contact and trade for so much of the eighteenth and nineteenth centuries, the assembly that met in the provincial capital of Canton was presided over by a *jinshi* degree holder and former official who had been active in nationalist agitations against the Portuguese in Macao and a leading member of the Guangdong Association for the Study of Self-Government. In the Hunan capital of Changsha, long a site of antiforeign unrest, the leader was a fine classical scholar who had received the *jinshi* degree in 1904 and had then been posted to the Hanlin literary academy. But as a director of schools for the Qing in Hunan, he had become antiforeign, antidynastic, and active in trying to defend the economic interests of the Hunanese. In Zhejiang, now a fruitful center of agriculture and foreign trade connected by myriad links to the growing metropolis of Shanghai, yet another pattern emerged. Here the leading figure in the provincial assembly was also a *jinshi* degree holder who had become affiliated with a radical academy in Hangzhou. While lecturing there he met fiery anti-Qing agitators and many radical students who subsequently went to Japan. In Fujian, several of the leading assemblymen were Protestant Christian converts, often with strong family or commercial ties to the Chinese in Southeast Asia. It was the Church that gave them experience in public speaking and introduced them to new social and organizational forms.[3]

It was impossible to tell precisely how these men and the assemblies they dominated were going to act, but one thing should have been clear to the Qing leaders: the Qing court had now effectively guaranteed that any actions it undertook in the future to strengthen its position would meet with sustained scrutiny from the very social strata that, in the past, had provided the dynasty with its most trusted supporters.

NEW RAILWAYS, NEW ARMY

Of the new technologies confronting the Qing, the railways proved to be the most troublesome. Many Chinese considered railways disruptive to the harmony of nature and of man: they sliced across the land, disturbing its normal rhythms and displacing its benevolent forces; they put road and canal workers out of jobs and altered established market patterns. Although some mid-nineteenth-century Chinese scholars pointed out that railways had been a main source of Western industrial development, the first short stretch of railway built in China, near Shanghai, was bought by the governor and torn out in 1877.

In 1880 Li Hongzhang had to use subterfuge to get a short length of track laid to move coal from the Kaiping mines at Tangshan to a nearby canal. This stretch of line was extended to Tianjin and adjacent towns in 1888, and a spur run into southern Manchuria in 1894, penetrating the pass at Shanhaiguan where Manchu troops had invaded China two hundred fifty years before. Despite the expressed willingness of many foreign powers to lend money to the Qing so that they might build a railway network, for a few years little further work was attempted, and at the end of 1896 China had only 370 miles of track. By contrast, the United States had 182,000 miles, Great Britain 21,000 miles, France 25,000, and Japan 2,300 miles.

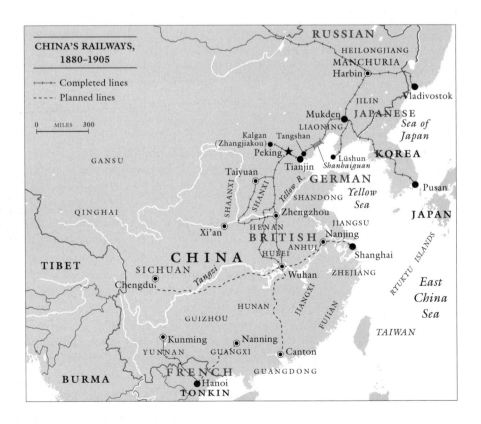

The pressures from foreign powers had been building up ever since China's defeat by Japan in 1894, but reached new levels in the five years following the Boxer Uprising. China, which now had the vast Boxer indemnity of 450 million taels to pay on top of all its other debts, began to find the proffered railway-development loans attractive, even if they came from foreigners. China's most ambitious railway scheme, the Peking to Wuhan* line, had already failed to lure enough active capital from Chinese shareholders, despite its integration with the newly founded Imperial Bank of China. The foreign powers, in turn, were making it clear that they would go ahead anyway and build railways in their areas of influence even if the Qing protested. Germany began to build lines in Shandong; the British drew up plans for lines in the Yangzi valley; the French projected a line from Hanoi north to Kunming; the Russians, who had already by treaty agreement driven a line straight across Heilongjiang province to their major port at Vladivostok, added a branch line to Lüshun; and the Japanese, as part of their military assault on Russia in the war of 1904–1905, drove lines north from Korea toward Mukden. After their victory, the Japanese took control of the main lines in the region and consolidated them as the Southern Manchuria Railroad Company. The results of foreign activity can be clearly seen in the mileage of Chinese track completed in this period: 280 miles between 1896 and 1899, and 3,222 miles between 1900 and 1905.

In this expansionist climate, China seemed a good target for railway investors; and through such new banking conglomerates as the British and Chinese Corporation (a key partner in which was the old opium trading firm of Jardine, Matheson), immense sums of money were offered for the basic development of a comprehensive system, the elements of which slowly began to take focus. The key north-south line, completed in 1905, linked Peking to Wuhan, and a second stage was planned to run from Wuhan to Canton. From Wuhan, another line was planned to run east to Nanjing and Shanghai, and one west to Chengdu in Sichuan province. The French-sponsored line into Kunming would be matched by another spur line from Indochina up to Nanning, in Guangxi province.

A strong mood of nationalism, however, had been growing in China; we have seen elements of it in Zou Rong's polemics, in antiforeign boycotts, as well as in antimissionary activity. As part of this new groundswell, people in many areas of China began to press for a "rights-recovery movement." The aim was to raise money through local bonds so that Chinese could buy back the railroad rights made available to foreign investors and thus regain

---

*Wuhan is a generic name, referring to the three linked mid-Yangzi cities of Wuchang, Hankou, and Hanyang.

complete control of their own transportation system. The confidence that suffused the movement partook of other economic and technological advances. One was the growth of new heavy industries in China run by Chinese entrepreneurs; another, the availability of a good deal of investment capital among the overseas Chinese in Southeast Asia; a third, the success of a new generation of Western-trained Chinese engineers in handling even the most difficult problems of railway construction in harsh terrain. Nineteen such railroad rights-recovery groups were chartered locally between 1904 and 1907, covering nearly all the provinces of China.

By 1910 the Qing government had decided that China's economic development and political stability required an efficient, centralized national railway network. The court therefore decided to buy out, in turn, the rights to railroad lines from their Chinese investors, and to nationalize the whole system under Qing control. They were drawn to this decision in part because those railways that were controlled by the new Qing Ministry of Posts and Communications (founded in 1906) were turning a handsome profit of around 8 million to 9 million taels a year. With annual budgeted expenditures by the Qing now running at 296 million taels on an income base of 263 million taels, this new source of funds made exciting news. The inexperienced Manchu regents for the boy emperor Puyi had little sense of how volatile an issue this had become to the Chinese, and were even told by their advisers that the Chinese investors need only be recompensed for part of their investments. The final edict on railway nationalization, promulgated in May 1911, stated in strong language the reasons for the decision:

> The Government must have in all directions extending to the borders of the Empire great trunk lines in order to carry on government effectively, and to maintain centralized authority. Hitherto the methods have been ill-conceived and there has been no fixed plan. . . . How can we contemplate the consequences of such mistakes? We now proclaim clearly to the whole Empire that the trunk railway lines are to belong to the Government.[4]

Only ten days later the Qing, who had just borrowed £10 million (around $50 million) from a British-American banking consortium, signed a new loan agreement with the same consortium for another £6 million to resume work on the Wuhan-Canton and the Wuhan-Chengdu lines. The many Chinese who believed that each province should have the right to control its own railway development, and that foreign powers should not be allowed a dominant role in the process, were outraged. Within weeks of the May 1911 decision, rallies and protests as angry as any once held against foreigners were being mounted against the Qing. Popular anger remained unabated throughout the summer, especially in Sichuan, where leaders of the provincial assembly and prominent stockholders vowed not to pay further taxes to the government and to fight for retention of their rights.

In the railway agitation of 1910 and 1911, the officers and soldiers of the newly reformed Chinese Army played a prominent role. Many of these troops were deeply nationalist and felt that the Qing were selling out the nation's resources to foreigners. At one railway rally, an army officer cut off his finger to protest his government's action. At another, a private soldier wrote a letter in blood to the Qing railway company, urging it to restore local control. In Sichuan itself, when a Qing general ordered those of his troops who were members of the antigovernment Railway League to step forward so they could be identified and expelled from the ranks, all the troops stepped forward in a show of solidarity, and the general had to rescind his order.

The officers and men in these armies represented a new element on the Chinese scene, the antecedents of which lay back in the 1850s, when Confucian generals like Zeng Guofan had formed locally recruited peasant armies, well drilled and ideologically loyal. Zeng had enhanced the military efficiency and moral rectitude of his troops by offering them decent wages and instilling in them a code of conduct designed to end the popular conception of Qing soldiers as the scourges of the countryside in which they fought. In the Beiyang (north China) armies developed by Li Hongzhang and others, with their officer-training schools, staff colleges, foreign instructors, and up-to-date armaments, the genesis of a modern army for China, to replace the Manchus' Eight Banners system, was firmly in place.

Starting in 1901 the Qing court made a concerted attempt to reorganize the armed forces and to develop what was termed "the New Army." So just as they had with the railway system, the Qing rulers tried to standardize and control the New Army on their own terms. Accordingly the various provincial New Army units were concentrated into 36 divisions under the direct control of the Peking-based Commission for Army Reorganization. With each division projected at 12,500, this would give the government a centrally directed New Army of 450,000 men. In 1906 the Qing also reorganized the Ministry of War, putting it under the direction of a senior Manchu officer served by two Manchu deputies. In 1907 a new position was created—comptroller of the army—and once again the incumbent was a Manchu. That same year the two most powerful provincial governors-general, Yuan Shikai and Zhang Zhidong, both of whom were Chinese, were transferred to Peking to be grand councilors, a technical promotion that took them away from their own troops. The dynasty clearly wished to show that final authority rested with the Manchus in Peking rather than with the Chinese in the provinces.

At many levels, Qing reorganization of the military was effective. A new system emerged that stationed divisions of the New Army at strategic locations across China, including cities where there were also garrisons of the traditionally organized Eight Banners, although these were now being slowly phased out. Qing troops had some dramatic successes in 1910 and 1911, the most spectacular in a series of campaigns in Tibet, where Qing influence had been waning in the face of the assertive independence of local princes and the maneuverings of the British in northern India. Qing forces dispatched to the region overcame the logistical and transportation problems posed by the harsh terrain and conquered portions of eastern Tibet, which were reconstituted as a new Chinese province called Xikang. Qing troops also occupied Lhasa, unseated several recalcitrant princes, garrisoned several towns, and forced the flight of the Dalai Lama to India. Qing soldiers even advanced to the borders of Nepal, Bhutan, and Sikkim to warn the British to ease their pressures on the region. To some Manchu leaders it must have seemed as if the grand old flames of Emperor Qianlong's eighteenth-century victories were being rekindled.

But many problems remained for the Qing military. The army command structure was still fragmented, especially in north China, where Yuan Shikai maintained a loyal following among the troops of the Beiyang army. The Manchus' only answer to Yuan's prestige was, in 1910, to have him removed from office on a trumped-up excuse of illness, which left him angry and his loyal senior officers disaffected. Among the New Army officers were many men who had embarked on military careers after the abolition of the traditional exams in 1905, since the army seemed to offer a swift and sure new channel of upward social mobility. Ambitious and restless, such men were actively involved in the agitations of the provincial assemblies, and New Army ranks were infiltrated with members of the revolutionary anti-Qing societies that owed allegiance to the exiled Sun Yat-sen.

As the troops and officers of the New Army began to adopt the drill, the khaki uniforms, and the modern weaponry of the European and Japanese troops they sought to emulate, they became more aware of the absurdity of certain customs that had hitherto been taken for granted. The Chinese practice of greeting a fellow gentleman by bowing slightly and repeatedly with one's hands clasped at one's chest, for instance, began to be replaced in the army by a crisp military salute. Of symbolically greater importance, the long queue of braided hair that the Manchu regent Dorgon had forced the Chinese to adopt in 1645 as a sign of loyalty and subservience looked ridiculous in modern combat situations. Soldiers who had first tucked their queues under their caps soon began to cut them off. With Taiping rebels in the 1850s, the cutting of the queue had been proof enough of rebellion against the state. Now, in 1910, the Manchu court took note of it but decided there was no disciplinary action that could be appropriately taken, and no alternative to grudging acquiescence.

NATIONALISTS AND SOCIALISTS

In the years between 1905 and 1911, as the Qing edged toward constitutional reform and tried to strengthen their control over the New Army and the railways, dissent in China continued to grow. Having begun to taste the excitement of new opportunities, assemblymen, overseas students, women, merchants, urban workers, and troops in the New Army all pushed both local authorities and the central government to respond more forcefully to their calls for reform. The government's failure to meet their varied demands provoked ever sharper criticism in which new concepts of China as a nation—and of the socialism that might transform it—began to emerge.

The Manchus' position was extraordinarily difficult. With the banner garrisons being slowly cut back or reassigned to civilian occupations and the planned New Army not yet under complete central control or up to full strength, the Qing had no clear military dominance over the country. Each fresh initiative—schools, public-works projects, diplomatic establishments overseas—brought rocketing expenses. When the Ministry of War drew up its first detailed budget in late 1910, it calculated that the expanding army would require expenditures of 109 million taels the following year (this huge sum did not include naval expenses), of which 54 million taels would go to the New Army units. In 1911, army expenditures alone represented almost 35 percent of the projected national budget of 338 million taels. This budgetary total was already 40 million taels higher than the deficit budget of 1910. The advisory national assembly, meeting in Peking, responded by slashing some 30 million taels from the army budget. Even so, the resulting budgetary deficit was huge and had to be met by increased agricultural taxes, a wide range of new duties on tea, wine, salt, and tobacco, higher transit and customs dues, and special taxes on all real estate and land-registration deals.

Aspects of these taxes angered almost everyone, and even when the Qing government was on the side of the angels—as, for instance, with its decision to stamp out opium smoking—it ran into problems. Opposition to the effort no longer came from the British, but from Chinese peasant cultivators of opium, who naturally resented the plowing under of their poppy fields. British opium sales had by now been thoroughly undercut by Chinese domestic production, which, confined early in the nineteenth century mainly to Yunnan and Guizhou, was now a vast enterprise in Sichuan, Shaanxi, and the coastal provinces of Zhejiang and Fujian. The Qing anti-opium drive antagonized people across a range of social strata, including distributors, transporters, opium-den managers and their staffs, and the millions of addicts themselves, many of whom were from the wealthiest classes. As if these problems were not enough, the very weather conspired against the Qing. Torrential rains in the Yangzi and Huai valleys during 1910 and 1911 caused catastrophic flooding, ruined millions of acres of crops, drove up grain prices, led to hundreds of thousands of deaths, and forced millions of refugees into major cities for relief.

The power of the state was nevertheless still strong within China itself— except in the treaty ports and concession areas—and it remained difficult for a concerted political opposition to flourish. Thus in the years after 1905, as before, much of the most effective political criticism came from Chinese living overseas, whether voluntarily or in exile. Among those offering significant critiques of the Qing, and backing them with their own original political programs, were the constitutional monarchists who followed the leadership of Kang Youwei, the nationalists influenced by Liang Qichao, various groups of anarchists and Marxists, and those held together in the Revolutionary Alliance directed by Sun Yat-sen.

Of all these critics, Kang Youwei enjoyed the greatest prestige among educated Chinese at home and overseas, since he was a distinguished classical scholar in his own right, had earned the *jinshi* degree (in 1895), and had been a personal adviser to Emperor Guangxu on the 1898 reforms. Right up to 1911 he continued to urge the Qing to reform their government and to modernize the country so that they could emulate the Japanese and make China strong enough to resist further foreign aggression. He formed various organizations to expound his views, the most important of which were the Society to Protect the Emperor and the Society for Constitutional Government. But as anti-Manchu sentiment grew stronger, Kang's position began to seem eccentric even to his personal supporters, while his various financial backers began to wonder where all their money had gone. Kang was personally extravagant and financially inept. He traveled widely and in style with a young female companion, lived in Paris for a time (where he saw the city from a balloon), and bought an island off the coast of Sweden as a summer retreat. His investments were erratic; he put much of his funds into shaky ventures in Mexico, where they were lost in the Mexican Revolution. Finally, his writings on politics, executed in elegant classical Chinese, began to seem out of place in the twentieth-century world. In his most visionary writings, he speculated on the possibilities of a unified world government that would end all nationalist antagonisms, and on the design of a comprehensive welfare state that would protect and nurture humans from birth to death. "It is as if we are all parts of an electrical force," as Kang put it, "which interconnects all things, or partake of the pure essence that encompasses all things."[5] He proposed the ending of gender discrimination at political gatherings by having all participants wear unisex clothing, and also suggested replacing current marriage arrangements with annual marriage contracts that each party could choose not to renew; such marriage contracts could also be made between two men or two women. But these visionary writings were kept mostly in manuscript, and few people at the time knew of the full range of Kang's thinking.

One of Kang's most loyal disciples, a fellow Cantonese who had sat for the same *jinshi* examinations in 1895, was Liang Qichao. Liang was less emotionally attached than Kang to the emperor Guangxu or to the Qing ruling house, and explored a greater range of political options. For a time he was even drawn to extreme ideas that prescribed "the medicine of liberty" as the cure for the "corruption and degeneration" of China. Yet he shied away from the violence of the French Revolution, noting that "the sacrifices of 1793 in France were rewarded only in 1870, and the rewards did not measure up to the expectations. If we now seek to purchase liberty at the price of infinite suffering, it may not be attained after seventy years, and even if it is, what will have happened to our ancestral country?"[6]

Liang worried, too, that the Chinese people were unprepared to assume democratic responsibilities. His pessimism was strengthened by what he saw of life in America's Chinatowns: Chinese behavior there seemed to him uncoordinated or cowardly, and the social conditions deeply unsatisfactory. So Liang used his great didactic powers at public meetings, and his forceful writing style in a wide range of newspapers (some of which he directed), to push for a stronger Chinese nation that would draw on all its people, including women, and develop an informed citizenry under the initial tutelage of tough natural leaders. To achieve this ideal of an active and unified community of citizens, China needed someone of iron discipline to curb its weaknesses, he wrote, like the Spartan leader Lycurgus or England's Oliver Cromwell, and should forget about the Jean-Jacques Rousseaus or George Washingtons of the world for the time being. But he could not condone Cromwell's execution of the English king, and Liang continued to extol the virtues of constitutional monarchy if it could go hand in hand with progress and economic development. He saw the Italian reunification movement of the nineteenth century as a possible model for China: in Italy military heroes, constitutional advocates, and skilled diplomats had combined their forces to oust foreign occupiers and to reassert a new national identity. Liang's political ideas, which he expressed in novels and plays as well as in essays, attracted a broad following among overseas Chinese and circulated widely within China itself, spreading a sense of disillusion about the Manchus' ability to lead the nation to reform and revitalization.

Far more radical, although less influential and often less elegantly expressed, were the feelings of a considerable number of Chinese who were drawn to various themes within European socialism and anarchism. The development and radical application of Marxist thought had been vigorous in Europe during the nineteenth century, and continued after Karl Marx's death in 1883. In 1889 a broad spectrum of Socialist parties and trade unions, many of them profoundly shaped by Marxist theories, were federated into the Second International, based in Brussels. Although this body supported the concept of parliamentary democracy, it also pledged to exploit the possibilities of international social upheaval brought about by warfare and to use every opportunity to advance the cause of socialist revolution. Members of the Second International accepted Marx's main premises concerning the inevitability of social revolution.

The first discussion of Marx in a Chinese publication appeared in 1899. Marx was summed up as saying that the poor would "continue to have many strikes to coerce the rich," and as believing that "the power of the rich will extend across state boundaries to all of the five continents."[7] Marx was also described, erroneously, as having been English. The attempted Russian revolution of 1905 was exciting to those Chinese who saw the tsars as parallel autocrats to the Qing emperors, and stimulated new interest in Marxist theories, which seemed to offer an opportunity to jolt China into the modern world. Several Chinese began to study an 1899 Japanese work, *Modern Socialism,* which had been translated into Chinese and stated that Marx "used profound scholarship and detailed research to discover an economic base" and that "socialism is easily grasped by the working people and receives the thunderous support of the majority."[8]

In 1906 a summary and partial translation of Marx's *Communist Manifesto* appeared in Chinese, with a rather more poetic and less violent touch than in the English or German version. The famous conclusion to the *Manifesto,* "The proletarians have nothing to lose but their chains. They have a world to win. WORKING MEN OF ALL COUNTRIES, UNITE!" emerged in Chinese as "Then the world will be for the common people, and the sounds of happiness will reach the deepest springs. Ah! Come! People of every land, how can you not be roused."[9]

Although there was no organized Chinese Socialist party until 1911, by

1907 the classical Chinese scholar Jiang Kanghu, whose reading abilities included Japanese, English, French, and German, began the scientific study of socialism. Jiang had served as educational adviser to Yuan Shikai and was an ardent feminist. In 1909 he attended the Congress of the Second International when it met at Brussels. Other Chinese were drawn to anarchism, specifically to the theories of Bakunin and Kropotkin, which criticized the entire contemporary structure of ideas about the state and stressed the role of the individual, the power of cultural transformation, and the importance of popular participation in all revolutionary processes. A group of Chinese living in Paris founded the anarchist New World Society in 1906 and published the journal *New Era*. Most of these Chinese were also connected to Sun Yat-sen's Revolutionary Alliance, but they were fortunate enough to have their own source of funding, since one of their number owned a bean-curd factory and a restaurant–tea shop. The anarchists' goals were broad and visionary: to abolish political authority and the military; to abolish all laws; to abolish class distinctions, and to abolish private property and capital. They advocated various ways of advancing toward revolution: written propaganda, mass associations, strikes, boycotts, mass uprisings, and assassinations when undertaken out of moral commitment. Another Chinese anarchist group flourished in Tokyo at the same time; this one focused more on the plight of women in traditional society, and embraced an antimodernist, agrarian position. Their hero was Tolstoy, and they took seriously the role of the peasantry in revolution, discussing such topics as communitarian life in the countryside and the possibilities of combining agriculture with industry in a rural economy.

Finally there was Sun Yat-sen himself, since 1905 the titular head of the broad spectrum of "revolutionary" and anti-Qing groups that were lumped together as the Revolutionary Alliance. Some of his adherents were drawn to terrorism and preached the use of assassination; most were completely committed to the idea of a republican revolution. They implacably opposed the Manchus and, as "nationalists," they sought China's release from what they considered the economic stranglehold of the West and Japan. Some were also determined socialists who wanted to move China away from what they saw as its "feudal" past into a new and advanced level of development that would avoid the ills of the capitalist system. A good many members of Sun's alliance were women with various agendas for strengthening the roles of women within a new Chinese state. Sun also had strong contacts with secret societies in southern China. He himself had been inducted into the Hawaii branch of the Triad society in 1904 and had relied on Triad support among overseas Chinese in the United States and Canada.

Sun also consistently sought the overthrow of the Qing with armed force.

Between 1906 and 1908, the Revolutionary Alliance directed or instigated at least seven uprisings against the government: three took place in Guangdong province, where Sun's contacts were strongest, and the others occurred in Hunan, Yunnan, Anhui, and Guangxi. Even though each uprising was suppressed by the Qing, Sun remained a charismatic figure to the overseas Chinese, wooing away many former supporters of Kang Youwei and attracting a steady stream of donations into his treasury. Much of this cash came in the form of outright gifts from those Sun had addressed in the United States (where he traveled on a false passport, claiming he was born in Hawaii), Canada, and Singapore, where he had strong backing from several wealthy Chinese entrepreneurs. Sun also sold bonds to those who supported his future regime, promising them a tenfold return on their investments if they would help him attain power. (Although Sun may not have realized it, Lin Qing had followed a similar strategy in his rebellion a century before.)

Despite his vague planning and many failures, Sun was kept going by his energy, persuasiveness, and the virulence of his hostility to the Qing. By the summer of 1911, the number of active Revolutionary Alliance members had grown from around 400 in 1905 to almost 10,000. Many of these were students who had been recruited in Japan by Sun or his affiliates, and had then returned to their home provinces to continue secret agitation against the state. Some had risen to be members of the new provincial assemblies, and others were soldiers or officers in New Army units, where they actively canvassed for further support with revolutionary rhetoric and by offering material inducements. The mix of anger, frustration, dreams, and hard cash was an explosive one.

QING FALL

The specific series of events that led to the fall of the two-and-a-half-centuries-old Qing dynasty was triggered by an accidental bomb explosion in Hankou, one of the three cities that composed the area of Wuhan, on October 9, 1911. This explosion might well have remained an isolated and forgotten incident, however, had it not been for the general agitation over constitutionalism, railways, the armies, Manchu power, and foreign encroachments.

Since at least 1904, groups of radical young Chinese—many of them students who had lived in Japan and a few of them affiliated with the Revolutionary Alliance—had formed revolutionary cells in Hankou and the neighboring city of Wuchang. These two cities, along with Hanyang, the third linked city, with their large numbers of industrial workers and Yangzi River boatmen, modern schools, New Army units, and Qing governmental staff, made the Wuhan tricity complex an exciting area for political and social experimentation. The long-range goal of the revolutionaries was to overthrow the Manchu state, "to avenge the national disgrace" (as they termed it), "and to restore the Chinese."[10] Their shorter-term strategy was to infiltrate the ranks of the New Army units and to coordinate political activities there with members of the various secret societies that had strong branches in the region. The revolutionaries' infiltration of these groups and recruitment of new members to their own ranks were carried out under cover of an elaborate net of allegedly literary or fraternal societies, which enabled small meetings to be held and individual prospects to be approached. When a particular society was investigated by local authorities, the revolutionaries would disband it and later regroup in another area under another name. By the fall of 1911, these various societies in the Wuhan tricity area had attracted 5,000 to 6,000 of the Hubei New Army troops, about one-third of the total force.

The explosion on October 9 occurred while a group of these revolutionaries were making bombs at their meetinghouse in the Russian Concession area of Hankou. Like earlier anti-Qing agitators in Shanghai, they had learned that the institutions of foreign imperialism could afford a measure of protection from Qing police, but on this occasion the size of the explosion brought the Russian authorities to investigate. As the most seriously injured conspirators were rushed to the hospital by their comrades, the Qing investigators who had been alerted by the Russians raided the headquarters and found three other revolutionaries, who were executed immediately. They also obtained the membership registers of the soldiers and others enrolled in the revolutionary societies. The revolutionaries understood that unless they could launch an uprising rapidly, their organization would be unraveled and many more members would lose their lives.

The first troops to take action were in the Wuchang Eighth Engineer Battalion, who mutinied on the early morning of October 10 and seized the ammunition depot. They were joined by transport and artillery units stationed outside the city. These troops launched a successful attack on Wuchang's main forts, and by the day's end troops from three other New Army regiments had come to their support. After trying in vain to muster loyal troops to defend the governor-general's offices, both the governor-general (a Manchu) and the Chinese divisional commander retreated from the city. On October 11, members of the revolutionary societies launched a successful uprising in the third of the tricities, Hanyang, across the Yangzi River from Wuchang, and, along with troops from the First Battalion, seized

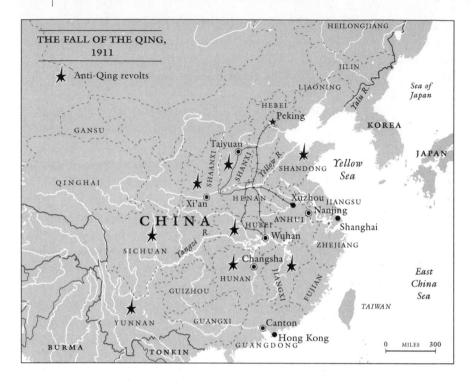

the Hanyang arsenal and ironworks. The Hankou troops mutinied on October 12.

It now became imperative that some prestigious public figure take over titular leadership of the mutinous Wuhan troops and guide the revolutionary movement. Since Sun himself was overseas and there were no senior members of the Revolutionary Alliance in the area, and no other local revolutionary society leaders considered suitable for the role, the rebellious troops approached the president of the provincial assembly, who cautiously declined. They then named the popular commander of one of the Hubei New Army brigades, Li Yuanhong, as military governor. No revolutionary himself (initially, he had to be forced at gunpoint to take the assignment), Li seemed a good choice because he was popular with the troops, had been an activist in the railway agitations, was well liked by the provincial assembly leaders (who agreed to serve in his "administration"), and spoke English, which reassured the large foreign community in Wuhan.

The Qing court responded vigorously to the crisis, ordering the Minister of War to coordinate a counterattack on Wuhan with two divisions of Beiyang army troops. At the same time the Manchus, swallowing their pride, summoned Yuan Shikai back from the "retirement" to which they had banished him in 1910. They believed that Yuan, with his long history of leadership over the Beiyang army and his strong personal ties to many of its senior officers, could muster those troops behind the Qing while the crisis in the south was stabilized. But Yuan was too canny to accept the appointment as military commander until he had a better sense of how the situation might develop.

Events now moved too swiftly to be controlled by any individual or political party. On October 22, 1911, the New Army mutinied in both Shaanxi and Hunan provinces: in the Shaanxi capital of Xi'an, large numbers of Manchus were massacred, and in Changsha, commanders loyal to the Qing were killed. In both cases the leading members of the provincial assemblies expressed their support for the revolution. During the last week of October, three other provinces rose against the Manchus. In Taiyuan, Shanxi, the governor and his family were killed, and the assembly joined with the mutinous New Army units; in Jiangxi province, a complex alliance of merchants, students, and teachers joined with assemblymen and army officers to assert independence of the Qing; and in Yunnan province, far to the southwest, the instructors in the officers' school rebelled and joined with New Army units in an attack on troops loyal to the Qing.

The military significance of railways, over which there had been so much debate in the later nineteenth century, now became apparent to both sides in the battle. While the Qing, using the Peking-Wuhan railway, sped troops south to quell the mutinies in Wuhan, rebellious units from Shanxi moved down the branch line from Taiyuan to cut that same route, thus severing the supply lines of the Qing army. At the end of October, a senior northern general rebuffed the Qing order that he lead his troops south by rail, instead joining with a number of other field commanders and issuing a circular telegram of twelve demands to the Qing court. The critical demands were to establish a parliament within the year, to promulgate a constitution through that same parliament, to elect a premier and have him ratified by the emperor, to deny the emperor all rights of summary execution of criminals, to declare a general amnesty for all political offenders, to forbid members of the Manchu imperial clan from serving as cabinet ministers, and to have the parliament review all international treaties before they were approved by the emperor.

Within a week the Qing court had complied with most of these demands. On November 11, three days after the members of the Peking provisional national assembly elected Yuan Shikai premier of China, the court issued a decree appointing him to the same office and ordering him to form a cabinet. Yuan complied, naming mostly his own partisans to key positions.

These developments were clearly moving China toward a constitutional monarchy under Manchu direction—the kind so long advocated by Kang Youwei and his supporters—rather than toward the republican form of government central to the demands of Sun Yat-sen and the Revolutionary Alliance. But Sun's supporters, although numerous, did not wield unified military strength in China, and Sun himself was fund-raising in the United States during the events of late 1911; he read the news of the Wuchang uprising in a Denver newspaper while en route to Kansas City. Sun saw his first priority as securing European promises of neutrality in the coming conflict, and accordingly traveled to London and Paris to confer with the foreign governments there before returning to China. In an important political success, he persuaded the British not to advance any more major loan payments to the Qing government.

Throughout November, Yuan Shikai performed a delicate balancing act, using his influence over the Beiyang army to pressure Manchus and revolutionaries alike. Qing forces managed, after heavy fighting, to recapture both Hankou and Hanyang (though not Wuchang, south of the Yangzi), but this was not much solace to the court as province after province declared its adherence to the revolution. Sun's Revolutionary Alliance turned out to have a startling degree of mass support, which the alliance's leaders skillfully exploited. Expanding its organization and focusing its goals, the alliance played a critical role in three provinces that went over to the revolution: Jiangsu (which declared its independence from the Qing on November 3), Sichuan (November 22), and Shandong (December 12). Elsewhere, the alliance remained part of a broader coalition of anti-Qing movements that continued to draw leaders mainly from the New Army, the provincial assemblies, and, in some cases, local merchants.

The Qing court's position was immeasurably weakened when Manchu and loyalist troops were defeated in Nanjing in early December after several weeks of heavy fighting. Nanjing had been China's capital in the fourteenth century, and since that time had always carried a symbolic importance lacking in other cities. Its fall now reminded Chinese of the failures of the prince of Fu's forces there in 1645 and of the great Taiping victory in 1853. Nanjing thus provided a truly national base for the Revolutionary Alliance to consolidate its position.

The mother of the five-year-old boy emperor Puyi now moved to the front of negotiations, pushing through the resignation of the current Manchu regent and authorizing Yuan Shikai to rule as premier while the emperor presided at audiences and state functions. But to many, this seemed like a return to the days of the empress dowager Cixi, and the compromise was not a popular one.

Sun Yat-sen returned to Shanghai by sea from France on Christmas Day, 1911. Four days later, the delegates from sixteen provincial assemblies, meeting in Nanjing, showed their respect for Sun's leadership and the influence of the Revolutionary Alliance by electing Sun "provisional president" of the Chinese republic. He assumed office in Nanjing on January 1, 1912, inaugurating the existence of the new republic, which was henceforth to follow the Western solar calendar with its seven-day weeks instead of the traditional Chinese lunar one with its ten-day periods. On that same New Year's Day, Sun sent a telegram to Yuan Shikai that acknowledged how weak his own military power base really was. In this telegram, Sun stated that even though he had accepted the presidency for the time being, "it is actually waiting for you, and my offer will eventually be made clear to the world. I hope that you will soon decide to accept this offer."[11]

China now had both a republican president and a Manchu emperor, an impasse that required some sort of resolution. Later in January 1912, the tension between the Manchu conservatives and ambitious Chinese politicians was underlined when a series of assassination attempts nearly took the lives of Yuan Shikai and several senior Manchu princes and generals. At the end of the month, a bomb killed the strongest remaining exponent of a tough Manchu line—the deputy chief of staff, who had endeavored to make the Imperial Guards Corps an elite Manchu military machine.

The final blow to the Qing came at the end of January 1912, when forty-four senior commanders of the Beiyang army sent a telegram to the Peking cabinet urging the formation of a republic in China. While the most intransigent Manchu princes retreated to Manchuria, where they tried to coordinate a resistance, the emperor's mother and her close advisers negotiated frantically with Yuan Shikai and the other Beiyang army leaders for a settlement that would guarantee their lives and a measure of financial security. When both Yuan and the senate of the provisional government in Nanjing agreed to guarantee to the boy emperor and his family the right to continued residence in the Forbidden City of Peking and ownership of its great imperial treasures, as well as a stipend of $4 million a year and protection of all Manchu ancestral temples, the court announced the abdication of the emperor Puyi on February 12, 1912. Refusing to recognize Sun Yat-sen's claims, a brief accompanying edict gave to Yuan Shikai full powers "to organize a provisional republican government"[12] and to establish national unity with the Revolutionary Alliance and the other anti-imperial forces in central and south China.

So, with a few simple words, the more than two millennia of China's imperial history were brought to a close. And with almost no experience whatsoever in the arts and institutions of self-government, the Chinese people were presented with the option of devising their own future in a watchful and dangerous world.

III | ENVISIONING STATE AND SOCIETY

ONE LATENT SOURCE of trouble during the Qing dynasty had been the balance between central and local power. The hope of China's more progressive politicians, as they struggled to establish a viable republic in the place of the discredited imperial system, was to create a new governmental synthesis that would transform China into a modern nation-state. A parliament in Peking composed of provincial delegates would link center and periphery together. A pool of almost 40 million voters would ensure wide representation for diverse regions and interests. A revitalized structure of local government would placate provincial interests and draw new revenues to the center so that urgent reforms could be undertaken and the power of the foreigners curbed.

The dream collapsed within a few months of China's first national elections in 1912. The leader of the majority political party was assassinated and his organization then outlawed by the provisional president, Yuan Shikai. Though Yuan had ambitious plans to revitalize China, he lacked the military power or the organizational skills to hold the center together. Political power, accordingly, flowed out either to the elites in the provinces—both rural and urban—or to the hundreds of military leaders who began to emerge as the dominant power brokers in China's localities. China's political weaknesses were underscored by international developments: Japan placed ever harsher demands on China, and even China's bold initiative of sending more than 100,000 laborers to work with the Allied powers in Western Europe during World War I failed to obtain the backing of those powers for China's territorial claims.

The result was a period of political insecurity and unparalleled intellectual self-scrutiny and exploration. Many educated Chinese were convinced that their country was about to be destroyed, and they began to study every kind of political and organizational theory, examine the nature of their own social fabric, debate the values of new forms of education and language, and explore the possibilities for progress that seemed to lie at the heart of Western science. Known generally as the May Fourth movement, such a concentrated outpouring of intellectual exuberance and doubt had not been seen in China for over two thousand years, although elements of the same search could be seen in the period of the Ming-Qing transition and in the debates over China's future at the end of the Qing.

From the many options explored by May Fourth thinkers, some of China's brightest minds were drawn to the doctrines of Marxist socialism, steered skillfully in this direction by international agents sent to China from the Soviet Union. By 1920 the nucleus for a Chinese Communist party was in place, and the first general meetings of the party were held in 1921. Although Sun Yat-sen's Guomindang (or Nationalist) party enjoyed a much wider prestige and following, the Communists were able to give cogent expression to China's aspirations in battling warlordism, landlordism, and foreign imperialism, and in addressing the plight of China's growing industrial working class. When Communist organizers joined with Guomindang activists, they were able to coordinate a number of impressive and effective strikes, though the strikers themselves sometimes paid for their boldness with their lives.

The alliance between the Communists and the Nationalists was born of a shared desperation and a shared hope. The desperation was over China's fragmented state, compounded by feuding militarist regimes and foreigners' special privileges. The hope lay in drawing on the spirit, skills, and intellectual powers of the Chinese people to create the strength necessary for lasting reunification. Despite competing long-range goals and clashing personalities, Communists and Nationalists could agree at least on the need to attempt reunification of the country through a mixture of military force and social reform. Working together in the southern city of Canton, they were able to train a new military elite and form rural associations that would add peasant numbers to the ranks of organized industrial workers. The military successes of 1926, which drove the newly combined armies to the Yangzi River, were astonishing. But the speed of victory over warlord forces only highlighted the depth of disagreement over social policy, and 1927 became a year of disaster for the Communists as they tried to outmaneuver their Nationalist allies and change the direction of the new state, only to see their movement all but crushed in the attempt.

While the Communists, driven out of the cities, tried to regroup in isolated rural areas, the Nationalists attempted to consolidate their hold over the entire country, and successfully brought China from Manchuria to Guangdong under one flag by the end of 1928. Juggling desperately with inadequate finances, Chiang Kai-shek concentrated on remolding the administrative organs of the state, and encouraging the development of an infrastructure of transportation, urban services, and educational facilities to go with them. During this same period, there were great changes in China's urban culture, which adapted many elements from the West, and many areas—especially Shanghai—took on a modern air. A number of foreign powers had particular importance in Chinese policy at this time. The United States offered money and technically skilled personnel along with its missionaries. Germany contributed military experts and proposed immense deals involving German armaments and rare Chinese minerals. But Japan continued intransigent, extending its hold over Manchuria through the creation of a puppet regime there, and pushing its forces south of the Great Wall until the Chinese agreed to declare northeast China a demilitarized zone. Dreams of a vibrant nation faded again as disgruntled intellectuals turned against the appeasement of the Japanese by the Guomindang, and the Communists began to create large and apparently viable rural governments based on their own radical mix of land reform and guerrilla armies.

For a brief period in the mid-1930s, Japan was the spur to Chinese national renewal as well as its gravest enemy. The Chinese Communists, driven out of their largest and best base, the Jiangxi Soviet, by Chiang's repeated and sustained assaults, retreated to the barren north in the Long March. But once there, they could appeal successfully to a public wearied by the constant spectacle of internecine warfare between Chinese. When Chiang Kai-shek was kidnaped by mutinous troops, the chance offered itself of once again declaring a united front, of reforging a single nation that would withstand the invader. Despite the terrible sufferings of so many Chinese people during the long years of fragmentation and reform, the idea of the nation had remained alive.

| # The New Republic

EXPERIMENT IN DEMOCRACY

The state of China as the last Manchu emperor abdicated in February 1912 bore many parallels to China's position when the last Ming emperor hanged himself in April 1644. The national finances were in disarray, with a depleted treasury in Peking and little money coming in from the provinces. Groups of scholars and bureaucrats had expressed a wide range of dissatisfactions with the defunct regime, and this discontent now had to be addressed. The army troops occupying Peking were numerous but hard to control, of doubtful loyalty, and liable to mutiny or desertion if their pay fell too long in arrears. Natural disasters had devastated the countryside, causing ruined harvests and starvation, and creating masses of refugees just when financial shortages made it difficult for local governments to offer famine relief. Many supporters of the defeated ruling house remained loyal and could be the focus for future trouble. Foreign pressure was intense, the possibility of invasion imminent. In the macroregions of central, western, and southern China, there was a strong chance that independent separatist regimes would emerge, further weakening central authority.

There were also, of course, numerous differences between the two transitional periods, of which four were probably the most significant. First, in 1912 there were at least seven predatory foreign powers with special interests in China, not just one, and China was already heavily in debt to them. Second, in 1912 the entire economic infrastructure of the country was being dramatically transformed by new modes of communication, transportation, and industrial development. Third, the significance of Confucianism as a central philosophical system with answers germane to all Chinese problems had been called into question. And fourth, although in 1912 many Chinese still favored a strong, central authority, the entire institution of the emperorship along with the compromise arrangement of a constitutional monarchy had been rejected by most educated Chinese. The most influential forces in the country sought to impose some type of republican government.

In this period of heightened tension, violence was unpredictable and common. Two men who were to become China's pre-eminent leaders in the second quarter of the century, and whose battles with each other were to affect the shape of the Chinese revolution, both had their first taste of violent conflict and political activity at this time. Mao Zedong, born in 1893 to a farming family in Hunan province, served with local student volunteer forces in the area of Changsha. He witnessed the speedy collapse of the Qing armies at firsthand, cut off his queue, and had the grim experience of seeing the murdered bodies of the two most prominent Revolutionary Alliance leaders lying in the city street. They had been killed not by Qing troops, but by republican supporters of the provincial assembly president Tan Yan-kai, who sought a more moderate path for China. Mao served briefly as a private in the Hunan republican army, and there came across pamphlets by the socialist thinker Jiang Kanghu, who founded the first Chinese Socialist party in November 1911. But Mao's own political stance was still cautious: he later told an interviewer that he had hoped for a government with Sun Yat-sen as president, Kang Youwei as premier, and Liang Qichao as foreign minister. Once the fighting ended, Mao embarked on a course of self-directed study of political and economic writings as preparation for playing a direct role in the reform of Chinese society.

The second man, Chiang Kai-shek,* had been born in 1887 to a salt-merchant family near the foreign treaty port of Ningbo in Zhejiang province. Following the route of many ambitious young Chinese of some means, he had gone to Japan to study in a military academy, where he stayed from 1908 to 1910. Chiang joined the Revolutionary Alliance, through which he became a close associate of the Zhejiang leader Chen Qimei; when Chen became military governor of Shanghai during November 1911, Chiang was promoted to be one of his regimental commanders. He served courageously in the attack on Hangzhou and in the effort to win the city over to the revolutionary cause. According to various accounts, Chiang's baptism of personal violence came when he instigated or performed the assassination

*This was the common romanization of his name. Drawn from the local dialect, it was used throughout his life by virtually all Western writers. Hence it is retained here, rather than the pinyin form of Jiang Jieshi.

of a dissident member of the Revolutionary Alliance who opposed both Sun Yat-sen and Chiang's mentor Chen Qimei.

The restoration of order to China required that Yuan Shikai link his Peking base and Beiyang army support to the Revolutionary Alliance and the Nanjing forces. It also hinged on the integration of the New Army units and the provincial assemblies into a national polity bound by a legitimate constitution. The first steps toward these goals were halting ones. Since his troops were no match for Yuan's, Sun Yat-sen, hailed by his supporters as provisional president on January 1, 1912, relinquished claims to the title just over a month later, on February 13, the day after the Manchu abdication; Yuan Shikai assumed the office in Sun Yat-sen's place. Leaders of the Revolutionary Alliance and their supporters had stipulated that Yuan Shikai govern from Nanjing, which would move him from his northern military base and mark an important symbolic step toward the formation of a viable civilian regime. But Yuan chose to remain in Peking, claiming that the unstable military situation demanded his presence there. A series of mutinies and outbreaks of violence in Peking, Tianjin, and Baoding during March 1912 seemed to confirm his view, although some cynics observed that it was probably Yuan who had instigated the trouble in the first place to prove his indispensability. Sun Yat-sen, for his part, showed the sincerity of his interest in a revitalized China by traveling to Peking, at Yuan's invitation, and drawing up a vast (and visionary) blueprint for the transformation of China's railway system.

The task now was to create a meaningful constitution, under which valid elections would be held across China for the new two-chamber parliament. The initial step toward this goal had been the convening of the National Assembly in Peking in October 1910. This was a one-chamber house, with its members either elected by the provincial assemblies or selected by the Manchu regent. The National Assembly at once joined with the provincial assemblies to press for the convening of a full parliament before the date of 1917 originally envisioned by Empress Dowager Cixi. In November 1910, the Manchu court agreed that a fully elected parliament should be convened in 1913.

Although a creation of the Qing court, 'the National Assembly swiftly moved to a position of importance for the future of constitutional government in China. On October 30, 1911, as the Manchus fought for survival, they authorized the National Assembly to draft a constitution, and the assembly produced the first version on November 3. Five days later, the assembly elected Yuan Shikai as China's first premier, conferring a form of democratic legitimacy on his rule.

Overlapping with these developments in Peking, however, came the meetings, at the instigation of the Revolutionary Alliance, of various groups of provincial delegates—first in Shanghai, then in Hankou, and finally in Nanjing. These delegates were formally convened as the National Council in Nanjing on January 28, 1912, with three delegates from each province. Their role was essential to the healthy growth of Chinese democracy, since Sun Yat-sen had stipulated that the National Council would ratify Yuan's election as provisional president. Yuan responded punctiliously by sending the council a formal message stating that "a republic is the best political system" and "we should never allow the Monarchic system to be restored in China."[1] At Sun's urging, the Nanjing council unanimously elected Yuan Shikai as China's provisional president on February 14.

Yuan Shikai's ascent to the top of the republican structure had come with dizzying speed. Born in 1859 into a lineage that had produced several successful officials, Yuan Shikai did not take the state examinations; instead he purchased a minor official title in 1880, a practice followed by many young men in the later Qing. Thereafter he served for over a decade in various military and commercial posts in Korea, during which time he had ample experience with Japan's expansionist aims in that country. After the Sino-Japanese War of 1894–1895, Yuan Shikai was appointed by the Qing to train the officers for China's first new modernized army corps, which gave him an important nucleus of military protégés. It is almost certain that he helped the empress dowager overthrow Emperor Guangxu and the Hundred Days' reformers, but he also successfully suppressed the Boxers in Shandong. After 1901, as governor-general of the Hebei region, he built the Beiyang army into China's finest fighting force (five of its seven divisional commanders and all the other senior officers were his protégés), and showed a real interest in reforms that strengthened his region, including development of local self-government, education, and a police force. Yuan's achievements in late Qing political life offered hope that as leader of the republic he might respond successfully to the challenges confronting China.

In his own letter of resignation as provisional president, Sun wrote that "the constitution of the provisional government was to be prepared by the Council, and the new president must obey it."[1] In accordance with these procedures designed to ensure the formation of a legitimate republican government, the council promulgated a new draft of the provisional constitution on March 11, 1912. It guaranteed all Chinese and minority peoples equality and protection of persons and property under the law, as well as freedom of worship and assembly, and stipulated that a full parliament must be convened within ten months. At that time the council would be dissolved, and Yuan would resign so that new presidential elections could be held.

The same council, with its representatives now increased to five from each province, voted on April 5 to move the provisional government to Peking, making China a united republic for the first time in word as well as deed. The old Qing national assembly had now been superceded.

Under the rules of this provisional constitution, the Chinese began to prepare for their first national elections. There were to be two chambers in the Parliament: one, a Senate, would comprise 274 members serving six-year terms, chosen by the provincial assemblies, with ten members from each province and the remainder representing the overseas Chinese; the other chamber would be a House of Representatives with 596 members serving three-year terms, and drawn more or less proportionately according to population on a basis of one delegate for each 800,000 people.

With the Qing dynasty at an end, Sun Yat-sen directed that the Revolutionary Alliance transform itself into a centralized, democratic political party that would run candidates for office in the December 1912 elections. The organization of this now renamed National People's party (Guomindang*) was placed in the hands of Song Jiaoren, one of Sun's most capable lieutenants during the years of exile. Song, only thirty years old in 1912, proved a naturally skillful political organizer, although his arrogant self-confidence alienated many. His main interest was to ensure that the powers of the president be limited and that the powers of the Parliament, with its elected representatives, be properly protected. It was clear to most observers in mid-1912 that Yuan Shikai completely dominated the cabinet he had named and wished to assert overweening presidential power. Traveling to many parts of China in 1912, Song Jiaoren made this point vehemently and in terms that often seemed to be directly critical of Yuan Shikai's ambitions. Song and other members of the Guomindang approached the December elections with an edge over their three main rivals: a group of loosely affiliated organizations known as the Progressive party (headed by Liang Qichao), the Republican party (which was strongly nationalistic in tone), and the Unification party. There were over three hundred other small political groups or parties that contested one or more seats in the elections.

Although the national elections drew more attention, political developments in the countryside were equally important. In the general discussion over local self-government during the last years of the Qing, there had been worries that the reform councils would merely serve to entrench the conservative gentry, who would now add official administrative power to the influence already conferred on them locally because of their education and landholdings. This fear was borne out in the months after the Manchu

*Until recently romanized as Kuomintang and abbreviated as KMT.

abdication, as old scores were settled and powerful local incumbents took over a range of new posts designed to bring the authority of the central government much deeper into the countryside than the old Qing magistrates had ever been able to do. Unless this trend were checked, it could undermine hopes for a working democracy in China. But in the excitement of the national race, this problem seemed peripheral and was not directly addressed by the Guomindang or their rivals, although the Guomindang platform did include remarks about the need to develop structures of local self-government.

New electoral regulations promulgated in 1912 gave the vote to Chinese males over twenty-one who held property worth $500 or paid taxes of at least $2, and held an elementary-school graduation certificate. Approximately 40 million men—around 10 percent of the population—could meet these requirements. Illiterates, opium smokers, bankrupts, and those of unsound mind were not allowed to vote. Chinese women had also failed to win the right to vote, despite their growing assertiveness in the late Qing, the support of several prominent intellectuals, the participation of many women as members and financial supporters of the Revolutionary Alliance, and the experiences of some as soldiers with the revolutionary armies or as nurses on the front lines. In 1912, the Peking suffragist Tang Junying led several women to the National Council in Nanjing, where they lobbied vigorously for the insertion in the new constitution of a statement on the equality of men and women, and on women's right to vote. Rebuffed, the women forced an entrance into the meeting chamber, shouting and breaking windows; they were unceremoniously evicted, neither of their requests granted.

The results of China's first national election were announced in January 1913, and they spelled a clear victory for the Guomindang. In the House of Representatives the party won 269 of the 596 seats, with the remainder divided up among the other three main parties. (In this initial election, many politicians maintained allegiance to several parties, so the seats claimed cumulatively by all four parties far exceeded 596.) In the Senate, of the 274 incumbents, 123 were Guomindang members. Under the provisional constitution, the Guomindang would now have a dominant role in selecting the premier and cabinet, and could proceed to push for the election of the president in a fully supervised parliamentary setting.

In the spring of 1913, China's newly elected representatives began to travel by rail, road, river, and sea to the Parliament in Peking. The victorious party leader, Song Jiaoren, went with his friends to the Shanghai railroad station on March 20. As he stood on the platform waiting to board the train, a man walked up and shot him twice at close range. Song was taken at once to the hospital but died two days later—two weeks before his thirty-first birthday. It was widely believed that he would have been named China's premier. It was also widely believed that Yuan Shikai was behind the assassination, since the trail of evidence led to the secretary of the cabinet and to the provisional premier. But the main conspirators were either themselves assassinated or else disappeared mysteriously, and Yuan was never officially implicated.

When the other Guomindang delegates had assembled in Parliament, they pressed to gain control over Yuan, to develop a permanent constitution, and to hold a full and open presidential election. The Guomindang members, in particular, were intensely critical of Yuan's handling of national finances: instead of addressing tax-collection problems directly, he had taken out another huge loan—a so-called "reorganization loan"—of over £25 million (approximately $100 million) from a consortium of foreign banks. Yuan interpreted these bitter protests as personal attacks and resolved to strike back. In early May 1913, he dismissed the leading pro-Guomindang military governors. In heavy fighting that summer, troops loyal to the Guomindang were routed by Yuan's forces, and in September, Nanjing was taken for Yuan by the reactionary general Zhang Xun, whose troops still wore their Manchu queues. In October, Yuan forced the members of Parliament to elect him president for a five-year term. (It took three ballots before he won a majority, however.) Finally, calling the Guomindang a seditious organization, he ordered the dissolution of the party and the eviction of its remaining members from Parliament. At the end of November, Sun Yat-sen left China for Japan, driven once more into exile from his own country, his republican dreams in ruins.

THE RULE OF YUAN SHIKAI

The foreign powers watched developments in China closely. They had realized that there was no sense in continuing the effort to keep the Qing dynasty alive in order to preserve the treaty rights they had won since 1842. As a result they followed a policy of strict neutrality in 1911 and 1912, while alerting their troops and ships to protect foreign nationals in China and guard a corridor from Peking to the sea to prevent any recurrence of Boxerlike antiforeign outbreaks. The main priority of the foreign powers was to protect their investments in China, which had totaled almost $788 million in 1902 and reached $1.61 billion by 1914. Foreigners were, therefore, likely to accept any government that created a favorable economic climate.

Although foreign investments were concentrated mainly in Shanghai and

FOREIGN INVESTMENTS IN CHINA, 1902 AND 1914[2]

	1902		1914	
	Millions of U.S. dollars	Percent of total	Millions of U.S. dollars	Percent of total
Great Britain	260.3	33.0	607.5	37.7
Japan	1.0	0.1	219.6	13.6
Russia	246.5	31.3	269.3	16.7
United States	19.7	2.5	49.3	3.1
France	91.1	11.6	171.4	10.7
Germany	164.3	20.9	263.6	16.4
Others	5.0	0.6	29.6	1.8
Total	787.9	100.0	1,610.3	100.0

southern Manchuria, they covered a wide spectrum of enterprises. Britain's approximately $608 million stake in China included the Hong Kong–to–Canton railway, shipping, public utilities (gas, electricity, and telephone), tramways, coal mines, cotton mills, sugar refineries, silk filatures, a rope factory, cement works, and real estate. Japan's $220 million investment (385 million yen) covered a similar range. American interests were much smaller, but nevertheless were estimated at around $49 million in 1914. The bulk of this was in mission properties (including hospitals and schools) and in Shanghai real estate, although when the first American chamber of commerce opened in Shanghai in 1915, thirty-two American firms took out membership right away.[3]

Japan and the European powers were initially skeptical about Yuan Shikai's new regime and held off from diplomatic recognition of the republic. In the United States, however, opinion was more favorable both to Yuan and to the idea of the new republic. A large number of American missionaries in China had been sympathetic to the republican movement, and many of the more reform-minded Chinese had been educated in mission schools. Sun Yat-sen was a Christian; and Yuan Shikai, even though he was no Christian, cleverly played on pro-Christian sentiments by asking American Protestants to pray for China in their churches as the new Chinese parliament convened in April 1913. The request made the headlines in American newspapers and received favorable attention from President Woodrow Wilson as well as his cabinet. Wilson observed that he did not know when he had been "so stirred and cheered," and his secretary of state, William Jennings Bryan, called Yuan Shikai's appeal "the most remarkable official document that had been issued in a generation." The *Christian Herald* compared

Yuan's action to Constantine's and Charlemagne's "in subjecting pagan nations to the yoke of Christ."[4] In May 1913, the American minister in Peking called on President Yuan, and full diplomatic recognition was extended to Yuan's government.

The British minister in Peking considered the American action "outrageous" since Yuan had not yet given formal guarantees on the preservation of foreign rights and investments. Britain was also anxious to ensure the autonomy of Tibet, which Yuan claimed—following late Qing precedent—was a Chinese dependency. Britain's intransigence on the matter was resented by the Chinese; but on October 7, 1913, Yuan did acknowledge Tibetan autonomy, although his decision was not ratified by either the cabinet or Parliament. The same day Britain extended diplomatic recognition to the Chinese republic. Japan extended recognition after China agreed to further large-scale railway deals, and Russia did the same after China acknowledged the autonomy of Outer Mongolia.

The fact that Yuan Shikai had now won foreign recognition for his regime did not mean that his government was secure. China's constitutional arrangements were in a shambles. As a prelude to purging the Guomindang members from the Parliament in late 1913, Yuan had ordered his police to conduct house-to-house searches of those representatives and senators believed to be Guomindang affiliates. The searches yielded up 438 members with Guomindang party cards, and these members were henceforth banned from the Parliament. Since the Parliament now lacked a quorum, in late November the speakers of both houses announced an indefinite adjournment; in January 1914, Parliament was formally dissolved, and in February similar dissolution orders were issued for the provincial assemblies and for local government organizations.

To give a semblance of legality to his regime, Yuan now convened a body of 66 men from his cabinet and from various posts in the provinces, and these men produced, on May 1, 1914, a "constitutional compact" to replace the provisional constitution. The compact gave Yuan as president virtually unlimited power over war, finance, foreign policy, and the rights of citizens. In explaining his action to one of his close advisers, Yuan observed: "Parliament was an unworkable body. 800 men! 200 were good, 200 were passive, 400 were useless. What had they done? They had not even agreed on procedure."[5] It was a suitably sardonic comment on the destruction of China's democratic hopes.

Deprived of any mass base of financial support, Yuan's government lived largely on loans. By 1913 only 2 million yuan or less were coming in from provincial land taxes, and the government was running a deficit of 13 million yuan each month. The revenue from tariffs on foreign trade was also mainly out of Yuan's reach, since in response to the unrest of the revolution, the Imperial Maritime Customs (now under Robert Hart's successor, Hart having died in 1911) deposited the customs revenues in foreign banks so they could be used to pay off the interest on China's rapidly accumulating foreign debts. Even the salt taxes were now under foreign supervision; they were either used to pay off debts or manipulated to put political pressure on Yuan.

Despite this trickle of funds, Yuan Shikai was ambitious, both for his country and for himself. Even as he subverted the constitution, paradoxically he sought to build on late Qing attempts at reform and to develop institutions that would bring strong and stable government to China. To prepare some of his reforms, he relied on a team of talented foreign advisers that included an Australian foreign-policy expert, a Japanese railway specialist, a French military attaché, and a Belgian jurist; most of these advisers, however, were by their own admission overpaid and underused.

Yuan continued to work for the development of an independent judiciary for China, not because he had any abstract love of justice, but because a firm, impartial system of courts would be China's best tool for ending the hated system of extraterritoriality. China's new Supreme Court—established in 1906 by the Qing dynasty—took vigorous steps forward in such areas as commercial law and married women's rights. All but three provinces had higher courts, as did many prefectures, although Yuan did not encourage county courts, preferring that judicial power at that level reside with local administration rather than special judges. To reform China's penal system, Yuan authorized an active prison-building program, the improvement of sanitary conditions in prisons, provision of work facilities for prisoners, and attempts at moral reform of criminals. In education, Yuan pushed for the nationwide expansion of primary schooling for males, which would be compulsory and free, and supported experimentation with alphabetized manuals and with teacher retraining. Yuan nevertheless insisted that, along with the new skills needed by China's citizens, the primary curriculum should include study of Confucius.

To develop the economy, Yuan ordered attempts at raising crop yields through irrigation and flood control, developing new strains of livestock, promoting afforestation, and speeding distribution of goods through low-interest loans and reduced railway freight rates. A national survey of China's geological resources was also begun under the direction of a Chinese scientist trained in Britain. The national currency was centralized, minting controlled, and millions of depreciated banknotes in the provinces recalled. Yuan Shikai also made an intensive effort to maintain the suppression of opium smoking and production that had begun in the late Qing. So effective was this plan—all county magistrates were evaluated according to their success at opium suppression—that opium dealers retreated into the foreign-concession areas, where they would be protected by foreign law.

It was to Yuan's initial advantage as he built his dictatorship that the First World War had erupted in Europe in August 1914, leaving France, Britain, Germany, and Russia too distracted to press for any more gains in China. Furthermore, in their desperate need for troops on the Western front, these foreign powers summoned home all their able-bodied nationals from China. This gave a new generation of Chinese entrepreneurs and managers a golden opportunity to take over the key functions in business and administration, to build up their private fortunes, and to gain invaluable financial experience. But unfortunately for Yuan, Japan was more than ready to pick up the slack. With formal ties of alliance to Great Britain that dated back to 1902, Japan had declared war on Germany in August 1914 and had immediately followed up by attacking the German concession areas in Shandong province.

In January 1915, Japan dealt China an even harsher blow when it issued Yuan's government the Twenty-one Demands. In these, the Japanese demanded far more extensive economic rights for their subjects in Manchuria and Inner Mongolia; joint Sino-Japanese administration of the huge Han-Ye-Ping iron and coal works in central China; nonalienation of any Chinese ports or islands to other foreign powers; the stationing of Japanese police and economic advisers in north China; and extensive new commercial rights in the region of Fujian province. Chinese hostility to these moves was expressed in nationwide anti-Japanese rallies and in a boycott of Japanese goods that was far more extensive and successful than the anti-American boycott of 1905. Still, Yuan felt he had to yield, although he did modify slightly some of Japan's conditions.

As Yuan's prestige and popularity sagged, his own intransigence hardened. His critics were harassed or silenced under the terms of censorship regulations imposed in 1914 on all newspapers and other publications; these regulations carried stiff penalties for anyone printing material "harmful to the public peace."[6] To build up additional support for his authority, Yuan had already begun to reinstitute elements of Confucian belief as China's state religion. As president, Yuan assumed the role of chief participant in important rituals at the Qing Temple of Heaven, to which he now drove in an armored car. By deliberately evoking Qing state religious observances, Yuan took on the trappings of emperor; in late 1915, Yuan indeed moved firmly in that direction, floating rumors that people wanted him to revive the institution. By August, official pressure to make Yuan emperor had taken on national dimensions, and in November a specially convened "Representative Assembly" voted—allegedly with the astonishing unanimity of 1,993 votes in favor and none opposed—to beg Yuan to become emperor. On December 12, 1915, Yuan accepted, inaugurating his new regime as of January 1, 1916. He placed an order at the former imperial potteries for a 40,000-piece porcelain dinner set costing 1.4 million yuan. He also ordered a large jade seal and two imperial robes at 400,000 yuan each.

Yuan Shikai and his advisers (one of them, Frank Goodnow, an American professor from Columbia University and former president of the American Political Science Association) believed that China was yearning for a symbol of central authority transcending the president and that, therefore, the restoration of the emperorship would be welcomed. But they had miscalculated. Many of Yuan's close political allies abandoned him, and the solidarity of his Beiyang clique of former military protégés was shattered. Throughout China there were mass protests matched by open actions in the provinces. The military leader in Yunnan declared that province's independence in December 1915; Guizhou followed in January 1916, and Guangxi in March. The foreign powers were aloof or openly hostile to Yuan and did not give him any of the support he expected. In March 1916, Yuan Shikai responded to the outcries by declaring that he would cancel the monarchy, but his prestige was now shattered, and province after province continued to declare independence of Peking. Yuan died of uremia—compounded, many thought, by anger and humiliation—on June 6, 1916, at the age of fifty-six.

The successor to the now tarnished presidency was Li Yuanhong, the reluctant ally of the Wuhan revolutionaries in October 1911 who had been serving since 1913 as the ineffective and equally reluctant vice-president. Li's power base was far weaker than Yuan's, and he had no Beiyang army standing behind him—only a sea of disaffected or independent provinces and an almost bankrupt treasury. Li's most important acts were to recall the members of the Parliament (who had been recessed over two years before) so that China might once again have representative government, and to reaffirm the provisional constitution of 1912 as the binding force on the nation. But both these steps were controversial: since the representatives elected in December 1912 had been voted in for three years only, it was not clear that any of them were now legally members; and since the 1912 provisional constitution had been replaced by Yuan's of 1914, it was not certain that it still had priority.

Li Yuanhong had been in office just over a year when a new military coup occurred, linked to yet another attempt at restoring the emperorship. This time the instigator was General Zhang Xun, who had been a fanatical supporter of the Qing ever since he had served as military escort to Empress

Dowager Cixi at the time of the Boxer Uprising. Zhang had fought loyally for the Manchus at Nanjing in 1911 and had remained a Manchu loyalist throughout Yuan's presidency, even ordering his troops to keep their queues in Manchu style. It was Zhang who had seized Nanjing back from the Guomindang troops in 1913, and despite the savagery of his army in looting the city after its capture, Yuan had named him a field marshal and inspector general of the Yangzi provinces. Allegedly acting as mediator between President Li Yuanhong and other feuding generals, Zhang led his army into Peking in mid-June 1917 and declared the restoration of the abdicated Qing emperor Puyi, now a boy of eleven. As bemused Peking residents searched for old Qing imperial banners to hang outside their houses, and the international diplomats tried to decide how to handle this new development, a small group of former Qing officials and scholars—among them the late emperor Guangxu's loyal supporter, Kang Youwei—hurried to the Forbidden City in official robes to serve the new emperor.

But the restoration never got off the ground. Other generals in the Peking region marched on the palace, and two aviators—in what may well have been China's first aerial action—dropped a bomb on the Forbidden City, killing three men. In mid-July, the troops of rival generals stormed Peking and defeated Zhang Xun, who was given political asylum in the Dutch legation and took no more active part in politics. Emperor Puyi was deposed once again, although not penalized, except by the order of the new president that he be given a modern education under Western tutors. (He continued to live in style in the Forbidden City until 1924, when another warlord evicted him from the palace and forced him to seek safety in the Japanese concession area in Tianjin. The Forbidden City was thereafter made into a public cultural and historical museum.)

With the collapse of General Zhang's insurrection at the hands of a group of other, rival generals, all pretense of real strength in the central government was gone. From now on both the presidency and the Parliament became the playthings of the militarists; and although able, intelligent men continued willing to serve in the government, they rose and fell at the behest of these outside forces. Democracy had vanished, and the era of "warlordism" had begun.

MILITARISTS IN CHINA AND CHINESE IN FRANCE

The men known as "warlords," who now controlled much of China, had a wide range of backgrounds and maintained their power in different ways.

A large number had risen through the ranks of the Beiyang army and had once been protégés of Yuan Shikai; many others had served in the provincial armies and had risen to positions as military governor or senior officer in late 1911 or early 1912. A number were simply local thugs who had seized an opportunity to consolidate a local base. Some dominated whole provinces and financed their armies with local taxes collected by their own bureaucracies; others controlled only a handful of towns and got their money from "transit taxes" collected at gunpoint or through confiscation. Some warlords were deeply loyal to the idea of a legitimate republic, continuing to hope that one day they would be reintegrated into a valid constitutional state; others believed that Sun Yat-sen and the Guomindang represented China's legitimate government. Out of choice or necessity, a number worked closely with foreign powers, whether it was the British in Shanghai, the Japanese in Manchuria, or the French in the southwest. Some controlled extensive lengths of railway line, drawing their revenues from passenger and freight services, and from the commerce of cities on the line. Some reinstituted opium growing in their domains and tapped the greatly expanded drug trade for revenues. Opium use once more began to attain the scale it had before the suppression campaigns of the late Qing and of Yuan Shikai's early presidency.

In character as well, the warlords differed greatly. Many, like the warlord who for a time dominated Shandong, were capable of a ferocious and erratic cruelty or of extremes of sensual indulgence, but many others were educated men who tried to instill in their troops their own vision of morality. This might be a kind of modified Confucianism, Christianity, socialism, or the curious amalgam concocted by the warlord of Shanxi, Yan Xishan, who drew on a wide array of heroes from Europe and the United States in pursuit of his ideal image. As Yan stated proudly, he had constructed a virtually perfect ideology to run Shanxi province, one that combined the best features of "militarism, nationalism, anarchism, democracy, capitalism, communism, individualism, imperialism, universalism, paternalism, and utopianism."[7]

No matter whether individual warlords were cruel or generous, sophisticated or muddleheaded, the fragmentation of China that was now beginning was to make any further attempts to unify the country even harder than it had been for those who inherited the mantle of leadership from the Qing. Nevertheless, a certain apparent coherence adhered to China's government because the warlords in north China never completely destroyed what remained of the presidency and the premiership. Instead, they placed their own supporters in these positions so that whatever prestige the offices preserved would redound back to the warlords themselves.

One man who assumed leadership under these conditions was Duan

Qirui, who became premier of China in 1916. Born in 1865, the year after the suppression of the Taiping rebellion, Duan in 1881 was among the first group of cadets to enroll in the new Beiyang military academy. Graduated top of his class, he was spotted by Li Hongzhang and sent to Germany for advanced study in military science. Thereafter, the course of his career mirrored the new opportunities and dislocations of China itself. His next sponsor, Yuan Shikai, made Duan head of the New Army's artillery battalion. Duan served with Yuan in Shandong during the Boxer Uprising and was given command of a division of Beiyang army troops in 1904. His appointment as head of the staff officers' college in 1906 provided him an admirable opportunity to build up his own clique of loyal young officers, just as he had served as a member of Yuan Shikai's loyal group of protégés. He commanded the Second Army Corps in Hubei during the 1911 revolution and was named military governor of Hunan and Hubei as a further reward for his loyalty to Yuan. In 1912, he was appointed to Yuan's cabinet as minister of war and served as acting premier during the 1913 purge of the Guomindang from the Parliament. With Yuan's death in 1916, Duan—who had opposed Yuan's imperial-restoration attempt—became premier, given crucial backing by other senior commanders from the old Beiyang army clique.

As Duan consolidated his complex civil and military power base in China, World War I began to reach its most crucial stage in Western Europe. Although there was no historical precedent for China's taking an active role in global events far from its shores, it fell to Duan to inaugurate a new era of overseas involvement. He and his advisers were intrigued by the possibilities of joining France and Britain in their fight against Germany, arguing that if Germany were defeated, then the strategically important German concession areas in Shandong province around Qingdao could be reclaimed by China. Duan was further pressured toward an anti-German declaration from two directions. One was from the United States, which in early 1917 was preparing to enter the war in response to German submarine attacks against neutral shipping in the Atlantic; the other was from the Japanese, who had abandoned various attempts to encourage separatist regimes in Manchuria, Mongolia, and southern China, and had decided to try to bribe Duan Qirui's regime into recognizing Japan's standing in north China at Germany's expense.

China's military strength was trivial compared to that of the European belligerents or of the United States, which had entered the war on the side of Britain and France in April 1917, but China had one crucial resource that the Allies lacked—namely, manpower. The slaughter in the European battlefields had been terrible: the British and French had lost over 600,000 men at the Battle of the Somme alone in 1916, and the following year the

British lost 250,000 more at the Battle of Ypres. In constant need of new men for the front, the Allies realized that if Chinese laborers could be used on the docks and on construction projects in Western Europe, it would free more European males for active combat.

Pursuing this harsh but accurate line of reasoning, the British and French had begun to negotiate with the Chinese as early as the summer of 1916. Well before the Chinese declaration of war, the result was the establishment of a processing plant for Chinese laborers in Shandong province, near the British naval base of Weihaiwei, with a second one added later at the port of Qingdao. Sarcastically referred to by the British as their "sausage machine,"[8] the processing system worked swiftly and smoothly. There were tens of thousands of Chinese volunteers, driven by the poverty of the region and China's political uncertainties, and lured by the generosity of the wages offered by the British. Each volunteer received an embarkation fee of 20 Chinese dollars, followed by 10 dollars a month to be paid over to his family in China; the volunteers were provided with clothing and meals as well. The Chinese were given medical examinations and checked specifically for trachoma (a contagious viral disease of the eyelids, especially common in Shandong), tuberculosis, and venereal disease. If accepted—and about 100,000 made it through the screening—they were issued dog tags with serial numbers, which were sealed with metal rivets on bands around their wrists. Then they were sprayed from head to foot with disinfectant and urged to remove their queues, which many had chosen to keep despite the revolution in 1911.

An initial boatload of Chinese laborers, traveling across the Indian Ocean and through the Suez Canal in 1916 on contract to the French government, had been sunk by German submarines in the Mediterranean; 543 Chinese lives were lost. New recruits were thereafter shipped over the Pacific to Canada, across Canada by train, and then reshipped in fleets accompanied by antisubmarine patrols for the final journey across the Atlantic. Although their employment had been protested by many French and British, particularly by labor-union members, the Chinese were soon at work, most of them in northern France. They were given such tasks as unloading military cargoes at the docks, building barracks and hospitals, digging trenches, and handling ammunition in the railway marshaling yards. They worked ten-hour days, seven days a week, with some time off allowed at the traditional Chinese festivals. The Chinese laborers remained nonbelligerents even after China's declaration of war, since there was no way Duan's regime could finance an army in Europe.

The presence of so many Chinese men in France—54,000 by late 1917, 96,000 by late 1918—brought both dangers and opportunities. Some of their camps were bombed by German planes or shelled, and on occasion they retaliated for their dead comrades by killing German prisoners of war. Some Chinese were blown up by unexploded mines or shells when cleaning battlefields or digging trenches. Many fell ill from the strange diet and the intense damp and cold, and on occasion they mutinied against their French and British employers or ransacked local restaurants in search of food. Sample sentences from a Chinese phrase book prepared by the British army for use by its staff in the camps hint at the levels of irritation or discrimination the Chinese labor corps experienced: "I want eight men to go over there quickly." "Why don't you eat this food?" "The inside of this tent is not very clean." "You must have a bath tomorrow." "This latrine is reserved for Europeans and is not available to Chinese."[9]

The most significant response to the bleak conditions came from representatives of the YMCA, who saw here a major opportunity for service. They focused especially on recreational activities and on problems of public education among the Chinese, designing special vocabularies and teaching techniques to spread literacy among the workers. Astonishingly, with the aid of such educated Chinese staff, as many as 50,000 letters a month were mailed from France to China, where they were read and reread aloud to the villagers. Brief, simple in vocabulary, and censored for military secrets by the Allies, these letters are nevertheless important signs of the growing literacy becoming possible for Chinese workers. One surviving letter ran as follows:

> For the inspection of my elder brother. I have come many ten thousand li* since I saw you. I am doing well and you need not have anxiety about me. I am earning three francs per day, but as living is expensive I cannot send many home yet. As to my quarrelling with you, that day at Yaowan, before I left, forget it! I did unworthily. Please take care of our parents and when I return in three or five years, I will bring enough money to help support them the rest of their days.[10]

The Chinese contribution to the war was not without its cost. In addition to the 543 lost at sea, almost 2,000 Chinese workers died in France and Flanders, and were laid to rest in a number of special cemeteries. There the long lines of gravestones, each neatly incised with the characters of their Chinese names and the serial numbers given to them by their Western employers, still bear mute testimony to China's first involvement in such a global conflict. More complex was the legacy of the tens of thousands of

*A *li* is one-third of a mile.

workers when they returned to China, literate and wise in the ways of the world, often with a decent balance of cash stored up safely with their families. They would be in a position to play a new kind of active role in Chinese politics, as some Chinese socialists observed.

After the armistice of November 11, 1918, ended the war with Germany's defeat, anticipation in China ran high. There were triumphant parades in Peking, and an exuberant crowd demolished the memorial that the Qing had been forced to raise in honor of the Germans killed by the Boxers. The Peking government was now headed by yet another Beiyang-faction president and premier; Duan Qirui had resigned in October 1918, but before doing so had used the huge Japanese loans to enhance his own military power and had continued to build a network of secret deals with the Japanese. The Chinese delegation to the postwar treaty negotiations at Versailles, sixty-two members strong, was headed by five capable diplomats who had never been fully briefed on what to expect. They were greeted at Versailles by the shattering announcement of the chief Japanese delegate that early in 1917, in return for Japanese naval assistance against the Germans, Great Britain, France, and Italy had signed a secret treaty ensuring "support [of] Japan's claims in regard to the disposal of Germany's rights in Shandong" after the war.[11]

As if that were not bad enough, the Japanese also announced that they had come to secret agreements with Duan Qirui in September 1918, while he was still premier. These agreements granted the Japanese the right to station police and to establish military garrisons in Jinan and Qingdao, and mortgaged to Japan, in partial payment for its loans to China, the total income from two new Shandong railroads the Japanese planned to develop. The Chinese delegates seem to have been genuinely unaware of these humiliating secret agreements. President Woodrow Wilson, who had earlier been sympathetic to China's desire to recover its Shandong rights, now felt that Japan had staked out a firm claim to them on the basis of international law. On April 30, 1919, he agreed with David Lloyd George of Britain and Georges Clemenceau of France to transfer all of Germany's Shandong rights to Japan.

As the nature of this new betrayal grew clear, urgent telegrams flew between Paris and Peking, and the Chinese public was aroused as rarely before. China's delegates at Versailles were bombarded by petitions and protests from political and commercial groups, from overseas Chinese communities, and from Chinese students at universities abroad. On May 1, the news reached Peking that the Chinese delegates acknowledged their case as hopeless because of the prior agreements. This news triggered mass protests in Peking on May 4, which were followed by demonstrations in cities all over China. While the government dithered, pressure on the Versailles delegates not to sign the treaty was unrelenting. With typical indecision, the Chinese president did at last telegraph an instruction not to sign, but the telegram was sent too late to reach Versailles before the June 28 deadline. However, Chinese students and demonstrators, by surrounding their nation's delegation in their Paris hotel, had forcibly prevented the delegates from attending the signing ceremonies. The Versailles treaty ended up without China's acceptance.

A new generation of Chinese activists was henceforth to direct probing questions at the nature of Western moral values, disgusted as much by the bloodshed of which Western nations had proved capable as by their duplicity. And the date of May 4, the day in 1919 on which the citizens and students of Peking protested publicly in the streets against the Versailles treaty, was to give its name to a new movement in China, one in which the juxtaposition of nationalism and cultural self-analysis took the Chinese people in yet another new direction.

CHAPTER 13

"A Road Is Made"

THE WARNING VOICE OF
SOCIAL DARWINISM

The fragmentation of authority under Yuan Shikai, the failure of the fledgling republic, and the betrayal of Versailles—all served to deepen a fear that had been latent among Chinese since the late Qing: that China was about to be dismembered, that it would cease to exist as a nation, and that the four thousand years of its recorded history would come to a jolting end. At the same time, analytical tools for probing China's plight had been made available by the spreading popularity of Western Social Darwinism; and even if the theories gave little solace to Chinese thinkers, these ideas nevertheless helped to bring some sense of method into a despairing debate.

The evolutionary theories of Charles Darwin, whose *Origin of Species* was first published in England in 1859, explained how the adaptive processes of natural selection determined which species managed to thrive and which were doomed to extinction. From the huge range of observations that he had made while sailing on the *Beagle* to the Cape Verde Islands, Chile, the Galápagos Islands, New Zealand, and Australia, Darwin came to realize that those organisms that were best fitted to survive in the constant struggle for the limited resources that made existence possible were the ones that did survive, and that in doing so they slowly ousted those less well fitted. Through the laws of heredity, furthermore, the degree of adaptation achieved by a species would be maintained or improved.

The British sociologist Herbert Spencer made his own creative adaptation of these theories. In *The Study of Sociology,* published in 1873, Spencer applied Darwinian theories to the development of human societies, arguing that the "survival of the fittest," a phrase Spencer coined in 1864, governed social as well as biological evolution. He declared that human societies evolved from the homogeneous to the heterogeneous and hence to a stage of increasing individuation. Societies were further divided between military ones obtaining cooperation by force and industrial societies in which voluntarism and spontaneity rose from the acknowledgment of individual consciousness. Spencer's theories were then reanalyzed and contested by the scientist Thomas Huxley, and encapsulated in 1893 in his book *Evolution and Ethics;* Yan Fu, a product of China's naval-school system during the self-strengthening period and later a student in England, read Huxley's book at the time of the Sino-Japanese War and translated it into Chinese in 1896—with his own added commentary and interpretations—under the title *On Evolution.* Partly because Yan Fu chose to give the work a nationalistic emphasis not evident in the original, it had an immense impact on Chinese scholars in the late Qing and early republic.

The message that came across from Yan Fu was that Spencer's sociological writings were not merely analytical and descriptive, but prescriptive as well, offering means to transform and strengthen society. Yan Fu summarized Darwin as follows:

> Peoples and living things struggle for survival. At first, species struggle with species; then as [people] gradually progress, there is a struggle between one social group and another. The weak invariably become the prey of the strong, the stupid invariably become subservient to the clever.[1]

Spencer, Yan Fu continued, "based himself on the theory of evolution to explain the origins of human relations and of civilization." Other late Qing thinkers were quick to see the significance of these ideas. In advocating the 1898 reforms, Liang Qichao observed hopefully that evolutionary theories allowed "the possibility of influence and change that can cause the species to steadily improve." Liang noted how heredity and education acted on human "thought, intelligence, physique and habits," and that the Chinese could strengthen their race to engage in the struggle for survival: "All countries that wish to have strong soldiers insure that all their women engage in calisthenics, for they believe that only thus will the sons they bear be full in body and strong of muscle."[2]

Social Darwinism inevitably led the Chinese to ponder problems of race and racial strength, and many Chinese combined the new theories from the West with the writings of seventeenth-century anti-Manchu nationalists like Wang Fuzhi. Writers reflected on whether there was an inherent Chinese essence and, if so, when it had developed. If all Chinese were descendants of the Yellow Emperor, had that noble progenitor sprung from peoples who had migrated to what was now China from somewhere else? Was their past history, therefore, one of creative adaptation that had only recently slowed because of the Manchus, perhaps, or the savage force of the foreign powers? China might well be doomed to extinction unless the nation evolved new strengths; a measure of hope lay in the belief that with will power and awareness that task could be achieved. "A nation with spirit will survive," a Chinese scholar wrote just before the 1911 Wuhan uprising; "a nation without it will perish. But where does the 'national spirit' lie? In national studies."[3]

The 1911 revolution briefly raised hopes that Social Darwinist ideas of harsh social competition were now discredited. Just before the 1912 elections were won by his reorganized Guomindang, Sun Yat-sen wrote:

> Before the twentieth century, the nations of Europe invented a newfangled struggle-for-existence theory, which for a time influenced everything. Every nation assumed that "the survival of the fittest" and "the weak are the meat of the strong" were the vital laws on which to establish a state. They even went so far as to say that "might is the only right, there is no reason." This kind of theory in the early days of the evolution of European civilization had its uses. But, from the vantage point of today, it appears a barbaric form of learning.[4]

But by 1913, Sun was writing sadly of a world dominated by struggles for survival from which no government or industrial enterprise could be exempt. Yan Fu, too, lost his enthusiasm for the theories he had so much helped to popularize in China, writing that the failures of the Chinese republic and the bloodshed of World War I in Europe showed that "three hundred years of evolutionary progress have all come down to nothing but four words: selfishness, slaughter, shamelessness, and corruption."[5]

Such pessimism might well lead to a refusal to strive anymore for social change, as indeed happened among Social Darwinists in the United States. This possibility lent added urgency to China's radical thinkers. As Chen Duxiu, later a cofounder of the Chinese Communist party, wrote to a friend just after Yuan Shikai's death: "The majority of our people are lethargic and do not know that not only our morality, politics and technology but even common commodities for daily use are all unfit for struggle and are going to be eliminated in the process of natural selection."[6] If that happened, China would die.

Elements of these strains of thought came together in the mind of another future leader of the Chinese Communist party, Mao Zedong. In 1917, when he published his first essay, Mao was twenty-four years old. He had rebelled against his father, rejecting both the rural life on the family farm in Hunan province and the marriage his parents had arranged for him with the daughter of a neighboring family. Instead, after serving briefly in the anti-Qing army in 1911, he had plunged into a life of study in Changsha, haphazard and eclectic. Having made his own way through Yan Fu's translations of Mill, Montesquieu, Rousseau, and Spencer, as well as a wide range of Chinese political philosophers, Mao was accepted as a student at the well-known First Normal School in Changsha, where he studied ethics as his major field. This deepened his knowledge of the works of Spencer and Rousseau, and introduced him to Kant, as well as to the ways that such thinkers could be usefully compared to figures from China's own past.

Mao's first approach to the problems of China's weakness was a literal-minded one. If China was weak, it was because the Chinese were weak. If the Chinese were weak, it was because their culture concentrated on building up the the mind and neglected strengthening the body. Mao tempered his own physique by swimming and exercising; in his essay "A Study of Physical Education," published in the journal *New Youth* in April 1917, he urged his countrymen to do the same. "Physical education not only harmonizes the emotions, it also strengthens the will," he wrote. The trouble was that the Chinese traditionally hated violent exertion and cultivated "flowing garments, a slow gait, a grave, calm gaze." All that must change: "Exercise should be savage and rude. To be able to leap on horseback and to shoot at the same time; to go from battle to battle; to shake the mountains by one's cries, and the colors of the sky by one's roars of anger"—that was what Chinese should strive for.[7]

In another essay, written two years later for a Hunan provincial journal and entitled "To the Glory of the Han People," Mao urged collective action on the Chinese race as a whole, using some of the rhetorical flourishes that had made Zou Rong's anti-Manchu diatribes in *The Revolutionary Army* so effective fifteen years before. If only the Chinese could truly combine, Mao wrote, if they could form a "union of the popular masses," then they could join the great tide of world change. This tide was "rolling ever more impetuously," and "he who conforms to it shall survive, he who resists it shall perish." If the Chinese people could so adapt, concluded Mao, "we should not fear the dead. We should not fear the bureaucrats. We should not fear the militarists. We should not fear the capitalists."[8]

As was true of many young Chinese at this time, Mao's main ideas were Darwinist and idealistic, and tinged with anarchist belief, but as yet not deeply affected by influences from Marxist-Socialism. As Mao wrote at this same time, he admired the anarchist Kropotkin more than Marx, for the key values in society were "mutual aid" and voluntary unions.[9] In a series of nine articles he wrote for a local Changsha newspaper in November 1919, Mao showed that he had combined his thinking on the need for collective struggle with the kinds of reflections on women and their rights that had been advocated by Liang Qichao, Qiu Jin, and others in the late Qing. They had argued that the energy of China's women should be harnessed to strengthen the state, enabling China to face the world with its full complement of 400 million people, rather than with the political resources of only its 200 million males. Mao's newspaper articles "On the Suicide of Miss Zhao" addressed an event that had occurred in Changsha that same month. A young woman from the Zhao family had been betrothed without her consent to a young man from the Wu family. Such arranged marriages were the norm in China, but what was unusual about Miss Zhao was that she objected so violently to the marriage that she slit her own throat inside the sedan chair carrying her to the marriage ceremonies in her future husband's home. Her death was followed by a grim tussle between the Wu and Zhao families as each tried to give the other responsibility for burying the corpse.

Writing with both passion and acuteness, Mao observed that this tragedy could have been avoided if any of three conditions had been different: if Miss Zhao's family had been more sympathetic, if the Wu family had not insisted on the letter of their marriage contract, and if the society of Changsha (and, by implication, of all China) had been more brave and open. Miss Zhao's death mattered, wrote Mao. "It happened because of the shameful system of arranged marriages, because of the darkness of the social system, the negation of the individual will, and the absence of the freedom to choose one's own mate." Yet Mao could not condone the act of suicide, even in such a state of despair. If the Chinese were to refuse to confront reality, they would achieve nothing. People commit suicide because society has deprived them of all hope, Mao argued; but even in a position of complete hopelessness, "we should struggle against society in order to regain the hope that we have lost. . . . We should die fighting."[10]

"We should die fighting." The words were bold ones, but the real difficulty lay in deciding who was the main enemy. Was it just an apathetic local society? Was it the local warlords who controlled Hunan? Was it corrupt politicians in Peking? Was it the gunboats of the voracious foreign powers, or the foreign businesses that were making ever further inroads into China? Or was it perhaps something even more complex: the whole structure of Chinese beliefs, and the economic system that went with it? For the young men and women of Mao's generation, the problems were baffling, but they had somehow to come up with a program for solving these difficulties if China were not to succumb to despair.

MARXIST STIRRINGS

Before the Bolshevik Revolution of 1917 in Russia, the Chinese had not shown much interest in Marxism. Almost none of Marx's work had been translated into Chinese, except for sections of *The Communist Manifesto.* Even Sun Yat-sen's socialist ideas came from a different tradition—that of Henry George, who had influenced British socialists by advocating state expropriation of all surplus value that accrued to landholders in the form of higher rents, which George saw as the unearned result of general social progress. At first, Marxism did not seem a useful analytical tool for China: Marx had shown little interest in China itself, apart from some writings on the Taiping, and his view of a passage for human societies from primitive communalism through an era of slavery to feudalism and capitalism did not appear to fit China's historical experience. And since China could hardly claim to be a capitalist society even in embryo, Marx's theory that the overthrow of capitalism was a prerequisite for the new era of socialism seemed to make that transition indefinitely remote.

So despite Chinese press reports of the victories of the Petrograd workers' soviet led by Trotsky, the overthrow of the liberal Kerensky government, and the formation of Lenin's revolutionary Soviet government, the news did not initially attract much attention. But slowly the Chinese began to realize that the events in Russia went beyond the experiences of France in 1789, and for many observers it was electrifying to see how the entrenched Russian autocracy, with all its embedded institutions, had turned out after all to have contained the seeds of the Soviet Union. A Guomindang newspaper in Shanghai took the lead in praising the Bolsheviks in January 1918, and Sun Yat-sen—who had returned to China after the death of Yuan Shikai—sent a personal message of congratulation to Lenin shortly afterward.

As the seriousness of the Bolsheviks' ongoing struggle with the conservative White Russian forces became apparent, and as hostile reactions from the Allied powers became more open once Lenin had made peace with Germany, greater numbers of Chinese began to reflect on the significance of what had occurred and to try and draw lessons from it for their own society. At the vanguard of this attempt was the head librarian at Peking University, Li Dazhao. Born in 1889 to a peasant family in Hebei province,

Li had sold what little property he owned to go to a modern school, and from 1913 to 1916 he studied political economy in Japan, earning a reputation there as a fine writer and editor. Because of these skills, in February 1918 he was appointed librarian of what had become China's most prestigious university.

Li Dazhao's initial salutation to the Russian Revolution was published in June 1918 against a backdrop of chaotic warlord politics, with Zhang Xun's restoration of Emperor Puyi only a few months in the past and with China's declaration of war on Germany still a burning issue in Peking. Li saw in the Soviet Union the promise of a new, third civilization rising to mediate between the East and West. Because of its geographical location, Russia had inevitably been influenced by both East and West; but now, wrote the euphoric Li, "we have only to raise our heads to welcome the dawn of the new civilization of the world, and turn our ears to welcome the new Russia that is founded upon freedom and humanism, and to adapt ourselves to the new tide of the world." Li felt that Russia was approaching a great surge of development: Britain and France had risen to splendid heights and were now sinking; Germany was at its peak and would soon, too, begin to fade; but Russia, "just because of its comparative slowness in the evolution of civilization," had "surplus energy for development."[11] Might not China also make such a leap?

Within six months, Li had established an informal study group at his library office in the university at which a dozen or so students and faculty would meet to discuss political developments. By the end of 1918, this group had acquired a semiformal identity as the "Marxist Research Society," with Li leading analytical discussions of Marx's *Capital.*

As interest grew, Chen Duxiu, who was dean of Peking University* as well as editor of the most influential Chinese journal of the day, *New Youth,* decided to run a special issue on Marxism with Li Dazhao as general editor. Originally scheduled for publication on May 1, 1919, printing delays kept the issue from the public until the fall. Most of the articles were scholarly analyses of specific Marxist concepts, and several were critical of Marx's methodology. But Li's essay, "My Marxist Views," gave the most careful analysis of the concept of class struggle and the problem of capitalist exploitation that had yet been published in China; and because of the journal's popularity, the message was immediately spread to an influential readership across the country.

Sympathy for the fledgling Soviet Union reached a new level when the Russian deputy commissar for foreign affairs, L. M. Karakhan, announced

---

*In March 1919 he was forced to resign by conservative opponents.

in July 1919 that the new government rejected the past policies of tsarist imperialism. Henceforth the Soviet Union would relinquish its special rights in Manchuria, cancel all former tsarist secret treaties with China, Japan, and the European powers, renounce all further indemnities due from the Boxer Uprising, and make no further claims on the Chinese Eastern Railway, returning the lines to the Chinese without any demands for compensation. This was in such marked contrast to the behavior of the other Western powers and Japan that the Soviet Union appeared as China's truest friend. Even though the Soviets later changed their mind and denied they had made the offer to return the railways without compensation (they claimed that this clause had been inserted by error in a French translation of Karakhan's message), the admiration for their earlier gesture was not much affected. The Chinese remembered Karakhan's generous words: the Soviet goal was to "free the people from the yoke of the military force of foreign money which is crushing the people of the East, and principally the people of China."[12]

By 1919, Li Dazhao's study group had attracted a broad circle of students. Some were wealthy, urban members of Peking University's elite student body, but others came from different backgrounds. One regular was Qu Qiubai, a young student from Jiangsu province who was a devout Buddhist and a fine classical scholar. Qu had become aware of the world's injustices after his mother—driven to distraction by an ineffectual opium addict of a husband and an uncaring clan—had committed suicide. Too poor to go to Peking University, he enrolled at the Russian language institute of the Ministry of Foreign Affairs, which was not only tuition-free, but even offered Qu a small stipend. Another was Zhang Guotao, son of a Hakka landlord from the Jiangxi-Hunan border. As a teenager, Zhang had smuggled guns for Sun Yat-sen's revolutionary organizations and later became an activist against Yuan Shikai.

Despite the initial enthusiasm these young men and other students showed for Bolshevism and Marxism, the need remained, if Marxism was to have any relevance to social conditions in China, to reformulate certain basic Marxist premises. Most vexing was the problem of the central role Marx ascribed to the urban proletariat and to the Communist party as the vanguard of that class, since China had such a small industrial sector. But it was encouraging that Russia had hardly fitted any Marxist model either; and by a certain intellectual sleight of hand, Li Dazhao developed an interpretation that brought China firmly into a Marxist arena of dialogue as a "proletarian nation." China, he observed, was at the mercy of foreign imperialist forces that had exploited all the Chinese people in ways similar to those in which capitalists exploited their workers—by owning the means of production and seizing the workers' surplus value for themselves.

Therefore, Li concluded of China that "the whole country has gradually been transformed into part of the world proletariat."[13]

As Li Dazhao was rethinking Marxist theory, he was urging his students to go out into the Chinese countryside and investigate the conditions of life there, for Li also believed in some of the fundamentally populist views that lay at the heart of the earlier phases of the Russian Revolution. By going to the peasants, Li said, the students would emulate their Russian predecessors who used their blood and sweat to "spread the principles of humanism and socialism." But this had even greater significance for China than for Russia, said Li, making a bold intellectual leap:

> Our China is a rural nation and most of the laboring class is made up of peasants. If they are not liberated, then our whole nation will not be liberated; their sufferings are the sufferings of our whole nation; their ignorance is the ignorance of our whole nation; the advantages and defects of their lives are the advantages and defects of all of our politics. Go out and develop them and cause them to know [that they should] demand liberation, speak out about their sufferings, throw off their ignorance and be people who will themselves plan their own lives.[14]

Li Dazhao also wrote powerfully on the need for intellectuals to dignify themselves through labor and to escape from the corrupting powers of city life by working alongside the farmers in the fields. He suggested that the presence of educated youth in the villages could gradually repair the wreckage of the constitutional system, for these urban students could explain to peasants the significance of the vote and the options within local government, and could look into the ways in which absentee financial interests dominated and exploited the local scene. By early 1920, Peking University students who had established a "Mass Education Speech Corps" were traveling to villages in the neighboring countryside, trying to live out Li's ideas.

The experience was not a mere academic exercise. In 1920 and 1921, much of Hebei province, along with the adjacent provinces of Shandong, Henan, and Shanxi, as well as Shaanxi to the west, were caught in a devastating cycle of famine caused by severe droughts in 1919. In farm villages where the average density of people per square mile was 1,230, the combination of withered crops and inadequate government relief was disastrous: at least 500,000 people died, and out of an estimated 48.8 million in these five provinces, over 19.8 million were declared destitute. Houses were stripped of doors and beams so that the wood could be sold or burnt for warmth; refugees crowded the roads and railway lines, and many lost limbs or were killed trying to force their way onto overcrowded trains; tens of thousands of children were sold as servants or, in the case of girls, as prostitutes and secondary wives. In one village, sixty homes out of a hundred had no food, and villagers were reduced to eating straw and leaves. Epidemics—typhus being the most dreaded and the most prevalent—decimated those already too weak to fight back. Those students who followed Li's call had an opportunity to learn something of the desperation and poverty that was endemic in their own society, and from which they had been sheltered hitherto. And some of them, as they pondered such misery and its context of governmental corruption and incompetence, began to wonder about the alternatives open to them personally, and to their country as a whole.

THE FACETS OF MAY FOURTH

Both the growing discussion of Social Darwinist ideas and the rise of interest in Communist ideology were symptomatic of a cultural upheaval that was spreading throughout China. This upheaval is often called the May Fourth movement, since in important ways it was intricately connected to the events that occurred in Peking on May 4, 1919, and to the effect that those events had on the country as a whole. The term *May Fourth movement* is therefore both limited and broad, depending on whether it is applied to the demonstrations that took place on that particular day or to the complex emotional, cultural, and political developments that followed.

Student representatives from thirteen area colleges and universities who met together in Peking on the morning of May 4, 1919, drew up five resolutions: one protested the Shandong settlement reached at the Versailles conference; a second sought to awaken "the masses all over the country" to an awareness of China's plight; a third proposed holding a mass meeting of the people of Peking; a fourth urged the formation of a Peking student union; and a fifth called for a demonstration that afternoon in protest of the Versailles treaty terms.

The fifth resolution was acted on at once. Defying a police order forbidding the demonstration, about 3,000 students assembled in front of the Forbidden City palace complex at Tiananmen Square—then a small walled park rather than the gigantic open space into which it was to be later transformed—and began to march toward the foreign-legation quarter. At the head of the procession fluttered two funeral banners on which were written the names of the most hated pro-Japanese members of the cabinet. As they marched, the students handed out broadsheets to the watching citizens, written in easy-to-read vernacular Chinese, explaining that the loss of the Shandong rights to Japan meant the end of China's territorial integrity, and calling on Chinese of all occupations and classes to join in protest. Barred from the legation quarter by foreign guards and Chinese police, the students marched instead toward the home of the minister of communications, who had been responsible for negotiating huge loans with Japan. Although the minister was away, some students broke into his house and set it afire while others accosted another prominent politician and beat him into unconsciousness. There were several violent clashes with police; one student, badly injured, died in a hospital three days later, the only fatality. The demonstrators had almost all dispersed by early evening, when police reinforcements arrived, arresting thirty-two of those still in the streets.

In the days that followed, the Peking students and some of their teachers proceeded to implement the rest of the resolutions that had been passed on the morning of May 4. They moved swiftly to establish a Peking student union that combined the middle-school and high-school students of the city with the college and university students. An important aspect of this new union was that it included women and gave formal support to the principle of coeducation as an alternative to separate girls' schools and women's colleges. (The first female students were admitted to Peking University in 1920.) The idea of broad-based student unions spread swiftly from Peking to Shanghai, Tianjin, Wuhan, and other cities. In June 1919, delegates from student unions in over thirty localities across China formed a Student Union of the Republic of China.

The student protesters were also successful in spreading their message to a wide circle of Chinese, once more reasserting the prestige of the scholarly elite that had been such a central part of Confucian-oriented education under the Qing dynasty, though now it was clothed in modern garb. The rash of student strikes and mass arrests led to a wave of national sympathy for the students' cause. Support came from the merchants and businessmen grouped in chambers of commerce in the major cities, from individual industrialists, from shopowners, and from the industrial workers. Although there was no central labor union organization at this time, and precise figures are hard to find, as many as 60,000 workers in 43 enterprises staged some form of work stoppage or sympathy strike in Shanghai alone. Work actions took place in textile plants, print shops, metal works, public utilities, shipping concerns, paper mills, petroleum works, and tobacco factories. Much of this radical activity was stimulated by numerous socialist clubs and study groups that had spread across the country during 1919.

Tied to the spreading protest against China's international position was the growth of a large number of new periodicals and newspapers that reached across China. Often written in simple vernacular style accessible to those with little education, they carried articles about a wide range of social and cultural problems, and pointed to the growth of a new force within China that bridged class, regional, and occupational lines, and drew millions of people together in a search for coherence and meaning in an apparently fragmenting world. Although many of these "May Fourth" journals did not last, their names still echo the excitement of the time: *The Dawn, Young China, New Society, People's Tocsin, The New Woman, Plain People, Upward, Strife*.[15]

The romantic poet Guo Moruo, recently returned from Japan, seemed to express all the explosive excitement of China's youth with the lines he wrote in 1919:

> I am the light of the moon,
> I am the light of the sun,
> I am the light of all the planets.
> I am the light of *x ray*,
> I am the total *energy* of the entire universe.

In his Chinese verse the words "x ray" and "energy" were printed in English script, giving the requisite touch of exoticism to the flamboyantly personal message.[16]

It was as if the far-off events at Versailles and the mounting evidence of the spinelessness of corrupt local politicians coalesced in people's minds and impelled them to search for a way to return meaning to Chinese culture. What did it now mean to be Chinese? Where was the country heading? What values should one adopt to help one in the search? In this broad sense, the May Fourth movement was an attempt to redefine China's culture as a valid part of the modern world. In the attempt, not surprisingly, reformers followed different avenues of thought and conduct. Some May Fourth thinkers concentrated on launching attacks against reactionary or irrelevant "old ways" such as Confucianism, the patriarchal family, arranged marriages, or traditional education. Some focused on reform of the Chinese writing style by using contemporary vernacular speech patterns in works of literature, thus putting an end to the inevitable elitism that accompanied the mastery of the intensely difficult classical Chinese. Some had a deep interest in traditional Western art and culture, while others looked to the avant-garde elements of that culture, such as surrealist and cubist painting, symbolist poetry, graphic design, realist drama, and new fashions in dress and interior decoration. Some sought to reinfuse Chinese traditional arts with a new spirit of nationalism by borrowing a selective range of Western painterly techniques.

Some writers advocated a problem-solving approach, developing techniques from such disciplines as sociology, economics, history, and philosophy in order to analyze China's problems and suggest ways to address them. Others took a similarly pragmatic approach, but thought the answer was to develop a sophisticated awareness of the achievements of Western science, engineering, and medicine. The pragmatists clashed with those who held a more ideologically oriented view of the world that drew inspiration from socialist, Marxist, and feminist critiques of society, and sought to change the world swiftly by radical activism. Some were drawn to the psychoanalytic theories of Sigmund Freud, now reaching their final formulation, and searched in Chinese vocabulary for ways to express such ideas as "Oedipus Complex," "penis envy," and "hysteria." And some sought a complete liberation of the human spirit, the realization of all human potential through a kind of promethean leap of romantic faith, in the face of which all barriers to love and progress would fall away.

Most of these reformers shared a central patriotic ground: they wished for a rejuvenated, unified China that would have the means to cope with the three great problems of warlordism, an exploitative landlord system now often described as "feudal" in nature, and foreign imperialism. The respect of reformers for Western technological power blended (rather as it had sixty years before in the minds of the Confucian scholar-officials of the Tongzhi Restoration) with a yearning to retain some essence of Chinese culture.

Although the May Fourth movement in this broad sense was a country-wide phenomenon, the formative thinking that lay behind the movement originated to a surprising degree with the faculty and students at Peking University. In the early years of the Chinese republic, Peking University had risen rapidly to prominence as China's leading center of learning, research, and teaching. This rise was attributable in part to the courageous leadership of the scholar-translator Yan Fu, who had served as the first president of the modernized institution in 1912. When the university faced severe budget cuts that year, Yan Fu had persuaded the relevant government ministries to maintain funding at a high level: "In today's world, every civilized country has many universities ranging in number from tens to many hundreds. If we cannot preserve even one, especially one already in existence, it is unfortunate indeed."[17] Yan Fu's success can be gauged by examining the lives of three men who achieved special prominence as May Fourth movement leaders and thinkers: Yan Fu's successor as president of the university, Cai Yuanpei; the dean of the university, Chen Duxiu; and the professor of philosophy, Hu Shi. Although no single person can encapsulate the turbulence and excitement of the movement, the backgrounds and activities of these three provide a useful index to a China in flux, show how widely perceptions of China's priorities varied, and demonstrate how the West could be both distrusted and revered, depending on the elements in view.

Cai Yuanpei, the oldest of the three, was the most distinguished: he had earned the classical *jinshi* degree in 1890, when he was only twenty-two, and been a member of the Hanlin Academy. In the last years of the Qing he had served as an educational official in his native Zhejiang, and then as a teacher and sponsor of radical schools and anti-Qing societies. He joined the Revolutionary Alliance, but was studying philosophy in Germany when the Wuhan uprisings began. Returning to China in 1912, he served briefly as the minister of education under both Sun Yat-sen and Yuan Shikai before traveling again to Germany (where he wrote a study of Kant) and to France, where he helped establish a work-study program for Chinese students. Appointed president of Peking University in 1917, Cai took a brave line with the military and civilian leaders who controlled the Peking government. He defended the rights of his faculty and students to speak out, claiming that they were all seeking "education for a world view" and that the function of a university president was to be "broad-minded and encompass tolerance of diverse points of view."[18] Four days after the May 4 demonstration, Cai resigned in protest at the arrest of his students. He was reappointed in late 1919 and continued as president of the university until 1922, guiding its students and faculty through stormy years and remaining a staunch defender of human rights and freedom of intellectual inquiry.

Chen Duxiu was of a different nature—volatile and emotional, an intuitive rather than an intellectual supporter of the underdog. Born to a wealthy official family in Anhui in 1879, Chen trained initially as a classical scholar but failed the province-level *juren* exams in 1897, later writing a caustic and amusing memoir about the filthy physical conditions, the dishonesty, and the incompetence that he felt pervaded the traditional examination system. He spent two extended periods of study in Japan, where he helped found radical political societies; he refused, however, to join Sun Yat-sen's Revolutionary Alliance, which he regarded as narrowly racist. Prominent in opposition to Yuan Shikai's imperial ambitions, he founded the journal *New Youth* in 1915 and joined the Peking University faculty as dean in 1917 at Cai Yuanpei's invitation. As editor of *New Youth,* which rapidly became the most influential intellectual journal in China, he espoused bold theoretical investigation, a spirited attack on the past, and a highly moralistic approach to politics through the cleansing of the individual character.

In leading an all-out attack on Confucian vestiges through the pages of *New Youth,* Chen argued that the key flaw in Confucianism was that it ran counter to the independence of individuals that lay at the center of "modern" life. To build a new state in China, said Chen in late 1916, "the basic task is to import the foundation of Western society, that is, the new belief in equality and human rights. We must be thoroughly aware of the incompatibility between Confucianism and the new belief, the new society, and the new state."[19] In other writings Chen urged the abandonment of the classical Chinese language in favor of the vernacular form, and espoused two concepts that he termed "Mr. Democracy" and "Mr. Science" as the key opponents to Confucian traditionalism. Chen was swiftly caught up by the enthusiasms of the May Fourth student demonstrations, and was jailed for three months by the Peking authorities on a charge of distributing inflammatory literature. The pamphlets he was circulating at the time of his arrest demanded the resignation of all pro-Japanese ministers and the guarantee of the rights of free speech and assembly. After his release Chen left Peking for Shanghai, becoming ever more interested in Marxism and eager for swift social change. In 1920 he was to become one of the first members of the new Chinese Communist party.

Hu Shi, the youngest of the group, had originally been a close friend and collaborator of Chen Duxiu. But though Hu also urged China to embrace the two concepts of "Science and Democracy," he later came to see Chen as an extremist who rejoiced in "isms" of all kinds without giving them adequate thought. Hu, also from an Anhui official family, studied in Westernized schools in Shanghai and traveled to the United States in 1910, when he was nineteen, on one of the scholarships that the Americans had established with Boxer indemnity money to bring bright young Chinese to U.S. schools. Hu took his B.A. in philosophy at Cornell University (he was elected to Phi Beta Kappa) and then enrolled at Columbia University to study philosophy with John Dewey among others. He began a thesis on the development of logical method in ancient China, but had not completed the dissertation when he returned to China in 1917 and was named by Cai Yuanpei to be a professor of philosophy.

Back in China, Hu became a strong backer of the movement to write in the vernacular cadences of ordinary speech. He also became an accomplished scholar of literary history, investigating the novels of the past as a source for narrative clarity and flexibility in language. In the early 1920s this work was climaxed by his pioneering study of the eighteenth-century novel *The Dream of the Red Chamber* by Cao Xueqin. Hu showed, among other findings, how the rich social fabric of the novel derived in part from the author's family, who had served Emperor Kangxi faithfully for many years and had lived in magnificent splendor in Nanjing before being disgraced and impoverished by Kangxi's son, Yongzheng.

Intellectually and emotionally, Hu Shi hewed to a difficult road. He clung to his belief in the advantages of Western methodology, and rejected Buddhist fatalism as he had rejected the Christianity he had briefly espoused in 1911. Emotionally, Hu was also cramped, feeling that he was a member of a transitional generation that had obligations both to the past and to the future, and was doomed to make sacrifices for both. His boldness in some cultural and historical matters existed side by side with his caution over speedy solutions. He followed the pragmatist philosopher John Dewey in seeking an "ever-enduring process of perfecting" rather than perfection. In the summer of 1919, he wrote a celebrated attack on Chen Duxiu and other radical intellectuals, which he entitled "Study More Problems, Talk Less of 'Isms.' " As Hu put it:

> We don't study the standard of living of the ricksha coolie but rant instead about socialism; we don't study the ways in which women can be emancipated, or the family system set right, but instead we rave about wife-sharing and free love; we don't examine the ways in which the Anfu Clique* might be broken up, or how the question of north and south might be resolved, but instead we rave about anarchism. And, moreover, we are delighted with ourselves, we congratulate ourselves, because we are talking about fundamental "solutions." Putting it bluntly, this is dream talk.[20]

Hu Shi stayed on at Peking University after the May Fourth demonstrations. He grew more politically conservative in the early 1920s, however, and tried to find a democratic middle way between competing factions. But Hu, like other May Fourth intellectuals, still found it difficult to resolve the tensions inherent in his visions of a new China. On the one hand, Hu Shi stayed with the wife he had acquired in an arranged marriage, even though he seems to have had no great affection for her and confessed that on occasion he found release by visiting prostitutes; on the other hand, he pressed for freedom from marriage constraints for others, and he acted as the interpreter for the famous American feminist and exponent of contraception techniques, Margaret Sanger, when she visited China on a lecture trip in 1922.

Sanger's visit highlighted the new issues that were constantly impinging on China. But she was only one of many foreigners whose visits to China in this period had enormous influence on May Fourth thinkers. The British philosopher Bertrand Russell traveled extensively in China in 1920 and 1921, even reaching cities like Changsha, far inland in Hunan province. Russell's brilliant expositions of mathematical logic enthralled his audiences, while his ideas on the importance of pacifism also found ready listeners. John

---

*A corrupt group of militarists and politicians who played a prominent role in Peking politics at this time.

Dewey lived in Peking during 1919 and 1920, taught several courses, traveled and lectured widely, and later wrote an influential account of China's intellectual life during the May Fourth movement. En route to Japan, Albert Einstein was invited to China in late 1922, just after completing his first work on general relativity theory. A little later, in 1923, Rabindranath Tagore, the Nobel Prize–winning Indian poet, gave a Chinese lecture tour to present his views on aesthetics, nonviolence, and the construction of rural communities based on principles of self-sufficiency and cooperative labor.

Through the force of such characters and ideas, the May Fourth movement brought changes in consciousnesses that in turn opened new possibilities for life and action in China. Another powerful influence in this regard was the work of the Norwegian dramatist Henrik Ibsen, whose plays were widely performed and admired in China at this time. In 1918, a special issue of *New Youth* that was devoted to Ibsen made a generation of young Chinese aware of the playwright's fundamental criticism of bourgeois hypocrisy and his powerful advocacy of women's emancipation. A full translation of Ibsen's play *A Doll's House* was printed in the 1918 issue, and the central figure of Nora, who decides at the play's end to leave her husband and go out into the world to find her own destiny, became a cultural and personal symbol to young Chinese women. Their mothers had unbound their feet and had begun to struggle for a basic education; *they* would go off to universities in other provinces and live with the young men or women of their choice. And many of them did so, attempting to live out a vision of romantic freedom as teachers, writers, journalists, artists, and political activists.

Bertrand Russell's companion in China, Dora Black, had been astonished that the girls she talked to in the Peking Girl's Normal School "would put to her every kind of question about marriage, free love, contraception, etc."[21] Lu Xun, observing what he called "the Nora phenomenon" with sympathy but also with some anxiety, addressed a woman's college on the theme "What Happens after Nora Leaves Home?" He warned his listeners not to forget the realities of the society in which they were still living. Women could overthrow some of the shackles of marriage and home; but until they gained a level of economic independence and equality, their sense of freedom would be a sham. For their part, men would not yield their economic control lightly, he pointed out. "I have assumed Nora to be an ordinary woman," Lu Xun added shrewdly. "If she is someone exceptional who prefers to dash off to sacrifice herself, that is a different matter."[22]

Lu Xun had unquestionably emerged as the most brilliant writer of the May Fourth movement, and his words were guaranteed an attentive audience. After so many years of apparently failed endeavor—as a medical student and a translator in Japan, as a minor bureaucrat and antiquarian in his native Zhejiang province and in Peking—he found his full voice in 1917, when he was thirty-five years old. Most of his greatest stories were published between that same year and 1921, including the famous "True Story of Ah Q," which portrayed the 1911 revolution as a muddled and inconclusive event, one controlled by charlatans and issuing in the deaths of the ignorant and the gullible. Lu Xun saw it as his task to direct the searching beam of his critical gaze onto the cultural backwardness and moral cowardice of the Chinese. He was harsh in his criticisms and often pessimistic in tone, even though his stories are full of compassion. He had come to understand his mission as a writer, he told a friend, through this image: he was a man standing outside a great iron box in which the people of China had fallen asleep. If he did nothing, they would all suffocate; if he banged and banged on the outside of the box, he would awaken the sleepers within, who might then be able to free themselves. Even if they could not escape, they would at least be conscious of their fate. The central idea here was not far from Mao Zedong's in his essays on Miss Zhao. But whereas Lu Xun believed that through his work the Chinese at least would die thinking, Mao had insisted that they die fighting.

Lu Xun hated the Confucian legacy and attacked it with bitter satire. He constantly reiterated the "Ah Q" theme, that the so-called "revolution of 1911" had changed nothing of significance in the Chinese character but had just brought a new set of scoundrels into office. He felt that revolutionary political activism might one day bring about constructive social change, but he feared that the admixture of progressive thought with superstition and apathy made that possibility problematic. He regretted bitterly the difficulties in China of speaking across class lines, and of keeping any hope alive in such a fragmented world. In the beautiful ending to one of his finest stories, "My Old Home," published in 1921, he mused aloud that "hope cannot be said to exist, nor can it be said not to exist. It is just like roads across the earth. For actually the earth had no roads to begin with, but when many people pass one way, a road is made."[23]

This was as much a central statement of May Fourth movement thinking as Hu Shi's, although more ambiguous and perhaps more pessimistic. But Lu Xun, like the other prominent figures in the movement who were aged thirty or older, largely confined his actions to the domain of words. When Chen Duxiu began passing out forbidden words with his hands and was arrested for it, this marked a new activism, a second stage. Younger students with a bolder vision of the future seized on this activist strain and claimed the need to expand it into a third stage. For them, it was gratifying that their predecessors had believed they could "overturn the earth with their pens." But for these younger radicals the true meaning of May Fourth lay in the recognition that the time had come "to struggle against the forces of darkness with our bare fists."[24]

THE COMINTERN AND THE BIRTH OF THE CCP

If China's youth were going to fight the forces of darkness with their bare fists, they would need a carefully thought out plan of attack. The outlines for one such plan were slowly becoming visible through the labors of the Communist party of the Soviet Union, even though the Russian revolutionaries had encountered difficulties enough to deter all but the most determined. Fighting against White Russian forces, especially in southern and eastern Russia, was bitter and protracted following the Bolshevik seizure of power in 1917. The hostility of many foreign nations was unremitting. Economically, the new Soviet Union was in chaos. Perhaps most disappointingly, workers' movements in Germany, Hungary, and Turkey were savagely suppressed by those countries' governments, and there was no succeeding wave of socialist revolutions elsewhere in the industrial world, as many theorists had posited there would be.

In an attempt to encourage socialist revolutions in other countries, Lenin established the Third International of the Communist party (the Comintern) in 1919, and its first congress was held in March that year.* Even though all the delegates were Russian or European, they issued a manifesto to the "proletarians of the whole world" in which they praised the Soviet form of government, urged other Communist parties to fight strongly against non-Communist labor movements, and expressed their support for all colonial peoples struggling against imperialist powers, including the Chinese seeking to resist Japanese encroachments. During this period when postwar territorial settlements were fueling nationalist movements in Europe and Asia, the strategic choice facing Lenin and the Comintern leaders was between supporting all efforts at socialist revolution overseas, even if that meant weakening a particular anti-imperialist nationalist movement, or supporting strong nationalist leaders, even if they were bourgeois reformers. At the second Comintern congress, held in July 1920, Lenin took the position that the capitalist stage of development need not be inevitable for backward nations if they were aided by the Soviet Union. Peasant soviets would be

---

*The Second Socialist International, with which Sun Yat-sen had been affiliated, had dissolved in 1915.

encouraged in such cases, along with "a temporary alliance" with bourgeois democratic parties.

Even before the second Comintern congress met, Lenin dispatched two Comintern agents—Grigori Voitinsky and Yang Mingzhai—to China to investigate conditions there and explore the possibility of setting up a Communist party. Voitinsky, aged twenty-seven, had been arrested by anti-Bolshevik troops in east Russia and imprisoned on Sakhalin Island; there he achieved fame leading a successful prisoners' rebellion, and was subsequently posted to the Siberian Comintern headquarters at Irkutsk. Yang was from a Chinese family that had emigrated to Siberia; he had spent the last decade of the tsarist regime living and studying in Moscow. Voitinsky and Yang reached Peking in 1920 and immediately contacted a Russian émigré who was teaching the Russian language at Peking University. On his advice they visited Li Dazhao, who in turn advised them to meet with Chen Duxiu.

After playing his leading role in the May Fourth demonstrations and subsequently serving a three-month jail sentence, Chen Duxiu had left Peking for Shanghai. He had settled in the French Concession and continued to edit *New Youth,* which had become politically leftist and been abandoned by many of its former liberal supporters like Hu Shi. When Voitinsky and Yang met Chen Duxiu in Shanghai that May of 1920, he was in a restless intellectual state, exploring a wide range of socialist options, including Japanese theories of model village formation, Korean-Christian socialism, Chinese proposals for "work-and-learning mutual assistance corps," and John Dewey's guild socialism. The Comintern agents gave Chen a clearer sense of direction and the techniques to bind together a political organization from the uncoordinated mixture of socialist groups that already existed in China. And it was on their urgings that Chen commissioned a friend—who happened to have just been fired from his teaching job for his "un-Confucian" attitudes—to undertake the first complete translation of *The Communist Manifesto* into Chinese. Chen arranged for the *Manifesto* to be published late in 1920. It was also on Comintern initiative that a nucleus of potential Communist party members met in May that same year. Drawn from a spectrum of socialist, anarchist, progressive, and Guomindang groups, they named Chen Duxiu secretary of their provisional central committee.

Over the next few months the movement took important steps forward. Two front organizations, a Sino-Russian news agency and a foreign-language school, were formed as covers for Communist recruiting activities. Yang and Mrs. Voitinsky, who had accompanied her husband to China, tutored a number of young Chinese in Russian; after gaining proficiency in the language, these young people were sent to the Soviet Union for advanced training as revolutionary organizers. The Comintern agents also formed a socialist youth league and founded a monthly socialist magazine. From these beginnings, the circles spread steadily outward. Under the direction of Mao Zedong, a Communist group was formed in Hunan; others were formed later that year in Hubei, in Peking, by Chinese students in Japan, and by the work-study students in France.

The French group was to be particularly important to the Chinese Communist party over the ensuing years. In 1919 and 1920, more than 1,000 young Chinese students volunteered for the work-study programs, which had grown out of a range of earlier programs (several developed by Chinese anarchists) that sought to mix advanced education with a morally rigorous, even ascetic, life-style. Among the group that traveled by sea to France in late 1919 were several of Mao Zedong's closest friends from the Changsha region of Hunan. They had been active in local labor agitations, in anti-warlord and anti-Japanese protests, and in local Hunanese follow-ups to the original anti-imperialist May Fourth demonstrations in Peking. Among those who went to France a year later was Zhou Enlai, leader of the Tianjin student protesters in the May Fourth movement, who had been jailed for his raid on a local government office earlier in the year. The youngest member of the French contingent was from Sichuan province, Deng Xiaoping, only sixteen but already a middle-school graduate who had spent a year in a special training school for Sichuan provincials planning to go to France.

In France, these students lived mainly in or near Paris, although others congregated at the university in Lyons. They studied French in special classes; when there were openings, some took jobs in factories—such as the Renault auto plant—where they were introduced to French labor organization and socialist doctrine. The most radical students, the ones from Hunan and Sichuan, ran their own underground journals (Deng Xiaoping was given the "honorary" title of doctor of mimeography for his efforts in this regard), attended demonstrations, and worked as political activists in other ways.

One of the Hunanese students in France, Xiang Jingyu, a young woman who had been a close friend of Mao's in Changsha, was active in the fight for women's rights as well as for socialism. Xiang contracted a "revolutionary" marriage with another Hunanese working in France: the two young lovers announced their union by being photographed together holding a copy of Marx's *Capital*. Xiang urged Chinese women to study science, argued that the government should not make women take the same exams as men since all women had been educationally deprived, and demanded equal numbers of women and men in the French work-study program.

The students were constantly plagued by financial problems and by arguments between rival ideological groups. A series of demonstrations outside the Chinese legation in Paris against low pay and poor work conditions had to be broken up by the police, and there followed in September 1921 an attempt by crowds of angry Chinese radicals to occupy the university buildings in Lyons. One hundred three protestors were arrested and deported. Among those who were able to stay on were Zhou Enlai and Deng Xiaoping, both of whom joined Communist youth groups in France and recruited actively and successfully among the ranks of Chinese in Europe.

Mao Zedong himself might well have gone to France had he had the contacts or the money, but he had little of either. Instead, for much of 1920 he drifted around Peking and Shanghai, discussing *The Communist Manifesto* and other Marxist books that had just been fully translated into Chinese, and working for some months as a laundryman. Mao then returned to Changsha in the entourage of influential Guomindang officials, and was appointed director of the primary school there. He now had the money to marry his former teacher's daughter, Yang Kaihui, which he did that fall, the same time that he established a Communist cell. Mao began to play a prominent part in Hunanese politics as a writer, an editor, and a leader of those workers struggling to achieve better labor conditions through the city's traditional workers' guilds. Because his name was now well known to party leaders, he was invited to be the delegate from Hunan at the first plenary meeting of the Chinese Communist party (CCP), held in Shanghai in July 1921.

The dangerous political climate of the time forced the CCP delegates to meet secretly. At first they met in the French Concession, on the top floor of a girls' school that was closed for the summer. After suspicious visitors began snooping around, they moved to a boat on a lake in Zhejiang, where they continued their discussions. For various reasons neither Chen Duxiu nor Li Dazhao could attend the meetings; and since Voitinsky had left the country, the leading role was played by a new Comintern agent who had recently arrived in China, a man working under the pseudonym "Maring." Maring and the thirteen Chinese delegates, who represented the approximately sixty CCP members in China, discussed the crucial issues of the day and worked to draw up a statement that would be in line with the Soviet Union's basic positions. If possible, they were also to develop an overall strategy for party development that could be applied to the "objective situation" that they had defined.

Probably because of Maring's influence, their final decisions on party role and organization took a conventional Leninist line. The delegates' summary of their discussions shows how a new type of political agenda had been transferred from the Soviet Union to China:

> In defining the tactics of the struggle in the transition period, it was pointed out that the Party not only cannot reject, but, on the contrary, must actively call on the proletariat to take part in and to lead the bourgeois democratic movement as well. The line was adopted demanding the organization of a militant and disciplined Party of the proletariat. The development of the trade union movement was put forward as a central task of the work of the Communist Party.[25]

On the question of a possible alliance with Sun Yat-sen there was protracted discussion. Some Communist delegates held that there should be no alliance with Sun because he was a "demagogue" and as bad as any of the Beiyang militarists. He and the CCP, therefore, "represented two diametrically opposed classes." This negative position was rejected by the majority of delegates, who declared that

> in general a critical attitude must be adopted toward the teachings of Sun Yat-sen, but his various practical and progressive actions should be supported, by adopting forms of non-Party collaboration. The adoption of this principle laid the basis for further collaboration between the Communist Party and the Guomindang and for the development of the anti-militarist and antiimperialist movement.[26]

Chen Duxiu was elected secretary-general of the CCP *in absentia*. The delegates then returned to their hometowns to share the conclusions with their comrades, to implement their findings where feasible, and to recruit new members into their party cells. Since the thirteen delegates were drawn from a wide geographical range—Guangdong, Hunan, Hubei, and Shandong, as well as Peking and Shanghai—they were able to spread the word swiftly. Even so, the CCP remained a tiny force on the national scene. By 1922 it counted around 200 members all told, not including those overseas.

That same year many of the Chinese Communists in France returned to their homeland, bringing welcome new strength to the CCP ranks. One of them, Xiang Jingyu, proved particularly adept at organizing women workers in China's factories. She thus brought a new dimension to the party's activities and identified another important source of party support, since the women (and child) laborers in the large spinning and weaving mills were among China's most cruelly exploited workers. But whereas her husband was swiftly elected to the newly formed Central Committee, she was only briefly appointed as an alternate member and then stayed in sideline positions connected with women's activities. Since Xiang also had two children—one born in 1922 and one in 1924—she could not devote all her attentions to party work; her case underlined the fact that CCP policies were directed almost exclusively by men.

In January 1922 the leaders of the Soviet Union thought it appropriate to invite about forty Chinese delegates to participate in a meeting of the "Toilers of the Far East" convened in Moscow. Despite the terrible conditions in Moscow and a serious shortage of food, the representatives from China, along with those from Mongolia, Korea, Japan, Java, and India, met at least ten times in plenary session. They were addressed by Grigory Zinoviev as spokesman for the Comintern. He told them that only a united world proletariat could overcome the forces of the capitalist powers:

> Remember that the process of history has placed the question thus: you either win your independence side by side with the proletariat, or you do not win it at all. Either you receive your emancipation at the hands of the proletariat, in cooperation with it, under its guidance, or you are doomed to remain the slaves of an English, American and Japanese camarilla.[27]

When one Chinese delegate, who was in fact a member of the Guomindang, was rash enough to suggest that the Soviets seemed now to be saying what Sun Yat-sen had been saying for twenty years, he was scolded by a delegate from Soviet Turkistan. "The Guomindang has done great revolutionary work," he was told, but in essence it was a "national democratic movement." As such, it was essential to the "first phase" of the revolutionary movement, but its struggle was not the true "struggle for the proletarian revolution."

Nevertheless, the question of allying in some way with Sun's Guomindang surfaced more and more frequently. Back in China, Maring pushed for the alliance, and it was adopted as part of the manifesto of the CCP at their summer 1922 congress in Hangzhou. Here the CCP announced they would seek a temporary alliance with the Guomindang in order to fight "against warlords of the feudal type." Once the democratic revolution had been successful, however, the stage of alliance would be over and the proletariat would "launch the struggle of the second phase," which would seek to achieve "the dictatorship of the proletariat allied to the poor peasants against the bourgeoisie."[28] In the eyes of those making these dogmatic and provocative statements, the amorphous preoccupations and slogans of the May Fourth movement were taking on a specific shape and focus.

CHAPTER 14

The Fractured
Alliance

THE INITIAL AGREEMENT

Despite the boldness of this united world rhetoric, Sun Yat-sen was not a very promising-looking ally. After being forced into exile in 1913 by Yuan Shikai, he had spent three years restructuring the Guomindang as a political party bonded to him by personal loyalty, and had greatly strengthened his personal leadership prerogatives. The party would be secretive and rigidly hierarchical; the revolution would be conducted in three stages, the first two directly under Sun's control. The first would be military, the second, one of "tutelage" for the Chinese people. Only when the tutelage was completed, Sun felt, would the Chinese be ready to move to genuine self-rule under a republican constitution. From the time of his return to China in 1916 down to the early 1920s, Sun Yat-sen barely managed to keep his hopes for political power alive as he shuttled between Shanghai and Canton according to the vagaries of the military situation. For a period in 1921 and 1922, under the protection of the Guangdong warlord Chen Jiongming, Sun was named "president" of a newly announced Chinese People's Government by surviving members of the old Peking Parliament who had moved south. But Chen disapproved of Sun's plans for using Canton as a base for a national unification drive and ousted him from that city in August 1922. Apparently Sun had fared no better than those early Qing predecessors who had tried to consolidate regimes in the same region—the Ming loyalist Prince of Gui or the southern Feudatory Shang Zhixin.

The Comintern agent Maring visited Sun in 1921, as Sun was trying to coordinate his national reunification drive in the south. Although their talks led to no specific agreements, Sun seems to have regarded the new economic policies launched by Lenin that year as a turn away from rigid state socialism on the Soviet Union's part, a step that he found promising. And Sun, who had long sought help from many other foreign governments and always failed to get it, was interested in the Comintern offer of financial and military aid. In the fall of 1922, with Sun settled in Shanghai, the Comintern dispatched more agents to China, and Sun agreed to allow Communists into the Guomindang. Finally in January 1923, Sun held extended meetings with a Soviet diplomat, Adolf Joffe. The two men issued a joint statement that, despite its guarded language, marked the emergence of a new policy both for the Soviet Union and for the Guomindang:

> Dr. Sun Yat-sen holds that the Communistic order or even the Soviet system cannot actually be introduced into China, because there do not exist here the conditions for the successful establishment of either Communism or Sovietism. This view is entirely shared by Mr. Joffe, who is further of the opinion that China's paramount and most pressing problem is to achieve national unification and attain full national independence, and regarding this great task, he has assured Dr. Sun Yat-sen that China has the warmest sympathy of the Russian people and can count on the support of Russia.[1]

Only a month later, so dizzying were the power shifts in warlord China that Sun was back in Canton, where a new consortium of militarists had ousted Chen Jiongming. One great irony here was that Chen Jiongming had been a believer in democratic procedures, and during his tenure of power had instituted elections for local government in both the cities he controlled and in the countryside. He had also urged that China's regions seek a federalist solution to the country's fragmentation, rather than pursuing a policy of compulsory military reunification. Sun saw this as a threat to his own leadership role, and he was backed by the Communists, who dismissed Chen's federalist dreams as "feudal."[2] On his 1923 return to Canton, Sun established a military government and named himself grand marshal, presumably in the hopes that this august title would give him ultimate leadership over his subordinate generals. Each of these militarists controlled men from his own native province, the most numerous being those from Guangdong itself, from Yunnan and Guangxi, and from Hunan and Henan. Sun's military government consisted of ministries for domestic and foreign affairs, finance, and national reconstruction. There was no longer any attempt to coordinate political decisions with the rump members of the old Parliament. Most of them had returned to Peking, where their presence was sought by successive presidents eager to acquire some legitimacy by convening a parliamentary quorum. By 1923 the parliamentarians were being paid

$20 for each meeting they attended to discuss a new constitution, and a bonus of $5,000 if they agreed to stay in Peking and vote as requested.

To stabilize the Canton military government, Sun needed assistance, and the Soviet Union was happy to provide it. The strategic thinking behind this Soviet position emerged from the tension between its twin desires to foster world revolution and to ensure the safety of its own borders. In east Asia, the greatest danger to Soviet security clearly lay with Japan, a staunchly anti-Communist society that had already defeated Russia in the war of 1904–1905 and was now becoming the dominant force in Manchuria, on the Soviet Union's southern frontier. Sun Yat-sen had expressed his support for joint Sino-Soviet management of the Chinese Eastern Railway, which ran straight across Manchuria and provided the main Russian link with Vladivostok. It was therefore in the Soviet Union's interest that China be strong enough to check Japan's ambitions. At the same time, the Soviet Union continued to conduct diplomatic negotiations with the various Peking regimes and with other northern warlords, winning diplomatic recognition by China in early 1924. But Soviet observers were not confident that there was anyone in the north strong enough to reunite the country. Indeed the manipulation of Duan Qirui by the Japanese, and the result of the Versailles negotiations, seemed to show that China was doomed to become Japan's pawn.

The CCP too needed the alliance. The party, which only had around 300 members by 1923, was still in a formative stage. Among the CCP's four priorities for China—national reunification, organization of the urban proletariat for socialist revolution, redress of the terrible poverty and exploitation in China's countryside, and eradication of the forces of foreign imperialism—it made sense for the party to address the national-reunification problem first, in order to give China some chance of proceeding with the other three. So the Comintern made the decision to work with the already existing Guomindang organization, which had national prestige because of Sun Yat-sen's name, and to strengthen it. Members of the CCP would keep their own party membership and also join the Guomindang, so that at some future time they could use the latter organization for their own purposes.

In addition, the nature of China's industrial labor force was in great flux at this time and made CCP plans to organize workers difficult to achieve. Many Chinese were drawn as laborers to the burgeoning new industrial enterprises; their numbers should not be exaggerated, however, since the bulk of China's 450 million people still worked the land in traditional ways. Half a million or more farm workers a year temporarily migrated into Manchuria, where they produced such cash crops as soybeans on a gigantic scale for the world market, forming a kind of mobile rural proletariat. (The crops reached the coast via the new Manchurian rail network.) Most of the workers that we might term "industrial," furthermore, were artisans who used customary methods in traditional crafts and were either self-employed or loosely bonded into groups. Such work was supervised by guilds, again of a kind that had existed in the Qing; the guilds offered some wage guarantees, upheld standards of quality, and regulated the entry of workers into a given line of work. Other workers, such as the rickshaw pullers and barge coolies, can only tangentially be called members of the proletariat, although some did form organizations and attempt strikes.

Every year a significant number of Chinese—perhaps a quarter of a million by 1922—were leaving the land or artisanal careers to find work in the new factories, docks, or railways of China's industrializing cities. Such a work force naturally posed problems for employers. Many, still linked to the seasonal rhythms of agriculture in their home villages, might simply collect their wages and quit at harvest time or during the spring planting. Others found it difficult to adjust to the repetitive precision of industrial labor and made careless mistakes or suffered accidents. Some, with no knowledge of machine-geared production, could not learn the new techniques at all.

If the ineptness of some workers disturbed their employers, this was more than matched by the indifference or callousness that employers showed their workers. Wages were low, hours extremely long, and vacations sparse or nonexistent. Medical help and insurance were usually not available, and housing—often in lodgings supplied by the factory or mineowners—was ghastly. Workers were frequently identified by numbers rather than by their own names. Harassment and bullying by supervisors on the shop floor were constant. Wages were docked for trivial reasons, kickbacks often demanded. Women workers frequently outnumbered men, forming 65 percent of the labor force in some textile factories, and their wages were even lower than that of their male counterparts. In many industries, but especially in the weaving mills, child labor was common. Girls as young as twelve were often set to work at such tasks as plucking the silk cocoons out of vats of near-boiling water with their bare hands, which led to terrible skin infections and injuries.

The strikes that many workers called in 1919 in support of the May Fourth student activists marked an important new development in Chinese history. Thereafter protesters regularly made effective use of strikes as a tool against injustice, even if initially these strikes were on a fairly small scale. From mid-1921 onward the fledgling CCP occasionally got involved, but often independent groups of workers took action on their own behalf. The pattern of small-scale strikes was sharply interrupted by the massive work stoppage that occurred in January 1922 in Hong Kong and Canton:

led by Guomindang activists, nearly 30,000 seamen and dockers struck, immobilizing over 150 ships that were carrying among them 250,000 tons of cargo. By March 1922, when the number of strikers—now joined by sympathetic vegetable sellers, tramway workers, and electricians—had risen to over 120,000, the owners capitulated. The seamen won raises ranging from 15 percent to 30 percent and, along with other material benefits, the recognition of their union's right to exist.

Shortly thereafter, in May 1922, two young Communists—Li Lisan (who had just returned from France) and Liu Shaoqi (who had been in the first group of Communist students sent to Moscow after the CCP first congress)—began forming "workers' clubs" as fronts for union organization among the Anyuan coal miners and the Daye steel foundry laborers. A host of similar clubs soon spread in scattered Chinese cities. Often with direct CCP leadership, these clubs were organized among lead miners, cotton balers, printers, powdered-egg makers, rickshaw pullers, and railway workers on the lines north and south out of Wuhan, to name just a few.

The costs of mounting a strike could be desperately high. Employers noted the names of strikers, who were often fired after their actions. Other strikers were threatened, savagely beaten, or killed in clashes with police. One grim example occurred among the strikers on the Wuhan-to-Peking railroad, which was controlled by the northern warlord Wu Peifu. Wu drew much of his income from freight on the line, as did the British who ran the Henan mines serviced by the railroad. As the time of the Guomindang alliance negotiations, the CCP had been actively encouraging the line's sixteen separate workers' clubs to solidify into one general union, which was achieved on February 2, 1923. Harassed by the police on Wu's orders, the new union called a general strike on the line on February 4, and effectively shut the railway down, After the workers ignored General Wu's orders that they return to work, on February 7 he ordered two of his subordinate generals to lead their forces against the strikers. Thirty-five workers were killed and many more wounded.

That same day the leader of the union's Wuhan branch, Lin Xiangqian—born in Fujian, a mechanic who had moved to Wuhan to work on the railway—was arrested at his home and told to order his union members back to work. When he refused, the workers were assembled on the platform, and he was beheaded in front of them. His head was hung on a station telephone pole. Despite a scattering of sympathy strikes from other unions, the railwaymen went back to work on February 9.

This grim outcome to the strike helped convince some wavering Communists of the need for the alliance. The coalition strategy was made all the more feasible because, in 1923, senior Guomindang politicians were sympathetic to the Soviet Union. Hu Hanmin, for instance, who had been made chief counselor to the Canton military government by Sun, felt that Lenin's anti-imperialist arguments formed an admirable basis for nationalist ideology. Hu also applauded the materialist conception of history and criticized Li Dazhao for not accepting the doctrine that all elements of a society's superstructure—political, intellectual, and spiritual—are merely reflections of the underlying economic base and modes of production. Furthermore, Hu had attempted to find precedents for aspects of Marxist-Leninist ideology in earlier schools of traditional Chinese thought. In the draft manifesto that Hu and Wang Jingwei wrote for the Guomindang at Sun's request in late 1922, they spoke of "the unequal distribution of property" as the critical defect in American and European societies, and pledged that China would "share in the new world era ushered in by the revolutionary changes in the rest of the world."

The CCP leader Chen Duxiu was more nervous about the alliance. He was just getting the CCP off the ground, and was skeptical of how useful or trustworthy the Guomindang might be as an ally, even though Maring insisted that the Guomindang "was not a party of the bourgeoisie, but the party of an alliance of all classes." Chen remarked that "an alliance between the parties would confuse the class organizations and restrain our independent policy." Li Dazhao, however, backed the alliance: he was less confident than Chen about the presence of a large Chinese urban proletariat ready for socialist revolution; he had also been expanding his concept of China as a "proletarianized" nation to one in which race was a central issue. Li felt that "the class struggle between the lower-class colored races and the upper-class white race is already in embryonic form," and that at such a moment Chinese solidarity against white imperialism was essential.[3]

The cementing of the alliance and the reorganization of the Guomindang were both achieved by the Comintern agent Borodin, who reached Canton on October 6, 1923, and was named "special adviser" to the Guomindang a week later by Sun. Borodin (his original name was Mikhail Gruzenberg), was born to a Russian Jewish family in 1884, grew up in Latvia, and began to work secretly for Lenin in 1903. Exiled after the failed 1905 revolution, he moved to the United States, took courses at Valparaiso University in Indiana, and became a successful schoolteacher for immigrant children in Chicago. After Lenin's seizure of power in 1917, Borodin returned to his homeland and undertook a number of secret assignments for the Comintern in Europe, Mexico, and the United States. By 1923 he was a veteran operative, and the new China assignment gave him a chance to prove his true mettle.

Borodin negotiated skillfully with all concerned. He convinced the CCP leaders that the policy of joining the Guomindang was in their own long-term interests and in the short run would allow them greater flexibility in organizing both urban and rural workers. At the same time, taking advantage of the imminent danger that Chen Jiongming's troops might recapture Canton, Borodin tried to push Sun Yat-sen to take a more radical stance. Workers and peasants would swiftly rally to Sun's armies, argued Borodin, if Sun backed a clear program for an eight-hour day and a fair minimum wage, and promised to confiscate landlords' holdings and redistribute them to the peasantry.

Sun did not dare alienate key allies by making such bold statements, but he did give Borodin the go-ahead to work on party reorganization and to summon an all-China Guomindang congress. Sun's basic justification for this was that Borodin understood the importance of nationalism in making revolution, and that the experience Borodin had gained in the Soviet Union was invaluable. The simple fact was that the Russian people were now free from foreign domination: "What our party and they advocate are the three Principles of the People: the ideologies are similar. But our party still lacks effective methods and should study theirs." When overseas supporters cabled Sun that he was being subtly "Sovietized," he answered that if the CCP were not allowed to cooperate with the Guomindang, then he himself would join the CCP. When others tried an anti-Semitic line of argument by asking if he knew Borodin's "real name," Sun replied that it was "Lafayette." And when Lenin's death was announced at the Guomindang conference in January 1924 (165 delegates had come, of whom about 15 percent were Communists), Sun delivered a public eulogy, calling Lenin a "great man" and exclaiming, "I wish to proceed along the path pointed out by you, and although my enemies are against this, my people will hail me for it."[4]

Borodin proceeded to strengthen Sun Yat-sen's position and the general disciplinary structure of the Guomindang. Sun Yat-sen's Three Principles of the People—anti-imperialist nationalism, democracy, and socialism—were declared the official ideology, and Sun himself was named party leader (zongli) for life. Borodin introduced the Soviet concept of "democratic centralism," under which any Guomindang decision, once reached by a majority of members of the relevant committees, would be wholly binding on all party members. He expanded the Guomindang party's organization into major cities, and actively recruited new members by coordinating operations of the regional party headquarters. Under the Central Executive Committee of the Guomindang he formed bureaus to deal specifically with rural and urban recruitment and policies, with youth, with women, and with the military. Special staff began compiling data on Chinese social conditions. Union organizing especially was intensified, and Communist members of the Guomindang began to propagandize actively among the peasantry in the countryside. The young Hunan communist activist Mao Zedong proved an adroit and able head of Sun's propaganda bureau, and he helped concentrate Sun's power and defuse that of the liberal opposition. The Communists acquiesced in Sun's further decision to abandon the old five-barred flag of the Chinese republic as his emblem, and instead to use a variant of the Guomindang symbol of a white sun on a blue background as the banner of the new regime.[5]

Just as important as these organizational changes was the Soviet decision to strengthen the Guomindang military, so that it could become a vigorous force in Chinese politics. The island of Whampoa, ten miles downriver from Canton, was chosen as the site for a new military academy, and Sun's friend Chiang Kai-shek, who had just spent several months in Moscow studying military organization as a member of a special Guomindang delegation, was appointed as its first commandant. Borodin cleverly kept a balance between Guomindang and CCP influences in the academy by having the Communist Zhou Enlai, who had just returned from France, named director of the political department there. The first cadets were mainly middle-class youths from Guangdong and Hunan (at least a middle-school graduation certificate was required for admission, which excluded nearly all workers and peasants); using good modern equipment, they received rigorous military training from highly skilled veterans like the Soviet adviser Vasily Blyukher.

The Whampoa cadets were also given a thorough indoctrination in the goals of Chinese nationalism and in the Three Principles of Sun Yat-sen. Although several of the cadets were already Communists or were recruited into the CCP—the young Lin Biao, for instance, a Hubei native who graduated with the cadets in 1925—the majority were not sympathetic to communism and became fiercely loyal to Chiang Kai-shek. This devoted group of tough young officers were to exert considerable influence in upcoming power struggles, and they gave the first proof of their efficacy on October 15, 1924. On that day the first class of 800, under Chiang's command and backed by local police and by cadets from other, smaller provincial military schools, routed a Canton force of the Merchant Volunteer Corps that had fired on Guomindang demonstrators and had tried to seize a shipment of confiscated arms.

The suppression of the Canton Merchant Corps made Sun deeply unpopular in the city, and when in November 1924 he was invited to join a "national reconstruction conference" in Peking, convened by the dominant warlord there, he consented. Traveling with his wife Soong Qingling and accompanied by Wang Jingwei and Borodin, he first visited Shanghai to talk with party loyalists. A side trip to Japan was abruptly terminated by illness, and he hastened to Peking. Doctors operated on Sun in January 1925 but found he had terminal liver cancer. He died in Peking on March 12, aged fifty-nine, leaving a brief, patriotic, and pro-Soviet last will and testament. Wang Jingwei was believed to have drafted this will for him, but it was not clear if Wang would inherit his mantle of leadership. Indeed it was unclear whether anyone could, since Sun's prestige had been a personal kind that accrued to him because of his long years building a revolutionary organization at the close of the Qing and during his exile in Japan.

Sun's death, along with that of Lenin, whom Sun had himself eulogized just fourteen months before, did not stop the momentum of the strategies they had developed. Even as Sun was dying, in February 1925, the Whampoa-led armies of Chiang Kai-shek, advised by Blyukher and supplied with recently received Soviet rifles, machine guns, and artillery, won a series of victories over the warlord Chen Jiongming near his main base of Shantou (Swatow), which Chiang's forces captured in March. Three months later, in another remarkable victory, they routed two other warlords who had tried to seize Canton; on this second occasion Chiang's troops took 17,000 prisoners and obtained 16,000 guns. They were now beginning to perform like an army ready for national endeavors, and Blyukher's early claim that he could sweep across China with three or four elite divisions began to seem less bombastic.

Once again it seemed that a new spirit of patriotism and determination was in the air in China, a feeling heightened by events that erupted at Shanghai in May 1925. This particular crisis was sparked by a group of Chinese workers who had been locked out of a Japanese-owned textile mill during a strike. Angry at the lockout, they broke into the mill and smashed some of the machinery. Japanese guards opened fire, killing one of the workers. In a pattern that was now familiar in China, the death was followed by a wave of public outrage, student demonstrations, further strikes, and a number of arrests. On May 30, in the Shanghai International Settlement, thousands of workers and students assembled outside the police station in the main shopping thoroughfare of Nanjing Road. They were there to demand the release of six Chinese students who had been arrested by the British and to protest against militarism and foreign imperialism. The situation was an inflammable one. Initially the demonstration, though noisy, was not violent; but as more and more Chinese converged on the police station and began to chant—"Kill the foreigners" according to some witnesses, harmless slogans according to others—the British inspector in charge of a detachment of Chinese and Sikh constables shouted at the crowd to disperse. Just ten seconds later, before the crowd could possibly have obeyed his instructions, he ordered his men to fire. They did so, firing a murderously accurate salvo of forty-four shots that killed eleven of the demonstrators and left twenty more wounded.

The outrage at the massacre was immediate and spread swiftly around China. At least twenty-eight other cities held demonstrations in solidarity with the "May Thirtieth Martyrs," and in several of these there were attacks on the British and the Japanese. A general strike was called in Shanghai, prompting the foreign powers hurriedly to bring in their marines and form volunteer corps to patrol the settlements. The tragedy of May 30 was compounded by events in Canton the following month, when Communist and other labor leaders combined protests against the Shanghai killings with the launching of a major strike in Hong Kong directed at the British. On June 23 a huge rally of Canton protestors was fired on by British troops as the demonstration passed close to the foreign concession area on Shameen Island. The rally had been formed from over a hundred different contingents of college students and soldiers, industrial workers and farmers, schoolchildren and boy scouts, and Whampoa cadets. The indiscriminate firing from Shameen killed 52 Chinese and wounded over 100. One foreigner was killed when some of the Chinese fired back.

The rage all over China was immense, and the strike in Hong Kong—which was to last sixteen months—grew in anger and intensity, backed by a massive boycott of British goods. There were echoes of May Fourth in the way May Thirtieth also became a symbol and rallying cry; but now—in 1925—conditions were different from those in 1919. Both the Guomindang and the CCP, or the combination of the two, stood ready to channel the rage and frustration of Chinese into their own party organizations. Indigenous nationalism could now call on Soviet organizational expertise to build for meaningful political action. Perhaps that was Sun Yat-sen's true legacy.

LAUNCHING THE NORTHERN EXPEDITION

In 1924, as the Guomindang-Communist alliance in Canton was beginning to produce its first impressive results, the situation in Peking also entered a new stage. The powerful warlord who controlled Manchuria, Zhang Zuolin, a free-lance soldier of the late Qing who had consolidated his power between 1913 and 1917, had for several years been involved in the north China fighting with various other warlords. Zhang was a tough, wily operator who had already shown the skills to maneuver between the Russians and the Japanese in order to protect his domain. In October 1924, after a coup in Peking had cut into the power base of his primary rival, Wu Peifu, Zhang

Zuolin sent his troops south through the pass at Shanhaiguan. Although it appeared unlikely that he would be able to use the preliminary Manchuria-to-Peking thrust as the basis for conquest of the whole country—as Dorgon and the Manchus had—his forces swiftly advanced down the Tianjin-Pukou railway line into the Yangzi River region. This success, when coupled with Zhang's development of a Peking power base, gave the Guomindang forces, as nationalists seeking Chinese unification, an additional sense of urgency. Their concern was heightened after 1926, when Zhang tightened his hold over north China through a new alliance with his former enemy, Wu Peifu, and began to take a strong anti-Soviet stand. Wu Peifu, in turn, consolidated his hold in central China, southern Hebei and Hubei.

Many intellectuals now despaired of seeing an end to the chaos. The writer Lu Xun, a sardonic observer rather than a political activist, was among those deeply moved. He was teaching in Peking on March 18, 1926, when several of his students were shot and killed in a demonstration against the Chinese politicians who had taken the spineless position of accepting Japanese demands for additional special economic privileges in northeast China. In all, forty-seven young people died that day, and Lu Xun, badly shaken, moved with his young wife first to Xiamen and then to Canton in search of some kind of security. As he wrote in a bitter essay: "I am always ready to think the worst of my fellow countrymen, but I could neither conceive nor believe that we could stoop to such despicable barbarism." He added sadly, "As for any deeper significance, I think there is very little; for this was only an unarmed demonstration. The history of mankind's battle forward through bloodshed is like the formation of coal, where a great deal of wood is needed to produce a small amount of coal."[6] Liang Qichao, who as a young man had been such a powerful spokesman for nationalism in the late Qing, and had continued to speak out for a strong China under the republic, now as a fifty-one year old mournfully watched these events from his home in Tianjin. Liang wrote to his sons, who were studying in the United States, that Peking was "like an enormous powder keg, just waiting for something to set it off."[7]

The problem of how to take effective action toward reuniting the country was widely discussed by the Guomindang, the CCP, and their Comintern advisers. If they launched a military campaign, they would face the fundamental problems of logistics, manpower, weaponry, and protecting flanks and rear in the advance. But theirs would also be a political campaign, and the problems of ideology and propaganda had to be considered with equal care. The Guomindang could not move too far to the Left politically or it would lose its main supporters, many of whom were landlords or industrialists and were not sympathetic to peasant demands for lower rents and taxes, nor to urban strikes for higher wages.

This lesson had been harshly demonstrated in the case of Liao Zhongkai, Sun Yat-sen's close friend, who by mid-1925 had become a member of the small Military Council that controlled the army, as well as minister of finance, governor of Guangdong, party representative to the Whampoa Academy, and head of the Guomindang workers' department. In this last capacity he had been largely responsible for organizing massive strikes and boycotts in protest against British abuses in both Hong Kong and Canton that summer. But on August 20, 1925, Liao was assassinated by a group of five or six gunmen as he arrived at a meeting of the Guomindang Executive Committee. Contemporaries speculated that the killers had been hired by antileftists in the Guomindang, perhaps in collusion with the British, or possibly by friends of Hu Hanmin, who was bitter not to have been given the title of "leader" of the Guomindang after Sun's death. The assassination remains unsolved.

Despite Liao's murder, Borodin's power and that of the Left in general seemed paramount in Canton. Indeed, with the protracted series of strikes against the foreigners, and the great number of armed workers' pickets patrolling streets and factories, Canton was called the "Red City" by some observers. Of 278 delegates at the second congress of the Guomindang, held in January 1926, 168 were leftists or Communists, with only 65 assigned to the center and 45 to the Right. With 7 of the 36 members of the Guomindang Executive Committee now Communists and another 14 on the Left, Borodin felt confident enough to placate the centrists by imposing a rule that would limit Communist spots on any given Guomindang committee to one-third.

Yet these appearances of leftist predominance were deceptive; at least four important indicators showed a countertrend. First, among the Whampoa cadets themselves a new group formed—the Society for the Study of Sun Yat-senism. This innocuous name initially concealed the fact that although the cadet members were nationalists and anti-imperialists, they were also strongly anti-Communist. Their view of a strong, united China did not draw on any Soviet model, and as they were appointed to their new posts they spread anti-Communist sentiment among other officers.

Second, the strongly leftist flavor of Canton after the middle of 1925 drove many businessmen and former Guomindang backers out of the city, to re-establish themselves in Shanghai or Peking.

Third, the success of the Whampoa-led armies in north and east Guangdong province began to bring newly surrendered warlord troops into the

Guomindang's National Revolutionary Army, as their forces were called from 1925 onward. Most of these troops could not be suddenly converted from their warlord ways; they lacked discipline, training, even courage. They were prone to desert if sent on dangerous missions, and some were also opium addicts. Although their presence made the Guomindang force look stronger on paper, they weakened that dream for a dynamic, ideologically charged, and technically trained elite force that Blyukher had conjured up. The historical record was ambiguous on such incorporations of surrendered troops. In the past, similar moves had both strengthened and weakened the Manchu armies in the 1640s, the Taiping in the 1850s, and the Revolutionary Alliance forces in 1911–1912.

Finally, the disaffected members of the Guomindang formed their own faction in late 1925 to try and steer their party off its leftward track. Called the "Western Hills" group from the area near Peking where they first met, they vowed to get the Communists out of the party, oust Borodin, and move the party headquarters to Shanghai from Canton. They preferred Hu Hanmin, who had been moving steadily to the right politically, to any of the other current Guomindang leaders.

On March 20, 1926, another incident occurred in Canton that showed the frailty of the Communist position and the dangers inherent in the alliance. A gunboat, the *Zhongshan,* commanded by a Communist officer, suddenly appeared before dawn off Whampoa Island. No one ever learned who had ordered it there, but the move was interpreted by Chiang Kai-shek and some of his supporters as the prelude to an attempt to kidnap him. Chiang at once invoked his powers as garrison commander and arrested the *Zhongshan*'s captain, put Canton under martial law, posted loyal cadets or police in crucial buildings, disarmed the workers' pickets, and arrested the more than thirty Russian advisers now in the city. A number of senior Chinese Communist political commissars were held in Whampoa for "retraining," and the publishing of CCP-affiliated newspapers was suspended. Within a few days Chiang slowly eased the pressures, and by early April he declared that he still believed in the alliance with the Soviet Union; but no one was sure how to interpret these statements.

Borodin had been away from Canton since February, holding a series of secret conferences on Comintern strategy with Russian colleagues in Peking. In late April he returned, and over the next few days he and Chiang reached a "compromise": in the future no CCP members could head Guomindang or government bureaus; no CCP criticism of Sun Yat-sen's Three Principles of the People was permitted; no Guomindang members could join the CCP; the Comintern had to share its orders to the CCP with a Guomindang committee, and a list of all current CCP members was to be given to the

Guomindang Executive Committee. Borodin accepted these terms because Stalin was just entering on a critical power struggle in Moscow and could not afford the blow to his prestige that would be caused by a complete eviction of the CCP and the Soviet advisers from Canton.

With a centrist position now staked out politically, Chiang and the other Guomindang leaders developed plans for a military campaign to unify China. The strategy for the Northern Expedition called for three armed thrusts: one up the completed sections of the Canton-Wuhan railway, or along the Xiang River, to the key Hunan city of Changsha; one up the Gan River into Jiangxi; and one up the east coast into Fujian. If all went well, the armies would then have two options: to push on north to the Yangzi River and consolidate in Wuhan; or to move east by river or railway to Nanjing and the rich industrial prize of Shanghai. A series of alliances would be worked out with various warlords along the way, and, where feasible, their troops would be incorporated into the Guomindang National Revolutionary Army.

Communist and Guomindang party members would move ahead of the troops, organizing local peasants or urban workers to disrupt hostile forces on the Guomindang line of march. This would have to be done, however, in such a way that it did not alienate potential allies, as had occurred in response to the efforts of Peng Pai, a Communist organizer on the coast above Canton in Haifeng County. Peng Pai created from 1923 onward a number of peasant associations that developed social services such as medical care, education, and information on agriculture, and he pushed for dramatic rent reductions—up to 25 percent in many cases. Peng also formed the peasants into self-defense corps to protect their territories against counter-attacking landlords. But such policies had provoked a savage backlash from local landlords and were too drastic for most Guomindang supporters.

The Guomindang and Communists also had to plan to provide large numbers of transport laborers to carry the army's military supplies over the great areas of country where there were neither railways nor adequate roads. Many of these men were recruited from among the Canton strikers, others from the peasantry on the line of march who were wooed by decent treatment and a high daily rate of pay, inducements never used by rival warlord armies. Railway workers were also organized to disrupt service on enemy-controlled railroads, to prevent the removal of basic rolling stock by hiding crucial parts, and, where possible, to cut off the enemies' retreat by sabotaging the track.

Two other central components in the planning were money and military manpower. Money problems had been greatly eased by the skills of T. V. Soong, Sun Yat-sen's brother-in-law, who, after graduating from Harvard

University and working three years at the International Banking Corporation in New York, had been made head of the Canton Central Bank in 1924. There he built up major reserves by skillful management; when he was promoted in 1925 to finance minister of the Guomindang government in Canton, he quadrupled revenues in the Guomindang-controlled areas. He relied on such devices as taxes on shipping and kerosene, which by late 1925 totaled over 3.6 million yuan per month. He also floated bond issues to raise money for the government.

As for manpower, 7,795 Whampoa graduates, mostly from well-off rural families, trained in both logistics and tactics, were ready for action by mid-1926. In a special report to the Guomindang congress in early 1926, Chiang Kai-shek estimated the number of men under arms and loyal to the Guomindang at 85,000. This figure included troops from Guangdong, Yunnan, and Hunan, many of whom were still led by the officers who had brought them to Canton but were now incorporated under the National Revolutionary Army. Another 30,000 Guangxi troops were soon added to this number, along with about 6,000 cadets still enrolled in the various military schools.

A series of changes in the military situation in Hunan during April and May 1926 gave added urgency to these hopes for a Northern Expedition. The feuding among the Hunan generals grew so intense that the powerful northern warlord Wu Peifu began actively campaigning against them, to protect his own southern flank. When one of the leading Hunan commanders expressed his sympathy for the concept of the Guomindang Northern Expedition, and agreed to incorporate his troops into the Guomindang army, the time for action had clearly come. The Canton government thereupon named Chiang Kai-shek commander in chief of these hybrid forces in June 1926, and the official mobilization order for the Northern Expedition was issued on July 1. The broad purpose of the expedition was defined as follows by the Guomindang Central Executive Committee:

> The hardships of the workers, peasants, merchants and students, and the suffering of all under the oppressive imperialists and warlords; the peace and unification of China called for by Sun Yat-sen; the gathering of the National Assembly ruined by Duan Qirui—all demand the elimination of Wu Peifu and completion of national unification.[8]

The obvious omission of Zhang Zuolin's name was presumably an invitation to that wily general to attack his erstwhile enemy from the north while the Guomindang advanced from the south. The Communists under Chen Duxiu were not happy over the timing of the Northern Expedition. Chen

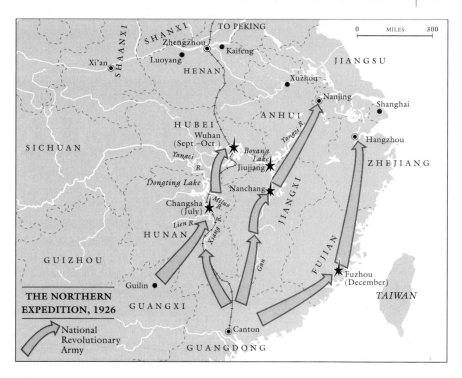

declared that the key goal should be to consolidate Guangdong itself against the "ruination from the force of the anti-red armies."[9] But it was impossible to check the new momentum, and on Comintern advice the Communists muted these criticisms and actively participated in the campaign.

As the troops commanded by Chiang pressed northward from Canton, their new Hunan allies fought a path through to Changsha, which they captured on July 11. Chiang Kai-shek reached the city in early August. Despite the floods, cholera, and transportation problems that hampered its progress, the National Revolutionary Army pressed northward until it caught up with the retreating enemy forces along the Miluo River, which flowed into the east side of Dongting Lake.

With new troops drawn to the ranks of the Guomindang force from Guizhou warlords impressed by the army's success, Chiang and Blyukher—the Russian now recovered from illnesses that had kept him on the sidelines—decided on a bold strike across the river before Wu Peifu could send heavy reinforcements south to bolster his Hunan allies. In Chiang's words to his generals, the battle would decide "whether or not the Chinese nation and race can restore their freedom and independence."[10] Between August 17 and August 22 the National Revolutionary Army brought off the gamble.

Cutting across the Miluo River in two places, they severed the Yuezhou garrison's rail links to Wuhan and surrounded the crucial tricity area. Some Yuezhou troops fled by boat, but others were trapped, and all their supplies and weapons fell into the Nationalists' hands.

In extremely heavy fighting during the last week of August, the Nationalists seized the bridgeheads—heavily fortified with barbed wire and machine guns—that guarded the approaches to Wuhan. General Wu Peifu had now reached the front and tried to rally his men by making an example of those who had lost the bridgeheads. Using the technique proven three and a half years before against the striking railway workers, he publicly beheaded eight of his commanders in the presence of their brother officers. The tactic did not work. In early September the tricities of Wuhan, where Wu Peifu planned a determined stand, began to fall to Guomindang forces. Hanyang, with its huge arsenal, fell first, betrayed by its own commander, who joined the Nationalists. Hankou followed, with its prosperous businesses and its large foreign concessions (despite his anti-imperialism, Chiang pledged to protect all foreigners in the city).

While the Wuchang defenders held out behind that city's massive walls, the Nationalists suddenly faced the threat of defeat from the warlord who controlled Jiangxi. His well-armed troops not only won several victories, but shattered Guomindang and Communist sympathizers by rounding up all known radicals, beheading them, and displaying the severed heads on stakes in the Boyang Lake cities of Jiujiang and Nanchang. To be considered "radical" it was enough for either male or female students to have cut their hair short in what was considered the Russian style. But these acts of terror backfired. The Wuchang commander, his city full of civilians near starvation, opened the city gates on October 10; while some Nationalist troops occupied the city, others pressed the counterattack back into Jiangxi. Fifteen years to the day after the original Wuhan mutinies, the tricity area had ousted its reactionary overlords and welcomed once again the forces of an unpredictable revolution.

SHANGHAI SPRING

In late 1926, the Guomindang and the Communists began to consolidate their hold over Wuhan, and Chiang Kai-shek shifted his attention to the Jiangxi campaign. The fighting was heavy, with key cities lost and taken several times. By mid-November, however, at a cost of 15,000 casualties, the National Revolutinary Army had firm control over both Jiujiang on the Yangzi, and Nanchang, the key road and rail junction on the west of Boyang

Lake. Here Chiang made his new base, joined by several members of the Guomindang Executive Committee. Other senior Guomindang leaders, however, especially the Communists and those sympathetic to the Left, settled in Wuhan, where antiforeign agitation and rapid gains in the urban labor movement offered the promise of social revolution.

The original Guomindang strategy for the Northern Expedition had called for three forward military thrusts, the last up the east coast. This offensive also proceeded successfully, partly through careful negotiations that induced various militarists to defect to the Nationalist side, and partly through military action. The coastal advance of the Nationalist armies was greatly aided by the defection to their side of key naval units that were able to cut off the enemies' retreat. Despite heavy fighting, in mid-December 1926 the troops of the National Revolutionary Army entered the Fujian capital of Fuzhou. The Nationalists now controlled seven provinces: Guangdong, their original base; Hunan, Hubei, Jiangxi, and Fujian, by conquest; and Guangxi and Guizhou, by negotiated agreements. The total population of these provinces was around 170 million. The world's view of these developments took dramatic shape when the British Foreign Office began to consider extending diplomatic recognition to the Guomindang government, and the British minister to China visited Wuhan in mid-December to hold talks with the Nationalist foreign minister. Until this moment the British had appeared to be firmly committed to Wu Peifu.

These victories brought the debate over the next phase of Guomindang strategy to a head. Chiang Kai-shek, at his Nanchang base, had decided on a drive to Shanghai by two routes—one east down the Yangzi, one northeast through Zhejiang—so that he could seize the industrial and agricultural heartland of China. The Guomindang leaders in Wuhan, agreeing with Borodin, who was ensconced there, supported instead a northern drive up the Wuhan-Peking railway. Their forces could then effect a junction with several northern warlords believed to be sympathetic to their cause, followed by a concerted assault on Peking and the final rout of Generals Wu Peifu and Zhang Zuolin. Tense arguments took place in January between the rivals, represented by the Provisional Joint Council in Wuhan and the Provisional Central Political Council in Nanchang. Chiang traveled to Wuhan on January 11, 1927, to state his case; instead he was not only rebuffed, but publicly insulted by Borodin and other leftists. He returned, angry, to Nanchang.

The spring of 1927 was henceforth to be dominated by the fate of Shanghai, but the outcome depended on the interconnections among a considerable number of factors: the reactions of various northern warlords to events in south China; the strength of the local labor movement; the nature of the antilabor forces in the city; the attitudes and actions of the foreign community and troops in the concessions; the position of the Guomindang leaders in Wuhan; and the long-range strategy for CCP action decided on by Stalin and relayed through the Comintern.

The speed of the Guomindang advance from Canton to the Yangzi gave pause to a number of the northern warlords. They had hitherto been engaged in complex maneuverings and alliances in the huge area stretching from Gansu province in the west, through Shaanxi and Hebei, and into Shandong and southern Manchuria. They had never formulated a common strategy or reached a binding agreement on how to carve up the territory, but all of them saw the Guomindang as a radical, even revolutionary, force, and they had to decide how to respond should the Guomindang seek to advance farther north. In the event, they remained divided. One of the three most powerful northern generals, Feng Yuxiang, decided after visiting Moscow to join the Guomindang and affirm his belief in its basic principles. From his base in Shaanxi, he pushed steadily into Henan province. Wu Peifu, smarting from the loss of Wuhan and the southern terminus of his railway empire, tried to shore up a new base at the railway-junction city of Zhengzhou, but he had been fatally weakened.

Zhang Zuolin, the Manchurian warlord who currently controlled Peking, had begun to show a grandiose side, having yellow earth—symbolic of an emperor's prestige—strewn across the roads he traversed, and offering sacrifices to Confucius in person. But his Peking government was ineffective, given to extravagant parties and lavish ceremonial affairs ordered by Zhang, who concentrated most of his own efforts on the game of mah-jongg.* Most importantly, although he had mobilized an army of 150,000 to march south to the Yangzi in late November 1926 to stem the advancing Guomindang armies, he suddenly countermanded the order.

It is possible that Chiang Kai-shek had negotiated secretly both with Zhang and the Japanese to protect his flanks as he attacked Shanghai. In any case, the Wuhan Communists attacked Chiang for his "crimes" in this regard, and there is no doubt that Zhang Zuolin had become a fanatical antileftist: his Peking headquarters were festooned with the slogan "Absolutely Destroy Communism."[11] In early April 1927, Zhang ordered his troops to raid the Russian embassy in Peking, and arrested all the Chinese who had sought shelter there. Among them was Li Dazhao, the former librarian and cofounder of the CCP. Zhang had Li Dazhao hanged along with nineteen of Li's arrested companions.

Despite these losses in the north, the labor movement all over central and

---

*A complex Chinese game played with small decorated tiles, often for high stakes.

southern China had been making headway since the National Revolutionary Army's successes and the formation of a General Labor Union to coordinate workers' actions throughout China. By late 1926 seventy-three unions were listed for Wuhan, with a membership of 82,000, and hundreds of thousands of workers were organized in Shanghai, despite the hostility toward them of the local warlord there. In February 1927 the Shanghai labor leaders, with the help of organizers from the General Labor Union, called a general strike in support of the National Revolutionary Army columns that had just captured Hangzhou to the south. The strikers managed to bring Shanghai to a standstill for two days, closing docks, municipal services, cotton mills, silk-reeling factories, public transport, and commercial centers. The strike was broken by warlord forces, who beheaded 20 strikers, arrested 300 strike leaders, and disrupted all workers' gatherings.

Worker morale and political concern nevertheless remained extremely high, bolstered by the lingering effects of the May Thirtieth Incident of 1925 and by the persistent efforts of Shanghai-based CCP leaders such as Zhou Enlai and Li Lisan. The General Labor Union continued with plans for a second major strike, organizing 5,000 pickets, hundreds of whom were armed. In the huge metropolis of Shanghai, organized workers were a volatile force, possibly capable of setting up a revolutionary workers' government, an urban soviet that might then trigger similar uprisings and the formation of soviets elsewhere, as had happened during the Bolshevik Revolution in Russia.

But there were plenty of people in the city anxious to defuse the strength of the labor movement. A loose confederation of factory owners and financiers, who had profited most from the dramatic expansion of the city as an industrial center and international port, stood to lose heavily if the waves of strikes continued. Some of these financial leaders were linked to the world of secret-society organizations such as the Green Gang (Qingbang), which had grown rich by controlling prostitution, gambling rackets, and opium distribution. For a price, Green Gang leaders could assemble squads to break up unions and labor meetings, and even kill recalcitrant workers. Many Green Gang leaders were also successful businessmen with established positions in the community, and some had strong links with the Guomindang, or had known Chiang Kai-shek in his Shanghai days.

At the end of 1926 the head of the Shanghai Chamber of Commerce visited Chiang Kai-shek at his Nanchang headquarters and offered the chamber's financial support. In other secret meetings, Chiang's intermediaries negotiated successfully with the heads of the powerful Bank of China in the city. They also held discussions with the chief of detectives in the French Concession—a major underworld figure in close contact with the

Green Gang—presumably concerning the suppression of labor agitation at a later date.

Since many wealthy Chinese businessmen lived in comfortable homes with gardens in the beautifully laid-out Shanghai foreign concessions, they had social contact with the foreigners and sometimes shared their business interests. The foreigners, few of whom spoke Chinese or knew or cared much about the details of the city's life, would often not be aware of the political or secret-society contacts of their Chinese acquaintances. Their main interest was to make sure that a reliable source of labor was available to work in their factories and on the docks, and that the social amenities revolving around their lavish clubs and the racecourse were not disturbed. They also wished to protect their investments—now approaching the $1 billion mark—from extremes of Chinese nationalist feeling that might lead to destruction of property or even confiscation.

But by early 1927 the foreign community in China was nervous. In January, fired up by the Communist party and Borodin, Chinese crowds had burst through barricades into the foreign-concession area of Hankou, causing considerable property damage and leading to the evacuation of all foreign women and children downriver to Shanghai; the men congregated in buildings near the shore, ready for swift escape. Similar disturbances took place in Jiujiang the same month. And most dangerously, in March 1927, Nationalist troops who had seized Nanjing from the retreating northern warlord armies looted the British, Japanese, and American consulates, killing several foreigners from those three nations as well as from France and Italy. American destroyers and a British cruiser in return shelled the area around the Standard Oil Company headquarters to allow an evacuation route for the foreign nationals, leading to several Chinese deaths. The British had shown, in the May Thirtieth Incident of 1925, that they would fire on threatening crowds; now they and the Americans had shown that they would shell a Chinese city. What they, the French, or especially the Japanese might do in the face of armed Guomindang opposition was unclear. There were by this time around 22,000 foreign troops and police in Shanghai, and 42 foreign warships at anchor, backed by an additional 129 warships in other Chinese waters.

The Guomindang leaders in Wuhan were meanwhile seeking to strengthen their own position politically and economically. The regular troops they controlled were fewer in number than those under Chiang Kai-shek's command, and they could hardly afford to alienate Chiang so completely that he became an open rival. They focused mainly on radical social reforms in the Wuhan area, on pursuing an alliance with General Feng Yuxiang that might make possible further advances northward from

Wuhan, and on public denigrations of Chiang Kai-shek for his attacks against labor organizations in Jiangxi, where he had been systematically suppressing the branches of the General Labor Union.

For Stalin, the stakes in the Chinese conflict had assumed a particular intensity. The reasons for this had more to do with Soviet politics than with events in China itself, for by early 1927 Stalin was locked in a bitter battle for power with Leon Trotsky. This battle was being fought in the ideological and bureaucratic arena rather than with troops, and the interpretation and direction given to the Chinese revolution were central to each man's arguments. Stalin insisted that the leadership provided by Chiang Kai-shek and his troops was critical in the "bourgeois-democratic" phase of the Chinese revolution. The CCP, by this reasoning, must "continue building up a four-class alliance of workers, peasants, intellectuals, and urban petty bourgeoisie within the Guomindang" in order to crush the feudal warlords and the foreign imperialists. In practical terms this meant that the CCP leaders in China must continue to cooperate with Chiang and the Guomindang.[12]

On March 21, 1927, the General Labor Union in Shanghai, under CCP direction, launched a general strike and an armed insurrection against the warlords and in support of the approaching Guomindang forces. Some 600,000 workers were involved, and again the city came to a standstill. Power and telephone lines were cut, police stations seized, and railway stations occupied, often after heavy fighting. There were strict orders not to harm foreigners, which the insurrectionists obeyed. The next day the first division of Nationalist troops entered the city, and on March 27 the General Labor Union, now with no need for concealment, held a public inauguration of its new headquarters in a former guild hall, with 1,000 delegates representing 300 union branches. In all, according to their released figures, there were now 499 unions in the city, representing 821,282 workers. There was also a workers' militia of 2,700 men, well armed with weapons and ammunition seized from the city's police stations and military depots.

Chiang Kai-shek himself entered the city at the end of March. He issued reassuring statements to the foreign community and praised the unions for their constructive achievements. While the CCP kept the union membership conciliatory and muted, pressed them to disarm, and withdrew their demands that the foreign concessions be returned to China, Chiang held meetings with wealthy Shanghai industrialists, centrist Guomindang figures like Wang Jingwei and former Peking University president Cai Yuanpei, and leading Green Gang and underworld figures. These Green Gang leaders formed a so-called Society for Common Progress, headquartered at the house of the chief of detectives in the French Concession. This was a front organization under cover of which a force of around 1,000 armed men was built up. At the same time, Chiang arranged for generous loans from Shanghai bankers, and transferred out of the city those army units known to be sympathetic to the workers.

At 4:00 A.M. on April 12, the men of the Society for Common Progress, heavily armed but dressed in civilian clothes of blue cloth with white arm bands, launched a series of attacks against the headquarters of all the city's large unions. These paramilitary anti-union groups operated with the knowledge (and at times the assistance) of the foreign-concession authorities, and as the fighting wore on through the day they were often assisted by troops from the National Revolutionary Army. Many union members were killed, hundreds arrested, and the pickets disarmed. When Shanghai townspeople, workers, and students staged a protest rally the next day, they were fired on by Guomindang troops with machine guns and almost 100 were killed. Arrests and executions continued over the next several weeks, the General Labor Union organizations were declared illegal, and all strike activity in the city ceased. The Shanghai spring was over.

WUHAN SUMMER, CANTON WINTER

The news of the April 1927 events in Shanghai caused anguished self-examination in Wuhan. Borodin and Chen Duxiu had the difficult task of fitting the killings of Chinese workers into some kind of convincing ideological scheme. To help them, they had only Stalin's late April analysis of the situation. In this, the Russian leader declared that it had been his goal, ever since March 1926, to prevent Chiang Kai-shek from driving the Communists out of the Guomindang; at the same time, he had worked to propagate "the withdrawal or the expulsion of the Rightists from the Guomindang." In Shanghai, Chiang had shown his true colors: he had emerged as a representative of the "national bourgeoisie" and defied the Guomindang by forming his own government in Nanjing (on April 18, 1927). Thus, Stalin concluded, the events of 1927 "fully and entirely proved the correctness of this line."[13]

This meant that the CCP now had to work closely with the Wuhan faction of the Guomindang, which was declared by Stalin and his advisers to be the "Left" or "revolutionary" Guomindang, the true inheritor of the Chinese revolution. Stalin hoped that these Guomindang members would lead the "masses of farmers and peasants" to crush the militarists, gentry, and "feudal landowners." Although with hindsight this hope seems absurd, many of the non-Communist Guomindang leaders in Wuhan did have fairly radical political views, and one can certainly say that they were to the left

of Chiang Kai-shek or Hu Hanmin. The most influential of these was Wang
Jingwei, who had won fame as a young polemicist and revolutionary in the
late Qing, and served Sun Yat-sen loyally in Japan and Canton. It was Wang
who had been with Sun during his last illness, and who had received the
leader's final advice and instructions. As chairman of the government in
Canton, he had sided with the Communists on many points, and had felt
it wise to travel to France with his family after Chiang's *Zhongshan* gunboat
coup of March 20, 1926. Wang had returned to China in April 1927 and
issued a joint statement with Chen Duxiu reaffirming ties between the CCP
and the Guomindang.

With Wang in Wuhan were such men as Sun Fo, Sun Yat-sen's son by
his first marriage (he had no children from his second marriage to Soong
Qingling). Sun Fo had political ambitions and a flair for city government.
A graduate of the University of California, he had risen through the Guomindang ranks to become mayor of Canton and a member of the Central
Executive Committee. Eugene Chen, a Trinidad-born Chinese whose father
had originally fled to the West Indies after being implicated in the Taiping
rebellion, was also a powerful force in Wuhan. He had been a confidant of
Sun Yat-sen, served as foreign minister for the Canton regime, and had
successfully negotiated the takeover of the Hankou and Jiujiang concessions
from the British. And Sun Yat-sen's widow, Soong Qingling, who had
dramatically flown by plane to Wuhan from Nanchang to show where her
political loyalties lay, had not only the prestige of her prior relationship with
Sun Yat-sen, but also natural intelligence, fluency in English, and a highly
developed social conscience, all of which made her influential in Guomindang party discussions.

The main goal for the Wuhan-based Guomindang leaders continued to
be the establishment of a firm political and economic base. They were not
the only power brokers in Wuhan, let alone in Hubei and Hunan, and they
had to deal with strong local warlords—nominally bound in alliances with
the Guomindang—as well as with the industrialists and wealthy landlords
of the region. In an attempt to win greater support for their regime,
Wuhan's Guomindang government had also tried to take over the Japanese
Concession area in Hankou. But the effort had been repulsed by machine-
gun fire, and a mile-long line of foreign warships were now anchored in
the Yangzi, ready to protect foreign property. The unrest in the city led to
the closing of most foreign shops and factories, throwing thousands of people
out of work. Needing 15 million yuan a month to run its offices and feed
its 70,000 troops, who were involved in heavy fighting in north China, the
Wuhan government could raise only a fraction of that sum and was reduced
to printing paper money, which banks finally refused to accept.

The Communists, had they been given a free hand, might have been able to foment real revolution in the countryside. In late 1926 and early 1927 there had been notable signs of peasant unrest in China. In some areas the peasants had seized the land for themselves, formed "poor peasants associations" to run their communities, and publicly paraded, humiliated, and in many cases killed the more hated of the local landlords. Peng Pai had had dramatic success in forming radical peasant associations near Canton, until they were counterattacked by landlord forces. Mao Zedong, who had risen while in Canton to become director of the Guomindang's Peasant Movement Training Institute, also had several opportunities in 1925 and 1926 to propagandize CCP views in the Hunan countryside, especially around Changsha. In February 1927, after the Northern Expedition had passed through the region, he took the time to study what was happening and wrote an excited report for a local CCP journal.

Mao was particularly impressed by the power of the poor peasants and their political consciousness. "They raise their rough, blackened hands and lay them on the heads of the gentry," he wrote. "They alone are the deadliest enemies of the local bullies and evil gentry and attack their strongholds without the slightest hesitation; they alone are able to carry out the work of destruction." The CCP, he noted, could take the initiative with these peasant stalwarts if it chose: "To march at their head and lead them? To follow in the rear, gesticulating at them and criticizing them? To face them as opponents? Every Chinese is free to choose among the three." Mao implied that it would be folly to ignore this immense potential force. If one assessed the 1926–1927 "democratic revolution" on a ten-point scale, he observed, then the "urban dwellers and the military rate only three points, while the remaining seven points should go to the peasants in their rural revolution."[14] But Mao's report was not practical in the context of Wuhan's political choices, and it did not fit the Comintern line of continued alliance with the petty bourgeoisie. Accordingly the Chinese Communists were told to dampen peasant ardor in order not to alienate the Guomindang and its remaining influential supporters, many of whom were landlords.

The final statement of the Wuhan-based Central Land Committee, issued in early May 1927, was the fruit of compromises among Wang Jingwei, Borodin, Chen Duxiu, Mao, and others. It proposed the establishment of self-government institutions at the local level to handle land redistribution problems, the guarantee of the land holdings of soldiers in the active pro-Guomindang forces, and—for soldiers with no such holdings—the promise of land once the war was won. The maximum size of a holding was to be set at 50 *mou* (each *mou* being one-sixth of an acre) of good land or 100 *mou* of poorer land. All those with larger holdings, unless they were revolutionary soldiers, would have the surplus confiscated.

As it happened, local military leaders solved these knotty problems for the leftists. On May 18, 1927, the Guomindang-allied general who controlled the Changsha-Wuhan stretch of railroad mutinied and marched on Wuhan, cutting a swathe of destruction among the members of the peasant associations he encountered. Although he was defeated, after heavy fighting, by Communist and Guomindang troops, his defection freed others to do the same. On May 21 the garrison general in Changsha raided the major leftist organizations there, ransacking their files, and arresting and killing nearly a hundred students and peasant leaders. Allegedly acting to forestall an armed attack on the city by the mobilized peasant associations, he ordered his men into the countryside to round up and kill the peasant forces. Thousands were slaughtered, often with atrocious cruelty, as the recently humiliated landowners—many of whom had seen their own relatives killed not long before—joined with army troops and members of local secret societies to exact vengeance on the peasant expropriators.

Guomindang leaders in Wuhan responded by blaming Communist "excesses" for the disaster. Wang Jingwei claimed that the military acted thus because they had been "backed into such a blind alley." Sun Fo argued it was the CCP's fault for "ranting and raving" about the possibility of a mass rural uprising.[15] When a peasant army did begin to form in order to attempt a counterattack against the militarists in Changsha, the gathering force was deflected by a cable from the Wuhan CCP asking it "to be patient and wait for the government officials in order to avoid further friction."[16] The "government officials" never arrived, and the peasant troops either disbanded or were killed.

The Wuhan Guomindang leaders seemed to acquiesce in this slaughter and to concentrate on strengthening their ties to those with military power. Still, Stalin responded to Trotsky's bitter mockery by proposing to deepen the CCP-Guomindang alliance, instead of proposing to abandon it and put new life into the peasant movement, so recently suppressed. He sent the Comintern agents Roy and Borodin a short cable, spelling out the need for the CCP to shift the Guomindang in a leftward direction while pretending to be firm backers of it. "Without an agrarian revolution victory is impossible," ran Stalin's message, received in Wuhan on June 1. "We are decidedly in favor of the land actually being seized by the masses from below." Since so many Guomindang leaders were "vacillating and compromising," large numbers of workers and peasants must be inducted into the party; "their bold voice will stiffen the backs of the old leaders or throw them into the discard." As if that were not enough, the CCP was also to mobilize 20,000 Communists and 50,000 "revolutionary workers and peasants" under student commanders into a "reliable army."[17]

Apparently thinking that this telegram would convince the Guomindang that the CCP was still a power to be reckoned with, and perhaps to steal a march on Borodin, M. N. Roy (a young Indian comintern representative) showed it to Wang Jingwei, Eugene Chen, and Soong Qingling. Wang, especially alarmed and startled, intensified his moves to dampen local revolution and curb CCP power, and began a series of negotiations to see if he could heal the rift with Chiang Kai-shek. Although the CCP issued a contrite statement promising to restrain labor and peasant activities even further, the Comintern agents could see the writing on the wall, and both Roy and Borodin began the long trek back by car and truck across the Gobi Desert to the Soviet Union. "The revolution extends to the Yangzi," said Borodin in a farewell interview with a foreign journalist; "if a diver were sent down to the bottom of this yellow stream he would rise again with an armful of shattered hopes."[18]

Among those now assigned the task of stirring up revolution in the countryside was Mao Zedong, whose Hunan report had gained little notice and who had spent the summer—in obedience to Comintern orders—making sure that the militarists' lands were not expropriated. As a loyal party member he did his best to re-arouse the peasants who had seen many of their friends and families killed, their homes ransacked, and their crops destroyed. By early September, Mao had managed to recruit an army of around 2,000 in the countryside and launched attacks on several small towns near Changsha. But his army, composed of some peasants along with disgruntled miners and Guomindang deserters, was a pale echo of the dedicated force of 100,000 armed peasants he had hoped to raise for these "Autumn Harvest Uprisings," and they were swiftly suppressed by local peacekeeping forces, with considerable losses.

More ambitious, and initially more successful, was a major insurrection in Chiang Kai-shek's former Jiangxi base of Nanchang. Here, in early August, close to 20,000 troops led by Communist generals—one of whom had kept his Communist ties secret for several years awaiting just such an opportunity—seized the city and expropriated the banks "under the banner of the Guomindang left." But they were defeated by a neighboring general whom they had just optimistically invited onto their Revolutionary Committee. Retreating southward, they briefly captured Shantou, the prosperous coastal city that had been Chen Jiongming's base in his battles with Sun Yat-sen. Driven from there, the remnants of the Communist force settled in the Haifeng area, where Peng Pai had managed to hold onto his radical rural soviet despite attacks from the local landlords and their backers in Canton.

The melancholy roster of setbacks for the CCP continued into December. That month, the fifteenth congress of the Russian Communist party was meeting in Moscow, and Stalin wanted a definitive victory in China to prove the superiority of his planning over the criticisms of Trotsky, whom he was hoping to crush once and for all. The Comintern passed the orders to the new CCP head, Qu Qiubai, that there must be an insurrection. Qu obediently directed the CCP to stage an uprising in the former revolutionary seedbed of Canton, where local workers, their ranks swelled by evicted strikers from Hong Kong, seemed to be primed for revolutionary action. At dawn on December 11, 1927, Communist troops and workers seized the police stations, the barracks, and the post and telegraph offices, and announced that authority in the city was now vested in a "Soviet of Workers', Soldiers' and Peasants' Deputies," just as Stalin and Qu had demanded.

But the organizers of this "Canton commune" were hopelessly outnumbered and outgunned by anti-Communist troops, who soon rallied. The commune lasted two days. Members of the Russian consulate who had let their building be used as a base for the insurrection were shot, as were all arrested workers and Communists who had joined in the "soviets." Many workers could be identified as radicals by the red marks left around their necks by the hastily dyed kerchiefs they had worn in their days of triumph. Finding that too much expensive ammunition was being wasted in executions, the local restorers of order had the rebels tied together in groups of ten or twelve, loaded onto boats, and pushed into the waters of the river below the city.

After an initial inclination to call this disaster a victory, Stalin and the Comintern accepted it as a serious blow to the CCP, but they also blamed the CCP for having caused it. The CCP, they charged, had not organized strikes properly, had overrelied on non-Communist workers, had not done adequate work among the peasants, and had not concentrated enough on subversion in the enemy armies. They must look at their strategy more carefully, they were told. As to the CCP itself, "its cadres, its periphery and its center" must all be strengthened. "To *play* with insurrections," they were chided, "instead of organizing a mass uprising of the workers and peasants, is a sure way of losing the revolution."[19]

CHAPTER 15

The Guomindang in Power

GUOMINDANG GOVERNMENT

These harsh and apparently successful moves to defuse the power bases of the Communist party did not of course mean that the Guomindang had solved all its own problems. National unification remained an elusive goal, and Chiang as commander of the northern expeditionary forces was desperately short of money. The Chinese bankers and industrialists of Shanghai would have been astonished had they known of Stalin's contention that Chiang Kai-shek had shown his true colors by allying with the forces of the national bourgeoisie. For in the months after his April 1927 coup, Chiang launched a reign of terror against the wealthiest inhabitants of the city. Initially he believed that this was the only way he could raise the millions of dollars he needed per month to pay his troops and maintain the momentum of the Northern Expedition. Chiang pressed the chairman of the Shanghai Chamber of Commerce to provide the bulk of a $10 million loan, and confiscated the man's property when he refused, driving him into exile. Businessmen were coerced into buying 30 million yuan of short-term government bonds, the bigger corporations each being assigned quotas of 500,000 yuan or more. Children of industrialists were arrested as "counterrevolutionaries" or as "Communists" and released only after their fathers gave "donations" to the Guomindang—670,000 yuan in the case of one cotton-mill owner, 200,000 in the case of a wealthy indigo merchant.

In June 1927, responding angrily to new Japanese pressures in Shandong, Chiang sponsored a League for the Rupture of Economic Relations with Japan and began to arrest and fine merchants for violating his boycott attempt. Fines as large as 150,000 yuan each were levied in the cases of one piece-goods dealer and one sugar merchant. Green Gang agents, moving at will through the Chinese city and the foreign concession areas, aided by thousands of beggars acting as spotters, made these arrests and acts of extortion possible. Green Gang leaders also organized a Labor Alliance, run by their own personnel, to replace the former Communist-dominated labor unions. And through the Guomindang's newly created Opium Suppression Bureau, the racketeers and the Guomindang in fact divided up the profits from the sale of the drug and from the "registration fees" paid by known addicts. At the same time, the Guomindang as a political party was actively encouraging the formation of ideologically nationalistic merchant associations—often opposed to the chamber of commerce—which were especially strident in the anti-Japanese boycott and strongly against the attempts of foreigners to collect real-estate taxes from those with businesses in the foreign-concession areas.

The influx of money was still not enough, and the Northern Expedition inevitably suffered from the effects of the split between Wuhan and Chiang's Nanjing regime. In July, Chiang's troops were badly defeated by warlord forces at the battle for the strategic rail junction of Xuzhou, and this, combined with the persistent personal hostility of Wuhan leaders and perhaps his own personal exhaustion, prompted Chiang to relinquish his posts in August. Ironically, in view of the boycott of Japanese goods for which he had just pushed so vigorously, he traveled to Japan, the purpose of his trip being matrimonial rather than political. For Charlie Soong's widow was living in Japan, and after protracted conversations Chiang finally received her permission to marry her youngest daughter, Soong Meiling, a Wellesley College graduate of 1917, YWCA activist, and member of the Shanghai Municipal Council's child labor committee. Since Meiling's two elder sisters were respectively Sun Yat-sen's widow and the wife of the financier H. H. Kong, Chiang had now secured himself important new connections.

The Chiang-Soong wedding, celebrated in Shanghai in December 1927, was an event that encapsulated many of the crosscurrents inside Chinese society. One traditional aspect of the event was that Chiang was still married to his first wife; their eldest son, by odd coincidence, was currently studying in Moscow. Although the Soongs were a Christian family, they apparently agreed to the bigamous marriage because Chiang promised "to study Christianity." In Shanghai, two ceremonies were performed. One, a Christian ceremony in the Soong home, was officiated by David Yui, a specialist in education who had received a Harvard University graduate degree in 1910, and then served as secretary to Vice-President Li Yuanhong before rising to be the highly successful general secretary of the YMCA in China. The

Chinese ceremony was held in the grand ballroom of the Majestic Hotel, presided over by Cai Yuanpei, the scholarly anti-Qing radical and former president of Peking University, now minister of education for the Guomindang.

In the course of Chiang's brief visit to Japan, the other Guomindang leaders had discovered that they could not raise money without him. Sun Fo, who had moved from the Wuhan regime to Nanjing as minister of finance for the reunited Guomindang, found it impossible to persuade the financial community to make further huge loans, and had to be content with small sums grudgingly provided. The Shanghai Chamber of Commerce became independent again, bonds were not paid up, opium revenue dropped to zero, and a plan to get rents forwarded from the foreign-concession areas failed. Unpaid, troops barracked in Shanghai refused to march north to continue the battle with Zhang Zuolin's forces.

In January 1928 Chiang was once again named commander in chief, and also a member of the standing committee of the nine-man Guomindang Central Executive Committee. He brought in his new brother-in-law, T. V. Soong, to run the government's finances. By a mixture of strong-arm methods and financial acumen, Soong was able, without a formal government budget, to get Chiang what he needed to resume the stalled Northern Expedition: 1.6 million yuan every five days.

Now Chiang worked to reactivate an alliance with the two most powerful warlords sympathetic to his reunification goals: one was Feng Yuxiang, the formerly Soviet-backed general who had played such a pivotal role in the 1927 negotiations and who was now firmly based in Henan, where he had defeated Wu Peifu; the other was the independent warlord ruler of Shanxi province, Yan Xishan. The leading Guangxi generals, who had backed the Northern Expedition from its early days and played a critical role in the capture and purging of Shanghai, were now on campaign in Hunan and not disposed to shift their forces to the north.

Heavy fighting began in late March 1928, with the Peking base of the Manchurian warlord Zhang Zuolin as Chiang's ultimate goal. Chiang's troops entered Jinan in Shandong province on April 30, 1928, and it seemed that final victory would soon be his. But at this point a severe setback to the renewed northern expeditionary drive occurred. The Japanese had 2,000 civilians residing in Jinan, and remembering how their concessions had been attacked by Guomindang troops in Hankou and Nanjing, the Japanese cabinet decided to send 5,000 regular army troops to Shandong to protect their nationals until the campaign was over. Five hundred of these troops were already in position as the Nationalists entered the city. When Chiang arrived in person and asked the Japanese to withdraw, it seemed at first that they

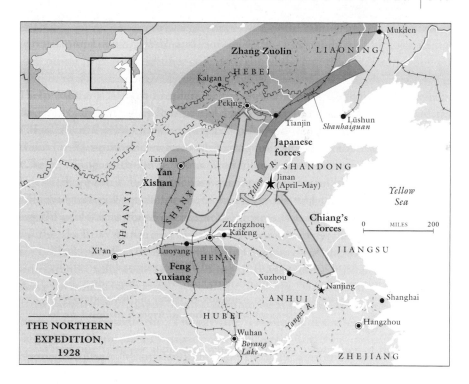

THE NORTHERN
EXPEDITION,
1928

would. But on May 3 fighting broke out, and the skirmish grew into a
devastating clash in which appalling atrocities, including castration and
blinding of helpless prisoners, were committed by both sides. The Japanese
ordered up reinforcements, and on May 11 the Chinese troops were driven
from the city. Appealing to the League of Nations, Chiang chose to duck
any further conflict and instead rerouted his troops across the Yellow River
west of the city and regrouped on the north bank. But a bitter sense of the
hostility between Chinese and Japanese lingered after the confrontation.

The plans designed by Chiang and Feng Yuxiang called for an immediate
joint attack on Tianjin to cut the railway that offered an escape route to the
Shanhaiguan pass for Zhang Zuolin's Manchurian troops, stationed in
Peking. But Tianjin was the site of five key foreign concessions with their
accompanying investments, and the foreigners wanted no trouble there.
Accordingly the Japanese took the lead in assuring Zhang Zuolin that if he
abandoned Peking and retreated peacefully back to Manchuria, they would
prevent the southern Guomindang armies from passing beyond the Great
Wall or through the Shanhaiguan pass. After frantic attempts to think up
other options, Zhang Zuolin gave in and on June 2 left Peking with his staff
in a luxury railcar.

As he approached Mukden on the morning of June 4, a bomb exploded, wrecking the train and killing Zhang. The assassination was carried out by Japanese officers and engineers garrisoned in southern Manchuria who disagreed with the more measured policy of the government in Tokyo. Their goal was to provoke a general crisis that would lead to widespread mobilization and an extension of Japan's northeast China power base. Instead the Shanxi general Yan Xishan occupied Peking, as planned by the Guomindang, while one of his subordinates peacefully occupied Tianjin. The Guomindang then pressed for an agreement with Zhang Xueliang, who succeeded to his murdered father's rule in Manchuria. While yielding to Japanese demands that he maintain the "autonomy" of Manchuria, Zhang also accepted an appointment to the State Council of the new National government formally proclaimed at Nanjing on October 10. At the end of 1928 he pledged allegiance to the National government and raised the Nationalist flag. Sun Yat-sen's dream seemed to have been realized after all, and the Guomindang flag, with its white sun on a blue and red ground, flew from Canton to Mukden.

The Guomindang's task was now to establish a political and economic structure that would consolidate this achievement. Since Sun Yat-sen had already laid down guidelines for the period of "tutelage" that would follow the military consolidation of the nation, there was little need for Chiang to worry about the trappings of democracy. Chiang's own title, conferred on him in October 1928, was chairman of the State Council, the ruling body of sixteen that constituted the top level of government. Five of the council-members served as heads, respectively, of the five main yuan* (bureaus) among which government tasks were divided: the Executive, Legislative, Control, Judicial, and Examination yuan. These represented the "five-power constitution" propagated by Sun Yat-sen, although establishing them in this hurried way, without a true backing of elective or popular support, ran counter to some of Sun's deepest ideas about the value of the system.

The Executive Yuan was the most important of the five. Its functions included direction of the central ministries, economic planning, general supervision of the military, relations with the provinces, and appointment of local government officials. Under Tan Yankai, its first head until his death in 1930, it had real prestige. Tan had risen steadily since the days when he had headed the Hunan provincial assembly at the end of the Qing, and was a fine administrator. But as the government was then constituted, Tan still had to follow instructions from the State Council.

*The character for yuan (bureau) is quite different from that for yuan (dollar), but confusingly they are rendered the same in English.

The Legislative Yuan also had an extensive role as a legitimizing device; the main job of its approximately eighty members was to debate and vote on new legislation. It also voted on proceedings of the Executive Yuan, especially as they pertained to budgets and foreign-policy matters. Under its first head, Hu Hanmin, it, too, had some prestige, but its ill-defined tasks and the erratic attendance of its members steadily reduced its power. The duties of the other three yuan, much like those of the former Qing Ministry of Punishments and related bureaus as well as the examination bureaucracy, were to supervise the selection and behavior of civil-service members and the proceedings of the judicial system.

Chiang Kai-shek's own power base remained in Nanjing, which was now officially named the capital of China in place of Peking.* This had been Sun Yat-sen's original goal in 1912, to lessen the power of Yuan Shikai and the northern generals. In Nanjing, Chiang established the Guomindang Central Political Institute and cadre training schools, the members of which would be firm in their personal loyalty to him, just as so many of the Whampoa cadets were. He entrusted the ideological molding of the students to the two Chen brothers, nephews of the same Chen Qimei who in 1911 had helped launch Chiang's career in Shanghai. (Chen Qimei himself had been assassinated in 1916, apparently on orders of Yuan Shikai, whose imperial ambitions Chen had opposed.) The basis of the training was an anti-Communist, anti-imperialist nationalism, into which was injected strong doses of a kind of reinterpreted Confucianism, a Confucianism concentrating on the virtues of order, harmony, discipline, and hierarchy. Since one Chen brother was in charge of the Control Yuan and the other of the so-called Investigation Division (i.e., anti-Communist counterespionage) of the Guomindang, the power at their disposal was enormous.

In all these aspects of his rule, Chiang was constantly invoking the closeness of his personal and political relationship to Sun Yat-sen. The building of Sun Yat-sen's mausoleum in Nanjing gave him a perfect opportunity to emphasize these links. Since Sun's death, the leader's body had been lying at a temple in the Western Hills outside Peking, the corpse oddly garnished with the trappings of modernity. The body was dressed in a Western suit, gramophone records of Sun's patriotic speeches played beside the bier, and movies displayed dramatic moments in Sun's life. But as soon as Chiang reached Nanjing in spring 1927, he arranged for a whole mountainside outside the city to be acquired as Sun's final resting place, and for a huge road to be driven through the congested city linking the Yangzi to the burial

---

*Peking's name was changed to Peiping (Beiping), which means "northern peace" as opposed to "northern capital." For simplicity, I retain "Peking" here.

site. In 1928 Chiang personally visited Sun's temporary bier near Peking, weeping aloud in a dramatic display of inconsolable grief. In 1929, with the lavish Nanjing tomb complex completed to truly imperial specifications, Chiang dispatched a special train to bring Sun's body—now decked in the robes of an imperial-era Confucian literatus—back to the revolutionary capital. And in the funeral ceremony at Nanjing in June 1929 Chiang took the leading role, carefully excluding his most important political rivals from this politically charged symbolic moment in China's history.[1]

Despite such flamboyant and extravagant displays of homage to the Guomindang founder, regular income for the Guomindang government remained as much a problem for Chiang as it had been for Yuan Shikai. Chiang had financed the later stages of the Northern Expedition in part by ruthless exploitation of the Shanghai Chinese industrialists, but that could not be the basis for a permanent policy. T. V. Soong worked hard to convince others that China must establish a central financial authority; he called for a powerful and independent budget committee that would allocate funds to the different branches of the government. But since the final budgetary decisions were still to be ratified by the State Council, problems of jurisdiction and special influence were bound to remain.

Soong estimated initially that total annual revenues after debt payment would be 300 million yuan. Since current military expenses had rocketed up to 360 million yuan a year, military demobilization and reorganization would be essential. It would also be necessary to sort out national and provincial revenues, a task further complicated by the fact that as of 1928 only four provinces—Jiangsu, Zhejiang, Anhui, and Jiangxi—could be considered fully under government control. Soong also served as the first head of the new Central Bank of China, incorporated in late 1928, with a capital of 20 million yuan. Its initial tasks were to pursue monetary reform and redeem bad notes issued by governments in Wuhan, Canton, and Nanjing itself. By vigorous negotiations with foreign powers, the Nationalists won full tariff autonomy in 1928 in exchange for abolishing internal transit taxes and a further range of special surtaxes that had been imposed since the Canton government of Sun Yat-sen. As a result customs revenues rose dramatically, from around 120 million yuan a year to 244 million yuan in 1929 and 385 million in 1931, far exceeding Soong's expectations.

Despite these attempts at reform, China's Guomindang government maintained a consistent budgetary deficit, as the accompanying table shows. There was no income tax, because of collection problems, until 1936. (An attempt in 1921 at a national income tax had yielded the Peking government only 10,311 yuan.) Nor was there a national land tax, since land revenues went to provincial authorities who were not controlled by the Guomindang.

And since it was impossible to tax the foreign corporations beyond a certain level, the brunt of industrial taxes fell on Chinese entrepreneurs. The paradoxical result was that some previously resilient Chinese companies like the Jian family's Nanyang tobacco firm, which had successfully competed with the mighty British-American Tobacco Corporation throughout the 1920s, were driven to virtual bankruptcy by constantly spiraling levies.

A further complication was the over-reliance of the Guomindang government on revenue generated within the lawless yet financially and culturally ebullient city of Shanghai, the population of which had grown to almost 3 million. Shanghai was divided into zones, two of which, the international and the French concession areas—descended from the old treaty port enclaves and protected under foreign laws by the system of extraterritoriality—were home to most of the foreigners and their businesses, as well as to hundreds of thousands of Chinese. A third zone was the main Chinese city, now a vast, sprawling metropolis, heavily industrialized; while the fourth was the aptly named "Badlands," west of the Chinese city and the Western enclaves, where criminal syndicates and a mixed overlay of police forces and paramilitary protection groups vied for control.

Shanghai was indeed a hybrid, its expanding new industries and bustling international harbor lending impetus to rocketing opium sales and addiction, rampant prostitution, and organized crime. The French had adapted

EXPENDITURES, REVENUES, AND DEFICITS OF THE NATIONAL GOVERNMENT, 1929–1937[2]

Year ending June 30	Expenditure excluding balances at end of the period, millions of yuan	Revenue, unborrowed, excluding balances at beginning of the period, millions of yuan	Deficit covered by borrowing	
			Amount, millions of yuan	Percentage of expenditure
1929	434	334	100	23.0
1930	585	484	101	17.3
1931	775	558	217	28.0
1932	749	619	130	17.4
1933	699	614	86	12.3
1934	836	689	147	17.6
1935	941	745	196	20.8
1936	1,073	817	256	23.8
1937	1,167	870	297	25.4

to Shanghai's seamy politics by making one of the leading Chinese racketeers the chief of detectives in their concession area: his job was to keep out all other hoodlums except for those connected with the city's most powerful criminal group—the Green Gang. There were undercurrents of connections between these men and Sun Yat-sen and his supporters, although they remain murky. Chiang Kai-shek, for example, who had been living in Shanghai on the edges of the criminal world during those years when he was not in Japan with Sun, was connected to members of the Green Gang and had a police record in the British files. Chiang was close to Du Yuesheng, who had risen through the opium-smuggling rackets to become one of the most important syndicate leaders in the international settlements. And after 1928 Chiang stayed in close contact with the Green Gang—some of whom began to pose more and more as conventional businessmen and philanthropists, without changing their true colors—and made massive sums of money for his own supporters by monopolizing opium distribution through licensing operations euphemistically called "opium suppression bureaus." To achieve a stable political structure, it was also imperative for the Guomindang government to re-establish effective administrative control over the countryside. This task had been too much for the late Qing rulers and for Yuan Shikai, and in the long run it proved too much for the Guomindang also. What they attempted to institute was a County Organization Law that maintained the old system of county *(xian)* units, governed by magistrates, and established within each county a group of wards consisting of ten to fifty townships. In each township were clusters of villages *(cun)* or urban neighborhoods *(li),* and at the base of the pyramid a household-responsibility system similar to the old Qing *baojia.* In time, the community groupings were supposed to elect headmen and councils; in practice, these officials were appointed from above by the county magistrates. Parallel to the magistrates' offices, there were specialized bureaus controlled by the provincial governments so that a magistrate's control even over his immediate resources was limited.

This administrative system left fundamental problems in the countryside unsolved, and in many rural regions life was little different from what it had been in the Qing. Local administrators were often tyrannical or corrupt, and were more sympathetic to local landlords than to the peasants, who often lived in dire poverty. Local officials insisted on tax collection and rent payments even in times of natural catastrophe, and used police or military power to enforce their demands. Crops were still sown and harvested by hand, produce was carried to market on human shoulders, infant mortality was high, life expectancy low. Many girls were still made to bind their feet, the traditional practice of arranged marriage endured, village localisms were perpetuated, education was minimal or nonexistent. The worldwide depression of the late 1920s brought disaster to many peasants who had over-concentrated on certain cash crops, and hundreds of thousands—perhaps millions—died when the markets in such crops as silk, cotton, soybeans, or tobacco suddenly plummeted. The need was therefore all the greater for strong political initiative. Rural reform required a plan for crop diversification, with fair divisions of landholdings, reasonable prices paid for produce, some form of local credit structure, universal education, and a measure of representative government.

Guomindang leaders were aware of these needs and did address them in a sporadic way. But money was always short and the government distracted by foreign pressures and internal dissensions. As a result, the Communist forces—though routed in the cities—still managed to find considerable support in the countryside, where they formed a number of rural revolutionary governments or "soviets." Chiang expended vast sums of money, and much of his political energy, on trying to eradicate these groups, but though almost successful he never succeeded entirely. Even in the areas he allegedly controlled, Chiang Kai-shek never held undisputed sway, and several times his supporters broke away to form their own temporary regimes: the Guangxi generals in 1929, Generals Feng Yuxiang and Yan Xishan in 1930, Hu Hanmin in 1931, a coalition of military and civilian forces in Fujian province in 1933. Perhaps not surprisingly, then, the main attempts at moderate land reform were carried out by dedicated individuals such as James Yen and Liang Shuming.

James Yen received his first challenge as a reformer and teacher working for the YMCA among Chinese laborers serving in France during World War I. Returning to China in 1921 he continued to work for mass literacy, concentrating his efforts in Ding County in Hebei. There, broadening his endeavors, he created a "model village" where the people were taught hygiene and agricultural technology in addition to the basic reading curriculum. By 1929, helped by international donations, James Yen had developed for over sixty villages and market towns in Ding County a fourfold program of reconstruction in the areas of education, public health, economic growth through light industry and agriculture, and self-government.

Liang Shuming, a noted Confucian scholar whose father had committed suicide in 1918 out of despair at China's plight, had gone on to become a professor of philosophy at Peking University during the May Fourth period. After experimental work in rural reconstruction in the south, Liang became director of the Shandong Rural Research Institute and attempted to develop Zouping and Heze counties as model communities. Here, in order to obviate the need for class struggle and draw the entire community into a self-governing enterprise, he concentrated on mutual economic assistance and educational projects that involved both the elite and the common people.

The very success of these private ventures showed what might have been accomplished. But there were few of these experiments in Guomindang China, a reflection not only of the prevailing practice of laissez-faire, but of something deeper as well: failure of will to confront China's problems directly.

CULTURE AND IDEOLOGY

At many levels, in the late 1920s and the 1930s when the Guomindang held sway, there was certainly immense change to Chinese life. Medical care became more sophisticated, new hospitals were built, schools and college campuses featured sports grounds and laboratories. The extension of metaled roads capable of carrying trucks and automobiles opened up new levels of social and commercial exchange. New power stations brought electricity to urban China; steamer transport expanded on the rivers and along the coast, cheapening interregional trade; faster trains traveled new track, and air transport became possible on certain national routes. Cinemas established themselves as part of urban life; radios and phonographs appeared in the richer homes; and Chinese men began sporting business suits, derbies, or cloth caps, the younger women short skirts and high-heels. Chic, sophisticated, and sexually suggestive advertising grew common in the new popular leisure magazines. Entertainment and shopping complexes grew more lavish, and popular singers and film stars became celebrities. Fascination with the private lives of the famous was linked to the availability of information on sexual matters through a dramatic rise in the sale and frankness of biological and sexual practice manuals. Cigarette smoking became a national fad. For the wealthier Chinese, life could be very good indeed, and to a Westerner living in China during this period these were truly "the years that were fat."[3] And yet a pervasive sense of malaise existed among many middle-class Chinese, who should have logically been the Guomindang's most loyal allies.

Ever since the feverish excitement of the May Fourth movement had dissipated amid the shocks of the late 1920s, most members of the generation of May Fourth iconoclasts had assumed one of five possible roles: as leaders in the CCP; as spokesmen for the Guomindang vision of an anti-Communist order; as defenders of a middle-of-the-road liberal tradition; as espousers of a rigorous academic methodology; or as exponents of a free-spirited and hedonistic way of life. In every one of these five postures they could live on the prestige brought by their past classical training, their participation—however remotely—in the drama of late Qing reform movements and the dynasty's fall, and their deep knowledge of one or more foreign cultures. Those who had been teenagers or younger at the time of the May Fourth movement faced the same general range of options as goals to be striven for, but the way toward these goals now seemed less clear. These people felt a deeper sense of dislocation than their elders, for the easier battles had been won; what on earth were they to do with the muddled legacy that seemed to have been left them?

The stakes were high, and the issues deadly serious, as can be seen from the case of two young gropers after truth: the writer Ding Ling and her husband Hu Yepin. Ding Ling, born to a gentry family in Hunan in 1904, had been educated in the modern schools of Changhsa; she and her mother had both been caught up in the dreams for a new China that lay at the heart of the May Fourth movement. They had been close friends with many of the students who went off to France in 1919, including several of those who joined the Communist party there. In 1922, Ding Ling said goodbye to her mother and friends in Hunan and traveled first to Nanjing and Shanghai, and then to Peking. There she lived an emancipated life with the aspiring poet Hu Yepin among a sprawling group of writers and artists, apparently the very model of a Nora who had successfully left home.

In late 1927 Ding Ling published her first major short story. It related the travails of Meng Ke, a naïve but attractive country girl who moves gingerly through the world of wealthy Shanghai sophisticates, over-Westernized aesthetes, and dogmatic radicals. She finally settles—by luck rather than good judgment—into a successful career as a movie actress, but in her triumph Meng Ke has been dehumanized, made into an object for the gratification of the male world. In an even more successful story entitled "The Diary of Miss Sophie" and published the following year, Ding Ling presented, through the eyes of the fictional Miss Sophie, a bitter view of loneliness and frustration. Sophie's restlessness is so deep that it makes her physically ill; her petulance tempts even the most loyal friend to shun her; she purposefully designs her erotic attachments so as to humiliate herself. In the remarkable closing lines of this powerful, dispiriting story, Miss Sophie reflects on what the future has to offer:

> I've defiled myself. Man is his own fiercest enemy. My heaven, how shall I begin to revenge and retrieve all I've lost? Life has been my own toy. I've wasted enough of it away, so it is of no material importance that this new experience has plunged me into a new abyss. I don't want to stay in Peking and I don't want to go to the Western Hills. I'm going to take the train

southward where no one knows me and waste away what's left of my life. Out of the pain, my heart revives. And now I look on myself with pity and I laugh.

Live and die your own way, unnoticed. Oh, how I pity you, Sophie![4]

As Ding Ling's reputation grew, Hu Yepin wrote poetry and short stories, too, which Ding Ling loyally helped him publish with her earnings. Both of them responded to the country's turmoil by moving left politically. Hu joined the Communist party first, in 1930, and wrote an emotional, exaggerated novel on the May Thirtieth Incident of 1925, which in fact he had not witnessed, since he was then already living in Peking. At the end of 1930, Hu determined to go to the Jiangxi Soviet to work on cultural affairs and literacy campaigns among the peasants. In January 1931, just after Ding Ling had borne their first child, he was arrested by British police at a secret meeting of the CCP in the British concession area of Shanghai and handed over to the Guomindang. There is evidence that Hu and his friends were betrayed to the police by a rival faction within the CCP. After a brief investigation he was shot, along with twenty-two comrades, on February 7, 1931, at the Guomindang garrison command headquarters near Shanghai. Ding Ling's response was to travel back to her home in Hunan and leave her baby with her mother, before returning to Shanghai and herself joining the CCP.

The young may have sought to further the cause of social justice by joining the CCP, but they found no cultural freedom once they became members. To the contrary, since 1930 the world of leftist creativity in China had been dominated by Soviet Russian views of political aesthetics as transmitted through the League of Left-Wing Writers. The Chinese leaders of this league meticulously followed the cultural line laid down by Stalin in the Soviet Union, which gave its own didactic definitions of how the world should be viewed and where political priorities lay. The basic Stalinist premise was that to be "correct," any depiction of social reality must illuminate the exact class relationships of the protagonists and leave no ambiguities about the direction and purpose of the socialist revolution. Ding Ling herself, after joining the CCP, wrote her new work according to league rules, although in most cases the stories about workers and peasants that she and her friends wrote were stilted and unconvincing.

Lu Xun, of all the senior May Fourth writers the most revered among the young, joined the league himself in 1930 but found it and its rules stifling. The Soviet idea of a perfect poem, Lu Xun wrote sarcastically, was

Oh, steam whistle!
Oh, Lenin![5]

and the Chinese members of the league, he observed, slavishly followed Russian guidelines while indulging in bitter and vengeful backbiting among themselves. Though constantly wooed by the CCP, Lu Xun refused to join their ranks. Instead, right up to his death from tuberculosis in 1936, he tried to encourage younger writers to hold onto a sense of the main issues in Chinese culture, to maintain an acute social conscience, and never to lose their sense of the ridiculous.

Another source of disillusionment, as Chiang Kai-shek and the Guomindang began to consolidate their power in the 1930s, was the disarray that characterized many universities in China. With the fading of the May Fourth exuberance came the realization for many students that, despite the genuine brilliance of some academics, a significant percentage of the faculty was politically timid, intellectually inept, and venal. These teachers claimed deep knowledge of foreign techniques which they did not possess, and even their vaunted foreign advanced degrees were sometimes false. It was hard for students to admire such badly paid, lackluster teachers. The seamier and sillier side of this intellectual milieu was later vividly caught by the writer Qian Zhongshu in his novel *Fortress Besieged*. Qian had grown up in such schools before going off to Europe to study comparative literature at Oxford and Paris. His bleak portrayal makes a fitting partner to Wu Jingzi's equally sardonic view of the world of fading Confucian literati, which Wu had captured in his novel *The Scholars,* written during Emperor Qianlong's reign nearly two hundred years before.

Yet many—perhaps most—educated young Chinese did not lose heart and hope. They were absorbed by the intellectual possibilities of the new age, and anxious to use their scholarship and skills. As one among other countless examples, we can point to Liang Qichao's own son, who learned to ride a motorbike in the narrow streets of Peking, and studied the architectural structures of China's ancient temples and palaces. With his wife, the scholar-poet and art historian Lin Huiyin, he embarked on far-flung travels across China to locate, photograph, sketch—and, if possible, preserve—the choicest items of China's own artistic heritage.

Yet even such free spirits operated in a coercive universe. Guomindang politicians, working through the Ministry of Education, as well as using pressure and intimidation, sought to tighten the educational system and develop a complex network of compulsory subjects and examinations that would keep students too busy studying to be able to foment social unrest. Some universities experienced a kind of reign of terror against radical students and faculty, with predawn raids and sudden searches and arrests. Although there are no official figures available for such attacks, in the spring and summer of 1932, after the protests against the Japanese assault on Shanghai, 22 students were killed in Peking, 113 expelled from various universities, and 471 arrested. During 1934, one college professor estimated, a further 300 teachers and students were arrested, and another 230 between the end of the year and March 1935. Government agencies also practiced a vigorous censorship of newspapers, journals, and books, as well as such new mass-media forums as the cinema. Some movie directors responded by couching their political polemics in allegorical terms, and the public was delighted when some clumsy censor failed to spot the hidden message and released the work.

It was obvious to Chiang Kai-shek and his close advisers that if the students, the intellectuals, and especially the urban workers were to be convinced by Guomindang claims that it was striving to fulfill its mission of national reunification and economic reconstruction, some means more effective than intellectual repression, repeated attacks on the Communists, and appeasement of the Japanese would have to be found. By early 1934 Chiang began to develop such a new unifying ideology, drawing partly on the doctrines of Sun Yat-sen, partly on the reformist social strategies of foreign missionaries, and partly on his own views of the central tenets of traditional Confucianism, especially with regard to the formation of a loyal and moral human character. Chiang named this set of beliefs the "New Life movement," and clearly expected great things from it. He declared that it would create "a new national consciousness and mass psychology" that, through the revived force of the virtues of "etiquette, justice, integrity and conscientiousness," would lead to "the social regeneration of China."

In presenting his doctrine, Chiang harked back to theories of Social Darwinism, writing that "only those who readapt themselves to new conditions, day by day, can live properly. When the life of a people is going through this process of readaptation, it has to remedy its own defects, and get rid of those elements which become useless. Then we call it new life."[6] Chiang started the movement during 1934 in Nanchang, where he was working on what turned out to be the final suppression campaign against the Jiangxi Soviet. From Nanchang the New Life movement was spread by Guomindang party organizations to other provinces, youth groups, and then the public at large. A wide range of mass communications were used to spread the word, including lectures, pictures, pamphlets, plays, and movies. Having absorbed the lessons of the movement, Chiang hoped, the country would be ready to solve the "four great needs" of the population, which he identified as clothing, food, housing, and transportation. Chiang's new ideology reflected this sense of national crisis, along with elements of fascism. He made clear that his goal, through the New Life movement, was "thoroughly to militarize the life of the people of the entire nation. It is to make them nourish courage and alertness, a capacity to endure hardship, and especially a habit and instinct for unified behavior. It is to make them willing to sacrifice for the nation at all times."[7]

Chiang hoped that by starting out with collective campaigns against such antisocial or undisciplined acts as spitting, urinating, or smoking in public, casual sexual liaisons, and provocative clothing, the country could gradually be drawn together to confront graver social and economic issues. But despite wide-scale publicity throughout the school system and such groups as the Boy Scouts and the YMCA, the movement never developed beyond its focus on these comparatively minor social peccadilloes. Still it managed a great deal of individual harassment and interference in private lives. Women especially were made to feel the whip of those who resented the changes in female behavior that had occurred since the fall of the Qing dynasty, and were frequently harried or even attacked if they wore immodest clothes or behaved flirtatiously. Younger Chinese women students in Jiangsu, for instance, were harangued by a Guomindang spokesman to act with "social decorum" because in the West "an unmarried woman, unless accompanied by a married woman, cannot participate in any public gathering. Men and women can only meet in the sitting room and cannot go together to the bedroom."[8]

Chinese women were urged to cultivate the "four virtues" of "chastity, appearance, speech, and work," and were told not to be hoodwinked into blindly following feminist ideas. "The women's movement in today's society is not a real woman's movement," the same Jiangsu lecturer explained. "It is a movement of imitating men." He left no doubt that Chinese women's central tasks were "to regulate the household" through chores, sewing, cooking, arranging the furniture, and designing the home and garden.[9] More detailed regulations promulgated in Jiangxi gave the exact dimensions for hem lines to fall below the knee (4 inches), for the slit in the traditional Chinese dress to rise above the knee (3 inches), and for a blouse worn with trousers to fall below the line of the buttocks (3 inches). Despite the seriousness of its original intent, instead of reviving the nation, the New Life movement gradually trickled away in a stream of trivia.

Also in the early 1930s, a much tougher organization was formed, spearheaded by Whampoa cadets of the earliest graduating classes, to steel the political and military leadership of China for the long struggles ahead. Pledging themselves to lives of ascetic rigor, rejecting gambling, whoring, or excessive consumption of food and drink, members of this group wore shirts of coarse blue cotton, which led to their being informally named "Blueshirts." Expanding in numbers, and with their own organizational structure, the Blueshirts were encouraged by Chiang, although their work and interests often cut across pre-existing bureaucratic or military lines. One

of Chiang's greatest political skills, indeed, was this ability to foster potentially clashing groups, whose existence reinforced his own indispensability
as the man in the middle.

One theorist for the Blueshirts spoke openly of their need to be like a
knife, an instrument that could kill in combat or harmlessly cut vegetables.
The precise act could be worried about once the knife was properly forged;
before that, neither task could be accomplished. The same theorist found
models for China to emulate in three societies: Stalin's Soviet Union, Hitler's
Germany, and Mussolini's Italy. In all three cases, he claimed, the purpose
behind slogans of national or state socialism was similar to that of Sun Yat-
sen's Three Principles of the People. He saw democracy as a sham that
could only damage a country like China, with its poverty and illiterate
masses. "If we were to implement democratic politics immediately," he
noted, "it would be just like giving a pair of high-heeled shoes to a girl with
bound feet from the countryside and then asking her to go out dancing."[10]

By 1934 other Chinese writers were openly praising fascism, particularly
that of Benito Mussolini. Admiration for Italy's nationalist reunification
under Giuseppe Mazzini and Giuseppe Garibaldi had initially been a focus
for some of Liang Qichao's writings in the late Qing, and the admiration
for Italy had revived when Mussolini's regime began to develop China's air
force in the early 1930s with planes, trainer pilots, and even the construction
of factories. To one writer in 1934, it was the context for the dictator's rise
that seemed to offer the closest parallels to China and Chiang Kai-shek:
"Two years after the European War, Italy, exactly like our country at present, was afflicted by internal disorder and foreign aggression. But she
obtained a Mussolini and after years of leadership and training, struggle and
hard work, and striving to seek a good system of rule, Italy was finally saved
from the near death she faced." Did China have such a leader? the writer
asked rhetorically. Yes, indeed: "Our own hardworking, highly meritorious,
outstanding revolutionary leader Generalissimo Chiang."[11]

With a fierce loyalty to the cult of Chiang as leader, with a strong base
in the administrative, military, and party machinery, and with its members
granted special roles in the anti-Communist campaign, the Blueshirt nucleus
developed into a disciplined military and secret-police apparatus that could
be used to investigate all kinds of domestic and foreign forces believed to
be subversive. The Blueshirt Dai Li, a Zhejiang-born Whampoa graduate,
became head of Chiang Kai-shek's Special Service Section in the euphemistically named Bureau of Investigation and Statistics. Initially supervising
about 145 operatives, by 1935 he had 1,700. Dai Li was believed to have
directed a number of political assassinations of those opposed to Chiang,
including the head of the Chinese League for the Protection of Civil Rights

(in 1933) and the editor of Shanghai's leading newspaper (in 1934).

But even though such men could have dissident individuals killed, frighten faculty and students into acquiescence, infiltrate labor unions, and gather intelligence from potentially restive rural areas, they could not remove the basic roots of discontent. The failures of the Guomindang's attempts at ideological indoctrination can be gauged through the wide-ranging observations assembled by the novelist Mao Dun in 1936. Building on an idea previously tried out by the Russian writer Maxim Gorky, Mao Dun and his associates, through widely distributed advertisements and announcements, asked people all over China to write in and say what had happened to them on a particular, randomly selected day—May 21, 1936. The resulting 3,000 replies, from almost every province in China and all social and occupational groupings, constituted a formidable criticism of Chiang's new policies and ideology. The respondents mocked the propaganda behind the New Life campaigns for its insincerity, and angrily criticized the disruption to rural life caused by compulsory land requisitions and the forced drafting of labor. They attacked those who collaborated with the Japanese, or presented specious arguments for avoiding conflict. One man wrote that China's "military and political authorities are walking away from North China, especially East Hebei, as though these were human excrement." Another writer, in one of the cleverest and saddest submissions sent to Mao Dun, played on the difference of accents that led Chinese in the north to misinterpret the sentiments of their fellow countrymen in the south. On one street, he observed, hung a sign with this uplifting message:

> Everything prospers, Heaven is protective.
> People are heroes. The place is famous.

But if read with a Cantonese accent, and then reinterpreted according to sound, the slogan became more depressing:

> Everything disintegrates, Heaven explodes.
> People are extinct. The place is bare.[12]

The author showed clearly that he felt it was the second version of the slogan that the Chinese should believe, not the first.

CHINA AND THE UNITED STATES

Given the realities of the world balance of power, much of the focus of the Guomindang had to be on the international diplomatic arena. Before turning to Japan, which represented the gravest threat, let us consider the United States, which also played a considerable role in Guomindang thinking.

In the chaotic decade that followed the end of World War I, important changes occurred in U.S. foreign policy toward China. The unfolding of events at the Versailles treaty negotiations had dramatically confirmed that Japan rather than China now played the dominant role on the international scene in east Asia. Ironically, in the negotiations President Wilson had been anxious to placate Japanese sentiment as much as possible because of his hopes for building a global league of nations that would guarantee lasting peace. But in 1919 and again in 1920, Congress refused to vote for U.S. entrance into the League, dooming Wilson's dream.

Cognizant of Japanese power, and uneasy at the expensive naval arms race that was developing, the United States decided to pursue new international agreements that would protect its own position in east Asia and the Pacific, cut back some of Japan's recent gains, and end the exclusivist British-Japanese alliance in Asia. Britain, equally worried about protecting her global empire with the diminished resources left her after World War I, was glad to join in discussions. So too were the Japanese, who were eager for further formal acknowledgment of their international status as a great power and all too aware that 49 percent of their budget was going for military expenditures.

The representatives of these three countries, along with France and five other states, met in Washington in November 1921 and continued their meetings until February 1922. The American goal of ending the exclusive alliance of Britain and Japan was met when a four-power agreement calling for "consultations" among the United States, Japan, Britain, and France in times of crisis was substituted for the former British-Japanese military-assistance treaty; all four powers agreed as well on the "nonfortification" of their Pacific islands. A follow-up Nine-Power Treaty (in which the above four states were joined by China, Italy, Portugal, Belgium, and Holland) condemned spheres of influence in China and gave rousing acclamation to the idea of maintaining the "sovereignty, the independence, and the territorial and administrative integrity of China."

In a third agreement, the navies of the three main signatories were fixed in relative size on a ratio of 5:5:3, measured in terms of tonnage of armored capital ships. The United States and Britain would have five units each to Japan's three. Although at first glance this agreement seemed to relegate Japan to a second-rank position, in fact because so much of the other two powers' fleets had to be concentrated in the Atlantic (and, for Britain, in the Mediterranean and the Indian Ocean), and because of the agreement by the two Atlantic powers not to build up major armed bases in the Pacific islands, the treaty was likely to assure Japan naval superiority in east Asia. Britain was content because the treaty did not affect her bases in Singapore, Australia, or New Zealand, and she had an advantage in gunnery on her existing ships. The Americans felt they had brought a new order and the possibility of peace to Asian international relations.

Japan appeared to be surprisingly flexible at the conference. On the understanding that its special position in southern Manchuria was not to be disturbed, Japan agreed to pull back from the Russian maritime provinces and Sakhalin, where Japanese troops had been opposing the Soviets. With respect to China, Japan agreed to back off from the Twenty-one Demands of 1915, restore management of the Qingdao-Jinan railway to the Chinese, and restore the Jiaozhou "leased territory"—seized from Germany in 1914—to the Chinese government.

Throughout the middle and late 1920s, U.S. policy toward China remained low-keyed. The gains initially made by the Comintern were watched cautiously by American officials, and there was general approval when Chiang Kai-shek moved decisively to crush the growing Communist power.

In the summer of 1928, T. V. Soong met in Peking with the American minister to China, and they signed a treaty in which the United States agreed to let China fix her own tariffs on foreign imports. The full revised tariff schedule, released later that year, raised rates to levels between 7.5 percent and 27.0 percent, bringing desperately needed revenue to the Guomindang government. In Washington's opinion, the signing of this treaty constituted *de facto* and *de jure* recognition of the Nationalist government; the ratification of the treaty by the Senate in February 1929 thus made the "recognition" official. Talks began soon after about ending extraterritoriality for Americans residing in China.

Americans were generally pleased by Chiang Kai-shek's marriage to Soong Meiling, whose degree from Wellesley College in Massachusetts enhanced her strong family ties to the United States. With her two younger brothers now both back in China to work alongside T. V. Soong, and her two sisters constantly in the public eye, Soong family members were effective lobbyists for American support. The popular image of this family in the United States was further strengthened in October 1930, when Chiang was baptized a Christian in Shanghai. With his young wife beside him they repeated their marriage vows and pledged to follow a life dedicated to Christian principles.

Reflecting this general satisfaction, American investments in China continued to grow steadily, although they still lagged in pace and scale far behind those of Britain and Japan. This disparity looks all the more graphic if one considers just foreign investment in manufacturing ventures, as opposed to the entire range of trading, banking, utilities, and real estate. The profitability of American investments compared well to those of Great Britain and Japan.

Much of America's involvement in China also represented an expansion of the earlier Christian missionary impulse, which in the late 1920s and early 1930s focused on education, medical care and training, and broad-based socially oriented programs such as the YMCA and YWCA. Many of the Christian schools were launched by American missionary societies, which tried to keep the enrollments small and the curriculum concentrated on Christian knowledge and principles. As Chinese nationalism grew, this focus inevitably caused explosive pressure to build in these institutions, leading to student riots, violence, and expulsions. Yet Yanjing (Yenching) University in Peking, an amalgam of what had originally been four colleges founded by Methodist, Congregational, and Presbyterian sponsors, was famous for its training in journalism and sociology. There generations of Chinese students learned to analyze and benefit their own society, whether through business, administration, or involvement in rural reconstruction projects.

The secular Nankai University in Tianjin, founded by a Chinese self-strengthening activist of the late Qing who went on to study at Columbia University's Teachers College, developed into a center for economic and social research thanks to gifts from private backers in the United States and the Rockefeller Foundation. Qinghua College—originally set up in Peking

FOREIGN INVESTMENTS IN CHINA BY COUNTRY, 1902–1936[13]

Country	1902	1914	1931	1936
Great Britain	260.3 (33.0)*	607.5 (37.7)	1,189.2 (36.7)	1,220.8 (35.0)
Japan	1.0 (0.1)	219.6 (13.6)	1,136.9 (35.1)	1,394.0 (40.0)
Russia	246.5 (31.3)	269.3 (16.7)	273.2 (8.4)	0.0
United States	19.7 (2.5)	49.3 (3.1)	196.8 (6.1)	298.8 (8.6)
France	91.1 (11.6)	171.4 (10.7)	192.4 (5.9)	234.1 (6.7)
Germany	164.3 (20.9)	263.6 (16.4)	87.0 (2.7)	148.5 (4.3)
Belgium	4.4 (0.6)	22.9 (1.4)	89.0 (2.7)	58.4 (1.7)
Netherlands	0.0	0.0	28.7 (0.9)	0.0
Italy	0.0	0.0	46.4 (1.4)	72.3 (2.1)
Scandinavia	0.0	0.0	2.9 (0.1)	0.0
Others	0.6 (0.0)	6.7 (0.4)	0.0	56.3 (1.6)
	787.9 (100.0)	1,610.3 (100.0)	3,242.5 (100.0)	3,483.2 (100.0)

*In millions of U.S. dollars; percent in parentheses.

FOREIGN INVESTMENTS IN MANUFACTURING IN CHINA
BY COUNTRY, 1936[14]

Manufacture	Britain	United States	Germany	France	Japan	Total	
Textiles	64.6*	1.2	3.9	0.0	112.4	182.1	(54.7)*
Metal, machinery, equipment	20.8	3.6	0.1	0.5	4.1	29.1	(8.8)
Chemicals	63.0	1.7	2.0	1.0	6.8	74.5	(22.4)
Lumber, woodworking	4.0	0.5	0.0	0.0	0.9	5.4	(1.6)
Printing, bookbinding	0.3	0.3	0.1	0.0	0.8	1.5	(0.5)
Food, drink, tobacco	23.3	1.1	0.9	0.5	5.8	31.6	(9.5)
Others	3.7	1.1	0.1	0.0	3.3	8.2	(2.5)
Total	179.7	9.5	7.1	2.0	134.1	332.4	
	(54.1)	(2.9)	(2.1)	(0.6)	(40.3)		(100.0)

*In millions of U.S. dollars; percent in parentheses.

to prepare Chinese students for study in the United States, where scholarships were provided from the almost $12 million accrued from the Boxer indemnity—trained 1,268 students between 1909 and 1929. The college was turned into a "National" Qinghua University by the Guomindang after the Northern Expedition, and added a fine College of Engineering to its already prestigious Colleges of Letters, Sciences, and Law.

Medical advances in China were also considerable, owing in large measure to the impact of private philanthropy—in particular the Rockefeller Foundation, which in 1915 made a major commitment to support a medical school in China. The Peking Union Medical College, fruit of this decision, became China's great center for medical research and teaching. Although the methodology was Western—eschewing the traditional Chinese concentration on diagnosis by pulses and cures through herbal treatments or acupuncture—and the language of instruction was English, the problems addressed were diseases unique to, or extremely prevalent in, China. Teaching procedures in the college's beautifully equipped hospital were meticulous, leisurely, and expensive: it took a faculty and administrative staff of 123 foreigners and 23 Chinese to oversee the graduation of 64 Chinese medical students between 1924 and 1930. But with a further grant of $12 million from the foundation in 1928, the college assured its status as the leader in China. The only close runner-up was the Japanese medical college in Manchuria, which was reserved for Japanese students.

The Xiangya medical college in Changsha, Hunan, experienced a different growth, although it too started with a sizable benefaction—from the American financier Edward Harkness. In this case the staff of a Yale University medical training school in Changsha pooled its resources with the Hunan governor and the local Chinese gentry to build and staff a training hospital. Chinese always figured prominently among the faculty, and in 1925 they assumed control of the administration. The joint Sino-American team achieved important results in smallpox and cholera research, rat extermination to combat an alarming spread of pneumonic plague, and remedies for opium addiction. The Changsha authorities did their part by guaranteeing an adequate supply of electricity so that the hospital's new X-ray machinery could function at all times.

Between 1921 and 1926, with a far smaller teaching staff than that at the Peking hospital, Xiangya graduated 43 Chinese doctors. One brief moment of glory for Xiangya came in 1926, when two of their doctors (one can imagine them working rather nervously together) extracted a painfully impacted wisdom tooth from Chiang Kai-shek, who was meeting with his generals in Changsha to plan the final stages of the Wuhan and Jiangxi campaigns. Several excellent medical colleges for women were also established at this time, most of them run by Christian colleges. And the Xiangya hospital developed an important nurses' training program in association with Yanjing University.

American influence spread also through the Chiangs' friendship with individual missionaries in China. Although the great majority of the close to 5,000 Catholic priests and nuns in China in the 1920s were European or Chinese, over half of the 6,636 Protestant missionaries resident in China were Americans grouped mainly in small mission stations scattered across the country. Once Chiang Kai-shek started his determined attempt to destroy the Jiangxi Soviet, the missionary influence grew, for Chiang and his wife made their summer home in the cool, breezy hills of Kuling (near Jiujiang), which had long been the chosen summer resort for the foreign community. The house the Chiangs rented belonged to the Nanchang Methodist Mission, and Madame Chiang in particular became a close friend of their landlord, William Johnson, a Methodist from Illinois who had been in China since 1910 and was especially interested in rural reconstruction. Although Chiang's closest foreign adviser was an Australian, W. H. Donald (who earlier had been a special adviser to Yuan Shikai), Chiang had lengthy discussions with many of the American missionaries. Later he was to draw more heavily on some of them, especially the Congregationalist missionary George Shepherd, a New Zealand–born naturalized citizen who was described as "the one trusted American" in Chiang's "innermost circle."

Another element making for harmonious relations was the muting of the problems of Chinese emigration to the United States. In the late Qing, America's exclusion laws and the Chinese boycotts of 1905 had soured relations between the two countries. But by the late 1920s, despite new American laws that forbade Chinese wives of American citizens to enter the United States and excluded Chinese children of couples nonresident in the United States even if they had citizenship, a kind of status quo had been established. The Chinese population in the United States, which had dropped dramatically with the exclusion laws, started slowly to climb again in the 1920s, and the gender imbalance gradually began to right itself as a new generation was born in the United States.

Although still mainly active in such enterprises as restaurants and laundries, some Chinese had moved into new careers in business, retailing, and manufacturing, and also spread out of the old Chinatowns on the West Coast into other parts of the country. The predominance of Chinese from around Canton also ended, and in 1929 a new fraternal organization was formed to support those who came from Jiangsu, Zhejiang, and Jiangxi. The year 1931 saw the last of the violent tong wars between rival Chinese neighborhood and dialect groups that had helped perpetuate the negative image of the Chinese in the United States for so long.

It was in this same period that Americans at home began to get some sense of the conditions of rural life in China. The most influential informant was the novelist Pearl Buck, whose *The Good Earth* was first published in 1931. This story of a Chinese peasant family caught in unending struggles with the land—fighting famine, experiencing Communist propaganda teams in Nanjing, and returning to the soil where they prosper once more—was based on careful observation. Buck, whose Presbyterian missionary parents were posted in Zhenjiang on the Yangzi River, grew up in China. She attended high school in Shanghai, and although in 1910 she left for college

CHINESE POPULATION IN THE UNITED STATES, 1890–1940[15]

	Total Chinese in United States	Number of women
1890	106,488	3,868
1900	89,863	4,522
1910	71,531	4,675
1920	61,639	7,748
1930	74,945	15,152
1940	77,504	20,115

in the United States, she returned to China in 1914 and later married John Lossing Buck, an agricultural specialist who conducted extensive research on the economic and social conditions of China's peasants. The Bucks lived for years in northern Anhui and later moved to Nanjing, which they had to flee for Shanghai during the antiforeign outbreaks of March 1927. The experience, the tensions, the excitement, and the yearning to write all came together for Pearl Buck in early 1928, and she wrote the entire novel in three months. *The Good Earth* sold 1.5 million copies, received the Pulitzer Prize, and was translated into thirty languages. It became a Broadway play in 1933, and four years later a movie that was seen in the United States by an estimated 23 million people. Americans clearly wanted to know about China if they could be entertained along the way, but they did not require an exotic or glamorous China. Perhaps, as the United States began to confront the Great Depression in all its complexity, it was comforting to know that in China things were even worse.

CHINA AND JAPAN

Japanese policy toward China after the beginning of the First World War underwent a number of swings. During 1914 and 1915, Japan's seizure of the German concessions in Shandong and issuing of the Twenty-one Demands had shown complete intransigence. The Washington Conference of 1921–1922 saw a more conciliatory Japan withdrawing its harsher demands and returning the former German possessions and railways to China. But in 1927–1928 the hard line resurfaced, partly in response to the belief that the Guomindang-Communist alliance would usher in a new era of antiforeignism that might damage Japan's privileged trading position in central China and its dominating military presence in southern Manchuria. The violent clash with National Revolutionary Army troops at Jinan in May 1928 and the assassination of Marshal Zhang Zuolin in June the same year gave ample proof of the new mood.

Tension between the Japanese army and the various governments in China mirrored growing problems in Japan itself. The enormous promise of rapid development that had lasted through the late nineteenth and early twentieth centuries began to waver and fade. Although the granting of full voting rights to all Japanese males in 1925 and the accession of the young and scholarly emperor Hirohito to the throne in 1926 seemed to augur continued vitality, the Japanese imperial-constitutional government had in fact entered a period of decline. The great government-backed industrial corporations were believed by many to have grown too powerful and corrupt, and to have undermined the integrity of elected politicians and the bureaucracy. Both the army and navy, well equipped and well trained, felt frustrated by international treaties and a foreign policy that seemed to deny them a meaningful role.

There was a pervasive fear of subversion within the country, and even though Japan's Communist party had been wholly ineffectual, tough new "peace-preservation laws" were passed in the late 1920s that gave special powers to the police in their hunt for domestic agitators. A population that had doubled in size since the Meiji reforms, reaching 65 million in 1928, began to face urban unemployment and agricultural depression. Both were exacerbated when the U.S. stock-market crash prefigured the collapse of the huge market for Japanese silks there, throwing thousands of Japanese workers out of jobs and costing farmers their main source of supplementary income. In 1929–1930 silk prices dropped to one-quarter of their previous levels, and Japan's exports to the United States dropped by 40 percent. Japanese exports of pearls, canned goods, and porcelain to the United States were all adversely affected by the Smoot-Hawley Tariff of 1930, which raised import duties by an average of 23 percent. In the same period, Japanese exports to China dropped by 50 percent.

There was, among many Japanese scholars and politicians, a complicated attitude toward China that combined admiration for past cultural attainments with patronizing contempt for its current predicaments. One of Japan's most famous China scholars and publicists, Naito Konan, was fully representative of these attitudes. On the first day of the Sino-Japanese War in 1894, as a young man of twenty-nine, Naito had written of Japan's new "mission" to spread "Japanese civilization and ways to every corner of the world." Since of all Asian nations China was the largest, naturally it "should become the primary target of Japan's mission." To Naito, this mission was special because Japan, in an inevitable process of diffusion and change, had become the possessor and developer of a cultural maturity once held by China.

The Jiangsu-Zhejiang dominance of Chinese culture in the late Ming and early Qing had been followed by a period of fluorescence for Guangdong— all three provinces had been originally inhabited by non-Chinese barbarians, Naito pointed out—until by the 1920s "the Oriental cultural center [had] shifted to Japan." Naito's language could at times be crudely dismissive: "We no longer need to ask when China will collapse," he wrote during the May Fourth movement in 1919. "It is already dead, only its corpse is wriggling." But more often he tried to spell out Japan's dreams for China by using protracted metaphors of progress and change:

> Suppose, with the intention to open up a huge rice field, you start digging irrigation canals. Eventually, you hit a big rock which must be cracked with

a hammer or even blasted by dynamite. What would you say if someone should disregard your ultimate objective, and criticize you for destroying the land?[16]

What this meant for China in economic terms fitted well with what the Southern Manchurian Railway Company, other Japanese industrialists, and the Japanese army were already contemplating or carrying out: "China must in the first place be so reorganized as to become a producing country of crude materials needed for manufacturing."[17] From the conjunction of such views emerged the idea of a Greater East Asian Co-Prosperity Sphere, in which China and Japan, under Japan's vigorous and martial leadership, would claim their rightful place in the world, even if it took war to persuade China of the correctness of this course.

Those Japanese army officers who had hoped that the 1928 assassination of Zhang Zuolin would spark a wider war in north China were disappointed. The Tokyo government took a watchful attitude and did not order general mobilization. Instead, Zhang Zuolin's son, Zhang Xueliang, succeeded to the leadership of his father's troops. Born in 1898, Zhang Xueliang had been an undistinguished officer in his father's Manchurian armies, an opium addict, and a social gadfly despised by many of his father's leading commanders. He could not have initially seemed much of a threat to the Japanese, and was dismissively called "the Young Marshal." But he showed surprising determination in the summer and fall of 1928 by bringing the three northeastern provinces that had constituted his father's domain—Heilongjiang, Jilin (Kirin), and Liaoning—into nominal unity with the rest of China under the Nanjing regime of the Guomindang. As an added inducement, Nanjing offered to let Zhang incorporate the province of Rehe (Jehol) into a Northeast Political Council that he would head. Despite Japanese warnings that they opposed the reunification of Manchuria with the rest of China, Zhang persisted, and pledged loyalty to the Nanjing government in December 1928.

Thereafter Zhang Xueliang began to show an alarming independence. The Japanese had hoped to influence or even dominate Zhang through two of his father's close confidants who had been important military and civil leaders in the northeast. Zhang, aware of this plan, invited the two men to dinner in January 1929 and had them shot during the meal; he excused himself from his guests to get an injection of his daily morphine while the killings were being carried out. Late that spring, in an echo of his father's 1927 raid on the Soviet embassy in Peking, Zhang raided the Soviet Union's consulate in Harbin and tried to take over the entire Soviet-controlled Chinese Eastern Railway while expelling all Soviet citizens from their posts on it. He had to retreat from these acts when Stalin ordered a strong military response. But in the fall of 1930, when a military-political coalition in the north tried to oust Chiang Kai-shek from power—Chiang's enemies were the formidable trio of Feng Yuxiang, Yan Xishan, and Wang Jingwei—Zhang Xueliang ordered his own troops south through the Shanhaiguan pass and occupied northern Hebei province. This move gave him control over the northern stretches of the Peking-Wuhan and Tianjin-Pukou railroads, and put the rich Tianjin customs revenues into his own pocket.

Chiang Kai-shek, preoccupied with breaking the hostile coalition, accepted Zhang Xueliang's extended base and confirmed Zhang's command over the Northeastern Border Defense Army that now numbered some 400,000 troops. The two men kept up steady pressure on the Japanese, refusing to negotiate new railway deals, actively working for the recovery of existing Japanese rights, demanding an end to extraterritoriality, and resuming development of a new port facility in south Manchuria to undercut the prosperity of the Japanese-controlled Lüshun. The Guomindang also waged a comprehensive economic boycott of Japanese imports, following serious anti-Chinese outbreaks in Korea.

Faced with intensifying domestic violence against politicians and industrialists, and an economy in decline, members of the War Ministry and the Foreign Ministry in Tokyo began moves to curb the actions of their army in Manchuria. In early September 1931 the Japanese government sent a senior general to Lüshun with orders that the commanding Japanese officer in Manchuria use "prudence and patience" in handling problems there. Once such orders had been formally issued, it would have been impossible for the Manchurian army to proceed as it chose. Alerted to the purpose of the general's visit by a secret cable from a junior staff officer in Tokyo, Japanese army officers in Mukden decided to act before they received the restraining orders.

On the night of September 18, 1931, they set off explosives on a stretch of railway line outside Mukden, selected because it was near the largest barracks of Chinese troops in the region. In the noise and confusion, skirmishes broke out between the Japanese and Chinese. The Mukden region's senior Japanese staff officer followed up by ordering a full-scale attack on the Chinese barracks, and the capture of the walled city of Mukden itself. The Japanese consul tried to remonstrate, but was silenced when one of the officers drew his sword. While the majority of the cabinet in Tokyo was urging restraint, and the Chinese and Americans requested the League of Nations to call for an end to the fighting, the Tokyo chief of staff sent ambiguous messages to his Manchurian forces. The Japanese commander in Korea independently ordered his troops across the border into south Manchuria, and the Mukden army used current guidelines for self-defense

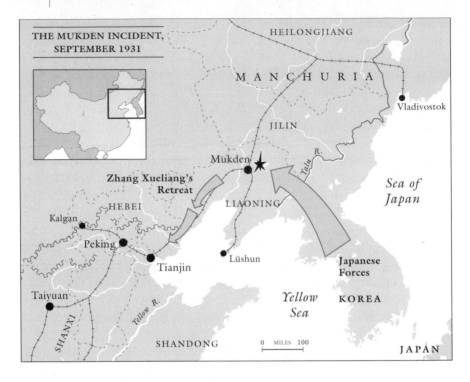

and bandit suppression to extend the scope of its actions. Chiang Kai-shek, who faced a crisis among his supporters because of his recent arrest of Hu Hanmin, could not afford another large-scale conflict. Instead he ordered Zhang Xueliang not to risk his troops in pitched battles and to withdraw them south of the Great Wall. By year's end, Manchuria was under complete Japanese control.

The question of who might lead this potential new "country" was swiftly solved. Since 1925 the ex-emperor Puyi had been living in the Japanese concession in Tianjin. In July 1931 his brother visited Japan and met with various politicians; only twelve days after the "Mukden Incident," representatives of the Manchurian army's general staff came to Tianjin to confer with Puyi. Talks on the future of Manchuria continued in October, with the Japanese assuring the twenty-five-year-old Puyi that they had acted merely against Zhang Xueliang and his troops, and that they wished to help the inhabitants of Manchuria create an independent state, although the Japanese were vague about whether the new state would be a monarchy or a republic. In November, Puyi, apparently convinced by these arguments, and perhaps stirred by dreams of restoring his family's Manchu heritage, allowed himself to be smuggled out of Tianjin on a Japanese motor launch, transferred to a Japanese freighter off Tanggu, and taken to Lüshun. In March 1932, after protracted negotiations with Japanese army representatives had failed to get them to agree to his being the "emperor" of a revived "Great Qing State," Puyi accepted the title "chief executive" of the state of Man-chukuo, which meant "land of the Manchus." A number of former Manchu grandees and conservative Chinese officials from the Qing court came to join him as he established his new regime.

Although it was slow to act, the League of Nations did not let these developments go unquestioned, and in November 1931 the League ordered a commission headed by the British statesman Lord Lytton to examine the situation. The United States, though not willing to risk armed intervention, attempted to influence other foreign powers to take a firm stance. President Herbert Hoover's secretary of state, Henry Stimson, announced in January 1932 that the Americans did "not intend to recognize any situation, treaty or agreement" in Manchukuo that defied the basic laws of peaceful inter-national behavior. But the British would not formally endorse this initiative for a "nonrecognition" doctrine, as it came to be called, on the grounds that "the present unsettled and distracted state of China" made it impossible to predict what might happen.[18]

"Unsettled and distracted" China might be, but the Mukden Incident prompted deeper levels of anti-Japanese and antiforeign feeling among Chi-nese. So serious did the boycotts become in Shanghai that on January 28, 1932, the Municipal Council of Shanghai declared a state of emergency and deployed troops for the defense of the various foreign concessions composing the International Settlement, so that they would not be caught napping as they had been in April 1927. On that same night Japanese marines, ordered ashore to secure their perimeter, exchanged fire with the Guomindang Nineteenth Route Army in the poor Chinese residential district of Chapei. Calling this clash an "insult" to the Japanese empire, the ranking Japanese naval officer ordered Chapei bombed on January 29.

The bombings—which roused passionate world opinion because of the number of innocent civilians killed—were followed by a full-scale Japanese attack on Shanghai's Chinese defenders. The Japanese committed three entire divisions to the battle, but the Chinese fought back with remarkable courage and tenacity. Their bravery under fire, when coupled with the determined defense of Heilongjiang by another Chinese army in the far north, renewed foreigners' respect for China's fighting capabilities. And since Japan's aggression was occurring in a context of growing disorder at home—the Japanese finance minister was shot and killed during the Feb-ruary elections, the head of the Mitsui corporation was assassinated in down-town Tokyo the same month, and another prime minister was gunned down in his official residence in May—Japanese claims of bringing order to a disintegrating China sounded specious.

The Japanese arranged an armistice in Shanghai in May 1932, forcing the Chinese to accept the drawing of a neutral zone around the city. Chiang Kai-shek transferred the Nineteenth Route Army, which had fought bravely in Shanghai, out of the city and down to Fujian because he did not trust the loyalty of the army's commander. Later that year the Japanese resumed an aggressive stance: in August the Japanese government announced its diplomatic "recognition" of Puyi's Manchukuo and expressed "fervent hope that the day is not far distant when Japan, Manchukuo, and China, as three independent powers closely linked together by a bond of cultural and racial affinities, will come to operate hand in hand for the maintenance and advancement of the peace and prosperity of the Far East."[19] In January 1933, after Japan learned that the Lytton commission report, though conciliatory in tone, was not going to acquiesce in the abandonment of Chinese sovereignty in Manchuria, Japanese troops were ordered to advance into Rehe (Jehol) on the pretext that "the affairs of Rehe province are unquestionably an internal problem of Manchukuo."[20] By April the Japanese had effectively conquered the whole province, consolidating their hold by occupying the strategic pass at the coastal end of the Great Wall in Shanhaiguan.

During February 1933, while the fighting in Rehe was raging, the League of Nations finally held its full debate on the Lytton report. The head of the Japanese delegation argued strongly that the League must understand the Japanese "desire to help China as far as is within our power. This is the duty we must assume."[21] He added a warning that failure to understand the logic of Japan's position might lead to a fateful alliance of a "Red China" with the Soviet Union. Unmoved, all the League countries but one—Siam abstained—endorsed the Lytton report, thus rejecting the concept of Manchukuo as an independent state. When the vote was announced, the Japanese walked out of the League, never to return.

The last stages in this drama of Japan's establishment of a base in northeast China came in May 1933. Finding, predictably, that they could not consolidate their forces along the north side of the Great Wall unless they cleared its south side of Chinese troops, the Japanese Manchurian army moved that month into Hebei province. They then attacked the Chinese troops in the province with a mixture of force, cunning, and psychological warfare. In a series of classic military engagements they pushed the Chinese armies back to the Bai River. Through a special agency based in Tianjin, they also bribed local generals and former warlords to defect or form rival government organizations. They encouraged resistance by local secret-society leaders and paramilitary forces. Setting up a radio station on Chinese

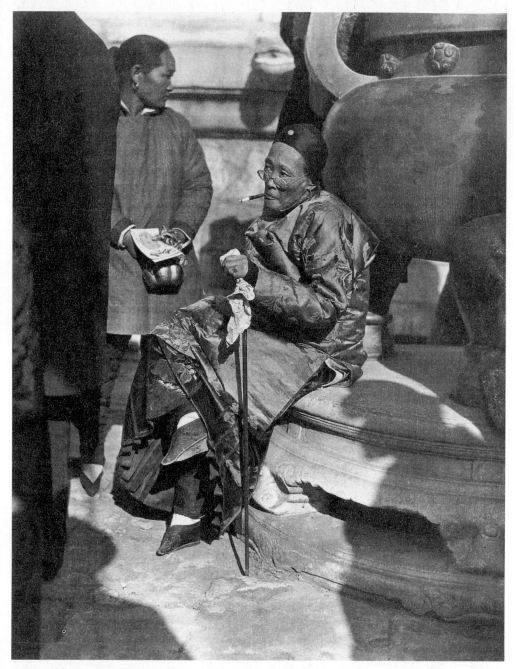

An old lady and her attendant, Forbidden City, Peking, 1918 (photograph by Sidney D. Gamble)   An elderly woman with bound feet observes the celebration of Armistice Day, November 13, 1918.

Chinese in France unloading artillery charges during World War I

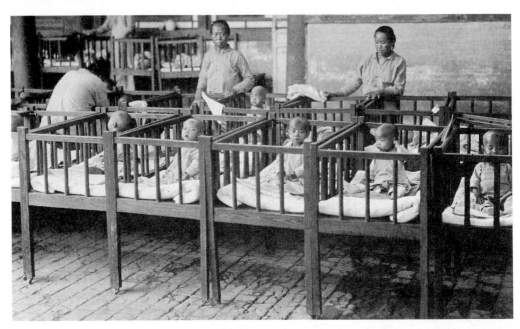

Foundlings' Home babies, Peking, 1919 (photograph by Sidney D. Gamble)   Gamble (1890–1968), sociologist, YMCA activist, and photographer, reported that 130 babies had been abandoned at the Foundlings' Home in the year 1917–1918. Of these, 111 were girls.

Hopeful Chinese assembling in Peking to celebrate the armistice ending World War I and press for China's territorial rights, November 1918 (photographs by Sidney D. Gamble)

Li Dazhao

Chen Duxiu

Cai Yuanpei

Hu Shi

Mao Zedong, c. 1919

Zhou Enlai (center) with other students in France, February 1921

A poster depicting the fate of Chinese patriotism at the hands of warlords and foreign imperialists in the aftermath of the May Thirtieth Incident (1925)

Students in Shanghai protesting the May 30, 1925 shooting of demonstrators in the International Settlement

Wu Peifu, whose stronghold—Wuhan—fell to Guomindang forces in the Northern Expedition

Feng Yuxiang, the powerful northern warlord who joined the Guomindang, 1928

Canton, December 11–13, 1927   Bodies of workers and Communists, executed in the aftermath of the failed Canton insurrection, lie in the streets.

Chiang Kai-shek at Whampoa, 1924

Leaders of the Green Gang, which controlled narcotics and other criminal enterprises in Shanghai in the late 1920s Members of the Gang cooperated with Chiang Kai-shek in the suppression of leftists in the city.

Li Lisan exhorting a mass rally in Hankou, 1927

Puyi, the last Manchu emperor of China, was made emperor of Manchukuo by the Japanese in 1934 Here Puyi (left) is pictured with the Japanese ambassador to Manchukuo, the real power in the region.

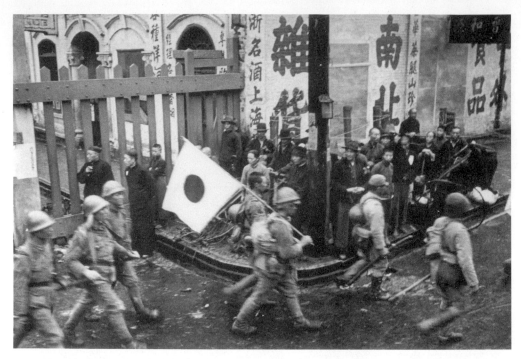

Japanese forces enter Hangzhou, 1930s

Chinese residents of Shanghai fleeing to the International Settlement and the French Concession, in fear of Japanese attack, 1935

The Nanjing Massacre, December 1937   These Chinese prisoners are about to be buried alive.

The grim march of surviving Communist forces across the "Great Snow" Mountains into northern Sichuan, May–June 1935

Communist leaders in Ya'nan, 1937: from left, Zhou Enlai, Mao Zedong, and Bo Gu

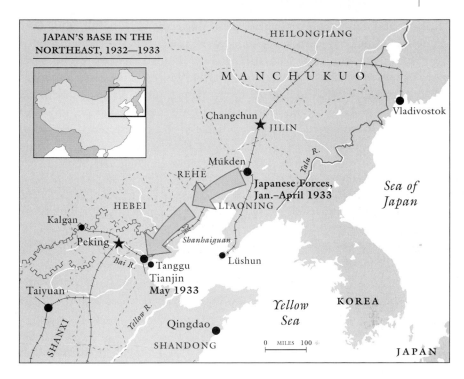

JAPAN'S BASE IN THE NORTHEAST, 1932–1933

HEILONGJIANG

M A N C H U K U O

Vladivostok

Changchun

★ JILIN

Mukden

REHE

Japanese Forces, Jan.–April 1933

Sea of Japan

HEBEI

LIAONING

Kalgan

Peking ★

Shanhaiguan

Bai R.

Tanggu

Tianjin

May 1933

Lüshun

Taiyuan

Yellow R.

KOREA

SHANXI

Qingdao

Yellow Sea

0   MILES 100

SHANDONG

JAPAN

military frequencies, they gave fake orders to Chinese field commanders, causing confusion in the Chinese battle plan. And by flying war planes low over Peking, they terrified the local population into a feeling of helplessness.

Routed, demoralized, and divided, the Chinese armies sued for peace at the end of May 1933. In the coastal town of Tanggu, under the guns of a Japanese battleship and destroyer squadron, the Chinese negotiators signed a humiliating truce. The Tanggu Truce stipulated that northeastern Hebei province, from a line just northeast of the Bai River, would be declared a demilitarized zone, to be patrolled only by Chinese police units that must "not be constituted of armed units hostile to Japanese feelings." In return, with the exception of the troops guarding the safe approaches to Peking, as stipulated long before by the Boxer Protocol, the other Japanese forces would retire back to the Great Wall, maintaining the right to fly spotter planes over the region to make sure there were no Chinese troop movements in violation of the truce.

Within weeks of the Tanggu Truce, the question of Manchukuo's form of government was discussed again—by Puyi and his advisers, the army, and ministers in Tokyo. The commander of the Japanese Manchurian army told Puyi that there was general agreement on restoring the emperorship.

Hearing this, Puyi made arrangements to have the imperial dragon robes of the last adult Qing emperor, Guangxu, shipped to him from Peking.

At special ceremonies in March 1934, Puyi donned his borrowed dragon robes to announce his accession at the Altar of Heaven in the eastern suburbs of Changchun, his new capital. He then changed into military uniform for his enthronement. For his new reign title he took the term *Kangde,* meaning "period of virtuous peace." The first syllable of this phrase was designed to evoke the power and prestige of Emperor Kangxi, who had unified the Qing state two hundred fifty years before, and consolidated Manchuria's borders against the Russians. Few of the Manchu and Chinese courtiers who were clustered with the Japanese officers around the ineffectual Puyi can really have believed that the great days of the early Qing were about to be re-enacted.

CHAPTER 16

Communist Survival

The Chinese Poor

The multiple changes and distractions confronting the Guomindang had made it impossible for them to tackle all the concerns of the Chinese people. Nanjing government statistics assembled in 1936 showed the population stood at just over 479 million, spread across about 86 million households. We are able to get some sense of what ordinary lives were like at this time, since the rapid growth of the social sciences in China, the proliferation of research institutes, the holding of surveys and the compiling of statistics, all meant that more data than ever before were available on the general population of China, both urban and rural. One can say with some confidence that conditions in China were satisfactory to the millions profiting from the continued growth of industry in the larger cities—despite the loss of Manchuria to the Japanese—or benefiting from the rising level of food production through new agricultural techniques and seed strains, and from the continuing expansion of road and rail transportation and distribution networks. At the same time, millions of Chinese people—perhaps tens of millions—lived in terrible and humiliating poverty, and were too preoccupied with the daily struggle for survival to look far ahead or brood about the national scene.

Workers with "elite" jobs in industries such as shipbuilding, railway machine shops, electrical plants, silk-weaving mills, thermos-bottle manufacture, and copper-sheet production might make as much as 100 yuan per month, even more. But monthly wages in most other industries were far lower, falling to 20 yuan or below in the manufacturing plants for lime, dyes, neon lights, cement, acid, starch, alcohol, cotton waste, batteries, and

INDUSTRIAL PRODUCTION OF CHINA PROPER AND MANCHURIA, 1926–1936*[1]

Commodity	China Proper			Manchuria		
	1926	1931	1936	1926	1931	1936
Coal	35.8	48.6	82.8	19.0	24.8	35.9
Iron ore	0.8	3.1	3.6	2.1	2.2	4.9
Pig iron	3.1	2.5	3.9	2.9	6.6	13.8
Steel	1.2	0.6	2.8	†	†	13.8
Antimony	2.8	2.0	2.2	†	†	†
Copper	†	0.1	0.1	†	†	†
Gold	7.8	4.8	8.8	3.4	4.9	6.3
Mercury	0.3	0.1	0.3	†	†	†
Tin	17.5	14.8	21.6	†	†	†
Tungsten	3.3	2.7	4.0	†	†	†
Cotton yarn	83.2	98.7	88.1	2.1	3.3	4.7
Cotton cloth	5.8	34.4	51.8	0.6	4.7	8.4
Cement	5.2	7.0	8.8	1.4	2.2	7.7
Crude oil	†	†	†	0.1	5.4	15.4
Electric power	16.4	26.8	62.1	10.6	19.5	48.6
Total	183.2	246.2	340.9	42.2	73.6	159.5
Index	100.0	134.4	186.1	100.0	174.4	378.0

*In millions of 1933 yuan.
†Less than 0.1 million yuan.

matches. Wages for women and for both male and female child labor were lower still, sliding down to 30 cents a day (for child labor in cotton spinning) and 24 cents (for women's work in the match industry.) For such workers, even on a six-day week if the work was available, it would be hard to make more than 7 or 8 yuan a month (between U.S. $2 and U.S. $3).* Despite the intensive labor agitation of the 1920s, hours for Chinese workers were still long—averaging 9.5 hours per day in Shanghai (the lowest recorded for any city), 10 hours per day in Peking and Wuhan, rising to 11, 12, or even 13 hours per day in some provincial industrial centers. And many other conditions of work made bleak lives bleaker: workers often had to live in company-run dormitories, accept their wages in company notes that could be redeemed only for food and necessities in company stores, or—in the case

*When the December Ninthers, in 1935, made their demands for united national action against Japan, the exchange rate of the Chinese yuan to the United States dollar had just been officially "stabilized" at a rate of 3.33 yuan to U.S. $1.

UNEMPLOYMENT IN CHINA, 1935*[2]

Place	Number
Hebei	49,750
Shandong	48,996
Henan	58,010
Jiangsu	411,991
Zhejiang	278,813
Anhui	5,545
Jiangxi	460,300
Hubei	233,391
Hunan	114,756
Sichuan	534,960
Guangdong	1,578,482
Guangxi	1,960
Nanjing	161,476
Shanghai	610,701
Peking	500,935
Total	5,050,066

*Partial returns only.

of women workers—yield up sexual favors in order to keep their jobs.

Work was not always available, however. As the table above shows, even an incomplete survey of Chinese workers, with entire provinces and many large cities not included, yielded a total of over five million unemployed in industrial areas in 1935. The same year saw, despite a tough government policy against such actions, a total of 275 industrial disputes, of which 135 led to full-scale strikes. These were spread across 53 different locations, and took in the range of issues and industries shown in the table on page 379. The available figures show an average of 2,600 workers involved in each strike for an average duration of almost eight days. Union organization was understandably weak, since in 1934 Chiang Kai-shek had moved—on the excuse of stopping the exploitation of workers—to forbid unions in five provinces (Henan, Hubei, Anhui, Jiangxi, and Fujian) as well as in Shanghai to collect any membership fees, and such unions that survived were often controlled by racketeers. During the same year, 1,506 workers died in industrial accidents and 4,123 were injured.

Shanghai remained the city with far the most industrial workers, and as a result was the area most thoroughly scrutinized by researchers. One housing-committee study of 390 families conducted in 1936–1937 showed how

Household Expenditures, Shanghai, 1936–1937[3]

Workers' degree of skills	Food	Rent	Clothing	Surplus	Total
Skilled (average wage = 45.82 yuan/month)	53.49%	13.50%	9.87%	23.14%	100.00%
Semiskilled (average wage = 29.55 yuan/month)	64.53	15.85	8.10	11.52	100.00
Unskilled (average wage = 21.24 yuan/month)	83.26	18.42	9.97	—	111.65

Shanghai households, categorized by average income and degree of work skill, spent their money. As a percentage of total income, the surplus expenditure of skilled workers in Shanghai compared well with that of American working-class families in the 1930s. The most common uses of this surplus, which came to around 10 yuan per month, were for recreation, religious offerings, public transport, reading material, medical needs, wine and tobacco, and weddings and funerals. For semiskilled workers, the "surplus" after meeting their basic monthly expenses was 3.55 yuan, a fraction over U.S. $1, which gave them little room for entertainment once basic necessities were met. Basic expenditures for necessities exceeded the average monthly incomes of unskilled workers by 11.65 percent, and the balance had to be made up by borrowing or by part-time work, if available, undertaken by other family members.

Of these 390 Shanghai families, none occupied more than one room. The survey gave a thorough description of one tenement house with a total floor space of 718 square feet. Despite its flat official language, the report still creates a vivid picture of what urban living was like for many of the poor:

> The courtyard has been covered in. The main ground floor room has been cut in two by a partition, and a passageway with a storage loft over made at the side. In the front part, about ten feet square, live the lessor and his family, five persons in all. He customarily pays the rent of the whole house to the landlord, letting out the rest to sub-tenants. In the back portion, about 10 ft. by 8 ft., live three persons. The kitchen has been sectioned off and three more live in a 9 ft.×9 ft. room. Upstairs, the large front room has been divided into two. The front part is the best in the house for it has light and air and runs the full width of the house—it is occupied by two persons.

The back part, smaller by reason of the passage, is home to three persons. The room over the kitchen has its advantages because it is secluded; this also is occupied by two persons. This was originally a two storeyed house, but two lofts have been made in the slope of the roof. The front one has a height of only 5 feet in front, 7 ft. 6 in. at the apex of the roof, and is about eight feet deep; it shelters two persons. The back room, about 10 sq. ft., is right under the roof slope, is only 3 ft. high at the back and is occupied by a single person. What was the drying stage has been enclosed, and two more people live in it—about 9 sq. ft.[4]

INDUSTRIAL DISPUTES (STRIKES), 1935[5]

Industry	Wages	Hours	Dismissals	Treatment	Other	Total
			Issues			
Agriculture	—	—	—	—	1 (1)	1 (1)
Mining	3	3 (2)	4 (2)	(3)	3	13 (7)
Factory						
Woodwork	2 (1)	—	3	—	—	5 (1)
Furniture	2 (1)	—	—	—	—	2 (1)
Metals	—	—	—	—	2	2
Machines	1	—	1 (1)	—	1	3 (1)
Vehicles	2 (1)	1 (1)	2 (2)	—	—	5 (4)
Bricks, glass	2 (1)	—	—	—	—	2 (1)
Houses, roads	3	—	—	—	—	3
Gas, water, power	—	—	—	1	2	3
Chemicals	5 (3)	1 (1)	5	2 (1)	3	16 (5)
Textiles	40 (24)	5 (4)	14 (10)	2 (1)	13 (8)	74 (47)
Clothing	7 (6)	—	—	—	1	8 (6)
Leather, rubber	3	—	1	—	—	4
Food, drink	8 (3)	—	4	1 (3)	7 (2)	20 (8)
Paper, printing	2 (2)	—	—	—	1 (1)	3 (3)
Clocks	1 (1)	—	—	1	—	2 (1)
Others	5 (1)	—	2 (2)	1	2 (1)	10 (4)
Transport	19 (6)	—	9 (4)	5 (1)	33 (21)	66 (32)
Commerce, finance						
General	5 (2)	—	4 (2)	1	4 (2)	14 (6)
Real estate	—	—	—	—	1	1
Banking	—	—	1	—	—	1
Hotel employees	5 (1)	2 (1)	—	—	4 (1)	11 (3)
Officials	1 (1)	—	—	1 (1)	2 (1)	4 (3)
Professional	2 (1)	—	—	—	—	2 (1)
Total	117 (55)	12 (9)	50 (23)	15 (10)	80 (38)	275 (135)

The same report added that these were by no means the worst conditions encountered. To examine those, one could go to the city's 5,094 huts of straw, bamboo, and reeds, where 25,345 people lived—mostly factory workers—paying anywhere from 40 cents to 3.00 yuan per "room" per month.

Just as the cities were coming under studious scrutiny, so was the countryside. A new generation of well-trained Chinese sociologists, such as Fei Xiaotong, conducted field studies of the rural areas, often at considerable personal risk: on his first research trip, to Guangxi province, Fei was caught in a tiger trap and his wife drowned while trying to get help. But Fei survived to produce a series of studies that analyzed China's rural predicaments in terms of the disintegration of a harmonious economic balance between the poor and the state. Fei believed such a balance had existed before foreign imperialism and the growth of a world market brought new types of financial pressure on rural areas, wrecking the rural handicraft and other sideline industries that kept peasant families above the poverty level. (We have seen, however, that as early as the first Qing emperors, Shunzhi and Kangxi, social tensions were already evident among different kinds of peasants and between those peasants and their landlords.) The British scholar R. H. Tawney surveyed China's agriculture in the early 1930s and concluded that it was beset by two interlocking crises: an ecological one characterized by soil exhaustion and erosion, deforestation, floods, and the pressures of the huge population on scarce available resources; and a socioeconomic one caused by exploitative land-tenure systems, abuses by moneylenders, poor communications, and primitive agricultural technology.

Another influential observer was the American missionary John Lossing Buck, who was largely self-taught in agricultural economics. (Until their divorce in 1933, Buck was married to the novelist Pearl Buck.) After being appointed to a professorship at the University of Nanjing, Buck wrote an extensive series of field studies based on data gathered by his own students when they went home on holiday. He subsequently built up a large corps of professional assistants, and in 1937 Buck published the fruits of this research on "land utilization in China." In one volume of text and two volumes of tables and statistics, Buck presented extensive data on 168 locations in 22 provinces, and almost 17,000 farms. Buck's figures provided a maze of detail not only on land, crops, and livestock, but on farm equipment, furnishings, even the clothing of the farmers' families. Although he found many prosperous families, others lived on the edge of destitution, with little land, food, or tools, and only the clothes they had on their back to call their own. Buck's work became a mine for other researchers, even though some of his findings were difficult to interpret and provoked considerable controversy.

The passion for empirical knowledge now took on major proportions, dwarfing the pioneering work conducted by the CCP. A Chinese scholar at Nankai Economic Research Institute in Tianjin—which had been given its start by grants from the Rockefeller Foundation and had gone on to produce some of the finest studies on the Chinese economy of the 1930s—noted in 1935 that no less than 102 monographs and 251 periodicals focusing on China's land problems had appeared in the last fifteen years. Eighty-seven percent of those periodicals had been founded after 1933. Cumulatively, these studies showed the amazing diversification of rural China and the difficulty of reaching judgments or offering solutions applicable to all areas. In certain regions strong lineage organizations dominated entire communities and created complex patterns of mutual support; in others, rural society was fragmented among poor tenant farmers who were easily exploited by absentee landlords. These landlords were backed by the police powers of the Guomindang state, and after 1934 by the control apparatus of the *baojia* mutual-security system, which was reinstituted by Chiang Kai-shek. In yet other areas, particularly in north China, the most successful "peasant" was the managerial farmer, who owned a farm of 20 to 40 acres, and worked it in part by himself and in part with the help of hired hands.

Many of these studies described conditions and even social tensions startlingly similar to those that had prevailed in the late Ming, suggesting that China's new levels of economic growth had as yet failed to reach hundreds of millions of people. The data amassed on rural China showed striking evidence of terrible poverty among large numbers of farmers in almost every area of the country. Millions of men lived at the subsistence level, working as carters and haulers in the slack season, or as agricultural laborers in the few hectic weeks of sowing and harvesting. At these times they joined scores of their fellows at 4:00 A.M. or earlier, waiting in anxious groups with their tools to see if any work would come that day. Few such men could ever afford to marry, and most died unnoticed after brief, miserable lives. Some of them "escaped" to the factories or became human horses, pulling two-wheeled rickshaws through the crowded streets of China's cities. These rickshaw men were constantly exploited by racketeers, and returned after each backbreaking day to grim tenements, where they slept in rows, packed side by side, in spaces just vacated by fellow pullers who had returned to the streets. The life of one such man was powerfully rendered by Lao She in his great novel *Rickshaw,* published in 1937.

Tens of millions more (the "poor peasants" of Mao Zedong's and other Communists' analyses) owned farms that were too small to be fully viable economically. These peasants perforce "overemployed" the labor of their family members on their farms, while to earn extra cash they hired out their own labor at the busiest moments of the farm year, even though that was when they were most needed on their own land. Still, many had to sell their children or watch them slowly starve. With the surplus of poverty-stricken labor available, few of the wealthier farmers went to the expense of mechanizing the farm work, even when machinery and fuel were available. Nor did they invest much in draft animals, since the wages paid to a hired laborer per day were the same as the cost of a day's fodder for a single donkey. The man could be laid off when the need for him was over, but the donkey had to be fed and sheltered for the whole year, even when it was not being used.

Poor women, too, sometimes fled the farms for work in the factories and mills of the big cities. Although they also experienced terrible work conditions as well as the effects of regional and sexual discrimination, they may have had a better life in the city than they would have had in the country, where they were bound to a world of arranged marriages, hard farm labor, child rearing, and handicraft work or silk-cocoon cultivation that filled in every spare moment. For even though they were badly paid in the cities and subjected to exploitative rhythms of work, they showed an astonishing skill at banding together in mutual support, sharing resources to make their lives a little brighter, and reinforcing each other in keeping the worst aspects of the male world at bay.

For the poor, a monotonous diet was an indelible part of existence. Getting food was the point, not its variety. One farm laborer in a village in Hebei, northeast of Tianjin, recalled his diet as follows:

> In the spring, gruel for breakfast, "dry" boiled millet for lunch, and gruel with vegetable for supper; in the summer, "watered" boiled millet for breakfast, "dry" boiled millet and bean-noodles in soup for lunch, and boiled millet and a vegetable for supper; in the fall, gruel for breakfast, "dry" boiled millet and bean-noodles in soup for lunch, and "watered" boiled millet for supper.[6]

For a Shandong farmer, it was sweet potatoes rather than millet that regularly punctuated the social world he inhabited:

> Among the poor, sweet potatoes are eaten at every meal every day throughout the year. From harvest time until the spring of the following year, they eat fresh sweet potatoes; when these are gone, they eat the stored dry slices. These are boiled, or ground into meal which is mixed with other flour to make bread or noodles. Supplementing the potatoes are, first, a kind of gruel made of barley flour and peanut powder; second, a kind of hash made of chopped turnips and soybean juice; and third, one or two kinds of pickles. Occasionally some kind of bread is served.[7]

One unexpected consequence of the spread of Japan's power in north China was that highly sophisticated surveys were produced by Japanese researchers, whose data—originally assembled for politico-military purposes—have retained immense value to this day. The first survey teams, drawn from military intelligence staff, the research division of the Southern Manchuria Railroad Company, and Japanese students working in China, were formed in 1935 and began work on 25 villages in north China the following year. In early 1937 another group of Japanese researchers (this time without military-intelligence involvement) selected 4 villages for more in-depth study, one of which was Michang, in Hebei.

The figures collected in these surveys rarely can be collated across a long time span for the same locality. It is therefore extremely difficult to know whether the poorer Chinese farmers and hired laborers were worse off than they had been a decade before, or doing about the same, or perhaps marginally more prosperous. It is equally hard to know how they stood in comparison to farmers of the mid-Qing period, or to those of the late Ming. Those analysts who contend that Chinese peasants were getting steadily poorer, and hence that some kind of revolutionary crisis was predictable, tend to rely on one of two main types of explanation. One holds that callous attitudes of the landlords combined with the pressures placed on China by foreign imperialism to worsen exploitation of the peasants. These two developments forced peasants who had formerly owned land into becoming tenants or hired laborers, and made them suffer the effects of an erratic world market. The second explanation suggests that population growth, primitive technology, and soil exhaustion—not the evils of the class structure—were responsible for the growing poverty in the Chinese countryside. Neither argument has been able to muster totally convincing evidence, giving rise to a third school, which suggests that with commercialization of agriculture and the changes in marketing and transport patterns brought about by the use of trucks, trains, and steamers, many farmers were doing better by 1920 than they had in 1900.

What does seem clear is that by the early 1930s, Chinese peasants were suffering a new wave of crises that forced many of them below the subsistence level. Devastating floods on the Yangzi River in 1931 created an estimated 14 million refugees and inundated an area the size of New York State. Japan's seizure of Manchuria broke the habitual patterns of hundreds of thousands of migrant workers, and the Japanese attack on Shanghai caused renewed dislocations in that highly populated area. Changes in the world economy caused by the depression slashed China's exports of cash crops and ruined local handicrafts. Guomindang military campaigns and

SAMPLE FARM INCOMES AND EXPENSES IN MICHANG VILLAGE,
HEBEI PROVINCE, 1937[8]

	Managerial farmer	Rich peasant	Middle peasant	Poor peasant
Farm size in *mou* (⅙ of an acre)	133	60	34	13
Adult male farm workers in household	2	3	2	2
Land rented from others (in *mou*)	0	8	7	7
Gross farm income in yuan	2,192	1,117	514	234
Net farm income (gross minus cost of fertilizer, rent, wages, taxes, etc.)	1,200	514	247	56
Fertilizer purchased (in yuan)	152	161	114	53
Fertilizer as percent of gross income	6.9	14.4	22.2	22.6
Rent for land paid to others (in yuan)	0	14	35	38
Rent paid as percent of gross income	0.0	1.3	6.8	16.2
Cash wages and board costs paid to others (in yuan)	550	259	80	66
Wages and board paid to others as percent of gross income	25.1	23.2	15.6	28.2
Taxes paid (in yuan)	113	41	22	6
Tax as percent of gross income	5.2	3.7	4.3	2.6

attempts at institutional and industrial rebuilding led to higher taxes. In the absence of accurate data, all one can do is acknowledge that the variations of suffering were endless, and that as impoverished families died out, others emerged to take over their land and struggle for survival in their turn. Nor can one tell with any precision if these poor peasant families—any more than their urban counterparts—knew or cared much about Communist policies or the threatening clouds of war. But it was in such a context of widespread poverty and frustration that the Communists—apparently almost wiped out in 1927—where able to regroup, and to rethink their revolutionary strategies.

Mao Zedong and the Rural Soviets

Because of the failure of the Autumn Harvest Uprisings and his abandonment of the attempt to seize Changsha, Mao Zedong was censured by the CCP Central Committee. In November 1927 he was dismissed from his position on that committee, and even from his membership in the Hunan provincial committee. But Mao probably did not even learn of these chastisements for several months, since he had taken the surviving Autumn Harvest troops—perhaps 1,000 in all—and marched south of Changsha up into the isolated Jinggang Mountains on the border between Hunan and Jiangxi, which he reached in October 1927. Just as in the Qing, so in the 1920s the safest place for fugitives was in those border regions where different administrative zones met, inhibiting coordinated counterattacks by the forces of the state. In this case the "state" was still a fragmented entity, and Mao's enemies were a variety of warlord troops bound by various types of alliance to the Guomindang forces, as well as the Guomindang itself.

Mao's own actions during this period were often dictated by practical rather than theoretical considerations. Just before the Autumn Harvest Uprisings he had told the CCP Central Committee that he favored the immediate formation of strong peasant soviets, that such soviets should be bonded together in revolutionary solidarity by a thorough confiscation and redistribution of land, and that he wished to give up all pretense that he still had any loyalty to the Guomindang flag. These positions were angrily rejected by the Central Committee at the time, but by the end of 1927, following changes in Stalin's stated policies, the Central Committee endorsed all three positions and added that the party should also support an uninterrupted series of uprisings in the countryside. The purpose of these uprisings would not be to establish stable bases, but to keep the masses at a high pitch of revolutionary awareness and to instill that same awareness thoroughly in the armed forces involved.

By the time the Central Committee had come to these decisions, however, Mao's practical experiences in Jinggang had led him to abandon essentially all of them. Although he did form CCP cells in the five villages within the 250 kilometer circumference that he controlled, ordered some landlords killed, and tried to organize soviets, he ran into sustained resistance from the richer peasants and from the lineage organizations that exercised control over their poorer neighbors. In the face of this opposition he did not try to redistribute all land in relation to each person's work capacity. Mao instead buttressed his strength by joining forces with two of the area's tough bandit chieftains, who were members of secret societies affiliated with the Triads. With their 600 men added to his own troops, Mao now stood at the head of a force drawn from the ranks of the dispossessed and "classless" members of society. Mao had written about these people with his customary vividness the year before:

> They can be divided into soldiers, bandits, robbers, beggars, and prostitutes. These five categories of people have different names, and they enjoy a somewhat different status in society. But they are all human beings, and they all have five senses and four limbs, and are therefore one. They each have a different way of making a living: the soldier fights, the bandit robs, the thief steals, the beggar begs, and the prostitute seduces. But to the extent that they must all earn their livelihood and cook rice to eat, they are one. They lead the most precarious existence of any human being.[9]

Nevertheless, Mao had added, "these people are capable of fighting very bravely, and, if properly led, can become a revolutionary force."

Although the Jinggang forces were greatly strengthened by the arrival of Communist fugitives from the south China fighting of 1927, they suffered constant attacks by Guomindang forces, and often had to send precious troops out of Jinggang to aid in CCP battles elsewhere. This was in line with the policies endorsed by the sixth CCP congress, which had had to meet in Moscow in the summer of 1928 because conditions in China itself were so dangerous. That congress, echoing Stalin's instructions, had dogmatically stated that even though at present there was no revolutionary rising tide, there must still be armed insurrections and more soviets formed under the leadership of the proletariat. Such orders were essentially meaningless, since union members still loyal to the Communists now numbered fewer than 32,000 in the whole country, and only 10 percent of the CCP were proletarians, according to Zhou Enlai. By 1929 the figure had dropped to 3 percent.

At the end of 1928 the sustained level of Guomindang attacks forced Mao to abandon the Jinggang Mountains. After moving steadily eastward, first across Jiangxi province and then into western Fujian, the Jinggang fugitives finally settled in a new border region—the mountainous area between

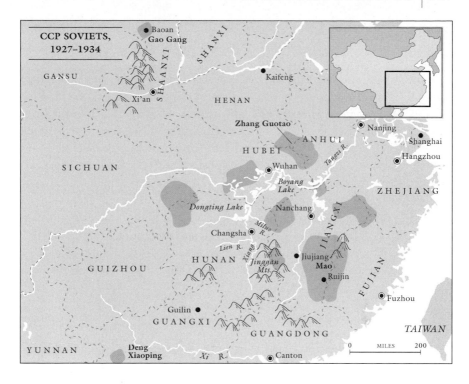

Jiangxi and Fujian provinces. Here they made the town of Ruijin their new base and the center of a new regime, the Jiangxi Soviet, which was to endure until 1934.

It should not be imagined that Mao, with preternatural cunning, had seized on the two places in China where speedy formation of peasant soviets was possible, nor, on the other hand, that the whole of rural China was seething with the hatred of peasants against their landlords. It is true that during the 1920s and early 1930s there were thousands of incidents in which peasants—either in small or large groups—out of anger or desperation used violence against local authorities. But these attacks were mainly against the representatives of the state: the civil and military officials who gouged them with high taxes and unexpected surcharges, conscripted their labor without adequate compensation, compulsorily purchased their land for public-works projects, or forced them either to plant or uproot their opium-producing poppies, depending on the vagaries of the local and national drug trade. There were, comparatively, far fewer cases of violent action against landlords, although these did occur. Since most resident landlords depended for their rents on some degree of tenant prosperity and contentment, such anger was usually directed against absentee-landlords' managers or bailiffs when they tried to extract high rents in periods of natural disaster. The skill of Communist organizers like Mao lay in transforming a largely fiscal discontent into class warfare, so as to push effectively for revolutionary change under CCP leadership.

Now Mao's policies grew more sophisticated. The experience in the Jinggang Mountains had shown that an extremely radical land policy alienated the wealthier peasants, who were the real force in local rural society, and left the CCP with support from only the poorest and least-educated peasants or from the impoverished, landless laborers. So it seems (the details are not all clear) that in Ruijin, Mao initially followed a policy that carefully avoided alienating the wealthier rural families. But such a policy was difficult, and in an April 1929 letter to Li Lisan—the former student in France who had been so active in Shanghai in 1927 was now secretary general—Mao tried to reassure the party of his orthodoxy while forcefully presenting his faith in the peasants:

> It would be wrong to abandon the struggle in the cities, but in our opinion it would also be wrong for any of our Party members to fear the growth of peasant strength lest it should outstrip the workers' strength and harm the revolution. For in the revolution in semi-colonial China, the peasant struggle must always fail if it does not have the leadership of the workers, but the revolution is never harmed if the peasant struggle outstrips the forces of the workers.[10]

In late spring 1930 Mao Zedong greatly strengthened his knowledge of rural conditions in Jiangxi by undertaking a meticulous examination of one particular county—Xunwu. From his report on this experience we can see how far he had advanced in analytical sophistication since he wrote the excited Hunan report on the peasantry in February 1927 or the ambiguous letter to Li Lisan in 1929. Now, in the Xunwu of 1930, Mao probed for the details of everyday life and searched for precise gradations within the complex layering of rural work and landownership. Broad generalizations about "the proletariat" and "expropriation" gave way to detailed explorations of the variety of local businesses in small county towns, and of the income to be derived from them. Mao studied salt, cooking oil and soybean sales, butchers and wine makers, the sellers of herbs, cigarettes, umbrellas, and fireworks, the makers of furniture and bean curd, boardinghouse keepers and ironsmiths, watch repairers, and prostitutes. He observed the rhythms of local markets, the relative strengths of different lineage organizations, the distribution and wealth of Buddhist and Daoist temples and of a host of other shrines and religious associations, as well as the number of active

Christian proselytizers (there were thirteen—ten Protestant and three Catholic).

Mao also tried to gauge levels of exploitation so that he could analyze class tensions more accurately. He computed the number of prostitutes in Xunwu city and discovered that there were about 30 in a total population of 2,684. He sought out poor peasants who had been forced to sell their children to pay their debts, and found out how much they got for the children and what ages the children were when they were sold. Boy children were sold for 100 to 200 yuan, and their ages when sold ranged from three to fourteen years old. (Mao found no cases in which girls were sold. This was probably because hard labor was the top priority in Xunwu, not domestic work or sexual services.) Mao noticed that when a child was sold to pay one lender, others rallied to the news. "On hearing that a borrower has sold a son, lenders will hurry to the borrower's house and force the borrower to repay his loan. The lender will cruelly shout to the borrower: 'You have sold your son. Why don't you repay me?'"[11] Mao also examined local landowning and tenancy practices, conveying his results in a detailed table with categories shrewdly based on rental income and means of subsistence rather than simply on acreage of individual holdings (see below).

In the past, temples, lineage organizations, and other groups owned 40 percent of Xunwu's land; landlords owned 30 percent; and the peasants themselves owned the remaining 30 percent. Mao showed an acute sense of the criteria that should be used in redistributing the land. While noting that in a revolutionary situation most land was redistributed simply on a per capita basis, he was aware of the arguments for distributing some land on the basis of ability to work. He also recognized the special needs of women, who often contributed more than men to the land (and endured harder lives), the problems posed by ex-monks and other categories of the needy, and difficulties in deciding how to divide up houses, fishponds, and mountainous or forested areas.

In the area of military planning, too, Mao had been growing more experienced—and more canny. His main teacher was Zhu De, a Sichuanese soldier of fortune and former opium addict who had mended his ways and gone to study in Germany during the early 1920s before returning to China to command a Guomindang officer-training regiment. Zhu had kept his Communist affiliations secret until the Nanchang army uprisings in August 1927, when he had been defeated and forced to flee, eventually joining Mao in the Jinggang Mountains. The "Red Army," as the two had structured it, now became a fast-moving guerrilla force that performed with great courage against the attacks of the Guomindang. Although only about 2,000 Red Army troops were left by early 1929, Mao and Zhu vigorously opposed the

XUNWU'S TRADITIONAL LAND RELATIONSHIPS[12]

Status	Percentage in each group
Large landlords	
Receive more than 500 dan* of rent	0.045
Middle landlords	
Receive 200–499 dan of rent	0.400
Small landlords	
Receive less than 200 dan of rent	
Of whom 1% are bankrupt families and 2% are newly rich families	3.000
Rich peasants	
Have surplus grain and capital for loans	4.000
Middle peasants	
Have enough to eat but do not receive loans	18.255
Poor peasants	
Insufficient grain and receive loans	70.000
Manual workers	
Craftsmen, boatmen, porters	3.000
Loafers	
No property	1.000
Hired hands	
Permanent and day laborers	0.300

*A dan was equal to approximately 133 pounds of rice or other grain.

directive by Li Lisan that they fragment their forces further by scattering them across the countryside in tiny units to foster local uprisings. As they wrote proudly to Li:

> The tactics we have derived from the struggle of the past three years are indeed different from any other tactics, ancient or modern, Chinese or foreign. With our tactics, the masses can be aroused for struggle on an ever-broadening scale, and no enemy, however powerful, can cope with us. Ours are guerrilla tactics. They consist mainly of the following points:
>
> Divide our forces to arouse the masses, concentrate our forces to deal with the enemy.
>
> The enemy advances, we retreat; the enemy camps, we harass; the enemy tires, we attack; the enemy retreats, we pursue.
>
> To extend stable base areas, employ the policy of advancing in waves; when pursued by a powerful enemy, employ the policy of circling around.
>
> Arouse the largest numbers of the masses in the shortest possible time and by the best possible methods.[13]

Their very success in consolidating and then expanding the Red Army in Ruijin paradoxically led to the optimistic view of the Central Committee that their troops had grown strong enough to fight outside the soviet area in conventional positional warfare. So in 1930, not long after the Xunwu investigation was completed, Mao and Zhu received direct orders, which they could not disobey, to attack Nanchang. These orders were part of an ambitious plan by Li Lisan to move the Communist struggle back to a revolutionary crest; assaults against Wuhan and Changsha were planned at the same time. All three ventures failed, although Communist forces held Changsha for ten days before the Guomindang retook it. When Mao and Zhu, defeated at Nanchang, were ordered to help the Communist troops at Changsha recapture the city, they reluctantly agreed; but faced with the annihilation of their carefully nurtured forces, they withdrew from the battle without permission and returned to Ruijin.

As well as concentrating on aspects of economic and military change while he was in Jiangxi, Mao also paid attention to social reform in areas such as women's rights. Since his frank writings on the suicide of Miss Zhao in 1919, Mao had shown a continuing awareness of the economic and family pressures that prevented any semblance of equality between the sexes in China. He had reiterated these feelings near the end of his 1927 report on the peasant movement in Hunan, writing that although the men suffered under three forms of authority—political, clan, and religious—the women had to endure a fourth—masculine authority. Mao felt that masculine authority was weakest among the poorer peasants, "because, out of economic necessity, their womenfolk have to do more manual labor than the women of the richer classes and therefore have more say and greater power of decision in family matters." Such women "also enjoy considerable sexual freedom." Mao hailed the formation of "rural women's associations" in parts of Hunan, which gave all women the chance "to lift up their heads."

So it was not surprising that one of Mao's important acts in the Jiangxi Soviet was to promulgate a new marriage law that forbade arranged marriages, encouraged free choice of spouses, and stopped "all purchase and sale in marriage contracts." Divorce was also made simple—to be granted at the request of either partner—although the language on continuing support was ambiguous: "On questions concerning divorce, it becomes necessary to protect the interests of women and place the greater part of the obligations and responsibilities entailed by divorce upon men."[14] An exception to the simple divorce rule was made in cases where the woman seeking divorce had a husband away on active military service.

One survey by Communist officials of two counties in the Jiangxi Soviet showed that in a period of three and a half months, 4,274 divorces were registered, 80 percent of them at the request of one spouse only, and that 3,783 marriages were registered for the same period. In nine cases the couple married *and* divorced on the same day. Mao's personal feelings may have played some role in this legislation, since he himself had separated from the wife he had wooed and won in the May Fourth period, along with their two children, and was now living openly with a second wife, He Zizhen, who had joined him in the Jinggang Mountains and followed him to Jiangxi.

But Mao also had a commitment to the men in his army, many of them desperately poor, who looked to the Communist government to help them find the wives that they could never have afforded under the system of arranged marriages. The result was that the women in the Jiangxi Soviet were often coerced into "marrying"—or possibly having physical relationships with several men—against their will. Male party cadres also abused their powers. Many widows were reported to have been pressured into remarrying within a few days of their spouse's death. But Mao held firm that minimum marriage ages should be held at twenty for men and eighteen for women. "Teams of laundresses" dispatched to certain units and used in recruiting suggest also that the Communist authorities countenanced a fair amount of not very clandestine prostitution.

By 1930, the attacks by the Guomindang and its allies on the Communists in the cities were becoming more savage and more successful. Attempts by the Communists to recoup their fortunes by sending assassination squads to murder former comrades who had defected to the Guomindang backfired badly. The Guomindang secret services were growing more canny and experienced, and successfully infiltrated many of the Communists' urban networks. (After 1932 the Guomindang's own terror squads were directed against those who collaborated secretly with the Japanese.) The labor organizations were in disarray, infiltrated by Guomindang agents and with their efforts at organized protest often wrecked by harassment or violence from secret-society members in the pay of the industrialists. Attempts at large-scale urban insurrections ordered by Li Lisan all failed. New leaders dispatched by Moscow to remedy the situation could do nothing. They were young, inexperienced, and doctrinally dogmatic, known sardonically in China as the "returned Bolsheviks." In 1931 a series of arrests and betrayals caused a growing number of senior Communists to abandon Shanghai altogether and join Mao in Ruijin. The more important "returned Bolshevik" leaders did the same in 1933, and temporarily pushed Mao into eclipse, accusing him of being too "rightist" in his policies of accommodation with the richer peasants. According to some sources, he was literally under house arrest during 1934 for his erroneous policies. (His obituary had already been published in the main Comintern journal in March 1930, suggesting that at least some senior party members wished him dead.)

Although it has received the closest attention because of Mao's role there, the Jiangxi Soviet was not the only rural Communist base at this time. There were at least a dozen regions in China where some form of CCP organization in the countryside held out against the Guomindang government or local military forces and tried to push through a variety of land policy and other social reforms. There were two other soviets at least partly in Jiangxi: one to the northeast of Ruijin, where the three provinces of Zhejiang, Fujian, and Jiangxi meet; and one to the northwest, where the borders of Hunan, Hubei, and Jiangxi converge. One of the largest of the other soviets was led by Zhang Guotao, like Mao a former member of Li Dazhao's Marxist study group who became a founding member at the 1921 CCP congress. Zhang's soviet was situated where the borders of Henan, Anhui, and Hubei meet, and flourished until fierce Guomindang attacks forced the retreat of the surviving troops into northern Sichuan.

One Communist general held onto another soviet base on the western-most edge of the shared Hunan-Hubei border; and in the only far-northern soviet, situated in the Shaanxi town of Baoan, Gao Gang dominated an area of poor mountain country that stretched, dependent on his military fortunes, from Shaanxi to Gansu. Gao Gang had been trained in a Xi'an military academy by Deng Xiaoping after Deng's return from France. Deng, after leaving Xi'an, had worked in yet another soviet, this one in southwest Guangxi, equidistant from the borders with Yunnan and Vietnam. According to an interview Deng gave later, the Chinese there cooperated with the Vietnamese who were launching their "worker-peasant" rebellion against the French. The Chinese gave them sanctuary, in retaliation for which French planes bombed the Guangxi soviet area. In late 1930, probably on orders from Li Lisan, Deng marched many of his troops northeast to help in the planned attacks on Changsha, Wuhan, and Nanchang. Having suffered heavy losses on the way, he arrived after the urban assaults were defeated, and his remnant troops were incorporated into Mao's and Zhu De's Jiangxi Soviet armies.

In the face of the Guomindang's military superiority in terms of conventional forces and modern weapons, the CCP had attempted a successful new strategy for survival, one in which it temporarily gave up its urban bases and reliance on the proletariat, and reconsolidated deep in the countryside. Living among poor peasants, on whose support they now depended, CCP leaders had to adjust their thinking. Chiang Kai-shek

THE NANJING GOVERNMENT'S MILITARY AND DEBT EXPENDITURES, 1928–1937*[15]

Fiscal year	Military expenditures		Debt service		Total military and debt expenditures	
	Amount	% of total expenditures	Amount	% of total expenditures	Amount	% of total expenditures
1928–29	210	50.8	158	38.3	368	89.1
1929–30	245	45.5	200	37.2	445	82.7
1930–31	312	43.6	290	40.5	602	84.1
1931–32	304	44.5	270	39.5	574	84.0
1932–33	321	49.7	210	32.6	531	82.3
1933–34	373	48.5	244	31.8	617	80.3
1934–35	368	34.4	356	33.2	724	67.6
1935–36	220	21.6	275	26.9	495	48.5
1936–37	322	32.5	239	24.1	561	56.6

*In millions of Chinese dollars.

also had to rethink his strategies and priorities. His Guomindang had won the cities, and defeated or allied with the strongest northern militarists. But to win over the countryside would take a massive and concerted military, political, and economic effort. To help in this endeavor, Chiang turned to a new source of aid and expertise, the Germans, hiring several of their military specialists to help him with logistical and long-range military planning. But it was only in 1932 that Chiang's growing political power let him move the relationship into high gear. In that year he had himself named both chief of the General Staff and chairman of the National Military Council, which commanded the army, navy, and air force. Further, in an attempt to speed the destruction of the Communists in their rural soviets—two major military campaigns in 1931 and 1932 had failed to dislodge them and had led to serious defeats at the hands of the Jiangxi Soviet forces—Chiang established, under the military council, a Bandit Suppression Headquarters, again with himself as its commander in chief. Since the commander in chief was empowered with complete civil, military, and party control in all areas where Communists were active, the five yuan of the national government had essentially no checks on his actions. Nor could they prevent an accompanying concentration of funds in the military. As the above table of government expenditures shows, when direct military costs were combined with accrued debt interest—often incurred for military needs as well—the amount left to the rest of the "government" for its expenses was never more than 20 percent of the total until 1934–1935. And these figures do not generally include provincial allocations for military defense and security.

The third "bandit suppression" campaign, directed by Chiang Kai-shek from his base at Nanchang between July and October 1932, was more successful, overrunning one of the central China soviets and driving deeply into the Jiangxi Soviet itself. Responding to German advice, Chiang and his staff now started to pay more attention to the psychological dimensions of the struggle through a program they termed the "3:7," meaning that three parts of the anti-Communist effort would be military and seven parts political. Under the "political" rubric they began to encourage the honesty and efficiency of local magistrates, readjust rents through mediation committees, and develop local cooperatives for advancing credit, making available food, seed, and tools, and marketing local goods. Chiang's forces also sought to indoctrinate the local peasantry with moral and patriotic values.

At the same time, the Guomindang put new demands on the people in the form of conscripted labor and heavy surtaxes as—again following the Germans' strategic suggestions—they began an ambitious program to build airfields and an encircling network of roads in the war zones. The Guomindang also set out to construct a line of sturdy stone or brick block houses around the entire Jiangxi Soviet area. The block houses both helped to consolidate an economic blockade and acted as defensive points, supply storehouses, emergency field hospitals, and the bases for forward operations. These tactics not only reflected German advice based on their World War I experience but were designed partially in emulation of Zeng Guofan's suppression of the Nian rebels seventy years before. To back up the fourth and fifth suppression campaigns undertaken in 1933 and 1934, 1,500 miles of new road were built, and 14,000 block houses.

Although a number of German officers were active as advisers in these campaigns, Chiang felt the need for a senior adviser whom he could really trust, a man with impeccable credentials who would give an intelligent overview of the entire Chinese military structure. The man he finally chose was General Hans von Seeckt, a distinguished World War I commander who had been responsible, between 1920 and 1926, for building the compulsorily streamlined German army—the Reichswehr—into a finely disciplined, spirited, well-equipped force.

Seeckt reached Chiang's mountain headquarters at Kuling, near Nanchang, in May 1933, and had several days of intense talks with him. Though Seeckt declined Chiang's request to become the permanent senior adviser of an expanded German mission, he agreed to write a detailed study of China's military needs for Chiang. Seeckt emphasized that the Guomindang-controlled army must be qualitatively excellent and led by a completely dedicated and professional officer corps, so that it could provide the "foundation of the ruling power." Chiang had too many troops, Seeckt wrote; an army such as the one he suggested need be no more than ten divisions. An elite training brigade should be developed first, which could also serve as a strike force in its own right. To achieve this and the logistical reform to go with it, Chiang "must ensure that the influence of the German advisers in fact prevails."[16] These advisers would also build up a standardized armaments industry for China using their own selected contractors. Seeckt broached the idea also of exchanging Chinese raw materials for the munitions and other goods that China would need from Germany.

The first step in this direction was taken in January 1934, when the German Military and Finance Ministry approved the formation of a single private corporation to handle military-industrial dealings with China. Seeckt made a second visit to China in the summer of 1934 as a lavishly feted guest of Chiang's on a monthly stipend of $2,000—"I am seen here as a military Confucius," the German wrote to his sister[17]—and a "strictly secret" treaty was signed in August 1934. Starting with a credit of DM 100 million, China was to obtain an iron and steel complex, ore-processing machinery, and modern arsenals from Germany. Seeckt had pointed out that the arms currently being made in China were "from 75 to 90 percent unusable" in a modern army such as the one he envisaged.

The Germans were to receive in return "high-quality ores." These ores were unspecified in the agreement, but referred mainly to antimony and tungsten, both of which were essential in modern warfare. Antimony was needed to harden lead alloys used in ammunition manufacture, especially for shrapnel shells and cartridge caps; tungsten (extracted from wolframite), with the highest melting temperature of any known metal, was used to cut steel and in making armor plate, armor-piercing shells, airplanes, light filaments, and telephone parts. Germany produced neither one of these minerals; China, in north and south Hunan, produced 60 percent of the world's supply of antimony (of exceptionally high purity) and, in Hunan and Jiangxi, half of the world's supply of tungsten. Whether or not Seeckt was a "military Confucius," the pressures being put on the Jiangxi Communists had become too great to withstand. And as the Guomindang and the Germans began to move their collaboration to an even higher level of ministerial exchange, the Communists secretly made their own decision to abandon their Jiangxi base altogether.

THE LONG MARCH

By mid-1934 Chiang Kai-shek's policy of combining an economic blockade of the Jiangxi Soviet region with a military encirclement based on coordinated road systems and blockhouses had made the position of the Communist forces extremely difficult. In August that year, the four men most dominant in the military planning of the Jiangxi Soviet—Red Army commander in chief Zhu De, the leading member of the returned Bolshevik group Bo Gu, Zhou Enlai, and the Comintern agent Otto Braun—reached general agreement that the soviet should be abandoned by the majority of the Communists, though the four disagreed about the timing of the move, how many people should be left as a rear guard, and the ultimate destination of the Communist forces. Mao Zedong, demoted in party councils because of disagreements over land policy, was not in the inner circle of decision-makers at this time.

Because the only hope of breaking through the Guomindang blockade hinged on the element of surprise, the planning took place in great secrecy, with most of the local Communist military commanders given only a faint idea of what was to be expected of them. There was, furthermore, no chance of coordinating final plans with the Soviet Union or the Comintern leadership, since a raid by Guomindang police in Shanghai had led to the seizure of the broadcasting equipment formerly used by the CCP to keep in touch with Moscow. Evacuation plans were spurred by the information that Chiang Kai-shek was planning a renewed offensive to take place in late autumn, and by the news that a Guomindang commander in northern Guangdong province might be willing to negotiate secretly with the Communists.

Probes by Communist troops suggested that the southwest corner of the Guomindang military blockade—between the Jiangxi cities of Ganzhou and Huichang—was the weakest, although even here there were four lines of north-south defenses to be breached, spread across a distance of 150 miles. But the local Guangxi and Guangdong troops defending this line were not as tenacious as those in Chiang Kai-shek's elite units; furthermore, if the Communists escaped through this southwest zone, they would have a running start over Guomindang troops campaigning in the northern areas of the Jiangxi Soviet. Accordingly in September, the Communist troops were readied for a breakout to the southwest. Food, ammunition, clothing, and medical supplies all had to be prepared and allocated, CCP documents and files packed or destroyed, and personnel winnowed to see who would join the marchers and who would stay behind.

The withdrawal strategy was coordinated by Zhou Enlai. The front thrust of the evacuation was to be given by the veteran troops of the First

Army Corps and the Third. These troops were commanded by two of the Communists' finest generals, who had earned their promotions on the Northern Expedition and in the early years of the Jiangxi Soviet: the First Corps was led by Lin Biao, a former Whampoa cadet, now aged twenty-seven, and the Third Corps by the thirty-six-year-old Peng Dehuai. Lin had around 15,000 combat troops in his corps and Peng 13,000, but they could not be armed adequately because of the Guomindang blockade. Each corps was equipped with only 9,000 rifles (each rifle with less than 100 cartridges), 2 field guns, 30 light mortars firing homemade shells, and 300 machine guns. There was a maximum of 500 or 600 rounds per machine gun, allowing for some ten minutes of high-speed firing per weapon in heavy combat. Most soldiers also carried 1 or 2 hand grenades.

Behind these two army corps came the bulk of the Jiangxi Soviet personnel. The "command column" with Central Committee members, intelligence staff, cadets, and a small anti-aircraft unit, was followed by the "support column," with more party and government personnel, field-hospital units, the supplies of silver bullion carefully hoarded by the CCP, some machinery for making simple arms and ammunition, along with printing equipment and political pamphlets. With their hundreds of recently recruited pack carriers, these two columns were slow and cumbersome to move, comprising around 14,000 men, only 4,000 of whom could be considered combat troops. Three other smaller and less-well equipped army corps defended the flanks and rear of the columns, making a grand total for the breakout of some 80,000 men, each carrying about two weeks' rations in rice and salt.

There were also about 35 women in these two columns, including Mao Zedong's young second wife He Zizhen, who was pregnant, and Zhu De's fourth wife, a young peasant woman. (Of Zhu's three previous wives, one had died after childbirth, one had been killed by warlords, and one had been executed by the Guomindang. Mao's first wife, Yang Kaihui, had also been captured and executed by the Guomindang in 1930.) But most of the women and their children—even those born to Red Army soldiers after the passage of the new, freer marriage laws—had to be left behind in Jiangxi at great personal cost and suffering during the Guomindang recapture of the area.

Also left behind was a rear-guard force of some 28,000 Communist troops, of whom as many as 20,000 were wounded and hence unable to make the necessary forced marches. Their goal was to fight as guerrilla units to retain scattered areas of the former Jiangxi Soviet, and to form an underground network for a possible return of main Communist forces at a later date. With this group was Mao Zedong's younger brother Mao Zetan as well as

Qu Qiubai, the party leader ousted after the second round of fighting in 1927, who had tuberculosis and was too ill to travel. Mao Zetan was later killed in action by Guomindang forces, and Qu Qiubai was captured and executed after writing a strange, poignant "last will and testament" that sketched his disillusionment with dogmatic Marxism and emphasized his yearning for a gentler, more romantic world.

The Communist break-out from Jiangxi began under cover of darkness on October 16, 1934. Thus was inaugurated the "Long March," one of the central heroic sagas in Chinese Communist history. Prompted by tactical defeats, the march ended as a strategic victory after the remnants of the Communist forces reached Shaanxi province on October 20, 1935, having trekked across almost 6,000 miles of hazardous country in the span of 370 days.

The initial phases of the march went almost as planned. The two leading army corps pierced the southwest perimeter of the Guomindang defensive rings, crossed the Tao River safely, and with the command and support columns close behind moved to the second ring, along the Jiangxi-Hunan border, just to the north of Guangdong province. Peng Dehuai's Third Corps rapidly broke the second defensive line, although Lin Biao's First

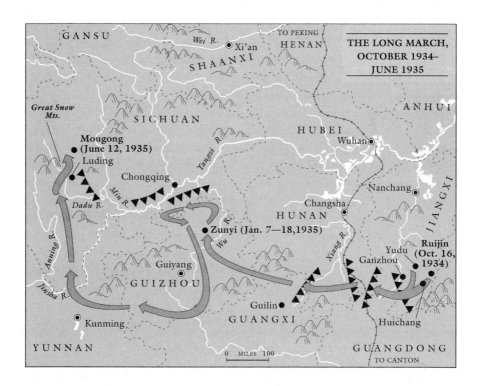

Corps took severe casualties in the mountains to the south. With both regional and Guomindang armies in close pursuit, the Long March forces adopted a round-the-clock policy of four hours' marching and four hours' rest, breaking through the third defense line on the Wuhan-Canton railroad. Held up by their bulky baggage trains and by the desertion of many of the carriers, plagued by poor maps and by the atrocious or nonexistent roads of the Guangxi-Hunan border regions, the Long March forces were almost trapped as they crossed the final defense line, along the Xiang River, in mid-December. Although the Guomindang and their allies had made it impossible for the main Jiangxi army to link up with other Communist forces in Hunan, they could not prevent the Communists' onward movement into Guizhou at the point where that province borders Hunan and Guangxi.

Over the next few weeks the Long March troops seized several Guizhou market towns, where they restocked their supplies and reorganized their columns after abandoning much of their heavy equipment, including artillery for which no more ammunition was available. Opposition was growing fragmentary, and after the Guizhou defenses of the broad Wu River had been overcome by the First and Third Corps' daring river crossing on bamboo rafts, on January 7, 1935, Communist advance troops entered the prosperous city of Zunyi before any of the wealthy merchants or Guomindang officials could escape. Here the Communists seized massive supplies of badly needed food and clothes, though the town's stores of ammunition were disappointingly low.

As the troops rested in Zunyi, party leaders moved to make the city the focus for radical change. They evoked some of the old excitement of their previous campaigns by holding mass meetings, discussing land reform, distributing confiscated goods to the poor, and forming revolutionary committees. It was also in Zunyi that a tense and important meeting of the highest-level Communist leadership took place. This Zunyi Conference of January 15–18, 1935, was attended by eighteen key Communist leaders: six members of the ruling Politburo group, four alternate members, seven senior army leaders, and the Comintern representative Otto Braun. In four days of protracted discussion these leaders thrashed over the reasons for the defeat of the party in the Jiangxi region and examined the political options now facing them. According to the "resolutions" issued after the conference had disbanded, the Jiangxi Soviet leadership was criticized for having followed a policy of "pure defense" instead of a more "mobile war," and for having conducted in early 1934 a "desperate, aimless fight against the enemy in the Soviet" that so wore out Communist strength that "the withdrawal from the Soviet became a flight in panic and a sort of house-removal operation."[18] Since these resolutions largely represented Mao Zedong's views, they marked an important step in his rise toward control of the Communist party. Mao was named a full member of the ruling Standing Committee of the Politburo, and the chief assistant to Zhou Enlai for military planning. The "returned Bolshevik" Bo Gu lost his position as "the person with overall responsibility in the Party Center," as he had been termed, and along with Otto Braun lost the controlling role in military decision making.

In the aftermath of the Zunyi Conference, Mao slowly moved to take over military leadership from Zhou Enlai. For the Communist forces it was a period of dangerous drifting across northern Guizhou province, northern Yunnan, and southern Sichuan, where they faced stubborn opposition from the warlords who still controlled most of those provinces, and from regular Guomindang troops. Some of the time Chiang Kai-shek, who flew to Guiyang, coordinated the counterattacks personally, and cleverly used the Communist presence in the southwest to build up his own political strength there at the expense of the local warlords.

The Long March troops avoided the fates that had long ago overcome both the Prince of Gui and Wu Sangui in these distant mountainous regions by making a daring move north into Sichuan and Xikang province (formerly eastern Tibet) in early May. After taking eight days to ferry their forces over the Jinsha River in small boats, they marched north through wild and mountainous terrain. At Luding Bridge, high over the Dadu River, the Communist forces performed one of the most daring acts of the Long March. The only crossing of this swift, wide river was by a chain suspension bridge with a plank floor. Hostile troops had removed most of the planks and commanded a clear field of fire over the bridge. But twenty of the Communist troops— carrying grenades—crawled 100 yards hand over hand across the chains and stormed the position on the other side, routing the defenders. The maneuver enabled the rest of the Communist forces to cross the river safely by the end of May 1935.

There followed a grim march across the "Great Snow" mountain ranges, during which Mao, sick with recurrent malaria, had to be carried in a litter at times, Lin Biao endured fainting spells from the thin air, and many soldiers suffered frostbite that later required foot or leg amputations. Harassed by Tibetan troops, sporadically bombed by the Guomindang air force, and climbing over terrain that reached 16,000 feet in places, the Long March troops at last reached the northern Sichuan town of Mougong on June 12, 1935. Their original number had been halved to around 40,000.

In north Sichuan, the Long Marchers joined forces with Zhang Guotao, who had abandoned his soviet areas in eastern Sichuan to lead his 50,000 troops to a new base. The union of these Communist forces should have been joyful, for Zhang and Mao had known each other long before at Peking University, and both had attended the founding meetings of the CCP in 1921 before going on to build their own base-area governments. But after weeks of strategic discussion the two leaders could only agree to disagree, Mao insisting on the need to drive yet farther north and east to Shaanxi or Ningxia, Zhang wishing to build an isolated and defensible soviet in the Sichuan-Xikang border region. Mao also expressed his intention to form a "united national defense government"[19] when he reached his new base area, so that all Chinese could join forces against Japanese aggression. This position in fact coincided with the Comintern's recent decisions in Moscow, although it is not clear if Mao was in touch with them or simply thinking along parallel lines. Zhang Guotao sought independence from the Comintern for the CCP, and was unhappy with this formulation. Even though Mao clearly emerged from these debates as the political and military leader of the CCP, he could not overcome Zhang's resistance. In a compromise, perhaps arranged by the commander in chief Zhu De, the two armies were both blended and redivided. Mao was given command of the reorganized "eastern column," which consisted of the survivors of Lin Biao and Peng Dehuai's First and Third Army Corps along with two corps of Zhang's troops. Zhang got Mao's former Fifth and Ninth Corps to add to his own forces, along with the services of Zhu De.

The Communist forces now split up again. Zhang moved southwest to rest his troops and prepare supplies and warm clothing for the coming winter, while throughout late August and early September Mao's exhausted column struggled across the bleak marshlands of the Qinghai-Gansu border region. Driving rain and hail, quicksandlike bogs, lack of food, and the impossibility of sleeping on the saturated ground except standing up, led to thousands of deaths from illness and exhaustion among the marchers. By day they groped their way forward, guided by thin grass ropes laid along the ground by advance scouts. Leaving the swamps, Mao's forces ran into renewed opposition from Gansu and Shaanxi troops as the column crossed below the western bend of the Yellow River and moved through the Liupan Mountains. At last on October 20, at Wuqizhen in northern Shaanxi, near the Ningxia border, Mao's troops met up with the north Shaanxi Communist guerrilla forces. About 8,000 to 9,000 of the 80,000 troops who had originally left Jiangxi were still with Mao. Over the course of the following year, surviving troops from Zhang Guotao's and Zhu De's "western column" (these units had been badly mauled in heavy fighting in western China) slowly straggled into the same area.

Summing up the experience in December 1935, Mao wrote: "The Long March is the first of its kind in the annals of History. It is a manifesto, a

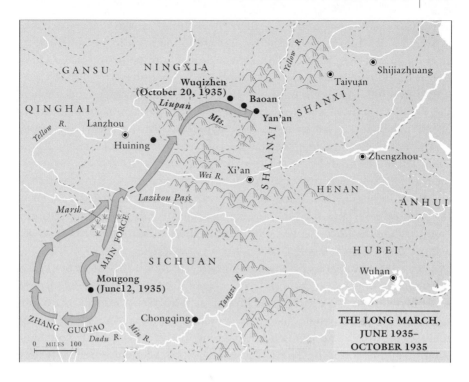

propaganda force, a seeding-machine. . . . It has proclaimed to the world that the Red Army is an army of heroes, while the imperialists and their running dogs, Chiang Kai-shek and his like, are impotent."[20] Brave words indeed, but they could not hide the fact that the Communist party had now lost virtually its entire structure of southern and eastern bases, urban and rural. Fifteen years of revolutionary endeavor appeared to have come to nothing, and rebuilding the shattered edifice would be profoundly difficult.

CRISIS AT XI'AN

One of the most popular writers in China during the 1930s was Lao She, a Manchu who had lived and worked six years in England before returning to China in 1930. An admirer of Charles Dickens, D. H. Lawrence, and Joseph Conrad, Lao She was influenced by the works of these three writers as he constructed his own novels, which were satirical yet tightly rooted in reality, socially sharp, and resignedly aware of the dissonances between East and West. While teaching in the Shandong city of Jinan during 1931, he became fascinated by local reminiscences of what had transpired in that city during the last phases of the Northern Expedition in May 1928, when the Japanese and Chinese had clashed so savagely, forcing Chiang Kai-shek to alter his line of march. So Lao She wrote a novel on the Jinan Incident and sent it to the well-known Commercial Press in Shanghai.

But by a bitter irony the only copy of the manuscript was destroyed when the Japanese bombed the press building during their January 1932 attack on Shanghai. Instead of trying to reconstruct the lost work, Lao She wrote a new novel, *Cat Country,* which was published serially in late 1932 and 1933. Although he did not consider the work an artistic success, no work of the 1930s succeeded in pointing out so well—nor so bitterly—the follies and the miseries of China's ongoing civil war, in which the struggle between the Communists and the Guomindang seemed to absorb all the nation's energy while the Japanese were building up their strength for further blows against Chinese sovereignty.

Cat Country was a transparent enough satire, presenting the story of a space traveler arriving on Mars to find the country of cats (China) being invaded by a tough nation of small people (the Japanese). The narrator details the bitter social and political divisions that separate factions of the cat people, preventing them from focusing any unified front against the aggressor. He reflects sorrowfully on what this must mean for those cat people, many of whom he has come to admire and respect, even to love. "War follows in the wake of every revolution," writes Lao She's narrator in a passage applicable to both the Guomindang and the CCP, "but it is the victorious ones who are helpless. Understanding only how to tear things down, they lack the imagination and ardor necessary to build things up again. And the only result of the revolution is to increase the number of soldiers in arms and the number of corrupt officials preying upon the common people. In this kind of situation the common people will go hungry whether they work or not." One had to reflect on the relationship between the individual and the nation when such a crisis was at hand, for "the 'death of a state' is not the catharsis of a tragedy; nor is it a poet's metaphor for righteousness; it is a cold and ugly fact; it is the steel logic of history."[21] At the end of Lao She's chilling novel the remaining cat people tear each other to death while the enemy soldiers watch.

Patriotic Chinese students responded to the harsh vision presented by Lao She. They had attempted anti-Japanese demonstrations during the 1930s, and the CCP had successfully boosted its popularity within China by "declaring war" on Japan from the Jiangxi Soviet base in 1932. When they reached Shaanxi at the end of the Long March, the Communists reiterated the need for a "united front" stance against Japan. Attacking the "closed-doorists"—as he called those in the CCP who damned all of China's bourgeoisie as being "entirely and eternally counter-revolutionary"—Mao

Zedong built on the line of argument that he had presented in Sichuan during the Long March. He called for a flexible approach that would draw together all those opposed to Japanese aggression, whether they were the wealthier urban classes, intellectuals, rich peasants, members of the government, Guomindang-controlled labor unions, or warlords. In so saying, he was once again echoing the position of the Comintern, as it struggled to find allies against the rising fascist powers in Europe.

One powerful figure who had come to agree with this position was Zhang Xueliang, "the Young Marshal" of Manchuria, whose father had been blown up in his train by the Japanese in 1928 and whose own army had been driven out of Manchuria in 1931. After curing his morphine addiction with the help of Western doctors in Shanghai, and taking a leisurely European tour in which he was deeply impressed by the military efficiency he witnessed in both Italy and Germany, Zhang Xueliang returned to China in early 1934 and offered his military services to Chiang Kai-shek. Chiang gave him the task of wiping out the Communist soviet in the Hubei-Henan-Anhui border region, which Zhang successfully accomplished. But Zhang Xueliang was dismayed that, at the very time he was using his troops to kill the Communists, the Japanese launched a new series of military threats. They were now planning to establish an independent regime in Inner Mongolia and extend the demilitarized zones established by the Tanggu Truce of 1933 to include all of Hebei province. In November 1935 eastern Hebei, controlled by a Japanese-backed Chinese general, was put under a so-called East Hebei anti-Communist and Self-Government Council that gave the Japanese decisive control in the area.

Despite the Guomindang's efforts to keep protesters quiet, on December 9, 1935, thousands of students rallied in Peking to protest Japanese power. The Peking police forces, by locking the city gates, turning water hoses on the demonstrators in the freezing weather, and clubbing or arresting those they could reach, hoped to intimidate the students and prevent further protests. But the "December Ninthers," as they were swiftly dubbed, had touched a national chord: just over a week later, more than 30,000 marched in a second demonstration, while thousands more protested in the Nationalist capital of Nanjing and in Wuhan, Shanghai, Hangzhou, and Canton. Communist organizers, active in many of these demonstrations and in coordinating follow-up activities, tried to broaden the base of the December Ninth movement by appealing for support from women, peasants, and even—on patriotic grounds—the police themselves.

The Young Marshal Zhang Xueliang, who had in the meantime been sent to Xi'an to coordinate the attacks on the Shaanxi Soviet, was among those instrumental in getting the arrested demonstrators released by the police. He was clearly moved by Communist appeals for united action against the Japanese, even as he continued to follow Chiang Kai-shek's orders on "bandit suppression." When Communist forces routed some of his best troops, causing heavy casualties, the Young Marshal confided to a friend that he had begun to wonder if the time had not come for "using 'peaceful' means to solve the communist issue." In January 1936 the Communists appealed directly to Zhang's troops—most of whom were in exile from their Manchurian homeland—to join "the workers' democratic government and the Red Army" so as "to fight the Japanese jointly."[22] By February Zhang had held at least one meeting with Communist negotiators, and in a brilliantly successful propaganda move the Shaanxi Communists released all the Manchurian army prisoners they had captured and indoctrinated with united-front anti-Japanese attitudes.

By the spring of 1936 Communist agents, with Zhang's knowledge and tacit acceptance, had organized an influential group of his young staff and army officers into a Society of Comrades for Resistance against Japan. And in late April or early May, Zhang Xueliang traveled to the Communist base area in the north Shaanxi mountains, where he had protracted conversations with Zhou Enlai on the possibility of concerted actions against Japan. Zhou had lived in Mukden as a child, and was emerging as a skillful diplomat; he charmed Zhang, who was convinced by the sincerity of the CCP's anti-Japanese sentiments.

The anti-Japanese movement gained further momentum in the summer of 1936, when the leading generals from Guangdong and Guangxi in the southeast, formerly allied with Chiang Kai-shek, marched their troops into Hunan and Jiangxi, demanding to be allowed to fight the Japanese in the north. That same summer Zhang Xueliang sent emissaries to confer secretly with the powerful warlord Yan Xishan, who had controlled neighboring Shanxi province since 1917 and had hitherto been a staunch anti-Communist ally of Chiang Kai-shek. Feeling pressured by the Japanese on his borders and anxious about the fate of China, Yan responded—guardedly—that he was not convinced of the correctness of the current focus on anti-Communist campaigns.

Although aware of these growing sentiments, Chiang Kai-shek continued to be tenacious in his desire to finish off the Shaanxi Communists before making any moves against Japan. He used the occasions of a visit to Xi'an in late October 1936 and the celebration of his fiftieth birthday at the end of the same month*—when many senior generals, including Yan and

---

*Chiang Kai-shek was born in October 1887, so by Western count the Chinese were honoring the beginning of his fiftieth year.

Zhang, were in attendance—to lash out at those who did not agree with him that "the communists are our greatest traitors." But the audience was no longer convinced by this familiar rhetoric, and Chiang returned to Nanjing leaving matters unresolved.

In late October and November 1936, troops from the Japanese puppet armies in Manchukuo as well as various Mongolian units launched a full-scale invasion of the northern province of Suiyuan, backed by Japanese planes and tanks. Chinese troops electrified the country by their heroic resistance. Elsewhere, Chinese workers went on strike in Japanese-owned factories, and leaders of the self-styled National Salvation Movement conducted vigorous campaigns in Shanghai. On the international scene, the signing of the Anti-Comintern Pact between Japan and Germany in late November made some people fear that Chiang Kai-shek, with his tradition of relying heavily on German military advice, might now become more pro-Japanese. The landing of Japanese marines in the former German leasehold city of Qingdao—where they helped enforce a lockout of striking workers, occupied public buildings, and arrested anti-Japanese agitators—inflamed the situation further.

In early December, Chiang Kai-shek flew back to Xi'an, despite warnings from close friends and others that it was a dangerous thing to do. There he conducted a series of private interviews with the generals in the Young Marshal Zhang Xueliang's army to test their loyalty, and moved decisively to break the Communists once and for all. Chiang ordered troops whom he could trust transferred to the Xi'an region and brought Chinese air-force bombers into the area, urging that "eight years of bandit suppression . . . be accomplished in two weeks, within a month at most." He remained adamant when thousands of Xi'an students rallied in the city on December 9, 1936, to celebrate the first anniversary of the 1935 December Ninthers. They tried to march on Chiang's headquarters but were turned back by police who fired on their ranks, wounding two students. Determined now to force Chiang to take an anti-Japanese stand, Zhang Xueliang and his senior officers held a final tense, protracted meeting on December 11, and at dawn on December 12 units of Zhang's Xi'an army stormed Chiang Kai-shek's headquarters in the hills outside the city. They killed most of Chiang's bodyguards and finally captured the shivering, injured generalissimo, who had escaped in his night clothes, scaled a back wall of his compound, and hidden in a cave on the mountainside before being seized by Zhang's men.

Later in the morning of December 12, Zhang and his supporters in Xi'an issued a circular telegram to all of China's central and provincial government leaders, the press, and various mass organizations. It listed eight key demands that they were putting to Chiang: to reorganize the Nanjing government into a broadly representative body to "save the nation"; to stop the civil war; to free the patriotic protestors arrested in Shanghai; to release political prisoners elsewhere; to encourage patriotic movements; to guarantee political freedoms of assembly; to carry out the will of Sun Yat-sen, and to convene at once a National Salvation Conference. At the same time Zhang tried to consolidate his military position, but failed to take the strategic cities of Tongguan (on the Yellow River–Wei River junction) and Luoyang, which guarded the approaches to Xi'an. He did succeed in capturing the Gansu capital of Lanzhou, to the northwest.

The next two weeks witnessed some of the most complex and delicate negotiations in China's modern history. The government in Nanjing, torn between choosing massive military reprisal or conciliatory negotiations to rescue Chiang, finally decided on both courses. Chiang's government mobilized the army and air force at Luoyang for a major assault on Xi'an, while sending Chiang Kai-shek's adviser, the Australian W. H. Donald (who had formerly been the personal adviser to Zhang Xueliang), to Xi'an. There he was joined by Madame Chiang, her brother T. V. Soong, and the Blueshirt leader Dai Li. Most of Chiang's warlord allies sat on the fence, anxious to see how events would develop; but a group of 275 young army generals, all graduates of the Whampoa military academy and claiming to speak for 70,000 other military graduates and students, sent a dramatic telegram to Zhang Xueliang. In it they assured Zhang that if anything happened to their leader "we, the alumni, swear that we shall deal with you with all our strength that is within us, and that we shall never live under the same sky and sun with you and with anyone related to you."[23]

In the Communists' Shaanxi base area, the news of Chiang's kidnaping caused excitement and confusion. As in the Nanjing government, there were divided opinions. Some saw this as a golden opportunity to have Chiang killed; others saw it as a chance to rally the country behind a united-front policy of anti-Japanese resistance and at the same time to strengthen the overall position of the CCP. While they debated and awaited Moscow's reaction—as they had told Zhang Xueliang they would have to do—a long telegram, believed to have been drafted by Stalin himself, reached Mao Zedong, Zhou Enlai, and the other Communist leaders. Stalin supported a united national front, but did not think Zhang Xueliang had the power or talent to lead it, the telegram explained. Despite everything that had happened during and since 1927, Stalin argued, Chiang Kai-shek remained the only man with the prestige for such a mission. Stalin also urged the CCP to try to secure Chiang's release. And in a surprising comment, which once again showed the tortuousness of Stalin's mind overbalancing his detailed control of the facts, he suggested that the whole Xi'an Incident might have been engineered by the Japanese to drive China deeper into a civil war that would further fragment the country.

On December 16, Zhou Enlai reached Xi'an as the chief Communist negotiator, flying in a plane sent for him by the Young Marshal. In several private talks with Zhang, Zhou argued in favor of a national united-front government under Chiang's leadership, rather than one based on Zhang's own armies in the northwest. On the nineteenth of December, the CCP issued a public declaration suggesting Tongguan as a demarcation point between the Guomindang and Zhang's forces, calling for a national conference that would include a CCP delegation, asking for careful discussion on the "disposition" of Chiang Kai-shek, and suggesting Nanjing as the best place to hold discussions.

Negotiations continued until Christmas Day 1936, when Chiang Kai-shek, who had steadfastly refused to issue any written statements since his kidnaping, offered a "verbal agreement" to Zhang and the other Xi'an leaders that he would review the situation. After more discussion, the other generals allied to Zhang Xueliang agreed at last to let Chiang fly out of Xi'an that Christmas afternoon. To prove the sincerity of his motives, and to remove any suggestion that he had been a "mutineer," as well as to hold Chiang to his word, Zhang Xueliang volunteered to fly out with him, and the party left Xi'an around 2:00 P.M. After various stopovers to refuel, Chiang reached Nanjing at noon on December 26, to a rapturous greeting from a crowd of 400,000. The kidnaping and his own steadfastness had clearly revived Chiang's popularity as a national leader.

At some levels, however, the subsequent events were anticlimactic. Zhang Xueliang was court-martialed for insubordination, tried in Nanjing, and sentenced to ten years in prison, soon commuted to house arrest. The Xi'an armies hostile to Chiang, after attempting further coups, were transferred to other regions, while troops of proven loyalty to Chiang were substituted. The CCP dramatically offered to submit its military forces to Guomindang leadership if a full national front against the Japanese were announced; but after extended meetings in February 1937, the Guomindang plenum responded by reiterating the need for anti-Communist vigilance and refused to make a full commitment to the united front.

Yet things *had* changed. The heat was now off the Shaanxi base area, where the Communists moved to consolidate their forces in the caves around the mountain-girded city of Yan'an. The country as a whole—with Madame Chiang, the Young Marshal, W. H. Donald, and T. V. Soong to bear witness—knew that Chiang Kai-shek had implicitly given his word to change the direction of his policies. There was now, suddenly, a chance that Lao She's direst fears would not prove true, and that the cat people might agree to confront their attacker together before they clawed each other to death.

IV | WAR AND REVOLUTION

THE ERUPTION OF full-scale war with Japan in the summer of 1937 ended any chance that Chiang Kai-shek might have had of creating a strong and centralized nation-state. Within a year, the Japanese overran east China, depriving the Guomindang of all the major Chinese industrial centers and the most fertile farmland, and virtually severing China's ties to the outside world. Chiang's new wartime base, a thousand miles up the Yangzi at Chongqing, became a symbolic center for national resistance to the Japanese, but it was a poor place from which to launch any kind of counterattack. Similarly, the Communist forces were isolated in their base at Yan'an in Shaanxi province, which, lacking even the agricultural resources of the Chongqing region, was one of the poorest areas in China, with no industrial capacity. It was not clear if the Communists would be able to survive there, and certainly it seemed an unpromising location from which to spread the revolution.

For the first few years of the war, the dream of national unity was kept alive by the nominal alliance of the Nationalist and Communist forces in a united front. While the Japanese ran the east of the country through an interconnected structure of puppet regimes headed by Chinese collaborators, the governments in Chongqing and Yan'an tried to find a meaningful common ground. The Communists muted their land-reform practices and tempered their rhetoric, while the Guomindang tried to undertake economic and administrative reforms that would strengthen China in the long term. But by early 1941 the two parties were once again at loggerheads, engaging in armed clashes with each other, and starting to position themselves and their forces in ways that looked more to the possibility of a future civil war than to the anti-Japanese exigencies of the present.

The entry of the United States into the war after the Japanese bombing of Pearl Harbor in December 1941 changed the equation.

China was now treated—on paper at least—as a "great power" by the Western Allies, and given military advice, massive loans, and such equipment and aviation fuel as could be flown over the mountains from India, which had become west China's last supply line. This assistance came to the Guomindang in Chongqing, as China's legally recognized government. The Communists in Yan'an had to survive with what crude weapons they could manufacture, or the matériel they could seize in raids on the Japanese. Making a virtue of necessity, the Communists honed their skills in guerrilla warfare and developed a maze of bases behind Japanese lines, using techniques of mass mobilization developed in the Jiangxi Soviet. They turned back to a more radical pattern of land confiscation and redistribution to strengthen their popular support in the countryside.

War's end in 1945 found the Guomindang demoralized by the long years of fighting, and its government weakened by personal conflicts and the serious inflation that affected the areas under its control. The party moved swiftly but ineptly to re-establish its control over the former Japanese-held areas, lacking the trained personnel to fill vacant positions and without the money to rebuild a war-shattered society. The Communists, also without resources, moved swiftly to seize what areas they could from the defeated Japanese and to secure a firm base of support among the people of north China. The Communists looked particularly to Manchuria as a promising location to build up their military forces for a final assault on Chiang Kai-shek. Their strategy was proved correct. By 1948 Chiang's forces in Manchuria were routed, and his own power base in China proper completely eroded by a now catastrophic inflation and by the defection from his side of a majority of China's intellectuals, students, professional classes, and urban workers. During 1949 his remaining forces simply disintegrated, and late that year, as Chiang retreated with his surviving supporters to Taiwan, Mao Zedong in Peking declared the founding of the new People's Republic of China.

Re-establishing order in China was not just a military matter. It demanded the complete restructuring of the bureaucracy and the governmental system, the integration of the CCP into that system, the curbing of inflation, the imposition of basic land reform, and the rooting out of domestic opposition. These tasks were vastly complicated by the Korean War, to which China contributed massively between 1950 and 1953, and in which it suffered enormous casualties. But the Korean War had the advantageous effect of highlighting the need for military reorganization and modernization. It also was used in domestic politics as a justification for investigating, harassing, and expelling foreigners, and for conducting a mass campaign against the Chinese themselves to ferret out all who might be secretly sympathetic toward or previously affiliated with the Guomindang or foreign powers. Other mass campaigns, conducted on a huge scale with much violence and intimidation, were directed against inefficiencies and corruption within the bureaucracy, against religious sects and other secret-society or labor-racketeering organizations, and against the urban bourgeoisie with its ingrained abuses and prejudices.

Once the war was over and the campaigns concluded, Chinese leaders worked to complete the first stage of their strategy for economic growth. They formulated a comprehensive five-year plan that was consciously based on the earlier experiences of the Soviet Union. The industrial growth projected by the plan was made possible in the main by extraction of a surplus from Chinese agriculture. To heighten that agricultural production and to prevent the re-emergence of old social patterns in the countryside, the government launched a second, more radical wave of land reform. The earlier program of partial land redistribution, which had left the idea of private ownership intact, was now replaced by a complete concentration of all agricultural land into large-scale cooperatives of around 200 to 300 households each. Almost all of China's peasants were enrolled in these cooperatives by the end of 1956, and Mao's vision of a truly Socialist China seemed to have been advanced a major step.

Overlapping with these great shifts on the land came changes in foreign policy and military organization. In both of these areas China in the mid-1950s took a highly pragmatic, professional stance, and seemed to be openly seeking to limit its revolutionary vision. China's students and intellectuals, too, were wooed by Mao Zedong and cajoled into venting any lurking grievances they might have against the state and the party. For a few heady weeks in mid-1957 the words flew and the party was shaken. As might have been expected, rather than responding creatively to the charges, the party struck back, the critics were labeled rightists, and hundreds of thousands were punished.

Now Mao and his fellow senior CCP leaders were at a crossroads. The country was under control and the economy growing steadily, but there had not been the exciting spurt of growth in the countryside that had been hoped for. To Mao, it became clear that releasing the full forces of the human will, not the cautious pragmatism of his central planners, was the way to economic breakthrough. In a wild and stirring campaign, the new cooperatives were merged into immense communes, and the Great Leap Forward was launched with the goal of galvanizing human life and the economy alike by ending all the old distinctions of gender, age, skill, and occupation. It was a fantastic dream, and it led to catastrophe for millions of people as famine followed euphoria.

Shaken to its roots, in the early 1960s the party sought to reorganize itself, reassert central control, and return the economy to a more predictable track. This had to be done with China's own resources, since the polemics with the Soviet Union, violent in the late 1950s, had resulted in an absolute break in 1960 and the return to Russia of all the Soviet advisers and technical personnel working in China. Once again, as in the First Five-Year Plan period, the careful orchestrations of comprehensive state planning came to the fore, and China's heavy industry, especially, was returned to a path of rapid and conventional growth. But the apparently routine and bureaucratic nature of these plans, coupled with party attacks on an older generation of revolutionary cadres— many of them rural—prompted Mao to attempt one more violent and radical reversal within China. Aided by the People's Liberation Army and by Defense Minister Lin Biao, who set himself up as the foremost promoter of Mao's political genius, Mao began to challenge his own entrenched party bureaucracy. Starting first in the cultural sphere, he expanded by 1966 into the political, the social, the educational, and the economic. Invoking the energy of youthful Red Guards against their elders, Mao and his close supporters launched the Great Proletarian Cultural Revolution, an immense and contorted movement that for years wrought terror and disorder on China. The party bureaucracy was challenged as it had never been before, and those who were not ousted were regrouped into "revolutionary committees" that allegedly instilled the new spirit of radicalism into every factory, commune, school, and work unit.

The turbulence brought new power to the PLA, which found itself playing a bewildering variety of new roles. Yet at the same time, Mao grew suspicious of the personal ambitions of Lin Biao, and Lin Biao grew fearful for his own future. In the most bizarre twist in a convoluted story, Lin Biao allegedly tried to assassinate Mao. The result was Lin's own death; but as the news of these machinations spread across China, it was Mao's credibility that suffered. What, now, were the Chinese to believe? What was left of their revolution? Where were they meant to be heading? Only perhaps by ending their long years of isolation and opening up to the skills and technologies of Japan and the West would they infuse new energy into their economy. Yet to do that would be to question many of the fundamental premises of Maoism itself. It was a harsh choice.

CHAPTER 17 | # World War II

THE LOSS OF EAST CHINA

During the spring of 1937 there was a period of calm, a deceptive respite before the cataclysm. While the Guomindang and the CCP sparred for the propaganda initiative in embracing the united front, the Japanese watched warily. Arguments and tensions within the Japanese cabinet and army led to a change of government in early 1937; the new premier was General Hayashi Senjuro—previously an effective and forceful war minister—who nevertheless claimed in Tokyo during his maiden address, "I have no faith in a pugnacious foreign policy." Hayashi's newly appointed foreign minister stated publicly that to "avert a crisis at any time" with China, Japan had simply "to walk the open path straightforwardly."[1] Ironically, during this lull, the Chinese army was growing more confident and more restive. In May 1937 the American ambassador in Nanjing worried that anti-Japanese sentiments had now at last become "a part of the Chinese racial consciousness," and his counselor in Peking commented that an explosion in Hebei might come from the Chinese armies' "growing belief in their own prowess."[2]

A number of large and small events then came together in what—cumulatively—turned out to be a fateful way. Premier Hayashi's government failed to get its economic policies through the Japanese parliament, and was replaced by a government headed by the influential but indecisive Prince Konoe. Japan's commanding general in north China suffered a heart attack, and had to be replaced by a less experienced subordinate. And Chinese troops in the vicinity of the "Marco Polo Bridge" (Lugouqiao) decided to strengthen some shore-line defenses on the banks of the Yongding River.

419

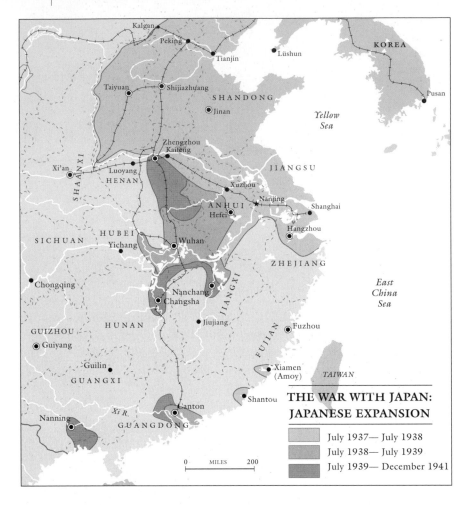

THE WAR WITH JAPAN: JAPANESE EXPANSION

July 1937— July 1938
July 1938— July 1939
July 1939— December 1941

This bridge—about ten miles west of Peking—had once been famed for its beauty; Emperor Qianlong wrote a poem on the loveliness of the setting moon when viewed there in the first light of dawn. Now a strategically important railway bridge had been built next to it, linking the southern lines with the junction town of Wanping. An army holding Wanping could control rail access to Tianjin, Kalgan, and Taiyuan, and for this reason the Japanese troops in north China often conducted maneuvers in the area, as they were entitled to do by the Boxer Protocol of 1901.

On July 7, 1937, the Japanese chose to make the bridge the base of a night maneuver by a company from one of the Peking garrison battalions. The troops were also authorized to fire blank cartridges into the air to simulate combat conditions. At 10:30 P.M. the Chinese fired some shells into the

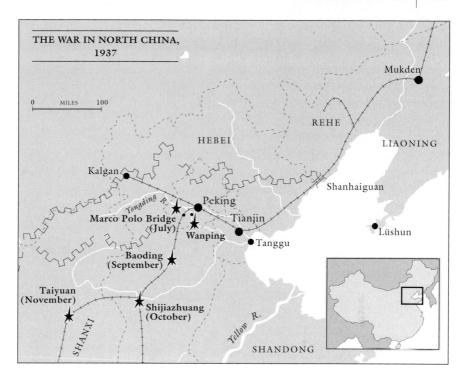

THE WAR IN NORTH CHINA,
1937

Japanese assembly area without causing casualties. But when one Japanese soldier was missing at roll call, the Japanese commander, thinking the Chinese had captured the man, ordered an attack on Wanping. This attack, which the Chinese beat back, can be considered the first battle of World War II.

The following day Chinese troops near the rail junction of Wanping launched an attack on the Japanese position, but were repulsed. Over the next few days, though the shooting had stopped, there was a flurry of often uncoordinated negotiations, statements, and counterstatements. These came from the local military commanders on both sides, the Chinese and Japanese authorities in Peking, the Chinese and Japanese regional commanders, and the governments in Nanjing and Tokyo. Feelings began to run high. The Japanese War Ministry called for the mobilization of five divisions within Japan to handle contingencies that might arise in north and central China, while Chiang Kai-shek ordered four divisions to move into the area around Baoding in southern Hebei. Prince Konoe, in a press conference, insisted that the incident was "entirely the result of an anti-Japanese military action on the part of China," and that "the Chinese authorities must apologize to us for the illegal anti-Japanese actions." Chiang Kai-shek, from his summer home in Kuling, announced that the previous agreements with the Japanese must stand as the *status quo:* "If we allow one more inch of our territory to be lost," said Chiang, "we shall be guilty of an unpardonable crime against our race."[3]

On July 27, just as the local military commanders seemed to be working out withdrawal arrangements, more fighting, fierce this time, erupted around the Marco Polo Bridge. Japanese troops seized the bridge and dug in on the left bank of the Yongding River. By the end of the month they had consolidated their hold over the entire Tianjin-Peking region. Hearing of the Chinese defiance, Prince Konoe called for "a fundamental solution of Sino-Japanese relations." Chiang responded: "The only course open to us now is to lead the masses of the nation, under a single national plan, to struggle to the last."[4]

In a major military and strategic gamble, Chiang Kai-shek decided to deflect the Japanese from their campaign in north China by launching an attack on their forces in the Shanghai area. It was here that Chiang had the bulk of his best German-trained divisions, primed for action since the Communists had been forced out of the Jiangxi Soviet onto the Long March. His forces outnumbered the Japanese in Shanghai by more than 10 to 1, and he had taken the precaution of constructing—again with German advice—a protective line of concrete blockhouses in the area of Wuxi on the railroad to Nanjing, should retreat become necessary.

On August 14, Chiang Kai-shek ordered his air force to bomb the Japanese warships at anchor off the docks of Shanghai. If he had hoped that this would be a triumphal revenge for the humiliating destruction by the Japanese navy of the Qing forces at Weihaiwei in 1895, he was sadly disappointed. Not only had the Nationalist air force lost the element of surprise when the Japanese intercepted and decoded a secret telegram, but the Chinese planes bombed inaccurately and ineffectively, missing the Japanese fleet and instead hitting the city of Shanghai, killing hundreds of civilians. Despite this tragic fiasco, the commanding Japanese admiral announced that "the imperial navy, having borne the unbearable, is now compelled to take every possible and effective measure." Prince Konoe declared that Japan was now "forced to resort to resolute action to bring sense to the Nanjing government."[5]

With the "war" still undeclared, the Japanese government sent fifteen new divisions to north and central China. Chiang ordered his troops to overcome the Japanese in Shanghai at all costs, but they failed in their early attempts to break the Japanese defensive perimeter. In late August and all through September and October, the Chinese, now on the defensive, fought with extraordinary heroism, even though they were shelled continuously by the heavy guns of the Japanese navy, bombed by Japanese carrier and land-based planes (including some from Japanese-occupied Taiwan), and attacked repeatedly by heavily armored Japanese marine and army corps. The casualties the Chinese absorbed, in answer to Chiang Kai-shek's call for an all-out stand, were staggering. As many as 250,000 Chinese troops were killed or wounded—almost 60 percent of Chiang's finest forces—while the Japanese took 40,000 or more casualties.

The Japanese finally broke the Chinese lines by making a bold amphibious landing at Hangzhou Bay, to the south of Shanghai, and threatening the Chinese from the rear. On November 11 the Chinese began to retreat westward, but in such bad order that they failed to hold the carefully prepared defensive emplacements at Wuxi. Instead they streamed back toward the capital of Nanjing.

Over the centuries, Nanjing had endured its share of armed attacks and the sustained propaganda campaigns that accompanied them: the Manchus in 1645, the Taiping rebels in 1853, the Qing regional armies in 1864, the republican forces in 1912. Now, in 1937, Chiang Kai-shek pledged that Nanjing would never fall, but he entrusted its defense to a Guomindang politician and former warlord, Tang Shengzhi, whose main claim to Chiang's faith was that he had led his troops in Hunan in the summer of 1926 to support Chiang's Northern Expedition plans. Tang's distinguishing feature was the abiding faith he held in his Buddhist spiritual adviser, whom he had used in the past to indoctrinate his troops in the ways of loyalty, and as a source of advice on career decisions. This Buddhist now advised Tang to accept the task of directing the city's defense, and Tang did so after the flight from Shanghai was in full swing. As the Japanese bombarded the city with leaflets promising decent treatment of all civilians remaining there, skeptical Chinese troops—fugitives from the Shanghai fighting—killed and robbed the people of Nanjing to obtain civilian clothing and make good their escape. On December 12 Tang himself abandoned the city; since he had vowed publicly to defend Nanjing to the last breath, he made no plans for the orderly evacuation of the garrison troops there, and his departure worsened the military confusion.

There followed in Nanjing a period of terror and destruction that must rank among the worst in the history of modern warfare. For almost seven weeks the Japanese troops, who first entered the city on December 13, unleashed on the defeated Chinese troops and on the helpless Chinese civilian population a storm of violence and cruelty that has few parallels. The female rape victims, many of whom died after repeated assaults, were estimated by foreign observers living in Nanjing at 20,000; the fugitive soldiers killed were estimated at 30,000; murdered civilians at 12,000. Other contemporary Chinese estimates were as much as ten times higher, and it is difficult to establish exact figures. Certainly robbery, wanton destruction, and arson left much of the city in ruins, and piles of dead bodies were observable in countless locations. There is no obvious explanation for this grim event nor perhaps can one be found. The Japanese soldiers, who had expected easy victory, instead had been fighting hard for months and had taken infinitely higher casualties than anticipated. They were bored, angry, frustrated, tired. The Chinese women were undefended, their menfolk powerless or absent. The war, still undeclared, had no clear-cut goal or purpose. Perhaps all Chinese regardless of sex or age seemed marked out as victims.

While the violence raged in Nanjing, the surviving Nationalist armies withdrew up the Yangzi to the west, with the goal of consolidating in Wuhan, site of the opening salvos of the birth of the republic and later seat of the Communists' brightest hopes. Fighting continued in central China throughout the first half of 1938. The string of Japanese victories was checked only occasionally, as at the southern Shandong town of Taierzhuang near the major railway junction of Xuzhou. Here in April, Li Zongren, one of Chiang's best generals, fought a brilliant battle, luring the Japanese army into a trap and killing as many as 30,000 of its combat troops, proving to the world that with inspired leadership and good weapons the Chinese could hold their own. But he could not sustain the victory and had to retreat. Xuzhou fell to the Japanese in May.

As the Japanese advanced yet farther west to the ancient capital of Kaifeng, which would win them control of the crucial railroad leading south to Wuhan, Chiang Kai-shek ordered his engineers to blow up the dikes of the Yellow River. The ensuing giant flood stalled the Japanese for three

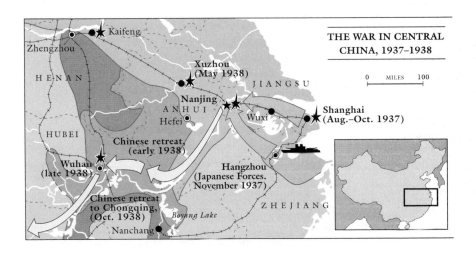

THE WAR IN CENTRAL
CHINA, 1937–1938

0   MILES   100

Kaifeng
Zhengzhou
HENAN
Xuzhou
(May 1938)
JIANGSU
Nanjing
ANHUI
Hefei
Wuxi
Shanghai
(Aug.–Oct. 1937)
HUBEI
Chinese retreat
(early 1938)
Wuhan
(late 1938)
Hangzhou
(Japanese Forces,
November 1937)
Chinese retreat
to Chongqing,
(Oct. 1938)
Boyang Lake
ZHEJIANG
Nanchang

months, destroyed more than 4,000 north China villages, and killed unknown numbers of local peasants. The destruction of the dikes changed the course of the Yellow River, which since the 1850s had flowed into the Yellow Sea north of the Shandong peninsula. Now the waters again followed the southerly course and flowed across the northern part of Jiangsu before reaching the ocean.

By the late summer of 1938, however, the Japanese had assembled the planes, tanks, and artillery needed for the final assault on the tricity area of Wuhan. Fighting took place at scores of locations north and east of the city for almost five months. The Japanese brought reinforcements by rail from the north, and by convoys of armored boats along the Yangzi, which they systematically cleared of Nationalist defense positions. Once they had assembled the vessels needed to sweep Boyang Lake, which the Nationalists had mined, they also were in a position to attack Wuhan from the south.

The tricities might have fallen far sooner had it not been for the heroic actions of the Russian pilots sent to China by Stalin, whose renewed concern for Nationalist China's survival could be traced to the anti-Comintern alliance of Germany and Japan. The Russian flyers' main base was at Lanzhou in Gansu, where they received supplies brought by truck and camel over the old Silk Road; in several pitched air battles—and on occasion through cunning ruses—they inflicted severe damage on the Japanese air force.

But by late October 1938 much of Wuhan was in ruins. Chiang Kai-shek, who had readied yet another wartime base, this time deep beyond the Yangzi gorges in the Sichuan city of Chongqing (Chungking), was flown out of the city to safety there, while those troops who could do so commenced their retreat. The Japanese took over the ravaged area on October 25, 1938, having (according to Chinese estimates) sustained 200,000 casualties and lost more than 100 planes. Only four days before, Japanese marine and naval units had landed and seized Canton. Chiang Kai-shek had now lost *de facto* control over the whole swathe of eastern China stretching from the passes at Shanhaiguan to the rich ports in the semitropical south, along with all the wealthy commercial and industrial cities lying in between. The area encompassed the most fertile of China's farmland and the ancient cultural heartland of the country.

CHINA DIVIDED

By 1938 the great expanse of territory that had once been a unified empire under the Qing was fragmented into ten separate major units: Manchukuo, the Inner Mongolian Federation, northeast China south of the Great Wall, east-central China, and Taiwan—all controlled in varying degrees by Japan—as well as the Guomindang regime in Chongqing, and the Communist base in Shaanxi. In addition, much of Shanxi province, especially around Taiyuan, remained in the hands of the warlord ruler Yan Xishan. Japanese-occupied Canton constituted yet another separate zone of authority, as did the great far-western expanse of Xinjiang. Here the predominantly Muslim population was controlled by an autonomous military governor who nervously sought aid and sponsorship first from Soviet Russia and then from the Guomindang. Tibet, too, had reasserted its independence.

Although China since 1911 had grown used to political fragmentation and civil war, this partial reconsolidation into large units, many as big as or bigger than whole countries, seemed to renew the threat that the pressures of foreign imperialism had posed in the late nineteenth century—that China might end up permanently divided. The solidification of such a group of new states would return China to the situation that had prevailed before the Qin conquests of 221 B.C., during the so-called Warring States period, when ten major regimes controlled the country among them; or it might bring a recurrence of the shifting patterns of authority and alliances that typified China's history from the third to sixth century A.D., and again from the tenth to the thirteenth.

The fall of Wuhan in late 1938 marked the end of Japan's first concerted assault on China, for the Japanese War Ministry's earlier plan to hold a ceiling of 250,000 Japanese combat troops in China had not proved feasible, and there was now a danger of becoming seriously overextended. Japan's goal in its China operations was to win an extensive base of natural resources that would fuel further industrial development—both for civil and military purposes—and to expand the "new order" in Asia under Japan's cultural leadership, a dream of the Japanese for forty years. There was no intention of tying down the cream of the Japanese army in a protracted occupation of all China; rather the plan was to develop an interlocking network of puppet regimes, on the model of Manchukuo, that would give Japan preferential economic treatment, be staunchly anti-Communist, and provide the puppet troops that would garrison and patrol their own territories in Japan's name. Japanese planners also hoped that by fragmenting China's economy further, and especially by weakening the comparatively successful *fabi* currency that the Nationalists had set up in reforms of 1935, Japan would undermine what little was left of China's financial stability. Without a decent financial base, the Chongqing regime would surely capitulate.

Japan's original puppet state, Manchukuo, which had been formed between 1932 and 1934, underwent rapid industrial and military expansion.

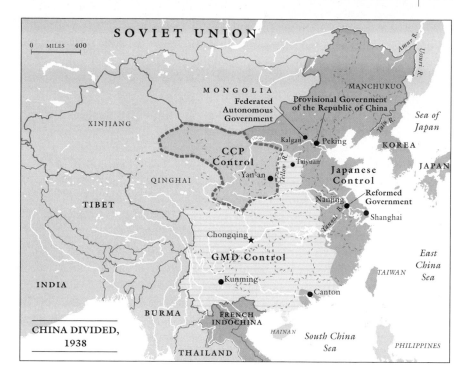

Formation of a second puppet state in Inner Mongolia, spearheaded by the Manchukuo armies in conjunction with Mongol troops and the Japanese, had initially been stalled by tough Chinese resistance. But after the crisis at Xi'an in 1936 and the attack on Shanghai in 1937, the Japanese strategy was to appease the powers of a rising Mongolian nationalism. Chiang Kai-shek had always refused to do this, fearing the area's complete secession from China. Bolder, the Japanese formed a Federated Autonomous Government under the leadership of a Mongol prince, aided by a Japanese "supreme adviser."

This new government was given control of the two provinces of Suiyuan and Chahar, as well as the northern section of Shanxi province around Datong, formerly dominated by the warlord Yan Xishan. With its capital in Kalgan, the new regime was linked economically by the Kalgan-Datong-Baotou railway line, and was designed to exploit the iron and coal resources of the region as well as develop the production of electrical power. The Japanese encouraged certain aspects of Mongolian nationalism by such devices as dating documents back to the era of the warrior-ruler Genghis Khan. But the incorporation of the population of northern Shanxi into the

Federated Autonomous Government meant that the already small Mongolian population was swamped by Han Chinese. Of the 5.25 million people who formed its constituency, over 5 million, or 95 percent, were Chinese; the Mongols accounted for 154,000, and the rest were Uighurs from the Xinjiang region, Koreans, or Japanese.

In mid-December 1937, while the rape of Nanjing was occurring, the Japanese army in north China moved to consolidate the various "councils" and "autonomous governments" south of the Wall into a third puppet regime, named the Provisional Government of the Republic of China. To serve as chairman of the new government's executive committee, the Japanese installed a former Qing dynasty *juren* degree holder, diplomat, and banker, Wang Kemin, who had been the Young Marshal Zhang Xueliang's financial adviser. This puppet government, with its base in Peking, worked closely with the newly formed North China Development Company to develop systematically a wide range of industries that had previously been managed by such Japanese corporations as Mitsui, Mitsubishi, Taido electric, and Asahi glass. With a capitalization of 350 million yen, the new company spun off subsidiaries such as the North China Transportation, Telephone, and Telegraph Companies, and took over responsibility for the area's iron and coal mines, steelworks, and harbor facilities.

Once Nanjing had fallen, the Japanese also moved to install a fourth puppet regime, this time for central China. It was hard to find any Chinese leaders of caliber willing to take the job, especially since it meant collaborating with those hated Japanese officers believed to have given full license to their troops during the Nanjing atrocities. But eventually another Qing *juren*-degree holder, Liang Hongzhi, who had lived in Nagasaki as a child and had served on the staff of the pro-Japanese premier Duan Qirui, accepted the post as president of the executive bureau of the new Nanjing-based "reformed government."

Like the Peking government, this regime comprised three main bureaus (yuan) and a cluster of subordinate ministries. Permanently short of money, it was forced to rely for much of its income on alliance with the still-powerful gangsters who ran the rackets of Shanghai. The Nanjing government made no serious effort to remove the Guomindang *fabi* currency from circulation, although with the help of the Japanese it did put steady pressure on the foreign customs service to yield up its share of the collected revenues. The British inspector general of the customs held firm for a while, and never gave over the backlog of collected duties; but to the deep disappointment of the Nationalist government in Chongqing, customs officials deposited newly collected dues in Japanese banks.

Again following precedents in the north, the Japanese established a Central China Development Company that supervised subsidiary firms useful to Japanese industrial development. Capitalized at 100 million yen (less than one-third the worth of its northern counterpart), the Central China company had the primary task of restoring the railway lines destroyed in the heavy Shanghai and Yangzi Valley fighting. Much of the track and many bridges had been demolished, and only 7 percent of the rolling stock was still functioning. Other operations controlled by the company were electrical power, waterworks, motor buses, and inland navigation. As they did in Tianjin, the Japanese pressured the foreign community of Shanghai's International Settlement to allow their troops in the area, after there had been assassinations of Chinese collaborators and industrialists, and attacks on Japanese military personnel and factory operatives.

The integration of the economic and political life of Taiwan, the fifth of these new regimes, with mainland Japan occurred far in advance of the other four because Taiwan had been a Japanese colony since the Shimonoseki treaty of 1895. Now Taiwan was supplying Japan with great amounts of industrial products, from wood pulp and chemicals to copper and foodstuffs. Its already impressive network of airfields was being expanded, as were the docking facilities at Keelung and Kaohsiung, and the entire railroad network. Chinese children on Taiwan were being thoroughly indoctrinated in the customs and values of Japanese life, and encouraged to learn the Japanese language rather than their own. Although the Taiwanese were thwarted in their attempts to set up a political assembly with its own representation, and even prevented from running their own independent newspapers, the economy of Taiwan was prospering in the dependency alliance with Japan.

The Chinese now living under either the Peking or Nanjing regimes, if they knew anything about Taiwan, might have seen it as an emblem of their future fate. Those who wanted to preserve their freedoms faced the choice—however risky—of joining one of the two other regimes that had established new temporary bases: the Guomindang in Chongqing, Sichuan, and the Communists in Yan'an, Shaanxi. The calls for united national resistance issuing from those two centers were powerful and emotionally compelling. Hundreds of thousands of Chinese chose to make the long and dangerous journey to new homes either in Sichuan or Shaanxi. Workers carried the machinery and spare parts of key factories across China. Whole classes of university students from Peking and Tianjin trudged across the country, with their books and personal belongings, to settle in the new Consolidated University (Lianda) at Kunming in Yunnan, which seemed for the time being safely beyond the reach of Japanese arms. These great treks by workers and intellectuals through unknown territory in some ways constituted a new version of the Long March. Urban Chinese, liberal intellectuals, and the young were introduced to patterns of poverty-stricken rural life or to the non-Han communities of the mountains, of whose existence—let alone customs, manners, and appearance—they had hitherto known nothing.

But most people in north and east China did not flee; they had not the strength, the resources, nor the will. They saw no great merit in the policies and the political practices of the Guomindang or the Communists, and preferred to face an uncertain future with the Japanese. This was true of industrial workers in the factories, as well as of the peasants in both north and south China. If they left their jobs or their land and took to the road, they had no guarantees of finding any work, unless they were conscripted into the armed forces. For their part the intellectuals had seen too much of the vindictiveness of the Guomindang and the Communists, however obscured for the moment by the rhetorical veneer of the united front.

Lu Xun's brother* was a case in point. A distinguished literary critic, translator, and essayist, he had studied in Japan as a youth along with Lu Xun, married a Japanese woman, and deeply admired both traditional and modern Japanese literature. He probably owed his life to the fact that during the bitter attacks against radicals launched by the warlord Zhang Zuolin in 1927, he was sheltered by the Japanese military attaché in Peking. It must have seemed natural for him to stay on in Peking after 1937, and he became in turn dean of the literature faculty at Peking University and director of the Bureau of Education of the Provisional Government.

Many other writers and intellectuals also stayed on in Shanghai after 1937, and continued to found literary societies, publish, and teach. The large International Settlement of Shanghai provided a haven for many Chinese, some of whom wrote anticollaborationist or anti-Japanese pieces, although such works were discouraged by the foreign Municipal Council, which was subject to continuing pressure by the Japanese to suppress all such criticisms. But in both Peking and Shanghai, the Japanese, despite their many inducements, were largely unsuccessful in persuading Chinese writers, filmmakers, or dramatists to produce pro-Axis works. Those works that did appear were stilted and insincere, and their authors were condemned even by others who had chosen to stay in the occupied areas. They were "a crossbreed of spiders and centipedes," as one Shanghai critic put it.[6] For Chinese of all political persuasions and economic backgrounds, the real question remained, Which of the regimes now getting established would have the strength to consolidate its forces and become a viable center for a true national reunification?

---

*Zhou Zuoren. Lu Xun was a pseudonym; his own original family name was Zhou Shuren.

CHONGQING AND YAN'AN, 1938–1941

While the Japanese consolidated their hold over northern and eastern China through the various puppet regimes, both the Communists in Yan'an and the Nationalists in Chongqing faced similar problems: how to protect their domains from further Japanese assaults, how to establish some form of viable governmental structure, and how to strengthen the loyalty of those living in the areas they ruled. Overlapping with these immediate needs each side had a longer-range goal—to build up support, through guerrilla forces or other means, inside the Japanese-dominated areas, so that later they might add these territories to their main centers of control.

Of the two, it was probably the Guomindang in Chongqing who had the harder time with these tasks, for they had lost more than the Communists. They faced a formidable problem of isolation, since they had no previous base of support in Chongqing, which was still in most ways a traditional city with little experience of modern industry or administration. If railways can be taken as one index for economic growth and integration, then the distance between Chongqing and any major railway line in 1937 shows how completely the Guomindang was now cut off from the patterns of development that this form of transportation had made possible (see the map on page 420).

Since Guomindang forces had entered Sichuan in 1935 while pursuing the Long March fugitives, the Nationalist government had sought to break the power of local warlords and implement a series of reforms that would bind Sichuan more strongly into the national fabric. A civilian provincial government was formed with centralized tax-collection powers, and new magistrates were transferred into the province to supervise local administration. An attempt was made to reduce the local armies by two-fifths and to send officers declared redundant to a new vocational training school in the city of Chengdu. Special inspectors designated by Chiang Kai-shek were to hunt down Communist remnants in the area. Provincial bonds were paid off with a gold loan worth 70 million yuan, secured on the local salt revenues, and a Chongqing branch of the Central Bank of China was issued 30 million yuan of the new *fabi* notes to redeem the variety of local note issues still in circulation. The Nationalists simplified taxes, launched a road-building program, and conducted an intensive opium-suppression campaign with the goal of ending all opium-poppy cultivation in the province by 1939. Considering the 1,300 or more opium dens in Chongqing alone, the reforms came none too soon.

These reforms were checked, however, not only by resistance from local militarists, but also by a series of catastrophic droughts that hit the province in 1936, causing the loss of most of the winter food crops. Women and children dodged police patrols to eat the bark of Chongqing's ornamental trees. In early 1937 the police, with their own hands, buried over 4,000 famine victims until special crematoria were built to speed the process. There were food riots in many Sichuan cities, and a predictable rise in banditry. When Chiang Kai-shek finally reached Chongqing on December 8, 1938, having flown from Wuhan via Guilin, it must have seemed a frail base of operations.

One of Chiang's first priorities was to align the neighboring province of Yunnan firmly with his Sichuan base. Yunnan had been run since 1927 as a virtually independent satrapy under the Lolo-tribesman warlord Long Yun. Despite his opium addiction, Long Yun had tried to build up the economic strength of Yunnan by developing mining and industry. Kunming, capital of a province two-thirds the size of France, had a population before the war of only 147,000; all the more dramatic therefore was the effect of the 60,000 refugees who streamed into the city in 1937 and 1938. Chiang Kai-shek confirmed Long Yun as governor of Yunnan, and the two worked together in uneasy alliance throughout the war. Long Yun refused to implement the tough censorship laws of the Guomindang, with the result that Kunming became a vital intellectual center and the wartime home of the new Consolidated University for refugee scholars and students from north China. As the projected terminus for a road being built over the mountains to Lashio in Burma, Kunming achieved further prominence once the Yangzi was closed to non-Japanese shipping and the French had been

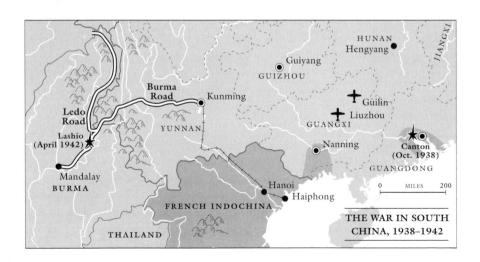

THE WAR IN SOUTH CHINA, 1938–1942

forced by Japanese pressure to stop carrying military supplies up the railway line that ran north from Hanoi.

The Burma Road now was south China's only link to the military supplies and gasoline needed to keep Chiang Kai-shek's resistance viable. Running about 715 miles (600 in China, 115 in Burma), the construction of this road, undertaken as the war flared in eastern China, caught the attention of the world. The popular Western stereotype of the patient, endlessly hard-working Chinese drew new force from the written accounts and photographs showing hundreds of thousands of Chinese laborers—men, women, and children—working by hand in the mountains and gorges, hauling rock and earth in baskets, blasting stubborn boulders with bamboo tubes full of gunpowder. Thousands died from accidents and malaria, and surely many others from malnutrition, for this was mainly a conscripted labor force, paid only with food, if at all. The Burma Road, officially opened on December 2, 1938, remained subject to a host of problems: landslides, stretches open only to one-way traffic, bridges that could bear only light loads, a mud surface dangerously slippery in wet weather, and an absence of telegraph communications centers or gasoline supply depots. But when the first supplies from Rangoon reached Kunming in December 1938, it marked a significant triumph.

With Sichuan as the central base and Yunnan as the conduit to the outside world, the Nationalists could keep a measure of control over the remaining provinces that marked the borderline between their mandate and that of the Japanese armies. These buffer territories included Guangxi, except for the area between Nanning and the coast, which the Japanese took over; Guangdong, except for the Pearl River delta around Canton; most of Hunan; southern Jiangxi; large areas of western Hubei and Henan, and southern Shaanxi. Most of Zhejiang and Fujian provinces were also free of Japanese occupation, but were so distant that it was hard for the Guomindang to exercise much control there. The only major Japanese thrust into Guomindang territories in 1939 and 1940 occurred along the Yangzi River to the distribution center of Yichang in Hubei. Japanese capture of the city seriously disrupted grain shipments from Hunan and Hubei upriver to Chongqing, causing even greater difficulties in the city.

The government set up by the Nationalists in Chongqing was directed by a Supreme National Defense Council, of which Chiang Kai-shek was chairman. Real power, however, was in the Military Affairs Commission, of which Chiang was also chairman, a role that made him commander in chief of the army and air force (as well as of the almost nonexistent navy), and gave him the statutory power to "direct the people of the entire nation."[7]

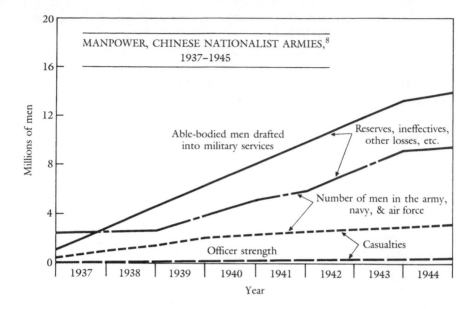

In 1938 Chiang had also been granted, by the Guomindang congress, the title of "director-general" of the party, formerly held by Sun Yat-sen.* And in 1943, after the death of the self-effacing politician who since 1932 had held the title of chairman of the Chinese republic, Chiang assumed that title as well.

But this vast apparent concentration of power, and the enormous size on paper of the Nationalist armies, could not hide the fact that Chiang actually served only as the presiding coordinator of a loose federation of forces. A parliamentlike body of 200 members, the People's Political Council, was designed to help him formulate policy, to give some scope for popular participation in the running of the government, and to embody the principles of the united front. Guomindang members were limited to 80 of the 200 seats on the council; independents held 70 seats, leaving 50 seats to the Communists and other small political parties. But such an organization could do little to pull together central policy, and the fragmented bureaucracy could not adequately coordinate the administration of the local officials across China who were meant to gather rural taxes and link the civil authorities to the military garrison commanders. Income shrank disastrously, and rocketing military expenses began to push Chongqing into an inflationary spiral. At the same time, huge military casualties hurt the regime's morale.

Paralleling the Guomindang's attempts at consolidation in south and cen-

*Chiang's title bore a slight difference of nomenclature, zongcai rather than zongli.

tral China were those of the Communists in their Yan'an base area to the north. By agreements reached between Chongqing and Yan'an in late 1937, after the Japanese assault on Shanghai, the Red Army was now constituted as the Eighth Route Army under nominal Nationalist command. In September of that year the two sides pledged "cooperation" in four critical areas, each of which represented concessions by the CCP: to work to realize Sun Yat-sen's Three Principles of the People—nationalism, socialism, and democracy; to give up armed rebellion, the forming of soviets, and the confiscation of landlords' holdings; to abolish the current autonomous government structure of the Shaanxi soviet; and to reiterate that the approximately 30,000 troops of the former Red Army would be under Guomindang command. Chiang correctly called this "a triumph of national sentiment over every other consideration,"[9] although the CCP was also here following the practice ordained by the Comintern for all Communist parties internationally.

The astonishing announcement in August 1939 that the Soviet Union had signed a nonaggression pact with Hitler's Germany did not alter this basic united-front policy. Mao Zedong greeted the Hitler-Stalin pact as a positive step that would frustrate the plans of the French and British "international reactionary bourgeoisie," and would "deal a blow against the Chinese capitulators."[10] Nor did this new web of international agreements, despite the earlier Guomindang-Soviet nonaggression pact, mean that the Germans would restore the great industrial-military deals that they had projected for China in the earlier 1930s. The Germans were now too committed to support the Japanese in their general east Asian policies.

Instead of organizing the areas they controlled into new soviets, the CCP, with Guomindang agreement, announced the formation of two border-region governments. One was named Shaan/Gan/Ning, from the first syllables of the northern provincial grouping of Shaanxi, Gansu, and Ningxia, and the second Jin/Cha/Ji, referring (less obviously, since these were archaic forms for the relevant provincial names) to the border region of Shanxi,

CHINESE BATTLE CASUALTIES, 1937–1941[11]

Year	Japanese estimates	Chinese estimates
1937	—	367,362 (July–Dec.)
1938	823,296 (July 1937 to Nov. 1938)	735,017
1939	395,166	346,543
1940	847,000	—
1941	708,000	299,483

Chahar, and Hebei. Japanese power was far stronger in the second border region than in the first; but since neither the Japanese, the provisional north China government, nor the Inner Mongolian Federation had complete control over its terrain, there was ample room for Communist political maneuvers, sabotage, and even the recruitment of new troops into the Eighth Route Army. In addition, the survivors of the Communist forces who at the time of the Long March had been left behind in central China to conduct guerrilla actions were now reorganized as the New Fourth Army. Since 1935 these guerrilla forces had lived an isolated, dangerous, and independent life, often sheltered in mountains and forests, operating by their wits, and developing their own ties with the rural poor and those who resisted first the Guomindang and then the Japanese. Drawn together again, after a three-year hiatus, into an organized force of 12,000 combat troops, this army was nominally subject to overall Guomindang direction but was actually commanded by veteran Communist officers.

In these early years at Yan'an the CCP tightened its organizational form—as the Guomindang had attempted to do—in each of three main areas: the party itself, the government, and the army. CCP membership increased dramatically in the period—from around 40,000 in 1937 to an estimated 800,000 in 1940—partly because of a sustained recruiting effort and search for new talent, but also because of the popularity of CCP united-front policies. Temporarily forbidden to pursue expropriation of the land, the CCP implemented a program of systematic rent reduction, and a graded-taxation system that made it uneconomical for many formerly rich landlords to keep large holdings and allowed many poorer peasants to increase their holdings to a profitable size. Thus villages could be rallied in loyalty to the CCP and to the anti-Japanese cause without divisive struggles. As for his own leadership position, Mao Zedong fought off two serious challenges—one by his Long March contestant Zhang Guotao, and one by Wang Ming, the most influential former member of the Comintern-dominated group known since their 1930 return from the Soviet Union as the "returned Bolsheviks." Thereafter, Mao and his confidential assistants worked steadily and effectively to denigrate the achievements of those former rivals, so as to suggest that it was Mao alone among the Communist leaders who had correctly foreseen the course that the revolution in China would take. These conclusions were then enshrined as the new historiographical orthodoxy among the Communists. The party expanded its power through regional branches spread across Shaan/Gan/Ning and the other border areas, as well as through groups divided according to tasks, such as propaganda, education, popular movements, women's affairs, press, and youth corps. The Resist Japan University (Kangda) in Yan'an served as a potent focus for cadre training and the refining of party views. Despite the poverty of the region, morale was high, and Yan'an seemed to many Chinese to be a new beacon of hope.

The Yan'an government consisted of the central administration with its subordinate ministries, and a network of representative assemblies that ideally—and in some cases actually—reached down to the county level. The united-front agreements were honored by implementation of the "three-thirds system": as a general rule, not more than one-third of positions in government bodies would be held by CCP members; this would leave, in Mao's words, one-third for "non-Party left progressives, and one-third for the intermediate sections who are neither left nor right." Mao's writings show that he believed this system would guarantee CCP dominance, since if Communists of high caliber were chosen for their third of the positions, "this will be enough to ensure the Party's leadership without a larger representation."[12] The table below indicates the social composition and party make-up of several representative assemblies at the county level.

SOCIAL COMPOSITION AND PARTY AFFILIATION IN YAN'AN
REPRESENTATIVE ASSEMBLIES, 1941[13]

Category	Suide	Qingyang	Heshui	Quzi	Xinzheng	Xinning	Zhidan
Landlord	23	12	7	47	—	14	2
Rich peasant	159	89	56	32	20	30	45
Middle peasant	578	325	166	181	185	115	101
Poor peasant	1,301	460	1,334	719	165	393	541
Tenant	—	—	—	—	13	19	—
Hired peasant	22	36	4	22	2	1	89
Worker	236	22	63	—	—	2	14
Merchant	127	27	6	—	1	—	3
Gentry	—	—	—	—	—	10	20
Total	2,446	971	1,636	1,001	386	584	815
CCP	400	196	219	257	124	151	386
Guomindang	161	41	58	—	2	2	—
Nonparty	2,075	732	361	744	188	487	439
Total*	2,636	969	638	1,001	314	640	825

*Party totals do not always correspond to category totals because of the number of nonrecorded or misrecorded cases.

The Communist military consisted not only of the Eighth and Fourth Route armies—with the Long March veteran Zhu De serving as commander in chief and Peng Dehuai as his deputy commander—but also of large numbers of local, full-time armed forces based permanently in their own home areas. These local regulars were supported by militia forces of men and women aged sixteen to forty-five who held down regular jobs in farms or the towns, and were poorly armed but invaluable in gathering intelligence and giving logistical support and shelter to the regular forces. The CCP devoted much attention to making sure that at all levels its military forces did not exploit the local farming communities, paid for the food and supplies they needed, and did not molest the local women. The CCP also worked carefully to gain the support of the local militarized secret societies that were strong in north China, such as the Elder Brothers' Society and the Red Spears, and to win them over to an anti-Japanese position. The result was a steadily widening popular base for the CCP.

Participation in the united front inevitably forced on many radicals a sharp break with their earlier ideological goals and aspirations: rent reduction and limited land redistribution had to replace the expropriation of wealthy landlords' holdings that had been practiced in Jiangxi and the other soviets. Gradualist approaches to education and indoctrination were substituted for confrontational strike action, and a cautious economic program of rural credits and development of local industries was designed to avoid alienating the wealthier farmers or townspeople in border regions. Such policies were not popular with many Communists, as can be seen in passages from a training manual written in question-and-answer form, and distributed by leaders of the CCP to their local cadres. A sample runs:

> Q: I feel that the united front and Guomindang-CCP collaboration are too great an about-face. It would be better to strike down the village bosses and divide the land. If we moved quickly, the revolution could easily be accomplished, isn't that so?
>
> A: This is incorrect, because to act in such a way today would certainly bring about the outbreak of civil war. If we fight each other, we won't be able to fight Japan. We would then be destroyed by Japan. Were the nation to perish and fall into Japanese hands, carrying out Communism would be very difficult. The realization of Communism requires national independence.[14]

While dampening social revolutionary forces in their border areas, in 1940 the Communists launched a series of attacks against Japanese strong points, roads, and railways in northern China. Called the Hundred Regiments Offensive—in fact as many as 104 regiments of CCP-affiliated troops were involved at different times—the attacks were coordinated by General Peng

Dehuai. There is disagreement about how the attacks were planned (some argue that Mao Zedong was not informed in advance) and what their purpose was: whether to damage the regular Japanese forces, stiffen national resistance as a whole, or deflect Guomindang attention from the strong expansion being made by the Communist New Fourth Army in central China.

Despite the courage with which the attacks were carried out, none of these objectives was attained. Though the Japanese did suffer heavy losses, the regular Japanese forces, with puppet troops as reinforcements, launched shattering counterattacks, often of immense cruelty, in which whole villages were destroyed to the last human being, farm animal, and building. As a result of the devastation, the population in areas more or less under CCP control dropped from 44 million to 25 million, and the Eighth Route Army lost 100,000 men to death, wounds, or desertion. Nor could it be said that national resistance as a whole was stiffened. In March 1940 Wang Jingwei, Sun Yat-sen's former lieutenant and one time second-in-command to Chiang Kai-shek, at last lent his prestige to the central China puppet regime—to the delight of the Japanese—by accepting the post as its ranking official. Wang's regime was accorded formal diplomatic recognition by the Japanese, while at the same time they strengthened their hold over the economies of central China. Despite concentrated attempts by Guomindang secret agents under Dai Li to assassinate prominent Chinese collaborators, Wang's regime survived, and was accepted as legitimate by millions of Chinese in the Shanghai-Nanjing region.

Nor did the events in north China stop Guomindang generals in central China from paying attention to the New Fourth Army. They were fully aware that the New Fourth Army gave the CCP a vital strategic presence in the Yangzi delta, which was China's richest food-producing area and the focus for much of China's heavy industry, now Japanese-controlled. The area was a maze of crisscrossing jurisdictions of Guomindang regular units, local militia, gangs of stragglers and deserters from regular units, and members of Green Gang and other criminal organizations. Some of these forces, coordinated by the Blueshirt leader Dai Li, were particularly resentful when the Communists edged into their zones of operations along the Nanjing-Shanghai railroad. Regretting the earlier united-front agreement that permitted some Communist units to regroup south of the Yangzi, the Guomindang generals in the area had been steadily trying to get them to comply with orders to move north. The Communists were reluctant, and in a series of skirmishes and one pitched battle, Nationalist troops trying to enforce the order suffered a serious defeat. In early December 1940, Chiang Kai-shek issued an ultimatum: any Eighth Route Army troops south of the

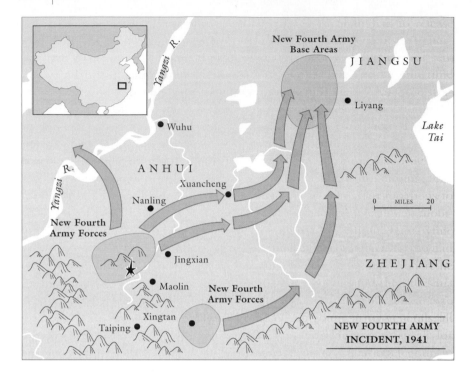

Yangzi must cross to its northern bank by December 31; during the same period the New Fourth Army troops must begin moving northward, and cross over the north bank by January 31, 1941.

Dilatory in carrying out these orders—and possibly not intending to do so—the New Fourth Army command dickered with the Nationalists over their route of march, safe conduct, and the supplies and gold reserves that they had with them. Aware that Guomindang armies were massing against it, the New Fourth Army held public rallies to explain its loyal intentions, although some units actually swerved south. In six days of fighting, from January 7 to January 13, 1941, this southern wing of the New Fourth Army was ambushed in the mountains by Nationalist forces, and around 3,000 of the Communist troops were killed. Many more were shot after arrest or taken off to prison camps.

The loss of men was a blow to the CCP, but the incident carried considerable propaganda value for the Communists. They could present the ambush as a cold-blooded plot by Chiang, whose arguments that CCP "insubordination" had to be punished sounded unconvincing to foreign and to Chinese ears. The CCP was also able to regroup the New Fourth Army in six separate areas just north of the Yangzi, and soon re-established a large guerrilla base to the south of the Yangzi, west of Lake Tai, in the very same area they had been before. The "New Fourth Army Incident," as it was soon termed, did not end the united front, but it certainly highlighted the tensions within it. From early 1941 onward the Communists and the Guomindang, though continuing to maintain their alliance against the Japanese, did so with even greater distaste than before.

CHONGQING AND YAN'AN IN THE WIDENING WAR

The eruption of World War II in Europe in the summer of 1939 strengthened Japan's hand in China. As in the Great War of 1914–1918, France, Great Britain, and Germany were now all preoccupied on their own fronts and had little time or energy to spare for east Asia. In that first world war, Japan had gained territory and concessions at the expense of Germany, while warily respecting British and French interests in east Asia; in the second, it became clear that Japan might be able to oust both Britain and France from their positions of power in the region. The force of "European imperialism," which had once affected China's history so crucially, suddenly began to shrivel.

We have seen how the Japanese were able to pressure the foreign customs service and the once sacrosanct foreign-concession areas in Tianjin and Shanghai; how they closed the Yangzi to foreign ships, at great financial loss to British trading firms; and how they forced France to close its railway lines in Vietnam to shipments of military aid for the Chinese in Kunming and Chongqing. Now in July 1940, as Britain tried to recover from the crisis of the Dunkirk retreat and to rally its forces for the aerial Battle of Britain, Prime Minister Winston Churchill announced to the House of Commons that he had yielded to a Japanese demand that the Burma Road be closed to all military supplies, trucks, and gasoline for three months. At the end of this period, with the battle against Germany going better, Churchill ordered the road opened, but Chiang Kai-shek remained bitter, noting that the closing of the road at such a difficult time had "permanently destroyed British prestige" in China.[15]

One American financial adviser now observed that "the situation in China is critical as to morale, since China seems almost alone for the moment, and American action of some sort must not be delayed beyond the point where China's morale would crack."[16] But the United States, preoccupied with Japan's expanding power—the Japanese army had entered French Indochina in 1940—did little between 1938 and 1941 but buy stocks of Chinese

China's Currency, 1937–1942[17]

	Nationalist-government expenditures (in billions of yuan)	Nationalist-government revenues (in billions of yuan)	Bank-note issues outstanding (in billions of yuan)	December retail-price indices, taking January 1937 as 1.00	Approximate value of yuan in U.S. cents
1937	1.16	0.87	2.06	1.18	.30–.29
1938	2.18	1.31	2.74	1.76	.29–.15
1939	2.80	0.58	4.77	3.23	.16–.06
1940	5.55	1.58	8.40	7.24	.08–.04
1941	10.93	2.02	15.81	19.80	.05–.03
1942	26.03	6.25	35.10	66.20	.03–.02

silver and grant the Nationalists loans in the $25 million to $50 million range. The loans could be used for nonmilitary purchases or price stabilization, and were offered against tin and tungsten exports as security. Nevertheless, China's currency began to slide badly, as the table above shows.

One of the Chongqing regime's most serious problems was its almost total lack of air power. An ex-U.S. Army–Air Force flyer, Claire Lee Chennault, had been in China since 1937 as adviser to Chiang Kai-shek, and after the fall of Wuhan he tried to persuade the Chinese to place major orders with U.S. factories for modern planes. The Chinese could have paid for these in part with the credits being established through their bulk sale of silver to the U.S. treasury; in 1937–1938 the Chinese sold 312 million ounces for U.S. $138 million. But arguments within the Chinese government over contractors, prices, and delivery dates dragged on, and no purchases were made.

Preoccupied by events in Europe, the Russians slowed down their aid to Chiang's air force and withdrew their "volunteer" pilots. The last German advisers had returned home in 1938, and Chiang's Italian air advisers had also left. The first airplane-producing factories constructed with Italian aid and advice were quickly bombed or destroyed by the Japanese air force. As a result Chongqing was almost defenseless, and from May 1939 on the Japanese subjected Chiang's wartime capital to systematic bombing. The initially high losses were checked only when the Chongqing authorities completed a network of underground shelters tunneled into the rock beneath the city, and established an early-warning system by which partisans with radios, behind Japanese lines, warned of Japanese bomber flights taking off.

When Chiang finally sent Chennault to Washington, in 1940, to request help, the Chinese had only 37 fighter planes left and 31 old Russian bombers that were not equipped for night flying. The Japanese had 968 planes in China—many of them the fast and effective new "zeros"—and another 120 in Indochina. The United States had few spare planes to sell, because of the immense demand from Britain. But after additional pressuring from T. V. Soong, who traveled to Washington as Chiang Kai-shek's personal envoy, and from the former leading May Fourth movement intellectual, Hu Shi, who was currently serving as China's ambassador to the United States, Franklin D. Roosevelt's administration agreed to ship 100 P-40 fighters to China. At the same time, by informal arrangement so as not to violate neutrality agreements with Japan, Chennault was allowed to recruit a large number of U.S. Army–Air Force pilots and take them to China as "volunteers," both to fly in combat and to train a new generation of Chinese pilots. Their combat feats made them famous as "the Flying Tigers," and they inflicted severe damage on the Japanese in late 1941 and early 1942, earning a bonus of $500 for every plane they shot down. In some ways their exploits echoed those of the Ever-Victorious Army over eighty years before.

[margin note: Chennault's Flying Tigers]

The Communists in Yan'an were denied even this small morale booster, since the Flying Tigers operated solely within the Chongqing orbit. The New Fourth Army Incident, which had hit the Communist forces south of the Yangzi so hard, was followed by an intensified series of Japanese attacks in the north after the Hundred Regiments Offensive. General Peng Dehuai attempted to combat the Japanese with the conventional techniques of modern warfare, but his forces could not overcome Japan's strength in manpower and supply. Chances of receiving help from the Soviet Union diminished following the signing of the Soviet-Japanese neutrality pact in early 1941 and Moscow's pledge to recognize the "territorial integrity" of Manchukuo. The CCP responded to this new blow with brave words: "We must return all the lost land of China. We must fight our way to the Yalu River and drive the Japanese imperialists out of China."[18] But they were in no position to act accordingly. The German invasion of the Soviet Union in June 1941 effectively ended any chance of China's receiving spare resources from the Soviet Union until the war in Europe was over.

Yan'an's isolation was strengthened by Chiang Kai-shek's decision, following the New Fourth Army Incident, to impose an economic blockade on the Shaanxi border-region government, to stop salt shipments to the region, and to end the subsidies that had been paid to the forces of the Eighth Route Army under the united-front agreements. The result was serious shortages in Yan'an accompanied by acute inflation. It is not surprising that the Communists, desperate for military supplies, instituted a reward system that encouraged the local civilian population to comb each battlefield for weapons once the fighting was over. Local peasants received 50 yuan for each machine gun they turned in to the Communists, 10 to 20 yuan for each rifle, and 5 for a pistol. But as a cadre's manual pointed out, it was not "absolutely necessary" to have modern weapons: "Old-fashioned firearms, spears, knives, poles, axes, hoes, and stones can all kill enemy soldiers."[19]

Communist attempts at organizing rural communities in opposition to the Japanese were met with ruthless counterforce under the program given the shorthand term "3-alls," standing for the Japanese army's orders, in certain areas, to "kill all, burn all, destroy all." When peasants, desperate to avoid discovery, crisscrossed the ground beneath their villages with mazes of tunnels, the Japanese responded by surrounding the villages with troops and pumping poison gas into the underground networks. One documented case of such an action states that 800 Chinese died. Another details the execution of 1,280 villagers and the burning of every house in an eastern Hebei village. A third describes a "mopping-up campaign" in north China between August and October 1941 that left 4,500 villagers dead and 150,000 homes burnt. Seventeen thousand other Chinese from the area were taken to Manchukuo to work as laborers. The purpose of such violence was to deter all Chinese from future collaboration with the Communist guerrilla forces. In many cases, it had that effect; but in countless others, it encouraged a deep and bitter resentment of the Japanese that the CCP was able skillfully to build upon.

The Japanese bombing of Pearl Harbor on December 7, 1941, was greeted with relief in Chongqing, because at last it heralded the full-scale involvement of the United States in the war with Japan. Ever since the Mukden Incident of 1931, Japan had been edging toward such a confrontation, and after the full outbreak of the war with China in 1937, Japan viewed the United States Pacific Fleet as a serious threat to its war aims. For if the U.S. fleet remained able to sail at will, Japan could neither enforce a total blockade of the China coast, nor consolidate its hold over Vietnam and Burma. But Japan's attack on Pearl Harbor guaranteed fresh support for the Chinese, whose war was now seen as part of the United States' own struggle. Aid to China came in the form of lend-lease supplies,* which from small beginnings rose to a total of a billion dollars by the end of the war, and large cash credits, which eventually reached a total of U.S. $500 million. This money came even though no one in the United States knew exactly

---

*"Lend-lease," as approved by the U.S. Congress in 1941, made military supplies available to Allied powers, stipulating that the supplies need not be paid for if they were used in the common cause against the enemy.

how it was to be used, and Chiang Kai-shek resolutely refused to give any guarantees or accept any strings.

President Roosevelt named a senior army officer, General Joseph Stilwell, to serve as his liaison with Chiang Kai-shek, as commander in chief of the American forces in the "China-Burma-India theater," and to have general supervision of lend-lease materials. Chennault's informal Flying Tiger squadrons were reorganized as a regular part of the Fourteenth Air Force, and Chennault himself promoted to general. Chinese morale was lifted further when a massive Japanese attack on Changsha in Hunan was halted by Nationalist troops, re-emphasizing in a timely way that China was a formidable ally. Despite British reluctance, China was accepted by President Roosevelt as one of the Big Four powers in the Allied war effort, the others being the Soviet Union and Britain itself.

The Chinese army was indeed playing a crucial role in the Allied effort, tying down about two-fifths of all the forces available to the Japanese. The potential importance of China's resistance was made even more vivid by the sudden and almost total collapse of the British forces in east Asia. It was not surprising that Hong Kong fell swiftly, since it was virtually indefensible. But Singapore had been regarded as an impregnable bastion that the Japanese would never dare attack, and its fall on February 15, 1942, after only a day's fighting, and the surrender of its 130,000 garrison troops, permanently damaged Britain's already weakened reputation with the Chinese. "Now that the British have been defeated by the Japanese," as Zhou Enlai put it in an April 1942 conversation with American officers, the Chinese "despise the British position."[20]

From the Chinese point of view, even worse than Great Britain's failure to secure Singapore was its inability to hold Burma and defend the supply road it had reopened in late 1940. Unwilling to coordinate their strategy with the movements of Chinese troops or with General Stilwell, the British

THE DISPOSITION OF JAPAN'S ARMY FORCES, DECEMBER 1941[21]

	China	Pacific and Southeast Asia	Manchuria	Japan	Taiwan and Korea
Army division (50)	21*	10**	13	4	2
Mixed brigade or equivalent (58)	20*	3	24	11	—
Army air squadron (151)	16	70	56	9	—

*Plus one cavalry group army and one army division at Shanghai under the direct command of the Imperial General Headquarters.

**Plus one special column. Of these ten divisions two were shipped from the China theater.

were outmaneuvered and outfought by Japanese forces. At the end of April 1942, after a five-hour battle with demoralized Chinese troops who were allegedly coordinating their campaign with the British, the Japanese seized the key Burmese town of Lashio, once again severing the Burma Road as a source of war materials for Chongqing (see the map on page 432). The Burma campaign cost Chiang Kai-shek many of the troops and most of the heavy equipment of the German-trained Fifth and Sixth armies, which had been a significant part of his power base, and constituted about one-third of his strategic reserves. From now on Chongqing would be almost as isolated as Yan'an, its only connection with the outside world being the dangerous air route over the Himalayas to India known as "the Hump."

A debate over military policy now erupted in Chongqing, pitting Chennault against Stilwell on the relative merits of air power versus conventional military power in containing the Japanese and working toward their defeat. The arguments for air power were convincingly made by Chennault, who pointed out to Chiang Kai-shek the comparative cheapness of this strategy, and the feasibility of flying in planes from India and supplying them with parts, gasoline, and ammunition airlifted over the Hump. Stilwell countered with the arguments that air forces had to be defended on the ground, and that the Nationalist armies were overofficered, underequipped, and undertrained. It would be far better to develop a smaller, elite Chinese army, training some of the troops at camps in India and some in west China, and then to work patiently to reopen the land route through northern Burma to Ledo, so that large-scale supplies could again reach Chongqing.

Chennault's arguments won out—he was both more tactful and more patient than "Vinegar Joe" Stilwell, and his flyers had notched up impressive victories. Stilwell, despite a good knowledge of the Chinese language and a deep affection for the Chinese common soldiers he had encountered, bore little but contempt for Chiang Kai-shek (whom he referred to in his dispatches by the code name of "Peanut") and despised most of Chiang's commanding officers for their reluctance to fight and their dishonesty. So while Stilwell made some progress in developing training programs for Chiang's armies, most of China's resources went into building up a line of airfields along the eastern edges of the territory controlled by the Chongqing regime, between Hengyang in southern Hunan province, and Liuzhou in Guangxi.

To pay for the enormous armies still under his nominal command and for the expenses of the enlarged air force, Chiang enforced a more rigorous tax system in the areas he controlled. With inflation eroding the value of Chinese currency (see the table on page 442), this tax was set at a grain equivalent of the prewar tax rate and was then collected in kind from the farmers, either in rice or wheat, or sometimes in beans, maize, millet, or even cotton. Over and above these taxes came a series of "compulsory bor-rowings" of food grains in the provinces to meet army and governmental needs. Those yielding up this extra food would allegedly be paid back at fair market price. Inevitably, however, there were delays and abuses, and when repayment was made it was often at low rates or in devalued currency. On top of this, the farmers had to meet the costs of transporting all this grain to the Nationalist collection stations.

In their border-region governments around Yan'an, the Communists also faced serious problems of revenue raising, social control, and morale. Their response, during 1942 and 1943, was to deepen the intensity of their involvement in the countryside through the mass mobilization of the whole population. There is also strong evidence that they eased their major finan-cial crisis by encouraging the peasants to resume opium production, which the Communists then shipped off to both Japanese- and Guomindang-controlled areas. (In their financial reports, however, the trade was disguised by such euphemisms as "special products" and "soap.") Peasants were also allowed to use opium revenues to meet some of the new tax demands.[22] Although taxes had to be collected even from the poor peasants, and at high rates, enforced rent reductions helped all but the poorest farmers who could not afford to rent anything. The Communists now paid less attention to the formalities of the united front or the three-thirds system in local govern-ment. Cadres went directly to rural areas to encourage formation of pro-ducer cooperatives for the purchase of grain and the advancing of credit. They sought to spur production by persuading peasants to pool labor, tools, and draft animals in mutual-aid teams, and by launching mass campaigns urging emulation of "labor heroes." Similar mass campaigns were begun, when feasible, in areas of east and central China where the Communists had fairly strong centers of support. Here, again, the Communists re-emphasized social struggle and targeted abusive landlords, harsh creditors, and corrupt local officials for public criticism, humiliation, and punishment.

Intellectuals, particularly those in Yan'an, were also introduced to the basic conditions of life in the countryside through specific campaigns that sent them "down to the villages" to learn from the peasants. From his earliest writings on, Mao Zedong had expressed disdain for the traditional-ist elites of China, especially their ignorance of rural poverty and their im-practicality. Like Chongqing, Yan'an had become home to thousands of refugees, and in an intensive campaign in 1942—the "Rectification Cam-paign"—people living in the Communist-controlled border regions were harshly reminded of the imperatives of socialist revolution. Those singled out for attack were criticized in mass forums for their views, forced to design their own self-criticisms, and transferred from positions of power to lower or menial jobs. Some were physically maltreated or driven to suicide. Among the victims were followers of Mao's main rival for party leadership, Wang Ming, who since his return to China from the Soviet Union had been trying to strengthen his own power base. The Rectification Campaign helped Mao preserve his dominance as party leader, and ensured the independence of CCP ideology from Soviet control.

Among the intellectuals demoted and sent to labor in the countryside was the writer Ding Ling, whose story "The Diary of Miss Sophie" had so well captured the anomie of China's youth in 1928, and who had joined the CCP after her husband's execution in 1931. Ding Ling had been held under house arrest in Nanjing by the Guomindang, but managed to escape and reach Yan'an in 1936. Yet once in Yan'an, Ding Ling began to write stories that criticized CCP cadres for insensitivity to women workers, and for enforcing an ideological outlook that destroyed individual initiative and opinion. She also argued that the party leadership was using the slogans of national resistance and party solidarity to undermine the recently hard-won rights of women.

In making an example of such people through the Rectification Campaign, Mao strongly reaffirmed the role of the CCP in defining the limits of intellectual expression and inquiry. To reinforce this role a number of essays—by Mao, Stalin, and others—were assigned to party members and intellectuals for general reading and discussion. In his own most detailed speeches of May 1942, Mao spoke of the social purpose of art and literature. Those in Yan'an must understand their duty to the masses; they must seek out the "rich deposits of literature and art [that] actually exist in popular life itself." These "deposits" had to be "the sole and inexhaustible source of processed forms of literature and art." Earlier Chinese artistic traditions, said Mao, and the foreign traditions that May Fourth intellectuals—and even Lu Xun—had espoused, must be kept firmly subordinate; they need not be completely rejected, but should be used "in a discriminating way . . . as models from which we may learn what to accept or what to reject." The intellectuals' task had to be to plunge into the war that was raging and to absorb it in all its terrifying complexity:

> Revolutionary Chinese writers and artists, the kind from whom we expect great things, must go among the masses; they must go among the masses of workers, peasants, and soldiers, and into the heat of battle for a long time to come.[23]

Hunger and oppression were everywhere, said Mao, and "no one gets upset about it." The true artist was the one who could change that attitude, who could "awaken and arouse the popular masses, urging them on to unity and struggle and to take part in transforming their own environment." Even in the midst of the day-to-day turmoils of the anti-Japanese war, Mao was saying, the intellectuals of China must keep in focus the necessities of long-term change for the Chinese people.

WAR'S END

In 1943 and 1944 the main pressures on the Japanese military, whose incredible successes had taken them far across the Pacific to the Gilbert Islands and through Southeast Asia almost to the Indian border, came from American rather than Chinese forces. China's greatest contribution continued to lie in holding down a large number of regular Japanese troops, for Japan never achieved its stated goal of using puppet troops to patrol and guard its areas of influence. Having won a spectacular naval victory in the Battle of Midway (June 1942), American forces were now involved in the slow and bloody ordeal of fighting their way back across the South Pacific, island by island. But as plans for the strategic bombing of Japan began to be developed by the U.S. Joint Chiefs of Staff, the possibility of deploying the powerful new B-29 bombers on Chennault's forward airfields became feasible, and at least kept China in the minds of the main American, Russian, and British planners.

A number of developments in 1943 showed how decisively Japan's military triumphs—and China's refusal to surrender—had altered the century-old patterns of Western exploitation of China. One important indicator of change was that, following protracted discussions among the Allies, in January 1943 the hated system of extraterritoriality was abolished by common agreement. After a full century of this humiliation, the Chinese would now be free to try all foreigners (except those with diplomatic immunity) under China's own laws.* In August 1943, in a move orchestrated by the Japanese, the collaborationist Nanjing regime of Wang Jingwei was allowed to take over both the former International Settlement and the French concession in Shanghai, and to administer them directly as Chinese territory. And in December 1943, Chiang Kai-shek joined Roosevelt and Churchill at the Cairo Conference, where the leaders stipulated the return of Manchukuo and Taiwan to Chinese Nationalist control after the war.

Another indicator of the West's diminished status lay in deliberate Jap-

---

*From June 1943 until the end of the war, however, U.S. service personnel in China were again put under American law.

anese wartime policies. After Pearl Harbor, the Japanese had allowed Westerners to continue to study and do business—albeit with restrictions—in
Peking and to a lesser extent in Shanghai. But in late March 1943, the foreign
community of Peking (excluding the Germans and a few other wartime
allies) were rounded up and marched—loaded down with their baggage,
golf clubs, and fur coats—in straggling lines to the railway station. A Chinese crowd, assembled for the occasion by the Japanese, watched silently.
"We provided precisely the ridiculous spectacle that the Japanese hoped for,"
recalled one American.[24] From Peking the foreigners were transferred to
the designated internment camp at Weixian, in north-central Shandong.
Here, in a ruined former mission compound, away from all their former
privileges and servants, over 1,000 Western adults and 500 children had to
forge a community of survival with grudging allowances of food, almost no
medical supplies, and only such social amenities, education, or recreation as
they could construct for themselves.

Americans and Europeans in Shanghai were interned under similar conditions at other camps in central China, but different treatment was meted
out to those from Jewish backgrounds. In mid-May, the great majority of
Shanghai's 16,000 Jews—refugees from persecution in Europe—were
moved by the Japanese to a designated ghetto in the poor "Hongkew" section of the city.* Forced to sell their hard-won homes and businesses at short
notice for pitifully low prices, the Jews were organized into mutual-security
baojia for their own policing and protection. Inside the ghetto, they were
completely dependent on the whims of a Japanese guards officer who gave
himself the sardonic title "King of the Jews" and had the power to issue
passes for all Jews wishing to leave the ghetto, whether on business or for
funerals or other emergencies.[25]

Many Jews were reduced to performing "coolie" labor for local Chinese
or eating in the soup kitchens that local charities kept going, and nearly all
suffered from malnutrition. Some took to begging and others to prostitution
in a grim coda to their earlier lives of hardship. But the Japanese never did
bow to Nazi proposals that the Shanghai Jews suffer the same terrible program of extermination that had been the fate of their fellows in Europe.

These humiliations of the Westerners in China occurred during a lull in
the heaviest fighting in the China theater, but the military stalemate ended
abruptly in 1944. While Stilwell and the British—with their retrained Chinese troops—had been fighting the Japanese in north Burma, and had begun
to construct a new road from Ledo that would eventually reconnect to the

---

*The ghetto order excluded Ashkenazic Jews, mostly from Russia, who had settled in China prior
to 1937.

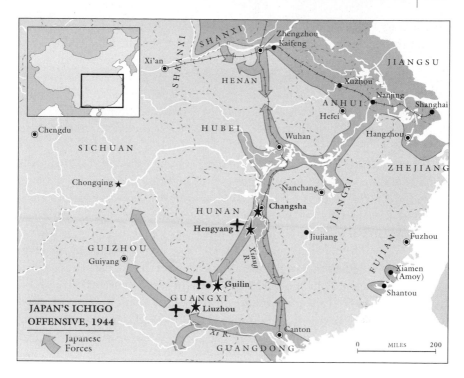

JAPAN'S ICHIGO
OFFENSIVE, 1944

Japanese
Forces

old Burma Road, Chennault's vision of the crucial importance of the air
war had been dramatically implemented, and tens of thousands of Chinese
laborers had been gradually expanding and improving China's net of airfields east of Chongqing. In early June 1944, B-29 bombers based on these
new Chinese airfields launched their first significant raid—in part a training
operation—against railway yards in Bangkok, Thailand. On June 15 they
reached the southern Japanese island of Kyushu, dropping 221 tons of bombs
on the Yawata steel plant there. More raids on Kyushu industrial targets
followed, along with raids on the Anshan steelworks in Manchukuo, an oil
refinery in Sumatra, and airfields in Taiwan.

As Stilwell had warned, the Japanese struck back, and with massive force.
In the summer of 1944, in an operation code-named Ichigo (meaning "Number One"), Japanese troops moved into Henan province to consolidate their
hold over the Peking-Wuhan railway, then moved southward down the
Xiang River to Changsha. This city, which had resisted so bravely in 1941,
now fell swiftly to Japanese forces. The only effective Chinese resistance
was offered around the city and airfield of Hengyang, but they too fell in
August. The Japanese army pushed on into Guangxi, seizing the air bases
at Guilin and Liuzhou in November. Two columns then swung westward,

threatening Guiyang and even Chongqing itself. At this point the Japanese halted the campaign, apparently content to have smashed the Chinese air-fields that had served as bases for the bombing of their homeland. At the very moment of this success, however, came fresh proof that the war was turning against Japan. In late November 1944, an intensive B-29 bomber attack was launched against Tokyo—not from east China, as Chennault had so long hoped, but from American bases in the newly recaptured Mariana Islands.

Japan's victories in the Ichigo campaigns seriously damaged Chiang Kai-shek's surviving military forces, and severed additional large areas of China from his control. At least as important, however, the Japanese victories contributed to a further deterioration of Chinese morale, and of American confidence in China's leadership. Wartime Chongqing had long been a center of gossip and malicious rumor, of stark contrasts of wealth and poverty, of financial speculation and price manipulation, of black-market goods and rumors of treason. A Chinese poet, in a variant of Western-style free verse, powerfully captured these contradictions in a 1944 poem that he concocted from movie advertisements, newspaper headlines, and official Guomindang press releases in Chongqing. He called his poem "Headline Music":

Tense, Tense, Tense
Bullish, Bullish, Bullish
Four thousand million dollars tumble in the gold market
Change, No change, Don't discuss national affairs
   Every tune grand, elegant, and elevating
   Every scene full of exquisite music and dance
   Sing in honor of schoolmates joining the army
   Dance for benefit of the refugees
A queue tens of miles long, spending the night in the cold wind
Peerless art on creamy artificial ice, spring color in the palace of the moon
Every word is blood and grief, moving the audience to tears
They carried and supported their old and young, we were deeply touched
   Domestically produced great film, a tragedy with costumes in the latest fashion
   The plot touchingly sad, tender, tense
   Ladies, old and young, are respectfully advised to bring more handkerchiefs . . . [26]

At this same time came the news that Chinese peasants in the former Guomindang-held areas had been killing, robbing, and disarming the Chinese troops retreating from the Ichigo attacks in pent-up rage at the callousness of those same troops a year earlier, when the troops had enforced tax collections in kind even in the midst of terrible famine. American reporters who traveled out of Chongqing to inspect the famine-stricken areas of

Hunan were shattered by what they saw. "The tear-stained faces, smudgy and forlorn in the cold, shamed us," wrote Theodore White,

> Chinese children are beautiful in health; their hair glows then with the gloss of fine natural oil, and their almond eyes sparkle. But these shrunken scarecrows had pus-filled slits where eyes should be; malnutrition had made their hair dry and brittle; hunger had bloated their bellies; weather had chapped their skins. Their voices had withered into a thin whine that called only for food.[27]

These journalists, angry and sickened when reports of such miseries were cut from their dispatches by Guomindang censors, ended up blaming the Chongqing regime for both the human and the military dimensions of the catastrophe.

Other Americans, including General Stilwell himself, were equally horrified at the campaigns of enforced conscription carried out by the Guomindang armies, and at the sight of ragged, barefooted men being led to the front roped together, already weakened almost to death by beriberi or malnutrition. Random executions of recruiting officers, occasionally ordered by Chiang Kai-shek, did nothing to end the abuses. It was estimated that of 1.67 million Chinese men drafted for active service in 1943, 44 percent deserted or died on the way to join their units. Those draftees who died *before* seeing combat between 1937 and 1945 numbered 1.4 million, approximately 1 in 10 of all men drafted.

In the face of this grim situation, it was not surprising that American officers began to look toward the Communist border base area of Yan'an for help. Both President Roosevelt and the Joint Chiefs of Staff discussed the possibility of arming the Communists to increase their effectiveness in combat against the Japanese. The War Department contemplated making some lend-lease equipment available to forces that included Communists, if not to individual Communist units. And despite Chiang Kai-shek's irritation, a small U.S. "observer group," under Colonel David Barrett, was sent to Yan'an in July 1944. Their mission was formally restricted to obtaining intelligence information on Japanese movements, gathering meteorological data, and aiding downed pilots to get back through Japanese lines to their units. Although under orders not to engage in "political discussion," the Americans inevitably got to know the Communist forces well, and to gain a high regard for their combat capabilities.

The presence of this American group in Yan'an was mainly the result of the urgings of Vice-President Henry Wallace, who visited Chongqing in June 1944. Further attempts at a rapprochement with the Communists were pushed by President Roosevelt's special envoy Patrick Hurley, who went to Yan'an in November. In between these two missions Roosevelt himself, drawing on the contrast between the second Burma campaign—in which Stilwell and the retrained Chinese troops were fighting with distinction— and the disasters of Ichigo, was becoming insistent that Stilwell be made commander in chief of all Chinese troops, including those within China. This was intolerable to Chiang and his senior Chinese advisers, and after some bitter lobbying and recriminations on both sides, Stilwell was recalled to the United States in October 1944 and replaced by General Albert Wedemeyer. Over the next three months, Chiang was also able to deflect all further plans for heightened American support to the Yan'an Regime.

The CCP were disappointed by this change of heart, but not surprised. They had been fighting on their own for a long time. So while as a propaganda ploy they continued to call for a coalition government that would unite all Chinese, and presented in their Yan'an base a smiling face to a growing stream of Western visitors and news reporters, they also worked systematically and determinedly to deepen their support in the Chinese countryside. Their policies became once again overtly radical, even if they showed a certain flexibility in defining class relations in the areas they controlled. Landlords were now strongly attacked, and once again peasants were precisely ranked according to the extent of their holdings.

By Yan'an definitions, "rich peasants" were those who earned more than half their income from the use of hired labor, but it was acknowledged that they might also be exploited as tenants at the same time. Therefore a key element in Communist social analysis and policy again became general living standards and the amount of livestock and tools owned. "Middle peasants" and "poor peasants" were defined in terms of subsistence as well as land-ownership: technically a "poor peasant" was one who could not reach subsistence level regardless of whether he owned or rented land, and so had to

THE RURAL POPULATION IN CENTRAL CHINA: SAMPLE CCP CLASSES OF HOUSEHOLDS BY PERCENTAGE OF POPULATION, 1941–1945[28]

Area	Landlord	Rich peasant	Middle peasant	Poor peasant	Hired hand	Others
Xinxin	7.6	4.8	31.0	40.0	16.6	—
Erlian	7.1	3.5	47.1	34.0	2.2	6.1
Zhangtang	2.3	7.0	34.5	50.5	3.6	2.1
Xinsi	9.0	10.0	30.0	51.0	0.0	—
Baishui	5.1	9.0	13.2	72.2	—	—

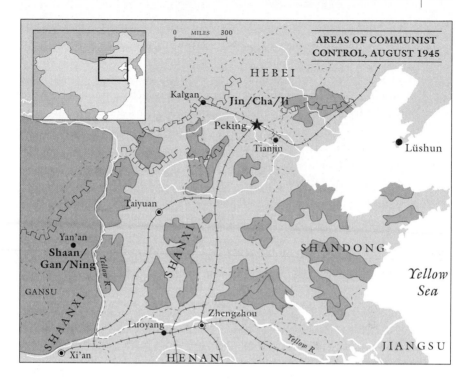

sell some of his labor; a "middle peasant" could sustain himself and his family by hiring other people's labor or occasionally hiring out his own. But who had the greater chance, in local eyes, of living a reasonably happy life? If, according to the community, it was the poor peasant, despite his poverty, and not the middle peasant, then the categories might be reversed. One example of this new flexibility was the case of a peasant widow with a five-year-old child. The widow, who owned 3.5 acres of land, 3 thatched houses, and 1 pig, was on the surface nothing but a landlord. She ended up, however, being classified as a "middle peasant" out of sympathy for her plight as a mother.

All over north China, in areas interspersed throughout nominally Japanese-controlled territory or puppet bases of power, and sometimes in areas where Guomindang pockets of resistance still lingered, the Communists continued this complex process of classifying and reclassifying, of analyzing rural social conditions and encouraging the breakdown of age-old patterns of deference through mass mobilization and public criticism. Foreign journalists, American military observers, and even Guomindang agents apparently knew virtually nothing about it.

In many communities, it was now the Communist cadres who instituted

a version of the traditional *baojia* mutual-security system. This was composed of five-person "mutual guarantee" groups, each group having been
formed voluntarily by those willing to pledge that no other member of the
group had indulged in wrongdoing. Not precisely linked to class analysis,
this system effectively left outside the community structure those who were
now identified by the CCP as "socially unreliable," and gave a great sense
of solidarity to the majority. Among the "socially unreliable" were those
who stole crops, worked as prostitutes, had ties to bandits or opium smugglers, frequented Japanese-occupied areas, were prominent members of
secret societies, or had once served in puppet forces. But vaguer categories
were also employed, showing how thoroughly CCP investigators questioned
villagers about their neighbors. For the same CCP surveys also warned
against those who had a "mysterious past," committed adultery, had bad
tempers, failed to attend political meetings, smoked opium, or had roving
wives.[29] The new Communists were to be disciplined people who could rise
above pleasure in the search for a new political order.

Satisfied with the growth of CCP power in north China—CCP membership now stood at 1.2 million, and over 900,000 troops were under arms
in the Eighth Route and New Fourth armies—Mao Zedong convened the
seventh national congress of the CCP at Yan'an in April 1945. (There had
been no such party gathering since the sixth congress had met in Moscow
in 1928.) No one challenged Mao's leadership now, and several of his former
rivals gave public self-criticisms. Both before and after the Congress, Mao
blamed himself in public for allowing excessive use of violence and terror
against loyal Communists, in the frenzied hunting for spies and traitors that
had been a part of the Yan'an experience for many. He even bowed in
contrition before his colleagues.[30] But Mao's "thought" was acknowledged
as the leading guide for the CCP in the text of the new party constitution,
and the foundations were firmly laid for what was later to become the "cult"
of Mao Zedong. In a report "On Coalition Government" Mao made some
gestures toward the Guomindang, but claimed that the government developed by the CCP in the border areas was the correct form, and one that
implemented each of the Three Principles of Sun Yat-sen. Since the Communists now controlled "liberated areas" with a total population of 95 million, Mao could afford to be self-congratulatory. The constitution strongly
centralized party power, and Mao assumed the newly formed post of chairman of the Central Committee. Certain other details stood out: strong representation was given to the rural areas, and references to the Soviet Union
and the world Communist revolution were dropped from the constitution.
The CCP seemed to be emphasizing its independence.

The seventh CCP congress had been deliberately staged to coincide with the sixth Guomindang congress held at the same time in Chongqing. Those sessions conspicuously failed to boost Chiang Kai-shek's position. Instead, strong criticism of the Guomindang came from the ranks of its own youth-corps members and from rival cliques within the party organization. Talk of corruption and demoralization was widespread. It was not clear if Chiang could keep the loyalty of even his own most prominent supporters.

Guomindang influence indeed seemed to be slipping not just in China, but overseas as well. Winston Churchill, who had never had much faith in China, wrote that to consider it still as one of the Big Four was "an absolute farce," and he noted China's "grotesque" military failures in the Ichigo battles. Meeting at Yalta in February 1945, Roosevelt, Stalin, and Churchill made no attempt to fill Chiang in on the momentous decisions they made: that the Soviet Union would enter the war in Asia within three months of Germany's surrender; that Russia would regain all territory lost to the Japanese, including Sakhalin and the Kuril Islands; that Russia would be able again to "lease" the great naval base at Lüshun and share in the benefits of an "internationalized" city of Dalian (Lüda), and that it would once more be given a preponderant interest in the formerly Sino-Russian railways in Manchuria. The last three clauses were all major blows to China's postwar aspirations.

With the war dragging on, the only sop to China came through the availability of large amounts of lend-lease supplies, and the careful way in which General Wedemeyer and his staff labored to improve the combat efficiency of thirty-nine specially selected divisions of Chiang's own armies, with no more unsettling talk of arming or training the Communists. Despite the U.S. Air Force's heavy bombing of Japan, and the land victories by Allied troops in Burma that led to the reopening of the Burma Road, the steady series of U.S. victories in the Pacific Islands were being won only at terrible cost in American casualties. Knowing nothing of the Yalta agreements or the atomic-bomb program—which was shrouded in secrecy—Wedemeyer thought, as did the Chinese, that the war would still take years to win. With Chiang's approval he drew up long-range contingency plans for a slow advance to the east coast of China and seizure of Canton in late 1945 or early 1946. A march northward toward Shanghai would follow, a plan that must have reminded Chiang of his Northern Expedition strategy of nineteen years before. In early August 1945, as an encouraging preliminary, Chinese forces recaptured Guilin and began to move south toward Hainan Island.

Germany's surrender in May 1945 cheered the Chinese but did not change their timetable. But on August 8, in response to the Yalta agreements, massive Russian forces moved into Manchukuo to attack the Japanese. Only two days before, the United States had dropped an atomic bomb on Hiroshima. The Americans dropped a second atomic bomb on Nagasaki on the ninth. Five days later the Japanese sued for surrender. With an extraordinary suddenness, and in ways no one in China was adequately prepared for, the whole structure of Asian power politics had changed.

CHAPTER 18

The Fall of the Guomindang State

THE JAPANESE SURRENDER AND THE MARSHALL MISSION

In a lengthy cable to the Joint Chiefs of Staff on the situation in the Chongqing war zone, written on August 1, 1945, General Wedemeyer noted that "if peace comes suddenly, it is reasonable to expect widespread confusion and disorder. The Chinese have no plans for rehabilitation, prevention of epidemics, restoration of utilities, establishment of balanced economy and redisposition of millions of refugees." In answer to his further questions over what his exact role should be in the event of Japanese surrender, Wedemeyer was given the confusing and overlapping instructions from Washington that he should help the Nationalists as much as possible without intervening on their behalf in a civil war, and should "assist the Central Government in rapidly moving its forces to key areas in China."[1]

Wedemeyer and Chiang Kai-shek had agreed that as American forces became available after the Japanese surrender they should move swiftly to occupy five key ports in this order: Shanghai, Pusan (in Korea), Dagu, Canton, and Qingdao. In the few weeks after Japan's surrender, the United States did occupy these and other ports, and U.S. Marines were sent in large numbers to Peking and Tianjin. But U.S. forces, following the orders of the Joint Chiefs, concentrated on airlifting as many of Chiang's troops as possible from the Chongqing region to north and east China, so that Nationalist forces could accept the Japanese surrenders in person. In the two months following Emperor Hirohito's surrender declaration, Dakota transport planes of the U.S. Tenth Air Force airlifted over 110,000 of Chiang's best

American-trained troops to key cities. Japanese commanders were told not to surrender to the Communists, and in many cases they continued to clash with Communist forces until Guomindang officials arrived. The Communists, for their part, were instructed by their commander in chief Zhu De to force Japanese officers to surrender directly to them wherever possible, after which the Communists would take on the task of maintaining local law and order.

The scale of the surrender operation was gigantic, and it took months to complete. There were close to 1.25 million Japanese troops in China proper, and another 900,000 in Manchuria, not counting all the puppet troops, armed or partially armed, and over 1.75 million Japanese civilians in the country. The Chinese Nationalist forces, despite their enormous losses, still numbered 2.7 million troops in 290 divisions. The Communists' Eighth Route Army and New Fourth Army contained close to 1 million troops. In some places the surrender was formal and dignified, as at Nanjing, where the Japanese commander in chief for the China theater yielded up his powers at the site specially designated for the ceremony by Chiang Kai-shek himself: the auditorium of the Whampoa cadets' Central Military Academy. In many other cities, however, there were clashes and violence. And in Shanxi the tenacious warlord Yan Xishan used Japanese troops to help him fight off the Communists and to preserve his power in Taiyuan.

In Manchuria, on the other hand, after arresting and deposing the Manchukuo Emperor Puyi, and accepting the Japanese surrender, the Soviet Union's troops allowed huge stockpiles of arms and ammunition to fall into the hands of the Chinese Communists. These Chinese troops had moved swiftly by forced marches into the area before Chiang could move his own forces there in sufficient numbers to deter them.

The lack of coordinated advance planning that had worried Wedemeyer so much in August turned out to have serious consequences for the Guomindang. As they took back city after city from the Japanese, and seemed to have the goal of reconstructing a united China once more within their grasp, their carelessness, their inefficiency, and often their corruption whittled steadily away at their basis of popular support. Many Chinese were outraged when puppet troops and politicians who had collaborated openly with the Japanese during the war were allowed to remain in their positions, just to prevent the Communists from expanding their territory. When anti-collaborator regulations were finally issued at the end of September, they were full of loopholes and promised leniency to those who had performed any patriotic acts during their term of office. And the effect of these orders was further nullified by the promotion to senior military rank in the Nationalist armies of numerous officers who had served in Manchukuo, the Inner

Mongolian Federation, or the Peking-area puppet regime. Yet when it suited their purposes, the Guomindang also accused some people who had not fled the Japanese-occupied areas as themselves having been collaborators, and punished them as such.

A number of scandals accompanied the freezing of assets that the Japanese or their collaborators had seized during the occupation and were now allegedly to be returned to their original rightful owners. Several overlapping and loosely supervised agencies were given the task of inventorying business premises and equipment, and of assessing claims. Factories and warehouses that were meant to be closed only a few days while handing-over formalities were completed remained closed for weeks in many cases, throwing thousands out of work and ruining local businesses. At the same time, robbery of closed properties was taking place everywhere, and squads of men with armbands identifying them as representatives of one of the government agencies could enter establishments at will, commandeer vehicles, and commit other abuses. Since those robbing public property included senior officers and even the chief of the Chapei police force in Shanghai, there was little chance of rectifying matters. In one incident indicative of many others, of the 3,438 motor vehicles taken over by officials in Hunan from the Japanese, every one was pirated for parts, which were then sold illegally to local dealers.

The Guomindang also mismanaged the difficult problem of stabilizing the currencies of China. It was essential to firm up the exchange rate of the Nationalist *fabi* currency, which had been used throughout the war in Chongqing, with the various currency notes issued by different puppet governments. By not acting decisively or promptly, the Guomindang allowed a chaotic situation to emerge in which exchanges varied wildly among cities; in one example, a given puppet currency traded at 40 to the yuan in Wuhan, 150 to the yuan in Shanghai, and 200 to the yuan in Nanjing. Exchange rates between *fabi* and U.S. dollars also veered sharply, holding for a time at 700 yuan to U.S. $1 in Tianjin and ranging from 1,500 yuan to 2,500 yuan in Shanghai. Naturally it paid speculators to shuttle between the cities, buying up U.S. dollars in Tianjin and selling them in Shanghai. Food prices also began to rise uncontrollably, and no central authority had the power to hold them at a reasonable level.

In this dispiriting context, the United States continued to push for some sort of Guomindang-Communist rapprochement that, it hoped, might prevent civil war from breaking out in China and guarantee at least some measure of democracy. In August 1945, Ambassador Hurley personally escorted Mao Zedong from Yan'an to Chongqing for negotiations with Chiang Kai-shek. These talks continued until October 10, during the very period in which the two sides were sparring for dominance in east and north China; they resulted in the publication of a set of principles that seemed a hopeful indication of future collaboration. Mao and Chiang announced that they agreed on the need for political democracy, a unified military force, and equal legal status for all political parties. A National Assembly or People's Congress should be convened promptly, to mark the end of the period of political tutelage that Sun Yat-sen had said would precede the transition to democracy. The government was to guarantee "freedom of person, religion, speech, publication and assembly" and would abolish "special service agencies," leaving law enforcement to duly constituted police and the courts. The principle of local government elections was also agreed to, although there was no agreement as to scope or timing.

It was harder to reach a satisfactory compromise over local militias and the Communist-controlled border-area governments. The Communists, who had already captured Kalgan, the main railway junction of the far north, were content to state that they would pull their troops out of southern China. Chiang, on the other hand, was determined to reassert his control over the entire country, and in November he launched a fierce attack on the Communists, sending many of his best troops north through the Shanhaiguan pass into Manchuria. He had not yet consolidated his hold over the south, and in his zeal for the appearance of unity he sacrificed the formation of a more genuine basis of power. As the fighting grew more bitter, Zhou Enlai, who had stayed on as mediator in Chongqing, flew back to Yan'an. And in a surprise move, Ambassador Hurley resigned in late November.

In his sharp letter of resignation to President Harry Truman, Hurley stated that American democratic ideals for China were being threatened by the twin forces of communism and imperialism. Moreover he added the serious charge against the American foreign-service officers in China that, out of sympathy for Yan'an, they had undermined U.S. attempts to prevent the collapse of the Nationalist regime, and had advised the CCP not to put its army under Nationalist command.

Apparently convinced that mediation was still possible, President Truman dispatched General George Marshall, the highly respected former head of the Joint Chiefs of Staff, as his envoy to China in December. The U.S. mandate for further involvement in China was unclear now that the anti-Japanese war was over, and the last of Chiang's thirty-nine divisions had received the training and materials promised by the United States in the war's closing years. Nor could the United States honestly claim that it was playing a neutral role, after helping Chiang to regain so many cities, advancing fresh credits to his government, and offering military equipment at bargain prices. Nevertheless Marshall got both parties to agree to a cease-

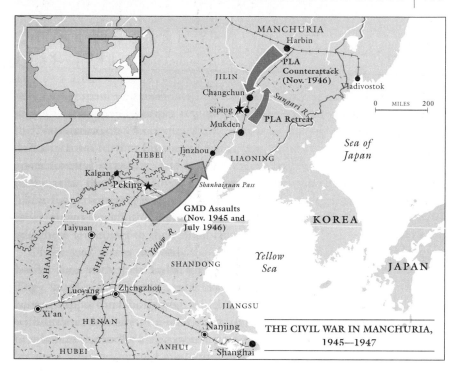

THE CIVIL WAR IN MANCHURIA,
1945—1947

fire beginning January 10, 1946, and persuaded Chiang Kai-shek to work toward convening the assembly he had discussed with Mao Zedong in the fall.

Accordingly thirty-eight delegates assembled in Nanjing for a "political consultative conference" on January 11. Among the thirty-eight were eight from the Guomindang, seven from the CCP, five from the newly formed Youth party (which was emerging as a powerful and vocal group clamoring for the peaceful reconstruction of China), and two from the Democratic League, which spoke for many of China's liberal intellectuals. The others were from various smaller political associations or were unaffiliated. In ten days of discussion that were widely reported in the press and that led to an upsurge of hope for the future, the delegates seemed to reach agreement on all the most important points concerning constitutional government, unified military command, and a national assembly. In late February a subcommittee named by the conference members announced detailed plans for troop reductions by both sides.

Unfortunately, these good intentions came to nothing—indeed perhaps had always been unrealistic. Military clashes between Communists and Nationalists continued in many parts of China, and the Central Executive

Committee of the Guomindang made crucial changes in the conference agreements. The committee limited the veto power of the Communists and the Democratic League in the projected State Council, reaffirmed presidential powers for Chiang Kai-shek rather than the genuine cabinet system called for in the new constitution, and reversed its stand on allowing more provincial autonomy. When the Communists and the Democratic League refused to cooperate further unless these changes were rescinded, the Guomindang went ahead without these groups and in late 1946 convened a national assembly and drafted a constitution, both without genuine democratic participation. The situation was reminiscent of Yuan Shikai's manipulation of the constitution and the assemblies in 1914 and 1915.

The whole point of democratic reconstruction had been undermined, and the random harassment and even assassination of leftists and liberals was resumed. The most prominent victim was Wen Yiduo, one of China's finest poets and a persistent critic of the Guomindang, who was gunned down in Kunming in the summer of 1946. Yet once again, in June 1946, George Marshall managed to get the two sides to proclaim a cease-fire, this time in Manchuria, and to push for reopening the war-damaged railway lines vital for China's economic health. (The CCP had cut some of the lines that were still intact after the war, because the Nationalists were using them for anti-Communist troop movements.) Even as the cease-fire was theoretically in effect, Nationalist troops were massing for a second assault on Manchuria, which commenced in July. The Communists, in the meantime, refused to give up their base areas in north China, reorganized their forces as the People's Liberation Army, and shifted the focus of land reform from rent reduction and redistribution to outright confiscation and violent punishment of class enemies.

One exception to the pattern of noncooperation between the Nationalists and the Communists was the mutual effort to rechannel the Yellow River into its northern bed, from which it had been blasted by Chiang Kai-shek's engineers in 1938. This work was directed by officials of the United Nations Relief and Rehabilitation Administration, who completed the huge task in 1947. But during this same period the verbal attacks by Chinese leftists against the United States for aiding the Guomindang and interfering in Chinese politics grew in intensity, and were accompanied by a mounting wave of demonstrations and riots. Several American servicemen were kidnaped by Communist forces, and in July 1946 a convoy of nine supply vehicles and its escort of forty marines were ambushed in Anping village as they journeyed from Tianjin to Peking.

The nature of this clash was indicative of the new levels of anti-American hostility, and in some ways echoed the Boxer attacks against Westerners making a similar journey nearly fifty years before. The motorized convoy of marines, slowed first by boulders placed in the road, next found their forward route blocked by some farm carts. Before they could retreat, a hail of fire wrecked the rear vehicles in the column, trapping all the rest. Communist troops, concealed by tall crops at the roadside, kept up fire much of the day. Three American marines were killed, one died later of wounds, and a dozen others were injured. An initial aerial reconnaissance showed fifteen or more Communists dead, and many more wounded. But when relief forces finally arrived, and the Americans advanced into the Communist positions, the Chinese troops had vanished, taking their wounded and even their dead with them. The nearby villagers, when questioned, claimed to have heard and seen nothing. Such incidents promised to make the American position untenable, especially since the U.S. government had no desire for wider involvement in another Asian war.

In sending his envoy to China, President Truman had stipulated that Marshall should be free to tell Chiang Kai-shek that "a China disunited and torn by civil strife could not be considered realistically as a proper place for American assistance"[2]—that is, U.S. aid would stop unless Chiang adhered to certain formal criteria for political reform. Tightening his stand in a letter of August 10, 1946, to Chiang Kai-shek, President Truman stated that "American faith in the peaceful and democratic aspirations of the Chinese people has not been destroyed by recent events, but has been shaken." If Chiang did not become more flexible, the president added, "it will be necessary for me to redefine and explain the position of the United States to the people of America." Chiang replied drily a few weeks later that "the desire for peace has to be mutual," and pointed to a variety of Communist cease-fire violations.[3]

Sporadic messages, polite enough and all urging reasonableness on the other side, flew back and forth among Zhou Enlai, Chiang Kai-shek, Marshall, and Truman for the rest of 1946. On October 10, 1946, Chiang used the thirty-fifth anniversary of the beginning of the 1911 revolution in Wuhan to present a major address. With sharp words he called on the CCP "to abandon its plot to achieve regional domination and disintegration of the country by military force." The CCP responded that the newly convened National Assembly was a "nation-splitting" fraud.[4]

One further incident helped aggravate tensions to a breaking point. On Christmas Eve 1946 a female Peking University student was raped by an American serviceman, while another U.S. serviceman held the young woman down. Shocking though the incident was in its own terms, it was rapidly raised by carefully orchestrated leftist propaganda into a major political and imperialist incident: by this interpretation, the young woman stood for China, and the American man's act was equivalent to imperialist invasion. The Guomindang attempts to present the case as simply a personal misfortune were shouted down by huge student demonstrations, and the once cheering crowds that had welcomed Americans as liberators in 1945 now became jeering mobs.[5]

If it had ever been possible for the United States genuinely to have helped ease the tensions in China, that time was clearly past, and the Chinese would now have to be left to fight out their own problems themselves. In a sad farewell statement issued in early January 1947, Marshall announced the failure of his mission. At the end of the month a terse ten-line press release from the State Department declared that the last American liaison groups trying to mediate between the Communists and the Guomindang had been disbanded.

LAND REFORM AND THE MANCHURIAN BASE

In the year following the Japanese surrender the Communists intensified their land-reform program in the areas where they were strong. At a conference of over 4,000 people interested in land reform, hosted by the Chinese Agricultural Association at Shanghai in 1946, a Communist representative spoke calmly and confidently about the CCP program. The Communists had moved on from the cautious united-front policies of rent reduction, he observed, and were working to abolish tenancy and return the land to the peasants who tilled it. The "redistributed" land, he claimed, was mainly land formerly owned by the Manchus during the Qing dynasty or by wartime "traitors," or was land unregistered by landlords to avoid taxation or wrongly seized from peasants because they had not been able to meet their loan payments. The Guomindang spokesman at the conference denied the need for drastic change, countering that conditions in the countryside were harmonious, and that rural education programs and improved agricultural technology would meet the needs of the time.

The CCP had been particularly active in northern Jiangsu, areas of Hebei, and Shandong, as well as in its original base area of Shaanxi. The Communists' success with land reform in these areas is remarkable considering the much lower incidence of tenancy in these provinces compared to most others. The tenancy rate was as low as 12 percent in both Hebei and Shandong, for instance, but as many as 56 percent of peasants were tenants in parts of the southwest. The Communist message was especially effective in the north in part because the devastation caused by Japan's "3-all" campaigns came on top of the flooding of the Yellow River and other natural disasters; moreover, the region's harsh winter climate exacerbated poverty, leading to even greater social misery. But there were also historical reasons for the Communist successes in these areas. The old social order, once bonded by lineage and religious associations, and by local leaders whose prosperity was linked to the community's welfare, had been steadily eroding. The reorganization of local administration first by the Guomindang and then by the Japanese had left rural communities institutionally weak, their social and economic lives fragile, their destinies often in the hands of new types of rural power brokers, whom villagers referred to simply as "local bullies."

The CCP moved fluidly into such fragmented communities. Realizing that their greatest allies were the poorer peasants and the landless farm laborers—whose plight had first been carefully analyzed in the 1930s by the Japanese and other scholarly investigators—the CCP, between 1946 and 1947, instigated a land program that, as their spokesman had promised, sought the elimination of tenancy and the equalization of both land and property within the villages.

Violence was an integral part of this process, as old scores were settled with village thugs and personal enemies as well as with landlords. Although figures vary wildly, one source gives a total of 19,307 "instances of struggle" within the CCP-dominated areas of Shandong alone in 1945, and many of these may have led to landlords' deaths. Accounts of village reform show how a whole community could be roused through mass meetings to attack its wealthier members, to kill the most hated, and then to redistribute all the confiscated property; often the seized food supplies were consumed in great celebrations by the poor, rather than sensibly hoarded to ward off the next bout of hardship. The head of the recently formed Peasant Association in a Shanxi village described the interrogation in January 1946 of a local landlord, Sheng Jinghe, against whom over a hundred charges of brutal treatment of villagers and tenants had been registered with local CCP cadres:

> When the final struggle began Jinghe was faced not only with those hundred accusations but with many many more. Old women who had never spoken in public before stood up to accuse him. Even Li Mao's wife—a woman so pitiable she hardly dared look anyone in the face—shook her fist before his nose and cried out, "Once I went to glean wheat on your land. But you cursed me and drove me away. Why did you curse and beat me? And why did you seize the wheat I had gleaned?" Altogether over 180 opinions were raised. Jinghe had no answer to any of them. He stood there with his head bowed. We asked him whether the accusations were false or true. He said they were all true. When the committee of our Association met to figure up what he owed, it came to 400 bags of milled grain, not coarse millet.

That evening all the people went to Jinghe's courtyard to help take over his property. It was very cold that night so we built bonfires and the flames shot up toward the stars. It was very beautiful.

Dissatisfied with the amount of grain that they found, the villagers beat Sheng Jinghe repeatedly and heated an iron bar in the fire to torture him with. Terrified, he at last confessed where his money was buried. The head of the Peasant Association concluded his account with these words:

> Altogether we got 500 yuan from Jinghe that night. By that time the sun was already rising in the eastern sky. We were all tired and hungry, especially the militiamen who had called the people to the meeting, kept guard on Jinghe's house, and taken an active part in beating Jinghe and digging for the money. So we decided to eat all the things that Jinghe had prepared to pass the New Year—a whole crock of dumplings stuffed with pork and peppers and other delicacies. He even had shrimp.
>
> All said, "In the past we never lived through a happy New Year because he always asked for his rent and interest then and cleaned our houses bare. This time we'll eat what we like," and everyone ate his fill and didn't even notice the cold.[6]

The land-reform programs in central and northeast China were subject, however, to a particularly grim corrective. Landlords who had been dispossessed and spared death—or the relatives of those who had been killed—could be expected to return in force, whenever possible, to seize back what their families had lost. The threat of such returns would always hang over the CCP as they worked in local communities. In the summer of 1946, for instance, the Guomindang massed 150,000 troops, many of whom now had excellent American or Japanese arms, equipment, and vehicles, to move on the 29 counties held by the Communists in Jiangsu province. All 29 were retaken by government forces. In the border area of Hebei/Shandong/Henan, where the Communists controlled 64 counties in 1946, 49 were recaptured by the Guomindang. Those who had sided with the Communists were held under what was euphemistically termed "voluntary surrender and repentance programs." They were jailed unless they could provide ransom money, and many were executed.

In such periods of restored power, landlords attended by armed guards went from house to house demanding the backlogs of overdue rent. In some cases returning government forces shot one member of every household that had participated in land reform; in others they buried alive the former peasant leaders and their relatives. Similar revenge was meted out on the peasants when in 1947 Guomindang troops—in a symbolic victory dear to

Chiang Kai-shek's heart—reconquered the Yan'an region, so long the base of the CCP's resistance. Although the violence intensified class rage and bitterness, it also made peasants resentful and deeply hostile to the Communist forces that had abandoned them to their fate.

Because of the danger of counterattack in central and northern China, Manchuria became all the more important to the future hopes of the CCP. Despite the ravages of war, Manchuria was an area rich in resources, with a population of over 45 million, large industrial cities, and extensive food reserves. Much of it forested and mountainous, the local topography also offered protection to guerrilla armies. Manchuria had a long history of social unrest, dating back to strikes that had been launched by Chinese—often in conjunction with the many Russian workers at Harbin or on the railways—as far back as 1906. In the earlier years of the Japanese occupation, a vigorous CCP organization there had pushed through land reform in more isolated areas, and carried out guerrilla activities against Japanese installations. Arrest records of Communists in Manchuria, kept by the Japanese authorities, show it to have been a young movement, with 29 percent of the members aged between twenty-one and twenty-five, and 29.5 percent aged between twenty-six and thirty. CCP members in Manchuria also represented a wide range of occupations and statuses: farmers, factory and railway workers, merchants, teachers and students, soldiers and policemen.

During the war with China, the Japanese—nominally working through the Manchukuo authorities—had become skillful at rounding up Communists in that region. Much of this success came through a ruthless policy of grouping more than 5 million peasants from isolated areas into some 10,000 "collective hamlets," where they lived under police supervision. Their original homes were then destroyed so they could give no shelter to the enemy. The terror had been intensified by the Japanese use of Communist prisoners—or those alleged to be Communists—in live human experiments conducted at secret camps in Manchukuo. The prisoners were infected with fatal strains of plague germs, subjected to vivisections, or used in "studies" on the effect of extremes of heat and cold on living test-subjects.

The scattered remnants of the region's Communist groups resurfaced in 1945, after Japan's defeat and the advance of Russian soldiers into Manchuria. These guerrilla forces were able to regroup with the arrival in late 1945 of the almost 100,000 Eighth Route Army troops who accompanied Lin Biao either overland from Yan'an through Suiyuan province, or by sea in junks from the north Shandong coast. The former guerrillas, by actively recruiting in the countryside, had meantime assembled a People's Self-Defense Army of around 150,000 men. Many of these troops were Koreans, fugitives from the Japanese occupiers of their homeland, who had stayed in

Manchuria after 1945 when their country was divided along the thirty-eighth parallel, the north now being in the Soviet camp and the south in the American. There were also about 25,000 troops from the Young Marshal's command who had been fighting in various regions of north China. They were led by the Young Marshal's younger brother, who had maintained their allegiance throughout the war.

As soon as Lin Biao's forces—many of whom were native to Manchuria—reached that area in the fall of 1945, they showed a determination to take and hold the key cities. In so doing they moved beyond the purely rural strategy that had been forced on them by the poverty of the Yan'an region and by their inability to hold any other large Chinese cities in the face of sustained attacks by either the Guomindang or the Japanese. As they arrived they found that the Soviet Union held the main industrial cities, the railways, and the mines, which it had occupied in August 1945. Soviet forces let stockpiles of Japanese weapons and equipment fall into Communist hands, and also hampered Chiang's efforts to move troops rapidly into the area. While in Manchuria, the Soviets seized rich stores of food and machinery for their own use and as reparations for their massive losses in the war against Germany. According to an American investigative team, they were especially thorough in removing power-generating equipment, transformers, electrical motors, laboratories and hospitals, and the latest and best machine tools. They also took U.S. $3 million in gold, and issued profuse runs of short-term bank notes. As a final gesture they stripped the generating plants and pumps from several of the largest Manchurian mines, causing severe damage in the shafts from flooding.

But Japanese investments in Manchuria in summer 1945 were estimated at 11 billion yen, and when the Soviet troops pulled out of Manchuria in 1946 much of this was seized by the Guomindang, including the huge Anshan steelworks, the Liaoyang cotton mills, the Fushun coal mines, and many hydroelectric stations. As in Shanghai and elsewhere, the arriving Guomindang officials were ruthless and wasteful in their takeover of industrial plants. Private profiteering was common, along with the renting out—for private gain—of public properties.

Chiang Kai-shek exacerbated these problems by assigning non-Manchurians to virtually all the key posts in the three provinces of Heilongjiang, Jilin, and Liaoning, which he subdivided into nine newly designated administrative districts in order to weaken local allegiances. In many of these, the new officials abused their powers and were content to sit snugly in their regional bases, allowing the Communists to roam almost at will through the rural counties. These Guomindang officials, unsure of the loyalties of other groups, tended to ally with former collaborators and landlords in the region. Also, the Manchurian economy was shaky because of Chiang Kai-shek's decision to issue a separate currency there in an effort to avoid the rapid inflation affecting *fabi*. But rocketing Guomindang military expenses and the payment of hundreds of sinecure salaries were eventually met only by bank-note issues of billions of yuan per month.

Local susceptibilities were irritated further by Chiang's decision to ship the Young Marshal Zhang Xueliang off to detention in the safer fastnesses of Taiwan, instead of releasing him from his decade of house arrest as many of his former troops had hoped. One newspaper correspondent commented from Mukden in late 1946, "As for the common people, they feel on the one hand that all under heaven belongs to the southerners and on the other that life today is not as good as it was in Manchukuo times."[7]

The Communists, still too weak to hold southern Manchurian cities against the numerically powerful and well-armed Guomindang forces, made their main urban base in Harbin, just north of the Sungari River. This industrial and commercial city of around 800,000 people became their revolutionary nerve center. The personnel to direct the expanding revolution were trained by veteran cadres in special institutes in the city, and all modern means of communication—newspapers, films, magazines, radio—spread the message of communism to the citizens. To ease the task of governing such a huge urban population, the CCP leaders divided the city into 6 districts, which were subdivided in turn into 58 street governments, each with a population of around 14,000 people. To cope with the large floating population in the city—laborers, hawkers, porters, droshky drivers—registration campaigns were conducted, bandits and destructive elements rounded up (the Russian secret police had already shipped back to the Soviet Union many fugitive White Russians), and 17,000 citizens organized into "night watchmen self-defense teams." When these organizations still could not control crime, each lane and alley was charged with forming its own patrols; as with the old *baojia* mutual-security system, any witness not reporting a crime would be treated as if he or she were the perpetrator of that crime. Travel was controlled by a rigidly supervised passport system.

In an emergency test of municipal governance, the CCP leaders in Harbin had to cope with an outbreak of bubonic plague in the city. The plague was spread by flea-infested rats that had been raised by Japanese military researchers conducting germ-warfare experiments. At war's end in August 1945 the Japanese had released the rats instead of destroying them; after an incubation period in 1946, the disease claimed over 30,000 lives in 1947. The casualties were not far higher because effective quarantine and inoculation measures were taken by the Communists, aided by health experts from the Soviet Union, and all road and rail traffic was strictly controlled to prevent those infected from spreading the plague farther afield.[8]

The party also exercised its municipal powers by mobilizing urban workers to help the People's Liberation Army carry goods, to drive carts, and to serve as stretcher bearers at the battle front. The urban economy was strictly monitored with graduated sales taxes, which were kept low for grain, fuel, and cooking oil, but levied at 40 percent for tobacco, and at 70 percent for luxuries and cosmetics. Businesses were also taxed, and all inhabitants of Harbin subjected to a barrage of campaigns calling for "voluntary contributions" to the Communist war effort. Using meetings, posters, banners, newspapers, and intimidation, the party raised at least 200 million yuan in Harbin in 1947. The Communists were now learning the full range of techniques and skills that they would need to govern China's major cities if they were to break out of Manchuria and join the guerrilla forces already scattered over the countryside of northern China. In a similar fashion in the 1620s and 1630s, Nurhaci and Hong Taiji had learned in Manchuria the skills of administration and politics needed to control the huge society of China lying to the south.

From its central Manchurian base in Harbin, the CCP sent teams of cadres into the countryside to draw the peasants to their cause with the promise of radical land reform. The Communists called for the confiscation of all land owned by the Japanese and by collaborators—a prodigious amount of land considering the nature and thoroughness of the Japanese occupation. There were so many huge estates in the area that the 12,000 land-reform cadres assigned to the work by Lin Biao rarely bothered with landlords holding less than 75 acres—a farm that would have seemed enormous in China south of the Wall. Manchurian landholding offered a number of special aspects befitting a "frontier society" that further taxed the ingenuity of land-reform leaders. One was the so-called "system of dependents," consisting of farm workers who were neither tenants nor day laborers, but people who lived with the landowner's family, ate with them, and worked the land in return for a percentage of the crop. Another was the "assignment system," by which a worker might be given his own land, tools, and house by the landlord, without being charged rent, in return for working a certain number of days per year for that same landlord without further compensation.

While urban and rural reform proceeded in the Communist-controlled areas, Lin Biao continued to build up the People's Liberation Army as a conventional—not a guerrilla—fighting force. The task was not easy. As a result of the Guomindang's assaults in 1945 and 1946, the Communists were pushed north across the Sungari River, while the Nationalists cleared a wide corridor along the coast north of Shanhaiguan, leading through Jinzhou to

Mukden and Changchun (see the map on page 463). Lin Biao however held onto Harbin, and astonished the Nationalist generals by crossing the frozen Sungari in November 1946 and attacking their armies in their winter quarters. Not allowing the Nationalist troops time to recover, Lin followed this up with a series of attacks across the river in early 1947, culminating in a massive attack on the railway junction of Siping in May with 400,000 troops. Beaten back with heavy losses by a concentration of Nationalist forces backed by air power, Lin was able to regroup and isolate the key Nationalist-held cities by destroying the railway lines that connected them. Morale among the garrison troops began to crack, and it became apparent how seriously Chiang had miscalculated in sending troops to Manchuria before consolidating his power in China proper. The Nationalist troops in the campaign abandoned huge amounts of arms and equipment, including whole depots and supply trains, which fell to the Communists. The Nationalists also showed a defensive attitude toward the war, digging in behind fixed emplacements rather than pursuing Lin Biao's forces.

The American consul general in Mukden cabled an excellent summary of the situation to the State Department at the end of May 1947. In condensed language the message drew together the many strands of the Guomindang predicament:

> There is good evidence that apathy, resentment, and defeatism are spreading fast in nationalist ranks causing surrenders and desertions. Main factors contributing to this are Communists ever mounting numerical superiority (resulting from greater use native recruits, aid from underground and Korean units), National soldiers discouragement over prospects getting reinforcements, better solidarity and fighting spirit of Communists, losses and exhaustion of Nationalists, their growing indignation over disparity between officers enrichment and soldiers' low pay, life, and their lack of interest in fighting far from home among 'alien' unfriendly populace (whereas Communists being largely natives are in position of fighting for native soil).[9]

Such observers were growing convinced that Chiang's attempt to hold onto Manchuria was doomed.

THE LOSING BATTLE WITH INFLATION

On the surface the most urgent aspect of the crisis facing the Guomindang was the steady loss of territory in the north to the Communists, and the attendant erosion of the morale of the Nationalist armies. But equally important was the growth of inflation in China, which wrecked all attempts of Chiang Kai-shek and his advisers at reinstituting viable central control.

The economic crisis confronting the Chinese government in the fall of 1945 had many sources, as we have seen: the muddle and graft involved in the return of Japanese and puppet businesses to their previous owners; wide-scale unemployment compounded by the cutting back of defense industries and the demobilization of many soldiers; the complexities of redeeming puppet-government currencies; speculation based on the regional variation of currency values; and the additional problem of the new currency intro-duced by Chiang in Manchuria. The common Guomindang response to money shortages was to print more bank notes, which merely contributed to the inflationary spiral. Taking September 1945 as the base line, the table below shows that wholesale prices in Shanghai had increased fivefold by February 1946, elevenfold by May, and thirtyfold by February 1947.

Anyone on a fixed income was disastrously affected by this precipitous price rise. Industrial workers protested with special vigor. Despite the Guomindang supervision of all labor-union activities during World War II, and the fact that the Guomindang-sponsored Chinese Labor Association was run by a Green Gang protégé of the Shanghai racketeer and Guo-mindang ally Du Yuesheng, soon after the war ended thousands of workers began to go out on strike. In 1946 there were 1,716 strikes and other labor disputes in Shanghai, all mounted in violation of the Guomindang laws requiring arbitration with official boards of mediators before work stop-pages began. The Communists had successfully infiltrated many unions, and although the information naturally was kept secret at the time, the CCP later revealed the pattern of influence that it had managed to develop in the closing year of the war and immediately afterward. Communist members were covertly installed in the Number 12 National Shanghai Textile Mill, the Shanghai Customs Collection Agency, the Dalong Machine Factory, the French Tram, Power, and Water Company, the Number 9 Cotton Mill, the Shanghai Power Company, and a number of Shanghai's large department stores. Similar patterns developed in other cities with industrial concentra-tions, such as Tianjin, Wuhan, and Canton.

The first significant strike of this postwar wave was at the Shanghai Power Company. The strike began in late January 1946 after several of the workers' representatives had been dismissed by the company. When fellow workers protested, they were locked out of the plant, but managed to pre-vent others from going in to keep the power station running. With power cut off, the negotiations had to be conducted by candlelight. Forty local unions joined in an initial protest demonstration in early February, which was followed by a show of solidarity involving representatives from seventy

The Course of *Fabi*
Depreciation, September 1945–
February 1947[10]
(September 1945=100)

Month	Shanghai wholesale price index
1945	
September	100
October	110
November	288
December	257
1946	269
January	
February	509
March	742
April	748
May	1,103
June	1,070
July	1,180
August	1,242
September	1,475
October	1,554
November	1,541
December	1,656
1947	1,990
January	
February	3,090

enterprises and businesses. The power company eventually yielded.

The government responded to this and other incidents with a softer line than its past record might have suggested, in what was clearly an attempt to buy off the workers. Despite the severe inflation, the government guaranteed to industrial workers wage rates primed to 1936 pay scales, multiplied by the current cost-of-living index. At the same time, the Guomindang tried to strengthen its hold over the labor movement by disbanding certain unions and re-forming them in more fragmented units that would be easier to supervise and manipulate. Unemployment continued to climb in late 1946, reaching around 8 percent of the population in Shanghai, 20 percent in Canton, and 30 percent in the capital of Nanjing.

The pegging of workers' wages to the spiraling price index failed to placate labor and displeased employers, who felt that China was now having to pay too much for its labor and thus was losing a competitive edge over other industrial countries. In February 1947 the government tried another tactic—imposition of price and wage ceilings. Wages were to be frozen on the basis of the January 1947 cost-of-living index, and in all large cities price controls were set on rice and flour, cotton yarn and cloth, fuel, salt, sugar, and edible oil. A meticulous system—at least on paper—stipulated exact amounts of each of these basic commodities that would be made available to each worker, along with an allowance of coal briquettes for cooking and heating. The controls had some positive effect during March 1947, thanks to vigorous police supervision; but inefficiencies in distribution, the spread of hoarding, and the drop in production of certain items (the response by producers to what they considered artificially low prices) soon brought a return of the old inflationary spiral. By April 1947 rice prices were almost double February's level, and edible oils were up two and one-half times. By May, in the face of mounting protests and evidence of failure, the freeze mechanisms were abandoned.

In the summer of 1947, as Chiang's Manchurian campaign was beginning

SHANGHAI WHOLESALE-PRICE AND COST-OF-LIVING INDEXES, 1947–1948[11]
(May 1947=100)

Year	Wholesale-price index	Cost-of-living index
1947		
June	112	107
July	130	122
August	141	131
September	179	146
October	282	208
November	319	226
December	389	290
1948	544	405
January		
February	780	642
March	1,260	923
April	1,460	1,100
May	2,100	1,432
June	7,650	3,022
July	11,100	5,863

to falter disastrously and General Wedemeyer returned to China, at President Truman's request, to evaluate the country's politics and economy, the Guomindang again acknowledged the financial crisis. This time, in July, they attempted to work through the Central Bank of China to offer a program for controlled distribution of food and fuel at artificially lowered prices. The beneficiaries of this plan were to be government employees, schoolteachers and students, factory workers, and those in certain cultural fields. This ambitious program, mainly confined to major cities, did not halt inflation; it did, however, force the cost-of-living index in Shanghai below the wholesale price index, suggesting partial success in helping people to survive. Allocations of raw materials for factories, along with coal and imported oil, were rationed among private firms and the public utilities, again with some effect. But the overall price rise continued at an alarming rate through the end of 1947 and into 1948. In the spring of 1948 the government began issuing ration cards for staple foods to citizens of the large towns, but this measure also failed to stop the price rises, although it did win the government some popularity for a brief time.

The indexed figures were dramatic enough, but what the inflation meant for the actual use of cash was becoming catastrophic. Even with notes issued in enormous denominations, and shopkeepers hurrying to change their price cards several times a day, there was little hope of coping with ordinary cash transactions. A standard large sack of rice (weighing 171 pounds in Western equivalents) sold for 6.7 million yuan in early June 1948 and 63 million yuan in August. In the same period, a 49-pound bag of flour went from 1.95 million yuan to 21.8 million yuan, and a 22-gallon drum of edible cooking oil rose from 18.5 million yuan to 190 million yuan. (The summer 1937 prices for the same volumes of these three commodities had stood at 12, 42, and 22 yuan respectively.)

In July 1948 Chiang Kai-shek met with T. V. Soong and his other senior advisers to discuss a bold plan to stem the chaotic financial slide. The decision was made to switch to a new currency, abandoning the old *fabi* yuan and inaugurating a gold yuan, at a conversion rate of 3 million *fabi* yuan to 1 new yuan. Several Guomindang advisers warned that the new currency probably could not hold firm unless the government drastically reduced its deficit spending, much of it the result of the huge military expenses to which Chiang was still committed. (The deficit in 1948 was 66 percent of total expenditures.) And many of them felt that the new measures would succeed only if the U.S. government agreed to extend a huge currency-stabilization loan to China—which in fact the United States refused to do.

Chiang Kai-shek used his emergency powers as president of the republic to declare a series of Financial and Economic Emergency Measures on

August 19, 1948. These measures, recognized by Guomindang ministers to be almost certainly the last chance to check the government's collapse, called for dramatic reforms. After a brief bank closure to prevent panic, all the old *fabi* notes were to be turned in to the banks and exchanged at a fixed rate of 3 million *fabi* to 1 gold yuan. To inspire confidence in the new notes, the government undertook not to print more than 2 billion of them. Wage and price increases were forbidden, along with strikes and demonstrations. And any gold and silver bullion, along with any foreign currency, held privately by Chinese citizens were to be turned in to the banks in exchange for the new currency, thus boosting the government's reserves of specie and foreign exchange. Sales taxes on commodities were sharply increased in order to raise more revenue. Yet, in what many considered a sellout to the wealthy, those Chinese with large bank accounts outside China—in such countries as Hong Kong, the United States, or Switzerland—were not required to exchange those funds for gold-yuan notes. Bank deposits overseas of over U.S. $3,000 were to be reported to the government, but there was no mechanism for assuring that this would be done.

The one place where the emergency laws seemed to have even a faint chance of succeeding was Shanghai. Here Chiang Kai-shek's son by his first marriage, the Soviet-educated Chiang Ching-kuo—who had returned to China from the Soviet Union in 1937 and worked several years as an administrator in Jiangxi—was appointed commissioner in charge of the reforms. He moved to the task with an immense amount of energy and sincerity, backed by tough implementation measures, a combination he had previously displayed in his attempts to modernize Jiangxi province. In Shanghai, Chiang mobilized criticism against hoarders and speculators, ordered the arrest and occasional execution of delinquents, and raided warehouses and suspects' homes, all to urge public compliance with the reforms. Chiang Ching-kuo himself employed local youth organizations along with the paramilitary forces of the newly established anti-Communist Bandit Suppression National Reconstruction Corps to help him in his task. "Secret-report boxes" were placed in the streets so that citizens could report speculators or anyone who defied the bans by raising prices in their shops. Loudspeaker trucks cruised the streets, reminding people of the new laws. Maximum publicity was given to important arrests. One of them was the Green Gang leader Du Yuesheng's own son, charged with black-market stock-exchange trading; other big financiers were jailed for foreign-exchange manipulation.

In some ways this assault on the Shanghai financial community echoed the tough measures that Chiang Kai-shek had taken in the summer of 1927 after smashing the city's union organizations. And as his father had, Chiang

Ching-kuo clearly saw the corrupting influence of foreign goods and manners. As he wrote of the wealthy Shanghai bourgeoisie in his diary at the height of his campaign:

> Their wealth and their foreign-style homes are built on the skeletons of the people. How is their conduct any different from that of armed robbers? Automobiles, refrigerators, perfumes, and nylon hosiery imported from abroad are like cells that thrive parasitically on this impoverished nation, or like opium that destroys the national economy, because using foreign currency to obtain high-class luxuries is a suicidal policy for the nation.[12]

But despite this moralistic dedication, and the strenuous attempts at enforcement, the gold-yuan plan failed. Shanghai was, in any case, not isolated from the rest of China, and the more successful Chiang Ching-kuo was, the greater the pressure on Shanghai businesses to sell their goods elsewhere, where prices were continuing to rise. It also made no sense for farmers to sell their produce in Shanghai at low prices when they could get much more elsewhere. Accordingly the city began to experience a desperate shortage of both food and manufactured goods. Nor did the government hold firm to its plan. When it imposed heavy new taxes on sales of certain consumer goods such as tobacco, shopkeepers simply closed their doors until they won permission to raise their prices by the same amount as the new taxes. News also spread rapidly that the note-printing program was accelerating, and promised soon to exceed the ceiling of 2 billion gold yuan pledged by the government. By October 1948, with shops emptied of goods,

SHANGHAI WHOLESALE-PRICE AND COST-OF-LIVING
INDEXES, 1948–1949[13]
(August 1948=100)

Year	Shanghai wholesale-price index	Shanghai cost-of-living index
1948		
September	106	N.A.
October	118	N.A.
November	1,365	1,170
December	1,921	1,670
1949		
January	6,900	6,825
February	40,825	52,113

restaurants closing, and medical supplies unobtainable, the failure of the reforms was clear.

For a moment in September and October, Shanghai had held firm, allowing hope that the economy could be turned around. What followed next is most simply shown by the figures themselves in the table above. The vaunted gold yuan began to follow in the steps of the old *fabi* currency. The Chinese republic had become, for all practical purposes, a barter economy.

DEFEAT OF THE GUOMINDANG ARMIES

It was in this context of a final loss of confidence in the economy and the political policies of the Guomindang that the Communists forged their conclusive military victory. In the spring of 1947 the Nationalists had managed to keep open four strategic corridors in north China: one running north of Peking through the Shanhaiguan pass to Mukden and Changchun in Manchuria; one southwest from Peking to Yan Xishan's armies in Taiyuan; one northwest from Peking along the Kalgan railway to Baotou; and one within Shandong linking Jinan to the port of Qingdao. They also held the key railway linking Xuzhou to Kaifeng, Luoyang, and Xi'an.

But the Communists now controlled most of the north China countryside. Peasant guerrillas constantly disrupted Chiang's supply lines, making relief of his beleaguered forces slow and dangerous. By May 1948 the situation of Chiang's armies was becoming hopeless. Both Mukden and Changchun were surrounded by Communist troops and could be supplied only by Nationalist air-force planes. There were 200,000 well-trained Nationalist troops in Mukden supported by artillery and tanks, but their slow strangulation was assured if the airfields fell. Yet Chiang Kai-shek consistently refused the proposals of the American military advisers still with him that he pull those troops back south of the Great Wall to invigorate his defenses in north China; he had invested too much of his waning prestige in the Manchurian campaign to back down now. The city of Luoyang, after changing hands three times in seesaw fighting, fell irrevocably to Communist forces in April 1948, severing Xi'an from the east. Major Communist victories in Shandong cut the Jinan-to-Qingdao corridor. This isolated the 100,000 Nationalist defenders in Jinan from supplies brought by sea into Qingdao, which was still being garrisoned by an American naval task force, backed by 3,000 marines and 50 planes. The Communists, under Peng Dehuai, also recaptured Yan'an in March, and that spring Peng made a bold thrust south toward Sichuan, although he was beaten back after heavy fighting.

Given added confidence by these remarkable victories, and by the quantities of vehicles, arms, and ammunition that had fallen into his troops' hands, Mao Zedong announced in 1948 that the Communist armies were going to shift from a strategy of predominantly guerrilla warfare to one of conventional battles in open country, employing massed armies of troops. The Communists had already conducted such campaigns in Manchuria, but now they were directed at Kaifeng, the city on the Yellow River that guarded the key railway junction of Zhengzhou, leading to Wuhan and to Xi'an. The Nationalists guarding the area numbered 250,000 regular troops, supported by 50,000 men in the Peace Preservation Corps. Against them the Communists threw 200,000 veteran troops in five groups. The Communists managed to seize and hold Kaifeng for a week in late June, but pulled back when Nationalist reinforcements counterattacked, aided by air strikes. The apparent Nationalist victory was hollow, however; they had suffered 90,000

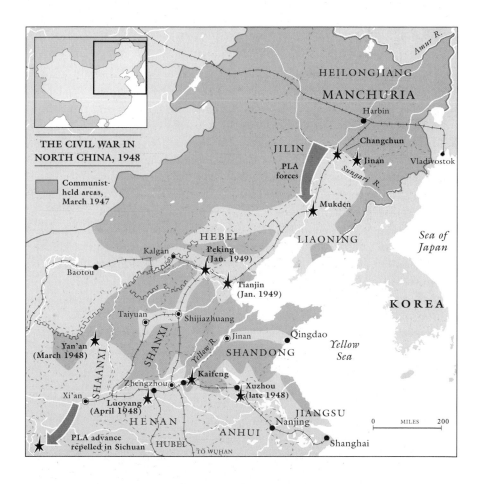

casualties, while the Communist troops won a propaganda victory by maintaining strict discipline and meticulously refusing to harm the civilian population. The Communist retreat therefore brought little lasting comfort to the Guomindang, whose senior military officers made a survey of relative troop strengths and came to the conclusion that the Communists were making relentless gains, as the table below shows.

This bleak assessment came at a troubled political moment. Chiang Kai-shek had been overwhelmingly re-elected president in spring 1948 by the new National Assembly—the one declared invalid as a representative body by both the CCP and the Democratic League—and had been given wide-ranging powers to by-pass the fledgling 1947 constitution in order to "take emergency measures to avert imminent danger to the security of the state."[14] But his power was eroding, and his waning popularity suffered further damage in July 1948 with the senseless killing of unarmed students by government forces.

This tragedy had its roots in the constant fighting that was filling northern Chinese cities with refugees, of whom the most vocal were students, displaced from their schools and campuses by Communist victories, and reassigned by the Guomindang into specified new locations. Given only a small subsistence allowance and then allowed to roam at will, such students became virtual beggars, sleeping out in parks or temples and sometimes turning to petty crime. Five thousand Manchurian students, flown south to Peking in a publicity-conscious gesture by the government, had been reduced to such a pass by July 1948 that they formed an angry demonstration and marched on the residence of the Peking Municipal Council's president. Instead of listening to their grievances, the authorities blocked their path with armored cars and fired at the demonstrators with machine guns. Fourteen students were killed and over 100 wounded, inevitably reminding people of the May Thirtieth demonstrations against the British in 1925, the warlord killings of Peking students in 1926, or the protests of the December Ninthers in 1935. By September 1948 the number of volatile student refugees had grown even higher; in Peking alone there were 20,000 to 30,000, with another 20,000 in Nanjing and 10,000 in Wuhan.

Shortly after this Peking massacre and the failure of the gold-yuan currency reforms, the heavily garrisoned city of Jinan fell, undermined from within by Communist subversion and troop desertions; thus Chiang lost his last main base in Shandong province. A series of tactically brilliant campaigns conducted by Lin Biao in Manchuria during September and October led to the fall of Mukden and Changchun, and the destruction, surrender, or desertion of 400,000 of Chiang's finest troops. Only 20,000 Nationalist

SHIFTS IN GUOMINDANG AND CCP TROOP STRENGTH, 1945–1948[15]

	August 1945	June 1948
Guomindang		
Well-armed troops	1,620,000	980,000
Poorly armed troops	2,080,000	1,200,000
Artillery pieces	6,000	21,000
CCP		
Well-armed troops	166,000*	970,000
Poorly armed troops	154,000	590,000
Artillery pieces	600	22,800

*This estimate is extremely low, given what we know of CCP power in Yan'an at the war's end.

troops escaped, evacuated by sea from south Manchuria.

Noting that the loss of Manchuria was "discouraging," but "relieves the government of a formidable burden, so far as military defenses are concerned," Chiang tried to regroup for a stand in north or central China. Zhu De, commander in chief of all the Communist armies, decided to commit 600,000 troops to the seizure of the railway junction of Xuzhou, opposing an equal number of Nationalist troops, who also had complete air superiority. In a sixty-five-day battle toward the end of 1948, the Communists showed a new mastery of massed artillery power and emerged victorious by completely outmaneuvering Chiang's generals. The Nationalist commanders were plagued by the contradictory and impractical orders personally issued by Chiang Kai-shek, and by the massive desertion of their troops. In this complex and protracted campaign, the extraordinary Communist effort at mobilizing upward of 2 million peasants in four provinces to provide logistical support was directed by Deng Xiaoping, once the youngest of the work-study students in France, now a veteran party organizer of forty-five.

In a third campaign, overlapping with these two, Lin Biao invested and captured Tianjin for the Communists in January 1949. Turning back west with the bulk of his forces and holding an overwhelming tactical advantage, he persuaded the Nationalist general commanding Peking to surrender. Communist troops entered the old imperial capital on January 31. North China was irrevocably lost to Chiang Kai-shek, who had resigned as president ten days earlier. Yet Chiang insisted on maintaining his position as head of the Guomindang political party, a separation of roles that would prove confusing and harmful to further resistance efforts.

The conquest of so many large cities in north China confronted the CCP with new administrative and economic problems. Mao Zedong acknowledged this in a report to the Central Committee delivered on March 5, 1949:

> From 1927 to the present the center of gravity of our work has been in the villages—gathering strength in the villages, using the villages in order to surround the cities, and then taking the cities. The period for this method of work has now ended. The period of the city leading the village has now begun. The center of gravity of the party's work has shifted from the village to the city. In the south the People's Liberation Army will occupy first the cities and then the villages.[16]

In practical terms this meant that the CCP must use its Harbin experience to the full and do everything possible to avoid the most serious administrative and financial mistakes that had been committed by the Guomindang in their return to east China in late 1945. The CCP insisted that the People's Liberation Army maintain strict discipline in the cities it occupied, that ordinary Chinese businesses not be disrupted, and that urban property not be redistributed to benefit the poor. Factories were patrolled and machinery guarded to prevent looting. A new "people's currency"—the *renminbi*— was introduced, with only a short term allowed in which to exchange gold yuan notes for the new ones. Thereafter trading in gold, silver, and foreign currency was to be explicitly forbidden.

CCP officials relocated Guomindang officers and soldiers to their homes, or incorporated them into the People's Liberation Army following a period of political education. The labor organizations were prevented from disruptive strikes by a web of mediation rules, and urged to accept "reasonable exploitation" by capitalists in the transition period. Refugees were fed and sent home whenever possible. Schools and colleges were kept open. Stockpiles of food and oil were kept in government deposits in order to stabilize prices during periods of shortage. City dwellers were encouraged to save through development of "commodity savings deposit units," cleverly designed to be safe from inflation. Depositors were promised that their savings would be computed in terms of the prevailing food and fuel costs, and at the time of withdrawal would be adjusted to yield the same amount of food and fuel, plus all accrued interest. Not all these measures succeeded at once, but the sincerity of the attempts was praised by both foreign and Chinese observers, regardless of their political sympathies.

Chiang Kai-shek, meanwhile, had roughly the same range of options that had faced the southern Ming court once the Manchus had seized Peking and the north China plain three hundred and five years before. He could

Children   Xiao Fang (1912–1937?) was a young photojournalist covering the outbreak of the Sino-Japanese War when he disappeared in July 1937. His photographs of China in the 1930s have recently been discovered.

*Teen-age coal miner (top); An announcement from
Generalissimo Chiang Kai-shek (bottom) (photographs by Xiao Fang)*

Female workers (top); students heading for an anti-Japanese demonstration, Peking (bottom) (photographs by Xiao Fang)

Communist cadres distributing food in their border region of Shaan / Gan / Ning (photograph by Wu Yinxian)

Armed only with red-tasseled spears, these young volunteers joined the Eighth Route Army, which became the Red Army, 1939 (photograph by Wu Yinxian)

Mao Zedong exhorting peasants to emulate "labor heroes," during a mass campaign in Shaan / Gan / Ning, 1943 (photograph by Wu Yinxian)

Crowds in Chongqing celebrating victory over Japan, August 1945

PLA forces attack Shenyang in Manchuria, 1948

Shanghai citizens desperately trying to reach a bank to change their depreciating currency, December 1948 (photograph by Henri Cartier-Bresson)

With the Guomindang regime in flight, refugees prepare to leave Nanjing, April 1949 (photograph by Henri Cartier-Bresson)

Exhausted troops of the People's Liberation Army, rice rations slung over their shoulders, entering Nanjing, 1949 (photograph by Henri Cartier-Bresson)

Mao Zedong declaring the founding of the People's Republic of China, Peking, October 1, 1949

The crowd greeting Mao's announcement

Chinese troops crossing the frozen Yalu River into North Korea, late 1950

The People's Liberation Army entering Lhasa, Tibet, 1951   The Tibetans protested the invasion, challenging the Chinese claim to be liberating the country: "Liberation from whom and what?"

Zhou Enlai at the Geneva Conference in 1954 ending France's war in Vietnam

Deng Xiaoping (left) and Liu Shaoqi, 1958   Deng, secretary general of the CCP, and Liu, at the time Mao's probable successor, lent their support to Mao's vision of heightened production by mass mobilization that underlay the Great Leap Forward.

Ding Ling   More than 30,000 intellecutals were branded "rightists" in the campaigns of 1957, and many were imprisoned or sent to labor camps. Ding Ling, the distinguished writer and early party member, was banished to a border farm in Heilongjiang.

A rally denouncing the Minister of Communications, Zhang Bojun, during the antirightist campaign, July 1957

Backyard steel furnaces during the Great Leap Forward, 1958 (photograph by Henri Cartier-Bresson)

try to consolidate a regime in central or southern China, perhaps in Nanjing, relying on the Yangzi River as a natural barrier; he could try to consolidate in the southwest, or establish a coastal base in the Xiamen region of Fujian or in Canton; or he could use Taiwan as a base, as Koxinga had done.

Despite Chiang's initial insistence that he would hold the Nanjing and Shanghai region to the bitter end, the Yangzi line was going to be hard to maintain against the imposing buildup of Communist troops on the north bank. The southwest might have offered Chiang a base for resistance had the commanding general there—who had succeeded to the dominant role held during World War II by the warlord Long Yun—shown any interest in cooperating. But Chiang was rebuffed, despite a personal visit to Kunming. The southeastern coastal areas were not solid bases of support for the Guomindang, nor were they easily defensible. Accordingly it was on Taiwan that Chiang concentrated as a final stronghold for his party.

The island of Taiwan, which had prospered economically as a colony under Japanese rule since 1895, was reclaimed by the Nationalist government late in 1945. In reasserting central government power, Guomindang officials behaved in a "carpetbagging" style similar to that followed in Shanghai and Manchuria. Often inefficient or corrupt, they failed to build up public support and managed to erode many of the more satisfactory aspects of Japanese economic development. The former Zhejiang militarist and governor of Fujian, Chen Yi, who was appointed chief administrator of Taiwan province by Chiang, roused strong local opposition because of his underlings' behavior. When Taiwanese anger broke out into antigovernment riots in February 1947, Nationalist troops fired into the crowd, killing many demonstrators. Over the following weeks, in a series of ruthless actions that recall Chiang Kai-shek's Shanghai tactics of 1927, Chen Yi attempted to break the spirit of the Taiwanese by ordering the arrest and execution of thousands of Taiwan's prominent intellectuals and citizen leaders.

With the Taiwanese opposition broken, Chiang recalled Chen Yi and replaced him with more moderate administrators, who slowly built up the island as a viable base for future mass Chinese occupation. In the months before the fall of Peking, furthermore, thousands of crates of Qing-dynasty archives were shipped to Taiwan along with the finest pieces of art from the former imperial-palace collections, in a clever propagandistic move to make the Nationalists seem like the preservers of the Chinese national heritage. A force of 300,000 troops loyal to Chiang was based on the island by early 1949, backed by 26 gunboats and some planes. The scene was set for Chiang's retreat to Taiwan, should he choose the option.

The spring of 1949 marked a waiting period in China, while the Communists regrouped, rested their troops north of the Yangzi, and formed a provisional people's government for north China. After his resignation in January 1949, Chiang had been succeeded as president by the Guangxi militarist Li Zongren. From his base in Nanjing, Li tried in vain to persuade Mao Zedong to compromise on the Communists' basic eight-point program for Guomindang surrender.

Mao's eight points were stark: (1) punish all war criminals; (2) abolish the invalid 1947 constitution; (3) abolish the Guomindang's legal system; (4) reorganize the Nationalist armies; (5) confiscate all bureaucratic capital; (6) reform the land-tenure system; (7) abolish all treasonous treaties; (8) convene a full Political Consultative Conference to form a democratic coalition government.

As Li Zongren was considering these terms, the Communist troops gave dramatic notice that they would not tolerate any involvement in the fighting by foreign imperialist interests. In making their point they echoed the actions of the Japanese, who in November 1937 had bombed, machine-gunned, and sunk the U.S. gunboat *Panay* when it was seeking to evacuate embassy personnel from the threatened city of Nanjing. This time it was the British who were put on notice, when in April 1949 they tried to move their armed frigate *Amethyst* up to Nanjing to take supplies to the embassy and evacuate British civilians if deemed necessary. As the *Amethyst* sailed up the Yangzi, it came under heavy fire from Communist batteries on the north bank and ran aground, with 17 dead and 20 wounded. The British navy ships sent to the rescue were beaten back. It was an extraordinary gesture of anti-imperialist activism that the British were powerless to counter, although they did eventually manage to rescue the ship itself.

Weary of further negotiations, the Communists in April 1949 gave President Li an ultimatum to accept their eight points of surrender within five days. When he refused, they recommenced their campaign. Nanjing fell without a fight on April 23, and Hangzhou and Wuhan shortly thereafter. Shanghai fell in late May after only token resistance. In the following months the Communist armies moved to consolidate their hold with a speed for which there had been no parallel since the victories of the Manchus and their Chinese collaborators in 1645–1646. Peng Dehuai's forces drove west, seized Xi'an, and, after being temporarily checked by the tough attacks of a Muslim general from Gansu, claimed Lanzhou for the Communists in August 1949. Lin Biao's troops took Changsha the same month, and marched rapidly south to Canton as Peng's armies in the northwest drove into Xinjiang. In September the Nationalist armies in Xinjiang surrendered, along with those in Suiyuan and Ningxia. Lin Biao's troops, who had faced considerable opposition in the southeast, took Canton in mid-October, as

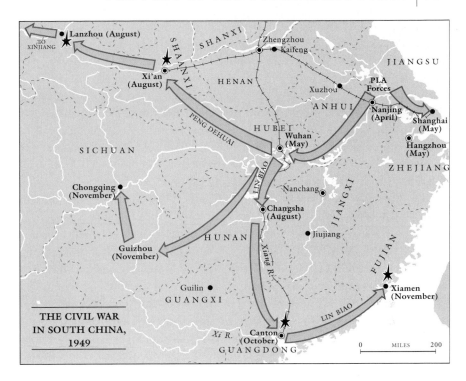

Lanzhou (August)

TO XINJIANG

SHANXI

SHAANXI

Zhengzhou
Kaifeng

JIANGSU

Xi'an
(August)

HENAN

Xuzhou

PLA
Forces

Nanjing
(April)

Shanghai
(May)

ANHUI

PENG DEHUAI

HUBEI
Wuhan
(May)

Hangzhou
(May)

SICHUAN

ZHEJIANG

LIN BIAO

Nanchang

JIANGXI

Chongqing
(November)

Changsha
(August)

Guizhou
(November)

HUNAN

Jiujiang

Xiang R.

FUJIAN

Guilin
GUANGXI

Xiamen
(November)

LIN BIAO

THE CIVIL WAR
IN SOUTH CHINA,
1949

LIN BIAO

Xi R.

Canton
(October)

GUANGDONG

0   MILES   200

well as Xiamen—which was stoutly defended as the last gateway for those retreating to Taiwan. Other Communist forces turned southwest, taking over Guizhou province in mid-November, and entering and seizing Chiang Kai-shek's wartime base of Chongqing at the end of the month.

Anticipating these final victories, Mao Zedong assembled a new Political Consultative Conference in Peking in late September. Appearing to be true to the announced principles of a "democratic coalition government," the body was dominated by the CCP but also consisted of representatives from fourteen other political parties, most of them small. They elected the members of the central government (Mao, predictably, became chairman and Zhu De senior vice-chairman); designated Peking as China's capital again, in place of Nanjing; chose the five-pointed gold star with its four subsidiary stars on a red ground as the national flag;* and ordered that each year now be designated in accordance with the Western Gregorian calendar.† At a

*The large star represented the CCP, and the four smaller stars the four classes that would constitute the new regime: the national and the petty bourgeoisie, the workers, and the peasants.

†The Guomindang had counted days and months according to the Western calendar, but had dated years by their distance from the 1911 revolution—e.g., 1948 had been termed "thirty-seventh year of the republic."

ceremony on October 1, 1949, from a reviewing stand atop the Gate of Heavenly Peace—once the main entrance to the Ming and Qing imperial palace—Mao Zedong formally announced the founding of the People's Republic of China.

The symbolism was appropriate, even though the violent acts of heroic self-sacrifice that had accompanied the fall of the Ming were absent. True, there had been many tough battles, and some members of Chiang's staff, as well as others deeply loyal to him, committed suicide. But there were few echoes of those seventeenth-century confrontations in which Confucian scholars had brought whole cities flaming down around their heads as they died to prove the rightness of their moral stance. Only in the Shanxi domain of the long-lived warlord Yan Xishan did a bizarre act of supreme sacrifice take place. Here it was not Guomindang regulars but a devoted leader of Yan's Patriotic Sacrifice League, Liang Huazhi, who took action. Liang, like Yan's other officers who had fought year after year against the Communists in Shanxi, was finally trapped in massively fortified Taiyuan city. The fighting was savage, and given an extra edge by the presence of thousands of Japanese troops who had stayed on at Yan's request, spear-heading the resistance. (Yan himself had abandoned his followers, after vowing to give his life in the fighting.) As the Communist troops finally broke into the city in April 1949, Liang Huazhi set fire to an entire jail full of Communist prisoners, and then committed suicide as the flames rose into the air.

But such acts were rare, and the country as a whole was watchful and nervous rather than in a mood for sacrifice. This had been a long, bloody, complex, and baffling civil war, full of heroism and cruelty, of dramatic social ideals and hideous abuses. We can catch some of the atmosphere of the time through the work of one of the West's great photographers, Henri Cartier-Bresson, who was in China in late 1949. His black-and-white images caught much of the doubt that flowed through Chinese hearts. The beggarwomen in the streets, the hungry children, the bent-backed coolies, the tired People's Liberation Army troops with their white bandoleers of rice rations slung around their shoulders, the equally tired Guomindang officers guarding their piled baggage on the docks, the mobs of peasant refugees, the citizens jammed together trying to reach a bank to change their constantly depreciating paper money, the students hurriedly erecting signboards to welcome their new conquerors—all of these Chinese had become parts of the revolution, and would now have to think their way into the new and uncertain future.

CHAPTER 19

The Birth of the People's Republic

COUNTRYSIDE AND TOWN, 1949–1950

In an essay he wrote in mid-1949 entitled "On the People's Democratic Dictatorship," Mao Zedong succinctly spelled out the ideas that would permeate the governmental policies of the new Chinese state. The experience of the revolution to date could be analyzed into two basic categories, wrote Mao. The first was the arousing of the nation's masses to build a "domestic united front under the leadership of the working class." This united front included the peasantry, the urban petty bourgeoisie, and the national bourgeoisie, as well as the working class, and would form the basis of a "people's democratic dictatorship" that the working class would lead. The second category embraced the international aspects of the revolution, including China's alliance with the Soviet Union, the countries in the Soviet bloc, and the world proletariat. This dimension of the revolution had taught the Chinese that they had to "lean to one side" or the other in their allegiances—either to socialism or to imperialism. The triumphs of the revolution had been attained under the leadership of the CCP, which, said Mao, "is no longer a child or a lad in his teens but has become an adult."[1]

Mao then elaborated on some of his main intentions. The new government would establish relations with any country willing to respect China's international equality and territorial integrity. China did not believe it could prosper without any international help. And China, in enforcing the people's democratic dictatorship, would "deprive the reactionaries of the right to speak and let the people alone have the right." In jocular style, Mao imagined critics protesting that he was being "dictatorial," to which he would reply, "My dear sirs, you are right, that is just what we are." He would be dictatorial to the "running dogs of imperialism," as well as to "the landlord class and bureaucrat-bourgeoisie" and to "the Guomindang reactionaries and their accomplices." But the rest of the people would enjoy the full range of freedoms, while China developed its potential through the twin policies of socialization of agriculture and "a powerful industry having state enterprise as its backbone."[2]

The constitutional structure that would make these changes possible was laid out in the Common Program for China announced by a group of delegates convened in September 1949 by Mao Zedong as the People's Political Consultative Conference. As in the ill-fated body of a similar name assembled in 1946, the delegates were drawn from a broad spectrum of political interests and parties. Chiang Kai-shek's former party, however, was now castigated as the "feudal, compradore, fascist, dictatorial Guomindang," with whose old programs the new ones were contrasted. In line with Mao's statement, Article 5 of the Common Program guaranteed to all, except for "political reactionaries," the rights of freedom of "thought, speech, publication, assembly, association, correspondence, person, domicile, moving from one place to another, religious belief, and the freedom to hold processions and demonstrations." It promised equal rights to women, and the end of their lives of "bondage." The program then outlined an ambitious plan for rural reform through rent reduction and land redistribution, and for the development of heavy industry. Here the framers clearly had the Soviet Union in mind as a model. They urged that work be "centered on the planned, systematic rehabilitation and development of heavy industry," defined as mining and the production of steel, iron, electrical power, machinery, and chemicals. The Common Program urged universal education to help meet these goals.[3]

In the first months of the People's Republic of China (PRC), the main focus had to be on the practical tasks of restraining inflation, building up agricultural production, restoring the dismantled heavy industries, and maintaining law and order. If there were to be a drastic remolding of the people's ideology, it would have to wait until the CCP had vastly increased the number of trained cadres it had at its disposal. The initial priority was to persuade the educated technical and managerial elites to serve the new state, regardless of their personal political beliefs or affiliations. Similarly, despite the rhetoric of anti-imperialism, foreign technical personnel and large foreign businesses already in China were encouraged to stay and work for the new society.

Countryside and city each had its own social rhythms and political pri-

orities. To cement the revolution in the rural areas, it was essential to institute some variety of land reform and to maintain the wide basis of peasant
support that had brought the CCP to power. Still, the party could not afford
to alienate the wealthier peasants, whose food production was necessary to
the life of the country as a whole. The result was a wide geographical
extension of land reform after mid-1950, but the restriction of land seizures
to a small fraction of the population. Although the holdings of the landlords
themselves were confiscated and redistributed, in many cases the land of
rich peasants was not touched. Mao justified this policy, in a report to the
party in early June 1950, as essential to economic redevelopment. He added
that rich peasants were no longer the danger they had appeared to be when
the People's Liberation Army was openly battling the Guomindang.

Land-reform work followed the practices that had been developed in
north China and Manchuria. It was coordinated at the local-administrative-
township level by work teams of anywhere from three to thirty people. Some
team members were veteran cadres, but others were young students, most
of whom had received only rudimentary training in the procedures to be
followed. To lend the reforms momentum, the work teams chose "key point
villages" in a given area that they worked in conjunction with the local and
equally newly formed Peasant Associations. Together they sought to identify
and then to isolate the landlords, and break the age-old patterns of deference
that were one of the props of landlord power. The work teams soon became
familiar with the complex deceptions that landlord families followed in the
countryside, whether it was dramatically dropping their standard of living
to appear poorer than they really were, consuming livestock that could not
then be counted as wealth, withholding fertilizer from land about to be
confiscated, or failing to perform customary charitable deeds that might
brand one as being of the landlord class.

Many women also began to benefit from land reform because a new
marriage law, promulgated in 1950, gave unmarried, divorced, or widowed
women the right to hold land in their own names. Also included in the
redistribution calculations were peddlers, monks, nuns, demobilized or
wounded soldiers, and émigrés from the villages who, now unemployed in
the cities, wished to return home. Exact figures on land reform for the whole
of China are hard to come by, but it is estimated that in central south China,
as the work teams fanned out across the country and reforms gained
momentum, about 40 percent of the cultivated land was seized from landlords and redistributed, and that 60 percent of the population benefited in
some way. The gain per head was between ⅙ and ½ acre, so that a family
of five might receive from below 1 to just above 2 acres. Such amounts could
not give families complete security, but for many it opened new possibilities

of survival, especially for those who had previously lived in atrocious poverty.

The reforms effectively wrecked the power base of the old landlord elite in the countryside. To ensure that this process firmed up class-based loyalties to the revolution, local CCP leaders encouraged violent confrontations between landlords and their tenants, the poorer peasants, and landless laborers. Indeed the violence attending the reforms probably matched in intensity the harsher days of the Japanese and anti-Guomindang fighting. Anecdotal figures suggest that around one landlord family out of six had a member killed in these confrontations; given the percentage of Chinese who could be classified as landlords, one can conclude that as many as 1 million or more people must have died during this phase of the revolution.

In the cities, by contrast, the first tasks for the Communist government were to prevent violent social confrontations, and to encourage industries to reopen and workers to stay at their jobs. The government promoted the formation of labor unions, but only with intense vigilance since secret-society members or racketeers connected to the old Shanghai and Tianjin criminal networks often used their contacts to build new power bases within the union organizations. Unless such people could be rooted out, it would be hard to instill confidence in the new regime. Here again the experiences of late 1948 and 1949 were valuable, but the CCP was short of cadres with urban backgrounds, and was often forced to rely on cadres from peasant families with little or no experience of city life. It was CCP policy to keep most city officials in their jobs—often as many as 95 percent—and to guarantee them, along with teachers and even the police, continued employment as long as they joined in group reform and discussion sessions, and studied the works of Mao Zedong.

The CCP tried to build a base for mass urban support by means of propaganda conveyed through newspapers, the theater, cinema, radio, and group meetings. Intensive campaigns were launched against financial speculators, and on behalf of the new government *renminbi,* or "people's currency." Webs of committees were established in large towns to deal with politics, military problems, arts, and education. Municipal government agencies with party representation were gradually extended down to the ward level. Citizens were also bunched into small study groups in which they labored to learn the new political vocabulary of communism and its significance. In imitation of the tactics of the Rectification Campaign of 1942 in Yan'an, group members were encouraged to explore their innermost thoughts as a preliminary step to transforming themselves from "experts" into "Reds."

As the party established control over cities and towns, the CCP leadership moved to set up a network of street-committee branches. These groups, each composed of the neighbors who lived in a close-knit section of streets and lanes, worked on such tasks as street cleaning, water supply, health and vaccination programs, running children's bookstores, and establishing night schools. They also had some responsibility for public security, and could be used to track criminals, enforce curfews, and even mount local patrols.

Partly under the aegis of these street committees, campaigns were launched against prostitution and opium addiction. Prostitution was effectively cut back through a system that registered all housing and monitored male visitors and their departure times. Known prostitutes, along with their madams or pimps, were enrolled in special prisonlike "schools," where they were lectured on the class contradictions that had led them to waste their lives, and were taught alternative ways of earning their livings. Though a significant number returned to prostitution after their release, the social controls and constant supervision did steadily reduce their numbers. Similarly, opium addiction was dramatically reduced with enforced methods of "cold turkey" withdrawal, and by making the former addicts' families responsible for their staying clean. Mass campaigns against addiction, the uprooting of poppy fields, and the execution of opium traffickers clinched the success of these measures. Street committees also exerted group pressure against flashy clothes or provocative hairstyles and make-up. With much greater thoroughness than had been possible in the 1930s, some of the elements of Chiang Kai-shek's New Life movement therefore came to be incorporated within the new Communist state.

This censoriousness was not surprising, for many peasant cadres, and those who had lived for long periods in Yan'an or as guerrilla fighters, were repelled by the corruption and the softness of China's cities. The veteran cadre Rao Shushi, for instance, who was the head of the Shanghai Municipal Committee and the senior government figure in the region, declared in 1949 that "the old Shanghai" had been "completely dependent on the imperialist economy for its existence and development." A Shanghai newspaper of August 1949, echoing this now fashionable criticism, wrote: "Shanghai is a non-productive city. It is a parasitic city. It is a criminal city. It is a refugee city. It is the paradise of adventurers."[4] Rao went so far as to suggest a dispersal of Shanghai's population into the interior of China, along with a transfer of schools and factories, and a focus on industries that would produce entirely for domestic consumption. His plan was not carried out, but that it could even be contemplated for the city in which the CCP had been founded suggests the ambivalence toward cities that was a feature of Chinese communism.

There were equally stubborn tensions among the local guerrillas in the south, many of whom had fought for years at great peril behind Japanese lines or against the Guomindang, and now found themselves pushed aside by cadres from the north. They were told that they had to learn northern "Mandarin" pronunciation in preference to their own local dialects if they wanted to regain their positions of power and influence. Many local cadres also found that CCP plans for efficient city government meant that they had to work in positions subordinate to the upper bourgeoisie they thought they were going to oust. A bitter saying that circulated in south China at the time highlights the ambiguity that for many lay at the center of this new stage of the revolution: "Old revolutionaries aren't treated as well as new revolutionaries, new revolutionaries aren't treated as well as non-revolutionaries, and non-revolutionaries aren't treated as well as counter-revolutionaries."[5]

THE STRUCTURE OF THE NEW GOVERNMENT

The establishment of an effective national government for China was Mao's paramount priority. Success here would bolster the Communists' claims to be representing the forces of a new order, and prove that the CCP had accomplished that reintegration of the huge country that had eluded Sun Yat-sen, Yuan Shikai, and Chiang Kai-shek, along with the Japanese and their surrogates. The new government was designed around a framework that nominally divided power among three central components: the Communist party, the formal governmental structure, and the army. This organizational form grew logically out of the Yan'an experience and the experiments of the civil-war period.

Supervising all aspects of ideology, and coordinating the work of the formal government and of the army, was the Communist party organization. The CCP had 4,448,080 members in October 1949, when the founding of the PRC was announced. The demands of governing the country led quickly to a massive jump in party membership, which reached 5,821,604 at the end of 1950. CCP members were integrated throughout all the governmental organs, the mass organizations, the courts of justice, the educational system, and the army. Regional branches of the party were coordinated at the top by the Central Committee, which had forty-four members in 1949; fourteen of those members constituted the Politburo, which was effectively run by its five-man "standing committee."

In 1949 this group consisted of the chairman of the CCP Mao Zedong, Liu Shaoqi, Zhou Enlai, Zhu De, and Chen Yun. The greater public prominence of Mao, Zhou, and Zhu De does not mean that the other two figures were of lesser importance; rather it suggests that their careers had focused on party organization and kept them out of the limelight. Liu Shaoqi, aged fifty, had been educated in the Soviet Union in the 1920s. Liu emerged later that decade and in the early 1930s as a masterful labor organizer; in the early 1940s he became a leading figure in organizing Communist groups in areas under Japanese occupation. His short book *How to Be a Good Communist,* originally delivered as lectures in Yan'an, became staple reading for Communist cadres in the 1940s and 1950s. The book was an intriguing mélange, blending Confucian traditions of morality and discipline with a standard Marxist-Leninist line, and presenting the whole in fervent revolutionary language. As Liu wrote:

> All those who have succeeded in becoming very good and experienced revolutionaries must certainly have gone through long years of steeling and self-cultivation in the revolutionary struggle. Hence, our Party members can make themselves politically inflexible revolutionaries of high quality only by steeling themselves, strengthening their self-cultivation, not losing their sense of the new and by improving their thinking ability in the course of the revolutionary struggle of the broad masses under all difficulties and hardships.
> Confucius said:
>
> > At fifteen, I had my mind bent on learning. At thirty, I stood firm. At forty, I had no doubts. At fifty, I knew the decree of Heaven. At sixty, my ear was an obedient organ for the reception of truth. At seventy, I could follow my heart's desire, without transgressing what was right.
>
> Here Confucius was relating the process of his steeling and self-cultivation. He did not regard himself as a born 'sage'.[6]

As a text, Liu Shaoqi's work spoke to a new generation in search of inner reasons to serve the revolution that had been so suddenly triumphant. Liu appealed to the "beauty" of the revolutionary vision, and contrasted it to the "ugliness" of the capitalist world. He emphasized selfless service as a goal and an ideal. And he spoke—reassuringly to upper-class intellectuals—of the mixed class backgrounds of party members. Few had ever been members of the working-class "urban proletariat," said Liu, and any class background could be transcended by piercing self-examination and prolonged study of Marxism-Leninism.

The fifth member of the inner group, Chen Yun, born in 1905, was a former Shanghai typesetter who joined the party in 1924 and became famous as a union organizer. Like Liu, he was considered a seminal party theorist, whose works were assigned in the 1942 Rectification Campaign. By 1949 he was also regarded as the CCP's leading economic planner, and was charged with the task of restoring China's shattered economy. Almost as powerful was Gao Gang, born in 1902, who had been one of the builders of the Gansu-Shaanxi border-area soviet in the early 1930s, and thus helped to create the relatively secure base to which Mao Zedong and the Long Marchers retreated in 1935. He served as political commissar of the Shaan/Gan/Ning border government, and as commander of the Jilin-Heilongjiang region during the Communist-Guomindang war in Manchuria. When Lin Biao's victorious troops moved south into China proper after defeating the Nationalists, Gao stayed on as military and political leader of Manchuria, with headquarters in Mukden. Even before the People's Republic was proclaimed, he led a delegation to Moscow to negotiate a trade agreement that would aid him in redeveloping the industry of the northeast.

These leaders of the Central People's Government were a formidable group with considerable military and administrative experience. They coordinated their work with the other main central government apparatus, the State Council (or cabinet), of which Zhou Enlai was premier. Under Zhou were twenty-four new ministries, the titles of which give a tidy summary of the problems considered of greatest importance in the nation's development: Agriculture, Communications, Culture (headed by the novelist Mao Dun), Education, Finance, Food Industries, Foreign Affairs (of which Premier Zhou Enlai was also minister), Forestry, Fuel, Heavy Industry, Internal Affairs, Justice, Labor, Law, Light Industry, Minority Nationalities, Overseas Chinese Affairs, Posts and Telecommunications, Public Health, Public Security, Railways, Textile Industries, Trade, and Water Conservancy. Two of these ministers, those of Justice and of Public Health, were women.

The formal governmental structure overlapped and interconnected constantly with the CCP organization, and both of them extended their influence through mass organizations that were intended to link the entire country across regional lines by dint of some special focus or shared interest: among these in 1949 and 1950 were the federation of literature and arts, the Sino-Soviet friendship association, the all-China federation of democratic youth, and the all-China federation of women. This last was headed by Cai Chang, a young radical from Changsha who had joined the group of students sent to France for work-study in 1919. A specialist in organizing women factory workers, she had served in the Jiangxi Soviet, survived the Long March, and become a prominent figure in Yan'an politics before being promoted to this important new post.

The power of the People's Liberation Army (PLA) was firmly embedded in Chinese society by the division of the nation into six massive regions, each with its own unified military command. These were directed by regional party bureaus that held both military and administrative power above the provincial governors, rather as in the Qing when the governors-general of groups of provinces had had jurisdiction over the individual governors. These regions developed out of the CCP's wartime border-government experience, and had some of the geographical and economic unity of the macroregions into which some analysts believe China naturally falls (see the map on page 77). These regions were grouped as follows:

1. *Northeast China Bureau:* Heilongjiang, Jilin (Kirin), Rehe (Jehol), Liaoning
2. *Northwest China Bureau:* Gansu, Ningxia, Shaanxi, Xinjiang, Qinghai
3. *North China Bureau:* Chahar, Hebei, Shanxi, Suiyuan
4. *East China Bureau:* Anhui, Fujian, Jiangsu, Shandong, Zhejiang
5. *Central-South China Bureau:* Henan, Hunan, Hubei, Jiangxi, Guangxi, Guangdong
6. *Southwest China Bureau:* Guizhou, Xikang, Sichuan, Yunnan

Each of these six regions had four main posts that followed the tripartite nature of the central government itself: a government chairman, a first party secretary, a military commander, and an army political commissar. Logically these powers might therefore have been divided among twenty-four senior incumbents, but in fact there were only thirteen incumbents, since so many men held two or more of the key posts.

Five of these men were particularly powerful in the regional governments. First, the Central People's Government Council vice-chairman Gao Gang had extraordinary power in Manchuria (the Northeast China Bureau), where he held all four of the key posts. Gao had close contacts with senior government and military men in the Soviet Union, and Russian interest in the railways and resources of Manchuria assured the importance of his role. Second, Peng Dehuai, the military commander who had shown great bravado in mounting fixed military campaigns (as in the Hundred Regiments Offensive of 1940 and the abortive attack on Sichuan in 1948), was both government chairman and military commander in the Northwest China Bureau. That area, too, because of its shared border with the Soviet Union and its mix of races and nationalities, was of critical importance in Sino-Soviet relations. Third, Rao Shushi, a veteran organizer of the New Fourth Army, had remarkable power in east China, where he held three of the key posts: first party secretary, government chairman, and army political commissar. He was also named party secretary of the Shanghai General Labor Union. Finally, Lin Biao and Deng Xiaoping had also obtained major

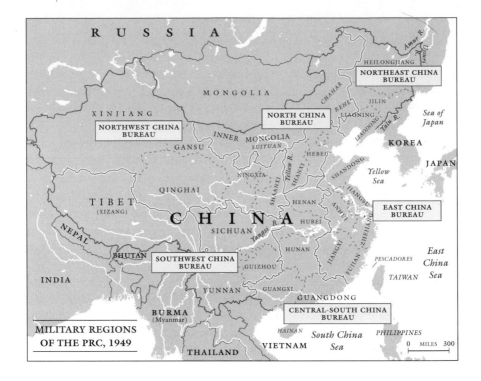

MILITARY REGIONS
OF THE PRC, 1949

regional power bases: Lin Biao held three of the four chief posts in the central-south China region, and Deng Xiaoping two of the four posts in the southwest bureau.

Each of these five was later to fall afoul of Mao Zedong and be purged. We can see with hindsight that despite the impressive restructuring of China's government, there were perennial problems embedded within the PRC. Tensions of regional and central authority, of crosscutting bureaucratic lines, and of individual ambitions and power bases, which in various ways had plagued China since the late Ming dynasty, were not going to be eradicated in any simple way.

THE KOREAN WAR

Even before all Guomindang forces within China had been eliminated, Mao Zedong followed up his statements about "leaning to one side" by traveling to the Soviet Union to meet with Stalin. He reached Moscow on December 16, 1949, just before Stalin's seventieth birthday. This was Mao's first excursion beyond China's borders. He had no firsthand knowledge of any of the countries that had so much influenced the Chinese among whom he had grown up. But now that the PRC was formally established, Mao had to enter the world of international diplomacy, and the sequence of nations granting recognition to the new state shows how swiftly many—and not just those in the Communist bloc—did swing to Mao's side.

Mao's experiences in the Soviet Union were baffling and contradictory. The initial meeting between the two leaders on the day of Mao's arrival seemed encouraging enough. Stalin expressed flexibility over aspects of the Yalta agreement that affected China adversely, and offered to help train China's air force and small navy. Stalin was cautious over agreeing to give Mao the "volunteer pilots or secret military detachments" that Mao sought in order to invade Taiwan, but he approved plans to use PLA troops to destabilize the Southeast Asian borders and added that China could also shake up Britain by fomenting trouble in Hong Kong. In a meeting the following month, Stalin also agreed to give serious thought to Mao's request for an air regiment to help China in its plans for "an attack on Tibet."[7] And yet after eight weeks of bargaining, all Mao gained was a security treaty that would protect China in the event of attack by Japan; credits valued at U.S. $300 million, to be paid in equal installments over five successive years; and a Russian promise to evacuate Lüshun and Dalian by 1952, when they would return to Chinese sovereignty. In a bitter blow, Mao was forced to

DIPLOMATIC RECOGNITION OF THE PRC,
1949–1950[8]

1949	
October 2	USSR
October 3	Bulgaria, Romania
October 4	Poland, Hungary, Czechoslovakia
October 5	Yugoslavia
December 9	Burma
December 30	India
1950	
January 4	Pakistan
January 6	(Great Britain),* Ceylon, Norway
January 9	Denmark, Israel
January 13	Finland, Afghanistan
January 14	Sweden

*The Chinese rejected Britain's January 6 offer, since the British maintained formal diplomatic ties with Taiwan.

acquiesce in the existence north of the Xinjiang border of an independent Mongolian People's Republic, which by definition was going to remain firmly under Russian influence. Mao had claimed several times that Mongolia would one day come under Chinese dominance; he now had to abandon any hope that China would regain western territories similar in extent to those controlled by the Qing at the height of their power.

The broad arena of foreign policy was not of central importance to the PRC leaders in the spring of 1950. Their main concerns were erecting a viable administrative structure, curbing inflation, and rebuilding domestic industry. With Hainan Island successfully captured by Lin Biao's troops in April, the military felt ready—even without any clear offer of Soviet assistance—to proceed with the two final aspects of territorial consolidation: the conquests of Tibet and Taiwan. The Tibetan operations, though logistically complex, were not expected to offer much challenge to the now seasoned PLA troops, especially since India had become independent in 1947 and the British had lost their paramount interest in maintaining Tibet's buffer status. Chinese Communist troops invaded Tibet in October 1950 in order to "liberate" the country from "imperialist oppression." Despite the poignant Tibetan protest, "Liberation from whom and what? Ours was a happy country with a solvent government,"[9] the United Nations took no action, nor would India or Britain intervene on Tibet's behalf. The Chinese occupied the key points in the country within a year and pressured the Dalai Lama's advisers into general acceptance of China's sovereignty over the region.

The Taiwan challenge was considered far more serious. Six months after relinquishing the presidency of China in January 1949, Chiang Kai-shek had retreated to Taiwan, where the Guomindang had stabilized its power following the riots and massacres sparked by Chen Yi in 1947. Taiwan had flourished economically under Japanese colonial administration between 1895 and 1945, and Chiang moved swiftly to reassert his leadership over the island's inhabitants, his own exiled Guomindang, and the 1 million Chinese troops who were already on Taiwan or who retreated there after the Communist victories of 1949. The PLA commanders were under no illusions that it would be easy to recapture the island. The PLA had already been defeated in its attempt of October 1949 to take the offshore island of Quemoy (Jinmen). In February 1950, the general commanding the units of the PLA Third Field Army in Fujian and Zhejiang, which were scheduled to make the assault on Taiwan, gave a frank assessment of the prospects:

> I must first of all point out that the liberation of the islands along the southeast coast, especially Taiwan, is an extremely big problem and will involve the

biggest campaign in the history of modern Chinese warfare. . . . [Taiwan] cannot be occupied without sufficient transport, suitable equipment, and adequate supplies. Furthermore a considerable number of Chiang Kai-shek's land, sea, and air forces are concentrated there together with a batch of the most intransigent reactionaries who have fled from China's mainland. They have built strong defense works, depending on the surrounding sea for protection.[10]

Because of these difficulties, Mao Zedong and other government leaders seem to have been torn about the correct course to follow. By the summer of 1950 the military consolidation over south China was complete, and a large force of veteran PLA troops were moved to the Fujian coastal region, but they were not ordered into action against Taiwan at that time. One possible explanation for the delay—apart from logistical and naval-transport problems—is that the CCP leaders were hoping that the Taiwanese themselves might stage an insurrection against the Guomindang occupiers. (Stalin himself had suggested this in December 1949 during his conversations with Mao, as an alternative to use of Soviet support forces.) Another possible explanation is that an epidemic raged through the PLA troops that summer, rendering many of them unfit for active duty.

Worried that military expenses would keep rising, yet mindful of the problems that the Guomindang had encountered when they demobilized too many troops too quickly after the Japanese surrender, the Central Committee of the CCP decided on a partial demobilization under close government supervision. In the Central Committee's words:

> The PLA, while preserving its main forces, should demobilize part of its troops in 1950, but only on condition that sufficient forces to liberate Taiwan and Tibet are guaranteed as well as sufficient forces to consolidate the national defense and suppress the counter-revolutionaries. This demobilization must be carried out with care so that demobilized soldiers can return home and settle down to productive work.[11]

There was at this same time nothing to suggest that the United States would intervene in the Chinese conflict any further, despite angry Republican party demands for enactment of a generous assistance program to aid Chiang Kai-shek in the eventual recovery of the Chinese mainland. In the summer of 1949, at President Truman's request, Secretary of State Dean Acheson had assembled what he considered all the documents relevant to China's wartime and civil-war experience, and to American involvement therein, writing in his letter of transmittal: "The Nationalist armies did not have to be defeated; they disintegrated. History has proved again and again that a regime without faith in itself and an army without morale cannot survive the test of battle."[12] Acheson concluded that further American aid or involvement would be as pointless as previous attempts had been. But not everyone agreed. The former Chinese ambassador to the United States, Hu Shi, who had been briefly drawn to Christianity in his pre–May Fourth movement days at Cornell University, jotted in the margin of his copy of Acheson's text the note "Matthew 27:24" ("So when Pilate saw that he was gaining nothing, but rather that a riot was beginning, he took water and washed his hands before the crowd, saying, 'I am innocent of this man's blood; see to it yourselves' ").[13]

In the meantime, State Department staff went ahead and drafted the official statement they would issue once Taiwan had fallen into Communist hands. Public declarations by both General Douglas MacArthur, the commander of occupied Japan, and Dean Acheson now defined the new American "defensive perimeter" in the Pacific as running along a line connecting the Aleutians, Japan, Okinawa, the Ryukyus, and the Philippines. The Chinese could take note that this definition of American strategic interests did not include Taiwan, nor did it include South Korea, which since 1945 had emerged as an independent state under American patronage, separated from Soviet-dominated North Korea along the thirty-eighth parallel. Once Taiwan was conquered, the PRC could therefore expect to take its rightful place in the United Nations, for which it was already actively lobbying.

The apparent harmony of these American and Chinese stances was shattered on June 25, 1950, when a massive force of North Korean troops crossed the thirty-eighth parallel and invaded South Korea. Within a few weeks, North Korean forces had advanced swiftly down the peninsula, capturing Seoul and forcing the South Koreans to a final desperate stand at the harbor of Pusan. By an ironic coincidence, the Soviet Union was at this time boycotting the United Nations Security Council because of the council's refusal to seat the PRC delegation in the place of Taiwan. With no threat of a Soviet veto, the other members of the Security Council acted swiftly to condemn the North Koreans and to urge UN members to give "such assistance" as "may be necessary." President Truman responded by ordering U.S. troops based in Japan to assist South Korea. Troops from fifteen other member nations joined the United States, including Great Britain, France, Australia and New Zealand, Thailand and the Philippines, Canada, Greece, and Turkey. Fearing that the Chinese might seize this moment to launch an attack on Taiwan, Truman also ordered the U.S. Seventh Fleet to patrol the Taiwan Strait as a "neutralization" move. The PRC now could not invade Taiwan even if it was ready to do so.

China's behavior over the next few months was a study in ambiguity.

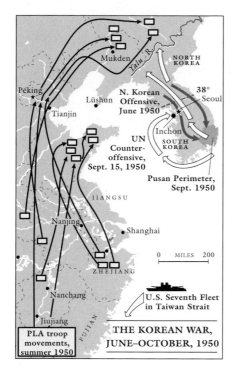

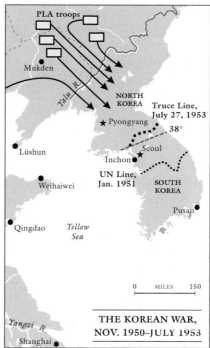

Though the North Korean leader had that spring briefed Mao on the possible invasion, and Zhou Enlai had said that China might intervene if the American troops crossed the thirty-eighth parallel, the Chinese remained muted about the conflict, and initially took no decisive action. Chinese criticisms of the patrol activities of the American Seventh Fleet were angrier and more determined. Zhou Enlai, in his capacity as foreign minister, issued a public statement calling the patrols "armed aggression against the territory of China."[14] Apparently acknowledging that the American deployment of the Seventh Fleet made any attack on Taiwan impossible, China's leaders ordered about 30,000 troops from the Third Army, who had been training on the coast in Fujian, transferred north to the Mukden area. Other troops were also moved north to the Shandong peninsula.

In August the United Nations hosted delicate negotiations, which included discussion of seating the PRC on the Security Council in exchange for its help in mediating the conflict. At the same time, General MacArthur, now commander in chief of United Nations forces in Korea, held cordial talks with Chiang Kai-shek; MacArthur reiterated his support for Chiang's regime, declaring now that Taiwan was part of the United States' "island chain" of air-power bases. (MacArthur did not, however, accept Chiang's offer of Nationalist troops to be used in the Korean fighting.) By late August, UN forces were winning major victories in South Korea, relentlessly bombing North Korean supply lines, and building up tactical superiority in tanks, artillery, and air power. Now China's verbal attacks on the United States began to grow harsher, and the whole country was spurred on by mass rallies condemning the United States and its allies for their role in the war. "The barbarous action of American imperialism and its hangers-on in invading Korea," ran one Chinese statement of late August, "not only menaces peace in Asia and the world in general but seriously threatens the security of China in particular." It continued, "North Korea's friends are our friends. North Korea's enemy is our enemy. North Korea's defense is our defense."[15] But in secret messages to Stalin, Mao continued to talk of North Korean military incompetence and their refusal to keep the Chinese properly informed of battlefield developments.

The crucial change in the war came in mid-September, when, in a daring and brilliantly executed amphibious maneuver, MacArthur landed his forces at the harbor of Inchon, to the rear of the North Korean lines, and threatened to cut off their retreat. As the North Korean troops began to break and retreat homeward, Zhou Enlai notified the Indian ambassador, who was acting as the conduit for Chinese messages, that China would have to intervene if the United States invaded North Korea. U.S. troops did cross the border on October 7, and pushed on northward to the Chinese border along the Yalu River. At this point both Stalin and Mao began to waiver, and in overlapping cipher cables argued the merits of leaving the North Koreans to their own devices, to fight whatever guerrilla war they were capable of. Only on October 13—allegedly won over by the passionate arguments of Peng Dehuai and Gao Gang—did Mao agree to allow Chinese "volunteers" to move across the North Korean border as long as the Soviet Union gave full air support. To this Stalin agreed.[16]

The commander of the Chinese forces, Peng Dehuai, coordinated his forces superbly, and in bitter fighting that December, the Chinese pushed the allies back once again to a line along the thirty-eighth parallel. In January 1951 the UN troops retreated farther south, as Chinese and North Korean units retook what was left of the burned-out shell of Seoul. Rallying, UN forces regained Seoul, and at this point the battle lines settled along the chains of hills that ran just north of the thirty-eighth parallel. Savage fighting for positional advantage continued, leaving both sides with heavy casualties. This phase of the war saw dogfights between squadrons of jet fighters, the first recorded in the history of warfare, and the pioneering use by the Americans of helicopters to move their troops swiftly into position. The war dragged on for a painful two years, ending with a truce signed in July 1953.

The armistice was due in part to the efforts of General Dwight Eisenhower, who in 1952 made a campaign promise to travel to Korea, but once elected president followed through by using the full weight of nuclear diplomacy to bring the Chinese and North Koreans to the final negotiating stage.

By that time U.S. casualties had reached over 160,000 (54,000 dead, 103,000 wounded, 5,000 missing), South Korean casualties 400,000, North Korean 600,000, and Chinese between 700,000 and 900,000. The Chinese never released exact figures since they claimed that all their troops in Korea were "volunteers," not regular army personnel. But the staggering losses of close to 1 million men, many of whom were killed in the last year of the war by the overwhelming fire power of the UN forces, gave Chinese military leaders pause. Peng Dehuai, especially, realized that China must develop a more modern, well-equipped army like the Soviet Union's if it were to confront the West in conventional war. Among the Chinese who died in the Korean conflict was the elder of Mao Zedong's two surviving sons by his first wife, Yang Kaihui. This son, Anying, born in 1922 when Mao was organizing Hunanese labor in the first strikes conducted by the newly formed CCP, had been a student in Moscow and a farm laborer in Yan'an. His body was buried on Korean soil. (Mao's only other son, Anqing, had a history of mental troubles and spent most of his life in institutions.)

The domestic significance of the war was profound. Uppermost was the suffering of hundreds of thousands of Chinese troops, who fought in harsh winter weather with inadequate clothing, insufficient food, and little ammunition, against an enemy with overwhelming superiority in air and artillery power. The courageous but costly charges that the Chinese mounted against well-entrenched enemy emplacements amazed the foreign troops who witnessed them. This very courage gave rise to a new mystique of Chinese endurance and heroism, which was elaborated in the People's Republic by an outpouring of literature, films, plays, and tales of model soldier-heroes that reinforced the values of sacrifice and revolution. China also drew closer to the Soviet Union, which appreciated China's loyalty to the Soviet bloc and made large amounts of military materials available—although the Chinese had to pay for the aid.

In addition, the events of the war were used to reinforce Chinese perceptions of the evils of Western imperialism, and particularly to isolate the United States as China's prime enemy. American involvement in Korea was pointed to as clear evidence of U.S. ambitions in east Asia, and of the implacable hatred of the United States for China and the Chinese people. Such themes were given strong play in the fictions and reportage about the war.

This led to another domestic effect of the war: the decision to turn against most of the Westerners who had stayed in China for business or religious reasons, and to force them to leave the country. A significant number, including some missionaries, were arrested and formally charged with being spies for the American imperialists. The Chinese government conducted mass campaigns to extend the ethos of the war into a passionate hunt for domestic spies and alleged or real enemy agents. This was accompanied by a general hardening of attitudes against all who had long been in contact with the Guomindang or had worked in foreign firms, universities, or church organizations. Finally, the government was forced to admit that it had failed to bring about a complete reunification of Chinese soil. Taiwan was not going to fall, but would remain a potential base for bombing raids and sabotage against China, and the focal point—with conspicuous American support—for all hostility to the PRC.

In the United States as in China, the effects of the war were serious, deeply harming the two countries' perceptions of each other. The "human wave" tactics of the Chinese in battle resurrected old stereotypes of an Asian contempt for life, linked now to the belief that the Chinese were robotlike followers of Soviet Russian orders, incapable of formulating their own independent policies. Revulsion and fear of the Chinese was heightened by what was learned of attempts to "brainwash" American or South Korean prisoners of war. And the fact that the Korean peace talks stalled for nearly two years because the People's Republic demanded that all Chinese prisoners be returned home, when over 14,000 had begged not to be sent back, showed how swiftly China had developed into a harsh dictatorship. The Chinese finally gave in on this issue, and the 14,000 prisoners were repatriated elsewhere—mainly to Taiwan.

Chinese Communist strength in the field also made Americans look afresh at the record of the 1930s and 1940s, much of which was now easily available in Acheson's lengthy report to President Truman, published in 1949 as a 1,054-page volume, replete with tables and appendices. For those who were drawn, either for partisan political reasons or out of inner conviction, to a deep antagonism to communism, the records of those Americans who had been sympathetic to Yan'an smacked of treason. Ambassador Hurley had introduced this idea at the time of his resignation in late 1945, and many others sided with it thereafter. The fact that both the president of the United States and the Joint Chiefs of Staff had thought seriously, if briefly, about arming Chinese Communists in 1944 to help the joint war effort was forgotten.

The corrosive period of domestic American anticommunism, which affected immigration laws, labor legislation, Hollywood screenwriters, and the media in general, and climaxed in the vague but damaging charges of subversion made by Senator Joseph McCarthy, precluded any firm or fresh look at American-Chinese relations for over a decade. Although conducted on a lesser scale than the contemporaneous Chinese hunt for domestic enemies, the campaign of allegation and innuendo launched by McCarthy and others had a profoundly damaging effect on many Americans. The leading China experts in the State Department were subjected to repeated loyalty investigations, and were dismissed or transferred out of their positions to backwaters of the world scene. Unable to get passports to travel to China, a generation of American scholars, students, and journalists was deprived of all personal contacts with that country.

It became ever more popular to say that the United States had somehow "lost" China—whether by deliberate treason, misrepresentation, or failure to provide crucial military and financial aid. The pervasiveness of this view made it difficult for the United States to withhold involvement in countries threatened with Communist subversion, even when it was generally known that their governments were corrupt, unpopular, and economically exploitative.

The Chinese Communists probably gained in the short run from participating in the Korean War, because if the United States had triumphed in October 1950 and been able to establish a unified and viable non-Communist Korean regime, the People's Republic would have had a hostile and powerful neighbor on its crucial Manchurian border, where so much heavy industry was concentrated. But the costs were high, as we have seen, and the longer-range tragedy was that China had lost all hope of the "new democracy" that had seemed implicit in the rhetoric and some of the policies of 1949.

MASS PARTY, MASS CAMPAIGNS

During the Yan'an period and the civil war, the Communist party continued to grow at a steady pace, passing the 1 million mark in early 1945, rising to 2 million in 1947, 3 million in 1948, 4 million in 1949, and 5 million in 1950. But there was not the enormous increase in numbers one might have expected in the first years of the People's Republic. Instead, the CCP leadership concentrated on raising the political awareness and expertise of those recent recruits to the party, weeding out incompetent or corrupt people who had been insufficiently scrutinized when they first joined, and broadening the class and occupational base of the party. The party had hitherto been predominantly rural, because of the nature of the Yan'an regime and the guerrilla warfare waged in the countryside against both the Japanese and the Guomindang. Now, as the CCP moved to the task of administering the cities of China, it desperately needed urban, educated cadres. One way to locate such potential cadres was to galvanize the cities through mass campaigns, and to see which people emerged as dedicated socialists and natural leaders.

The CCP had learned, during the Yan'an Rectification Campaign of 1942, how to scrutinize itself, force its members into self-criticism, and use group pressure and intimidation to arrive at an apparent consensus. In the early 1950s these experiences surfaced again in four major campaigns involving the mass mobilization of the Chinese people. The first of these was the Resist America and Aid Korea campaign, noted above, which focused on foreigners in China. The party ordered police searches of alleged spies, confiscated objects such as radio receivers and firearms, and investigated public associations that included or had contact with foreigners—whether these associations were involved in cultural, business, health, or religious pursuits. These investigations scared away many Chinese who had formerly associated with foreigners. Foreign business assets were frozen in December 1950, and foreign businesses—although not wholly expropriated—were pressured into selling out, often at artificially low prices. Some gave up their assets altogether to meet enormous demands for "back taxes" imposed on them by the Chinese. Workers in foreign-owned factories and businesses aired their grievances against their employers at public meetings, and in some cases mass rallies were held to accuse the foreigners of cruel behavior.

In a dramatic confrontation that recalls the anti-Christian agitations of the Confucian gentry or the Boxers in the later nineteenth century, five Canadian nuns who ran an orphanage in Canton were accused in early 1951 of having killed over 2,000 babies entrusted to their care. Although the nuns were not killed, immense rallies were staged to protest their alleged cruelty. Other foreigners were imprisoned and forced—through the physical and mental pressures of brainwashing techniques—to confess to espionage. By late 1950 almost all foreigners had left the country. Chinese Christians, most of whom remained in China, were registered and organized into the Three Selfs movement, so-called for its firm commitment to free the Chinese Church from foreign funds, foreign influence, and—in the case of Catholics—from Vatican control.

Given momentum by the anger and excitement of the Korean War, a second mass campaign was directed at domestic "counterrevolutionaries." Millions of Chinese who had been in Guomindang party or youth organizations, or had served in Guomindang armies, had stayed on in their homeland when the Communists took over. They had never been thoroughly investigated, and some of them no doubt harbored pro–Chiang Kai-shek sympathies. A few secretly aided the sabotage expeditions that were sent from Taiwan to the Chinese mainland in attempts to disrupt the regime. In the summer of 1951 the CCP leadership launched a series of mass rallies in large cities to publicize this new campaign against domestic subversion, and held exhibitions to brand the counterrevolutionaries' activities. As the campaign grew in intensity it became brutal and terrifying. For millions of Chinese the violence and humiliation of these days effectively ended any hope that they would be able to live out their lives peacefully under the Communist regime, whatever their past histories might have been.

The state also used the campaign against counterrevolutionaries to disarm the local populace of the bewildering mass of weaponry that had been passed out during the long years of warlord and guerrilla fighting and rule by the various separatist regimes. In Guangdong, for example, over 500,000 rifles were collected in the course of the campaign. As a similar security measure—and this despite the provisions in the Common Program of 1949 guaranteeing freedom of movement from one locale to another—all people over fifteen now had to obtain official residence certificates from the police, and get permission if they wished to move somewhere else.

The CCP leadership had already been planning a third mass campaign—this one against corruption within their own party. Even before the Suppression of Counterrevolutionaries campaign was over, the party was mobilizing for what was termed the Three Anti campaign, which was directed against three sets of vices stated to be common among three occupational groups: the three vices were corruption, waste, and obstructionist bureaucracy; the three targeted groups were Communist party members themselves, the wider circles of bureaucratic officials (many of whom were not party members, and some of whom had served the Guomindang), and the managers of factories and other businesses.

The Three Anti campaign was first launched in Manchuria—perhaps as a trial run—under the direction of the party chief there, Gao Gang. At the end of 1951 it spread to the rest of China, and even though it was not conducted with the violence of the Suppression of Counterrevolutionaries campaign, it did lead to thorough investigations of offices and enterprises, and to the humiliation or expulsion of many senior figures—some of whom had indeed, according to what seems solid evidence, benefited financially from their privileged positions. The Three Anti campaign was also used to strengthen the government's control over labor. In cities whose job contractors and tough local bosses had continued to dominate the assignment of labor, the mass meetings of the Three Anti campaign enabled the CCP to educate workers about this pattern of discrimination. Enraged workers were then mobilized to turn on their own bosses and join in expanded state-supervised labor organizations that would, the party promised, end the decades-long practice of local graft and influence.

The Three Anti drive drew much of its energy from a fourth mass campaign that was waged concurrently—the Five Anti campaign. This campaign was designed as an all-out assault on the bourgeoisie in China, an act of class war that mirrored in scope, rage, and effectiveness its counterpart in the countryside—the campaign against rural landlords. The targets of the Five Anti drive were specifically identified as those Chinese industrialists and businessmen who had stayed on in China after the Communist takeover, and also those who "represented" the capitalist class, a vague definition that could incorporate anyone the state chose to charge. The five vices that were to be expunged were "bribery, tax evasion, theft of state property, cheating on government contracts, and stealing state economic information."

The Five Anti campaign was launched in January 1952, as the Korean War settled into a protracted stalemate. It took place in cities all across China, but the movement in Shanghai can serve as a case study since the city's size and the wealth of its business community meant that coverage of events in press and radio was especially thorough. In tracking the growth of the Five Anti movement, we can see how all the elements of group mobilization and self-criticism—developed in Yan'an and Manchuria and honed in the other mass campaigns—were now brought to a smoothly manipulated consummation.

As a preliminary stage in the campaign, in 1951 CCP cadres in Shanghai had carefully coached workers' organizations to look into their employers' business affairs and search out evidence of tax evasion or other wrongdoing. This tactic had indeed a perfectly legitimate goal—that of raising national revenues and curbing inflation—and involved some 20,000 cadres and 6,000 specially trained shopworkers. Propaganda networks were also developed, consisting of trained experts who could work through the media—especially radio and newspapers—and through small discussion groups to encourage compliance with the government's policies. By late 1951 there were about 15,000 trained propagandists in Shanghai whose work was coordinated by the growing numbers of the Communist Youth League. One function of these cadres and propagandists was to break down the often tight personal, emotional, and family bonds that united workers to their employers, especially in the smaller businesses. Even if wages were desperately low, personal bonds often crossed class lines, and many employers were not dramatically wealthier than their workers. The situation paralleled that in the countryside, where it was hard to get peasants to speak out in public bitterness against people they had known and worked with all their lives.

China's business leaders were forced to undergo group criticism sessions and to confess their past economic crimes. Some did confess to actual financial malfeasance, although many tried to write bland self-criticisms that dodged all the major issues. To weaken the business leaders' sense of solidarity, they were encouraged by the party to denounce each other. At the same time, the class-war element in the campaign was deepened by the city-wide convening of shopworkers' committees for the purpose of assembling mass meetings and drawing together public denunciations against carefully targeted business figures. The business leaders of China had been harshly treated by the Guomindang in 1927. Now they were once again to suffer intimidation from the state.

In early February 1952 over 3,000 meetings were held in Shanghai, and an estimated 160,000 workers attended one or more of them. Parades with drums and banners, door-to-door visits by squads of activists, and the use of radio and then of loudspeakers set up at key street junctions all over the city mobilized the whole community and put immense psychological pressure on individual business leaders. In addition, newspaper reading groups were formed in most neighborhoods, where cadres would read to the illiterate and explain the finer points of the campaign.

By March, the CCP was ready to hot up the pace. Twelve thousand specially trained cadres were now available for the dramatic phase of the campaign. After a smaller number had experimented with amassing evidence and leveling charges at certain workplaces known as "test key points"—in emulation perhaps of the "key point" villages used in rural land reform—Shanghai workers were organized into Five Anti work brigades, subdivided by their wards, their type of work, and the individual firms that employed them. These brigades were small—each had fewer than twenty members—and were bound together by oaths of allegiance to the party. Their job was to spearhead the final identification of victims by assembling the workers for struggle sessions at different plants. In meetings throughout April, business leaders were forced to endure the open meetings and denunciations, and publicly to confess all their "crimes."

The owner of the Dahua copper company provides an example of how a prominent industrialist could be brought to heel. He initially tried to duck further criticism by confessing to illegally obtaining 50 million yuan,* but his employees kept after him to confess to greater crimes. At home, his mother-in-law and daughter also urged him to confess, as did a number of

---

*Chinese dollars in the new currency of *renminbi.*

prominent capitalists who had recently had their own confessions accepted. After falling ill with worry, he finally "reconfessed," more contritely acknowledging graft totaling over 2 billion yuan.

The "basic victory" of the campaign was announced on April 30, 1952, and the final evaluations for the small and medium firms revealed in early May (see the table below). Other cities ended up with harsher assessments of their business communities: in Tianjin, at the end of a similar pattern of mass mobilization, investigation, confession, and judgment, only 10 percent of enterprises were classified as "law-abiding," 64.2 percent as "basically law-abiding," 21 percent as "semi law-abiding," and 5.3 percent as being "serious lawbreakers."[17]

In China as a whole, the Three Anti and Five Anti campaigns had an immense effect. The CCP revealed that it was not going to protect private businesses any longer, nor tolerate the maze of semilegal practices that had continued in China after 1949. Chinese capitalists were now threatened just as foreign capitalists had been the year before, and enormous fines were levied on them for what were often baseless charges. The Korean War contributed to the scope of the campaigns, for the war created new employment and procurement opportunities for firms in north China (hence Tianjin's harsher evaluations than Shanghai's) even as it brought the government huge new expenses. Sometimes the government even lent capitalists the money to pay their fines, leading to a complex pattern of subservience and indebtedness.

The main purpose of the campaigns was to assert government control over workers' organizations, and to end the independent modes of operation of capitalists and bureaucratic functionaries. In sharp contrast to the Suppression of Counterrevolutionaries campaign, few of the Three Anti and Five Anti victims were killed. Almost all were terrified or humiliated or both, and many had not only to pay their fines but also to repay all money

RESULTS OF THE FIVE ANTI MOVEMENT
IN SHANGHAI, 1952[18]

	Small firms	Medium firms
Law-abiding	59,471 (76.6%)	7,782 (42.5%)
Basically law-abiding	17,407 (22.4%)	9,005 (49.1%)
Semi law-abiding	736 (0.9%)	1,529 (8.3%)
Serious lawbreakers	2	9
Total	77,616	18,325

they had allegedly taken in graft or withheld from their taxes; some had their property confiscated and were sent to labor camps.

The techniques of group pressure employed in the Three Anti and Five Anti movements did not end with the campaign in April. On the contrary, worker-employer meetings now became a regular part of most businesses, and the pressures brought by workers and party cadres prevented employers from running their own businesses in their own way. Meticulous examinations of class status were carried out around China, with the result that urban dwellers were classified as precisely as rural workers had been in the Xunwu investigation or in the later land-reform programs. Among the sixty new categories into which "class" was now divided, one could find such labels as "enterprise worker," "handicraft worker," "pedicab worker," "idler," "urban pauper," "peddler," "small shop owner," "office employee," and so on. Furthermore, a whole new group of activists had now been identified by the state. In Shanghai alone, 40,000 workers who had proven themselves effective in the Five Anti struggles were enrolled in new propagandist corps, ready to serve the state again when needed, and large numbers were similarly recruited in other cities. At the end of 1952, the CCP leadership felt confident in swelling the ranks of the party as a whole to 6 million. Even those who had never seen a guerrilla unit or experienced life in the countryside now had had at least a taste of revolution.

CHAPTER 20

Planning
the New Society

THE FIRST FIVE-YEAR PLAN

With the first phase of land reform complete, the economic base of the bourgeoisie broken, and the Korean War over, the CCP was free in 1953 to develop an integrated plan for the nation's economic development. The model adopted was that of the Soviet Union, where state-controlled industrial production in a sequence of five-year plans was believed to have been responsible for the nation's emergence as a world-class power in the 1930s, with the ability to withstand and repulse the full force of Germany's attack in World War II. That victory in turn allowed the USSR greatly to expand its influence in Europe at war's end, despite the United States' efforts to the contrary.

Exactly why the Chinese chose the Soviet model, the specific workings of which they knew very little about, is a key question that remains difficult to answer. Perhaps the Soviet model seemed the only logical choice after the failure of Guomindang attempts at reform along Western lines, and after the Korean War and the mass campaigns against foreigners left China further isolated from Western powers. China's use of the Soviet model was certainly one way of emphasizing the anticapitalist and anti-imperialist nature of the new Chinese state. And the CCP, having seized power in a violent revolutionary confrontation, needed some model for exercising that power as it set out to build socialism in the poverty-stricken country.

To prepare for the task of restructuring the economy, China's leaders set standards for bureaucratic recruitment and pay scales, introduced regular administrative procedures, and organized the people of China according to the local units in which they worked (*danwei*) so as to increase the efficiency of social control and indoctrination. In 1954, during difficult discussions at the highest political levels, the structure of the government was reorganized to do away with the six basic military-political bureaus (regions) into which the country had been divided in 1949. The army was placed under a newly formed Ministry of Defense, itself subordinate to the State Council in Peking. For implementation of party decisions, China moved to a tightly centralized system, in which provincial party secretaries supervised the dissemination of Central Committee orders through an elaborate chain of subprovincial party offices. China was now to be administered through 21 provinces,* 5 autonomous regions (Xinjiang, Tibet, Inner Mongolia, Ningxia, and Guangxi), and 2 municipalities—Peking and Shanghai.† Below these units were approximately 2,200 county governments, which in turn supervised about 1 million branch offices of the CCP in towns, villages, army units, factories, mines, and schools.

Interconnected with these basic shifts in political organization was the first major purge to occur in the CCP since the founding of the People's Republic. The purge took place during late 1953 and early 1954, and the two main victims were Gao Gang and Rao Shushi, who had respectively been serving as the political commissars in the Manchurian and Shanghai regions. Both men were members of the key State Planning Commission, which was currently reviewing the country's future direction. Although they had been two of the most powerful figures in China, no precise reasons for their fall were given beyond the vague charges that they had tried to develop "independent kingdoms" or to follow "erroneous" economic policies. At a December 1953 meeting of the Politburo, where Gao was present, Mao claimed that there were now "two headquarters in Peking. The first, headed by me, stirred up an open wind and lit an open fire. The second, headed by others, stirred up a sinister wind and lit a sinister fire; it was operating underground."[1] After making these vague charges, Mao disappeared from public view for three months, allegedly "on holiday," leaving Liu Shaoqi to spearhead the ensuing investigation on party unity that led to the dismissals of Gao and Rao. Deng Xiaoping, in his capacity as secretary-general of the CCP, later announced that Gao Gang had "committed the ultimate treason"—suicide. No word was given as to the fate of Rao Shushi.

Despite these crises at the very center of the party's power structure, the First Five-Year Plan achieved a dramatic increase in industrial production across a broad sector of goods. (See the table below.) The plan was designed to cover the years from 1953 to 1957, although exact details were released

*Taiwan was listed as the twenty-second.
†Tianjin was later added as a third municipality.

THE FIRST FIVE-YEAR PLAN, 1953–1957[2]

Indicator (unit)	1952 Data	1957 Plan	1957 Actual	1957 Actual as percentage of plan
Gross output value (in million 1952 yuan)				
Industry (excluding handicrafts)	27,010	53,560	65,020	121.4
Producer sector	10,730	24,303	34,330	141.0
Machinery	1,404	3,470	6,177	178.0
Chemicals	864	2,271	4,291	188.9
Producer sector less machinery and chemicals	8,462	18,562	23,862	128.5
Physical output				
Coal (mmt)	68.50	113.00	130.00	115.0
Crude oil (tmt)	436	2,012	1,458	72.5
Steel ingot (mmt)	1.35	4.12	5.35	129.8
Cement (mmt)	2.86	6.00	6.86	114.3
Electric power (billion kwh)	7.26	15.90	19.34	121.6
Internal combustion engines (thousand hp)	27.6	260.2	609.0	234.2
Hydroelectric turbines (kw)	6,664	79,500	74,900	94.2
Generators (thousand kw)	29.7	227.0	312.2	137.5
Electric motors (thousand kw)	639	1,048	1,455	138.8
Transformers (thousand kva)	1,167	2,610	3,500	134.1
Machine tools (units)	13,734	12,720	28,000	220.1
Locomotives (units)	20	200	167	83.5
Railway freight cars (units)	5,792	8,500	7,300	85.9
Merchant ships (thousand dwt tons)	21.5	179.1	54.0	30.2
Trucks (units)	0	4,000	7,500	187.5
Bicycles (thousand units)	80	555	1,174	211.5
Caustic soda (tmt)	79	154	198	128.6
Soda ash (tmt)	192	476	506	106.3
Ammonium sulphate (tmt)	181	504	631	125.2
Ammonium nitrate (tmt)	7	44	120	272.7
Automobile tires (thousand sets)	417	760	873	114.9
Sulphuric acid (tmt)	149	402	632	157.2
"666" insecticide (tons)	600	70,000	61,000	87.1

Note: mmt = million metric tons; tmt = thousand metric tons.

only in 1955 because of continuing internal debate over procedures. Most of its targets had already been fulfilled by the end of 1956. Even if the output figures for 1952 are considered artificially low because of the long periods of industrial disruption brought on by the Japanese war, the civil war, and the first period of Communist retrenchment, the plan was still a formidable achievement.

This was the period of closest collaboration between China and the Soviet Union. Thousands of Soviet technical advisers came to China to help with factory building, industrial planning, the development of hydroelectric power, the extension of the railway network, and even urban architecture—where their massive structures failed to harmonize with China's urban landscape. The Soviet technique for rapid industrial growth has been summarized as containing five basic elements: an emphasis on the need for high growth across the entire plan period, a focus on heavy industry as the index of meaningful growth, insistence on high rates of saving and investment to make that growth possible, institutional transformations in agriculture, and a bias toward capital-intensive methods. In all these ways the Chinese followed their Soviet mentors. The Chinese also added a rigorous policy of "primitive accumulation" that forced the peasantry to sell more than a quarter of their total grain production to the state at extremely low prices. This policy left the peasants at subsistence level while it enabled the government to guarantee food supplies in the cities and keep wages down.

The government had prepared the economy for the five-year plan by curbing inflation, which was achieved by 1952 despite the pressures for military production brought on by the Korean War. Use of the new *renminbi* currency was enforced throughout China, a process completed when the separate currency that had been circulating in Manchuria was withdrawn

DISTRIBUTION OF GOVERNMENT BUDGET EXPENDITURES, 1950–1957[3]

Expenditure category	1950	1952	1957
Economic construction	25.5%	45.4%	51.4%
Social, cultural, and educational outlays	11.1	13.6	16.0
National defense	41.5	26.0	19.0
Government administration	19.3	10.3	7.8
Other	2.6	4.7	5.8
Total in percent	100.0	100.0	100.0
Total in millions of yuan	6,810	16,790	29,020

in March 1951. The state produced a balanced budget by ruthlessly controlling government spending and reorganizing the tax system to raise rates on urban dwellers. Particularly striking here was the reduction in the percentage of the budget that was allocated to the government's own administration, and the effective reduction of military expenses (see the table below). The other side of this coin was the low level of investment in public health and welfare undertaken during this phase of rapid industrial growth, as the table below shows. Despite this small investment, with the conclusion of the terrible wars that had racked China for so long, and the adoption of basic measures of hygiene and disease and pest control—both by voluntary means and through mass campaigns—the population of China expanded rapidly, growing dramatically in each province except Guangxi. This is known with some certainty because in 1953 the first full-scale Chinese census was taken using comparatively modern methods.* The census figures showed that China's population had grown by well over 100.0 million since the late Qing, and now numbered 582.6 million; by 1957, the population had risen to 646.5 million.

The government met its budgetary deficits not by issuing new notes—as the Guomindang had—or by borrowing large sums from powerful credi-

DISTRIBUTION OF FIXED CAPITAL INVESTED BY THE STATE, 1952–1957[4]

Economic sector	1952	1955	1957
Industry	38.8%	46.2%	52.3%
Construction	2.1	3.9	3.3
Prospecting for natural resources	1.6	3.2	2.2
Agriculture, forestry, water management, and meteorology	13.8	6.7	8.6
Transport and communication	17.5	19.0	15.0
Trade	2.8	3.7	2.7
Culture, education, and research	6.4	6.3	6.7
Public health and welfare	1.3	1.1	0.9
Urban public utilities	3.9	2.4	2.8
Government administration	0.4	1.5	1.3
Other	11.4	6.9	4.2
Total in percent	100.0	100.0	100.0
Total in million yuan	4,360	9,300	13,830

*Some demographers say that the 1953 figures may have been undercounted by anywhere from 5 percent to 15 percent, which would make the subsequent rise less dramatic.

tors, but by sale of government bonds and the encouragement of "contributions," stimulated by mass patriotic campaigns. Since consumer goods were deliberately kept in short supply, saving was further stimulated. The Bank of China was also able to bring interest rates down dramatically, strengthening faith in the economy. Bank interest rates that had been 70 percent to 80 percent per annum in December 1949 were brought down to 18 percent in 1950, and to 3 percent in 1951. To heighten confidence further, all wages were paid out to workers, and savings received into the state banks, on the basis of "commodity basket" values—that is, on the basis of the cost of a typical package of food staples, cloth, coal, and cooking oils. The cost of such a package was announced in all major cities every seven to ten days, and those withdrawing from savings would be given the new cash equivalent to the commodity-basket units they had originally deposited, plus accumulated interest. Retail price rises were held to between 1.5 percent and 2.0 percent per year between 1952 and 1957.

China's state planners were often ignorant of basic procedures, and the planning process itself was marred by numerous errors, production bottlenecks, and disagreements between the industrial ministries in Peking and the local producers. Threatened by production-quota deadlines, many managers were encouraged to build up unofficial stockpiles of goods. Furthermore, there was a minimum of cooperation among industries, and fierce competition for emergency supplies and repair services. Tensions with private firms lessened, however, as partial state involvement spread to ever more of the private enterprises. This trend continued through the Five Anti campaign and into the First Five-Year Plan, until at the end of 1955 an official shift to the nationalization of private industry abolished all wholly private enterprises, leaving China with only two forms of industrial organization: the completely state-controlled and the mixed public and private.

The complexity of the government's task in trying to coordinate all levels of production, supply, and distribution is well shown by the new ministries that were constantly being added to the original ones formed in 1949. In 1955, for instance, four new ministries were added to manage agricultural supplies, coal, electric power, and petroleum industries. Many of the personnel in the technically most demanding of these new ministries—those of electric power and petroleum—had been trained in the Soviet Union and were later to attain an extraordinary influence in the government and party. In 1956 no fewer than nine more ministries were established to administer aquatic products, building-materials industries, chemical industries, metallurgical industries, power equipment, state farms and land reclamation, the timber industry, urban construction, and urban services.

For the urban workers, increases in production brought material benefits and a measure of job security, but at the cost of personal mobility. It was hard to change assigned jobs, and strict controls were placed over travel into the cities by country dwellers. Through its own union organizations and party apparatus the government controlled the workers much more effectively than the Guomindang had ever been able to do. A careful comparison of annual food consumption by Shanghai families shows that living standards in 1956 were considerably higher than those characterizing the city's residents in 1930 (see the table below). But the people of Shanghai still were far from living in comfort.

The industrial side of the First Five-Year Plan was, given the nature of China's economy, intimately connected with agricultural developments. Indeed most of the resources needed for industry had to be extracted from

PER CAPITA ANNUAL CONSUMPTION, SHANGHAI, 1929–1930 AND 1956[5]
(in *catties,* except as noted)

Commodity	1929–1930	1956	% increase
Rice	240.17	270.74	12.5
Wheat flour	15.17	15.68	3.4
Pork	9.78	16.21	65.7
Beef, mutton	1.89	2.29	21.2
Chicken, duck	0.76	2.70	255.3
Fish, shellfish	10.17	27.39	169.3
Eggs	1.85	7.02	379.5
Vegetables	159.57	193.50	21.2
Vegetable oil	612.58	10.20	−18.9
Animal oil	0.47	0.71	73.2
Sugar	2.40	4.17	73.8
Cigarettes (20)	24.21	32.36	33.7
Alcoholic beverages	13.43	6.46	−51.9
Tea	0.55	0.15	−72.3
Cotton fabrics (m²)	6.43	14.00	117.7
Kerosene	19.17	0.40	−91.9
Coal and charcoal	43.14	228.17	428.9
Combustible grasses	242.77	78.24	−67.8
Leather shoes (pair)	0.17	0.27	58.8
Rubber shoes (pair)	0.10	0.51	410.0
Stockings (pair)	1.26	2.08	65.0
Living space (m²)	3.22	4.78	48.5

Units: 1 *catty* = 1.1 lb. or 0.5 kg.

the agricultural sector; some of this investment came in the form of taxes and savings, but the great bulk came from the meeting of government procurement quotas at artificially low prices. Once the first land-reform drives had broken the landlords, the state began methodically to group the peasantry into forms of cooperative labor. The first stage was to encourage peasants to join mutual-aid teams, which built on the social consciousness developed in land reform by showing the heightened productivity that could be obtained by pooling certain quantities of labor power, tools, and draft animals. Such teams usually included 6 or 7 households; by excluding rich and even middle peasants, they drove home to members of those groups the ambiguous and potentially dangerous nature of their position as affluent members of their villages. To further emphasize this point, the same meticulous scale of class status that was being followed in the cities was now applied to the countryside. Mao's essays on class in Chinese society were widely circulated, since most people in rural society were ignorant of the terminology, and special attention was paid to the rural "semifeudal" class relationships that Mao discussed. Land-reform experiences from the Jiangxi Soviet, Yan'an, and the civil-war period were analyzed. Landlords were given a variety of designations—"hidden," "bankrupt," "enlightened," "overseas Chinese," "despotic"—and middle peasants were subdivided into "old," "new," and "well-to-do." As discussion deepened, the mutual-aid teams, which had initially been disbanded after each harvest season, were gradually solidified on a year-round basis.

In 1952 and 1953, the government tentatively experimented with bonding peasant workers from mutual-aid teams into cooperative units of 30 to 50 households. Land as well as labor was pooled in these cooperatives, even though each peasant family kept its title to the plots it contributed. This consolidation gained extra acreage for the cooperative by abolishing the strips that had separated the myriad tiny plots into which a peasant's holdings were traditionally divided, led to some improvements in labor productivity by eliminating the tiresome travel between plots, and in some cases allowed for use of mechanized techniques in farming. At the end of each year, after the government procurement quotas had been met and some money set aside for investment in the cooperative, the balance was divided between a "land share" based on the acreage contributed to the cooperative by each family and a "labor share" based on the daily amount of work each family performed. This was only a semisocialist arrangement, since richer peasants, by contributing more land, also gained a greater reward, for which reason these were often termed "lower-stage cooperatives."

The steady shift to cooperative organization involved enormously complicated decisions, not only about class status and work methods, but about the ideal size of plots for specific crops, the scope or feasibility of mechanization, and the exercise of authority within the cooperatives. The rhythms of rural campaigns had to be integrated with the mass drives in urban areas, so that the whole country was not in upheaval at once. By late 1955, however, after extensive propaganda campaigns and careful experimentation in target areas, the state began to whittle away at the land share, and increase the percentage that went into the labor share. To persuade the rich or middle peasants that this was to their advantage, the government withheld state credit and other facilities from them, so that they might come to see an economic gain in contributing to such "higher-stage cooperatives" in which labor performed became the sole criterion for remuneration. These higher-stage cooperatives were organized on a much larger scale, often including 200 to 300 households. They thus exceeded the size of most traditional rural villages, and demanded more full-time administrators and party representatives. By 1956 this shift was well under way, and the lowerstage cooperatives began to shrink in number as the higher-stage cooperatives gained (see the table below). At the same time, the government dropped its emphasis on mutual-aid teams, which then ceased to be a significant factor in rural life.

Peasants, however, still technically held title to the land they contributed to the cooperatives, and they were also allowed to keep private plots for their own use, which further preserved a sense of individual ownership and gave them scope for their own entrepreneurial skills. Such plots were not meant to constitute more than 5 percent of a given higher-stage cooperative's land area, but they were tilled with great fervor since the produce they yielded could be sold in rural markets by the producers themselves, who could thus supplement the income they received from the labor they contributed to the cooperative. Peasants generally used the plots to raise vegetables, which could be sold for several times the price of food grains. As much as 20 percent to 30 percent of farm income came from these private plots in 1956, and an astonishing 83 percent of all hogs in China were raised with feed purchased with this surplus income, supplemented by vegetable scraps. The same combination of foods was used to raise much of China's poultry. The livestock in turn produced valuable fertilizer, which went to further raise the yields of fruit and vegetables on these private plots.

The resulting surge in private production began to alarm Mao Zedong and others in the government who feared the resolidification of the traditional two-or three-class system in the countryside, in which a new generation of enriched peasantry might begin to rise at the expense of their less able, or fortunate, or ruthless fellows. In 1956 and 1957 the peasants were

SHARE OF PEASANT HOUSEHOLDS IN DIFFERENT TYPES OF
OWNERSHIP UNITS, 1950–1959[6]

| Year | Mutual-aid teams | Agricultural producer cooperatives | |
		Lower stage	Higher stage
1950	10.7%	negl.%	negl.%
1951	19.2	negl.	negl.
1952	39.9	0.1	negl.
1953	39.3	0.2	negl.
1954	58.3	1.9	negl.
1955			
End of autumn	50.7	14.2	0.03
Year end	32.7	63.3	4.00
1956			
End of January	19.7	49.6	30.70
End of July	7.6	29.0	63.40
Year end	3.7	8.5	87.80
1957	None	negl.	93.50

eating better than they had in the early 1950s, and their per capita consumption of grain was higher than that of urban workers. At the same time, it is clear with hindsight that the poultry and hogs raised on private plots contributed heavily to the availability of chicken, duck, eggs, and pork that was such a conspicuous feature of the industrial worker's fattened consumption basket. There was a paradox in the making, and how the government responded to the increasing success of private production would be of crucial importance to the next stage in the history of the People's Republic.

FOREIGN POLICY AND THE NATIONAL MINORITIES

During the early and mid-Qing dynasty, China had sought to perpetuate the image that the court at Peking was the cultural center for the bordering nations and the countries of the southern seas, that China's virtues drew those from afar into her orbit. The power of the Chinese emperor radiated outward, manifested in the influence of such cultural artifacts as the works of Confucius, the Chinese calendar, and the Chinese writing system. The offering of "tributary gifts" from the more dutiful nations acknowledged this image, which China occasionally reinforced by the dispatch of embassies to oversee a royal investiture or scout out trade opportunities, although those embassies were short-term affairs and usually not led by senior officials. However, any universalistic pretensions the system might have had were always limited by the difficulty of controlling the nomadic tribes and Muslim peoples to the north and west of China, and were completely destroyed by the incursions of Europeans after their brief early years of deference.

It was a central goal of China's leaders in the 1950s to re-establish the international prestige that had dwindled to almost nothing under Yuan Shikai and the warlord leaders, and during the last years of Guomindang rule. As Churchill had warned, China's role in World War II did not echo in reality the great power status the Allies had conferred on China in words. The Korean War further complicated China's international status by fixing the United States in a position of hostility, which in turn ensured that Taiwan would remain outside the control of the PRC and the PRC outside the United Nations.

China's international prestige nevertheless grew swiftly in the 1950s, at the same time that the First Five-Year Plan was being implemented. This was a period of optimism for China, and by presenting the PRC as a new yet responsible member of the world community, Chinese leaders modified the sense of extremism generated by their domestic policies. The architect of this new foreign policy was Zhou Enlai, who held the dual offices of premier of the State Council and foreign minister, and could coordinate all decisions with the apex of the leadership through his position as a member of the five-man standing committee of the Politburo. A seasoned Communist revolutionary and the veteran negotiator at Chongqing during World War II, Zhou Enlai had a remarkable presence as a diplomat that came in part from his prosperous background, in part from his years in France as a young man, and in part from his flexibility in pursuing his desired ends. Initially he concentrated on relations with India and developed a warm friendship, based on mutual respect, with India's postindependence leader, Jawaharlal Nehru. Zhou managed to persuade the Indian government to accept China's occupation of Tibet in 1950 and 1951, and Indian officials acted as the go-betweens for China and the United States during many difficult phases of the Korean War truce negotiations.

The death of Stalin in March 1953, which led the Soviet Union to modify some of its belligerent postures, also broke the impasse over the Korean War negotiations and ended the threat—posed by Eisenhower—that nuclear weapons might have to be used to conclude the fighting once and for all. Zhou Enlai attended Stalin's funeral in Moscow—Mao Zedong chose not to go, possibly because no senior Soviet leader had yet made a ceremonial visit to the People's Republic—and was treated with considerable respect by Soviet officials while he was there. He was permitted to stand with the new leaders of the USSR—Nikita Khrushchev, Georgi Malenkov, and Lavrenti Beria—instead of with the groups of "foreign" dignitaries, and walked with the same three directly behind the gun carriage bearing Stalin's coffin. These meetings bore fruit in late 1954, when Khrushchev himself visited Peking to take part in the fifth-anniversary celebrations of the People's Republic.

Both before and after this visit to Moscow, Zhou had been working to tighten relations with the other key Communist states on China's borders, in line with Soviet policies promoting solidarity among the socialist ranks. In late 1952 he signed an economic and cultural agreement with the Mongolian People's Republic,* as well as a formal agreement with Kim Il Sung to help in postwar reconstruction of the shattered North Korean economy. China forged close ties with the insurgents in Vietnam as well, building up the road and rail transport system in Guangxi province in order to send bulk supplies to Ho Chi Minh, now involved in the last stages of his struggle for independence against the French. These supplies matched the support that the French were receiving from the United States, and helped Ho Chi Minh's forces survive their costly and protracted war. As the Soviet Union began to show greater flexibility toward neutralist countries, Zhou also furthered ties with India and had amicable talks with Prime Minister U Nu in Burma,† all under the newly coined slogan of "Peaceful Coexistence."

The first great shift in China's diplomatic visibility came when Zhou Enlai traveled to Geneva, Switzerland, in April 1954, to attend the international meetings convened there to settle the Franco-Vietnamese War. Zhou walked a delicate line between Soviet, French, American, and North Vietnamese demands and counterproposals, and his patience and shrewdness were credited with helping the powers iron out an agreement. In this, the Communist Vietminh obtained independence for their state in North Vietnam, and the parties pledged to hold elections at a future date (not more than two years off) to create a coalition government of a united Vietnamese state. In exchange, despite their fears that this yielded up too much under Chinese pressure, the Vietminh stopped their subversive activities in the

---

*This agreement was also a *de facto* acknowledgment of the independent status of Outer Mongolia (i.e., the Mongolian People's Republic), and hence of the loss of territory that once had been more or less under Qing control.

†Since 1989 renamed the Union of Myanmar.

south and withdrew their forces from Laos and Cambodia, which were to be allowed to form independent regimes.

During one early meeting in Geneva, Zhou Enlai found himself in the same room with President Eisenhower's secretary of state, the staunchly anti-Communist John Foster Dulles. In a confrontation that swiftly became famous, Zhou held out his hand to Dulles, but Dulles rudely turned his back on Zhou and walked out of the room, uttering the words "I cannot." With a Gallic-style shrug of the shoulders at this behavior, Zhou delighted onlookers and made a small victory out of a moment of possible humiliation. He handled with equal aplomb Dulles's insistence that the Chinese delegate never be allowed to chair the Geneva sessions, and furthered the impression of urbanity and flexibility he conveyed by having lunch with Charlie Chaplin, who was living in Switzerland following his black-listing in the United States because of his radical politics.

Of even greater political importance, however, was Zhou Enlai's prominent participation in the Bandung conference held in Indonesia in 1955. Behind the calling of this conference lay an intricate skein of international relationships. More impressed by the considerable fire power and effective insurgent strategy that had led to the Vietminh victory at Dien Bien Phu than by Zhou Enlai's statements on peaceful coexistence, a number of anti-Communist countries had formed a new alliance. This was the so-called SEATO (Southeast Asia Treaty Organization) agreement, which was signed in Manila in September 1954 by the United States, Britain and France, Australia and New Zealand, and the Philippines, Pakistan, and Thailand. The goal of SEATO was to build an international alliance for stopping further Communist revolts in Southeast Asia. The member nations were particularly concerned about Laos and Cambodia, although they also harbored fears over growing Communist threats to South Vietnam and the Philippines. The SEATO powers did not maintain their own standing force, but pledged to aid each other with their conventional forces; they established the SEATO headquarters in Bangkok, Thailand, and developed subordinate bureaus in charge of public relations, area security, cultural affairs, and some areas of economic collaboration.

Zhou Enlai complained vociferously that while China was working for "world peace and the progress of mankind," the "aggressive circles" in the United States were aiding the Nationalists on Taiwan and planning to rearm the Japanese. China responded energetically in fall 1954, beginning a sustained shelling of the offshore islands near the Fujian coast that still harbored Guomindang army garrisons, and flying a reconnaissance plane over Taipei. Taiwan in turn mounted numerous air raids on the Chinese mainland, using advanced model U.S. fighter-bombers. The United States then signed a mutual-defense treaty with Taiwan in December 1954.

In response to this heightening of area tensions, the five countries known as the Colombo Powers—India, Burma, Indonesia, Pakistan (also a SEATO member), and Ceylon (Sri Lanka)—invited China to join them at a spring 1955 conference in Bandung, Indonesia, which drew delegates from twenty-nine Asian and African nations. Zhou, as head of the Chinese contingent, skillfully gave the conference a neutralist stance that made the United States appear as the major threat to the stability of the area. With the support of Nehru, Gamal Abdel Nasser, Sukarno, and others, the conference delegates produced strong declarations in favor of peace in the region, the abolition of nuclear weapons, the principle of universal representation in the United Nations, and arms reductions. Particularly telling to the assembly was Zhou's remark that "the population of Asia will never forget that the first atom bomb exploded on Asian soil."

One important sideline to Bandung was China's effort to resolve problems arising from the large numbers of Chinese living in Southeast Asian countries. The income that these Chinese sent back to their families at home was an important source of China's foreign exchange, and the last thing China wanted to do was weaken the loyalty of these overseas citizens to their native land. On the other hand the very large communities of Chinese in countries such as Indonesia (where they numbered more than 3 million), Malaya, Vietnam, and the Philippines, and their dominant position in many retail operations and other businesses, were considered by their host countries as potential threats to national security.

It was in Malaya that this threat seemed most serious. The Malayan Communist party had been trying since 1948 to destroy the British colonial government there by terrorist attacks on planters, police, and their associates, and by clearing "liberated areas" in the countryside as the Chinese had done during their resistance to Japan. Because the Malayan Communist party was more than 90 percent Chinese, it was easy to think of it as being manipulated from Peking, and to ignore the refusal of most Chinese settlers in Malaya and Singapore to join or help the party. In other areas of large Chinese settlement where local Communist forces, although scattered, were strong, such as the Philippines or Indonesia, the Chinese formed only a minority in the Communist parties and often faced discrimination prompted by the overwhelmingly nationalistic thrust of those insurrectionary movements.

One curious anomaly in this pattern of feared Chinese Communist subversion was the threat posed by tens of thousands of Guomindang troops who, defeated by the Communists in 1949, had retreated south and west, into Thailand or the Shan states of northern Burma. When Burma achieved independence from Britain in 1948, the Guomindang general Li Mi established an independent Shan regime for his Anti-Communist National Salvation Army. This army was partially supported with funds and advisers supplied by the United States, although most of its money came from opium-poppy production and distribution. Over 7,000 of these troops were repatriated to Taiwan in 1953; but at the time of the Bandung negotiations, 7,000 troops were still ensconced on the Burma-Laos border, and thousands more in northern Thailand.

China's stance had traditionally been that overseas Chinese remained citizens, and owed ultimate obedience to the Chinese state, now the People's Republic. But in light of these fears of Chinese subversion, and after protracted negotiations conducted largely by the Chinese ambassador to Indonesia, in 1955 the Chinese government signed its first dual-nationality agreement, in which it authorized Chinese to choose either their own or their host country's nationality during the next two years. In fact, the agreement was not ratified as a formal treaty until 1957, and the promise of harmony was undercut in 1959 when Indonesia decided to close many Chinese businesses and schools, and condoned widespread anti-Chinese incidents.

But those difficulties lay in the future and did not tarnish Zhou's image at Bandung as a flexible and open-minded negotiator. Zhou also showed great subtlety over the Taiwan and offshore-islands crisis. As it became apparent that the Americans—and perhaps even the British—would guarantee Taiwan's independent existence if Taiwan would abandon the offshore islands, which were a potential powder keg, Zhou persuaded the Chinese government to back off from confrontation and let Chiang Kai-shek keep Quemoy and Matsu. In May 1955 Zhou Enlai issued a formal statement declaring that the PRC would "strive for the liberation of Taiwan by peaceful means so far as it is possible."

Although it did not fall under Zhou Enlai's personal purview, the problem posed by China's minority peoples was comparable to that of the overseas Chinese. By Chinese computation, there were fifty-four such minority nationalities with a population of around 30 million. They occupied many of China's strategically important border regions, where indeed in the Qing they had served a buffer function between the Han Chinese and inhabitants of other lands. The CCP had actively recruited among such minorities, and Mao Zedong's second brother had been killed in Xinjiang while working among the Muslims there. Minority people who had become prominent members of the Communist party before 1949 included Mongols, Bai (from southwest China), Koreans in Manchuria, Uighurs and *hui* (Muslims) in the far west, and a number of Tibetans who had joined the Long March and stayed in Yan'an.[7]

Those Han Chinese cadres dispatched to work in these non-Han regions, where the local minority party members were too few to be effective on their own, experienced some of the elements of travel to a foreign country and some of the first stages of land reform in the guerrilla areas. Work teams sent into minority regions would seek out amenable local headmen, and if possible find someone who spoke Chinese. In the carefully articulated government descriptions of these relationships, it was claimed that the Han work teams were meticulous in observing minority customs and brought important benefits, such as the draining of swamps to control malaria, or construction of small irrigation works. By day, work-team members would undertake the boring, routine tasks of farm living—fetching water in buckets, perhaps, or gathering firewood. In the evenings they would perform simple plays to explore ideas of class exploitation, not hesitating to portray the villain as a Han Chinese official who had to be overthrown by revolutionary forces.

The work teams encountered deep distrust on the part of minority peoples. "A rock does not make a good pillow, nor a Han Chinese a friend" went one local saying. "If we read our stomachs will ache, our crops won't grow, and our women will become barren" went another. As late as 1957 one slave-owning member of the Yi minority in the southwest was his area's delegate to the National People's Congress. Nomads would quietly decamp at night, leaving startled cadres to find themselves alone at dawn. Some Tibetans who collaborated with Han Chinese on road-building projects were killed or mutilated by their fellow villagers. Problems in Muslim areas of Gansu in the early 1950s echoed those in the same area at the time of the great 1870 rebellions. *Hui* were forbidden to enter certain cities, allowed only a few posts in the local militia, and were even fired on by Han Chinese settlers. And in art and fiction the idea of the sensual and free-spirited minority peoples—especially their women— was given constant exposure in China, and contrasted with the sober, hardworking, and politically more dedicated ways of the Chinese Communist cadres.[8]

Yet despite tensions, confusions, and outright hostility, the CCP forged slowly ahead with local recruitment and party training. The admission of the first group of new Tibetan recruits into the ranks of the party (as opposed to those who had joined during the Long March) was proudly announced in the summer of 1956. In 1957 the journal *Nationalities Solidarity* saluted the party's reaching its goal of 400,000 CCP members in all the minority areas combined (the national membership total by then was 12,720,000), and of a further 600,000 in the Communist Youth League. To the leadership of the PRC, progress in integrating China's long-troubled border areas appeared as encouraging as their success in establishing ties with the bordering countries.

ARMY REFORM

The People's Liberation Army (PLA) performed bravely in the Korean War, but took a terrible mauling. Chinese casualties were calculated between 700,000 and 900,000. Medical services had been inadequate, food in short supply, and even clothing unfit for the Korean winter. Almost 90 percent of Chinese troops were reported to have suffered from frostbite in the harsh winter campaigns. Weapons had been a motley assemblage of American, Japanese, Russian, German, and other materials—often all four types being used in the same regiment—and most infantrymen were issued eighty bullets or less. Only slowly in 1951, as the Soviet Union made MiG fighters available, did the Chinese get any parity in the air. And they never had any effective naval forces to counteract the formidable sea power of the United States.

Even before the 1953 truce and the return home of its troops, China began a massive military reorganization in an attempt to develop a professional army that could compete with others in the modern technological world. Peng Dehuai, the commander of the Chinese forces in Korea who subsequently was named minister of defense, believed that the best hope for rebuilding the PLA lay in following the Soviet Union's lead and developing well-armed conventional forces, rather than relying on the kinds of guerrilla strategies that had served Mao so well in the 1930s and 1940s. This decision was accepted by the rest of the Chinese leadership, and in 1953 Mao called for "a tidal wave of learning from the Soviet Union on a nation-wide scale," even though the Soviets had proven at best a grudging friend during the early stages of the Korean conflict. The language used in a PLA training manual showed a pragmatic modification of Mao's earlier dismissal of American imperialists, despite their atomic bombs, as "paper tigers."

> The American army is politically a reactionary military organisation of the imperialists, and basically is a 'paper tiger.' But it is an army with modernized equipment and fighting power. Its training and equipment are very different from that of the reactionary nationalist [i.e., Guomindang] troops. To destroy thoroughly such enemy troops, it is necessary to build up a strong modernised national defence army, and responsible officers should give an all-out and correct understanding of the American army to every soldier of the PLA.[9]

One crucial decision that the party leaders made early on was that the PLA must cut back its numbers and focus on building a well-trained force that could be adequately outfitted and supplied. This was something Chiang Kai-shek had never been able to carry out with his own armies, despite the attempts of his various U.S. advisers. Even while the Korean War was in progress, the PLA began to demobilize large numbers of troops inside China, as soon as provision had been made for them to find employment in the cities or in their native areas in the countryside. By 1953 the size of the PLA was down to 3.5 million from its 1950 peak of 5 million, close to 3 million having been demobilized and 1.5 million new recruits brought into the ranks. By 1956 PLA strength was 2.75 million, and in 1957 2.5 million. Despite this demobilization, China's military budget remained surprisingly constant, and declined significantly as a percentage of the national budget only when that budget began to expand dramatically with the First Five-Year Plan.

The purges of Rao Shushi and Gao Gang in 1954 most probably meant that a significant number of China's leaders felt that too much power had been accruing to the six vast regional bureaus into which China had been subdivided during the early years of the PRC. In 1954 that structure was abolished, and the military was redivided into thirteen regional commands

CHINA'S MILITARY BUDGET, 1950–1960[10]

	Million yuan	Percent of budgetary expenditure
1950	2,827	41.53
1951	5,061	42.52
		48.00
1952	4,371	26.04
1953	5,680	26.43
	6,176	28.00
1954	5,814	23.60
1955	6,500	24.30
		22.10
1956	6,117	19.91
1957	5,509	19.24
	5,523	18.85
1958	5,000	15.12
1959	5,800	11.20
1960	5,826	8.30

under the direction of the PLA general headquarters, which reported both to the newly established Military Affairs Commission (of which Mao Zedong was chairman) and to the Ministry of Defense headed by Peng Dehuai. Although these were still large units—a typical military region comprised two or more provinces—the new organization allowed far more effective central control. The shape of a professional army began to emerge, especially with the development of technical arms such as the engineering corps, railway and signals corps, and the "ABC" corps, so named for its attempt to master the techniques of anti-atomic,-biological, and-chemical warfare. The Chinese believed the United States might use all or any of these if there were an all-out attack on China. Also closely coordinated in these regional commands were the Public Security Forces of the PLA, under a formidably effective Red Army veteran who later became PLA chief of staff.

By carefully integrating their needs with the industrial priorities of the five-year plan, the army was supplied with a wide range of modern infantry weapons, including rifles, machine guns, mortars, rocket launchers, and medium artillery. Because of the cost involved, however, the PLA remained poorly equipped with self-propelled artillery, military transport vehicles, heavy engineering equipment, and tanks. The caliber of officers improved as military academies in Peking, Nanjing, and Dalian began to train a new generation in the techniques of modern war. A significant number of Chinese officers were also sent for advanced training to the Soviet Union's military staff college in Kiev.

An adequate flow of personnel into the army was guaranteed by a conscription law, promulgated officially in 1955 following two years of experimentation. All able-bodied men between eighteen and twenty had to register, except for criminals and those "deprived of their political rights." Local authorities then chose those slated for military service according to a national quota system designed to furnish about 800,000 recruits each year. Those who were only sons, along with high-school or college students, could get exemptions from conscription; but the majority of those chosen for military service, especially from poor rural areas, were happy to take the assignment, which offered a prime chance for upward career mobility and acquisition of special skills. The huge pool of nonconscripted registrants, along with those who had served their three-year terms, were formed into reserve units. The CCP maintained a flow of propaganda about the glorious service to the nation that conscription in the PLA made possible, and issued vivid accounts designed to show how different conditions now were from the days of Guomindang conscription. Nevertheless, army life was still tough, and complaints about hardship and unfairness within the military system were widespread.

Because of the length of time needed to acquire new technical skills, conscription into the air force meant a term of four years, and in the navy a term of five. Both these arms, considered crucial to PRC defenses after China's experiences in Korea, had to be built up from a weak base, since most of the matériel left after the anti-Japanese war had ended up in Guomindang hands. Suitably enough, the deputy director of the air force training department was a former Guomindang air captain who had defected with his new American B-24 bomber from Chengdu to Yan'an in 1946. Other leading officers were those who had been allowed to take over Japanese planes in Manchuria by the Russian armies in 1945. After initial caution, the Soviet Union began making large numbers of MiG-15 jet fighters available to China in 1951, along with a small number of light jet bombers. But, anxious to avoid giving China any chance to escalate the war, the Soviets did not provide China with any medium or heavy long-range jet bombers that might have been able to strike more distant targets. From 1954 onward the air force concentrated its effort on building up a net of airfields along the coast near Taiwan, and it seemed clear that the purpose of this investment was to speed the recapture of the island. But the air force was not used to supplement the shelling of the offshore islands of Quemoy and Matsu, as if acknowledging that such acts might bring a dangerous U.S. response.

From 1955 on, the Soviets permitted the Chinese to manufacture the more advanced Soviet MiG-17 jet fighters under license at their own plants in Manchuria. The Chinese made no attempt to design new aircraft for themselves, apparently lacking the research staff or the design capability. If China still labored under a burden of technological backwardness, it was eased that same summer of 1955 when the rocketry expert H. S. Tsien was finally allowed to leave the United States, where he had been detained by the Immigration Department for five years under proceedings of dubious legality. Under Tsien's direction, the Chinese began assembling the staff to develop their own rocket and ballistic-missile program. At the same time, other Chinese nuclear physicists were working partly independently and partly in collaboration with Soviet scientists at the Dubna nuclear research institute near Moscow to build up China's own nuclear capabilities, and Soviet leaders promised to provide China a prototype atomic bomb at a future date.

The self-strengthening experts of the later Qing had considered the development of a modern navy central to China's defense against foreign powers and to the success of China's reform program; in the PRC this was no longer considered a high priority. China's small navy focused its energies on acquiring and manning fast coastal patrol vessels, the main goal presumably being to interdict commando squads from Taiwan that were still active on China's eastern coast, or to prevent smuggling and the illegal escape of defectors. The Soviet Union also made available some pre–World War II submarines. When, in 1955, the Soviets finally abandoned Lüshun, as they had promised to do, they handed over some vessels as well—including two destroyers and five newer-model submarines, of which two had long-range ocean-going capability. But it was obvious that, for a time, the Chinese navy was not going to figure prominently on the world scene.

The general growth of professionalism within all branches of the PLA had a profound impact on Chinese society and on the CCP itself. Particularly troubling was the problem of re-emerging elitism. In the countryside and in the towns, the protracted and often violent campaigns against the landlords and the capitalists had reasserted values of equality and cooperative labor. But in the army, where once in guerrilla days decisions were supposed to be made after group discussion, and ideological mobilization was as important as military tactics, all the steps in the mid-1950s seemed to move in the opposite direction. The last traces of the old camaraderie vanished as fourteen precise grades of officers' ranks were introduced in 1955, along with insignia and uniforms distinguishing officers from their rank-and-file troops. Pay scales became harshly differentiated, with a lieutenant getting ten times more than a private, and a colonel close to three times more than a lieutenant. Higher education and scientific abilities could lead swiftly to staff school and senior promotions.

Even more seriously, the combination of high status with the garrison mentality of troops away from home led to a range of abuses that, taken cumulatively, showed a slide away from the standards of local solidarity that the Red Army had depended on for survival in the areas where it operated its guerrilla campaigns. These new PLA troops were beginning to act like the Nationalists, or even like Qing bannermen. In the guarded words of the head of the PLA's political department in summer 1955, some officers now felt "no need for the tradition of unanimity of army men and civilians, and support of the government and love of the people."[11] In practical terms this meant that the PLA were requisitioning land, living in a luxurious style, ignoring road safety in their army vehicles, and taking over private homes without permission (no less than 72,400 homes, according to one estimate). Officers took their children to school in military vehicles, and used their status to reserve theater and cinema tickets for themselves and their families. The practice of abusing women in the local communities was also widespread, as is clear in the report of a senior and much decorated Red Army officer who was investigating charges of PLA misconduct. As he expressed his worries in 1957:

The officers of some units sought too many spouses in one area to the dissatisfaction of the local populace. It has been suggested that the officers must observe the following three points in seeking wives. First, they must not seek wives in schools. Second, they must not use money or other material goods as their means in getting wives. Third, they must not interfere with other people's marriages.[12]

The response to these and other abuses was an attempt by the CCP to bring the erring officers to heel by having them involve themselves and their units in the day-to-day life of production and work in the countryside; PLA officers were expected to contribute their physical strength and technology especially to the transition from low-level to higher-level cooperatives. An elaborate code of twenty shifts in behavior was drawn up by the PLA political department and promulgated to all units in February 1956. It is not hard to imagine how some officers, serving in what they had hoped would become elite, technologically advanced careers, responded to the directives, among which were the following: All officers' dependents should be persuaded to join in the work of the cooperatives. Work teams of officers and men should be placed under local party committees to help in agricultural work, and should contribute five to seven free labor days a year to local projects. On their holidays, the PLA were to join all local peasants in hunting down the "four pests"—rats, sparrows, flies, and mosquitoes. All PLA human excrement should be collected and given to local cooperatives as fertilizer. Every fifty PLA members must jointly raise one hog. All army men must learn the standard northern pronunciation of Chinese (which in the West is usually termed "Mandarin") and should help in primary and night schools. Military engineering workshops should be made available to peasant communities for the repair of their farm tools, and military signals units should allow their equipment and poles to be used to expand local communications networks.

In many areas the meticulous performance of such acts would surely increase popular support for a PLA presence, and lead to some mitigation of former hardships. But among some in the army the regulations would arouse profound antipathies and even undermine their obedience to the party. One of the most famous quotations from Mao Zedong's works, much in vogue in the West to prove the bellicose nature of his thinking, was that "political power grows out of the barrel of the gun." Taken that far, it did seem to confirm Mao—at one level at least—as a kind of heir to the warlord leaders and Guomindang generals who for so long had fought over China's wasted body. But what Mao had actually said was this: "Political power grows out of the barrel of the gun. Our principle is that the party commands the gun and the gun shall never be allowed to command the party."[13] As army officers and even regular troops began to gain new technical skills that Communist cadres had not yet mastered, tensions between army and party had to be reckoned with. It was not clear in which direction the predominant tilt would go.

THE HUNDRED FLOWERS

During the first years of the People's Republic, the intellectuals of China struggled to find a satisfactory position under the new regime. The substance and methods of traditional Chinese learning had been thoroughly attacked by the May Fourth generation of social critics; but if anything, the ensuing intellectual climate was even more complex, since layers of modern Western disciplines and concepts now subsisted alongside the traditional ideas without effectively replacing them. Education remained a time-consuming and costly process, and most intellectuals continued to come from families that had made or inherited money from landholdings or business. Those with staff positions in the government bureaucracy, or who worked in the teaching or legal professions, had inevitably had extensive contacts with, or been employed by, the Guomindang. Those in universities and the medical and scientific professions had often obtained their advanced degrees overseas or been taught by Westerners in China.

Since such backgrounds were now considered "feudal," "reactionary," "comprador," or "capitalist," it was incumbent on the intellectuals to show their loyalty to the CCP. Most were ready to make the effort to help the new regime because they had become sick of the inefficiencies of the old China and had lost any faith that the Guomindang could bring enduring, constructive change. The CCP's promise that even Guomindang officials might stay on at their jobs had been reassuring. Not only did the bulk of the Chinese intellectual elite not flee the country to Taiwan or the West, but distinguished figures living overseas returned to China in late 1949 and 1950 to help in the creation of the new order. Among them were many scientists and economists, along with members of the diplomatic corps who had been serving the Guomindang in China's various embassies and consulates. Even those who had seen the faults of both the CCP and the Guomindang were drawn home out of patriotism and a sense of new opportunities. Lao She, author of *Rickshaw* and *Cat Country*—who had been living in New York since 1946 and was famous throughout the United States, where *Rickshaw* had been a best seller—returned home in 1950 despite the warnings of his friends that he might find life there difficult.*

During 1950 and 1951 tens of thousands of Chinese intellectuals of all ages were given six-to eight-month-long "courses" at "revolutionary colleges." These courses, carried out on pre-existing campuses or at sites in specially designated cities, were an attempt to lead the intellectuals to a true understanding of their class background and the sheltered nature of their lives hitherto. As well as being lectured by veteran CCP cadres on the nature of the revolution, and introduced to the thought of Mao Zedong along with the basic works of Marx, Engels, Lenin, and Stalin, they met with small groups of other intellectuals in joint sessions for discussion and self-criticism, and prepared "autobiographies" in which they analyzed their own past failings and those of their parents. This last requirement caused profound crises for many who had been brought up believing in the strict tenets of filial piety as derived from the Confucian tradition, and in general the entire process subjected the intellectuals to severe mental stress. As the process advanced, they moved from an excited appreciation of the shared group solidarity, through a period of intense isolation and guilt, followed by fear and insecurity, to a final "resolution" in which they both acknowledged and expressed their gratitude to the CCP for making their new lives possible.

The eleven-page confession of a distinguished professor of philosophy who had studied at Harvard University before returning to take up his post in China offers a good example of the final result. The professor began by criticizing the life of ease he had spent with his "bureaucratic landlord family," went on to analyze the "crust of selfishness" that enclosed him, to condemn his interest in decadent bourgeois philosophy and his wish to remain above politics, and finally to hail his sense of new purpose in life granted him by the Communist party and by the "miracles" of the People's Liberation Army.[14] The most distinguished alumnus of the process—in terms of former rank—was the former Qing emperor and Manchukuo ruler, Puyi. Returned to China by the Soviet authorities who captured him in 1945, he was subjected to "remolding" in a camp for war criminals in Fushun, Manchuria, and began to draft his first full confession in 1952.† It is impossible to tell if such confessions were sincere or not. The party rejected confessions it regarded as insincere or self-censored, but the use of irony was always hard to catch.

---

*The best-selling English edition of *Rickshaw* was given an upbeat, romantic ending by its translator, without Lao She's permission. The original Chinese novel ended with a pessimistic view of the future.

†Because of the complexities of his experiences, Puyi was not finally released by the Communists until 1959. In 1960 he was assigned a job at a machine repair shop in a Peking botanical garden. He died of cancer in 1967.

Intellectuals, like other members of society, participated in the confrontations of the Three Anti and Five Anti campaigns. Struggling to prove their loyalty to the new regime, they also volunteered to participate in land-reform teams, and worked to promote the party's policies. The need for "correct" thinking was made clear to them in a campaign the CCP officially launched in 1951 against a highly praised film released in 1950 on the late Qing self-strengthener, Wu Xun. Wu Xun had risen from the life of a beggar to become a landlord, and used his money and his influential contacts to help found schools to educate the very poor so that they in turn could help the nation. But CCP theorists pointed out that such reformist action discouraged revolution. Study groups all over China were ordered to attack the film, and its writer-director had to make a public recantation.

During the early stages of the First Five-Year Plan, Mao Zedong began to see that intellectuals—writers as well as scientists and engineers—of all political persuasions would be needed if there were to be a surge in China's productive capacities. These creative people could not be terrorized by campaigns like that launched against Wu Xun's film, or else the country would suffer. Cadres were told that they were wrong to "take the ability to grasp Marxist-Leninism as the sole criterion on which to base their judgments." Intellectuals who "are capable of working honestly and of knowing their work" must be encouraged.[15]

Yet when writers went too far in following up the logic of these remarks, they met ferocious opposition. The author and editor Hu Feng, who was a party member himself and held seats on the executive board of the writers' union and in the National People's Congress, wrote that the kind of control exercised by the party over culture "exhausted" people so that they could no longer think straight. The party's use of Marxism to judge works of art was "crude sociology" and "not based on reality." "This weapon is frightening, because it can stifle the real feelings of creativity and art."[16]

In 1955 Hu Feng himself became the target for a countrywide criticism campaign, and he was dismissed from the writers' union and his other posts. As the campaign deepened in intensity and spread to struggle groups all around the country, the accusations against Hu Feng grew more serious. Charged first with ideological deviation, he was next accused of being a counterrevolutionary and an imperialist, and finally cast as an agent of the Guomindang secret service and commander of an anti-Communist underground. Despite their wildness, the charges against Hu Feng became the focus for countless meetings to deepen political consciousness; these sessions were held, by design, while the rural reform campaign was being geared up for the move from lower-level agricultural cooperatives to higher-level cooperatives in 1955 and 1956. Thus the countrywide search for "Hu Fengism" became a way of detecting whether anyone dared overtly oppose the role of the party in speeding land reform at the cost of private initiatives. Hu wrote three lengthy self-criticisms, which the party rejected as inadequate. He was tried in secret—presumably on charges of counterrevolutionary activities—and sentenced to prison. Hu was to remain in jail, with one short hiatus of freedom, until 1979.

A curious situation now developed in which China's leadership became bitterly divided over how to deal with its own demoralized intellectuals. Of the wide spectrum of positions on the matter, two polar views stood out. One favored continuing the united-front alliance of the CCP with the intellectuals, arguing that their skills were desperately needed in the drive to achieve the First Five-Year Plan and in the transition to collectivized agriculture, and that their loyalty could ultimately be trusted even if they did criticize the party. The other held that the unity of the CCP was paramount, that the CCP had led the revolution and could not now be criticized from outside without fatal effects on party effectiveness and morale.

The tortuous course of what came to be called the Hundred Flowers movement emerged slowly from these political divisions. The decision to launch the movement was part of the attempt by PRC leaders to understand the significance of Khrushchev's secret attacks on Stalin's memory, made in January and February 1956 at the twentieth congress of the Soviet Communist party, which both Deng Xiaoping and Zhu De attended. It was a time when many felt that things were going well in China, a feeling expressed in a loosening of the drab dress codes, a brief blooming of flowered blouses and slit skirts, and even the staging of an officially sanctioned fashion show. Khrushchev's statement that war was not predestined between the great opposing powers also reinforced the views Zhou Enlai had been expounding at Bandung concerning the importance of peaceful coexistence. In a speech he delivered on May 2 to a closed session of party leaders, Mao elaborated on the idea of "letting a hundred flowers bloom" in the field of culture, and "a hundred schools of thought contend" in the field of science.[17]

There followed a lull while party leaders continued to brood about the problem in private. Mao was ebullient at the general successes of his policies, as we can judge by a triumphant poem he wrote in the summer of 1956, after he took three lengthy swims in the Yangzi to register his continuing good health—he was now sixty-two—with the country at large. But in the fall, things began to go poorly as the attempt to impose cooperative agriculture led to chaos and waste, compounded by bad management and contradictory orders. The rapid growth of the First Five-Year Plan period was clearly going to be hard to repeat, and the difficulties confronting China's leaders were becoming apparent. At the eighth party congress in September

1956—the first since the congress held just prior to the ouster of the Guomindang nine years before—Mao's most dramatic plans for faster economic
growth in agriculture were shelved in favor of stronger planning controls.
And in the new draft of the party constitution all references to the importance of Mao Zedong thought were dropped, as was perhaps inevitable after
the Soviet attacks on Stalin's cult of personality.

In explaining this decision, Liu Shaoqi was quoted as saying that "if one
is always repeating something so that people get accustomed to hearing it,
it does not serve any purpose." Statements by Mao that he might "retire to
the second front" seemed to imply that he was looking for a peaceful succession to his leadership, a theory reinforced by the introduction into the
constitution of a new post—honorary chairman of the Central Committee.
The general tenor of the congress opposed so-called united-front policies,
and favored stricter party discipline and supervision. Chinese leaders were
also concerned over the political riots that occurred in Poland that June, and
their worries were reinforced in October 1956 by the Hungarian uprisings
against the Soviet Union. At the same time, major demonstrations occurred
in Tibet protesting the presence of Chinese troops on Tibetan soil.

Mao had to use all his influence to get a full Hundred Flowers campaign
going. In a free-wheeling and often utopian-sounding speech of February
1957, delivered to a large group of intellectual and Communist leaders, Mao
tried to instill the idea of flexibility and openness into the minds of his
captive audience, in sharp contrast to what had become the party's more
authoritarian mode—one which he himself had helped to create. Other
party leaders successfully prevented the draft of this speech, "On Contradictions," from being published in the party press.[18] Only in late April of
1957, after months of pressure against foot-dragging party secretaries around
the country, did the full weight of the press and other propaganda organs
swing in favor of the campaign. It was now couched in the rhetoric of a
full rectification movement, in which intellectuals were encouraged to speak
out against abuses within the party. The campaign took aim at the CCP's
own "bureaucratism, sectarianism and subjectivism" in a deliberate echo of
the 1942 Rectification Campaign in Yan'an against similar vices. The language of the campaign directive, however, tried to reassure cadres that they
would be gently treated. This was to be a campaign for unity that would
bind all in common progress. It would be, said Mao,

> a movement of ideological education carried out seriously, yet as gently as a
> breeze or a mild rain. It should be a campaign of criticism and self-criticism
> carried to the proper extent. Meetings should be limited to small-sized dis-
> cussion meetings or group meetings. Comradely heart-to-heart talks in the

form of conversations, namely exchange of views between individuals, should be used more and large meetings of criticism or 'struggle' should not be held.[19]

Convinced that permission to air their grievances against the CCP was now official, the intellectuals of China responded with enthusiasm across a five-week period from May 1 to June 7, 1957. In closed forums attended by CCP delegates, in the state-controlled press, in magazine articles, in posters glued onto the walls of their campuses, and at rallies in the streets, people began to speak out. Mao and other high officials tried to lead the way by concentrating on such issues as reintroducing a measure of constructive physical labor for party cadres to keep them in touch with the masses, or allowing economic issues to get a proper airing before decisions were made. But the public criticisms immediately broadened the scope of the dialogue. They protested CCP control over intellectuals, the harshness of previous mass campaigns such as that against counterrevolutionaries, the slavish following of Soviet models, the low standards of living in China, the proscription of foreign literature, economic corruption among party cadres, and the fact that "Party members enjoy many privileges which make them a race apart." The earlier mass campaigns were called "a serious violation of human rights" by one professor of accounting at Hankou. He added, "This is tyranny! This is malevolence!" The voting system of ratifying party slates was a farce. "Today we do not even know the height or size of a person we elect, let alone his character or ability. We have simply become ballot-casting machines."[20]

"There seems to be an invisible pressure which compels people to say nothing," observed a Shaanxi professor, describing normative life under the CCP. "It is not true that all the peasants consciously want to join the cooperatives," said a Mukden teacher. "As a matter of fact, the majority of them are forced to join." Another Manchurian professor wrote that the administration at his university was "absolutely littered with feudal princes and stinking charlatans." A former friend of Lu Xun's wrote that there had been more freedom of speech for writers in Chongqing under Chiang Kai-shek than in today's Peking. "The communist party is at the end of its tether," ex-landlords in Henan allegedly said. "The time for our liberation has come."[21]

In the heart of Peking University, the students created what they called a "Democratic Wall" and covered it with posters critical of the CCP. Addressing students there in late May, a young woman from another campus defended Hu Feng, blasted the Yan'an campaign for the restrictions it had imposed on literary and poetic production, and urged the students to coordinate their protest movement with actions already occurring in the northwest, Nanjing, and Wuhan. In fact protests had already erupted in far more cities than that, and soon from Chengdu to Qingdao there were reports of excited groups of students rioting, beating up cadres, ransacking files, calling on other colleges and secondary schools to join them in sympathy strikes, and urging new educational policies. Not since the spread of the May Fourth movement in 1919 had there been such a concerted cultural and political outcry.

Some of China's most famous scholars began to publish articles of astonishing frankness. Fei Xiaotong, a pioneering sociologist whose essays and books on rural China and the traditional gentry system had been famous in the 1930s and 1940s, was among the most outspoken. In June 1957 he published an account of his return visit earlier that year to Kaixiangong village in a remote part of Jiangsu, where he had done important field work in the 1930s. Fei pointed out numerous problems that still existed in the area, including irrational planning practices, disregard for local industries, failure to raise livestock suited to the environment, and total neglect of children's education. Fei's implication was that in the mid-1950s many aspects of life in Kaixiangong were no better than they had been in the mid-1930s, and he included several reflective passages in which his uneasiness with current Maoist policies shone through his circumlocutions:

> To doubt the superiority of collectivization is incorrect. But to recognize the superiority of collectivization and at the same time believe that it solves all problems is in my opinion incorrect as well. The one way is as incorrect as the other. If we think too simplemindedly, we will be in greater danger of error. Please excuse me if I go on about this: I hope that I can keep the reader from seizing on one or two of my sentences to argue that I am being negative.[22]

The party secretaries in at least nine of China's provinces had never backed the Rectification Campaign, and many others were doubtless only reluctant participants. Their backlash began in June. They were supported by those in Peking who had always opposed the campaign but had been temporarily overruled by Mao. Realizing that the tide was now going against him, Mao swung to the side of the hard-liners. He altered the text of "Contradictions" so that it read as if the promised intellectual freedoms were to be used only if they contributed to the strengthening of socialism, and this revised version was published and widely disseminated. It now appeared that the speech was a censure of intellectuals rather than the encouragement of public criticisms that Mao had originally intended it to be. In July, an intensive propaganda assault against critics of the party was mounted in all major newspapers across the country, and the CCP announced the start of an "antirightist campaign." In early August Peng Zhen accused the CCP's critics of behaving like the "anti-communist, counter-revolutionary 'heroes' Chiang Kai-shek and Wang Jingwei" during 1927; should the CCP in 1957, he asked rhetorically, behave as Chen Duxiu, the party leader, did in those dark days of the Shanghai and Wuhan massacres, and "with 'great magnanimity' 'forgive' the anti-communist, anti-people, counter-revolutionary crimes . . . and suffer the ferocious onslaughts of the bourgeois rightists?" His answer was preordained: "Very definitely, we cannot."[23]

By the end of the year, over 300,000 intellectuals had been branded "rightists," a label that effectively ruined their careers in China. Many were sent to labor camps or to jail, others to the countryside not just to experience life on the land for a year, but into what was essentially a punitive exile that might last for life. Among them was Ding Ling, her Stalin prize and her reaffirmed loyalties forgotten, banished to a border farm in Heilongjiang. A whole generation of bright young party activists were similarly penalized, among them some of China's finest social scientists, scientists, and economists. Fei Xiaotong himself gave an abject public confession to the National People's Congress, which still met occasionally in formal session, allegedly keeping some form of democratic participation alive on a countrywide scale. Fei repudiated his Kaixiangong report, and confessed he had been "doubting and opposing the goals of socialism," had "incited a worsening of relations between the Party and the peasants," and "even planned to use these materials to write yet another piece of propaganda for foreigners."[24] Fei lost his various honorific posts, was labeled a "rightist," and was forbidden to teach, publish, or conduct research on Chinese society. Still he was more fortunate than many other professors and students who were driven to suicide by the incessant pressure of public struggle sessions. Three student leaders in the Hanyang First Middle School who had triggered a bitter protest against the CCP administration of their school were tried and shot; according to the New China News Agency the executions were carried out at the start of the new school year and in the presence of 10,000 people, many of them presumably fellow students. The blooming of the Hundred Flowers had ended with a vengeance, leaving China poised for a new era of sharp revolutionary struggle.

CHAPTER 21

Deepening the Revolution

THE GREAT LEAP FORWARD

The Hundred Flowers campaign was not a simple plot by Mao to reveal the hidden rightists in his country, as some critics later charged and as he himself seemed to claim in the published version of his speech "On . . . Contradictions." It was, rather, a muddled and inconclusive movement that grew out of conflicting attitudes within the CCP leadership. At its center was an argument about the pace and type of development that was best for China, a debate about the nature of the First Five-Year Plan and the promise for further growth. From that debate and the political tensions that accompanied it sprang the Great Leap Forward.

Despite the speed of compliance with the call for higher-level cooperatives, agricultural production figures for 1957 were disappointing. Grain production increased only 1 percent over the year, in the face of a 2 percent population rise. Cotton-cloth rations had to be cut because of shortages. Indeed although the First Five-Year Plan had met its quotas well enough, it had also revealed disturbing imbalances in the Chinese economic system. While industrial output rose at about 18.7 percent per year during the plan period, agricultural production rose only about 3.8 percent. Per capita grain consumption grew even less, at just under 3 percent per year. With rural markets booming, local purchasers bought up most of the grains, edible oils, and cotton that was for sale, decreasing the amount available for state procurement or for urban consumers. At current levels of agricultural production, it was hard to see how more could be extracted from the peasantry to pay for the heavy industrial growth that was mandated by the Soviet model, unless China were treated to the same ruthless program of enforced agricultural procurement that had caused such terrible famine in the USSR in the early 1930s. But this was an unlikely measure, since in the 1950s China's per capita grain production was far lower than the Soviet Union's had been in the 1930s. Moreover, the CCP membership was almost 70 percent rural (the Soviet party was 70 percent urban) and would not be enthusiastic about such a policy if it led to misery in the countryside.

Mao's emerging response to the disappointing agricultural production on the cooperative farms was a strategy of heightened production through moral incentives and mass mobilization under the direction of inspirational local party leaders. Mao's vision, which drew on memories of methods used in Yan'an, was endorsed by Deng Xiaoping as party secretary-general, and by Liu Shaoqi, Mao's probable successor. By decentralizing economic decision making, this strategy would lead to even greater CCP power in the countryside and a corresponding decline in the influence of professional economic planners in the ministries. China's economic woes would be solved by the spontaneous energizing of the whole nation.

This debate over China's growth strategy, which unfolded during 1957 and 1958, took place in a period of ambiguous Sino-Soviet relations. The Soviets were making China pay dearly for aid in industrial development, and one reason China needed an even greater agricultural surplus was to meet the terms for repayment of Soviet loans. Yet Soviet technology, which had already mastered the production of the atomic and hydrogen bombs, seemed triumphant with the successful testing of an intercontinental ballistic missile (ICBM) in August 1957 and the launching of the Sputnik satellite only six weeks later. In early November 1957, when Mao made his second (and last) trip to the Soviet Union for economic and political talks, a second Soviet satellite was launched into orbit, this time with a live dog on board.

The Soviet achievement came only a few months after Mao had lost all hopes for a peaceful reunification with Taiwan. A series of anti-United States riots in Taiwan had been rigorously suppressed by Chiang Kai-shek, who publicly apologized to the Americans for the disturbances. Chiang's government thereafter allowed the United States to deploy Matador surface-to-surface missiles in Taiwan, from which the missiles could easily deliver nuclear warheads hundreds of miles into Chinese territory. Now, in Moscow, Mao told Chinese students that, weighing the state of international competition, the "forces of socialism surpass the forces of imperialism" and that "the East wind [China and the USSR] was prevailing over the West wind." This conclusion led Mao to the view that in a nuclear war the Chinese would triumph. "If the worst came to the worst and half of mankind died, the other half would remain while imperialism would be razed to the ground and the whole world would become socialist."[1]

Mao Zedong was troubled, however, by the loss of vitality as the Chinese revolution moved inexorably into a phase of cautious long-range planning. The roots of Mao's radical thinking had always lain in the voluntaristic, heroic workings of the human will and the power of the masses that he had celebrated in his earliest writings forty years before. Then he had seen his friends go off to early work-and-study programs that blended intellectual activity with manual labor, and he himself had plunged into the exciting task of organizing basic labor groups in which unlettered workmen were swiftly taught to master new skills and to seize their destinies for themselves from their capitalist exploiters. Following these experiences, Mao had felt the euphoria of working with emerging peasant associations in 1926 and 1927, when once again the simplest of illiterate peasants seemed able to grasp complex problems of strategy and politics and to apply them to their own grim circumstances.

In the circumstances of China in 1957, as Mao disappointedly told a gathering of CCP officials in Qingdao, the peasants and rural cadres had fallen into a pattern of "individualism, departmentalism, absolute egalitarianism or liberalism." This was shorthand for saying that the peasants were too concerned with gaining a better living after collectivization, that cadres concealed true output figures and exaggerated shortages in order to pay less to the state and get more from it, and that peasants and rural cadres alike resented the higher living standards of urban workers and urban cadres. This rhetoric was accompanied by police action, as groups of internal security agents fanned out across the country, hunting down those criticizing the government or those whose behavior could in any way be described as "capitalist." Unlicensed traders, peddlers, vagrants, and "delinquents" were all caught in the net, given long sentences in detention camps, and in some cases publicly shot.[2]

On a different tack, but still veering in the same direction, Mao sorted out his thoughts on the idea of continuing revolution. In the Soviet Union the theory of "permanent" revolution had been repudiated as a Trotskyist heresy that denied the validity of correct revolutionary stages and the leadership role of the party. Mao boldly seized on a similar concept with a different label in an attempt to give "continuing revolution" new respectability as a Chinese contribution to revolutionary theory and practice. The idea could draw on all of China's revolutionary experiences to date, and could be invoked to mobilize the activities of the masses yet again. Here it is worth quoting Mao's own words, in this instance from a list of "Sixty Points on Working Methods" that he circulated as an internal document to senior Communists in January and February 1958:

Continuing revolution. Our revolutions come one after another. Starting from the seizure of power in the whole country in 1949, there followed in quick succession the anti-feudal land reform, the agricultural co-operativization, and the socialist reconstruction of private industries, commerce, and handicrafts. ... Now we must start a technological revolution so that we may overtake Britain in fifteen or more years. ... After fifteen years, when our foodstuffs and iron and steel become plentiful, we shall take a much greater initiative. Our revolutions are like battles. After a victory, we must at once put forward a new task. In this way, cadres and the masses will forever be filled with revolutionary fervour, instead of conceit. Indeed, they will have no time for conceit, even if they like to feel conceited. With new tasks on their shoulders, they are totally preoccupied with the problems for their fulfilment.[3]

In elaborating on this idea of continuous revolutionary upsurge, Mao also emphasized the need for all Chinese to be both "red and expert," to forge a true synthesis of their socialist commitment and their technical skills. Mao celebrated the fact that China's 600 million people were "poor and blank," as he phrased it, for "poor people want change, want to do things, want revolution. A blank sheet of paper has no blotches, and so the newest and most beautiful words can be written on it, the newest and most beautiful pictures can be painted on it."[4] From this, as the vision soared, it was a short leap of memory back to the most utopian and finely phrased passage of Marx's *The German Ideology,* which was to become the most quoted passage of Marx in the China of 1958. Writing of the future joys of a communist society, Marx exclaimed that it would be a world in which

nobody has one exclusive sphere of activity but each can become accomplished in any branch he wishes, [a society that] regulates the general production and thus makes it possible for me to do one thing today and another tomorrow, to hunt in the morning, fish in the afternoon, rear cattle in the evening, criticize after dinner, just as I have a mind, without ever becoming hunter, fisherman, shepherd or critic.[5]

In late 1957, the leaders of the CCP began to experiment with a new scale of social organization by mobilizing the peasants for gigantic new tasks in water control and irrigation, as if to prove that human will and strength could vanquish all natural and technical challenges. By the end of January 1958, 100 million peasants had allegedly opened up 7.8 million hectares of land through irrigation work. If China's people could be galvanized in this way, surely they could transform agricultural production equally; it was just a question of finding the right organizational forms and maintaining mass commitment. But the almost military dragooning of labor on the irrigation projects led to new social problems as men were taken away from their cooperatives to work at some distance from home. One solution to this problem was to persuade women in the countryside to take a greater role in farm labor outside the home. Since it was essential to release them from domestic work to do this, there were attempts to centralize childcare and household tasks, including preparation of meals. This centralization of domestic tasks became even more urgent when, to raise industrial production nationwide, party leaders ordered some industries relocated to the countryside. This would enable the peasants both to learn new techniques and to benefit from their productive labor in the slacker periods of the farming year.

Thus did the massing of higher-level cooperatives into much larger units become an accepted part of Chinese revolutionary thinking. The goals were to increase rural productivity in order to boost China's industrial growth, as well as to realize new human potential and flexibility. In the fall of 1957 the CCP Politburo ordered formerly urban-based cadres to "go down" to the countryside in person and examine conditions there, and work to increase production under the campaign slogan "More, faster, better, cheaper." Cowed by the mass rural hunts for dissidents, and manipulated by their local political leaders who were often fighting their own career battles, local peasants dared not dispute even the most fanciful claims for higher agricultural yields. The term "people's commune" *(renmin gongshe)* was not used in party journals until July 1958, but as early as April the trial abolition of private plots and the amalgamation of 27 Henan cooperatives into one immense commune of 9,369 households were carried out.

By the summer of 1958, after a fine harvest had dramatically raised everyone's hopes, the campaign to end private plots and to organize all of rural China into people's communes began, with extraordinary apparent success. Without exactly endorsing the policy, which had raced ahead under radical rural leadership with Mao's obvious if distant blessing, the Central Committee of the CCP, meeting at the seaside resort of Beidaihe near Tianjin in August 1958, acknowledged that "the people's communes are the logical result of the march of events." They attributed this to "the all-round, continuous leap forward in China's agricultural production and the ever-rising political consciousness of the 500 million peasants." Evidently dazzled by claims that rural production under commune management had doubled, increased tenfold, or even "scores of times," the Central Committee issued this ecstatic vision of the Great Leap process:

> The people have taken to organizing themselves along military lines, working with militancy, and leading a collective life, and this has raised the political

consciousness of the 500 million peasants still further. Community dining rooms, kindergartens, nurseries, sewing groups, barber shops, public baths, happy homes for the aged, agricultural middle schools, "red and expert" schools, are leading the peasants toward a happier collective life and further fostering ideas of collectivism among the peasant masses . . . .

In the present circumstances, the establishment of people's communes with all-round management of agriculture, forestry, animal husbandry, side occupations, and fishery, where industry (the worker), agriculture (the peasant), exchange (the trader), culture and education (the student), and military affairs (the militiaman) merge into one, is the fundamental policy to guide the peasants to accelerate socialist construction, complete the building of socialism ahead of time, and carry out the gradual transition to communism.[6]

At their next meeting, held in Wuhan during December 1958, the Central Committee claimed that this "new social organization," which had "appeared, fresh as the morning sun, above the broad horizon of East Asia," was now in place. Across China, 740,000 cooperatives had been merged into 26,000 communes; these comprised 120 million rural households, or 99 percent of the peasant population. The triumph of production in the communes was such, the committee added, that China need no longer worry about overpopulation, as some had been doing. To the contrary, the forthcoming problem would be "not so much overpopulation as [the] shortage of manpower."[7]

The vision was altogether intoxicating, and seemed a complete vindication of Mao's views on the possibility for sustained growth through the mobilization of mass will and energy, especially when freed of the constraining effects of overcautious planning and an entrenched bureaucracy. For several months the euphoria was self-sustaining as the astounding production figures prepared by local rural cadres continued to pour into provincial offices, to be relayed thence to Peking. The language also was self-sustaining as observers caught the mood that they knew party leaders wanted. One example, from a reporter observing conditions in Jiangxi in the fall of 1958, can serve for a myriad others.

Small red flags fly overhead indicating the sections belonging to the various companies and squads of farmer-steelworkers, who are organized like militia units. The air is filled with the high-pitched melodies of local operas pouring through an amplifier above the site and accompanied by the hum of blowers, the panting of gasoline engines, the honking of heavily-laden lorries, and the bellowing of oxen hauling ore and coal.[8]

It does not belittle the vision—which was as rich or richer than anything expressed in China since the Taiping Heavenly King, Hong Xiuquan, ruled

over Nanjing just over a century before—to say that it did not coincide
with reality. The grain-production figures had been disastrously over-
inflated. The announced total for 1958 of 375 million tons of grain had to
be revised downward to 250 million tons (Western economists later guessed
that actual production was around 215 million tons). Not only had no cadres
dared to report shortfalls of the procurement quotas they had been given
out of fear of being labeled "rightists" or "defeatists," but many of the best-
trained statisticians from state bureaus, having been removed in the 1957
antirightist campaign (along with the most able demographers), were no
longer around to issue words of caution even had they dared. Furthermore,
the diversion of resources into local backyard steel furnaces—1 million had
been scattered across the face of China—did not pay off, since the furnaces
were not able to produce a high-standard product.

The Great Leap did bring several fundamental changes to China. The
pooling of all household, child-raising, and cooking arrangements had significant effects on family structure, even as it showed that the independent
nuclear family remained a more popular form of social organization. The
massing of huge numbers of rural and city workers for giant irrigation,
terracing, and construction projects changed the face of China's landscape
and brought prosperity to previously infertile regions. Thousands of peasants were given simple training and instructions and then sent out into
isolated areas of China to prospect for uranium and petroleum. The aim
was to prove that Chinese self-reliance could speed the country's development of a nuclear weapon, and end China's recurrent fuel shortages. In
several cases, the peasant prospecters made important finds. Cities were also
transformed, sometimes at great aesthetic cost; in Peking, for instance, the
last of the great city walls were demolished to create flat new boulevards,
and the city itself was honeycombed with a maze of underground shelters
in case of nuclear attack from the United States. The huge people's militia
that was developed during the Great Leap—when 220 million people had
allegedly been organized into militia units, and 30 million furnished with
modern or primitive firearms—brought new strength to local areas and
provided a potential rival to the PLA. The attempt also to mobilize a great
leap forward in poetry encouraged millions of men and women, who had
always thought poetry to be the preserve of a scholarly elite, to try their
hands at it, and spurred the collection by diligent fieldworkers of hundreds
of thousands of folk tales and songs. Perhaps this aspect of the Great Leap
came closest, briefly, to realizing a fragment of Marx's dream about developing fully rounded human beings with access to all their latent talents.

But criticism of Mao Zedong, and an attempt to constrain the communes
and return to central planning and allocation, had begun even before the

Central Committee's Wuhan meeting in December 1958. The rhetorical flourishes of those proceedings did not hide the conviction of most party leaders that they had moved too far too fast, and that the long-term prospects for the Great Leap were dim. These leaders refused to assert as forcefully as Mao had done that the communes marked China's transition from the stage of socialism to that of communism. By early 1959 some communes were already returning to their earlier cooperative forms, and their smaller subcomponents—the production brigades—were being acknowledged as the new units of accounting. In many areas, private plots were once again allocated to individual families. Mao stepped down as head of state during the Wuhan meetings, and in the spring of 1959 Liu Shaoqi was named to his place. Mao had earlier announced that he might step down, but the timing implied a measure of coercion, even though he kept his other powerful positions as chairman of the CCP and of the Military Affairs Commission.

Despite the chaos caused by the Great Leap, there was only one attempt to censure Mao for the extremism of his plan. This criticism came from the army marshal Peng Dehuai at a conference of China's top leaders (Chen Yun and Deng Xiaoping were absent, attending to other duties) held at Lushan in Jiangxi during July 1959. In informal discussions at Lushan, Peng Dehuai pointed out some of the Great Leap's problems, and also observed that Mao's home village in Hunan had received more state aid than Mao realized. Peng had already voiced grave doubts about the accuracy of the enormous grain-harvest figures (375 million tons) that had been reported for 1958, and in a private letter he delivered to Mao at Lushan, Peng spelled out his worries over the misreporting of conditions in the countryside, and its potential effect on the nation.

Instead of treating the letter as a private communication from a trusted colleague, Mao circulated it to all the senior cadres present, and launched a personal denunciation of Peng. He accused Peng of forming a "right opportunist clique" and of "unprincipled factional activity,"[9] and made it clear that he believed Peng, who had just been visiting the Soviet Union, had given negative information about the communes to Khrushchev. The Soviet leader had then used this information in a speech deriding the idea of communes. The bitterness of Mao's attack startled those at Lushan, and marked a key juncture in CCP history. Criticism of policy within senior party ranks had now been treated by Mao as an attack on his own leadership and foresight. Peng was removed from his post as minister of defense, and the other party leaders were cowed into accepting Mao's interpretations of recent events.

In a speech he made to his Lushan colleagues, Mao took a bellicose and self-justificatory position on the Great Leap and the communes. Confucius, Lenin, and Marx had all made mistakes, he said, so why be surprised that he had too? If everyone insisted on emphasizing nothing but the negative side, then he himself would "go to the countryside to lead the peasants to overthrow the government. If those of you in the Liberation Army won't follow me, then I will go and find a Red Army, and organize another Liberation Army." As for the communes, said Mao, "up to now not one has collapsed. We were prepared for the collapse of half of them, and if seventy percent collapsed there would still be thirty percent left. If they must collapse let them." He ended caustically, addressing those at the conference with language drawn from the rural people, as if to emphasize that he came from the masses whereas so many of the other leaders present did not: "The chaos caused was on a grand scale and I take responsibility. Comrades, you must all analyze your own responsibility. If you have to shit, shit! If you have to fart, fart! You will feel much better for it."[10]

The scatological metaphor was designed to shock the audience, and perhaps to defuse the tension of the moment with laughter. But in the context of the crisis in the countryside, the metaphor was crueler than Mao seems to have realized. At the time he was delivering his earthy remarks, peasants within fifty miles of Peking, like those in many other parts of China, were starving in their villages. One young party activist, branded as a rightist after the Hundred Flowers movement and exiled to the countryside to reform herself through labor, recalled later how she combed the mountainsides for apricot pits fallen from the trees, so that they could be pressed for oil or boiled for porridge. The other food of the villagers was rice husks or crushed corncobs, with apricot leaves dried in the sun and ground into "flour" before being mixed with powdered elm-tree bark to make another kind of "porridge." Since pigs, too, were starving in the new commune piggery, they were let out and allowed to roam the communal latrines. As the commune members squatted there, swollen with malnutrition and constipated from the grim diet, the pigs would jostle them with their snouts, trying to get at the excrement before it had even fallen from their bodies.[11]

The victory over Peng Dehuai at Lushan gave Mao renewed confidence in his revolutionary vision, and a determination to reassert the primacy of the commune system, bureaucratic decentralization, and mass mobilization. The organizational form of the commune was now spread to many cities in an effort to encourage factory workers to reach new heights of production. Far from responding to worries over grain shortfalls by remitting procurement quotas to desperate areas, Mao insisted on the heightened extraction of a dwindling peasant surplus. Still believing the wildly exaggerated reports of local grain production, many cadres even ordered fields left fallow to prevent crises caused to local communities by a shortage of storage facilities for the anticipated giant surpluses.

As China's investment in industry rose to an amazing 43.4 percent of national income in 1959, grain exports to the Soviet Union were also increased to pay for more heavy machinery. The average amount of grain available to each person in China's countryside, which had been 205 kilos in 1957 and 201 kilos in 1958, dropped to a disastrous 183 kilos in 1959, and a catastrophic 156 kilos in 1960. In 1961 it fell again—to 154 kilos. The result was famine on a gigantic scale, a famine that claimed 20 million lives or more between 1959 and 1962. Many others died shortly thereafter from the effects of the Great Leap—especially children, weakened by years of progressive malnutrition. In the China of 1957, before the Great Leap began, the median age of those dying was 17.6 years; in 1963 it was down to 9.7. Half of those dying in China that year, in other words, were under ten years old. The Great Leap Forward, launched in the name of strengthening the nation by summoning all the people's energies, had turned back on itself and ended by devouring its young.

THE SINO-SOVIET RIFT

The planning and implementation of the Great Leap Forward, and the subsequent Communist party debates about the reasons for its failure, took place at the same time that relations between China and the Soviet Union entered a catastrophic decline. In important respects, indeed, these two events must be linked together. For the Great Leap—a desperate Maoist attempt to break through economic constrictions and to reassert the centrality of revolutionary social change—stood in opposition to the Soviet Union's more cautious approach to economic development and mass mobilization.

Behind the Soviet-Chinese disagreements that emerged in the late 1950s lay a tangled history of friendship and distrust. Ever since the later 1920s, Mao Zedong had differed with Stalin by asserting his own interpretations of the need for a mass-based rural revolution, whether in Hunan, in the Jiangxi Soviet, in Yan'an, or during the closing year of the civil war. At the same time, he and Stalin had joined in the call for an aggressive wariness in dealing with the capitalist world, which each described—with a mixture of rhetoric and conviction—as the tenacious enemy of socialist development in both China and the Soviet Union.

In its early years, the People's Republic of China depended heavily on Soviet technical assistance to develop its own industry, communications networks, and power supplies. Soviet influence was also strong in such areas as architecture and city planning, higher education, and the arts and literature. After Stalin died in 1953, Soviet influence seemed to continue unabated, and the heavy Chinese losses in the Korean War required an intensified Soviet involvement in building up China's army, navy, and air force. This technical interconnection was valued and deepened by Marshal Peng Dehuai, veteran leader of the World War II Hundred Regiments Offensive against the Japanese, commander in chief of the Chinese forces in Korea, and the incumbent minister of defense. The Chinese accepted the fact that the Russians for the time being were their only shield against the threat of possible nuclear attack by the United States, a point that became especially important in 1957 when the United States announced that it would deploy Matador missiles in Taiwan. At the same time, Mao was anxious to advance China's development of an atomic bomb in order to reduce what might become a dangerous overreliance on the Soviet Union.

Nikita Khrushchev, one of the leading contenders to succeed Stalin, visited Mao in China during 1954, and some analysts have guessed that Mao subsequently used what influence he had to support Khrushchev, who was battling for leadership with Georgi Malenkov. If that was so, Mao was rudely shocked in early 1956, when Khrushchev launched his attack on Stalin's memory in a speech to the delegates at the twentieth Soviet party congress. Before making his charges, which had disturbing implications for those party leaders throughout the Communist world who had previously praised and venerated Stalin, Khrushchev had made no attempt to warn Mao in advance of what he intended to do. Indeed Mao's key general from Yan'an days, Zhu De, who was in Moscow as China's representative, had just praised Stalin in a speech at the same congress. The Chinese press proceeded to ignore Khrushchev's attacks in its own coverage of the congress.

Khrushchev underlined the new approach he wanted for Soviet-bloc relations in June 1956, when he invited Yugoslavia's famous former anti-Nazi guerrilla leader and current Communist chief, Marshal Tito, to visit Moscow. It was hard for the Chinese to accept this offer of an olive branch to a "revisionist" who had held his country aloof from the Soviet Union during the postwar Stalin years. Chinese leaders were further dismayed but probably not surprised when, in a bid for greater freedom and flexibility, the Hungarians rose in revolt against the Soviet Union that autumn. After weeks of bloody street fighting, the revolt was smashed by the might of Russian tanks.

There was still no overt clash between China and the Soviet Union, even after Mao published the emended version of his ideas on the theory of contradictions in the summer of 1957. By suggesting the inevitability of "nonantagonistic contradictions" even within socialist countries, and the need for their careful acknowledgment and resolution, Mao's speech could be seen as a rebuke to the Soviets for allowing the situation in Hungary to get out of control. Khrushchev nevertheless invited Mao to visit Moscow in October 1957 for the celebration of the fortieth anniversary of the Bolshevik Revolution. Mao's visit marked the second and last time he traveled outside China; the first had been his trip to the Soviet Union in 1949. On October 15 the two countries signed a secret agreement on "the new technology for national defense," in which, Mao later claimed, the Soviets promised to give China "a sample of an atomic bomb and technical data concerning its manufacture." After Marshal Peng Dehuai, who had accompanied Mao to Moscow, and various senior Chinese army officers and scientists had conferred with their Russian counterparts, the details of the assistance were refined, and over the next two years the Soviets helped the Chinese design and develop uranium mines in Hunan and Jiangxi, construct a gaseous diffusion plant near Lanzhou in Gansu province, and build a nuclear testing site in the Lop Nur desert of Xinjiang. The Chinese in turn reorganized their research structures to speed the independent development of a nuclear-weapons and a missile program should the Soviet decide after all not to help them.

Mao believed that the Communist bloc should now prepare for a vigorous challenge to the capitalist West, but Khrushchev showed no inclination to back away from the stance he had publicly taken at the twentieth congress in 1956, when he had declared that "the Leninist principle of peaceful coexistence of states with different social systems has always been and remains the general line of our country's foreign policy," and reasserted his faith in the basic principles espoused by India and China in 1955 at the Bandung conference. "There is, of course a Marxist-Leninist precept that wars are inevitable as long as imperialism exists," Khrushchev admitted, but this principle was now outdated. Pointing out the rise of numerous socialist states, and the power of the labor and the peace movements within capitalist countries, Khrushchev concluded that "war is not fatalistically inevitable." The peaceful transition of capitalist societies to socialism must also be seen as feasible, said Khrushchev, and "need not be associated with civil war under all circumstances." If backed by the proletariat, "the winning of a stable parliamentary majority" could lead to a country's securing "fundamental social changes."[12] True to this spirit, Khrushchev refused to respond actively to the United States' dispatch of marines to Lebanon, or to support the Chinese when they began to bombard the offshore island of Quemoy, still occupied by troops from Chiang Kai-shek's army on Taiwan. He also made it clear that the Soviet Union would not provide the Chinese with a prototype atomic bomb.

Khrushchev's caution angered the Chinese leaders, who felt defenseless on many levels. Their control over their nation's economy was shaky; they faced a Taiwan armed with the latest American weapons; and they confronted a U.S. government that remained unremittingly hostile and, they were convinced, might at any time use nuclear weapons against China. U.S. policies had combined with China's own to isolate China from world markets and Western technology, leaving her overly dependent on the Soviet Union for rare favors and for nuclear retaliatory power. The Chinese desperately needed Soviet aid to supplement the Great Leap strategy, yet they found Khrushchev to be grudging with spare resources as he struggled to raise living standards in the USSR. In 1959 Chinese leaders backed off from their earlier claims, made during the Great Leap, that they were nearing a rapid transition to communism; they noted, but did not explicitly comment on, Khrushchev's remarks to American leaders that the communes were in essence "reactionary" institutions that sought to boost production without adequate economic incentive.

Also in 1959, a wide range of global events began to impinge on China just when the country could least muster effective leadership to cope with them. In Laos, the coming to power of an elected Communist government was thwarted by a right-wing coup, with tacit and probably actual U.S. encouragement. In Tibet, a surge of protests against the Chinese occupation burst into armed rebellion in March. Many Tibetans were killed by Chinese troops in bitter fighting, and some of the most beautiful Lamaist monasteries were destroyed by the Chinese. The Tibetans' spiritual leader, the Dalai Lama, fled to India where he was given sanctuary despite Chinese protests. The apparent Chinese military victory in Tibet did not stop the insurgency there, in part because of the activities of the Central Intelligence Agency, which was training Tibetan rebels at camps in Colorado before flying them back to their homeland.

In addition to problems in Laos and Tibet, a crisis arose in Indonesia. After negotiations with the Indonesian government over Chinese trade and residence rights ended in failure, anti-Chinese riots erupted in many parts of Indonesia, thousands of Chinese were killed or injured, and the survivors were forced to abandon their money and property and flee the country. The confrontation was exacerbated for China when Khrushchev flew to Jakarta and offered Indonesia a $250 million credit package. Finally, the threat of war with India emerged after it was revealed that several stretches of a strategic road that the Chinese had built south of the Kunlun Mountains to

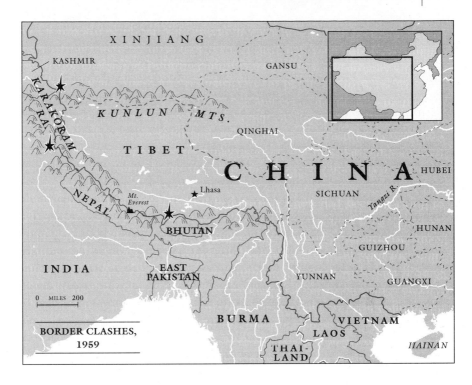

link Xinjiang with Tibet in fact ran across territory claimed by India. The conflict flared to include disputed Sino-Indian border territories in Bhutan as well, and in 1959 fighting broke out between troops of the opposing countries. With a major war apparently looming, Khrushchev expressed his views by extending generous credits to the Indian government, refusing to endorse China's territorial claims, and describing the fighting as "sad" and "stupid."

While the events at the Lushan plenum were unfolding in China, Khrushchev followed up on his coexistence initiatives by traveling to the United States to meet with President Eisenhower for protracted talks at Camp David. Immediately after returning to Moscow that September, Khrushchev changed planes, flew to Peking, and presented his case to the Chinese, repeating that "we on our part must do all we can to exclude war as a means of settling disputed questions."[13] Though Mao met Khrushchev at the Peking airport, he made no public comment on the Soviet leader's American journey, the withdrawal of the atomic-bomb offer, or Khrushchev's coexistence pronouncements. The party journal *Red Flag,* however, had already clarified official policy by remarking that some socialist leaders (i.e., Khrushchev) mistakenly believed that the Americans would "lay down their butcher knife and become Buddhas." Home in Moscow that November, Khrushchev responded by comparing Mao's belligerent attitudes to Trotsky's in 1918.[14]

Throughout 1960 the relationship between the two giant socialist states deteriorated. Charges and countercharges were bandied at international Communist meetings. Albania and Yugoslavia, oddly, became central to the polemic. Since China supported the Albanians in their bid for independence from Moscow, to criticize Albania, as the Soviet Union did with ever greater sharpness, was, in the eyes of informed observers, to criticize China. The Chinese responded by denouncing Yugoslavia, but choosing issues and attitudes that made it clear that they were really attacking the Soviet Union. While the Soviet-bloc countries issued statements concerning the horrors of nuclear war and the "annihilation of whole states," the Chinese press— echoing the statements made in 1957 by Mao—continued to insist that the Chinese were not frightened. After a nuclear war, ran an essay in *Red Flag,* "on the debris of a dead imperialism, the victorious [socialist] people would create very swiftly a civilization thousands of times higher than the capitalist system and a truly beautiful future for themselves. The conclusion can only be this: whichever way you look at it, none of the new techniques like atomic energy, rocketry and so on has changed, as alleged by modern revisionists, the basic characteristics of the epoch of imperialism and proletarian revolution pointed out by Lenin."[15]

That summer of 1960 the Soviet Union declared its intention of removing all its 1,390 experts and advisers working in China, a threat that was carried out in September when they were all summoned home, taking their blueprints with them and leading, the Chinese claimed, to the cancellation of 343 major contracts and 257 other technical projects. Among the departing Soviet scientists were two nuclear-weapons experts who had consistently refused to give information on atomic-bomb construction to the Chinese, and were derided by the Chinese as "mute monks who would read but not speak."[16] As they left, the two men tore to shreds all the documents they could not take with them. Painstakingly reconstructing the shredded documents, the Chinese found in them crucial information on atomic implosion. When, in November 1960, the Soviet Union called for a meeting of the Communist parties from 81 countries, Mao declined to attend.

Yet, as the Chinese had asserted in a statement after the November 1960 meeting, "the imperialists will never succeed in their hopeless scheme to split the unity between the Chinese and the Soviet Parties and between the two countries,"[17] and there may have been some lingering desire to retain working relations. For whatever reasons, when invited to attend the October 1961 congress of the Soviet party in Moscow, the Chinese not only agreed, but sent Mao's close collaborator and confidant, Premier Zhou Enlai, as their representative. At the conference, however, Khrushchev delivered a blistering attack on both Albania and Stalin. The allegories had simply worn too thin to be taken any more. Zhou Enlai walked out of the Moscow congress and returned to Peking.

POLITICAL INVESTIGATION AND "SOCIALIST EDUCATION"

In the confusing months of 1959 following the ouster of Peng Dehuai and the growth of tensions with the Soviet Union, Chinese leaders jostled for new roles in the ruling hierarchy, and the people at large struggled for survival. But by late 1960 the Great Leap strategy was discredited in most eyes; and while Mao "retired from the front line," as he put it, other Chinese leaders assessed strategies for recouping the nation's economic losses and rebuilding public morale.

One strategy they followed, which in a sense recalls the days of Mao Zedong's careful on-the-spot examination of local conditions in Hunan and Jiangxi in 1927 and 1930, was to have individual leaders travel to the countryside to inspect conditions for themselves. A crucial investigation of this type was made by Chen Yun in the early summer of 1961. Chen was one of the most respected and experienced CCP leaders, and was currently ranked number five in the ruling Standing Committee of the Politburo's Central Committee. A truly old-guard proletarian who had been a typesetter and union organizer in the 1920s, he had joined in the Long March, then studied in the Soviet Union, and been prominent in the Yan'an Rectification Campaign of 1942–1944. Since 1949 he had been the CCP's foremost spokesman on problems of economic development. In late June 1961, Chen traveled to a people's commune near Shanghai in Qingpu county, an area he chose in part because he had been born there and had organized peasants in the county as a young party activist in 1927. In two weeks of intensive discussions with local peasants, Chen quizzed them about their pig-raising procedures, crop-growing patterns, use of private plots, remuneration for labor performed, and involvement in local commerce and handicraft work. He also asked about their state purchase quotas, the behavior of the local CCP cadres, and problems of local crime.

Chen Yun was reassured that the peasants remembered his record in the area and therefore "dared speak the truth." This made their disclosures all the more worrying. Even in this commune, which should have been extremely prosperous because of its proximity to the huge urban market of

Shanghai, the peasants did not have enough to eat. Because the commune's collective agriculture had been badly supervised, they had no enthusiasm for it, preferring to work on their own private plots and on "sideline production" for the market. They believed that the Communist cadres in their commune had given wrong orders and then stubbornly refused to make self-criticism. And after having set arbitrarily high production quotas and procurement demands for peasants, the same cadres "have failed to participate regularly in work and have led privileged lives."[18]

In a hundred ways, Chen observed, the local peasants seemed to know those small details of ordinary rural life that were ignored by the party cadres who tried to make the peasantry conform to national norms and follow allegedly "logical" plans for collectivized development. It was the local farmers, he noted, who understood how to protect the weakest piglets from death by attaching them to the sow's third nipple, the one with the richest milk supply. It was these farmers who knew how to keep a sow from heatstroke in summer by using waterweeds as her bedding base. The locals knew that combining broad green beans with a single rice crop was far more productive than double-cropping rice or adding wheat. The locals knew that if their bamboo groves were chopped down to make room for intensive cereals production, then there would be not only much less fuel but fewer weeding rakes and handles for the simple harrows which they all used.

Drawing on these and other observations, Chen came up with five basic recommendations. Since agricultural recovery would take many years and conditions in the cities were also deteriorating, the 30 million peasants who had drifted into the cities since 1957 should be relocated back to their families in the countryside, and unemployed urban youths should be sent to work there as well. Thousands of inefficient Great Leap industrial enterprises should be dismantled. Although the principle of collective work was preserved, 6 percent of rural land was to be restored to peasants in the form of private plots. Private rural markets should be reopened. And individual households should again be made responsible for the fixing of output quotas. Chen Yun's pessimistic assessments as well as his recommendations were conveyed to Mao Zedong by three of China's most powerful leaders: Liu Shaoqi, head of state; Zhou Enlai, premier of the State Council; and Deng Xiaoping, secretary-general of the CCP. Mao agreed to let Chen Yun's views be circulated even though he himself felt that China was well on the way to economic recovery, and despite his strong opposition to any policy of dismantling the collectives.

During 1962 and 1963, as the party followed a policy of economic retrenchment, more and more evidence showed how bad morale was in the countryside and how frequently cadres abused their positions. It was the Great Leap famine that had sparked this corruption. Given enormous local autonomy in decision making to meet unrealistic national quotas, cadres adjusted to famine conditions by ruthlessly protecting themselves and those in their favor, while confiscating grain from the weaker or those they did not favor. Once the famine conditions eased, they continued to behave in high-handed ways. Numerous cases were reported of cadres who gambled, traded illegally, were corrupt, or arranged "marriages by sale." Fourteen-year-old girls were being sold for 750 yuan, and one girl was "married" thirteen times. Peasants often responded by retreating into the banned worlds of "spiritualism and witchcraft," or by cynically concentrating all their labor on their own small plots at the expense of the collective.

So serious were these problems that a range of leaders including Mao, Liu Shaoqi, Zhou Enlai, and Deng Xiaoping seem to have agreed on a comprehensive new program to reintroduce basic socialist values into Chinese society. Under the Socialist Education Campaign, class struggle was to be re-emphasized across the land as all joined in the fight for "four cleanups" *(siqing)*: in the spheres of accounting procedures, granary supplies, property accumulation, and in the system of allocating compensatory work points in return for hours and types of labor performed in the communes. Tens of thousands of cadres were to be relocated into the countryside, both to learn from the peasants by manual labor and to purify the peasants' understanding of the "mass line." The collective was to be placed ahead of the individual, public property ahead of private. With the formulaic use of numbers beloved by party theoreticians, there were to be "three threes": the first to promote three "isms" of collectivism, patriotism, and socialism; the second to oppose three "bad styles"—the capitalist, the feudal, and the extravagant; the third, to implement the "three necessities" of building socialism, loving the collective, and operating communes "democratically and frugally."[19]

The Socialist Education Campaign moved the struggles at the upper levels of leadership out into the countryside, as can be seen in the example of Liu Shaoqi and his wife Wang Guangmei. Wang Guangmei traveled to Taoyuan in Hebei province in November 1963 and stayed there until April 1964. Wearing ordinary working clothes, disguising her identity under a pseudonym and her face under a gauze mask (often worn locally as protection from dust or germs), she took part in mass meetings and slowly built up a circle of trusted local informants. Without telling even the local party officials who she was, she painstakingly compiled dossiers concerning graft and incipient capitalism among the local cadres, concluding harshly that in Taoyuan "the four uncleans exist universally among the cadres. All of them, big or small, have problems and cannot be trusted." Among the peasants, too, she uncovered no less than 66 forms of incipient capitalism, from selling chickens to building independent family businesses. When her report was submitted to her husband Liu Shaoqi, he instructed her to initiate public struggle sessions against the miscreants. Forty out of the forty-seven ranking cadres in Taoyuan were publicly criticized or removed from office. That summer of 1964, Liu and his wife made a well-publicized tour of central and south China (stopping in Hubei, Hunan, Guangdong, and Henan provinces) to spread their warnings against party corruption and to urge the need for stern correctives. Here again, especially in Guangdong, they found examples of spectacular abuses by allegedly "model cadres."

The harshness of Wang's condemnation could be interpreted as an assault on those very cadres who had risen to power initially in the early days of Mao's rural revolution, and then had consolidated their hold there during the First Five-Year Plan and the Great Leap Forward. Of these cadres, none was more famous than Chen Yonggui, the leader of a production brigade in the mountainous and impoverished Shanxi commune of Dazhai, in Xiyang county. By the dramatically hard work of its residents, under Chen's leadership, this bleak and eroded area had allegedly blossomed, increasing production fivefold, and proving to all the truth of Mao's vision of rural self-reliance and revolutionary zeal as the keys to China's future. Because of his achievements, Chen Yonggui was elected to the Xiyang County People's Congress, and in 1964 he was sent as a Shanxi delegate to the National People's Congress in Peking. Then followed a dizzying spate of honors: Chen was placed in the prestigious presidium of the People's Congress, publicly praised by Zhou Enlai, given a private audience with Mao, and allowed personally to address the congress delegates on his chosen theme— that "Self-Reliance Is a Magic Wand" for implementing Mao's policies. In late December 1964, Chen's photograph appeared beside Mao's on the front page of *People's Daily.* The caption repeated Mao's declaration of earlier the same year: "In agriculture learn from Dazhai."

What was especially significant about these public gestures was that during late 1964 an investigative work team—similar in composition and operation to the one run by Wang Guangmei in Taoyuan—had been looking into Chen's leadership in Dazhai. The team concluded that many of Chen's dramatic claims were spurious, based on inflated production figures, the underreporting of available land, and exaggerated grain sales figures, and that the people of Dazhai did not have enough to eat. "There are woodworms in the staff of the red banner of Dazhai. If they are not eliminated, the banner cannot be raised high."[20] In normal circumstances, Chen could have expected to be disciplined or dismissed like the condemned rural cadres of Taoyuan and scores of other scrutinized communities. But boosted by

Mao's declaration of faith, he returned to Dazhai in triumph and it was the investigative work team that retired, discomfited.

A different type of ambiguity was at the heart of Mao's call, issued in late 1963, that in industry China should "learn from Daqing." The huge Daqing oilfields in Heilongjiang, first explored by technicians and squads of peasants in the Great Leap period, had swiftly become one of China's major economic assets. The oilfields, which were developed along "self-reliance" lines by workers with primitive equipment, often laboring at sub-zero temperatures with only the vaguest sense of the purpose of their efforts, had indeed been an example of Chinese daring and tenacity. And yet, knowing Mao's ideological propensities, the senior party personnel at the oilfields had chosen to overemphasize the local people's untrained contributions to the oilfield's development, and had completely played down the fact that the managers of Daqing had relied as well on foreign technology, including prospecting and refining equipment that they had bought on the international market. Ecstatic at their success—by 1963 Daqing produced 4.4 million metric tons of oil, over two-thirds of China's total—Mao began to transfer staff members from Daqing and the Petroleum Industries Ministry into his top economic-planning institutions. By 1964 these people were well entrenched, helping Mao formulate ambitious development plans that undercut his more cautious planners.[21]

Mao's struggle with Liu Shaoqi over the investigative work teams was a subtle yet important one. Liu continued to believe that correction of CCP abuses was an internal party affair, and should be handled by party members themselves, so as to maintain prestige in the eyes of the public. With so many cadres discredited by their ruthlessness or corruption in the Great Leap period, this approach was more essential than ever. Mao felt that if the party showed serious signs of weakness, it should be rectified through open debate and criticism, with the "masses" involved in the process. Thus Mao believed that he was calling for a *socialist* campaign that would pit the genuine proletariat against the bourgeoisie, while Liu and his friends were sidetracking the issue by concentrating on the "four cleanups" or comparatively minor economic faults. By using investigative work teams in such a dictatorial manner, and discrediting huge numbers of Communists, Liu was in fact working *against* socialism. As Mao phrased it, "Though you repeat day after day that there must be democracy, there is no democracy; though you ask others to be democratic, you are not democratic yourselves."[22]

The party secretary-general Deng Xiaoping was equally guilty of this kind of behavior, said Mao in January 1965. By shrouding the investigations in secrecy, by not bringing the common people of the area themselves into the investigative process, Deng was being "placid"; by this Mao meant that

Deng did not really have faith in the judgment of the masses, and shied away from a genuine mass movement. Of course such a process was unpredictable, but that was what revolutions were all about. As Mao chided another senior party leader who was a close friend of Liu Shaoqi: "When you go out to develop and engage in a mass movement, or to lead a mass struggle, the masses will do as they wish and they will create their own leaders in the course of the struggle. . . . Whether one is a professional or an amateur, one can only learn by fighting." When the party leader concerned argued that the party members must "control the temperature" in such situations to prevent excess, Mao retorted sharply, "It is necessary to give the masses a free hand."[23]

The language about learning by "fighting" came straight from Mao's past as a young radical protesting the tragic suicide of Miss Zhao in 1919; the objection to reducing revolutionary temperature was delivered by one who had seen, in 1927, what happened to the workers of Shanghai and the peasants of Hunan when their excesses were prevented; the appeals to the innate integrity of the masses were reprises of Yan'an and the euphoric beginnings of the Great Leap. But to China's economic planners, who felt they were getting the country back on its feet, the rhetoric must have sounded tired. For them, the achievements of the years 1962 to 1965 were palpable. The initial retrenchment proposed by Chen Yun had been accomplished, leading to the removal of millions of unproductive urban workers from state payrolls and the closing of over 25,000 enterprises. Although this led to corresponding drops in coal, cement, and steel production, the 1960 budget deficit of 8 billion yuan was replaced by a 1962 surplus of close to 1 billion yuan. Spared the huge grain procurement demands of the Great Leap period, peasant production teams of 20 to 30 households working within smaller communes were given new economic initiatives and allowed to produce for the open market on their own plots. By 1965 agricultural production levels had returned to around the pre–Great Leap levels of 1957, while the output of light industry was expanding at 27 percent a year and heavy industry at 17 percent. Thanks to the incredibly rich deposits found at the Daqing wells in Heilongjiang, domestic oil production was up tenfold since 1957, freeing China from her long reliance on Soviet oil supplies, and natural gas was up fortyfold. If such steady advances could continue, China might have a chance to enter an era of unspectacular yet real economic progress under the leadership of the CCP. The party professionals and the planners— not Mao and the masses—would be pointing the way to China's future.

| # Cultural Revolution

THE CULT OF MAO AND THE CRITICS

The divided opinions that had surfaced among the leadership of the People's Republic concerning the Hundred Flowers, the Great Leap, relations with the Soviet Union, continuing American hostility, and the pacing and focus of the Socialist Education Campaign left Mao feeling threatened. Liu Shaoqi, Deng Xiaoping, Chen Yun, and Zhou Enlai, veteran revolutionaries all, seemed less and less to share his vision of governance through continuing struggle; indeed they barely seemed to need his presence or his inspiration. Mao himself had developed a personal life-style that was out of touch with many of his political colleagues. He had come to value the trappings of power, whether it was swims in the private pool built for him in the Zhongnanhai residence compound, the privilege of summoning his staff to meetings at any time of day or night, the pleasant sojourns in various villas (to which he could travel in his special train), or the sexual companionship of a succession of young women—whom he met either at the weekly Zhongnanhai dances or amidst the enthusiastic youthful followers he encountered on his train journeys.[1] But these diversions, and his long periods of private reading and reflection in his book-lined study, could not disguise the fact that his policies of the late 1950s had failed, and his reputation in the early 1960s was not as high as once it had been.

One man who helped to rebuild Mao's sense of self-esteem was Lin Biao, the veteran army commander from the days of Yan'an and the civil war. Born in 1907 and educated among the first military cadets at the Whampoa Academy, Lin had consistently been a loyal Communist, although ill health had often kept him on the sidelines of the great political events of the 1950s.

After the dismissal of Marshal Peng Dehuai, however, Mao Zedong chose Lin Biao to be the new minister of defense and the *de facto* head of the People's Liberation Army.

In the early 1960s, while the economic planners were trying to work out ways to restabilize the economy after the crises of the Great Leap, within the army Lin Biao moved to strengthen the vision of Mao as a great leader. He did this by making a compilation of aphorisms from among the huge body of papers and speeches that Mao had produced over the previous thirty years and more. By 1963 these *Quotations from Chairman Mao* (in reference to Mao's role as chairman of the Communist party) were being studied and discussed throughout the PLA. Though the ideological significance of this collection, with its constant exhortations to self-sacrifice, self-reliance, and the maintenance of revolutionary impetus and ongoing struggle, was not apparent to most CCP leaders, first thousands and then millions of soldiers began to study and memorize Mao's sayings, raising him to a new level of reverence. The special role of Mao's works was underlined in 1962, when projects to publish the collected works of Head of State Liu Shaoqi and the economic planner, Chen Yun, were both shelved.

Lin Biao rapidly increased the number of Communist party members in the army. He also renewed aspects of the first organizational structure installed by the CCP when they took power in 1949, including his own role in the Central-South China Bureau, by making sure that generals in charge of certain military regions were concurrently designated the secretaries of the regional party bureaus. Other party secretaries were appointed PLA political commissars to ensure an even tighter meshing of the civilian and military spheres. Mao furthered this blurring of organizational lines by calling for the formation of a gigantic civilian militia that would be able to coordinate its defense of China in depth, down to the village level, with the PLA.

In early 1963, Lin Biao intensified the degree of indoctrination in the army by starting a mass campaign within the PLA to emphasize the basic values of service to the party. The center of this campaign was the life of a young PLA soldier named Lei Feng, who had recently given his life for his country. The posthumously discovered *Diary of Lei Feng* emphasized again and again the soldier's undying love for the revolution, for his country, and for his comrades, as well as his unswerving devotion to Chairman Mao. The fact that the "diary" was fictitious, concocted by PLA propaganda writers, should not conceal its basic significance, which was to launch an attack against the lack of revolutionary fervor displayed by many intellectuals and writers in the People's Republic.

Those writers had been starting once again, especially after the Great

Leap, to concentrate on some of the ambiguities of the revolutionary experience, on problems that peasants faced in responding to economic hardship or that workers and teachers faced in analyzing their tasks in the new society. Lei Feng's life allowed no such ambiguities. He was pledged to service and obedience. His life was presented as honest and sincere, but without great drama except for his own family's suffering at the hands of Japanese invaders, Guomindang rightists, and rapacious landlords. Lei Feng himself drove an army truck, and yearned to see China's countryside "mechanized," but his example was hardly a vivid argument for new technological development. And he died, selflessly but unheroically, in an accident as he was trying to help a comrade in trouble. The study of Lei Feng's diary was introduced into China's regular school system, and Mao consolidated its impact when, in late 1963, he graced the diary's title page with his own calligraphy. Mao called on the whole country to "learn from the PLA," implicitly undercutting the basic understanding hitherto that the country should be "learning from the party."

The idea of self-reliance and sacrifice was again underscored in 1964, when the growing threat that the Vietnam War would spread to China led Mao to order a speedy development of industry and transportation systems in the southwest. This would enable the Chinese people, if threatened by U.S. invasion, once again to retreat deep into their own heartland, as they had in the face of the Japanese in 1937 and 1938. This time, however, unlike Chiang Kai-shek's Chongqing regime, the Chinese would be properly prepared for a protracted resistance. Initially Mao seems to have chosen the disgraced Peng Dehuai to supervise this inland rebuilding, but that choice was prevented, perhaps by Lin Biao's intervention. In any case, little could check Lin's prestige, especially since the PLA had performed extremely well in renewed border wars with India in 1962, and scientists working on a crash program under PLA supervision at secret bases in Qinghai and Ningxia had designed, built, and successfully tested China's own atomic bomb in October 1964.* The nuclear device was exploded just two days after Khrushchev had been toppled from power in a Soviet coup, underlining China's new-found technological powers.

Lin Biao had also been extending his power base beyond the army by making important contacts in China's internal-security apparatus and in the cultural bureaucracy, and by placing PLA-staffed political bureaus in many schools and factories. Matters of internal security and culture were closely connected in the PRC, just as they had been throughout the Qing and

---

*The first Chinese atomic bomb was code-named "596," in sardonic reference to the month of June 1959 in which Khrushchev had informed the Chinese that the Soviets would not give them a prototype of the bomb.

republican periods. It was often through their paintings or literary works that opponents of government policies chose to voice their criticisms, using a measure of historical allegory or poetic allusion to get across negative or sarcastic points that no one could dare issue openly. Lin Biao's attempts to indoctrinate the PLA with Maoist ideology and to control potential dissent through the broader institutional base he was forging made him a formidable force.

A natural ally for Lin was Mao Zedong's third wife, Jiang Qing, who was beginning to play an active part in cultural politics. Born in 1914, Jiang Qing had been a stage and screen actress in Shandong and Shanghai during the early 1930s. Among her roles was the part of Nora in Ibsen's *A Doll's House,* and she performed in the Shandong countryside to spread the message of socialist revolution. Traveling to Yan'an in 1937, she soon became Mao's companion and by 1939 was regarded as his third wife. (Mao's second wife, He Zizhen, who had borne a child on the Long March, had fallen mentally and physically ill and been sent to the Soviet Union for medical treatment.) Jiang Qing, who bore Mao one daughter, kept out of politics until the early 1960s. It was at this time, she later stated, that she became deeply disturbed by the "traditionalist" or "feudal" content of much contemporary Chinese art, including the plays she saw in Shanghai in the early 1960s, and was eager to do something about the situation. A third figure, Kang Sheng, shared the same ideological goals. Kang had emerged as a force in the Chinese national security system, and had become Mao's closest adviser on problems of interpreting Soviet ideological policies and pronouncements. Kang had been trained by the Soviet NKVD secret service in the 1930s, and served as a prominent leader in the Yan'an Rectification Campaign. By the 1960s he also was convinced that Chinese culture was being permeated with an unhealthy spirit of criticism toward the Communist party and even toward Chairman Mao. Kang urged that Chinese literature and art return to a purer vision of revolution that would draw its inspiration from the ranks of the workers and peasants, and in turn encourage writers and artists to emerge from the ranks of the workers rather than from the old intellectuals who still seemed to dominate so much of the Chinese cultural world. Lin Biao's use of Lei Feng's life to inspire the masses fitted in well with that approach.

There could hardly have been a more suitable victim for these radical ideologues than the talented historian and writer Wu Han. An expert on the history of the Ming dynasty, Wu Han as a young man had used examples drawn from Ming history in order to criticize Chiang Kai-shek and the Guomindang during World War II. In the midst of the Great Leap Forward, he was invited by Mao Zedong to write on the celebrated Ming official

Hai Rui, who had fought stubbornly for the people's economic rights against shortsighted and conservative bureaucrats. Wu Han concentrated in his first essay on the way that Hai Rui, though loyal to his emperor, criticized the monarch for wasting the country's resources while the famished population was driven to the edge of rebellion. In September 1959 Wu Han published another essay on Hai Rui in the newspaper *People's Daily*. This time, Hai Rui was praised as a man "of courage for all times" who remained "unintimidated by threats of punishment." The emperor whom Hai Rui served, however, was described as "craving vainly for immortality" and as "being self-opinionated and unreceptive to criticism." The average official who served the emperor, in his turn, was called the type of person who would not "dare to oppose anything even though he knew it was bad."[2]

In 1965 both Mao and Jiang Qing were to seize on these essays as Wu Han's attempt to link Peng Dehuai allegorically to the virtuous Hai Rui. However, these two essays were not publicly criticized at the time, and during the early 1960s Wu Han was one of a number of intellectuals who published short pieces in the Peking newspapers, using historical or other social themes that were obviously critical of many Communist government policies, and of Mao's isolation from an accurate reading of public opinion. These intellectuals wrote under the joint pseudonym of Three-Family Village, referring to a Song dynasty official who, dismissed from the government, had retired to a village of that name. One of the group, Deng Tuo, was especially sharp in the way he praised the Donglin partisans of the late Ming dynasty for their courage in opposing the court's injustice. As Deng wrote in a poem to the Donglin martyrs' memory:

> Do not think of them as mere intellectuals indulging in
>   empty talk;
> Fresh were the bloodstains when the heads rolled.
> Fighting the wicked men in power with abiding will,
> The Donglin scholars were a stout-hearted generation.[3]

Wu Han developed the theme of Hai Rui into a full length play, *The Dismissal of Hai Rui from Office,* which was staged in Peking in February 1961 and published the summer of the same year. By this time all Chinese concerned with politics knew that Peng Dehuai had criticized Mao for the Great Leap, so Hai Rui's words of protest must have had sharp relevance to Wu Han's audience:

> You say the common people are tyrannized,
> but do you know the gentry injures them?

> Much is made at court of the gentry's oppression,
> but do you know of the poverty
> endured by the common people?
> You pay lip service to the principle
> that the people are the roots of the state.
> But officials still oppress the masses
> while pretending to be virtuous men.
> They act wildly as tigers
> and deceive the emperor.
> If your conscience bothers you
> you know no peace by day or night.[4]

The Three-Family Village writings and Wu Han's play were but parts of a broad-based flow of allegorical and critical works that angered many leading political figures. These leaders were, however, unclear about how to forbid the publication of such pieces, which often were carried in party-controlled newspapers and magazines. Mao himself called for a wave of criticism against "reactionary bourgeois ideology" in September 1965. Apparently angered at the weak response, and unable to get as wide a forum for his views as he had hoped because many journals were controlled by his opponents, Mao left Peking that November and disappeared from public view altogether. It later emerged that he had moved to Shanghai, where a group of hard-line Communist intellectuals were assembled, determined to bring what they saw as socialist order and rigor back into the intellectual life of the country.

In 1965 Lin Biao shifted the PLA itself further left not only by reaffirming the importance of Mao's thought, but by taking the extreme, egalitarian step of ordering all ranks and insignia abolished in the PLA. Henceforth PLA officers and men would be indistinguishable from each other in uniform, and would share many of the common tasks of daily life. At the same time, Lin Biao engineered large-scale shifts in personnel that ensured PLA control over the public-security apparatus. And in November 1965, coinciding with Mao's withdrawal, a close colleague of Jiang Qing's named Yao Wenyuan—who had allied himself with those backing the call for "proletarian writers" of purity—published in Shanghai a strong attack on Wu Han's play, *The Dismissal of Hai Rui from Office*. In this article, Yao stated that Wu Han had been guilty of denying the key premise of Mao's thought—that the masses of the people constitute the motive force of history. Instead, Wu Han had tried to insist that individual "moral" men could somehow transcend the economic and social realities of their time.

Just as serious, said Yao, was Wu's call for "redressing injustices" in the countryside at the very time that "the peasants of our country have already realized socialism, possess everything, and have established the great People's Communes." Could it be, Yao asked rhetorically, that Wu and his supporters wished "to replace the state theory of Marxism-Leninism with the state theory of the landlord and bourgeoisie"?[5] It was twenty days before Yao's Shanghai essay was picked up by the Peking press and published in the capital, attesting to the uneasiness there over the implications of this first salvo. Now sides were going to have to be taken publicly by the most powerful political figures in the country. Were they for or against Wu Han? By implication, for or against Peng Dehuai? And, not so transparently, for or against Mao Zedong and Lin Biao?

LAUNCHING THE CULTURAL REVOLUTION

As the year 1966 began, two quite different groups met to discuss the Wu Han case and related matters. One was the Group of Five—though its active membership was far larger than the name implied—which met under the direction of Peng Zhen, a veteran party leader who was currently mayor of Peking and a member of the Standing Committee of the Politburo. This group included senior staff from the press, party academics, and members of the Ministry of Culture, almost all of whom could be regarded as professional party bureaucrats and intellectuals who embraced the *status quo* and were close to Liu Shaoqi and Deng Xiaoping.

The second group met in Shanghai under the general guidance of Jiang Qing, who led a forum to discuss the political purposes of literature and the performing arts. Members of this group may be loosely called radical or nonestablishment intellectuals; they were pushing for socialist purification of art, and generally favored the search for new dramatic forms untainted by either so-called feudal or Westernized May Fourth elitist values. Members of this group would all have approved of Mao's sarcastic observation that because of its fascination with past glories, the Ministry of Culture in Peking should be renamed "the Ministry of Emperors, Kings, Generals, and Ministers," "the Ministry of Talents and Beauties," or "the Ministry of Foreign Mummies."[6] They were aware of the new opportunities that arose for spreading their radical views on the content and form of art when Lin Biao formally invited Jiang Qing to coordinate the new cultural policies for the PLA in February 1966.

Peng Zhen's conservative Group of Five tried to defuse the Wu Han case by treating it as an academic debate rather than as a political matter involving the crucial factor of class struggle. They issued a cautious report that criticized Wu Han but did not push for a comprehensive assault on China's cultural system. Acknowledging the importance of Wu Han's case, they nevertheless noted that "we must carry out this struggle under leadership, seriously, positively and prudently," especially since "problems of academic contention are rather complicated, and some matters are not easy to define within a short time." This gradualist approach was reinforced by the group's use of language drawn from the more moderate phases of Chinese land reform in its calls for "mutual-aid teams" and "cooperatives" of academic workers. They pointed out, in what could be seen as a jab at Mao or Jiang Qing, that "even some staunch revolutionary leftists . . . can hardly avoid saying something wrong."[7] Much as Mao might have disliked this analysis, on February 12, 1966, the Central Committee of the CCP approved it for distribution as a policy discussion document.

That same February, Jiang Qing and cultural workers from the PLA were meeting at their Shanghai forum. The delegates saw numerous finished films and the rushes of works in progress, attended three theatrical performances—including new, radicalized versions of several traditional Peking operas—and joined in group readings of Mao Zedong's works. Mao's writings on culture, they concluded, marked a "new development of the Marxist-Leninist world outlook." They claimed that China, despite Mao's achievement, was still "under the dictatorship of a sinister anti-Party and Anti-Socialist line which is diametrically opposed to Chairman Mao's thought. This sinister line is a combination of bourgeois ideas on literature and art, modern revisionist ideas on literature and art and what is known as the literature and art of the 1930s." They branded Wu Han's work as a perfect example of this politically erroneous writing, and warned that the Chinese cultural garden was overgrown with "anti-socialist poisonous weeds." But the recent radicalization of Peking opera showed that even the "most stubborn of strongholds" could "be taken by storm and revolutionized." In this cultural fight the PLA—"the mainstay and hope of the Chinese people and the revolutionary people of the world"—would play a crucial role, and help "destroy blind faith in Chinese and foreign classical literature." In warmly endorsing the final report of the forum, which spelled out all these ideas, Lin Biao noted that "if the proletariat does not occupy the positions in literature and art, the bourgeoisie certainly will. This struggle is inevitable."[8]

So were the lines at last drawn, beyond effective mediation, for the cataclysmic central phase of what Mao and his supporters called the Great Proletarian Cultural Revolution. This movement defies simple classification, for embedded within it were many impulses at once feeding and impeding each other. There was Mao Zedong's view that the Chinese revolution was losing impetus because of party conservatism and the lethargy of the huge and cumbrous bureaucracy, which had lost its ability to make speedy or innovative decisions. Mao declared that many party bureaucrats "were taking the capitalist road" even as they mouthed the slogans of socialism. There were, too, Mao's sense of his advancing age—he was now seventy-three—and his concern that his senior colleagues were seeking to shunt him aside. There were straightforward elements of factional struggle pitting Jiang Qing and the Shanghai radicals against those in the Peking cultural bureaucracy who wanted to maintain their own power bases. There were the political strategies of those who diverged sharply with Mao over the pace and direction of change, among whom were such veteran Communists at the apex of the government as Liu Shaoqi, Deng Xiaoping, Chen Yun, and Peng Zhen. There were the personal political ambitions of Lin Biao and those who supported him in his efforts to expand the role of the army into politics, and make the PLA a centerpiece of cultural change.

These factional fires were fueled by the anger of students frustrated over policies that kept them off the paths of political advancement because the students had the ill fortune to be born to parents who had had connections with the Guomindang, the landlords, or the capitalist "exploiters" of the old regime and were therefore classified as "bad" elements by the CCP. There were as well millions of disgruntled urban youths who had been relocated to the countryside during the party campaigns of earlier years, or in line with the plans of Chen Yun and others to save the cost to the state of providing subsidized grain supplies for such city residents. There were those, within the largest cities, who were denied access to the tiny number of elite schools that had become, in effect, "prep schools" for the children of influential party cadres. (With the shortage of colleges in China, and the thickets of complex entrance examinations that still stood in the way to them, only education in this handful of schools could assure access to higher education.) There were industrial workers who felt trapped in dead-end jobs and were excited by the possibilities for changing their fortunes. And finally there were those who felt that party positions were monopolized by the uneducated rural cadres of Mao's former peasant guerrilla days, and that these people should now be eased out to make way for newer, more educated recruits.

In the late spring and summer of 1966, events moved to a swift yet unpredictable climax. In May the report of the Group of Five, calling for caution in cultural reform, was repudiated by the Central Committee—clearly at Mao's urging—and a purge of the cultural bureaucracy commenced. Peng Zhen was ousted, other key figures in the Ministry of Culture removed, and attacks launched against the writers of the Three-Family Village articles and against Wu Han and his family.* The protests and criticisms spread throughout China's university system after Nie Yuanzi, a radical philosophy professor at Peking University, wrote a large wall poster attacking the administration of her university. Attempts by Deng Xiaoping, Liu Shaoqi, and others to send "work teams" onto the campuses to quell the disturbances backfired as more and more radicals among faculty and students turned on party members. Turmoil spread swiftly to the Peking high schools, and squads of students were issued arm bands by the Cultural Revolution radicals declaring them to be "Red Guards"—the vanguard of the new revolutionary upheaval.

To underscore his vigor and health, Mao Zedong took a July swim in the Yangzi River near Wuhan, where the 1911 revolution had first erupted. The swim was given euphoric coverage in the party press, which presented it as an event of huge significance to the Chinese people. Back in Peking, Mao heated up the revolutionary rhetoric even further by declaring that Professor Nie's "big character poster" was "the declaration of the Paris Commune of the sixties of the twentieth century; its significance far surpasses that of the Paris commune." The Paris Commune of 1871, about which Marx had written with great passion, had been considered a pinnacle of spontaneous socialist insurrection and organization in Western history. Now Mao was claiming that China would exceed it. Of course there would be hostile forces, he noted, just as there had been in France. "Who are against the great Cultural Revolution? American imperialism, Russian revisionism, Japanese revisionism, and the reactionaries." But China would "depend on the masses, trust the masses, and fight to the end."[9]

In early August 1966, the Central Committee issued a directive of sixteen points on the Cultural Revolution, calling for vigilance against those who would try to subvert the revolution from within. Still there were enough cooler heads in office for a sentence to be inserted suggesting that debates "be conducted by reasoning, not by coercion or force," and that "special care" be taken of scientists and technical personnel. But as August drew on, Mao Zedong, from a stand atop the Tiananmen gate, entrance to the former imperial Forbidden City in Peking, began to review gigantic parades of chanting Red Guards, all waving their copies of his little red book of quotations. Initially composed largely of students from the elite schools, the Red Guard ranks were now swelled by other disaffected and frustrated students, and by those from the provinces drawn by the revolutionary rhetoric and their reverence for Mao as father of the revolution. Lin Biao heightened the

---

*Wu Han died in 1969 of illness following the brutal treatment to which he was subjected.

public euphoria with his own declarations. "Chairman Mao is the most outstanding leader of the proletariat in the present era and the greatest genius in the present era," Lin told a Red Guard rally on August 18. What Mao had done was to create "a Marxism-Leninism for remoulding the souls of the people." By the end of August, Lin had developed a formulaic description of Mao as "our great teacher, great leader, great supreme commander and great helmsman" that became standard usage in China.

In the autumn and winter of 1966, the struggles grew deeper and more bitter, the destruction and loss of life more terrible. With all schools and colleges closed for the staging of revolutionary struggle, millions of the young were encouraged by the Cultural Revolution's leaders to demolish the old buildings, temples, and art objects in their towns and villages, and to attack their teachers, school administrators, party leaders, and parents. Under the direction of a small group of Mao's confidants, along with his wife Jiang Qing and other Shanghai radicals, the party was purged at higher and higher levels until both Liu Shaoqi and Deng Xiaoping were removed from their posts and subjected to mass criticism and humiliation, along with their families.

The leaders of the Cultural Revolution called for a comprehensive attack on the "four old" elements within Chinese society—old customs, old habits, old culture, and old thinking—but they left it to local Red Guard initiative to apply these terms. In practice what often happened was that after the simpler targets had been identified, Red Guards eager to prove their revolutionary integrity turned on anyone who tried to hold them in check, anyone who had had Western education or dealings with Western businessmen or missionaries, and all intellectuals who could be charged with "feudal" or "reactionary" modes of thinking. The techniques of public humiliation grew more and more complex and painful as the identified victims were forced to parade through the streets in dunce caps or with self-incriminatory placards around their necks, to declaim their public self-criticisms before great jeering crowds, and to stand for hours on end with backs agonizingly bent and arms outstretched in what was called "the airplane position."

With the euphoria, fear, excitement, and tension that gripped the country, violence grew apace. Thousands of intellectuals and others were beaten to death or died of their injuries. Countless others committed suicide, among them Lao She, the author of the novel *Cat Country,* which had spoken so eloquently in 1932 against the Chinese who turned on each other. Many of the suicides killed themselves only after futile attempts to avoid Red Guard harassment by destroying their own libraries and art collections. Thousands more were imprisoned, often in solitary confinement, for years. Millions were relocated to purify themselves through labor in the countryside.

The extent of this outpouring of violence, and the rage of the young Red Guards against their elders, suggest the real depths of frustration that now lay at the heart of Chinese society. The youth needed little urging from Mao to rise up against their parents, teachers, party cadres, and the elderly, and to perform countless acts of calculated sadism. For years the young had been called on to lead lives of revolutionary sacrifice, sexual restraint, and absolute obedience to the state, all under conditions of perpetual supervision. They were repressed, angry, and aware of their powerlessness. They eagerly seized on the order to throw off all restraint, and the natural targets were those who seemed responsible for their cramped lives. To them Mao stood above this fray, all-wise and all-knowing. The disasters of the Great Leap had never been widely publicized, and in any case could be attributed to inept bureaucrats or hostile Soviets and Americans. Mao spoke still for hope and freedom, and in the absence of any convincing counterclaims, the wild rhetoric about his powers was accepted as true.

Another explanation for the extent of this violence can be found in the nature of Chinese politics and personal manipulation over the past seventeen years. All Chinese were now enmeshed in a system that controlled people by assigning class labels to them, by making them totally dependent on the "bosses" of their particular units, and by habituating them to mass campaigns of terror and intimidation. Such a system bred both fear and compliance.

Embedded within this frenzied activism was a political agenda of great significance, what might be called a "purist egalitarianism" that echoed the values of the Paris Commune of 1871 so vividly evoked for China by Mao Zedong. This involved much more than the confiscation or destruction of private property: demands were heard now for the complete nationalization of all industrial enterprises, the abolition of all interest on deposits in the state banks, the eviction of all landlords from their own houses, the elimination of all private plots and a restrengthening of the commune system, and the ending of all traces of a private market economy—down to the poorest peasant selling a handful of vegetables from his wheelbarrow at the village corner.

The peak of this profoundly radical program came during the first month of 1967, in what has been termed the "January power seizure." Backed by the Cultural Revolutionary group in Peking, a variety of militant Red Guard organizations attempted to oust party incumbents and take over their organizations all over China. The campaign was triggered by New Year's Day editorials in the press that called for "worker-peasant" coalitions to "overthrow power holders in factories, mines and rural areas," and urged these worker-peasant groups to ally with "revolutionary intellectuals" in the struggle. Ambitious workers seized on this opportunity to leapfrog up the political ladder into leadership positions. The Red Guards were told to view the Cultural Revolution as the struggle of one class to overthrow another, and to exempt no one in that struggle; unlike 1949, they were told, when the CCP had had to show some caution in taking power so as not to alienate the centrists and liberals, in 1967 "everything which does not fit the socialist system and proletarian dictatorship should be attacked."[10]

The result was a bewildering situation in which varieties of radical groups, not coordinated by any central leadership, struggled with party leaders and with each other. The battles at the provincial level show this best. One seizure attempt, in Heilongjiang province, northern Manchuria, was led by a former opponent of the Great Leap Forward who now tried to prove his loyalty to Mao by showing his revolutionary fervor. In Shanxi, the vice-governor of the province joined with Red Guards to oust the other party leaders. In Shandong, the second secretary of the Tianjin municipal committee worked with a member of the Shandong party committee to found a Provincial Revolutionary Committee. In Guizhou, it was the deputy political commissar of the province who allied with the Red Guards.

It was difficult in many such cases to tell if these were real or sham power struggles—whether "the masses" were really seizing power or whether party leaders were merely pretending to hand over power while in fact continuing to exercise all their old functions under loose Red Guard supervision. This latter was clearly the case in Guangdong province, where the first party secretary, Zhao Ziyang, handed over his seals to the "Red Flag faction," a loose federation of railway workers, demobilized soldiers, teachers, college and high-school students, and film-studio workers. Having made his gesture, Zhao and his staff continued to run the province.

The word *radical* was used in many ways at this time. In Shanghai, for instance, where the power seizure was defined as successful, it was the 500,000 strong Scarlet Red Guards, a workers' organization, who began by making the strongest demands for better wages, working conditions, and the right to leave their work and participate in "revolutionary experiences" without losing pay. Similar demands were launched by millions of other workers around China, from pedicab drivers to cooks, from street peddlers to train engineers. Workers on short-term contracts and other temporary laborers were especially vocal, often demanding permanent job status and awards of several years' back pay. But such actions, initially radical-seeming, were soon branded by leaders of the Cultural Revolution as "economism." The Scarlet Red Guards' stance was labeled "conservative" by other groups, such as the equally huge Shanghai Workers' General Headquarters, which claimed the radical label for themselves. During the last months of 1966, battling factions of both student and worker Red Guards had managed virtually to paralyze Shanghai: the shipping of goods on the wharves was completely disrupted; railway service was in chaos or, in some cases, stopped entirely when lines were cut; the city was jammed with millions of Red Guards, returnees, or fugitives from the countryside; and stores opened for shorter and shorter hours as food supplies fell to dangerously low levels. In this context, the January 1967 "radical" power seizure in Shanghai can also be seen as a successful attempt to prevent the workers from gaining truly independent power.

This stage of struggle began when one of Jiang Qing's closest allies, Zhang Chunqiao, traveled to Shanghai in early January 1967. After gaining control of the most influential newspapers and ordering the workers to return to their jobs, Zhang held a series of mass meetings and rallies to criticize and humiliate members of the Shanghai party leadership who were accused of "economism" for giving in to workers' demands for better pay. Joined by Yao Wenyuan (who had fired the first major shots against Wu Han the year before), Zhang used the PLA to restore order in the city and to develop the new slogan "Grasping Revolution and Promoting Production." While PLA troops guarded airfields, banks, freight terminals, and docks, student Red Guards were used in place of workers still refusing to return to their jobs.

Zhang and Yao, however, also had to fight militant student Red Guards who wished to maintain solidarity with the workers. In late January mass student groups held a struggle session against Zhang and Yao themselves, and also "arrested" the latter's main propaganda writers. Only in early February, with massive military support, was order restored to the liking of the Cultural Revolution leaders. On February 5, Zhang announced the formation of a new institution, the Shanghai People's Commune, which created a truly paradoxical situation. For under the guise of this most revolutionary sounding of titles, those who had so thoroughly purged their own party tried now to bolster their own positions as China's new leaders, and to force a return to obedience of the very students and workers who had sought to usher in a new age of freedom.

PARTY RETRENCHMENT AND THE DEATH OF LIN BIAO

At first the formation of the Shanghai People's Commune was hailed in Peking. But Mao seems to have rapidly moved away from his initial desire to make such communes models for development nationwide, and in mid-

February 1967 he issued a more cautious set of guidelines. Because these new policies cut against the dramatic power seizures of January, the radical group referred to them as the "February adverse current." Mao may also here have been directly opposing his wife Jiang Qing, who had openly declared that "the title of chief should be smashed in pieces." Mao responded that "actually 'chiefs' are necessary. The question lies in the content," which was a reassertion of the need for cadres in leadership roles, as well as of his own indispensability.[11] Mao announced that "power seizures" would no longer be legitimated after the fact, but must receive prior party approval.

In late February, Mao told Zhang Chunqiao to transform the Shanghai Commune into a "Revolutionary Committee." Such committees, whether in large urban areas, in the rural communes, or in such institutions as universities, schools, and newspapers, were henceforth to consist of a "three-way alliance" comprising representatives from the masses, members of the PLA, and those cadres who had been found "correct" in attitude and behavior. In practice, this meant an important reduction in the representation of industrial workers in the local leadership.

Under the "February adverse current" guidelines, "power seizures" were often coordinated by central party leaders themselves, as was dramatically shown in Premier Zhou Enlai's ability to manipulate an intricate series of assaults on the various ministries in the central government bureaucracy. In an attempt by Zhou to dampen the extent of disruptive violence, students were told to "resume classes and carry on revolution," army personnel were to extend military training into all colleges and schools down to the primary levels, and cadres were to be permitted "to reform themselves and redeem their mistakes by making contributions." The result was a period in which the more extreme forms of "radical" disruption were muted, although the country remained in a turbulent state.

The PLA in particular, as a key component of the new three-way alliance, began to play an expanded role in the structure of government. Not only were PLA troops fully represented on all the new revolutionary committees, they also used force of arms to suppress militant radicals who tried to disrupt or purge the PLA's own organization. Throughout the Cultural Revolution, both Lin Biao and the PLA had taken a highly complicated hand in the struggles. The leaders of the "radicals" in one sense, champions of the *Quotations of Chairman Mao* and the drive to overthrow all feudal, bourgeois, and Western elements, apparently egalitarian in organization and procedure, the PLA was also a professional army committed to defending China's borders and preventing civil war. Thus the PLA, while apparently supporting the radical excesses of the militant Red Guards, had kept its own ranks closed to their interference, along with its military installations, confidential files, and production plants. PLA troops also protected the technical installations at the huge Daqing oilfields from Red Guard takeover, and kept Red Guard units—even one led by Mao Zedong's own nephew—from entering the secret facilities where many of China's brightest physicists were working on the hydrogen bomb.

When Jiang Qing attacked the chief of the PLA propaganda department for having "changed the army into an army of bourgeoisie," Red Guards picked up her lead and raided the man's house. This brought an instant response from Zhou Enlai, who, at a meeting of 900 senior military leaders in late January 1967, issued a broad criticism of those who sought to "lower the prestige of the Army." In early February, army leaders followed up on Mao's promise that frontier military regions should not all experience the Cultural Revolution "simultaneously" by virtually excluding these regions from the process, and forbidding interference with the navy fleet and the naval and air-force training schools.

The PLA had been given the task, at the end of January 1967, of disbanding all "counter revolutionary organizations." They chose to interpret this as a call to break up all militant revolutionary organizations that took a line sharply opposed to their own (or their political allies') organizational interests. The numbers of those killed by the PLA in these various confrontations is unknown, but there were eyewitness reports of rivers blocked with bodies, and many corpses washed up on the shores of Hong Kong. The backers of the Cultural Revolution in Peking, in their turn, were dismayed by the severity of the PLA's attacks on those who were, after all, often responding to the center's own call to purify the ranks of the bureaucracy. Numerous instructions went out to the PLA, urging them to be more restrained and to understand the true meaning of the Cultural Revolution.

The most important clash between the army and the radicals occurred in Wuhan during the summer of 1967. Earlier that spring, the PLA had arrested at least 500 leaders of radical Red Guard and workers' groups that claimed to speak for 400,000 militants. A struggle ensued in Wuhan that moved via public protests and hunger strikes to massive labor stoppages, and finally to armed clashes in which a thousand or more protesters were killed by the army. When two senior members of the Cultural Revolution leadership traveled from Peking to Wuhan in July and condemned the army for its behavior, one of them was kidnaped from his hotel by supporters of the PLA, while the local troops did nothing to rescue him. He was released only when airborne units, a naval vessel, and other military reinforcements were ordered to the city by the Peking authorities.

The Wuhan incident prompted a period of renewed violence and confrontation between the PLA and a wide range of "radical rebel" groups that continued in many parts of China throughout the summer. Opposing worker and student factions continued also to attack each other, often with deadly results, using arms and ammunition seized from raided PLA depots. The violence was especially bad in Peking and Canton. These confrontations escalated at last into the upper ranks of the government itself. In August 1967 a genuine power seizure occurred when radicals took over the Ministry of Foreign Affairs, disrupted all its routine operations, and began to "appoint" radical diplomats to posts around the world. Perhaps to justify these actions on "anti-imperialist" grounds, the radicals attacked the British embassy and set it on fire.

So serious was the chaos by September 1967 that most leaders from Mao through Zhou Enlai to Lin Biao and Jiang Qing seem to have agreed that it had reached an intolerable level. Jiang Qing, formerly the key spokeswoman for the radicals and their urge to push the struggle on to the end, now denounced "ultra-left tendencies" and praised the PLA as a champion of "proletarian dictatorship." While student factions continued to battle each other, the leadership turned to workers' organizations as a means of curbing student excesses and returning the campuses to order. PLA propaganda across the country called now for an intensive study of Mao's works rather than an all-out assault on "people taking the bourgeois road." Complex negotiations were carried on with warring factions in several provinces, and as agreements to end hostilities were reached, energies previously devoted to conflict began to go into contests for representation on the various revolutionary committees. Following the pattern established at Shanghai in early 1967, these revolutionary committees would each constitute a "three-way alliance" of the PLA, the masses, and "correct" cadres. Membership in the committees would determine who held the deciding voice in communes, schools, and factories, as well as in the centers of provincial government and the Peking ministries. The winners in those contests would be able to prevail politically in China until the system changed yet again. Nevertheless it was not until the summer of 1968—with hundreds more dead in armed clashes, including five workers (sent by Mao to restore order) who were shot by students on the Peking campus of Qinghua University—that something approaching order was restored.

These divisive events shattered China's educational system, placed immense strains on the army, and crucially weakened the CCP's efficiency and morale. In an attempt to restore order to the party and to political life, a new campaign was launched during the period from late 1967 into 1969. Known as the Campaign to Purify Class Ranks, it was coordinated by a loose coalition of leaders that included Mao, Jiang Qing and her supporters, the PLA, and those cadres they considered loyal or who had managed to win control of the local three-way alliance committees. This campaign focused on the millions of cadres who could be suspected of having been "bad elements" because of prior connections with the bourgeoisie, on "renegades and spies" (i.e., those once connected to the Guomindang or to Westerners), and on landlords and unrepentant rightists. Suspects were thoroughly investigated by newly formed Workers' Mao-Thought Propaganda Teams drawn from the "revolutionary masses," in conjunction with the PLA and the relevant revolutionary committees.

There was enormous room to maneuver in these investigations, and the precise balance between one's background, past performance, and current behavior was carefully weighed by the investigative teams. Grim and tense though these procedures were, they at least eventually issued in clear verdicts. One might be "graduated" from the study classes, and hence freed to go back to work; or ordered to study further, which could lead to eventual release; or ordered out of the class, which meant that one was purged from the party.

For hundreds of thousands of cadres and intellectuals, these investigative sessions were held not in their own hometowns, but at special May Seventh Cadre Schools, so named for a crucial directive issued on that day by Mao Zedong early in the Cultural Revolution. These "schools" combined hard agricultural labor with constant self-evaluation and study of Mao's works, allegedly to instill in "students" a deeper understanding of the socialist revolution. In fact they were as much prisons as schools, in which all freedoms to move around or dispose of one's own time were severely restricted. Families were often split apart, the frail and elderly set to work along with the strong, and living conditions were harsh, with "students" given minimal food allowances and the barest of dormitory accommodations. The work, too, was often simply pointless since the cadres and intellectuals could not conceivably compete in rural production with the local peasants, on the edges of whose fields their "schools" were often placed. Although the "students" learned much about the bleakness of rural conditions, it is probable that few had their thinking fundamentally changed. Yang Jiang, a sixty-year-old professor of English in Peking, was sent to such a school for two years with her elderly husband, the novelist and scholar Qian Zhongshu (whom she called Mocun). As she described their departure from their first May Seventh school in southern Henan:

> In the New Year, at the beginning of April on the Qingming Festival Day, the cadre school moved to a new location in Minggang. Before going, our whole brigade assembled in the vegetable garden one last time to tear down everything that had been put up and pull out whatever could be moved. When

we had finished, a tractor came and turned the ground over so that not a trace of the fields or trenches was left. As we were about to set out, Mocun and I sneaked back to have one last look: The hut, well-stand, irrigation ditches, fields—everything had disappeared. Even the flat mound of earth over on the bank of the stream had gone. All that was left was a large area of freshly turned soil.[12]

This combination of incessant indoctrination with hard labor was also the norm in ordinary villages all over China during the Cultural Revolution. A detailed study done of one small village community in Guangdong province illuminates this clearly. Chen Village had its share of political tensions and upheavals, which took place at two overlapping levels. One power struggle pitted two village farmers, both locally well known, who switched in leadership roles according to whether they could or could not successfully defend their records of socialist loyalty to Mao and the community. (At times no one in the village wanted any kind of leadership position, so volatile had the situation become, just as under the Qing, villagers had sometimes fled rather than assume the responsibilities—and perils—of being the *baojia* head.) The other struggle was between educated youth "sent down" to live and work in Chen Village and the native villagers. These rusticated young men and women often led the political discussion because of their superior education (many of the Chen Villagers were illiterate), and used loudspeakers—newly available after the electrification of the village in 1966— to maintain an intense level of political criticism and public awareness. Within these two levels of conflict were countless other small divisions; and as for victims, the villagers found their representatives of the "four olds" and the students found their "rightists," who could be isolated in a special run-down hut known as the "cow shed" and struggled against at regular intervals.

Amid the political chaos, however, the rhythms of agricultural work and family life with its joys and sorrows continued in Chen Village under the painted wall slogans, the countless stenciled portraits of Mao, the blare of loudspeakers, and the constant injunctions to "emulate Dazhai." In line with directives that they give up "selfish" or private production, the villagers returned to the general ethos of the Great Leap period and yielded up to communal ownership their fruit trees and small bamboo groves, their fishing nets, even their breeding sows. For a time, too, the small work teams in which all the peasants knew each other well had to forfeit to the higher level of the production brigade their accounting procedures and powers to allocate work points and distribute land. Despite local worries about these changes, individual incomes for the best agricultural workers in Chen Village were higher in 1968 than at any time in the preceding four years. And the new resources made possible by their collective labor led to useful diversification that promised the villagers higher incomes in the future. In the space of a few years Chen Village built a brick factory, a grain mill, a peanut-oil press, a small sugar and alcohol refinery, and a processing plant for yams.

Before every meal, the Chen villagers held what was almost a service for Mao, reciting some of his quotations, singing verses from the Red Guard anthem "The East Is Red," and offering a little prayer aloud:

> We respectfully wish a long life to the reddest red sun in our hearts, the great leader Chairman Mao. And to Vice Chairman Lin Biao's health: may he forever be healthy. Having been liberated by the land reform we will never forget the Communist Party, and in revolution we will forever follow Chairman Mao![13]

The reference to Lin Biao was by no means just formulaic. Lin Biao's stock had risen ever higher since 1969, when he was declared Mao's chosen successor at the national party congress. That same year, the PLA engaged in a number of serious military clashes with troops from the Soviet Union on the two countries' shared borders. The Soviets had been massing more and more troops both on China's western Xinjiang frontier and in northern Manchuria along the Ussuri River, and tensions with China had risen accordingly. Although the clashes did not lead to full-scale war, around 100 Russians were killed or wounded, and as many as 800 Chinese. In China, the major impact of the fighting was on domestic politics. News of the battles, dramatically retold, produced an outpouring of popular excitement over PLA heroism, intensified anti-Soviet antagonisms, and made it appear that Lin Biao's troops were literally saving the Chinese people. Lin's prestige seemed at its zenith in Chen Village as throughout China. It was therefore completely bewildering when in late 1971 party leaders from the village were rushed to the commune headquarters and returned, shocked and initially pledged to secrecy, with the astonishing news that Lin Biao had betrayed Chairman Mao and met his death in a plane crash.

What the Chen villagers did not know was that Mao had begun to have second thoughts about Lin, and about the way the PLA was handling the protracted purges and investigations of veteran party cadres. Mao was seeking once again to strengthen the party, feeling it had been shaken up adequately, and he and others began to suggest that in their arrests and interrogations the army had been guilty of "carelessness" and "arrogance." In March 1970, Mao decided to remove the post of chairman of the state, vacant since Liu Shaoqi's arrest, from the draft constitution, which meant not only that Lin could not succeed to such a post, but that Zhou Enlai as premier would continue to outrank Lin.

In August 1970, Mao put forward new instructions on rebuilding the CCP that dropped the criteria of revolutionary zeal and ideological purity that Lin and the PLA had propagated so assiduously since the early 1960s. Over the course of 1971 Mao began to pursue a three-part policy he later referred to as "throwing stones, adding sand to mud, and undermining the cornerstone."[14] The "stones" were thrown at the senior army officers directly under Lin, who were all made to issue public self-criticisms. The "sand" was added by altering the personnel in the Military Affairs Commission of the CCP Central Committee, to remove some of Lin's supporters. The "cornerstone" comprised the armed forces of the Peking military region, where Mao also replaced key personnel. Still moving circumspectly, Mao stepped up the criticism campaigns against "defective work styles" in the PLA, and himself visited the regional military commands in Nanjing and Canton, presumably to reassure himself of their commanders' loyalty.

According to documents later released by the CCP, Lin Biao, driven to desperation by the collapse of his high political ambitions, sought support among his closest friends for an assassination attempt on Mao. Unable to implement this plan, Lin panicked and fled China, along with his wife and son, in a military Trident jet. The party documents added that the plane was making for the Soviet Union but was inadequately fueled for such a trip; it also had on board neither navigator nor radio operator. It crashed in Mongolia on September 13, 1971, burning to death all on board. This story is essentially beyond verification, since the photographs later released by the Chinese authorities are of dubious authenticity, and details on Lin's exact plans and on the other plotters are blurred. But it was clear to all that Lin's political life—and presumably his physical one as well—was now dramatically over.

At the apparent height of his power, in an address to the ninth party congress on April 1, 1969, Lin had told the assembled delegates that China's former head of state Liu Shaoqi had "betrayed the Party, capitulated to the enemy and became a hidden traitor and scab." In 1972 Premier Zhou Enlai announced that it was Lin Biao who had been the "renegade and traitor." Not surprisingly, the Chen villagers were as puzzled as anyone. "I had felt faithful to Mao," said one Chen Village peasant, recalling this period in a later interview, "but that Lin Biao stuff affected my thinking." Or as one of the urban youths assigned to live in the village put it:

> When Liu Shaoqi was dragged down we'd been very supportive. At that time Mao Zedong was raised very high: he was the red sun and what not. But the

Lin Biao affair provided us with a major lesson. We came to see that the leaders up there could say today that something is round; tomorrow, that it's flat. We lost faith in the system.[15]

The bewilderment of the villagers is fully understandable. The credulity of the Chinese people had been stretched beyond all possible boundaries as leader after leader had first been praised to the skies and then vilified. The most violent strains in Chinese society had been given free rein and the basic organizational structures stretched to the breaking point. The Great Leap Forward had at least had a meaningful economic and social vision at its heart. The Great Proletarian Cultural Revolution showed that neither Mao nor the CCP seemed to know how or where the nation should be heading.

V | RE-ENTERING THE WORLD

DURING THE LATE 1960s, the leaders of the Cultural Revolution had firmly turned their backs on both the Soviet Union and the Western powers. China was to call on its own resources to create a new, purified society and to implement a creative form of Marxism imbued with the vigor of Mao Zedong thought. Yet this involuted approach could not be maintained for long, especially if China's new technical challenges—such as exploiting its offshore oil resources—were to be met. So even as the purist rhetoric continued, feelers went out to the United States and came to fruition in 1972 when President Richard Nixon traveled to China and met with Mao. The two men issued a joint communiqué on the current state of U.S.-Chinese relations and their attitudes to Taiwan, and China signed a number of massive deals with the United States as well as Japan, Britain, West Germany, and France for imports of advanced technology.

China's leaders, however, remained divided as to the wisdom of this course, especially once they discovered the cost of the new imports and saw the nation's balance of payments fall into deficit. The Cultural Revolution's leaders continued to invoke Dazhai and Daqing as models of self-reliance, even as the government edged toward acknowledging the usefulness of foreign technology. A new ideological campaign, ostensibly aimed against "Lin Biao and Confucius," highlighted the worries that many ideologues felt about over-Westernization and the abandonment of Marxist values.

At the same time, the Chinese people themselves showed a growing willingness to criticize the party, and in the spring of 1976 the largest genuinely spontaneous demonstration to occur in the history of the PRC up to that time took place in Peking. The demonstrators were appealing for more openness in government, an end to dictatorship, and a return to the true spirit of Marxism-Leninism. Suppressed by police, the demonstrators were vindicated by the government in 1978, which led to a new and even greater upsurge of demands for political and intellectual freedoms known as the Democracy Wall protests. In the meantime, Mao Zedong had died and the country had embarked on a new course of speeded-up economic development—though still following the now-conventional line of combining self-reliance with the Four Modernizations in industry, agriculture, science and technology, and national defense.

By the late 1970s, a new trend had emerged in China's economic life: the old ideal of self-reliance within the collective was replaced by a strategy of heightened local initiative and worker responsibility. In pilot programs that proved dramatically effective, rural families were allowed to increase vastly the amount of land they could till as private plots and to sell the produce on the open market at unpegged prices. On a smaller scale, urban entrepreneurs were encouraged to experiment with nonexploitative businesses.

The most careful census ever made in China was carried through in 1982, and showed that China's population had now passed the 1 billion mark. The implications of this were grave, for unless population growth could be checked, even the most dramatic changes in rural and industrial production would not raise the country's standard of living. The census highlighted a number of other problems, such as the high mortality rates among China's minority populations and the growing population density on a slowly shrinking acreage of farmland. Sex ratios analyzed by age also suggested that China's attempts to enforce a policy of one child per family, when coupled with the new economic incentive systems in rural areas, were leading many families to practice female infanticide in the hopes of having a son as the next child.

To steer China along its perilous new course there stood a government with structural problems. Leadership in the PRC had never been completely unified, despite the extraordinary prestige of Mao Zedong. But in the years following his death it became apparent how much the workings of the Chinese government depended on connections, favors, bargains, and trade-offs, and how hard it was for all sectors of the bureaucracy and the provincial governments to act in concert. In China's new world of complex, long-term deals with foreign corporations, which placed billions of yuan at risk, these structural problems threatened further to impede China's growth.

Even as the last elements of Cultural Revolution rhetoric and practice were laid to rest, the new developments in the economy triggered alarming new cases of corruption, while the reintroduction of Western literature, films, art, and music stirred disillusion with the conventional tenets of Marxism-Leninism among China's intellectuals and youth. The outpouring of cultural exuberance that followed was met, once again, by harsh government reaction in what this time was termed the antispiritual-pollution movement. Yet even as that campaign was cowing many intellectuals, the government issued a ringing reaffirmation of the new individual rights in industry and agriculture, and moved to reintroduce a system of law designed to reassure foreign investors and Chinese entrepreneurs alike.

These mixed signals were one indication that, with the demise of the Maoist utopian vision and the public discrediting of so many members of the CCP during the Cultural Revolution, there was no clear focus of authority left. Petty peculations had no doubt often been practiced in the past by CCP members, but by 1985 it was becoming corruption on an enormous scale. The newly affluent Chinese who were able to benefit from the economic reforms were thirsting for consumer goods, and the temptation to reroute scarce imports their way in black-market deals was hard to resist. The government seemed caught in a curious posture—peering toward the future while tilting back into the past.

Frustration among students and intellectuals with their government reached an explosive point by the end of 1986. In a series of demonstrations, students defied government bans and demanded that democratic rights be granted to the Chinese people so that the economic modernizations could proceed in a more open atmosphere. The government's response, as it had been in the past, was to launch an attack on the students for being disloyal to the party and the state, and to reinvoke hallowed (but by now shopworn) stereotypes of revolutionary unity and self-sacrifice. The secretary-general of the CCP was himself dismissed for failing to prevent the disturbances from occurring. But while repressing all calls for democratic freedoms, the government adopted constitutional protections for the new industrial and agricultural enterprises.

Many of China's old revolutionaries stepped down (or were shunted aside) in the late 1980s, but the new leaders called in to replace them could do nothing to solve the inconsistencies that so plagued Chinese society. Areas of extraordinary wealth and the most advanced new technologies coexisted with primitive living conditions, calls for more openness went unanswered by the party, and rampant economic corruption was linked to an ingrained system of contacts and nepotism that left those on the outside resentful and frustrated. In 1989, less than two years after the suppression of the most recent demonstrations, these tensions again burst into the open. But now the confrontations grew in intensity, reaching a scale unprecedented in the history of the PRC. In mid-May, over 1 million Chinese from all walks of life assembled in and around Peking's Tiananmen Square, calling for dialogue with the government leaders over democracy and an end to the corruption that seemed to taint all areas of life. Completely eclipsing the visit to China of the leader of the Soviet Union, which ended the thirty-three-year rift between the two nations, the Peking demonstrators pushed their demands ever more strongly, adding a prolonged hunger strike to their arsenal of pressure tactics.

The PRC government responded with a declaration of martial law, enforcement of which was at first prevented by the spontaneous courage of the inhabitants of Peking, who blocked PLA soldiers from entering the heart of the city. Finally, the hard-line leaders, having outvoted or outmaneuvered their more conciliatory colleagues, ordered newly summoned battalions of heavily armed troops, backed by tanks, to smash their way through to Tiananmen. The resulting massacre shocked China and the world, and highlighted the distance that lay between those seeking a greater pluralism in Chinese life and expression, and those who sought still to funnel programs through the control mechanisms of the single-party state. But as continuing proof of the government's coercive power, those who had lost loved ones were forbidden to mourn, hospitals were prevented from issuing casualty figures, most fugitive dissidents were rounded up and sentenced to long prison terms, and Deng Xiaoping publicly praised the PLA for its courage.

With the suppression of the broad-based pleas for greater democratic participation, the party reconsolidated its power. At the same time, it allowed maximum leeway in economic growth, both to distract the populace from making more political demands and to strengthen the nation as a whole. China embarked on a heady period of fast economic growth, which changed the face of the cities completely and also steadily increased rural industrialization. Foreign investment soared, and foreign countries—especially the United States—began to experience major trade deficits with China. Long anticipated, Deng Xiaoping's death came in the spring of 1997, accompanied by no massive demonstrations. Instead, the leaders brought to power as hard-liners in 1989 seemed to consolidate their power, and gloried in the peaceful return of Hong Kong to the mainland regime on July 1, 1997, symbolically and literally ending a century and a half of Western imperialism in China. Dampening opportunities for democracy in Hong Kong, the leaders seemed determined to maintain a path of economic growth without social dislocation, impossible though that seemed to many observers. And the problem of Taiwan's reunification, muted as a topic for many years, now came to the fore as the focus for the kind of decision that had to be faced in the future. Would China stay in the world as a modern nation at last? Or would its rulers seek to perpetuate policies that would place China at odds with the other developed nations?

CHAPTER 23 | # Reopening the Doors

THE UNITED STATES AND THE NIXON VISIT

During the early years of the Cultural Revolution, despite the efforts of Zhou Enlai to maintain some continuity with the past and to protect senior personnel in the Ministry of Foreign Affairs from criticism and dismissal, the rhetoric of China's foreign policy grew defiantly revolutionary. In 1965 Lin Biao had declared that just as the rural revolutionaries had surrounded and strangled China's cities in 1948 and 1949, so now would the impoverished Third World countries surround and strangle the superpowers and the rest of the advanced capitalist nations. This statement became a basic formula for Chinese foreign policy during the Cultural Revolution, and was interpreted by many Western observers to mean that China sought to play a dominant role in creating global upheavals that might lead to a weakening of the capitalist nations.

But the rhetoric was not backed by any overt military actions and turned out to be largely meaningless. It merely underlined China's inability to help other struggling nations in any significant way. Lin Biao's formula was, however, used to justify China's reaching out to a wide range of radical opposition groups abroad, to poor nations in Africa and the Middle East, and to such Arab nationalist groups as the Palestine Liberation Organization, despite their espousal of terrorism. Visionary statements appeared in China's press of the inherent oneness of her people with the oppressed of the world. For some older intellectuals these statements might have evoked the language of Li Dazhao during the May Fourth period, when he had talked of foreign imperialism having "proletarianized" the Chinese people.

595

Despite their own internal turmoil, the Chinese continued to give aid to conspicuous development projects in Third World countries. Chairman Mao's thought was held up as an international guide to revolution, and the Little Red Book of his quotations was translated into scores of languages, with millions of copies distributed around the world. In perhaps the most graphic attempt at historical universalism, some Chinese analysts even argued that Charles Gordon, the British officer whose Ever-Victorious Army had been helpful to Zeng Guofan and Li Hongzhang in their suppression of the Taiping, and who was subsequently killed by Sudanese rebels at Khartoum in 1885, had met his doom because the African masses had intuitively understood the need for vengeance against Gordon felt by his Chinese Taiping victims.

But during the late 1960s China had also been lobbying intensively to win the seat in the United Nations, and the accompanying Security Council vote, that had been held since 1949 by the Guomindang government on Taiwan. With the help of some nonaligned powers, the claims of the PRC were advanced each year, and the U.S.–backed position of boycotting the PRC slowly eroded, despite heavy U.S. pressure on its own allies. In 1971 the United States finally gave up its opposition as futile, and in October of that year the PRC was admitted to the China seat in the UN, and Taiwan forced to withdraw.

Well before this, the United States had been edging toward renewed contacts with the PRC. For many years, relations between the two had been conducted only through the roundabout means of having the American ambassador to Poland meet at intervals with Chinese diplomats in Warsaw. Some gestures by the Kennedy administration toward rethinking American intransigence to China were halted after the president's assassination in 1963. By 1966 the momentum had built up again, and in the summer of 1966 the secretary of state suggested to the Chinese Communist government that some Chinese scientists and scholars be allowed to visit the United States. The gesture, however, coincided with the opening acts of the Cultural Revolution, and was angrily rejected by the Chinese as a meaningless propaganda ploy by the hostile superpower.

But by 1970 Mao himself had grown deeply worried both by the continuous buildup of Soviet troops on China's borders since the 1969 border clashes, and by Lin Biao's ambitions. The idea of reopening some avenues of contact with the United States was accordingly discussed by members of the Chinese leadership, despite the ongoing revolutionary and anti-imperialist rhetoric of Jiang Qing and other leaders of the Cultural Revolution. Members of the technically sophisticated staffs of the Daqing oilfield and the Ministry of Petroleum Industries also lobbied actively for ending

China's rejection of advanced Western technology. Many of these men, brought in by Mao between 1964 and 1966 to be senior economic planners, had been harried by Red Guards or sent to May Seventh Cadre Schools in the late 1960s. Now, as the oilfields they had developed proved to be one of the only growth sectors of the Chinese economy, and Mao began to turn against Lin Biao and some of the more insistently radical exponents of complete self-reliance, the "Petroleum Group" (as some called them) came back into favor. They knew that if China were to continue to expand oil production at the rate desired by the top leadership, it would require major initiatives in offshore exploration and drilling, and for this China had neither the resources nor the technology. Foreign skills would be essential, and in petroleum technology the United States was the proven world leader.

In January 1970, at the one hundred thirty-fifth regular Warsaw meeting, the Chinese broke the routine pattern of angry exchanges over the status of Taiwan and mentioned the possibility of having further talks "at a higher level or through other channels acceptable to both sides." After additional behind-the-scenes maneuverings on both sides, in April 1971 the Chinese suddenly invited the U.S. table-tennis team, which was competing at the time in Japan, to visit China on a good-will mission. The gesture was overt and clear, the opportunity too good to let by. Within days, the era of "ping-pong diplomacy" was declared to be at hand.

By dint of negotiations that were initially concealed from the public, the Congress, the State Department, and even the secretary of state himself, President Nixon's national security adviser Henry Kissinger, traveled to China in July 1971 to meet privately with Zhou Enlai and plan the details of a visit by President Nixon. Negotiations were aided by decisions of the treasury and other departments to end the ban on the transfer of U.S. dollars to China—Chinese-Americans could now send money to relatives on the mainland—to allow American-owned ships under foreign flags to transport goods to China, and to allow Chinese exports into the United States for the first time since the Korean War. On July 15 the public announcement of a presidential visit, scheduled for an unfixed date "before May 1972," was made on radio and television by Nixon himself in California. The Chinese also mentioned the upcoming visit in a small box on the front page of *People's Daily*.

As Kissinger later noted in his memoirs, "no government less deserved what was about to happen to it than that of Taiwan."[1] Ever since the decision of President Truman to protect Taiwan against a possible PRC invasion in the first year of the Korean War, Taiwan had been a strong ally of the United States, had provided a valuable Pacific base for U.S. missiles, and had also benefited from massive American aid and trade. The issue of Taiwan was also volatile in the United States, since a highly vocal "China lobby" had continued to press for the need to defend Chiang Kai-shek at all costs against threats from the mainland, and any charges of being "soft" on Chinese communism could once again rekindle the smoldering ashes of the McCarthy period. Perhaps only a Republican president like Richard Nixon, with a well-documented past of intense—even unrelenting—hostility to communism, could have made such risky decisions in secret and avoided a political confrontation with Congress. But since both the People's Republic and Taiwan were implacably opposed to a "two Chinas" solution that would deny the basic right of either side to represent the whole, no easy compromise was going to be possible. Nixon's announcement of his China trip had a foreseeable effect in the UN. In late October the General Assembly, by a tally of 59 to 55 with 15 abstentions, voted against the U.S.-sponsored procedural motion that would have allowed Taiwan to keep its UN seat; by a formal vote, the People's Republic of China was then granted that seat, which meant the expulsion of the Taiwan delegation.

President Nixon was not met in Peking, as he and some of his advance planners had hoped, by large crowds of cheering Chinese who would boost his wavering image back home via American television. Instead, when he stepped onto the tarmac of Peking airport on the morning of February 21, 1972, and publicly shook hands with the waiting Premier Zhou Enlai—to assuage the slight made by Dulles at Geneva eighteen years before—there was only a small line of Chinese officials and a plainly dressed though impressive honor guard. The motorcade to the guesthouse where the Americans were lodged drove down empty streets, and the massive Tiananmen Square, in front of the Forbidden City, was similarly deserted.

Nixon was taken to meet Mao Zedong that afternoon. Mao explained the cautious welcome in part by observing that a "reactionary group" had been "opposed" to any official contact with the United States, and then made it clear that he was referring to Lin Biao, among others. Mao also joked that Chiang Kai-shek disapproved of the meeting as well. In other informal remarks—though they might well have been carefully prepared beforehand—Mao said to Nixon, "I voted for you during your election," and went on to clarify this by pointing out that "rightists" were comparatively predictable. When Nixon sought to flatter Mao by saying that Mao's writings had "moved a nation" and "changed the world," Mao responded, "I have not been able to change it. I have only been able to change a few places in the vicinity of Peking."[2] In a reversal of normal Chinese practice, this meeting with Mao was filmed, and a ten-minute segment carried on Chinese national television. Chinese newspapers also carried pages of photographs.

The diplomatic substance of Nixon's visit was hammered out in long private sessions by Chinese and American negotiators, while the president and his escorts enjoyed their visits to the Great Wall and the Ming tombs outside Peking, and endured an endless round of banquets. The central issues were how to handle the status of Taiwan and the possible effects of a changed China policy on the Soviet Union, with which an American summit meeting was already planned for May. The resulting statement, which marked a major policy shift for both countries, was issued at Shanghai, during Nixon's visit there, on February 28, 1972. Presented in the form of a "joint communiqué," this document summarized both the American and Chinese points of view on global politics without attempting to reconcile them. The "U.S. side," as the document termed it, reaffirmed the American opinion that the role of the United States in the Vietnam War did not constitute "outside intervention" in the affairs of Vietnam, and restated U.S. commitment to "individual freedom." The United States also pledged continued support for South Korea. The "Chinese side" declared that "wherever there is oppression, there is resistance," and that "all foreign troops should be withdrawn to their own countries." Korea should be unified along lines proposed by North Korea.

On the matter of Taiwan, the Shanghai communiqué carefully continued, there were obvious differences of opinion rooted in the different "social systems and foreign policies" of China and the United States, and complete agreement was not possible. As the Chinese phrased their side of the argument:

> The Taiwan question is the crucial question obstructing the normalization of relations between China and the United States; the Government of the People's Republic of China is the sole legal government of China; Taiwan is a province of China which has long been returned to the motherland; the liberation of Taiwan is China's internal affair in which no other country has the right to interfere; and all U.S. forces and military installations must be withdrawn from Taiwan. The Chinese Government firmly opposes any activities which aim at the creation of "one China, one Taiwan," "One China, two governments," "two Chinas," an "independent Taiwan" or advocate that "the status of Taiwan remains to be determined."

The United States wrote its own interpretation into the communiqué:

> The United States acknowledges that all Chinese on either side of the Taiwan Strait maintain there is but one China and that Taiwan is a part of China. The United States Government does not challenge that position. It reaffirms

its interest in a peaceful settlement of the Taiwan question by the Chinese themselves. With this prospect in mind, it affirms the ultimate objective of the withdrawal of all U.S. forces and military installations from Taiwan. In the meantime, it will progressively reduce its forces and military installations on Taiwan as the tension in the area diminishes.[3]

The closing sections of the communiqué suggested the desirability of more "people-to-people contacts and exchanges" in "science, technology, culture, sports and journalism," agreed that trade between the two countries should be increased, and that "a senior U.S. representative" should visit Peking "from time to time." (China would have its own UN delegation in New York, and thus would have senior diplomats permanently on American soil. Since the United States still recognized Taiwan diplomatically as representing China, the Taiwan government would keep its embassy in Washington.) Finally, both China and the United States would work for "the normalization of relations between the two countries" as a contribution toward "the relaxation of tension in Asia and the world."

It was a remarkable moment in diplomatic history. Mao was struggling to reassert some order after the ravages of the Cultural Revolution and Lin Biao's death, and already showing the advanced symptoms of debilitating illness. Nixon was watching his popularity wane in domestic hostility over the Vietnam War, and already displaying that deeply suspicious view of the American opposition that was to plunge him into Watergate and shatter his presidency. Yet the opportunity for global realignments had been noted by both men, and rather than let it slip by, they decided to seize it. Perhaps the Treaty of Nerchinsk in 1689, the Treaty of Nanjing in 1842, and the Treaty of Shimonoseki in 1895 had had more dramatic immediate consequences for the Chinese people. But this agreement of 1972, cautious and elliptical though it was, marked a turning point of parallel significance in China's foreign relations.

ATTACKING CONFUCIUS AND LIN BIAO

As if to emphasize the importance of the leaders of the Cultural Revolution in China's current and future politics, it was the Shanghai politician and theorist Zhang Chunqiao, in his capacity as chairman of the Shanghai Revolutionary Committee, who hosted the farewell banquet for President Nixon and his entourage on February 27, the eve of the announcement of the Shanghai communiqué. In his speech Zhang made the claim, which he described as springing from Mao's teachings, that the people of Shanghai were "maintaining independence and keeping initiative in our own hands and relying on our own efforts."[4] This reassertion of the Maoist value of self-reliance was mandatory in the context, but presumably Zhang and his listeners understood that the United States would be used to strengthen China's economic and strategic position in its ongoing hostility to the Soviet Union.

In China's cities and villages, furthermore, political expectations were different from what they had been only a few years previously. When Liu Shaoqi had been ousted in 1966, the news was accepted across China without great excitement, even though Liu had been head of state and one of Mao's close associates for over forty years. But, as the peasants of Chen Village had so clearly stated, the ouster of Lin Biao, and his alleged treason and death, were much harder to understand. Lin had appeared to be at the very center of the Cultural Revolution's planning and euphoria, Mao's Little Red Book carried Lin's personally written introduction, and the 1969 constitution had named him as Mao's chosen successor. How was the party to vilify him convincingly and still keep its credibility?

The stakes involved in this question were particularly high for Mao Zedong, who had lost credibility himself over the way Lin's death had been presented, as well as for Jiang Qing and her supporters. The stakes were considerable also for the hundreds of thousands of others who had come to power during the same period, and the millions of new members who had been admitted to the party. CCP enrollments in this period strongly suggest a seesaw pattern of rapidly rising numbers of new recruits in the early years of the Cultural Revolution, followed by a purge of those hostile to the movement, followed in turn by a swelling of membership again. This second jump, in 1972 and 1973, was caused both by the enrollment of additional new recruits to strengthen the power base of those leaders hoping to succeed Mao as rulers of China, and also by the return to party ranks of previously disgraced members such as Deng Xiaoping.

CCP ENROLLMENT, 1966–1976[5]

Year	China's population	% change	CCP members	% change
1966	750 million (approx.)		18 million	
1969	806 million	7.5	22 million	22.2
1971	852 million	5.7	17 million	−22.7
1972	870 million (approx.)	2.1	20 million	17.6
1973	892 million	2.5	28 million	40.0
1976	925 million (approx.)	3.7	34 million	21.9

The party's response to the difficult task of maintaining its prestige can be traced through the crosscurrents of its campaign against Lin Biao. Initially, in the first months after his death, Lin Biao was not officially referred to by name, although local party leaders had been alerted to the planned campaign at special briefings. Instead the press, party journals, and radio stations began a series of attacks on unnamed people defined as "swindlers like Liu Shaoqi" or as "sham Marxist political swindlers." The crime of these "swindlers" was that they "wanted to use the spectre of anarchism to stir up disorder and poison the masses in order to oppose the revolution," and that they "cunningly incited ultra-'left' trends of thought, wanting democracy without centralism and freedom without discipline."[6] By early 1973, some leaders of the Cultural Revolution must have realized that such a campaign of vilification would backfire, for the charges sounded uncannily as if they applied to the behavior they had practiced themselves. Now the Chinese people were warned that the swindlers' line was revisionist, not leftist, and that those same swindlers had "at certain times and on certain issues... put on an extreme 'Left' appearance to disguise their Right essence." One goal of these swindlers, among others, was a "counterrevolutionary desire for the restoration of the overthrown landlord and bourgeois classes."[7] Although everyone in China must have realized the charges referred to Lin Biao, it was not until the tenth party congress in August 1973 that Zhou Enlai said so officially and in public. But Zhou made no convincing attempt to explain exactly what Lin had done and how he had been allowed to do it, nor what historical precedents there could have been for his actions, which must surely have sounded absurd to most listeners.

At almost the same time that the tenth congress was convening, a new mass campaign was launched, the ostensible target being no less a personage than Confucius himself, and the humanistic and conservative values that he represented. Scholars in China began to publish articles on Confucius that had clear implications for the Cultural Revolution, the bureaucracy, and the role of labor in society: Confucius was described as a representative of the declining slave-owning aristocracy who hated the emerging feudal landlords and their supporters, the legalist philosophers. Since in the context of economic and social development in the fifth century B.C. it was "progressive" to move from a slave-owning to a feudal society—as later it was progressive to move from feudalism to capitalism—obviously Confucius was a reactionary.

Other essays published in late 1973 linked the attack on Confucius to praise for China's first emperor, the celebrated Qin Shihuang, who unified all China under his rule in 221 B.C. Though Qin Shihuang had been vilified in the past as an absolute tyrant who brought terrible suffering in the name of centralized order, scholars in 1973 urged the people to praise him along with the legalists who supported him. The scholars argued that even such Draconian actions as his burning of the Confucian books and burying alive of scholars had been necessary in order to consolidate the "dictatorship of the landlord class." Lin Biao, it was firmly stated (in case anyone had missed the point), was one of "the Confuciuses of contemporary China."[8]

By 1974 the "Anti-Lin Biao anti–Confucius" movement had become a mass campaign all across China. In ways that recalled the anti–Hu Feng campaign during the consolidation period of the early 1950s, or the anti-Wu Han campaign that led into the Cultural Revolution, the Lin-Confucius campaign was made the focus for mass rallies and intense group discussions in party cells and universities, in the PLA and the local militia units, in communes and factories. Even if made weary or cynical by the plethora of such campaigns, there was nothing that the Chinese could do but attend the study groups and read along in the required texts with their local cadres. Western visitors and academics, now beginning to appear in China in some numbers, were subject to endless briefings on the nature and importance of the campaign, and its significance to understanding recent events in Chinese history.

In a parallel cultural attack, a documentary film on China made by the Italian director Michelangelo Antonioni was bitterly denounced by Chinese critics for failing to pay attention to the dramatic achievements of the "new" China, and for its passion for traditional patterns of farming, old buildings, and primitive housing. Antonioni, who had claimed to admire China, was now accused of "using the camera to slander the Cultural Revolution, insult people and attack the leadership."[9] Foreign visitors in China were startled to see huge banners attacking Antonioni hanging above the machinery in factories and displayed in communes, for the message seemed to be all too clear that foreigners were not welcome unless they praised what they saw. But the government could not always anticipate how its propaganda might be used. Some Chinese professors quietly observed that they were using the campaign against Confucius to reintroduce the teaching of classical Chinese literature in their classes. Study of such classical texts had not been favored during the high tide of the Cultural Revolution; but now, teachers asked visitors in mock innocence, how could the students criticize Confucius with maximum effect if they could not use every nuance of his reactionary language?

Behind these cultural tensions, which reflected disagreements within the Chinese leadership fed perhaps by the views of Jiang Qing, there also lay problems with the restructuring of China's educational system. Schools and colleges had been reduced to shambles in the early years of the Cultural

Revolution, with buildings closed for years, students deployed as Red Guards or reassigned to the remote countryside, administrators and teachers humiliated or dismissed, and new books and materials unavailable. The reopening of high schools and colleges in the late 1960s and early 1970s, and especially the reappearance in 1973 of examinations for university entrance, were met with mixed reactions among students who had now tasted a different kind of learning. One case, that of Zhang Tiesheng, an educated youth who had been sent to Liaoning province in the northeast for five years and had risen to become head of his production team, received national attention when it was reported that he had handed in a blank examination paper to a college admissions committee. In a note to the examiners, Zhang wrote that he was too busy working eighteen-hour days on the commune to devote time to academic study, and that he had "no respect for the bookworms who for many years have been taking it easy and have done nothing useful." It was unfair, noted Zhang, that after all the work he had put in for his country "a few hours of written examination may disqualify me for enrollment in college."[10] The national publicity given Zhang's case showed that many in leadership positions were trying to protect the policy of admission to college based on the "revolutionary purity" so extolled in the Cultural Revolution.

Even more media coverage was given to a philosophy student named Zhong who resigned from Nanjing University in his second year. Zhong, who had been working on a commune, had been admitted to this prestigious college on the basis of a telephone call made to the admissions committee by his father, a Long March veteran and senior military cadre. Zhong now realized, he wrote, that the use of such "connections" (guanxi) and "back door influence" (houmen) was improper and unfair to the masses. His resignation was approved and he returned to his work in the countryside, loaded down with the presents bestowed on him by admiring friends: the works of Marx, Engels, Lenin, and Mao; a full package of materials on the struggle to criticize Lin Biao and Confucius; and a hoe, a chisel, scissors, and a sturdy pair of straw shoes.[11]

The students Zhang and Zhong, with their contrasting modes of approach to university entrance and their common experience of work in the rural communes, were the most publicized voices to emerge from the immense body of youthful Chinese who had been sent to the countryside— allegedly to boost production there but also to ease overcrowding in the cities—during the Cultural Revolution. Over 16 million urban youths were resettled in these years, 1 million of them from Shanghai. Yunnan in the southwest had absorbed 600,000 youths from various cities, and Heilongjiang in the far northeast, on the Soviet border, 900,000. This vast program of relocation might have eased some social problems caused by crime and overcrowding in the big cities, but it also led to terrible personal dislocations and hardship for those unused to rural labor, and brought a new range of social and political conflicts into the countryside. Few of those ordered to live out their lives in impoverished rural areas can have shared the cheery official estimate that these young people were "growing healthily in the vast and resourceful rural areas."

DEFINING THE ECONOMY, 1974–1975

By 1974 it was clear that there would soon be significant changes in China's leadership. Zhou Enlai was seriously ill with cancer, and although he continued his intensive schedule of work as premier, he was often in the hospital for treatment; Mao Zedong could no longer control the symptoms of Lou Gehrig's disease, never appeared without nurses in attendance, and spoke more and more of being interested only in philosophical rather than practical administrative problems, and of "preparing to meet god." Zhu De, the builder of the Red Army, was in his late eighties, and had long retired from an active public role.

Amid the figures now jockeying for position, the four leaders of the Cultural Revolution constituted an energetic and forceful bloc, supported in the provinces and in the state-controlled media by others who had risen to power in the years since 1966. Despite a grudging acceptance of China's partial opening to the West, they continued to push for what can be called a "radical" line. This meant continuing the system of communes as it had been consolidated in the years after the Great Leap Forward, with the peasants organized into a hierarchy rising from a base of millions of small production teams of a dozen or so families, which were consolidated into the larger production brigades of 200 or 300 families, and then combined again into around 200,000 communes. Senior cadres represented Peking in the communes, wielding their bureaucratic mandates to enforce production quotas, their allocation of development funds and heavy machinery, and their control over local education, health-care facilities, and militia.

The radical line also meant continued exhortations to "learn from the model of Dazhai," the production brigade in Shanxi province that had survived its near demystification in the early 1960s and was once again extolled in the media as the true model for heroic local initiative through incessant hard work and the Maoist virtue of self-reliance. Along with praise for Dazhai as the great example of self-sustaining rural development came continued invocations of the great oilfield at Daqing, northwest of Harbin in

Heilongjiang province, as an example of how a major industrial enterprise employing tens of thousands of workers should grow. At Daqing, it was alleged, the emphasis was still on self-reliance and independence, and on mobilizing the work force to its fullest extent through constant political training and indoctrination with Mao's thought. Ironically, such self-reliance could be extremely expensive. Reports from the same period noted that while grain was still sold to urban dwellers at 1950 prices, the state was paying communes twice as much for their grain as it had then. This strategy of keeping urban wages low by subsidizing grain sales was costing the state billions of yuan a year.

The radicals also continued to insist on the right of Chinese from "good class backgrounds," such as those whose fathers had been poor peasants and industrial workers, to be admitted without formal examination to college, where their political correctness would have the chance to flourish. They continued as well the compulsory relocation of educated youth from the cities to the countryside. They fostered further self-reliance in health systems through the use of "barefoot doctors" or paramedic personnel—of whom there were over 1 million by 1974—rather than highly trained Western-style physicians and surgeons with their expensive hospitals and equipment. And in line with Jiang Qing's earliest expressed views on the cultural scene, they wished to keep tight control over the political content of art, drama, and literature so that class lines would not be blurred nor the moral force of the socialist message blunted by ambiguity. An attempt to do this was made by limiting dramatic performances to a handful of allegedly "model" works, such as *The White-haired Girl* and *The Red Lantern,* which gave didactically "correct" interpretations to the purity of revolutionary activism.

In growing opposition to this rigidly indigenous program for national development were the Chinese planners who hoped for a more dynamic economic growth that would draw on foreign technology and expertise while continuing to preserve China's economic and political integrity. This had been the goal of the nineteenth-century self-strengtheners, and although those statesmen had failed, their Communist successors in the 1970s were confident of success. Zhou Enlai himself was a supporter of this strategy. Another proponent of this approach was Deng Xiaoping, who had maintained a strong group of supporters in the CCP hierarchy despite his disgrace in 1966. Now restored to power as a vice-premier, Deng, in a speech he delivered at the United Nations in 1974, gave a succinct definition of what China was attempting. While apparently praising the "self-reliant" aspects of development so touted by the Cultural Revolutionaries, he added important modifications:

Self-reliance in no way means "self-seclusion" and rejection of foreign aid. We have always considered it beneficial and necessary for the development of the national economy that countries should carry on economic and technical exchanges on the basis of respect for state sovereignty, equality and mutual benefit, and the exchange of needed goods to make up for each other's deficiencies.[12]

And the Petroleum Group, though risen from Daqing ranks, as we have seen, were also drawn to the outer world. A natural part of this development must be "technology transfer," which could be expected to include low-interest loans, international trade, and the employment of foreign experts. Another component of technology transfer was the purchase by China of entire industrial plants.

The Chinese advocates of growth had originally intended to offset much of the cost of importing foreign plants by increasing the production of oil for export from the Daqing fields and by boosting other exports. What Chinese planners had not anticipated was a combination of worldwide recession and inflation, which by 1974 was beginning to shrink the market for China's exports and dramatically raise the costs that China had to meet for its technological imports. The result was a $760 million trade deficit for China in 1974, which led to a spirited counterattack by the radicals against

Chinese Trade and Complete Plant Purchases[13]
($ millions)

Year	Total exports	Total imports	Balance of trade	Machinery and equipment imports	Complete plant contracts
1966	2,210	2,035	175	455	0
1967	1,960	1,955	5	380	0
1968	1,960	1,825	135	275	0
1969	2,060	1,835	225	240	0
1970	2,095	2,245	−150	395	0
1971	2,500	2,310	190	505	0
1972	3,150	2,850	300	520	0
1973	5,075	5,225	−150	860	1,259
1974	6,660	7,420	−760	1,610	831
1975	7,180	7,395	−215	2,155	364
1976	7,265	6,010	1,255	1,770	185
1977	7,955	7,100	855	1,200	80
1978	10,260	10,650	−390	2,500	6,934

the "worship of things foreign" and those who followed a "slavish comprador philosophy."

As was done so often in the past, historical "analysis" was used to make
the necessary critical point. One such essay, which accused the self-
strengthener Li Hongzhang of accepting high technology from foreigners
and allowing them to run China's factories in the nineteenth century, was
clearly directed at Premier Zhou Enlai. Another essay attacking the last of
the important Qing self-strengtheners, Governor-General Zhang Zhidong,
who had popularized the influential *ti-yong* ("essence" and "practical use")
theory, was transparently aimed at Deng Xiaoping. In the fall of 1975 a
number of similar critiques were synthesized in an essay that appeared in
China's foremost historical journal under the pseudonym Liang Xiao, the
name used by a group of Peking intellectuals who acted as the defenders of
the radical policies of the Cultural Revolution leaders. Allegedly referring
to the nineteenth century, the article stated:

> Politically, "wholesale Westernization" meant loss of sovereignty and national
> humiliation, total sell-out of China's independence and self-determination. . . .
> Ideologically "wholesale Westernization" was meant to praise what is foreign
> and belittle what is Chinese and propagate national nihilism in order to under-
> mine the national consciousness of the Chinese spirit. . . . Economically "whole-
> sale Westernization" was aimed at spreading blind faith in the Western
> capitalist material civilization so as to turn the Chinese economy into a com-
> plete appendage of imperialism.[14]

The scope of the radicals' counterattack can best be seen in the pomp
surrounding the First National Conference on Learning from Dazhai in

CONTRACTS FOR WHOLE PLANTS, BY INDUSTRY[15]
($ millions)

	1973	1974	1975	1976	1977	1978	Total
Petrochemicals	698	114	90	136	39	3,325	4,402
Iron and steel		551		40		2,978	3,569
Fertilizer	392	120		8			520
Coal and electric power	161	46				202	409
Transport			200			79	279
Communications and electronics						217	217
Nonferrous metals						127	127
Manufacturing	8		74	1	21	6	110
Petroleum and gas					20		20
Total	1,259	831	364	185	80	6,934	9,653

Agriculture, which was convened in Shanxi province in September and October 1975. Among the 7,000 dignitaries in attendance were both Jiang Qing and Deng Xiaoping, who were bitter political enemies and stood for opposite strategies of national development. The keynote speech however was made neither by Jiang nor Deng, but by the former party secretary from Mao's home province of Hunan, Hua Guofeng, who had recently been named a vice-premier of the State Council and placed in charge of China's agricultural development. Born in Shanxi in 1920 and posted to Hunan in the early 1950s, Hua laid the basis of his rise to power by reassuring Mao Zedong with favorable assessments of the progress of the Great Leap Forward in Hunan province during 1959. Hua further ingratiated himself with Mao in 1964 by founding a model "Dazhai" brigade in Hunan, and by orchestrating Red Guard visits to Mao's home village, which became almost a shrine to worshipful crowds in the late 1960s. Hua complemented the achievement by overseeing the development of a factory in Hunan that could produce 30 million Mao buttons a year. Hua had then developed his political strength through his role in investigating Lin Biao's alleged assassination attempts on Mao, and in January 1975 he was promoted to minister of public security.

Part of the success of Dazhai, noted Hua, lay in its self-reliance and high production yields, part in its advanced levels of mechanization. Claiming that over 300 counties had now achieved similar levels of mechanization and organization, Hua threw out the challenge that one-third of all China must attain this level by 1980. Hua observed that such gains could be achieved only if the collective sector of the economy were steadily expanded, if all party members took on active leadership roles, and if "the dominance of the poor and lower-middle peasants as a class" were established by the local party committees, so that they could jointly "wage resolute struggle against capitalist activities." Hua was not referring here to the activities of industrialists or foreigners, but to "well-to-do middle peasants" whom he claimed had never ceased to be influenced by their own acquisitive drives. In other words, there was to be no freeing up of the market economy, and no change in the policy of rigidly curtailing the size of private plots and the degree of family production from those plots. If modernization of agriculture were achieved in this way, noted Hua, it would "more effectively push forward and guarantee the modernization of industry, national defence and science and technology."[16] Zhou Enlai and Deng Xiaoping had already suggested that these were the four main areas in which modernization should be concentrated, but now Hua was carving out terrain for himself as an advocate of compromise by invoking Maoist rhetoric on the communes while supporting practical policies for economic growth.

Within days of the closing of the Dazhai conference on October 19, 1975, articles, essays, and broadcasts throughout the country were picking up these main themes and hammering their radical message home. At meetings and rallies, Hua's points were repeated and local production studied with a view to achieving the new goals. At year's end, by means of work teams and propaganda teams at all levels, at least 1 million cadres had been sent "to the front line" in their own communities, and numerous other leaders were reported to be receiving "rectification."

This attempt to resurrect the whole gamut of Maoist revolutionary arguments and images was spread over China just after two quite different critics of Mao's message had passed from the scene. One was Peng Dehuai, whose career as one of China's leading military men had been wrecked in 1959 by his criticism at Lushan of Mao's Great Leap Forward; the other was Chiang Kai-shek, who had battled Mao's rural revolution for twenty-two years before leading his Taiwan exile bastion through a successful land reform of its own. Neither man was there to read the glowing press reports of China's retrenchment. Peng Dehuai had died in November 1974 at the age of seventy-six, and Chiang Kai-shek just a few months before the Dazhai conference opened at the age of eighty-seven.

1976: THE OLD GUARD DIES

Death was now in the air for China's aging revolutionary leaders. Zhou Enlai succumbed first, dying on the morning of January 8, 1976, at the age of seventy-eight, from the cancer that he had battled for four years. To the surprise of many, Mao Zedong had not visited Zhou in his last months, nor did he issue any personal message on Zhou's achievements and contributions to the revolution. Mao sent no public condolences to Zhou's widow, herself a formidable revolutionary with a lifetime of service to the party behind her. And he did not attend the imposing funeral ceremonies in the Great Hall of the People the following week. Perhaps Mao himself was too ill, although he had not been too ill to receive the president of São Tomé and Príncipe two weeks before Zhou's death, nor was he too ill to receive the now former President Nixon in February. Perhaps Mao had grown to distrust Zhou's sincerity in all the complex swings of Cultural Revolution politics.

But whatever Mao's attitude may have been, the country as a whole seemed plunged into mourning. Peking was described by foreign correspondents as looking like a ghost town, and the news that Zhou had willed that his ashes be scattered across the rivers and hills of his beloved land, rather than buried in some mausoleum, was received with deep emotion. With Zhou gone it suddenly emerged how many people had revered him, and regarded him as a symbol of an ordered life and of a measure of decency in deeply troubled times.

At Zhou's state funeral on January 15, it was Vice-Premier Deng Xiaoping who gave the eulogy. Though much of his eulogy echoed the wording of the official Central Committee statement issued on the day of Zhou's death, or else gave a meticulous summation of Zhou's remarkable, committed, and active political life, near the end Deng offered a more personal tribute to the character of the man he had served for many years, one that seemed to speak from the heart even while using the rhetoric of a ceremonial state occasion:

> He was open and aboveboard, paid attention to the interests of the whole, observed Party discipline, was strict in "dissecting" himself and good at uniting the mass of cadres, and upheld the unity and solidarity of the Party. He maintained broad and close ties with the masses and showed boundless warmheartedness toward all comrades and the people.... We should learn from his fine style—being modest and prudent, unassuming and approachable, setting an example by his conduct, and living in a plain and hard-working way. We should follow his example of adhering to the proletarian style and opposing the bourgeois style of life.[17]

If one wished to, one could see this brief passage as a controlled yet biting criticism of Mao Zedong and of the leaders of the Cultural Revolution, for none of them could possibly be praised for being "open and aboveboard," "good at uniting the mass of cadres," for displaying "warmheartedness," or for his or her modesty, prudence, or approachability.

Whether Deng's speech intensified already deep antagonisms toward him or whether his political enemies simply determined to force him once again into obscurity cannot be exactly known. But in the first week of February 1976, after the Central Committee named Hua Guofeng acting premier, the campaign against Deng Xiaoping that had begun in late 1975 was significantly intensified. As has happened so often in China's recent past, it started with wall posters and rallies, and kept the true target in the shadows: students at Peking and Qinghua Universities, demanding the rights of those from poor rural and urban backgrounds for advanced education, began to suggest that a group of "revisionists" and "capitalist roaders" were insisting on reinstituting the old intellectual elitism, and were ignoring "experience as the basis for developing science in favor of closeting scientists behind closed doors." In March the Chinese Academy of Sciences issued a formal denunciation of China's "capitalist roader," while an essay in *Red Flag* directed a vigorous attack against a man who could only be Deng, although he still was not named. The content of this essay suggests that it was written on instructions from Jiang Qing herself, and that she had been particularly chagrined at Deng's refusal to respond to the radical people's opera she had been staging. The article stated:

> Not only does he still refuse to watch the model revolutionary theatrical works, but also he dislikes the fine works created after learning from the experience of the model revolutionary theatrical works. He watched the film "Spring Shoots" but left half-way through in displeasure, criticizing it as ultra-leftist. As for those works airing an opposing view against the model revolutionary theatrical works or those distorting the image of workers, peasants and soldiers, he loves them at first sight and personally sponsors and supports their production. In short, what the proletariat supports, he opposes; what the proletariat opposes, he advocates.[18]

The campaign had reached this stage when one of the most extraordinary events in the history of the PRC up to that time occurred. It was an event that—like others to follow over the next thirteen years—showed how spontaneous mass emotions and unplanned actions could fuse with decisive significance despite the state system that was trying to impose revolutionary unanimity on its people. On April 4, 1976, the eve of China's annual Qingming festival of homage to deceased ancestors, thousands of people gathered around the memorial to the martyrs of the Chinese revolution, which stands on a massive pediment in the center of the vast Tiananmen Square in front of the Forbidden City. It was in this square in 1966 and 1967 that Mao Zedong and Lin Biao had saluted millions of Red Guards passing in review; now the people of Peking used the occasion to pay homage to the dead Zhou Enlai with wreaths, banners, poems, placards, and flowers.

On the morning of April 5, fresh crowds gathering at the memorial found that all the tributes from the previous day had been removed by the police. Their protests led to scuffles and blows. Police cars were set on fire, and as the crowd swelled to 100,000 or more it forced entry into several of the government buildings that surround the square. Most of the crowd dispersed around 6:00 in the evening after being warned in a broadcast speech by the head of the Peking Municipal Committee not to be "duped" by the "bad elements carrying out disruption and disturbances and engaging in counter-revolutionary sabotage."[19] But a hard-core group remained until 10:00 P.M. At that hour security forces backed by "tens of thousands of worker-militiamen" moved in on the demonstrators and arrested a reported 388 people, although the actual figure was certainly far higher. Several of those arrested were subjected to a mass "people's trial" at Peking University, and others were sent to prison camps to "reform themselves through labor." Demonstrations in homage to Zhou, although not on this scale, took place in many other areas of China as widely scattered as Zhengzhou in Henan, Kunming in Yunnan, Taiyuan in Shanxi, Changchun in Jilin, and Shanghai, Wuhan, and Canton.

Among the provocations that had especially angered the authorities were the demonstrators' shouts and placards claiming that the rule of Qin Shihuang was now over, and demanding a return of "genuine" Marxism-Leninism. Clearly these were criticisms of Mao and the radical leaders of the Cultural Revolution, and whether or not they had been orchestrated in any way by Deng and his supporters, the Central Committee decided, apparently on the urgings of Mao himself, to strike back. A terse announcement of April 7, in the name of Mao and the Central Committee, removed Deng Xiaoping from all his posts "inside and outside the Party," although he was allowed to keep his party membership. An equally brief announcement the same day named Hua Guofeng first vice-chairman of the CCP Central Committee (a position second only to Mao's) and premier of the State Council.

Over the following months the case against Deng was deepened by nationwide meetings and study sessions. The Tiananmen incident was likened to the Hungarian uprising of 1956, Deng denounced as the new Imre Nagy, and the poems posted on the memorial equated with the counterrevolutionary "vicious language" used by Lin Biao in his secret assault on Mao. As the campaign against Deng spread, it coalesced around charges that he believed the class struggle was over in China, that he was attempting to reverse the achievements of the Cultural Revolution, that he desired to restore capitalism, and that he was convinced of the need, if China were to achieve the four modernizations mentioned at the Dazhai forum, "to rely on those proficient in technical or professional work and to introduce more and more advanced foreign techniques."[20] Deng had given plenty of ammunition for such a campaign by his outspokenness over the previous two years, in which he had attacked Maoist "sectarians," mocked the cycles of political purges, and said sadly of his own land: "Everyone here is scared—the youth, even more the elderly. That is precisely why our technology is so far behind."[21]

While the anti-Deng campaign raged and Hua Guofeng consolidated his power, it became clear that Mao had not much longer to live. He performed his last official function on May 27, 1976, when he received Prime Minister Zulfikar Ali Bhutto of Pakistan. That June the Central Committee declared he would receive no more foreign visitors, and there were rumors that a famous neurologist had been flown in from Europe to attend him. The country's attention was caught at this point by another death—that of Zhu De, which came in early July shortly after his ninetieth birthday. In his role as the new premier, Hua Guofeng delivered the eulogy, which summarized Zhu's extraordinary career as an army general, military strategist, and builder of the Red Army in the 1930s and 1940s.

Less than three weeks later, on July 28, 1976, one of the worst earthquakes in China's recorded history occurred, with its epicenter in Tangshan, Hebei. The main shock waves were so immense that heavy damage was done in Tianjin, 60 miles to the southwest, and even in Peking, 100 miles away. The city of Tangshan was virtually obliterated, and the death toll was later officially reported as 242,000, with 164,000 seriously injured. (The initial estimates by the Hebei Revolutionary Committee were far higher: 655,000 dead and 779,000 injured.) In either case, it was a colossal human tragedy. True to the radical spirit of self-reliance, China declined foreign and UN offers of humanitarian aid. Instead, a national relief campaign was launched, spearheaded by 56 medical teams that arrived from Shanghai the day after the disaster. Medical and rescue teams from virtually every province and autonomous region of China were sent to Tangshan. The PLA played an important role in the rehabilitation effort, partly restoring an image that had been badly tarnished by its killing of Red Guards in the Cultural Revolution, and by the alleged treason of its leader Lin Biao.

China's ability to recover from the disaster, to rebuild the shattered river and rail bridges, speedily reopen the Tangshan coal mines, and restore and refire the furnaces in the Tangshan steel plant were all cause for national debate and celebration. The occasion of a relief conference convened on September 1 allowed Hua Guofeng, "on behalf of Chairman Mao," to use the earthquake to make a political point. The natural disasters of 1960 that followed the Great Leap Forward, he pointed out, had been exploited by Liu Shaoqi and Deng Xiaoping as a pretext for expanding private plots, opening free markets, and encouraging household production and small enterprises. In 1976, by contrast, socialist principles had been the key to handling the disaster. It was interesting that Hua should invoke Mao in this context, for in traditional Chinese historiography the imminence of profound political upheavals leading to dynastic collapse was usually heralded by a cataclysmic natural event such as an earthquake or flood, or by some celestial portent. Such gross superstitions, of course, were now consigned to the dustbin of history, but when Mao Zedong died of complications following his long illness, on September 9, at ten minutes after midnight, many Chinese must have linked the two events in their minds.

A week-long period of mourning was declared, and Mao's body was placed in a casket in the Great Hall of the People for the crowds to file past. Some 300,000 did so, but even though people were shocked and silent, in Peking there was none of the rush of emotion that had occurred in response to Zhou's death. The expressions of grief and respect from elsewhere in China and around the world were, however, moving, the signal exception being the Soviet Union, which placed the news of Mao's death on the bottom of page 3 in *Izvestia* and refused to send a message of condolence at the "state to state" level. The Russian "party to party" message was rejected by the Chinese as improper. The Central Committee's public eulogy, and Hua Guofeng's own speech before 1 million Chinese assembled in Tiananmen Square, gave fulsome praises to Mao's extraordinary achievements, but also had a direct political message: they praised as one of Mao's greatest accomplishments the suppression of a series of both "Right and 'Left' Opportunist lines in the Party," a list that began with Chen Duxiu, Qu Qiubai, and Li Lisan, and ended with Peng Dehuai, Liu Shaoqi, Lin Biao, and Deng Xiaoping.

The demands for national mourning were made in almost peremptory terms by the Central Committee. All over China, at 3:00 P.M. on September 18, as the final ceremonies began, people were to stop their work and stand at attention, in silence, for three minutes. The phrasing of this statement reminds us that despite its over 3,000 mile extent from east to west, all of China is kept on Peking time, which provides the pulse for the whole nation. At the same moment all trains, ships, military vessels, and factories were to sound their sirens for three minutes. All government organs, factories, mines, army units, schools, communes, and neighborhood groups were to assemble to hear the live broadcasts or watch the televised version of the Peking ceremonies.

If it was Hua Guofeng who made the final eulogy and thus received the greatest public attention, the four radical leaders of the Cultural Revolution were also plainly visible. Wang Hongwen presided over the final ceremonies, and Zhang Chunqiao was a director of the funeral committee. Jiang Qing, accompanied by her own and Mao's surviving children, was prominent at the funeral, and cameras also focused on Yao Wenyuan. Yet in the final startling event of an already dramatic year, all four radical leaders of the Cultural Revolution were suddenly arrested without warning by Hua Guofeng's orders on October 6, and placed in detention at an unknown location. They were accused of having constituted a clique or "Gang of Four," and of having persevered in their evil conduct despite stern warnings from Mao himself.

Hua Guofeng's success in routing his political enemies was due less to his political acumen than to the support of senior PLA generals and the key military commander in Peking, Wang Dongxing. Fanatically loyal to Mao Zedong ever since he joined the Jiangxi Soviet in 1933 as a seventeen-year-old orphan from a poor peasant family, Wang had served as Mao's bodyguard on the Long March and protected him in Yan'an and during the civil war. After 1949, Wang developed an elite military force known as Unit 8341, which was responsible for protecting China's top leaders; Wang's command of this unit, when combined with his other official posts in the public-security apparatus, gave him enormous power. Unit 8341 oversaw the arrests and confinement of such Cultural Revolution victims as Peng Zhen, Liu Shaoqi, and Deng Xiaoping. Troops from Unit 8341 guarded secret party files and in 1967 reasserted "order" in Peking by forcibly occupying the most militant factories and universities. Wang himself allegedly helped break Lin Biao's plot against Mao. And Wang, having come to believe that Hua Guofeng was Mao's true heir, ordered the troops of Unit 8341 to arrest the Gang of Four on October 6 as they were assembling for a party meeting. Although much about Wang's career remains obscure, the extent and nature of his power hints at the conspiratorial substructures that bonded military men and secret police at the very center of the CCP.

As more and more charges were brought against them in October and November, the phrase "Gang of Four" became known to everyone in China. Cumulatively they were accused of almost every possible crime in the political book, including factional attacks on Zhou Enlai, forging Mao's statements, diluting the criticism of Lin Biao to save their own skin, organizing their own armed forces, tampering with education (and concocting the story of Zhang Tiesheng's blank examination paper), inciting the masses to fight each other, supporting inefficient techniques by such spurious claims as "a socialist train behind schedule is better than a revisionist train on schedule," attacking worthy government cadres, criticizing Dazhai and Daqing, disrupting industrial production, hindering the earthquake relief work, defaming Hua Guofeng, slandering army veterans, producing subversive films, criticizing worthy schoolteachers, sabotaging foreign trade, leading the young to oppose Marxism, and using the public-security apparatus for their own purposes. The members of the group that had proved so ingenious in thinking up a miasma of charges against prominent CCP leaders and intellectuals during the Cultural Revolution now found themselves on the receiving end of the same process.

Those who had been baffled by the fall of Lin Biao would now have further food for thought, but they would not be encouraged to show their doubts in public. For on October 7, 1976, Hua Guofeng was also named to succeed Mao as chairman of the Central Committee of the CCP and chairman of the Military Affairs Commission. He thus seemed to stand at the apex of each section of that three-part structure of army, state, and party that constituted the government of China.

At the end of October 1976, rallies of over 1 million Chinese in both Shanghai and Peking saluted the beginning of Chairman Hua's era. And in November Hua formally laid the foundation stone for the new mausoleum in Tiananmen Square that would receive the remains of Mao Zedong. The mausoleum was to rise exactly on the old central axis radiating out from the Forbidden City, an axis that in olden days had carried the eye southward through gate after gate, as in imagination the central force of imperial China spread through the city and beyond the outer wall to the people of the country as a whole. Now the shrine for Mao's embalmed corpse would form a permanent barrier to that vision.

CHAPTER 24 | # Redefining Revolution

The Four Modernizations

With Mao Zedong embalmed and at rest, the struggle for power in the CCP gained new intensity. Wisely leaving Peking in the spring of 1976, the vilified Deng Xiaoping had sought shelter far to the south, in Canton. Protected there by the military governor of the region, General Xu Shiyou, Deng carefully planned his political comeback. Xu was a tough military veteran who had begun his career by serving the warlord Wu Peifu before switching to the Communist party. Although he had been loyal to Mao after a mutiny attempt in 1937, he was no lover of the Gang of Four or of Hua Guofeng; most important politically, Xu not only held the key military power in Guangdong, he also had a second power base in east China, where he had previously served as the military chief of the "Nanjing region" for nineteen years (1954 to 1973). This pivotal region comprised the wealthy provinces of Jiangsu, Anhui, and Zhejiang. Accordingly when in early 1977 Xu, backed by the first party secretary of Guangdong, began pressuring the Central Committee to rehabilitate Deng Xiaoping, Xu carried the day. In July 1977, Deng was reappointed to his vicepremiership, to the Politburo, and to the Military Affairs Commission, although Hua Guofeng still held onto the senior positions he had acquired during the previous year.

Not surprisingly, given the different political philosophies of Deng and Hua, China's direction in both domestic and foreign policy remained ambiguous throughout 1977 and 1978. While the communes continued to be the main form of rural social organization, and peasants were still criticized or penalized for engaging in excessive side-line production, and while industry

618

remained tied to inflexible government plans, China was scoring a number of signal achievements requiring high levels of technological skill. The PRC dramatically developed its domestic and international airline systems, completed an immense dry-dock facility at the Hebei port of Shanhaiguan (where Dorgon's troops had entered China to "avenge" the Ming in 1644), built and launched its first oil tanker in the 50,000-ton class, and completed a linkage to Japan via seabed cable. The state conducted several hydrogen-bomb and other nuclear tests, both in the atmosphere and underground, and successfully continued the active satellite-launching program begun in 1975. Work also began on the development of China's own ICBM warhead delivery system (the first successful launching was announced in May 1980). And although economic exchanges with the United States were slow to develop, the negotiation of a new $10 billion industrial agreement with Japan, along with joint Sino-Japanese exploration for oil in the Bohai (North China Sea), when coupled with extensive new commercial agreements with Great Britain and France, showed that China was far from withdrawing from the international scene.

Domestically, Chairman Hua was allegedly in command, still championing the radical programs of "learning from Dazhai and Daqing" in agriculture and industry. He claimed this was the true way to obtain the "Four Modernizations," as they were now regularly termed, in agriculture, industry, national defense, and the linked areas of science and technology. At the same time, Deng Xiaoping was maneuvering with growing success to bring back ever more of the CCP cadres ousted in the Cultural Revolution, and to move toward full implementation of a modernization plan that would incorporate foreign investment and technology along with the training of Chinese students overseas. During a National Science Conference held in Peking in March 1978, at which both Deng and Hua made speeches, this modernization plan gained momentum. To achieve development in the high-priority areas of energy sources, computers, laser and space technology, high-energy physics, and genetics, it was announced there would be a crash training program for 800,000 scientific research workers in China, along with the development of new research centers integrated into a national system.

Over the following months, policies were drawn up for the development of eighty-eight "key universities," with admission only by rigorous competitive examinations, and for a number of lower-track technical colleges. Schools were instructed to identify gifted children early and give them advanced training. Scientists sent to the countryside over the previous years were to be recalled and reassigned to professional jobs. A new Chinese constitution, adopted in March 1978, specifically addressed the needs of tech-

FIELDS OF STUDY FOR PROJECTED CHINESE STUDENTS IN THE UNITED STATES, 1978–1979[1]

Fields	Students
Mathematics	30
Physics	58
Chemistry	30
Mechanics	10
Material sciences and technology	15
Astronomy and astrophysics	6
Meteorology	7
Life science	25
Medical sciences	29
Radioelectronics	50
Computer sciences and engineering	45
Control engineering	15
Aeronautical engineering	15
Space technology	15
Nuclear engineering	10
Construction technology	10
Mechanical engineering	8
Metallurgical engineering	10
Chemical engineering	10
Agricultural sciences	11
Other subjects	24
Total	433

nical personnel and the protections to be afforded these people. During 1978 a preliminary group of 480 able Chinese students was dispatched to twenty-eight countries to study; as the "normalization" talks with the United States moved into high gear in late 1978, the Chinese presented a much larger list of requests for higher technical training to the American Committee on Scholarly Communication with the People's Republic of China. Though not all these requests could be immediately met, the list is indicative of the priority placed in the post-Maoist era on technical training.

In the latter part of 1978 the Chinese government followed up these initiatives with an extraordinary range of important decisions in both foreign and domestic policy. The foreign-policy events were the ratification of the Sino-Japanese Treaty of Peace and Friendship (October 23); Deng Xiaoping's denunciation of the new Soviet-Vietnamese Treaty of Friendship and

Cooperation as a threat to the peace and security of the Pacific (November 8); the announcement (December 15 and 16) that the United States and China would establish full diplomatic relations on January 1, 1979, and exchange ambassadors on March 1 that same year; and the condemnation of Vietnam for backing a "Kampuchean national united front" to overthrow Pol Pot's regime (also December 16).

Domestically, the key contextual events were the announcement by the Peking Municipal Communist Party Committee that the Tiananmen demonstrations in memory of Zhou Enlai, held in April 1976, should be viewed favorably as a "completely revolutionary action" (November 15); the rehabilitation of many of those wrongly condemned, going back to the year 1957, the original focus of the antirightist campaign (also November 15); and the public posting in Peking of a long wall poster declaring that Mao Zedong had been a supporter of the Gang of Four and hence responsible for the ouster of Deng Xiaoping after the Tiananmen incident (posted November 19). At the same time, in 1978, a host of new writings was given wide circulation through the state-controlled press and journals. Focusing on the horrors and tragedies experienced by many in the Cultural Revolution, this "literature of the wounded," as it was called, stimulated debate and reflection about China's past and its future prospects. Dozens of other signs seemed to point to a new cultural thaw, among which one could include the decision to stage Wu Han's play, *The Dismissal of Hai Rui from Office*, in Peking, along with Bertolt Brecht's *Galileo*. Another was the convening of a conference (in far-off Kunming in Yunnan, admittedly) to study the long-taboo subject of comparative religion, with papers delivered on Buddhism and Daoism, Islam and Christianity.

But it was the events of December 1978, at the meetings formally known as the Third Plenum of the Eleventh Central Committee of the CCP, that were to mark the most important change in overall Chinese Communist policy since the outbreak of the Cultural Revolution. And in their long-run effects, the decisions at the Third Plenum were to have greater impact even than that earlier cataclysm. First, the Plenum laid out the requirements of the Four Modernizations in relation to industrial production, stating that since the struggle against Lin Biao and the Gang of Four could now be seen to have been victorious, it was therefore suitable to move "the stress of the Party's work" to socialist modernization "as of 1979." The decision would not be a light one.

Third Plenum

> Carrying out the Four Modernizations requires great growth in the productive forces, which in turn requires diverse changes in those aspects of the relations of production and the superstructure not in harmony with the growth of the

productive forces, and requires changes in all methods of management, actions and thinking which stand in the way of such growth. Socialist modernization is therefore a profound and extensive revolution.[2]

One problem facing this new revolution was familiar—the continuing presence in China of "a small handful of counter-revolutionary elements and criminals who hate our socialist modernization and try to undermine it"—but could be taken care of. It might be more difficult to handle the problems plaguing the current bureaucracy, especially the "over-concentration of authority." In words that could be interpreted as hinting at critical changes to come, the plenum noted that authority should be shifted "from the leadership to lower levels," and that clear distinctions should be made among the three elements in the production equation —namely, the CCP, the local government, and the enterprises themselves. The party must not usurp government functions, nor the government hamper the enterprises. "Managerial personnel" should have greater responsibilities in defining efficiency, rewarding good work, and penalizing bad through "punishment" or "demotion."

Second, referring to agricultural policy, the plenum added this important observation:

> The rapid development of the national economy as a whole and the steady improvement in the living standards of the people of the whole country depend on the vigorous restoration and speeding up of farm production, on resolutely and fully implementing the policy of simultaneous development of farming, forestry, animal husbandry, side-occupations and fisheries, the policy of taking grain as the key link and ensuring an all-round development, the policy of adaptation to local conditions and appropriate concentration of certain crops in certain areas, and gradual modernization of farm work.[3]

The key phrase here was "side-occupations," those myriad of local initiatives in growing and marketing grains, fruit, vegetables, livestock, and poultry that had so often been the target of "leftist" planners and cadres seeking to root out a stubborn peasant "capitalist streak." Such small plots of land, the plenum statement added firmly, along with "domestic side-occupations" and "village fairs," were necessary to socialist production and "must not be interfered with." In an even more immediate gesture to China's peasants, the plenum recommended that the price paid by the state for quota grain be raised by 20 percent following the summer 1979 harvest, and that the state price for grain harvested over and above the quota be raised by 50 percent. Such a shift in grain policy had major effects on the economic life of all

Chinese. At the same time, the plenum proposed that the prices of farm machinery, chemical fertilizers, insecticides, and plastic goods needed for farm use and made by state factories be cut by 10 percent to 15 percent. To protect urban workers from the effects of these reforms, state subsidies of food prices would be raised proportionately so that workers would pay no more than they had before for their basic food rations.

Third, the December 1978 plenum called for a new effort to combine "centralism" with "people's democracy" in order to ensure the success of modernization, and affirmed the importance of law in maintaining that success. Hinting at other key shifts, the plenum declared that judicial organizations "must maintain their independence as is appropriate." They must both "guarantee the equality of all people before the people's laws and deny anyone the privilege of being above the law."[4] What exactly this meant, given the absence of an independent judiciary in China, was far from clear, but the plenum was acknowledging that a new world of local commercial initiatives and independent production, not to mention increased foreign contacts, was bound to bring new demands for adjudication. To avoid the legal disputes that had plagued the Qing state and led to the imposition of extraterritoriality by the West, the PRC government would have to offer new kinds of safeguards.

The plenum added in conclusion, but in what to many must have seemed like a dutiful afterthought, that all of its central recommendations were premised on the "indelible" achievements of Mao Zedong's thought. More germane to the young in China was the admission that Mao had not been free of "all shortcomings and errors." The basic point was simply for the Chinese people to "integrate the universal principles of Marxism–Leninism–Mao Zedong thought with the concrete practice of socialist modernization and develop it under the new historical conditions."[5]

The Third Plenum adjourned on December 22, 1978. Three days before, on December 19, executives at the gigantic Boeing aircraft plant in Seattle, Washington, announced that China had ordered three jumbo 747 jet airliners. Also on the nineteenth, the chairman of Coca-Cola in Atlanta, Georgia, announced that his corporation had reached agreement to sell the soda inside China, and would open a bottling plant in Shanghai.

Thereafter events continued their headlong pace. On Christmas Day, a large Vietnamese force invaded Cambodia to oust Pol Pot's regime. On January 1, 1979, as planned, the United States and China announced the opening of full diplomatic relations, and Washington severed its formal ties with Taiwan. On January 28, the same day that the Central Committee ordered the ending of discrimination against all those who were children of landlords or rich peasants, Deng Xiaoping flew to Washington, D.C. He was greeted by ecstatic crowds and an eager press, pictures of which were duly beamed back by satellite to Chinese television, the first such media bonanza in China's history. In Washington, Deng visited President Carter and influential congressional leaders, and was given a gala reception at the Kennedy Center for the Performing Arts. He then traveled to the Houston Space Center, where he observed the training facilities for American astronauts, as well as to Atlanta and Seattle to view the production facilities that went along with China's new corporate agreements with Coca-Cola and Boeing. On February 8, after a two-day visit to Tokyo to brief the Japanese prime minister, Deng was back in Peking.

One might have thought that at this point China would have done everything possible to assure the world of its pacific nature so as to encourage foreign investment and international confidence. But at dawn on February 17, a large force of People's Liberation Army troops crossed the Chinese border into the northern part of Vietnam. The Chinese claimed that their invasion was a response to a series of border provocations, and a protest against both Vietnam's actions in Cambodia and the country's dramatic tilt toward the Soviet Union. One can also see another motive for the Chinese display of force. At a time when domestic economic expansion was being given so much prominence, the Chinese leaders were determined to show that in their focus on agricultural reform, technical training, and industrial development—all of which had received major emphasis at the Third Plenum—they were not neglecting the fourth modernization: national defense.

THE FIFTH MODERNIZATION

The Third Plenum of the Eleventh Central Committee of the CCP and Deng's visit to the United States took place in what initially seemed to be a new atmosphere of intellectual freedom in the PRC. For over two decades almost no one in China had felt free to speak out against the state that constrained them; the Red Guards were no exception, since they spoke out against one orthodoxy in the name of another, and rationalized their critiques with the thought of Mao Zedong. But in November and December 1978, stimulated in part by the "reversal of verdicts" against the Tiananmen demonstrators of 1976 and in part by the new opening of China to the West, thousands of Chinese began to put their thoughts into words, their words onto paper, and their paper onto walls to be read by all who passed by. The most famous focus for these displays became a stretch of blank wall just to the west of the former Forbidden City in Peking, part of which was now a public museum and park, and part the cluster of residences for China's most senior national leaders. Because of the frankness of some of these posters, and the message of many that some measure of democratic freedom should be introduced in China, this Peking area became known as Democracy Wall.

The main modes of expression in the attempted Democracy movement were wall posters—composed of either essays or poems—and a wide range of small magazines, usually run by groups of friends and printed or mimeographed in limited editions on paper that was always difficult to obtain. Just as the flurry of new publications in the May Fourth movement had done, so did the names of these magazines evoke the emotions they aroused and represented: *China's Human Rights, Exploration, Enlightenment, April 5 Forum, Harvest, Science, Democracy and Law, Masses' Reference News, Today, Peking Spring.* Some of the poems in these magazines were openly political paeans of Deng Xiaoping, China's emerging new leader, and showed little or no aesthetic subtlety.

Deng Xiaoping

Wise and talented, like the Duke of Zhou,*
 he's Hua's right hand.
He'll chat and laugh easily, and by lifting a finger
 make people and country happy and peaceful.
Don't be surprised that he's fallen twice and risen
 three times,
There are always traitors on the road to revolution.[6]

Other poets spoke bitterly of Mao's effect on China, likening him to the tyrants of the past:

Chairman's tomb and Emperor's palace
 face each other across the square,
One great leader in his wisdom
 made our countless futures bare,
Each and every marble staircase
 covers heaps of bones beneath,
From the eaves of such fine buildings
 fresh red blood drops everywhere.[7]

But some young poets were drawn by the moment to explore themselves and their world with a freedom that had not been permitted to appear in

---

*The "Duke of Zhou" had been the sagelike adviser to the founder of one of China's earliest dynasties, and a figure extolled by Confucius in his writings. The name had also been allegorically used to refer to Premier Zhou Enlai in the anti-Confucius campaign of 1973–1974.

print since the founding of the PRC, in part because such emotions were oblique, ambivalent, beyond class analysis, aloof from political programs. Here is the poem "Let's Go," by one of the finest poets to emerge in the Democracy movement, Bei Dao:

> Let's go—
> Fallen leaves blow into deep valleys
> But the song has no home to return to.
>
> Let's go—
> Moonlight on the ice
> Has spilled beyond the river bed.
>
> Let's go—
> Eyes gaze at the same patch of sky
> Hearts strike the twilight drum.
>
> Let's go—
> We have not lost our memories
> We shall search for life's pool.
>
> Let's go—
> The road, the road
> Is covered with a drift of scarlet poppies.[8]

Of all the flood of words that appeared in this period, none had more impact than those of a young man called Wei Jingsheng. Wei's influence came partly through the force of his ideas and partly through the inspired title he chose for his Peking wall poster of December 5, 1978: "The Fifth Modernization." This was obviously a gauntlet flung in the face of the CCP hierarchy—including Deng Xiaoping himself, who had declared the Four Modernizations a sufficient basis for transforming China. Wei insisted that until China embraced a fifth modernization, the other four would be "merely another promise." For Wei, the fifth modernization was democracy, the "holding of power by the laboring masses themselves," rather than by the corrupt representatives of the party state who had imposed a new "autocracy" on the workers and peasants of China. "What is true democracy?" asked Wei rhetorically in his poster. "It means the right of the people to choose their own representatives [who will] work according to their will and in their interests. Only this can be called democracy. Furthermore, the people must also have the power to replace their representatives any time so that these representatives cannot go on deceiving others in the name of the people."[9]

Articulate, courageous, and angry, Wei was very much the voice of a new China. The son of an ardent Maoist revolutionary who held a good job in the party bureaucracy, Wei was born in 1950 and raised having to learn a page of Mao's works each day before he would be given his dinner. He was a Red Guard in one of the prestigious Peking units, composed largely of cadre children, that emerged in mid-1966. But Wei's unit fell afoul of rival groups loyal to Jiang Qing. Arrested and jailed for a four-month period, Wei subsequently read up on international politics, using his father's access to restricted party journals to get at scarce materials. He trained and worked as an electrician, and joined the PLA, serving for four years before returning to his electrician's job. Deeply moved by the April 1976 demonstrations, he also fell in love with a young Tibetan woman living in Peking whose father had been persecuted politically. Wei's 1978 writings were drawn from this emotionally charged background.

Wei wrote as an ardent socialist and as one who saw much good in the earliest phase of the Cultural Revolution, before it was co-opted by the "autocratic tyrant." For he felt that in its first stage the Cultural Revolution showed the strength of the Chinese people as a whole, the force of their struggle for democracy. Wei also wrote as one who had observed the terrible poverty all around him in China but did not accept that such poverty was inevitable, considering the talents, skills, and resources of the Chinese themselves. In pursuit of his analysis, he dared to challenge the basic assumptions of Lenin as well as Mao. Wei wrote that democracy was not solely the *result* of social development, as Lenin had claimed; it was also the *condition* for the development of higher productive forces. "Without this condition, the society will become stagnant and economic growth will encounter insurmountable obstacles."[10]

In two addenda to his opening poster, which were published in the December 1978 and January 1979 issues of *Exploration* (*Tansuo*), Wei took these arguments further. Most of the justifications for China's austerity could be turned back on themselves, he wrote; one had only to look at Chinese slums, the prevalence of prostitution (or its close copy—the sexual abuse of women by Communist cadres), and the omnipresence of grinding poverty and begging to see that the Communist party had not solved China's problems. It was an awful fact that the great social novels of the nineteenth-century West (was Wei thinking of Dickens? of Balzac? of Zola?), which were used in China to show the rottenness of Western civilization, "could perfectly well have drawn upon our present situation for their examples; it is almost as though history had stood still." The vaunted collectivism of the world's "socialist" countries—which by no coincidence also happened to be the world's poorest—was flawed because it allowed "no room for the independent existence of individualism." The Chinese must fight for their right "to live a meaningful life," concluded Wei, and upon that freedom build their nation's modernization. "We must never be enslaved again."[11]

The Democracy movement was fought with more than words. On December 17, 1978, twenty-eight young people held a demonstration in Tiananmen Square to protest living and working conditions in rural southwest China. Though that number seemed pitifully small, the protesters claimed to speak for 50,000 youths who had been "sent down" to do farm work in Yunnan, and had been holding a "general strike" since December 9 in opposition to local CCP leaders who had "trampled on their human rights." (The date of December 9 had presumably been chosen to echo the courage of the December Ninthers of 1935 who had marched in Peking to protest Guomindang ineffectiveness.) In another incident, on January 8, 1979, several thousand people who had been sent down to the countryside around Peking held a demonstration in the city, carrying banners that read "We don't want hunger" and "We want human rights and democracy." In late January, an estimated 30,000 more sent-down workers and their children entered the capital, camping out around the railway station and in side streets, many wearing only rags in the subzero weather, attempting to petition their government leaders for help. At least eight died from exposure to the cold. In Shanghai, rusticated youth marched into the city and besieged the party headquarters for several hours. In Hangzhou, posters went up demanding "the right to live as human beings" and protesting China's astounding housing shortage, which made it difficult even for married couples aged thirty or older to find a single room of their own in which to enjoy some privacy.

The predictable government crackdown began in mid-January 1979, before Deng Xiaoping left for Washington. It seems possible that Deng had initially encouraged the Democracy Wall posters because their views on modernization often coincided with his own, and because they criticized or mocked the attitudes of Hua Guofeng and other radical Maoists. But when they went too far, challenging the fundamental premises of the CCP itself, he turned against them. Deng's actions thus ran parallel to Mao's in 1957, when Mao unleashed the antirightist campaign in order to smother the Hundred Flowers movement that he had just set in motion. Deng himself, as secretary-general of the CCP, had also played a major part in enforcing the massive purge of China's intellectuals in 1957.

The first victim of the 1979 anti-Democracy crackdown was a young woman, Fu Yuehua, arrested and accused of having instigated and organized the rusticated youth who were demonstrating in Peking. Fu had had a tragic life, suffering a broken marriage and repeated rape attempts by her unit boss, who finally dismissed her her job. Her appeals for an investigation of his behavior had gone unanswered, and it is probable that she had turned to helping the demonstrators out of her personal anger and sorrow. Fu Yuehua was given a two-year jail sentence for her disruptive behavior.*

Other arrests followed, many involving underground journal writers and editors. In a dangerous shift of government policy, they were accused not just of "impairing the state system," but of doing so with the "aid of foreigners," which seemed to edge their activities toward the category of treason. In late March 1979, Wei Jingsheng, who in the meantime had written several more provocative pieces—one sharply challenging Deng Xiaoping's insensitivity to China's needs, and one exposing conditions in China's maximum-security political prisons—was arrested and brought to trial. Charged not only for his writing, but with espionage for leaking information on the Sino-Vietnam war to a foreign journalist, he was convicted and sentenced to fifteen years in prison. Wei's appeals, based in part on his claim that he had no access to confidential information of this kind, were rejected.

The special irony of this charge was that China's war with Vietnam—designed as a short, sharp surgical strike to teach the Vietnamese a lesson for invading Cambodia, and to demonstrate the effectiveness of the modernizing PLA to the Soviet Union and the rest of the world—had been extremely costly. (The commander in chief of the Chinese forces was Deng's protector of two years before, General Xu Shiyou, but he proved an inept tactician and subsequently was demoted.) After absorbing heavy casualties and experiencing paralyzing logistical difficulties, the Chinese had begun their withdrawal on March 5, 1979, completing it by March 16, almost two full weeks before Wei's arrest. In subsequent developments, following a condemnation of the Democracy movement's excesses by Deng Xiaoping himself, the remaining journals were closed one by one, and on April 1 the right to hang wall posters was withdrawn, except at a few specified locations under police supervision. By the time of the 1979 Qingming festival of April 5, when huge demonstrations along the lines of those in 1976 might have been expected, the supporters of China's Democracy movement were too beaten down to react, and the day passed uneventfully.

Some of the responses to the brief movement's passing were extraordi-

---

*At the end of her jail term she was not released, but was sent to a labor camp. She was never cleared or allowed to restate her case.

narily articulate, however, and gave warning to the government that the forces briefly released here could not be suppressed indefinitely. One protester, arrested in May 1979, wrote that he had been trying to speak for China's "second generation" that had grown up under the Communist rule of the PRC and had "spontaneously" decided to challenge it. He noted shrewdly that the critics of the PRC were of two kinds: those who believed the CCP had failed because it had not been true to Marxist-Leninist principles, and those who believed that the CCP *had* been properly Marxist-Leninist. In this second case, "the terrible thing [is] that it is precisely this Marxism-Leninism itself which is absurd and erroneous." The Democracy movement might have done far more, he believed, if the intellectuals en masse had joined in, but on the whole they had stayed aloof, unwilling to risk the pleasant "tidbits" that the ruling party casually flung into the air to them. The main achievements of the movement had been made by those between ages twenty and thirty, "young workers who had not been to university," who had only a middle-school education. Nevertheless, the anonymous writer concluded, the movement had shown its potential strength. For despite the apparent omnipotence of the CCP and its huge bureaucracy and army, "a few little sheets of paper and a few lines of writing, a few shouts and they're frightened out of their wits."[12]

Others preferred to abandon political analysis and return to poetry. Just after the announcement of the April 1, 1979, crackdown, according to observers, a young Chinese man pushed through the onlookers at Democracy Wall and posted one final poem, now forbidden, on the once crowded wall, before walking swiftly away without saying a word. He signed his poem with the pseudonym "Icicle" (Ling Bing), and entitled it "For You":

> My friend,
> Parting time is pending.
> Farewell—Democracy Wall.
> What can I briefly say to you?
> Should I speak of spring's frigidity?
> Should I say that you are like the withered wintersweet?
>
> No, I ought instead to talk of happiness,
> Tomorrow's happiness,
> Of pure orchid skies,
> Of golden wild flowers,
> Of a child's bright eyes.
> In sum we ought
> To part with dignity,
> Don't you agree?[13]

TAIWAN AND THE SPECIAL
ECONOMIC ZONES

The opening up of China to the United States, and the challenge to Communist government authority posed by the Democracy movement activists, occurred as Taiwan was entering a new era of prosperity and struggling to redefine its own future. In their official statement on "normalization" of relations with the United States in 1979, the Chinese Communists had made this declaration:

> As is known to all, the Government of the PRC is the sole legal government of China and Taiwan is a part of China. The question of Taiwan was the crucial issue obstructing the normalization of relations between China and the USA. It has now been resolved between the two countries in the spirit of the Shanghai communiqué and through their joint efforts, thus enabling the normalization of relations so ardently desired by the people of the two countries. As for the way of bringing Taiwan back to the embrace of the motherland and reunifying the country, it is entirely China's internal affair.

The U.S. statement had a different flavor, since it included additional sections concerning the termination of diplomatic relations with Taiwan and the cancellation of the mutual-defense treaty between Taiwan and the United States. It also declared that the United States would withdraw its remaining military personnel from Taiwan within four months of the January 1, 1979, signing of the agreement with China. On the question of Taiwan's future, the United States had joined with China in declaring that it recognized "the Government of the PRC as the sole legal government of China," although it elaborated what this meant for Taiwan in a separate passage:

> In the future, the American people and the people of Taiwan will maintain commercial, cultural, and other relations without official government representation and without diplomatic relations. . . .
> The USA is confident that the people of Taiwan face a peaceful and prosperous future. The USA continues to have an interest in the peaceful resolution of the Taiwan issue and expects that the Taiwan issue will be settled peacefully by the Chinese themselves.[14]

The PRC statement that "bringing Taiwan back to the embrace of the motherland" was "China's internal affair" made sense only if Taiwan was considered part of China, a province that had temporarily lost its home. In fact, although Taiwan still claimed that *its* government represented the Chinese people, its course of development since 1949 had made it, in important ways, a fully independent society with its own economic and political structures. Chiang Kai-shek, acting partly on advice from the United States and partly in the interests of his own survival, had in the 1950s and 1960s instituted thoroughgoing and successful reforms on the island. The government of Taiwan remained dominated by the 2 million Chinese supporters of the Guomindang who had fled from the mainland in 1948 and 1949; the earlier Taiwanese settlers, subjugated by the Japanese from 1895 to 1945, found themselves once more barred from any independent political life, although they flourished economically under the new reforms and could advance up through the ranks if they joined the Guomindang.

At the time of the normalization announcements, Taiwan's population stood at 17.1 million, 1.8 percent of the PRC's estimated population of 950 million. Yet Taiwan's per capita GNP by 1979 was around six times that of the PRC, having risen 416 percent between 1952 and 1979. This growth had not been easy to achieve, and had initially been carefully fostered by the United States, especially through the Joint Commission on Rural Reconstruction, which in the 1950s supervised a land-rent-reduction program and a land-sale program to help owner-cultivators in Taiwan. Essential to the success of these programs was control of the hyperinflation that had afflicted Taiwan along with China in the 1940s. The substitution of a new currency in Taiwan, at an exchange rate of 40,000 yuan of the old currency for $1 of the new, was carried through successfully in 1949 (unlike the disastrous gold-yuan experiments in 1947 on the mainland), in large part because Taiwan's comparatively small size made it possible to check speculation and control gold sales. A 1949 inflation rate of around 3,400 percent was reduced to 306 percent in 1950, 66 percent in 1951, and from 1952 onward dropped slowly to an annual rate of 8.8 percent. By 1961 it had been forced down to 3 percent.

The techniques used to battle inflation were initially not wholly dissimilar to those used in the PRC. By instituting interest rates on savings of around 10 percent and controlling specie circulation, the government kept a grip on the new currency. Under the Taiwan government's land-to-the-tiller program, shares in state enterprises were distributed to farmers to help give them security, and tenant farmers were promised title to the land they worked if they contracted to provide the state quota payments of grain for a decade. Since Taiwan was also a one-party state—controlled by the mainland refugees through the Guomindang, which was still dominated by

Chiang Kai-shek—no democratic process was required to institute these reforms.

But as agricultural production in Taiwan rose encouragingly to meet domestic needs, the government made a determined effort to shift the economy from its base in exporting mainly rice and sugar, developed during the Japanese occupation of 1895 to 1945, to a focus on advanced industrial production. The results were startling, especially in Taiwan's export sector, as shown in the table below. The economy's focus in the 1960s was largely on electronics and other technologically advanced industries, but there was also a dramatic increase in production of textiles, as well as of rubber, chemicals, and plastics. The 1973–1974 world oil crisis brought serious disruptions to Taiwan's economy, with its overdependence on oil imports, but food-price subsidies during the emergency period, coupled with extremely severe monetary policies, kept the crisis from becoming a catastrophe.

In comparison to growth rates in the PRC, Taiwan's were similar during the mainland's First Five-Year Plan, but broke away swiftly with the post–Great Leap Forward economic disruptions, and held that lead during the Cultural Revolution. (The figures for Japan show that Taiwan almost matched Japanese growth rates in this period. See the table on page 634.)

As much as it could, the government on Taiwan had restricted imports of products that would worsen its balance-of-payments problems, especially products that could be considered luxury goods or competed directly with Taiwanese manufactures. But the state actively promoted exports by making cheap credit available to manufacturers of export goods, and by giving these firms special economic support in a series of export processing zones. The first of these was established in 1966 at the southern Taiwan port of Kao-

TAIWAN'S ECONOMIC BASE, 1953 AND 1962[15]

	1953	1962
Percent of employment		
Agriculture	61	55
Industry	9	12
Percent of gross domestic production		
Agriculture	38	29
Industry	18	26
Percent of export		
Agricultural goods and products	93	49
Industrial products	7	51

hsiung, which had been developed into an active harbor with U.S. aid. Two more such zones were established in 1969. In these zones, industrial parks were supervised by a streamlined bureaucracy to avoid government red tape, and both foreign and Taiwanese firms were given tax incentives and exemptions from import duties on special machinery if they exported all their finished products.

Although the Shanghai communiqué of 1972 did not decisively affect Taiwan's economic status, the absence of any consultations with Chiang's government prior to its announcement was humiliating. And when the Taiwanese pondered this humiliation along with the loss of Taiwan's UN seat, their sense of anger and rejection mounted. Anti-U.S. riots erupted in Taiwan during 1971–1972, fed as well by protests against the ossified Chiang regime, the unrepresentative nature of the Guomindang government, and the severe restrictions on individual freedom that were still a part of Taiwan life. Underlying the discontent was the feeling of powerlessness that oppressed the majority of the population—those Chinese who had settled on the island before 1945 and had continued to resent the occupation by post-1949 refugees from the mainland. Acute differences between these two constituencies spilled over into everything from marriage patterns to education, and there was a distinct possibility of serious violence. Chiang's government feared that the widespread protests might encourage the growth of the small but articulate Taiwan Independence movement, a potential threat to Guomindang power. But the Guomindang was able to suppress domestic dissent through strict police and political control, which could be backed, when necessary, by overwhelming military force. Torn by its own

GROWTH RATES: TAIWAN, PRC, AND JAPAN, 1952–1972[16]

	1952–1960	*1960–1965*	*1965–1972*
Percentage rates of overall GNP growth			
Taiwan	7.2	9.6	10.1
PRC	6.0	4.7	5.7
Japan	8.3	9.8	10.8
Percentage rates of per capita GNP growth			
Taiwan	3.6	6.4	7.3
PRC	3.6	2.9	3.3
Japan	7.2	8.8	9.5

troubles, the PRC was not able to exploit Taiwan's divisions for political ends.

The 1979 Carter-Deng normalization agreements, however, seemed more threatening to Taiwan—at least in the eyes of Guomindang supporters in the United States. Chiang Kai-shek had died in 1975, and though his son Chiang Ching-kuo soon took over the island's presidency, there was concern that he might not have the prestige to hold Taiwan together. The ending of all official American diplomatic concourse with Taiwan meant that henceforth relations would be conducted only through two "institutes," one in Taipei and one in Washington, D.C., although these were staffed mainly by professional foreign-service personnel considered to be on leave during their assignments. Particularly threatening, in the eyes of Taiwan's supporters, were the U.S. offer to withdraw all its military personnel from the island within four months, the abrogation of the mutual-security treaty, and the agreement reached with the PRC by which the United States would not supply new offensive arms to Taiwan and would gradually reduce overall military support.

The result was that in April 1979 Congress passed a strong Taiwan Relations Act that reflected the worries of pro-Taiwan forces by reaffirming the U.S. commitment to Taiwan, and especially by underlining that "the future of Taiwan will be determined by peaceful means" and that any "boycotts and embargoes" by the PRC against Taiwan would be considered a "threat to the peace and security of the Western Pacific." Furthermore, Congress emphatically undertook "to provide Taiwan with arms of a defensive character," and pledged to "resist any resort to force or other forms of coercion that would jeopardize the security, or the social or economic system, of the people on Taiwan." The only real sop to the broader-based Carter position on China was the statement in the act that the United States would also work for the "preservation and enhancement of the human rights of all the people on Taiwan."[17]

In the event, the loss of U.S. diplomatic recognition in 1979 did not affect the Taiwanese economy adversely. On the contrary, 1979 proved to be an exceedingly strong year as Taiwan's GNP grew by 20.3 percent to an all-time peak of $32 billion. Although Taiwan cut back its reliance on U.S. trade to some extent—which was in any case a practical move—overall trade, conducted with 120 different countries, rose 31 percent the same year. Foreign investment *in* Taiwan also rose dramatically—by over 50 percent, from $213 million in 1978 to $329 million in 1979. Taiwan's main problem continued to be its dependence on oil imports, which at 380,000 barrels a day cost Taiwan over $2 billion a year; but the expansion of the island's nuclear-power facilities promised to offset this problem to some extent. (In 1980 Taiwan lost both its International Monetary Fund and its World Bank seats to the PRC, but this also had no apparent adverse effect on the economy.)

The leaders of the PRC were aware of Taiwan's prosperity, and slowly began to realize that however strong their rhetoric concerning "reunification" might be, there was no realistic expectation for it whatever if the economic disparities between the two countries remained as broad as they were. The table that follows compares the purchasing power of Shanghai and Taipei workers for food, clothing, and consumer goods in the mid-1970s. It shows that as a percentage of workers' income, product prices in Taipei (Taiwan's capital) were generally lower than in Shanghai. The Taiwanese worker was almost invariably able to afford to purchase more, despite attempts in the PRC to subsidize food prices for city dwellers. Since a comparison of monthly family budgets in Shanghai and Taipei shows that roughly the same percentage of total income was spent on food, the implication is that workers in Taipei ate far better than their counterparts in Shanghai—something apparent without the aid of statistics to most casual observers. Housing and health care, in comparison, absorbed a higher percentage of the Taiwan workers' earnings.

The challenge for the PRC was to adopt some means for implementing the Four Modernizations (the "fifth" was not in question here) at a swifter rate, and one that would gain China freer access to the world financial community. It seems to have been two party officials from Guangdong who first suggested to Deng Xiaoping the idea of instituting "special zones" that would be used to develop the particular economic resources of their province. So secretive were many aspects of Chinese politics, however, that it has been plausibly suggested that Deng sent these two men to Guangdong so that they could then *seem* to be urging their own province's claims when in fact they were echoing Deng's own intentions. In either case, Deng Xiaoping pushed the idea at a work conference of the Central Committee in April 1979, when the brief China-Vietnam war had ended and the democratic protestors been largely silenced. A work team was accordingly sent to the two south coastal provinces of Guangdong and Fujian, and in July 1979 the Central Committee moved to establish four "special zones for export." The following year the name was changed to "special economic zones" to suggest their broader range of economic activity, and perhaps to make them sound less like Taiwan's "export processing zones."

The four areas were carefully chosen for their proximity to foreign-capital sources and their accessibility. Zhuhai is adjacent to Macao, Shenzhen just over the northern border of Hong Kong, Shantou and Xiamen are opposite

COMPARATIVE PURCHASING POWER IN SHANGHAI AND TAIPEI, MID-1970s[18]

Item	Price Shanghai (SH yuan)	Taipei (NT$)	Income price* SH (%)	TP (%)	SH/TP
Food					
Rice (kg.)	0.28	16.90	1.04	0.88	1.18
Wheat flour (kg.)	0.28	13.30	1.04	0.69	1.51
Pork (kg.)	1.80	78.00	6.67	4.04	1.65
Chicken (kg.)	2.50	110.00	9.26	5.70	1.62
Fish (cheapest) (kg.)	0.44	37.00	1.63	1.92	0.85
Hen eggs (kg.)	1.60	35.50	5.93	1.84	3.22
White sugar (kg.)	1.45	15.80	5.37	0.82	6.56
Soy sauce (kg.)	0.54	16.70	2.00	0.86	2.31
Salt (kg.)	0.28	5.00	1.04	0.26	4.00
Potatoes (kg.)	0.06	12.80	0.22	0.66	0.34
Scallions	0.15	10.00	0.56	0.52	1.07
Bean curd (kg.)	0.52	12.50	1.93	0.65	2.97
Red beans (kg.)	0.11	18.30	0.41	0.95	0.43
Bok choy (cabbage) (kg.)	0.06	15.00	0.22	0.78	0.29
Clothing					
Socks (m.; pr.)	2.50	16.00	9.26	0.83	11.17
Polyester shirt (m.)	6.00	150.00	22.22	7.77	2.86
Cotton jacket (m.)	12.50	240.00	46.30	12.43	3.72
Plastic sandals (pr.)	4.50	35.00	16.67	1.81	9.19
Sneakers (m.; pr.)	9.50	130.00	35.19	6.74	5.22
Cloth coat (w.)	66.00	400.00	244.44	20.72	11.80
Consumer goods					
Bicycle	120.00	2,400.00	444.44	124.25	3.57
Basketball	15.00	280.00	55.56	14.51	3.83
Electric fan	179.00	864.00	662.96	44.76	14.81
Electric clock	19.00	683.00	70.37	35.39	1.99
Sewing machine	150.00	2,725.00	555.56	141.18	3.93
Television (11")	700.00	5,000.00	2,592.59	259.05	10.01
Transistor radio	30.00	320.00	111.11	16.58	6.70

*"Income price" is the percentage of monthly per capita income needed to purchase one unit. Monthly income figures are 27 yuan for Shanghai and NT $1,930.10 for Taipei. "SH/TP" is the ratio of income prices between Shanghai and Taipei.

ALLOCATION OF MONTHLY FAMILY
BUDGET IN SHANGHAI AND TAIPEI,
MID-1970s[19]

Item	Shanghai	Taipei
Food	38.55%	36.24%
Clothing	15.06	4.30
Housing	5.62	17.54
Furniture	5.95	2.05
Utilities	5.30	4.38
Medical	1.20	3.25
Education	4.22	4.25
Transportation	6.02	2.33
Entertainment	6.02	1.77
Savings	6.02	16.46
Taxes, interest	0.00	3.45
Remittances	6.02	0.00
Other	0.00	6.14

Taiwan. In their nineteenth-century British romanizations, Shantou (Swatow) and Xiamen (Amoy) had been among the treaty ports forced on the Qing dynasty by the British. Those imperialist echoes might have bothered some, but China's leaders seem to have been confident they could avoid foreign dominance over these zones by vigorously maintaining Chinese control and supervision. Nevertheless, the facilities extended to foreigners and overseas Chinese in the four zones were considerable. The PRC offered to build plants to the specifications of foreign investors, and provide a well-trained (and presumably obedient and nonunionized) labor force at competitively low wages. They also offered investors preferential tax rates and a number of other financial incentives, including the development of transportation networks in the zones.

Investors did respond, but not as quickly as the Chinese had hoped, nor with the commitment of advanced technology that had been expected. The Chinese work force was often not as skilled as the foreign investors had hoped, the bureaucracy remained cumbersome, and quality standards were low. The zones did take off—especially Shenzhen, which grew to look almost like the less affluent sectors of its high-rise neighbor, Hong Kong— but the boom was expensive to PRC planners, who had to invest far more state funds in construction and other support systems than they had expected. The planners were surprised too when imports *into* Shenzhen grew at an alarming rate. At the same time, a maze of social problems began to appear in the zones, from the regular use of Hong Kong currency, black markets, and corruption among officials to street crime and prostitution. High government leaders in China—some perhaps already wary of Deng Xiaoping's ambitious plans—began to grow anxious about the accelerated pace of change.

As early as July 1979 the National People's Congress had argued for readjusting the economy to pay more attention once again to agriculture, and suggested caution over the other three of the Four Modernizations. The veteran economic planner Chen Yun, raised to the Standing Committee of the Central Committee's Politburo in 1979, called late the following year for a period of retrenchment. One factor in this decision was the discovery that, exciting though the prospects for economic growth might be, and however potentially profitable the special economic zones, the foreign-trade deficit for the year 1979–1980 had turned out to be $3.9 billion, by far the largest in China's history. Integration into the world of technologically advanced trading nations was clearly going to be an expensive business.

At a different level of magnitude, but equally disturbing in its way, was the announcement in *People's Daily* on April 23, 1979, of the worst case of corruption yet uncovered in the PRC. A CCP middle-level cadre named Wang Shouxin, working in northerly Heilongjiang province with a group of associates, many of whom also held party and bureaucratic positions, had managed to embezzle state property worth at least 536,000 yuan in a series of scams and thefts spread over seven years. Wang Shouxin's case was a convoluted one, involving her manipulation of the coal company she supervised and the distribution system that went with it. The case attracted the attention of one of China's shrewdest writers, Liu Binyan, who had suffered in the antirightist campaign and the Cultural Revolution for his outspokenness. The profession of "investigative reporter" was, in the late 1970s, being encouraged as one way of airing popular complaints against corrupt cadres, and Liu was a dramatic example of how effective such a role could be, even in the world of China's state-controlled press. He traveled to Heilongjiang to interview people in Wang's unit and to try and unravel the details of the case. His remarkable exposé, a sixty-page essay that he entitled "People or Monsters," was published in *People's Literature* in September 1979. Since this was an "official journal," the CCP cultural authorities obviously agreed with Liu's basic indictment of certain echelons within the CCP itself.

Wang Shouxin, in Liu's sardonic portrayal, was "a warmly sentimental woman with clearly defined likes and dislikes. Her tens of thousands of tons of coal and her nine trucks were the brush and ink that she used every day to compose her lyric poems." The "poems" that Wang composed were designed to protect and promote her own family, and to ingratiate herself with party members and cadres at all levels through selective manipulation and corruption. Wang was not in fact so special, Liu observed in passing; only the scale of her operations was unusual. She was merely a symptom, a dishonest person whose behavior had for years been "covered up by the general decline in social morality, by the gradual legalization of criminal activity, and by the people's gradual acclimatization to the moral decay around them."[20] If Wang was indeed a symptom rather than an isolated case, then the opening up of China to the West was going to offer as many temptations as opportunities.

"Truth from Facts"

The ups and downs in Chinese economic policy during the four years after Mao's death in 1976 reflected disagreements at the center of the government between Deng Xiaoping and Hua Guofeng. Considering the importance of the stakes, and the absence of any precise mechanism for peaceful transitions at the top of the power structure, either Deng or Hua was going to have to shunt aside his rival. In the event, it was Deng who succeeded in the power struggle.

Although Hua Guofeng apparently held the more impressive formal positions—as chairman of the CCP, premier of the State Council, and chairman of the Military Affairs Commission—Deng had the more powerful connections in the party and in the army, as well as among leading intellectuals. Hua had based his climb to power on his contention that he was Mao's chosen successor; but after the arrest of the Gang of Four, as criticism of Mao began to be voiced publicly, Hua discovered that this was not a helpful legacy. Furthermore, Deng Xiaoping worked patiently in the late 1970s and in 1980 to discredit Hua. Hua's rash statement, made after he had attained power in 1976, that all the Chinese needed to do to achieve a happy future was to "obey whatever Mao had said and to ensure the continuation of whatever he had decided" caused him and his close associates to be dubbed believers in "the two whatevers," and to be mocked in private even as they held forth grandiloquently on the need for pure Maoist principles. Deng, publicly espousing the Maoist slogan to "seek truth from facts," energetically pushed the image of himself as a pragmatist, and broadened the whole sense of Mao's phrase by adding the crucial clause "and make practice the sole criterion of truth."

Deng consolidated his victory over Hua by grooming two protégés for power. The two men Deng selected, Hu Yaobang and Zhao Ziyang, could claim stronger revolutionary credentials than the discredited Gang of Four. Although they had not participated as adults in the early years of the revolution, their lives echoed in different ways the many levels of struggle that China had experienced over the past half century. The elder of the two, Hu Yaobang, was born in Hunan in 1915 (some sources say 1913) to a poor peasant family, and had been recruited as a boy to serve in Mao's ill-fated Autumn Harvest Uprisings of 1927. He joined the CCP in the Jiangxi Soviet in 1933, fought on the Long March, and rose steadily in the party ranks during the Yan'an and civil-war periods, becoming director of the Communist Youth League. He was ousted from power in 1966 when the Red Guards targeted the league—by then some 30 million strong—as a potential rival in the Cultural Revolution's struggle for leadership. Returned to office in 1975 as party secretary of the prestigious Academy of Sciences, Hu speedily developed a reputation as a tough defender of the sciences and of the rights of talented scholars to uninterrupted research time. Always salty and outspoken, his words had a directness that was refreshing to many after decades of Maoist rhetoric about serving the people. "The Academy of Sciences is the Academy of Sciences," as Hu put it once. "It is not an Academy of Production. It is a place where one studies, not a place where one plants cabbages. It is not a potato patch, it is a place where one does science, the natural sciences."[21] Disgraced along with Deng Xiaoping in 1976, Hu returned to even greater power in 1977 as codirector of the Central Party School and director of the Central Committee's organization department. In late December 1978 he was named to the Politburo, and in 1980 elected to the key Standing Committee of the Politburo. Later that year Deng arranged for Hu to be named general secretary of the party, a key move toward the eventual removal of Hua Guofeng from power, which was achieved successfully in 1981.

The second man groomed for power by Deng Xiaoping was Zhao Ziyang. Zhao was from a completely different background than Hu and experienced a different career pattern, but like Hu he was a fine administrator and a seasoned political operator. Born in 1919 to a landlord family in Henan, Zhao joined the Communist Youth League as a schoolboy in 1932. At nineteen he entered the CCP, and served as a guerrilla-base organizer during World War II and the civil war, working especially in that troubled border zone where Shandong, Henan, and Hebei meet. In the 1940s that area was still—as it had been when Lin Qing made it the base of his Eight Trigram rebellion in 1813—fertile ground for recruitment of the dissident and the dispossessed. After the Communist victory, Zhao was transferred to Guangdong and rose steadily in the provincial hierarchy there, becoming party secretary in 1961. Adaptable to new political winds, he pushed land reform vigorously in the early 1950s, defended family-unit production after the Great Leap disasters, and rode out the first phase of the Cultural Revolution by posing as a leader of the Red Guards in Canton, until he was ousted by more radical Red Guards in 1967. By the mid-1970s, after a brief spell of service in Inner Mongolia, Zhao was back in Canton.

But it was after his transfer to Sichuan in 1975 as party secretary and political commissar to the Chengdu region that Zhao's career really took wing. Sichuan, traditionally one of China's most prosperous and productive province, with a population of 97 million in mid-1970, had suffered disastrous setbacks during the Cultural Revolution. The zeal with which radical cadres promoted extremist policies in the province severely disrupted agriculture and industry, and for the first time in decades Sichuan—customarily China's supplementary "rice basket"—ceased to be self-supporting in food grains. The complex politics of the province also allowed it to remain a bastion for Lin Biao supporters long after he had died and his supporters been ousted elsewhere in China.

As party secretary, Zhao had to overcome this troubled legacy, and in late 1976 he began to implement a series of policies designed to reverse the economic radicalism that had marked first the Great Leap period and then the decade of the Cultural Revolution. Realizing that local farmers were once again working hard on private plots, and thus dramatically increasing production, Zhao authorized up to 15 percent of the land in Sichuan communes to be farmed privately and the produce of those plots to be sold in private markets at noncontrolled prices. He also authorized a host of smaller "side-line industries" by which individual families could supplement their incomes. The result was a spectacular leap in production as private economic initiative found a new freedom; grain production in Sichuan jumped 24 percent between 1976 and 1979.

Zhao was equally flexible with state industries based in the province. Plant managers were given virtual financial autonomy, allowed to negotiate their own access to markets, and permitted to combine with other sectors in joint industrial ventures. The work force was offered bonuses for high production, and factory operations were tightened up. The result was an even more extraordinary jump of 80 percent in industrial production during the same three-year period of 1976–1979. A folk saying punning on the similar pronunciation in Chinese of the word "to look for" and Zhao's surname began to circulate in China at this time: "If you want to eat, go and look for Ziyang" (*"Yao chi liang, zhao Ziyang"*). When Deng Xiaoping, himself a Sichuanese, returned to power in 1977, he named Zhao an alternate member of the Politburo, and thereafter Zhao's rise was swift: in 1979, he was made a full member of the Politburo; in February 1980, he was appointed to the

Standing Committee of the Politburo; and in April 1980, he became vice-premier of China. In September that same year, he was made premier in Hua Guofeng's place. Reviewing this remarkable record of successful innovation, we can see how the example of what Zhao had achieved gave Deng Xiaoping the confidence he had needed to draw up the guidelines for change at the Third Plenum of the Eleventh Central Committee.

Deng Xiaoping, who in 1978 had himself taken over the post of chairman of the Military Affairs Commission from Hua, had by 1980 apparently achieved his goal: each part of the three key elements of the Chinese state was now in his hands or in those of his two protégés. Hua Guofeng was not penalized further, but allowed to keep some rank and dignity as an ordinary member of the Central Committee. His chance of running the country as Mao's successor, however, was ended, and to emphasize the break with the past Deng Xiaoping led the party in the delicate task of evaluating Mao's legacy. It was an operation fraught with problems if the party was not to undermine its prestige or yield important theoretical ground to the officially discredited Democracy movement. The party began by publicizing harrowing cases of those who had tried to criticize aspects of Mao's policies in the 1960s and 1970s, and had been persecuted or even tortured and killed for their stubborn determination to right the record. Then the Central Committee conducted its own careful analysis, which it completed in the summer of 1981. Mao was blamed for certain "leftist" excesses in his later years, such as his beliefs that the bourgeoisie could continue to exist inside the party, that mass revolution against revisionism should be encouraged, and that there was need for "continuing the revolution under the dictatorship of the proletariat." The final summation was that Mao had been correct 70 percent of the time and incorrect only 30 percent of the time, with most of those errors bunched near the end of his life. But using these mistakes to "try to negate the scientific value of Mao Zedong thought and to deny its guiding role in our revolution and our construction" would be "entirely wrong," the Central Committee concluded. "Socialism and socialism alone can save China."[22]

As this political struggle was slowly reaching a conclusion, the state-controlled press began to issue reports emphasizing examples of local initiative in China and showing how certain types of small enterprise could flourish. The initial examples were modest, as in the 1980 story of an elderly couple who had apparently for decades been running a small guesthouse in a former general store. The couple's little "Heavenly Justice Guest House," which was used by peasants and others visiting Peking who were too poor for the regular hotels, could sleep eight men at a time on a *kang* (the raised brick platform, heated from below and covered with bedding, that was the customary sleeping place in north China). Women guests had to sleep with the guesthouse owner's wife, while her husband moved in with the men. Across a span of thirty years, the press related, the couple had in this simple way cared for 46,000 guests, apparently oblivious to all the shifts in the political wind. Their venture was not to be considered "capitalist," argued the party press, since the couple always "relied on their own labor and did not exploit anyone."[23]

In another much-publicized story that same year, several Sichuan families near Chengdu were awarded certificates for achieving "wealth through diligent labor." Such families used the new "responsibility system" to contract for the right to work a given plot of commune land. All surplus produced above the state-imposed quota could be sold on the free market locally. Sideline production included raising silk cocoons for the commune's silk spindles and raising pigs for sale. Families engaged in these activities might make as much as $700 a year, and since the per capita income in Sichuan's richest communes was $160 a year and the average for the province as a whole $55, this new system represented a startling opportunity. By the end of the year, such stories of commercial success in the countryside were becoming commonplace to Chinese readers. The only minor villains in these vignettes were the local cadres, who often dithered over bureaucratic niceties and took months to process the necessary paper work.

In this same atmosphere of growing euphoria over independent enterprise, the once-disgraced party leader Liu Shaoqi was formally vindicated of all the charges leveled against him during the Cultural Revolution. Liu himself had died years before, in 1969, allegedly from pneumonia; but his widow, Wang Guangmei, who had so angered Mao by her participation in the investigative work groups of the post–Great Leap Forward period, was still alive and present to hear the speeches in her late husband's honor. The vindication of Liu must have seemed as baffling to many young party members as the original charges had been to their parents. Since Liu's disgrace the CCP had more than doubled in size—from 18 million in 1966 to 38 million in 1980—so that half the membership had spent their entire party lives in the belief (or at least the public appearance of belief) that Liu Shaoqi had been "a traitor, a scab, and a number one person in authority taking the capitalist road." As with the story in 1971 of Lin Biao's death, party credibility was once more stretched to the limits.

It was apt that during this transitional year of 1980 the Gang of Four should finally be brought to trial. There were ten defendants in all: the Gang of Four, five senior army officers accused of complicity in Lin Biao's plot, and Mao's former secretary and ideological expert, Chen Boda, who had been a leading figure in the early years of the Cultural Revolution.

National and international interest in the trial focused on the Gang of Four themselves, who were accused of "persecuting to death" an estimated 34,800 people during the Cultural Revolution, and of having "framed and persecuted" 729,511 others during their years in power. In concentrating on crimes committed during the later 1960s and early 1970s, the prosecutors moved away from earlier criticisms of the Gang of Four that had sought to undermine their political character by digging up (or fabricating) charges that went far back into the past. At the time of her original arrest, for instance, Jiang Qing was accused of cooperating with the Guomindang in 1934–1935 and betraying members of the underground to Chiang Kai-shek's police. Similarly, Zhang Chunqiao was accused of having joined the Guomindang Blueshirts in the mid-1930s, and of having continued working secretly for the Guomindang after reaching Yan'an in the early 1940s. Yao Wenyuan was accused of covering up the fact that his family had been landlords for five generations in Zhejiang province, and of being the godson of a senior officer in the Nationalist Secret Police. Wang Hongwen, the youngest of the group, who had not even been alive in those dramatic early days of the revolution, was charged with having wangled a change of assignment during his service in the Korean War—from signalman to trumpet player in the band.

During the trial Mao's widow, Jiang Qing, was defiant, shouting at witnesses, calling the judges "fascists and Guomindang," and requiring removal from the courtroom at times. She clung consistently to her defense that Mao had supported her activities in the Cultural Revolution and that ultimately she was merely obeying his will. Zhang Chunqiao held stubbornly aloof from the proceedings, refusing to answer the prosecutor's questions. Most of the other defendants were more docile, apparently beaten down by their long years of harsh detention in prison. But the trial did little to reassure observers that the rule of law was returning to China. In fact the proceedings were a bizarre public spectacle that many Chinese discounted, even though they were glad to see these particular former leaders brought low.

In the formal sentences, handed down on January 25, 1981, the two most stubborn of the Gang of Four, Jiang Qing and Zhang Chunqiao, were condemned to death, but with a two-year reprieve during which time they might "repent" and thereby avoid execution. Wang Hongwen was given life imprisonment; Yao Wenyuan got eighteen years in prison. Chen Boda and the five army officers all received prison sentences of sixteen to eighteen years.

With these sentences and the clear political demise of Hua Guofeng, a political era of Chinese "leftism" seemed to have ended. This was underlined not only by the rehabilitation of Liu Shaoqi, but also by the favorable reassessment of such long-vilified party leaders of the late 1920s and early 1930s as Qu Qiubai and Li Lisan. It seemed that the party leaders now realized that if they were to restructure the country's socialist economy, they were also going to have to restructure the party's didactic vision of its own past.

CHAPTER 25

Levels of Power

ONE BILLION PEOPLE

By the year 1981, despite the continuing disagreements among the leadership over the proper pace of economic change, a consensus had emerged that without a vigorous plan for population control, China was going to eat up whatever material gains it might achieve, just as a number of other developing nations were doing. There had been two previous censuses in the PRC, one in 1953 that showed a total Chinese population of 582.6 million, and one in 1964 that yielded a figure of 694.6 million. But neither of these had been monitored with precision, and to make intelligent plans for the future, the leadership realized, it was essential to know the precise size of China's population and the speed of its growth. Accordingly, a target date for a full national census was set: July 1, 1982.

The results of the census confirmed what Chinese demographers and planners had expected: China's total population was now more than 1 billion. Although foreign demographers questioned some aspects of the methodology employed, especially in areas where the stated totals seemed to match projected totals too neatly, the figures were accepted as generally reliable. For the census was carried through with advice from United Nations experts on population, and had been carefully planned several months in advance; population data were gathered by over 5 million canvassers and digested by 29 colossal computers. The final figure of 1,008,175,288 Chinese in the PRC was therefore believed to be as accurate as possible, given the circumstances. Because political necessity required counting Taiwan as part of China, the full figure released was 1,031,882,511, which included the estimated populations of Taiwan, Hong Kong, and Macao.

AGE COMPOSITION OF THE TWO SEXES IN CHINA'S POPULATION, 1982[1]

Age group	Total	Male	Female	Sex ratio (female=100)
Total	1,008,152,137*	519,406,895	488,745,242	106.27
0–4	94,704,361	48,983,813	45,720,548	107.14
5–9	110,735,871	57,026,296	53,709,575	106.18
10–14	131,810,957	67,837,932	63,973,025	106.04
15–19	125,997,658	64,420,607	61,577,051	104.62
20–24	76,848,044	40,300,907	36,547,137	110.27
25–29	93,142,891	48,310,132	44,832,759	107.76
30–34	73,187,245	38,153,148	35,034,097	108.90
35–39	54,327,790	28,669,005	25,658,785	111.73
40–44	48,490,741	25,878,901	22,611,840	114.45
45–49	47,454,949	25,123,395	22,331,554	112.50
50–54	40,856,112	21,568,644	19,287,468	111.83
55–59	33,932,129	17,530,819	16,401,310	106.89
60–64	27,387,702	13,733,702	13,653,367	100.59
65–69	21,260,370	10,171,973	11,088,397	91.74
70–74	14,348,045	6,434,731	7,913,314	81.32
75–79	8,617,043	3,496,703	5,120,340	68.29
80+	5,050,091	1,765,823	3,284,268	53.77

*In some cases the precise age was unclear; hence this figure is slightly lower than the total census figure.

One fact emphasized by the 1982 census was the extraordinary youthfulness of China's population. The figures showed that around 60 million Chinese women were currently in their thirties, 80 million in their twenties, and 125 million between ten and twenty—already (or soon to be) of marriageable age (see the table above). At the same time, life expectancy was also rising dramatically.

This enormous potential pool of childbearing women gave added urgency to the arguments of those seeking a stronger family-planning policy in China. Ever since the founding of the PRC there had been a tension in this policy debate between socialist optimism and the pessimism of the "Malthusian" laws of population limitation,* which implicitly contradicted the

*According to Thomas Malthus (1766–1834) in his *Essay on the Principle of Population* (1798), the population of a given country was doomed to be checked by famine, disease, war, or other catastrophes when it pushed too hard against the limits of available resources. At almost the same time, late in Qianlong's reign, the scholar Hong Liangji had also warned that rapidly rising population might harm China.

hope that socialism would bring the most dramatic changes in human life. In the early 1950s, some of China's foremost economists had warned of trouble if close attention was not paid to the nation's overall population picture. A host of factors supported this conclusion: the new marriage law of 1950 that allowed women as well as men the opportunity to leave uncongenial partners and find new ones; the drop in infant mortality because of improved health care; a rise in life expectancy because of better diet and health care for the elderly; the closing of monasteries and convents; the banning of prostitution, which brought even more women into the marriage market; and the persistence of the Chinese people in seeking prosperity and lineage continuity alike through numerous progeny, including several sons.

These warnings prompted the approval in 1953 of laws on birth control and abortion, and the formation in 1954 of birth-control study groups. In 1956 Zhou Enlai urged limitations on childbirth. But the more influential economists holding such views were purged in the antirightist campaign of 1957 (Zhou survived in power), and during the politically extremist years of the Great Leap Forward and the Cultural Revolution little attempt was made to analyze or limit China's population growth. Throughout the 1960s and early 1970s many families had five or six children. Had it not been for the catastrophic famines of the post–Great Leap years, and the dismal health conditions afflicting the so-called "minority" regions and the poorer parts of rural China, the rate of population growth would have been even higher.

But whereas in 1974 Chinese spokesmen at international conferences could still assure their listeners that "population explosion" theories were a "fallacy peddled by the superpowers,"[2] the government had already begun to check population growth through mass propaganda and the spread of birth-control devices. The fertility rate of Chinese women, which stood at 4.2 percent in 1974, dropped to 3.2 percent in 1976 and 2.2 percent in 1980. In September 1980 Hua Guofeng, who still served as the government spokesman on some important matters, told the National People's Congress that henceforth Chinese families must strive to limit the number of children they bear to one, and that family planning must be built into China's long-term development strategy. Exceptions would be allowed only for the "minority peoples."

Following Hua's speech, a "revised marriage law" of the PRC was promulgated, fixing the earliest marriage age permitted for men at twenty-two and for women at twenty. (It had been twenty and eighteen respectively in the 1950 marriage law.) Because of government policies urging late marriage, actual marriage ages for men and women had been considerably higher than these new levels. The intent of the law was to formalize the rules and prevent earlier marriages while encouraging "later marriage, later childbirth." The law's recommended guidelines for women were first marriage at twenty-four, first (and ideally last) childbirth at twenty-five.

Reinforcing Hua's statements, the State Family Planning Commission pointed out that studies made of births during 1981 showed almost 6 million babies had been born to families who already had one child, obviously threatening the policy of one child per family. In an alarming 1.7 million cases, new babies had been born to families who already had five or more children. As a result, the government intensified the rigor of its birth-control programs, ordering compulsory IUD insertion for women who had borne one child, and compulsory sterilization of either husband or wife after the birth of a second child. Provinces were assigned sterilization quotas, which were then passed down to the counties and municipalities for implementation, and in many cases women were coerced into having late-term abortions. Furthermore, many party administrators handed out land contracts to peasant families only if the peasants signed a second contract undertaking not to have a child while they worked the land. Such families would be fined or even forced to forfeit the land if they bore a child. There were reports of couples fleeing as local sterilization teams entered their villages, and some birth-control cadres felt so threatened that they requested armed escorts. In all, between September 1981 and December 1982, 16.4 million women underwent sterilization by tubular ligation, and 4 million men received vasectomies. In response to these new zones of governmental interference in their lives, villagers began to offer either abortion or sterilization ritual gifts to affected families, showing both the persistence and the internal flexibility of the traditional rural patterns of exchange.[3]

The one-child family also posed new problems in the countryside. Since the household incentive system put a premium on family-based work power, many rural families came to see that it was more important to have several children to work on the land and care for them in old age than to follow the state's call to limit family size so drastically. And although a wide range of family-planning aids were easily available in the cities, these were less easily obtainable in the countryside. Furthermore, the breakup of the hierarchically integrated system of teams, brigades, and communes made the state's implementation of its population-control message much harder to achieve.

The state introduced severe penalties for families who violated the one-child limit. Whereas families with only one child received special economic, educational, and housing benefits, those with several children were punished with fines and the withholding of rights to housing and education. In many tragic instances, desperate families resorted to female infanticide. This practice was harshly condemned by the state, but the very harshness of the

critique hinted at the scale of the problem, believed by some Western analysts of Chinese demographic data to be in the region of 200,000 female
babies in a single year. Some parents used the newly available technique of
amniocentesis to detect the gender of the fetus early in pregnancy, and then
obtain an abortion if the tests showed the baby to be female. A number of
seriously ill girls were just left to die.

Another way out of the predicament of overpopulation, some analysts
might have suggested, would have been to encourage more Chinese women
or men not to marry at all. Some women had followed this route in the late
nineteenth and early twentieth centuries, when they had formed "sisterhoods" whose members lived in common and shared incomes and employment opportunities, often relying on Buddhist-inspired beliefs to give them
courage. But marriage had become an expectation for virtually every woman
in the PRC, as is sharply shown in another set of figures developed from
the 1982 census. Marriage rates were also high for men. In the Qing and
republican periods many poor men had not been able to marry for economic
reasons, while other men who had the money found that because of multiple
concubines among the wealthy and the practice of female infanticide among
the most desperate of the poor, marriageable women were just not available.
Social changes in the PRC had essentially obliterated such patterns, though
with a male-female ratio for those in their twenties and thirties that ranged
between 102 and 107 males to 100 females, it continued to be impossible for
some men to find wives even if they wanted to.

Among the many other factors that had to be taken into careful account

PERCENTAGE OF CHINESE WHO NEVER MARRIED, BY AGE GROUP, 1982[4]

Age group	Total	Male	Female
15–19	97.38	99.07	95.62
20–24	59.45	71.98	46.45
25–29	14.72	23.59	5.27
30–34	4.93	8.84	0.69
35–39	3.70	6.77	0.28
40–44	3.13	5.71	0.20
45–49	2.39	4.37	0.18
50–59	1.66	2.98	0.21
60–79	1.37	2.56	0.30
80+	1.11	2.63	0.29

by Chinese planners as they pieced together a new policy of population control, perhaps five were the most important: the availability of land suitable for agriculture throughout China, the overall age profile of the population, the balance of urban and rural growth, the characteristics of the labor force, and the levels of education attained by the population. In all these areas the 1982 census figures offered new and significant details.

First, in its amount of agricultural land per capita, China compared unfavorably with many other parts of the world, and enjoyed little room for imaginative maneuver. China's land area was larger than the United States' (960 million hectares* compared to 930 million), but comprised only around half as much cultivated land (99 million hectares against 186 million in the late 1970s). When this smaller area of cultivated land was combined with China's vastly larger population, the resulting *per capita* amount of cultivated land stood at only 0.25 acres for China, compared to 2.10 acres for the United States. Furthermore, China's available agricultural land had been slowly shrinking since it peaked in size just before the Great Leap. This was the result in part of a number of government decisions that had disastrous effects on the country's ecology and environment—such as uncontrolled deforestation, poorly planned hydroelectric dams, and massive industrial pollution—and in part of the ongoing construction of new homes, factories, roads, and rail lines. Though new crop strains, more intensive and efficient land use, irrigation, and chemical fertilizer could all offset this loss to some extent, the shrinkage of the land available to the peasants actually working the fields with their hands was alarming. It meant that the new system of agricultural incentives was going to have to be successful indeed for productivity to increase, given such small amounts of arable land. The table below tells the story clearly enough.

Second, the overall age profile of the population was rising rapidly with the eradication or effective control of many of the most dangerous infectious and parasitic diseases in China. By 1982, over 63 percent of the deaths in China's cities came from "cerebral diseases" (i.e., strokes), heart disease, or malignant tumors (cancer), and the same three causes accounted for 53 percent of all deaths in the countryside. Respiratory diseases were the fourth most frequent killer in both town (8.7 percent) and country (11.5 percent). Partly because of these changes in disease patterns, by 1981 the life expectancy for Chinese men was sixty-nine in the cities and sixty-five and a half in the countryside, that for women seventy-two and a half in the cities and sixty-eight and a half in the country. (The comparable figures for 1957 had been sixty-three and a half and fifty-nine and a quarter for men, and sixty-

---

*A hectare is a unit of land measurement equivalent to 2.47 acres.

three and fifty-nine and three-quarters for women.)

In the third area, the urban/rural balance, it was clear that China's population was gradually becoming more urban. The process had been slower than in many other developing nations because of effective Chinese control over mobility through the registration of all persons, police supervision, tying of food and clothing rations to one's registered location, and the compulsory dispatching of millions of urban young (as well as "rightist" intellectuals and disgraced cadres) to the countryside. But considering China's population size, the shift in urban/rural composition was still drastic, despite officials' success in holding the line during the Cultural Revolution.

For many—perhaps the majority—of peasants, the dismantling of the communes and the establishment of a contract system operating at the household level brought new freedom and new profits. But the changes were not universally welcomed. Those peasants who had thrived in the collective structure of the communes and production brigades, who believed the political rationalization for that form of social and economic organization to be convincing, and who considered the communes the main benefit brought by China's long and bloody revolution, now found that they had to abandon their former lives and go into contract farming with their families or on their own if they had no families. With rural production brigades no longer guaranteeing a minimum grain allowance to members of the rural community, those who could commute to nearby market towns often did so to earn a basic wage, leaving subcontracted grain production to women workers, children, or the elderly. Within this overall picture, the 1982 census

CHANGES IN THE AREA OF CULTIVATED LAND IN CHINA, 1949–1978[5]

Year	Total cultivated area (1,000 hectares)	Average per capita amount (acre)	Per capita average for agricultural population (acre)	Per capita average for able-bodied peasants (acre)
1949	97,881	0.44	0.54	—
1952	107,919	0.46	0.54	1.53
1957	111,830	0.42	0.51	1.43
1962	102,903	0.38	0.45	1.19
1965	103,594	0.35	0.42	1.09
1970	101,135	0.30	0.36	0.89
1975	99,708	0.27	0.31	0.83
1977	99,247	0.26	0.30	0.83
1978	99,389	0.25	0.31	0.82

CHINA'S URBAN/RURAL POPULATION BALANCE, 1949–1983[6]

Year	Total city and town population (10,000)	Urban proportion in nation's total population (%)	Total rural population (10,000)	Rural proportion in nation's total population (%)
1949	5,765	10.6	48,402	89.4
1958	10,721	16.3	55,273	83.7
1966	13,313	17.9	61,229	82.1
1976	16,341	17.4	77,376	82.6
1981	20,171	20.2	79,901	79.8
1983	24,126	23.5	78,369	76.5

highlighted regional disparities. It showed, for example, that around six times more infants died before the age of four in certain poor areas than in China's large cities, with their superior health-care facilities.

In the fourth vital area, China's labor force, there were also challenging circumstances to be confronted. Compared with workers in Japan or the United States, China's work force started young and retired early. According to the 1982 census, 18.09 percent of China's work force fell within the fifteen-to nineteen-year-old age bracket. (By contrast, 3.25 percent of Japanese workers and 7.94 percent of American workers fell within this category.) These young workers had no chance for advanced education. Because of the age curve of China's total population, only 38.15 percent of the work force were in the thirty-five-to sixty-year-old range, where one would expect a high level of experience and perhaps responsibility and competence. (The comparable figure for Japan was 53.57 percent and for the United States, 54.41 percent.) Within the 1982 Chinese work force of 521.5 million, 56.3 percent were men and 43.7 percent were women. Men were heavily concentrated in such manual trades as construction (81.13 percent male) and in mining and lumber work (80.64 percent male). Despite the claims made for women's parity in education and in government employment, positions in what the Chinese termed "Government Organs, Party and Mass Organizations," where physical strength was not at a premium, also went mainly to men, who held 79.55 percent of the posts; and of those held by women, the majority were at the lower end of the spectrum. There was near parity between the sexes in the catering trades, commerce, public-utilities work, and neighborhood services, as there was in basic agricultural work.

The census also documented low levels of education in the overall labor force, which came as a shock to many observers, especially to those in the

West who had believed the emphatic Chinese claims that illiteracy had been virtually eliminated in the PRC. Only 0.87 percent of China's work force had college degrees, 10.54 percent a senior-middle-school (i.e., high school) education, and 26 percent a junior-middle-school education; 34.38 percent had stopped their education after primary school, and 28.2 percent were classified as "illiterates or semi-illiterates."

As the census computers teased out these various figures, making different types of analysis possible, China's leaders may have accepted with equanimity that 73.69 percent of the nation's peasants had still not progressed beyond primary school, despite the fact that it was now thirty-three years since the "liberation" of 1949. More unsettling, certainly, must have been the finding that of China's bureaucratic and party cadres, 26.96 percent had never progressed past primary school, and 42.78 percent had ended their education at the junior-middle-school level. That left only 21.87 percent who had received a senior-middle-school education, and 5.85 percent with some kind of college degree. Such figures would have been irrelevant in the days of mass mobilization for guerrilla warfare, and in the early stages of land reform, the Great Leap, or the Cultural Revolution. But in the context of China's new ambitions for achieving the Four Modernizations, the figures could not but appear daunting.

GOVERNING CHINA IN THE 1980s

By the late 1980s, the government of the PRC faced the task of controlling 1 billion people, handling foreign contracts worth several billion yuan, completely restructuring its economy, and restoring its shattered schools and universities to make them places where intellectual and scientific research could flourish at accepted international standards. But the governmental system that now ran China was a sprawling one, full of overlaps and inconsistencies, and not necessarily equipped to meet the extraordinary challenges facing it. Furthermore, the PRC government had been shaken to the core several times in its short life. The Great Leap Forward and the Cultural Revolution had been the most dramatic examples, but other events had also shown how deeply divided the leaders often were over fundamental political, economic, or intellectual issues: the Gao Gang and Rao Shushi crisis of 1953–1954, the antirightist campaign of 1957, the arguments in the Socialist Education Campaign of 1964, Lin Biao's death in 1971, the purge of Deng Xiaoping and arrest of the Gang of Four in 1976, the dramatic policy turnarounds of the Third Plenum in 1978. The bitterness of the arguments on these occasions, the dismissals, arrests, and deaths, emphasized the extent to which the PRC was, of its own choice, a government above the law, a one-party state that allowed no public or impartial forum for the airing of grievances and no effective mechanisms for the peaceful transition of power. It is worth looking at the shape of this government during the early to mid-1980s in order to see how, in the absence of formal checks and balances, countervailing sources of power in China made it hard for any individual leader to implement particular reforms or projects in a timely fashion.

At its summit, China was run by a shifting group of between twenty-five and thirty-five people, of whom all but one were men.* This ruling group was not formally acknowledged as such, and its members could not necessarily be identified by office or titular rank. One had to be moderately familiar with Chinese politics to know who was in this circle—most members of which lived or worked in the walled and closely guarded Zhongnanhai compound to the west of Peking's Forbidden City.[7]

Within this ruling group were four categories of leader. One category consisted of four or five party elders so experienced and prestigious that even if they held no substantive office their advice was generally heeded.† Their contacts with other senior party and military comrades, deeply imbued with revolutionary memories, were essential to the implementation of most key decisions. The second category consisted of the figure identified as the pre-eminent leader, whose contacts and experiences were so encompassing and whose prestige within the party was so high that his views could never be ignored, even if they might not always be followed. From 1978 onward, with his victory over Hua Guofeng, this leader was indubitably Deng Xiaoping. Even if Deng never had Mao Zedong's prestige, and had himself twice been purged and publicly vilified (in 1966 and 1976), his revolutionary credentials were impeccable, from his work-study sojourn in France, through the Jiangxi Soviet, the Long March, and Yan'an. Furthermore his long years of service as secretary-general of the CCP, and subsequently as chairman of the Military Affairs Commission, had enabled him to accumulate a vast range of friends and colleagues who were permanently in his debt.

The third category of the ruling group comprised specialists who had a particular training essential to the ruling group's ability to make effective decisions; the most important areas of expertise were the economy, the energy sector, the military, and propaganda and internal security. These

---

*The lone woman to be in or on the edge of this inner circle was Qian Zhengying, appointed minister of water resources and electric power in 1982. Born in 1922, Qian had studied engineering in college and served with the New Fourth Army in World War II. She subsequently rose swiftly in the energy bureaucracy.

†In the early 1980s this group included Li Xiannian, Peng Zhen, Chen Yun, and Ye Jianying.

leaders might be members of the Standing Committee of the Politburo, the premier or one of the vice-premiers of the State Council, heads of the PLA or other armed services, or heads of important ministries or commissions. The same offices provided bases for most of those in the fourth category of the ruling group: the generalists, whose broad-based political experience, it was hoped, made them adept at long-range policy planning that could cut across special-interest lines. Prominent in this group by the mid-1980s were Zhao Ziyang, Hu Yaobang, and a younger man—Li Peng—who was the generalist in charge of coordinating energy policy.

The immense range of problems that these leaders had to address meant that they could not handle them on their own, as had been almost possible in the days of Yan'an or the civil war, and to some extent in the simpler economic and technical universe of the 1950s. Thus by the 1980s, the ruling group had come to rely on networks of research institutes and personal experts—the prestige of individual leaders was often mirrored in the extent and complexity of their support systems—and on four institutions that worked closely with the leaders and their staffs to evaluate and coordinate national policy: the State Planning Commission, the State Economic Commission, the State Science and Technology Commission, and the Ministry of Finance. These four institutions, which competed energetically to attract talented and technically trained graduates to their staffs, outranked the other government ministries and were expected to make projections and feasibility studies that were unaffected by the special interests of the other ministries. In 1973, as we've seen, the State Planning Commission drew up a 4.3 (later raised to 5.1) billion yuan blueprint for technology transfers to China; the commission's mandate covered all so-called "category 1" goods, such as petroleum, electricity, cement, and steel. The job of the State Economic Commission was to work out how to implement the Planning Commission's recommendations, and to do this the commissioners studied technological and managerial improvements, raw-material distribution and exports, and energy allocations.

Plans approved by the leaders and their staffs, and deemed feasible by the commissions and fundable by the Ministry of Finance, would then be passed on to the thirty-eight regular-line ministries in Peking for discussion and implementation. Each of these ministries had its special area of expertise, its own staff and budget. Since these ministries were considered equal in rank to the individual provinces, no ministry could simply impose its will on a given province. To carry out "national policy," a ministry always had to negotiate carefully with the province that was affected by, or expected to contribute to, that policy decision.

The provincial governments had their own structures and their own priorities, which did not necessarily mesh with the structures and priorities of Peking. Political life in a given province was directed by three officials: the first party secretary, the governor, and the ranking military officer from the PLA—the regional commander if the provincial capital was his headquarters, otherwise a senior officer from the military region in which the province was located. These three officials took responsibility for different aspects of the province's life. The party secretary oversaw ideological work, mass campaigns, rural policies, and personnel assignments; the governor supervised education and economic development; the PLA officer saw not only to military needs, but also to various economic endeavors (factories, mines, communications) when these were linked to specific PLA needs and strategic programs. He also oversaw the PLA cultural troupes and many aspects of internal security.[8] (This division was based on an administrative logic that had changed little over time; Qing provinces had similarly been ruled by a governor who oversaw the general management of his province, a financial commissioner, and the ranking military officer from the banner or Green Standard organization.) The balance of power among the three top officials would vary from province to province according to whether the party, government, or military leader was the predominant personality or had the best contacts with the Peking bureaucracy.

The three main provincial leaders each had his own expert staff and bureaucracy that oversaw the running of the province through descending levels of command from cities to counties and communes or townships. At the base of the structure every working Chinese man or woman was registered in the unit with which he or she worked (the *danwei*), whether that be a city ward, factory, rural production brigade, hospital, school, or office. The party leaders in each *danwei* had immense power over their *danwei* members, since their approval was needed in such areas as job assignments, educational opportunities, travel at home or abroad, or for permission to marry and to have a child. Students were registered by household and by school affiliation. Thus every Chinese man and woman was bound into a chain of command that reached from house, room, or apartment through the provincial hierarchy and up to the central leaders in Peking. (Such had been the goal, too, of the Qing emperors—and later the Guomindang—in their use of the *baojia* registration system, but those governments had never operated so effectively to ensure ideological cohesion and police control.)

Demographic factors, personal interests, long-term relationships, and local contacts all played an important part in this complex pull of forces between central and provincial power. Some provinces were more populous than others—by the mid-1980s the leaders were Sichuan with 100 million people, Henan and Shandong each with 75 million, and Jiangsu and Guangdong each with just over 60 million—and hence had greater claims to central government attention. Some had crucial reserves of raw materials that brought entire subbureaus of the three national commissions or the ministries into their provincial capitals: the Ministry of Petroleum Industry directly supervised its own oil wells in Heilongjiang, Liaoning, Shandong, and Henan, while in the south newly formed government corporations looked to the development of new oilfields off the coasts of Guangdong and Fujian. The Ministry of Coal had special subbureaucracies to oversee the mines in Shanxi, Jiangsu, and elsewhere. In turn, the provinces kept bureaucratic staffs in offices in the capital so they could lobby for their province's cause directly. Some members of the central ruling group in Peking had particularly fond memories of their native provinces and could be expected to edge favors their way. As one provincial official commented in the early 1980s:

> No unit or individual lets you have something strictly according to regulations. Rather, you must have *guanxi* or you come up with nothing. This is true everywhere but especially in the South. The *guanxi* does not refer to old school ties and so on. Rather, the *guanxi* is based on interest—strictly a you scratch my back and I scratch yours situation. The exchange of goods and favors seals the deal. This situation is pervasive because that is the way things are done at higher levels, and until they do things differently, nobody else will change.[9]

What these political arrangements meant in practice can be seen through three examples of the 1980s, in coal-mining, dam-building, and oil production each one of which was important to the potential long-term growth both of the Chinese economy and of the region concerned. In Shanxi province, where Deng Xiaoping had personally expressed an interest in using foreign technology to develop huge open-pit mines, the central government could not simply enforce its will over coal production as a whole. Coal mines in the province fell into three quite different administrative categories, each subdivided into further classifications, and all with their own subbureaucracies, specialized staffs, supervisors, and workers. Seven large mines were run by the Ministry of Coal through a subsidiary office called the Shanxi Coal Management District; 209 smaller mines were administered by a separate Shanxi Local Coal Management Bureau; and these mines were organized into 5 subgroups distinguished by their type of management. One subgroup was jointly managed by municipal or county governments, but shipped all its coal out of the province. One subgroup was locally managed and kept most of its production for use in Shanxi. A third subgroup was jointly managed by the relevant commune bureaucracies and by the Shanxi

Number Two Light Industry Department. A fourth group was co-managed by the Provincial Labor Reform Bureau; the miners in this group were convict laborers undergoing "reform." The fifth subgroup was coadministered by the PLA, and all its outlay went to military needs. A further 3,000 small mines were run by local townships, their production coordinated by yet another agency, the Shanxi Township Enterprise Management Bureau.

Cutting across all these divisions were the various national, provincial, and municipal bureaus that supervised transportation of the coal and determined its allocation, so crucial to China's heavy industrial and electrical-power needs as well as to household cooking and heating. Such details as the production and distribution of railway cars to haul the coal became of great significance in this system. On many occasions, smaller mines might "hijack" rail cars for a week or two to move their own coal to local or national markets, only later returning them to the larger mines that technically owned the rail cars. A central decision to reallocate coal or open a major new mine was thus not a simple act, and although Deng Xiaoping finally succeeded in getting the mine he wanted operational, it took years of bargaining and trade-offs.[10]

These potential tensions between the center and the provinces, and within the hierarchy of each province, could have a paralyzing effect on state planning. Often the planning process itself had to run through a maze of channels before reaching the localities. One of the greatest projects ever envisioned in China, the Three Gorges Dam on the upper Yangzi River above Yichang, though first discussed in the mid-1950s was still under process of evaluation all through the decade of the 1980s (and construction only at last began in 1995). The dam was designed to end the Yangzi flooding that had plagued China for millennia—the most recent catastrophic flood had been in 1870, with serious floods occurring in 1931, 1935, 1949, and 1954—and to increase China's hydroelectric power by an annual 64.9 billion kwh. But the dam was inevitably controversial for its ecological and scenic impact, and because of the potential for disaster for cities lower down the river, should the dam be breached.

By the 1980s, as thirty years of inconclusive debate continued concerning the feasibility of the dam, its exact location and height, and the desired depth of the water level above the dam, the following actors were involved: the Yangzi Valley Planning Office (which alone had a staff of 12,000 as of 1985); numerous ministries (those of Finance, Water Resources and Electric Power, Electronics, Communications, and Machine Building being particularly involved); members of the central ruling group, their staffs, and the key commissions in Peking; the governments of all the affected Yangzi provinces from Sichuan to Jiangsu, along with the independent municipality of Shanghai; Chongqing city; all the major towns between the potential dam sites and Chongqing that might either be flooded or chosen as sites for the relocation of people displaced from other areas; 58 units and factories that specialized in relevant research, design, and construction; 11 research institutes and universities; and numerous consultants and entrepreneurs from the United States, Japan, and other countries.[11]

Only slightly less complicated were the bureaucratic structures responsible for developing China's offshore oil resources in the southeast, involving as they did the same central commissions, a range of key ministries (especially the Ministry of Foreign Relations and Trade), the Bank of China, and the China National Offshore Oil Corporation (founded in 1982 as an offshoot of the Ministry of Petroleum Industry). This corporation spawned its own host of subsidiary organizations up and down the east coast to coordinate its work with foreign firms and with scores of Chinese local municipalities ranging from Canton to small, strategically placed harbors or communications hubs. Virtually anyone at any point in these intermeshing networks could stall or block plans considered crucial by someone else. For Chinese officials, frustration levels ran high, as did the possibilities for enormous profits and graft.

The rulers of the Qing dynasty had struggled for two centuries of their rule to streamline bureaucratic procedures, marshal and supervise errant bureaucrats, subordinate the provinces to the center, and defuse the social bitterness caused by corrupt behavior. Under the Guomindang, the battle was even harder as the bureaucracy grew and the central government weakened, contributing to the dishonesty, the malaise, and the inefficiencies. The PRC leadership, having tried to dissociate itself completely from such past abuses, now found that even the most advanced levels of technological planning were subject to the same tenacious tugs of localism and human frailty.

THE PROBLEMS OF PROSPERITY, 1983–1984

It was Deng Xiaoping, the pre-eminent leader of this sprawling network of competing interests, who had to try and maintain the forward momentum of the Four Modernizations in the face of inevitable setbacks and criticisms. From 1977 to early 1982, Deng had concentrated his energies on making sure that China did not fall under the sway of a residual Maoism, and that it prepared itself to take part in the complex arenas of international business, diplomacy, and technology. In 1983 and 1984 his task was more delicate, premised in part on the successes of the previous five years. For now he had to try to steer a mediating position between those who favored accelerated reform for China and those who advocated a more cautious pattern of change that would maintain the central authority of the party and minimize the corrosion of Chinese Marxist values by Western influence. Since the exponents of both views were strongly represented at the highest levels of the party hierarchy, the result was a series of swerves, retreats, and sudden jumps in policy rather than any simple linear progression toward a "modernized" China.

The courses taken by these policies can perhaps best be charted by following several groups of economic and social indicators. Three of these were broad in nature and drew on a richly patterned historical background: the eclipse of the old revolutionary models, the acceptance of economic growth itself as a fundamental goal, and the accompanying shifts in culture and the arts, which culminated in the "antispiritual-pollution campaign." The other four were more precisely tied to current issues, and consisted of the paired developments of the responsibility system in agriculture and the incentive system in industry, the ratification of these changes in "Document Number 1" of January 1984, the extension of the special-economic-zone concept, and, finally, the emergence of disturbing new patterns of corruption, which most glaringly highlighted the problems of prosperity.

By 1982 the idea that it might be permissible to criticize Mao Zedong— first broached at the time of the Third Plenum—had become generally accepted in China. The consensus was that he had been a fine leader during the formative years of the revolution, but that from the Great Leap onward his policies had been erratic and at times destructive. The huge stockpiles of his works now went largely unread, languishing in the corners of bookstores, while slowly around the country his portrait came down from walls and public places. Many of the concrete statues of his coat-draped form, one arm raised in salute, that had dominated urban landscapes and public squares were removed. The spirit of Dazhai, publicly denigrated in 1980 by a *People's Daily* article that described new economic projects in the brigade as "folly," was laid to rest when the revolutionary leader of the Dazhai brigade, Chen Yonggui—who in 1966 had stood at Mao's side, in 1969 been elected to the Central Committee, and in 1973 been named to the Politburo—lost the last of his posts and his Politburo seat in 1981. And the PLA's revolutionary model-hero, the selfless Lei Feng, after being briefly and unconvincingly resurrected by the army in the early 1980s, also passed once more from the scene. His message of uncompromising self-reliance did not mesh easily with the current goals of acquiring the latest high technology from the West.

With these once potent symbols of revolutionary dedication now deprived

A mass rally in the early stages of the Cultural Revolution, Heilongjiang (photograph by Li Zhensheng)

Labor in the countryside, Hebei, 1965 (photograph by Marc Riboud)

Wuhan University students cultivating the land, 1965 (photograph by Marc Riboud)

At a Red Guard rally in Harbin, Heilongjiang province, September 1966, party and state officials suffered public humiliation The provincial party secretary is fitted with a dunce's cap (top). The longtime provincial governor, identified by the sign around his neck as "a member of the Black Gang," that is, the enemy of the Cultural Revolution, has his hair shorn for wearing it in a style similar to Mao's (bottom).

A labor camp in the frozen wastes of Heilongjiang province during the Cultural Revolution (photograph by Shi Zhimin)

In their drive against the "four olds"—old customs, habits, culture, and thinking—Red Guards caused vast destruction to buildings, art objects, and temples such as this one, August 1966

Mao (left), Lin Biao (center), and Jiang Qing (right) with cast members at the premier of the revolutionary opera "The Red Lantern," July 1968

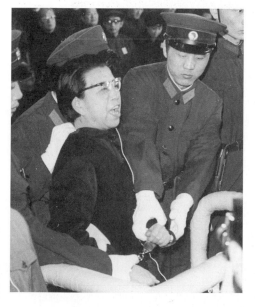

Jiang Qing (left) and other members of the Gang of Four were arrested in October 1976 and convicted in 1981 of crimes committed during the Cultural Revolution. Jiang Qing, defiant throughout, was imprisoned and held under house arrest until 1993, when it was announced that she had committed suicide.

Crowds gathered in Tiananmen Square on April 5, 1976, to mourn the death of Premier Zhou Enlai

Deng Xiaoping emerged as China's paramount leader in 1978 Here, at age eighty, he reviews an honor guard on the thirty-fifth anniversary of the founding of the People's Republic, 1984.

A young Peking couple delighted at having acquired one of the "eight bigs" : television, refrigerator, stereo, camera, motorcycle, furniture set, washing machine, and electric fan

Dazibao ("big character" posters) at Democracy Wall, 1979

The Goddess of Democracy and Freedom, modeled after the Statue of Liberty, erected in Tiananmen Square during the spring 1989 protests by students of the Central Academy of Fine Arts

The massacre, Peking, June 3–4 More than 700 protesters were killed as tens of thousands of well-armed PLA troops crushed the demonstration in the area of Tiananmen Square and other sections of Peking.

An unarmed Chinese civilian halts a tank convoy heading for Tiananmen Square, June 5, 1989 After speaking to the crew of the lead tank, he was pulled away to safety. His fate is unknown.

of their power, economic growth itself became the prime focus of attention, with only its speed and intensity subject to debate. Following the first boom of economic optimism in 1979 and the huge trade deficit that resulted in 1980, the years 1981 and 1982 marked a period of more cautious development, the course favored by the party elder Chen Yun. Investments were cut back, many costly foreign contracts canceled, the domestic budget trimmed, and the trade deficit overcome by vigorous export policies. The PRC was able to announce a trade surplus of $6.2 billion in 1982, and $5.2 billion in 1983.

In culture and the arts, furthermore, there was a party backlash against the burst of innovation and excitement that had been sparked in part by Western movies, exhibitions of Western abstract painting, and performances of Western plays, and in part by the kind of critical self-exploration that had appeared in the days of Democracy Wall. The most notorious case was that of the scriptwriter Bai Hua, whose brilliant screenplay for *Bitter Love (Kulian)* caused the film to be suppressed in 1980, despite its popularity, because of its "negative" message. In this film, Bai Hua presented the fictional story of Ling Chenguang, a young Chinese revolutionary activist and artist, courageous and radical during World War II, who in 1946 leaves China for the United States to flee Guomindang repression. Becoming a fashionable painter in San Francisco, Ling nevertheless chooses to return to the PRC in 1950, bringing his wife (originally raised in China, but of the boat-dwelling minority peoples) and their newborn daughter with him to serve the revolution. Happy and prosperous in the early years of the PRC, Ling and his family are brutalized in the Cultural Revolution because of his earlier Western contacts. Unable to bear his treatment any longer, Ling runs away one winter from his labor camp and dies from exhaustion fleeing those he thinks are his pursuers. In fact, they are not pursuers but cadres charged with telling him that after all his sufferings he has finally been exonerated by the state. At the film's end, as the camera pans upward from Ling's dead body lying sprawled in the snow, the audience can see that his crumpled corpse forms a black question mark against the whiteness.

Almost immediately the film drew sharp criticism, especially in the PLA political journals, and after an initial silence both Deng Xiaoping and Hu Yaobang joined in the negative chorus. Their criticism gradually expanded to include written works such as a series of bleak poems, which appeared at the same time, about the victimization of the Chinese people at the hands of CCP cadres and PLA generals. By 1982 the configurations of a new campaign were clear, and these various complaints were drawn together by the CCP into a blanket condemnation of what was called "spiritual pollution," a term designed to suggest the extent of the damage wrought by decadent influences from the West. Just as Bai Hua's film had been a kind of echo, three centuries later, of the analysis of the loyalty and duty to self, to loved ones, and to the state that had lain at the heart of Kong Shangren's *Peach Blossom Fan,* so was the antispiritual-pollution campaign an echo of the conservative self-strengtheners' attempts in the late Qing to maintain a pure Chinese-Confucian "essence" even as they espoused elements of Westernization for "practical purposes."

The antispiritual-pollution campaign dismayed intellectuals, both inside China and abroad, because it reinforced the view that the CCP did not intend to relax its control over the lives of its citizens in any significant way. Coming at a time when thousands of Westerners were traveling to China and in many cases living there for long periods to conduct business, work in joint ventures, do research, or teach, the campaign dampened an enthusiasm for China that had been approaching levels not seen since the French philosophers had sung Confucius's praises in the eighteenth century. But as if to emphasize yet again the paradoxes at the center of the Chinese experience, overlapping with the antispiritual-pollution campaign began a new phase of reform that was, finally, to implement fully the range of economic ideas sketched out at the Third Plenum of 1978, to shake up the whole Chinese economy, and to dismantle the collective system that had dominated economic life for almost thirty years.

A New Year's Day editorial published in *People's Daily* on January 1, 1983, set the tone with the promise that this would prove a significant year in China's modernization program. The national priorities would be completing "structural reforms ... to improve Party work style" at the provincial, prefectural, and city levels, and maintaining economic development at a level equal to 1981. While Premier Zhao Ziyang called for deeper economic change, other party theorists pushed for the promotion of younger cadres to positions of power, urging that cadres with college education or professional training be rapidly given leading provincial positions in both the CCP and the government. Sichuan again proved the pacesetter, as it had been for economic reform; provincial leaders claimed to have slashed the number of administrative personnel, dropped the average age for incumbent officials from 60.6 to 52.5, and raised the college-educated proportion of the government from 16.8 percent to 32.2 percent. The municipalities were made the administrative seats of prefectures and counties in a new system that completely undercut the role of the communes. Each municipality *(shi)* was now declared to be the "political, economic, financial, scientific, cultural, educational and medical center of its neighboring areas," its most important feature being its role in exercising economic leadership. Administrative townships *(xiang)* took the place of communes, and villages *(cun)* began to supplant production brigades at the subcommune (now subtownship) level. There were reports that these initiatives were also being followed in Liaoning, Jiangsu, and Guangdong.

Much attention was given to local successes in attaining the Third Plenum goals of "speeding up" and "modernizing" farm work through the new rural contract system, or the "agricultural production responsibility system" as it was officially titled. By 1983 at least three variants had emerged. One was a labor-contract system under which small groups of families, individual households, or even individual laborers contracted with their local village to do specific farm work (sowing, transplanting, harvesting, etc.) to fixed levels of performance in terms of quantity, quality, and cost. Their payoff was a higher work-point allocation—and hence more cash or food—if they were successful, a lower allocation if they failed in some way. Second, there was the output-contract system in which households undertook to produce a given amount of crop on a specified area; they could keep the surplus if they achieved one but had to make up the shortfall if they failed. Third, in the net-output delivery system, again undertaken by the household, a contract required the family to meet state quotas and provide a surplus for the collective in return for granting the contractors complete freedom over production methods and what amounted to ownership over the farm implements and draft animals made available to them.[12]

"Document Number 1," so-called because it was the first document issued by the Central Committee in 1984, gave a clear summary of the new economic policies and their rationale:

> Extending the period for which land is contracted will encourage peasants to increase investment, conserve the natural fertility of their land and practise intensive farming. In general, the period for which land is contracted should be more than 15 years. Where production is of a developmental nature or takes longer to be realized—for example fruit growing, forestry or the reclamation of barren hillsides and wasteland—the period should be even longer. However, before extending the contract period, any popular demands for land readjustment should be fully discussed and a unified decision on such action [be] taken by the collective in accordance with the principle of "small readjustments in the interests of broad stability."

The crucial point here was that by stipulating a contract period of fifteen years or more, the government came closer than ever to restoring private control over land use and production. As a palliative to this extreme interpretation, Document Number 1 emphasized the role of the collectivity, and specifically stated, a few lines further on, that "private plots and land under contract may not be bought and sold," nor could they be leased to third parties, used as building sites, or put to nonagricultural uses. But the overall message was still clear.

Equally important was Document Number 1's statement about rural capital:

> Capital belonging to peasants and the collective should be allowed to flow freely, or in an organized manner, without any geographical restriction. Peasants should be encouraged to invest and become shareholders in all manner of enterprises; and on the principle of voluntary participation and mutual benefit, both peasants and collective should be encouraged to pool funds and set up various joint enterprises. In particular, support should be given to promoting ventures of a developmental nature. The legal rights and interests of investors must be protected by the state.

Although Document Number 1 then reiterated certain safeguards against the exploitation of labor hired by the contractors to help them meet their obligations, it was clear that the state would now accept considerable wage differentials between such laborers and their "managers." And the homage paid to these new rural entrepreneurs showed that the Central Committee was not worried about unfortunate parallels being drawn with an earlier world of rich peasants and their exploited landless laborers, in the name of whom many must still have remembered that the revolution had been fought in the countryside:

> The specialized households, which have emerged in the countryside in the wake of the output-released contract responsibility systems, are something new in our rural development. They have taken a lead in making themselves rich through hard work, developing commodity production and improving production techniques. We should cherish and treasure them and give them our active support. The most effective way of extending such support is to give them the necessary social services and meet their demands in the areas of information, supply and marketing and technical progress.[13]

In all these areas of rural economic growth, as later analysts noted, the government was taking credit for processes that had been initially implemented by the most entrepreneurially minded farmers themselves.

In industry, there were also important reforms. Enterprises were now to pay the state a 55 percent tax on total annual revenues, but were allowed to keep half the profits that remained after deducting production costs, with the other half going to the state; previously they had passed on all profits to the state. This incentive system, it was hoped, would bolster industrial production as much as the rural incentive system had inspired peasant families. Tentative steps were taken to establish a contract system in some industries, and there was talk of an expanding management-responsibility system.

A number of key areas were designated as experimentation centers in which factory directors and managers *alone* would take responsibility for the productivity and administration of their plants. This reform effectively cut against the idea of collective leadership under party supervision that had been the basis of industrial organization in the PRC since the mid-1950s. Because the experimentation centers contained most of the bases for heavy industrial production in China's heartland—including Dalian and Shen-yang, Peking, Tianjin, and Shanghai—it was clear that these reforms were going to become standard. Other directives from the State Council gave managers some power to appoint factory heads, punish incompetent workers by dismissal (this had been virtually impossible under the earlier PRC system of the "iron rice bowl" for factory workers), and reward outstanding work-ers with promotions or bonuses. These bonuses would, however, be subject to taxation.

Two well-publicized cases showed how local commercial initiatives might flourish. In one, a floundering Anhui pharmaceutical company was taken over by a thirty-four-year-old female engineer and eight other employees; by branching into new products and introducing more efficient manufac-turing methods, they made a profit of 200,000 yuan their first year. In another, the newly appointed director of a bankrupt shirtmaking factory in Zhejiang saved the business and made it the most prosperous in the province through three techniques: introducing material incentives that specifically linked wages to output; building morale by composing a company song that all workers learned and sang together; and firing inept employees.

In another key decision of the Central Committee in 1984, the concept of special economic zones was extended to fourteen more coastal cities and to Hainan Island, which was to remain a part of Guangdong province but to be boosted as a development and tourist center. These cities would set up special high-technology development areas and be permitted to offer tax exemptions and other benefits to foreign investors. In addition, three "devel-opment triangles" were targeted for rapid economic growth: the Pearl River delta in Guangdong, the Min River delta in Fujian, and the Yangzi River delta. These were designated "trade and investment promotion zones," and in language that once again echoed the earlier self-strengtheners, they were declared to be "filters" that would "digest" modern science and technology "so as to discard the dross and select the essential."[14]

Such statements were not just made in an economic vacuum, but reflected a number of changes going on in related areas. Thus direct foreign investment in China in 1983 was estimated at $910 million, and the PRC had taken out a further $1.05 billion in international loans. The impressive total of 9,477,000 foreign visitors had come to China since 1979 (on tours, for trade, or for academic and other exchanges). Also, 11,000 Chinese students were studying at government expense in 54 foreign countries, and an additional 7,000 were attending schools overseas at their own expense. The Shenzhen economic zone especially was thriving; heads of enterprises there had made 2,500 agreements of various kinds with foreign firms, bringing an estimated investment of $1.8 million. Customs duties on Hong Kong/Shenzhen trade were abolished. (Duties with Taiwan had already been abolished on the grounds that "Taiwan was part of China"; but since there was no direct legal trade between the two states this point remained moot.)

The emerging patterns of corruption, to which the government began to react with alarm, were seen by some leftist critics as an inevitable concomitant to such rapid and often unmonitored changes. When Liu Binyan in 1979 had electrified his readers by discussing the crooked ways of Wang Shouxin, he was presenting the scandal as emblematic of the bad old days of Gang of Four turbulence and the Cultural Revolution's laxity. But in the 1980s, with Wang Shouxin dead from a firing squad's bullets and the Gang of Four all behind bars, the crimes continued. No less than 45,000 embezzlement and other economic crimes were reported in 1983 and 1984. Some were startlingly new.

A Canton factory deputy director, for instance, accepted a U.S. $42,000 bribe from a Hong Kong businessman, who then cheated the PRC out of $2.97 million. (The deputy director of the factory was sentenced to death, the businessman given life imprisonment.) Even worse was the Hainan Island case, which came to light in early 1985. A group of officials—some stationed on Hainan Island, others in China's inland provinces—had conspired to exploit the "enterprise zone" aspect of China's economic growth. Using money raised as development loans from Peking banks, the Hainan officials bought overseas products and then sold them to buyers all over China. The goods the officials had imported for illegal resale between January 1984 and March 1985 included 89,000 motor vehicles, 2.9 million television sets, 252,000 video recorders, and 122,000 motorcycles; their fraudulent schemes involved sums in excess of $1.5 billion.

According to the facts discovered by the hundred-person investigation team belatedly commissioned by Peking, the corrupt Hainan officials found willing purchasers in twenty-seven out of China's twenty-nine provinces and metropolitan regions. At least $700 million of the money was unrecoverable, and hundreds of Japanese trucks and cars rusted in Hainan's sea air as the probe continued. Because it was hard to pinpoint the legal parameters of such trading, and perhaps also in order to downplay the incident and avoid discrediting the whole enterprise-zone structure of the Four Modernizations movement, the principal offenders were treated far more leniently than the principal figures in the Canton case. They were demoted for "serious mistakes" and for having ignored government warnings that they must not resell their imported goods. (Many of the confiscated cars that remained in good condition were subsequently shipped to Peking and sold by other officials.)

Some saw dangerous signs here, as the Chinese celebrated the centennial of Marx's death with speeches and meetings, but the secretary-general of the CCP, Hu Yaobang, was unruffled. As he succinctly put it in a briefing to Communist cadres during an inspection tour of Henan and Hubei, "Do not fear prosperity."[15]

REBUILDING THE LAW

The various shifts in the implementation of reform in China did not end with the bold decisions of 1984. The reforms led to such overheating of the economy, coupled with problems of unemployment, inflation, and renewed trade deficits, that a second period of retrenchment (matching that of 1981–1983) was demanded by the more cautious faction among the Chinese leaders in 1985. This lull was brief, however, and in 1986 those seeking speedy change, presumably led by Zhao Ziyang and Hu Yaobang, with Deng Xiaoping's encouragement, returned to the attack: price controls were dropped from a range of manufactured goods, bold experimentation with labor-incentive systems was again encouraged, more rural production came into the hands of family contracting units, the need to allow open markets for the raw materials of production became a subject for debate and experiment, and some state or collective enterprises were leased to individual entrepreneurs or groups of workers. In some cases these enterprises raised funds by floating stock issues and forming their own boards of directors, and in Shanghai a small stock exchange was established.

But whether the pace of change was speeded up or slowed down, one fact was inescapable: the Chinese government had now, of its own choice, entered a world where law, in all its manifold complexities, would have to be studied, understood, and practiced. There were so many facets to this problem that it defied simple solution. But by looking briefly at four areas—the training of lawyers, the nature of tax law, the enforcement of family law, and the study of international law—we can get a general sense of what this major adjustment to living in the world entailed.

As an essential preliminary step in developing and implementing a legal code, China had to train its own lawyers. This offered special challenges to the PRC rulers, since the steady growth of legal expertise in the later years of Guomindang rule had effectively ceased after the Communist victory of 1949, when all private practice of law was banned and the application of legal expertise limited to those in certain government ministries and within the state-controlled judiciary. At the time of the Hundred Flowers movement there were some 800 "legal adviser's offices" served by 2,500 full-time and 300 part-time lawyers. Most of these skilled practitioners were dismissed during the antirightist campaign of 1957, and in 1959 the Ministry of Justice was abolished altogether, along with any forums for organizing lawyers as a group. Though some law schools remained open, they had few students and concentrated on political rather than professional legal training. In serious criminal cases the "law," such as it was, was handled by a system of state courts and state prosecutors. In national-security matters the Ministry of Public Security was in control, and for party members who transgressed there was a separate system of review and punishment meted out by the provincial party committee structure. Most of what might be called civil cases were handled at the local city-ward or rural-brigade level by mediators. Early in the Cultural Revolution the few remaining law schools were closed, their libraries dispersed or destroyed and their faculty sent to the countryside.

This situation lasted just over ten years, until 1979, when the government began to reassemble the rudiments of a legal system. Law schools were reopened, rusticated legal personnel were rehabilitated, the Ministry of Justice was re-established, and the four-tiered system of state courts was revamped, though the regulations stipulating that "counterrevolutionaries and antisocialist reactionaries" could be sent to labor camps without public trial showed the continuing party control of this system. "Provisional regulations on lawyers" were adopted in 1980, and by 1982 there were 5,500 full-time lawyers once again working in China, and 1,300 part-time lawyers.

To bring more personnel into the legal profession, an ingenious linkage was made with the PLA, which the government was currently trying to cut back in size. The Ministry of Justice announced in 1982 that no less than 57,000 "outstanding army officers" were being transferred to the civilian sector and given legal training, prior to being assigned to the court system or Public Security Departments. And in emulation of the "bare-foot" doctors charged with extending the range of the medical profession, 200,000 "judicial workers" with some government experience were assigned to the legal system.

By 1982, twenty universities and institutes were offering some form of four-year undergraduate legal training, and 2,000 students were enrolled. To become lawyers, these favored students had to complete their course work, prove that they "cherished the PRC and supported the socialist system," serve at least a two-year apprenticeship in some kind of judicial work or legal research, and pass a bar examination. One hundred other colleges and the Ministry of Justice itself offered some legal training by correspondence or on a part-time basis.

A sample of the examination questions used by the Ministry of Justice to determine which applicants should be accepted for legal training shows that students still had to be alert to the nuances of the current political line. The general questions posed in 1979 included the following:

> What are the four basic principles we must adhere to in order to achieve the four modernizations?
> What is the correct method for handling the two different kinds of contradictions?
> Use the theory of the dialectical relationship between democracy and centralism to analyze and criticize the fallacy of ultra-democracy.
> What is the basic difference between materialist dialectics and metaphysics? Criticize the "gang of four" for spreading the fallacy of metaphysics.

The questions grouped in the section on history show that the aspiring law students also had to know how to interpret Qing, republican, and World War II history:

> On the basis of the changes in political and economic conditions before and after the Opium War, analyze how our country began to sink into the condition of a semi-colonial, semi-feudal society.
> Pick out and describe Comrade Zhou Enlai's important revolutionary activities during each period of our country's democratic revolution.
> Give three examples of sudden attacks launched by the imperialist countries during the Second World War, and explain the historical lessons they convey.[16]

Despite the politicization of the entrance exams, once admitted to law programs the students gained a good general grounding. Most of their teachers were survivors from a much older generation, many of them trained in Europe, Japan, the United States, or the Soviet Union, and they offered in each school a core curriculum of Chinese constitutional law, legal theory and jurisprudence, and civil and criminal law. Some schools had additional specialities: Peking University and the East China Institute in Shanghai offered courses in international law and economic law. In Shanghai students were also required to take an environmental-law course, and in Nanjing marriage law was the required option.

Overlapping with the development of the law schools came the drafting of the rules of Civil Procedure for the PRC, a process that began in 1979 and ended only in 1986 after numerous discussions, changes, and study-group sessions by China's jurists and political figures. Revisions of the procedures were accompanied by the enactment of a host of new civil-law statutes and the thorough revision of the Marriage Law (1980), Economic Contract Law (1981), Trademark Law (1982), Patent Law (1984), and Inheritance Law (1985). The Code of Civil Procedure dealt with such matters as the capacities and responsibilities of citizens (as compared to those of minors and the mentally impaired), legal partnerships, the definition of "Enterprises" as "Legal Persons" with rights to equal treatment under the laws, the obligations under the law of Sino-foreign joint ventures and of "wholly-foreign-owned enterprises," which were to be completely subject to Chinese law unless formally exempted by treaty. Individuals working land on contract from their collectives were specifically promised protection of the law, as long as the land they had contracted for was not "bought and sold, leased, mortgaged, or by other means illegally transferred." The elderly, mothers, children, and the handicapped were promised protection of the law, and freedom of marriage was guaranteed; "buying, selling or arranging marriages" were all forbidden.[17]

Special areas of the law rapidly assumed importance and reinforced the realization of the Chinese that the new reforms were no simple matter. One was tax law, now crucial since bonuses and certain types of profits made under the reform guidelines were to be taxed, as would the profits on Sino-foreign joint ventures and on wholly foreign-owned enterprises. The PRC's first income-tax laws, enacted in 1980, excluded most Chinese individuals by allowing a deduction of 800 yuan a month when monthly incomes rarely reached above 50 yuan for city workers and around 15 yuan in the countryside. These early tax laws were directed largely at foreigners resident in China and perhaps specifically Americans, since the details of the code closely followed current Internal Revenue Service stipulations. Chinese citizens mainly paid commercial and agricultural taxes, and occasionally salt taxes, customs duties, vehicle taxes, and urban-real-estate taxes. But as certain Chinese began to make large incomes from their new enterprises, the government instituted stricter "income regulation taxes" in an attempt to syphon off the excess.

Another area of emerging complexity was that of marriage and inheritance law. The supportive words about marriage rights for women in the Code of Civil Procedure were echoes of those used in the Marriage Law of

1980, but in fact they were frequently violated. Sale of women and girls into marriage, forcible remarriage of widows, purchase of brides, or parental negotiation of children's marriages in exchange for various forms of "bride price" remained common in China. Cases publicized in the early 1980s showed the grim results when relatives interfered with their children's love matches for financial reasons. Legal disputes frequently arose over broken marriage contracts, and the amounts concerned were large considering the incomes then available. "Betrothal gifts" could run from 1,000 up to 5,000 yuan, and in one case it was found that the bride's family had demanded from the groom a 125 yuan watch, 19 *jin* (a *jin* being 1.3 pounds) of husked rice, 19 ducks, and 109 *jin each* of pork, eggs, and oranges, plus cash to the tune of 1,900 yuan. (The prevalence of the auspicious number 9 here seems to hark back to earlier geomantic ideas of good fortune as well as to the merely mercenary.) These changes in bridal-gift patterns showed clearly how the old reciprocal dowry structure of the once parentally dominated joint family had been replaced by the financial imperatives of the conjugal family unit.[18]

Effective enforcement of the 1980 Marriage Law was crucial, since in many cases husbands could be forced to stop beating, and even torturing, their spouses only when brought to court. (Some Chinese decisions would still have been considered unusual in most Western courts, as in the case of a Jiangsu judge who convicted a husband for marital rape.) With the law's reassertion of the right of women to obtain divorce (the 1950 law had also provided for this), the incidence of divorce rose to about 5.5 percent of all marriages for 1983 (in 1979 it had been 3.0 percent); over 70 percent of the divorce petitioners in 1983 were women. The 1980 Marriage Law also allowed divorced women a greater chance to sue for the joint property once shared in marriage. (Rights of individuals to property owned before marriage remained, however, a vexing legal question.) Divorcing couples who together had contracted out for farmland or orchards under the new economic system had to subdivide them in some way that would not affect their financial obligations to the state.

As a general rule, the local prosperity brought about by the economic reforms, and the dismantling of the communes, enormously increased the stakes over property in divorce cases. Similarly, in families that adhered to the one-child policy, the fights over child custody in divorce cases became extraordinarily bitter. As they grew in numbers and intensity, divorce cases were handled in a variety of ways that included formal court appearances, the use of legal advisers or mediators, or simply the application of pressure by family or work-unit. To handle the increasing caseload, the Chinese government pledged to train more lawyers, and when the First National

Congress of Lawyers assembled in July 1986, it claimed to speak for 20,000 legal professionals. The state goal was to train 50,000 lawyers by 1990.

One other area of Chinese jurisprudence, international law, underwent significant changes in the 1980s. Despite their entry into the United Nations in 1971 and the Shanghai communiqué of 1972, it was only in 1978 that the Chinese launched a concerted attempt to develop an international legal expertise that would enable them to take proper advantage of the new opportunities and challenges facing them. (So had the Zongli Yamen under Prince Gong moved in the early 1860s to publish and distribute W. A. P. Martin's translations of international law works so that the Qing could better contend with the foreigners.)

This push came at the same December 1978 Third Plenum of the Eleventh Central Committee in which so many other shifts in social, economic, and cultural policy were debated. In March 1979 a follow-up planning conference on the study of law, held in Peking, listed international law as one of China's priority areas, and the following September Peking University admitted thirty students as undergraduate majors in international law—the first such comprehensive program in China's history. Scholarly works proliferated swiftly. Between 1965 and 1978 there were no articles on international law published in China. In 1979 there were 13; in 1982, 73; and in 1984, 110.[19] A definitive textbook of international law, with contributions from twenty senior Chinese jurists, was published in 1981, and gave direction to the development of the field as a whole. Peking officials also invited numerous foreign legal experts to visit China and help them analyze international procedures, as in the case of the 1986 "Law of the PRC on Enterprise Bankruptcy."

China's international lawyers generally stayed away from theory and followed instead Deng Xiaoping's challenge to "seek truth from facts." There was now little attempt to insist on polemical Marxist premises of international relations and law. The Chinese government realized that to achieve the Four Modernizations they would have to accept international economic practice and gain membership in world economic organizations. Within two years of the 1978 Third Plenum, the PRC entered the International Monetary Fund (IMF) and the World Bank, fulfilling the difficult financial and technical requirements; Taiwan was forced to withdraw from the same organizations. The PRC moved aggressively to take up its new rights, bargaining its share of IMF allocations up from Taiwan's seventeenth place to eighth and gaining access to U.S. $1.56 billion. By 1983 the allocation for China had risen to U.S. $2.63 billion. China also negotiated vigorously with the World Bank, receiving loans of $200 million in 1981 for a Universities Development Project intended to raise scientific standards and enrollments in twenty-six major universities. A 1982 World Bank loan of a further $60 million was earmarked for irrigation and drainage facilities in the North China Plain. There followed other loans and grants for expansion of the Daqing oilfield, land reclamation in Heilongjiang, and the development of a television university.

In the international arena as a whole, perhaps the most significant symbol of China's break with Maoist ideological principles was the election of a Chinese delegate, Ni Zhengyu, to the International Court of Justice at The Hague, and his acceptance of the honor. Ni, a pre–World War II graduate of Stanford University Law School, was seventy-five at the time of his election; his acceptance of the honor—and the dedicated work he performed on the court—signaled China's return to the international world order. In the United Nations General Assembly, China tended to vote with the Soviet Union and a majority of the Third World countries, despite Peking's ongoing rhetoric of hostility toward Moscow.

Perhaps no example of China's new international status was more striking than the accord it reached with Great Britain over Hong Kong. During 1983 and 1984 the Chinese government negotiated firmly and tenaciously to fix the future status of the British colony, that "barren and uninhabited rock" the seizure of which in 1840 had been reluctantly ratified by the Qing two years later in the Treaty of Nanjing. In 1898 the British had bolstered the colony's strength by "leasing" for ninety-nine years an area of the Chinese mainland adjacent to Hong Kong island known as the New Territories. When early in the 1980s the British raised questions about the future status of the colony, the PRC government made it clear that they would not renew the lease on the New Territories in 1997. The British, knowing Hong Kong was not defensible militarily—it even drew almost all its drinking water from the PRC—decided they had little choice but to comply with the Chinese demand that they also cede back Hong Kong island by the same date.

The freewheeling, speculative economy of Hong Kong made it difficult to see exactly how it would fit into the PRC's evolving system, but both the British and the Chinese stalled on that question and the Hong Kong Chinese, who had only minimal electoral representation in the colony's government, were barely consulted. The agreement, signed by the British and Chinese in Peking on September 26, 1984, stipulated that sovereignty over Hong Kong would revert to China on July 1, 1997, but that for fifty years after that date the former colony would become a "special administrative region" with a capitalist economy under the formula "one country, two systems." Peking would control foreign and defense policy, but the island would be largely autonomous economically, continuing as a free port and world financial center. Its residents would not pay taxes to the PRC, and

English would remain the official language during that fifty-year period.

Two clauses in the agreement attempted to reassure Hong Kong's residents that their rights would be protected. Clause 3 stated firmly that "the laws currently in force in Hong Kong will remain basically unchanged," and clause 5 was even more sweeping:

> The current social and economic systems in Hong Kong will remain unchanged, and so will the life-style. Rights and freedoms, including those of the person, of speech, of the press, of assembly, of association, of travel, of movement, of correspondence, of strike, of choice of occupation, of academic research and of religious belief will be ensured by law in the Hong Kong Special Administrative Region.[20]

These were the same rights that the PRC government had guaranteed to its own subjects in its various constitutions, and yet had consistently withheld. It remained to be seen if the Chinese government had now reconsidered the meaning of law so thoroughly that it might indeed be willing to protect such basic freedoms, or whether it would continue, as it had done since 1949, to disregard all laws when they happened not to suit its purposes.

CHAPTER 26 | # Testing the Limits

DEMOCRACY'S CHORUS

Initially almost forgotten in the race for new entrepreneurial arrangements in the countryside were the residue of the millions of urban youth sent to rural areas over the previous decades who had not been permitted to return home. Some had been radical Maoists and had found meaning in the commune system; now they were simply exiles from their homes and families, the men often unable to find wives locally because of their uncertain status, and less skilled at rural work than the peasants born on the land. In April 1985, hundreds of Chinese who had marched as young-sters to Shaanxi seventeen years before to serve Mao Zedong in the coun-tryside returned to Peking illegally. Defying the ban on such activities, they staged a sit-in on the steps of the CCP headquarters, and appealed to Deng Xiaoping to hear their case. They were not seriously harassed by police, but received no clear answers to their requests to be allowed to return to the capital. Since they claimed to speak for 20,000 such "urban exiles" in Shaanxi, and over 400,000 young people had been sent to Shaanxi in all, their requests presented the government with a knotty problem, especially since waiting lists for even minimal housing in Peking were already several years long.

Other public protests in 1985 were staged by those who had come to oppose the new atmosphere associated with the Four Modernizations. Some of this unrest was fed by resentment of public slights, as in the case of China's first-ever soccer riot, which broke out in Peking after the Hong Kong team defeated the PRC in an international challenge match. Others felt a different and understandable hostility to "progress," such as the thousands of Uighur minority people from Xinjiang who demonstrated boldly in Urumchi, Shanghai, and Peking against China's continued atmospheric nuclear testing in the Xinjiang testing grounds of Lop Nur. Many Chinese also began to express concern over Japan's growing economic influence in the PRC, referring sarcastically to "Japan's second occupation." Near year's end in 1985, when it appeared that student groups were preparing protest demonstrations, the government announced its own rallies for December 9, apparently to pre-empt any flare-up of antistate hostility similar to that staged by the December Ninthers against Chiang Kai-shek exactly fifty years before. But such games had to be played with caution. The last thing that Deng or the other veterans of the Cultural Revolution purges wanted was a new wave of youthful violence that would pit one wing of an uncontrollable mass movement against another, leaving the CCP fractured and impotent in the middle. They had already seen where that could lead.

Although Deng calculated correctly on this occasion, and there were no large antigovernment demonstrations on December 9, 1985, the general malaise continued to grow. It was slowly becoming clear that millions of Chinese—students especially, but also many of their teachers and growing numbers of unemployed youth—found it difficult to get their bearings in China's shifting landscape or to see where they were going. Many now began to express their bafflement in stories, plays, rock lyrics, poems, paintings, cartoons, and films, some of which were censored by party officials but most of which circulated with greater freedom than had been allowed at any time since 1949. Disconsolate Chinese began to express their doubts and insecurities aloud. Some, like the authors of the "Not-Not Manifesto" proclaimed in Chengdu, Sichuan, on May 4, 1986, saw current politics as absurd, and responded with imagery and logic that seemed to be drawn in part from Daoism and in part from the Western Dadaist movement of the 1920s.

> Not-Not: a blanket term covering the object, form, contents, methodology, process, way and result of the principles of Pre-cultural Thought. It is also the description of the primordial mien of the universe. Not-Not is not "no."
> After deconstructing the relationship between man and objects to their pre-cultural state, there is nothing in this universe that is not Not-Not.
> Not-Not is not the negation of anything. It is only an expression of itself. Not-Not is aware that liberation exists in the indefinite.[1]

Writing from Xi'an in Shaanxi, in the fiftieth anniversary year of Chiang Kai-shek's kidnaping, the poet Li Shan presented the country he called "Endland" as a sad place:

The emblem flies
The stars ripen
Rotten on the ancient secret-covered pond
The black spirit speeds past—
    close-up of doomsday

Awakening a wilderness of wolfbones
    sad beauty
Ten thousand leagues of hatred
    unfurled
Mollified by a chromosome

Ants mawing hair and nails
Bringing rotten news from below ground ... [2]

A dark view of China's potential for creative change, and a condemnation of Chinese character as a whole, were provided by an extraordinary pamphlet that began circulating in China in 1986. This was *The Ugly Chinaman,* written in 1984 by a Taiwan-Chinese using the pseudonym Bo Yang. That this sardonic work could circulate at all in the PRC was surprising, since Bo Yang attacked the Chinese for their failures and self-inflicted degradations with an energy and bitterness that recalled Zou Rong's *Revolutionary Army* of the late Qing, or Lu Xun's biting essays of the 1930s. "What makes the Chinese people so cruel and base?" asked Bo Yang. "What makes the Chinese people so prone to self-inflation?" His answers were harsh:

> Narrowmindedness and a lack of altruism can produce an unbalanced personality which constantly wavers between two extremes: a chronic feeling of inferiority, and extreme arrogance. In his inferiority, a Chinese person is a slave; in his arrogance, he is a tyrant. Rarely does he or she have a healthy sense of self-respect. In the inferiority mode, everyone else is better than he is, and the closer he gets to people with influence, the wider his smile becomes. Similarly, in the arrogant mode, no other human being on earth is worth the time of day. The result of these extremes is a strange animal with a split personality.[3]

Yet the despair suggested by the writings of Bo Yang, the Not-Nots, and Li Shan was not shared by all their compatriots. Despite their sufferings, the Chinese were resilient and showed an irrepressible awareness of the zany paradoxes of life. In one exemplary exploration of this mood, two Chinese writers traveled their own country by train and on foot, interviewing men and women from all walks of life and transcribing their interviews from tape recorders into printed form. Though some of those interviewed asked to be protected by anonymity, their trenchant stories and views were received with fascination by Chinese readers when they appeared in small-circulation literary journals in early 1985 and in book form in 1986. Now Chinese from all backgrounds could see how their fellow citizens reacted to the circumstances of their lives. The chief hair stylist at a once-fashionable beauty salon in Chongqing, for instance, gave his own inimitable view of Chinese politics:

> I tell you, nobody can beat a hairdresser when it comes to spotting political changes. Take the campaign against Hu Feng. All the educated people stopped coming to get their hair done right away. They were like rats, terrified of being noticed, remembered and dragged into the case. If you ask me, that campaign was what started educated people on the downward slope. Every time there was a movement our business fell off—the anti-rightist movement, class struggle in 1962, the "four clean-ups" in 1964, and so on till the beginning of the Cultural Revolution in 1966. By then the only women's style left was bobs.[4]

A former peasant who survived as a twelve year old in the famine year of 1960 by begging in the streets, and kept comfortably alive during the Cultural Revolution by pretending to believe in every single faction so he could get handouts from all of them, now sold polyvinyl moldings from his hometown factory and hustled on the side. This was his view of surviving the Four Modernizations:

> Tricks of the trade? Plenty! I don't rely on a notebook. If you lose it you're sunk. I keep everything in my head—what everyone else's job is, what they like eating, what they want, what I can get from them. When I go to a new place I find out what's in short supply—it's scarcity makes things valuable. Isn't that what the national economy and the people's livelihood is all about? They look after the national economy with their state plans, and I sort out the people's livelihood—food, clothes, consumer goods, entertainment.[5]

And a quietly proud mother reflected on her daily two hours of bicycling in Peking to get to and from her factory job:

> None of us riders know each other, we don't talk to each other, we all ride our different ways. I think all cyclists are the same, workers, students and ordinary cadres going to work or back. I once had the idea that someone

should make a film of us and show it to our children and grandchildren in twenty or thirty years' time. They should see how we raised them, cycling like this, taking our licences, ration books, grain coupons and oil coupons with us. . . . From morning till night, for the sake of the country and our families, we weave in and out of the traffic on our bikes to help modernize China.[6]

And the children being raised by such mothers also spoke out clearly as they responded honestly and often humorously to interviewers, sharing their sense of the strains and joys within their own families and trying to place their lives of incessant and competitive schoolwork in the broader context of an open future. "I think a lot about traveling to the moon and other planets," as one nine-year-old boy put it. "It would be fun to go there. On the moon the gravitational force is weak, so a person can jump very high and then come down slowly. That sounds like a lot of fun." "I want to be an athlete, a runner," said a second child, a girl of thirteen. "I want to run faster; I want to get better. Also I want to study medicine. I want to become a doctor." "When I am at home all by myself," said a third, a boy of twelve, "I imagine I can invent things. I imagine these things, but I can't really build them." "I fantasize about everything," said a fourth, a boy of fifteen. "My ambition is to become a high official. You probably think it's funny, but I really mean it. I want to become a high official. . . . Sometimes I fantasize that I have conversations with foreigners. I want to know all about world affairs, about U.S. politics, for example. I am interested in their presidential election."[7]

Self doubt, cynicism, pride, and hope—each here expressed by different voices from a range of generations—found a curious unity in the mind of Fang Lizhi. Born in 1936, a brilliant student who entered Peking University at sixteen to study astrophysics, only to be disgraced and dismissed from the party in the antirightist campaign of 1957, Fang had been rehabilitated in the late 1970s and become one of China's best-known professors. Appointed vice-president of the University of Science and Technology, once a branch of Peking University but now transferred to Hefei in Anhui, Fang was instrumental in reshaping the school in a new, more open mold, one that reflected his views on the fundamental premises of democracy. For Fang, power had to be shared in order to prevent abuses, decisions had to be made openly, differences had to be confronted honestly, and free speech had to be protected. Thus could the university best contribute to the nation's life and advance the cause of the Four Modernizations. Fang openly told students in Hefei and Peking that "unethical behavior by Party leaders" was especially to blame for "the social malaise in our country today." Elaborating on this theme, Fang told the students:

Another cause is that over the years our propaganda about communism has been seriously flawed. In my view this propaganda's greatest problem has been that it has had far too narrow an interpretation—not only too narrow but too shallow. I, too, am a member of the Communist Party, but my dreams are not so narrow. They are of a more open society, where differences are allowed. Room must be made for the great variety of excellence that has found expression in human civilization. Our narrow propaganda seems to imply that nothing that came before us has any merit whatsoever. This is the most worthless and destructive form of propaganda. Propaganda can be used to praise Communist heroes, but it should not be used to tear down other heroes.[8]

Fang Lizhi was touching a major national chord with these words. When even children were intrigued by American elections, it was not surprising that college students would be too. Rhetoric from Deng Xiaoping, Zhao Ziyang, and others had called for "reforms" in government, but nothing concrete had been done to open up the system to genuine mass participation. The electoral laws, established for China in 1953 and modified in 1979, had set up a four-tier system of allegedly representative government. At the base were congresses in each of the communes (by 1986 these had become administrative townships or *xiang*) elected every two years. Above these were 2,757 county congresses elected for three-year periods. Then came the congresses with five-year terms in China's 29 provinces, autonomous regions, and the 3 urban areas of Shanghai, Peking, and Tianjin. At the top was the National People's Congress, which convened in Peking. The party defined this system as "democracy under the leadership of centralism,"[9] and made sure that all congressional candidates followed the CCP line. Students trying to give real force to these elections had occasionally fought for seats as deputies to the commune-and township-level congresses—they had waged especially vigorous campaigns in Peking and Changsha in 1980. But even when elected, these students were prevented from taking their seats, and the CCP had effectively clamped down on such disputed elections in 1982 and again in 1984 by insisting on their proposed slates.

Party leaders who assumed they had done so again in 1986, however, miscalculated. At Hefei on December 5 and again on December 9, 3,000 or more students rallied vociferously against the manipulated elections in their city and university. Their slogans and wall posters once more echoed the past while addressing the present: "No democratization, no modernization"; "Almost every day the newspapers talk about democracy. But where can we actually find any?"[10] At least 5,000 more marched in Wuhan that same week. News of the disturbances soon reached Peking, where posters demanding democracy also began to appear on campuses along with others complaining about poor living conditions and low pay for graduates. The

posters were removed overnight by university authorities, but were replaced
with new ones—and in greater numbers—on successive days. Since both
demonstrations and the display of unauthorized posters were forbidden after
the constitutional revisions of 1980 that followed the dramas of Democracy
Wall, all these dissident students faced prospects of negative entries in their
dossiers, suspension, ruined career chances, and even imprisonment.

Undeterred, on December 20, 1986, at least 30,000 students marched in
Shanghai, parading through People's Square and the "Bund," where party
and government offices were housed in the massive stone buildings raised
long before by British financial firms. The students were joined by an estimated 30,000 to 40,000 townspeople. Among the banners, the most common
proclaimed "Long Live Freedom" and "Give Us Democracy." The main
demonstrations proceeded without harassment by police, but students
attempting sit-ins at municipal buildings were forcibly removed. Other protests were reported at Kunming, Chongqing, and the Shenzhen economic
zone. Some students in Shanghai had prepared a brief manifesto, recalling
in tone and content the one put forward by the May Fourth demonstrators
so long before, which the students now printed on 3"×5" slips of paper and
handed out to the crowd.

> To our countrymen:
>   Our guiding principle is to propagate democratic ideas among the people.
> Our slogan is to oppose bureaucracy and authoritarianism, and strive for
> democracy and freedom. The time has come to awaken the democratic ideas
> that have long been suppressed.[11]

Other Shanghai posters and slogans flung their messages with a directness
that raised the debate to a confrontational level:

> "When will the people be in charge?"
> "If you want to know what freedom is, just go and ask Wei Jingsheng."
> "To hell with Marxism–Leninism–Mao Zedong Thought."[12]

Government officials prevented mass-media coverage of the students' views,
and tried to keep the rest of the country ignorant of what was happening.
Ingeniously, the students avoided the news black-out by mailing hundreds
of letters and manifestoes to friends across China and to students on other
campuses. Other students ringed the railway stations asking departing passengers to spread the word, and assembled outside the United States consulate shouting that their views should be heard abroad. Finally, after three
days of demonstrations, the Shanghai police issued an official ban on all such

assemblies. The official government statement tried to discredit the protest movement by blaming it on a few troublemakers.

> A tiny number of people are attempting to disrupt stability and unity, derange production and social order by taking advantage of the patriotic zeal of students and their longing for democracy.[13]

Despite the bans and condemnations of the authorities, fresh demonstrations broke out in Tianjin and Nanjing. And in Peking itself, although threatened with jail if they did so, thousands of students from at least four of the major universities continued to march and demonstrate in the bitter winter cold and in the face of large forces of police.

The meaning of the call for "democracy" was hotly debated by the students themselves: some saw it as a meaningless slogan; others picked up the ideas of the students at Hefei and invoked the term in conscious opposition to the government's insistence on running elections from prepared slates of candidates. Students argued that these elections were mockeries of a perfectly valid political idea. Yet others saw it as the crucial second component to that call for liberation through "science and democracy" that had lain at the center of the May Fourth movement.

In a chilling follow-up to the demonstrations, a small number of political leaders in Peking began to issue condemnations of the students' behavior and demand greater discipline and political indoctrination on campuses. In early January 1987, after Peking students defied police bans yet again and held a massive rally in Tiananmen Square itself, a member of the Politburo forcefully defended the hard-liners' common stand:

> The Chinese Communist Party is a great, glorious and politically correct party that has always retained its revolutionary vigor. The leadership of the Communist Party is not granted by heaven, but by countless revolutionary martyrs who, wave after wave, shed blood and sacrificed themselves for half a century.[14]

Thereupon the party hard-liners (who could be called "conservatives" or "radicals" according to one's interpretation of their actions) moved swiftly to quash the burgeoning student movement, striking not at the students themselves, but at those the students found most inspirational. One of these was Fang Lizhi. In announcing Professor Fang's dismissal from the CCP, his removal from all teaching duties, and his assignment to a research position, the secretary of the Anhui provincial CCP committee sharply attacked Fang's political doctrines:

> Fang Lizhi advocated bourgeois liberalization, defamed the party's leadership and party officials, negated the achievements of the party over the past decades, and slandered the socialist system. He also sowed discord among the party and the intellectuals, especially the young intellectuals.[15]

The second prominent victim was the writer Liu Binyan, whose exposé of the corrupt Heilongjiang cadre Wang Shouxin in "People or Monsters" had been so influential in 1979. Liu had followed that essay with other widely read descriptions of party insensitivities and corruption, and had charged party conservatives with obstructing reforms and failing to see the value of a loyal opposition. Such opposition was essential to a healthy nation, he argued in an incisive story entitled "A Second Kind of Loyalty." Liu's dismissal from the party on grounds of oversympathy to capitalism and bourgeois ideas, and of "violating party principles and discipline," was particularly ironic.

The purges of these popular figures at first diverted attention from the fact that the secretary-general of the CCP, Hu Yaobang, had not been seen at any public functions in January 1987. When Deng Xiaoping, in mid-January, joined in the general attacks on "bourgeois liberalization" it became apparent that Hu Yaobang himself would be made the scapegoat for the unrest. Hu's outspokenness on the need for rapid reform and his almost open contempt of Maoist excesses had made him a controversial leader of the party in any case. In one well-known example, Hu had told the graduates of the party training school never again to espouse the "radical leftist nonsense" of preferring "socialist weeds to capitalist seedlings."[16] On January 16 it was announced in Peking that Hu had "resigned" as secretary general of the CCP after making "a self-criticism of his mistakes on major issues of political principles." Although Hu Yaobang was allowed to keep his place among the members of the Standing Committee of the Politburo, Premier Zhao Ziyang took over Hu's duties as secretary-general on an acting basis until a full-time successor was found.

A few days later the government announced the creation of a new state agency whose express role was to control all publications and press in the PRC, and oversee distribution of all supplies needed in printing, including ink, paper, and presses. A number of "troublemakers" in cities where the demonstrations had taken place were identified, arrested, and given long prison sentences for "counter-revolutionary activities." In early February, the head of the CCP's propaganda department—a former protégé of Hu Yaobang—was dismissed from his post and replaced by the deputy editor of the hard-line party journal, *Red Flag*. Bowing to the times, Premier Zhao Ziyang, though still wearing the elegant Western-style suits and ties that had become one of his hallmarks, attacked the "pernicious" influence of Western ideas and declared that the two central tasks facing China were first to "increase production and practice economy," and second to "combat bourgeois liberalization."

In a gesture that showed how little it was interested in the pro-democracy demonstrators' arguments, the party yet again held out the image of Lei Feng as a model. A national campaign was launched to remind the Chinese people of the simple PLA soldier's spirit of self-sacrifice. Lei Feng's original image builders, in the days of Lin Biao, had made the young man say of himself, "I will be a screw that never rusts and will glitter anywhere I am placed." In 1987 this metaphor again made the rounds.[17] As the head of the PLA Political Department told the senior leaders of the CCP, who assembled in March 1987 inside their walled Zhongnanhai compound for a well-publicized "Lei Feng Spirit Forum":

> The Lei Feng spirit is the Communist spirit, the spirit of serving the people wholeheartedly, and the spirit of warmly loving the Party wholeheartedly, and the spirit of warmly loving the motherland and socialism, of studying painstakingly, of waging arduous struggle, of being selfless, and of taking pleasure in helping others. . . . It is representative of the advanced ideology of the young generation and has become a vital part of the great spirit of our times.[18]

There could hardly be a sharper way of saying that the democracy demonstrators were not only not "advanced," but were running contrary to the true needs of the nation.

BROADENING THE BASE

These power shifts and countershifts seemed to suggest that Deng Xiaoping had been checked in his moves for a sustained level of rapid change. Yet an alternative hypothesis is that Deng remained an ideological conservative where party organization was concerned, and saw his role as a mediating one between the more cautious forces in the Politburo who wanted to maintain a planned economy guided by sternly enforced Leninist principles, and the eager prophets of reform. To hold this balance, Deng was willing to sacrifice his friend Hu Yaobang, if necessary; but that did not mean he would not also curb the hard-liners, if they threatened the policy of opening up to the West and developing substantial free enterprise within China's socialist economy. It was apparently along these latter lines that Deng worked through the summer and fall of 1987.

The forum for these critical decisions on the direction of PRC policy was the CCP's thirteenth congress, which convened in Peking on October 25, 1987 (the twelfth congress had met in 1982). The determination to keep lines open to the West was manifested by the willingness of party leaders to admit Western reporters to the congress for the first time. This was more than a mere gesture, since following a major uprising in Lhasa by hundreds of Tibetans protesting China's presence there, grim scenes of which had been photographed by Western journalists and circulated abroad, the Chinese government had imposed martial law in Lhasa and ordered all Western journalists out of Tibet. They had subsequently imposed an effective news embargo on the region.

Addressing the 1,936 party delegates in Peking's Great Hall of the People on October 25, 1987, Zhao Ziyang insisted on the need to maintain market pricing for all save a few staple items. He suggested further that the CCP should slowly separate itself from the administration of government and industry, leaving leadership there in the hands of professional civil servants and managers. At a press conference the next day, the director of China's Rural Policy Research Bureau announced that the government was considering allowing the peasants to buy and sell rights in the land they had contracted to work, and also to pass on such land rights as inheritances to their children.

The presence of foreign journalists at the congress ended abruptly after only two days, when all foreigners were banned from the proceedings, suggesting the seriousness of the deliberations that were now under way following Zhao's speech and the statement on the possible sale of land rights. Rumors swept Peking that Deng Xiaoping, now eighty-three, was battling to ensure implementation of his policies and would agree to leave the Central Committee if he felt his policies were safely in place. The November 1 announcement of Deng's resignation from the Central Committee, along with the resignations of hard-liners Chen Yun and Peng Zhen, who had been cautious about the pace of the reforms, seemed to confirm these rumors. Four other senior Standing Committee members also resigned. The following day Zhao Ziyang was formally elected secretary-general of the CCP—now comprising 46 million members—which he would have to prune and reduce to a manageable number of better-educated members.

Four new members were elected to serve with Zhao Ziyang on the Politburo Standing Committee. They represented a substantially younger age group than the retiring old guard, for though one of them was seventy the other three were in their late fifties or early sixties. Of the four, Li Peng had the best connections.* A Sichuanese, born in 1928, Li had been only seven when his father was killed by the Guomindang. The childless Zhou Enlai personally befriended the boy in Chongqing during 1939, and later looked after him in Yan'an. After the war, Li was sent for advanced training in energy-related engineering to Moscow, where he spent the late 1940s and early 1950s. In the late 1950s and the 1960s, Li Peng was carefully groomed for leadership by powerful figures in the energy bureaucracy, who systematically promoted him until he was named minister of electrical power in 1979, and served as the expert on energy matters within the small ruling group. (He had survived the Cultural Revolution without harm because he was in charge of Peking's power supply at that time.)[19] Informed observers were not surprised when Zhao Ziyang named Li Peng acting premier in late November 1987.

But Deng Xiaoping remained China's pre-eminent leader, and continued to serve as the chairman of the Military Affairs Commission, which gave him ultimate control over the PLA. Deng also arranged for the eighty-four-year-old Yang Shangkun to be named China's president. Yang had powerful connections throughout the party and the army: his brother was the chief of the PLA propaganda department, and he himself had served for years as director of personnel for the Central Committee, and as vice-chairman of the Military Affairs Commission under Deng. Furthermore, like Deng, Yang Shangkun was a Sichuanese whose entire life embodied the country's revolutionary history. He had worked in Shanghai as a young labor organizer in 1927, had studied in Moscow and been one of the "returned Bolsheviks" of 1930, and had risen through the party ranks in Yan'an and during the civil war.

With such powerful backing, Zhao Ziyang and Li Peng had an excellent chance to forge ahead with China's economic reforms. There was urgency to this task, since the economic indicators in early 1988 were not encouraging. Prices continued to rise, and agricultural production of staple food crops was declining once again as peasants moved to work in factories or raised more lucrative cash crops. Highly unpopular rationing of such items as pork, sugar, and eggs had to be reintroduced.

After preliminary discussions of the most pressing issues in early 1988, the new party leaders decided to use the March and April sessions of the seventh National People's Congress as the forum for cementing the desired changes. These congresses had generally acted as rubber stamps for prede-

---

*The other three were Yao Yilin, Qiao Shi, and Hu Qili.

termined party decisions; however, the seventh congress became a focus for real debate and discussion. Seventy-one percent of the 1,970 delegates were newly elected, and many of them expressed independent and assertive views. In a total break with precedent, by which an automatic show of raised-hand unanimity had terminated all policy discussions, delegates now began to cast negative votes. This trend was started by a lawyer from Hong Kong, attending as a member of the Guangdong delegation, who complained that she could not vote on a certain slate of committee candidates because she had no knowledge of how they had been selected. A former resident of Taiwan, now living and working as a scientist in China, also spoke out, urging delegates not to vote for an eighty-nine-year-old candidate for a committee chairmanship. "He is too old and should be given more time for a rest," said the delegate; after a startled pause a burst of clapping came from his fellow delegates.[20] Encouraged by these examples, more delegates began to speak up and cast negative votes on other candidates—as many as 200 in the case of the vice-presidential candidate Wang Zhen, who had been one of the most hard-line critics of the student demonstrators the previous year.

In a new departure, segments of the congress were shown on Chinese national television, lending a participatory sense to the occasion and allowing viewers to see that a lively debate was indeed possible. Foreign journalists were permitted to attend all the main sessions (not first invited and then banned, as they had been the year before at the party congress), and there were frequent press conferences and public discussions.

The most important issues before the seventh congress were presented by Li Peng, and though he sometimes hedged his statements with qualifications and calls for caution, he seemed to convey a strong endorsement of the central ideas guiding the accelerated race to the Four Modernizations as opposed to the slower pace desired by many senior party members. Most radical in its implications was the decision that constitutional protection would henceforth be given to the freedom of people to buy and sell their land-use rights or their stakes in enterprises. (Since 1985 such rights could be inherited in the case of the contractor's death, but now transfers would be much more flexible.) Also of great potential importance was Li Peng's determination that housing too should be a market commodity, freely bought and sold like agricultural produce in the free markets or the industrial production of the new urban enterprises. Li suggested that housing be treated in this regard like "refrigerators or bicycles," but such a parallel understated the significance of what he was really proposing. Decent housing in China was in agonizingly short supply, and obtaining good housing was a key measure of power and status. If housing were now to come on the market freely, it would place great pressures on the system of party patronage and also cement emerging economic inequalities in both city and countryside.

Of equal importance, were they to be fully implemented, were plans for restructuring the bureaucracy that were presented to the congress by another member of the Politburo. Building on ideas formulated by Zhao Ziyang, these plans called for a 20 percent cut in personnel throughout the bureaucracy, to be accomplished mainly by ending the final control of enterprises by government departments and investing the enterprises themselves with responsibility for both management and profits. Such cuts would remove millions of Chinese from the contacts and perquisites they had enjoyed, in many cases for decades. Four central ministries in charge of managing the heart of China's energy and transportation systems—those for railways, petroleum, coal, and nuclear power—would be abolished and replaced by corporations with their own independent managements. The streamlined Chinese bureaucracy would then—in this visionary plan—become a true civil service, staffed by those chosen on the basis of merit rather than party service.

In two of these ministries, institutional change was already under way. As we've seen, there were ongoing experiments with reorganizing coal production, and in the petroleum industry Chinese corporations were operating extensive joint ventures with Japanese, British, and American companies. But the problem of how an independent civil agency might run China's fledgling nuclear industry, in a world just coming to grips with the implications of the nuclear accidents at Chernobyl and Three Mile Island, was an inordinately complex one. Similarly, the huge scale of China's railway network, which had been expanded enormously since 1949, made the idea of corporate management problematical. The need for reform in the railway system was highlighted, however, by the news—released while the seventh congress was still meeting—that 290 people had been arrested in a giant train-ticket scalping operation in Shanghai. Buying up blocks of tickets, the scalpers then sold them to desperate passengers for up to six times their nominal price.

The PLA was undergoing institutional changes of its own. In the mid-1980s a plan had been made to demobilize almost one quarter of the 4.2 million members of the armed forces. Forty-seven thousand elderly officers were edged into retirement. The last traces of Lin Biao's egalitarianism vanished when full insignia for all ranks were restored. In order to encourage the army to take an innovative role in weapons and delivery-systems development, the Chinese government allowed the PLA to sell its weapons worldwide and to keep for its own use a large proportion of any foreign currency obtained through such deals. The fruits of this policy could be seen in early 1988 as both Iran and Iraq, ravaged by their almost decade-long war, began to bombard each other's cities with Chinese computer-guided, short-range "silkworm" missiles, either sold directly to them by the Chinese or filtered through intermediaries. Between 1984 and 1987 China had signed arms deals with Iran worth some $2.5 billion, and with Iraq for $1.5 billion. By the summer of 1988 the Chinese were discussing the sale to Syria of a new 375-mile-range M-9 missile, capable of delivering chemical warheads. Libya was reportedly negotiating for the same missile, and had invested large sums in a Chinese silk factory in Zhejiang to prove its good intentions. China also sold ballistic missiles to Saudi Arabia.* In a world in which French *Exocet* rockets launched by Argentineans had almost wiped out the British fleet in the Falkland Islands, and "Irangate" funds were filtered through American dummy corporations to deliver arms to Nicaraguan Contras, the Chinese showed the West that they had also come to understand this particular aspect of international life and trade.

How any of these institutional changes and proposals would address China's inflation—which was running 20 percent or higher in the cities during the first quarter of 1988—was not clear. But the standing commitment to develop independent zones of enterprise was reaffirmed by the final act of the seventh congress, taken after it had approved all the proposals on constitutional, economic, and institutional reform presented to it by Li Peng and others. By this final vote, Hainan Island was to be removed from the jurisdiction of Guangdong and made a separate province. As such, the island would be given wide autonomy in developing foreign investment, expanding the tourist trade, and allowing a virtually free flow of goods and services. Foreign visitors to Hainan province would not even require visas. This decision—a bold one in view of the notorious Hainan import scandals revealed the year before—could be seen either as a trial balloon for learning how to handle Hong Kong, or as an experiment in developing separate administrative and economic structures that might in the long-term heighten China's attractiveness to Taiwan. If successful, the model would also be adopted in major Chinese cities.

The issue of Taiwan had become all the more relevant when Chiang Kai-shek's son, Chiang Ching-kuo, president of Taiwan since 1978, died in early

---

*Imaginative uses were also being found for computers in many areas outside China's military and space programs. At the university of the new economic zone of Shenzhen, for instance, the Chinese literature department had combined with the computer science department to develop a word-retrieval program for the whole of Cao Xueqin's eighteenth-century novel, *The Dream of the Red Chamber,* so that within a few seconds seekers after Qing sensibility could locate any word cluster or association of images that they chose.

1988 shortly before the congress convened, changing the tenor of Taiwan-PRC relations. During the last years of his presidency, Chiang Ching-kuo had carried through democratic reforms of considerable significance. The Taiwanese themselves were now running much of their country. Chiang Ching-kuo's vice-president, who under Taiwan's constitution took up the position of president, was a native Taiwanese, Lee Teng-hui. Born in 1923 to a rural family of rice and tea farmers, Lee grew up under the Japanese occupation of Taiwan and received his college education in Japan before returning to study agricultural economics in Taipei. He subsequently enrolled in graduate programs in the United States, receiving an M.A. from Iowa State University and a Ph.D. from Cornell.

On taking office, President Lee continued to invoke Chiang Ching-kuo's rhetoric about there being only one China, and made it clear he was not in sympathy with the anti-Chinese policies of the Taiwan Independence movement. Within a few months of his accession, all travel restrictions were lifted on Taiwanese who wished to visit their relatives in the PRC. The result was an amazing rush of Chinese visitors from Taiwan to the mainland that reached 10,000 people a month by May 1988. Taiwan businesses that for years had surreptitiously been routing their dealings with the PRC through Hong Kong agents or subsidiaries began openly to move productiion to China, taking advantage of the tax incentives in the special economic zones and of wage rates that in some cases were as little as one-tenth those they paid their workers on Taiwan.

Nevertheless, these expanded contacts emphasized the immense disparities between the two societies, as much as their shared heritage, and there seemed little likelihood of speedy reunification, even on a variant of the Hong Kong model. In July 1988 President Lee was elected chairman of the Taiwan Guomindang; this greatly strengthened his power base, and promised to bond the Taiwanese and the post-1949 Chinese refugees and their families on the island into an even more prosperous union. Taiwan, which had seemed almost a pawn of American policy makers in 1972 and 1979, was now a fully independent and capable actor on the international scene. Before Taiwan developed any closer political ties with the mainland, the PRC would have to prove through its performance that it could indeed achieve a sustained level of economic growth and development.

SOCIAL STRAINS

While repression continued in China against those who spoke of democracy or who allegedly were prey to "bourgeois-liberal" values, it nevertheless

appeared that millions were benefiting from the reforms and becoming una-
bashedly materialistic. As a lighthearted popular slogan put it, mocking the
earlier Maoist inclination to list categories of political behavior by number,
what you needed in China if you were a man nowadays were the "Three
Highs" and the "Eight Bigs"; the "Four Musts" were no longer enough.
The "Four Musts" that had set the outer limit of materialist yearnings under
Maoism had been a bicycle, a radio, a watch, and a sewing machine. In the
new world of Deng Xiaoping they were replaced by the "Eight Bigs": a
color television, a refrigerator, a stereo, a camera, a motorcycle, a suite of
furniture, a washing machine, and an electric fan. As for the "Three Highs,"
those were what a man needed to get a wife: a high salary, an advanced
education, and a height of over five feet six inches.

The Chinese and foreign media in early 1988 emphasized this optimistic
approach by extolling individual entrepreneurs who were making a success
of the new flexibility, either by privatizing previously bankrupt state industries and running them efficiently, or by mechanizing agricultural production and applying scientific methods in cultivating the land held on contract
from the state. But late in 1988 and early in 1989, it became clear that these
encouraging entrepreneurial case studies were taking place in an economic
and bureaucratic context that was suffering great tensions and problems.
Taken cumulatively, these problems showed how difficult it was for China
to contain the new forces that the decisions of Deng Xiaoping and his allies
had set in motion. Among the difficulties that the government began to
discuss at the plenum of the Central Committee in late 1988 and in the
National People's Congress of early 1989, and which were extensively covered in the Chinese press, seven seemed paramount: inflation, low grain
production, labor unrest, graft, unregulated population movements, rapid
population growth, and illiteracy.

The amount of income now accruing to those Chinese benefitting from
the Four Modernizations and the new economic liberalization had led to an
insatiable demand for consumer goods, and for new housing and capital
construction. For a time, this level of demand led in turn to more employment opportunities and greater options for workers and peasants; but at the
same time it pushed inflation, which had been around 20 percent earlier in
1988, up to 26 percent or more in urban areas by year's end. Living standards
fell for many in the cities, and retrenchments in capital projects ordered by
the government threw many out of work. Panic buying and hoarding
affected a wide range of products, from grain and edible oils to toothpaste
and soap.

Hoarding exacerbated the problems created by the decline in grain production in 1988. The reasons for the decline were many. State procurement

prices for grain, though raised by the government in answer to peasant unrest, were still unrealistically low when compared to free-market prices and the profits that could be gained from cash crops like sugar and tobacco (production of which rose dramatically in the same period). The government was so short of cash that it began paying peasants with scrip or promissory notes for their compulsory procurement quotas; yet the peasants were not allowed to use these IOUs in trade for essential fuel and foodstuffs, and much bitterness resulted. The available amount of arable land continued to shrink in the face of alternative land uses—80 percent of all new enterprises, for instance, were situated in rural areas. Peasants themselves began to stockpile their own grain when they saw the surplus grain they sold to township governments resold at markups of two and a half times or more.

Labor unrest sprang in part from urban inflation and in part from the harsh work conditions imposed by the new breed of entrepreneurial managers. These managers in fact worked closely with the local party bureaucracy in most cases, and continued to rely on local political leaders for lucrative contracts, access to raw materials, transportation of goods, and favorable tax rates that increased investment profits. As wages lagged and workers were laid off, many began to strike. Though not on a scale familiar from the republican era, the extent of some strikes in 1988 was considerable: 1,500 workers at a Zhejiang textile mill, for instance, walked out for two days; 1,100 workers at a medical-appliance factory stayed out for three months.

Graft and corruption among CCP members—many of them the associates of local managers—continued to grow. Figures for 1987 released in 1988 showed that 150,000 CCP members—out of an unknown number investigated or charged—had been punished for corruption or abuse of authority. Over 25,000 of these had been dismissed from the party. Half of all enterprises in the same year had dodged taxes in various ways, as had 80 percent of individual entrepreneurs. In rural areas, agricultural production further suffered from the authorized sale of substandard insecticides, chemical fertilizers, and seed. The government ordered that henceforth every CCP member would have to face an annual review of his or her honesty and party loyalty.

Internal migrations of part-time workers and disaffected or unemployed rural and urban populations were also reported to be uncontrollable. Tentative government figures suggested 8 million Chinese a year were moving to urban areas, and that 400 million Chinese were now residing in China's 365 largest cities, marking another decided increment in the shift away from rural residence shown in the 1982 census. Thirty thousand migrant workers of various kinds were reported *daily* in Sichuan rail stations; the "floating population" of unemployed or laid-off workers was said to be 1.8 million in Shanghai and over 1.1 million in both Peking and Canton. Such huge migrations were themselves only part of a larger problem, since changes in rural land use and production methods, coupled with government retrenchments and a freeze on new capital construction projects, had made 180 million farm workers "redundant"; 200 million more were expected to be in the same plight over the next decade.

The overall population-growth figures gave little solace to government planners. Taking into account the size and youthfulness of China's child-bearing population, the relevant state bureaus estimated that 20 million babies would be born each year for at least the next eight years. With a current urban birth rate per thousand of 14.3, and a rural birth rate of 24.94, China's population would inevitably reach 1.3 billion by the year 2000. The policy of one child per family was proving hard to enforce: 32.33 percent of all current births were second children; 14.95 percent were third children. Although China was already importing far more grain than it should have been in light of its $3 billion trade deficit, per capita annual grain consumption was falling steadily: down 40 kilos (from 400 to 360) between 1984 and 1988. It was also likely that much of this rising population would be less well educated than preceding generations in the PRC. Two hundred thirty million people in China (95 percent of them rural and 70 percent of them female) were defined as "illiterate" by the State Statistical Bureau; the State Education Commission noted a growing resistance even to universal primary education among parents and employers seeking cheap child labor for their farms and enterprises. More than 7 million children dropped out of Chinese schools in 1988: this figure included almost 7 percent of China's 40 million junior middle-school students and 3.3 percent of all those in primary school.[21]

As if all these domestic problems did not make government planning for China's transformation seem inextricably mired, the foreign news was not much better. Although there was an overall foreign investment in the PRC of some $5.2 billion in 1988, and close to 6,000 joint-venture contracts of various kinds, this was not nearly as much as the Chinese had hoped for. China's exports for 1988 were $47 billion, but imports totaled $54 billion. As a world exporter, China ranked sixteenth, whereas Hong Kong was eleventh, and Taiwan twelfth. In many cases, official figures of foreign investment in China, when carefully scrutinized, turned out to be greatly inflated. A number of the most publicized joint ventures—such as that of American Motors and Beijing Jeep—had run into major crises, marked by low production levels, delays and evasions by Chinese managers (matched by American intransigence and unrealistic expectations), and a sullen hostility among workers on the shop floor. Oil drilling by joint-venture corporations off the southeast coast had not yielded the immense discoveries confidently expected a few years before. And the special economic zones themselves were often mismanaged and graft-ridden. So many of the enterprises in the zones were run by the children or relatives of the most senior party politicians that those Chinese outside this inner charmed circle began to talk openly and bitterly of a "clique of heir apparents" and "the princes' clique." Contacts and *guanxi* seemed for disillusioned young educated Chinese to be the only way to advance in the society. They felt correspondingly threatened by the new "freedoms" they were offered to find their own employment, for without connections there were no lucrative jobs to be had. To compound the disillusion, persistent government cost cutting had left the facilities of many colleges and universities so run-down, and the dormitories and dining halls so badly dilapidated, that both students and professors complained that it was impossible to do work effectively in them. The dream of reforming China's economy and modernizing the whole nation seemed to be disintegrating before people's eyes.

THE BREAKING POINT

Nineteen eighty-nine promised to be an anniversary year of special significance for China: the year would mark the two hundredth anniversary of the French Revolution, the seventieth anniversary of the May Fourth movement, the fortieth birthday of the People's Republic itself, and the passage of ten years since formal diplomatic relations with the United States had been reinstituted. A number of China's most prominent scientists and writers—including the dismissed party member Fang Lizhi and the poet Bei Dao—sent letters to Deng Xiaoping and other leaders asking them to seize this opportune moment to take steps that would emphasize the flexibility and openness of Chinese politics. They urged that Wei Jingsheng, who had now served ten years in prison for his role in the 1978 Democracy Wall movement, be granted amnesty, along with others who were in prison solely for their dissident political views. They also urged the government to grant the rights of freedom of expression that would allow the kind of lively intellectual exchange considered essential to real scientific and economic progress, and to put more money into education for the sake of the country as a whole. Delegates to the National People's Congress suggested that a "socialist democracy" promised a solution if it could combine "political, social and cultural democratization" with the economic reform currently under discussion. Other intellectuals urged a return to the kind of pragmatism that had seemed to be implied by Deng Xiaoping's famous remark from the late 1970s: "It does not matter whether a cat is black or white: as long as it catches mice it is a good cat." Others went further, like the former head of the Marxism–Leninism–Mao Zedong Thought Institute, Su Shaozhi, who suggested that the divorce between theory and practice was now a "chronic malady" in China. Echoing the disgraced party secretary-general Hu Yaobang, he pointed out that Marxism in China currently seemed frozen in the grip of "ossified dogmas." Surely genuine reform could invigorate Marxism while rejecting all "ideological prejudices and bureaucratism," all "cultural autocracy."

Such voices were a reaffirmation of what the massed students in Hefei had called for in 1986, and of what Wei Jingsheng had himself boldly suggested in 1978 and 1979: without abandoning the spirit of Marxism itself, there was still room for creative growth and change. Neither Deng Xiaoping, Li Peng, or Zhao Ziyang responded publicly to these various overtures, leaving the task to their subordinates, whose response was harshly dismissive. Such requests and critiques, they observed, were "incitements" to the public and an attempt to exert "pressure" on the government. Since there were no political prisoners in China, the request to "release" Wei Jingsheng and others was a meaningless one.

In this uneasy atmosphere, on April 15, 1989, Hu Yaobang suddenly died of a heart attack. Hu, the feisty Long March veteran and Communist Youth League leader, had been Deng Xiaoping's handpicked secretary-general of the CCP until he was made the scapegoat for allowing the 1986–1987 student demonstrations to spread. At the time of his dismissal from his party posts in 1987 the Central Committee had made him issue a humiliating "self-criticism"; the nature of this disgrace and the way Deng condoned or even encouraged it had left a bad taste in Chinese mouths. As soon as the news of Hu Yaobang's death was released, students in Peking saw a means of pressuring the government to move more vigorously with economic and democratic reforms. It was Deng Xiaoping, after all, who in 1978 had "reversed the verdicts" on the Tiananmen demonstrations of 1976 in homage to the deceased Zhou Enlai, thus openly acknowledging the legitimacy of such actions. By launching a pro–Hu Yaobang demonstration, and demanding a reversal of the verdict against him too, the students would ensure that all the issues of the 1986–1987 pro-democracy protests, and perhaps also those of Democracy Wall in 1978–1979, would once more be at the forefront of the nation's attention.

This idea seems to have originated with students in the party-history department at People's University in Peking. Many of these students were themselves party members and the children of senior Communist cadres, and could be expected soon to be embarking on careers in the party bureaucracy or the new economic corporations. They understood how to apply political pressure and how to maintain it. Thousands of students from the other Peking campuses, including Peking University itself, joined them in a rally that was held in Tiananmen Square on April 17. Their purpose was to mourn Hu's passing and to call for an end to corruption and nepotism in government, for more democratic participation in decision making, and for better conditions in the universities. Wall posters—declared illegal by the party since 1980—appeared in many places, openly praising Hu and his support of liberalism and political and economic reform. After class, and when the libraries closed, excited groups of young people would join together spontaneously and share their feelings; from such gatherings sprang new, autonomous student associations. Students in Shanghai and other cities caught the mood and took up the same cry. On April 18, students held a sit-in near the Great Hall of the People in Tiananmen Square; that night, with bravado unparalleled under the PRC, they staged sit-ins at the party headquarters and in front of the most senior party leaders' residences in the Zhongnanhai compound on the edge of the Forbidden City. The government declared April 22 to be the official day for Hu Yaobang's funeral ceremonies; demonstrations were forbidden and plans made to cordon off the whole of Tiananmen Square. But by clever preparation and inspired coordination, Peking students entered the square before the police had taken up their positions and held a large, peaceful demonstration. In a ritualistic but sincere gesture, reminiscent of Qing practice, several students knelt on the steps of the Great Hall and begged Premier Li Peng to come out and talk to them. He declined to do so. On April 24, students began a mass boycott of classes in an attempt to pressure government leaders into hearing their requests.

Up to this point, compromise of many kinds appeared possible, even if the demonstrators had gone beyond anything attempted in 1976, 1978, or 1986. Zhao Ziyang was believed by students to be receptive to dialogue over changes, as were many of his senior staff, and in his position as secretary-general of the CCP he could presumably urge the party in the same direction. Zhao, for his part, may have seen the students' demonstrations as a potential political force that could strengthen his own party base and enable him to shunt aside Li Peng and perhaps even Deng Xiaoping himself. (In 1978 Deng Xiaoping had successfully used the Democracy Wall protests to cement his position against Hua Guofeng.) But in late April the students and their supporters were stunned by a strong editorial in *People's Daily* that referred to their movement as a "planned conspiracy," firmly implying that all those following the current action might be subject to arrest and prosecution. Zhao himself was away on a state visit to North Korea at the time, and the *People's Daily* editorial obviously represented the views of a tougher group of party leaders, perhaps Premier Li Peng or Deng Xiaoping himself.

Instead of being intimidated, the students reacted with anger and defiance. They were joined now by many of their teachers, by scores of journalists, and by citizens of Peking. The rallies and marches grew larger, the calls for reforms and democratic freedoms more bold. The government leaders appeared paralyzed, for any use of force on the anniversary of the May Fourth demonstrations would immediately lead to reminders of the warlord era. May 4 came and went peaceably, though over 100,000 marched in Peking, dwarfing the student demonstrations of 1919. Similar rallies and parades were held in cities throughout China, but it was Peking that remained the focus for world media attention, not only because of the demonstrations, but because the secretary-general of the Soviet Communist party, Mikhail Gorbachev, was due in Peking in mid-May for a crucial and long-planned summit meeting with Deng Xiaoping. This summit was expected to mark the end of the rift between the Soviet Union and China that had lasted for thirty-three years, ever since Khrushchev had shocked Mao with his "secret speech" attacking Stalin's memory.

Gorbachev was enthusiastically welcomed by the Peking demonstrators, not least because his own attempts to introduce a range of new political and intellectual freedoms in the Soviet Union could be contrasted sharply with the Chinese leaders' obvious resistance to such change. But the significance of Gorbachev's visit and the benign light this might have cast on Deng Xiaoping was overshadowed as the student demonstrators introduced a new tactic—the hunger strike—to emphasize their pleas for reform. Tiananmen Square became a vast camp as close to 3,000 hunger strikers lay out in makeshift tents, surrounded by tens of thousands of their classmates, Peking citizens, and curious visitors and onlookers. Students all over Peking were kept in touch with the latest developments by a squad of volunteer motorcyclists who proudly named themselves the "Flying Tigers." Planned ceremonies for Gorbachev had to be canceled or changed by the Chinese government, and as television cameras broadcast the scene around the world, ambulances raced in and out of the square attending to those now so dangerously weakened by their fast that there was a real chance they would die.

Nothing like this had been seen in China before, for although crowds as large had assembled during the Cultural Revolution, those gatherings had been orchestrated by the state and were held in homage to Mao Zedong as supreme leader of the party and the people. Now, even though Zhao Ziyang still tried to mute the conflict, and suggested that the *People's Daily*'s condemnation of the students had been too harsh, the demonstrators began openly calling on Deng Xiaoping and Li Peng to resign. Boisterous and angry, sometimes chanting and dancing, at other times deep in political discussion or sleeping in exhaustion, the students and their supporters were at once a potent political challenge to their government and an endlessly engrossing spectacle to the rest of China and the world. Li Peng did invite the hunger-strike leaders to one meeting, but it went badly. Li found the students rude and incoherent, while they found him arrogant and aloof. On May 17 and again the following day, the number of demonstrators in and around Tiananmen Square passed the 1 million mark. Muzzled until now by government controls, journalists and editors of newspapers and television news threw off their restraints and began to cover the protests as honestly and comprehensively as they could. On May 19, appearing close to tears, Secretary-General Zhao Ziyang visited the hunger strikers and urged them to end their fasts. Li Peng also briefly talked with strikers, but made no pleas and no promises. On May 20, with no published comment by Zhao Ziyang, Premier Li Peng and the president of China, Yang Shangkun, declared martial law and ordered units of the People's Liberation Army brought into Peking to clear the square and return order to the city.

But for two weeks the soldiers could not clear the square, their efforts stymied by the courage and unity of the citizens of Peking. Workers, initially sought out as allies by the students, now organized themselves into their own groups to join in the protests and to stem the soldiers' advance. With a kind of fierce yet loving solidarity, the people of Peking took to the streets and erected makeshift barricades. They surrounded the army convoys, sometimes to let the air out of tires or stall engines but more often to argue with or cajole the troops, urging them not to enforce the martial-law restrictions and not to turn their guns on their fellow Chinese. For their part the troops, seemingly embarrassed by their assignment, practiced considerable restraint while the central leadership of China, both in the party and the army, was clearly divided. Enraged by the students' intransigence and the mounting disorder in the streets, which surely reminded him of the Cultural Revolution, Deng Xiaoping lobbied for hard-line support and ordered each of the regional PLA commanders to send a certain number of their seasoned troops to the capital. Zhao Ziyang found himself without a sufficient base of support among his colleagues, and was unable to check the hard-line approach from gaining ground.

The students who had emerged as leaders of the demonstrations over the previous month now found themselves in charge of a huge square crammed with their supporters but also awash with dirt and garbage that threatened the outbreak of serious disease. At May's end they began to urge their fellow students to end the hunger strikes, return to their campuses, and continue to attempt a dialogue with the government from there, and the great majority of the Peking students did so. But there were new recruits—often from other cities where major demonstrations were occurring—to take their place. Speakers espousing a tougher stance urged that retreat would mean a betrayal of their principles, and that the government would never speak to them openly unless they maintained the pressures they were currently exerting through their numbers and tenacity. A group of Peking art students provided the faltering movement with a new symbol that drew all eyes—a thirty-foot-high white plaster and Styrofoam statue of their version of Liberty, fashioned as a young woman with head held proudly aloft, clasping in both her hands the torch of freedom.

Late at night on June 3, the army struck. These were not inexperienced and poorly armed soldiers like those called in up to this time, but tough, well-armed troops from the Twenty-seventh Army (whose commander was a relative of President Yang) and from other veteran units loyal to Deng. Backed by scores of heavy tanks and armored personnel carriers that smashed through the barricades, crushing those who fell in front of them or tried to halt their progress, the troops converged on Tiananmen Square down the wide avenues to its east and west. Armed with automatic weapons, they fired at random on crowds along the streets, at anyone who moved in nearby buildings, and at those who approached too close to their positions.

In the small hours of June 4, troops blocked off all the approaches to Tiananmen Square, and turned off all the lights there. After protracted and anguished debates, the remaining students and demonstrators decided to leave. As they walked out in bedraggled but orderly formation, troops and tanks overran their encampments and crushed the liberty statue to pieces. There followed a period of macabre and terrifying chaos in Peking, as the army gunned down students and citizens both near the square and in other areas of the city. Screams echoed through the night, and flames rose from piles of debris and from army trucks or tanks hit by homemade bombs. Hospitals were overwhelmed by the numbers of dead and wounded, but in many cases were forbidden to treat the civilian casualties. PLA soldiers also died, some killed in terrible ways by enraged crowds who had just seen unarmed demonstrators mowed down. Rumors spread swiftly that the fires in Tiananmen Square were piles of corpses burned by the army to hide the evidence of their cruelty. Whether that was true or not—and no one could get past the troops to check—there were enough bodies in full view elsewhere, lying in the roads, in hospitals, or tangled up in their bicycles where they had fallen, to indicate the scale of the violence. Many hundreds were dead and thousands more wounded. The callousness and randomness of the killings evoked memories of the worst episodes of China's earlier civil wars and the Cultural Revolution.[22] Similar violence was meted out to civilian demonstrators by the armed police in Chengdu and perhaps other cities, but the thoroughness of the government's news blackout made it hard to gauge the scale. Foreign journalists were forbidden to take photographs or conduct interviews, and satellite links abroad were cut.

For a few days rumors swirled that other units of the PLA, shocked by the massacre, might attack the Twenty-seventh Army and start a civil war, or that China's workers would unite in a general strike, or that sympathy riots in other major cities would bring down the government, but none of those things happened. The hard-liners had "won," if that was the right word. Zhao Ziyang was dismissed, the second of Deng's hand-picked "successors" to meet that fate. Li Peng and Deng Xiaoping, in the presence of the most influential party elders—all dressed once again in the traditional high-collared "Mao suits" that were meant to represent a revolutionary simplicity of life-style—publicly thanked the PLA officers and soldiers for clearing the square, and praised their courage. To head the Communist party in Zhao's stead, Deng turned to a comparatively unknown figure, the sixty-three-year-old party boss of Shanghai, Jiang Zemin. A Russian-trained electrical engineer, Jiang had had an unspectacular but steady rise through the party ranks, from student activist and factory director, to ministerial positions in the industrial sector, and thence to mayor of Shanghai in 1985, and Shanghai party secretary in 1987. Jiang had been summoned to Peking in the spring of 1989 to help control the demonstrations, and his main claim to his new office was that he had at the same time successfully kept Shanghai's demonstrators from getting out of hand. Now Jiang joined in dutifully as the party launched a concerted campaign in press, radio, and television blaming the demonstrations on counterrevolutionaries and "hooligans," and mounted an extensive hunt for the student leaders and their main supporters. Many of the "most wanted" students eluded the police for weeks, and several managed to leave China secretly, suggesting the range of public support for their actions and the efficiency and solidarity of their organizations. But thousands of other students were arrested and interrogated. The government also determined to avoid the formation of any autonomous unions of workers, and showed special ferocity toward workers who had joined in the protests. Many were arrested and executed.

Foreign governments were stunned by these events, though uncertain how to act. Many of them expressed outrage, ordered their nationals home, imposed economic sanctions, and talked of barring China from various international associations. But they did not break diplomatic relations with

China, even when trigger-happy troops sprayed the buildings where foreigners lived with fire from automatic weapons. The U.S. embassy did give sanctuary to Fang Lizhi and his wife when they requested it, an act blasted by the PRC government as unwarranted interference in Chinese internal affairs.

On June 9, Deng Xiaoping himself issued a harsh attack on the demonstrators in a speech that became the mandatory text for study sessions and party discussions all over China, and clearly represented the official interpretation of events. In its idiosyncratic way, the speech summed up the long years of revolution that China had endured, while also showing the difficulty of relating those experiences to the turbulent present. What the government had suppressed, said Deng, was nothing less than a "counterrevolutionary rebellion." Moreover, it was a rebellion "determined by the international and domestic climate, it was bound to happen and was independent of man's will." Yet while offering this long-range, almost cosmic interpretation of events, Deng told the assembled party leaders and army officers that it was the "dregs of society" who had been seeking to overthrow both state and society in order to "establish a bourgeois republic entirely dependent on the West."

Deng did not make clear who these dregs were, but they were to be distinguished from the "masses," the "young students," and the "onlookers." The army's courage in suppressing the rebellion had been exemplary, Deng said, and showed that even new PLA recruits aged eighteen or nineteen understood how to defend socialism and their country. Deng made no attempt at all to suggest why the students had been demonstrating with such protracted tenacity, nor why so many citizens supported them, but he did insist that any effort to discredit CCP leadership and the paramountcy of "Marxism, Leninism, and Mao Zedong Thought" must always be resolutely quashed, along with any move to introduce "the American system of the separation of the three powers." Yet this did not mean China should again become a "closed country," or that the government leaders should go "back to the old days of trampling the economy to death." Deng's speech concluded with a ringing affirmation of the needs of rapid national economic growth: more railways, more ships, more roads, more steel, more electric power. He called for a doubling of the gross national product in twelve years followed by fifty years of 2 percent annual growth, so that China would reach the level of a "moderately developed nation" by the year 2050.

In his assessment of the "crux of the current incident," as he referred to the crackdown of June 3 and 4 in the context of the events of April and May, Deng did grope toward wider ideological themes. China was facing a great struggle, he said. It was between socialism on the one hand and the forces of "bourgeois liberalization and spiritual pollution" on the other. This was the battle that the Chinese, under the leadership of the CCP, would be fighting into the foreseeable future. Nostalgic for the austere yet exciting days of the Jiangxi Soviet, of Yan'an, and of the founding years of the PRC, Deng called for a return to simple values and standards, for "plain living" and the "enterprising spirit in hard struggle." Only so could China achieve its own vision of "reform and openness" without "importing evil influences from the West."[23]

It was not only that nothing had changed, Deng seemed to be telling the nation, it was as if nothing of any real significance had even occurred. The course that China must take had been set for a decade; now all the Chinese had to do was follow it to its logical conclusion.

CHAPTER 27

Century's End

RETURNING TO GROWTH

Despite Deng Xiaoping's expressions of confidence, the crisis of 1989 showed that aspects of China's past were still much in evidence. To take one short-term parallel, the political maneuvering by Deng Xiaoping proved how far the Communist party still was from solving its leadership and succession problems. Deng's rejection of his two chosen heirs, Hu Yaobang and Zhao Ziyang, and his sudden benediction of the previously little-known Jiang Zemin as party secretary-general was eerily reminiscent of Mao's attempt to install Hua Guofeng after he had turned against Liu Shaoqi and Lin Biao. In a longer historical context, Deng's insistence that economic reforms and the dramatic changes they brought should still be kept totally separate from any changes in the political superstructure and modes of public expression reawakened historical memories of the late Qing dream—that China could join the modern world entirely on its own terms, without sacrificing its prevailing ideological purity. Some Chinese even noticed parallels between Deng's suppression of the Democracy movement in 1989 and the Empress Dowager Cixi's countercoup in the face of Emperor Guangxu's ambitious reform program of 1898.

The Chinese scholars and students who had joined together to vent their frustrations in the spring and summer of 1989 also raised echoes of their own, echoes of earlier groups of Chinese who had taken great personal risks in order to emphasize that educated Chinese had a moral obligation to criticize the shortcomings of their rulers even if those rulers warned them that such criticisms were unacceptable and that they would be punished. Wittingly or not, the Chinese who marched and spoke out in 1976, 1978,

1986, and 1989 shared a great deal with the anti-Guomindang Nationalists of the 1930s, the May Fourth experimenters of the 1920s, the anti-Qing activists of the later nineteenth century, certain "evidential research" scholars of the eighteenth century, and both the Donglin partisans and the Ming loyalists of the seventeenth century.

At a different level, the outbursts of vindictive rage on the part of some Chinese citizens and workers, however much they had been provoked to such acts by the very soldiers they killed, pointed to a different kind of tradition. Again and again, ordinary Chinese people with little or no education and no particular guiding ideology had risen against those who oppressed or exploited them. Vague dreams for a better life, an inner sense of hopelessness, and bitterly impoverished living conditions—these had proven potent goads to action against apparently unyielding and uncaring governments. And those with no weapons who wished to kill soldiers had to use their bare hands until they had seized their enemies' arsenals. Late-Ming peasant rebels; desperate followers of Wang Lun, Lin Qing, or the White Lotus sects; the Nian; the Boxers; peasants and urban workers in Hunan or Shanghai in the twentieth century all showed that there were limits to the indignities they would endure.

Finally, one other set of echoes seemed, in mid-1989, as if it too could have considerable resonance. While many of the student leaders on the government's "most wanted" list and some of the well-known intellectuals critical of the Communist regime managed to evade the police cordons and make their way to sanctuaries overseas, it seemed that they might be able to establish a potent base in exile from which to launch their criticisms of the state. Such criticism might, in turn, bring down the current government, or at least lay the groundwork for a series of reforms that would prepare the way for a successor regime more sympathetic to these exiles' aspirations for change. Constitutional reformers like Kang Youwei and Liang Qichao, Sun Yat-sen and the leaders of the Revolutionary Alliance, young Communists in the 1920s (including both Zhou Enlai and Deng Xiaoping himself) had all found shelter and ideological freedom to develop their ideas in foreign countries, from Japan to Mexico, and from the United States to Great Britain and France.

But though various foreign powers initially gave considerable financial and moral support and media attention to the exiled groups of 1989 dissidents, enthusiasm and support both waned as the dissident groups quarrelled among themselves, competed for attention with each other, and failed to come up with any particular leaders or effective organizational structures that would focus their energies. For a time they lobbied, with near success, to pressure individual corporations and foreign governments to cut back trade and investment in China unless flagrant Chinese human rights abuses were corrected. Through newsletters and other writings they also awakened Western consciences to the continuing crackdown against all dissidents, to the horrors of Chinese forced labor systems, to the tens of thousands of political prisoners who were incarcerated in such camps on the flimsiest charges under a special branch of "administrative laws" that by-passed the court system altogether, and to the role that the products of prison labor played in China's growing export trade. But in the long run, though many of the criticisms were solidly based, the economic arguments for continuing trade with China overwhelmed the moral ones, and by 1991 the levels of foreign investment in China first returned to the pre-1989 levels, and then began to rapidly exceed them.

Deng Xiaoping's position however had been seriously weakened by the events of 1989, and he was now placed more on the defensive then he had been before. The second half of 1989, as well as much of 1990, were occupied with rounding up the pro-democracy protesters and their supporters in the media and the bureaucracy, and attempting to render them powerless. Many thousands were arrested and jailed or sent to labor camps, and several— mainly workers—were executed. Thousands of party cadres were purged from government research institutes, from various academies teaching Marxist-Leninist (and Maoist thought), and especially from various "think-tanks" established by Zhao Ziyang—who, according to rumor, had refused to issue a self-criticism of his attempted leniency during the demonstrations. Zhao was removed from all official posts and placed under house arrest in Peking, where he remained even after Deng's death.[1]

Deng's critics within the Chinese Communist leadership pointed out that the headlong rush to embrace the West had led to an erosion of Chinese Communist values, produced severe imbalances within the Chinese economy, and threatened serious inflation. Li Peng, the premier who presided over the formation of day-to-day party planning, urged hewing to a rigid annual growth limit of 6 percent per year, to avoid the inflationary crises that had helped spark the disorders of 1989. As if current problems were not enough, the erosion of communist states all across Eastern Europe, the sudden fall of Gorbachev, and the subsequent swift collapse and fragmentation of the Soviet Union itself seemed terrible harbingers to many Chinese Communist leaders of China's own impending fate. Absolute suppression of domestic dissidents, tightened security in border areas with large "minority" populations such as Tibet and Xinjiang, and the reining in of economic change, all became government priorities. A group of thirty-two senior party members even suggested that the special economic zones be abolished altogether.

In the year or so following the bloody suppression of China's diffuse Democracy movement, there was a passion outside China for charting various scenarios of what the future might hold for the country: the options discussed ranged from internal political upheavals by students or workers leading to the ouster of Li Peng and the return of Zhao Ziyang, to a military coup, or even to the fragmentation of China along regional lines, and a return to something approaching the warlordism that followed the collapse of the Qing dynasty. What most people did not anticipate was that the Communist government under Deng would be able to hold onto its power and perquisites—and vastly increase its members' wealth—through a delicate balancing act of selectively stifling domestic criticism and dissent while at the same time allowing rapid economic growth for large sectors of the country as a whole.

Because no one could doubt Deng's own long loyalty to the revolution, his many years in Mao's confidence, and his active roles in the antirightist campaigns and the Great Leap Forward, Deng was able to steer around people like Chen Yun who wanted to continue strong centralized planning, and some of the tougher-minded Maoists who wished to return to rigorous public programs of ideological indoctrination. The hard-liners knew too that Deng's Cultural Revolution experiences had soured him on youthful enthusiasms in the name of revolution. At the same time, Deng's reiterated public praise for the PLA in June 1989 and thereafter for its steadfastness in the face of "hooligans," along with his support of the ambitious and profitable PLA patterns of international arms sales and domestic investments, assured him of the support of the armed services.

The forces inhibiting rapid economic growth showed surprising tenacity, however. The "gold-digging" attitudes of the young workers in Shenzhen came under harsh criticism, and the August 1991 coup against the Soviet leader Gorbachev by senior figures in his own party showed the vulnerability of even the most powerful leaders pushing for economic change.[2] So in January 1992 Deng decided to take a bold initiative in which he would use all his remaining prestige to reassert the economic validity and viability of China's greatest centers of economic dynamism and change, the special economic zones in China's southeast. In 1984 Deng had made a brief trip to Shenzhen to emphasize his faith in the new zone there, but the 1992 visit was more elaborate and took place in a more critical environment. Curiously, Deng described his 1992 visit as being an "inspection visit to the South," exactly the same term that Emperor Kangxi had used for the six tours of the South that he made between 1684 and 1707. When Kangxi said the "South" he had meant the key Yangzi Valley economic centers of Yangzhou, Nanjing, Suzhou, and Hangzhou; the emperor never went further south, into the subtropical region of Guangdong province itself. Deng Xiaoping, in his Southern tour, included Shanghai and the huge inland Yangzi industrial region of Wuhan, but he concentrated his attention on the deep South, Guangzhou (Canton), Zhuhai (near Macao), and Shenzhen right across the border from Hong Kong. Specifically referring to certain "conservative forces within the party," Deng noted that "ideology cannot supply rice." He praised the region of Guangdong for being a "leading force in economic development" and urged that the region soon catch up with the "four little dragons," by which he referred to Hong Kong, Singapore, Taiwan, and South Korea.

The levels of hostility to Deng—perhaps even the overt threat that he posed to several party seniors—is evident in the silence with which the Chinese media initially greeted this tour. But later in the spring Deng not only succeeded in having the significance of the tour and information about the crucial economic role of the new regions widely disseminated in the press but also formally incorporated in the public proceedings of the National People's Congress and in Central Committee documents. The PLA played its part, too. During the spring of 1992 the military commanders of all seven of China's military regions, along with fifty-seven other army generals, dutifully visited the Shenzhen and Zhuhai special economic zones, and allegedly returned from the visits "convinced of the success" of the zones and determined "to learn from the experience" there. Not to carry out "reform and opening," not to "develop the economy" could "only be the road to ruin," noted Deng. In addition, *rapid* development was essential to China: "low-speed development is equal to stagnation or even retrogression."

It was overly "leftist," Deng also observed, to see such reforms as being capitalist or as a corrosive form of "peaceful evolution" that would have dangerous consequences on China as a whole. "Socialism's real nature is to liberate productive forces, and the ultimate goal of Socialism is to achieve common prosperity." In an only thinly veiled reference to the crises of 1989, Deng added his own promise that all Chinese people conducting advanced study overseas would be welcomed if they came home to contribute their skills to the economy. To underline this point, he added that Hu Yaobang and Zhao Ziyang had fallen from power not because they had pushed for rapid economic growth, but because they had "stumbled on the issue of opposing bourgeois liberalization."[3]

ZONES AND GAMES

On his Southern tour, Deng Xiaoping had mused aloud that Shanghai should have been included in the list of the first designated special economic zones. Once he had consolidated his views in the spring of 1992—and even won the grudging acquiescence of his leading senior opponent within the party, the redoubtable Chen Yun (who had predicted that Deng's policies would lead to the collapse of the party along Russian or East European lines)—Deng moved to correct this lapse. He declared Shanghai to be the new "Dragon Head" of the Yangzi, the anchor for trade of five major river cities that were now to be opened to foreign investments.* At the same time, five other cities in Manchuria, the northwest, and the southwest were also to be developed as "open cities" for foreign trade and investment, along with various "border regions" in Xinjiang, Fujian, and Yunnan.†

The geographical spread of the areas now opened to the world's trade thus replicated the range of treaty ports at the peak of their growth in the late nineteenth century, though Deng was clearly confident that there would be no return to the world of special privileges and exploitation that had marked that period of Western arrogance and declining Qing power.

Mao Zedong had consistently shown his suspicion of the disruptive potential of Chinese cities—especially Shanghai—and though he had been willing to use the Shanghai-based radical faction of the early Cultural Revolution period to foster his own view of continuing revolution, the city had remained into the 1980s a vast and lumbering metropolis, with its huge population living in desperately poor housing, served by antiquated transport and harbor facilities, and working for the most part in vast, inefficient, and old-fashioned collective factories. Nevertheless, experience in Shanghai administration had proved crucial to Jiang Zemin, who found himself plucked by Deng Xiaoping from the city's party secretaryship in the summer of 1989 to take over the entire Chinese Communist party of 52 million members. Deng used Jiang in two capacities at once: first, to disarm the critics of fast growth by launching a campaign against "mammonism, hedonism and ultraegoism" within the Communist party—in a rather blunter moment Jiang dropped the euphemism and explained that he meant "exchanging money for power and indulging in lavish eating and illegal sex"—and by backing up the threats with arrests and executions.[4] Second, by having Jiang use his party office to endorse the 1992 Southern tour and to issue a new definitive version of Deng's economic goals for the nation. Jiang was rewarded for his loyalty by receiving two new appointments in 1993: as chairman of the Military Affairs Commission, and as president of the Chinese Republic. (The last person to hold these offices while also heading the party had been Hua Guofeng.)

---

*The five cities were Wuhu, Jiujiang, Wuhan (Hankou), Yueyang, and Chongqing.

†This second group of five cities consisted of Harbin, Hohhot, Urumchi, Kunming, and Nanning.

In the summer of 1992 Deng reached out to another Shanghai official, Zhu Rongji—a Hunanese, born in 1928 and trained originally as an electrical engineer before becoming Shanghai's mayor in the 1980s—and made him one of the architects of Chinese economic growth. Zhu became in rapid succession a vice-premier, a member of the ruling Standing Committee of the Politburo, and governor of the Bank of China (which had assets of 1,107 billion yuan at the time, with annual profits of 9 billion yuan). In his policy statements, Zhu emphasized that to foster growth the managers of Chinese enterprises must be able to fire workers and to assume responsibility for profit and loss, just as directors must be able to make key decisions without constant outside interference. Enterprise-wage increases should be "strictly in line with enterprise returns." To put such concepts in the context of population growth, reports in that same summer of 1992 noted that the fourth national census (based on China's population at midnight on July 1, 1990) had been 1.13 billion people. 318 million Chinese women were currently at childbearing age, and it seemed unlikely China could hold to the State Family Planning Commission goal of a population under 1.3 billion by the year 2000. Other figures suggested China's current "floating population" of those away from their officially registered permanent residence was about 70 million.

The Chinese economy was beginning to overheat. The growth of China's gross domestic product (GDP)—which had risen from the cautious post-1989 6 percent, to 12 percent in 1992—rose again in 1993, to 14 percent, and remained at 12 percent in 1994. One result of this growth was inflation, which reached 25 percent in 1993; others included wild speculation in real estate in Peking, Shanghai, and other cities, exacerbated by many banks' willingness to grant enormous loans for the flimsiest of reasons and with the weakest of collateral to those who had good party connections. Zhu Rongji sought to control these dangers by reducing GDP growth to 8 or 9 percent through a policy of cutting government spending, curbing luxury imports, checking speculation in stocks, firming up tax collection, hiking savings through forced purchase of government bonds, and raising interest rates.

Zhu's policies clashed with Deng Xiaoping's now apparently unstoppable optimism about growth. Although the two men avoided open conflict, Deng's new slogan that "Slow growth is not socialism," clearly militated against austerity, especially when coupled with a final visit of the now ninety-year-old Deng to Shanghai in 1994. Even though the national TV coverage made it clear that Deng was very frail and unable to speak clearly, his mere presence in Shanghai was enough to make the economy again grow dramatically. For a brief time inflation rose to a dangerous 30 percent in major cities, and reached 22 percent for the country as a whole. At the same time, foreign investment continued to pour into China, the number of joint ventures and their geographic distribution increased rapidly, and countries like the United States that erected no tariff barriers against China began to experience enormous trade deficits. Figures issued for the calendar year 1991 had already shown a trade surplus for China of U.S. $12 billion, listed 37,215 foreign-funded enterprises active in China, and showed that 33 million visitors from overseas had traveled to China in that year alone.

The Chinese government's success in curbing social unrest after the spectacular public demonstration and crackdown of 1989 undoubtedly boosted its self-confidence. Even if China was not yet a modern nation in the sense of permitting true pluralism, freedom of conscience and belief, or valid legal protections, it was still undergoing astonishing changes in the larger cities, in architecture, automobile traffic, storefront displays, advertising, and the range of permitted dress, all of which gave an appearance of modernity.

In this ambiance of heightened foreign visibility, and growing international interconnections, China sought to have its new-found self-identity as an emerging great power ratified in some dramatic way. By mid-1993 the leadership had seized on the goal of making Peking the site of the Olympic games for the year 2000—a symbolic and literal entry into the new millennium that would prove conclusively that China had arrived. To this end, the government conducted an energetic and at times flagrant lobbying program with all the major national delegations that would have the final say in the selection process. China's own athletes were themselves becoming world-class competitors in many sports, especially diving, track and field, and gymnastics. In addition, with the successful hosting of the Asian games in 1992, China had demonstrated the ability to construct top-level sports facilities, and provide adequate hotels and communications. Peking and other Chinese cities, by late 1993, were awash with billboards and posters stating that China was the natural site for the Olympics, and the Olympic logo with Chinese lettering was everywhere on display.

When foreign Olympic delegations were present, the government made special efforts to curb the serious pollution from Peking's factories by temporarily closing some of them; it banned the cheaper taxis and many private automobiles from the streets as well. Schoolchildren were assigned to clean the traffic signs, and shop assistants were given lessons on posture and friendliness. In similar vein, peddlers, poor migrant laborers, and beggars were kept out of sight, and the People's Liberation Army and the police forces were at pains to demonstrate that they would be able to maintain a high level of public security for visiting athletes and dignitaries.

To underline the general message of China's new openness, the prominent dissident Wei Jingsheng, author of "The Fifth Modernization" who had been in prison and forced labor camps ever since 1979, was suddenly released on September 14, 1993, a year short of his full fifteen-year sentence. This release was well publicized to coincide with the Chinese representatives' final lobbying of the Olympic delegates while the voting began in Monaco, on September 23. The successive votes to whittle down the possible sites were breath-takingly close: the rival cities of Istanbul, Manchester, and Berlin were defeated one by one, leaving Peking still in the running by the fourth and final ballot. Because China had invested so much emotional and real capital in a favorable outcome, their ultimate loss to Sydney in Australia, by a total of two votes (45 to 43, with 1 abstention), was a shattering blow to its self-esteem.

One immediate scapegoat was Wei Jingsheng, who was arrested again shortly after the negative vote and held secretly in detention, on the grounds that he had plotted against the state. Wei had in fact met with several of the 1978 and 1989 dissidents after his release, and had also spoken to foreign journalists. Furthermore, though just before the Olympic vote he had dodged journalists' questions about whether or not his release was connected to the Olympic games, once the vote was over Wei wrote a spirited essay on China, the United States, and the human rights issues. In this essay, entitled "The Wolf and the Lamb," he explained that the Chinese rulers found it difficult to accept that other countries really cared about human rights; they also believed President Clinton's remarks on the topic were "just an affectation." Washington's mistake, wrote Wei, lay in thinking that "the Communist Party resembles a bunch of slow-witted rulers of a backward culture and that China doesn't comprehend that violations of human rights are evil." In fact, China's leaders knew full well what they were doing, which was deliberately "to deprive the people of their freedom." Wei noted that the Americans were acting like the lamb in Aesop's fable: "After the wolf accuses the lamb of fouling his drinking water, the lamb protests: 'I could not have fouled your water because I live downstream from you.' The wolf eats the lamb anyway."[5]

Wei's essay was published in the *New York Times* on the "Op Ed" page in November 1993, and he also talked with President Clinton's deputy assistant secretary in charge of human rights. It was clearly these two events within the context of the Olympic Games' rejection that led to Wei's arrest and the severity of the charges. After a long period of secret incarceration, Wei was given a trial as manipulated as his first one in 1979; but this time none of his friends was able to smuggle a tape recorder into the courtroom. Wei was given little chance to speak in his defence and was sentenced to fourteen more years in prison. The tensions between the party's nationalistic pride on the world stage and its continuing harshness at the level of the obdurate individual dissenter had rarely been shown with such clarity. Only in 1997, after Deng Xiaoping's death, was Wei again released, and allowed to settle in the United States.

Little Dragons

Despite the government's inflexible stance towards those like Wei who tried to call openly for more democracy, there were signs within China that gradual change might be stirring from within. For example, when the huge and controversial project for the Three Gorges Dam on the Yangzi River was brought in final form before the National People's Congress of 1992, backed with the full authority of Premier Li Peng and other party elders, debate was extremely lively, and both the safety factors and the environmental and social impact of the dam were heatedly discussed. When the final vote was tallied, although 1,767 delegates voted in favor, 177 had the courage openly to vote against it, while a further 664 delegates abstained, and several others cast no vote at all. To have close to a third of the members of this normally acquiescent body register disapproval of such a major government-sponsored project was an extraordinary new development. Over the following years critics within China continued to express open opposition to many aspects of the dam, to interview those who might be adversely affected by its construction, and to circulate negative reports from engineers and bureaucrats who opposed the project. Similarly, in village "elections" where there had normally been automatic acceptance of candidates from the party's designated list, in several cases party nominees were rejected and more popular local candidates were substituted.

But such scenarios were still highly unusual in China and were dependent on the personal commitment of a few remarkable individuals. The most important models for shifts in a democratic direction from within Chinese communities came from two of those "four little dragons" that Deng Xiaoping had called on the Chinese to emulate economically, namely Taiwan and Hong Kong.

Of the two, it was Taiwan that had been making the most dramatic changes. The crucial event here was the decision by Chiang Kai-shek's son Chiang Ching-kuo, Taiwan's president, to move toward full and open democratic elections for the island's two chambers, the Legislature (where seats changed every three years) and the National Assembly (where many old Guomindang members still held their seats on the basis of their mainland elections back in 1947). Chiang Ching-kuo determined to encourage all the aspects that went with full democracy: truly competing political parties, clear and fair electoral rules and procedures, interparty coalitions, and an open, broad-based electorate of all adult citizens. He took the first key step in 1987 by officially ending martial law in Taiwan, legalizing opposition parties, and removing most press curbs and sedition laws. After the death of Chiang Ching-kuo in 1988, the domination of the Guomindang by mainland-born party elders was ended. In a crucial change of direction for Taiwan, the Taiwan-born Lee Teng-hui, whom Chiang had carefully prepared for the role, succeeded to the presidency. A new stage was reached with the 1991 decision of Taiwan's Council of Grand Justices that the surviving 1947 mainland-elected members of the National Assembly should retire that same year, opening up the institution to a new flock of representative candidates. This move was followed by the decision to have open elections for the president and vice-president by all Taiwanese citizens, as opposed to the past practice of ratifying those leaders by an Assembly vote. In a supplementary gesture designed to help heal old wounds, the Guomindang not only agreed to permit full and public study of the February 1947 massacre of Taiwanese people by the post-war Guomindang occupying forces but also expressed regret for the tragedy.[6]

The main rival to the Guomindang, the Democratic Progressive Party (DPP), which had been openly advocating an independent Taiwan, won 20 percent of the seats in the National Assembly elections of 1991, and 31 percent of those for the Legislature in 1992. In 1993 a third "new party" split off from the former Guomindang, making the competition even more lively. In 1994 the DPP candidate won the politically major office of mayor of Taipei over the Guomindang's chosen candidate. The climax to this process came with the first full election for Taiwan's president in 1996, in which candidates from all the major parties ran for office. An impressive 76 percent of eligible Taiwan voters went to the polls, and Lee Teng-hui won a majority with 54 percent of the total vote. The Chinese Communist government lost considerable prestige and respect by its attempt to intimidate any potential supporters of Taiwan independence during these elections by holding missile tests and conducting fleet maneuvers in the waters around Taiwan, which almost brought trade to a standstill. With this vote one could fairly say that the "tutelage system" envisioned by Sun Yat-sen as the crucial intermediary stage on China's march towards democracy had at last ended—at least for this Chinese society on China's periphery.

Taiwan thus seemed established as the kind of society that Deng Xiaoping hoped the mainland would become: in the mid 1990s its population of 21 million enjoyed a per capita average income of U.S. $10,556, ate an average of 3,000 calories per day, had life expectancies of seventy-one for men and seventy-seven for women, and an annual population increase below 1 percent. Fifty-seven percent of Taiwanese received some form of post-secondary-school advanced education, and more of its bureaucrats and legislators had advanced degrees than the comparable group in any other society. Unemployment in the 9-million-strong labor force stood at 0.9 percent.

By contrast, Hong Kong's road toward democracy was slower and more limited, conducted as it was under the shadow of the Sino-British Joint Declaration of "one country, two systems" that assumed the 1997 reversion of Hong Kong to the mainland. It was in the summer of 1991 that the British loosened their colonial grip by allowing the first open elections for eighteen of the seats on Hong Kong's sixty-member Legislative Council (Legco). The other forty-two seats were filled half with government-appointed members, and half from indirectly elected "constituency groups," such as doctors, lawyers, teachers, trade unionists, and businessmen. At least ninety-five candidates ran for office from a wide spectrum of pro-Peking, pro-business, pro-democracy groups, and from those with individual agendas of their own. The elections gave a strong majority to a party known as the United Democrats of Hong Kong, led by the articulate lawyer Martin Lee, who had been openly critical of Chinese mainland human rights abuses and of mainland interference in Hong Kong's affairs. The pro-Chinese Communist candidates were almost all defeated.

In October 1992 the newly appointed British governor, Christopher Patten, announced plans to open the constituency seats to elections as well, at the same time increasing the number of such seats and reducing those directly appointed by the governor. He stated that this would be followed by a full and open election by all Hong Kong residents eighteen and older to the Legislative Council, scheduled for 1995. Patten claimed these changes did not violate the basic law of 1984, but China disputed his contention. In addition, the appointed seats (now reduced to ten) were also to be chosen from a more widely based group of elected representatives. Responding angrily, the Chinese government announced that it would abolish such an openly elected Legislative Council when the Communists assumed power on July 1, 1997, and as an interim move named its own Advisory Panel on the transition, composed entirely of its own nominees. In the preliminary elections held in September 1994, the United Democrats gained twice as many seats as the pro-China parties. When the final, greatly anticipated elections were held in 1995 for the Legco, they gave a strong victory yet again to the United Democrats and a near-rout to the pro-China groups. But the total election turnout this time was only a disappointing 35 percent of those eligible. The Chinese government reiterated its vow to cancel the body after Hong Kong returned to Chinese control on July 1, 1997.

The Chinese government's attitude thus closely reflected the ideas expressed by Deng Xiaoping: the economic achievements of the Chinese people in Hong Kong and Taiwan were clearly a source of pride to China and were even seen as worthy of emulation, in terms of trade and investment strategies and independent management practices. But if those Chinese moving to new levels of prosperity sought valid democratic reforms, they were to be deflected—whether by threat, by force, or by simple abrogation once the Chinese Communist government was able to control the situation on its own terms. For China itself, the period of tutelage was unquestionably still in existence.

INTO THE SEA

It was not just the opposition to these borderland ventures in democracy that gave China a hard-edged look in these last years of Deng Xiaoping's rule as "paramount leader"; a whole slew of policies and pronouncements in China seemed to suggest that confrontation with Western powers—especially the United States—was now as much in the air as accommodation. It was in early 1994 that China shifted the basis of its rhetoric by branding the United States as the new "hegemonist" power, an abusive label that from the 1960s to the 1980s had been used to describe the Soviet Union and its various alleged attempts to sabotage the Chinese Revolution. By some accounts, Deng Xiaoping tried to stop this shift of the old polemical terminology from the Soviet Union to the United States, but he was unsuccessful, proving that his personal power was waning. The attacks on the United States were linked to insistent pressure from senior Chinese party leaders and generals—spurred on by what they had seen of the military technology used in the Gulf War—to give the People's Liberation Army more money to modernize and adapt its forces to the demands of a confrontational world. It was the "blatant interference by the American hegemonists," as the PLA chief of general staff put it in May 1994, that was offering "open support for the debilitating activities of hostile elements inside our country as well as opposing and subverting our socialist system." A member of the Politburo Standing Committee underlined the message, noting that the American goals were no less than "subverting the Chinese government and strangling China's development."[7]

Surely more was meant here than the United States' willingness to allow its officials to meet with Wei Jingsheng and discuss human rights violations, and more than injured dignity over the rejection of Peking as the Olympic games site for the year 2000. Looming larger were the protracted debates in the United States over withdrawing the "most-favored-nation" trading status for China, offering moral support to the exiled Dalai Lama in his quest for an end to Chinese exploitation of Tibet, and charges that China was defying international agreements by selling nuclear technology to countries such as Iran and Pakistan. Chinese responses to these and other "hegemonic" threats ranged from shadowing American warships in the Yellow Sea region with nuclear-powered submarines, to persecuting and fining Chinese Christians, re-arresting and resentencing many of the 1989 dissidents, arranging for the purchase of large quantities of Russian fighters and transport planes, and building an early warning radar net in the disputed area of the Spratly Islands (lying between Vietnam and Indonesia), to which China laid claim despite the Islands' enormous distance from the mainland.

But in truth, significant though the perceived threats from the West may have been, if any forces were conducting "debilitating activities" and "subverting the socialist system" of China, they were forces within China itself, and mostly without any overt or even covert Western support. It was changes in the nature of party rule, a growing popular awareness of the party's past lies and inconsistencies, and the influx of new hopes and ambitions among China's people that were putting the party so much on the defensive. Though adulation of Mao Zedong was still being expressed, it now often took on the dimensions of a pop cult rather than of a deeply held and passionate belief. A new Chinese cinema, the so-called "Fifth Generation" of filmmakers, used aesthetic evocations of old China to underline its messages of the unnecessarily bitter suffering in the People's Republic and to outline the inconsistencies and fallacies in current party attitudes toward ideas of justice and history. Swaggering novels and stories of street-smart Chinese youth, iconoclastic Chinese versions of rock and rap, sardonic cartoons and witty graffiti all carried their own messages of decay and change. A wry joke circulating in China caught these levels well: after shouting in the streets that Premier Li Peng was a "melonhead," a Chinese man was arrested and sentenced to twenty years in prison. The sentence was arrived at by combining two separate charges: one of five years for the expression of counterrevolutionary sentiments, and one of fifteen years for revealing state secrets.

At the same time, the urban and rural landscapes of China were in constant change. Roads were rammed through city neighborhoods, and whole villages were demolished, without any regard for historical preservation, local life-styles, or aesthetic considerations. Like Taiwan and Hong Kong, but without the benefit of either city planning or gracious architecture, huge forests of high-rise hotels and business towers—many owned and financed

China's emerging modernity reflected itself in additional material, rather than political, freedoms. Many newly accepted styles of dress were showcased on the catwalk of China's first major fashion show, April 1991.

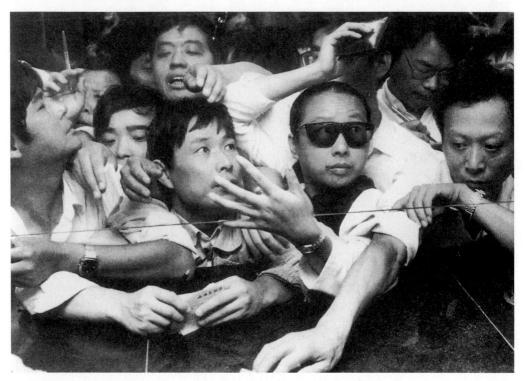

The opening of a stock exchange in Shanghai in the early 1990s set off a speculative mania in which every stock offer was snapped up

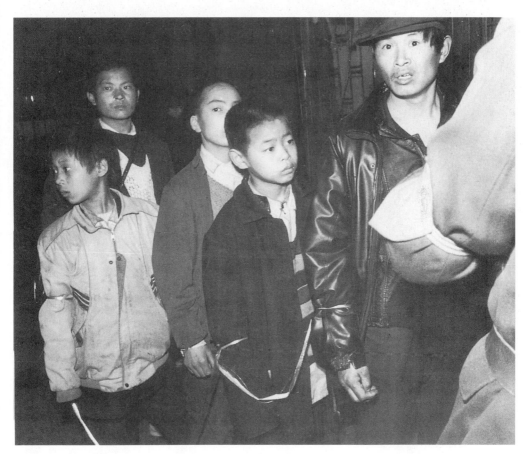

By 1992 over one million people—children as well as adults—were illegally migrating across China, mainly into the cities, in search of jobs

Wuhan Bridge   Since the 1979 passage of the "Sino-Foreign Joint Firms Law," foreign investment in China has supported China's economy and opened doors to the outside world. The Wuhan Bridge, completed in 1995, was a joint venture among investors in China, Japan, and Hong Kong.

The Three Gorges Dam   A massive flood control and hydroelectric project under construction on the upper Yangzi River above Yichang, the dam required the forced relocation of millions of residents along the river and the flooding of the beautiful, culturally significant gorges.

Lee Teng-hui. In March 1996, Lee, a Taiwan native, won re-election as Taiwan's president in the first free and direct presidential election on the island.

Zhu Rongji. Hand-picked by Deng Xiaoping to bolster China's economic situation, Zhu, now premier of the National Peoples Congress, struggled for years to maintain a robust economy in the face of rapid inflation.

Jiang Zemin, now president of the Peoples Republic of China With the end of Li Peng's term and the death of Deng Xiaoping, President Jiang Zemin quashed the authority of the former party leaders and assumed the role of the next generation of leaders.

On July 1, 1997, Hong Kong was returned to China, after more than 150 years of British colonial rule

A young couple in the coastal town of Xiamen, preparing for married life, embark on a quest for a decent material life

by the army or the internal security bureaucracy—began to ring not only Beijing and Shanghai, but to change the skylines of even small provincial towns, far from any special economic zones. Corruption cases became almost routine: there were 140,000 "legal and disciplinary cases" involving party members just in the first six months of 1994. Even as urban unemployment spread, and the outmoded collective industries struggled to survive in the newly competitive marketplace, agricultural life-styles changed too, sending millions of former farmers into the cities to find work at the booming building sites and in a new generation of sweatshops. Shanghai's migrant labor force swelled to 2.81 million; 60,000 were entering Peking in search of work in a single day: Jilin province in Manchuria issued a call of alarm when over 10 percent of its rural workers had migrated elsewhere. Thousands of academics and civil servants found their slender pay totally inadequate in the world of sharply rising prices and new consumer patterns. They added second or even third jobs to their schedules, in the race to exploit the current moment by "venturing out into the sea" (*xia hai*), as the common phrase put it.

The temper of the times can also be gauged by another phenomenon, the rising number of those who took the idea of getting "into the sea" with a new literalness. These were a new generation of Chinese migrants—many from Fujian province—who found the world of fast money hard to take, in the context of their own extreme poverty, and accordingly tried illegally to buy their way overseas. The case of the *Golden Venture*, a vessel loaded with Chinese illegal immigrants that ran ashore on Long Island near New York City in the summer of 1993, revealed dramatically that thousands of Chinese were promising payments of U.S. $20,000 or more to Chinese smugglers for a chance to get to the United States. Each time one route was cut by American immigration authorities and the coastguard, others opened up: first through the Caribbean by air, and then via complex trails through Southeast Asia. The scale of these operations revealed the power of Chinese organized crime, often linked (at least by name) to the old secret societies such as the Triads, which had been so powerful in the later Qing.

Only individual life stories can give a sense of this mix of turmoil, disequilibrium, excitement, and opportunity. Recent interviews conducted in rural China have highlighted the factors at work here. They show how once illiterate peasants, reared in the sufferings of the 1920s and 1930s, who had seen their families starve, the Japanese invade their land, and the Communists infiltrate their villages, gladly worked with the Communist party after 1949, and lived for and by the voice of Chairman Mao. But under the new policies of Deng Xiaoping, they had to venture out into the unknown once again, as they witnessed the breaking up of their communes and the decentralization and decollectivization of agriculture. Parallel stories from industrial workers remain to be told, though the general parameters can be gauged from "confessions" taken from such workers during the Cultural Revolution. A wide range of unofficial sources also show that in the 1990s there were clearly many more attempts at strikes, and far more serious industrial unrest, than the party has so far been willing to admit to. Many of the highly educated victims of the antirightist campaign and the Cultural Revolution have also written their stories, but usually these focus on their grim experiences in the 1960s and 1970s rather than on their subsequent attempts at readjustment in the Deng Xiaoping years.

For the young and middle-aged urban professionals of the 1990s, tension was endemic. Many spoke of their lives as a constant flux: though to some extent anchored by parents and spouses, they also felt the need to cope as loners in an unsettled society. Young couples often hedged their bets, with one family member venturing out into the unknown worlds of higher technology, marketing, or foreign trade, while the other spouse stayed tight within what was left of the socialist net, willing to work unproductive hours at low pay in return for health and social benefits, and access to adequate (if not spacious) housing. Most such couples had only one child in obedience to party dictates, but that single child was passionately cherished, though paradoxically often looked after by grandparents or sent to weekly boarding school because of the insistent work pressures on the parents. These young professionals read widely, thought freely, and were sarcastic about the party, even while admiring many of its past achievements. They felt it still had some role to play in stopping the country from sliding into anarchy. They saw the Democracy movement, at least as manifested from 1986 to the mid-1990s, as having little to offer China at the current time. They were starting to think of personal appearance, of family vacations, of surrounding themselves with aesthetically beautiful objects, and they were both frugal and shrewd. Those who had been teenagers in the Cultural Revolution remembered their parents' humiliations as strongly as they remembered their own, but they felt well steeled by those past deprivations to cope in the current world.

The parents for their part, especially those who were born in the 1920s or 1930s and had joined the party at the end of World War II or during the civil war, were often nostalgic for the clarity of choice that the world had offered in those days, for the promise of a better society that then seemed within reach. They vividly remembered the sharpness of the transition they had lived through, and their youthful sense that they were in the mainstream of history. They were saddened in the 1990s by the tumult and the lack of vision; they watched with bemused affection as their children floundered.

The generational sequencing was stark: one generation in the republic having large landholdings, or perhaps studying overseas; the next joining the party, working underground, building the revolution, and living in comparative security during the 1950s; a third weathering the Cultural Revolution, studying with passion through college, and then plunging into a succession (or often an overlapping sequence) of varying jobs.

To take just one example, a child born in 1955 was left to fend for himself in 1966, when his parents were arrested, and he subsequently worked in a steel mill and as an educational cadre. Acquiring a job in a state-run venture-capital firm, he went from there to assemble real-estate packages for a Hong Kong conglomerate, before creating a business selling TV advertising time to domestic and foreign sponsors. With money from these ventures came capital to design and patent automobile accessories, to found a social club for wealthy Communist cadres, and to set up a massage parlor, as well as making other forays into retailing apparel, publishing, and information storage on the Internet.[8] The lives of his contemporaries, who were drawn to the scholars' life, were equally filled—by the pursuit of knowledge for its own sake (with homage duly paid to the past complexities of Chinese history and culture), by deep respect for their own teachers, a tireless willingness to work, an astounding control of sources and bibliography, and strong ambitions to make a mark in the national and international world of letters.

If such men and women subverted the state and party, it was through their energy, independence, and integrity, not from deliberation or in pursuit of nefarious ends. Their goal was to find an opening for their hopes inside a China that they knew was changing, under leaders they could no longer admire.

DENG'S PASSING

An intriguing book that appeared in China in late 1994 gave a strange kind of focus to the country's mood. Entitled *Looking at China through a Third Eye*, the book was allegedly authored by a German scholar, but this fabrication was soon exposed, and the author was found to be a close friend of the son of the veteran party leader Chen Yun. The book boldly asserted that Deng's policies had led China into the trap of revering rapid and uneven economic growth; the result, however, had been to leave China's 800 million peasants "a living volcano" that could erupt at any time. It was this volatile force that was already flooding China's cities. The author sketched in vivid detail how Deng had laid the groundwork for a potential catastrophe even worse than Mao's Great Leap Forward, which had led to 30 million deaths.

Deng's polices would lead to an apocalypse of uncontrollable lawlessness in China that would dwarf Mao's disasters.[9]

The leadership scenario in China had indeed become increasingly bizarre to outside eyes, as had the setting in which the largely silent leadership struggle was taking place. While individual thugs (with or without party backing) were taking over many industries and even whole rural communities [10], China was now operating two major nuclear power plants, foreign exchange reserves were over U.S. $30 billion, and the United States trade deficit with China close to U.S. $20 billion. At the same time, the PLA was making gigantic purchases of advanced tanks, air-defence missile systems, and inflight refueling aircraft from the assembled stockpiles of the now defunct Soviet Union.

It was in this world of change and turbulence that the last living representatives of Mao's central legacy passed slowly from the scene, the roster of their names providing a cumulative summary of the revolution's tortuous history. It was in 1992 that Li Xiannian and Nie Rongzhen died, Li at the age of eighty-three and Nie at ninety-three. Li, a carpenter from Hubei, had joined the Communist party as a teenager in 1927, and was a key leader of the anti-Japanese guerrilla forces in Central China, before becoming the Communist Minister of Finance, and finally president of the People's Republic from 1983 to 1988; Nie, from a Sichuan landlord family, traveled to France in 1920 with the work-study group that included Deng Xiaoping, joining the party there in 1923. A fine scientist and intuitively brilliant military strategist, Nie played a leading part in the Long March, the Yan'an years, and the civil war, before becoming a marshal of the PLA and director of the Special Technology Commission that guided China's nuclear weapons and missile programs. The following year, 1993, the Hunan-born railroad worker Wang Zhen, who rose to be the logistical chief of the PLA and China's vice-president, and became the hardest of hard-liners, died at eighty-five.

Perhaps most importantly for Deng Xiaoping and his own close followers was the death of Chen Yun in 1995 at the age of eighty-nine. A typesetter with the Shanghai Commercial Press in the early 1920s, Chen joined the party in 1924 and became a major labor organizer. He helped to orchestrate the great Shanghai strikes of 1927, was made a member of the Central Committee in 1931, serving subsequently as Mao's most important economic advisor and as the architect of the post-1949 socialist reconstruction in China. From the 1980s onward, he had emerged as the most important critic of economic decollectivization and unchecked growth, and of what he saw as the accompanying erosion of moral and spiritual values in China. His death removed the main center of support and prestige for those Chinese planners who still espoused what they considered the fundamental Marxist-Leninist values, and who looked to ideological discipline, fiscal egalitarianism, and restraint as the keys to an ordered future for China.

During the mid-1990s, Deng Xiaoping's exact role was an enigma to most political observers. After his 1992 Southern tour, he made no more dramatic public gestures or statements. And the blurred pictures from his 1994 Shanghai visit were the last ones publicly circulated. Deng's personality cult was fostered in his old age by the government now headed by Jiang Zemin and Li Peng, who made sure that the "works of Deng" were widely disseminated and discussed, and who constantly referred to him as China's "paramount leader" despite his relinquishment of all formal government posts. But if Deng was paramount leader, it was mainly as an offstage presence, almost beyond speech, hearing, and gesture, whose often enigmatic remarks were filtered through the lips of close family members, especially his daughters and a small group of senior generals. There were few references any more even to the competitive bridge games with a small circle of friends, which had long been his recreational passion—though to the end Deng retained his title as "Honorary Chairman of the China Bridge Association." Deng was said to be keeping up with events in a general way, and enjoying the company of his grandchildren.

In the meantime, the leadership of the country seemed to be on hold, even as the frenzied and uncoordinated spate of economic growth and change continued. Premier Li Peng—whose own term of office was due to end in March 1998—issued a public statement in April 1995 that a transition "from the second-generational central leading collective, with Deng Xiaoping at the core," was underway "smoothly" and that the "third-generational leading collective, with Comrade Jiang Zemin at the core," was now in place. Behind these remarks lay some tough and complicated political maneuvering. Almost immediately after Chen Yun's death, Jiang Zemin had forced the resignation of one of his own key rivals, the powerful Peking Party Secretary Chen Xitong (whose own deputy-mayor had just committed suicide in the midst of a major corruption scandal). As Peking party head, Chen Xitong could have called on the services of tens of thousands of police and security forces in the capital. With Chen's removal, Jiang brought to completion a series of preventive moves to ensure that he would not follow the fate of the Gang of Four after Mao's death. He had already appointed his own personal head bodyguard, You Kexi, to be the commandant of the Peking-region Central Guards Regiment, with the rank of lieutenant general. This regiment was the famous "Unit 8341," which back in 1976 had spearheaded the coup against the Gang of Four.[11]

Thus when the death of Deng Xiaoping on February 19, 1997, from a lung infection and complications of Parkinson's disease, was announced to the nation, there was a strange sense of uncertainty as much as loss. The government moved at once to make sure that demonstrators would not use the pretext of mourning Deng to raise major political criticisms of the regime, as they had done so conspicuously on two previous occasions: in April 1976, in the mourning for Zhou Enlai, and in April 1989, in the mourning for Hu Yaobang. The first of these cases, that of April 1976, grew into an open attack on Chairman Mao and his policies, and Deng Xiaoping himself was blamed for the upheaval by his political enemies; once Deng regained power in 1979, he "reversed the verdicts" on 1976, claiming that the demonstrations were justified as criticisms of the excesses of the Gang of Four and the Cultural Revolution. But Deng had never reversed the verdicts on the events of 1989, nor expressed any contrition for the deaths of students and civilians that occurred at that time. Police controls were tight in 1997, to make sure that his memory neither be excoriated nor yet overpraised in what might be seen as a slap to China's current president and party secretary-general, Jiang Zemin. So muted, indeed, was the public response, that the government had to encourage limited and carefully controlled displays of emotion on the day of Deng's funeral, but only for delegations from state enterprises and work units specially invited by the government. By Deng's own previous request, after the ceremony his ashes were scattered over the sea, as Zhou Enlai's had been in 1976.

The muted funeral also served to accentuate a more subtle political point, one that Jiang Zemin was anxious to establish in the nation's mind: Deng Xiaoping had been on the sidelines for several years, and the *de facto* transfer of power had been quietly, yet effectively, carried out. To emphasize this further, Jiang in his funeral oration expressed the hope that the remaining elderly former leaders of the party—several of whom were at the funeral ceremony—should now step aside and not seek tenure of power for life. This would remove from influence the last figures such as Peng Zhen (ninety-five), Bo Yibo (eighty-nine), and Yang Shangkun (ninety) who had all been close to Mao and whose long revolutionary lives gave them a historical resonance that the much younger Jiang Zemin—who was seventy-one—could never aspire to. Jiang's own revolutionary credentials were limited to his work as a student leader in the later 1940s, followed by a career as an energy expert in the party bureaucracy. Such retirements would also mean that the more senior military officers who currently controlled the PLA would also have to step down, thus giving Jiang Zemin a much stronger base on the all-important Central Military Commission.

The timing of Deng's death ensured Jiang Zemin the freedom to enjoy the limelight at midnight between June 30 and July 1, 1997, when, by the prior 1984 agreement with Great Britain, Hong Kong reverted to Chinese control. As the Union Jack and the former colonial Hong Kong flag were lowered, and the red flag with gold stars of the People's Republic was raised aloft next to the newly designed red pauonia-blossom flag of the Hong Kong administrative region, Jiang Zemin sat next to Britain's Prince Charles on the stage of the vast new convention center, which was just being completed by a group of Hong Kong and Chinese real estate developers on a controversial landfill site on the edge of the main harbor.

China's own choice for the new chief executive of Hong Kong, who would replace the departing British governor Christopher Patten, was the articulate, crew-cut Chinese businessman Chee-hua Tung, who went by the name of "C. H." Tung was born in 1937 to a wealthy Shanghai family that had built up a shipping business before and after World War II; after the Communist victory the family emigrated to Hong Kong and their business expanded rapidly both there and in Taiwan (where they received Guomindang support). C. H. himself went to university in Britain and worked for a decade with corporations in the United States, before returning to Hong Kong to join his father. When the family business was threatened with collapse in the early 1980s, C. H. Tung staved off bankruptcy by negotiating a $120 million loan from Peking. He owed his new position to his prominent role among the elite group of Hong Kong's Chinese business leaders who were well known in Peking, and because his views seemed to coincide with what could loosely be called the "new authoritarianism" that now was fashionable: thus, C. H. Tung publicly espoused the values of law and order, denigrated any excessive race towards democracy, praised Singapore's centrist government as a suitable model, and publicly endorsed the stated Chinese decision to abolish the democratically elected Legislative Council. But at the same time, C. H. Tung reassured the people of Hong Kong that he would protect their distinctive way of life, faithfully enforce the Basic Law, and maintain the independence of the judiciary.

What all this said about the previous decades of Communist rule was of course not lost on China's satirists, who were themselves once again ready to speak out with vigor and freshness. It was the veteran writer of irreverent Peking street-life stories Wang Shuo who caught the mood most perfectly. As a little boy, wrote Wang in an essay published three days before the handover, he had been taught clearly that "the Chinese people had all stood up, but Hong Kong people still served the British as their cows and horses." His boyish heart used to fill with pity as he heard that the Hong Kong people had no shoes, and lived on fishbones. But now there was a bit of a mystery. Apparently these Hong Kong people did wear shoes after all, and leather ones at that. They were also very rich, so rich that by their loose and lascivious ways they had changed the "good old adultery" of the "pure and honest mainlanders" into prostitution. Some of his muddled friends, Wang Shuo continued, said Hong Kong's prosperity showed that China might have done better in the past to leave Qingdao in German hands, and Dalian in Japanese, and let them become wealthy "cash boxes" like Hong Kong. Nothing would have been lost: "The motherland would still be the great motherland." But perhaps at that point he had better stop, said Wang. "Poor dad still has a bad temper, and he'll beat his kid over any little thing." The best policy remained, as it had been before: "Be like the Shanghainese: Work hard, then send your own people to Beijing to take over the Politburo."[12]

Looming behind this celebration of the end of foreign control over Hong Kong lay the question of Taiwan. Weeks before the Hong Kong transfer, as a giant clock specially erected in Tiananmen Square counted down the days, hours, and minutes, banners displayed in Peking carried slogans stating that "China was eagerly welcoming the return to the motherland of Hong Kong, Macao, and Taiwan." Macao's return, after more than four and a half centuries of total or partial Portuguese control, was already set for 1999. But the case of Taiwan was infinitely more complex. Even as Chinese authorities were citing pro-Taiwan independence rallies as the kind of demonstrations that would not be tolerated in Hong Kong, any more than those demanding independent rights for the people of Tibet or the Muslim inhabitants of Xinjiang would, the government of President Lee on Taiwan was working with a coalition of rival parties to end the system by which a "provincial government" of Taiwan coexisted with the central Taiwan government. The significance of this change was that the separate provincial government was a throwback to the period of the civil war and the early fifties, when Taiwan claimed to be merely the temporary base for a Chinese national government in exile. With the abolition of this provincial representation, Taiwan would become, in effect, a completely independent political unit, with no more formal governmental interdependence with the mainland. Thus the Peking government attacked the decision as a dangerous provocation.

The facts were curious. If China now stood on the edge of modernity, as its people had long hoped, it would be propelled forward by twin legacies to which it had long been opposed: one, the very system built up in Hong Kong under British Imperialism against which the Communist party had fulminated since its inception; the other, the Taiwan economic and political dynamo that had sprung out of Japanese colonialism by way of half a century of rule under the Communist party's bitterest domestic enemy, the Guomindang.

No one could doubt that Hong Kong and Taiwan had made the transition into being modern Chinese societies, with all the economic and cultural possibilities and challenges that such a label signified. But with 6.3 million and 21.6 million people respectively, the two societies were utterly dwarfed by the close to 1.3 billion population of the People's Republic. And China itself was still facing the future on the basis of the state's dominance over key areas of the economy. In mid-1997, state-owned enterprises still employed 67 percent of China's urban work force and contributed 60 percent of the state's revenues; in key industries, state control was even higher: 77 percent in chemicals, 79 percent in metallurgy, and over 90 percent in both electrical power and oil production. Deciding to confront this anomaly directly, in September 1997 China's leaders announced their decision to sell off at least 10,000 of the remaining 13,000 large and medium state-owned enterprises. Dodging the word "privatization" they argued that selling stock in those companies would constitute "public ownership." The decision was a bold one, for it would take the most imaginative and courageous planning to sell off these companies without raising industrial unemployment to explosive levels and without producing further environmental imbalances in a country already suffering dangerous levels of water shortage, soil erosion, shrinking arable land, and air and rain pollution.

In public, some Chinese party stalwarts continued to express their belief in the socialist values with which they had been raised. As one acerbic party member noted in an anonymous special report, "the mentality of imitating Hong Kong and Taiwan culture, worshipping everything foreign, and yearning for the capitalist world has been passed from ignorant young people to some intellectuals and party and government cadres." The author conjured up a Chinese world of "speculation in stocks and real estate, trading of false invoices, pornography, production and selling of counterfeit goods, and even smuggling," within a society where a mere 2 percent of all bank depositors now contributed 80 percent of the total deposits. The author of the report went on to paint a scenario of industrial strikes, violence, rural impoverishment, and weakened cultural morale coexisting in close proximity with the world of "nightclubs, golfcourses, saunas, massage parlors, and brothels." In his view, "almost all ugly phenomena of the old society prior to the establishment of the Republic have been revived."[13]

Irresponsible leaders, a luxury-loving elite, a morally lax middle class, and an exploited rural and manufacturing sector living on the edge of direst poverty: this was also close to the social scene invoked not only by Ming patriots as in anguish they watched their dynasty fall to the upstart Qing, but also by Chinese revolutionaries at the Qing dynasty's end and by the Communists as they marshalled their disciplined forces against the world of perceived republican decadence. From such a viewpoint, the negative forces now confronting the party and the people of China were little different from what they had been in the bad old days. But there was something too tidy about such a pattern of argument and criticism. As a book published in late 1996 by a Chinese student recently returned from an American university had explained, the United States was not merely a country suffused with "singing, laughter, and the smell of barbecue at parties." It was also living proof that Chinese themselves could have "a different kind of life, free from the repetitious political movements in the past and life-and-death struggles." It was not a "natural and absolute" truth that China's leaders had to "control the people."[14]

On an official visit to the United States in October 1997, president Jiang Zemin seemed implicitly to support a more open stance, as he included both Independence Hall in Philadelphia and the New York Stock Exchange in his itinerary. A few weeks later, just after Chinese construction workers had completed their diversion of the Yangzi River so that work could begin on the second stage of the Three Gorges Dam project, the dissident Wei Jingsheng was released from prison and allowed to go abroad. A few months later, in March 1998, in his inaugural speech as China's new premier, Zhu Rongji spoke at length of China's economic challenges, but never once mentioned the name of Mao Zedong. Such juxtapositions of a pragmatically developmental attitude with a more open ideological one seemed to offer a constructive road into the rapidly approaching new century. Perhaps, once again, the skills and the insights of China's people would be allowed full range to grow, so that some sense could be made of both the legacies and the wreckage of the past. If this were to be the case, then there was indeed a chance that something at once modern, harmonious, and perceptive would emerge, offering to the world a new kind of vision of what it was to be Chinese.

APPENDIXES

Notes and Permissions

CHAPTER 1 *(pages 7–25)*

1. Tang Xianzu, *The Peony Pavilion,* trans. Cyril Birch (Bloomington: Indiana University Press, 1980), pp. 14 and 32.

2. G. William Skinner, ed., *The City in Late Imperial China* (Stanford: Stanford University Press, 1977), p. 351.

3. Tang Xianzu, p. 34.

4. Wang Yangming, *Instructions for Practical Living and Other Neo-Confucian Writings,* trans. Wing-tsit Chan (New York: Columbia University Press, 1963), p. 146 (modified).

5. L. Carrington Goodrich and Fang Chao-ying, eds., *Dictionary of Ming Biography* (New York: Columbia University Press, 1976), p. 708.

6. This is the first period in which China's interconnectedness with an emerging global economy can be charted. For details of the crisis theory of silver see William Atwell's "International Bullion Flows and the Chinese Economy circa 1530–1650" (*Past and Present* 95 [May 1982]: 68–90) and the same author's "Some Observations on the 'Seventeenth-Century Crisis' in China and Japan" (*Journal of Asian Studies* 45, no. 2 [February 1986]: 223–224). Also see Frederic Wakeman's "China and the Seventeenth-Century Crisis" (*Late Imperial China* 7, no. 1 [June 1986]: 1–26). This crisis theory is modified in Richard von Glahn, *Fountain of Fortune: Money and Monetary Policy in China, 1000–1700,* (Berkeley: University of California Press, 1996), 237–245.

7. Helen Dunstan, "The Late Ming Epidemics: A Preliminary Survey," *Ch'ing-shih wen-t'i* 3, no. 3 (1975): 29–30.

8. *Ibid.,* 39–40. The basic premises of traditional Chinese medicine are presented in Nathan Sivin, *Traditional Medicine in Contemporary China* (Ann Arbor: University of Michigan Press, 1987).

CHAPTER 2 *(pages 26–48)*

1. Franz Michael, *The Origin of Manchu Rule in China* (New York, 1965), p. 121.

2. Gertraude Roth, "The Manchu-Chinese Relationship," 1618–1636," in Jonathan Spence and John Wills, eds., *From Ming to Ch'ing* (New Haven: Yale University Press, 1979), p. 9.

3. *Ibid.,* p. 18.

4. *Ibid.,* p. 30.

5. Lynn Struve, *The Southern Ming, 1644–1662* (New Haven: Yale University Press, 1984), p. 129.

6. Frederic Wakeman, *The Great Enterprise* (Berkeley: University of California Press, 1985), pp. 55–58; Struve, pp. 47 and 58–61.

7. Robert Oxnam, *Ruling from Horseback* (Chicago: University of Chicago Press, 1975), pp. 52 and 56.

8. "Biography of Ch'in Liang-yü (Qin Liangyu)," in *Eminent Chinese of the Ch'ing Period,* ed. Arthur Hummel (Washington, D.C., 1943), pp. 168–169.

CHAPTER 3 *(pages 49–73)*

1. Jonathan Spence, *Emperor of China: Self-Portrait of K'ang-hsi* (New York, 1974), p. 32.

2. Willard Peterson, "The Life of Ku Yen-wu, 1613–1682," *Harvard Journal of Asiatic Studies* 28 (1968): 142.

3. Kong Shangren (K'ung Shang-jen), *The Peach Blossom Fan,* trans. Chen Shih-hsiang and Harold Acton (Berkeley: University of California Press, 1976), p. 278.

4. Richard Strassberg, *The World of K'ung Shang-jen: A Man of Letters in Early Ch'ing China* (New York: Columbia University Press, 1983), p. 275.

5. *Ibid.,* p. 219.

6. Spence, p. 165.

7. Richard von Glahn, *Fountain of Fortune: Money and Monetary Policy in China* (Berkeley: University of California Press, 1996), pp. 211–215.

8. Spence, pp. 148–149.

CHAPTER 4 *(pages 74–95)*

1. These three macroregion case studies are drawn from Susan Naquin and Evelyn Rawski, *Chinese Society in the Eighteenth Century* (New Haven: Yale University Press, 1987), ch. 5. The basic works introducing and expanding the macroregion concept are the essays by G. William Skinner in the volume he edited, *The City in Late Imperial China* (Stanford: Stanford University Press, 1977).

2. Figures for Hebei and Shandong are from Philip Huang, *The Peasant Economy and Social Change in North China* (Stanford: Stanford University Press, 1985), p. 322. "All China" figures from Ho Ping-ti, *Studies on the Population of China, 1368–1953* (Cambridge: Harvard University Press, 1959), p. 281.

3. From James Lee and Robert Eng, "Population and Family History in Eighteenth Century Manchuria: Preliminary Results from Daoyi, 1774–1798," *Ch'ing-shih wen-t'i* 5, no. 1 (June 1984): 31. Also see James Lee and Cameron Campbell, *Fate and Fortune in Rural China: Social Organization and Population Behavior in Liaoning, 1774–1873* (Cambridge: Cambridge University Press, 1997), chapters 4 and 5.

4. Madeleine Zelin, *The Magistrate's Tael: Rationalizing Fiscal Reform in Eighteenth-Century Ch'ing China* (Berkeley: University of California Press, 1984), p. 80.

5. This paragraph and the rest of this section are based on the material in Beatrice S. Bartlett's *Monarchs and Ministers: The Rise of the Grand Council in Mid-Ch'ing China, 1723–1820* (Berkeley: University of California Press, 1990).

6. Cited (with slight modifications) from Beatrice S. Bartlett, "The Vermilion Brush: The Grand Council Communications Systems and Central Government Decision Making in Mid-Ch'ing China" (Ph.D. diss., Yale University, 1980), pp. 57 and 61.

7. Antonio Sisto Rosso, *Apostolic Legations to China of the Eighteenth Century* (South Pasadena, 1948), p. 405.

8. Fu Lo-shu, *A Documentary Chronicle of Sino-Western Relations, 1644–1820,* 2 vols. (Tucson: University of Arizona Press, 1966), vol. 1, p. 164.

CHAPTER 5 *(pages 96–116)*

1. On Qianlong's Muslim consort see James A. Millward, "A Uygher Muslim in Qianlong's court: The Meanings of the Fragrant Concubine," *Journal of Asian Studies* 53, no. 2 (1994): 427–458.

2. The *I-ching* or *Book of Changes,* trans. Richard Wilhelm and Cary Baynes (Princeton: Princeton University Press, 1950), pp. 213 and 670.

3. The key study of the *kaozheng* movement, on which these paragraphs are based, is Benjamin Elman, *From Philosophy to Philology* (Cambridge: Harvard University Press, 1984).

4. The analysis of women as writers has been greatly enriched by Susan Mann in *Precious Records: Women in China's Long Eighteenth Century* (Stanford: Stanford University Press, 1997).

5. Cao Xueqin, *The Story of the Stone [Dream of the Red Chamber],* trans. David Hawkes, vol. 1 (New York, 1973), pp. 51 and 55 (slightly modified).

6. *Ibid.,* vol. 3, p. 31.

7. Susan Naquin, *Shantung Rebellion: The Wang Lun Uprising of 1774* (New Haven: Yale University Press, 1981), p. 60.

8. *Eminent Chinese of the Ch'ing Period,* ed. Arthur Hummel, 2 vols. (Washington, D.C., 1943), vol. 1, p. 223.

9. Harold Kahn, *Monarchy in the Emperor's Eyes* (Cambridge: Harvard University Press, 1971), p. 255, and J. L. Cranmer-Byng, ed., *An Embassy to China: Lord Macartney's Journal, 1793–1794* (London, 1962), p. 120.

10. Cranmer-Byng, pp. 281–283.

CHAPTER 6 *(pages 117–137)*

1. J. L. Cranmer-Byng, ed., *An Embassy to China: Lord Macartney's Journal, 1793–1794* (London, 1962), p. 340. On the kowtow compromise see Joseph Esherick, "Cherishing Sources from Afar," *Modern China* 24, no. 2 (April 1998): 151–152.

2. Cranmer-Byng, pp. 191, 212–213.

3. Derk Bodde and Clarence Morris, eds., *Law in Imperial China* (Cambridge: Harvard University Press, 1967), p. 390.

4. Randle Edwards, "Ch'ing Legal Jurisdiction over Foreigners," in *Essays on China's Legal Tradition,* ed. Jerome Cohen, Randle Edwards, and Fu-mei Chang Chen (Princeton: Princeton University Press, 1980), pp. 222–269.

5. *Ibid.,* p. 229.

6. Figures drawn from Hosea Ballou Morse, *The International Relations of the Chinese Empire,* 3 vols. (Shanghai and London, 1910–1918), vol. 1, pp. 173 and 209, and Chang Hsin-pao, *Commissioner Lin and the Opium War* (Cambridge: Harvard University Press, 1964), p. 223.

7. Jonathan Spence, "Opium Smoking in Ch'ing China," in *Conflict and Control in Late Imperial China,* ed. Frederic Wakeman and Carolyn Grant (Berkeley: University of California Press, 1975), pp. 143–173 (slightly modified).

8. François Marie Arouet de Voltaire, *Essai sur les moeurs et l'esprit des nations* (Geneva, 1771), vol. 1, p. 36.

9. Nicolas Antoine Boulanger, *Recherches sur l'origine du despotisme oriental* (Paris, 1763), trans. John Wilkes (Amsterdam, 1764), p. 260.

10. Adam Smith, *An Inquiry into the Nature and Causes of the Wealth of Nations,* ed. Edwin Cannan (Chicago: Chicago University Press, 1976), p. 70.

11. *Ibid.,* pp. 71–72, 95.

12. Georg Wilhelm Friedrich Hegel, *The Philosophy of History,* trans. E. S. Haldane and Frances Simon (New York, 1956), pp. 18–19.

13. *Ibid.,* pp. 87, 90–91.

14. *Ibid.,* quotations in order: pp. 116, 138, 101.

CHAPTER 7 *(pages 145–166)*

1. Wolfgang Bauer, *China and the Search for Happiness,* trans. Michael Shaw, (New York, 1976), p. 257.

2. Li Ruzhen (Li Ju-chen), *Flowers in the Mirror,* trans. Lin Tai-yi (Berkeley: University of California Press, 1965), p. 113.

3. Shen Fu, *Six Records of a Floating Life,* trans. Leonard Pratt and Chiang Su-hui (New York, 1983), p. 73, and Lin Yu-tang's rendering in *T'ien Hsia Monthly* 1 (1935): 316.

4. Two recent dissertations cause re-evaluation of previously accepted views of the silver problem and the Hong merchants: Lin Man-houng, "Currency and Society: The Monetary Crisis and Political-Economy Ideology of Nineteenth Century China" (Harvard, 1989), and Chen Kuo-tung, "The Insolvency of the Chinese Hong Merchants, 1760–1843" (Yale, 1989).

5. H. B. Morse, *The International Relations of the Chinese Empire,* vol. 1 (Shanghai, 1910), p. 126.

6. Chang Hsin-pao, *Commissioner Lin and the Opium War* (Cambridge: Harvard University Press, 1964), pp. 134–135.

7. Arthur Waley, *The Opium War through Chinese Eyes* (London, 1958), pp. 44, 46, 49.

8. *Ibid.,* p. 47, and quotation from Chang Hsin-pao, p. 160.

9. Morse, p. 622.

10. Chang Hsin-pao, p. 191; Morse, p. 253.

11. Chang Hsin-pao, pp. 206–207.

12. Morse, p. 241.

13. *Ibid.,* p. 661–662.

14. The history of the *Nemesis* and the Chinese copies are detailed in Gerald Graham, *The China Station: War and Diplomacy, 1830–1860* (New York: Oxford University Press, 1978), pp. 117–118, 183, 215–218.

15. The full text of the Treaty of Nanjing is from Godfrey Hertslet, *Treaties etc. between Great Britain and China and between China and Foreign Powers,* 2 vols. (London, 1908), vol. 1, pp. 7–12.

16. Morse, p. 330 on Wanghia.

17. Joseph Fletcher, *The Heyday of the Ch'ing Order in Mongolia, Sinkiang and Tibet,* vol. 10 of *The Cambridge History of China* (Cambridge, 1978), pp. 377–383.

18. John K. Fairbank, *Trade and Diplomacy on the China Coast* (Cambridge: Harvard University Press, 1953), p. 113.

CHAPTER 8 *(pages 167–191)*

1. Susan Naquin, *Millenarian Rebellion in China: The Eight Trigrams Uprising of 1813* (New Haven: Yale University Press, 1976), pp. 72–77.

2. *Ibid.,* p. 83.

3. *Ibid.,* p. 93.

4. Frederic Wakeman, *Strangers at the Gate* (Berkeley: University of California Press, 1966), p. 89.

5. Jen Yu-wen (Chien Yu-wen), *The Taiping Revolutionary Movement* (New Haven: Yale University Press, 1973), pp. 93–94.

6. Franz Michael and Chang Chung-li, *The Taiping Rebellion: History and Documents,* 3 vols. (Seattle: University of Washington Press, 1966–1971), vol. 2, p. 314.

7. The analysis of the events and social attitudes in Taiping-occupied Nanjing is drawn from John Withers, "The Heavenly Capital: Nanjing under the Taiping, 1853–1864" (Ph.D. diss., Yale University, 1983).

8. Michael and Chang Chung-li, vol. 3, p. 767.

9. *Ibid.,* vol. 1, pp. 168 and 174.

10. H. B. Morse, *The International Relations of the Chinese Empire,* vol. 1 (Shanghai, 1910), pp. 671–672.

11. *Ibid.,* p. 579.

12. Elizabeth Perry, *Rebels and Revolutionaries in North China, 1845–1945* (Stanford: Stanford University Press, 1980), p. 130.

13. Teng Ssu-yu, *The Nien Army and Their Guerrilla Warfare, 1851–1868* (Paris, 1961), p. 169.

14. Chu Wen-djang, *The Moslem Rebellion in Northwest China, 1862–1878: A Study of Government Minority Policy* (The Hague, 1966), pp. 57 and 69.

15. *Ibid.,* pp. 91–92, citing Wang Boxin.

CHAPTER 9 *(pages 192–214)*

1. Cited from Andrew Cheng-kuang Hsieh, "Tseng Kuo-fan, a Nineteenth Century Confucian General" (Ph.D. diss., Yale University, 1975), p. 23.

2. Teng Ssu-yü and John K. Fairbank, *China's Response to the West: A Documentary Survey, 1839–1923* (Cambridge: Harvard University Press, 1954), pp. 53–54.

3. *Ibid.,* p. 62.

4. Yung Wing, *My Life in China and America* (New York, 1909), p. 168.

5. Mary Wright, *The Last Stand of Chinese Conservatism: The T'ung-chih Restoration, 1862–1874* (Stanford: Stanford University Press, 1957), p. 213.

6. Masataka Banno, *China and the West, 1858–1861: The Origins of the Tsungli Yamen* (Cambridge: Harvard University Press, 1964), p. 228.

7. Teng and Fairbank, pp. 47–48.

8. H. B. Morse, *The International Relations of the Chinese Empire,* vol. 2 (Shanghai, 1910), p. 37.

9. Morse, p. 38.

10. Immanuel Hsü, *China's Entrance into the Family of Nations: The Diplomatic Phase, 1858–1880* (Cambridge: Harvard University Press, 1960), p. 132.

11. *Ibid.,* pp. 133–134.

12. Fred Drake, *China Charts the World* (Cambridge: Harvard University Press, 1975), pp. 159 and 164–165; pp. 187 and 245 for details on the Washington Monument.

13. Wright, p. 252.

14. G. E. Moule, "The Obligation of China to Europe in the Matter of Physical Science," *Journal of the North China Branch of the Royal Asiatic Society* n.s. 7 (1871): 150–151.

15. Yung Wing, pp. 3–4.

16. Katherine F. Bruner, John K. Fairbank, and Richard Smith, eds., *Entering China's Service: Robert Hart's Journals, 1854–1863* (Cambridge: Harvard University Press, 1986), pp. 230–232.

17. Frederick Wells Williams, *Anson Burlingame and the First Chinese Mission to Foreign Powers* (New York, 1912), pp. 136–139.

18. Michael Hunt, *The Making of a Special Relationship: The United States and China to 1914* (New York: Columbia University Press, 1983), p. 92.

19. *Ibid.,* p. 93, citing James G. Blaine.

CHAPTER 10 *(pages 215–242)*

1. H. B. Morse, *The International Relations of the Chinese Empire,* vol. 3 (Shanghai, 1910), p. 35.

2. Joseph Esherick, *The Origins of the Boxer Uprising* (Berkeley: University of California Press, 1987), pp. 299–300.

3. Victor Purcell, *The Boxer Uprising, a Background Study* (New York: Cambridge University Press, 1963), p. 225 (modified).

4. Zou Rong (Tsou Jung), *The Revolutionary Army: A Chinese Nationalist Tract of 1903,* trans. John Lust (The Hague, 1968), p. 122.

5. *Ibid.,* p. 126.

6. W. H. Brewer Papers, Yale University Archives, 1/6/185/18v.

7. Don Price, *Russia and the Roots of the Chinese Revolution, 1896–1911* (Cambridge: Harvard University Press, 1974), p. 215.

CHAPTER 11 *(pages 243–263)*

1. Roger Thompson, "Visions of the Future, Realities of the Day: Local Administrative Reform, Electoral Politics, and Traditional Chinese Society on the Eve of the 1911 Revolution" (Ph.D. diss., Yale University, 1985), p. 45.

2. *Ibid.,* p. 111.

3. Ryan Dunch, "Piety, Patriotism, Progress: Chinese Protestants in Fuzhou Society and the Making of Modern China, 1857–1927" (Ph.D. diss., Yale University, 1997).

4. Ralph Huenemann, *The Dragon and the Iron Horse: The Economics of Railroads in China, 1876–1937* (Cambridge: Harvard University Press, 1984), p. 79.

5. Jonathan Spence, *The Gate of Heavenly Peace* (New York, 1980), p. 34.

6. Don Price, *Russia and the Roots of the Chinese Revolution, 1896–1911* (Cambridge: Harvard University Press, 1974), p. 130.

7. Martin Bernal, *Chinese Socialism to 1907* (Ithaca: Cornell University Press, 1976), p. 37.

8. *Ibid.,* p. 95.

9. *Ibid.,* p. 117.

10. Edmund Fung, *The Military Dimension of the Chinese Revolution* (Vancouver: University of British Columbia Press, 1980), p. 138.

11. Li Chien-nung, *The Political History of China, 1840–1928,* trans. Teng Ssu-yü and Jeremy Ingalls (Princeton, NJ, 1956), p. 260.

12. *Ibid.,* pp. 266–267.

CHAPTER 12 *(pages 271–289)*

1. Li Chien-nung, *The Political History of China, 1840–1928,* trans. Teng Ssu-yü and Jeremy Ingalls (Princeton, NJ, 1956), p. 268, replacing "senate" by "council" to avoid confusion.

2. From C. F. Remer, *Foreign Investments in China* (New York, 1933), p. 76.

3. *Ibid.,* p. 430.

4. James Reed, *The Missionary Mind and American East Asia Policy, 1911–1914* (Cambridge: Harvard University Press, 1983), pp. 36–37.

5. Cyril Pearl, *Morrison of Peking* (Sydney, Australia, 1967), p. 289.

6. Lee-hsia Hsu Ting, *Government Control of the Press in Modern China, 1900–1949* (Cambridge: Harvard University Press, 1974), p. 13.

7. Donald Gillin, *Warlord: Yen Hsi-shan in Shansi Province, 1911–1949* (Princeton: Princeton University Press, 1967), p. 63.

8. Michael Summerskill, *China on the Western Front: Britain's Chinese Work Force in the First World War* (London, 1982), p. 69.

9. *Ibid.,* p. 166.

10. *Ibid.,* p. 102.

11. Chow Tse-tsung, *The May Fourth Movement: Intellectual Revolution in Modern China* (Cambridge: Harvard University Press, 1960), p. 86.

CHAPTER 13 *(pages 290–313)*

1. Benjamin Schwartz, *In Search of Wealth and Power* (Cambridge: Harvard University Press, 1964), pp. 45–46.

2. James Pusey, *China and Charles Darwin* (Cambridge: Harvard University Press, 1983), pp. 101–103.

3. Martin Bernal, *Chinese Socialism to 1907* (Ithaca: Cornell University Press, 1976), p. 100. And on the "national essence movement" see Tang Xiaobing, *Global Space and the Nationalist Discourse of Modernity* (Stanford: Stanford University Press, 1996).

4. Pusey, p. 435.

5. *Ibid.,* p. 439.

6. Lin Yü-sheng, *The Crisis of Chinese Consciousness: Radical Anti-traditionalism in the May Fourth Era* (Madison: University of Wisconsin Press, 1979), p. 59.

7. Stuart Schram, *The Political Thought of Mao Tse-tung* (New York, 1972), pp. 157, 158, 160.

8. *Ibid.,* p. 163.

9. Stuart Schram, *Mao's Road to Power*, 2 vols. (Armonk, NY, 1992 and 1994), vol. 1, *The Pre-Marxist Period, 1912–1920; vol. 2, National Revolution and Social Revolution, Dec. 1920–June 1927.* Citation, vol. 1, p. 380.

10. Schram, *Political Thought*, pp. 335–336, and Roxane Witke, "Mao Tse-tung, Women and Suicide in the May Fourth Era," *China Quarterly* 31 (1967): 142.

11. Maurice Meisner, *Li Ta-chao and the Origins of Chinese Marxism* (Cambridge: Harvard University Press, 1967), pp. 64–65.

12. Robert North, *Moscow and Chinese Communists* (Stanford: Stanford University Press, 1963), p. 45.

13. Meisner, p. 144.

14. *Ibid.,* pp. 80–81.

15. As listed in Chow Tse-tung, *The May Fourth Movement: Intellectual Revolution in Modern China* (Cambridge: Harvard University Press, 1960), p. 179.

16. Julia Lin, *Modern Chinese Poetry: An Introduction* (Seattle: University of Washington Press, 1972), p. 209.

17. Vera Schwarcz, *The Chinese Enlightenment: Intellectuals and the Legacy of the May Fourth Movement of 1919* (Berkeley: University of California Press, 1986), p. 44.

18. *Ibid.,* p. 48.

19. Lin Yü-sheng, p. 76.

20. Jerome Grieder, *Hu Shih and the Chinese Renaissance: Liberalism in the Chinese Revolution, 1917–1937* (Cambridge: Harvard University Press, 1970), p. 124.

21. Bertrand Russell, *The Autobiography of Bertrand Russell, 1914–1944* (Boston, 1967), p. 183.

22. Spence, *The Gate of Heavenly Peace* (New York, 1980), p. 217.

23. Lu Hsün (Lu Xun), *Selected Stories* (New York, 1977), p. 64 (modified).

24. Schwarcz, p. 7.

25. North, p. 58.

26. *Ibid.,* p. 59.

27. *Ibid.,* p. 61.

28. *Ibid.,* p. 63.

CHAPTER 14 *(pages 314–341)*

1. Xenia Eudin and Robert North, *Soviet Russia and the East, 1920–1927: A Documentary Survey* (Stanford, CA, 1957), p. 141.

2. John Fitzgerald, *Awakening China* (Stanford: Stanford University Press, 1996), pp. 147–159.

3. Lee Feigon, *Chen Duxiu, Founder of the Chinese Communist Party* (Princeton: Princeton University Press 1983), p. 169, and Maurice Meisner, *Li Ta-chao and the Origins of Chinese Marxism* (Cambridge: Harvard University Press, 1967), pp. 191 and 222.

4. C. Martin Wilbur, *Sun Yat-sen, Frustrated Patriot* (New York: Columbia University Press, 1976), p. 178, and Dan Jacobs, *Borodin: Stalin's Man in China* (Cambridge: Harvard University Press, 1981), p. 132.

5. Fitzgerald, pp. 180–185

6. Jonathan Spence, *Gate of Heavenly Peace* (New York, 1980), p. 197.

7. *Ibid.,* p. 207.

8. Donald Jordan, *The Northern Expedition: China's National Revolution of 1926–1928* (Honolulu: University of Hawaii Press, 1976), p. 64 (modified).

9. *Ibid.,* p. 63.

10. *Ibid.,* p. 76.

11. Gavan McCormack, *Chang Tso-lin in Northeast China, 1911–1928: China, Japan and the Manchurian Idea* (Stanford: Stanford University Press, 1977), p. 210.

12. Eudin and North, pp. 292–294.

13. Robert North, *Moscow and Chinese Communists* (Stanford: Stanford University Press, 1963), p. 98 (modified).

14. Stuart Schram, *The Political Thought of Mao Tse-tung* (New York, 1972), pp. 250–254.

15. Roy Hofheinz, *The Broken Wave: The Chinese Communist Peasant Movement, 1922–1928* (Cambridge: Harvard University Press, 1977), p. 47.

16. Harold Isaacs, *The Tragedy of the Chinese Revolution* (Stanford: Stanford University Press, 1961), p. 236.

17. North, pp. 105–106.

18. Jonathan Spence, *To Change China* (Boston, 1969), p. 204.

19. North, p. 120.

CHAPTER 15 *(pages 342–374)*

1. For the tomb see Liping Wang, "Creating a National Symbol: The Sun Yatsen Memorial in Nanjing," *Republican China* 21, no. 2 (1996): 23–63.

2. Arthur N. Young, *China's Nation-Building Effort, 1927–1937: The Financial and Economic Record* (Stanford: Hoover Institution Press, 1971), p. 38, table 15:1.

3. George Kates, *The Years That Were Fat: The Last of Old China* (Cambridge: MIT Press, 1967 reprint).

4. Harold Isaacs, *Straw Sandals: Chinese Short Stories, 1918–1933* (Cambridge: MIT Press, 1974), p. 169.

5. Jonathan Spence, *Gate of Heavenly Peace* (New York, 1980), p. 215.

6. Michael Lestz and Cheng Pei-kai, "Fascism in China, 1925–1938: A Documentary Study" (unpublished ms.), pp. 311–314, (cited with permission).

7. *Ibid.*, pp. 328, 331, 334–335.

8. *Ibid.*, p. 368.

9. *Ibid.*, pp. 372–373.

10. *Ibid.*, p. 240.

11. *Ibid.*, pp. 243 and 246.

12. Sherman Cochran and Hsieh Cheng-kuang, with Janis Cochran, trans. and eds., *One Day in China, May 21, 1936* (New Haven: Yale University Press, 1983), pp. 210–211, 245.

13. Hou Chi-ming, *Foreign Investment and Economic Development in China, 1840–1937* (Cambridge: Harvard University Press, 1965), p. 17, table 4.

14. *Ibid.*, p. 81, table 18.

15. W. L. Tung, *The Chinese in America, 1820–1973: A Chronology and Fact Book* (Dobbs Ferry, NY, 1974), pp. 18–31.

16. Okamoto Shumpei, "Japanese Response to Chinese Nationalism: Naitō Konan Torajirō's Image of China in the 1920s," in F. Gilbert Chan and Thomas Etzold, eds., *China in the 1920s: Nationalism and Revolution* (New York, 1976), pp. 164 and 167; Tam Yue-him, "An Intellectual's Response to Western Intrusion: Naitō Konan's View of Republican China," in *The Chinese and the Japanese,* ed. Akira Iriye (Princeton: Princeton University Press, 1980), pp. 172 and 175.

17. Tam Yue-him, p. 178.

18. James Crowley, *Japan's Quest for Autonomy: National Security and Foreign Policy, 1930–1938* (Princeton: Princeton University Press, 1966), pp. 155–156.

19. *Ibid.*, pp. 182–183.

20. James Morley, ed., *The China Quagmire: Japan's Expansion on the Asian Continent, 1933–1941* (New York: Columbia University Press, 1983), p. 19.

21. Crowley, pp. 185–186.

CHAPTER 16 *(pages 375–409)*

1. J. K. Chang, *Industrial Development in Pre-Communist China* (Edinburgh: Edinburgh University Press, 1969), p. 103, table 28.

2. Reworked from *China Year Book, 1936* (Shanghai, 1936), p. 322.

3. Drawn from Augusta Wagner, *Labor Legislation in China* (Peking: Yenching University, 1938), p. 47, and Sidney D. Gamble, *How Chinese Families Live in Peiping: A Study of the Income and Expenditure of 283 Chinese Families . . .* (New York and London, 1933), ch. 9.

4. Wagner, p. 50, citing p. 99 of the report.

5. *China Year Book, 1936,* p. 321 (combined tables).

6. Philip Huang, *The Peasant Economy and Social Change in North China* (Stanford: Stanford University Press, 1985), p. 189.

7. Martin Yang, *A Chinese Village: Taitou, Shantung Province* (New York: Columbia University Press, 1945; 1968 reprint), p. 32.

8. Adapted from Huang, table 11:1 on p. 186, and table 11:2 on p. 188, extracting data on households 1, 5, 8, and 10.

9. Stuart Schram, *The Political Thought of Mao Tse-tung* (New York, 1972), pp. 245–246.

10. Mao Tse-tung, *Selected Works of Mao Tse-tung,* 5 vols. (Peking, 1975–1977), vol. 1, p. 123.

11. Roger Thompson, trans. and ed., *Mao Zedong: Report from Xunwu* (Stanford: Stanford University Press, 1991).

12. *Ibid.,* table on Xunwu county, p. 116.

13. Mao Tse-tung, p. 124.

14. *Ibid.,* pp. 45–46. Also Schram, pp. 258, 337.

15. Tien Hung-mao, *Government and Politics in Kuomintang China, 1927–1937* (Stanford: Stanford University Press, 1972), p. 83.

16. Kirby, pp. 111–119.

17. *Ibid.,* p. 117.

18. Benjamin Yang, "The Zunyi Conference as One Step in Mao's Rise to Power: A Survey of Historical Studies of the Chinese Communist Party," *China Quarterly* 106 (1986): 263–264.

19. Lyman Van Slyke, *Enemies and Friends: The United Front in Chinese Communist History* (Stanford: Stanford University Press, 1967), pp. 403–419.

20. Mao Tse-tung, *Selected Works of Mao Tse-tung,* 5 vols. (Peking, 1975–1977), vol. 1, p. 160.

21. Lao She, *Cat Country,* trans. William Lyell (Columbus: Ohio State University Press, 1970), pp. 268–269, 280–281.

22. Wu Tien-wei, *The Sian Incident: A Pivotal Point in Modern Chinese History* (Michigan, 1976), pp. 25–26.

23. *Ibid.,* p. 92

CHAPTER 17 *(pages 419–458)*

1. James Crowley, *Japan's Quest for Autonomy: National Security and Foreign Policy, 1930–1938* (Princeton: Princeton University Press, 1966), pp. 316–317.

2. *Ibid.,* p. 319.

3. *Ibid.,* pp. 331 and 335.

4. *Ibid.,* pp. 338–339.

5. Hata Ikuhiko, "The Marco Polo Bridge Incident," in *The China Quagmire: Japan's Expansion on the Asian Continent, 1933–1941,* ed. James Morley (New York: Columbia University Press, 1983), p. 454, n. 71; Crowley, pp. 342–343.

6. Edward Gunn, *Unwelcome Muse: Chinese Literature in Shanghai and Peking, 1937–1945* (New York: Columbia University Press, 1980), p. 53.

7. Lloyd Eastman, "Nationalist China during the Sino-Japanese War, 1937–1945," *Cambridge History of China,* vol. 13, pt. 2 (Cambridge, 1986), p. 559.

8. F. F. Liu, *A Military History of Modern China: 1924–1949* (Princeton: Princeton University Press, 1956), p. 133.

9. Lyman Van Slyke, *Enemies and Friends: The United Front in Chinese Communist History* (Stanford: Stanford University Press, 1967), pp. 92–93.

10. Robert North, *Moscow and Chinese Communists* (Stanford: Stanford University Press, 1963), pp. 185–187.

11. From Liu, p. 145.

12. Van Slyke, pp. 141–144.

13. Material selected from Van Slyke, p. 148.

14. *Ibid.,* p. 113.

15. Arthur Young, *China and the Helping Hand, 1937–1945* (Cambridge: Harvard University Press, 1963), pp. 114–115.

16. *Ibid.,* p. 114.

17. *Ibid.,* pp. 435–437.

18. James Reardon-Anderson, *Yenan and the Great Powers: The Origins of Chinese Communist Foreign Policy, 1944–1946* (New York: Columbia University Press, 1980), p. 12.

19. Chalmers Johnson, *Peasant Nationalism and Communist Power: The Emergence of Revolutionary China, 1937–1945* (Stanford: Stanford University Press, 1962), p. 86.

20. Young, p. 229.

21. Liu, p. 209.

22. Chen Yung-fa, "The Blooming Poppy under the Red Sun," in Anthony Saich and Hans van de Ven, eds., *New Perspectives on the Chinese Communist Revolution* (Armonk, NY, 1995), pp. 263–298.

23. Bonnie McDougall, *Mao Zedong's "Talks at the Yan'an Conference on Literature and Art": A Translation of the 1943 Text with Commentary* (Ann Arbor: University of Michigan Press, 1980), pp. 69–70.

24. Langdon Gilkey, *Shantung Compound* (New York, 1966, 1975), p. 4.

25. David Kranzler, *Japanese, Nazis and Jews: The Jewish Refugee Community of Shanghai, 1938–1945* (New York: Yeshiva University Press, 1976), pp. 489–502.

26. Hsü K'ai-yu, ed. and trans., *Twentieth Century Chinese Poetry: An Anthology* (Ithaca: Cornell University Press, 1970), p. 403. The poet is Yuan Shui-p'ai.

27. Theodore White and Annalee Jacoby, *Thunder out of China* (New York, 1946, 1961), p. 169.

28. Drawn from Chen Yung-fa, *Making Revolution: The Communist Movement in Eastern and Central China, 1937–1945* (Berkeley: University of California Press, 1986), p. 133.

29. *Ibid.,* pp. 103–104.

30. Frederick Teiwes with Warren Sun, "From a Leninist to a Charismatic Party: The CCP's Changing Leadership," in Saich and Ven, pp. 339–387, especially 373–375.

CHAPTER 18 *(pages 459–488)*

1. Charles Romanus and Riley Sunderland, *Time Runs Out in CBI* (Washington, D.C., 1959), pp. 390 and 394.

2. U.S. Department of State, comp., *United States Relations with China, with Special Reference to the Period 1944–1949* (Washington, D.C., 1949; Stanford: Stanford University Press, 1967), p. 606.

3. *Ibid.,* p. 653.

4. *Ibid.,* pp. 671 and 683–685.

5. James A. Cook, "Penetration and Neo-Colonialism: The Shen Chong Rape Case and the Anti-American Student Movement of 1946–47," *Republican China* 22, no. 1 (November 1996): 65–97.

6. William Hinton, *Fanshen: A Documentary of Revolution in a Chinese Village* (New York, 1966), pp. 137–138 (modified).

7. Suzanne Pepper, *Civil War in China: The Political Struggle, 1945–1949* (Berkeley: University of California Press, 1978), p. 177.

8. This summary of events in Manchuria is all drawn from Steven Levine, *Anvil of Victory:*

The Communist Revolution in Manchuria, 1945–1948 (New York: Columbia University Press, 1987). The bubonic-plague information is in pp. 148–150. For comparable handling of an earlier Manchurian plague crisis, see Carl Nathan, *Plague Prevention and Politics in Manchuria, 1910–1931* (Cambridge: Harvard University Press, 1967).

9. U.S. Department of State, p. 316.

10. Lloyd Eastman, *Seeds of Destruction: Nationalist China in War and Revolution, 1937–1949* (Stanford: Stanford University Press, 1984), p. 174.

11. Chang Kia-ngau (Chia-ao), *The Inflationary Spiral: The Experience in China, 1939–1950* (Cambridge: MIT Press, 1958), p. 356.

12. Eastman, p. 182.

13. Chang Kia-ngau, p. 359.

14. Howard Boorman, comp., *Biographical Dictionary of Republican China* (New York: Columbia University Press, 1967–1971), vol. 1, p. 335.

15. Lionel Chassin, *The Communist Conquest of China: A History of the Civil War, 1945–1949,* trans. Timothy Osato and Louis Gelas (Cambridge: Harvard University Press, 1965), p. 177.

16. Mark Selden, *The People's Republic of China: A Documentary History of Revolutionary Change* (New York, 1979), p. 180.

CHAPTER 19 *(pages 489–513)*

1. Mao Zedong, *Selected Works,* vol. V (Peking, 1977), p. 411.

2. *Ibid.,* pp. 417 and 419.

3. Mark Selden, *The People's Republic of China: A Documentary History of Revolutionary Change* (New York, 1979), pp. 187–193.

4. Richard Gaulton, "Political Mobilization in Shanghai, 1949–1951," in *Shanghai: Revolution and Development in an Asian Metropolis,* ed. Christopher Howe (Cambridge, 1981), p. 46.

5. Ezra Vogel, *Canton under Communism: Programs and Politics in a Provincial Capital, 1949–1968* (Cambridge: Harvard University Press, 1969), p. 53.

6. Liu Shaoqi (Liu Shao-ch'i), *How to Be a Good Communist* (Peking, 1951), p. 8.

7. *The Cold War in Asia,* Cold War International History Project, *Bulletin* 5–6, Woodrow Wilson International Center for Scholars (Winter 1995–1996): 5–9.

8. From Lionel Chassin, *The Communist Conquest of China: A History of the Civil War, 1945–1949,* trans. Timothy Osato and Louis Gelas (Cambridge: Harvard University Press, 1965), p. 243.

9. Shakabpa Tsepon, *Tibet, a Political History* (New Haven: Yale University Press, 1967), pp. 299–305.

10. Allen Whiting, *China Crosses the Yalu: The Decision to Enter the Korean War.* (New York, 1960), p. 21 (modified).

11. *Ibid.,* p. 18.

12. U.S. Department of State, comp., *United States Relations with China, with Special Reference to the Period 1944–1949* (Washington, D.C., 1949; Stanford: Stanford University Press, 1967), p. xiv.

13. Howard Boorman, comp., *Biographical Dictionary of Republican China* (New York: Columbia University Press, 1967–1971), vol. 2, p. 173.

14. Whiting, p. 58.

15. *Ibid.,* pp. 84–85.

16. *The Cold War in Asia*, pp. 38–47, 87–89, 112–119.

17. Kenneth Lieberthal, *Revolution and Tradition in Tientsin, 1949–1952* (Stanford: Stanford University Press, 1980), for full details on the Tianjin campaign. The classification of firms is on p. 168, table 8.

18. The material in this section is drawn from John Gardner, "The *Wu-fan* Campaign in Shanghai: A Study in the Consolidation of Urban Control," in *Chinese Communist Politics in Action,* ed. A. Doak Barnett (Seattle: University of Washington Press, 1969), pp. 477–539. For the table, see p. 522 (percentages slightly adjusted).

CHAPTER 20 *(pages 514–543)*

1. Frederick Teiwes, *Politics and Purges in China: Rectification and the Decline of Party Norms, 1950–1965* (White Plains, NY, 1979), ch. 5, on the Gao-Rao purge. Teiwes cites Mao's comments on pp. 172–173.

2. Thomas Rawski, *China's Transition to Industrialism: Producer Goods and Economic Development in the Twentieth Century* (Ann Arbor: University of Michigan Press, 1980), table, p. 39.

3. Alexander Eckstein, *China's Economic Revolution* (Cambridge: Cambridge University Press, 1977), table, p. 186.

4. *Ibid.,* table, p. 187.

5. Bruce Reynolds, "Changes in the Standard of Living of Shanghai Industrial Workers, 1930–1973," in *Shanghai: Revolution and Development in an Asian Metropolis,* ed. Christopher Howe (Cambridge, 1981), table, p. 223.

6. Eckstein, table, p. 71.

7. This discussion of minority policies is drawn from June Dreyer, "Traditional Minorities, Elites and the CPR Elite Engaged in Minority Nationalities Work," in *Elites in the People's Republic of China,* ed. Robert Scalapino (Seattle: University of Washington Press, 1972).

8. On the stereotyping of minorities and the sensual exaggeration, see Dru Gladney, "Reproaching Nationality in China: Refiguring Majority/Minority Identities," *Journal of Asian Studies* 53, no.1 (1994): 92–123.

9. John Gittings, *The Role of the Chinese Army* (New York: Oxford University Press, 1967), p. 126.

10. *Ibid.,* table, p. 309.

11. *Ibid.,* p. 189.

12. *Ibid.,* p. 190.

13. Ellis Joffe, *Party and Army: Professionalism and Political Control in the Chinese Officer Corps, 1949–1964* (Cambridge: Harvard University Press, 1965), p. 57.

14. Jin Yuelin in Robert Lifton, *Thought Reform and the Psychology of Totalism* (New York, 1961), pp. 473–484.

15. Merle Goldman, *Literary Dissent in Communist China* (Cambridge: University Press, 1967), p. 109.

16. *Ibid.,* pp. 131 and 145.

17. Roderick MacFarquhar, *The Origins of the Cultural Revolution,* vol. 1: *Contradictions among the People, 1956–1957* (New York: Columbia University Press, 1974), pp. 48–52, and 337 n. 89 on Liu.

18. The transcript of the original version of this speech is in MacFarquhar, Timothy Cheek, and Eugene Wu, eds., *The Secret Speeches of Chairman Mao from the Hundred Flowers to the Great Leap Forward* (Cambridge: Harvard University Press, 1989), pp. 131–189.

19. MacFarquhar, I, pp. 185 and 212.

20. Roderick MacFarquhar, ed., *The Hundred Flowers* (London, 1960), pp. 92 and 94.

21. *Ibid.,* pp. 98, 105, 109, 177, 238.

22. James McGough, *Fei Hsiao-t'ung: The Dilemma of a Chinese Intellectual* (White Plains, NY, 1979), p. 62.

23. MacFarquhar, *Origins of the Cultural Revolution, I,* pp. 289–290.

24. McGough, p. 81.

CHAPTER 21 *(pages 544–564)*

1. Stuart Schram, *The Political Thought of Mao Tse-tung* (New York, 1972), pp. 408–409.

2. For Henan, this is vividly portrayed in Jean-Luc Domenach, *The Origins of the Great Leap Forward* (Boulder, CO: Westview, 1995), pp. 128–129.

3. Jerome Ch'en, *Mao Papers: Anthology and Bibliography* (New York: Oxford University Press, 1970), pp. 62–63.

4. Schram, *Political Thought,* p. 352, and Maurice Meisner, *Mao's China: A History of the People's Republic* (New York, 1979), p. 213.

5. Meisner, p. 234.

6. Mark Selden, *The People's Republic of China: A Documentary History of Revolutionary Change* (New York, 1979), p. 402.

7. *Ibid.,* p. 410.

8. *Ibid.,* p. 413.

9. Kenneth Lieberthal, "The Great Leap Forward and the Split in the Yenan Leadership," in *Cambridge History of China,* vol. 14 (Cambridge, 1987), pp. 313 and 317; and Nicholas Lardy, "The Chinese Economy under Stress, 1958–1965," *ibid.,* pp. 379–382.

10. Schram, *Chairman Mao,* pp. 139, 142, 146.

11. Yue Daiyun, with Carolyn Wakeman, *To the Storm: The Odyssey of a Revolutionary Woman* (Berkeley: University of California Press, 1985), pp. 80 and 82.

12. G. F. Hudson, Richard Lowenthal, and Roderick MacFarquhar, *The Sino-Soviet Dispute* (New York, 1961), pp. 42–45.

13. *Ibid.,* pp. 58 and 62.

14. Allen Whiting, "The Sino-Soviet Split," in *Cambridge History of China,* vol. 14, pp. 513–514.

15. Hudson et al., pp. 93–94, citing *Red Flag.*

16. John Wilson Lewis and Xue Litai, *China Builds the Bomb* (Stanford: Stanford University Press, 1988), p. 160.

17. Hudson et al., p. 224.

18. Nicholas Lardy and Kenneth Lieberthal, eds., *Chen Yun's Strategy for China's Development: A Non-Maoist Alternative* (Armonk, NY, 1983), p. 156.

19. Richard Baum and Frederic Teiwes, *Ssu-Ch'ing: The Socialist Education Movement of 1962–1966* (Berkeley: University of California Press, 1968), pp. 55–56.

20. Richard Baum, *Prelude to Revolution: Mao, the Party, and the Peasant Question, 1962–66* (New York: Columbia University Press, 1975), pp. 117–121 (quotation from p. 119, modified).

21. Kenneth Lieberthal and Michel Oksenberg, *Policy Making in China: Leaders, Structures, and Processes* (Princeton: Princeton University Press, 1988), pp. 175–183, on Daqing oilfield.

22. Baum, p. 124.

23. *Ibid.,* p. 126, quoting Liu Zihou.

CHAPTER 22 *(pages 565–586)*

1. For Mao's personal life see the provocative and intimate account by Mao's doctor Li Zhisui, *The Private Life of Chairman Mao* (New York: Random House, 1994).

2. Merle Goldman, *China's Intellectuals: Advise and Dissent* (Cambridge: Harvard University Press, 1981), pp. 32–34.

3. Merle Goldman, "The Party and the Intellectuals, Phase Two," in *Cambridge History of China,* vol. 14, p. 446.

4. Clive Ansley, *The Heresy of Wu Han: His Play "Hai Jui's Dismissal" and Its Role in China's Cultural Revolution* (Toronto: University of Toronto Press, 1971), p. 76. A careful evaluation of the exact nature of Wu Han's work is given by Tom Fisher, " 'The Play's the Thing': Wu Han and Hai Rui Revisited," in Jonathan Unger ed., *Using the Past to Serve the Present* (Armonk, NY, 1993), pp. 9–45.

5. *Ibid.,* p. 90.

6. Lin Biao (Lin Piao), *Important Documents on the Great Proletarian Cultural Revolution in China* (Peking, 1970), pp. 29–30.

7. *CCP Documents of the Great Proletarian Cultural Revolution, 1966–1967* comp. Union Research Institute (Hong Kong, 1968), pp. 8, 9, 11.

8. Lin Biao, pp. 199, 208–215, 221.

9. Ch'en, pp. 24–25.

10. Lee Hong-yung, *The Politics of the Chinese Cultural Revolution: A Case Study* (Berkeley: University of California Press, 1978), p. 154.

11. *Ibid.,* p. 169.

12. Yang Jiang, *Six Chapters from My Life "Down Under"* (Seattle: University of Washington Press, 1984), p. 50 (translation modified).

13. Anita Chan, Richard Madsen, and Jonathan Unger, *Chen Village: The Recent History of a Peasant Community in Mao's China* (Berkeley: University of California Press, 1984), p. 170.

14. Philip Bridgham, "The Fall of Lin Piao," *China Quarterly* 55 (1973): 435.

15. Lin Biao, p. 14; Bridgham, 441; Chan et al., p. 231.

CHAPTER 23 *(pages 595–617)*

1. Henry Kissinger, *White House Years* (Boston, 1979), pp. 733.

2. *Ibid.,* pp. 1060–1063; Richard Nixon, *RN: The Memoirs of Richard Nixon* (New York, 1978), pp. 560–564.

3. "Quarterly Documentation," *China Quarterly* 50 (April 1972): 402.

4. *Ibid.,* p. 392.

5. Lee Hong-yung, "The Changing Cadre System in the Socialist State of China" (unpublished ms., 1988), p. 246 (cited with permission).

6. "Quarterly Documentation," *China Quarterly* 53 (January 1973): 192–193.

7. "Quarterly Documentation," *China Quarterly* 54 (April 1973): 408–409.

8. "Quarterly Documentation," *China Quarterly* 57 (January 1974): 207–209.

9. *Ibid.,* citing *Peking Review* no. 5 (1974).

10. "Quarterly Documentation," *China Quarterly* 56 (October 1973): 809–810.

11. "Quarterly Documentation," *China Quarterly* 58 (April 1974): 414–415.

12. "Quarterly Documentation," *China Quarterly* 59 (July 1974): 644.

13. Shannon Brown, "China's Program of Technology Acquisition," in *China's Four Modernizations,* ed. Richard Baum (Boulder, CO, 1980), p. 159.

14. *Ibid.,* p. 161. On the work and identity of "Liang Xiao" see Yue Daiyun, with Carolyn Wakeman, *To the Storm: The Odyssey of a Revolutionary Woman* (Berkeley: University of California Press, 1985), pp. 375–362.

15. *Ibid.,* p. 163.

16. "Quarterly Documentation," *China Quarterly* 65 (March 1976): 168–173.

17. "Quarterly Documentation," *China Quarterly* 66 (June 1976): 423.

18. *Ibid.,* p. 432.

19. "Quarterly Documentation," *China Quarterly* 67 (September 1976): 607.

20. *Ibid.,* 673.

21. Lucien Bianco and Yves Chevrier, *La Chine: Dictionnaire bibliographique du mouvement ouvrier international* (Paris, 1985), p. 169.

CHAPTER 24 *(pages 618–646)*

1. Richard Baum, ed., *China's Four Modernizations: The New Technological Revolution* (Boulder, CO, 1980), p. 170.

2. "Quarterly Documentation," *China Quarterly* 77 (March 1979): 168.

3. *Ibid.,* 170.

4. *Ibid.,* 172.

5. *Ibid.,* 173.

6. David Goodman, *Beijing Street Voices: The Poetry and Politics of China's Democracy Movement* (London, 1981), p. 79.

7. *Ibid.,* p. 95.

8. Bei Dao, *The August Sleepwalker,* trans. Bonnie S. McDougall (London: Anvil Press, 1988), p. 34.

9. James Seymour, *The Fifth Modernization: China's Human Rights Movement, 1978–1979* (Stanfordville, NY, 1980), p. 52.

10. *Ibid.,* p. 54.

11. *Ibid.,* pp. 63–64, 69.

12. Goodman, p. 142.

13. *Ibid.,* p. 122.

14. *China Quarterly* 77 (March 1979): 216.

15. James C. Hsiung, ed., *The Taiwan Experience, 1950–1980: Contemporary Republic of China* (New York, 1981), p. 132.

16. *Ibid.*

17. *Ibid.,* p. 437.

18. James E. Nickum and David C. Schak, "Living Standards and Economic Development in Shanghai and Taiwan," *China Quarterly* 77 (1979): 40 (selected items).

19. *Ibid.,* p. 42.

20. Liu Binyan, *"People or Monsters?" and Other Stories and Reportage from China after Mao,* trans. Perry Link et al. (Bloomington: Indiana University Press, 1983), pp. 23 and 51.

21. Lucien Bianco and Yves Chevrier, *La Chine: Dictionnaire bibliographique du mouvement ouvrier international* (Paris, 1985), p. 246 (translated).

22. Andrew Nathan, *Chinese Democracy* (New York, 1985), p. 103.

23. *New York Times,* March 31, 1980.

CHAPTER 25 *(pages 647–676)*

1. *New China's Population* (New York: China Financial and Economic Publishing House and Macmillan Publishing Company, 1987), p. 117, table 8:14.

2. Colin Mackerras, *Modern China: A Chronology from 1842 to the Present* (San Francisco, 1982), p. 578 (August 21, 1974).

3. Judith Banister, *China's Changing Population* (Stanford: Stanford University Press, 1987), 215. In *The Flow of Gifts: Reciprocity and Networks in a Chinese Village* (Stanford: Stanford University Press, 1996), pp. 54–55, Yan Yunxiang gives a careful examination of such gifts in a north China village in the PRC.

4. *New China's Population,* p. 132, table 9:2.

5. *Ibid.,* p. 215, table 12:2.

6. *Ibid.,* p. 102, table 7:6, amending 1983 rural percentage.

7. For this method of describing Chinese leadership I am indebted to Kenneth Lieberthal and Michel Oksenberg, *Policy Making in China: Leaders, Structures, and Processes* (Princeton: Princeton University Press, 1988), pp. 35–42.

8. *Ibid.,* pp. 339–344.

9. *Ibid.,* p. 339.

10. On coal and offshore-oil data, *ibid.,* chs. 5 and 7.

11. On Three Gorges, *ibid.,* esp. pp. 283 and 320.

12. Y. Y. Kueh, "The Economics of the 'Second land Reform' in China," *China Quarterly* 101 (March 1985): 123.

13. "Document Number One" *China Quarterly* 101 (March 1985): 133–134. Kate Xiao Zhou, *How the Farmers Changed China: Power of the People* (Boulder, CO, 1996) emphasizes the local farmers' initiatives.

14. Harry Harding, *China's Second Revolution: Reform after Mao* (Washington, D.C., 1987), p. 167.

15. Stuart Schram, " 'Economics in Command?' Ideology and Policy since the Third Plenum, 1978–1984," *China Quarterly* 99 (September 1984): 454.

16. Richard Herman, "The Education of China's Lawyers," *Albany Law Review* 46 (1982): 793–794.

17. Whitmore Gray and Henry Zheng, trans., "General Principles of Civil Law of the People's Republic of China," *American Journal of Comparative Law* 34 (1986): 715–743.

18. Jonathan Ocko, "Women, Property, and Law in the Ch'ing and the PRC" (unpublished ms.), p. 13 (cited with permission). See Yan, *Flow of Gifts,* pp. 176 204, on the shifts to conjugal giving.

19. Samuel S. Kim, "The Development of International Law in Post-Mao China: Change and Continuity," *Journal of Chinese Law* 1, no. 2 (1987): 117–160.

20. Text in *China Quarterly* 100 (December 1984): 920–922.

CHAPTER 26 *(pages 677–704)*

1. *Seeds of Fire: Chinese Voices of Conscience,* ed. Geremie Barmé and John Minford (New York, 1989), p. 405.

2. *Ibid.,* p. 410.

3. *Ibid.,* p. 174.

4. Zhang Xinxin and Sang Ye, *Chinese Lives: An Oral History of Contemporary China* (New York, 1987), p. 174.

5. *Ibid.,* p. 313.

6. *Ibid.,* p. 153.

7. Chin Annping, *Children of China: Voices from Recent Years* (New York, 1988), pp. 53, 103, 201.

8. Orville Schell, *Discos and Democracy: China in the Throes of Reform* (New York, 1988), p. 132.

9. Andrew Nathan, *Chinese Democracy* (New York, 1985), p. 197.

10. Schell, pp. 213–214.

11. *New York Times,* December 11, 1986.

12. Schell, pp. 224–225.

13. *New York Times,* December 11, 1986.

14. *Ibid.,* January 3, 1987, citing *People's Daily.*

15. *Ibid.,* January 13, 1987.

16. *New York Times,* January 6, 1985, and February 21, 1985.

17. Schell, pp. 134 and 291.

18. *Ibid.,* p. 292.

19. Data on Li Peng drawn from Kenneth Lieberthal and Michel Oksenberg, *Policy Making in China: Leaders, Structures, and Processes* (Princeton: Princeton University Press, 1988), pp. 51–58.

20. *New York Times,* March 31, 1988, and April 9, 1988.

21. All figures from "Quarterly Documentation," *China Quarterly* 117 (March 1989): 180–195, and 118 (June 1989): 391–407. Trade figures following from *MOR China Letter* 3, no. 3 (April 1989): 7, and courtesy James Stepanik. On American Motors and China, see Jim Mann, *Beijing Jeep* (New York, 1989).

22. A careful narrative with key accompanying documents is in "Quarterly Documentation," *China Quarterly* 119 (September 1989): 666–734. Dramatic photographs of the demonstrations and the victims are shown in David and Peter Turnley, *Beijing Spring* (New York, 1989).

23. *New York Times,* June 30, 1989.

CHAPTER 27 *(pages 705–728)*

1. Maurice Meisner, *The Deng Xiaoping Era: An Inquiry into the Fate of Chinese Socialism, 1978–1994* (New York: Hill and Wang, 1996), pp. 474–475.

2. Luo Xu, "The 'Shekou Storm': Changes in the Mentality of Chinese Youth Prior to Tiananmen," *China Quarterly* 142 (June 1995): 541–572.

3. *China Quarterly* 130 (June 1992): 454–56, and *ibid.* 131 (September 1992): 860.

4. *Ibid.* 136 (December 1993): 1040–1041.

5. *New York Times*, November 18, 1993, "Op Ed" by Wei Jingsheng, "The Wolf and the Lamb."

6. *China Quarterly* 148 (December 1996), Special Taiwan issue, especially Ramon Myers, "A New Chinese Civilization" and Hung-mao Tien and Yun-han Chu, "Building Democracy in Taiwan."

7. This and the following paragraph drawn from Richard Bernstein and Ross H. Munro, *The Coming Conflict with China* (New York: Alfred Knopf, 1997), pp. 72–76.

8. For this particular case study see Jonathan Spence and Annping Chin, "Letter from Beijing: Deng's Heirs," *The New Yorker*, March 10, 1997, pp. 68–77. Other cases based on the same authors' unpublished interviews and impressions.

9. *New York Times*, October 8, 1994, Richard Baum, "China after Deng: Ten Scenarios in Search of Reality," *China Quarterly* 145 (March 1996): 153–175.

10. A vivid example is the case of Wang Zhiqiang in Henan, as recorded by Sheryl Wu Dunn, *New York Times*, May 16, 1993.

11. Wei Li, "The Security Service for Chinese Central Leaders," *China Quarterly* 143 (September 1995): 814–827, at p. 823.

12. Wang Shuo, "Welcome, Cash Box," *Asian Wall Street Journal*, June 27, 1997.

13. Anonymous [?Deng Liqun], "Ten Thousand Character Statement," *China Quarterly* 148 (December 1996): 1426–1441.

14. "Beijing Journal," by Patrick E. Tyler, *New York Times*, July 21, 1997. The author of the book was Qian Ning, son of China's foreign minister Qian Qichen.

PERMISSIONS

The publisher gratefully acknowledges the following for their generous permission to reprint copyright materials: Indiana University Press for excerpts from Tang Xianzu, *The Peony Pavilion*, trans. Cyril Birch; University of California Press for excerpts from Kong Shangren, *The Peach Blossom Fan*, trans. Chen Shih-hsiang and Harold Acton, and for data from Chen Yung-fa, *Making Revolution: The Communist Movement in Eastern and Central China, 1937–1945*; Columbia University Press for excerpts from Richard Strassberg, *The World of K'ung Shang-jen: A Man of Letters in Early Ch'ing China*; Stanford University Press for data from Philip Huang, *The Peasant Economy and Social Change in North China*, for data from Roger Thompson, ed. and trans., *Mao Zedong: Report from Xunwu*, for data from Tien Hung-mao, *Government and Politics in Kuomintang China, 1927–1937*, for data from Lyman Van Slyke, *Enemies and Friends: The United Front in Chinese Communist History*, and for data from Lloyd Eastman, *Seeds of Destruction: Nationalist China in War and Revolution, 1937–1949*; Harvard University Press for data from Ho Ping-ti, *Studies on the Population of China, 1368–1953*, for data from Chang Hsin-pao, *Commissioner Lin and the Opium War*, for data from Hou Chi-ming, *Foreign Investment and Economic Development in China, 1840–1937*, for data from Arthur Young, *China and the Helping Hand, 1937–1945*, and for data from Lionel Chassin, *The Communist Conquest of China: A History of the Civil War, 1945–1949*; James Lee and Robert Eng for data from "Population and Family History in Eighteenth-Century Manchuria: Preliminary Results from Daoyi, 1774–1798," *Ch'ing-shih wen-t'i*, 5, no. 1 (June 1984); Princeton University Press for excerpts from the *I-Ching*, trans. Richard Wilhelm and Cary Baynes, and for data from F. F. Liu, *A Military History of Modern China, 1924–1949*; University of Washington Press for excerpts from Guo Moruo in Julia Lin, *Modern Chinese Poetry: An Introduction*, and for data from John Gardner, "The *Wu Fan* Campaign in Shanghai: A Study in the Consolidation of Urban Control," in *Chinese Communist Politics in Action*, ed. A. Doak Barnett; Edinburgh University Press for data from John K. Chang, *Industrial Development in Pre-Communist China*; Cambridge University Press for data from *The Cambridge History of China*, vol. 13, for data from Alexander Eckstein, *China's Economic Revolution*, and for data from Bruce Reynolds, "Changes in the Standard of Living of Shanghai Industrial Workers, 1930–1973," in *Shanghai: Revolution and Development in an Asian Metropolis*, ed. Christopher Howe; Hoover Institution Press for data from Arthur N. Young, *China's Nation-building Effort, 1927–1937: The Financial and Economic Record*; Cornell University Press for excerpts from Hsu K'ai-yu ed. and trans., *Twentieth-Century Chinese Poetry: An Anthology*; W. L. Tung for data from *The Chinese in America: A Chronology and Fact Book*; Random House for excerpts from William Hinton, *Fanshen: A Documentary of Revolution in a Chinese Village*; MIT Press for data from Chang Kia-ngau (Chia-ao), *The Inflationary Spiral: The Experience in China, 1939–1950*; University of Michigan Press for data from Thomas Rawski, *China's Transition to Industrialism: Producer Goods and Economic Development in the Twentieth Century*; Oxford University Press for data from John Gittings, *The Role of the*

Chinese Army; University of Toronto Press for excerpts from Clive Ansley, *The Heresy of Wu Han: His Play "Hai Rui's Dismissal" and Its Role in China's Cultural Revolution;* Anvil Press for excerpts from David Goodman, *Beijing Street Voices: The Poetry and Politics of China's Democracy Movement,* and for excerpts from Bei Dao, *The August Sleepwalker,* trans. Bonnie S. McDougall; *China Quarterly* for data from James E. Nickum and David C. Schak, "Living Standards and Economic Development in Shanghai and Taiwan," 77 (1979); Praeger for data from James C. Hsiung, ed., *The Taiwan Experience, 1950–1980: Contemporary Republic of China;* Macmillan for data from *New China's Population;* Hill and Wang excerpts from Geremie Barmé and John Minford, eds., *Seeds of Fire: Chinese Voices of Conscience;* Panda Books for excerpts from Zhang Xinxin and Sang Ye, *Chinese Lives: An Oral History of Contemporary China.*

Further Readings

CHAPTER 1

Ming Society: Timothy Brook, *The Confusions of Pleasure: Commerce and Culture in Ming China* (Berkeley: University of California Press, 1998); Craig Clunas, *Superfluous Things: Material Culture and Social Status in Early Modern China* (Urbana: University of Illinois Press, 1991); Craig Clunas, *Fruitful Sites: Garden Culture in Ming Dynasty China* (London, 1996); Dorothy Ko, *Teachers of the Inner Chambers: Women and Culture in Seventeenth-Century China* (Stanford: Stanford University Press, 1994).

Ming Elite Life and Culture: W. T. deBary, ed. *Self and Society in Ming Thought* (New York: Columbia University Press, 1970); *Journey to the West,* trans. Anthony Yu, 4 vols. (Chicago: University of Chicago Press, 1977); Tang Xianzu, *The Peony Pavilion,* trans. Cyril Birch (Bloomington: Indiana University Press, 1980); Patrick Hanan, *The Chinese Vernacular Story* (Cambridge: Harvard University Press, 1981); Jonathan Spence, *The Memory Palace of of Matteo Ricci* (New York, 1984); Joanna Handlin, *Action in Late Ming Thought* (Berkeley: University of California Press, 1983); Willard Peterson, *Bitter Gourd: Fang I-chih and the Impetus for Intellectual Change in the 1630s* (New Haven: Yale University Press, 1979).

Ming Biographies: L. Carrington Goodrich and Fang Chao-ying, eds., *Dictionary of Ming Biography, 1368–1644,* 2 vols. (New York: Columbia University Press, 1976); Huang Tsung-hsi (Huang Zongxi), *The Records of Ming Scholars,* ed. Julia Ching (Honolulu: Hawaii University Press, 1987).

Ming Government: Charles Hucker, ed., *Chinese Government in Ming Times* (New York: Columbia University Press, 1969); Ray Huang, *1587, a Year of No Significance: The Ming Dynasty in Decline* (New Haven: Yale University Press, 1981).

Ming Social Problems and Rebellions: James Parsons, *Peasant Rebellions of the Late Ming Dynasty* (Tucson: University of Arizona Press, 1970); Linda Grove and Christian Daniels, eds., *State and Society in China: Japanese Perspectives on Ming-Qing Social and Economic History* (Tokyo: University of Tokyo Press, 1984); *The Cambridge History of China,* vol. 7: *The Ming Dynasty, 1368–1644, Part I,* ed. Frederick Mote and Denis Twitchett (New York: Cambridge University Press, 1988).

CHAPTER 2

The Manchu Conquest and Consolidation: Pamela Crossley, *The Manchus* (Oxford: Blackwell, 1997); Frederic Wakeman, *The Great Enterprise: The Manchu Reconstruction of Imperial Order in Seventeenth-Century China,* 2 vols. (Berkeley: University of California Press, 1985); Jonathan Spence and John Wills, eds., *From Ming to Ch'ing: Conquest, Region, and Continuity in Seventeenth-Century China* (New Haven: Yale University Press, 1979); Robert Oxnam, *Ruling from Horseback: Manchu Politics in the Oboi Regency, 1661–1669* (Chicago: University of Chicago Press, 1975).

Ming Loyalism: Lynn A. Struve, *Voices from the Ming-Qing Cataclysm: China in Tigers' Jaws* (New Haven: Yale University Press, 1993); Lynn A. Struve, *The Southern Ming, 1644–1662* (New Haven: Yale University Press, 1984); Jerry Dennerline, *The Chiating Loyalists: Confucian Leadership and Social Change in Seventeenth-Century China* (New Haven: Yale University Press, 1981); Kang-i Sun Chang, *The Late Ming Poet Ch'en Tzu-lung: Crises of Love and Loyalism* (New Haven: Yale University Press, 1990); Wang Fangyu, Richard Barnhart, and Judith Smith, eds., *Master of the Lotus Garden: The Life and Art of Bada Shanren (1626–1705)* (New Haven: Yale University Press, 1990).

Qing Biographies: Arthur Hummel, ed., *Eminent Chinese of the Ch'ing Period (1644–1912),* 2 vols. (Washington, D.C., 1943).

Social and Economic Aspects: Philip Huang, *The Peasant Economy and Social Change in North China* (Stanford: Stanford University Press, 1985); Hilary Beattie, *Land and Lineage in China: A Study of T'ung-ch'eng County, Anhwei, in the Ming and Ch'ing Dynasties* (New York: Cambridge University Press, 1979); Sung Ying-hsing, *T'ien-kung K'ai-wu: Chinese Technology in the Seventeenth Century,* trans. E-tu Zen Sun and Shiou-chuan Sun (University Park: Pennsylvania State University Press, 1966).

CHAPTER 3

Kangxi as Ruler: Jonathan Spence, *Emperor of China: Self-Portrait of K'ang-hsi* (New York, 1974); Silas Hsiu-liang Wu, *Communication and Imperial Control in China: Evolution of the Palace Memorial System, 1693–1735* (Cambridge: Harvard University Press, 1970); Silas Hsiu-liang Wu, *Passage to Power: K'ang-hsi and His Heir Apparent, 1661–1722* (Cambridge: Harvard University Press, 1979); Jonathan Spence, *Ts'ao Yin and the K'ang-hsi Emperor, Bondservant and Master* (New Haven: Yale University Press, 1988); Lawrence Kessler, *K'ang-hsi and the Consolidation of Ch'ing Rule, 1661–1684* (Chicago: University of Chicago Press, 1978).

Maritime China and Foreign Powers: Ng Chin-keong, *Trade and Society: The Amoy Network on the China Coast, 1683–1735* (Singapore: Singapore University Press, 1983); John Robert Shepherd, *Statecraft and Political Economy in the Taiwan Frontier, 1600–1800* (Stanford: Stanford University Press, 1993); Ralph Croizier, *Koxinga and Chinese Nationalism: History, Myth and the Hero* (Cambridge: Harvard University Press, 1977); John Wills, *Embassies and Illusions: Dutch and Portuguese Envoys to K'ang-hsi, 1666–1687* (Cambridge: Harvard University Press, 1984); Mark Mancall, *Russia and China: Their Diplomatic Relations to 1728* (Cambridge: Harvard University Press, 1971); Johanna Meskill, *A Chinese Pioneer Family: The Lins of Wu-feng, Taiwan, 1729–1895* (Princeton: Princeton University Press, 1979).

Culture and the Arts: James Cahill, *The Compelling Image: Nature and Style in Seventeenth-Century Chinese Painting* (Cambridge: Harvard University Press, 1982); Irving Lo and William Schultz, *Waiting for the Unicorn: Poems and Lyrics of China's Last Dynasty, 1644–1911* (Bloomington: Indiana University Press, 1980); Ellen Widmer, *The Margins of Utopia: Shui-hu* *hou-chuan and the Literature of Ming Loyalism* (Cambridge: Harvard University Press, 1987); Richard Strassberg, *The World of K'ung Shang-jen, a Man of Letters in Early Ch'ing China* (New York: Columbia University Press, 1983); Patrick Hanan, *The Invention of Li Yu* (Cambridge: Harvard University Press, 1988); Judith T. Zeitlin, *Historian of the Strange: Pu Songling and the Chinese Classical Tale* (Stanford: Stanford University Press, 1993).

CHAPTER 4

Eighteenth-Century Social Structures: Susan Naquin and Evelyn Rawski, *Chinese Society in the Eighteenth Century* (New Haven: Yale University Press, 1987); James Lee and Cameron Campbell, *Fate and Fortune in Rural China: Social Organization and Population Behavior in Liaoning, 1774–1873* (Cambridge: Cambridge University Press, 1997); G. William Skinner, ed., *The City in Late Imperial China* (Stanford: Stanford University Press, 1977); Mark Elvin, *The Pattern of the Chinese Past* (Stanford: Stanford University Press, 1973); Lloyd Eastman, *Family, Fields and Ancestors* (New York: Cambridge University Press, 1988); Ho Ping-ti, *Studies on the Population of China, 1368–1953* (Cambridge: Harvard University Press, 1959).

Yongzheng as Ruler: Madeleine Zelin, *The Magistrate's Tael: Rationalizing Fiscal Reform in Eighteenth-Century Ch'ing China* (Berkeley: University of California Press, 1984); Beatrice S. Bartlett, *Monarchs and Ministers: The Rise of the Grand Council in Mid-Ch'ing China, 1723–1820* (Berkeley: University of California Press, 1990); Huang Pei, *Autocracy at Work: A Study of the Yung-cheng Period, 1723–1735* (Bloomington: Indiana University Press, 1974).

Rural China: Peter Perdue, *Exhausting the Earth: State and Peasant in Hunan, 1500–1850* (Cambridge: Harvard University Press, 1987); Evelyn Rawski, *Agricultural Change and the Peasant Economy of South China* (Cambridge: Harvard University Press, 1972); Hsiao Kung-chuan, *Rural China: Imperial Control in the Nineteenth Century* (Seattle: University of Washington Press, 1960).

Elite and the Bureaucracy: John Watt, *The District Magistrate in Late Imperial China* (New York: Columbia University Press, 1972); Chang Chung-li, *The Chinese Gentry: Studies on Their Role in Nineteenth Century Chinese Society* (Seattle: University of Washington Press, 1955); Ho Ping-ti, *The Ladder of Success in Imperial China: Aspects of Social Mobility, 1368–1911* (New York: Columbia University Press, 1962); Thomas Metzger, *The Internal Organization of Ch'ing Bureaucracy: Legal, Normative and Communication Aspects* (Cambridge: Harvard University Press, 1973); Ch'ü T'ung-tsu, *Local Government in China under the Ch'ing* (Cambridge: Harvard University Press, 1962).

CHAPTER 5

Philosophy and History: Chow Kai-wing, *The Rise of Confucian Ritualism in Late Imperial China: Ethics, Classics, and Lineage Discourse* (Stanford: Stanford University Press, 1994); Benjamin Elman, *From Philosophy to Philology: Intellectual and Social Aspects of Change in Late Imperial China* (Cambridge: Harvard University Press, 1984); Thomas Metzger, *Escape from Predicament; Neo-Confucianism and China's Evolving Political Culture* (New York: Columbia University Press, 1977); David Nivison, *The Life and Thought of Chang Hsüeh-ch'eng (1738–1801)* (Stanford: Stanford University Press, 1966); R. Kent Guy, *The Emperor's Four Treasuries: Scholars and the State in the Late Ch'ien-lung Era* (Cambridge: Harvard University Press, 1987); *Tai Chen's Enquiry into Goodness,* trans. Cheng Chung-ying (Honolulu, 1971); Chin Annping and Mansfield Freeman, *Beyond Reason and Proof: Tai Chen's Evidential Study of the Meaning of Terms in the Book of Mencius* (New Haven: Yale University Press, 1990).

Culture, Women, and the Arts: Susan Mann, *Precious Records: Women in China's Long Eighteenth Century* (Stanford: Stanford University Press, 1997); Ellen Widmer and Kang-i Sun Chang, eds., *Writing Women in Late Imperial China* (Stanford: Stanford University Press, 1997); Colin Mackerras, *The Rise of the Peking Opera, 1770–1870: Social Aspects of the Theatre in Manchu China* (New York: Oxford University Press, 1972); Arthur Waley, *Yuan Mei, Eighteenth Century Chinese Poet* (London, 1956); Maggie Keswick, *The Chinese Garden: History, Art and Architecture* (New York, 1978); Cao Xueqin, *The Story of the Stone [Dream of the Red Chamber]*, trans. David Hawkes and John Minford, 5 vols. (New York, 1973–1982); Cécile and Michel Beurdeley, *Giuseppe Castiglione: A Jesuit Painter at the Court of the Chinese Emperors* (Rutland, 1972); Evelyn Rawski, *Education and Popular Literacy in Ch'ing China* (Ann Arbor: University of Michigan Press, 1979).

Dissenting Voices: Philip Kuhn, *Soulstealers: The Chinese Sorcery Scare of 1768* (Cambridge: Harvard University Press, 1990); Paul Ropp, *Dissent in Early Modern China: Ju-lin wai-shih [The Scholars] and Ch'ing Social Criticism* (Ann Arbor: University of Michigan Press, 1981); Susan Naquin, *Shantung Rebellion: The Wang Lun Uprising of 1774* (New Haven: Yale University Press, 1981); Wu Jingzi, *The Scholars*, trans. Yang Hsien-yi and Gladys Young (Peking, 1957); Dian H. Murray, *Pirates of the South China Coast, 1790–1810* (Stanford: Stanford University Press, 1987).

The Emperor's World: Harold Kahn, *Monarchy in the Emperor's Eyes: Image and Reality in the Ch'ien-lung Reign* (Cambridge: Harvard University Press, 1971); Preston Torbert, *The Ch'ing Imperial Household Department: A Study of Its Organization and Principal Functions, 1662–1796* (Cambridge: Harvard University Press, 1977).

CHAPTER 6

Handling the Foreigners: John K. Fairbank, ed., *The Chinese World Order: Traditional China's Foreign Relations* (Cambridge: Harvard University Press, 1968); John K. Fairbank, ed., *The Cambridge History of China,* vol. 10: *Late Ch'ing, 1800–1911, Part 1* (New York, 1978), essays by Joseph Fletcher on Inner Asia and Tibet; John Wills, *Pepper, Guns, and Parleys: The Dutch East India Company and China, 1662–1681* (Cambridge: Harvard University Press, 1974); Fu Lo-shu, *A Documentary Chronicle of Sino-Western Relations (1644–1820)* (Tucson: Arizona University Press, 1966); Mui Hoh-cheong and Lorna Mui, *The Management of Monopoly: A Study of the English East India Company's Conduct of Its Tea Trade, 1784–1833* (Vancouver: University of British Columbia Press, 1984).

Qing Law: Philip C. C. Huang, *Civil Justice in China: Representation and Practice in the Qing* (Stanford: Stanford University Press, 1996); Kathryn Bernhardt and Philip C. C. Huang, eds., *Civil Law in Qing and Republican China* (Stanford: Stanford University Press, 1994); Jerome Cohen, Randle Edwards, and Fu-mei Chang Chen, eds., *Essays on China's Legal Tradition* (Princeton: Princeton University Press, 1980); Derk Bodde and Clarence Morris, *Law in Imperial China, Exemplified by 190 Ch'ing Dynasty Cases* (Cambridge: Harvard University Press, 1967); Jonathan Spence, *The Death of Woman Wang* (New York, 1978); Sybille van der Sprenkel, *Legal Institutions in Manchu China* (London: University of London, 1962).

Western Attitudes: Jonathan Spence, *The Ch'an's Great Continent: China in Western Minds* (New York, 1998); Colin Mackerras, *Western Images of China* (New York: Oxford University Press, 1989); David Mungello, *Curious Land: Jesuit Accommodation and the Origins of Sinology* (Stuttgart, 1985); Hugh Honour, *Chinoiserie: The Vision of Cathay* (New York, 1962); John Witek, S.J., *Controversial Ideas in China and in Europe: A Biography of Jean-François Fouquet, S.J. (1665–1741)* (Rome, 1982); Jonathan Spence, *The Question of Hu* (New York, 1988).

CHAPTER 7

Social Contexts in Early Nineteenth-Century China: *Cambridge History of China,* vol. 10: *Late Ch'ing, 1800–1911, Part 1* (New York, 1978), essays by Joseph Fletcher; *ibid.,* vol. 11: *Late Ch'ing 1800–1911, Part 2* (New York, 1980), essays by Philip Kuhn and Susan Mann, and Frederic Wakeman; Frederic Wakeman, *Strangers at the Gate: Social Disorder in South China, 1839–1861* (Berkeley: University of California Press, 1966); Benjamin Elman, *Classicism, Politics and Kinship: The Ch'ang-chou School of New Text Confucianism in Late Imperial China* (Berkeley: University of California Press, 1990); Li Ruzhen (Li Ju-chen), *Flowers in the Mirror,* trans. Lin Tai-yi (Berkeley: University of California Press, 1965).

Studies of Lin Zexu: Arthur Waley, *The Opium War through Chinese Eyes* (London, 1958); Chang Hsin-pao, *Commissioner Lin and the Opium War* (Cambridge: Harvard University Press, 1964).

Military and Diplomatic Dimensions: John K. Fairbank, *Trade and Diplomacy on the China Coast* (Cambridge: Harvard University Press, 1953); Michael Greenberg, *British Trade and the Opening of China, 1800–1842* (New York: Cambridge University Press, 1951); Peter Ward Fay, *The Opium War, 1840–1842* (Chapel Hill: University of North Carolina Press, 1975); Gerald Graham, *The China Station: War and Diplomacy, 1830–1860* (New York: Oxford University Press, 1978); Hosea Ballou Morse, *The International Relations of the Chinese Empire,* 3 vols. (Shanghai and London, 1910–1918); Teng Ssu-yü, *Chang Hsi and the Treaty of Nanking, 1842* (Chicago: University of Chicago Press, 1944).

CHAPTER 8

Sects and Secret Societies: David Ownby, *Brotherhoods and Secret Societies in Early and Mid-Qing China: The Formation of a Tradition* (Stanford: Stanford University Press, 1996); B. J. Ter Haar, *The White Lotus Teachings in Chinese Religious History* (Leiden: E. J. Brill, 1992); Dian H. Murray and Qin Baoqi, *The Origins of the Tiandihui: The Chinese Triads in Legend and History* (Stanford: Stanford University Press, 1994); Daniel Overmyer, *Folk Buddhist Religion: Dissenting Sects in Late Traditional China* (Cambridge: Harvard University Press, 1976); Fei-ling Davis, *Primitive Revolutionaries of China: A Study of Secret Societies of the Late Nineteenth Century* (Honolulu: Hawaii University Press, 1977); Susan Naquin, *Millenarian Rebellion in China: The Eight Trigrams Uprising of 1813* (New Haven: Yale University Press, 1976); Jean Chesneaux, ed., *Popular Movements and Secret Societies in China, 1840–1950* (Stanford: Stanford University Press, 1972).

The Taiping: Franz Michael and Chang Chung-li, *The Taiping Rebellion: History and Documents,* 3 vols. (Seattle: University of Washington Press, 1966–1971); Jonathan Spence, *God's Chinese Son: The Taiping Heavenly Kingdom of Hong Xiuquan* (New York: Norton, 1996); Jen Yu-wen (Chien Yu-wen), *The Taiping Revolutionary Movement* (New Haven: Yale University Press, 1973); James Cole, *The People versus the Taipings: Bao Lisheng's "Righteous Army of Dongan"* (Berkeley: University of California Press, 1981); Vincent Shih, *The Taiping Ideology, Its Sources, Interpretations, and Influences* (Seattle: University of Washington Press, 1967); C. A. Curwen, *Taiping Rebel: The Deposition of Li Hsiu-ch'eng* (New York: Cambridge University Press, 1977).

The Taiping and Foreign Powers: Richard Smith, *Mercenaries and Mandarins: The Ever-Victorious Army of Nineteenth-Century China* (Millwood, NY: KTO Press, 1978); John Gregory, *Great Britain and the Taipings* (London, 1969); Eugene Boardman, *Christian Influence upon the Ideology of the Taiping Rebellion, 1851–1864* (Madison: University of Wisconsin Press,

1952); Rudolf Wagner, *Reenacting the Heavenly Vision: The Role of Religion in the Taiping Rebellion* (Berkeley: University of California Press, 1982).

The Nian and Muslim Rebellions: Teng Ssu-yü, *The Nien Army and Their Guerrilla Warfare, 1851–1868* (Paris, 1961); Elizabeth Perry, *Rebels and Revolutionaries in North China, 1845–1945* (Stanford: Stanford University Press, 1980); Chu Wen-djang, *The Moslem Rebellion in Northwest China, 1862–1878: A Study of Government Minority Policy* (The Hague, 1966); Chiang Siang-tseh, *The Nien Rebellion* (Seattle: University of Washington Press, 1954).

CHAPTER 9

Confucian Resistance and Restoration: Mary Wright, *The Last Stand of Chinese Conservatism: The T'ung-chih Restoration, 1862–1874* (Stanford: Stanford University Press, 1957); Jonathan Ocko, *Bureaucratic Reform in Provincial China: Ting Jih-ch'ang in Restoration Kiangsu, 1867–1870* (Cambridge: Harvard University Press, 1983); Stanley Spector, *Li Hungchang and the Huai Army: A Study in Nineteenth-Century Chinese Regionalism* (Seattle: University of Washington Press, 1964); Philip Kuhn, *Rebellion and Its Enemies in Late Imperial China: Militarization and Social Structure, 1798–1864* (Cambridge: Harvard University Press, 1970).

China's Growing Knowledge of the West: Jane Kate Leonard, *Wei Yuan and China's Rediscovery of the Maritime World* (Cambridge: Harvard University Press, 1984); Fred Drake, *China Charts the World: Hsü Chi-yü and His Geography of 1848* (Cambridge: Harvard University Press, 1975); Masataka Banno, *China and the West, 1858–1861: The Origins of the Tsungli Yamen* (Cambridge: Harvard University Press, 1964); James Reardon-Anderson, *The Study of Change: Chemistry in China, 1840–1949* (Cambridge: Cambridge University Press, 1991); Immanuel Hsü, *China's Entrance into the Family of Nations: The Diplomatic Phase, 1858–1880* (Cambridge: Harvard University Press, 1960); Teng Ssu-yü and John K. Fairbank, *China's Response to the West: A Documentary Survey, 1839–1923* (Cambridge: Harvard University Press, 1954); Thomas La Fargue, *China's First Hundred: Educational Mission Students in the United States, 1872–1881* (reprint, Pullman: Washington State University Press, 1987); Paul Cohen, *Between Tradition and Modernity: Wang T'ao and Reform in Late Ch'ing China* (Cambridge: Harvard University Press, 1974); J. D. Frodsham, *The First Chinese Embassy to the West: The Journals of Kuo Sung-t'ao, Liu Hsi-hung, and Chang Te-yi* (New York: Oxford University Press, 1974).

The Missionary Impact: Daniel H. Bays, ed., *Christianity in China: From the Eighteenth Century to the Present* (Stanford: Stanford University Press, 1996); Edward Gulik, *Peter Parker and the Opening of China* (Cambridge: Harvard University Press, 1973); Paul Cohen, *China and Christianity: The Missionary Movement and the Growth of Chinese Antiforeignism, 1860–1870* (Cambridge: Harvard University Press, 1963); Knight Biggerstaff, *The Earliest Modern Government Schools in China* (Ithaca: Cornell University Press, 1961); John K. Fairbank, ed., *The Missionary Enterprise in China and America* (Cambridge: Harvard University Press, 1974); Susan Wilson Barnett and John K. Fairbank, eds., *Christianity in China: Early Protestant Missionary Writings* (Cambridge: Harvard University Press, 1985); Jane Hunter, *The Gospel of Gentility: American Women Missionaries in Turn-of-the-Century China* (New Haven: Yale University Press, 1984); Irwin Hyatt, *Our Ordered Lives Confess: Three Nineteenth Century American Missionaries in East Shantung* (Cambridge: Harvard University Press, 1976).

Robert Hart: Katherine F. Bruner, John K. Fairbank, and Richard Smith, eds., *Entering China's Service: Robert Hart's Journals, 1854–1863* (Cambridge: Harvard University Press, 1986); John K. Fairbank, Katherine Bruner, and Elizabeth Matheson, eds., *The I.G. In Peking:*

Letters of Robert Hart, Chinese Maritime Customs, 1868–1907, 2 vols. (Cambridge: Harvard University Press, 1975).

Chinese Overseas in the Nineteenth Century: G. William Skinner, *Chinese Society in Thailand: An Analytical History* (Ithaca: Cornell University Press, 1957); Yung Wing, *My Life in China and America* (New York, 1909); Yen Ching-huang, *Coolies and Mandarins: China's Protection of Overseas Chinese during the Late Ch'ing Period (1851–1911)* (Singapore: Singapore University Press, 1985); Robert Irick, *Ch'ing Policy toward the Coolie Trade* (Taipei, 1982); Chan Sucheng, *This Bittersweet Soil: The Chinese in California Agriculture, 1860–1910* (Berkeley: University of California Press, 1986); Alexander Saxton, *The Indispensable Enemy: Labor and the Anti-Chinese Movement in California* (Berkeley: University of California Press, 1971); James Loewen, *The Mississippi Chinese: Between Black and White* (Cambridge: Harvard University Press, 1971); Watt Stewart, *Chinese Bondage in Peru, 1849–1874* (reprint, Westport, CT, 1970).

CHAPTER 10

Late Qing Self-Strengthening: Samuel C. Chu and Kwang-ching Liu, eds., *Li Hung-chang and China's Early Modernization* (Armonk, NY, 1994); Kwang-ching Liu, *Anglo-American Steamship Rivalry in China, 1862–1874* (Cambridge: Harvard University Press, 1962); John Rawlinson, *China's Struggle for Naval Development, 1839–1895* (Cambridge: Harvard University Press, 1967); Daniel Bays, *China Enters the Twentieth Century: Chang Chih-tung and the Issues of a New Age, 1895–1909* (Ann Arbor: University of Michigan Press, 1978); William Ayers, *Chang Chih-tung and Educational Reform in China* (Cambridge: Harvard University Press, 1971); Albert Feuerwerker, *China's Early Industrialization: Sheng Hsuan-huai (1844–1916) and Mandarin Enterprise* (Cambridge: Harvard University Press, 1958).

Economic Developments: Hao Yen-p'ing, *The Commercial Revolution in Nineteenth-Century China: The Rise of Sino-Western Mercantile Capitalism* (Berkeley: University of California Press, 1986); Wellington Chan, *Merchants, Mandarins and Modern Enterprise in Late Ch'ing China* (Cambridge: Harvard University Press, 1977); Hao Yen-p'ing, *The Comprador in Nineteenth Century China: Bridge between East and West* (Cambridge: Harvard University Press, 1970); Rhoads Murphey, *The Treaty Ports and China's Modernization: What Went Wrong?* (Ann Arbor: University of Michigan, 1970); Michael Godley, *The Mandarin-Capitalists from Nanyang: Overseas Chinese Enterprise in the Modernization of China, 1839–1911* (New York: Cambridge University Press, 1982); Samuel Chu, *Reformer in Modern China: Chang Chien, 1853–1926* (New York: Columbia University Press, 1965); Susan Mann, *Local Merchants and the Chinese Bureaucracy, 1750–1950* (Stanford: Stanford University Press, 1987); William Rowe, *Hankow,* vol. 2: *Conflict and Community in a Chinese City, 1796–1895* (Stanford: Stanford University Press, 1989).

1898 Reforms: Joan Judge, *Print and Politics: Shibao and the Culture of Reform in Late Qing China* (Stanford: Stanford University Press, 1996); Luke Kwong, *A Mosaic of the Hundred Days: Personalities, Politics and Ideas of 1898* (Cambridge: Harvard University Press, 1984); Hsiao Kung-chuan, *A Modern China and a New World: K'ang Yu-wei, Reformer and Utopian* (Seattle: University of Washington Press, 1975).

Emergent Nationalism: Lloyd Eastman, *Throne and Mandarins: China's Search for a Policy during the Sino-French Controversy, 1880–1885* (Cambridge: Harvard University Press, 1967); Stewart Lone, *Japan's First Modern War: Army and Society in the Conflict with China, 1894–95* (London, 1994); John Schrecker, *Imperialism and Chinese Nationalism: Germany in Shantung* (Cambridge: Harvard University Press, 1971); Philip Huang, *Liang Ch'i-ch'ao and Modern*

Chinese Liberalism (Seattle: University of Washington Press, 1972); Chang Hao, *Liang Ch'i-ch'ao and Intellectual Transition in China, 1890–1907* (Cambridge: Harvard University Press, 1971); Joseph Levenson, *Liang Ch'i-ch'ao and the Mind of Modern China* (Cambridge: Harvard University Press, 1953); Tang Xiaobing, *Global Space and the Nationalist Discourse of Modernity: The Historical Thinking of Liang Qichao* (Stanford: Stanford University Press, 1996); Zou Rong (Tsou Jung), *The Revolutionary Army: a Chinese Revolutionary Tract of 1903,* trans. John Lust (The Hague, 1968).

The Boxers: Paul A. Cohen, *History in Three Keys: The Boxers As Event, Experience, and Myth* (New York: Columbia University Press, 1997). David Buck, *Recent Chinese Studies of the Boxer Movement* (Armonk, NY, 1987); Joseph Esherick, *The Origins of the Boxer Uprising* (Berkeley: University of California Press, 1987);

Sun Yat-sen's Early Years: Yen Ching-hwang, *The Overseas Chinese and the 1911 Revolution, with Special Reference to Singapore and Malaya* (Kuala Lumpur, 1976); Harold Schiffrin, *Sun Yat-sen and the Origins of the Chinese Revolution* (Berkeley: University of California Press, 1970); J. Y. Wong, *The Origins of a Heroic Image: Sun Yat-sen in London, 1896–1897* (New York: Oxford University Press, 1986).

CHAPTER 11

Central Forces in the Revolution: Harold Schiffrin and Eto Shinkichi, eds., *China's Republican Revolution* (Tokyo, 1994); Mary C. Wright, ed., *China in Revolution, the First Phase* (New Haven: Yale University Press, 1968); Ralph Powell, *The Rise of Chinese Military Power, 1895–1912* (Princeton: Princeton University Press, 1955); Ralph Huenemann, *The Dragon and the Iron Horse: The Economics of Railroads in China, 1876–1937* (Cambridge: Harvard University Press, 1984); Roger R. Thompson, *China's Local Councils in the Age of Constitutional Reform, 1898–1911* (Harvard Council on East Asian Studies, Cambridge, MA, 1994); Stephen MacKinnon, *Power and Politics in Late Imperial China: Yuan Shi-kai in Beijing and Tianjin, 1901–1908* (Berkeley: University of California Press, 1980); Li Chien-nung, *The Political History of China, 1840–1928,* trans. Teng Ssu-yü and Jeremy Ingalls (Princeton, NJ, 1956); Edmund Fung, *The Military Dimension of the Chinese Revolution* (Vancouver: University of British Columbia Press, 1980).

Regions and Elites in the Revolution: Min Tu-ki, *National Polity and Local Power: The Transformation of Late Imperial China,* trans. and ed. Philip Kuhn and Timothy Brook (Harvard Council on East Asian Studies, Cambridge, MA, 1989); Edward Rhoads, *China's Republican Revolution: The Case of Kwangtung, 1895–1913* (Cambridge: Harvard University Press, 1975); Joseph Esherick, *Reform and Revolution: The 1911 Revolution in Hunan and Hubei* (Berkeley: University of California Press, 1976); Mary Rankin, *Early Chinese Revolutionaries: Radical Intellectuals in Shanghai and Chekiang, 1902–1911* (Cambridge: Harvard University Press, 1971); Mary Rankin, *Elite Activism and Political Transformation in China, Zhejiang Province, 1865–1911* (Stanford: Stanford University Press, 1986); Roger Des Forges, *Hsi-liang and the Chinese National Revolution* (New Haven: Yale University Press, 1973); R. Keith Schoppa, *Chinese Elites and Political Change: Zhejiang Province in the Early Twentieth Century* (Cambridge: Harvard University Press, 1982); John Fincher, *Chinese Democracy: The Self-Government Movement in Local, Provincial and National Politics, 1905–1914* (Canberra, 1981).

Intellectual Shifts: Benjamin Schwartz, *In Search of Wealth and Power: Yen Fu and the West* (Cambridge: Harvard University Press, 1964); Michael Gasster, *Chinese Intellectuals and the Revolution of 1911: The Birth of Modern Chinese Radicalism* (Seattle: University of Washington

Press, 1969); Frank Dikötter, *The Discourse of Race in Modern China* (London, 1992); Joseph Levenson, *Confucian China and Its Modern Fate,* 3 vols. (Berkeley: University of California Press, 1958–1964), reissued as *Modern China and Its Confucian Past;* Martin Bernal, *Chinese Socialism to 1907* (Ithaca: Cornell University Press, 1976); Don Price, *Russia and the Roots of the Chinese Revolution, 1896–1911* (Cambridge: Harvard University Press, 1974); Paula Harrell, *Sowing the Seeds of Change: Chinese Students and Japanese Teachers, 1895–1905* (Stanford: Stanford University Press, 1992); Douglas R. Reynolds, *China, 1898–1912: The Xinzheng Revolution and Japan* (Harvard Council on East Asian Studies, Cambridge, MA, 1993).

CHAPTER 12

The Early Republic: K. S. Liew, *Struggle for Democracy: Sung Chiao-jen and the 1911 Chinese Revolution* (Berkeley: University of California Press, 1971); Ernest Young, *The Presidency of Yuan Shih-k'ai: Liberalism and Dictatorship in Early Republican China* (Ann Arbor: University of Michigan Press, 1977); George T. Yu, *Party Politics in Republican China: The Kuomintang, 1912–1924* (Berkeley: University of California Press, 1966); Edward Friedman, *Backward toward Revolution: The Chinese Revolutionary Party* (Berkeley: University of California Press, 1974); Franklin Houn, *Central Government of China, 1912–1928: An Institutional Study* (Madison: University of Wisconsin Press, 1959); C. Martin Wilbur, *Sun Yat-sen, Frustrated Patriot* (New York: Columbia University Press, 1976); Andrew Nathan, *Peking Politics, 1918–1923: Factionalism and the Failure of Constitutionalism* (New York: Columbia University Press, 1976).

Warlordism: Edward A. McCord, *The Power of the Gun: The Emergence of Modern Chinese Warlordism* (Berkeley: University of California Press, 1993); Ch'i Hsi-sheng, *Warlord Politics in China, 1916–1928* (Stanford: Stanford University Press, 1976); Lucian Pye, *Warlord Politics: Conflict and Coalition in the Modernization of Republican China* (New York, 1971); Diana Lary, *Warlord Soldiers: Chinese Common Soldiers, 1911–1937* (New York: Cambridge University Press, 1985); Robert Kapp, *Szechwan and the Chinese Republic: Provincial Militarism and Central Power, 1911–1938* (New Haven: Yale University Press, 1973); Donald Gillin, *Warlord: Yen Hsi-shan in Shansi Province, 1911–1949* (Princeton: Princeton University Press, 1967); James Sheridan, *Chinese Warlord: The Career of Feng Yü-hsiang* (Stanford: Stanford University Press, 1966); Donald Sutton, *Provincial Militarism and the Chinese Republic: The Yunnan Army, 1905–1925* (Ann Arbor: University of Michigan Press, 1980).

The Business World: Sherman Cochran, *Big Business in China: Sino-Foreign Rivalry in the Cigarette Industry, 1890–1930* (Cambridge: Harvard University Press, 1980); Andrea Lee McElderry, *Shanghai Old-Style Banks (Ch'ien-chuang) 1800–1935* (Ann Arbor: University of Michigan, 1978); S. A. M. Adshead, *The Modernization of the Chinese Salt Administration, 1900–1920* (Cambridge: Harvard University Press, 1970); Albert Feuerwerker, *The Foreign Establishment in China in the Early Twentieth Century* (Ann Arbor: University of Michigan, 1976); Mark Elvin and G. William Skinner, eds., *The Chinese City between Two Worlds* (Stanford: Stanford University Press, 1974).

Foreign Elements: Cyril Pearl, *Morrison of Peking* (Sydney, Australia, 1967); James Reed, *The Missionary Mind and American East Asia Policy, 1911–1915* (Cambridge: Harvard University Press, 1983); Hou Chi-ming, *Foreign Investment and Economic Development in China, 1840–1937* (Cambridge: Harvard University Press, 1965); C. F. Remer, *Foreign Investments in China* (New York, 1933); Michael Summerskill, *China on the Western Front: Britain's Chinese Work Force in the First World War* (London, 1982).

CHAPTER 13

General Analyses of the May Fourth Movement: Chow Tse-tsung, *The May Fourth Movement: Intellectual Revolution in Modern China* (Cambridge: Harvard University Press, 1960); Lydia H. Liu, *Translingual Practice: Literature, National Culture, and Translated Modernity, China, 1900–1937* (Stanford: Stanford University Press, 1995); Vera Schwarcz, *The Chinese Enlightenment: Intellectuals and the Legacy of the May Fourth Movement of 1919* (Berkeley: University of California Press, 1986); Merle Goldman, ed., *Modern Chinese Literature in the May Fourth Era* (Cambridge: Harvard University Press, 1977); James Pusey, *China and Charles Darwin* (Cambridge: Harvard University Press, 1983); Lin Yü-sheng, *The Crisis of Chinese Consciousness: Radical Anti-traditionalism in the May Fourth Era* (Madison: University of Wisconsin Press, 1979).

Lu Xun: Leo Ou-fan Lee, *Voices from the Iron House: A Study of Lu Xun* (Bloomington: Indiana University Press, 1987); Leo Ou-fan Lee, ed., *Lu Xun and His Legacy* (Berkeley: University of California Press, 1985); William Lyell, *Lu Hsün's Vision of Reality* (Berkeley: University of California Press, 1976).

Founding the CCP: Anthony Saich, *The Origins of the First United Front in China: The Role of Sneevliet (Alias Maring)*, 2 vols. (Leiden, 1991); Marilyn Levine, *The Found Generation: The Chinese Communists in Europe during the Twenties* (Seattle: University of Washington Press, 1993); Yeh Wen-hsin, *Provincial Passages: Culture, Space, and the Origins of Chinese Communism* (Berkeley: University of California Press, 1996); Christina Gilmartin, *Engendering the Chinese Revolution: Radical Women, Communist Politics, and Mass Movements in the 1920s* (Berkeley: University of California Press, 1995); Maurice Meisner, *Li Ta-chao and the Origins of Chinese Marxism* (Cambridge: Harvard University Press, 1967); Arif Dirlik, *The Origins of Chinese Communism* (New York: Oxford University Press, 1989); Robert North, *Moscow and Chinese Communists* (Stanford: Stanford University Press, 1963); Lee Feigon, *Chen Duxiu: Founder of the Chinese Communist Party* (Princeton: Princeton University Press, 1983); Frederic Wakeman, *History and Will: Philosophical Perspectives of Mao Tse-tung's Thought* (Berkeley: University of California Press, 1973).

Influential May Fourth Figures: Jerome Grieder, *Hu Shih and the Chinese Renaissance: Liberalism in the Chinese Revolution, 1917–1937* (Cambridge: Harvard University Press, 1970); Charlotte Furth, *Ting Wen-chiang, Science and China's New Culture* (Cambridge: Harvard University Press, 1970); Joey Bonner, *Wang Kuo-wei: An Intellectual Biography* (Cambridge: Harvard University Press, 1986); David Roy, *Kuo Mo-jo, the Early Years* (Cambridge: Harvard University Press, 1971); Laurence Schneider, *Ku Chieh-kang and China's New History: Nationalism and the Quest for Alternative Traditions* (Berkeley: University of California Press, 1971); William Duiker, *Ts'ai Yüan-p'ei, Educator of Modern China* (Philadelphia: University of Pennsylvania Press, 1977); Leo Ou-fan Lee, *The Romantic Generation of Chinese Writers* (Cambridge: Harvard University Press, 1973).

CHAPTER 14

Urban Life and the Labor Movement: Elizabeth Perry, *Shanghai on Strike: The Politics of Chinese Labor* (Stanford: Stanford University Press, 1993); Jean Chesneaux, *The Chinese Labor Movement, 1919–1927*, trans. H. M. Wright (Stanford: Stanford University Press, 1968); Lynda Shaffer, *Mao and the Workers: The Hunan Labor Movement, 1920–1923* (Armonk, NY, 1982); Nicholas R. Clifford, *Shanghai, 1925: Urban Nationalism and the Defense of Foreign Privilege*

(Ann Arbor: University of Michigan, 1979); David Strand, *Rickshaw Beijing: City People and Politics in the 1920s* (Berkeley: University of California Press, 1989); Shirley Garrett, *Social Reformers in Urban China: The Chinese YMCA, 1895–1926* (Cambridge: Harvard University Press, 1970); Colin Mackerras, *The Chinese Theatre in Modern Times, from 1840 to the Present Day* (Amherst: University of Massachusetts Press, 1975); E. Perry Link, *Mandarin Ducks and Butterflies: Popular Fiction in Early Twentieth Century Chinese Cities* (Berkeley: University of California Press, 1981).

Rural China and the Peasant Movement: Fernando Galbiati, *P'eng P'ai and the Hai-lu-feng Soviet* (Stanford: Stanford University Press, 1985); Roy Hofheinz, *The Broken Wave: The Chinese Communist Peasant Movement, 1922–1928* (Cambridge: Harvard University Press, 1977); Angus McDonald, *The Urban Origins of Rural Revolution; Elites and the Masses in Hunan Province, China, 1911–1927* (Berkeley: University of California Press, 1978); Robert Marks, *Rural Revolution in South China: Peasants and the Making of History in Haifeng County, 1570–1930* (Madison: University of Wisconsin Press, 1984); R. Keith Schoppa, *Xiang Lake—Nine Centuries of Chinese Life* (New Haven: Yale University Press, 1989); Phil Billingsley, *Bandits in Republican China* (Stanford: Stanford University Press, 1988).

The United Front and the Northern Expedition: John Fitzgerald, *Awakening China: Politics, Culture, and Class in the Nationalist Revolution* (Stanford: Stanford University Press, 1996); Donald Jordan, *The Northern Expedition: China's National Revolution of 1926–1928* (Honolulu: University of Hawaii Press, 1976); Dan Jacobs, *Borodin: Stalin's Man in China* (Cambridge: Harvard University Press, 1981); F. Gilbert Chan and Thomas Etzold, eds., *China in the 1920s, Nationalism and Revolution* (New York, 1976); Harold Isaacs, *The Tragedy of the Chinese Revolution* (Stanford: Stanford University Press, 1961); Xenia Eudin and Robert North, *M. N. Roy's Mission to China: The Communist Kuomintang Split of 1927* (Berkeley: University of California Press, 1963); Gavan McCormack, *Chang Tso-lin in Northeast China, 1911–1928: China, Japan and the Manchurian Idea* (Stanford: Stanford University Press, 1977); S. Bernard Thomas, *"Proletarian Hegemony" in the Chinese Revolution and the Canton Commune of 1927* (Ann Arbor: University of Michigan, 1975); *Cambridge History of China*, vol. 12: *Republican China 1912–1949, Part 1,* (New York, 1983), essays by Jerome Ch'en, C. Martin Wilbur, Marie-Claire Bergère; C. Martin Wilbur and Julie How, eds., *Documents on Communism, Nationalism, and Soviet Advisers in China, 1918–1927* (New York: Columbia University Press, 1956).

Biographical Collections: Howard Boorman, ed., *Biographical Dictionary of Republican China,* 4 vols. (New York: Columbia University Press, 1967), vol. 5, Janet Krompart, *A Personal Name Index* (1979); Donald Klein and Anne Clark, *Biographic Dictionary of Chinese Communism, 1921–1965,* 2 vols. (Cambridge: Harvard University Press, 1971).

CHAPTER 15

The Guomindang Government: Tien Hung-mao, *Government and Politics in Kuomintang China, 1927–1937* (Stanford: Stanford University Press, 1972); William Wei, *Counterrevolution in China: The Nationalists in Jiangxi during the Soviet Period* (Ann Arbor: University of Michigan Press, 1985); Lloyd Eastman, *The Abortive Revolution: China under Nationalist Rule, 1927–1937* (Cambridge: Harvard University Press, 1974); Parks Coble, *The Shanghai Capitalists and the Nationalist Government, 1927–1937* (Cambridge: Harvard University Press, 1986); Joseph Fewsmith, *Party, State and Local Elites in Republican China: Merchant Organizations and Politics in Shanghai, 1890–1930* (Honolulu: University of Hawaii Press, 1985); Akira Iriye, *After*

Imperialism: The Search for a New Order in the Far East (Cambridge: Harvard University Press, 1965); Ch'ien Tuan-sheng, *The Government and Politics of China, 1912–1949* (Stanford: Stanford University Press, 1970).

Republican Shanghai: Frederic Wakeman, *Policing Shanghai* (Berkeley: University of California Press, 1995); Frederic Wakeman and Wen-hsin Yeh, eds. *Shanghai Sojourners* (Berkeley: Institute of East Asian Studies, 1992); Brian Martin, *The Shanghai Green Gang: Politics and Organized Crime, 1919–1937* (Berkeley: University of California Press, 1996); Bryna Goodman, *Native Place, City, and Nation: Regional Networks and Identities in Shanghai, 1853–1937* (Berkeley: University of California Press, 1995); Gail Hershatter, *Dangerous Pleasures: Prostitution and Modernity in Twentieth-Century Shanghai* (Berkeley: University of California Press, 1997); Christian Henriot, *Shanghai, 1927–1937: Municipal Power, Locality, and Modernization* (Berkeley: University of California Press, 1993); Emily Honig, *Sisters and Strangers: Women in the Shanghai Cotton Mills, 1919–1949* (Stanford: Stanford University Press, 1986).

Cultural Life under the Guomindang: Wilma Fairbank, *Liang and Lin: Partners in Exploring China's Architectural Past* (Philadelphia: University of Pennsylvania Press, 1994); Frank Dikötter, *Sex, Culture, and Modernity in China* (Honolulu: University of Hawaii Press, 1995); Jay Leyda, *Dianying, Electric Shadows: An Account of Films and the Film Audience in China* (Cambridge: MIT Press, 1972); Christoph Harbsmeier, *The Cartoonist Feng Zikai: Social Realism with a Buddhist Face* (Oslo, 1984); Ralph Croizier, *Art and Revolution in Modern China: The Lingnan (Cantonese) School of Painting, 1906–1951* (Berkeley: University of California Press, 1988); Holmes Welch, *The Buddhist Revival in China* (Cambridge: Harvard University Press, 1968).

The United States and China: John K. Fairbank, *The United States and China* (Cambridge: Harvard University Press, 1948, and later eds.); Dorothy Borg, *American Policy and the Chinese Revolution, 1925–1928* (New York: Columbia University Press, 1947); Dorothy Borg, *The United States and the Far Eastern Crisis of 1933–1938* (Cambridge: Harvard University Press, 1964); Peter Conn, *Pearl S. Buck: A Cultural Biography* (Cambridge: Cambridge University Press, 1996); Lian Xi, *The Conversion of Missionaries: Liberalism in American Protestant Missions in China, 1907–1932* (University Park: Pennsylvania State University Press, 1997); James Thomson, *While China Faced West: American Reformers in Nationalist China, 1928–1937* (Cambridge: Harvard University Press, 1969); Philip West, *Yenching University and Sino-Western Relations, 1916–1952* (Cambridge: Harvard University Press, 1976); Jessie Lutz, *China and the Christian Colleges, 1850–1950* (Ithaca: Cornell University Press, 1971); John Bowers, *Western Medicine in a Chinese Palace: Peking Union Medical College, 1917–1951* (Philadelphia: Josiah Macy Foundation, 1972); Mary Bullock, *An American Transplant: The Rockefeller Foundation and the Peking Union Medical College* (Berkeley: University of California Press, 1980); Randall Stross, *The Stubborn Earth: American Agriculturalists on Chinese Soil, 1898–1937,* (Berkeley: University of California Press, 1986); Stanford M. Lyman, *Chinese Americans* (New York, 1974); Paul Siu, *The Chinese Laundryman: A Study of Social Isolation* (New York: New York University Press, 1987); Renqiu Yu, *To Save China, To Save Ourselves: The Chinese Hand Laundry Alliance of New York* (Philadelphia: Temple University Press, 1992).

Japan and China: Parks M. Coble, *Facing Japan: Chinese Politics and Japanese Imperialism, 1931–1937* (Harvard Council on East Asian Studies, Cambridge, MA, 1991); Akira Iriye, ed., *The Chinese and the Japanese: Essays in Political and Cultural Interactions* (Princeton: Princeton University Press, 1980); James Morley, ed., *The China Quagmire: Japan's Expansion on the Asian Continent, 1933–1941* (New York: Columbia University Press, 1983); Joshua Fogel, *Politics and Sinology: The Case of Naitō Konan (1866–1934)* (Cambridge: Harvard University Press, 1984); James Crowley, *Japan's Quest for Autonomy: National Security and Foreign Policy,*

1930–1938 (Princeton: Princeton University Press, 1966); Ito Takeo, *Life Along the South Manchurian Railway,* trans. Joshua Fogel (Armonk, NY, 1988).

Germany and China: William Kirby, *Germany and Republican China* (Princeton: Princeton University Press, 1984); Liang Hsi-huey, *The Sino-German Connection: Alexander von Falkenhausen between China and Germany, 1900–1941* (Amsterdam, 1978); Bernd Martin, ed., *The German Advisory Group in China* (Düsseldorf, 1981).

The Late Manchus: Pamela Kyle Crossley, *Orphan Warriors: Three Manchu Generations and the End of the Qing World* (Princeton: Princeton University Press, 1989); Lao She, *Beneath the Red Banner (An Autobiographical Manchu Novel),* trans. Don Cohn (Peking, 1982); Puyi Aisin-gioro, *From Emperor to Citizen (The Ex-Emperor's Autobiography),* 2 vols. (Peking, 1964); Lee Chong-sik, *Revolutionary Struggle in Manchuria: Chinese Communism and Soviet Interest, 1922–1945* (Berkeley: University of California Press, 1983).

CHAPTER 16

Rural China and CCP Survival: Roger Thompson, trans. and ed., *Mao Zedong: Report from Xunwu* (Stanford: Stanford University Press, 1990); Ilpyong Kim, *The Politics of Chinese Communism: Kiangsi under the Soviets* (Berkeley: University of California Press, 1973); Benjamin Schwartz, *Chinese Communism and the Rise of Mao* (Cambridge: Harvard University Press, 1958); Stuart Schram, *Mao Tse-tung* (Harmondsworth, 1966); Jerome Ch'en, *Mao and the Chinese Revolution* (New York: Oxford University Press, 1965); Hsiao Tso-liang, *Power Relations within the Chinese Communist Movement, 1930–1934: A Study of Documents* (Seattle: University of Washington Press, 1961); Richard Thornton, *The Comintern and the Chinese Communists, 1928–1931* (Seattle: University of Washington Press, 1969).

Perspectives on the Long March and the Xi'an Incident: Tony Saich and Hans van de Ven, eds., *New Perspectives on the Chinese Communist Revolution* (Armonk, NY, 1995); Gregor Benton, *Mountain Fires: The Red Army's Three-Year War in South China, 1934–1938* (Berkeley: University of California Press, 1992); Lyman Van Slyke, *Enemies and Friends: The United Front in Chinese Communist History* (Stanford: Stanford University Press, 1967); Otto Braun, *A Comintern Agent in China, 1932–1939* (Stanford: Stanford University Press, 1982); Chang Kuo-t'ao, *Autobiography: The Rise of the Chinese Communist Party, 1921–1938,* 2 vols. (Lawrence: University Press of Kansas, 1972); Edgar Snow, *Red Star over China* (New York, 1938); John Israel, *Student Nationalism in China, 1927–1937* (Stanford: Stanford University Press, 1966); Agnes Smedley, *The Great Road: The Life and Times of Chu Teh* (New York, 1956); Dick Wilson, *The Long March of 1935: The Epic of Chinese Communism's Survival* (New York, 1971); Wu Tien-wei, *The Sian Incident: A Pivotal Point in Modern Chinese History* (Michigan, 1976); James Bertram, *First Act in China: The Story of the Sian Mutiny* (New York, 1938).

Maintaining Confucian Values: Guy Alitto, *The Last Confucian: Liang Shu-ming and the Chinese Dilemma of Modernity* (Berkeley: University of California Press, 1979); Jerry Dennerline, *Qian Mu and the World of Seven Mansions* (New Haven: Yale University Press, 1988); Susan Chan Egan, *A Latterday Confucian: Reminiscences of William Hung (1893–1980)* (Cambridge: Harvard University Press, 1987); Charlotte Furth, ed., *The Limits of Change: Essays on Conservative Alternatives in Republican China* (Cambridge: Harvard University Press, 1976).

Writers of the 1930s: Ting, Lee-hsia Hsu, *Government Control of the Press in Modern China, 1900–1949* (Cambridge: Harvard University Press, 1974); Mao Dun (Mao Tun), *Midnight,* trans. Hsu Meng-hsiung (Peking, 1957); Lao She, *Rickshaw,* trans. Jean James (Honolulu:

Hawaii University Press, 1979); David Pollard, *A Chinese Look at Literature: The Literary Values of Chou Tso-jen in Relation to Tradition* (Berkeley: University of California Press, 1973); Paul Pickowicz, *Marxist Literary Thought in China: The Influence of Ch'ü Ch'iu-pai [Qu Qiu-bai]* (Berkeley: University of California Press, 1981); Tani Barlow and Gary Bjorge, eds., *I Myself Am a Woman: Selected Writings of Ding Ling* (Boston, 1989); Yi-tsi Mei Feuerwerker, *Ding Ling's Fiction: Ideology and Narrative in Modern Chinese Literature* (Cambridge: Harvard University Press, 1982); Tsi-an Hsia, *The Gate of Darkness: Studies on the Leftist Literary Movement in China* (Seattle: University of Washington Press, 1968); Jeffrey Kinkley, *The Odyssey of Shen Congwen* (Stanford: Stanford University Press, 1987); Olga Lang, *Pa Chin and His Writings: Chinese Youth between Two Revolutions* (Cambridge: Harvard University Press, 1967); Hsü Kai-yu, *Twentieth Century Chinese Poetry, an Anthology* (Ithaca: Cornell University Press, 1970); Hung Chang-tai, *Going to the People: Chinese Intellectuals and Folk Literature, 1918–1937* (Cambridge: Harvard University Press, 1985).

The State of the Peasantry: Kenneth Pomeranz, *The Making of a Hinterland: State, Society, and Economy in Inland North China, 1853–1937* (Berkeley: University of California Press, 1993); Ralph A. Thaxton, Jr., *Salt of the Earth: The Political Origins of Peasant Protest and Communist Revolution in China* (Berkeley: University of California Press, 1997); Prasenjit Duara, *Culture, Power, and the State: Rural North China, 1900–1942* (Stanford: Stanford University Press, 1988); Ramon Myers, *The Chinese Peasant Economy: Agricultural Development in Hopei and Shantung, 1890–1949* (Cambridge: Harvard University Press, 1970); Fei Hsiao-t'ung (Fei Xiaotong), *Peasant Life in China* (London, 1939); R. H. Tawney, *Land and Labor in China* (London, 1932); John Lossing Buck, *Land Utilization in China: A Study of 16,786 Farms in 168 Localities . . .* , 3 vols. (Shanghai and Chicago, 1937); Philip Huang, *The Peasant Economy and Social Change in North China* (Stanford: Stanford University Press, 1985); W. E. Willmott, ed., *Economic Organization in Chinese Society* (Stanford: Stanford University Press, 1972); Daniel Little, *Understanding Peasant China: Case Studies in the Philosophy of Social Science* (New Haven: Yale University Press, 1989); David Faure, *The Rural Economy of Pre-Liberation China: Trade Expansion and Peasant Livelihood in Jiangsu and Guangdong, 1870–1937* (New York: Oxford University Press, 1989).

The Urban Labor Force: S. Bernard Thomas, *Labor and the Chinese Revolution: Class Strategies and Contradictions of Chinese Communism, 1928–1948* (Ann Arbor: University of Michigan Press, 1983); Augusta Wagner, *Labor Legislation in China* (Peking: Yenching University, 1938); Emily Honig, *Sisters and Strangers: Women in the Shanghai Cotton Mills, 1919–1949* (Stanford: Stanford University Press, 1986); Gail Hershatter, *The Workers of Tianjin, 1900–1949* (Stanford: Stanford University Press, 1986); David Buck, *Urban Change in China: Politics and Development in Tsinan, Shantung, 1890–1949* (Madison: University of Wisconsin Press), 1978.

CHAPTER 17

The Military History of the War in China: Charles Romanus and Riley Sunderland, *United States Army in World War II: China-Burma-India Theater,* vol. 1: *Stilwell's Mission to China,* vol. 2: *Stilwell's Command Problems,* vol. 3: *Time Runs Out in CBI* (Washington, D.C., 1953, 1956, and 1959); Maochun Yu, *OSS in China: Prelude to Cold War* (New Haven: Yale University Press, 1996); F. F. Liu, *A Military History of Modern China: 1924–1949* (Princeton: Princeton University Press, 1956); Christopher Thorne, *Allies of a Kind: The United States, Britain, and the War against Japan, 1941–1945* (New York: Oxford University Press, 1978); Milton Miles, *A Different Kind of War: The Little-Known Story of the Combined Guerrilla Forces Created in China by the U.S. Navy and the Chinese during World War II* (New York,

1967); Joseph Stilwell, *The Stilwell Papers,* ed. Theodore White (New York, 1948); Barbara Tuchman, *Stilwell and the American Experience in China, 1911–1945* (New York, 1970); Claire Lee Chennault, *Way of a Fighter* (New York, 1949).

The Chongqing Government and Politics: Chang-tai Hung, *War and Popular Culture: Resistance in Modern China, 1937–1945* (Berkeley: University of California Press, 1994); James C. Hsiung and Steven I. Levine, eds., *China's Bitter Victory: The War with Japan, 1937–1945* (Armonk, NY, 1992); Lloyd E. Eastman, *Seeds of Destruction: Nationalist China in War and Revolution, 1937–1949* (Stanford: Stanford University Press, 1984); Ch'i Hsi-sheng, *Nationalist China at War: Military Defeats and Political Collapse, 1937–1945* (Ann Arbor: University of Michigan Press, 1982); Michael Schaller, *The U.S. Crusade in China, 1938–1945* (New York: Columbia University Press, 1979); Arthur Young, *China and the Helping Hand, 1937–1945* (Cambridge: Harvard University Press, 1963); Paul Sih, ed., *Nationalist China during the Sino-Japanese War, 1937–1945* (New York, 1977).

The Japanese Occupation of China: Edward Gunn, *Unwelcome Muse: Chinese Literature in Shanghai and Peking, 1937–1945* (New York: Columbia University Press, 1980); Lincoln Li, *The Japanese Army in North China, 1937–1941: Problems of Political and Economic Control* (Tokyo: Oxford University Press, 1975); Alvin Coox and Hilary Conroy, eds., *China and Japan: A Search for Balance since World War I* (Santa Barbara, CA., 1978); John Boyle, *China and Japan at War, 1937–1945: The Politics of Collaboration* (Stanford: Stanford University Press, 1972); Gerald Bunker, *The Peace Conspiracy: Wang Ching-wei and the China War, 1937–1941* (Cambridge: Harvard University Press, 1972); David Kranzler, *Japanese, Nazis, and Jews: The Jewish Refugee Community of Shanghai, 1938–1945* (New York: Yeshiva University Press, 1976); Langdon Gilkey, *Shantung Compound* (New York 1966, 1975); Martha Smalley, ed., *American Missionary Eyewitnesses to the Nanking Massacre, 1937–1938* (New Haven: Yale Divinity School, 1997); Frederic Wakeman, *The Shanghai Badlands: Urban Terrorism and Urban Crime, 1937–1941* (Cambridge: Cambridge University Press, 1996).

Yan'an Government and Politics: Mark Selden, *The Yenan Way in Revolutionary China* (Cambridge: Harvard University Press, 1971); Kataoka Tetsuya, *Resistance and Revolution in China: The Communists and the Second United Front* (Berkeley: University of California Press, 1974); Chalmers Johnson, *Peasant Nationalism and Communist Power: The Emergence of Revolutionary China, 1937–1945* (Stanford: Stanford University Press, 1962); Chen Yung fa, *Making Revolution: The Communist Movement in Eastern and Central China, 1937–1945* (Berkeley: University of California Press, 1986); S. Bernard Thomas, *Season of High Adventure: Edgar Snow in China* (Berkeley: University of California Press, 1996); James Reardon-Anderson, *Yenan and the Great Powers: The Origins of Chinese Communist Foreign Policy, 1944–1946* (New York: Columbia University Press, 1980); Bonnie McDougall, *Mao Zedong's "Talks at the Yan'an Conference on Literature and Art": A Translation of the 1943 Text with Commentary* (Ann Arbor: University of Michigan Press, 1980); John Service, *Lost Chance in China: The World War II Dispatches of John S. Service,* ed. Joseph Esherick (New York, 1974); David Barrett, *Dixie Mission: The United States Army Observer Group in Yenan, 1944* (Berkeley: University of California Press, 1970); Kenneth Shewmaker, *Americans and Chinese Communists, 1927–1945: A Persuading Encounter* (Ithaca: Cornell University Press, 1971); Raymond F. Wylie, *The Emergence of Maoism: Mao Tse-tung, Ch'en Po-ta, and the Search for Chinese Theory, 1935–1945* (Stanford: Stanford University Press, 1980).

CHAPTER 18

The CCP in the Civil War: Steven Levine, *Anvil of Victory: The Communist Revolution in Manchuria, 1945–1948* (New York: Columbia University Press, 1987); Lionel Chassin, *The*

Communist Conquest of China: A History of the Civil War, 1945–1949, trans. Timothy Osato and Louis Gelas (Cambridge: Harvard University Press, 1965); William Hinton, *Fanshen: A Documentary of Revolution in a Chinese Village* (New York, 1966).

The Guomindang in the Civil War: Suzanne Pepper, *Civil War in China: The Political Struggle, 1945–1949* (Berkeley: University of California Press, 1978); Chang Kia-ngau (Chia-ao), *The Inflationary Spiral: The Experience in China, 1939–1950* (Cambridge: MIT Press, 1958); Chou Shun-hsin, *The Chinese Inflation, 1937–1949* (New York: Columbia University Press, 1963); Donald Gillin and Ramon Myers, eds., *Last Chance in China: The Diary of Chang Kia-ngau* (Stanford: Hoover Institution Press, 1989); George Kerr, *Formosa Betrayed* (Boston, 1965).

U.S. Policies: U.S. Department of State, comp., *United States Relations with China, with Special Reference to the Period 1944–1949* (Washington, D.C., 1949; rpt., Stanford: Stanford University Press, 1967); William Stueck, *The Wedemeyer Mission: American Politics and Foreign Policy during the Cold War* (Athens: University of Georgia Press, 1984); Ernest May, *The Truman Administration in China, 1945–1949* (New York, 1975); William Leary, *Perilous Missions: Civil Air Transport and CIA Covert Operations in Asia* (Tuscaloosa: University of Alabama Press, 1984); Wilma Fairbank, *America's Cultural Experiment in China, 1942–1949* (Washington, D.C.: U.S. Department of State, 1976); Forrest Pogue, *George C. Marshall: Statesman, 1945–1959* (New York, 1987); Dorothy Borg and Waldo Henrichs, eds., *Uncertain Years: Chinese-American Relations, 1947–1950* (New York: Columbia University Press, 1973); Nancy Tucker, *Patterns in the Dust: Chinese-American Relations and the Recognition Controversy, 1949–1950* (New York: Columbia University Press, 1983); Tsou Tang, *America's Failure in China, 1941–1950* (Chicago: Chicago University Press, 1963).

Border Regions: Andrew Forbes, *Warlords and Muslims in Chinese Central Asia: A Political History of Republican Sinkiang 1911–1949* (New York: Cambridge University Press, 1986); Melvyn Goldstein, *A History of Modern Tibet: The Demise of the Lamaist State* (Berkeley: University of California Press, 1989).

Foreign Observers of the Civil War: John Melby, *The Mandate of Heaven, Record of a Civil War: China 1945–1949* (Toronto: University of Toronto Press, 1968); Derk Bodde, *Peking Diary, 1948–1949: A Year of Revolution* (New York, 1967); A. Doak Barnett, *China on the Eve of Communist Takeover* (New York, 1963); Henri Cartier-Bresson, *From One China to the Other* (New York, 1958).

CHAPTER 19

Consolidating the People's Republic: A. Doak Barnett, *Communist China: The Early Years, 1949–1955* (New York, 1955); Mark Selden, *The People's Republic of China: A Documentary History of Revolutionary Change* (New York, 1979); Ezra Vogel, *Canton under Communism: Programs and Politics in a Provincial Capital, 1949–1968* (Cambridge: Harvard University Press, 1969); Kenneth Lieberthal, *Revolution and Tradition in Tientsin, 1949–1952* (Stanford: Stanford University Press, 1980); Robert Lifton, *Thought Reform and the Psychology of Totalism: A Study of "Brainwashing" in China* (New York, 1961); *Cambridge History of China*, vol. 14: *The People's Republic, Part 1: The Emergence of Revolutionary China 1949–1965* (New York, 1987), essays in Pt. I; Maurice Meisner, *Mao's China and After: A History of the People's Republic* (New York, 1986).

Analyses of PRC Structure: John Wilson Lewis, *Leadership in Communist China* (Ithaca: Cornell University Press, 1966); Richard Kraus, *Class Conflict in Chinese Socialism* (New York: Columbia University Press, 1981); Richard Solomon, *Mao's Revolution and the Chinese Political*

Culture (Berkeley: University of California Press, 1971); A. Doak Barnett, *Cadres, Bureaucracy and Political Power in Communist China* (New York: Columbia University Press, 1967); A. Doak Barnett, ed., *Chinese Communist Politics in Action* (Seattle: University of Washington Press, 1969); John Lindbeck, ed., *China: Management of a Revolutionary Society* (Seattle: University of Washington Press, 1971); Robert Scalapino, ed., *Elites in the People's Republic of China* (Seattle: University of Washington Press, 1972).

The Korean War and the PLA: Chen Jian, *China's Road to the Korean War: The Making of the Sino-American Confrontation* (New York: Columbia University Press, 1994); *The Cold War in Asia*, Cold War International History Project, *Bulletin 6–7*, Woodrow Wilson International Center for Scholars (1995–1996); Shu Guang Zhang, *Mao's Military Romanticism: China and the Korean War, 1950–1953* (Lawrence: University Press of Kansas, 1995); Allen Whiting, *China Crosses the Yalu: The Decision to Enter the Korean War* (New York, 1960); John Gittings, *The Role of the Chinese Army* (New York: Oxford University Press, 1967); William Whitson, *The Chinese High Command: A History of Communist Military Politics, 1927–1970* (New York, 1972); Harvey Nelson, *The Chinese Military System: An Organizational Study of the People's Liberation Army* (Boulder, CO., 1977); Michael Ying-mao Kao, *The People's Liberation Army and China's Nation Building* (White Plains, NY, 1973); Callum MacDonald, *Korea: The War before Vietnam* (Basingstoke, Eng., 1986).

U.S. Responses: Edwin Martin, *Divided Counsel: The Anglo-American Response to Communist Victory in China* (Lexington: University Press of Kentucky, 1986); Ross Koen, *The China Lobby in American Politics* (New York, 1974); Lewis Purifoy, *Harry Truman's China Policy: McCarthyism and the Diplomacy of Hysteria, 1947–1951* (New York, 1976); Stanley Bachrack, *The Committee of One Million: China Lobby Politics, 1953–1971* (New York: Columbia University Press, 1976); Gary May, *China Scapegoat: The Diplomatic Ordeal of John Carter Vincent* (Washington, D.C., 1979); Robert P. Newman, *Owen Lattimore and the "Loss" of China* (Berkeley: University of California Press, 1992).

CHAPTER 20

Rebuilding the Economy: Alexander Eckstein, *China's Economic Revolution* (New York: Cambridge University Press, 1977); Thomas Rawski, *China's Transition to Industrialism: Producer Goods and Economic Development in the Twentieth Century* (Ann Arbor: University of Michigan Press, 1980); Theodore Shabad, *China's Changing Map: National and Regional Development, 1949–71*, rev. ed. (New York, 1972); Dwight Perkins, *Market Control and Planning in Communist China* (Cambridge: Harvard University Press, 1966); Audrey Donnithorne, *China's Economic System* (New York, 1967); Peter Schran, *The Development of Chinese Agriculture, 1950–1959* (Champaign: University of Illinois Press, 1969); Cheng Chu-yuan, *Communist China's Economy, 1949–1962* (South Orange, NJ: Seton Hall University Press, 1963).

Early PRC Foreign Policy: Michael H. Hunt, *The Genesis of Chinese Communist Foreign Policy* (New York: Columbia University Press, 1996); R. G. Boyd, *Communist China's Foreign Policy* (New York, 1962); James Chieh Hsiung, *Law and Policy in China's Foreign Relations: A Study of Attitudes and Practice* (New York: Columbia University Press, 1972); Jerome Cohen and Hungdah Chiu, *People's China and International Law: A Documentary Study*, 2 vols. (Princeton: Princeton University Press, 1974); Garth Alexander, *Silent Invasion: The Chinese in Southeast Asia* (London, 1973); Mary Somers Heidhues, *Southeast Asia's Chinese Minorities* (Melbourne, Australia, 1974); Robert Randle, *Geneva 1954: The Settlement of the Indochinese War* (Princeton: Princeton University Press, 1969); King C. Chen, *Vietnam and China, 1938–1954* (Princeton: Princeton University Press, 1969); Thomas E. Stolper, *China, Taiwan, and* *the Offshore Islands* (White Plains, NY, 1985); Alice Langley Hsieh, *Communist China's Strategy in the Nuclear Era* (Englewood Cliffs, NJ, 1962).

China's Minorities: June Dreyer, *China's Forty Millions: Minority Nationalities and National Integration in the People's Republic of China* (Cambridge: Harvard University Press, 1976); Donald McMillen, *Chinese Communist Power and Policy in Xinjiang, 1949–1977* (Boulder, CO., 1979); Chang Chih-i, *The Party and the National Question in China,* ed. and trans. George Moseley (Cambridge: MIT Press, 1966).

The Hundred Flowers: Roderick MacFarquhar, ed., *The Hundred Flowers* (London, 1960); Roderick MacFarquhar, *The Origins of the Cultural Revolution,* vol. 1: *Contradictions among the People, 1956–1957* (New York: Columbia University Press, 1974); Merle Goldman, *Literary Dissent in Communist China* (Cambridge: Harvard University Press, 1967); Nieh Hualing, ed., *Literature of the Hundred Flowers,* vol. 1: *Criticism and Polemics,* vol. 2: *Poetry and Fiction* (New York: Columbia University Press, 1981).

CHAPTER 21

The Great Leap Forward: Roderick MacFarquhar, *The Origins of the Cultural Revolution,* vol. 2: *The Great Leap Forward, 1958–1960* (New York: Columbia University Press, 1983; Jean-Luc Domenach, *The Origins of the Great Leap Forward: The Case of One Chinese Province* (Boulder, CO: Westview, 1995); Jasper Becker, *Hungry Ghosts: Mao's Secret Famine* (New York, 1996); Roderick MacFarquhar, Timothy Cheek, and Eugene Wu, eds., *The Secret Speeches of Chairman Mao: From the Hundred Flowers to the Great Leap* (Cambridge: Harvard University Press, 1989); Franz Schurmann, *Ideology and Organization in Communist China* (Berkeley: University of California Press, 1966); *Cambridge History of China,* vol. 14: *The People's Republic, Part 1: The Emergence of Revolutionary China, 1949–1965* (New York, 1987), essays in Pt. 2, by Kenneth Lieberthal, Nicholas Lardy, Suzanne Pepper, Merle Goldman and Allen Whiting.

The Sino-Soviet Rift: Donald Zagoria, *The Sino-Soviet Conflict, 1956–1961* (Princeton: Princeton University Press, 1962); G. F. Hudson, Richard Lowenthal, and Roderick MacFarquhar, *The Sino-Soviet Dispute* (New York, 1961); Donald Treadgold, ed., *Soviet and Chinese Communism: Similarities and Differences* (Seattle: University of Washington Press, 1967); John Wilson Lewis and Xue Litai, *China Builds the Bomb* (Stanford: Stanford University Press, 1988); Andrew Wedeman, *The East Wind Subsides: Chinese Foreign Policy and the Origins of the Cultural Revolution* (Washington, D.C., 1987).

Mao and the Intellectuals: Li Zhisui, *The Private Life of Chairman Mao* (New York: Random House, 1994); Stuart Schram, *Chairman Mao Talks to the People: Talks and Letters, 1956–1971* (New York, 1971); Jerome Ch'en, *Mao Papers: Anthology and Bibliography* (New York: Oxford University Press, 1970); Clive Ansley, *The Heresy of Wu Han: His Play "Hai Rui's Dismissal" and Its Role in China's Cultural Revolution* (Toronto: University of Toronto Press, 1971); Merle Goldman, *China's Intellectuals: Advise and Dissent* (Cambridge: Harvard University Press, 1981).

CHAPTER 22

The Early 1960s: Party and Politics: Roderick MacFarquhar, *The Origins of the Cultural Revolution,* vol. 3, *The Coming of the Cataclysm, 1961–1966* (New York: Columbia University Press, 1977); Richard Baum, *Prelude to Revolution: Mao, the Party, and the Peasant Question,*

1962–66 (New York: Columbia University Press, 1975); Richard Baum and Frederic Teiwes, *Ssu-Ch'ing: The Socialist Education Movement of 1962–1966* (Berkeley: University of California Press, 1968); Timothy Cheek, *Propaganda and Culture in Mao's China: Deng Tuo and the Intelligentsia* (Oxford: Clarendon Press, 1998); Nicholas Lardy and Kenneth Lieberthal, eds., *Chen Yun's Strategy for China's Development: A Non-Maoist Alternative* (Armonk, NY, 1983); John Bryan Starr, *Continuing the Revolution: The Political Thought of Mao* (Princeton: Princeton University Press, 1979); Jonathan Unger, *Education under Mao: Class and Competition in Canton Schools 1960–1980* (New York: Columbia University Press, 1982); Chalmers Johnson, ed., *Ideology and Politics in Contemporary China* (Seattle: University of Washington Press, 1973).

The Cultural Revolution: Analyses and Documents: Michael Schoenhals, ed., *China's Cultural Revolution, 1966–1969: Not a Dinner Party* (Armonk, NY, 1996); Lynn White, *Policies of Chaos: The Organizational Causes of Violence in China's Cultural Revolution* (Princeton: Princeton University Press, 1989); Elizabeth J. Perry and Li Xun, *Proletarian Power, Shanghai in the Cultural Revolution* (Boulder, CO, 1997); Byung-joon Ahn, *Chinese Politics and the Cultural Revolution: Dynamics of Policy Processes* (Seattle: University of Washington Press, 1976); Lee Hong-yung, *The Politics of the Chinese Cultural Revolution: A Case Study* (Berkeley: University of California Press, 1978); Parris Chang, *Radicals and Radical Ideology in China's Cultural Revolution* (New York: Columbia University Press, 1973); Andrew G. Walder, *Chang Ch'un-ch'iao and Shanghai's January Revolution* (Ann Arbor: University of Michigan, 1977); Lars Ragvald, *Yao Wen-yuan as a Literary Critic and Theorist: The Emergence of Chinese Zhdanovism* (Stockholm, 1978); Roxane Witke, *Comrade Chiang Ch'ing* [Jiang Qing] (Boston, 1977); Anne Thurston, *Enemies of the People: The Ordeal of the Intellectuals in China's Great Cultural Revolution* (New York, 1987); Margie Sargent, Vivienne Shue, Thomas Matthews, and Deborah Davis, *The Cultural Revolution in the Provinces* (Cambridge: Harvard University Press, 1971); Anita Chan, *Children of Mao: Personality Development and Political Activism in the Red Guard Generation* (Seattle: University of Washington Press, 1985); Stanley Rosen, *Red Guard Factionalism and the Cultural Revolution in Guangzhou* [Canton] (Boulder, CO, 1982); David Raddock, *Political Behavior in Adolescents in China: The Cultural Revolution in Kwangchow* [Canton] (Tucson: University of Arizona Press, 1977); Lin Biao (Lin Piao), *Important Documents on the Great Proletarian Cultural Revolution in China* (Peking, 1970); *CCP Documents of the Great Proletarian Cultural Revolution 1966–1967,* comp. Union Research Institute (Hong Kong, 1968); Lowell Dittmer, *Liu Shao-ch'i and the Chinese Cultural Revolution: The Politics of Mass Criticism* (Berkeley: University of California Press, 1974).

The Cultural Revolution: Chinese Participants and Victims: Gao Yuan, *Born Red: A Chronicle of the Cultural Revolution* (Stanford: Stanford University Press, 1987); Liang Heng and Judith Shapiro, *Son of the Revolution* (New York, 1983); Yue Daiyun, with Carolyn Wakeman, *To the Storm: The Odyssey of a Revolutionary Chinese Woman* (Berkeley: University of California Press, 1985); Nien Cheng, *Life and Death in Shanghai* (New York, 1986); Yang Jiang, *Six Chapters from My Life "Downunder"* (Seattle: University of Washington Press, 1984); *The Wounded: New Stories of the Cultural Revolution,* trans. Geremie Barmé and Bennett Lee (Hong Kong, 1979); Bei Dao, *Waves,* trans. Bonnie McDougall and Susette Cook (London, 1987); Jung Chang, *Wild Swans: Three Daughters of China* (New York, 1991); Liu Sola, *Chaos and All That* (Honolulu: University of Hawaii Press, 1994); Rae Yang, *Spider Eaters, A Memoir* (Berkeley: University of California Press, 1997).

Labor Camps: Jean-Luc Domenach, *Chine: l'archipel oublié* (Paris, 1992); Harry Wu, *Laogai: The Chinese Gulag* (Boulder, CO, 1992); Harry Wu and Carolyn Wakeman, *Bitter Winds:*

A Memoir of My Years in China's Gulag (New York, 1994); James Seymour and Richard Anderson, *New Ghosts, Old Ghosts: Prisons and Labor Reform in China* (Armonk, NY, 1998).

CHAPTER 23

Foreign Policy and the United States: Peter Van Ness, *Revolution and Chinese Foreign Policy: Peking's Support of Wars of National Liberation* (Berkeley: University of California Press, 1971); Bruce Larkin, *China and Africa, 1949–1970: The Foreign Policy of the People's Republic of China* (Berkeley: University of California Press, 1971); Henry Kissinger, *White House Years* (Boston, 1979); Richard Nixon, *RN: The Memoirs of Richard Nixon* (New York, 1978).

Campaigns and Cadres: Thomas Bernstein, *Up to the Mountains and Down to the Villages: The Transfer of Youth from Urban to Rural China* (New Haven: Yale University Press, 1977); B. Michael Frolic, *Mao's People: Sixteen Portraits of Life in Revolutionary China* (Cambridge: Harvard University Press, 1980); David Lampton, *The Politics of Medicine in China: The Policy Process, 1949–1977* (Boulder, CO, 1977); Susan Shirk, *Competitive Comrades: Career Incentives and Student Strategies in China* (Berkeley: University of California Press, 1981); Harry Harding, *Organizing China: The Problem of Bureaucracy, 1949–1976* (Stanford: Stanford University Press, 1981); Michael Oksenberg, ed., *China's Developmental Experience* (New York, 1973); Stuart Schram, ed., *Authority Participation and Cultural Change in China* (New York: Cambridge University Press, 1973).

Rural Life: Dali L. Yang, *Calamity and Reform in China: State, Rural Society, and Institutional Change since the Great Leap Forward* (Stanford: Stanford University Press, 1996); Richard Madsen, *Morality and Power in a Chinese Village* (Berkeley: University of California Press, 1984); John Burns, *Political Participation in Rural China* (Berkeley: University of California Press, 1988); Gordon Bennett, *Huadong: The Story of a Chinese People's Commune* (Boulder, CO, 1978); William Parish and Martin Whyte, *Village and Family in Contemporary China* (Chicago: University of Chicago Press, 1978).

Urban Life: John Wilson Lewis, ed., *The City in Communist China* (Stanford: Stanford University Press, 1971); Martin Whyte and William Parish, *Urban Life in Contemporary China* (Chicago: Chicago University Press, 1984).

PRC Culture: Ellen Johnston Laing, *The Winking Owl: Art in the People's Republic of China* (Berkeley: University of California Press, 1988); Lois Snow, *China on Stage: An American Actress in the People's Republic* (New York, 1972); Bonnie McDougall, ed., *Popular Chinese Literature and Performing Arts in the People's Republic of China, 1949–1979* (Berkeley: University of California Press, 1984); Richard Kraus, *Pianos and Politics in China: Class, Nationalism and the Controversy over Western Music* (New York: Oxford University Press, 1989); Simon Leys, *Chinese Shadows* (New York, 1977).

Women in the Revolution: Judith Stacey, *Patriarchy and Socialist Revolution in China* (Berkeley: University of California Press, 1983); Kay Ann Johnson, *Women, the Family and Peasant Revolution in China* (Chicago: University of Chicago Press, 1983); Elisabeth Croll, *Feminism and Socialism in China* (London, 1978); Elisabeth Croll, *The Politics of Marriage in Contemporary China* (New York: Cambridge University Press, 1981); *Contemporary Women Writers* (*Renditions* nos. 27 and 28, Chinese University of Hong Kong, 1987); Margery Wolf and Roxane Witke, eds., *Women in Chinese Society* (Stanford: Stanford University Press, 1975).

CHAPTER 24

The Four Modernizations: Richard Baum, ed., *China's Four Modernizations: The New Technological Revolution* (Boulder, CO., 1980); Andrew Walder, *Communist Neo-Traditionalism: Work and Authority in Chinese Industry* (New York: Columbia University Press, 1986); John Burns and Stanley Rosen, eds., *Policy Conflicts in Post-Mao China* (Armonk, NY, 1986); Colin Mackerras, *Modern China: A Chronology from 1842 to the Present* (San Francisco, 1982); Leo Orleans, *Chinese Students in America* (Washington, D.C., 1988); Helen Siu, *Agents and Victims in South China: Accomplices in Rural Revolution* (New Haven: Yale University Press, 1989); William Joseph, *The Critique of Ultra-Leftism in China, 1958–1981* (Stanford: Stanford University Press, 1984); David Lampton, *Paths to Power: Elite Mobility in Contemporary China* (Ann Arbor: University of Michigan, 1986).

The Democracy Movement and the "Fifth Modernization": Anita Chan, Stanley Rosen, and Jonathan Unger, *On Socialist Democracy and the Chinese Legal System: The Li Yizhe Debates* (Armonk, NY, 1985); David Goodman, *Beijing Street Voices: The Poetry and Politics of China's Democracy Movement* (London, 1981); James Seymour, *The Fifth Modernization: China's Human Rights Movement, 1978–1979* (Stanfordville, NY, 1980); Bei Dao, *The August Sleepwalker,* trans. Bonnie McDougall (London: Anvil Press, 1988); Liu Binyan, *"People or Monsters?" and Other Stories and Reportage from China after Mao,* trans. Perry Link et al. (Bloomington: Indiana University Press, 1983); Andrew Nathan, *Chinese Democracy* (New York, 1985); Perry Link, ed., *Stubborn Weeds: Popular and Controversial Chinese Literature after the Cultural Revolution* (Bloomington: Indiana University Press, 1983); Wei Jingsheng, *The Courage to Stand Alone: Letters from Prison and Other Writings* (New York, 1997); H. Lyman Miller, *Science and Dissent in Post-Mao China: The Politics of Knowledge* (Seattle: University of Washington Press, 1996).

Taiwan: Linda Chao and Ramon H. Myers, *The First Chinese Democracy: Political Life in the Republic of China on Taiwan* (Baltimore: The Johns Hopkins University Press, 1998); John Cooper, *A Quiet Revolution: Political Development in the Republic of China* (Washington, D.C., 1988); Thomas Gold, *State and Society in the Taiwan Miracle* (Armonk, NY, 1986); James C. Hsiung, ed., *The Taiwan Experience, 1950–1980: Contemporary Republic of China* (New York, 1981); Victor H. Li, ed., *The Future of Taiwan: A Difference of Opinion* (White Plains, NY, 1980); Hungdah Chiu, ed., *China and the Taiwan Issue* (New York, 1979); John Fei, Gustav Ranis, and Shirley Kuo, *Growth with Equity: The Taiwan Case* (New York: Oxford University Press, 1979).

The Development of Special Economic Zones: Harry Harding, *China's Second Revolution: Reform after Mao* (Washington, D.C., 1987); Samuel S. Kim, ed., *China and the World: Chinese Foreign Policy in the Post-Mao Era* (Boulder, CO, 1984); A. Doak Barnett, *The Making of Foreign Policy in China: Structure and Process* (Boulder, CO, 1985); Zbigniew Brzezinski, *Power and Principle: Memoirs of the National Security Adviser, 1977–1981* (New York, 1983).

Biographies: Wolfgang Bartke, *Who's Who in the People's Republic of China* (Armonk, NY, 1980); Lucien Bianco and Yves Chevrier, *La Chine: Dictionnaire bibliographique du mouvement ouvrier international* (Paris, 1985).

CHAPTER 25

Population and Environment: Vaclav Smil, *China's Environmental Crisis* (Armonk, NY, 1993). Judith Banister, *China's Changing Population* (Stanford: Stanford University Press,

1987); *New China's Population* (China Financial and Economic Publishing House and Macmillan, New York, 1987); Penny Kane, *The Second Billion: Population and Family Planning in China* (Ringwood, Australia, 1987); Steven Mosher, *Broken Earth: The Rural Chinese* (New York, 1983).

Governing China in the 1980s: Kenneth Lieberthal and Michel Oksenberg, *Policy Making in China: Leaders, Structures, and Processes* (Princeton: Princeton University Press, 1988); Tony Saich, *China's Science Policy in the 80's* (Manchester, Eng.: Manchester University Press, 1989); Victor Falkenheim, ed., *Citizens and Groups in the Policy Process of the People's Republic of China* (Ann Arbor: University of Michigan Press, 1987); David Goodman, ed., *Groups and Politics in the People's Republic of China* (Armonk, NY, 1985); Vivienne Shue, *The Reach of the State: Sketches of the Chinese Body Politic* (Stanford: Stanford University Press, 1988); Elizabeth Perry and Christine Wong, eds., *The Political Economy of Reform in Post-Mao China* (Cambridge: Harvard University Press, 1985).

Chinese Law in the PRC: Jerome Cohen, ed., *Contemporary Chinese Law: Research Problems and Perspectives* (Cambridge: Harvard University Press, 1970); Victor Li, *Law without Lawyers* (Stanford, CA, 1977); David Buxbaum, ed., *Chinese Family Law and Social Change in Historical and Comparative Perspective* (Seattle: University of Washington Press, 1978); R. Randle Edwards, Louis Henkin, and Andrew Nathan, eds., *Human Rights in Contemporary China* (New York: Columbia University Press, 1986); Henry Zheng, *China's Civil and Commercial Law* (Singapore, 1988); Michael Moser and Winston Zee, *China Tax Guide* (New York: Oxford University Press, 1987).

Chinese Writers: Merle Goldman, with Timothy Cheek and Carol Hamrin, *China's Intellectuals and the State: In Search of a New Relationship* (Cambridge: Harvard University Press, 1987); Jeffrey Kinkley, ed., *After Mao: Chinese Literature and Society, 1978–1981* (Cambridge: Harvard University Press, 1985).

Hong Kong: Frank Welsh, *A Borrowed Place: The History of Hong Kong* (New York, 1993); Jan Morris, *Hong Kong* (New York, 1997); Chiu Hungdah, Y. C. Jao, and Yuan-li Wu, eds., *The Future of Hong Kong: Toward 1997 and Beyond* (Westport, CT, 1987).

Life and Health: Yunxiang Yan, *The Flow of Gifts: Reciprocity and Social Networks in a Chinese Village* (Stanford: Stanford University Press, 1996); Gail Henderson and Myron Cohen, *The Chinese Hospital: A Socialist Work Unit* (New Haven: Yale University Press, 1984); Arthur Kleinman, *Social Origins of Distress and Disease: Depression, Neurasthenia, and Pain in Modern China* (New Haven: Yale University Press, 1986); Arthur Kleinman and Tsung-yi Lin, eds., *Normal and Abnormal Behavior in Chinese Culture* (Dordrecht, Holland, 1981); Deborah Davis-Friedmann, *Long Lives, Chinese Elderly and the Communist Revolution* (Cambridge: Harvard University Press, 1983).

Westerners in China: Arthur Miller, *Salesman in Beijing* (New York, 1984); Tani Barlow and Donald Lowe, *Teaching China's Lost Generation: Foreign Experts in the People's Republic of China* (first printed as *Chinese Reflections*) (San Francisco, 1987); Mark Salzman, *Iron and Silk* (New York, 1986); Vera Schwarcz, *Long Road Home: A China Journal* (New Haven: Yale University Press, 1984); Jim Mann, *Beijing Jeep: A Case Study of Western Business in China* (Boulder, CO, 1997).

CHAPTER 26

A Range of Voices: Zhang Xinxin and Sang Ye, *Chinese Lives: An Oral History of Contemporary China* (New York, 1987); *Seeds of Fire: Chinese Voices of Conscience,* ed. Geremie Barmé and John Minford (New York, 1989); Chin Annping, *Children of China: Voices from Recent*

Years (New York, 1988); Emily Honig and Gail Hershatter, *Personal Voices: Chinese Women in the 1980's* (Stanford: Stanford University Press, 1988); Perry Link, Richard Madsen, and Paul Pickowicz, eds., *Unofficial China: Popular Culture and Thought in the People's Republic* (Boulder, CO, 1989); Nick Browne, Paul Pickowicz, Vivian Sobchak, and Esther Yau, eds., New Chinese Cinemas: Forms, Identities, Politics (Cambridge: Cambridge University Press, 1994).

Economics and Politics: Carol Hamrin, *China and the Challenge of the Future: Changing Political Patterns* (Boulder, CO, 1989); Bruce Reynolds, ed., *Chinese Economic Policy: Economic Reform at Midstream* (New York, 1989); Orville Schell, *Discos and Democracy: China in the Throes of Reform* (New York, 1988); June Dreyer, ed., *Chinese Defense and Foreign Policy* (New York, 1989); Jim Mann, *Beijing Jeep* (New York, 1989).

The Peking Demonstrations and Massacre: The Photographers and Reporters of Min Pao News, *June Four: A Chronicle of the Chinese Democratic Uprising,* trans. Zi Jin and Qin Zhou (Fayetteville: University of Arkansas Press, 1989); David and Peter Turnley, *Beijing Spring* (New York, 1989); Roger Des Forges, Luo Ning, and Wu Yen-fo, eds., *Chinese Democracy and the Crisis of 1989: Chinese and American Reflections* (Albany: State University of New York Press, 1993); Han Minzhu, ed., *Cries for Democracy: Writings and Speeches from the 1989 Chinese Democracy Movement* (Princeton: Princeton University Press, 1990); Timothy Brook, *Quelling the People: The Military Suppression of the Beijing Democracy Movement* (Oxford: Oxford University Press, 1992).

CHAPTER 27

Central Government: Kenneth Lieberthal, *Governing China, from Revolution through Reform* (New York, 1995); Maurice Meisner, *The Deng Xiaoping Era: An Inquiry into the Fate of Chinese Socialism, 1978–1994* (New York, 1996); Yan Sun, *The Chinese Reassessment of Socialism, 1976–1992* (Princeton: Princeton University Press, 1995); Alan P. L. Liu, *Mass Politics in the People's Republic: State and Society in Contemporary China* (Boulder, CO, 1996); Bruce Gilley, *Tiger on the Brink: Jiang Zemin and China's New Elite* (Berkeley: University of California Press, 1998).

Cultural Critiques: Jianying Zha, *China Pop: How Soap Operas, Tabloids, and Bestsellers Are Transforming a Culture* (New York: The New Press, 1993); Jing Wang, *High Culture Fever: Politics, Aesthetics, and Ideology in Deng's China* (Berkeley: University of California Press, 1996); Howard Goldblatt, ed., *Chairman Mao Would Not Be Amused: Fiction from Today's China* (New York, 1995); Geremie Barmé and Linda Jaivin, eds., *New Ghosts, Old Dreams: Chinese Rebel Voices* (New York, 1992); Geremie Barmé, *Shades of Mao: The Posthumous Cult of the Great Leader* (Armonk, NY, 1996).

Military and Strategic: Michael Pillsbury, ed., *Chinese Views of Future Warfare* (Washington, D.C.: National Defense University Press, 1996); Andrew J. Nathan and Robert Ross, *The Great Wall and the Empty Fortress: China's Search for Security* (New York, 1997); Richard Bernstein and Ross H. Munro, *The Coming Conflict with China* (New York, 1997).

Economic Prospects: Kate Xiao Zhou, *How the Farmers Changed China: Power of the People* (Boulder, CO, 1996); Deborah Davis, Richard Kraus, Barry Naughton, and Elizabeth Perry, eds., *Urban Spaces in Contemporary China: The Potential for Autonomy and Community in Post-Mao China* (Washington, D.C.: Woodrow Wilson Center Press, 1995); Lester R. Brown, *Who Will Feed China?* (New York, 1995).

Glossary

Amherst, Lord William (1773–1857): Leader of the second British diplomatic and trade mission to China. In 1816 Amherst attempted to meet with the Jiaqing emperor, but due to misunderstandings in protocol, his mission was refused.

Anhui: Province in east-central China, over 50,000 square miles in area, with a population of 59,000,000. Capital: Hefei (population: 93,000).

Annam: The central region of present-day Vietnam.

Anti-American boycott of 1905: Boycott of all American goods organized in response to the mistreatment of Chinese in the United States. The first united economic expression of Chinese nationalism against a foreign power.

Anti–Lin Biao, Anti–Confucius campaign: Mass propaganda movement launched in late 1973 that linked the disgraced (and dead) Lin Biao to Confucius and called for mass criticism of the reactionary, feudal aspects of Chinese society that the two figures allegedly symbolized.

Antispiritual pollution campaign: Movement launched in 1982 by the CCP under Deng Xiaoping to criticize what was seen as Western-influenced decadence in writing and other arts.

Autumn Harvest Uprisings (September 1927): Series of unsuccessful attacks made on Comintern orders by peasant forces on several small towns near Changsha, Hunan province, led by Mao Zedong.

Bandung conference (1955): Meeting of delegates of Asian and African countries held in Bandung, Indonesia, in which Zhou Enlai called for Asian-African solidarity and won international recognition of China's new diplomatic role.

banner system: Method of military organization applied by the Manchus whereby fighting men (and their families) were grouped in divisions identified by different colored banners. Eight banners were devised, using the colors red, blue, yellow, and white: four solid and four bordered. The system, begun by Nurhaci, was phased out in the early twentieth century with the development of the Qing New Army.

baojia: Method of household organization and control, based on a system described in ancient texts and employed with varying degrees of success from the Song dynasty through the Qing. One hundred households were organized into a *jia*. Ten *jia* made a *bao*. The leaders of the units, elected on a rotating basis, were charged with maintaining local order, supervising community works, and enforcing tax collection.

Bei Dao [Bay Dow] (b. 1949): Poet, coeditor of the underground literary journal *Today.*

Blueshirts: Paramilitary organization formed in the 1930s that functioned as Chiang Kai-shek's "secret police." Led by Dai Li and other Whampoa graduates loyal to Chiang, the Blueshirts gathered intelligence on "subversive" activities and orchestrated assassinations of those thought to oppose Chiang.

Bogue: British corruption of the Portuguese *Boca Tigre,* "Tiger's Mouth," the name for the mouth of the Pearl River at Canton.

bourgeois liberalization: General term used by the CCP to describe and criticize the demands made by those calling for democracy and human rights in the student protests of 1986 and 1989.

Boxer Protocol (1901): Demands of foreign powers agreed to by the Qing government (represented by Li Hongzhang) after the suppression of the Boxer Rebellion, which included the payment of an indemnity that amounted to almost half of the Qing annual budget. Indemnity payments were later used by the United States to establish a fund to allow Chinese students to study in America.

Boxer Uprising (1900): Anti-Christian, antiforeign peasant uprising that originated in northern Shandong and ended with the siege of the foreign legation in Peking. Participants were mostly poor peasants who practiced a type of martial art that gave the name "boxer" to the movement. The uprising ended when a combined Western military expedition entered Peking, forcing the empress dowager Cixi and her court to flee to Xi'an.

Buddhism: Religion of compassion and salvation based to some extent on the teachings of the Indian prince Siddhartha ("the Buddha," 563–483 B.C.). Influential in Chinese society since its introduction during the Han dynasty (206 B.C.–220 A.D.), Buddhism at various times contested against and blended with the two indigenous schools of Chinese religious and philosophical thought, Confucianism and Daoism.

Burma Road: Overland passage running 715 miles from Lashio in Burma to Kunming in the southwestern province of Yunnan. Used by the Allies in the early part of World War II to send supplies to Chiang Kai-shek's government in Chongqing. Closed in 1942 when Britain lost Burma to Japan.

Cai Yuanpei [Tsi Yu-en-pay] (1868–1940): President of Peking University from 1916 to 1926. Important supporter of the May Fourth movement.

Campaign to Purify Class Ranks: Movement launched during the Cultural Revolution to investigate the class background of all cadres suspected of having "bad" elements in their past. Cadres "studied" their faults in May Seventh Schools set up throughout the country.

Canton: Major southern city in the Pearl River delta, known as "Guangzhou" in Mandarin. Capital of Guangdong province.

Canton commune (December 11, 1927): Communist-led workers' uprising ordered by Qu Qiubai at the command of Stalin. Put down two days later by an anti-Communist warlord and Guomindang troops.

Central Committee: Central coordinating organ of the Chinese Communist party. The powerful Politburo and its Standing Committee are drawn from its members.

Chen Duxiu [Chun Doo-shee-o] (1879–1942): Important figure in the May Fourth movement; founded the journal *New Youth* in 1915 upon his return from studies in Japan. One of the earliest Chinese Marxists and, with Li Dazhao, a founder of the Chinese Communist party.

Chen Yonggui [Chen Yohng-gway]: Leader of a production team in Dazhai; became nationally famous in 1964 when he was praised by Mao for using elements of Mao Zedong thought to achieve dramatic increases in agricultural production. Chen lost his high government appointments in the 1980 criticism of Dazhai.

Chen Yun (1905–1995): Shanghai typesetter who joined the Communist party in 1924 and went on to become the CCP's foremost economic planner after 1949. Helped orchestrate China's economic recovery after the Great Leap Forward. Criticized during the Cultural Revolution, he returned to high-level government positions in the 1980s as a conservative opponent of rapid economic change in China.

Chiang Ching-kuo [Jee-ang Jing-gwo] (1910–1988): Soviet-educated son of Chiang Kai-shek. He served under his father in various Guomindang positions, including commissioner in charge of Guomindang financial reforms in the 1940s. Inherited his father's position as president of Taiwan from 1978 to his death ten years later.

Chiang Kai-shek (1887–1975): Military and political leader of the Guomindang after the death of Sun Yat-sen. Joined the anti-Manchu Tongmeng hui as a military student in Japan. Sent by Sun Yat-sen to the Soviet Union for military training in 1923 and named leader of the Whampoa Academy upon his return. After leading the Northern Expedition, he set up a Nationalist government in 1928 and fought for the next twenty years against warlords, the Japanese, and the Communists for the control of China. President of the Guomindang government on Taiwan from 1949 until his death twenty-six years later.

Chongqing: Port city on the Yangzi River in Sichuan province. Served as the location of Chiang Kai-shek's Nationalist government during World War II.

Cixi [Tse-shee] (1835–1908): Concubine to Emperor Xianfeng; mother of Emperor Tongzhi; known to Westerners as "the empress dowager." From the time she became regent to the boy-emperor Tongzhi in 1861 until her death forty-seven years later, she held *de facto* power over the Qing government, naming two successive emperors to the throne.

Cohong [gong-hang] ("combined merchant companies"): Chinese merchant guild, formally established in 1720, with a monopoly over maritime trade with Western countries. From 1760, when all trade was restricted to Canton, the Cohong acted as agents of the Qing government, collecting duties and handling all negotiations with foreigners. The system was abolished in 1842 with the Treaty of Nanjing.

Confucianism: System of ethics based on the teachings of Kongfuzi (tr. 551–479 B.C.), who held that man would be in harmony with the universe if he behaved with righteousness and restraint, and adhered properly to specific social roles. With its emphasis on the study of the Classics, the worship of ancestors, and the submission to authority, Confucianism formed the dominant ethic of Chinese social units from the imperial government to the peasant family.

Cultural Revolution: Complex social upheaval that began as a struggle between Mao Zedong and other top party leaders for dominance of the CCP and went on to affect all of China with its call for "continuing revolution." Dates for the movement are usually given as 1966 to 1976.

Dai Zhen [Die Jun] (1724–1777): One of the most important and influential *kaozheng* scholars of the eighteenth century. Served as a compiler of the *Four Treasuries.*

Dalai Lama: Supreme spiritual leader of Tibetan Buddhism; also the supreme political leader of Tibet from 1642 to 1959. In various periods through Tibetan history, Chinese policy has had considerable influence on determining the placement and the power of the Dalai Lama. The Dalai Lama fled Tibet in 1959 and now lives in exile in India.

danwei [dahn-way]: Place of work in post-1949 China; a company or an organization that functions as an employer and often provides housing and social services for its employees.

Daoguang [Dow-gwang] (1782–1850): Reign name of Minning, second son of Emperor Jiaqing; became the sixth emperor of the Qing dynasty in 1821. His reign saw the worsening of conflicts between foreign powers and Chinese interests that culminated in the Opium War (1839–1842).

Daoism: School of philosophy based on the writings of Laozi (tr. 604–521 B.C.) and Zhuangzi (369–286 B.C.), which teaches that liberation is achieved when man is in harmony with the empty, spontaneous, and natural essence of "the way."

Dazhai: Rural brigade in Shanxi province, led by Chen Yonggui. Used in the early 1960s and again in the mid-1970s as a model for socialist agricultural production achieved through the application of Mao Zedong thought.

December Ninth movement (1935): Series of protests against Japanese aggression and Chiang Kai-shek's inability to check that aggression. It was touched off by student demonstrations held in Peking on December 9, 1935, and helped generate a climate sympathetic to the second Communist-Guomindang united front.

Democracy Wall: Stretch of wall edging the Forbidden City in Peking, where posters that called for democratic freedom were displayed in 1978–1979. The most famous of these posters, composed by Wei Jingsheng, proposed the adoption of democracy as the fifth modernization.

Deng Xiaoping [Dung Shee-ow-ping] (1904–1997): Son of a Sichuanese landlord family, he joined the Communist party while on a work-study program in France in the 1920s. A veteran of the Long March, Deng rose to high positions in the Central Committee during the 1950s and early 1960s, and returned to power after a period of persecution during the Cultural Revolution, replacing Hua Guofeng as premier in 1980. He was instrumental in implementing the Four Modernizations, and crushing the 1989 democracy protests.

Ding Ling (1904–1986): Feminist writer and Communist party member whose famous works include "The Diary of Miss Sophie" and *The Sun Shines over the Sanggan River.* She was criticized during the Rectification Campaign of 1942, and imprisoned in the anti-rightist campaign following the Hundred Flowers movement and again during the Cultural Revolution.

Donglin ("Eastern Grove") Society: Academy founded in the early seventeenth century in Wuxi by a group of scholar-officials. The society was dedicated to the restoration of "orthodox" Confucian morality as found in the Classics, which would counter what the members perceived to be the "degenerate" effects of the intuitive philosophy of Wang Yangming. As a political faction, members of the society struggled against the power of the eunuchs in the imperial court. Many from the academy suffered torture and death in a purge ordered by the powerful eunuch Wei Zhongxian in 1625.

Dorgon (1612–1650): Manchu military leader, the fourteenth son of Nurhaci, and half brother of Hong Taiji. Led the first Manchu attacks on China inside the Great Wall, capturing Peking in 1644. Dorgon exercised power over the first Qing court in his role as coregent to Hong Taiji's son, the boy emperor Shunzhi.

Dream of the Red Chamber, The *(Hong Lou Meng):* Novel, also known as *The Story of the Stone,* written by Cao Xueqin during the reign of Qianlong. This tragic love story of the hero Jia Baoyu and Lin Daiyu is set amid courtyards of a large wealthy family in the Yangzi delta region.

Duan Qirui [Dwan Chee-ray] (1865–1936): Premier of China after the death of Yuan Shikai in 1916. Accepted loans and bribes from the Japanese government, which he used to build up his own military strength. The secret agreements he made with Japan at the end of World War I became the basis of the Allies' decision to transfer Germany's Shandong rights to Japan in the 1919 Treaty of Versailles.

Du Yuesheng [Doo Yweh-shung] (1888–1951): Shanghai racketeer, banker, financier, leader of the Green Gang secret society; friend and important ally of Chiang Kai-shek.

Eighth Route Army: Name given to the Communist Red Army placed under nominal Guomindang command during the second Communist-Guomindang united front against Japan (1937–1945).

Elliot, Charles: Named in 1836 as second British superintendent of foreign trade after the death of Lord Napier. Dismissed during the Opium War for not extracting enough concessions from the Chinese in initial treaty negotiations.

Ever-Victorious Army: Foreign-officered mercenary army that fought alongside Qing forces to repel Taiping attacks in the lower Yangzi delta. The army's successful use of steam-driven gunboats and advanced artillery helped cause the Qing to consider adopting Western military technology.

fabi [fah-bee]: Unit of currency issued by the Nationalist government beginning in 1935. Runaway inflation after World War II prompted the government to abandon *fabi* in 1948 and establish a new currency, the gold yuan, whose exchange rate was 1 yuan for 3 million *fabi*.

Fang Lizhi [Fahng Lee-jir] (b. 1936): Prominent Chinese astrophysicist and dissident, expelled from the Communist party for "bourgeois liberalism"—that is, he supported student demonstrations for democracy in 1986.

Fei Xiaotong [Fay Shee-ow-tohng]: Sociologist whose pioneering field work in the 1930s and 1940s explored the patterns of social change in rural China.

Feng Yuxiang [Fung Yu-shee-ahng] (1882–1948): Warlord whose power base in the 1920s ranged from the northwestern province of Shaanxi to Peking. Influenced by the Soviet Union, he decided to join the Guomindang against other northern warlords during the Northern Expedition.

Feng Zikai [Fung Tz-kye]: Illustrator and cartoonist whose simple line drawings accurately portrayed and criticized Chinese society of the 1930s.

fifth modernization: Another name for "democracy," taken from the title of a wall poster written by Wei Jingsheng calling for the addition of democracy as the "fifth modernization," without which the Four Modernizations would not succeed.

Five Anti campaign: Struggle launched in 1952 by the Communist party against Chinese industrialists and businessmen who had stayed on in China after 1949. The movement ended the independent operation of capitalists and helped consolidate CCP power over the Chinese economy.

Five Classics: Five works (*The Book of Rites [Li Ji]*, *Spring and Autumn Annals [Chun Qiu]*, *The Book of History [Shujing]*, *The Book of Poetry [Shijing]*, and *The Book of Changes [Yi-Jing]*) said to have been edited by Confucius. Together with the Four Books, they formed the central canon of Confucian learning.

Flying Tigers: "Volunteer" force of U.S. Army–Air Force pilots who fought for China against Japan in World War II. Led by former U.S. Army pilot and adviser to Chiang Kai-shek, Claire Lee Chennault. Also used for couriers in 1989 Peking.

Four Books: *Analects* (sayings of Confucius *[Lun Yu]*), *Mencius [Mengzi]*, *The Doctrine of the Mean [Zhong Yong]*, and *The Great Learning [Da Xue]*, which formed the center of Confucian education along with the Five Classics.

"Four cleanups" *(siqing):* Action to eradicate rural corruption in the areas of accounting, granary supplies, property accumulation, and work-point allocation. Part of the Socialist Education Campaign begun in 1963 by Mao and others in the CCP to re-establish socialist morality in the countryside.

Four Modernizations: Goal of Chinese domestic policy, announced in 1978, to develop the four areas of agriculture, industry, national defense, and science and technology. In pursuit of this goal, China under Deng Xiaoping implemented an open-door policy toward the West, developing special economic zones and sending students abroad.

Four Treasuries: Massive anthology, compiled under Qianlong, of China's most famous literary and historical works. One of the great achievements of Chinese bibliography.

Fu, prince of (d. 1646): Title of a grandson of the emperor Wanli and claimant to the Ming throne. Was proclaimed emperor in 1644 in the original Ming capital of Nanjing. Manchu armies captured him in 1645 and sent him back to Peking, where he died the next year.

Fujian: Province on the southeastern coast of China, 46,300 square miles in area, with a population of 31,500,000. Capital: Fuzhou.

Fu Yuehua [Foo Yweh-hwa]: Young woman arrested in 1979 for leading peasant demonstrations in Peking during the crackdown against the Democracy Wall movement.

Gang of Four: Group consisting of Yao Wenyuan, Zhang Chunqiao, Wang Hongwen, and Jiang Qing, who were officially blamed for creating and directing the Cultural Revolution. Arrested under Hua Guofeng's orders in October 1976, the four were tried and convicted in nationally televised proceedings in 1980.

Gansu: Province in north-central China, 174,000 square miles in area, with a population of 23,500,000. Capital: Lanzhou. Much of Gansu is barren plain and desert.

Gao Gang (1905–1954): Communist leader responsible for planning the economic recovery of Manchuria after World War II. Accused during a party purge in 1954 of attempting to set up his own power base in the northeast. His death by suicide was announced the same year.

Golden Lotus (Jin Ping Mei): Considered one of the major works of Chinese fiction, first published in the late Ming. Follows the businessman/official/scholar Qing Ximen's hedonistic pursuits, many of them erotic, among his five consorts.

Gong, Prince (1833–1898): Sixth son of Emperor Daoguang, important figure in the Qing dynasty's late attempts at revitalizing its power and regaining its dignity in the face of foreign aggression. Was called upon in 1860 to negotiate the Convention of Peking with invading British forces on behalf of his exiled half brother, Emperor Xianfeng. In 1861 became adviser to the empress dowager Cixi and leader of the newly formed Office for the Management of the Business of All Foreign Countries (Zongli Yamen), a position he held until 1884 and then again from 1894 to 1898.

Grand Canal: System of waterways connecting Peking to the Yangzi River delta, allowing for the shipment of rice and other products from the south to the imperial capital.

Grand Council: Small chamber of highly trusted advisers to the emperor. First formed by Emperor Yongzheng as a secret council to expedite military planning and established as a formal institution under his son, Emperor Qianlong. The power of the Grand Council superceded that of the Grand Secretariat and the six ministries.

Grand Secretariat: Administrative body of the central imperial government, consisting of a small group of Manchus and Chinese whose function was primarily to handle routine memorials passed up from the six ministries.

Great Leap Forward (1958–1961): Attempt launched by Mao Zedong to heighten economic productivity dramatically in China through mass organization and the inspiration of revolutionary fervor among the people. Exaggerated reports of the success of policies such as the radical collectivization of peasants into large "people's communes" and the decentralization of industrial production temporarily masked the actual economic disaster and widespread famine brought by the Great Leap.

Green Gang: Secret society that dominated organized crime in Shanghai before 1949. In the 1920s and 1930s Green Gang ties were exploited by business and Guomindang to control workers' strikes and suppress CCP activities.

Guangdong ("Broad East"): Province in southeastern China, 81,000 square miles in area, with a population of 66,100,000. Capital: Guangzhou (Canton).

Guangxi ("Broad West"): Zhuang autonomous region in southwestern China, 89,000 square miles in area, with a population of 44,400,000. Capital: Nanning.

Guangxu [Gwang Shu] (1871–1908): Reign name of Caitian, nephew of Emperor Xianfeng, chosen at the age of four by his aunt Cixi to be the ninth emperor of the Qing dynasty after the death in 1875 of his cousin, Emperor Tongzhi. Sympathetic to the appeals of Confucian reformers such as Kang Youwei, Guangxu helped launch the Hundred Days' Reforms of 1898, but was imprisoned by Cixi that same year for supposedly plotting to remove her from power.

Gui, prince of (1623–1662): Title of the last known surviving grandson of the emperor Wanli and last major claimant to the Ming throne. Assumed the title of Ming emperor in 1646 from his court-in-exile in Guangdong. Forced by pursuing Manchu troops into Burma, where he was finally captured and executed by Wu Sangui.

Guizhou: Mountainous province in southwest China, 65,000 square miles in area, with its capital at Guiyang. Many of its 34,100,000 people are members of the Miao and Zhuang minorities.

Gujin tushu jicheng ("Complete Collection of Illustrations and Writings from the Earliest to Current Times"): Encyclopedia, 800,000 pages long, of writings on natural phenomena, history, literature, and government. Compiled by the scholar Chen Menglei under the patronage of Emperor Kangxi and published later as the work of Kangxi himself during the reign of Yongzheng.

Gu Yanwu [Goo Yen-woo] (1613–1682): *Kaozheng* scholar of the early Qing, revered by later scholars as a model of intellectual precision and integrity. Avoiding Confucian metaphysical speculation, he instead conducted pragmatic scholarship on such themes as government, ethics, history, and geography.

Hakkas *(Kejia):* Ethnic minority people of south-central China. Famous Hakkas include Taiping leader Hong Xiuquan and the Soong family.

Hebei ("River North"): Province in northeastern China, 69,500 square miles in area, with a population of 63,300,000. Capital: Shijiazhuang.

Heilongjiang ("Black Dragon River")ʻ Northeastern-most province in China, 180,000 square miles in area, with a population of 36,400,000. Capital: Harbin. Place of vast wilderness and harsh, long winters.

Henan ("River South"): Province in east-central China, 61,800 square miles in area, with a population of 89,500,000. Capital: Zhengzhou. Much of Henan is situated on the broad, flat plain of the Yellow River.

Heshen (1750–1799): Powerful minister and adviser to the emperor Qianlong, accused at Qianlong's death of corruption and contributing to the decline of the empire. In one year he rose from imperial bodyguard to the highest positions in the government, where he used his power to enrich himself and his followers. Arrested and forced to commit suicide after the death of Qianlong.

He Zizhen [Huh Tz-jen] (1909–1984): Second wife of Mao Zedong, his companion on the Long March and in Yan'an until he left her for his third wife, Jiang Qing.

Hong Taiji (1592–1643): Sometimes known as Abahai. Eighth son of Nurhaci, emperor of the Manchus for seventeen years after the death of his father in 1626. With the help of Chinese advisers and troops, he extended Manchu rule east over Korea and south to the Great Wall. He died in 1643, leaving the final conquest of Peking to his younger half brother, Dorgon.

Hong Xiuquan [Hong Shee-o-chwen] (1813–1864): Leader of the Taiping rebellion, an aspiring scholar from a poor Hakka family. Believing himself to be the brother of Jesus Christ, entrusted by God to drive the demon Manchus out of China, he formed the Society of God Worshipers in Guangxi province, proclaimed himself emperor of the "Heavenly Kingdom of Great Peace" (Taiping Tianguo), and led a rebellion against the Qing that almost ended the dynasty.

Hoppo: Derived from *Hubu,* or "Ministry of Revenue." Official head of Maritime Customs for the Qing government before the Opium War. The Hoppo did not deal directly with foreigners, but received duties and all communiqués from foreigners through Cohong merchants.

Hua Guofeng [Hwah Gwo-fung] (b. 1921): Former party secretary of Hunan province who rose to the position of premier of China and head of the CCP after the death of Mao in 1976. Hua ordered the arrest of the Gang of Four in order to consolidate his power, but was in turn edged out of his central positions in 1980 by an ascendent Deng Xiaoping.

Huai River: One of the major waterways of China, approximately 625 miles long, flowing west to east through the central provinces of Jiangsu, Anhui, and Henan.

Hubei ("Lake North"): Province in central China, 69,500 square miles in area, with a population of 56,500,000. Capital: Wuhan. The middle reaches of the Yangzi River run through this province.

Hu Feng: Poet, friend of Lu Xun, and Communist party member. Object of a major rectification campaign in 1955 for his insistence on the freedom of artistic expression.

Hunan ("Lake South"): Province in south-central China, 81,000 square miles in area, with a population of 63,100,000. Capital: Changsha.

Hundred Days' Reforms (Summer 1898): Three-month period during which Kang Youwei and his supporters influenced Emperor Guangxu to issue edicts on political and economic reform. Ended when Cixi staged a coup, imprisoning the emperor and executing six reformers, including Kang Youwei's younger brother.

Hundred Flowers movement (1957): Brief period of liberalization begun in May 1957, when Mao encouraged the "blooming of a hundred flowers and the contending of a hundred schools of thought" and called for the nation's intellectuals to criticize the Communist party. The resultant outpouring of expression was swiftly cut off by the end of June, when an "antirightist campaign" was launched against those who had spoken out.

Hu Shi [Who Shir] (1891–1962): Writer, philosopher, leading figure of the May Fourth movement. Later served as the Nationalist government's ambassador to the United States from 1938 to 1942.

Hu Yaobang [Who Yow-bahng] (1915–1989): Protégé of Deng Xiaoping who rose from leader of the Communist Youth League in the 1950s to secretary-general of the CCP in 1981. Dismissed from this position in 1987 for supposedly supporting the student democracy protests of December 1986. His death in April 1989 served as a rallying point for the renewed student democracy protests that culminated in the Peking massacre of June 4, 1989.

Hu Yepin [Who Yeh-pin] (1907–1931): Poet, Communist, member of the League of Left-Wing Writers, and companion of Ding Ling. Executed by Guomindang authorities in Shanghai.

imperial household *(nei wu fu):* A self-contained bureaucracy within the imperial palace, staffed by bannermen and bondservants who managed the financial and personal affairs of the emperor and the imperial family.

Inner Mongolia *(Nei Menggu):* Autonomous region of deserts and grassland in northern China, 463,000 square miles in area, with a population of 22,300,000. Inner Mongolia shares a long border with Soviet-allied Mongolia to the north. Capital: Hohot.

Inspectorate of Customs: Foreign-managed service that collected maritime customs fees for the Qing court. Established in 1854 during the Taiping rebellion to reorganize the Chinese customs in accordance with Western international trade protocol. Under Robert Hart, the Inspectorate successively channeled large sums of money into the imperial treasuries.

Jehol (Rehe): City 100 miles northeast of Peking, site of the summer palaces of the Qing emperors. Now the city of Chengde in Hebei province.

Jiang Qing [Jee-ahng Ching] (1914–1991): Third wife of Mao Zedong, a former Shanghai movie actress who rose in the late 1960s and early 1970s to become a major political figure of the Cultural Revolution. Arrested in 1976, after the death of her husband, on charges that as the leader of the Gang of Four she was personally responsible for directly persecuting hundreds of party members and indirectly causing the suffering of millions of Chinese. Her death sentence was commuted to life under house arrest. She committed suicide in 1991.

Jiangsu: Province on the eastern coast of China, 38,000 square miles in area, with a population of 69,700,000. Capital: Nanjing. Bordering the municipality of Shanghai, Jiangsu is traditionally a center of Chinese culture and business.

Jiangxi ("River West"): Province in southeastern China, 61,800 square miles in area, with a population of 39,700,000. Capital: Nanchang.

Jiangxi Soviet: Experimental rural Communist government led by Mao Zedong, centered in the town of Ruijin on the mountainous border between Jiangxi and Fujian provinces. Established in 1928, it lasted until a Guomindang blockade of the area forced the Communists to escape north in 1934 on what became the Long March.

Jiang Zemin (b. 1926): Received training in the Soviet Union as an electrical engineer, before embarking on Chinese political bureaucratic career. Mayor of Shanghai 1985, and promoted to head CCP in summer 1989 after dismissal of Zhao Ziyang. In 1990s appointed president of the PRC and head of Military Affairs Commission.

Jiaqing [Jee-ah-ching] (1760–1820): Reign name of Yongyan, fifth son of Emperor Qianlong. Named fifth emperor of the Qing dynasty in 1796, he took full power after his father's death in 1799. During his rule China was plagued by pirates, internal rebellions, and natural disasters. Jiaqing himself was the target of an assassination attempt in 1813, when followers of the Eight Trigrams religious-cult leader Lin Qing broke into the Forbidden City.

Jingdezhen: City in Jiangxi province, famous since the Yuan dynasty for its imperial porcelain factories.

Jinggang Mountains: Isolated area on the Jiangxi-Hunan border where Mao Zedong, after the failed Autumn Harvest Uprisings of 1927, attempted to set up his first rural soviet.

jinshi: Highest degree attainable through the imperial examination system. Candidates sat for the test in Peking, where it was given once every three years throughout the Ming and Qing dynasties until the abolition of the examination system in 1905. Holders of the *jinshi* degree were assigned to high offices in the provinces and the imperial capital.

Journey to the West (Xiyou Ji): Major work of Chinese fiction, based on the pilgrimage of the Tang dynasty monk Xuan Zang to India in search of Buddhist sutras. First published in novel form in the late Ming.

Kangxi [Kahng-shee] (1654–1722): Reign name of Xuan Ye, third son of Emperor Shunzhi, who came to the throne at the age of seven and for sixty-one years ruled China as the second emperor of the Qing dynasty. Saw to the consolidation of Manchu rule over China, personally leading successful military campaigns to the northwest border areas while his generals subdued the rebellious Three Feudatories in the south and captured Taiwan. During his reign China was the largest and one of the most prosperous unified empires on earth.

Kang Youwei [Kahng Yo-way] (1858–1927): Confucian scholar, influential in late Qing reform movements, who held that economic and political modernization could take place within a Confucian political and moral framework. His plans for reform were supported by Emperor Guangxu in the Hundred Days' Reforms of 1898.

Koxinga (1624–1662): Naval commander, supporter of the Ming cause who fought the Manchus through the 1650s along the southeastern coast of China. Defeated by Manchu troops at Nanjing in 1659, Koxinga went on to establish a powerful military and commercial base on Taiwan.

Lao She [Laow Shuh] (1899–1966): Novelist and playwright whose works criticized the corruption and injustice of Chinese society of the 1920s and 1930s. His most famous works include *Cat Country* and *Rickshaw.* Driven to suicide by Red Guards in the Cultural Revolution.

League of Left-Wing Writers: Organization of poets, novelists, and essayists, many of whom were Communist party members, formed in Shanghai in the 1930s. Members included Ding Ling, Hu Yepin, Qu Qiubai, and Lu Xun.

Lee Teng-hui (b. 1923): Native Taiwanese politician who succeeded Chiang Ching-kuo to the presidency of Taiwan in 1988. Concerned with reopening contacts between Taiwan and the PRC, one of the first major actions of his presidency was to lift all restrictions on Taiwanese traveling to the mainland to visit relatives.

Lei Feng [Lay Fung]: Young PLA soldier whose humble demeanor and selfless death in the service of Mao Zedong and the Communist party has been upheld as a role model in various propaganda campaigns of the past twenty-five years, the first of which was launched by Lin Biao in 1963 in a campaign to "learn from the army."

Liang Qichao [Lee-ahng Chee-chow] (1873–1929): Student of Kang Youwei. Exiled to Japan after the conservative coup of 1898, he used his writings to raise support for the reformers' cause among overseas Chinese and foreign governments. Initally a supporter of Kang Youwei's ideas of constitutional monarchy, he later split with his teacher and advocated a liberal republicanism.

Liaoning: Province in northeastern China, 54,000 square miles in area, with a population of

40,400,000. Its capital, Shenyang (Mukden), is one of the major heavy-industry centers in China.

Liao Zhongkai [Lee-ow Johng-kye] (1878–1925): American-born, Japanese-educated associate of Sun Yat-sen. Early Tongmeng hui member. Managed financial affairs for the Guomindang from 1914 until his death. Assassinated in 1925, perhaps by right-wing Guomindang members, for his support of the Hong Kong–Canton workers' strike.

Li Dazhao [Lee Dah-jow] (1889–1927): Important figure in the May Fourth movement, early Chinese Marxist, and one of the founders of the CCP. Studied in Japan, returned to China in 1918 as director of the Peking University library and co-editor of *New Youth* magazine. Went on to become an influential Communist party leader during its first united-front alliance with the Guomindang (1923–1927). Captured and executed in Peking by the warlord Zhang Zuolin.

Lifan Yuan ("Office of Border Affairs"): Established in 1638 by Hong Taiji to handle relations with Mongols and other non-Han peoples in northwest China. (Relations with more sinified countries such as Korea, Vietnam, Burma, and Thailand were handled through the Ministry of Rituals.)

Li Hongzhang [Lee Hong-jahng] (1823–1901): General/official in the service of the Qing dynasty and a major figure in the self-strengthening movement of the late nineteenth century. Came to prominence in the 1860s under the tutelege of Zeng Guofan as leader of the provincial Huai army against the Taiping. Later went on in the 1870s and 1880s to help develop railways, telegraph lines, shipping companies, and arms manufacture.

Li Lisan [Lee Lee-sahn] (1900–1967): Early Communist labor organizer, selected in 1928 to replace Qu Qiubai as leader of the Communist party. Li was criticized and removed from his leadership position in 1930 for insisting that the urban proletariat, not the peasantry, would be the dominant force of the Chinese revolution.

Lin Biao [Lin Bee-yow] (1907–1971): Military leader who helped to transform the PLA into a conventional modern army; succeeded Peng Dehuai in 1959 as minister of defense. An ardent supporter of Mao, Lin compiled the influential *Quotations from Chairman Mao* and was named to be Mao's successor in 1969. Supposedly died two years later in an airplane crash after having escaped a failed coup against Mao.

Lin Qing [Lin Ching] (1770–1813): Leader of the Eight Trigrams millenary Buddhist cult who organized his followers to stage anti-Qing uprisings in Henan in the early 1800s. Some of his supporters broke into the Forbidden City in an attempt to assassinate Emperor Jiaqing.

Lin Zexu [Lin Dze-shu] (1785–1850): Scholar-official from Fujian province, appointed in 1838 as imperial commissioner to end opium trade. He led a moral campaign aimed at domestic users of opium and at the same time attempted to stop foreign importation of the drug. His confiscation and destruction in 1839 of 3 million pounds of opium from British warehouses in Canton outraged British trading concerns and helped trigger the Opium War (1839–1842).

Li Peng (b. 1928): One of several orphans protected by Zhou Enlai, he was a Soviet-trained engineer who became premier of China in 1988. Initially seen as a supporter of Deng Xiaoping's policies of rapid economic change, he emerged as a major hard-liner in 1989.

Liu Binyan [Lee-o Bin-yen] (b. 1925): Writer and journalist, famous for his *People or Monsters?*, an exposé of the economic crimes of Wang Shouxin. Expelled from the Communist party in 1987 in the campaign against "bourgeois liberalization."

Liu Shaoqi [Lee-o Shaow-chee] (1898–1969): Soviet-educated Communist organizer and theorist, author of *How to Be a Good Communist*. Publicly recognized in the early 1960s as Mao's successor to party leadership, Liu was severely criticized as a "capitalist roader" and purged from the party during the Cultural Revolution.

Li Zicheng [Lee Dze-chung] (1606–1645): Post-station attendant and deserter from the Ming army who in 1644, with his own rebel forces, overthrew the Ming dynasty. From his base of power in Shaanxi province, Li established his rule over much of northern and central China. He finally marched unopposed into Peking in 1644, bringing to an end a dynasty already weakened by threats from the Manchus and from other rebel armies.

Long March (1934–1935): Journey of 6,000 miles made by Communist forces escaping the suppression campaign of Chiang Kai-shek. Only 8,000 to 9,000 of the original 80,000 who began the year-long trek out of the Jiangxi Soviet area in 1934 lived to establish a new Communist base at Yan'an in the northwestern province of Shaanxi.

Lu Xun [Loo Shun] (1881–1936): China's most famous short story writer. His works criticized, with dry, sardonic wit, the traditional culture and mentality of his fellow Chinese. Among his most famous works are "The True Story of Ah Q" and "My Old Home."

Macao: Port city in southern China, 50 miles southwest of Hong Kong, under Portuguese territorial rule 1557–1999.

Macartney, Lord George (1737–1806): Leader of the first official British diplomatic mission to China. Sent in 1793 by the British East India Company with the cooperation of the court of George III to establish formal "Western-style" trade and diplomatic relations with the court of Qianlong. Macartney managed to meet with the emperor in the Manchu summer palaces in Jehol, but his demands were politely refused and the mission returned a failure.

macroregion: Area consisting of a central "core" of heightened population density and trade, surrounded by a "periphery" of weaker economic development. Used to analyze economic structures of Chinese society.

magistrate: Head administrator of a county, the lowest appointed official of the central government in imperial China. Responsible for the collection of government revenues, the execution of public works, and the administration of justice in the towns and the countryside.

Manchukuo ("Land of the Manchus"): Name given by the Japanese to the puppet regime they established in Manchuria in 1932. The Japanese placed the deposed Qing emperor Puyi as "chief executive" of the government and retained control of the area until the end of WWII.

Mao Dun [Mao Dwun] (1896–1981): Leftist writer, author of the novel *Midnight,* depicting the corrupt capitalist society of Shanghai in the 1930s. Served as the minister of culture in the Communist government after 1949.

Mao Zedong [Maow Dzuh-Dohng] (1893–1976): Peasant from Hunan who became an early member of the CCP while working in the Peking University library under Li Dazhao. Rose to party leadership by the 1930s, advocating that China's Marxist revolution would be won by the peasants, not by an urban proletariat. Led the CCP on the Long March and then to establish the People's Republic of China in 1949. Until his death in 1976 he was the paramount political leader and theorist of Chinese communism.

March 18, 1926: Date of mass demonstrations in Tiananmen Square in which forty-seven students protesting against Japanese aggression were killed by warlord troops.

Marco Polo Bridge incident: Refers to the Japanese taking of the Marco Polo railway bridge near Peking on the night of July 7, 1937. The fighting that followed this maneuver marked the beginning of open hostilities between China and Japan and can be seen as the first battle of World War II.

May Fourth movement: Term used to describe student demonstrations that took place in Tiananmen Square on May 4, 1919, in protest against the unfair terms of the Treaty of Versailles. Also refers to the period of iconoclastic intellectual ferment that followed the protests, which included movements to adopt the use of vernacular Chinese in literature and the exploration of different forms of Western cultural and political models.

May Seventh Cadre Schools: Labor camps established during the Cultural Revolution that combined hard agricultural work with the study of Mao's writings in order to "re-educate" cadres and intellectuals in proper socialist thought.

May Thirtieth Incident: Incident of 1925 in which the British-led police fired on unarmed student and worker protestors in the International Settlement in Shanghai. Many demonstrators died, setting off a wave of demonstrations and strikes that expressed solidarity with the antiforeign nationalistic cause of the "May Thirtieth martyrs."

memorial: Form of communiqué written by imperial government officials conveying information to the emperor for his review. Usually mediated through the Grand Secretariat, the common memorial lacked speed and confidentiality. The "palace memorial" system, a form of confidential, direct communication between trusted ministers and the emperor, was established by Kangxi and used extensively by his son, Yongzheng.

mou: Traditional Chinese measure of land; equals one-sixth of an acre.

Mukden: Manchu name for the city presently known as Shenyang, in the northeastern province of Liaoning. Made the capital of Nurhaci's Manchu Empire in 1625.

Mukden Incident: Refers to an outbreak of fighting between Chinese and Japanese troops on September 18, 1931, instigated by Japanese officers alleging that Chinese attacked them along a railway line outside of Mukden (Shenyang). Following this incident, Japan quickly mobilized its troops to take control of all of Manchuria.

New Army: Modern system of military organization, based on the model of the Western-influenced provincial armies of Zeng Guofan and Li Hongzhang, launched by the Qing government in 1901 to replace the traditional Eight Banners system. Eventually the New Army fragmented into splinter groups under control of their influential regional commanders, such as the Beiyang army of Yuan Shikai.

New Fourth Army: Communist guerrilla forces that had been left behind in central China during the Long March, reorganized during the second united front. The tenuous nature of the united front was demonstrated in 1941 when 3,000 troops of the New Fourth Army were killed by Guomindang forces in an ambush that became known as the New Fourth Army Incident.

New Life movement: Set of beliefs, part fascist, part Confucian, part Christian, formulated by Chiang Kai-shek's government during the 1930s to change the moral character of the Chinese and create an alert, "militarized" society.

Nian rebellion (1851–1868): Led by Zhang Luoxing, a guerrilla war fought mostly by impoverished peasants against the Qing in the area north of the Huai River (including parts of Shandong, Henan, Jiangsu, and Anhui). Defeated by the local Huai Army under the leadership of Li Hongzhang, protégé of Zeng Guofan, the general who had suppressed the Taiping rebellion.

Ningxia: Autonomous region in north-central China, 60,000 square miles in area, with a population of 5,000,000. Capital: Yinchuan. Many of the people of this dry, barren region are of the Muslim *hui* minority.

Northern Expedition (1926–1928): Military campaign, undertaken by allied Guomindang-Communist forces (the National Revolutionary Army) under the leadership of Chiang Kai-shek, to free China from fragmented warlord rule and unify it under one government. Two years after the launching of the campaign from his base in Canton, China as far north as Mukden was under the nominal control of Chiang, who then established the capital for his Nationalist government in Nanjing.

Oboi (d. 1669): Manchu general who struggled for and achieved considerable power in the imperial court after the death of Dorgon in 1650. In 1661 became coregent for the seven-year-old emperor Kangxi. During his regency, Oboi reversed the benevolent policies of Kangxi's father Shunzhi, and vigorously pushed for clear reassertion of Manchu power over the Chinese.

Opium War (1839–1842): Fought between Britain and China; triggered by British outcry against Lin Zexu's confiscation of British opium, and by Chinese anger at the murder of a Chinese by the British. Hostilities were initially confined to Canton and to the east China coast as far north as Tianjin. When British forces threatened the Yangzi delta city of Nanjing, the Qing sued for peace, signing the Treaty of Nanjing in 1842.

Peking convention (1860): Treaty between Britain and China, "negotiated" between Lord Elgin and Prince Gong after British troops entered Peking, razed the summer palace, and forced the Qing court to flee to Jehol. In addition to reconfirming the terms of the Treaty of Tianjin, the convention stipulated the ceding of the Kowloon peninsula to Hong Kong, the opening of Tianjin as a treaty port, and the payment of an additional 8 million taels in indemnity to Britain.

Peking massacre (June 4, 1989): On orders of CCP hard-liners, thousands of pro-democracy demonstrators and Peking citizens were killed by PLA troops following six weeks of rallies in Tiananmen Square.

Peng Dehuai [Pung Duh-hwye] (1898–1974): Communist general, leader of the Chinese forces in the Korean War. A trusted and venerated veteran of the Long March, Peng was purged in 1959 from his senior position in the party for criticizing Mao's Great Leap Forward policies at Lushan.

Peng Zhen [Pung Jen] (1902–1997): Mayor of Peking from 1951 to 1966, demoted and criticized during the Cultural Revolution. Returned to Chinese politics as member of the Central Committee. Known as a hard-liner who opposed rapid change in China.

people's commune (*renmin gongshe*): Central unit of economic and political organization in the countryside, some consisting of tens of thousands of families, introduced in the Great Leap Forward and popularized again in the Cultural Revolution. Communes were further divided into brigades and production teams that directed labor and divided work points.

picul: Unit of weight, equaling approximately 130 pounds, used as a measure for both grain and opium.

PLA (People's Liberation Army): Name given to the armed forces of China. Begun as the Red Army famous for its guerrilla fighting tactics in the 1930s, the PLA has evolved into a modern military organization of approximately 3 million soldiers in the late 1980s.

Pottinger, Sir Henry (1789–1856): Appointed in 1841 as superintendent of trade and sole plenipotentiary of Chinese affairs for the British government, replacing the dismissed Charles Elliot. Presided over the signing of the Treaty of Nanjing.

Puyi [Poo-ee] (1906–1967): Tenth and last emperor of the Qing dynasty. Ascended the throne in 1908 at the age of two, formally abdicating four years later. Installed by the Japanese as the figurehead of their puppet regime in Manchukuo from 1932 to 1945. After 1945 he underwent over ten years of "rehabilitation" in a CCP prison, and ended his life quietly in Peking.

Qianlong [Chee-en-lung] (1711–1799): Reign name of Hongli, fourth son of Emperor Yong-zheng, who assumed the throne in 1736 as the fourth emperor of the Qing dynasty. His sixty-three-year reign saw a large growth in the Chinese population, the military conquest of Xinjiang, the compilation of the *Four Treasuries,* and the first British diplomatic mission to China under Macartney.

Qinghai ("Green Sea"): Province in west-central China, 278,000 square miles in area, with a population of 4,700,000. Capital: Xining. Most of Qinghai is covered by inhospitable mountains and desert, and is the site of many Chinese labor-camps.

Qiu Jin [Chee-o Jin] (1875–1907): Anti-Manchu feminist revolutionary. Fled an arranged marriage and went to Japan to study. Returned to native Zhejiang province and established a school for girls, from which she launched an unsuccessful uprising against the Qing. She was captured and promptly executed by Manchu authorities.

queue: Manchu men's hairstyle that consisted of a high shaved forehead and a long braid down the back; originally developed to keep long hair out of the face in battle. By Manchu decree issued by Dorgon in 1645, all Chinese men had to adopt the hairstyle upon risk of execution. Anti-Manchu activists would often cut the queue braid as an act of defiance against the Qing.

Qu Qiubai [Chew Chee-o-bye] (1899–1935): Early Chinese Communist who lived in Moscow in the early 1920s. As head of the Communist party from 1927 to 1928, he bore the blame for a year of disastrous worker and peasant uprisings, including the Canton Commune. Too ill to join the Communists on the Long March, he was captured and executed by Guomindang forces in 1935.

Rape of Nanjing: Period of seven weeks in December 1937–January 1938 during which Japanese troops plundered Chiang Kai-shek's capital city, killing an estimated 50,000 and raping tens of thousands of women.

Rectification Campaign (1942): Political struggle launched by Mao Zedong in order to strengthen the dominant role of his ideology in the Communist party. Major targets of the criticism in Yan'an included rival party leader Wang Ming and the feminist writer Ding Ling.

Red Guards: Groups of university and middle-school students who claimed allegiance to Mao and acted as the executors of the Cultural Revolution directives to attack "feudal" and "reactionary" elements of society. Lack of organization and overzealous revolutionary fervor led to violence among Red Guard factions and between Red Guards and the PLA in the late 1960s.

renminbi ("people's currency"): Official unit of exchange in China. Informally known as yuan.

Revolutionary Alliance (Tongmeng hui): Anti-Manchu group founded in 1905 in Tokyo by the exiled Sun Yat-sen and Chinese students studying in Japan, including Liao Zhongkai and Wang Jingwei. It sponsored propaganda, fund-raising, and insurrectionary activities that culminated in 1911 with the Wuhan uprising and the fall of the Qing dynasty.

revolutionary committees: Small groups created during the Cultural Revolution to lead local urban governments, rural communes, universities, and other institutions. Each group consisted of representatives from "the masses," the PLA, and select cadres.

rites controversy: Conflict between the Catholic church and Emperor Kangxi over the nature of Chinese rites of ancestor worship and homage to Confucius. Kangxi insisted, and

Jesuits in the court agreed, that such rites were civil, not religious, and that missionaries should allow Chinese Christian converts to practice them. The Vatican disagreed and prohibited missionaries from following Kangxi's order. The controversy resulted in the expulsion of many Catholic missionaries from China.

Sacred Edict: List of Confucian maxims on morality and social relations compiled by the emperor Kangxi in 1670 and promulgated throughout China. Kangxi's son Yongzheng elaborated on his father's edict and had it read in colloquial Chinese to ensure its transmission to all his subjects.

Shaanxi: Province in north-central China, 73,000 square miles in area, with a population of 34,400,000. Capital: Xi'an. Located in the dry plain of the Yellow River.

Shandong ("Mountain East"): Province in eastern China, 58,000 square miles in area, with a population of 86,400,000. Capital: Jinan.

Shanghai communiqué: Document issued on February 28, 1972, at the end of President Nixon's visit to China, stating the positions of China and the United States on questions such as the status of Taiwan and calling for the beginning of work toward the normalization of Sino-American relations.

Shanxi ("Mountain West"): Province in north-central China, 73,500 square miles in area, with a population of 30,100,000. Capital: Taiyuan.

Shunzhi [Shwun-jihr] (1638–1661): Reign name of Fu Lin, ninth son of Hong Taiji and the first emperor of the Qing dynasty. Was placed at the age of six upon the throne of Peking under the regency of his uncle Dorgon. Fond of Chinese literature and culture, Shunzhi adopted a benevolent policy toward his Chinese subjects after the death of his uncle.

Sichuan ("Four Rivers"): Province in southwestern China. Its 220,000-square-mile area includes fertile river valleys farmed by Han Chinese and towering foothills of the Himalayas inhabited by ethnic minorities. The total population of this prosperous province is 111,000,000. Capital: Chengdu.

single-whip reforms: Attempt made by the Ming government in the mid-sixteenth century to simplify the collection of tax revenues, whereby all levies previously collected in kind were merged into one tax, payable in silver.

six ministries: The major units of central government in Peking. Modeled on a system first established in the Tang dynasty, they included the Ministries of Civil Office, Revenue, Rituals, War, Public Works, and Punishments.

Socialist Education Campaign: Movement begun in 1963 by the CCP under Mao to revive socialist values in Chinese society. Urban cadres were sent to work in the countryside, and emphasis was placed on class struggle and collective economic activity.

Song Jiaoren [Soong Jee-ow-ren] (1882–1913): Early leader of the Guomindang. An ardent critic of Yuan Shikai, Song was assassinated on his way to assuming his leadership role in the first nationally elected parliament.

Soong, T. V.: Harvard-educated brother of the Soong sisters. Helped his brother-in-law Chiang Kai-shek finance the Northern Expedition and later served as minister of finance in the Guomindang government.

Soong Ailing [Soong Eye-ling]: Eldest of the three Soong sisters, wife of financier/industrialist H. H. Kong.

Soong Meiling [Soong May-ling]: Youngest of the Soong sisters, wife of Guomindang leader Chiang Kai-shek. An American-educated Methodist, Soong Meiling played an active role in the Guomindang war effort in the 1930s and 1940s, sponsoring refugee relief efforts and women's organizations as well as acting as spokesperson to the West for her husband's cause.

Soong Qingling [Soong Ching-ling]: Middle Soong sister, became wife of Sun Yat-sen in 1914. After the death of her husband, she supported the alliance of the Guomindang left with the Chinese Communist party. Soong Qingling remained in China after 1949 and was named to several nominal positions within the Communist government.

special economic zones: Cities targeted by the CCP to accept direct foreign investment; designed to increase Chinese exports and act as a bridge for the adoption of foreign technology. The first four special economic zones—Shenzhen, Zhuhai, Shantou, and Xiamen—were established in 1979 and were followed by fourteen other cities plus the island of Hainan in 1986.

Stilwell, Joseph ("Vinegar Joe"): U.S. Army general; after Pearl Harbor was named commander in chief of U.S. forces in the China-Burma-India theater and acted as President Roosevelt's liaison with Chiang Kai-shek. Personal animosity between Chiang and Stilwell was a factor that led to Stilwell's being replaced by General Albert Wedemeyer in 1944.

Sun Yat-sen (1866–1925): Considered the father of the Chinese republican revolution. Educated in medicine in Hong Kong, he became an anti-Manchu activist and through his Tongmeng hui helped to overthrow the Qing dynasty. As leader of the Guomindang, Sun struggled against warlord factions to try to unite China throughout the 1910s and early 1920s. Accepted the help of the Soviet Union and entered into a united-front alliance with the CCP in 1923. Died in 1925; leadership of the Guomindang passed to Chiang Kai-shek.

Suppression of Counterrevolutionaries campaign: Mass movement launched by the Communist party in 1951, aimed at rooting out Guomindang sympathizers, secret-society members, and religious-sect adherents. Thousands were arrested and executed during the year-long mobilization.

tael: One ounce of silver; unit of exchange (most importantly, unit of tax payment made to government treasuries) in imperial China.

Taiping uprising (1851–1864): Led by Hong Xiuquan, a military and social movement that sought to overthrow the Qing and establish a "Heavenly Kingdom of Great Peace" (Taiping Tianguo) in China. With a combination of quasi-Christian beliefs and communal vision, the Taiping armies spread northeast through the middle Yangzi valley from their base in rural Guangxi province, capturing Nanjing in 1853, where they made their capital for eleven years. They were finally defeated in Qing counterattacks spearheaded by the Xiang provincial army led by Zeng Guofan. It is estimated that as many as 20 million Chinese died in the thirteen years of the rebellion.

Tang Xianzu [Tahng Shee-en-zoo] (1550–1617): Playwright, author of the romantic late Ming masterpiece *The Peony Pavilion.*

Three Anti campaign: Mass movement begun by the Communist party in 1951, aimed at eliminating the three vices of "corruption, waste, and obstructionist bureaucracy" among party members, government administrators, and factory managers. Held in conjunction with the Five Anti campaign.

Three Feudatories: Refers to (1) the area of south and southeast China, stretching from Sichuan to the eastern coast, left by the Qing government to the control of the three generals (Shang Zhixin, Geng Jingzhong, and Wu Sangui) who had helped subdue the region during the Manchu conquest, and to (2) the generals themselves. Wu rebelled against the Qing, announcing the establishment of his own "Zhou" dynasty in 1673. The ensuing civil war ended with Manchu victory in 1681.

Three Principles of the People: "Nationalism, democracy, and people's livelihood," formulated by Sun Yat-sen as the basis of Guomindang ideology.

Tiananmen Incident: Mass demonstrations that occurred on April 5, 1976, in Tiananmen Square expressing grief over the death of Zhou Enlai, held on the traditional holiday of Qingming, when the Chinese pay respects to their dead ancestors. Interpreted as a criticism of Mao and the Cultural Revolution.

Tianjin massacre (1870): Incident sparked by conflict between Catholics and Chinese in Tianjin in which angry crowds killed the French consul Fontanier along with fifteen other French men and women.

Tibet (Xizang in Mandarin): Taken over by the Chinese in 1950 and named an "autonomous region." 1,200,000 square miles in area, with a population of 2,320,000. Capital: Lhasa. Tibetans protested violently against the Chinese in 1959, and again in 1988.

ti-yong [tee-yong]: Formulation composed of two Chinese words—*ti,* meaning "essence," and *yong,* meaning "practical use." Used to describe the method of self-strengthening envisioned by Confucian reformers of the late nineteenth century: Chinese learning for the underlying "essence" of society, and Western learning for "practical application" in economic development. A similar concept informed China's opening to the West after 1972.

Tongzhi [Tongjir] (1856–1875): Reign name of Caichun, only son of the emperor Xianfeng. Became the eighth emperor of the Qing dynasty in 1862, at the age of six. His mother, Cixi, ruled for him as regent until he reached his seventeenth birthday, and continued to exercise power over his decisions until his death at the age of nineteen.

Tongzhi Restoration: Period from the late 1860s to the late 1870s named after the Tongzhi reign of this time, during which the Qing attempted to revitalize the government and the nation through a combination of Confucian morality and Western technology. Major figures in this "self-strengthening" movement included Zeng Guofan, Li Hongzhang, and Prince Gong.

Treaty of Nanjing (1842): Most important treaty settlement of Chinese history, signed by the British and the Qing governments to end the Opium War. Its twelve articles included the opening of five treaty ports (Canton, Fuzhou, Xiamen, Shanghai, and Ningbo) to unrestricted British trade and residence; the cession of Hong Kong; the payment of a 21 million tael indemnity; and the abolition of the Cohong monopoly. It was supplemented in the following year by the Treaty of the Bogue, which contained the most-favored-nation clause, automatically giving to Britain any privilege granted by the Qing to another nation in a treaty agreement.

Treaty of Nerchinsk (1689): Treaty negotiated between the Qing court of Kangxi and Russia, setting the north-south border between the two countries at the Gorbitsa and Argun rivers. A major departure from the usual Qing management of foreign affairs, the treaty was signed as an agreement between two equal sovereign states.

Treaty of Shimonoseki (1895): Disastrous treaty for China, ending the Sino-Japanese War (1894–1895). Under its terms Korea effectively became a Japanese protectorate. China ceded to Japan Taiwan and the Pescadores, added four more treaty ports, and promised to pay Japan 200 million taels in war indemnities.

Treaty of Tianjin (1858): Agreement between Britain and the Qing court after the British, angered by the Qing refusal to renegotiate the Treaty of Nanjing, sent forces north to threaten the port city of Tianjin. The treaty forced the Qing to accept the establishment of a British ambassador in Peking, the unrestricted preaching of Christianity, and the opening of ten new treaty ports both on the coast and inland.

Triads: Secret society, originating in Taiwan and Fujian during the late eighteenth century, also known as the Heaven and Earth Society. Triad activity combined organized crime and banditry with anti-Manchu sentiments. Their ties with local bureaucracy and militia made them an important force in Chinese society.

Tung Chee-hua (b. 1937): Hong Kong financier, trained in England and United States, returned to head his father's shipping business. Conservative politically, effective entrepreneur, chosen by Peking to be the first chief executive of the new Hong Kong administrative region in 1997. Known as "C. H."

Twenty-one Demands: Issued by Japan in January 1915, in which Japan demanded economic rights for Japanese in Manchuria, the right to station police and economic advisers in Manchuria, and major economic concessions in China proper. Demands accepted by the government of Yuan Shikai in spite of popular Chinese protest.

united front: Term used to describe a tenuous policy of cooperation between the usually antagonistic Chinese Communist party and the Guomindang, effected twice for the purpose of realizing national goals. The first united front (1923–1927) aimed at reclaiming China from warlord forces (*see* **Northern Expedition**); the second united front (1937–1945) sought to resist Japan in World War II.

Unofficial History of the Scholars *(Rulin waishi):* Published in 1768, one of the major literary works of the Qing dynasty. The novel describes the plight of the degree-holding elite, many unemployed, in the eighteenth century.

Wang Guangmei [Wahng Gwahng-may] (b. 1921): Wife of Liu Shaoqi. In 1964 led an investigation of rural cadre corruption in Hebei province as part of the Socialist Education Campaign. Severely criticized along with her husband during the Cultural Revolution, which she managed to survive, although her husband did not.

Wang Hongwen: Former cadre from a textile mill in Shanghai who rose to become a close associate of Shanghai party secretary Zhang Chunqiao during the Cultural Revolution. Tried and convicted in 1980 as part of the Gang of Four.

Wang Jingwei [Wahng Jing-way] (1883–1944): Early associate of Sun Yat-sen who helped found the Tongmeng hui as a student in Japan in 1905. Held several top positions in the Guomindang during the first Communist-Guomindang alliance (1923–1927) and in Chiang Kai-shek's Nanjing government (1928–1937). In 1940 Wang agreed to be titular head of a collaborationist regime in Nanjing that cooperated with invading Japanese forces.

Wang Yangming [Wahng Yahng-ming] (1472–1529): Philosopher-official of the early Ming who held that it was not study of the Confucian classics but the cultivation of the intuitive knowledge inherent in everyone that led to the understanding of Confucian truths. Accused by later scholars of fostering eccentric individualism and initiating the breakdown of Confucian moral standards that contributed to the fall of the Ming court.

Wanli [Wahn-lee]: Reign name of Zhu Yijun (1563–1620), the thirteenth emperor of the Ming dynasty. The beginning of his forty-eight-year rule saw the height of Ming glory, but by the time of his death, internal disorder and court intrigues had set the stage for the fall of the dynasty.

Wei Jingsheng (b. 1950): Worker and former PLA member active in the Democracy Wall movement of 1978–1979. His writings on the fifth modernization and on party corruption led to his arrest and trial, at which he was sentenced to fifteen years hard labor. In 1995 sentenced to a further fourteen-year term for continuing to criticize the government. Released and came to the United States in 1997.

Whampoa: Military academy near Canton, established by Sun Yat-sen in 1924 to train officers for the Guomindang. Many of its graduates were personally loyal to the academy's first leader, Chiang Kai-shek, and immeasurably strengthened his political power base.

White lotus rebellion: Sporadic uprisings in north-central China in the late eighteenth–early nineteenth centuries by followers of a millenary folk-Buddhism cult that evoked the powers of "the Venerable Eternal Mother" to overthrow Manchu rule and establish a new order on earth.

Wu Han (1909–1969): Writer and historian, was deputy mayor of Peking under Peng Zhen in the early 1960s when he wrote the controversial play, *The Dismissal of Hai Rui from Office,* an allegorical criticism of Mao's purge of Peng Dehuai. The attack against the play by Yao Wenyuan was one of the acts that heralded the beginning of the Cultural Revolution.

Wuhan uprising (October 1911): Triggered when explosives kept by Revolutionary Alliance members accidentally went off in the city of Hankou, uncovering their activities and forcing them to launch their uprising. New Army troops joined the mutiny against the Qing, beginning the revolution that led to the fall of the dynasty in 1912.

Wu Peifu [Woo Pay-foo] (1874–1939): Most powerful warlord in the east-central area of Hubei and Hunan in the 1920s. Ordered the violent suppression of the Peking-Hankou railway strike in 1923. His hold on central China ended when Chiang Kai-shek's National Revolutionary Army took the city of Wuhan in 1926 as part of the Northern Expedition.

xian [shee-en] ("county"): Unit of government administration below the level of province.

Xianfeng [Shee-en-fung] (1831–1861): Reign name of Yiju, fourth son of the emperor Daoguang. Became the seventh emperor of the Qing dynasty in 1850 at the age of nineteen. Ruled during a period of continuing Sino-English conflict over treaty concessions. Finally forced in 1860 by invading British troops to flee to Jehol, where he died the following year, leaving power over the throne to his consort, the empress Cixi.

xiang ("township"): Unit of local government below the level of *xian* ("county").

Xi'an Incident (December 1936): Refers to the kidnaping of Chiang Kai-shek by the warlord Zhang Xueliang in Xi'an. Attempting to force Chiang to agree to a united Chinese effort against the Japanese, Zhang held Chiang until negotiations between the Guomindang and the CCP (represented by Zhou Enlai) resulted in Chiang's release on Christmas Day.

Xinjiang ("New Territories"): Autonomous region in northwestern China, 617,000 square miles in area, with a population of 16,100,000, including a number of central Asian Muslims known as Uighurs. The region's vast deserts contain valuable mineral resources and China's nuclear testing zones. Capital: Urumqi.

yamen: Word designating residence and office of Chinese provincial officials.

Yan'an: Poor mountain-region town in Shaanxi province; base for CCP activities from the end of the Long March (1936) to its seizure by Guomindang forces in 1947.

Yan Fu [Yen Foo] (1854–1921): Qing naval student sent to England in 1877 to study naval science; later went on to translate influential works by Darwin, Huxley, Spencer, and Adam Smith. Became the first president of the modernized Peking University in 1912.

Yang Xiuqing [Yang Shee-o-ching] (1822–1856): Orphaned illiterate charcoal maker who joined the Taiping rebellion and became chief military adviser to its leader, Hong

Xiuquan. Later attempted to usurp power from Hong and was killed on Hong's orders in a palace coup.

Yangzi (Chang Jiang in Mandarin ["Long River"]): One of the major waterways of the world and the longest (3,430 miles) in Asia, flowing from Qinghai out to the East China Sea at Shanghai. Often thought of as the dividing line between north and south China, the Yangzi cuts through treacherous gorges in its upper reaches, while its fertile eastern delta fosters one of the most prosperous and populous regions of China.

Yan Xishan [Yen Shee-shahn] (1883–1960): Tenacious warlord who controlled the province of Shanxi from 1912 to 1949. Cooperated with Chiang Kai-shek in opposing Communist activities, even employing Japanese soldiers against CCP forces as late as 1949.

Yao Wenyuan: Colleague of Jiang Qing, author of an article attacking Wu Han's *The Dismissal of Hai Rui from Office,* which was considered the "first shot" of the Cultural Revolution. Tried and convicted in 1980 as a member of the Gang of Four.

Yellow River (Huang He): The second longest waterway in China, flowing 2,900 miles from Qinghai north through Inner Mongolia and then bending south and east out to the Gulf of Bohai at Shandong province. Heavy silting caused constant floods.

Yen, James: Leader of mass-education movements in China and among overseas Chinese. After graduating from Yale in 1918, he went to France, where he established a newspaper for Chinese workers there. Continued his work through a YMCA-sponsored literacy and rural reconstruction program in Ding county, Hebei.

Yongzheng [Yong-jung] (1678–1735): Reign name of Yinzhen, fourth son of Kangxi, and third emperor of the Qing dynasty (ruled 1723–1735). Deeply committed to direct involvement in government affairs, Yongzheng launched a vigorous reform of the Qing tax structure. To manage his military campaigns more efficiently in the northwest, he bypassed the cumbersome regular bureaucracy and formed a group of his most trusted grand secretaries which became known as the Grand Council under Yongzheng's son, the emperor Qianlong.

yuan: (1) "Institution" in Mandarin. Used for the five main bureaus of Chiang Kai-shek's Nationalist government: the Executive, Legislative, Control, Judicial, Examination yuan. (2) A monetary unit of China; also known as Chinese dollars.

Yuan Shikai [Yuen Shir-kye] (1859–1916): Leader of the powerful Beiyang (North China) army, initially loyal to the empress dowager Cixi, later instrumental in arranging the abdication of the Qing in 1912. Because of Yuan's military strength, Sun Yat-sen offered Yuan the presidency of the new republic. Yuan abused the office, purging the Parliament and proclaiming himself emperor in 1915. He died six months later, in 1916.

Yung Wing (1828–1912): First Chinese to graduate from an American university (Yale, 1854). With his knowledge of the West, he served in Qing self-strengthening efforts such as assisting Zeng Guofan in buying machine equipment and arms from the United States.

Yunnan ("South of the Clouds"): Province in southwestern China, 168,000 square miles in area, with a population of 38,900,000. Capital: Kunming.

Zeng Guofan [Dzung Gwo-fan] (1811–1872): Confucian statesman/general/scholar; leader of the Hunan provincial army (Xiang) that defeated the Taiping forces in Nanjing and put an end to the rebellion. Played an important role in Qing self-strengthening efforts, advocating the use of modern military technology and enlisting a group of talented men around him to serve the Qing cause. Adhered to strict Confucian standards of discipline, diligence, and loyalty to the emperor.

Zhang Chunqiao: Head of the Shanghai CCP and close ally of Jiang Qing in the Cultural Revolution. Tried and convicted in 1980 as a member of the Gang of Four.

Zhang Xianzhong [Jahng Shee-en-jong] (1605–1647): Shaanxi native and Ming army deserter; leader of an anti-Ming rebel army that controlled parts of central and south-western China. Established himself in 1644 as "king of the Great Western Kingdom" with his capital in Chengdu. Three years later he and his kingdom were eliminated by Manchu armies.

Zhang Xueliang [Jahng Shweh-lee-ang] (b. 1900): Son of the northern warlord Zhang Zuolin. In 1928, after his father's assassination, he was given the name "the Young Marshal," inherited his father's forces, and established his own power base in Manchuria. Pledged allegiance to Chiang Kai-shek's Nanjing government in 1928, but kidnaped Chiang in 1936 (*see* **Xi'an Incident**) to force a united Chinese front against the Japanese.

Zhang Xun [Jahng Shun] (1854–1923): Chinese general who remained loyal to the Manchus even after the fall of the dynasty in 1912. Led coup in 1917 to restore the boy-emperor Puyi to the throne. Restoration attempt failed when the troops of other generals attacked Peking, driving Zhang into political retirement.

Zhang Zhidong [Jahng Jir-dong] (1837–1909): General/official in the Qing government who was appointed to the governorship of several provinces, including Shaanxi, Guangdong/Guangxi, and Hubei/Hunan. Like Zeng Guofan and Li Hongzhang, Zhang was active in the late Qing self-strengthening efforts, building textile factories, arsenals, and rail-roads, and fostered the *ti-yong* idea for China's development.

Zhang Zuolin [Jahng Dzwo-lin] (1875–1928): Warlord who came to prominence during the presidency of Yuan Shikai and later went on to control Manchuria, eastern Mongolia, and finally Peking with his armies. Staunchly anti-Communist, he ordered the execution of Li Dazhao in 1927. Defeated by Chiang Kai-shek's New Revolutionary Army in 1928. Killed in Manchuria by a bomb planted by Japanese army officers.

Zhao Ziyang [Jow Dz-yahng] (b. 1919): Protégé of Deng Xiaoping who rose from secretary of the Guangdong province CCP in the 1960s to premier of China and then secretary-general of the CCP in the mid-1980s. Considered an advocate of economic change and expanded contacts with the West. Removed from his party posts in 1989 for supporting student demonstrations that followed the death of Hu Yaobang.

Zhejiang: Province in eastern China, 38,600 square miles in area, with a population of 42,700,000. Capital: Hangzhou.

Zhou Enlai [Joe Uhn-lye] (1898–1976): One of the most powerful and respected leaders of the CCP from the days of the Long March to his death nine months before that of his colleague Mao Zedong. Served as premier of China from 1954 and was influential in Chinese foreign policy for three decades. In the Tiananmen demonstrations of April 5, 1976, the Chinese people expressed their admiration for Zhou as a moderating element in the Cultural Revolution.

Zhu De [Joo Duh] (1886–1976): Mao Zedong's chief military adviser from the days of the Jiangxi Soviet. Zhu was commander in chief of the People's Liberation Army and long-time member of the Standing Committee of the Communist party Politburo.

Zhu Rongji (b. 1929): Electrical Engineer, denounced in 1957 antirightist campaign, reha-bilitated 1978. Rose rapidly in Communist bureaucracy. Mayor of Shanghai, 1987; named to Politburo Standing Committee, 1992; deputy prime minister, head of eco-nomic and trade office, director of Bank of China, 1993. Skillful and forceful economic planner, succeeded Li Peng as premier in 1998.

Zongli Yamen [Dzong-lee Yah-mun] ("Office for the Management of the Business of All Foreign Countries"): Established by the Qing in 1861 in an attempt to deal with the crises presented by Western foreign powers. Under the leadership of Prince Gong and Wenxiang, the Zongli Yamen was involved not only in treaty negotiations with Western countries, but in self-strengthening efforts including the establishment of language schools with Western curricula, the research of Western forms of government, and the investigation of international law.

Zou Rong [Dzo Rong] (1885–1905): Anti-Manchu revolutionary educated in Japan; author of *The Revolutionary Army* (1905), which called for the overthrow of the Qing and the establishment of democracy. Died in prison at the age of nineteen.

Zuo Zongtang [Dzwo Dzong-tahng] (1812–1885): Leader of the Qing armies that suppressed the Muslim revolts in northwestern China (1862–1873). Zuo, who had also led his own local Hunan militia against the Taiping, was appointed to important government and military posts by the Qing in spite of having never received the *jinshi* degree.

Note: Where given, population statistics are from *Chinese Business World*'s website (www.cbw.com), as of April 1997.

Illustration Credits

For illustrations between pages 38 and 39:

1) The Art Museum, Princeton University. Du Bois Schanck Morris Collection.
2) *Top, middle, and bottom:* The Shanghai Museum, photographed by David Allison for The Asia Society, New York.
3) *Top and bottom:* By permission of the British Library (15226.b.19).
4) Collection of the National Palace Museum. Taiwan, Republic of China.
5) © The British Museum.
6) *Top and bottom:* From *The Great Enterprise: The Manchu Reconstruction of the Imperial Order in Seventeenth-Century China,* Frederick E. Wakeman (Berkeley, 1985).
7) *Top and bottom:* Courtesy, Peabody Essex Museum, Salem, MA.
8) *Top:* The New York Public Library, Astor, Lenox and Tilden Foundation; *bottom:* Private Collection.
9) Courtesy, The Palace Museum, Beijing, China.
10) Collection of the National Palace Museum. Taiwan, Republic of China.
11) *Left:* Private Collection, Canada; *right:* The Spencer Collection, The New York Public Library, Astor, Lenox and Tilden Foundation.
12) Courtesy, The Palace Museum, Beijing, China.

For illustrations between pages 132 and 133:

1) *Top and bottom:* Collection of the National Palace Museum. Taiwan, Republic of China.
2) *Top and bottom:* By permission of the Houghton Library, Harvard University.
3) Lang Shih-ning (Giuseppe Castiglione), Chinese, 1688–1768, Qing

A71

Dynasty. *Inauguration Portraits of Emperor Qianlong, The Empress, and the Eleven Imperial Consorts*, 1736. Handscroll, ink and color on silk, 52.9 x 688.3 cm. © The Cleveland Museum of Art, John L. Severance Fund, 1969.31.

4) *Top:* © The British Museum; *bottom:* The New York Public Library, Astor, Lenox and Tilden Foundation.

5) "Grossmogul"—The Emperor on His Travels (detail), Bamburg Residenz. Bayerische Verwaltung der Staatlichen Schlösser, Garten und Seen. Photographed by Ingeborg Limmer.

6) *Top:* Courtesy, Peabody Essex Museum, Salem, MA; *bottom:* Courtesy, Winterhur Museum.

7) *Top and bottom:* The Martyn Gregory Gallery, London.

8) Harvard-Yenching Library, Harvard University.

9) Collection of the National Palace Museum. Taiwan, Republic of China.

10) *Top:* From *From Bondage to Liberation: East Asia 1860–1952*, Nigel Cameron (Hong Kong, 1975); *bottom:* Mansell/Time, Inc.

11) Beato, Felice, *Interior of the English Entrance to North Fort on 21st August, 1860*. The Museum of Modern Art, New York. Purchased as the gift of Shirley C. Burden and the Estate of Vera Louise Fraser. Copy print © 1998 The Museum of Modern Art, New York.

12) Courtesy, Bibliothèque nationale de France.

13) The Bancroft Library, University of California, Berkeley.

14) Courtesy, The Palace Museum, Beijing.

For illustrations between pages 228 and 229:

1) Zhejiang Provincial Museum.

2) Michelangelo Durazzo/Magnum Photos.

3) *Top:* The J. Paul Getty Museum. Thomson, John, *A Mandarin's House* from *Illustrations of China and its People, Vol. IV*, c. 1871–72, autotype, 71.7 x 22.1 cm.; *bottom:* L'Illustration/Sygma.

4) *Top:* The Palace Museum, Beijing; *bottom left:* General Commission on Archives and History, The United Methodist Church; *bottom right:* The J. Paul Getty Museum. Thomson, John, *Prince Kung* from *Illustrations of China and its People, Vol. 1*, c. 1871–72, autotype, 29 x 19.7 cm.

5) *Top and bottom:* General Commission on Archives and History, The United Methodist Church.

6) *Top left, top right, and bottom:* The Warder Collection.

7) *Top:* UPI/Corbis; *bottom:* National Archives #111-SC 74985.

8) *Top left: Twilight in the Forbidden City,* R. F. Johnston (London, 1934); *top right:* The Warder Collection; *bottom:* The Camera Press.

9) *Top:* The Palace Museum, Beijing; *bottom:* General Commission on Archives and History, The United Methodist Church.
10) *Top left:* The Warder Collection; *top right:* General Commission on Archives and History, The United Methodist Church; *bottom:* Ullstein Bilderdienst.
11) Harlingue-Viollet.
12) General Commission on Archives and History, The United Methodist Church.

For illustrations between pages 372 and 373:

1) The Sidney D. Gamble Foundation for China Studies.
2) *Top:* YMCA of the USA Archives, University of Minnesota Libraries; *bottom:* The Sidney D. Gamble Foundation for China Studies.
3) *Top and bottom:* The Sidney D. Gamble Foundation for China Studies.
4) *Top left and right:* Museum of the Revolution, Peking; *bottom left:* The Warder Collection; *bottom right:* Library of Congress.
5) *Top:* JAF Collection/Magnum Photos; *bottom:* The New York Public Library, Astor, Lenox and Tilden Foundation.
6) *Top:* Library of Congress; *bottom:* From La Cina edi Cinesi loro leggie Constumi, Giuseppe Domenico Musso (Milan 1926).
7) *Top:* UPI/Corbis-Bettman; *bottom:* AP/Wide World Photos
8) *Top and bottom:* Jay Calvin Huston Collection; Hoover Institution Archives, Stanford University.
9) *Modern China Rare Photograph Library, Sun Yat–sen and the Guomindang Party,* The Commercial Press (Hong Kong), Ltd., 1994.
10) *Top: Modern China Rare Photograph Library, Chiang Kai-shek and the Guomindang Party,* The Commercial Press (Hong Kong), Ltd., 1994; *bottom:* Milly Bennet Collection, Hoover Institution Archives, Stanford University.
11) Collection Viollet.
12) *Top:* Walter Bossard/Magnum Photos; *bottom:* Photoworld.
13) *Top:* Hulton Getty/Tony Stone Images; *bottom:* Museum of the Revolution, Peking.
14) The Lattimore Foundation, photograph courtesy of The Peabody Museum of Archaeology and Ethnology, Harvard University.

For illustrations between pages 484 and 485:

1) Photographers International Magazine.
2) *Top and bottom:* Photographers International Magazine.
3) *Top and bottom:* Photographers International Magazine.

4) *Top and bottom:* Wu Yinxian/Magnum Photos.
5) Wu Yinxian/Magnum Photos.
6) *Top:* Wedemeyer Collection, Hoover Institution Archives, Stanford University; *bottom:* From *From Bondage to Liberation: East Asia 1860– 1952,* Nigel Cameron (Hong Kong, 1975).
7) Henri Cartier-Bresson/Magnum Photos.
8) *Top and bottom:* Henri Cartier-Bresson/Magnum Photos.
9) *Top:* Eastfoto; *bottom:* Xinhua News Agency.
10) *Top:* Xinhua News Agency; *bottom:* Museum of the Revolution, Peking.
11) *Top:* Hulton Getty/Tony Stone Images; *bottom:* New China Pictures/ Magnum Photos.
12) The Warder Collection.
13) Xinhua News Agency.
14) Henri Cartier-Bresson/Magnum Photos.

For illustrations between pages 622 and 623:

1) *Top:* Li Zhensheng.
2) *Top and bottom:* Marc Riboud/Magnum Photos.
3) *Top and bottom:* Li Zhensheng.
4) *Top:* Shi Zemin; *bottom:* AP/Wide World Photos.
5) *Top:* From *China This Century,* Rafe de Crespigny (Melbourne, 1975); *bottom:* Xinhua News Agency.
6) Xinhua News Agency.
7) New China Pictures/Magnum Photos.
8) *Top:* Marc Riboud/Magnum Photos; *bottom:* Inge Morath/Magnum Photos.
9) AP/Wide World Photos.
10) *Top and bottom:* AP/Wide World Photos.

For illustrations between pages 718 and 719:

1) Eastfoto.
2) Yong He.
3) Yong He.
4) Eastfoto.
5) AP/Wide World Photos.
6) *Top:* AP/Wide World Photos; *bottom left:* Eastfoto; *bottom right:* East- foto.
7) Eastfoto.
8) Xu Yong.

A Note on the Calligraphy

Jacket and title page

The character *zheng,* "struggle," written in *cao shu* or "cursive" style.

Part I

The inscription reads: "Wu you yi ri zhong," "Be not sad; be like the sun at midday." Quote from the *Yi Jing,* written in *bianti xiaozhuan* or "modified small seal" style.

Part II

The ancient commentary on the above inscription from the *Yi Jing: ri zhong ze ze,* "When the sun stands at midday, it begins to set," also written in modified small seal style.

Part III

The two characters *sai* and *de,* used by writers in the May Fourth movement to represent "science" and "democracy," respectively. Written in *heiti xiangxing* or "bold ideograph" style.

Part IV

The single character *fan,* "to turn over or upside down," written in a dramatic form of *cao shu* or "cursive" style.

Part V

The characters *yan bo,* "extending the waves," written in ultra-rapid cursive style.

ABOUT THE CALLIGRAPHER

Liang Minwei was born in Canton, People's Republic of China, in 1962, and studied painting at the Yuexiu Art Institute. He was head of design at a major Canton retail firm for several years before continuing his study of Chinese painting under Ke Hejun at the Canton Academy of Fine Arts. Since his arrival in the United States in 1987, Liang Minwei's calligraphy and abstract landscapes have been exhibited widely in and around the New York metropolitan area. He lives in New Haven, Connecticut, with his wife and three cats.

Index

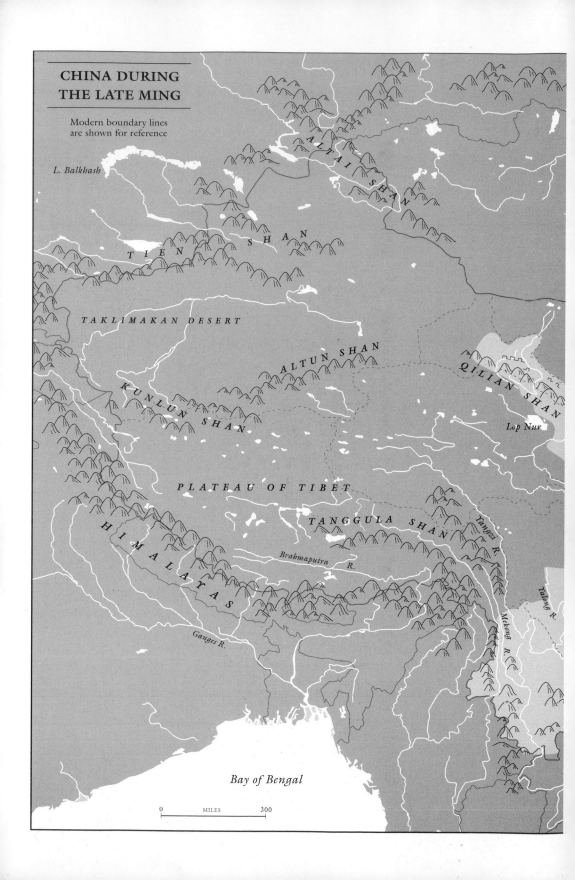

CHINA DURING
THE LATE MING

Modern boundary lines
are shown for reference

L. Balkhash

ALTAI SHAN

TIEN SHAN

TAKLIMAKAN DESERT

ALTUN SHAN

QILIAN SHAN

KUNLUN SHAN

Lop Nur

PLATEAU OF TIBET

TANGGULA SHAN

Yangzi R.

Brahmaputra R.

HIMALAYAS

Ganges R.

Talong R.

Mekong R.

Bay of Bengal

0   MILES   300

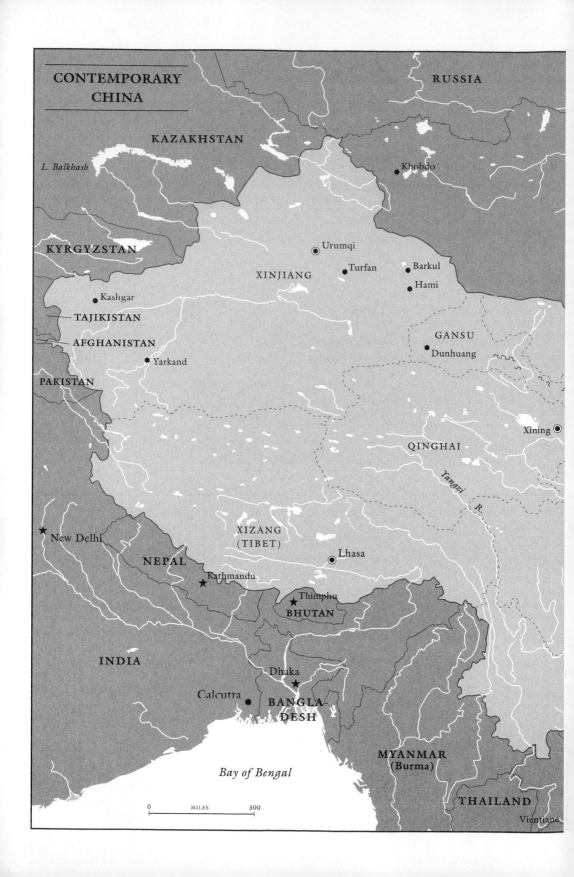

CONTEMPORARY
CHINA

RUSSIA

KAZAKHSTAN

L. Balkhash

Khobdo

KYRGYZSTAN

Urumqi

Turfan

Barkul
Hami

XINJIANG

Kashgar

TAJIKISTAN

AFGHANISTAN

Yarkand

GANSU

Dunhuang

PAKISTAN

Xining

QINGHAI

Yangzi R.

New Delhi

XIZANG
(TIBET)

Lhasa

NEPAL

Kathmandu

Thimphu
BHUTAN

INDIA

Dhaka

Calcutta

BANGLA-
DESH

MYANMAR
(Burma)

Bay of Bengal

THAILAND

Vientiane

0   MILES   300

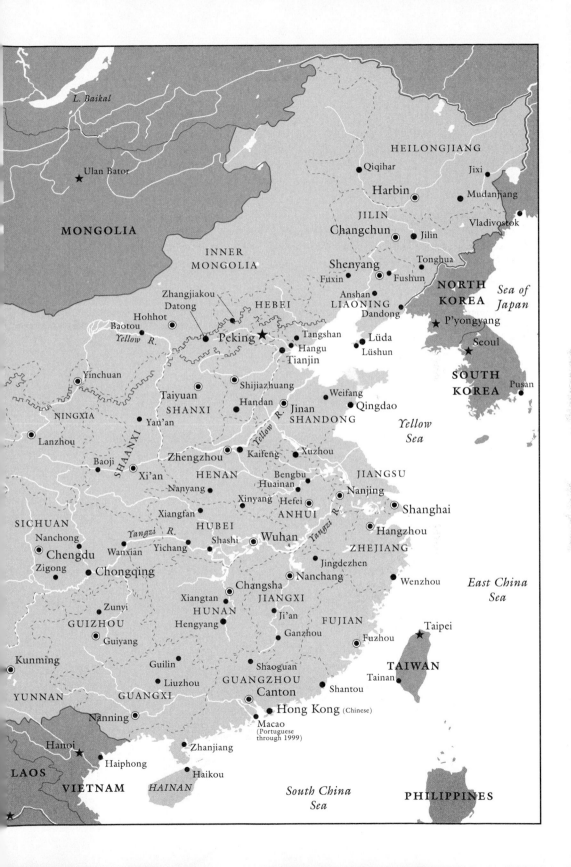

JONATHAN D. SPENCE is Sterling Professor of History at Yale University. Born in England in 1936, he was educated at Winchester College and Cambridge University. He commenced graduate work at Yale in 1959, and earned a Ph.D. in history in 1965. He is the author of many acclaimed works on China, including *Emperor of China: Self-Portrait of K'ang-hsi, The Death of Woman Wang, The Gate of Heavenly Peace* (awarded the *Los Angeles Times* Book Prize for history and named one of the best nonfiction books of the year by the *New York Times Book Review*), *The Memory Palace of Matteo Ricci, The Question of Hu,* and *God's Chinese Son.* His most recent book is *The Chan's Great Continent: China in Western Minds.*